THE 16TH MICHIGAN INFANTRY IN THE CIVIL WAR

THE 16TH MICHIGAN INFANTRY

IN THE CIVIL WAR

revised and updated

Kim Crawford

Michigan State University Press | *East Lansing*

∞ The paper used in this publication meets the minimum requirements
of ANSI/NISO Z39.48-1992 (R 1997) (Permanence of Paper).

Michigan State University Press
East Lansing, Michigan 48823-5245

Printed and bound in the United States of America.

28 27 26 25 24 23 22 21 20 19   1 2 3 4 5 6 7 8 9 10

LIBRARY OF CONGRESS CATALOGING-IN-PUBLICATION DATA
Names: Crawford, Kim, 1957–
Title: The 16th Michigan Infantry in the Civil War / Kim Crawford.
Description: Revised and updated. | East Lansing : Michigan State University Press, 2019.
| Includes bibliographical references and index.
Identifiers: LCCN 2018059362| ISBN 9781611863338 (cloth : alk. paper) | ISBN 9781609176112 (pdf)
| ISBN 9781628953749 (epub) | ISBN 9781628963755 (kindle)
Subjects: LCSH: United States. Army. Michigan Infantry Regiment, 16 th (1861–1865)—History.
| United States—History—Civil War, 1861–1865—Regimental histories.
| Michigan—History—Civil War, 1861–1865—Regimental histories.
Classification: LCC E514.5 16th .C73 2019 | DDC 973.7/474 –dc23
LC record available at https://lccn.loc.gov/2018059362

Book design by Charlie Sharp, Sharp Des!gns, East Lansing, Michigan
Cover design by Erin Kirk New
Cover art is "Bring Up the Colors (the 16th Michigan at Little Round Top,
battle of Gettysburg)" © 1994 by Todd Price and is used courtesy
of the artist. All rights reserved. (www.nightowlstudio.net).

Michigan State University Press is a member of the Green Press Initiative and is committed to developing and encouraging ecologically responsible publishing practices. For more information about the Green Press Initiative and the use of recycled paper in book publishing, please visit *www.greenpressinitiative.org.*

Visit Michigan State University Press at *www.msupress.org*

CONTENTS

PREFACE

Before Colonel Thomas B. W. Stockton faced his former West Point colleague, Robert E. Lee, and his wife's nephew by marriage, James Longstreet, on Virginia battlefields in the Civil War, he battled governmental authority in his own state, Michigan, to command a Union regiment. That outfit—initially called Stockton's Independent Regiment, and later the 16th Michigan Infantry—would begin as an anomaly of the conflict—a battalion of volunteers like scores of others, but one formed by him over the objection of Michigan's governor, Republican Austin Blair, despite the fact that President Abraham Lincoln wanted the colonel to form and lead a regiment in the spring of 1861.

A War Democrat, Flint resident, and veteran who had owned a slave as a young U.S. Army officer on the 1830s frontier, Stockton had deep family roots in American history. But it was only after the stunning defeat of the Union army at the battle of Bull Run that Lincoln's War Department directly authorized him to organize his own regiment. Ultimately enrolled a few months later as a state command, the 16th Michigan, these volunteers from Detroit, Saginaw, Adrian, Ionia, Lansing, Ontonagon, and scores of small towns would fight as part of the Army of the Potomac in some of the bloodiest battles of the war—Gaines' Mill, Malvern Hill, second Bull Run, Fredericksburg, and Gettysburg, to name a few. Far more of them would die in battle and from their wounds than from disease, typically the biggest killer of soldiers.

This day-to-day narrative of the 16th Michigan in the Civil War is based on the letters, diaries, reports, and reminiscences of the officers and common soldiers who served in this notable combat unit, but one that was historically shamed by certain critics because of the regiment's right breaking and retreating when it was flanked and overwhelmed by Confederates at a hill near Gettysburg called Little Round Top. Because of this onus, Col. Norval Welch of Ann Arbor, a handsome young lawyer and the regiment's second commander, would later pay with his life, redeeming his reputation for what occurred in the fateful, vicious fight at Gettysburg, explained here in a blow-by-blow account.

It was this question—what really happened to the 16th Michigan in the fight for Little Round Top—that sparked the following research into this controversial outfit. But a regiment's history is more than a single battle or the record of individual officers, and this narrative illustrates the many experiences, observations, hardships, friendships, rivalries, opinions, and lives and deaths of these Michigan citizen-soldiers, from the regiment's founder, Stockton, on to his men's beginnings as raw recruits in late summer of 1861, to Lee's surrender at Appomattox Court House in April 1865.

This is their story.

ACKNOWLEDGMENTS

The idea for this narrative history of the 16th Michigan Infantry goes back to the early 1990s and my newspaper days, when colleagues Larry Kasparek and Dave Larzelere suggested I take this on. A variety of people then guided me to and shared important materials about this regiment, in those days before Internet search engines were commonplace, and I still owe them my thanks: Dennis Spiekerman, John Gibney, Donald M. D. Thurber, Evelyn Ziehm, Kim Leese, Don Harvey, Edward Parker and John Parker, and Leo Wiegant; also Don Farrant, Ophelia Parrish, Florence Lembeck, Betty Melson and Eric Melson, Roger Vance, Marjorie Neufer, and Brian Russell.

I also had assistance back then from Tod Butler, then of the National Archives, and historians Scott Hartwig, Donald Pfanz, and John Heiser of the National Park Service. More recently, John, and Patrick Schroeder, of the Appomattox Court House National Park, have graciously helped with their expertise and encyclopedic knowledge, and for that I am grateful.

It is a near certainty that no one taking on a true story of Michigan soldiers in the Civil War will have much in the way of pictures without the help of a group of dedicated collectors, and thankfully they have been in my corner. Many of the portraits appearing in this book are courtesy of Dale Niesen, Paul Mehney, Mike Waskul, Dave Parks, Dave Finney, Bob Coch, and Jeff Kowalis. Other portraits appear thanks to Clayton Lewis and Louis Miller at the University of Michigan's Clements Library; Andy Clark, Monroe County Museum; Bill Gainey and Freeman Greer of Flint's Stockton Center; Geoffrey Reynolds at Hope College; Justin Sielder, Albion College; Brittany Phalen of Sloan Museum's Perry Archives; and the staff at the Grand Rapids Public Museum. Some portraits are here thanks to skillful photo editing by Mary Chaney (Mary Olivia Photography), and by Mark McFadden. My thanks to them all.

Of course, I once again thank the staffs at the U.S. Army Heritage and Education Center (USAHEC); the Archives of Michigan; the Bentley Historical Library; the Burton

Historical Collection of the Detroit Public Library; the Flint Public Library and Saginaw's Hoyt Library; the Clarke Library, Central Michigan University; and Western Michigan University's Archives and Regional History Collection. And I express my appreciation to my editor, Julie Loehr, and the staff at Michigan State University Press, for giving me the opportunity to tell the remarkable story of these soldiers.

Lastly, thanks to my wife Kelly and daughters Ellie and Mary, whose love and support made this possible when I first took this project on, twenty years ago.

1.

APRIL–SEPTEMBER 1861

THE TIME FOR ACTION HAS ARRIVED

He was one of Michigan's most experienced military men—a West Point graduate who had commanded state volunteers for the Mexican War. An experienced engineer, he worked on important projects for the U.S. government, traveling the Great Lakes region as an officer and a civilian agent in the era of Jackson, building and improving bridges, harbors, and roads. And when news of the Rebel attack on the federal island base called Ft. Sumter in Charleston harbor reached him in Flint, that former U.S. Army officer, Thomas B. W. Stockton, quickly wrote out an order to the farmers, mechanics, laborers, and store clerks who served in volunteer militia companies under him:

Flint, April 16, 1861

GENERAL ORDER NO. 1

The President of the United States having made a request upon the Governor of this State for one regiment of Infantry to aid in suppressing the combinations &c. against the Union . . . I deem it proper to direct that immediate and prompt efforts be made by each of said companies to fill up to the war standard (100 men rank and file), tender their services and hold themselves in readiness to move as soon as ordered. . . .

Commanders of Companies will report to me by letter as soon as the order is complied with.

T. B. W. Stockton
Major and commanding the 1st Saginaw Valley Battalion[1]

Stockton was a local businessman, 55, about 5 feet, 8 inches tall and tending toward stockiness, with graying auburn hair; a Maine soldier who would serve under him in the Civil War described him simply as "a short, thick, gray-haired man." A lifelong Democrat,

Stockton was certain that Michigan's new governor, Republican Austin Blair, would want him to command this newly requested state regiment—one of many new military units President Abraham Lincoln needed to confront the seceding Southern states, to suppress their rebellion. The United States had only a small standing army, and the government did not have the power and central authority in national security matters that it would eventually take on. In times of war, presidents necessarily turned to governors to raise state regiments for federal service.

The authority to create this new Michigan command and to commission or appoint its officers, therefore, rested with Gov. Blair. The same day Stockton issued his order to the militia companies of his part of the state, he wrote to Blair, asking to lead the 1st Michigan Infantry Regiment. After all, he had been commissioned colonel of a regiment of the same designation some thirteen years earlier during the Mexican War, though the conflict was over by the time they got to the scene. But Stockton pointed out that he had the "experience perfectly competent to command and perform all the duties of a regiment which others would have to learn." He enclosed for Blair's consideration an endorsement by leading citizens from his area. "Col. Stockton's known military skills and experience are a sufficient guarantee that he will discharge the duties of that position [as colonel of the 1st Michigan Infantry Regiment] with honor to himself and credit to the state," his supporters wrote, "[we] cheerfully and earnestly urge his appointment."[2]

But Stockton's request to command a new regiment hit a brick wall with Blair. A specific reason for Blair's lack of confidence in the colonel was never publicly discussed in Michigan newspapers, or in later accounts of Stockton's life. Perhaps the political differences between an abolitionist Republican governor with power to appoint Michigan officers and a conservative Democrat who longed for a command were enough to explain it. But there was an aspect of Stockton's past, undiscussed, that would have mattered greatly to Blair, who saw the conflict as a "sacred war" that would end American slavery: Stockton himself had been a slave owner.

Thomas Baylis Whitmarsh Stockton was born in 1805 and raised in small towns in New York's Catskill Mountains, part of a family with roles in American history long before the Civil War. His father's cousin, Richard Stockton, was a signer of the Declaration of Independence, locked up and mistreated by the British. Richard's grandson, Commodore Robert F. Stockton, was a senator, slave owner, and controversial naval war hero who served from the War of 1812 on through the conquest of California during the Mexican War; he was part of a commission that tried to head off the Civil War.[3]

Young Tom Stockton chose an army career, accepted to West Point at age 17 and graduating in 1827. A second lieutenant, he was sent to Jefferson Barracks at St. Louis and then to Ft. Snelling (now St. Paul, Minnesota), serving under future war hero and president Zachary Taylor. There Stockton met his wife, Maria Smith, the teenaged daughter of a Detroit fur trader named Jacob Smith. Smith had been an unofficial agent of influence for the United States among Michigan's Chippewa and Ottawa tribes before and after the

War of 1812; Smith and his wife died when Maria was a child, so the girl had lived with her eldest sister, Harriet Smith Garland, and Harriet's husband, then-Captain John Garland of the U.S. Army. Lt. Stockton and Maria were married in the spring of 1830 at Ft. Crawford at Prairie Du Chien, Wisconsin, then part of the Michigan Territory.[4]

Soon Maria was pregnant. Life on the wilderness frontier was difficult and uncomfortable for the toughest of characters, and this may have been the reason that Stockton, like other officers, bought a slave. He arranged the purchase of a teenaged "mulatto" named Rachel in St. Louis that fall, a domestic servant for Maria. The northern forts were home to small communities of slaves because of this practice—Stockton's brother-in-law, Garland, a Virginian, was a typical example of an army officer-slave owner. Rachel was brought to the Stocktons as they were on their way back to Ft. Snelling, and she was their servant for the next four years, accompanying them to Washington and back to Ft. Crawford. But Rachel got pregnant and gave birth to a son, James Henry, in the spring of 1834. Now Stockton decided he no longer needed a slave. "I sold Rachel having taken her with me to St. Louis, Missouri for that purpose," he wrote later. Undoubtedly, he thought this was the last he would hear of Rachel.[5]

Stockton had been a quartermaster, or supply officer, in the early years of his career, but soon he was assigned to supervise building projects as a topographical engineer in the Great Lakes region, work he continued as a civilian agent of the War Department after resigning from the army. He was elected mayor in Michigan City, Indiana, and eventually moved to Flint, Michigan, where he, John Garland, and other heirs of controversial fur trader Jacob Smith claimed ownership of land due his actions. Smith, who died in 1825, had lined up property there for his children in his dealings with the U.S. and the Chippewa leaders in the early 1800s, and his heirs won the subsequent legal and political struggle for that land; it was why Stockton eventually moved to Flint in the late 1830s, to sell and develop his wife's property.[6]

In the meantime, the young woman who'd been Stockton's slave did not disappear into obscurity—at least not yet. Rachel had been sold by Stockton to an intermediary in St. Louis, who in turn sold her to a slave dealer named William Walker; Rachel claimed Walker beat and assaulted her, and intended to sell her and her young son "down the river" to New Orleans. But Rachel learned about the experiences of other slaves taken north into states and territories where slavery was illegal under federal law; incredible as this may seem, she started a legal battle for her freedom since Missouri allowed slaves, as "poor persons," to bring suit. Stockton's involvement in this case was only a letter in which he described his purchase of Rachel as a personal servant for his family, and how he took her to what became Wisconsin and Minnesota, and to the nation's capital, before selling her.

Rachel's attorney argued that because she had been brought North to "free soil" by Stockton, she was now free. Stockton, he charged, did not have the right to violate federal law by expanding slavery to a place where it was not allowed. Walker's lawyer countered that Stockton, as an army officer, had no choice as to his duty assignment; he should not have to forfeit his "property"—Rachel—because he had been temporarily detained on free soil, a place that was not his permanent residence. Rachel therefore remained a slave, Walker's counsel maintained.

Rachel lost her case in the local circuit court, but appealed to the Supreme Court of Missouri, which ruled in her favor in 1836—she was free. *Rachel v. Walker* was an important legal precedent for the next twenty years, establishing that a slave, outside of states or territories where slavery was allowed, *was no longer a slave.* Rachel became, for a time, the embodiment of the tenet "once free, always free."[7]

What became of Rachel after her victory is unknown, but her former master, Stockton, continued working as an engineering officer and civilian agent over the next decade. Biographical materials say he was "applying to go back into the army" when war broke out with Mexico in 1846, probably meaning he offered to command a new regiment forming after the border dispute in Texas between Mexico and the Democratic administration of James A. Polk turned violent. But it was not until the fall of 1847 that Michigan Gov. William Greenly, also a Democrat, was asked by the War Department to raise a full regiment from Michigan; he commissioned Stockton colonel to command the 1st Michigan Infantry, the only state regiment sent to the conflict.

It was a painfully slow process, recruiting soldiers and traveling to the scene of the war, and it was over as the 1st Michigan arrived in Mexico. The regiment served as an occupying force and supply train guard, with Stockton appointed military governor of the town of Cordova. Though they were never in combat like other state men who served in companies that fought and defeated the Mexican army, scores of 1st Michigan soldiers died of disease—the terrible reality for so many nineteenth-century armies. Stockton's brother-in-law in the regular army, now brevet Brigadier General John Garland, was severely wounded by what today would be called guerilla sniper fire. Garland's soon-to-be sons-in-law, brevet Majors James Longstreet and George Deas—future Confederate officers of importance—were both wounded in combat in Mexico. The subsequent marriages of Longstreet and Deas to Garland's daughters, Louisa and Bessie, nieces of Maria Stockton, meant Col. Stockton was an uncle of sorts to the young soldiers.[8]

Stockton returned to Flint after the war and then moved his family to California in the Gold Rush era of the early 1850s, building telegraph lines and engineering mines, and holding the federal post of customs collector in San Francisco. By the time he moved back to Michigan in 1858, the Supreme Court of the United States had handed down one of the most infamous and controversial decisions in its history—a case in which the 1830s circumstances of Stockton and his former slave Rachel were part of the argument over legal precedent.[9]

That overtly political and stunning court decision was, of course, the 1857 Dred Scott case. Like Rachel, Scott was a slave who had been taken into a Northern state or territory where slavery was illegal, by a physician who received an appointment as an army doctor. But at the Supreme Court, Chief Justice Roger Taney and a majority of justices, who favored slave owners, rejected and wiped out previous case law, and all state and federal laws that extended any rights to blacks. Slaves or ex-slaves had no rights, they ruled, and any law restricting slavery was unconstitutional. Taney thought he was putting an end to the increasingly divisive question of slavery in the United States, but the decision, with its hard reactionary and sectional turn, only inflamed feelings among abolitionists and Northerners unsympathetic to slave owners. It galvanized Republicans, contributing to Lincoln's election in 1860, which in turn led the Southern slave-holding states to secede, their leaders convinced that the election of a "Black Republican" was the first step in the North's ending slavery.

Was it Stockton's past slave ownership that tainted and disqualified him, in the eyes of Austin Blair, from leading a Michigan regiment as the Civil War began? Stockton and the case of Rachel were only mentioned in the hundreds of pages of the Dred Scott decision. Yet it is hard to imagine that Blair, a founding member of the Republican Party, dedicated abolitionist, lawyer, and politician, who had spent his earliest professional life fighting for equal rights for African-Americans, did not know or hear about Stockton's history, especially given that *Rachel v. Walker* had been an important "freedom case" and precedent for two decades.

A Democrat, Stockton almost certainly had not supported Lincoln or Blair in 1860, and his war diary and letters would show that he was not sympathetic to abolitionists or slaves. Yet he felt secession was treason and had to be stopped. Men of this view were soon called "War Democrats." In Flint, his party's newspaper, the *Genesee Democrat,* noting his military qualifications, wrote a brief endorsement of Stockton, a short editorial that was copied and republished without comment by the paper's arch-rival, the Republican *Wolverine Citizen.* The governor was not moved. "Quite a number of gentlemen have made a like tender [offer] with yourself," Blair diplomatically replied, "and I think it advisable to take a little time for consultation before offering a commission."[10]

Stockton figured that Blair would consult with the Michigan's new adjutant general, Detroit's John Robertson, about such appointments—the adjutant general was the state's military affairs administrator and advisor to the governor. "Now as he will of course consult with you among others," Stockton wrote Robertson, "I would be gratified if *you* who have known him for so long would give your influence. This regiment is to be called into *immediate* service and you will know that its field officers at least should be perfectly competent to drill and command. . . . There will be little or no spare time to learn. It may be called into action within ten days after muster. With inexperienced commanders, what will be the result?"[11]

But when Robertson issued to him his first official assignment of the war four days later, it was far short of what Stockton had in mind: "I have appointed you Depot Quartermaster and assigned you to duty according to your rank, subject to orders of the Quartermaster General," Robertson wrote. In other words, Stockton was being put in charge of managing military supplies coming into Michigan on trains.[12]

April turned to May, and Michigan's contribution to the war effort grew to four infantry regiments with state plans for more. But while other Michigan men who were Democrats got commissions (like Dwight Woodbury of Adrian, to command the 4th Michigan), Stockton received no appointment. Even Stockton's hometown militia company was chosen to go into the new 2nd Michigan Infantry Regiment as he waited. He pressed the governor again, but Blair's next response left Stockton furious: The governor claimed he had heard Michigan volunteers were not willing to serve under the colonel. In response, Stockton visited seven of the ten companies that were forming the new 5th Michigan Infantry Regiment, asking these men to sign statements that they would serve under him.

"Enclosed I present to you several acquiescences [sic, approvals] of the *ten* companies attached to the 5th Infantry indicating their *desire* to serve the United States for *three* years *under* me as their *Colonel,*" he wrote to Blair, "thus complying on my part with your request and proving, I trust, that the rumors none were willing to serve under me *are and were false*. . . . I have not had time to see the other three. As however, these seven are clear and over the majority, I presume it will be unnecessary for me to go further and satisfy you. I am *not* so very *unpopular* as has been represented to you."[13]

The War Department had just lengthened the term of enlistments of volunteers from three months to three years, and some men willing to serve ninety days reportedly balked at the prospect of a three-year hitch. Stockton's point was that the men of these companies, knowing about the longer enlistment term, did not object to him as their commander. But this was not enough for Blair. May passed into June, and Stockton had time to leave Detroit's busy military camps to return to Flint and complain to the city council about a street drain that was damaging his property.

The next day, June 5, Stockton's brother-in-law, widower and veteran U.S. Army officer John Garland, died in New York City. According to family lore, Garland, though a Virginian, remained loyal to the United States to the end, and counseled his soldier sons-in-law, James Longstreet and George Deas, not to join the rebellion. But they ignored his counsel, resigned from the army, and became officers of the Confederacy. Stockton would face Longstreet in the coming battles of Gaines' Mill and Fredericksburg, Virginia. Because these Confederates jointly owned property in Flint and elsewhere in Michigan through their wives, along with other Garland family members, U.S. marshals from Detroit in the near future would file writs seizing their interest in these lots.[14]

Days after John Garland's death, he was buried with military honors in Georgetown's Oak Hill Cemetery, Washington, D.C., next to his wife Harriet, the eldest sister of Maria Stockton. Accompanying his casket and firing the graveside salute were the 12th New York Militia Regiment under Col. Dan Butterfield and a light artillery battery commanded by Capt. Charles Griffin, prominent commanders in the Union army in the months ahead.[15] Whether the Stocktons got to Washington in time to attend Garland's funeral is not clear. Regardless, Stockton had important business in the nation's capital. Three days after his brother-in-law was buried, Stockton took his case for a regimental command to the president of the United States.

Postwar accounts of Stockton say he met face-to-face with Abraham Lincoln to offer his services to lead a regiment in this new war. A presidential memorandum dated June 13 suggests Lincoln was impressed. "I think it entirely safe to accept a fifth regiment from

Michigan," the president wrote to Secretary of War Simon Cameron, "and with your approbation I should say a regiment presented by Col. T. B. W. Stockton, ready for service within two weeks from now, will be received. Look at Colonel Stockton's testimonials." One of Stockton's supporters was the Rev. Henry Ward Beecher, a leading abolitionist cleric, who personally directed Stockton to the president. "Ought not such a man as the one I send to you, Col. T. B. W. Stockton, of Michigan, a *West Point graduate,* a colonel in the *Mexican War,* to have a chance in this great war, with a thousand men at his back?" Beecher asked Lincoln. How Beecher knew Stockton is not clear, but Beecher said he wanted *all* soldiers available to come to the aid of the U.S. government, whether they were sent by governors or not.[16]

The secretary of war telegraphed Gov. Blair the day after Lincoln and Stockton met. "Sir; a regiment under the command of Col. T. B. W. Stockton, of Michigan, has been offered to this Department for acceptance to serve for three years or during the war," Cameron wrote. "The President is willing to accept this regiment if it meets with your approbation, and if it can be got ready for service, full, thoroughly organized and uniformed within two weeks from this date."[17]

Stockton returned to Detroit with a copy of Cameron's message—proof that the president himself wanted Stockton to lead a state regiment for federal service. As a veteran soldier, the colonel probably could not imagine that Blair would say no to the president in this time of crisis. But Cameron's telegram and Lincoln's message were not orders, only requests—and Austin Blair was not changing his mind. It was after this rejection, according to a history of Stockton's hometown, that the governor finally said Stockton could form and lead his own regiment, but with a key condition: The state of Michigan was not paying for it. Unlike other regiments organized in his home state, Stockton would have to put up collateral to cover the cost of organizing and supplying his regiment until it was mustered into federal service.[18]

Of course, simply feeding and supplying the basic needs for hundreds of men, even short term, would cost a huge sum. Stockton could not agree to this—to him, this was another insult and obstacle placed in his path by Gov. Blair. It seemed then, in the summer of 1861, that Stockton was going nowhere.

Then the Union army's crushing defeat at the battle at Bull Run in Virginia on July 21 changed everything. The rout of Northern soldiers left Washington vulnerable; with that disaster, the question of a regiment led by Stockton was wrested out of the hands of Austin Blair. The federal government needed soldiers, and right away. The next day the secretary of war telegraphed Stockton, bypassing the governor. "I will consent to accept a full regiment under your command and request that you will use every effort to have it mustered into service in three weeks from this date," Cameron messaged the Flint colonel.[19]

With those words, Blair's opposition to Stockton no longer mattered. Though the Lincoln administration did not necessarily want to trump Blair's authority, the national crisis and the need for troops mattered more than the governor's prerogatives and prejudices. The Democratic *Detroit Free Press* urged volunteer companies to rendezvous, or gather, for the formation of Stockton's regiment. But it would take time for the government to send supplies and equipment to the new regiment, so "all expenses, until mustered into service, will have to borne by the company," a newspaper reported. In other words, Stockton's officers and men still had to pay their own way until they were sworn into U.S. service. But quickly the paper said "some of our most prominent citizens" stepped up to support Stockton's forming regiment.[20]

Notices went out around the state, urging volunteers to join Stockton's regiment, and recruiting offices opened in Detroit and Flint. The *Free Press* hailed the news. "He [Stockton] understands his duty, which is far more than can be said of many called to command of regiments," the paper sniffed, referring to Union officers who had not been able to keep their men from fleeing at Bull Run. Stockton also asked certain Michigan men to raise companies.[21]

As volunteers and companies came to Detroit to join Stockton's regiment, the feud between Stockton and Blair burst into the partisan press. The colonel's supporters noted that he had the endorsements of prominent men, both Republicans and Democrats, yet the governor had refused to let him lead state troops. Blair soon was hearing of some voters' anger about his treatment of Stockton.[22]

That same day, in a telegram sent to the governors of Michigan and the Northern states, an anxious secretary of war stressed that Lincoln wanted *all* available regiments immediately sent to Washington. In words that could have applied directly to Stockton's regiment, Cameron reminded the governors the Union needed soldiers as soon as possible. "To ensure the movement of troops more rapid than might otherwise be done," Cameron suggested, "you will please confer with and aid all officers of independent regiments." In a second telegram that day Cameron stressed the point directly to Blair. Blair was furious. He thundered back:

> I desire to say a word which is not appropriate for the telegraph. It is to make an earnest appeal to you to recognize no more independent regiments in this state. They are introducing confusion and discord into all our affairs. Companies are divided and officers in unseemly quarrels. I will furnish all the troops you call for much sooner and in better order than these independent regiments can do, and thus avert a great amount of local ill feeling.[23]

Was there discord and chaos in independent regiments? Or was the governor concerned that "local ill feeling" about Stockton's regiment was political damage to himself? If Blair was concerned that Stockton was once a slave owner, why didn't he say so publicly? Even if Stockton's previous slave ownership somehow did not enter in to Blair's opposition, Stockton was a Democrat, and hard-line abolitionists like Blair, soon called "Radical Republicans," distrusted northern Democrats; for decades Democrats had favored compromise in the struggles between slave states and free states, or had supported slave-holding interests.

There can be little question that Blair was also unhappy that the Lincoln administration allowed Stockton to form his own regiment. Issuing commissions to Michigan men, such as local politicians, business men, lawyers, and others who wanted to serve as officers in state regiments, was a potent political tool for the governor. Michigan's Bruce Catton wrote that the system of creating state regiments and then "federalizing" them was cumbersome, but the power to appoint officers "provided a governor with a handy form of political patronage." But not in the case of Stockton; perhaps to soothe angry feelings in the colonel's hometown, the governor gave command of another new regiment, the 8th Michigan Infantry, to a leading local Democrat and former lieutenant governor, William M. Fenton.[24]

Stockton enjoyed his moment of triumph, pledging to "*prove* myself, in *every way*." He installed himself at the Michigan Exchange hotel as volunteers for his regiment arrived in Detroit; they were sent to a camp set up on the state fairgrounds, and it was here that the companies of Stockton's regiment rendezvoused. In Flint, attorney Thomas C. Carr built a company around a village militia outfit grandly called the Flushing Light Artillery. For recruiting purposes, Carr renamed the company the Genesee Light Guard to encompass the county. But company names like this meant nothing to the U.S. Army, and these Flint area volunteers were soon designated Company C in Stockton's command.[25]

At 5 feet, 4 inches tall, the youngest and smallest member of Company C was a blue-eyed, dark-haired 16-year-old from Shiawassee County, George Sidman, who had come with his family from Onondaga County, New York. Sidman first tried joining, as a drummer boy, a local company called the Ingersoll Rifles in April, but it was not mustered into service (meaning it had not been formally placed in a Michigan regiment) until months later. Sidman's parents were divorced, and he had a record of running away from home; fearing he might miss all the excitement, he joined Stockton's regiment. "Having a suspicion that my mother might interfere with my ardent wishes, I left the Rifles and went to Flint, where on Aug. 1, 1861, I enlisted as a drummer," Sidman recounted later. Of course, the lad lied about his age. "I gave my age as 18 to the mustering officer," he admitted, "but I was not yet 17." Many youths did the same, he said; it was necessary for adventuresome boys to get into the army without their parents' permission.[26]

A prominent Detroit man from the city's Fifth Ward, Thomas Barry, who had served in the ninety-day 1st Michigan Infantry, traveled to the mining districts of the Upper Peninsula along with men named George Swan and George Prentiss to recruit most of the men who would make up Company A of Stockton's regiment. One recruit living in Ontonagon was John G. Berry, 23, a farm laborer who, like so many Michigan residents of that time, was born in New York; he would keep a diary through most of the war. Thomas Barry became captain of the company, with Swan and Prentiss his lieutenants. These recruits called themselves the Lake Superior Light Guard, and many were of German descent; ninety of them sailed down to Detroit on the *City of Cleveland*. An editor hailed the Upper Peninsula's "noble example, for all portions of the state to imitate."[27]

Benjamin Franklin Fisher, a 40-year-old insurance man and captain of the Saginaw Valley Guard Company from East Saginaw, figured he and his men would join the 8th Michigan Infantry Regiment, then forming. They ended up designated for Stockton's regiment. "The company is composed of seventy-nine strong, able-bodied men and sixteen officers," a newspaper said. "Many of them have been engaged as lumbermen and thereby become *disciplined* to the most severe hardships." The company boarded the steamship *Forest Queen* after speeches and band music and pulled into Lake Huron for Detroit "amid cheers and touching adieus."

There they were joined by a group of Lenawee County men under Theodore S. Mahan, their leader from the town of Adrian and son of the president of the local college. With the Saginaw men, they became Company D in Stockton's regiment, with Fisher as their captain and Mahan as first lieutenant.[28]

A member of Company D was 20-year-old Francis D. Keeler, whose father was a contractor and commissioner of streets in Saginaw, a salt mining and lumber town of 1,500. His friends of course called him Frank. "We arrived this morning at the foot of Woodward Avenue with ninety-three men, all well and cheerful," Keeler wrote his parents.

> Col. Stockton came on board and told us our quarters were ready so we formed in a double file and marched up to the fairgrounds through the rain. . . . Breakfast was soon announced and we were marched into an adjoining building and seated at a rough table without spread. Our breakfast consisted of good [soft] bread, hard bread, beef steak, liver, boiled potatoes, butter and coffee all of which were as good as we could expect, so no fault was found. We are well quartered in a comfortable board shanty, shingled, battened and floored, and everything is as comfortable as circumstances will permit.[29]

These quarters were in the Floral Hall on the state fairgrounds, said a comrade from Saginaw County, 18-year-old Alfred Wellington. Wellington enlisted with his older brother Sam, 25; he disagreed with Keeler, declaring that "most of us can't eat" the fresh meat and questioning whether the coffee and tea served at meals, prepared by twenty black employees, was *really* coffee and tea at all. By that second week of August, there were about 350 men in the camp so far, Keeler wrote, "some drilling, some making bunks, etc., none drunk."[30]

An Irish-born Detroiter, 42-year-old Stephen Martin, immediately opened a recruiting office on Michigan Avenue; he called his new company the Willcox Guard in honor of Orlando Willcox, a lawyer and veteran who'd just commanded the 1st Michigan Infantry Regiment and was captured at Bull Run. Martin brought into the service his son John, who'd been born in Brooklyn. Martin's men would become Company H in Stockton's command. Stephen Martin was its captain, though at least one conflicting report stated this company, however briefly, was led by a man from Lansing.

Some of this company were Detroit men, but one enlistee who ended up serving in it was a farm boy from near Grand Ledge, a small town about twelve miles from Lansing. His name was George Washington Ervay; according to family historians he was 16 and had a third-grade education. Like other young volunteers, he lied about his age to enlist, initially in his regiment's Company E and later transferring to "H." His letters would soon reveal he was thrilled, at first, to be a solider in what he considered a great adventure.[31]

Detroit's Charles H. Salter, 21, had just served as a private in the ninety-day 1st Michigan that got a taste of combat at Bull Run. Like many of these veterans, Salter was considered officer material because he had three months of army life and experience under fire. Salter spent the early years of his life with his grandparents in Albion, New York, after his mother died; his father moved to Detroit, remarried, and eventually sent for Charles, then six. The lad worked as a grocery store manager before enlisting in the Detroit Light Guard, a militia unit that became Company A in the 1st Michigan.[32]

After Bull Run and the mustering out of that ninety-day regiment, Salter returned to Detroit with his comrades on August 1. Less than a week later, he was made a second lieutenant in Stockton's regiment in a company called the Ruehle Guards, named for the colonel's second-in-command, Lt. Col. John V. Ruehle, a Mexican War veteran, Detroiter, and German-born immigrant. The Ruehle Guards became Company E, led by Robert T. Elliott of Detroit, another veteran of the 1st Michigan and a former leader in Detroit's "old Number 2 fire company." In accepting his position with Stockton's regiment, Salter went to work as a recruiter at 38 Woodward Avenue. For the next four years, Salter would regularly write letters to his friends, the prominent Duffield family of Detroit.[33]

Company F was a mix of men, some recruited in Detroit, Calhoun County, and other communities by James Dafoe and William B. Rowe of Plymouth and Solomon P. Brockway of Albion. None of these officers would serve long with Stockton's regiment. Dafoe, their captain, would resign in less than a year—he would give illness as his reason, though a letter sent to Gov. Blair indicated he disagreed with Col. Stockton's constant criticism of Republican leaders. Brockway, son of the regiment's chaplain, would resign because of a seniority dispute with another officer, while Roe would soon find himself "detached" or reassigned to the Union army's signal service.

One man who was soon in Company F, a dry goods clerk from Hillsdale, at first hoped he could be one of the traveling merchants who accompanied regiments into the field. "Is there any chance of a person, properly recommended, getting the position of sutler in one of the three regiments now formed in the state?" Butler Brown asked the state adjutant general. But instead of becoming a sutler, Brown and others from his area joined another independent regiment forming there under Col. William May. The formation of that independent regiment, however, was stalled by the objection of Gov. Blair, so Brown and some of his fellow volunteers were soon assigned to Company F of Stockton's regiment.[34]

Like Company F, Company G's officers and men came from different towns—Capt. Charles Meyers was from Detroit, another veteran sergeant from the 1st Michigan; Lt. Jacob Webber or Weber, a militia officer from Lansing; and Lt. Frank Eddy from Flint. Webber had been trying to get a military appointment from Blair since April, when he organized what he hoped would be an artillery company, but now took his men into Stockton's regiment. Some of Col. May's recruits from south-central Michigan also ended up in Company G.[35]

Other men wound up in Stockton's outfit more by accident than by choice. The colonel had been after Thomas Morris, a 26-year-old Saginaw man probably known to Stockton through the militia, to be his regiment's adjutant (a kind of military executive assistant).

Morris was hoping for an officer's position in whichever regiment was leaving first for the fight, and he consented to go with Stockton's regiment a few days after Bull Run.[36]

In the wake of that Union defeat, the citizens of Greenville, Michigan, wrote to the governor in support of a commission for Michael Chittick, a 38-year-old veteran of the Mexican War; he did not get it. But Chittick soon signed on to a company that was forming with men from Ionia and surrounding communities under Capt. Henry Sibley and his lieutenants, Guy W. Fuller and Morris B. Wells. They called themselves the Ionia Union Guards but were soon Company B in Stockton's regiment. Chittick was fated to die at the second battle of Bull Run.[37]

Stockton's regiment got its own musicians in September when the Steuben Guards Band of Ann Arbor joined. Some of its members had belonged to the band of the ninety-day 1st Michigan, an ensemble reported to have been one of the Union army's finest, as well as a favorite of President Lincoln's when the regiment arrived in Washington back in the spring. The Steuben Guards Band surely impressed Frank Keeler. "We have got a band that can almost raise a person off his feet," he told his parents. Not everyone agreed. "We have got a band in our regiment that can't play worth a cuss," complained Private Marion Munson of Company E, a more critical young farmhand from Avon Township in Oakland County.[38]

But what would be the name of this new, independent regiment? Regiments authorized by the state were numbered; Stockton's regiment was not, since it had been formed on the authority of the U.S. government. Initially, Detroit's Democratic newspaper referred to Stockton's regiment as the "Cass regiment," named for Lewis Cass, Michigan's once formidable but now elderly national statesman.[39] Cass had been an architect of political compromise on the issue of slavery, and a one-time presidential candidate. A leading Democrat in his day, he had resigned as secretary of state from the cabinet of Lincoln's predecessor, President James Buchanan. When Buchanan refused to take action against the secessionists, Cass returned to Detroit, infirm and despairing of the coming war. But the name "Cass" did not stick, perhaps dropped by Stockton. Capt. Stephen Martin, one of the first to recruit for the regiment, posed the question to the colonel: What was this regiment going to be called? Stockton, apparently impressed with Martin, replied that he would have the privilege of giving the regiment its name. "Then it shall be Stockton's Independent Regiment," Martin reportedly said.[40]

For his regimental staff, Stockton chose John V. Ruehle, a friend and fellow veteran of the Mexican War, as his lieutenant colonel. His regimental surgeon was an old Democratic Party friend and pioneering Michigan physician, Dr. Isaac Wixom, who lived in Genesee County's Argentine Township. Wixom was "acknowledged to be most heroic of surgeons and a man of large experience," the *East Saginaw Courier* wrote. Wixom, 58, had already secured a place in Michigan's medical history by performing what his associates and friends believed (wrongly, as it turned out) the first successful amputation of a man's leg at the hip joint in 1845. In fact, the procedure had been done by another surgeon back in 1824. Wixom served in the state legislature for years, but now he actively recruited for Stockton's regiment, bringing in men of his community for whom he had provided medical care all their lives.[41]

The regiment's assistant surgeon, William Butler, came from upstate New York and probably knew Stockton or Wixom. The chaplain was William Brockway, a Michigan Methodist leader, former missionary, and state legislator from Albion, while the adjutant was Thomas Morris, the young man from Saginaw who had some military schooling experience under his belt.

But there was a delay in the announcement of Stockton's major, the third-highest officer's post in a regiment. The name of the major was left blank when Stockton announced his other appointments in mid-August, and it was not until five days later that he revealed his choice: Norval E. Welch, a handsome, strong-willed lawyer, 26, from Ann Arbor, who had once served as an assistant to Lewis Cass. According to a man who knew him, Welch was "the embodiment of physical beauty, ruddy with health, overflowing with animal spirits, ready for a frolic, apt with the dumb-bells or boxing gloves."[42]

That description came from James Kidd, who would finish out the Civil War as a cavalry general. Kidd told of how Cass had hired Welch "on the spot" to be his personal secretary a few years before the war. "It is related of him that on an occasion when he [Welch] was in Detroit, he happened to walk by the residence of General Cass, who was then, I believe one of the United States senators from Michigan," Kidd wrote. Cass was supposedly so impressed that he immediately offered the young man a job. Welch served him until the old man went into the cabinet of James Buchanan, when Welch returned to study law at the University of Michigan, class of 1860. He was one of three children, but after his father's death in 1855 he was said to have solely provided for his mother; by 1861, he was living in Detroit and involved in local courts.[43]

However impressive Welch had seemed to Cass, he may not have been Stockton's first choice for major. A Detroit newspaper mentioned a different local man was going to get that appointment, but he instead became an officer in a cavalry regiment.[44] Did Stockton have to be persuaded to give Welch that appointment? The colonel appointed friends and acquaintances to other staff posts, yet there is nothing in the historical record to suggest such a relationship with Welch, other than that both men were War Democrats.

Perhaps it was only a coincidence, but an August newspaper advertised that a "Mr. Welch" was holding a weekend "trotting match"—horse racing—at Detroit's riding park on Woodward Avenue, located at the state fairgrounds where Stockton's regiment was rendezvousing. Was "Mr. Welch" Norval Welch? Had he and Stockton met at an afternoon horse race?[45]

However it happened, the relationship between Stockton and his major would prove to be a strange subplot in the regiment's story. Within a short time of the regiment taking the field, relations between the men would turn cool, then rocky and finally adversarial. In the months ahead, Stockton would try to have Welch cashiered, while Welch would suffer the hard judgment of history for his conduct at what for years was considered a critical moment of the Civil War.

As soon as companies arrived in Detroit, training began for the raw recruits. For Stockton's men, this was at the new military base at the fairgrounds, now called Camp Backus after Lt. Col. Electus Backus of the "regular army," a veteran and War Department liaison. One of Backus's jobs was to muster state volunteers into the federal service, swearing them in to serve three years. "Today we commenced drilling," Frank Keeler wrote the day after arriving, "and we were marched up in front of the quarters and examined one by one. We all passed with the exception of about six or eight of them, and among them was Charley Voorheis, who was too young." The recruits reformed into line and the Saginaw men were administered the oath by Backus. "Not one refused," Keeler wrote, though six men from what he called "the Plymouth company" (probably Company F) refused to be sworn. Keeler did not say what happened to these men, but they were probably ejected from camp.

The volunteers soon learned the facts of army life. Stockton ordered that bunks and tents were to be put in order immediately after reveille, with the grounds and buildings swept clean; a general inspection followed. And there was to be no loud talking during meals, and "all or any disorderly conduct" was to be promptly reported. Frank Keeler did not mind. "Our officers are kind and considerate, careful to keep the quarters clean and to require the men to keep clean and neat," he wrote. Stockton wanted the men's hair cut short and combed. Drilling—the fundamental army exercise of marching, turning, and shifting into different formations—took up hours each day, but with decent food and accommodations, Keeler had no complaint. "Each officer takes a squad and drills about an hour and a half or two hours, and then rests half an hour, just as they feel. I find I can drill a squad as well as any of them." Like many young volunteers, he was proud of his company and felt "we make the best appearance of any of the five companies in camp."[46]

Not all the enlistees had the clothing and personal supplies they needed, because some recruiting notices said, wrongly, the men would "immediately" be issued uniforms and equipment. Hurrying to Detroit and expecting to be provided with everything they would need, some men arrived at Camp Backus with nothing more than the clothes on their backs. Unfortunately, uniforms and other essentials, particularly washcloths and towels, had not arrived. Stockton turned to the public for help. "I appeal to the liberality and kindness of all, and more especially to the ladies," he wrote, "to supply whatever shirts, cotton or woolen, also a small sponge or two coarse towels to each man." These were indispensable for the men's cleanliness and health, he noted. "As *my* regiment is not supplied with any of the many conveniences provided by the state to state troops," he continued with a dig at Gov. Blair, "I trust that individuals will feel more liberal to these who have so patriotically joined my regiment."

Women from Detroit, Flint, Flushing, Parma, Wayne, and the Saginaw Valley and the citizens of Albion responded with blankets, clothes, bandages, hospital shirts, and other items. "The ladies of the city bring in shirts, socks, delicacies for the sick and many other little comforts for our men, visit the men in their bunks," Frank Keeler observed, "and I tell you they receive the gratitude of the soldiers." The clothing shortage eased in September when government supplies arrived, Stockton wrote, thanking the public for the contributions, though he noted that his men still required more "towels and sponges, which are still wanted."[47]

The arrival of regular army uniforms was news. "The coats and pants are of dark blue, the hat black felt and the overcoats of a light blue material," one paper noted. "They are much more handsome than the common blue or gray uniforms, provided for the other regiments, and said to be more durable."[48]

Sickness went hand-in-hand with military service. Perhaps Col. Stockton's requirement that his men wash and keep their hair short kept the sick list down that summer, but Frank Keeler noted there were "six or eight men" ill by mid-August; by the end of the month Maj. Welch set up a small hospital in a "neat little white house" about 700 feet away from the recruits' quarters, where the sick received care. Keeler felt that the change in drinking water and the consumption of apples were the causes of the men's "complaint" (meaning diarrhea). He felt the water at the camp was good, though he did not drink much of it. "I drink scarcely a pint of water though the 24 hours, but have good coffee with milk and sugar and all I want," he said.[49]

Young Keeler was made corporal, and he enjoyed the perquisites of rank. "I find that my office secures to me a great many privileges," he told his parents. "I am entitled to the counter-sign (password). Last Thursday and Thursday night, I served as corporal of the guard. My business was to change signals every two hours during the twenty-four. The next twelve I was corporal of police; my duties were light."

Camp was quiet on Sunday mornings. Keeler told his parents he hadn't the opportunity to feel homesick, but he admitted on his second week away that he missed them. "I just heard a baby crying, which sounded like Hattie's voice, which being engaged in writing to you made me involuntarily lookup to satisfy myself I was not at home," he wrote. "There are a great many ladies in the camp and if there is one thing that will make me home-sick sooner than another, it is the sight of a baby." He had to shake those feelings off, he knew. "I hope for the best, determined to meet the trials and difficulties as bravely as I can." He added an odd anecdote about a minister from Pennsylvania who had preached to the men, then enlisted, and somehow managed to get drunk.[50]

As September came on there were presentations of swords and sashes by citizens from Detroit and elsewhere to favorite sons in the new regiment. A delegation came from the Flint area to present a sword and belt to Lt. Randolph W. Ransom, from Flushing, in Company C. Another group came from Detroit's Fifth Ward to the parade grounds to present a sword and sash to Capt. Thomas Barry, and so did the friends of Stephen Martin. These ceremonies were marked by patriotic speeches. "Now that our beloved country is in danger . . . I feel called upon to hasten to the aid of my country in this hour of peril," Barry said to his friends. "Now as I go forth with the brave men who are with me, this mark of your confidence and regard inspires me with a new determination to do my duty faithfully." Barry was a better speech maker than Martin, who said he lacked the words to thank his supporters. Drawing his new sword from its scabbard, Martin commented on "its spotless purity," and that it should return "without a stain upon its surface," perhaps a pledge that he would not dishonor the gift from his friends.[51]

But the regiment's time in Detroit was ending as mid-September approached. Stockton knew his regiment was leaving soon, so he directed the men spend all available time in drill. "No furloughs or leaves of absence will be granted for longer than during the day," he ordered, "and that [will be] limited from after guard mounting until evening parade, except for some extreme and urgent cause."[52]

That day, the secretary of war wired Austin Blair and other Northern governors: Put in rapid march to Washington "all organized regiments under your control." Blair, perhaps still smarting from the editorial and political criticism Stockton's regiment caused him, questioned the semantics of Cameron's directive. "By the words, 'organized regiments,'" Blair asked, "do you intend me immediately to forward all state regiments, whether full or part full, and also independent infantry and cavalry regiments raising within the state by direct instructions to the colonels from the war department?"

Blair had been avoiding any involvement with Stockton, but Cameron's answer was sharp: The federal government expected Blair to immediately start for Washington the reorganized 1st Michigan Infantry (now a 3-year regiment) and Stockton's regiment. "Use such authority as may be necessary to fill these regiments from any men now mustered into service," Cameron directed, perhaps annoyed he still had to explain that the government needed all available soldiers. "Secure transportation and forward immediately. Answer what we may expect from Michigan."[53]

Adjutant General John Robertson immediately sent instructions—Stockton's regiment was to depart for Washington on the following Monday. But in passing along the instructions, Robertson's order made no mention to the first part of the order from the secretary of war—the filling up of Stockton's regiment with companies of Michigan troops who mustered into federal service, but who had not yet been assigned to a regiment. As Stockton's regiment prepared to leave, it had a total of 761 troops. With the addition of 80-some men from the independent regiment that was forming in south central Michigan under Col. William May, Stockton would soon have 840 men—still short of the 1,000-man standard. Stockton would later accuse Blair of ignoring the first part of Cameron's message.[54]

But at last they were leaving. On the evening of September 15, a large crowd came to camp to watch the regiment's final Sunday battalion parade. "I begin to think a soldier is no ordinary man when I see the crowd gathered on the ground to witness our parade," Keeler said. "I will venture to say there were over a thousand persons facing our battalion tonight counting women and children and all, and when our band marched down and back in front, the scene was well worth coming two or three miles to witness."[55]

The next day the regiment quickly packed. "We left in such a hurry that I had no time to ever bid you goodbye," Lt. Charles Salter of Detroit later apologized to friends. "The notice was entirely unexpected," the *Free Press* reported,

> but it very suddenly infused new vigor into the men and they were about making their preparations with an alacrity that overcame all obstacles. . . . The scene at the camp was necessarily a busy one. The men worked with a will and the officers with the double burden of their private affairs and official duties, for once, dispensed with the usual custom of eating thrice a day and from morning until night labored without a moment's cessation.[56]

At 4 p.m. on the 16th, the regiment marched onto the parade ground as the crowd pressed around. The soldiers created a space in the throng and into it stepped a federal official, Judge Ross Wilkins, and several prominent Detroit women and kin, with a grand new regimental flag for Stockton's regiment. Wilkins, holding the flag in his hands, stepped onto a platform set up for the occasion. The banner was made of heavy blue silk, six feet-by-six-and-a-half feet; on one side was the state seal with the words "Stockton's Regiment" beneath. The other side was the national eagle and shield, with the words "Stand by the Union and the Constitution" on a scroll. The flag's edges were mounted with a heavy gold fringe, and a carved eagle with outstretched wings perched on the flag staff.

Wilkins addressed the regiment. "This ensign combines the insignia of the state and the Union blended in harmony together," the judge said, "representing state sovereignty of the Union. They must stand or fall together; they breathe the same spirit, and have the same object in view—protection to civil and religious liberty and to the rights of property, and individual industry, and they both exist by and in and through the Union of all the States." The Constitution and the Union had to stand together, Wilkins continued; destroy the Union and there would be no government. "Destroy the government and the Union is severed forever. Stand then, by both. There is no middle course. No compromises can be made with armed rebellion." The soldiers, he said, must uphold the constitutional authority of the government.[57]

Wilkins passed the flag to Mrs. Charles Dunks, the leader of the women's flag donation effort, who presented it to Stockton. "Ladies," he said, "in behalf of my regiment and myself I accept this honor as a token of your regard and confidence for myself and those under me. It is more the duty of a solider to act than to speak, and as the time for action has arrived you must expect no lengthened remarks from me. When we return—if we ever do return—I hope we shall, in defending that banner and the Union of the States, have reflected honor upon ourselves, our state and you." Stockton turned to Company C. "Sgt. McDowell," he said to a 42-year-old man who'd enlisted a month earlier. "You have been selected to bear these colors, and sir, never let them be lowered in the face of the foe or surrendered to rebel or traitor while life shall be given you."[58]

The band played and the chaplain gave a benediction, and then another Detroit resident, George M. Danforth, stepped forward for one last presentation—a sword for Maj. Norval Welch from his friends. "We go forth to fight for the Constitution and the Union," Welch said after thanking them, "and if it is necessary to sacrifice my life in assisting, with this bright blade, to shield my country from death and dishonor, willingly will I yield it up."

There was only an hour left before their departure, so the men were dismissed to say their goodbyes to friends and family. At 6 p.m. they reformed and, led by their band, marched down Woodward Avenue to the docks on the Detroit River. Rain was falling now, but the sidewalks were crowded with well-wishers, and so were the wharves where the steamers *May Queen* and *City of Cleveland* were moored. Guards had to be posted to prevent civilians from rushing up the gangplanks to shake hands with the men "one last time." The *May Queen* left anchor first, about 7:30 p.m., as the band played "The Star-Spangled

Banner." Detroiters cheered from the docks while the departing soldiers cheered back from the deck rails. The steamer stopped briefly at a nearby dock for freight while her sister ship got underway. As darkness fell the steamers disappeared down the river, carrying the men of Stockton's Independent Regiment to war.[59]

2.

SEPTEMBER 1861–MARCH 1862

STOCKTON'S WORM-EATERS

The steamers arrived in Cleveland the next morning and Stockton's regiment boarded the train for Pittsburgh. "All along the route we were cheered by the people," Frank Keeler said. "Not a house did we pass but that somebody was at the door waving handkerchief, towel, dish cloth or anything else available, at all the stations we were cheered until we were out of hearing. Young ladies came to the cars when we stopped and shook hands with us, threw us kisses and waved their handkerchiefs."

Their cars clattered into Pittsburgh that night; the men were fed supper and immediately left for Harrisburg, arriving late in the afternoon of September 18. Here Stockton had been instructed to telegraph the adjutant general and the quartermaster general of the Union army; the regiment stayed here nearly twenty-four hours, joined by the additional volunteers assigned to Stockton. "The company from Col. May, only 83 strong, arrived this morning," he reported to Michigan's adjutant general. "Have the residue [rest] ordered on." What Stockton would soon realize is that the governor of Michigan was not sending him more men. It would take action by the federal government in the coming weeks to add more soldiers to his regiment.[1]

The rocky vistas on the way to Washington were striking for a young man who'd spent most of his life in the comparatively flat land of Saginaw Valley. "The scenery through Pennsylvania, I tell you it was GRAND," an enthusiastic Keeler wrote. "I can give you no idea of what I saw; mountains which reached above the clouds, to valleys down, down, oh, it was grand . . . I never expected to see so much in my life as I did from Detroit to here." At Harrisburg the men boarded the train for Baltimore, a city that had been the scene of violence against Northern soldiers traveling to Washington early in the war. Volunteers traveling through Baltimore that spring and summer were usually convinced they would be attacked by rabid secessionists, and Stockton's regiment was no exception. But when the soldiers decanted at 1 a.m. to march to another train station (where the tracks went south to Washington), all was calm since Rebel sympathizers had been suppressed. "As we passed down the street the stars and stripes were waved at us from every window, and the only exclamation or speeches heard were 'hurrah for Uncle Sam,'" Keeler noted. The regiment stopped in front of city hall for coffee, hard crackers, "and such cakes and gingerbreads as we had brought along," and then boarded the cars at daylight for Washington, where they arrived around noon of September 20.[2]

"We were fed, took a little rest and a good wash," Keeler continued. "Sgt. Silliman and myself, not being very tired, started up town to see the sights." (Sheffield Silliman, of Saginaw County, would survive the war and leave at the expiration of his three-year hitch.) They met a man who showed them through the Capitol building and again the sights thrilled Keeler, who called the House of Representatives and Senate chambers "gorgeous." He was "dazzled" by the paintings, marble walls, statues, gilded ceilings, and stained-glass windows.

From the unfinished dome Keeler could see more landmarks, including the Arlington home of Robert E. Lee, the former federal army officer who had sided with his home state of Virginia and the Confederacy back in the spring. He could also see a Rebel camp on Munson's Hill, Alexandria, in the distance, a reminder of just how close Confederate forces were, though now Union guns and infantry were posted to protect Washington. "All around the city are camps of soldiers, on the hills, in groves and out in the sun," he said. But his tour came to an end and the regiment marched 1½ miles to a location on Meridian Hill called Camp Casey, on the grounds of the Smithsonian Institution. As he did previously from Detroit, Keeler reported home about the food and housing:

> We have good bread, corned beef, coffee, sugar, soup, rice, soap, candles, bacon and ham. The meat has to be good or Col. Stockton won't have it issued. Our tents are comfortable and it rained last night but we slept dry in our canvas houses. Our men are nearly all well. . . . I suppose there will be a report at home that two of Capt. Fisher's men were poisoned here; it is not so. Two of our men had the cholera morbus as soon as they arrived . . . but they are both most well enough for duty today. . . . Our regiment officers are liked more and more every day; the men speak of Col. Stockton on the highest terms. He does everything he can for the comfort of the men. The Lt. Colonel [Ruehle] is said to be a good soldier; the men are ready to follow him anywhere. The adjutant [Morris] and the major [Welch] have the name of being expert and sharp figurers as well as good military men.[3]

Stockton was acting commander of a new brigade, a grouping or command of three to five regiments. A rumor circulated that his position would be permanent. Keeler wondered: Who would be the regiment's new colonel if that happened? There was also the question of weapons; the regiment still had no arms, and the men were looking forward to being issued rifles. "Then after a month's drill we will be ready to go over into 'Secesh,'" he wrote confidently. The world of soldiering for Keeler and the new volunteers, without bloodshed so far, was alive with excitement—the pounding of artillery somewhere on the other side of the Potomac, and the observation balloon rising into the sky from Washington's Chain Bridge to reconnoiter Rebel positions; rumors of spies added to the intrigue. "Yesterday some of the Zouaves [probably Pennsylvanian or New York troops wearing French Foreign Legion-style uniforms] captured three women 'seceshers' who were poisoning a spring close by," Keeler wrote as September waned, repeating what was likely one of the rumors the soldiers soon called "camp stories." "One of the women turned out to be a man. Four men, it is reported died from drinking from the poisoned spring. Sunday night a man was caught close by our regiment who is supposed to be a spy; I do not know what they have done with him."

The men drilled, marching, turning, and shifting in and out of various formations, six hours each day. Keeler's parents were concerned about reports of tragic incidents where Union pickets shot their own comrades, but he assured them there was little danger. And there was no way the Rebels, though close, could attack their encampment because of Union fortifications on Arlington Heights, he claimed. "If I live through this war and get an honorable discharge, I will have accomplished more than I ever expected to do in Saginaw," Keeler wrote.[4]

The regiment stayed on Meridian Hill for two more days, when Stockton received orders to move his regiment across the Potomac; the Michigan men marched first to the arsenal and at last received their weapons—Lt. Salter said these were muskets, but Frank Keeler would specify they were "the old Harper's Ferry musket." Arriving at Washington's Long Bridge, the officers learned that the heavy military traffic had been too much for the structure and part of it had collapsed. The men again camped on the Smithsonian's lawn, rising before dawn and crossing the next morning, passing the 2nd and 3rd Michigan regiments as they marched up the river to Ft. Corcoran, opposite Georgetown.[5]

Stockton's regiment was assigned to a brigade under Gen. Fitz John Porter, but within a short time Porter was made a division commander, a division being made up of three or more brigades. That meant Stockton's men served in Brig. Gen. Dan Butterfield's brigade of Porter's division—the same Butterfield who had led the funeral detail of Stockton's brother-in-law, John Garland, back in June. For four days the regiment camped near Ft. Corcoran, with the lights of Georgetown shining at night across the river. Pvt. George Ervay, the youth from Oneida Township, near Grand Ledge, was supremely confident as he wrote to friend, and could not wait to go into battle. "I do not think that the ball [bullet] was or ever will be molded to kill me," he boasted. "I like to be a soldier very well. . . . I would not give one cent to come home now, but would give ten cents if I could get site of a rebel that belongs to the South, and more too [if] I could get site of old Jeff Davis, the old devil."[6]

From Ft. Corcoran the regiment was ordered to Hall's Hill (now part of Arlington, Virginia), about five miles west of the Long Bridge. Here the other brigades of Porter's division encamped in what Frank Keeler called pleasant country with groves of trees. "Our tents are shaded by beautiful cedars," he wrote, "and we sleep on beds of cedar boughs. There are lots of chestnuts here. John Weller caught an eel in a brook close by." Drummer boy George Sidman of Owosso remembered a fierce storm descended on them. "We first encountered a tornado and a flood of rain, which gave some of us the first genuine bath we had had for several days," he said later.[7]

Col. Stockton began to keep a diary, briefly listing events from his regiment's departure from Detroit to their arrival at Hall's Hill. "Ever since we have been here, we have and are still keeping up a thorough course of drilling and daily exhibition in tactics," he wrote. "General Butterfield appears to be an efficient and able officer and will have one of—if not the best—brigades in the service. We are drilling at company, battalion and [the] brigade is practicing all the evolutions of the line and making every possible preparation for a forward movement; when that will be remains to be seen."

Corporal Keeler thought his regiment was a fine group of clean-cut lads; "I don't think our boys are growing rough or boisterous at all," he told his parents. "There are no Germans, Irishmen or any other foreigners except for three or four Canadians in our companies; they are most all Yankee farmers. There is not a drunkard in the company, and if there was he could not get any liquor in this country." Pvt. Marion Munson agreed with his colonel about the extensive training. "We have drill from daylight to dark, company drill and battalion drill and brigade drill," he wrote a friend. He was sure they would soon be fighting, but he was concerned about the slow pace of the Union army moving into the Virginia countryside around Washington. "If we don't move faster than that, we will have to enlist for five years more before we close the war," he said. In fact, the Union army was moving out to hold the land around the Washington area for defensive purposes.[8]

Two infantry regiments, the 12th New York and the 17th New York, made up Butterfield's brigade with Stockton's, and now the 83rd Pennsylvania joined them, followed later that month by the 44th New York. Soon the daily schedule of drill, camp chores, and picket duty—a kind of advanced sentry duty out in the countryside, to ensure that an army would not suffer a surprise attack—was routine. Keeler heard about an incident where men of the 5th Michigan Infantry confronted and drove away nearby Rebel pickets without firing a shot. "They won't stand and fight," the Saginaw man bragged somewhat prematurely. "Our troops are constantly making advances into the enemy's territory."[9] But again, the "advances" were the Union forces being sent into the surrounding country by their commander, Gen. George B. McClellan, where they built forts to protect the capital; the truth was that McClellan had no intention of conducting a major offensive yet.

The Stockton regiment's brigade commander Daniel Butterfield was not a West Point graduate, but he'd been a serious militia officer for some time and was familiar with military maneuvers, tactics, and practices, right down to bugle calls, which the army used to signal and direct its soldiers, whether in camp or on the battlefield. Though he could not read music, Butterfield could play traditional army bugle calls, and it seems it was here on Hall's Hill that he introduced the first of his own compositions—a six-note bugle call that employed the three tones of the major scale's triad to assemble his brigade. This phrase sounded like a musical recitation of his own name—"Dan-Dan-Dan But-ter-field." It was a simple clarion call, easy for his brigade buglers to play and just as easy for his soldiers to recognize.[10]

Though Lt. Charles Salter, Sergeant Major William Kydd, and some other men who had been in the original 1st Michigan experienced combat at Bull Run, most of the soldiers had only seen Confederates from a distance, if at all. On October 9, Salter was sent out three miles with Capt. Tom Barry and ninety men to cut down trees to ensure Union artillery had a clear field of fire on a hill near Fall's Church. "We saw a large body of rebels about a half mile distant," he said. "We sent a messenger back for our brigade and in a short time Gen. Butterfield came out with 2,500 men and three cannon." The Confederates withdrew "without giving us a chance to give them battle," Salter wrote, seemingly disappointed.[11]

These picket line alarms continued periodically, as did rumors of a forward movement, Frank Keeler wrote. "There seems to be little prospect of a fight," he observed, correctly. "McClellan's policy seems to be HOLD ON." Picket-duty rotation was such that his company went out every ten days. "I do not have to stand guard," he bragged. "It is my business to relieve sentinels and while privates are standing on guard, the corporal can be seen among the reserves—a hundred men from which the sentinels are relieved." It was serious duty and periodically men traded shots with their Rebel opposites. One October night saw a Michigan picket shoot himself in the hand, while another nodded off while on duty. "A guard sleeps on his post, and he is sent back arrested," noted John G. Berry, the 24-year-old diarist in Company A.

Soldiers not on picket or sentry duty managed to amuse themselves. Oliver Norton, a still-green private with the 83rd Pennsylvania, put together outlandish costumes with two of his friends and then, as a joke, went over to Stockton's regiment to be challenged by the Michigan sentries. When the guard demanded "Who goes there?" the Pennsylvanians gave replies such as "a flock of sheep," or "the devil." "We made quite a round and had a lot of fun and came back with something to laugh over," Norton wrote.[12]

Picket duty in the countryside brought the soldiers face to face with secessionists and also with slaves, and some Michigan men were not very understanding of the difficult position of enslaved blacks. When a detail was sent nine miles west to Fairfax Court House to search some houses, Pvt. Marion Munson said the soldiers threatened a black servant who was apparently uncooperative. "There was one girl and her mother, her husband was in the South[ern] army," he told friends about the residents of one house. "She said that she was not afraid of us Yankees, but she was afraid of our guns."[13]

The men were reasonably healthy that fall—only one man had died of illness since they'd left Detroit and only a handful more were sick. Lt. Salter, who was more religious than many soldiers, approved of Chaplain Brockway's holding services in a grove near their camp. He had his portrait taken by a photographer to send back to his friends, and thanked them for sending useful gifts—towels. They were, he said, "very useful indeed now that we are so far from home, and I assure you we are truly grateful for them." Col Stockton, as a commanding officer, suffered less inconveniences and, like many others, moved his wife Maria to Washington, where he could visit her or bring her to camp. "Went to town in the afternoon and stayed all night," he noted on an early November Sunday. "Found wife well."[14]

In the meantime, the regiment had been regularly at target practice with their older model muskets, and Keeler said the men "did well for the first time" in a brigade firing drill late in October. This was an impressive sight—watching two regiments at a time advance in columns and form a line of battle, while two other regiments moved up behind them.

"Ready. Aim. Fire. Load," Gen. Butterfield ordered; then the regiments in the advance would close in column formation to withdraw, while the next two regiments stepped forward to take their place and fire. Best of all for Keeler, he did not have to stand, march, and shoot in these formations, since he was in the color guard during these drills.[15]

The still-inexperienced soldier expressed shock at the "ravages" of war he witnessed (though in truth they were mild compared to the terrible things that lay ahead for many civilians of the Confederacy). Some Union cavalry troopers unconcernedly tied their horses to a line of cherry trees at a nearby house, and the horses gnawed on them so that "nearly every tree was PEELED FROM THE GROUND TO THE LIMBS," the shocked Keeler wrote. "The soldiers spare nothing except when restricted by special orders. Our drummers were all put in the guard house the other day for taking some tomatoes." Marion Munson, the young soldier from Oakland County, felt nothing was happening fast enough, and he wondered about the lack of a real Union offensive. "This is a war of speculation [rather] than the patriotism of '76," he complained. "The officers are unqualified and un-drilled so that makes it bad. . . . They are fighting for money and not for our country. . . . The grub is bad and the prospects is poor for getting better. If we go do anything this fall, we have to do it soon."[16]

Rains came in November, halting drills and bringing more illness. "There is a good deal of sickness in our regiment," Lt. Salter noted, "more, I think, than in any other regiment in our division and no less than thirteen of our men have died since crossing the Potomac." Two were the brothers from northern Saginaw County.

> Last Sunday we buried a young man named [Sam] Wellington of Capt. Fisher's Saginaw company; he had a brother [Alfred] die in the hospital at Georgetown only a few days before this, and today another man belonging to the St. Johns company [Company B] was buried. They were none of them sick but for a short time. Fever and the measles appear to be the principal complaints amongst the sick.[17]

Sgt. William H. Borden, 20, was also a member of Company B, and for the moment, a lucky one. "I did not have the measles as the doct[or] thought—I am well," he wrote his father back in Ionia. "But Bill Brown does not gain very fast. He is a very sick boy. I don't know what his complaint is." Brown, 19, did not last much longer in the service. Within several weeks, he was discharged on a surgeon's certificate for disability.[18]

There were grim developments in October when a Union probing action of Confederate positions ended up in disaster at a place several miles away called Ball's Bluff, Virginia, where poorly led, rookie Union soldiers were chased back to the Potomac by the Rebels; those who did not surrender drowned or were shot in the water as they tried to escape. The defeat was a national scandal and Col. Stockton recorded in his diary how corpses floated down the river. "Potomac banks very high, and many bodies of soldiers who were killed and drowned in the late fight have been picked out as they were floating by," Stockton wrote.[19]

Despite the rains, some 14,000 men were marshaled for a grand review on November 9 by Major General George B. McClellan, who had been promoted to command of the entire Union army. "It rained quite hard," wrote Lt. Salter, "but the review passed off the same as if it had been fair weather, though to be sure it was not quite as pleasant for us. As the general entered the field, the artillery saluted him and three times three cheers from the whole division greeted him. In fact he is very popular with all the troops here and they recently received the news of his promotion to the command of the Army with great enthusiasm."[20] Reviews were generally good for the morale of soldiers, since they showed the men that they were part of a huge force, and this helped to instill confidence and pride in them.

As soldiers drilled and trained, Stockton moved his wife into camp when the house where she stayed in Washington was turned into a hospital. But the first intimations that all was not well between the colonel and Norval Welch now appeared in Stockton's diary. "Major Welch and a party of 20 men sent out to scout tonight by order of General Porter—evidently done at the request of the Major!" Stockton wrote, apparently surprised or peeved. "Delightful evening," he continued. "Hope the major will meet some of the Rebels, just to try him and his party." Two days later, Welch again seemed to cause the colonel consternation as their brigade drilled. "Major sent for his envoy!" Stockton wrote, learning Welch had gone to the capital with the brigade commander, Butterfield. "Has been to Washington with General B!"[21]

There was news from home. Michigan women were forming Soldiers Aid Society chapters, whose aim was to make the lives of the troops more comfortable. Lt. Salter was glad to hear it, and hoped their work would ease the towel shortage that had plagued the regiment since its formation. "We have an account of the meeting held by the society in the Woodward Avenue M. E. Church on the 2nd [of November] and I have no doubt it will accomplish much good. . . . Our regiment is very well provided with about everything with the exception of towels." Salter told his friends that men who wanted to have church services were raising money for a large tent so that services would not have to be held out in the elements. He hoped that would check the men's vices like gambling and cursing. "I have notice that the bad habit of swearing has become quite common in the army and most of the officers are doing as much as they can to put a stop to it," he said. Pvt. Marion Munson told his friend and former boss that he was not gambling at cards with his comrades. "Your advice was pretty good," Munson wrote. "I am pretty well clear from the evils, most soldiers gambling all the spare time they have. I don't play at all." Munson admitted he had briefly tried smoking tobacco—someone told him it would relieve heartburn, which he believed came from eating "raw meat" (meaning salt pork) and half-cooked coffee.[22]

The men drew their pay on November 16, a cold, clear Saturday. "I received $31 and 55 cents, paid the sutler $1 which was all I had drawn on him," Frank Keeler wrote his parents. "I have $30 in U.S. Treasury notes and the balance in specie. After figuring the matter over I concluded I had drawn all that was due me, and I will send you $25. I have $8.88, which I think will carry me through to next payday. The $11 I brought from Saginaw lasted me well." Sutlers were, of course, the camp-following merchants who trailed the army almost everywhere. Keeler described them to his parents in a Christmas letter: "Traders are numerous, all about here," he wrote. "Every little hut, hovel, corn-house and barn is a 'store' where the soldier may get rid of his change for boots, shoes, Yankee notions, press, cakes, cigars and the like commodities at generally reasonable prices. Selling liquor is a dangerous branch of trade. The dealer is pretty sure to get into the guard house as soon as his business is known."[23]

Col. Stockton, meanwhile, worried about the pending inspection of his regiment by Lt. Col. Strong Vincent of the 83rd Pennsylvania, while Maj. Welch went off to inspect the 17th New York. Inspection, of course, was a military tradition long before the Civil War, and how his regiment stood up to an inspection by another commander mattered to him very much. "All passed off well," Stockton recorded after the inspection.[24] Vincent, a lawyer like Welch, would become an acquaintance if not a friend to the major from Ann Arbor.

Shipments of clothing and new uniforms arrived in time for the regiment to turn out in new dress for another grand review of divisions on Munson's Hill by President Lincoln and General McClellan on November 20. Frank Keeler described the uniform's head gear, but that was all: a tall, brimmed, black felt hat "with a brass eagle on the right side which holds the brim turned up."

Thousands of soldiers participated, and the grandeur of it struck officers and soldiers alike. Salter thought it was "undoubtedly the largest review that has ever taken place in this country." Farm boy George Ervay also told his family about it. "I wish you could have been with me last Saturday," he wrote. "If I ever saw a crowd of men, I saw it then." Stockton was proud his men looked sharp. "My regiment was in new uniform and appeared so well as to elicit praise," the colonel wrote. Maria Stockton was there on horseback to witness the event, attended by Dr. Wixom, the regiment's surgeon.[25]

Young Keeler was happy with army-issued garments—"Uncle Sam furnishes good clothing and plenty of it," he wrote. "We get white flannel undershirts, good socks and good shoes. In fact, most of our men were never so well clothed as they have been since they came into the army." But not all soldiers were as satisfied: On the night of November 24, some men in Company A got drunk and angry and complained to Stockton about rations and other shortcomings of army life. Unhappy with his response, they threatened to mutiny, John Berry recorded. Officers finally responded by calling the company out for roll call, and mutinous or not, the men responded. As the company stood in line, their bayonets and cartridge boxes were confiscated, and the rest of the regiment was called out—under arms. This made the point to the troublemakers of Company A that they were unarmed and outnumbered. Order was restored, but John Berry thought this would not have been needed, if only the malcontents had been firmly dealt with in the first place. "All of this is done on account of three or four drunken men and the cowardliness of our officers," he complained.[26]

The regiment was still shorthanded, and Col. Stockton tried again to pressure Michigan Adjutant General John Robertson to provide more volunteers. He notified Robertson he was sending three officers back to Michigan to recruit; he had to do this, since he had not heard "whether the Governor intends to send on any men for my regiment." The colonel reminded the adjutant general that he had promised Stockton he would send another company. "We are expecting to be moving south or else forward very soon," Stockton wrote. "I wish to have my regiment full. I have, like every other regiment, a large sick list, but all are now recuperating." He also bragged about his regiment's successful inspection and drill performances. "My regiment is in one of the best divisions and brigades," Stockton continued, "and what is more, my regiment is considered *as good* as the best in the brigade."[27]

Yet Stockton's claim that he must have a full regiment quickly was strictly a bluff. By late November, temperatures at times dropped to near freezing and the rain would have made moving thousands of men, guns, and supplies difficult. At this point in the war, campaigning was expected to stop during the winter months. The same day the colonel sent his letter for more troops, he recorded in his diary that his orders "seem strongly to point to a truce soon." The truth was his regiment was not going anywhere. He had his tents arranged "so that today we are much more comfortable." The men did the same. "The weather is growing wintry and the nights frosty," said Frank Keeler, "but our tent is very comfortable. We raised it up by building a sort of embankment about two feet high of poles and mud, then set the tent on top of it. In the center we made a fireplace with a chimney leaning outside and thus we are as comfortable as a tent can be made."[28]

Young George Ervay misplaced his gear, and it cost him. "I had the luck to lose my knapsack with my shirts and blanket and overcoat, and everything that was in it," he complained, "I had to pay for them, and it drawed very hard on my pay. All I got was five (dollars) and 67 cents, and I shall want that before I get any more pay." But the cold weather caused Sgt. William Borden to think about his ice skates, and the possibility that his folks might let someone back home borrow them. "I don't want you to lend my skates for I don't know what day I shall be home to use them," he cautioned them. "Lend them red ones, if any."[29]

On the afternoon of November 26, a Union cavalry patrol was attacked and driven back to the safety of their pickets in the Virginia countryside, where men from Stockton's regiment were the reserve picket. Anticipating an attack, the regiment moved out under arms and spent a cold but uneventful night, since nervous officers forbade campfires. The next day, the day before Thanksgiving, Frank Keeler was put on guard duty at the hospital "on a little hill about 40 rods northeast of camp at Hall's Hill."

It consists of a farmhouse and outbuildings, mostly of logs, pleasantly situated and

> I must say that this change from camp life was very enjoyable to me. The clean, fresh garden, though sere and frost-browned, was an agreeable contrast to the hard-trodden streets of the regimental camp. I went over a few rods beyond to a farmhouse and had dinner with the family of Virginians. It was the first time I have set down to a table since I left Detroit.[30]

There were still nights when it was warm enough that fires were not necessary, he assured his parents, and he gently explained to them that, no, he did not need them to send a pillow. "I should like a pillow very much," he wrote, but it would be in the way and burdensome on a march. . . . A soldier finds his knapsack will answer for many purposes."

> It makes a good pillow with a coat spread out, makes a tolerably fair table for some purposes, answers for a stool, and is a trunk, wardrobe, bureau, etc. When we get on our knapsack and haversack, packed, canteen, cartridge box, belt, cap, pouch, bayonet scabbard and musket, we have everything which is necessary for the soldier and do not feel or appear burdened.
>
> Mother, I wish you could look into my tent tonight. We are seated around the fireplace not because it is cold, for the fireplace is in the center of the tent and besides, it is so warm that we have no fire in it. Seven of the ten are writing letters, one is reading and the other two are sleeping.
>
> There is no card playing in the tent; there seems to be no inclination for such amusements but writing and reading fill up the leisure time pretty well and we have plenty of reading supplied us by the chaplain, such as tracts, little books, religious newspapers, etc. . . . Besides all this, we can buy the latest papers every day. I should like a [Saginaw] Courier once in a while if you can send one conveniently.[31]

Pvt. George Ervay's account of life in a tent at mealtime was far less tranquil. "I would like it if you could look into my tent about the time that we are eating dinner or supper," he wrote. "One will holler, 'Git your darn coat tail out of my coffee' and another 'git your foot off my bread' and another there, 'you have got your head in my soup, git off my potato. Wish the devil had you if you cannot [sit] without getting into my vittles.'"[32]

Ervay walked to the camps of other nearby Michigan regiments in his spare time, looking for friends, news, and gossip from back home. He told his parents he wanted a pair of gloves, but he knew it would be hard for them to send any since they were not near a railroad. It appears that officers and soldiers alike had an easy time of it on Thanksgiving, which Col. Stockton noted was celebrated by general order; he went on a leisurely horseback ride with his wife, Dr. Wixom, and other officers toward Fall's Church, having a "first rate dinner" and later having an evening meal with Gen. Butterfield. Though inclement weather might keep an army from some activities as December came, it could not stop inspection, that fundamental exercise in army neatness and order. "Col. Lansing (of the 17th New York) pronounced my regiment and camp, etc. all in fine order," Stockton noted proudly. "Co. 'E' (Capt. Elliott's) the best in regiment."[33]

The food prepared by their kitchen, or "mess," might have clinched that title for Company E. Lt. Salter reported that their cook got a glowing review from Lansing. "The colonel passed by our company cook just as the men were eating dinner," the Detroiter said of the inspection. "He tasted their soup and pronounced it was as good as could be obtained at any hotel in New York and better than he had at his table." But a "cold north wind" visited northern Virginia, and the men saw a newspaper report that the regiment was being sent to South Carolina. The report was not true, but the men were angry that the source of the story was one of their lieutenants, trying to lure new Michigan recruits into the service with promises of warmer climates. "The whole regiment feels very indignant that he should have done so as it must cause considerable anxiety on the part of the friends and relatives of all," Salter complained.[34]

Many more soldiers were sick now, he told his friend, with an average of about 150 to

200 men ill since the regiment had arrived at Hall's Hill. In the meantime, the usual camp stories circulated. For example, Frank Keeler of Saginaw wondered if he would be coming home soon. "I shall be back in the spring, I believe," he wrote his parents. "One of our men told me he overheard Gen. Butterfield say that he would bet a thousand dollars that before February, we would all be home." At the same time, Col. Stockton was longing for a promotion to brigadier general, not just a temporary brigade command he held when Butterfield was away. He went to Washington to talk with politicians who would have a say in the matter. "All seemed friendly," he wrote, "and said there would be no more general[s] made until a fight, and then only some who deserved [promotion]," he wrote.[35]

Most of the regiment was ordered out into the countryside on a mild December Saturday, and Stockton wondered if it was an important mission (which he hoped would lead to his brigadier general appointment). But it ended up being a three-day foray to check on nearby residents, some of whom were suspected of spying. Charles Salter characterized it as a welcome change of scene. A young soldier from Flint in Company C, Henry "Tip" Aplin, said he saw a "rebble spy" while he was on picket—probably meaning they were watched from a distance by a Confederate officer or cavalry trooper. Though he heard stories of other nearby Union pickets being driven back by the enemy, his regiment had no such scrape. But Aplin did manage to visit Washington early that month, visiting the Capitol, the White House, and other government buildings and seeing President Lincoln, too.[36]

Col. Stockton was called back to Washington to serve as a member of courts-martial, and he sometimes lobbied politicians. That was fine by his regiment. "In his absence we do not drill much and have quite an easy time," Lt. Salter wrote. But the fact that Michigan authorities still had not provided him with additional companies continued to irk the colonel; he wrote to the secretary of war, charging that his nemesis, Gov. Austin Blair, was responsible for short-changing his regiment's manpower. "On the 14th Sept. you directed Gov. Blair of Michigan (by telegraph) to 'start today for Washington the [new three-year] First [Michigan Infantry] and Stockton's Regiments,'" he wrote, reminding Simon Cameron of that order, "'—use such authority as may be necessary to fill these regiments from any men now mustered into service.'"[37]

Blair had complied with the first part of the telegram, but failed to fulfill the second part, the colonel noted. The regiment left Detroit nearly 300 short. Since then, Blair had provided

> only 77 men and three officers and has not yet sent any more, but on the contrary, has authorized and permitted three or more other regiments to be raised since. . . . I most respectfully ask that you will require the governor of the state of Michigan to comply with your instructions of Sept. 14th and at once fill up my regiment to the maximum standard.
>
> Had he not thrown every obstacle in my way, I could have easily filled up my regiment within thirty days from the time you granted me the authority to raise it. I will defer until I can have a personal interview with you and attempt to explain all the difficulties I had to encounter bringing into the field my regiment—having you to judge, from the reports of my superior officers, whether I have proved myself thus far worthy of the trust you place in me.[38]

By now the federal government decided it would form no more independent regiments, probably because of the objections of governors like Blair. Yet Stockton's complaints found a sympathetic ear at the War Department. Before winter camp was struck and the Army of the Potomac headed into the field, Stockton would at last receive more men. One body of troops was an independent company composed of men described as some of the best marksmen in Michigan; the other was a group of men who had initially signed up to fight in the manner of the European knights of old—with lances.

Perhaps the approaching holiday caused Stockton to think of absent family, recording on December 19: "Wrote today to my very silent boy urging him to come home." The colonel had a son named Baylis Garland Stockton, then living in California, but his diary also mentions a step-son who does not seem to appear in family papers. A week or so later, Stockton was surprised to get a letter from this step-son, who had gotten married.

But the war was at a standstill. The regiment's band went to the Capitol to play for the Michigan congressmen and to perform before lectures on the war. The soldiers played ball or organized their own music and dances. "We have in our tent a violin player and he can play pretty good," Marion Munson told his friend back home. "We have a dance three or four times a week and it livens up the boys greatly. All the difficulty is that we hain't got any ladies; the boys all look alike; it is with some difficulty we dance."[39]

Another review of troops, more bad weather, more rumors about which regiments would be shipped further south continued as Christmas drew nearer. Lt. Salter struggled to stay well after getting a severe cold and sore throat while his company did camp guard duty on the 23rd, and he complained he was not able to shake it. "Yet however I have attended all drill to the same as usual," he wrote with pride. Christmas at Hall's Hill was subdued, at first; Frank Keeler said it was quiet in camp and that the regiment's sutler "treated the boys [to] cider and cakes." Other men left the camp to buy their dinner from locals who turned their "homes into restaurants, boarding houses and cake shops."[40]

But Keeler said the men of the 44th New York, with the permission and cooperation of their officers, cut loose with a comedic satire on army life:

> I wish I could describe for you the burlesque parade of the 44th New York on Christmas. The men were dressed in the most grotesque and ludicrous manner imaginable. Officers took places in the ranks as privates and privates and non-commissioned officers from the colonel down to the corporal. Our regiment tried to get up a similar show but the officers would not consent to the changes.[41]

The Stockton regiment's chaplain, William Brockway, was traveling back from Michigan, so the men had no church service, Lt. Salter wrote. But like Keeler, he mentioned the 44th New York's antics. "The men had a mock fancy dress parade in the afternoon," Salter said, "electing officers of their own and conducting the parade in the manner best calculated to ridicule the usual form of the regular dress parade." Chaplain Brockway, however, wrote that he got back to the regiment in time to bring blankets and other Christmas presents donated by people back in Michigan, and that "many a soldier's heart was made glad when those boxes were opened, and such kindness will not be forgotten by the men."[42]

Frank Keeler also wrote at Christmas that when men from their brigade died from illness at Hall's Hill, they were being buried at the Mt. Olivet Church at a nearby crossroads. Gen. Butterfield proposed the men raise money to rebuild the church, in bad shape even before it had been stripped by the soldiers. Keeler liked the idea, since two of his Company D, Alfred Wellington of Saginaw County and Francis Briggs of Birch Run, were interred there. But this plan was never put into effect.[43]

The day after Christmas, Col. Stockton was injured with a painful sprain to his right knee and ankle when his horse balked as he dismounted, disabling him temporarily. But the most important event for the soldiers was that they got newer, better weapons on New Year's Day. "The boys are all well and in good spirit as we have just received new guns, beautiful rifled muskets from the Springfield factory," Frank Keeler told his family, "smaller and lighter than the old Harper's Ferry musket which we laid by. Yesterday we mustered for pay and the inspecting officer said we have the best arms in the service."[44]

The celebration on New Year's Eve for officers in the Third Brigade, thrown by Col. John McLane of the 83rd Pennsylvania, featured an excellent supper served in large tents decorated with evergreen branches, Chinese lanterns and chandeliers with glistening bayonets, Lt. Salter said. Col. Stockton also enjoyed the party, though he was ordered to keep his regiment ready for action. He suspected this was a ruse to keep the men in camp and sober, though no one was really sure what was happening when artillery and small arms sounded in the distance.

At 2 a.m. on New Year's Day, the long roll of the drums sounded—the army's alarm signal—calling out the men to immediately assemble with their weapons. There had been a report of a Confederate advance near Centreville, but Keeler thought it was possible the noise was "just a loud celebration on the east side of the Potomac." Stockton thought the alarm and order for the troops to be ready for action was just an attempt by commanders to keep order on a holiday when men wanted to get their hands on alcohol. Highlights that day included yet another comic dress parade by the 44th New York, and the arrest of a peddler who hid liquor among the pies and baked goods on his wagon. "Our colonel takes charge of the liquor and the pies is confiscated—not by Uncle Sam but by the guards," John Berry said.[45]

A new round of rumors passed through the soldiers—they were soon going on a new expedition, by land, or by sea; to South Carolina, or to Virginia's York River; or to the coast of Georgia, or Alabama. The truth was that no one knew. "All things considered," Chaplain Brockway wrote as freezing rain and snow hit Hall's Hill, "I would prefer to go to South Carolina or Georgia." Lt. Charles Salter also wondered about being sent further south, but he figured the Rebels were suffering far more than the Michigan men, given the cold, stormy weather, "as they are said to be quite destitute of clothing and cannot bear the cold as well we northerners can anyway."[46]

Corporal John Berry of Company A managed, after a great deal of trouble, to get an order signed by Gen. Butterfield and Col. Stockton, his own captain and the regimental adjutant, that allowed him to go to Washington for a day. He walked to Georgetown, took an omnibus into the capital, and had breakfast in a hotel. He went shopping for members of his company, admired exhibits at the Smithsonian, and toured the Patent Office and Post Office. He was searched for liquor as he went back into Virginia, but it hardly mattered. "A very pleasant and agreeable visit," Berry said about his trip. But the feeling could not last, for that night a snowstorm blew in and a soldier on guard duty accidentally shot off one of his own fingers.[47]

The excitement of soldiering had worn off for young Pvt. George Ervay of Company H. A late January inspection revealed that many soldiers' rifles were not clean. For that, he said, they had caught "Hail Columbia" from the officers. "I would put them, all of the little petty officers, in the guard house until they would get enough of it," Ervay groused. Nor did he like having to fall out to assemble twice a day in full gear. "It is not a very pleasant thing to be [a] soldier," he wrote. Marion Munson, the teenaged private in Company E, was also unhappy—with the regimental band, the chaplain, and the Congress that was making the decisions that paid for everything. The band, he complained, was supported for the most part by taxpayers, but was in part paid for by a tax on the regiment itself. In addition, Munson claimed the regiment supported the chaplain to the tune of $7 a day, but was not getting its money's worth. "All he does is to go to Washington for the mail and preach a sermon, one a week. It hain't preaching either; he gets up and yam[s] it a spell and sing[s] a patriotic song and dismiss[es] them." It would be better, he wrote, if the officers tended to their business "instead of being in their tents drunk and drinking champagne and whiskey." Munson's pointed observation may have been about his own captain, Robert T. Elliott of Detroit, who would develop a reputation as drinker.[48]

Stockton heard more talk that he was going to be promoted. "Capt. Carr and others who returned from Washington bring rumor that I am surely to be a brigadier general," he noted. "Only rumor, I fear." But just as Stockton longed for his brigadier's star, the officers of his regiment wanted commissions, and of course, they had none. At a time when a man's home state was a proud and defining part of his identity, Stockton's officers got their appointments from the colonel, as authorized by the federal government, but not from the state of Michigan.

This, they felt, was a slight against their honor and service—some of these officers had been civilian leaders, men of business and law, some politicians, in their communities back home; they wanted to be able to say or to show that they had been commissioned by the governor, and that they represented their state. But they could not—Gov. Blair was dead set against Stockton and his regiment. This was also a practical problem for ambitious officers who hoped to rise to higher rank when opportunities opened in other Michigan regiments as the war went on. By now there were at least ten infantry regiments from

Michigan, as well as some cavalry regiments and artillery batteries. But since Stockton's officers held no commissions from the governor, it was hardly conceivable Blair would consider promoting them as vacancies appeared in other state regiments.

Letters that came into Stockton's hands that season showed Blair's antipathy toward him had not lessened. "Dear sir," the governor wrote to a man who had inquired about Stockton's regiment. "The conduct of Col. Stockton has been such of late that I have determined to have nothing more to do with him. He does not hold a commission and has no claim upon the state." To another, Blair wrote: "I have nothing to do with Stockton's regiment. He does not hold a Michigan commission. Having started 'independently' I intend to let him remain so."[49]

The officers of Stockton's regiment petitioned Blair directly. The colonel, Lt. Col. Ruehle, Maj. Welch, Adjt. Morris, and 24 captains and lieutenants asked for commissions matching their rank, retroactive to the dates they mustered into the service of the United States. But their request was met with silence from the governor's office.[50]

"We went out to practice target firing this afternoon," Cpl. Frank Keeler wrote that month, "but the fog and the smoke was so dense that we could do but little. We had 44 men and three sergeants. Each one fired at a target about the size of your closet door at a distance of 35 rods and FORTY-SIX balls were put through the target. . . . I rather think that if we get a chance to fire into secesh ranks we shall worry them some." He said that a case or two of smallpox in camp caused the entire regiment to be marched to the surgeon's tent for vaccinations. "Shortly after this there occurred another case and again the regiment was marched up and vaccinated. Nothing more has been seen or heard of the disease."[51]

As the month ended Stockton ordered his men to again raid more merchants who engaged in selling contraband—alcohol—to the soldiers. "Today [I] had arrested a nest of traders, etc. over at Brinkhurst," he noted. "Found liquor, etc. Seized six persons and nearly $900 in money and goods, [a] span of horses, 10 cows and pretty good haul!" Drill—the seemingly endless exercise of marching men in squads, companies, battalions, and even the entire brigade—was sometimes canceled because of bad weather. But picket duty went on regardless, and sometimes soldiers got the chance to visit nearby farms and plantations. Just as Lt. Salter had described earlier in the fall, John Berry also told of a household where the owner had joined the Rebels, though his attractive daughter remained at home. "By what I could learn the folks of the house are secessionists, the man of the house is in the Confederate army," he wrote. "Amongst the family is the daughter, who is quite an intelligent young lady, from whom we glean some quite interesting stories of the neighborhood. We all pronounced her to be the picket belle and the prettiest girl we have seen in Virginia."[52]

But Grand Ledge teen George Ervay was on picket duty about six miles from camp when he and another soldier used deadly force, shooting down a man and a woman they suspected of spying and who would not surrender once confronted. The soldiers, unseen by the couple, had watched the pair approaching through the countryside:

> My partner says to me, "Let's not shoot them unless they run before they see us." They came up within five rods of us and then they saw us and turned away. I halted them and they did not stop. I shot and hit the man through the leg and the woman received a ball through the arm, and she stayed by the man that could not run. One of the men on the other posts came up and he and me went to them and we had to kill the woman before we could take them prisoners and we had a hard time to take them.
>
> The [wounded] man hit me in the face and made me a black eye. We dragged him by the arms to the post and our relief came and carried them to the camp. Today the woman was buried and four shots passed over her grave [apparently in salute]. I tell you, when I took hold of the man [i.e., aimed my rifle at him] my hair stood up.[53]

Men from Stockton's regiment and their brigade were detailed to help build a military road from Ft. Corcoran to Fall's Church, since conditions were so muddy that the route nearly impassable. By now the regiment had a nickname of sorts—"Stockton's Worm-eaters." The name probably derived from the fact that thick army crackers called "hardtack" often contained tiny worms. Hardtack could be nearly impossible to bite and chew, so soldiers broke the crackers up in their coffee, or dunked them to soften them. This made hardtack edible, but resulted in larvae rising to the surface of their cups; experienced soldiers skimmed the worms off with their spoons. Perhaps the nickname was a joking reference to a time when Stockton's green soldiers did not know about scooping bugs out of their coffee, or that it was a humorous matter of pride that the men were so tough, they consumed their coffee and crumbs, worms and all. Marion Munson of Company E, writing home, urged his friend to tell the men at home about the regiment. "If those boys has got good teeth they can enlist and they can stand the war pretty well," Munson said. "But if they can't eat there is a poor chance in Dixie, especially in Stockton's worm eaters, as we call ourselves."[54]

Whether that nickname stuck is open to question. Only one other mention of the name "Stockton's Worm-eaters" appears in the available record, when an officer of the regiment, Ziba Graham, of Flint, claimed three decades later the nickname referred specifically to Company C, the Genesee County company. Col. Stockton was also given a nickname by the men who served under him, though exactly how and when he got it, and what it meant, is not clear. In 1862, brigade bugler Oliver Norton of the 83rd Pennsylvania, would write that Stockton was called "Jack o' Clubs."[55]

In February, Stockton and his friend Lt. Col. Ruehle rode to Washington, had their portraits taken, and met with various senators. But Norval Welch's actions again bothered or offended the colonel. "Returning home [to camp] on account of inquiry called on Major Welch!!" Stockton wrote, with two exclamation points. "If he does not look sharp he will be court-martialed." Meanwhile, both the regiment's surgeon and its assistant surgeon were granted leaves—Dr. Wixom to return to Genesee County to attend his dying son, and Dr. Butler for thirty days away. Butler, however, resigned and never returned to the regiment. Wixom signed up a civilian contract physician, a Dr. Thomas W. Seeley, to take his place while he was gone. Seeley would stay on after Wixom returned to the regiment, temporarily taking the place of Butler.[56]

On February 10, Stockton's regiment finally grew when fifty-five men and two officers from an independent company of marksmen, called sharpshooters, arrived in camp at Hall's Hill. A short time later they were joined by twenty-eight more of these riflemen and their leader, Capt. Kiniston S. Dygert, 38, of Detroit, who had initially stayed behind in Michigan to finish up contracts he let for arms. This company was known as Brady's Sharpshooters, or alternately, the Brady Sharpshooters. Their name came from Gen. Hugh Brady, a U.S. Army hero of the Indian campaigns in the Ohio Valley after the Revolutionary War, as well as the War of 1812 and the "Patriot War," a period of civil unrest on the Canadian border from 1836 to 1838. Brady spent much of his career as the federal army's commander in Detroit before his death in 1851, and for years a local militia company bore his name.

Kin Dygert, listed as an accountant in 1860 Detroit, had been a member of the Brady Guards militia company since 1843, so he took the name for his new company of marksmen. They came from around the state—Michigan-born men, Germans, natives of England, and men who'd come with their families from New York and points east—farmers, coopers, harness makers, and even a lawyer. Like Stockton's regiment, the sharpshooters company was raised in the fall of 1861 under the authority of the secretary of war and independently of the state of Michigan. After some sort of indecision as to where the company was to go and with whom they would serve, they had been sent to Stockton's regiment by Lt. Col. Electus Backus, the U.S. Army officer in Detroit.[57]

A recruiting announcement for the Brady Sharpshooters laid down strict marksmanship requirements. "No man will be accepted or mustered into service who cannot, when firing at a rest at a distance of 40 rods, put ten consecutive shots in a target of an average space of not to exceed five inches from the center of the bull's eye to the center of the ball [bullet]," the poster read. One article about the company said these were the same shooting requirements for joining Col. Hiram Berdan's companies of U.S. Sharpshooters, federal army marksmen. It reported that Dygert was "an expert rifle shot" and that he had signed on "some 50 or more of the best shots in the state."

Initially the members of the Brady Sharpshooters Company furnished their own weapons, wrote Pvt. Edwin Farmer from Decatur, for which the government would pay them $55. Another sharpshooter said years later they were first outfitted with "heavy target rifles, afterward exchanged for Sharp's breech-loaders." Farmer wrote late in November 1861 that the gathering sharpshooters drilled at the Detroit Firemen's Hall and at least some of the company was quartered at the Franklin Hotel. "We have got the best company of men that was ever collected in the State of Michigan," he bragged, "and we have a first rate captain."[58]

One of the sharpshooters was a diminutive man, Sgt. Rufus W. Jacklin, 19, a member of the old Detroit Light Guard militia company that had gone into the ninety-day 1st Michigan Infantry Regiment. Jacklin had been born in England but worked as a clerk for a notable Detroit gunsmith named William Winegert. But because Jacklin was only 5 feet, 2 inches tall, he had not been mustered into that 1st Michigan regiment. He was, however, accepted into the Brady Sharpshooters and he would quickly rise in rank.

Another sharpshooter was a 25-year-old Grand Rapids man, Alfred M. Apted, another English-born immigrant who had come to Michigan as a child. Before he enlisted in the

Brady company, he had made a return trip to visit England and twice journeyed to Pike's Peak, Colorado, in search of frontier gold. But his civilian life had been for the most part far less adventurous, with Apted working as a carpenter and millwright before becoming a soldier. He would begin to keep a diary in the coming summer, his sharpshooting company playing important roles in the battles his regiment would fight in the months ahead.[59]

Winter dragged on into 1862. Stockton hailed the news of Gen. Grant's victory at Fort Donelson on the Cumberland River in Tennessee; Frank Keeler complained that he still had not seen a Rebel, let alone been in a skirmish, but then George McClellan was not going to start the Army of the Potomac on the offensive until he felt his men were fully trained and ready for combat. Stockton's men continued working on the road to Georgetown, with the regiment divided into right and left wings that alternated between target practice and fatigue (work) duty.

John Berry's Company A managed to hold a ball in a local house to which the regimental band and the officers were invited, though he did not say whether they managed to invite any women. Keeler, on the other hand, said "there were quite a number of ladies in camp, captains' wives, sutler's wife, Mrs. Stockton and also several children who run about the camp laughing and playing." Keeler also listened as Capt. Ben Fisher interviewed a slave from a nearby residence—the man reminded Keeler of the character "Uncle Tom" from Harriet Beecher Stowe's powerful antislavery novel. "He said his master treated him well, he had not a wife, but as to running away, he only laughed and shook his head," Keeler wrote.[60]

As the winter waned Stockton got news he'd been waiting for—another two companies of soldiers were joining his ranks, which, with the addition of the Brady Sharpshooters, brought his regiment to the proper standard of manpower. Marion Munson heard about this early in February. "There is 225 men a-coming to this regiment out of the Lancers and then we will have a good a regiment as ever came out of Michigan," he wrote. "And I think that they will do as good execution as any regiment on the Potomac, and about the first of March, we will have a chance to know what we can do to the rebels."[61]

The first of these new Michigan soldiers arrived on March 8. Because of the unusual circumstances of their origins, and how they were assigned to Stockton's regiment, the story of these Michigan Lancers is an important part of the history of the 16th Michigan Infantry. Serving as foot soldiers had not been the first choice of these men—they had originally signed up to be cavalry troopers of sorts. Strange, too, was that their controversial first commander had not been a U.S. citizen, but a Canadian.

3.

SEPTEMBER 1861–MARCH 1862

THE MICHIGAN LANCERS

Late in the summer of 1861, Canadian Col. Arthur Rankin of Windsor, across the river from Detroit, offered his services to Governor Blair and President Lincoln to aid the United States in putting down the rebellion of the slave states. Rankin traveled to Washington in early September, where he received approval to form a lancer regiment—a kind of cavalry outfit—in Michigan. His plan was not only accepted by the state and federal governments, it also received hearty support from Michigan residents who lived in close proximity to Rankin.[1]

There were similarities between Rankin and Thomas Stockton, who was then organizing his independent regiment. Rankin was a man of means, military training, and experience. He held the rank of colonel in the Ninth Division of the Canadian militia, and was a member of Canada's Parliament, representing Essex, and Rankin had also held provincial office. But unlike Stockton, Rankin had the support of Michigan Governor Austin Blair.

Rankin's regiment was to be based on English lancers—mounted troops armed with long-shafted wooden spears. Lancers carried this weapon upright as they rode, resting the handle on their stirrups. When they charged, they of course lowered the lances with the metal point thrust forward toward their foe—a terrifying vision for soldiers who faced being impaled. The lancers would also have firearms and sabers, for conventional cavalry combat. According to Rankin's proposal, there were to be 1,600 lancers ready to leave the state by December 1861; recruiting offices opened around Michigan. In response to announcements in the press, some 683 men enrolled that fall in the regiment that was to be called either the Michigan Lancers or the U.S. Lancers.[2]

In Detroit there were no doubts about placing a friendly foreigner at the head of a regiment filled with Michigan men. Rankin, the *Free Press* said, "possesses all the requisites of experience and military training to take command of this novel corps."[3] Canadians also came over to join the lancers. This was not unusual, for already men from Canada joined other Michigan regiments, including Stockton's. But to some Canadians, the idea of Rankin going to war for the United States was not acceptable: Col. Rankin was an important political and military leader in his region of Canada, yet he was inserting himself into the United States' war. Almost immediately, there were objections from some of his countrymen about his plan to organize a regiment for the United States. "No man can serve two masters," the *Quebec Chronicle* warned. "Allegiance to the Foreign Government of the Northern States and allegiance to the government of Great Britain cannot co-exist."

Of course, what was left unsaid in such editorials was the ambivalence of Britain, which did not mind seeing the United States weakened by civil war. On one hand, English textile mills relied on Southern cotton, yet Britain had herself outlawed slavery long ago. There was also a long tradition of British officers serving in the militaries of other countries, though that was not mentioned in the *Chronicle,* either. But dark rumors quickly circulated in Canada that U.S. gold was being sent over to pay bounties for their men to join the lancers; other stories claimed that menacing Americans, armed and searching for deserters, had been confronted near Windsor.[4]

Rankin's troubles were just beginning. When he visited Toronto that week, he was arrested on charges that he had violated the Foreign Enlistment Act, a law that was said to date back to the reign of King George III. Released on bond, Rankin said that, contrary to sensational stories that his enemies printed, he did *not* have large sums of U.S. money at his disposal for the "furtherance of the (lancer) scheme." His lawyers argued there was no evidence he had hired or enlisted Canadians to join his regiment—if countrymen had done so, they did it on their own volition, and not because of American intrigue. Though some Canadians expressed support for the colonel, authorities agreed that Rankin could not serve two masters; a bulletin in the newspapers showed they were not going to stand by while Rankin pledged himself to fight for the United States. "Montreal, October 19," a dispatch in the *Free Press* began. "Col. Rankin has been dismissed from the [Canadian] militia and Lieut. Clark [serving as major with the lancers] from the cavalry service, being charged with enlisting men for the [U.S.] Federal service."[5]

The dismissals of Rankin and Clark from Canada's military did not cause them to stop, and their plans for a Michigan lancer regiment went forward. Though they could not know it then, as recruiting officers signed up volunteers in towns like Monroe, Adrian, Bay City, Milford, and many others, events were in motion that would overtake their plan for the Michigan Lancers.

By early November, then, some 250 or more lancer recruits had come to Detroit; they were to rendezvous at Ft. Wayne, the U.S. Army base about two of miles from the city's downtown on the Detroit River. Some of them were staying, on a temporary basis, on a steamship called the *Mississippi,* docked nearby until adequate quarters could be arranged. No horses had yet been acquired, let alone all the other equipment the lancers would need, and Rankin himself spent part of that month in Washington, returning in the third week of November. The local press welcomed him back, expressing satisfaction that now the lancer commander was present, active drilling would commence.[6]

Thanksgiving Day was quiet for the volunteers. One was Joseph Stanfield, 25, a serious-minded, religious man from the Ann Arbor area; he wrote that he thought back to

Thanksgiving of 1860, when a Baptist minister had passed the hat to help the poor people of "bleeding Kansas," torn by violence and hatred over slavery. "But how changed the scene today," Stanfield wrote in his journal, "now that the war for the Union and liberty is being resolved in every breast, and what a day it would be should peace with them be restored."[7]

But an international crisis was unfolding that would directly affect the lancers and their colonel: Suddenly the United States and Great Britain were only steps away from war. Earlier in November a U.S. warship stopped a British steamer, the *Trent,* at sea. Navy officers arrested Confederate envoys James Mason and John Slidell and removed them back to the United States as prisoners. This was explosive, a direct insult and outrage to British prestige. For days, and then weeks, there was talk of war over the matter. Of course, if it came to that, Canada, as part of the British Empire, would be at war with the United States just as it had been in the War of 1812 and the American Revolution. In Virginia, where Stockton's regiment was encamped, Michigan soldiers heard Stockton wonder whether they would have to go home to battle Canadians. "The colonel said the other day that he thought we should go back to Ft. Wayne [Detroit] to defend Michigan," young George Ervay wrote.[8]

Within two weeks of the arrest of the Confederate envoys, federal officers in Detroit had serious reservations about the Michigan lancers' Canadian connections. Lt. Col. Electus Backus learned that while Canadians were being recruited for the lancer regiment, the movement of these men on Canadian railroads was being "disguised" by one James Tillman of Detroit. Tillman was a prominent businessman and Republican, but more importantly, he was the second-in-command of the lancers. Why was this railroad matter a problem? Backus learned that Tillman was furnishing certain railway certificates—a kind of a free pass for traveling recruits—that were for use on the Detroit & Milwaukee Railroad. These passes were *not* for travel on the Canadian railroad lines, yet they were being used by Canadian recruits to reach Detroit; worse, Backus charged, these railroad passes were being altered and sold illegally, and he called this "bare-faced swindling." He warned that the recruitment and transportation of Canadians, thinly disguised with U.S. railroad passes, was more than just fraud—it could turn into an ugly and embarrassing scandal just as tensions between the federal government and the British were already so severely strained. Backus turned this information over to the U.S. Army Adjutant General. "Lieutenant Colonel Tillman is the author of this dangerous experiment, and in my opinion has willfully endangered the peace of the United States and Great Britain," Backus warned. He was obliged to report this, "at a time when it is presumed the Government does not desire to give her Britannic Majesty a just cause of complaint."[9]

It is not clear whether army officials investigated Backus's complaint, but either way the *Trent* crisis and the talk of war with Britain were overwhelming the goodwill and support Gov. Blair and Michigan newspapers expressed for the lancer regiment. Despite this, the lancer officers and Detroit military authorities planned to shift the recruits from their "unpleasant quarters" at Ft. Wayne to Camp Backus at the state fairgrounds as the month ended. At the same time, the War Department handed down an order that no more cavalry regiments were going to be accepted. Did this order apply to the lancers? Did it mean they would have to disband? Blair said he did not think so, but recruiting fell off dramatically once the *Trent* affair exploded in newspapers.[10]

"They have nothing to do, and time hangs heavy on their hands," one journalist wrote of the lancer volunteers. He noted that while most of the privates were U.S. citizens, the commissioned and noncommissioned officers were "foreigners"—Canadians. It was an obvious inference that at a time of the fear of war with Britain, command of the lancers would be in the hands of men who could soon be at war with the United States. Meanwhile, Ft. Wayne, the military base that the lancers had just left, was reported to be on a "war footing" because of the threats of Britain over the *Trent* crisis. Yet a rival newspaper denied there was any problem in the lancer regiment.[11]

Within the lancers, though, morale plummeted, according to Stanfield and letters by a recruit named Gershom W. Mattoon from Shiawassee County. Mattoon wrote that he and his comrades "had a very good time, but we did not drill much," while fights between lancer volunteers at Ft. Wayne were frequent. "Perhaps you have heard that there is six or eight hundred men here," Mattoon wrote to his sister, "but if you have, there is not, for they desert as fast as they come in." Lancer officers like Capt. Judd Mott did their best to keep the men's spirits up and maintain order by conducting drill, living in the same barracks as the men, and sleeping on beds of straw. Mott, 27, was a Vermont native who'd come to Detroit; he was later said to have been a University of Michigan graduate traveling in Europe in the spring of 1861 when the news of the outbreak of war reached him. He returned home, and that fall was commissioned as a lancer officer.[12]

Major Clark, the Canadian cavalry officer who had lost his commission from his own country, reassured the men that the lancer regiment was still on track. The federal government, he said, had promised to "render every possible assistance to the regiment." Probably to boost morale, the enlistees were allowed to go home on furlough for either Christmas or New Year's, and it was as the holidays approached that the *Trent* crisis was resolved. The nation learned that President Lincoln ordered the release of Mason and Slidell rather than risk war with Britain. But on December 26, as newspapers still wrote of the possibility of war, Arthur Rankin resigned from the Michigan lancer regiment.

"I feel constrained from a sense of duty," he wrote, "not only as a British subject but as a member of the Canadian Parliament, to withdraw from the service of the United States and return to Canada, my native land, determined to share the fate of my countrymen, whatever their destiny may be." He stressed that he had offered his services to the United States "in the spirit of a friendly neighbor" and not out of discontent as a British subject. He would never be hostile to his own country, and having been a neighbor to Detroit for more than twenty years, no one could contemplate the possible rupture of U.S.–Canadian relations with more regret. Rankin then went back to Canada, where he was "cordially received" as he offered his services to the Deputy Adjutant General of the province of Lower Canada, to defend their border if war broke out with the United States.[13]

So Rankin was gone, but his proposed lancer regiment lingered on. Uniforms arrived in January, and soon after, 200 men marched to the factory on Woodbridge Street that made their lances. These were morale boosters for the men. "They marched back to quarters in great spirits, the red and white pennon of the lances fluttering in the breeze," said one newspaper. "The lance blades are made of the best sword steel, highly polished. The shafts are Michigan white ash of the clearest grain and best quality." The uniformed men got compliments as they strolled down Woodward Avenue, Lt. Col. Tillman having allowed them to attend local church services. But the status of the regiment remained unsettled, with newspapers complaining about the cost of their uniforms and lances, and that the officers were "neglecting" the men.[14]

Good news and bad came in rapid succession. In mid-January, federal army officers received a telegram from the War Department that the lancers were to "be immediately mustered out of service," followed by another message countermanding that order. "Such a state of suspense as the officers and men have been kept in for the past ten days by the contradictory rumors and orders that have reached must here be anything but pleasant," commented the *Free Press*. "It is to be hoped that something definite in regards to the regiment may be arrived at ere long."[15]

Recruit Joseph Stanfield recorded the unrest in the lancer camp, though some recruits continued to obey orders to drill and carry out their guard assignments. Several of the volunteers were sick that season and sent to St. Mary's Hospital; Stanfield sometimes got passes to visit them, writing a letter for a young man named James Bogart, 22, to his parents in Pinkney, a small town in Livingston County. Bogart's face was swollen and he'd been diagnosed with measles and other maladies, yet the doctor was sure he'd recover.

But the fact the U.S. government was wrestling with the lancers' future was depressing and aggravating to the men, and then came an editorial in the *Free Press* that held Lt. Col. Tillman responsible for the lancers' problems, accusing the well-connected Republican businessman of profiting from supplying the regiment. Other newspapers, without naming Tillman, agreed. What could be done with these lancer recruits, who wanted to serve? A suggestion about this matter appeared in a column headlined "Local Intelligence" in the newspaper. "Colonel Stockton's regiment left here lacking two companies of its complement," the column noted, after outlining the lancers' problems:

> There is a splendid opportunity for two entire companies retaining their officers and company organization to be at once mustered into service. This regiment is under the command of popular and experienced officers, and has already by its precision in drill and soldierly bearing won the high encomiums of its brigade and division commanders.
>
> It is rumored that one or two companies of the Lancers have already partially decided upon entering Col. Stockton's regiment. No better choice could be made.[16]

Where this suggestion originated was not revealed, but Lt. Col. Backus, the federal army officer in Detroit, was familiar with Stockton's complaints about Gov. Blair's failure to send him more men. Within weeks, orders from the War Department would make this suggestion a reality. In the meantime, order and discipline broke down in what was left of the lancers. Joseph Stanfield noted that two volunteers, apparently drunk one night, ran from the camp guard, fell into the Detroit River, and drowned. One newspaper reported others made a dummy representing the officers and hung it in effigy, and that they got drunk and would not follow orders. Arguments raged in the press about whether these reports were true (they were); who was to blame for what had happened to the regiment; and whether these volunteers could still make good soldiers.[17]

Now Secretary of War Edwin Stanton sent Thomas Scott, an assistant secretary, to Michigan to "examine the condition of Michigan troops, particularly the Rankin Lancers." This was probably the final nail in the coffin for the lancer regiment. Scott almost certainly conferred with Backus, even as a newspaper claimed that the lancer men "are utterly demoralized and worthless at best." A few days later, Backus was ordered to organize two companies of infantry and two smaller detachments from the lancers, "to join General Fitz John Porter's division at the earliest possible moment." Stockton's regiment, of course, was part of that division and it seems obvious that was where they were headed. The rest of the remaining officers and men who had wanted to be lancers were to be mustered out of the service, though they were free to enlist in another regiment. "What will be done with the six or seven thousand dollars' worth of spears," one paper wrote about their lances, "remains a mystery."[18]

Now it was just a matter for the remaining lancers to await their final pay day. Stanfield and another volunteer, Orville Greene, went to visit sick comrades at the hospital. They found James Bogart much improved though weak, but that a "Mr. Eddy" from the lancers' Company G had died early that morning. Bogart sat with the dying man, and told his comrades how a few hours before the end, Eddy saw a vision of his mother, who had been dead for several years. "He aroused from his slumber while James was at his bedside," Stanfield wrote, "and looking upward he said, 'There is my mother. Don't you see her? She has come to take me home.'" Eddy died peacefully a short time later. Bogart would soon join Stockton's regiment, as would Stanfield and Greene, 21, of Ann Arbor.

Back in the lancer camp, military discipline for many or most of them ceased to exist. "Before [receiving the order to disband] we had some order," said Gershom Mattoon, "if a man got drunk, he was put in the guard house. We had twelve sentries on at once and three reliefs [*sic*] making thirty-six men every day, and if a man passed [through] the lines, [he needed] a written pass signed by one of their commissioned officers, or the counter-sign. But now we have no guards and all the men go where and when they have a-mind to."[19]

The lancers' companies D and E were designated as those that would be assigned to Stockton's regiment, though Mattoon noted that the men of Company D would "not go one inch" until they were paid off and discharged from the lancers. Many of them would reenlist, he said, "but they will not go under the officers they have now." Mattoon was correct; the captain of that company, an unpopular Canadian, did not lead those lancers into Stockton's command. In the days ahead, that role was instead filled by Capt. Mott and Lt. Edward Hill, 27, a New York state native and Detroiter. Among the lancer recruits following them into Stockton's regiment, which was soon to be enrolled as a state command, the 16th Michigan Infantry, was Stanfield, the serious and religious Ann Arbor area volunteer; Bogart, from Livingston County; and Wallace Jewett from Saginaw. All these men were fated to die in the months ahead: Bogart would be killed in action at

Gettysburg, Pennsylvania, on a hill called Little Round Top; in the National Cemetery there his name is misspelled "James Bags" on the stone marker.

On March 2, Mott led the first sixty volunteers, "men transferred from the lancers, and are composed of the best material of that regiment," on a three-day journey to join Stockton's Independent Regiment at Hall's Hill, Virginia. Mott would soon return to Detroit to take more ex-lancers, along with Lt. Benjamin F. Partridge. John Berry, one of the soldiers from the Upper Peninsula in the Stockton regiment, recorded the coming of the ex-lancers along with morning's hard frost and regiment's bayonet drill. "A co. of Lancers arrived today from Detroit to fill up our regiment," he noted. Frank Keeler also mentioned their arrival that week in a letter back to Saginaw. Ex-lancer Joseph Stanfield expressed satisfaction with the new camp and comrades.[20]

For him and some 200 former lancers, this was their revised starting point as soldiers in the Civil War, in what would soon be two companies in Stockton's regiment in the Army of the Potomac. In particular, officers Mott, Partridge, and Edward Hill would prove able leaders in their new regiment in the months ahead.

In the meantime, the fact that Col. Stockton and his officers held no commissions from Michigan got the attention of the generals. Men like Fitz John Porter and George McClellan, professional soldiers (and Democrats), were sympathetic to these officers of volunteers, since a commission from one's home state was an honor and point of pride. But not only did Stockton's men not have commissions, it was obvious that Gov. Blair would not consider promoting them when leadership vacancies appeared in other Michigan regiments. The idea that Stockton's officers would be denied the chance for promotion was probably anathema to military professionals, since they knew these men were risking their lives in the service of their country. But how could this be resolved? The answer was twofold: by changing the rules and by applying political pressure to the governor of Michigan.

On February 10, McClellan recommended to Secretary of War Edmond Stanton that the federal authority, given previously to men like Stockton who raised independent regiments, be revoked. That would mean Stockton could no longer bring new officers and recruits into his regiment on his own authority, but it necessarily meant that the governor would have to do so. This new rule would end independent regiments, essentially turning them into state regiments after the fact. It would also force Blair to commission the officers of Stockton's regiment or create massive headaches and political problems for himself. Less than two weeks later, the War Department issued orders to this effect—the governors alone were the legal authorities to raise volunteer regiments and commission volunteer officers.[21]

In the meantime, Col. Stockton took the matter of his regiment's officers not having proper commissions to President Lincoln. On February 24, with the approval of generals Butterfield, Porter, and McClellan, Stockton made his case. "The Governor has always shown the utmost hostility to us—using from the beginning every means in his power to prevent us from raising this regiment," the colonel wrote. Stockton included for the president's consideration the two letters from the governor to "C. Sykes" and "Witherell," where Blair stated he would have nothing to do with Stockton and his regiment. These letters, the colonel said, showed the governor's "*present* feelings toward myself and regiment and his determination *not* to *recognize* us, or grant us commissions."[22]

Surely his officers were "entitled to commissions from some source," Stockton wrote; perhaps the president could grant them. "I respectfully refer to my Brigade and Division commanders, as to the manner that myself and those under me have been performing our duties."

> Unaided and strongly opposed by all the executive influence of my state, I nonetheless succeeded in raising my regiment, brought it on and am now ready with it, and prove our loyalty whenever and as soon as our gallant commander deems it proper to give us an opportunity to do so. In the chances of war, my officers should have his [*sic*] commission as proof of his rank. It is for that reason that myself and subordinates present our position.[23]

Gen. Fitz John Porter, the commander of the division of which Stockton's regiment was part, supported Stockton in a note to the president. "I have asked Gov. Blair to commission the officers of this regiment and to otherwise recognize it by numbering the regiment with the others from the state and supply it colors," Porter wrote. "He pays no attention to my appeal nor to Col. Stockton. As I presume no power can compel action from him, I respectfully ask the rights of these officers to be recognized by the United States and that they may be also commissioned by the government."[24]

Lincoln sent Stockton's request on to Gov. Blair through the secretary of war, who asked the governor to provide commissions to the officers of the Stockton regiment. Faced with these pressures, Blair would soon at last give in, and Stockton's regiment would be formally enrolled as a state command. But winter was giving way to spring in Virginia now, and the war was about to resume.

Just a week after the first of the ex-lancers arrived, most of Stockton's Independent Regiment moved out with their brigade and division. "On Sunday night [March 9] about 2 o'clock, the orders came to us in camp at Hall's Hill for a *real* move," wrote an officer. "The camp in a moment was all astir." This was probably Maj. Norval Welch, sending a letter back to the Democratic newspaper in Detroit. At last the tedium of winter camp life was ending. McClellan had vowed there would be no more embarrassing defeats like Bull Run, which occurred before he was given command of the Union army; the soldiers army must be well trained, properly equipped and prepared before he went on the offensive. But months had passed, and Lincoln demanded McClellan move against the Confederacy. Now the Army of the Potomac was about to advance toward enemy positions a day's march away on the road to Richmond.

The new men who had recently joined Stockton's regiment—the ex-lancers who did not know infantry movements, and the Brady Sharpshooters who did not yet have all the necessary gear—stayed behind as camp guard. Some of these men watched with envy as their new comrades marched out. “I enlisted months ago for this good war,” one sharpshooter complained, “and have waited patiently for this hour to come, and now, when I would give everything to go with you, I am deprived just for the want of equipments.”[25]

The troops were sure this was the “on to Richmond” movement some Northern newspapers were demanding, and they would soon meet the Rebel force that McClellan thought was waiting for them in defenses at Manassas and Centreville. The marching columns of Porter’s division passed through Fall’s Church that morning, and John Berry of Company A found the going slow and tiresome, what with the muddy road and heavy packs and provisions.[26]

“It commenced raining and continuing all afternoon, the roads very bad,” Col. Stockton agreed. His regiment was at the rear of their division and the twelve-mile march brought them to Fairfax Court House that night. “Having only taken five tents, the men used them for shelter bunks and we encamped in a lonely grove just east of town.” But Stockton recorded the news of the day in an understated fashion: “On arriving, we ascertained that the Rebels had evacuated Centreville and Manassas.”[27]

The reluctant McClellan had believed faulty intelligence reports that these were fortified, heavily manned positions. Instead his troops found empty works and logs propped up in gun emplacements to look like cannon—“Quaker guns.” The Confederate commander here, Joseph Johnston, recognizing he did not have adequate forces to hold their long line and anticipating a Union advance, pulled his force back to the Rappahannock River. The men of the brigade in which Stockton’s regiment served and other Union soldiers cheered, considering this a bloodless victory. But McClellan’s critics were outraged. They had been impatient for an offensive to punish the Rebels and take Richmond, the Confederate capital, but the town remained well protected.

McClellan, they charged, had been fooled and accomplished nothing. Stockton, a Democrat like McClellan, sided with his general against the Radical Republicans who derided him. When the colonel looked at the abandoned Rebel positions, he felt McClellan was right in exercising caution. “With Major Welch visited the Centreville and [Manassas-Bull Run] battlefield,” Stockton noted in his diary. “Found the former strongly fortified, some at various points toward the battlefield. Found larger encampments of well-built log huts, far more comfortable that any we have had. Every evidence that the Rebels left us on Sunday [March 9] in great haste.”[28]

Another officer from the regiment, probably Maj. Welch again writing to Detroit, maintained the Quaker gun issue was being used by abolitionists to attack McClellan when the fake cannon had been put there, as a joke, by Union cavalry troopers. “The ruse of the wooden cannon, ‘Quaker guns,’ was perpetrated by our own men,” he wrote. “The regiment that arrived first . . . placed some pine longs in the embrasures to terrify, if possible, the regiments that came after them.” He said the story told by McClellan’s critics that he’d been fooled by these was “absurd and shameful.” He claimed the Confederate troops left their strong defenses at the last moment, and went on to say that the soldiers supported McClellan wholeheartedly. “I do not know an abolitionist or an emancipationist among us,” the officer insisted.[29]

Stockton's regiment remained with its brigade at Fairfax Court House for a few days and the colonel used the time to continue to drill the brigade. McClellan reviewed Porter's division on the evening of March 12, but no longer was he in charge of all the Union forces; his command was reduced by Lincoln to that of the Army of the Potomac alone. Now he would start his men on a new but plodding offensive against the Confederacy and its capital.

Back in Michigan, Gov. Austin Blair had been feeling the pressure to officially recognize the officers of Stockton's regiment with state commissions; Lincoln and the generals wanted it, and the officers of the regiment (with all their friends and families back home) wanted it. In addition, there were almost certainly complications arising. Consider the example of Capt. Judd Mott, formerly of the lancers (which Blair had supported). Would Mott be deprived of a commission for taking his men, at the order of the War Department, into Stockton's Independent Regiment (which Blair had opposed)? It may have been pointed out to Blair that he had gotten what he wanted, after all. He had demanded the federal government stop authorizing the formation of independent regiments, and it had. Now he, in turn, would have to do something about the resolving the question of the status of Stockton's regiment and its officers, despite his animosity toward the colonel.

Blair messaged State Adjutant General John Robertson on March 19. "Please issue commissions to Capt. Mott and his lieutenants and attach them to Col. Stockton's regiment, which I think you had better number the 16th Infantry." With that memorandum, the governor seems to have accepted that which he had so long opposed—a state regiment under Thomas Stockton, authorized after the fact. Now that the once-independent regiment was an official state command and Michigan entity, the next logical stop was that its other officers should also have the honor of state commissions, though Gov. Blair did not like that idea, either. A week later, he relented on that point. "Dear sir," Blair wrote to Robertson, "In accordance with the request of the War Department, issue commissions to Stockton and his officers. I presume the public service requires it."[30]

With the addition of two companies of former lancers and the Brady Sharpshooters company, Stockton now had, at least on paper, a full-strength regiment, though illness and casualties would very soon slash away at the ranks of these men and their officers. Now the war in the Virginia theater would begin again as McClellan moved his army by sea to the peninsula formed by the York and James Rivers.

4.

MARCH–MAY 1862

VICTORIES WITHOUT BLOOD IS McCLELLAN'S PLAN

Before dawn on Saturday, March 15, Brig. Gen. Fitz John Porter's division rose and began the march from Fairfax Court House. Their destination was Alexandria, where ships waited to take the Army of the Potomac down the Virginia coast for McClellan's new offensive. "Began to rain about 8 [a.m.] and poured down most of the day," Col. Stockton wrote. "All of my men perfectly well." The men's morale was not so positive. Some accounts of their brigade said the troops were disappointed in the failure of the previous week's "on to Richmond" march, and the mood was gloomy as they moved sixteen miles in what Pvt. Henry "Tip" Aplin called "awful bad marching."

"The road was completely lined with soldiers," he continued. "Clothes of every description, knapsacks, were thrown away by the hundreds. I stood the march first rate and kept all that I started with, which was not much." Outside of Alexandria, Stockton's regiment took possession of tents that had been occupied by the 53rd Pennsylvania. "They were most acceptable to us, all wet and tired," Stockton wrote. One of the regiment's clerks did not agree. "Camp very bad," wrote that chronicler, "named Camp Misery, very properly." Some members of the Brady Sharpshooters and ex-lancers fared better; Capt. James Dafoe of Company F was in charge of a number of the soldiers who had to initially remain behind at Hall's Hill, but now when they arrived at Alexandria he found them temporary quarters in a large brick building, apparently a warehouse.[1]

The men who did not go to Alexandria were those who were too sick, like Warren Heald, a 22-year-old farmer from Ionia. "It was on the account of our regiment having orders to move, and I not able to go, so I was sent here," he wrote to his family from a government hospital in Philadelphia. Heald eventually rejoined his regiment, but by the fall would be hospitalized again. That was the beginning of the end of his service; before the year was over, he was mustered out. Illness did not just take more lives than combat in the war in the Civil War, it also debilitated thousands of men like Heald.[2]

Alexandria was crawling with Union soldiers, boarding or waiting to board transports. Stockton's officers tried to keep the men busy with drill as they bivouacked on a hill west of town near the Fairfax Seminary in a muddy assemblage called Camp California. In their spare time the men looked for friends from home as hundreds of ships were loaded for the journey, though they had not been told where. The loading was slow and the wet weather turned cold. Stockton's regiment moved closer to town to another hillside called Camp Kearney, but it was impossible to stay dry or comfortable in poncho tents. John Berry of Company A said he heard Col. Stockton complain to Gen. Butterfield about the terrible conditions the men were experiencing, but Butterfield said no to the request for better quarters—perhaps because of orders that the private property of Rebel sympathizers and civilians had to be respected, or perhaps because there was simply no place to put entire regiments, brigades, and divisions. Faced with yet another miserable night, many of the Michigan soldiers walked away from camp to find better shelter and the officers did not stop them. "Towards night, two-thirds of the regiment take French leave and find their own quarters," Berry wrote. "Some go to Alexandria, some camp in the woods. I stay in camp, rains all night."[3] "French leave," of course, meant unauthorized leave.

At noon on March 21 the regiment began to file toward the docks with hundreds if not thousands of others, waiting and standing for hours and sinking into mud that was said to be a foot deep. Most of Stockton's men crowded aboard a steamship called the *Nantasket* while the remaining companies boarded the *William R. Frazier.* The men by this point guessed that their destination was the Union stronghold down the Virginia coast called Fortress Monroe. But the rain kept falling that night—a miserably uncomfortable one for the soldiers—as the ships pulled away from shore to await the other transports that were still loading.[4]

Around noon the next day the fleet bearing the Army of the Potomac sailed into Chesapeake Bay, past the massive masonry Fort Washington and abandoned Rebel batteries. The journey down the coast took a day and a night in clearing weather, with the ships, escorted by U.S. Navy gunboats, arriving on the afternoon of March 23 at Fortress Monroe at the tip of the York-James Peninsula and across the harbor from Norfolk. Frank Keeler was impressed with the sight of the famous new naval craft that had done battle earlier that month with the ironclad *Merrimac*—"the great iron gunboat Monitor, which looks, as the rebels say, 'like a cheesebox on a plank,'" he wrote.[5] The *Monitor* had fought its opponent, renamed the *Virginia* by the Confederates, to a draw. The battle ended the era of the wooden ship navy.

Here from the ruined town of Hampton, Virginia, close by Fortress Monroe, McClellan planned to advance his army to Richmond. After dreary hours of delay and waiting, the ships docked and unloaded on the morning of March 24; the town had been burned to the ground months before. Stockton's regiment marched out of Hampton and camped that night in the fields, moving again the next day with its Third Brigade of Porter's division in the heat to the edge of a pine forest. Gen. Butterfield passed on the order that civilian property was to be spared, so no more fence rails were to be turned into firewood. Worse for the men, it would take days to establish new, working supply lines. "We have had very hard living since we left Hall's Hill," complained John Berry. "We have had nothing but hard bread, salt pork raw and coffee, and the last few days nothing but hard bread and not enough of that."[6]

With nowhere to go as the unloading of ships continued, the next day the men drilled, though Company A received new lessons—aiming, loading, and firing cannon. "Officers and men of Company A have an artillery drill," Berry said. "The officers of the artillery of our brigade instruct us, the reason of our learning this drill is in case the cannoneers [*sic*] get killed in action, we can take their place." On March 27 Stockton's men moved out with their division in pleasant weather through farm country to a town called Big Bethel, where a large force of Rebels was thought to be waiting. At 11:30 a.m. the Confederate breastworks came into view, but the Rebel skirmishers fell back as the Union soldiers advanced. The Confederates withdrew further up the York-James peninsula, and there was no clash that day. Stockton's regiment and their comrades marched back to their camp, tired and hungry as the sun went down. "We returned . . . much disappointed in not getting a sight at the Rebels," Stockton wrote. He thought the enemy would give a "great fight," perhaps at Yorktown.[7]

The rains returned and for several days the soldiers drilled, did washing and guard duty, and underwent inspections, their camp sometimes shifting as they tried to get out of standing water. As March ended and April began, ships continued to bring what amounted to more than 100,000 men and ton after ton of supplies, wagons, horses, and artillery batteries. Now Captain Judd Mott and Lt. Edward Hill, former lancers, showed up in Stockton's camp within hours of each other, bringing more of their men for the regiment. There were probably about 180 ex-lancers in Stockton's regiment at this point, and most of them would serve in two new companies—Company I under Mott, and Company K, initially under Capt. Gustav Kast of Detroit, a former officer in the 2nd Michigan Infantry Regiment who was related by marriage to Lt. Col. John V. Ruehle. Kast would only be with Stockton's regiment until his resignation in three months' time, when Ruehle also resigned from the army.

Frank Keeler noted that one of the new noncommissioned officers from the lancers was from his hometown. "Wallace Jewett of Saginaw City is the orderly sergeant of Company K," he wrote that week. It would turn out that Jewett had only fifteen months to live; he would reach the rank of lieutenant and die in battle on a rocky hill in Pennsylvania called Little Round Top.[8]

The regiment moved out with its brigade and division on the morning of April 4. On days such as this when the troops were on the march, passing groups of curious soldiers would ask each other the identities of their regiments. Edward Hill recalled, decades later, his comrades' answer; when soldiers from Ohio or Massachusetts or New York asked them what regiment they were, they replied "Stockton's, old Stockton's."[9]

If the colonel heard these exchanges, he was undoubtedly proud. That was changing, however, as the regiment's new state identity, the 16th Michigan Infantry, took hold. But the Union troops moved up the peninsula on the road to Yorktown that morning, with the Rebels withdrawing as they advanced. Stockton's men and their comrades camped on the ground the Confederates vacated. The rain returned, and the next day the roads turned to deep mud as Stockton's regiment continued on that afternoon. "The roads are in awful condition," John Berry recorded. "Our regiment being on the left flank of the left brigade [in the moving column of troops], is the rear of the whole division & consequently we have the worst road." It was the hardest march they had yet experienced as they drew closer to the town, the eastern-most point of the Rebel defensive position across the narrow York-James peninsula. "We halted in front of the rebel fortifications in shelling range, with a clump of woods between us and the enemy, so we did not get shelled out," Cpl. Frank Keeler said. The Union batteries in front started firing back but Stockton's regiment did not participate in this clash, and only moved by it with their brigade. "We could see the firing on both sides," Keeler said, "and the shells bursting and cutting the trees and bushes over our batteries."[10]

They marched on, now directly south of Yorktown, where the Confederate infantry and artillery covered the approaches from both land and sea. At about 4 p.m. Stockton's regiment was ordered out of the brigade to make a reconnaissance; the colonel said his orders were "to find if there was any new way to approach Yorktown than the one in front"—that is, other than the road running directly to the town. His men moved to the edge of a pine woods and formed in line. The small-statured Sgt. Rufus Jacklin of the Brady Sharpshooters said later he was ordered to reconnoiter to the right, nearest to the banks of the York River, where he was to communicate his findings to Union gunboats. "I performed my duty by deploying the company as skirmishers, crossing the bayou, driving back the enemy and firing the first guns upon the works at Yorktown," he later boasted. Perhaps it was his performance directing these skirmishers that would, in just over a month's time, earn him promotion to second lieutenant.[11]

The confrontation as recorded then by John Berry of Company A was not so dramatic. He said squads from the regiment crossed a creek or mill dam, but they were spotted by the crew of a Rebel battery in the Yorktown defenses, which opened fire. "We beat a retreat in hurry," Berry admitted. Tip Aplin from Company C said he stood in a skirmish line with his comrades that afternoon within "100 rods" of a large fort. There were Confederate rifle pits here, what modern soldiers would call foxholes or perhaps trenches. "Their pickets and ours were from 20 to 80 rods apart and the way the bullets whistled around our heads was not slow." Aplin said he saw "two or three" Rebels fall in the exchange of rifle fire.[12]

This was a baptism of fire for some of the regiment, though not a true test of the Yorktown defenses. Stockton's officers said that the Confederate positions in front of them were strong; reconnaissance by other Union units had found vulnerable points but McClellan decided no assault would take place. Just before dark the weary men ended their probe of the enemy's line. Stockton's regiment marched back to bivouac with their division as a Union observation balloon floated above them. That night Stockton recorded the situation as Gen. McClellan presented it to his officers: The Rebels had built a strong crescent-shaped line of forts from the York to the James, and these were manned by 50,000 troops with more arriving each day. The colonel bemoaned that Northern politicians were not united in support of McClellan, who was under constant criticism by Republican leaders and press who felt that the war was about slavery, and that McClellan was too cautious in his tactics.

In truth, the Confederate general in charge of the Yorktown defenses, John Bankhead Magruder, only had a fraction of that number, though he was receiving reinforcements that would eventually bring his forces up to 70,000 men. McClellan, on the other hand, had 53,000 soldiers and 100 cannon—a far more powerful force than the one he faced as his men reached Yorktown. The skirmishing that day marked the start of what Stockton called "a pause in operations" while large siege guns were brought up to shell the Yorktown defenders. Though many soldiers like Stockton were sure a large battle would soon take place, McClellan did not intend to attack these fortifications with infantry.[13]

THE SIEGE OF YORKTOWN

Stockton's men pitched their tents, underwent inspections, heard dueling cannon, and suffered some hunger pangs until supplies arrived. But the colonel's prediction that "the conflict must open soon" at Yorktown was limited to picket fire and periodic shelling. "Very pleasant to look at," Stockton wrote about the jetting plumes of artillery smoke, "but not so pleasant when shot at. Both [sides] fire with great accuracy and strike or explode very close. Five or six gunboats up here and firing at the town or enemy."[14]

The spring rains opened up again, turning the Union camps into swamps. Fitz John Porter's division, of which Stockton's regiment was part, moved back out of artillery range, making room for the placement of Union guns. Though the colonel waxed dramatically that some "200,000 men" on both sides were ready to "spring to arms and unite in mortal combat," the truth was that a kind of trench warfare was taking place, with the Union soldiers digging rifle pits and gun emplacements, and building roads and bridges so heavy siege batteries could come up. "It is said that their entrenchments here are the strongest they have, and that we will have a hard time taking them," Lt. Charles Salter wrote. He, too, heard the story that the Rebels had 100,000 men and hundreds of cannon in those defenses, and it was clear his generals accepted this was true. "Great preparations are being made for a heavy siege," Frank Keeler wrote. "The battle will undoubtedly be mainly with artillery. Mortars are being landed below [just south of Yorktown] and planted for action."[15]

Shot and shell flew as the soldiers dug or manned rifle pits within sight of the Confederate forts, sometimes working near sites where soldiers dug trenches more than eighty years previously as the Revolutionary War was coming to a close at Yorktown. A Rebel sharpshooter fired at Lt. Col. Ruehle, Stockton's old friend. "Close, but missed him," Stockton noted. John Berry said enemy fire was routine. "While I am on post the balls fly all around me, one passing a foot from my head, but a 'miss' is as good as a mile," he wrote. Tip Aplin from Flint said that in trenches closest to the enemy "a half a dozen bullets was sure to come in close proximity with our heads" if a man showed himself.[16]

The marksmanship of the Brady Sharpshooters of Stockton's regiment and the U.S.

Sharpshooter regiments posed deadly danger to Confederates on the fortifications. "Our sharpshooters are picking them off with precision all the time at a distance of 800 yards," Berry recorded proudly. "This is not very encouraging to them." Lt. Salter said skirmish fire by pickets at about 400 yards was routine.[17]

The weather turned hot and muggy. When off duty the men could gather oysters from the small creek nearby; there was also laurel growing around the camp, so many soldiers worked on wood carving projects in their spare time. "Almost every soldier is whittling out a pipe or a ring," Keeler wrote. But artillery fired regularly, sometimes through the night; Tip Aplin said he was used to it. "The noise does not disturb my nightly dreams in the least," he claimed. "I can sleep as sound as if I was in a feather bed." Col. Stockton recorded that he was suffering "cutting pains" in his right side and back and he treated them with liniment, but he did not ask medical leave since he was convinced a battle could start at any moment.[18]

An unhappy officer from Stockton's regiment was also putting pen to paper that day. Thomas Barry of Detroit, captain of Company A, complained to the Michigan Adjutant General—something he could not do before Stockton's regiment became the state's 16th Michigan Infantry. Barry explained that he had organized his company at Stockton's request and so had Stockton's friend from Flint, Thomas Carr. But Carr only managed to sign up forty men for Company C initially, so his men had been mustered in with Barry's.

"I asked Col. Stockton if I could be mustered as I supposed I would," Barry wrote. "He said it did not matter—wait a day or two weeks." The captain said he did not think anything of it, and he had done the work of senior captain since then. But now that they were an enrolled state regiment, Stockton's roster of regimental officers showed that Carr, not Barry, was listed as senior captain. Why was this important to Barry? Say for example that because of death, severe illness, or resignation, the position of major became open in the regiment. Barry knew Stockton, a West Point graduate and former army officer, would by seniority promote Carr since Stockton decided he was the "senior" captain. "It is the general opinion of the officers of the regiment that I am entitled to it," Barry said about the designation of senior captain.[19]

It was an example, he continued, of Stockton's favoritism toward his friends and acquaintances from Flint and Genesee County in Company C, and Barry claimed he was not alone in this feeling; officers and men in the rest of the regiment resented that choice assignments were given to these men. "Quartermaster, commissary Sergeant, assistant [quartermaster,] wagon master [are] all from Flint, which seems to run the regiment," he complained. Barry said he would resign if it were not for the fact that the regiment could be called into battle soon, "for I can assure you that it takes me all the time and constantly fighting to get my rations for my men and they go hungry half the time. I have heard we were numbered the 16th Infantry from Michigan for which I am very glad for now perhaps, we will be looked after somewhat better than we have been."[20]

Was Company C getting special treatment? Better food, or more food? As did John Berry of Company A, Tip Aplin, a member of Company C, complained his rations were "hard bread, coffee, and beef, and sometimes nothing but hard bread." In truth, many soldiers felt like they were not getting enough to eat at Yorktown as commissaries (food supply officers) struggled to organize new supply lines out of the confusion of the army's big move. The fact that Stockton's regiment was only recently enrolled as a state regiment had no bearing on this, for all the regiments were in the federal service. "If you happen to come down this way, you had better fetch along a file to sharpen your teeth with," Aplin joked about eating hardtack, an army staple. "Mine are getting rather dull." Aplin asked his brother to send him cash, "for nothing comes so handy as money while we are on the march. We don't draw anything but hard crackers and a little meat. If I had a little money, I could by a piece of cheese, a little butter, cakes or something else."[21]

Clearly Stockton's decisions giving certain jobs to men from Company C had nothing to do with the issuing of the regiment's rations, or whether one company got more food than another. Jobs and assignments within a military unit were the province of the commanding officer; if Stockton gave choice assignments to men who had been friends and neighbors back home, it was his prerogative. Jealousies and complaints like Barry's seem to have poured into state adjutant generals' offices during the Civil War, and there is no evidence that Michigan's John Robertson took any action on Barry's complaints.

For the soldiers, the main tasks were picket or fatigue in the near constant rain. Stockton's men, who were learning about their new 16th Michigan designation, incurred no fatalities or even wounds from Confederate guns of Yorktown—only injuries they inflicted on themselves. "There was no accident on our side, I think," former lancer Joseph Stanfield about a day-long picket duty, "except that a drummer boy of Company F shot off his own thumb with his pistol." Marion Munson of Company E was standing guard in the brush when the drummer, standing behind him in a ravine, was "a-fooling" with his pistol. "He got shot through the thick of his thumb and the ball just went over my head," Munson said.[22]

That night the regiment moved up an old road going to the northeast, closer to Yorktown defenses, so close they could hear a Rebel band concert. "They have some excellent musicians, and it sounds most beautiful in the still of the night," said John Berry. Company D, which had scores of Saginaw men, went with three other companies into the no man's land between the lines, passing through a peach orchard and establishing a picket in an estate called the Moore mansion, a picturesque colonial-era farm. There were no Rebels here, so the officers posted guards while the rest of the men stacked arms and rested in the darkness. Frank Keeler and his friend Heber Woodruff explored the old mansion, which had been stripped to bare walls and floors.[23]

The Michigan soldiers were in the unenviable position that men in wartime often face. They were tired, and it was dark; their position was dangerous—well within artillery range—but quiet. Men could rest, but they could not build a fire or get too comfortable. One of the men was having too much fun, however, to be bored. "Among the most wakeful was Cordell Green of Bridgeport," Keeler said, "a thorough clown, never tired, and always up to mischief. His delight was to frighten the timid at every opportunity." Six men who were not on guard duty climbed into an omnibus, or enclosed carriage, parked on the grounds. These soldiers "entertained themselves with frightful stories in low tones till after 2 a.m. when sleep began to make them a trifle unconscious of everything but the ever present sense of danger."

Green, then about 18, saw his comrades nodding off and gathered several of his friends over to watch him scare the daylights out of the men dozing in the omnibus. He quietly reached into the carriage, "caught hold of the one nearest the door with a sudden shake, at the same time uttering the frightful warning, 'fall in, fall in!' in a loud whisper.'" His friends observing the prank withdrew to a safe distance, trying to suppress convulsing laughter as they watched "six men try to see who could get out of the omnibus door first." They "could not have been more frightened if a dozen rebels had jumped on them 'with both feet,'" Keeler laughed. The prankster Green would be wounded later that year at Second Bull Run, but he survived and was mustered out of the army at the end of his enlistment in 1864.[24]

The night was uneventful, and the men moved out before daylight, marching back to camp for a rest. Late that afternoon, 300 of Stockton's men went out again with 500 soldiers from their brigade, digging trenches in the rain. That pattern continued, though temperatures at last began to rise again. The men placed their rifles on the ground behind them as they dug, throwing dirt in front (toward the Rebel positions) to make a parapet. Sometimes work stopped when Confederate gunners fired on them, at least until the Union gunboats could answer, suppressing the Rebel fire.

Yet another of Stockton's men proved he may have learned to handle a rifle, but not his own revolver. Pvt. Daniel Manchen of Company E shot himself in the knee while demonstrating how his pistol worked as he tried to sell it to another soldier. That was enough for Col. Stockton; Marion Munson said the colonel ordered all privates and noncommissioned officers to turn any sidearms over to the quartermaster. The men could have their revolvers back after the war was over, Stockton ruled.[25]

By now there was a Union network of newly constructed roads and trenches spreading through the countryside at Yorktown, "so that artillery, cavalry or infantry can be brought up in front of the enemy at a dozen different points without their having intimation of your approach," Frank Keeler wrote as April ended. "Once Yorktown is reduced and the army in it captured, the war in Virginia will be about closed." Not all their engineering efforts went smoothly. One side of a bridge that Marion Munson worked on collapsed as it was finished. "I believe they have made it a pontoon bridge now," Munson wrote, probably with sarcasm.[26]

The rain let up briefly, but the work went on nonstop. John Berry had a close call when a cannonball plowed into the ground, throwing mud and dirt over him and another soldier. Still, he thought, "the explosion of shells looks very beautiful in the night." The Union siege guns were coming up now with long wagon trains of ammunition, though fatigue continued. Corporal James Worth, 30, from Flushing, died suddenly of an apparent heart attack as he sat down to smoke his pipe after their work was over one day. At almost the same time, Col. Stockton wrote, probably to state Adjt. Gen. John Robertson, defending Gen. McClellan. He was sure that a "big fight" would now take place, one that could end the rebellion, but with little loss of life because of McClellan's careful approach. "He is doing wonders and his strategy is the best that can be," the colonel wrote. "I trust all will wait a short time yet, before they condemn him for being so slow."[27]

Suddenly the Confederate artillery opened a furious barrage, not just a few volleys at the pickets or working soldiers, but an ongoing shelling, sending more projectiles flying than before. "The Rebels throw shells around our camp but accidentally do not do any damage," John Berry wrote on May 2. His colonel also recorded this: "The enemy has fired very often today, and in all directions," he wrote. "They are emboldened by our silence."[28]

The firing died off and the next morning was clear. As Stockton's regiment left camp for entrenching work, the Rebel guns cut loose again. One soldier, John Hodgkins, 29, of Lapeer, who was likely with the lancers before joining the regiment, was struck on the shoulder by a spent piece of shell—that is, a flying fragment that had lost velocity to the point where it did not tear into Hodgkins or break his bones when it hit him. "The Rebels did not fire until about 9 a.m., leading many to suppose that they might be evacuating," Stockton wrote, "but they soon heard very different for they kept up a very continuous firing." The big Union guns, now in place, replied; Corporal Frank Keeler said their firing seemed to shake the earth.[29]

But Stockton was wrong—the Confederates were indeed leaving their Yorktown defenses under the cover of their artillery bombardment, hoping it would keep Union soldiers' heads down as they withdrew. That afternoon, Gen. Fitz John Porter decided to go up in the observation balloon and see for himself. The balloon was still anchored only a couple hundred feet from Stockton's camp. "At once the balloon became a target," Stockton wrote, "and as my regiment is in front and nearly in the line of fire, shot and shell fell in and around my camp. One piece struck [a] sergeant's tent and broke things generally, another missed [the] adjutant's horse." But the balloon came quickly down, and the regiment emerged unscathed. The only casualty in their vicinity was a mule, grazed by a projectile.[30]

The artillery firing continued into the early morning of May 4 as the Rebels successfully withdrew the last of their soldiers from the Yorktown line. For nearly a month they had stalled McClellan while fortifying Richmond's defenses. At 7 a.m. Stockton's men heard the cheering from Union trenches: The enemy was gone! Some of McClellan's force quickly moved out in pursuit; Frank Keeler wrote that the pounding drums and bands, the cheers, and the army in motion "make up a scene I am unable to describe." Stockton, like McClellan and his supporters, viewed the Confederate evacuation as a victory, though he knew the general's critics would be angry. "I suppose our abolition friends will say that we have not had a fight and half of us killed," he grumbled. "But I look upon such a victory, a bloodless one, as the most glorious one. Honor to him, who had by his strategy brought it about."[31]

Stockton's regiment was not part of the force that pursued the Confederates—Porter's division was held in reserve. For the next day or so, the men could hear cannonading up the river, and they avoided small white flags that other Union soldiers had planted to mark the presence of land mines, then called "torpedoes" and made with artillery shells. They heard about the battle of Williamsburg, where the Rebels fought a tough rear-guard action about 15 miles to the north. Stockton's men were now under marching orders—that is, they had to be prepared to move out at any moment—but the regiment and its division did not leave Yorktown till May 8.

That afternoon the soldiers marched past the fortifications and flag-marked torpedoes to the York River. At 8 p.m. some boarded the steamboat *Long Branch* and others the *Spaulding* as their brigade and division prepared to sail up the river twenty-five miles to the town of West Point. They arrived that night, at the point where the Pamunkey and Mattaponi rivers met and formed the York. In the morning they left the ships and camped by the river.[32]

The men heard rumors about the Williamsburg battle and a clash that took place on May 7 there where they had landed—Stockton himself heard gossip about Col. Henry Terry, commander of the 5th Michigan Infantry, yelling with pain at a nonexistent wound to his foot (a recurring tale among Civil War soldiers). Stockton also heard a false report that his niece's Rebel husband, Gen. James Longstreet, had been killed. "Poor Louise," Stockton wrote, thinking the story true. "What a blow that will be to her."

One of the most shocking stories, at least part fiction, recorded by Stockton and two of his men, was that soldiers from a what was supposedly a black Confederate regiment had committed atrocities, stabbing to death or cutting the throats of several wounded Union soldiers. The colonel wrote that a Rebel deserter, a "Negro sergeant" from that regiment, was hung in retribution for the murders. James M. Hollister, 20, a former lancer from Utica, gave an even more ghastly account to his sister of the murders of black Rebels who, he claimed, admitted to the atrocities. "We caught 4 of them & they confessed they did it," Hollister wrote. "We hung them up until they were half dead, cut them down & burnted [*sic*] the other half." Yet the identity of these murdered men and their regiment is not mentioned in the various versions of the story that circulated. In truth, Union battle reports written about the clash on May 7 stated that one soldier was found with his throat cut and another who had been killed by multiple stab wounds, with no indication whether those who committed these atrocities were black or white.[33]

It was during these few days of waiting at West Point that the officers and men finally parted with their original name, "Stockton's Independent Regiment." Governor Blair had agreed to enroll and number it as a state command back in mid-March, and for some weeks now, army reports had been referring to Stockton's regiment as the 16th Michigan, though Stockton for a time continued to refer to it by his name. That would suggest he did not like the change, but then he and his men had asked for state commissions. The name "Stockton's regiment" would linger for a while, but the reality was that his regiment was now the 16th Michigan Infantry Regiment. Benjamin Partridge, the ex-lancer from Bay City, would later complain that being labeled as "the 16th Michigan"—a "high" number—made it seem the men had been laggards about signing up to serve their country. "In consequence of our not having been numbered when leaving the state," he said, "we were classed among the last regiments that left the state under the demand for 300,000 [troops] while in reality, we were among the first and should have been numbered as such."[34]

The men bathed and washed clothes and returned to a schedule of drill and inspection in pleasant weather in an area of orchards, marshes, and woods across the river from West

Point, until the Army of the Potomac could reassemble and resupply. Joseph Stanfield, who had followed Capt. Judd Mott from the lancers, saw some soldiers placing fences around the graves of New York soldiers under the shade of two elm trees. "How glorious to die on the battlefield in a good and noble cause," he concluded in his diary entry that evening.[35]

McClellan arrived the next day "and was charmingly received," Col. Stockton wrote. "It is supposed and believed that the Rebels will make yet another strong stand, somewhere before we reach Richmond." That was true. Confederate forces under Gen. Joseph E. Johnston had pulled back to the Chickahominy River to make their defenses just outside of town. On a more personal level, Stockton had broken his spectacles and "was in a bad fix" but remarkably, his wife was able to send him two pairs of glasses that reached him nine days later while his regiment was encamped nearby at Turnstall's Station. This was a testament to the efficiency of the Union's logistical organization that, once established, moved tons of supplies, rations, and ammunition, as well as soldiers' mail.[36]

The men enjoyed their rest until the offensive began again and got their orders on May 12: The army would march west toward Richmond. Before dawn the next day, the 16th Michigan rose, ate breakfast, and fell in after daylight. Thousands of men marched out into the morning sun through forest and farm fields as the day grew hot and dusty. "We suffer a great deal from thirst," John Berry wrote, "water being very scarce on the road." Marion Munson learned that if he was careful in sipping from his canteen and rinsing his mouth (while also avoiding the heavily salted pork and beef the army issued), he could ease his thirst without consuming all his water on the march. "If you go according to the directions in the book, one canteen full will last you one day," he wrote; by the end of the day he still had enough water left to make coffee.[37]

Their column marched through Kent Court House and reached Cumberland that night. In the morning they waited in the rain as thousands of men went by since the 16th Michigan was now holding the place of the last regiment of their division. Secretary of State William Seward arrived to review the troops that evening and was greeted with cheers. When the 16th Michigan marched through the mud and woods on May 15, there was little progress as soldiers helped push struggling wagons and batteries. The men were issued whiskey that evening to try to ease their discomfort in wet tents, Frank Keeler wrote; in the morning they covered the last three or four miles on the terrible road, emerging from the woods into fields of red clover of the White House plantation on the Pamunkey River.

This was the home of Mary Custis Lee, granddaughter of Mrs. George (Mary Custis) Washington, and wife of Gen. Robert E. Lee, who would soon become the commanding general of the Confederate army. Now it was owned by the Lees' son, Col. W. H. F. "Rooney" Lee of the Rebel cavalry. This place on the river was being turned into an important communications and supply base as the Union army advanced, and barges, gunboats, and transports moved back and forth on the water. "The masts of the vessels in the river as seen from our camp look very strange in a clover field, and are the only indication of navigable water so nearby," Keeler wrote.[38]

Earlier in the spring the Union army had been organized into four corps, composed of two or more divisions. Divisions, in turn, were generally made up of three or four brigades, while a brigade, as noted previously, usually comprised three or more regiments. Stockton's regiment had been part of Butterfield's brigade in Fitz John Porter's division, and these had been part of the Third Corps. McClellan had not been happy with the organizing of the army's corps by President Lincoln, and he was dissatisfied with some of his corps commanders. Now authorized to make changes, he created a Fifth Corps and placed it under the command of Porter, whose old division was now called the First Division of the Fifth Corps. This division would be commanded by Brig. Gen. George Morell. Thus, the 16th Michigan, for the rest of the war, served in the Third Brigade of the First Division of the Fifth Corps of the Army of the Potomac.[39]

Like hundreds of other soldiers, Col. Stockton fell ill as the regiment halted, and feared he contracted typhoid. Young George Ervay, the teen from Grand Ledge, wrote home; at Yorktown, he had been given a job with the butchers of the Third Brigade, tending cattle to keep soldiers fed. "I have all that I can eat," he happily reported, telling of driving the herd over the Williamsburg battlefield. "I saw as much as it would take to make a regiment of men laying scattered on the ground of dead and wounded," he wrote. "It was an awful site but I think that before next week is even over we shall have Richmond. I think they cannot hold out much longer."

He told his family a tale of an improbable message that Confederates had left for the Union soldiers earlier in the month on an unexploded bomb: "At Yorktown, they wrote on a shell that our gunboats throwed in their fort—it did not burst," he explained, "—it said, 'You God damn Yankees, you sent this shell over five miles and now we are a-going to leave, but when we get you Yankee sons of bitches where your gunboat can't help you, well, we will give you hell.'"[40]

John Berry got word of the death of a Company A comrade, William Gilland. After the Confederates left Yorktown, Gilland, a Washtenaw County man about 21, had been put on a medical ship. "He was sent with the rest of the sick on board one of the floating hospitals to New York," Berry wrote. "He died on the way there." But the regiment marched five miles west the next day to the burned-out hamlet called Turnstall's Station on the Richmond & York Rail line, and Col. Stockton, unwell, wrote that he was sure the army would be at the Confederate capital soon.[41]

Sgt. William Borden, an Ionia man about 20 or 21 years old in Company B, used the pause to write a letter home about the near-daily rain and explaining his pay, personal finances, and business dealings. "I hear people say, 'how does Bill send home so much money? Does he gamble?'" Borden wrote. "Don't say that I don't play cards. There is one thing sure, I don't make any money at it." The soldier said he only played occasionally; he really made money by lending to his fellow soldiers at a usurious interest rate, loaning $10 now for $15 later. He had also sold, on installment plans, a revolver and a couple of watches his family sent. As a result, he sent home $100 yet still had cash left over. "[I] think it is nobody's business if I spend it playing bluff or any other game, or if I spend it for something to eat, which I am pretty apt to do," he wrote.[42]

As the regiment camped with its division at Turnstall's Station, John Berry was sent with a group of soldiers to lead a wagon train to a river landing to meet a steamship that was bringing up supplies. They stopped at a plantation owned by a Confederate officer named Garlick, and as they waited for the supplies to arrive, Berry talked with Garlick's slaves. They had been told by their master that the Union soldiers would maim and brand and kidnap them, but they quickly realized that these Yankees would pay them for hoecakes and chicken. "In fact the Negroes were making more money than they had ever seen before," he wrote. "Whether the Negro is capable of self-government or not, they appeared to be going on in their own responsibility not only here but, by what I can learn, on all the neighboring plantations." Some of the younger slaves were choosing to marry now that the master was gone, and some hired on as servants and cooks for the Union soldiers. Older slaves with families were staying on to harvest plantation crops, and Berry noted that a few young slaves showed "considerable mixture with the Anglo-Saxon race."[43]

Now the march toward Richmond resumed, the 16th Michigan's division covering only a few miles each day for the next few days in weather alternately humid, stormy, and fine, with nights that were wet and cold—first to a place called Kidd's Mill, where there was plenty of spring water and fields of grain; to Goodly Hole Swamp, where the men had a bath in a millpond; and finally to a mill owned by a certain virulent secessionist, Dr. Gaines, on a tributary that flowed into the Chickahominy River on May 26. It had been tortuously slow going as thousands of men jammed the road that week, but now the 16th Michigan joined 100,000 Union troops, some just a few miles from the Confederate capital. The river ran across much of the York-James Peninsula, and went by Richmond at an angle from northeast to southwest; the Confederates had destroyed the bridges over it, presenting a natural obstacle to the Union army.[44]

Soon Union engineers repaired the bridges and even the local rail line back toward the White House; shortly before the arrival of the 16th Michigan with their brigade and division at the Chickahominy, McClellan pushed two of his corps across the flood-prone river, dividing his army but threatening Richmond. In the last week of May the Army of the Potomac's position stretched for several miles from a wooded crossroads a few miles from the city called Seven Pines north across the Chickahominy to the village of Mechanicsville, northeast of Richmond. The 16th Michigan and its brigade camped near Gaines' Mill in an area of old farms and fields, about two miles from the river and a crossing called New Bridge, a few miles east-southeast of Mechanicsville.

On the way to this place, Stockton, though not sure what sort of Confederate defenses waited ahead, expressed confidence that his men and the Army of the Potomac would not be thrown against the enemy's fortifications at Richmond. He was sure McClellan would again carefully prepare before committing his men to battle. "We know the General will do so," the colonel wrote. "'Victories without Blood' is his plan.'"[45]

McClellan had continued to receive intelligence reports that wildly inflated Confederate troop strength at Richmond and he demanded that reinforcements be sent to him. After haggling with Lincoln and his military advisors, who were concerned that an adequate force must be left to defend Washington, the general received reports that there was a large enemy force twenty miles or more north of his position outside of Richmond—Confederates who could threaten his army's supply line stretching back to White House Landing.

Historians say these couple of Rebel brigades were in that area protecting a railroad that ran to Richmond.[46]

The Fifth Corps was the nearest of McClellan's forces to these Confederates. This corps was commanded by Fitz John Porter, a McClellan favorite, and Porter chose his old First Division, of which the 16th Michigan was part, for the mission to drive away this Confederate force. In the evening of their arrival at Gaines' Mill, Third Brigade commander Dan Butterfield summoned Stockton and his other colonels for instructions: At 4 a.m. their regiments must be ready to advance with two days' provisions. As part of Gen. George Morell's First Division, they would move north to attack the Rebels there and destroy the railroad they were using. "We go to fight to victory or death," Col. Stockton proclaimed dramatically in his diary. "God watch and protect me for my beloved wife's sake." As rain fell that night, he prepared a letter that Maria was to give to their son in the event he was killed.[47]

It was still raining when the regiment was called up at 3 a.m., hard enough that Gen. Butterfield noted that his brigade could not build fires. "In consequence, many started on the march without coffee," he wrote sympathetically. One of those coffee-deprived soldiers, John Berry, also glumly made note of that fact in his diary. The march was wet, muddy, and miserable, up the New Bridge Road to the Hanover Turnpike. The rain stopped three hours into the march and the sun came out, Lt. Charles Salter said; the steamy heat was stifling. Men threw away their coats, and officers and men alike fell out (that is, dropped out of the marching columns, exhausted). By noon the 16th Michigan's brigade was about three miles from Hanover Court House, "but our fatigue was soon to be forgotten," John Berry wrote; ahead there was the crackle of skirmish fire.[48]

HANOVER COURT HOUSE

This was a neighborhood of farms and woods. The regiments of the Third Brigade of Morell's division hurried forward, but the 16th Michigan's marching position was toward the rear of the column. Finally arriving at a crossroads south of Hanover Court House and coming out of a belt of woods, the men could see their comrades and batteries firing across open ground at the Rebels on the other side of the fields, Lt. Salter said; their brigade was ordered to wait in support of the Union guns. On the other side, the Confederates were posted at the edge of more woods and by the home of a local resident, a Dr. McKinney. For more than an hour, this fighting went on when the 16th Michigan and the other regiments from the left wing of their brigade were marched out and around to flank the Rebel positions; the Confederates were badly outnumbered. "When we came out into the field again, we found our troops had already put the rebels to flight and captured one of their cannons," Salter said.[49]

The soldiers of Butterfield's brigade, including the 16th Michigan, pursued the withdrawing Confederates, who made a brief stand near Hanover Court House and then seemed to scatter, Salter continued; his regiment had had no real part in this fighting nor suffered any casualty. Now the 16th Michigan and the 83rd Pennsylvania were ordered to advance north along the railroad, to the depot about a mile ahead where there were freight cars loaded with Confederate supplies.

But while they did so, the main part of the Rebel force, a brigade composed of untried North Carolina troops and Georgia regiments, had remained hidden in the woods off the main road. General Butterfield reported that he learned from a prisoner that they intended to strike back at the Union troops. Meanwhile, the Michigan and Pennsylvania soldiers continued along the rail line to the local depot. By now it was late afternoon and the men were in a "tired out condition," John Berry said. Then orders arrived ordering the soldiers back to join the rest of their division. "Immediately we heard firing in the direction of [John C.] Martindale's [First] Brigade," Stockton said of this moment.

The tired men were energized when they heard rifle fire behind them in the near distance—the Confederate counterattack on their division comrades—and ran toward the sound. Some soldiers from the 16th Michigan who fell out on the tiring march that day had not caught up with their regiment; they took part in this fight by joining the 2nd Maine, Joseph Stanfield said; some fired forty rounds, or all the cartridges that they had been issued. It appeared that John Hodgkins, the Lapeer man who had been struck by a piece of shell at Yorktown and just returned to duty, was one of these men; he was again wounded and relatively lucky—a bullet hit the tip of his thumb.[50]

The rest of the 16th Michigan was trying to get back to the scene of this fight. "We first ran across corn fields and wheat fields, and there our road lay through the woods and a swamp," Lt. Salter said about the dash back to the new battle line. Stockton ordered his regiment to the right (west), hoping he could catch the enemy in the flank or rear, but an aide brought orders from Butterfield ordering Stockton to bear to the left, since the general was concerned Stockton's men would arrive at the battleground too much in front of the soldiers from the First Brigade now firing at the Confederates.

In following Butterfield's direction, the 16th Michigan had to cross back over the railroad, which was at this point built on a high embankment—and on the other side of it was a swamp. The officers had to dismount their horses and tie them to trees or fence posts; Stockton slid into the mire, where soldiers sank up to their waists. Marion Munson said that the colonel, "although old in years," struggled through as well as any of the men, and took his position in front, sword in hand, as they pushed into the woods."[51]

Slogging through the swamp, the 16th Michigan's men could hear cheering up ahead, and some thought, correctly, that it was charging Union troops. But Butterfield thought these were "the cheers of the enemy, with their unceasing volleys of musketry." Munson said Stockton called for his men to yell their own hurrahs as they were about to reach the scene. "Now, my brave boys, let us give three cheers for the stars and stripes," he shouted. But as they arrived, the North Carolina brigade (made up of inexperienced soldiers) and Georgians, outnumbered, broke and scattered through the woods, having paid a heavy price for their attack on the First Division. "Before we got to the firing," Joseph Stanfield wrote, "it ceased."

The sun was going down and the fight at Hanover Court House was over. Morell's division's mission, in hindsight, had not been a critical one and the engagement there would go down in history as a mere skirmish, not a battle. Some of the 16th Michigan's stragglers had been in the fight, and so had some of their brigade comrades, but the regiment, as a whole, was not. They had come through it with almost no casualties. Still, the men were proud and exhilarated. "The day's work was a complete triumph," Thomas Frank Powers remembered years later, "and that night we bivouacked for the first time on a field we had won." At the time of fight, Powers was an ex-lancer and sergeant in Company K, but he recalled it with pride.[52]

Frank Keeler and Marion Munson believed, naively, that it was the 16th Michigan's cheering that terrified the Rebels into retreating—that the enemy heard the approaching troops and thought they were about to be flanked by the "entire Army of the Potomac." In truth, the Confederates had been hammered that day by a much larger and slightly more experienced force. But the Michigan soldiers stacked arms and prepared to bivouac for the night. "Being tired and worn out, each regiment collected together," John Berry wrote, "and we lay down for the night on the battlefield amongst the dead and the dying."

Col. Stockton was less satisfied with the events of the day, unhappy that he was not allowed by Gen. Butterfield to follow his intended course of action to try to strike the Confederate flank. "The result was that when I came out at the scene of action, the enemy had fallen back, laying in trenches, whereas had I been left to my own pursuit I would have been put in line to have taken the flying [retreating] foe in the rear and taken many prisoners," he complained. "So much for luck."[53]

The 16th Michigan bivouacked on a nearby farm. Soldiers were busy the next day burying the dead and caring for the wounded, except for a black man named Walker from Company K, who had quite an adventure. Whether Walker was a soldier is not clear, since records for the only man named Walker to serve in that company was white; it could be the African-American Walker was civilian employee of the company, perhaps a cook or servant. "He is a good natured fellow and a great favorite among the men," Joseph Stanfield said of Walker.

Presumably one of the commanders of the Hanover Court House mission, perhaps Gen. Butterfield or Gen. Morell, sent Walker out into the countryside "on a scout" or to gather intelligence, and he soon discovered a company of Rebels who were not far off. Of course, in the slave-holding South, a black man in civilian clothes was assumed to be a slave; Walker was not challenged, and he returned to camp knowing where the Confederates could be found. Provided a horse, he led a Union cavalry detachment to capture them; they took the Rebel soldiers by surprise without firing a shot. "The whole co. was taken," Stanfield wrote. "Capts., Lieuts., and about 90 men."[54]

Lt. Charles Salter of Detroit walked over the Hanover Court House battlefield and was shocked by the sight of dead, sometimes mangled, Union soldiers. "The appearance of the dead left lying upon the ground was very sad to behold," he told friends. "The most mutilated state of those killed by artillery was the most shocking to behold of anything I have seen." It was the true ugliness and horror of war, what really happened to men struck by flying metal. He visited the wounded, taken to nearby houses, and found a friend, Lt. Halpin of the 25th New York. Wounded in a fierce fight as his skirmish line was being overwhelmed, Halpin shot down two Rebels with his revolver before being fatally wounded. "He lived until noon the next day," Salter wrote. "He was one of my best friends."[55]

The soldiers had been issued two days' rations for this mission, so the food they brought had been consumed. Thomas Frank Powers recalled the officers "suggested" the men take care of themselves by "foraging"—a euphemism for taking foodstuffs, sheep, cattle, or pigs from nearby residents and farms. "Here for the first time the regiment had a taste of living on the enemy," he wrote later. "Through some strange freak, the commanding officers winked at it. Beef, pork, dried fruits and preserves—in fact, everything that an epicure could crave—were procured in abundance." Joseph Stanfield, writing that night, said he and comrades had pork and mutton "and milk in our coffee for supper."[56]

Since the end of winter camp back in March, the regiment had marched scores of miles, participated in a siege, and been involved in skirmishes, picket firing, and reconnaissance missions. They had been under artillery fire and come through it with barely a scratch so far. Still, the 16th Michigan had not yet been truly tested in battle. But now as the Army of the Potomac truly stood at the gates of Richmond, it was only a question of when.

5.

MAY–JUNE 1862

THE BULLETS RAINED IN RANKS AROUND ME

The 16th Michigan started with its division back to the camp near Gaines' Mill, marching on May 29 from Hanover Court House in good spirits, though the men's attitude likely wore down with the constant stops and starts in the muggy heat; the day turned into a long night, so their brigade arrived before dawn the next morning. As the month ended, Tip Aplin told his mother that he had gotten the hang of soldiering and learned how to effectively handle and prepare his rations, or allotments of flour, bacon, and coffee. "When I first came to Washington I almost suffered for enough to eat," he wrote. "Then I did not know how to cook what I did get, nor how to get something when I had nothing, but now I manage things first rate."

Aplin had learned a soldier's skills, but also found that the regiment's quartermaster kept a stock of foodstuffs on hand; if a man could get an order from a commissioned officer in his company, the quartermaster would sell him items—a pound of sugar or ham for 10 cents, or a pound of hardtack for 15 cents, tea for 75 cents, and molasses syrup for 60 cents a gallon. "It is against orders to sell any of these things to a private or a non-commissioned officer," Aplin noted. But officers like his lieutenant, if asked, would get the items for his men. "So you see, I do not need anything except medicine."[1]

Severe thunderstorms blew in that night and the quartermaster sergeant in the 44th New York, camped just up the hill from the Michigan soldiers, was killed by lightning. Frank Keeler's Company D was posted at dusk along the north bank of the Chickahominy River and he thought the Rebels engineered the flood that cut their picket off from dry ground, forcing them to wade through the water. But it was the heavy rainfall, and not Confederate mischief, that caused the flooding.[2]

The next day the 16th Michigan was the reserve picket for their area of the river—that is, they would back up the soldiers doing picket duty. It was quiet until the afternoon, when a rising din of musketry and cannon sounded in the distance, just a few miles away. This was the start of a large attack by most of the Confederate army at Richmond under Gen.

Joseph Johnston on two Union corps on the south side of the river, east of the Rebel capital, near the hamlets of Seven Pines and Fair Oaks Station. Johnston and Gen. Robert E. Lee, then an advisor to Confederate president Jefferson Davis, believed the Union's attack at Hanover Court House four days earlier represented the start of a menacing link of the Army of the Potomac with tens of thousands more Union soldiers coming down from the north—a force that, combined with McClellan's, could crush Richmond's defenses. This joining of Union forces was not really happening, but Lee was convinced it was—and that the Confederate army must stop it. The Rebel assault east of Richmond on May 30 drove Union soldiers back, but reinforcements passed over one of the Chickahominy bridges damaged by the flooding and helped fight the Confederates to a standstill.

The men of the 16th Michigan heard this combat raging while they were on picket, and the next morning, June 1, they returned to their camp and heard the battle starting again. Almost immediately they and their entire division were issued provisions for three days and told to be ready to march at a moment's notice—"battle orders," John Berry said. But they were never sent to join the fight. "[Our] Loss very great, supposed over 5,000 killed and wounded," Col. Stockton wrote in his diary, an accurate assessment of Union casualties at Fair Oaks-Seven Pines. "At first our forces were driven back, but after reinforcements, our forces drove the enemy."[3] The Confederate commander, Gen. Johnston, was wounded in this battle and he was replaced, at the direction of Jefferson Davis, by Lee, a distinguished former U.S. Army officer and Mexican War hero.

A tense calm returned to the Richmond front and early June was uneventful, except for two more heavy showers. McClellan prepared, as he had at Yorktown, to bring up siege guns and large mortars, but for the moment life was comparatively easy for the 16th Michigan. "We have been enjoying ourselves pretty well as we have had no long marches or hard duties to perform," Sgt. Hubbard Barrett of Ionia wrote to friends. "There was a hard battle fought between here and Richmond last Saturday and Sunday," he continued, referring to Fair Oaks-Seven Pines, "but we had nothing to do with it except to listen to the firing which was about four miles away." Stockton wrote to his wife Maria. "Nothing near yet," he told her, referring to the lack of a fight for his regiment, "so I write this on a sheet of paper which I picked up at 'Hanover' on the campground of Secesh camp." Stockton sent her $400. "Don't want but a little about me," he explained, "lest the Secesh might get it!" He reminded Maria that both of their birthdays were coming up. "Then or before I hope to have you with me. I surely want to spend these days with you."[4]

Stockton gossiped about Col. Stryker of the 44th New York, who was soon removed from command by Brig. Gen. Dan Butterfield, and he noted that fatigue details now began—the building and repair of roads and bridges for placement of the big guns. Stockton sent out Lt. Col. John Ruehle and Maj. Norval Welch taking 600 men to work, leaving himself in camp with the guard and the "old soldiers"—a term for men who were too sick for duty, or who claimed to be. "It is wonderful how sick men always happen to be when any fatigue parties are called for," he wrote. "Well, I would prefer it that way rather than reverse." Men who tried to dodge the work, but who were not excused by the doctors, had to clean up the camp. "You would laugh, dear wife, if you could see the lieutenant colonel, major and myself, and in fact nearly all my officers," he continued. "We have had our hair cut as short as a convict's. Mine seems to be renovating. Would you not be agreeably surprised if all the gray hair disappeared? You would have a young looking husband."[5]

He chided his wife because he had not received a letter for some days, and he asked if she had her photograph taken. "Look as natural and calm as you can," he told her. "I want it much—but oh! How much more the original! The lips that move and speak, the eye that sparkles and gives animation to the 'heart.'" Stockton enclosed a picture of McClellan and told her to keep the letter as a memento of the fight at Hanover Court House.[6]

Pvt. George Ervay also wrote home. "My brigade had a hard battle the other day," he said about Hanover Court House, without providing detail. He thought his picture was appearing in a popular publication, since he had been standing near Prof. Thaddeus Lowe's observation balloon as it was prepared for launch while an artist sketched the scene. "If you see the picture of the balloon in Frank Leslie's [newspaper] and you see a man with his shirtsleeves rolled up, you can reckon it is me," he wrote.[7]

For the next two weeks the regiment was on picket or fatigue. "Built about one-half miles of corduroy road in the cussedest mud hole in Virginia," complained Private Alfred M. Apted of the Brady Sharpshooters on June 8, a Sunday. "There is no Sunday in the Army, 'tis not known." There was a visit by a Spanish general and an eclipse of the moon as the work went on. "'Tis said we are getting siege guns in place near Fair Oaks," Col. Stockton wrote.[8]

Pvt. Marion Munson of Oakland County, also building roads through swamps, could hardly believe the war was still dragging on. "Who would think for one moment over a year ago that it would last so long as it has," he wrote. "Six months ago we thought it would be settled by the Fourth of July and all the troops sent to their respective homes in honor." They had thought the Rebels were hanging on by a thread, but that had not been the case. Now that the Union army was in striking distance of Richmond, the men wondered. Would the Confederacy last another week? Another month? "Has it got so strong," Munson asked prophetically, "that it may last us three years?"[9]

Their First Division of the Fifth Corps was called out 4 p.m. on June 13 on a report that the Rebels were launching another attack, but it did not materialize in their vicinity. In fact, the dashing Confederate cavalry officer Gen. J. E. B. "Jeb" Stuart was on the move, raiding and disrupting Union supply and communications lines, his troopers on a daring three-day ride and reconnaissance around McClellan's army. It was during this raid that the first member of the 16th Michigan, a young man from Saginaw, was killed.

Stuart's troopers were in the middle of their mission, galloping south to the place called Garlick's Landing, one of the important links in the Union supply line on the Pamunkey River near White House, the Lee family home. Here rations and ordnance were unloaded from barges or transports, and then carried west to the front by wagon or the local railroad, reactivated by McClellan's engineers. Stuart ordered Col. W. H. F. "Rooney" Lee of the 9th Virginia Cavalry, the son of the new Confederate army commander, "to destroy whatever could be found at the landing."[10]

Col. Lee dispatched two squadrons of troopers to Garlick's Landing, where members of Butterfield's Third Brigade supply train, including personnel from the 16th Michigan, were sitting down to supper, having loaded their wagons for the return trip to their camp near New Bridge. "A band of guerillas, 100 strong, came dashing down upon them, shooting and firing as they advanced," wrote Sgt. Wallace Jewett of Saginaw about the raid. (Union soldiers often referred to Confederate cavalry as "guerillas," though Stuart's report makes clear the raiders were members of the 1st and 9th Virginia cavalry regiments.) The 16th Michigan's quartermaster sergeant, Drowne Potter, and some other Union soldiers jumped on one of the river transports, called a "schooner," and pushed off into the river to escape. But defying the troopers cost Potter his life. Lee wrote that his squads "met with a slight resistance from a part of about 100 men, but a few shots soon brought the matter to an end, and they captured almost all of them." Though that schooner seems to have escaped the Confederates, one of the shots struck Sgt. Potter in the head. He was 23.

The troopers set the supply wagons and two transports on fire, took scores of U.S. army mules, and captured a number of Union soldiers. The raiders rode to the nearby train depot and fired on the passing train (now being operated by McClellan's troops), killing and wounding several more men. Then they continued on their way, successfully riding around the Army of the Potomac and providing Lee with important information about its position.[11]

Stockton sent two men to investigate Potter's death and soon had a report of the incident. Edward Hill, who joined the 16th Michigan from the lancers, as did Potter, remembered him as a "brilliant young law student." Sgt. Wallace Jewett, writing to a Saginaw newspaper, called Potter a soldierly and talented man who, had he lived, would have gone far in the army. Ex-lancer Joseph Stanfield also knew and liked Potter. "He was promoted about two weeks ago," he recorded. "I was a little acquainted with him. He was a scholar and a gentleman in every sense of the word. His loss is felt by all who knew him."[12]

Lt. Charles Salter also told of the raid and Potter's death in a letter home. The regiment had been lucky to have not lost anyone to gunfire so far, but now the first of them had died violently—not in battle or in some heroic action, but only trying to escape the raiders. Potter was buried at nearby White House Landing. Stockton, who apparently thought the wagon crews should have put up a fight, wrote to the young man's mother. "Wrote to wife and [to] Mrs. Potter, breaking the thing to her by saying her son was brave," he recorded. "Must never write the facts. Poor woman."[13]

Stockton turned 57 on June 18. "Pleasant and quite warm," he wrote. "Just received orders again to be ready at any moment." But they did not move and that week he loaned $10 to a sergeant from Detroit, one William Kydd, 23, who apparently worked as a molder, perhaps making castings or molds for some industry, before joining the army. His commanding general, meanwhile, had continued to demand that Lincoln send him more troops—he got thousands—but now McClellan believed, wrongly, that the Confederates had 200,000 soldiers in the Richmond defenses. McClellan pulled all his men but the Fifth Corps over to the south side of the Chickahominy. The Fifth Corps, to which the 16th Michigan belonged, remained east-northeast of Richmond, the "right wing" or right-hand portion of the Army of the Potomac in positions outside of town.

The quiet the 16th Michigan enjoyed was broken briefly when artillery shells fell into camp as the Rebels attempted to shoot down the Union's observation balloon on June 20, but there were no injuries. Private George Ervay got the news that his father acquired some cattle in a trade with another farmer, and George offered to buy some since he was sure the war would soon end. "I think that it will do no harm to have a pair and a young cow when I return home," he said, "which I think it will not be long, if we continue much longer to whip the rebs."[14]

The regiment's camp was moved on June 21 to a field of oats on a large plantation, seemingly a short distance down the Chickahominy from New Bridge. Alfred Apted of the Brady Sharpshooters was delighted by the plentiful fruit in the local orchards, and he ate all he could. And though some Union and Rebel pickets had been exchanging shots at night, John Berry of Company A recorded that they had reached an understanding with their Confederate opposites not to shoot at one another—a common agreement that often occurred between soldiers on picket.

Stockton, like hundreds of soldiers in their division, continued to suffer illness and Dr. Wixom treated him with quinine. But his biggest worry came when he saw a newspaper article about the Hanover Court House fight that was inaccurate and potentially harmful to him, since it made it sound as if he had been tardy or in the wrong place. The colonel promptly wrote to Gen. Butterfield about the article, but he waved off Stockton's concern. "Newspaper reports, if we allowed them to trouble us, would keep us awake nights and busy day times," he replied. "I don't think anybody would ever accuse you of being out of the way in the hour of duty."[15]

There were critical developments that week that soon affected thousands of soldiers on both sides. First, McClellan was planning to seize more ground east of Richmond on the south side of the Chickahominy. This would allow him to bring the large-caliber artillery even closer and it would reduce the isolation of Fitz John Porter's Fifth Corps, alone on the other side of the river. Second, reliable information reached him that Gen. Stonewall Jackson's force was on the march from northern Virginia south to Richmond to join Robert E. Lee. Though McClellan continued to wrongly believe his army was outnumbered two-to-one, he was correct in understanding that Jackson could soon attack the Fifth Corps and cut the supply line of the Army of the Potomac going back to the east.

Another powerful thunderstorm pounded the countryside on the night of June 24—Col. Stockton said it was one of the most terrific storms he had ever heard—and their brigade received orders: The first was to detail 500 men to guard New Bridge; the second, for the remainder of the brigade to be ready to march north for Mechanicsville at daylight to join Fifth Corps comrades there. McClellan correctly expected the Confederates to attack at that point. The next day, June 25, battle indeed erupted, but initiated by McClellan himself toward the other end of the Union positions near the Confederate capital, a few miles away.[16]

Here elements of three Union army corps fought Rebels in positions south of Richmond, in a reconnaissance-in-force. This fighting went on all day but did not break the Confederate line in a battle known as Oak Grove. The weather was fine and cool as the men of the 16th Michigan heard the cannonading, and one stray projectile came their way. "A shell came whizzing over my head and struck in the dirt," wrote sharpshooter Apted. "Nobody hurt, but many scared."

The regiment did not move, but remained at the ready on June 26, until Stockton decided, in the rising heat of that day, the men should drill. Pvt. Berry recorded that he was getting sick, though he tried to keep up with the exercise. It was likely drilling in the heat that angered Apted with his own company's leaders. "We have the poorest lot of officers in the regiment," he complained. "[They] do not have any feeling or care for the uniform or for the men."[17]

But several miles to the north, Lee's attack on their Fifth Corps comrades began outside of Mechanicsville. The aggressive Rebel general was determined to drive McClellan away from Richmond, and the division commanded by Gen. A. P. Hill started the assault on strongly posted Union positions in fighting that lasted until dark. Again, the men of the 16th Michigan, with their brigade comrades, heard the sound of the guns and were told to get ready to move.

Col. Stockton was by now so ill that Brig. Gen. Butterfield urged him to go by ambulance to McClellan's field headquarters, south across the river. "This the colonel did not do, probably thinking we would cross the river that day," wrote Capt. Robert T. Elliott of Company E. Though he would not leave, Stockton temporarily placed Lt. Col. John Ruehle in command of the regiment. Between 2 and 3 p.m., orders came to strike the tents, load the regiment's wagons, and get them moving east to White House Landing. These preliminary moves were the first indications that Gen. McClellan was going to give up his offensive to take Richmond and move the Army of the Potomac in retreat, south to the James River.[18]

The regiment, with the Third Brigade, marched three or four miles east to the town of New Cold Harbor, where those elements of the Fifth Corps not in the fight at Mechanicsville took positions. One soldier who did not make it was diarist John Berry of Company A, who was ill. "On the way there I am sun-struck," he wrote, "but after a while [I] recover and follow the brigade to Gaines' Mill, but then I am ordered back to camp, the doctor pronouncing me not in a condition to go with the regiment."

That order may have saved Berry's life; he waited with the teams and medical wagons with the sick as they prepared to cross the Chickahominy for a railroad hamlet called Savage's Station. The afternoon and evening of June 26 were tense as the soldiers of the 16th Michigan waited in line of battle near New Cold Harbor and listened to the guns, but it turned out that their Fifth Corps comrades at Mechanicsville blunted the Confederate attack. As darkness fell, the brigade was sent back to the site of its camp near the Chickahominy.[19]

The men stacked arms, assuming there was nothing more they would do that night, but once again they were assembled and marched a half-mile before stopping and sleeping on their arms in a field about a mile from New Bridge, Capt. Elliott wrote later. Col. Stockton, weak and weary, rested in the nearby camp of the 4th Michigan Infantry.

GAINES' MILL

At dawn on June 27, the regiment and its brigade were pulled back into a new line of battle formed by the Fifth Corps, which was now the rear guard of the entire army as McClellan began moving his men south. Lee had correctly gambled that if he attacked McClellan's flank, the conservative Union commander would give up the initiative.[20]

So even though the Fifth Corps had defeated the Confederates at Mechanicsville, inflicting 1,400 casualties on them, Fitz John Porter's men marched back in the early morning hours of June 27 to this place chosen by the generals—some low hills south of Gaines' Mill and the town of New Cold Harbor, overlooking a swampy Chickahominy tributary called Boatswain's Creek. Porter's defensive line stretched for more than a mile along the hills, mostly open ground with farm fields, but with tangled woods, brush, and thickets in the swamp, along the creek, and on the margins of the fields.

The Third Brigade of Gen. Morell's First Division was posted on the extreme left of this line, or furthest west, not far from the farm of a family named Watt; their line curved from west to north, the direction from which the Confederates would come. About a mile behind them was the Chickahominy. The 16th Michigan's position shifted a few times that morning, but as a hot sun beat down in the early afternoon, the regiment was in reserve about 150 yards from the front, where the 83rd Pennsylvania and the 44th New York were building breastworks of tree limbs. The Brady Sharpshooters were sent out ahead to the swamp, with other companies from the brigade, as pickets.

Capt. Elliott saw that Col. Stockton was even sicker today than he had been previously, and again the brigade commander, Butterfield, advised him to leave the field. Stockton, nearly deaf from the effects of quinine, refused, "and remarked that he might as well die there as anywhere else, and would stay with the regiment," Elliott said. Despite illness, Stockton was in good spirits and "sanguine that the regiment would behave well and establish their reputation as one of the best regiments in the Army of the Potomac," the captain wrote.[21]

Confederate skirmishers approached from the north and probed the Union positions, Lt. Charles Salter wrote, and Rebel artillery opened fire. Because most of the 16th Michigan's men were lying down on the back, southern slope of the Third Brigade's hill, where there were some woods, they were initially protected. "My regiment occupied its position until somewhere near 3 o'clock p.m., when the skirmishing beginning intimated that the enemy was approaching," Stockton wrote in his battle report. "It grew louder and louder, and soon the battle began in good earnest along our whole front. The enemy's artillery opened with shot and shell, evidently trying to drive us from the shelter of the woods where our line was posted."[22]

Confederate Gen. Ambrose P. Hill's division began the attacks on the Fifth Corps, and

Hill was eventually joined that afternoon by the division of Gen. James Longstreet. The Third Brigade's skirmish line, including the Brady Sharpshooters Company, was driven in. The Rebel brigades came through brush, forest, and swamp to assault the Union line, wading the creek and moving up a steep bank, exposed to terrible fire as they came into view. Porter's men were dug in on higher ground and had strong artillery support; they cut down Rebels by the score. Some historians said the Confederate attacks came in a piecemeal fashion, given the difficulty of crossing the swamp, and that their brigades lacked coordination until early in the evening. But they were looking for a weak spot in the Fifth Corps line, and they kept coming.

As more Confederates joined the battle, Stockton reported that Brig. Gen. Butterfield became concerned about the portion of the Union line held by another brigade in their First Division, to the right, and that Butterfield sent the 16th Michigan to support it. Stockton proudly claimed his men "most gallantly charged [advanced], thereby sustaining our line and compelling the enemy to fall back." Butterfield, however, said other regiments managed to hold that line, and he ordered the 16th Michigan back to await developments. Stockton moved his regiment to the Third Brigade's position, again in reserve behind the 83rd Pennsylvania.[23]

As they waited at the edge of the patch of woods behind their brigade, the fighting intensified. At about 5 p.m. Rebel artillery projectiles ripped through this stand of trees, killing Capt. Thomas C. Carr, 35, of Company C; he was hit in the heart by a piece of grape shot, said Ziba Graham of Flint. "He was within a foot of me when he fell," Graham told Carr's widow. "He died without a groan." Stockton reported that four or five soldiers were mortally wounded at the same moment, probably by the round metal shot fired from cannon like huge shotgun blasts. "They assaulted us with great fury all afternoon," Lt. Salter said, referring to his division's line of battle, "making no less than six bayonet charges on us with their whole force of infantry. At the same time, their artillery kept up a heavy fire of solid shot all the while, but they could not force us to give way a single inch."[24]

Stockton, with Gen. Butterfield's approval, moved his regiment behind the 44th New York; he thought they remained here for an hour. The 16th Michigan had been mostly in reserve, but now the regiment went into the front line. Lt. Col. John Ruehle said that two companies from the 16th Michigan, B and F, took positions in rifle pits on the left of the 44th New York, but Capt. Elliott indicated the entire regiment went into the trenches. Butterfield reported that he "brought forward my two reserves"—meaning the 16th Michigan and the 12th New York—so that his entire brigade was in the battle line.

Now the whole Fifth Corps line was fiercely engaged, and further to the right of the 16th Michigan's position, charging Confederates were said to be close enough to fight hand-to-hand, men stabbing their foe with bayonets and using rifles as clubs. No specific description of this part of the battle from any member of the 16th Michigan seems to exist—it may have been out of their line of sight. But then Stockton saw Union troops to his right running from the fight—the Rebels broke the line between their First and Second Brigades, and further east at part of the line held by other elements of their Fifth Corps.

It was about 6 p.m. Pressing hard on the First Brigade in the division of which the

16th Michigan was part, troops under Gen. John Bell Hood forced these Union soldiers to retreat, driving them back. Over the next hour, Confederates pushed through the hole they had punched in the corps' line, forcing Porter's men to retreat when they were hit by fire from the front and side. It was a deadly and untenable situation for them; ideally, these soldiers would get away from this danger and form a new line to resume fighting, but panic set in and some soldiers simply fled. The Union line was unraveling. "The rebels, then rushing through the gap thus made in immense numbers, soon had us outflanked and slowly regiment after regiment of our troops gave way and retreated," Lt. Salter said.[25]

While some accounts said Col. Stockton was on horseback that evening, Capt. Elliott said that Stockton was so sick he was unable to ride, and the colonel later agreed that he was on foot. Stockton said he was with Gen. Butterfield when they saw the Union position begin to break. From the trenches near the 44th New York, Capt. Robert Elliott also saw Union troops retreating, some running toward the Chickahominy bridges, and he knew it was only a matter of time before the advancing Rebels would flank the Third Brigade. Butterfield ordered his regiments to shift to meet this threat—"refusing" or reforming his line at an angle to face these Confederates. Elliott said the regiments turned and marched into the adjacent wheat field—the 12th New York was just ahead of the 16th Michigan, while the 83rd Pennsylvania was on its right and the 44th New York on its left. "We changed our position twice, no Rebels coming from our front, but pouring in on us from the right flank by brigades and masses," Elliott said. "I think we fired four volleys."[26]

Then they were ordered to about face, and cross a ravine; beyond it was Woodbury's Bridge over the Chickahominy. The 16th Michigan was briefly sheltered from fire as they marched down the back of the hill, "to save from being flanked," Stockton reported. But it was not enough. The colonel reported that Maj. Barnum of the 12th New York, the brigade's field officer of the day, rode up and urged him to hold on a few minutes longer, probably because Butterfield ordered that a new defensive line be formed. Stockton said he ordered his regiment to resume firing, but then Maj. Norval Welch rushed up and warned him that if they "remained a minute longer we would be all cut to pieces—that the enemy were close upon us in overwhelming force. I thereupon faced my regiment to the rear, still intending to fall back fighting, but I had no sooner given the command to march than all started in double-quick, leaving me at once in the rear."[27]

Stockton had command of the right half, or wing, of his regiment that day, while Lt. Col. John Ruehle commanded the left. Certainly the 16th Michigan's line was disrupted by other Union soldiers trying to get away, and some of Stockton's men joined them in flight. But some of these troops heeded their officers' shouts to halt and reform their line. The sun was dropping in the sky as their brigade retreated, and Capt. Elliott saw Stockton trying unsuccessfully to stop soldiers running for the Chickahominy bridge. Meanwhile, Maj. Welch and other officers moved back about 150 yards and reformed some of the regiment with the 83rd Pennsylvania and the 44th New York. Lt. Salter said that it appeared the entire corps fled, "until finally there were none of ours left, but one brigade, who were on the extreme left of the line."[28]

The Third Brigade was going to be flanked again as the Confederates came on, and

Butterfield sent aides to his regiments with orders to retreat. Capt. Hugh Campbell of the 83rd Pennsylvania rode up to the 16th Michigan, and Welch, excited and proud of their regiments' performance, rushed over to greet him. "Campbell, haven't we done splendid?" he shouted. The men there cheered, but the orders were to retreat. It was an opportune time, because there was a lull in firing as the men formed in marching order in the haze of smoke that settled over the field in the shallow valley in which they stood, behind the high ground where the front line had been previously. Then Confederates appeared, coming over the hill, moving toward them.

Regiments from a South Carolina brigade, part of the division of Gen. James Longstreet, given the job of protecting the Confederate right, moved up and over the slope from Boatswain's Swamp into the farm fields, not expecting there were any Union forces left in this corner of the battlefield. Rebel witnesses writing after the war said they saw columns of marching men before them, but in the smoky haze and the twilight, could not tell if these troops were friend or foe. Nor could the Union soldiers be sure who was advancing at them; there was a moment of uncertainty in the sulfurous, sweltering atmosphere as the remaining regiments of the Third Brigade marched across the field in front of the South Carolinians.

Col. Micah Jenkins of the Palmetto Sharpshooters now shouted a demand: "Identify yourselves." One Confederate veteran, G. G. Buchanan, said Jenkins got his answer when a Union officer shouted, "16th Michigan." But another former Rebel comrade, James S. Hoyt, said Jenkins did not get an answer—only that an officer from the unidentified regiment (the 16th Michigan, he thought later), shouted for his men to halt, turn and fire. At practically the same moment, the South Carolina troops also fired.[29]

Thomas R. Lackie of Detroit, who was in the 16th Michigan's Company F, remembered it differently. He said that a Rebel officer, probably Col. Jenkins, realized it was Yankees in his front and demanded that they "surrender or be destroyed." Major Welch shouted back: "Damned if we do." Bay City's Benjamin Partridge, a lieutenant at the time, later agreed that Welch cursed at the Rebel who ordered them to give up. However this confrontation unfolded, the evening exploded in volleys of musketry, which Lt. Col. John Ruehle described as "terrible fire." "The regiment now halted, fronted and poured its fire into the Rebel ranks at close range," he reported.[30]

The Confederates charged, driving the Michigan and Pennsylvania soldiers back, but a Union battery opened up on the advancing Rebels and Butterfield's brigade got a bit of breathing room as the 16th Michigan retreated, firing, toward Woodbury's bridge, Lt. Col. Ruehle reported. George Prentiss, then a lieutenant in Company A, later indicated the retreat was disorganized until he, Lt. Butler Brown, and another officer formed some men into yet another line. "Everything was in utter confusion," Prentiss wrote. "Bullets flying thick and fast." But he, Brown, and that third officer "made a stand behind a brook, got a few men into line, opened fire on the disorganized Rebels and soon our regiment was rallied and the ground lost by our brigade was recovered."[31]

That third officer, unnamed by Prentiss, was probably Maj. Norval Welch. Other accounts say Welch planted the colors—apparently the national flag—on the bank of a ditch and shouted for the regiment to gather around. Benjamin Partridge of Bay City said later he recorded this in his diary that night. "Maj. N. E. Welch deserves great credit for his good behavior this day," Lt. Partridge wrote, "for mounting a stump and calling for the men to stand firm and beat the enemy back." Partridge guessed there must have been 1,000 men from the 16th Michigan and other regiments of the Third Brigade and various stragglers rallied on the hillside. Gen. Butterfield ordered a last advance as reinforcements arrived; Lt. Col. Ruehle reported that "the order was received by Major Welch, who gallantly led it back up the hill."[32]

Fresh Union troops also reached the field, having come over the bridges from the south side of the Chickahominy, just before what was left of the 16th Michigan and their brigade charged. "Word was brought that Meagher's Irish Brigade and Sickle's Excelsior Brigade had crossed the river and were charging the Rebels on our right," Lt. Charles Salter wrote. "And soon we saw the Irish Brigade with their coats off, sleeves rolled, charging the Rebels and driving them back in confusion. We then rallied and charging upon the enemy, drove them back and regained most of our original position."[33]

Capt. Robert Elliott looked around for Stockton as their charge went forward, but the colonel was nowhere to be seen. Darkness was falling and most of their comrades had retreated across the Chickahominy. These last fifteen minutes of the battle, Thomas Lackie claimed, were when the casualties dramatically mounted for the 16th Michigan. "The rebels opened on the whole line again, mowing men down like grass," Ben Partridge agreed. Under intense fire and nearly surrounded, there was nothing left for the men to do now except save themselves. The firing tailed off and the Union troops withdrew as night came on.

"It was now growing dark and we had held our position longer than it had been intended we should," Lt. Salter wrote. "Therefore, as the Rebels were still pressing upon us with overwhelming numbers, we retreated across the Chickahominy after having fought one of the hardest battles for the numbers engaged that was ever fought on this continent."[34]

The Third Brigade's retreat across the river at Woodbury's Bridge that night was no simple matter. The Confederates brought artillery to bear on the bridges, some that were already partly destroyed by Union soldiers to prevent pursuit. "Crossing the log bridge, Lt. (Byron) McGraw, walking with Lt. Partridge, lost his right leg, hit by a shell," according to an unpublished account probably written by Partridge years later. Partridge went with McGraw, a young man from Pontiac, in an ambulance to Savage's Station, where his leg was amputated below the knee. McGraw, 22, died two days later.

By the time some soldiers made it to the Chickahominy that night, where Union forces held the south bank, there was no bridge to cross. "The bridge had already been destroyed, but the regiment crossed the swamps and reached the opposite side shortly after dark that night," Lt. Col. Ruehle reported. Capt. Elliott agreed. He brought about twenty of his men over, slowly and carefully, through water that was in places over the men's heads. It took them until about 10 p.m. to get across. The men, dazed, grimy, exhausted, and hungry, searched the darkness for comrades.[35]

The 16th Michigan probably barely existed as a military command that night. The regiment had been mauled, its survivors scattered in small groups. More than 230 of the regiment had been killed, wounded, or were missing and the dead numbered about fifty, as far as the survivors knew at that moment. But the death toll was higher. In addition to Capt. Carr, killed early in the battle, Lt. Richard Williams, who had originally joined Company A and recently transferred to Company C, had been killed in action (regimental records gave for him, alternately, Detroit and Saginaw as his place of residence). All told, seventy-eight men from the 16th Michigan had been killed or mortally wounded. Gaines' Mill, the regiment's first true battle, would prove to be its worst, though it was even worse for the 83rd Pennsylvania: Their colonel was killed and they lost more men killed and wounded than any regiment in the battle.[36]

The 16th Michigan's commander, Col. Stockton, was missing, possibly dead or wounded as far as the survivors knew. Several other officers were missing or wounded: Capt. Charles Meyers of Detroit was wounded, his military service ended; Lt. Gilbert Chandler of Saginaw had to have his shattered arm amputated; Lt. Frank Eddy from Flint was luckier, suffering three grazing wounds. Corporal Frank Keeler of Saginaw was so convinced that his company commander, Capt. Ben Fisher, was killed that he sent Fisher's wife a letter informing her so. "If there was a chance for our hope of his being alive yet we would gladly encourage it," Keeler wrote. "But it would be cruel to raise hopes which must eventually be crushed." In fact, Keeler was wrong—Fisher was alive and a prisoner.[37]

"How I ever escaped and got out is more than I can tell," Keeler wrote to his family. "The bullets rained in ranks around me, men fell on my left and right. Lt. (Gilbert) Chandler was wounded in the left arm and I helped him along." Company D, made up mainly of Saginaw area men, had gone into the battle with fifty-three men; it came out with twenty-six. "Eleven of our men were found on this side of the Chickahominy, wounded," he said about the battle's aftermath. "The other 16 were missing, having been left on the battlefield." Sgt. Ziba Graham of Flint sent a similar note home. "Out of 49 men who went into the engagement of last Friday, nine were killed, twelve were wounded, five missing—being about one half our number," he wrote about Company C.[38]

One of the wounded men from his company was 17-year-old George Sidman from Owosso, who had joined as a drummer, but by his own admission had turned out not to be very good at it. Sidman had traded his sticks for a rifle. Struck in the hip by a bullet at the battle, he broke his rifle over a stump and crawled into the Chickahominy swamp. He was captured the next day and spent several weeks as a prisoner of the Confederacy, first at Libby Prison, then at Castle Thunder, and finally Belle Isle. Sidman was released in a prisoner exchange on August 18 and sent to Point Lookout Hospital in Maryland; soon after he left without authorization, stowing away on a steamer to Washington. Still on crutches, he would be sent to a convalescent camp that fall. But that was still weeks and months away.[39]

In Company E, a second lieutenant or noncommissioned officer charged with record keeping noted that it had lost nineteen men killed, wounded, or missing; in Company H, the casualties were twenty-five. John Berry recorded that his Company A lost ten men killed, twelve wounded and twelve missing, although some of the missing were among those killed or who died from their wounds. Among the regiment's dead at Gaines' Mill was 26-year-old Sgt. Joseph Stanfield, from the Ypsilanti area, the studious ex-lancer. Like Lt. McGraw, he was retreating with his regiment, going back to the bridge with Lt. Partridge and others when he was killed. Stanfield had written in his diary that it was noble to die on the battlefield for one's country and he had done exactly that.[40]

Colonel Stockton was not among those who made it across the Chickahominy. Thinking that the Confederates would cut off those who ran over the field for the bridges, he and several others headed for the woods along the river's swamp to find a way across. But he was weak and exhausted, and in the darkness he and his group were separated from the regiment before their last rally and charge. "After struggling all night through mud and water," Stockton later reported, "we were suddenly captured just after daylight on Saturday morning and immediately sent to Richmond."[41]

The 16th Michigan had also lost its regimental colors, captured by the South Carolina regiment of Palmetto Sharpshooters. With Stockton was the captain of Company D, Ben Fisher, wounded. So was Capt. Judd Mott, the ex-lancer officer whom Joseph Stanfield had followed into Stockton's regiment. Also captured was Dr. T. W. Seeley, the contract surgeon who was filling in for Dr. William Butler, the assistant surgeon who had resigned.[42]

But Stockton's fate was a mystery to most of the men who escaped across the river. Some thought he had been captured, but others believed he was surely severely wounded or killed in the heavy rifle fire. Lt. Col. Ruehle sent his old friend's effects back to Washington to Maria Stockton, and even the colonel's horse, "Old Billy," was safely removed from the battlefield and eventually returned to her. But Capt. Robert Elliott was convinced Stockton was alive. Elliott said that after the survivors got over the Chickahominy, he and four men quietly recrossed to the Confederate side to try to find and rescue the colonel early on the morning of June 28. They were unsuccessful—and fired upon by Confederate pickets—but came back to the Union-held side of the river sure Stockton had been captured.[43]

Lt. Col. Ruehle, Maj. Welch, and Col. Stockton were among many officers lauded in Gen. Butterfield's report of the battle; he said "they behaved well and deserve credit." Welch and Major Barnum of the 12th New York, however, were singled out by Butterfield for having "rendered me invaluable assistance throughout the entire fight, exposing themselves to danger by carrying orders and bringing information with unsurpassed coolness and bravery." Others echoed that compliment. "It gave me great pleasure to notice the gallant conduct of Major Welch, of the 16th Michigan," wrote Lt. Col. Robert Richardson of the 12th New York, "who held his men steady under the hill in the rear of the woods, and who, afterward advanced them with some of my own men under Capt. Randall against the enemy, covering the retreat of the brigade."[44]

These compliments were reported in the days ahead. That night after the battle, the soldiers of the 16th Michigan and their comrades had almost nothing in the way of tents or rations as they rested near another Union division on the south side of the Chickahominy. In the light of morning, the regiment reformed and joined its brigade and division for the march to McClellan's field headquarters, which he was now giving up as he retreated south. Offensive operations by McClellan's Army of the Potomac against the Confederate capital were over.

Very much intact, the army trudged south, and eventually Lee's army pursued. "On the 28th, we gathered our little regiment together and marched towards the James River," Frank Keeler wrote. That day, the First Division of the Fifth Corps moved in the heat to Savage's Station and crossed the White Oak Swamp. Some of the regiment's men were put to work building bridges or causeways to get troops over the swamp, where they camped before sunset. That night, a storm opened up on them, adding to the misery and discomfort of tired and hungry soldiers.[45]

Wounded men who could not be moved were left behind and soon 2,000 or more of them were in Confederate hands. "Lt. Chandler bade me a cheerful goodbye at Savage's Station," Keeler said about his wounded officer. "His arm has been amputated and he seems in fine spirits." One of the men staying behind there with the wounded was Henry "Tip" Aplin, even though he knew he would be made prisoner. Sgt. Ziba Graham of Company C wrote to Aplin's brother Tom, telling him of Tip's decision. "I with my lieutenant (Ransom) remained at the station until Sunday morning (June 29) with the boys, we both being sick," Graham said. "We left them about 9 a.m. . . . all in good spirits. Henry was not wounded but merely remained voluntarily to look after and care for his wounded comrades. It was a noble act, well worthy of him."[46]

The soldiers of Butterfield's brigade marched from the swamp and formed in a partial line of battle to prepare for another possible Confederate attack at the intersection of the New Market and Charles City roads, but it did not come. Instead, to the north on June 29, other Union troops fought a rearguard battle at Savage's Station. Pvt. John Berry, who had missed the battle of Gaines' Mill because he was ill and sunstruck, had spent the 28th with the sick and wounded wagon train, but found his regiment on the 29th. He felt well enough to march and stand picket. "We are making tracks for the James River," he wrote that night. "The enemy are close upon us." In truth, the Confederates were not looming behind Berry, yet the mood was tense.[47]

The Fifth Corps made a tiring and sometimes confusing march south that night through the woods. Pickets from the 16th Michigan returned to the site of their bivouac near White Oak swamp at daybreak, June 30. Within an or hour or so, they joined their comrades on the march on the Quaker Road to a landmark called Malvern Hill, on the last leg of their retreat to the James. There Union gunboats on the river could provide protection as the Army of the Potomac withdrew per McClellan's order—a depressing surprise to his soldiers.

Another terrible battle was shaping up, meanwhile, and soon raging a few miles to the north, where most of the rest of the Union army formed roughly into a semicircle facing north and west, protecting the intersections of the roads leading south to the James River as the retreat continued. This was the battle of Glendale; here Lee wanted the combination of his divisions to destroy the Union forces. Again, the Rebels got so close at points that men fought hand-to-hand. But Stonewall Jackson, who may have been suffering from exhaustion, did not send his men into the fight as Lee directed, and that night the Union soldiers withdrew to the open ridge called Malvern Hill.[48]

The 16th Michigan heard the fighting to the north and briefly came under fire from some nearby Confederate artillery, though no member of the regiment was hurt. But they had no combat on June 30. The regiment arrived with its brigade late that morning near a sharp turn in winding James River called Turkey Bend; the river here wound just south of Malvern Hill, a prominent plateau, higher than the rest of the countryside. The men rested briefly, for soon commanders sent them up the hill, which from the north gradually inclined up from woods and fields to high crests and even cliffs on its sides toward the river on the south. "We reached the Malvern Hill," Lt. Charles Salter wrote, "there halted and formed a line of battle in a good position, and then waited for the coming of the enemy."[49]

The wide ridge rose to a reported height of about 150 feet from the low ground and creek beds at its margins; the slope to its first (northern) crest was uneven, with gentle hills and shallow valleys. Overall, Malvern Hill stretched more than a mile from north to south. The higher, open crest of the hilltop was less than a mile across from east to west, and the James River was less than a mile behind it. Union generals had already recognized it was an excellent defensive position; as some of the first Union troops to arrive, the division of which the 16th Michigan was part was placed on the center left, or western, portion of the crest. Meanwhile, the battle of Glendale spread along the main Union lines on the important roads to the north, eventually reaching the Malvern neighborhood late that afternoon of June 30 when Confederate forces comprising Lee's right struck briefly at the Fifth Corps' salient. "The rebels were coming down the river road [from the west] in an immense force and soon their artillery was planted and throwing shell right amongst us," Lt. Charles Salter wrote.[50]

Lt. Col. Ruehle stated two Confederate divisions approached through the countryside that afternoon, and Union reports reflect that officers thought this amounted to over 20,000 Rebels. Their artillery opened fire on Union soldiers and guns on Malvern Hill with six batteries at 4 p.m., and the 16th Michigan was ordered to take a position behind some of the Union cannon. "We were in column doubled on the center, just below the summit of the hill," Ruehle wrote, "when General Butterfield led us to the crest, and the battalion was deployed under a severe fire from the enemy's rifled field pieces." From the top of Malvern Hill, there were no targets for the 16th Michigan, so the men were ordered to stack their rifles and lie down. "We remained in this position a quarter of an hour or more."[51]

Though Rebel shelling forced the Michigan soldiers to keep low, Lt. Salter indicated he had a view of what was happening as Confederates probed the Fifth Corps defenses being positioned on the ridge. But the answering Union guns quickly stifled this firing. "Our artillery was not idle either," Salter wrote, "and as we had the advantage of position, they caused great havoc among the rebels." Union gunboats also opened fire on the Confederate batteries west of the hill, ending their bombardment in short order. Now the 16th Michigan was ordered to move out, down the back of the hill and around to the front to support the 83rd Pennsylvania, which, with their division, would back up some of the Union batteries positioned down the slope.

"On the side [where Union positions were] furthest from the river, however, the fighting had been more desperate and the loss on our side considerable," Salter said about the bitter battle of Glendale to the north that day. "And it was on this side [at Malvern Hill] that the Rebels determined to make their principal attack the next a.m., July 1st." The ridge would give its name to the next battle.[52]

6.

JULY–AUGUST 1862

IT WAS AWFUL TO LOOK UPON

The morning of July 1 was quiet for the men of the 16th Michigan until they heard Confederate artillery somewhere to the right, Lt. Col. John Ruehle wrote later. This was not the actual start of the battle—just periodic cannon and picket fire that did no damage to the Army of the Potomac, strongly positioned across Malvern Hill. But it foreshadowed a terrible storm of lead and iron soon to be unleashed; first, though, there were the were the preliminaries. "The regiment was ordered toward a belt of woods that skirted the field upon the east, upon which we lay and through which a small stream ran," Ruehle continued. "We were deployed on the left of the 44th New York Volunteers, and threw a platoon of our rifle company, Brady Sharpshooters, [under] Captain Dygert, out as skirmishers through the woods to cover our front." This seems to have been near the center of the long hillside, not far from the intervening crest that locals called Crew's Hill; again, the ground sloped gently downhill before them to the north, but rose behind them to the south, to the top of Malvern Hill.

Ruehle's regiment, with its Third Brigade of the First Division of the Fifth Corps, comprised part of the Union left or its western portion, and now the entire position across the ridge bristled with guns and lines of troops. The Fifth Corps was not alone; as night had fallen on June 30, the rest of the Army of the Potomac had moved south from the Glendale battlefields, taking positions on the eastern or right side of the hill, down to the river. Union gunners and infantry did not return the fire of the probing and testing by the Rebels that morning, but in the afternoon—some said 1 p.m., others thought 2 p.m.—the artillery available to the attacking Confederates increased their fire. Lee's army had followed the Union army south to Malvern Hill, still hoping to destroy their foe, and now the assault began.

On the western part of Union position, the 16th Michigan was ordered forward along the side of a country lane called the Quaker Road to support the 83rd Pennsylvania, posted ahead in the lines of infantry and artillery, facing north. Before their brigade on the brow of Crew's Hill, looking further down the slope, was a line of Union field guns. These batteries were only a small part of the total artillery forces; more batteries stood to their right, with more positioned higher on the hillside behind them. And there was still more Union artillery in reserve. But the Confederates brought artillery, too, and now their gunners made their presence known.[1]

"The rebels had a large number of cannon, planted around in every direction they could possibly, to bring them to bear upon us," Lt. Charles Salter wrote of the Confederate bombardment. His lieutenant colonel, in command of the regiment since Thomas Stockton was missing at Gaines' Mill, said the men had some protection in the "undulating" landscape, "but the cross-fire from their guns was exceedingly severe, and some of our men were killed and wounded by solid shot and shell."

Confederate infantry could be seen moving through the trees down the slope; at the point where the 16th Michigan waited with comrades, they were about half a mile away when they emerged from the trees, marching over open ground. Though Lt. Col. Ruehle did not mention the Brady Sharpshooters falling back to the regiment to get out of the way, at some point the skirmishers necessarily retreated to avoid being hit by their own gunners or captured by the approaching Confederates. "When the rebels would advance from the cover of the woods, our artillery would open on them with canister and grape shot, mowing down immense numbers of them at every discharge," Salter said.[2]

Fitz John Porter, commander of the Fifth Corps, would call these first piecemeal Rebel attacks along the front line "spasmodic, but sometimes formidable." The soldiers of the 16th Michigan had so far been under some Confederate shelling but not involved in the fight. But by evening, the Confederates, as they had done at Gaines' Mill, launched a more coordinated attack to overwhelm the Union line. The Fifth Corps' commander remembered there was a kind of lull before this massive assault began—and then it came with a fury; the Confederates again opened fire with their artillery, trying to do as much damage as they could to the Union guns, to protect their advancing infantry. But it did not work.

"It was awful to look upon," said Cpl. Frank Keeler of Saginaw. "The graybacks coming out of the forest to make a charge seemed determined to crush us, but our brass guns opened on their double ranks at five hundred yards, and every shot of double canister made a wide gap in them." John Berry of Company A agreed. "Our batterys [*sic*] pour the grape & canister right into them," he wrote in his diary.[3]

"The hardest fighting of all took place after 6 p.m.," Salter agreed. "That is the time the enemy advanced upon us in greater numbers than ever before. They came out of the woods with a long line in front that looked splendid whilst after this came a large number of them from the wood like a swarm of bees. We had brought up some of our siege guns and these being placed about a half-mile in the rear of our field artillery, soon opened upon them with their 100 lb. shell."

"Toward 6 p.m. we were ordered to advance to the brow of a hill 500 yards in advance, to the support of a battery just on the left of the road," Lt. Col. Ruehle reported, referring to the Union guns on Crew's Hill. "This was done under a bitter fire of shell and spherical case-shot, wounding several men." The generals had seen how a massive Confederate infantry attack had broken the Fifth Corps line at Gaines' Mill, and no one wanted a recurrence of such a disaster. Gen. Dan Butterfield sent the 16th Michigan and the 83rd Pennsylvania to support the middle of the Union line. As the 16th Michigan moved to back up the gunners there, the men on the left wing of the regiment stepped over the prone bodies of two companies of men from the 22nd Massachusetts, who were also waiting. The Michigan soldiers were ordered to halt between the guns on the crest of that hill and the artillery caissons behind them. Here they waited; some of the soldiers helped carry ammunition to the battery, while two 16th Michigan men (perhaps men who had instruction in loading and firing cannon back in the spring) took the place of wounded gun crew members. Lt. Col. Ruehle identified this artillery unit as Wolcott's Maryland Battery.[4]

Once the battery was out of ammunition, Ruehle wrote, it was "limbered up," or withdrawn by its crew and their teams; the 16th Michigan moved up to where those guns had stood and opened fire. The lieutenant colonel said the regiment fired "about 40 rounds" before another battery arrived to take the regiment's place. Lt. Salter said the 16th Michigan assisted these gunners and cannons, too, that he identified as a battery of the 5th U.S. Artillery, a regular army unit attached to their division. As gun crew members were killed or wounded, some of the Michigan soldiers were sent to help. "We detailed 50 men from our regiment to assist them," Salter said. One of the men was Josiah Wadsworth of Company D, from Saginaw County, who was killed in action.

Lt. Col. Ruehle said that the Confederate firing tailed off, ending the battle as darkness came on, though Salter gave a much more dramatic account of his brigade comrades closing out the fight. "The [artillery] firing was very rapid, at every discharge immense gaps were made in the ranks of the rebels[. B]ut no sooner [were these gaps] seen than they were instantly filled up again, and on they came apparently determined to crush us at once," the lieutenant from Detroit wrote. As this last advancing line of Confederates came within rifle range, he continued, the Union batteries on the hill ran out of ammunition and withdrew. Salter's comrades in the battle line fired rapidly, but still the Rebels came on. "And everything looked dark enough for us, but our Gen. Butterfield soon remedied this error. 'Charge,' he shouted, and we did charge with terrible effect upon the enemy." Salter used the editorial "we," meaning his brigade; specifically, Butterfield sent the 83rd Pennsylvania and the 44th New York to charge, supported by the 12th New York, to stop the oncoming Confederates, and they did so. Salter wrote that the Rebels withdrew back toward the woods down the hill, and fresh Union artillery pulled up onto the crest and commenced firing after the retreating infantry. Night fell over the battlefield littered with thousands of dead and wounded men. Line after line of Confederate soldiers had been wiped out by the batteries that afternoon and evening as they marched up those slopes.[5]

Fifteen Confederate brigades attacked Malvern Hill that day, and they had lost over 5,000 men, killed, wounded, and missing. Union casualties were slightly more than 2,000. The Rebels, Salter wrote, "had not succeeded in forcing us to give way a single inch, whilst the rebels had lost more men killed and wounded than they did in the great battles of Shiloh and Fair Oaks." Frank Keeler agreed. "Their charge was a failure and when they withdrew from range the field was covered with their dead," he wrote. "We are bound to say that the rebs fought with a desperate determination." Only two soldiers from the 16th Michigan had been killed in action that day, but the number of the regiment's dead in the battle would rise to ten, as eight of the thirty-seven wounded soldiers died in the days that followed; three men were missing.

Another regiment in their brigade, the 83rd Pennsylvania, which charged the attacking Confederates, suffered nearly forty men killed and more than 100 wounded; their death toll rose as some of the wounded succumbed in the days that followed. In the 16th Michigan, Capt. Gustav Kast, commanding Company K, recognized Lieutenants Edward Hill and Lewis Webster and Sergeants Wallace Jewett and Frederick Forsyth, all former lancers, in a brief summary of his company's performance. Webster, a Saginaw man, had been detailed that day to command Company D, the Saginaw company.

Keeler said the Confederate prisoners told their Union captors that they had drunk liquor fortified with black powder before the charges they had made, almost certainly an exaggeration meant to impress and baffle the Yankees. "Many people will not believe that the Johnnies in this fight mixed gun powder with the whiskey in their canteens," he wrote. "A prisoner showed us the contents of his canteen, and it was as I state. He said he had not taken any water that day, that their officers filled their canteens with the mixture and used every means to keep them away from water! Many of the prisoners begged our men to give them water and take their whiskey."[6]

Throughout the Seven Days, the Army of the Potomac had consistently inflicted higher casualties on the Confederates than their enemy had on them. The Rebel army did *not* outnumber them two to one, as McClellan and his officers on down believed (Union enlisted men thought it was an even worse ratio, some inflating it to ten to one). And the Army of the Potomac had fought from defensive positions, giving them the decided advantage. But under the cover of darkness, the Union soldiers, at McClellan's order, moved off the ridge and walked down a muddy road along the James River in retreat, going several miles to a place called Harrison's Landing. The 16th Michigan remained on the Malvern Hill battlefield on picket, until they too were told to march early in the morning of July 2. As they did so, tired and hungry, the rain came down.

"We were almost the last ones on the field," Brady Sharpshooter Alfred Apted wrote. They rejoined their brigade and division moving on the road to the Harrison's Landing, arriving there several hours later. Men had lost or thrown away their equipment on the retreat from Gaines' Mill and mountains of Union supplies had been destroyed, so there was no shelter except what the men could throw together, and little if anything in the way of rations. One report said they had only received rations once between June 27 and July 1. "Marching night and day," wrote Company B's Sgt. Hubbard H. Barrett, 27, of Ionia, describing the retreat of July 2, "and I am sore and lame and used up."[7]

"We stack arms in the rain, and having lost our tents, blankets and even overcoats and knapsacks in the late battles, we make large fires," wrote John Berry of reaching Harrison's Landing. "Besides this we are hungry and have nothing to eat. We pass a very miserable day and still more miserable night." An officer who kept records for Berry's company noted his satisfaction with his men's performance during the withdrawal from the Chickahominy, the battles, and the retreat to Harrison's Lansing. "The behavior of the company in those actions was very [creditable] to them," he wrote. "They were cool and firm, obeying every order with alacrity."[8]

The Confederate cavalry managed to move a battery into position near the encampments of the Union army and opened fire that night or early on the morning of July 3. The bombardment did no real damage and stopped when Union gunboats pounded back at the Rebels with overwhelming force. The 16th Michigan was called out ready to fight, but other soldiers briefly skirmished with the Rebel troopers, who were not looking to have a battle in any event. But supplies started to arrive, the camps were moved to higher ground, and it was generally a time of rest, though thousands of Union soldiers were sick.[9]

Some accounts suggest men of the Army of the Potomac were dispirited and glum after the retreat from Richmond ordered by McClellan, but the generals nevertheless marked the 4th of July with reviews, patriotic speeches, and artillery fire. This reminded the soldiers that they were still part of a huge and powerful force and, hopefully, restored their pride and morale in this difficult period. Pvt. Apted of the Brady Sharpshooters called it "the dullest Fourth of July I ever spent in my life," while Berry recorded, word for word, the proud speech read to the men from McClellan.[10]

As affairs settled down in their camp at Harrison's Landing, Salter wrote to his friends in Detroit, telling them about the events of late June and early July. "We have passed through more battles and skirmishes than I had ever seen before since the war broke out, and although at times I have thought that I could not go through with the severe fighting we had and not get killed or wounded, I find myself uninjured and in as good health as ever." Salter wrote of the battles and the retreat, but he stressed that the Union army had not given up hope of victory. "Here we do not, any of us, feel discouraged or lonely as everybody is too busy here, scarcely spare time to think of such things," the Detroiter said. "As for myself, I know that I am doing my duty here and doing more for the benefit of my country in my present situation, than I could do in another other. . . . [I] think that is about the way most of us think about it."[11]

Rain was setting in as Salter finished his letter, and he closed it with a remonstration to his civilian friends that heroic descriptions and accounts of battles that appeared in the newspapers did not reflect what soldiers really experienced. "I can assure you no matter how grand it may be for people up north to read accounts of splendid victories," he wrote, knowing of the scores of casualties in his company and regiment, "it is not very pleasant for those engaged in it."

Sgt. Hubbard Barrett wrote to his folks back in Ionia about the familiar faces of men from his company now missing from the ranks. "When I look through our company and find lots of them gone, I can't say they are not dead," he said. "But it makes me feel sad to think that their bodies are on the battlefield, and then to think that perhaps I will have to follow them next battle."[12]

George Ervay of Company E wrote home to Grand Ledge. "We have had an awful battle," the teenager told his parents, referring to Gaines' Mill. "There was 96 men in our company and now there is 13 left. There was an awful slaughter in it. We had a great retreat and I do not know how it stands for we have not had any papers." A farm boy who would soon transfer into Company H, Ervay had been detached from his regiment to tend the brigade's beef cattle herd, but he had come under artillery fire and witnessed the combat. "I lost everything that I had, for the boss with his wagon was in the rear and had to throw [away] everything it had in it to get away," he explained about Gaines' Mill. "I had a horse that I was riding and a shell struck his hind legs and broke them from under me. The tree tops [hit by artillery] was a-falling on both sides of the road."[13]

When Ervay's parents asked to hear more about the battles, he replied: "It was an awful scene to witness, I tell you that, when a man has to go up within 5 to 25 rods apart and haul up and shoot each other right down. The rebels were 10 to 1 of our men, and it was a miracle that we was not all taken prisoners." He continued:

> I suppose that the folks in Michigan think that the Army of the Potomac is all cut to pieces and whipped, but I tell you that if you tell a soldier of the army that, you might just as well knock him flat to the ground, for he will knock you down as quick as the words is out of your mouth. The last day of the fight, the boys would charge bayonet with as much courage as the first day's fight. I tell you that when a person can see his comrades fall on the right and left and musket balls passing through his pants legs and other parts of his clothes, that looks as if it would scare a man to death. But a man gets harden[ed] to it after the first two or three shots; a man thinks no more of it than if he was shooting at a mark.[14]

Pvt. Marion Munson, who like Lt. Salter served in Company E, also wrongly believed the Confederates had a ten-to-one advantage or more during the battles. He wrote to his friend at Stony Creek that though he had lost everything he owned after Gaines' Mill, he was glad to have escaped the Seven Days with his life. "If it had not been for artillery," he said, "we would have been annihilated." Though some Republican politicians were critical of McClellan for his failure to capture the Confederate capital and crush their army, Munson said those leaders had thought the rebellion was "a one-horse concern, that it could be put down by a turn of the wrist." The Peninsula Campaign had proved them wrong.[15]

The day after the battle of Gaines' Mill, Col. Thomas Stockton, a prisoner of war removed to Richmond's Libby warehouse, wrote to his wife, telling her he was alive and unhurt. "What the loss in killed and wounded on either or both sides I do not yet know," he wrote Maria, "but it was large." The minié balls had whistled around him, but he had been preserved, he told her; and when he had given the order for his regiment to withdraw, the men broke into a run and fled. Still, he claimed that his regiment was the last of the Third Brigade to give way. He was sure that Maj. Norval Welch had escaped capture, but he feared his friend Lt. Col. John Ruehle had been killed. Of course, both Welch and Ruehle had escaped with their lives.

There were about a hundred Union officers confined to one large room, he said of the Confederate accommodations, and one of his fellow prisoners was Brig. Gen. John

Reynolds, a brigade commander who would survive the war for just another year, becoming a corps commander and losing his life in action on the first day of the battle of Gettysburg. Also with Stockton were his captains Judd Mott and Ben Fisher, both slightly wounded. The rebel wardens provided the prisoners with a cot and two quilts. "They seem to be doing all they can for our comfort, under the circumstances," Stockton wrote. "I shall need clothing next."[16]

Of course, Stockton had family connections in the South—his wife's nieces were married to important Confederate officers, Gen. James Longstreet and Lt. Col. George Deas—the sons-in-law of Stockton's brother-in-law, the late Brig. Gen. John Garland of the U.S. Army. Stockton had known both soldiers and been friendly with them in days gone by. In his letter to his wife, Stockton thought it better not to mention Longstreet by name, but used only the first and last letters with dashes between. He was sure that he and other Union officers would not be detained long. "I have written to L——t, and trust he will aid me soon to get off," the colonel wrote. Life as a prisoner was monotonous. "The only thing we fear is sickness," he told her. "We hear we are to be moved to better quarters. Hope so. But some say that a grand fight is going on today. All I desire is to return."[17]

Stockton's family connections, and perhaps his West Point connections, did not fail him. Consider that the Confederate commander, Robert E. Lee, graduated from West Point two years behind Stockton in 1829, and of course Lee was a hero in the Mexican War. According to one of Stockton's letters, an aide to Gen. Lee called on him in prison on July 13, accompanied by Gen. Longstreet's 13-year-old son, Garland, who was in Richmond with his mother, Louise. Garland Longstreet had lost three younger brothers to scarlet fever early in 1862, and their mother was still grieving. Though the Longstreets were dealing, as were so many others, with heartbreak, loss, and the uncertainty of life in wartime, they made sure that her Uncle Tom Stockton had what he required. "He [Garland Longstreet] told me his father had received your letter and had considered it," the colonel told Maria. "Louise and the general isn't [*sic*] sure they would call [but] that they would see that I was supplied with whatever I wanted. I am well and only need some change of clothes if I remain long. I shall also need funds. If you have the opportunity, send me $100 in gold. Of course, it will have to be sent through proper channels and your letter open."[18]

Shortly after Stockton sent his letter, Mrs. Longstreet visited him at the prison. Mary Louise (or Louisa, as her relatives called her) and her sister, Bessie, who married soldier George Deas, had grown up in the same frontier households with their Aunt Maria, since their parents, the Garlands, had raised Maria from the time she was a few years old, and she was part of the household since before her nieces were born. It is not too much to suppose that their family relationships were close and strong, even if Maria's husband and those of the Garland daughters were on opposite sides in this war. Stockton wrote to his wife again after Louise Longstreet's visit to the Libby warehouse prison on July 16. "She told me [that] you had written to her husband and that he had answered and that he would aid me to be exchanged at the earliest moment," he told Maria. "She will forward this and write you also. Be of good cheer. Before many weeks I trust I will be with you."[19]

Stockton had heard that Maria was fearful about what had happened to him in the days after the battle, but eventually saw that his name was on the list of prisoners. In the meantime, Louise Longstreet "has called on me a number of times [and] supplied me with some changes of clean clothes," he wrote. The Union and the Confederacy were establishing a formal prisoner exchange at that point, but the colonel wrote that Gen. Lee and the Confederate secretary of war "promise to me exchange in case no general exchange has [been] agreed upon"—a remarkable statement suggesting that the personal connection between the officers on opposing sides could trump the lack of a formal prisoner swap arrangement. Stockton would be formally exchanged some days later on August 12 with other officers under the procedure set up by the two sides.[20]

But what truly upset Stockton was the news that came in another officer's letter—his old friend and second-in-command, Lt. Col. John Ruehle of Detroit, "had resigned & was on his way home!!!" The colonel was shocked. "How is that?" he demanded. "I cannot understand why he would resign at this *crisis* & especially when I was *prisoner!*" Stockton also made clear he was unhappy with Maj. Norval Welch. "I am sorry to have my Regt. under the command of the Major," he continued. "By his folly our flag was lost."[21]

In addition to seeking the help of the Longstreets, Stockton also wrote to the Confederate married to his wife's other niece. This was George Deas, a career U.S. Army officer until his resignation in February 1861. A Pennsylvanian by birth and promoted for his gallantry in the Mexican War, Deas had married Bessie Garland; now he was a lieutenant colonel in Virginia, where he served as a staff officer. It seems that Stockton and Deas had known each other well, but Deas made clear he was not going to intervene to help Stockton for old times' sake. "Sir," he replied to Stockton in early July, "My fixed determination is to hold no personal intercourse with any man, for the present, who had volunteered his services to fight against an unoffending people in this infamous war which is now carried on by the United States."

> An interview between us could not be an agreeable one. I must there decline to accede to your request that I should visit you. The very fact of our former intimate acquaintance would be an additional feeling of repugnance to a renewal of any social relations.
>
> Not withstanding, however, that I have these personal feelings, which I can assure you are universally entertained throughout this Country, I yet can never be blind to the dictates of humanity and if you should be suffering in any way, it will give me pleasure to assist you.
>
> My stock of clothing is by no means large. But if you will let me know how I can send you some articles of convenience, I will do so immediately.
>
> I have no communication with Washington, but if an opportunity should occur, you may rest assured that Mrs. Stockton will be informed of your safety. But in this respect I think you need give yourself no uneasiness as your name has been published in the papers here, and unquestionably will be copied into the papers of the United States.[22]

The days in the Libby prison were long and boring, and the officers with Stockton played chess, cribbage, and euchre, held religious services, read, and carved ornaments;

they walked around the room for exercise and of course talked. Stockton, hearing that his friend John Ruehle resigned, soon wrote to Michigan Adjutant General John Robertson, concerned that the authority to recommend officers for promotion in the 16th Michigan now fell to Maj. Norval Welch, who naturally recommended himself to replace Ruehle and others for vacancies in the regiment. The colonel was suggesting that because he would soon be released from Confederate prison, the adjutant general and the governor should wait for his return and *his* recommendations for promotions. As soon as he was exchanged, Stockton wrote, "I will send you a full report and names for promotion."[23]

But Maj. Welch was not waiting for Stockton to return. He quickly sent up his own name for promotion to the post of lieutenant colonel and that of Capt. Thomas Barry, who had complained about Stockton to the state adjutant general, to be major. Thus, when Stockton returned to command the 16th Michigan in September, he would find his two top officers were men he did not choose.[24]

Another member of the 16th Michigan who spent time in Rebel prison that summer was Tip Aplin, captured with the wounded and the medical personnel who had stayed behind at Savage's Station during the retreat from Richmond. Aplin wrote to his mother in Flint on August 5, and Elvira Aplin passed the news to her son George, serving in the 10th Michigan Infantry. "He did not complain of ill treatment while he was a prisoner," she wrote. "He said all he had to eat per day was a half a loaf of bread and a small slice of fresh beef or a little soup without any salt that you know would hardly make a man lunch between meals."

Tip Aplin got sick before he was released from prison on July 31, and he believed he would have died had he been kept longer. "He said all the prisoners shouted with all the strength they had when they came within sight of the old stars and stripes," Elvira Aplin reported about Tip's arrival on a James River transport to Union-held territory. "When they came near Gen. McClellan's headquarters, the general came on board the transport and shook hands with the men who had been prisoners."[25]

In the meantime, Col. Micah Jenkins of the South Carolina Palmetto Sharpshooters thought it would be a noble gesture to present the Yankee flag his men had captured at Gaines' Mill—the flag that had been presented to Stockton's regiment in Detroit back in the fall of 1861—to the governor of South Carolina. Jenkins made his request to his division's commander, Gen. James Longstreet, who in turn wrote on July 11 to Robert E. Lee about Jenkins's request. Lee approved.

"The Secretary of War has authorized me to comply with the request of Colonel Jenkins, as to retaining the regimental standard of the 16th Michigan Regiment for presentation to the Governor of his State," Lee wrote. And so Stockton's regimental flag was turned over to Jenkins.[26] Later a Confederate brigadier general, Jenkins would be mortally wounded in the confused fighting in the battle of the Wilderness in May 1864—the same incident in which Longstreet was wounded.

But within days of Lee's letter, the 16th Michigan's flag was in South Carolina. The

Charleston Mercury reported the gift of the soldiers to their governor. "The flag is of blue silk, six feet by four, with a gold fringe and mounted on a staff which has lost its spearhead in the fight," the paper wrote. "One side exhibits the Goddess of Liberty and the inscription 'Stand by the Constitution and the Union'; the other shows the State arms of Michigan and the name, 'Stockton's Regiment.'" The flag was placed in the state house at Columbia and never returned to Michigan; according to James Hoyt of Greenville, South Carolina, that flag and other captured Union flags were destroyed when the state house burned down by the "careless" handling of fire by Gen. William T. Sherman's soldiers as the war came to a close in 1865.[27]

The 16th Michigan Infantry Regiment remained near Harrison's Landing through July and into early August, camped on a ridge on the north side of the James River at plantation called the Berkley estate, a two-story brick mansion that was once the home of President William Henry Harrison. The house now served as a hospital tended in part by the Sisters of Charity. "These ladies are a curiosity to us soldiers," Corporal Frank Keeler wrote. "We haven't seen a woman since we left Alexandria except for some of the 'poor white trash,' as they are called down here."

Lt. Charles Salter wrote home about the state of the 16th Michigan. "Our regiment at Yorktown numbered 1,040 men and was the largest in our brigade," he said. "This is quite a reduction in our regiment; in three months. . . . 300 have been killed or wounded in different battles we have been in, and the rest, some are sick in northern hospitals, some prisoners in Richmond, and the others we do not know what have become of them." Now the regiment stood at 340 men.[28]

John Berry of Company A and Alfred Apted of the Brady Sharpshooters hoped to see President Lincoln when he came to visit the troops on July 8, but it was night by the time he reached their division—"so we have a review by moonlight," Berry wrote. Bands played and the soldiers cheered the president. Alfred Apted was disappointed he could not get a good look at Lincoln. "'Twas dark when he reached where I was," the sharpshooter complained, "so [I] could not get a chance to see the old fellow." Having come through the Seven Days unscathed, young George Ervay of Grand Ledge wanted to do some fishing, but had no hooks. "We are within 100 rods of the James River," he wrote to his parents late in July. "Next time you write to me I wish you would send me a small line and two or three fish hooks, for if I had them I could catch fish to eat."[29]

The days were dull and oppressively hot, though supplies and equipment soon replaced what the soldiers had lost, worn out, or thrown away. Being so close to the James meant the men could, when they had the time and inclination, take baths. They learned that Norval Welch had been promoted from major to lieutenant colonel; Alfred Apted thought Welch was "a fine, safe man" to command the 16th Michigan. Apted himself suffered fever and headaches, and he recorded the temperature at 104 degrees one day near the Berkley estate, while John Berry got the news that he was promoted to corporal. The regiment's camp was shifted about a half mile to a higher ridge, less prone to flooding and better suited to catch any breeze that might come by.

It was during one of these sweltering July days at Harrison's Landing that their brigade commander, Gen. Dan Butterfield, composed, or perhaps adapted, a bugle call that would forever change the way the army and, in time, all the armed services, signaled "lights out." Oliver W. Norton of the 83rd Pennsylvania, who was the bugler for the Third Brigade, said he was summoned to Butterfield's tent to play a short tune the general had scribbled on the back of an envelope. Between Butterfield whistling and Norton bugling, the general made changes in his small tune until he was satisfied.

Norton played Butterfield's new bugle tune that night, the general having ordered that his new "Taps," or "extinguish lights" call, replace the old traditional drumbeat pattern or nonmusical bugle call used previously. Butterfield's "go to sleep" tune was simple but hauntingly beautiful, even moving. It was an immediate hit with other buglers in the brigade and the division, and it spread rapidly through the entire army. Little did those soldiers from Michigan, Pennsylvania, and New York realize as they bedded down on those July nights that a new military tradition had been created.[30]

On the night of July 31, Confederate troops quietly moved a battery into position on a high ridge overlooking the James River from the south and opened fire on the Union encampments and ships on the north side. "We had not placed any troops on that side of the river and didn't suppose the Rebels would dare make their appearance there because we supposed the gunboats would keep them away," Lt. Salter said. He thought the enemy must have had 24 cannon, but a Union gunboat and batteries down the river were brought to bear on the Confederates and ended the bombardment. Still, it killed ten Union soldiers. "They didn't do much damage as their shot, almost all, went over into the swamp," claimed Sgt. William Borden.[31]

Union troops, including the 16th Michigan and 4th Michigan infantry regiments, crossed the James the next day on steamers. The Rebel pickets fled, and the men cut down trees and demolished buildings that provided cover to the guns the Confederates had positioned on this bluff across the river from Harrison's Landing, called Coggin's Point. The Michigan soldiers destroyed a plantation that someone said belonged to the ardent secessionist Edmund Ruffin, who had fired the first gun at Ft. Sumter and begun the hostilities of the Civil War, but that was not the case, wrote Oliver Norton of the 83rd Pennsylvania; Ruffin's plantation was nearby, however. But the men leveled the plantation from where the Confederates had fired on the Union camps.

"The house, being situated on a bluff overlooking the river[, was] surrounded with the most beautiful grounds I have ever seen," Lt. Salter wrote. "By sunset, we had every building afire and the entire place was made a desert." Men helped themselves to the farm's livestock, and plundered nearby farms, including what was said to be Ruffin's massive library. "Some captures were made," joked a soldier-historian of the 4th Michigan. "Among the trophies were a considerable amount of geese." One of the raiders was Pvt. Alfred Apted, the Grand Rapids area man in the sharpshooter company, who returned to Coggin's Point and what he said was Ruffin's estate a week later with a party of men. Again, they cut down more trees to give Union artillerists clear lines of fire in case the Rebels came back. Apted helped himself to the remains of the secessionist's library. "Was out to the house of Dr. Ruffin and found a number of books," he wrote.[32] Ruffin would commit suicide after Lee's surrender in 1865, citing his hatred of the Yankees and their victory.

The hot summer air was thick with mosquitoes and flies. Late in July the regiment's surgeon, Dr. Isaac Wixom, took a leave of absence of Michigan. With the contract surgeon, Dr. Seeley, captured and not yet released by the Confederates, this left the 16th Michigan without a doctor at a time when nearly a third of the men were ill, though Frank Keeler wrote home that month that the regiment's sick were attended by a hospital steward and "a Dr. Clark," whom he did not identity but who was probably the former surgeon of the 4th Michigan. Each day, Lt. Salter told his friends, an entire ship of sick men from the Union army was sent north to hospitals, and Sgt. William Borden of Company B figured that "someone dies out of our regiment almost every day."

But for those who were well, at least, now better food was arriving—some of it fresh, like potatoes and onions, and also dried fruit. Borden wrote that the men did not get all of they would like, but it was better than nothing (or getting only hardtack and salt pork). "I have no fault to find, am perfectly willing to stay," he wrote about army service. "As long as the war lasts I don't want to come home until it is over; as long as they give me enough to eat, I will stay."[33]

Though soldiers like Sgt. Borden could not know it, President Lincoln and his advisors, in the wake of McClellan's retreat from Richmond, were wrestling with questions about how the war should now be prosecuted and whether it was time to find another general to command the Army of the Potomac. While common soldiers loved McClellan, many Union officers and corps commanders were critical of him and his reluctance to attack the Confederate army during the Peninsula Campaign; McClellan himself continued to urge Lincoln to take a very conservative policy in the direction of the war, recommending that slaves should not be freed and that civilian Confederates not be subjugated or mistreated.

Of course, leading Republicans were taking the very opposite view of what needed to be done. After meeting with some of the generals and holding discussions with his advisors, Lincoln decided that if McClellan would not move against the Rebel capital, then the Army of the Potomac, or most of it, would be pulled from the York-James Peninsula. And within days of writing that letter back to Ionia County, Sgt. Borden and his comrades would again be in motion with their division and corps as the army's fumbling generals sought a victory in Virginia.[34]

7.

AUGUST–SEPTEMBER 1862

HURRAH FOR HELL

With the losses the 16th Michigan had suffered in battle and to illness, and other state regiments suffering similarly, Lt. Charles Salter felt that Gov. Austin Blair should use new recruits to fill in the gaps in existing commands, rather than create new regiments.

> I should really like to see every young man between the ages of 18 and 30 that is unmarried in Michigan drafted and sent right here, especially those behind the counters of stores, measure tapes, etc. and keeping books, and all such work that might just as well be done by the ladies. And I think the young ladies of Detroit ought to take some measures to drive these cowards off to war. If they would, they would do more for the benefit of the brave men who have fought so long, than they could in any other way.[1]

Salter's comment on conscription, written at Harrison's Landing while his regiment and the Army of the Potomac waited for their commander to act, was prompted by a draft law passed by Congress that summer, and the fact that Lincoln had asked the Northern governors for thousands more recruits. This new draft system, however, was slow, cumbersome, and probably not what Salter envisioned; the 16th Michigan would, in time, receive conscripts and men prompted by the draft to enlist. But at that particular moment in the stifling August heat, Capt. Thomas Barry, soon to become major, was in charge of the regiment, while Lt. Col. Norval Welch returned to Michigan to recruit men to replace some of the scores lost to the summer's battles and disease.

Another change for the 16th Michigan and many other regiments was the discontinuing of regimental bands. Many regiments had them and most soldiers liked them. But their day was largely over and the 16th Michigan's band mustered out of the service on August 11. Alfred Apted noted that men from his regiment were sent on a reconnaissance beyond the Union picket lines and put to work cutting down trees around Harrison's Landing.

The most exciting events for the soldiers were probably a fight between a couple of men, the heat-induced collapse of another, and the capture of three Rebels while some of the Michigan soldiers were on patrol on the south side of the James.[2]

The regiment's contract surgeon, Dr. Thomas W. Seeley, was released by the Confederates and rejoined the regiment on August 5. He was soon joined in camp by Dr. William F. Breakey, a physician who was about to turn 27, from Salem Township near Ann Arbor. Breakey had first volunteered his medical services to the Sanitary Commission after the battle of Shiloh in the western theater of the war; he was briefly assigned to the 3rd Michigan Cavalry Regiment at Corinth, Mississippi, but the experience, he said, "increased my desire for more." Returning to Michigan in that summer in 1862, Breakey applied for an officer's commission in a state regiment and was immediately appointed assistant surgeon in the 16th Michigan, a position vacant since Dr. Butler's resignation in the spring. He was told to report to the regiment in four days. A native of New York state who graduated from the University of Michigan's medical school in 1859, Breakey promptly married his sweetheart and took a quick honeymoon to New York before starting for Harrison's Landing.[3]

Breakey arrived shortly before Col. Stockton, whose release from Confederate prison came on August 12. After forty-five days as a prisoner he was exchanged for Col. L. B. Williams of the 1st Virginia Infantry. Captains Ben Fisher and Judd Mott, recovered from light wounds, were also returned to Union hands. Stockton quickly applied to Gen. McClellan for a twenty-day furlough, which was granted. He headed for Washington, where his wife Maria was waiting.[4]

At about the same time, McClellan, after days of delay, enacted important orders he had received from the new general-in-chief of the Union army, Henry W. Halleck: The Army of the Potomac must move back toward Washington, where the troops could be used by other Union generals contending with Stonewall Jackson. Once McClellan had withdrawn his army from Richmond in early July, Robert E. Lee reorganized his army and sent Jackson's corps back to northern Virginia; there, Jackson's troops clashed with a force south of the Rapidan River, part of a newly formed Union army under a cocky commander from the west, Gen. John Pope.

Lincoln, his advisors, and Republican leaders were appalled that McClellan's Richmond offensive accomplished nothing, so they were hoping the tough-talking Pope would prove to be McClellan's successor. But when Lee understood that the Confederate capital was safe from any further Union advance, he had moved his own army's other corps to north-central Virginia, to join Jackson, crush Pope, and end the war on the Confederacy's terms.[5]

Now the 16th Michigan and most of the rest of what had been McClellan's command at Harrison's Landing started on their way to join the Union's Army of Virginia, which Pope had ordered into positions along the Rappahannock River. Some soldiers from the Army of the Potomac boarded steamboats, but the men of the 16th Michigan were disappointed when they and their comrades were ordered to march back across country on the road to Williamsburg. "On August 14th, we were marching down the peninsula," Dr. Breakey wrote later, "almost reversing part of the route by which portions of the army had gone towards Richmond." They broke camp but did not get started until the next day, crossing the Chickahominy River on a pontoon bridge at the point where it joined the James and covering twenty-five miles.[6]

The regiment reached Williamsburg on August 16. "The town was a mere hamlet with many deserted buildings," Breakey remembered. The soldiers raided local fruit trees, though in theory they were not supposed to be foraging from the civilians. "At Williamsburg a cavalry colonel placed a guard over an orchard with orders to allow no one to touch the fruit," said Frank Keeler of Saginaw, who was promoted to sergeant that month. "Capt. Fisher, hearing of it, told me to gather a squad and go with him for some apples. We drove the guard away and took away all we could carry." The next night the 16th Michigan bivouacked on the site of its old camp during the siege of Yorktown, Camp Winfield Scott. "Not one of us expected to see Yorktown (again) until we had taken Richmond," Brady Sharpshooter Alfred Apted noted. "But alas for human calculations, Richmond is still in the hands of the rebels."[7]

Though a newcomer to the 16th Michigan, the assistant surgeon remembered the regiment's stay at Yorktown as an emotional experience for those who had been through the Peninsula Campaign—nearly a hundred of their comrades had been killed and scores more wounded since they had come this way in the spring, not counting those who died of disease. "In the evening the regimental glee club sang 'Tenting on the Old Camp Ground,' and many other army songs, the circumstances and surroundings contributing to make the effect indescribably sweet and touching," Breakey remembered; patriotic songs like the National Anthem and "Rally Round the Flag" were sung "with vigor and received loud applause, while the songs that told of comrades lost and 'Home Sweet Home,' sung with pathetic feeling, caused many a heart to throb with tenderness, and many a tear was stealthily wiped away in the dim light of the camp."[8]

The regiment, with thousands of other soldiers, marched back through Little Bethel and Big Bethel, reaching Fortress Monroe on August 18, and "slept under the protecting shadows" of the Union stronghold, Frank Keeler wrote. They moved to Newport News the next day and embarked on the steamboat *Louisiana,* sailing up the Potomac to Aquia Creek on the 20th. From this point the soldiers traveled by railroad to the town of Fredericksburg on the Rappahannock River about ten miles away. In this region now were moving and gathering tens of thousands of Union soldiers under Gen. John Pope and his commanders Irvin McDowell and Ambrose Burnside as their next confrontation with the Confederate army began to take shape.

"The tall spires are the first things visible as we approach over a ridge," Sgt. Keeler said about Fredericksburg. "From our military depot, at the summit of a ridge on the north side of the river, the compact and regularly laid-out city seems to lay at our feet and presents a very attractive appearance." This part of northern Virginia reminded Pvt. Apted of home. "The country around [is] quite hilly and rolling, more like Michigan than any that I have seen," he wrote.[9]

In the meantime, Col. Thomas Stockton, back in Washington on sick leave, wrote his belated report of the battle at Gaines' Mill. Stockton angrily took issue with a statement he had seen in newspapers—that Welch had led the 16th Michigan in the Seven Days' battles. The words that infuriated Stockton so much had been printed in the *New York Herald* and reprinted in the *Detroit Free Press* and other papers. "I have seen editorials, which had remained uncontradicted [*sic*, uncorrected] by the major, that he, the major, 'led his regiment in all the recent fights, Colonel Stockton having been taken prisoner in the very beginning of the Gaines' Mill battle'; a statement entirely false," Stockton charged.

To Stockton and his supporters, Welch had slighted him by minimizing his role at Gaines' Mill (though it was clear that, after the regiment's right broke, Welch led the rest of the 16th Michigan in the bold counterattack). Furthermore, Lt. Col. Ruehle was in command of the 16th Michigan, not Welch, at Malvern Hill. But there had been no apology or correction from Welch, who felt he had done nothing wrong. Stockton would not forget this; the rift between him and Welch was widening. For the men of the regiment, however, another battle with the Confederate Army of Northern Virginia was in the offing.[10]

On the evening of August 21, the 16th Michigan moved northwest from Fredericksburg with its division along the river, marching and countermarching, or shifting back and forth, until a few days later they reached Kelly's Ford, a river crossing point. They did not move far or fast during these hot and humid days. "It seems as though our division is acting as a kind of reserve to be ready to strengthen any point where strength is needed," Sgt. Frank Keeler wrote. Sharpshooter Alfred Apted also recorded that the regiment was shifted backward and forward in this area, adding: "Lord only knows where."

On August 26, as their division marched again to Kelly's Ford, Apted got sick and dropped out. His Brady Company commander, Capt. Kin Dygert, was also ailing; he left the regiment and was gone till the end of October, but the army ruled him absent without leave. It would take Dygert months to clear his name. But the back-and-forth movement of their brigade and division, Lt. Charles Salter thought, was because elements of their corps were acting as the extreme left of Gen. Pope's army, which was widely spread out over the countryside, watching the fords on the Rappahannock where it was thought Stonewall Jackson (or another approaching Confederate force) might cross the river.[11]

But Jackson's corps had crossed the river at an unguarded ford and moved north. Lee then ordered Jackson to make a sweeping march around Pope's right along the Rappahannock; Jackson did so, striking the Union supply depot on the Orange & Alexandria Railroad line at Manassas Junction on the 26th, very near the place where the Rebels had first defeated the Union army in July of 1861. The surprise raid that evening was successful, with Jackson's men helping themselves to stacks of Union supplies and destroying the rest.[12]

The 16th Michigan, with its division about twenty-five miles away, got word that night to be prepared to move. The next morning the soldiers marched for that rail line; they were among thousands of soldiers, Union and Confederate, converging on the Manassas area, where Jackson had hidden his army in woods near a hamlet called Groveton a few miles from the smoldering ruins of the railroad depot at Manassas Junction. Veteran soldiers were stunned to learn that they were right back where the Union army had been slightly more than a year before—Bull Run—despite the hundreds of miles they had marched and the thousands of casualties suffered.

Dr. Breakey wrote to his father-in-law about this. "We learned that the enemy were at Manassas and had destroyed several bridges and portions of the [rail] road—not very cheery news for the men who six months ago started out to go to Richmond," the doctor said. It was disturbing and ironic that after all the millions of U.S. tax dollars spent and the lives lost, the armies of the Confederacy were again near Bull Run and the Confederate capital was safe. "Soldiers think all of this, and talk of it, too," Breakey continued. Since the regiment marched from Fredericksburg on August 21, he noted, "we have fared hard, marched much, and a good deal at night, slept without tents . . . [Men] quarreled for a 'hardtack' and officers were glad enough to get one and a drink of coffee."[13]

With rations running out, the two divisions of their Fifth Corps present marched eighteen miles to Warrenton Junction, and then another fifteen miles in the early morning hours of August 28 to within two miles of Manassas Junction. Though the army was composed of tens of thousands of volunteers in scores of regiments, batteries and cavalry troops, it was not uncommon for soldiers to come across friends and acquaintances from back home. A Detroiter and commander of a division in another corps, Brig. Gen. Alpheus S. Williams, recorded that he met several 16th Michigan officers he knew that morning, including captains Robert Elliott and Tom Barry; Barry was commanding the regiment. Williams remembered that Barry had been a clerk in a business owned by James W. Tillman (of the ill-fated lancers) in pre-war times.[14]

The 16th Michigan remained in the vicinity of the railroad junction with the First Division as Union generals serving under Gen. Pope received from him confusing and sometimes contradictory orders over the course of the next twenty-four hours. These orders reflected that Pope did not know where elements of his army were, nor did he have a clear notion of where they should go as the mass of Confederate forces were assembling before him in what historian Jeffry Wert called "a brilliant maneuver, and offensive masterpiece" by Gen. Lee. A few miles northwest of where the 16th Michigan waited with its brigade that evening of August 28, elements of Stonewall Jackson's force attacked Union troops from Pope's army who had been trying to find them. It was the beginning of another major battle, one in which Pope was being lured into a trap of Lee's making.

Now on the morning of August 29, the Fifth Corps commander, Gen. Fitz John Porter, received orders from Pope to march northeast to the town Centreville (where there were no Confederates), only to have Pope change his mind and reverse their course, causing some of Porter's soldiers to have to take a ten-mile detour back to Manassas Junction. Pope had decided to send them west toward the town of Gainesville, where he believed his force would cut off a retreating Stonewall Jackson, though in fact Jackson was *not* retreating. In truth, Gen. James Longstreet's corps was advancing toward that point, joining Lee and Jackson.[15]

Thus, the 16th Michigan with their brigade and division marched again that day, heading west along the Manassas Gap Railroad and watching for Rebels. Soon the men saw rising clouds of dust—a sign that Longstreet's corps was arriving in the woods ahead of them, linking with Jackson. "On Aug. 29 we moved out from Manassas [Junction] two or three miles and formed line of battle," Frank Keeler wrote to his parents. Lt. Charles Salter thought they moved seven miles, perhaps including the back-and-forth march of the early morning. He and his comrades were facing the southern end of a line of enemy troops and guns that they could not see, but that soon stretched along the slope of a wooded ridge for more than two miles.

The 16th Michigan's assistant surgeon recalled that day well, for he nearly became a casualty. "On the 29th our brigade . . . had halted and was resting in a cover of a wooded slope overlooking a valley and facing a wooded ridge half to three-fourths of a mile to the south, in the edge of which some indications of the enemy were reported," Dr. Breakey wrote years later.[16]

At this particular moment, some of the soldiers and Breakey himself were thinking about food, for their rations were consumed and they had not been resupplied. Looking down the hill, some of the men spotted a cabin and foragers from the regiment started for it. "As we were short on rations I left my horse in [the] charge of a hospital attendant, and started for the cabin, hoping to get some fresher food and milk for some of our men who were ill," Breakey wrote. As he reached the cabin, others were leaving with a turkey, chicken, bread and milk. "The cabin was occupied by an old colored woman and her little boy about eight years old, and she explained that she did not 'see no difference between the secesh and the Yanks,' for whichever side came along took all she had." The doctor figured that some of the soldiers did not pay her anything while they raided her pantry, and all that she had left was "a solitary frightened chicken and a half-baked hoecake"[17]

Dr. Breakey said he paid the woman a half-dollar for the bird, some milk, and butter while the corn meal cake was still baking over a fire. But he grew uneasy as he waited, for his brigade moved out of sight and suddenly the explosion of artillery sounded close by. When the woman finally gave him the food moments later, he started out the door and saw three or four Rebel cavalry troopers riding straight for him. He ran through the woman's garden as bullets whistled "uncomfortably near"; then he jumped a ditch and scrambled up the slope into the woods. Fortunately for Breakey, the Confederates did not pursue him. The doctor, "chagrined at the ludicrous outcome" of his foraging effort, sat and ate what food survived his run and rejoined his regiment and brigade. Though Lt. Salter said there was some skirmishing that day with the Rebels before them, Sgt. Frank Keeler wrote that the enemy fired "several shots and became quiet."[18] Waiting in the woods ahead were thousands of Confederate soldiers under James Longstreet, joining Jackson. Historian Stephen Sears wrote that "Lee with his two lieutenants had formed the wide-open jaws of a trap for a stubbornly unwary John Pope."

SECOND BULL RUN OR SECOND MANASSAS

But it was not quiet two or three miles north of their position. Here the second battle of Bull Run (or second Manassas) began that morning of August 29. Gen. Pope ordered his soldiers forward to attack, and Stonewall Jackson's men fell back "along and behind the old railroad embankment extending along his entire front," Pope wrote later. The Union troops crossed open fields to strike the Rebel position and they were killed and wounded by the score as the hours dragged on. Historian Jeffry Wert wrote that Pope had throughout the campaign "misinterpreted intelligence or misjudged Lee's intentions" and this day was tragically no different. Needing more soldiers to throw into this battle, Pope ordered Gen. Fitz John Porter's Fifth Corps, of which the 16th Michigan was part, to advance from its position at the south end of the Union line to flank Jackson's position, to attack it from the left. But Porter was not near Jackson's line, and he saw that if he moved his 9,000 men past Longstreet's position, he would open *his* Fifth Corps up to a devastating flank attack by Longstreet's much larger force. Pope, a favorite of Radical Republican politicians, was furious and disbelieving, and he would soon cause Porter to be cashiered for not following his order. Porter, a Democrat who was close to George McClellan, was made the scapegoat by Pope and the Republicans for the loss of this battle. It would take him decades to get official vindication.[19]

The 16th Michigan withdrew with its brigade and the divisions of its corps from the wooded ridge south of the main battlefield that night outside of Manassas Junction. "We remained there and at midnight drew rations; at 3 a.m. [August 30, we] started for Bull Run," wrote Sgt. Frank Keeler. Finally resupplied, the regiment marched with its brigade and division east back along the railroad line and then north to Groveton and the main body of Pope's army.

But night marches could be confusing affairs, the general commanding the 16th Michigan's First Division, George W. Morell, missed the turn to Groveton and mistakenly marched with part of his command east to Centreville. That left the 16th Michigan's Third Brigade with only one other brigade from their division, now under the command of Brig. Gen. Dan Butterfield, as they arrived on the battlefield that morning. These soldiers were considered "fresh," Dr. Breakey wrote, because they had not been in the fighting here. But in fact, with all the marching and countermarching they had done over the past days, the men did not feel like they were "fresh troops."[20]

"I went with the regiment into the field," the assistant surgeon wrote, "where they were ordered to lay down beside a cornfield under a brow of a hill." Soon artillery was firing, and late in the morning or in the early afternoon the 16th Michigan was moved with its Third Brigade to a skirt of woods, facing west—the open battlefield. "We received many compliments from the enemy in the shape of bursting shells and solid shot," wrote Capt. Stephen Martin, the Irish-born Detroiter of Company H, who had been lightly wounded at Gaines' Mill. Across the rolling fields less than a mile away, the Rebels waited.[21]

Pope foolishly believed that he had Stonewall Jackson on the ropes, and that the Union troops were fighting a Confederate rear guard as Jackson retreated. In reality, Jackson was there with the Lee's entire army. Pope continued to send Union brigades and divisions in piecemeal only to be defeated, and now it was the turn of the 16th Michigan and its comrades. They were near the center of the Union line when they were ordered to advance. "[We] were in a wood, in front of which was a ridge where the enemy had their batteries planted," Lt. Charles Salter wrote to his friends. "In another place [nearby], there was a railroad embankment behind which rebel infantry was concealed, or rather protected."[22]

Salter continued: "Our artillery were in the rear of us, on high ground from whence they were firing at the rebels over our heads. During all the day, so far as we had noticed, that [Union Gen. Irwin] McDowell [to the left,] had not advanced, nor had he even fired a gun, and we had not seen Gen. Pope at all." But these two men, proving to be lackluster generals at best, ordered Salter's regiment and their comrades into the fight. "McDowell seeming in command, he sent an order to Gen. Porter to send one division to charge the rebel batteries in front of us, but Gen. Porter sent back word it was useless to attempt to take them in that manner—'Flank them first on the right,' he advised," Salter said. "However, there came another pre-emptory order to charge, and Gen. Porter had to order our two brigades to do it."[23]

The 17th New York moved out first in line of battle, with other regiments—the 44th New York, the 83rd Pennsylvania, the 12th New York and the 16th Michigan—in doubled columns behind them. Since Col. Stockton was on leave and Lt. Col. Welch was back in Michigan recruiting, the regiment was under the command of Capt. Thomas Barry, soon to be major at Welch's recommendation. Because of the losses the regiment suffered during the Seven Days, some officers were responsible for two companies. One was Lt. Edward Hill, the former lancer, in Company K. He turned to a soldier named Frederick J. Forsyth, an old sergeant from Bay City considered to be one of the great characters of the 16th Michigan, and delegated command of a company to him. Forsyth had fished on Saginaw Bay as a civilian, and claimed to have fought Indians with Kit Carson and served in the navies of Brazil, Spain, and the United States.

Hill would later say that Forsyth lied about his age to enlist—he was actually in his 60s and too *old* to be in the army—but he had done his job so well that Col. Stockton ordered him exempt from all camp guard duty. As their attack on Rebel positions was about to begin, old Forsyth had only fifteen seconds to address his men. "Attention, company!" he shouted. "Who's afraid of fire? Hurrah for hell! Forward, march! Double quick! Charge!" The men started forward on the run.[24]

As they charged with a yell, Captain Martin said, they were in column formation, a fact reflected in the subsequent reports of Capt. Robert Elliott of the 16th Michigan and others. "As soon as we came out of the wood, we were exposed to the full fire of the enemy, but we advanced steadily on, keeping up a continual fire on the rebels," Lt. Salter wrote. "Meanwhile, we soon saw we were getting into a very bad place, for the enemy's battery were planted in the form of a half circle and we were advancing right into that." Capt. Martin said the regiment was hit by musketry as well as grape and canister shot "thrown into us with profusion. . . . The ground around was [torn] and had a resemblance as though . . . rooted by a drove of hogs."

Martin felt the regiment should deploy, or break out of columns into a line of battle. In column formation, the soldiers could easily be killed and wounded *en masse* since a single shell or cannon ball could strike many down like bowling pins. "I requested Barry to deploy the regiment, stating that if we got within grapeshot range, we would be blown to atoms," Martin wrote. "He declined to do so. I commanded the first division [or wing of the regiment] and willing to abide the consequences, I gave them the command to deploy." Although the men were moving on the double-quick—a jogging pace—they immediately formed into a battle line as "a tremendous firing commenced. The battery was too well protected."[25]

George Prentiss, then a lieutenant and acting adjutant, later agreed. "The enemy at the time in question were in a deep railroad cut parallel to our line, or nearly so, and we in line of battle, firing at these at very close quarters [were] under great disadvantage—they being well protected, and we having no protection." Martin saw men falling around him, struck by Confederate rifle fire. "Captain [Randolph] Ransom of Company C was the first officer killed," the captain wrote. "He was shot in the right temple and fell by my side. Lt. [Michael] Chittick was also killed, shot in the head. Sgt. [Jeremiah] Kitchen, the color sergeant, was killed, shot in the head."

The mayhem continued as the regiment advanced into the field alongside the 2nd Maine, firing at the well-protected Rebels. "Corporal [Henry Everington] of Co. H (my company), was killed, shot in the head," Martin continued. "I next gave the flag to a non-commissioned officer whose name I don't recollect. He was killed, shot in the head. As he was falling, I caught the flag and gave it in charge of a corporal, ordering him to part with it only with his life."[26]

Lt. John Ruby, 27, of Plymouth was killed and several of the other officers were wounded, including captains Barry and Robert Elliott and lieutenants Patrick McLaughlin and George Swan. "But still we kept steadily on," said Lt. Salter, "expecting our batteries to be advanced and also that we would be reinforced by infantry. But no reinforcements came." Capt. Martin said two additional regiments did come out to support those on the battlefield, "but they were so severely shelled that they thought it prudent to retreat, which they done in great disorder." Worse, what is known today as "friendly fire," or ordnance fired by Union gunners, was hitting them. "When we were about ½ mile in advance of the wood," Lt. Salter wrote, "we found that our artillery had not been advanced and could not reach the enemy. But many of their shells were bursting in our own ranks."[27]

Sgt. Keeler agreed. "Many shells falling in our midst [were] from our own batteries," he wrote. "We were halted on the crest of a small plateau at the further side of which were the Johnnies, strongly posted behind an old railroad bank. We fired as rapidly as we could into their faces and received their fire ourselves." Soon it was clear that nearly half of their small force of their short-handed division had been killed and wounded, Salter said; they were running out of ammunition and men from the 16th Michigan took cartridges from the dead and wounded in the field. Officers knew that their beleaguered force must retreat.

The original blue "Stockton's Regiment" flag, donated to the regiment back in the fall of 1861, had been captured at Gaines' Mill, so the 16th Michigan that day fought under the U.S. flag it brought from Detroit. Martin looked around for the corporal holding that flag and ordered him to about face. "He did not hear me, nor did he hear me until I placed my hand on his shoulder and turned him 'round," Martin continued. "We started on the double quick."[28]

As the regiment turned and ran, the Confederate troops stood, rising above the embankment to fire down on the retreating Union soldiers. "It seemed to me that the firing at our flag might be compared to a shower of hail stones," Martin wrote. George Prentiss later claimed that ten men fell around the colors that day; the death that pained him for years to come was that of Jeremiah Kitchen, a Detroiter about 27 years old, a slight fellow and, Prentiss thought, the first of the color bearers to die that day. "For I had doubted him," Prentiss said, "he being small and modest."

"Men were falling on the right and left, before and behind," Keeler told his family. "The wounded and killed were lying everywhere and our only course was to get out of range as soon as possible." Reeling and in retreat, with no other Union commands covering their withdrawal, the 16th Michigan was vulnerable to a Confederate charge, should Jackson's men come over the embankment to try to capture their U.S. flag. The idea of losing another banner must have been anathema to the officers. George Prentiss claimed that when the order for retreat came, he shouted, "Save the colors."[29]

Officers and men of the regiment began to gather near the flag bearer as they retreated. Capt. Martin said that Sgt. William Kydd was first, and then his own son, Lt. John Martin, and then Capt. Barry, who was in command of the regiment. They were almost out of range of the Rebels when he was struck on the leg by a spent piece of shell. Martin was able to limp off the field with the color bearer but by the time the regiment was out of rifle range this flag had been shot full of holes.

Gen. Porter, their corps commander, and his staff watched as the 16th Michigan walked off the battlefield. Martin claimed that Capt. Barry, of whom he obviously thought little, physically stepped next to the flag carrier, crowding him away from the colors. According to Capt. Martin, Barry said, "I am in command of the regiment, I will conduct these colors." In response, Martin said he angrily pushed Barry away. "I have risked too much in saving them to yield the honor to you in the presence of the general," he reportedly said to Barry.[30]

Stephen Martin claimed he assumed his position with the flag-carrying corporal who had borne the colors off the field. Though he could not remember that man's name in the account he said he took from his diary nearly twenty years later, he recalled that "at my request, Col. Stockton promoted him to the rank of sergeant for bravery on the battlefield." For the record, that soldier was Francis Fairbanks, 22, of Company G. Just one month later, Stockton promoted Fairbanks to sergeant for distinguished bravery.

Thomas Barry, one of the walking wounded, became major and left the service some months later. He vehemently denied Capt. Stephen Martin's version of his conduct at the second battle of Bull Run; he said he had received "a bullet through the ribs" that day and protected the flag with a nucleus of sixty men. Both Martin and Barry offered transcriptions of what they said were their 1862 diaries as proof of their separate versions of events, and both claimed they could produce witnesses to support their respective accounts. For the record, Lt. Col. Norval Welch, though he was not present that day, later credited Martin for "rescuing" the 16th Michigan's flag at this battle.[31]

The fight was over for the 16th Michigan and the Third Brigade. Yet the disaster for the Union Army of Virginia was far from over, for now James Longstreet's Confederate corps struck from the southern part of the battlefield, collapsing that portion of the Union position. "Now the rebels attacked our left wing, [where Gen] Irwin McDowell's Corps [was] stationed," Lt. Salter wrote about the defeat. "It appears that McDowell had not even had skirmishers thrown out in front of his troops as his corps officers informed me, and the rebels had brought up their artillery and placed in position where they could fire right into his troops. And also the rebels had brought up large numbers of infantry so that when they did commence the attack, they took them [McDowell's men] by surprise, and in a few minutes McDowell's entire corps were in full retreat and we received orders about sundown to fall back to Centreville."[32]

Pvt. George Ervay's job of tending brigade cattle had ended after the losses of the Seven Days, so he was back with his company carrying a rifle at Manassas when he had been struck by a piece of spent shell than knocked him down and left his side black and blue. He cursed the general responsible for the Union left, now regarded as a traitor by the soldiers. "Old McDowell, the cuss, let them flank us so that they fired on us from three sides and they would not send us any reinforcement," Ervay wrote. "They say that Gen. Sigel put him under arrest. I hope God it is so and I hope they hang him."[33] But these last sentiments were just soldiers' rumors; McDowell, who had support of Republican leaders, was heavily criticized, but he was neither charged with a crime nor hung. Only Gen. Fitz John Porter of the Fifth Corps would be blamed, wrongly, by Pope, for the disaster.

As the regiment had moved forward that morning, Dr. William Breakey was with their corps' First Division hospital set up near the banks of Bull Run, behind the battlefield. The operating tables were set up in the shade of a tree and a force of Union cavalry stood by in reserve. From this point the assistant surgeon experienced his first battle as part of the 16th Michigan. "The roar of the battle came back to us, but the only information that reached us was through ambulance drivers and wounded soldiers," the doctor wrote. After an hour or two shells began to fall nearby and the surgeons and their assistants started packing. Before they could move, "a confused broken, irregular wavy line of men came over the ridge," Breakey said. "Fragments of our brigade and regiment came down the roadway near to our hospital."

> An officer, whose name I will not mention, as the disordered mass came drifting rapidly along, was making a great outcry about being wounded in the foot and unable to walk. I got down off my horse and helped him on. After he was safely mounted he seemed to forget his wound and pain and was loudly boasting of his prodigies of valor he had performed while others of known bravery were quiet. After wading the stream while he rode, I insisted upon learning the extent of his wounds. The heel of his shoe showed quite a wound but not a scratch on his body.[34]

The hospital personnel fell back, up the hill to the old Stone House that had been a landmark in the first battle of Bull Run, not far from Gen. Pope's headquarters. The wounded were gathering in the rooms and under the trees. As shells exploded near the house, Breakey said that an ambulance driver with a rig full of wounded men jumped down from his seat and began to cut loose a member of the mule team to ride off and escape. But a lieutenant drew his pistol and leveled it at the driver, ordering him to stay until he was told otherwise. Breakey tended those wounded that he could, but "then was obliged to leave those of them who could not march or get in the ambulance, and fall back with my regiment."

Mounting his horse to leave the house on the hill, the doctor looked back and saw a view of thousands of Union troops retreating. By now the flight was more confused than before. "Rev. Dr. Winslow, chief agent [of the] Sanitary Commission of the Potomac, acting as a volunteer aide on General [Gouverneur] Warren's staff, rode across the ebbing tide fragments of commands, trying to stem the tide," Breakey wrote. From his horse, the gray-bearded Winslow shouted "This is not a retreat." But it was a retreat and every surviving soldier knew it, as the Union army left Bull Run once more.[35]

The regiment crossed the run with thousands of other Union soldiers. Darkness was falling and the army "converged into a deep narrow road cut down a somewhat steep descent to the narrow bridge across the stream of Bull Run—at this point narrow, but deep with muddy banks," the assistant surgeon wrote. As he rode, he carried many personal items that tired officers and men asked him to take, including a coat for Lt. Frank Eddy of Flint. In the darkness it caught on a tree branch or a passing wagon and was torn away from Breakey's saddle. Of course, it was impossible to recover it, in that mass of soldiers crowding down and over the bridge.

On the retreating soldiers walked to Centreville, where the Union officers formed their men into defenses to halt the advancing Confederates. The 16th Michigan reached the village at 10 p.m. "Thus ended all that I saw of the battle of Manassas," Lt. Salter wrote, "a battle that has been the most disastrous of any that has occurred to us during the war, and it is the universal opinion of the army that it lost to us by the treachery of McDowell." Soldiers and officers alike were denouncing him, and hoping he would be dismissed from the service. Capt. Stephen Martin said he was ordered into an ambulance and sent to Georgetown Seminary Hospital, and his military career would end with his resignation in several months in April 1863. "A more disgraceful defeat is not recorded in the world's history," he said about second Bull Run, "and *it was not the soldiers' fault.*"[36]

With Thomas Barry also wounded, Capt. Robert T. Elliott of Detroit was temporarily in command of the regiment a few days later when he wrote a terse report about the battle. "The behavior of the regiment, both officers and men, was good, not a single one flinching," he stated. The 16th Michigan had gone into battle with 290 men; sixteen of them had been killed in action, but this number would rise to twenty-five as wounded men died and additional bodies were later discovered on the battlefield. Some sixty others were wounded, with several listed as missing. Nearly 14,000 Union soldiers had been killed, wounded, or missing in the two-day battle, while the Confederates lost just under 8,500.[37]

The next day, September 1, Dr. Breakey went back to the Manassas battlefield near Groveton under a flag of truce with a party of surgeons and ambulances to pick up the wounded and bury the dead. Thirty-four years later, he described what he saw to a meeting of veterans.

> I followed the route taken by our own regiment and brigade, reaching the line in front of a cut in the Manassas Gap Railroad, where the slaughter had been so terrible.
>
> All across an open field of sixty rods or so, the bodies of brave soldiers lay as they had fallen, like sheaves of human grain cut down by some monster reaper. Within a space not larger than this room, and within two to four rods of the sunken cut—unseen in the slight ascent until close upon it—lay the bodies of four of the color bearers of our own regiment, one after another having taken the flag as it fell from the hands of a fallen comrade.[38]

Graves were quickly dug for these men, not far from the Confederate breastworks; to the rear was their deadly battery, protected in the trees. But it would turn out that these graves were too shallow. In 1863, Lt. Salter of Detroit would write that while camping at Bull Run, the skeletons of Capt. Ransom, Lt. Chittick, and one of the flag bearers were discovered at the ground's surface, identifiable by their still-intact uniforms. But that day after the battle, Breakey found the Union dead bloated and dark, stripped of their clothes and shoes. Many of the wounded had also been stripped and left on the field. The doctor found one man from the 16th Michigan sitting under a tree; he had been shot through the legs and without water for nearly twenty-four hours. His comrades' bodies were nearby. The wounded soldier smiled when he recognized Breakey, who gave him water and brandy before he was removed on a stretcher.[39]

Dr. Thomas W. Seeley, the contract surgeon who was working with the 16th Michigan medical staff, was supposed to have been in camp with the regiment that day, but for some reason he appeared on the battlefield. Breakey thought his colleague was "somewhat eccentric" but now the hired doctor became one of the mysteries of the 16th Michigan. Whether he had had enough of the bloodshed and pain of wounded and dying men, or whether he walked into enemy lines and was again captured, no one knew. Perhaps he made up his mind that he was going no further and went home of his own accord. Whatever the reason, Seeley vanished that day and was not seen again by the regiment. "His absence left me without help and considerably increased by work," Dr. Breakey complained.[40]

A hard rain fell after the Union army's retreat to Centreville and the 16th Michigan had rested with rifles at hand, ready to fight should the Confederate pursue them, and that night the men were on picket duty. At 2 a.m. on September 2 the regiment rose and marched through the towns of Fairfax, Vienna, and Lewinsville on the way to Washington, covering about thirty miles. They halted in darkness near the Chain Bridge. Late that day the regiment, along with thousands of other troops, learned that the command of their army had once again fallen to Gen. George B. McClellan. Dr. Breakey wrote of it in his sketch of his service:

> On the night march in from Centreville we first learned of the reinstatement of McClellan in command of the Army of the Potomac. He had come out with a brilliant staff and met the tired and dispirited soldiers. His reception was an ovation and cheers resounded along the line as soon as his presence was known. Whatever else might be said of McClellan, there was no doubt about his popularity in the Army of the Potomac at that time, and his appearance and the knowledge of his return to command was an inspiration in itself.

Gen. John Pope, who had performed so badly throughout the second Bull Run campaign, was dismissed, though his charges against Fifth Corps commander Fitz John Porter would soon end that officer's career. Lincoln's cabinet was against restoring overall command of Pope's force to McClellan, but the president felt he had no other choice.[41]

On the evening of September 3, the weary men of the 16th Michigan marched to Hall's Hill, the site of its old winter camp. "Since we left Harrison's Landing we have not slept two consecutive nights in the same place," complained Saginaw's Sgt. Frank Keeler. "We have moved every day except the one day we lay in line of battle at Centreville." He, like thousands of other, wondered: What had been accomplished since the regiment had marched away from this place, with the rest of the army, six months ago?

The same thought occurred to Brady Sharpshooter Alfred Apted, the English-born volunteer who had come from western Michigan. Apted got sick and dropped out of the regiment before the second Bull Run battle, and had walked with other sick men to Fredericksburg; from there they had been shipped to Camp Convalescent in Alexandria. Now as he rejoined his regiment at Hall's Hill, he was struck by the fact that the ranks of the 16th Michigan were so depleted that it and two other regiments could camp on the same space that the Michigan soldiers had needed for themselves during the previous winter.[42]

The 16th Michigan had arrived at Washington in the darkness, so when Dr. Breakey awoke on the morning of September 4 he got a look at the city from a hill across the Potomac. He saw "for the first time . . . the unfinished done of the Capitol and the stump of the Washington Monument, about 150 feet high." These were impressive sights but he soon had more pressing concerns as sickness swept through the ranks. One of the sick was Lt. Charles Salter, who suffered a fever and was carried in an ambulance a few days later when the regiment went with its division to the Alexandria Seminary, where they camped for two days before going back to Fort Corcoran near Georgetown. Dr. Breakey also contracted a fever, probably because he was caring for the regiment's sick with no other physician to help. The 16th Michigan's surgeon, Dr. Isaac Wixom, was only now about to return to the regiment. But Breakey became so dizzy he could not walk or ride, and he and Salter were among the thousands of men taken to Washington area hospitals.

Breakey's illness began his separation from the 16th Michigan that would last until 1864. As he recovered in the coming months, he received a series of assignments detaching him from his regiment: He would be placed in charge of the Baptist Church Hospital in Alexandria; assigned to the 20th Maine; and placed in a division hospital specifically for men who contracted smallpox. Lastly, he would serve as surgeon to Battery D of the 5th U.S. Artillery and Bigelow's 9th Massachusetts Battery before ultimately rejoining his regiment.[43]

Col. Thomas Stockton returned to duty that first week of September, from the sick leave he had been granted after his stay in Libby Prison. Since Brig. Gen. Dan Butterfield was sick, Stockton commanded the Third Brigade of their First Division of the Fifth Corps. On September 9 and 10, the 16th Michigan briefly shifted camps to Arlington Heights and briefly to Arlington House, the former home of Robert E. Lee. Dr. Wixom returned from Michigan that week, bringing with him his son-in-law, the soon-to-be-commissioned Lt. James Topping, and some new recruits. Lt. Col. Norval Welch also came back from Michigan after recruiting.[44]

The return of these officers was fortuitous, for their corps was about to march into Maryland with the newly reformed and reorganized Army of the Potomac, again under George McClellan. After defeating Pope's army at Bull Run, Gen. Robert E. Lee decided it was time for his Army of Northern Virginia to press on, crossing the Potomac River into Maryland upstream from Washington. Just before the 16th Michigan moved out with thousands of other Union troops on the road to Frederick, a new regiment joined their Third Brigade. This was the 20th Maine Infantry, under a Col. Adelbert Ames, a West Point graduate, artillerist, and professional soldier who would be overshadowed historically by his second-in-command, a Bowdoin College professor named Joshua Chamberlain; Chamberlain, in time, became one of the most popular heroes of the Civil War.

Lt. Salter, writing from a hospital bed in Washington, found it difficult to imagine the 16th Michigan, as depleted as it was, could go into combat. "They numbered when they left here but 166 men, so that they cannot be expected to do a great deal of fighting this time," he told friends as he recovered from illness at Carver Barracks Hospital on the city's 14th Street. "Our brigade of five regiments was so reduced in numbers by the many battles they have been in, that when they left here they only numbered 750 men altogether, less than any one of the new regiments."[45]

Pvt. George Ervay from Grand Ledge wrote to his parents three days before he moved out with his division on September 13. "I saw in the paper this morning that the Rebels had cross[ed] the Potomac at Rock Point and that their plan was to surround Washington and cut off their supplies," he said, "and if they succeed in their plan, that President Lincoln would have to recognize them as a nation. It is hard telling which way it will go, but if the men in the North think anything of the Union, they must try and save it now."[46]

Even before Ervay finished his letter, the Army of the Potomac began cautiously moving out toward Lee in three wings, covering the area between Baltimore and Washington. The division of which the 16th Michigan was part marched north and then west in good weather to Rockville, and over the Catoctin Mountains to Middletown and South Mountain. Here on September 14, one of the army's new regiments, the 17th Michigan Infantry, was in a fierce fight along with other Union troops, suffering 150 men killed and wounded when the rookie soldiers charged and helped to defeat Confederate artillery and infantry trying to block and delay the Union advance on the main body of Lee's forces.

"It speaks well for a new regiment like the 17th to fight so well as they did," wrote Lt. Salter, "and I think they have taken all the feathers out of the cap of their more favored rival, the 24th Michigan." (In fact, the 24th Michigan eventually became known as one of the most famous Union regiments for their role in the fighting at the battle of Gettysburg in the coming year.) But on September 15, Col. Stockton could hear the firing on the road up ahead as Robert E. Lee's trusted lieutenants were bringing their forces to a ridge above a small tributary of the Potomac called Antietam Creek, near the Maryland village called Sharpsburg. The next day, Stockton and his regiment joined the rest of the Army of the Potomac on the Boonsboro Road to that town.[47]

The 16th Michigan and its brigade and division would not fight the next day, September 17, and from that standpoint, they were lucky. "Never before in America had a single day been drenched in so much blood," Jeffry Wert, a historian of the Army of the Potomac, would write about the battle of Antietam. Saginaw's Frank Keeler summed up the terrible battle briefly, but he probably saw little if any of it. "Our division reached here on Tuesday evening and on the following morning was in line of battle, our corps being in reserve. Batteries posted in front kept up heavy firing on the enemy all day." The division of which the 16th Michigan was part was placed behind hills just east of Sharpsburg, near the Middle Bridge that ordinarily bore the traffic of the Boonsboro Road over Antietam Creek. They waited in reserve as the battle raged.[48]

From morning until dark, to their right and to their left, thousands of Union soldiers charged toward the Rebel positions in nightmarish combat—Gen. George McClellan had about 60,000 soldiers at hand, while Lee had about 40,000, though once again McClellan wrongly believed he was significantly outnumbered. "The enemy having chose [*sic*] to give fight," Col. Stockton wrote in his diary, "the battle opening at daylight and continuing all day." Stockton was commanding the Third Brigade, and late in the day the order came for his regiments to get into position to advance into the battle. "Moved my brigade, the first reserve, ordered forward just before sundown," Stockton wrote, "but the order was countermanded and we returned to our position and bivouacked."[49]

Historians say that if McClellan had sent those reserves, including the division that included the 16th Michigan, the Confederates simply did not have the forces to meet them. At least theoretically, Lee's line would have been broken and the Army of Northern Virginia destroyed. But the Union reserves were not sent in, with the Fifth Corps commander, Fitz John Porter, agreeing with McClellan that it was just too risky to send in those reserves. The Confederate invasion of Maryland had been blunted in horrific bloodshed, but that was all. McClellan's handling of Union troops was poor, historians say, though McClellan himself thought he had won a great victory.

More than 3,700 men, North and South, had been killed or mortally wounded and more than 18,000 wounded. In the days that followed the battle, McClellan did not push after Lee, and once again he would lose the support of President Lincoln. Even Stockton, a McClellan supporter, wondered about the lack of another assault on the Confederates. "If we would have attacked them yesterday [September 18] we would have captured many, for they were out of ammunition," the colonel wrote of the battle's aftermath.[50]

Stockton's comment about the lack of an aggressive assault on Lee's army seems to be the only surviving comment that a soldier of the 16th Michigan made about the terrible battle of Antietam. Lt. Salter, who usually wrote letters to Detroit, was absent sick, and diarist Pvt. Apted of the sharpshooters had sprained his knee on the march; in the case of the diary kept by John Berry of Company A, pages from his journal that covered this time are missing. It may be that men who experienced Gaines' Mill and second Bull Run simply did not feel compelled to record much about it; they had not been in the battle themselves, and only glimpsed it from shelter behind the hills and batteries. Of course, they were aware that newspapers would write about the battle. Sgt. Frank Keeler seems to have made no comment on the battle, only noting afterward that the locals in Sharpsburg sold baked goods to the Union soldiers. "We live pretty well here," he wrote home, "we buy bread, cookies and pies from people in the village."[51]

The First Division of the Fifth Corps was finally ordered on the morning of September 20 south across the Potomac after the enemy, who had already withdrawn from the Maryland side to Virginia. Here, near the village of Shepherdstown, the river could be crossed—a place called Boteler's Ford. Other units had waded across when the Third Brigade, commanded by Col. Stockton, started over. Suddenly he was ordered to pull his men back, warned "that the rebels were approaching in force," he wrote. Another of the brigades in their division, already across, was hit hard and a new regiment called the 118th Pennsylvania "was very seriously cut up." It had been a trap; the Pennsylvanians, also called "the Corn Exchange regiment" because of the regiment's organization by a banking firm, had been among the first to cross the river. Their men had been given defective and obsolete rifles, and they were hammered by the veteran Rebels, losing over 300 men killed, wounded, and missing.[52]

The Confederates kept up a harassing fire from across the river that night and into the morning, answered by pickets of the Third Brigade; Stockton had a battery shell the Rebels, driving them away. His men helped ninety wounded Pennsylvanians back from the Virginia side of the Potomac and Stockton sent forty men over under a flag of truce to bring back the dead. One of the officers in the detail was from Pvt. George Ervay's Company H. "My first lieutenant went across the river yesterday, and he seen a lot of the rebels," Ervay wrote, "and he said they were dirty and ragged and half-starved at that." As September drew to a close and the 16th Michigan's brigade moved to a new camp on a nearby hill, "the regular routine of camp life resumed," the colonel wrote. It was obvious that no pursuit of Lee was being contemplated and on a fair day Stockton rode up to the battlefield outside of Sharpsburg. "The graves are many, the trees cut off by shot from our batteries," he wrote that evening. "Found one poor female weeping over the graves where some of her relatives were buried. How many other desolate ones this battle has made."

Almost an afterthought, his next line reflected the routine business of picket duty and of rounding up soldiers who had gone astray, whether they had fallen out on the march to Sharpsburg or roamed away to find more pleasant distractions. It was another reflection of the strange nature of life and death in Civil War, and how, even though unimaginable numbers of men had been killed and maimed from the summer through the fall, the orders, duties and procedures of the army went on regardless. "Ordered to furnish 800 men for picket tomorrow," the colonel noted. "Also to send one officer from each regiment to Washington to collect stragglers."[53]

8.

SEPTEMBER–DECEMBER 1862

FAREWELL, McCLELLAN, YOU ARE ABOUT PLAYED OUT

Alfred Apted, the English-born Grand Rapids resident and sharpshooter, had not been with the 16th Michigan as it waited in reserve at Antietam. He had sprained his knee on the march and was sent to the hospital set up at Columbia College at 14th Street and Madison Hill; there, he noted in his diary, he had seen the president passing by with a body of cavalry. "Abe Lincoln rode past here twice today, so we a have a good chance to see the old fellow," Apted wrote. Lincoln reminded the young soldier of a hotel operator back home. "He looked somewhat like M. L. Sweet of Grand Rapids."

Grand Ledge's George Ervay of Company H, still a teenager, had also been hospitalized in Washington. He said he heard the assurance of the president that he and his comrades would soon be going home, since Lincoln believed, wrongly, his army would soon destroy Lee's. "I am well and in good spirits and Mr. Lincoln says that he is a-going to have us all home to eat dinner next New Year's," Ervay wrote. Like thousands of others, Ervay had suffered typhoid fever. "I was very sick for two weeks, but had a good doctor and good nurse . . . I was crazy as a loon, but I am all right now," he assured his family.[1]

Pvt. Henry "Tip" Aplin from Flint had spent most of the summer in Confederate custody after being captured at Savage's Station. Aplin was now in Annapolis, Maryland, in a camp where paroled prisoners sent from Rebel prison were supposed to wait until the exchange system formally processed their return to the Union army. Some men who had been prisoners of the Rebels were in no hurry to go back to their regiments, and this system was reportedly often abused by soldiers. Aplin was well enough to make business trips out of the camp to buy items to resell to his comrades there, according to his mother. "Tip has been keeping a sutler's shop on a small scale and has made good wages (He sent me $100 last week)," Elvira Aplin wrote to her son George, serving in another Michigan regiment. "He goes to Baltimore to buy his goods."[2]

Col. Thomas Stockton, in the meantime, at the camp of the Third Brigade with his regiment near the Potomac and the Antietam battlefield, was dealing with a spate of resignations and promotions in the 16th Michigan. Though Stockton was in command of the brigade, he obviously still thought of the regiment as his own, and was dealing with its vacancies himself rather than delegating these decisions to Lt. Col. Norval Welch. Of course, it was not unusual for a regimental commander to have to deal with vacancies—for example, John V. Ruehle had resigned from the post of lieutenant colonel immediately after the Seven Days; Lt. Morris Wells of Ionia also resigned and became adjutant in the 21st Michigan (Wells would become lieutenant colonel of that regiment, dying in action at Chickamauga, Georgia, in 1863). But now came a round of new resignations: Henry Sibley of Ionia resigned as captain of his company, and so did Capt. Ben Fisher of Company D, who got a new appointment in the 23rd Michigan; Solomon Brockway, now a captain, also resigned, apparently angry that Stockton had ruled that Capt. Judd Mott, who had come into the regiment from the Lancers, outranked Brockway in seniority. And Lt. Thomas Morris, the regimental adjutant, left to become the major in the 15th Michigan. Stockton, who had asked Morris to be in his regiment a year earlier, accepted Morris's resignation with contempt. "Good riddance," he grumbled to his diary. "Wish some others would do the same."

Nor had relations between Stockton and Gov. Blair improved. On October 1, Stockton hurried to Washington when he heard Blair was in town, but the governor left before the colonel could get there. No doubt Stockton knew he would need Blair's blessing if he was ever to be promoted to the post of brigadier general. For while the Congress had to approve such an appointment, the political truth of the matter was that no such promotion could occur in the Union army without the favor of the appointee's home state governor and senators.[3]

Stockton quickly sent off a letter to Blair, asking him to send more men to fill his regiment and to work out the details of pending promotions and vacancies. He also pointed out that he had been busy commanding the Third Brigade in the absence of Gen. Dan Butterfield, indicating he was capable and deserving of a promotion to the rank of brigadier general. He hinted that he did not necessarily agree with the promotions of Norval Welch to lieutenant colonel and Thomas Barry to major—the colonel had been in Rebel prison when Blair approved their commissions for these promotions, recommended by Welch. But Stockton had to accept them.

Sgt. Frank Keeler confirmed there was tension in the regiment about some of the promotions, and this probably contributed to some of the resignations. Keeler wrote that their corps commander, Gen. Fitz John Porter, had recommended certain soldiers be promoted for gallantry during the battles of the summer, though Porter's recommendations probably meant little to Blair, especially since Republicans were blaming Porter, a Democrat, for the Union defeat at second Bull Run. The sergeant's words also reflected that promotions recommended by Norval Welch while Stockton had been a prisoner were also points of contention.[4]

Stockton stayed in Washington with his wife for a few days before returning to camp, which was shifted to a ridge about three miles down the Potomac, near the point where

Antietam Creek flowed into it. The colonel worked on his own much-hoped-for promotion, gathering recommendations from his commanders. He thought about bringing his wife to camp and heard the news about Confederate cavalry commander Jeb Stuart making a raid into Maryland, taking horses, shoes, and pistols, among other prizes, again embarrassing the Union army. He also wrote to Michigan Adjutant General John Robertson, telling him where state authorities could find soldiers who had gone absent, and that his regiment required nearly 400 men to bring the 16th Michigan up to minimum strength.

The colonel noted that he had three lieutenants' posts open because of resignations and promotions. "Some of these I desire to fill with outsiders, if by doing so, it will bring in thirty or more recruits each, making it a condition that they first furnish their quota of men." Specifically, Stockton wanted commissions for James Topping from Genesee County, son-in-law of regimental surgeon, Dr. Isaac Wixom, and also a man named Martin Borgman of Detroit. Borgman was a former lancer, as was Borgman's friend and new brother-in-law, English-born James Beckett. Beckett had already served with the 16th Michigan for several months in 1862 before being released on a medical discharge that fall. Now, less than a month later, Beckett returned to the 16th Michigan with Borgman—the two friends had just married a pair of sisters. But Beckett was fated to die in the year ahead in the coming battle on Little Round Top, a rocky hill just south of Gettysburg, Pennsylvania, where Borgman would be wounded.[5]

Giving commissions to Borgman and Topping—newcomers who had not been in battle—did not sit well with veteran Second Lt. Charles Salter, back with his regiment after recovering from sickness. "Our colonel now proposes to bring on recruits and give them the vacant offices to pay them for bringing the recruits, whilst the officers think that the vacant places should be filled by promotion of the officers and such non-commissioned offers as deserve it," he complained. Salter said he did not want to resign in protest, but he had been through battles and hardships for a year and a half. "If I cannot get the promotion, but have seen some men that has never seen a battle and knows nothing about military affairs sent on from Michigan and placed over me, I would be disgraced by remaining in the regiment."

He assured friends he would wait to see what Stockton did in his own case; he also told them that the appearance of the Antietam battlefield was surprisingly scenic, given the terrible bloodshed that took place. "A person coming here now can scarcely realize that it was so recently the theater of such a heavy battle," he wrote, "but for the graves that are so thickly scattered for miles around Sharpsburg and the marks of the cannon balls and shells upon the houses of the village." Some of the Union dead had been recovered by friends and relatives who sent their coffins north for burial at home, and other soldiers "were buried properly with headboards to designate their names," Salter explained. But the Rebel dead went into mass graves.[6]

The weather turned raw and wet, but Salter said he was comfortable. "The tent I live in is a small one, called by us a poncho tent," he explained. "It is 6 feet long, 4 feet wide and 3 feet high. I have cedar boughs spread on the ground to sleep on." The lieutenant from Detroit had the luxury of his own tent, while other officers were sharing them. But he thought the changing weather meant it was too late for another advance by the Army of the Potomac as winter drew nearer. "When the rainy season sets in, it is impossible to move an army in Virginia," he wrote. He also figured the thousands of new troops who had come into the army would have to be well drilled before they could go on the offensive. "There has been one new regiment added to each brigade in our corps," he continued. "The 20th Maine has joined us and the other day when the President received us, their line was longer than that of the five old regiments."[7]

Salter mentioned a conspiratorial view of the conduct of the war by the U.S. government, an idea that was not uncommon when soldiers talked amongst themselves or wrote to family. "The Capitol and the patent office and several other public buildings are now being used as hospitals," he explained. If it was strange that the Capitol was housing sick and wounded soldiers, Salter wrote, it was a better use of the building "than it was last summer, when the politicians were in it, plotting how they might best prevent our army from taking Richmond."[8]

Some of the new enlistees were coming into the regiment, and Stockton sarcastically recorded the failure of Lt. Col. Welch to drum up the numbers he had promised. "Nine recruits arrived yesterday from Borgman," the colonel wrote. "Welch has sent but one, leaving 199 of his promised [number] to come yet." He recorded that an acquaintance from his days in California, a "Mr. Kelly," showed up in camp, and promised to give Stockton an interest in a lead mine he owned out west. Kelly's son was a sergeant in the 44th New York, so Stockton gave the young man a position at their division headquarters, seemingly his end of the *quid pro quo*.[9]

The colonel, also thinking the army would be going into winter camp, had his tent fixed up with a fireplace and a double bed to accommodate his wife Maria, but the war intruded on his plans. On October 23, he received orders to be ready to move the Third Brigade. As he made his preparations, he was angered to hear some of his officers having a drunken party the next night. "Loud singing, carousing, etc. tonight in [Lt. Guy] Fuller's tent *after tattoo,*" Stockton noted, referring to a term for the old "taps," or "lights out" signal. "[Capt. Robert T.] Elliott there and evidently under the influence of liquor! Fuller is officer of the day [and responsible for keeping order in the regiment]. It pains me much to do it, but I cannot overlook such conduct. They know better, and the sooner I use stringent measures, the better it will be for my regiment, them, and myself."

Whatever disciplinary action Stockton took against the officers, it did not result in their dismissals. Several soldiers of the 16th Michigan landed themselves in trouble three days later when they protested a sutler's exorbitant prices. "Some of the men of the regiment rally in [disrupt] his establishment, upsetting his tent and destroying some of his goods," Cpl. John Berry of Company A wrote. "Two or three of them get arrested and are lodged in the guard house."[10]

Preparations for the march were halted while their brigade said goodbye to their former brigade commander, Gen. Dan Butterfield, as the Army of the Potomac was reorganized by McClellan. "I had each regiment turn out, and rode with him after all called on him," Stockton wrote. "Butterfield's gold spurs that Major Welch got were presented to him, tho' I believe they are not yet paid for by those subscribing," he added, perhaps with sarcasm. Col. Strong Vincent of the 83rd Pennsylvania presented the spurs, with Butterfield expressing thanks. After the ceremony Stockton and captains Stephen Martin and Judd Mott accompanied Maria Stockton to Harper's Ferry, where she boarded the train to Washington. Returning at that moment was Brig. Gen. Charles Griffin, a gruff professional soldier, artillery officer, and brigade commander in their corps' First Division, and he rode back to camp with Stockton. Griffin told him of the rumors of impending changes in the army command—that McClellan was about to be replaced again. "This constant changing will ruin our cause," Stockton fretted.[11]

Three days later, on October 30, the Fifth Corps broke camp as McClellan, under pressure from an impatient Lincoln, started the Army of the Potomac on a half-hearted pursuit of Lee's army. The 16th Michigan and the brigade of which it was part moved out that evening and encamped halfway to Harper's Ferry. The march resumed the next day on the Leesburg turnpike—"up and down ravines and hills," Sgt. Frank Keeler said. They crossed the Potomac and then the Shenandoah on pontoon bridges and followed a winding road up a rugged cliff called Loudoun Heights. Now back in Virginia, the Fifth Corps headed toward the Blue Ridge Mountains, and some of the soldiers were sure there would be a battle fought soon. There was skirmishing ahead that did not involve the 16th Michigan and its brigade, and the soldiers stayed in camp until the morning of November 6 as the weather turned cold. Stockton used this time to inspect his Third Brigade and recommend men for promotions in the 16th Michigan, including Sgt. Ziba Graham of Flint (to lieutenant) and Lt. Rufus Jacklin of the Brady sharpshooters (to the post of regimental adjutant); the colonel told the governor he needed another assistant surgeon, since Dr. William Breakey had become ill.[12]

For Saginaw's Frank Keeler, this was a particularly lucky moment—he was appointed commissary sergeant, which meant he drew and issued rations for the 16th Michigan's enlisted men. "I like the position, very much; don't have to carry thirty or forty pounds and march all day, but get up on a high seat with any of our teamsters and ride," he bragged. The job also took him out of much routine duty and also the firing line; because long trains of supply wagons were constantly moving back and forth from ports or railroad depots to wherever the army was at the front or in camp, the commissary sergeant was often dealing with the matter of keeping soldiers supplied with food.[13]

But now that the Union troops were back on Confederate soil, they helped themselves to the food and livestock of Virginia's farmers—they would "live off the land." In the years ahead, Capt. Thomas Frank Powers of the 16th Michigan would recall this time fondly. "So well was the regiment supplied with poultry, fresh meats, honey and preserves, that the commanding officer of the division made a sly insinuation to Col. Stockton that the 16th must have had a lax training in its youth to so soon forget the high moral culture that had made the Army of the Potomac so fond of furnishing food for the powder of Rebel bushwhackers." Of course, this joking remark centered on the fact that the Union army had lost so many supplies to raiding Confederates in previous months, and now the Michigan soldiers were helping themselves, taking from the farms of Rebellion supporters. John

Berry recorded this in his diary. "The men spend most of the day in foraging amongst the secesh farmers," he noted. "In Maryland we respected everyone's property, but in Virginia, hogs, sheep, chickens and vegetables have to suffer as soon as it is known the owner is a secessionist."[14]

On the evening of November 5, the 16th Michigan and other regiments received orders to march the next day. It troubled Stockton, who from the heights could see Rebel positions and artillery on the east side of the Shenandoah River. "This looks suspicious," the colonel wrote, "as if we were retreating." In fact, over the next four days, their corps moved east, back toward Washington. The nights were frosty and the roads were bad, but the regiment was rejoined by Maj. Thomas Barry, recovered from his wound at second Bull Run and back from recruiting in Michigan. At the town of Warrenton, Stockton got the news that his beloved commander had been replaced—again. "Rumor that Gen'l McClellan has really been superseded," Stockton noted. "Wrote to wife, in case 'tis true, that I wish to resign." The news was true, and he received orders for the men to be drawn up for a review the next day.

With McClellan fired by Lincoln, Stockton called November 10 "the saddest day" of his life as 50,000 soldiers were drawn up in columns to "bid a sad farewell to their chosen and honored commander." The colonel wrote that it was fortunate for Lincoln and the Radical Republicans that the general was a patriot—otherwise, he would march his army back to Washington to demand his restoration. "McClellan's own soldiers wept as he bade them adieu," Sgt. Keeler wrote about the review. "He looked every inch a hero yesterday as he rode along our front in advance of his staff, cheered by his troops, such cheers as I never heard before." Berry agreed. "They cheer him loudly and wave the tattered banners as he rides through our ranks," he wrote. "Farewell, McClellan, I am afraid you are about played out."[15]

Though his Republican enemies had wanted Gen. Fitz John Porter dismissed in the wake of the second battle of Bull Run, McClellan had protected him and kept him in command of the Fifth Corps. Now the officers of the corps were invited to say their goodbyes to McClellan at Porter's headquarters. "We saw emotions and demonstrations [of officers' respect]," Stockton wrote. "What were his feelings, I can only judge." But the colonel was sure that McClellan would soon run for and be elected president, and that even his enemies—Republicans—would soon turn to the general to save the country. Lt. Salter wrote that the emotional general shook hands with the assembled officers, reminding them they were proud members of the Army of the Potomac. [16]

No sooner had McClellan left the army than Porter was also removed, blamed by Gen. Pope and the Republican leadership for losing the second Bull Run battle by disobedience and disloyalty. "Another of our old and beloved generals taken from us," an angry Stockton wrote, "Gen. Porter relieved by Gen. [Joseph] Hooker and ordered to Washington for trial!" He considered the removals of Porter and McClellan the result of "mistrust and jealousy" by Radical Republican leaders. The Fifth Corps was drawn up in formation to bid Porter goodbye. "As he passed our division the soldiers manifested their sympathy for him by cheering vociferously and throwing their caps in the air," Salter wrote. "It seemed to us as if we were losing our best friend." Of course, Republicans looked at this as the beginning of an effort to remove McClellan's Democratic supporters and influence from the army.

Back in October, the news had reached the soldiers that Lincoln was issuing the Emancipation Proclamation to take effect on January 1, 1863—that slaves in Confederate-held states and territories were now free. Of course, there was the matter that most slaves under the close control of their masters were not likely to throw off their chains, and that slaves held in border states that were not part of the Confederacy were *still* slaves. Many Union soldiers shrugged off the proclamation, hoping that it would perhaps help their cause, even though most of them felt they had not signed up to abolish slavery. Of course, both Porter and McClellan were Democrats who felt the war was not, and should not be, about abolition. Sgt. Frank Keeler, writing at the time of the removal of these generals, mentioned the Michigan soldiers' view of the war. "We, that is those who are Republican, are sometimes called abolitionists by certain northern newspapers," he said. "We are not abolitionists in the sense those papers would convey, but if emancipation becomes a military necessity, if slavery is a benefit or aid to the Rebels, then we soldiers say abolish it.

"But if it is not a help to them," he continued, "then pass it by, leave it to be considered when we shall have ceased this struggle for the life of our country, when peace is restored and the authority of our Constitution re-established, when our laws are obeyed and respected in every state of the Union—then we will turn our attention to the rabid radicals and treat them as they deserve." Of course, Keeler seems to have missed the point that the war *was* in fact about slavery—that the country had broken up because the leaders of Southern states feared Lincoln's election meant slavery would be banned in new territories and states. Yet Keeler echoed the common sentiment—that the war was about the defeating secession and not abolition. "We are fighting to SAVE THE UNION," he wrote. "If the administration considers it wise and expedient to abolish slavery in order to hasten or insure an end to the war, we will support such a measure willingly. This I believe is the prevailing political sentiment in the army of the United States in relation to slavery."[17]

The new commander of the Army of the Potomac was a McClellan friend, Maj. Gen. Ambrose E. Burnside, who previously commanded the Ninth Corps. He reorganized the army again, creating a new system of "grand divisions." The Fifth Corps, of which the 16th Michigan was part, was joined with another corps, and this giant unit would be commanded by Gen. Joseph Hooker. Col. Stockton was not impressed. "Now we do not know or have much confidence in either of our new generals," he wrote, "though we trust that both are equal to the positions they are promoted to."

In addition, the commander of their corps' First Division, Gen. George Morell, was transferred and replaced with Gen. Charles Griffin, who had commanded a brigade alongside Col. Stockton. The Third Brigade's original commander, Gen. Dan Butterfield, was put in charge of the Fifth Corps in Hooker's grand division. Stockton paid a visit to Hooker within two days of his appointment. "He is evidently no friend of McClellan's, as he said, 'he [McClellan] was no soldier.' He assured me we would move in a few days to Fredericksburg." Indeed, that day, two corps, part of the Army of the Potomac, left the huge camp near Warrenton, marching south toward Fredericksburg, with more soon to follow. "We are destined undoubtedly to have some fighting somewhere in that direction," the colonel predicted. As Union forces began the move toward the Rappahannock River, the men understood a fight was in store. "When we do advance again we shall have another great battle," Lt. Salter wrote, "for we cannot advance much further without being met by the rebels in force."[18]

As the 16th Michigan waited at Warrenton to move out, Brady Company sharpshooter Alfred Apted recorded his surprise at seeing women of the town freely mingling with soldiers, and at the high prices of bread for sale by the locals—"$11 for eight small biscuits," he wrote. Lt. Salter, from Detroit, learned he was being made a first lieutenant in the new round of promotions, and moved from Company E to Company B, "the Ionia company." His new commission was dated from the second Bull Run battle. "I prize it very highly as it is a promotion made on the field of battle," he wrote. Less happy were those involved in rivalries over promotions and other flaps. Capt. Guy Fuller of Company B preferred a charge against Capt. George Swan of Company A, apparently forced to do so by Col. Stockton even though Fuller apparently also wanted to resign. "I am resolved to put a stop to this slandering of one another behind one's back," Stockton wrote. "I will catch some of them at it in regard to myself."[19]

The changes in personnel continued. Capt. Solomon Brockway, who had resigned from the regiment, went back to Michigan and was appointed to a new cavalry regiment; his father, Chaplain William Brockway, also turned in his resignation. "I am glad to be rid of them both," Stockton wrote. At the same time, Dr. Isaac Wixom handed in his resignation for reasons that are not clear, but probably because as a Democrat he disapproved of the removals of McClellan and Porter and with Lincoln's Emancipation Proclamation. It is also possible that Wixom was aware that Lt. Col. Norval Welch, who was nominally in charge of the 16th Michigan while Stockton commanded the Third Brigade, was investigating whether Dr. Wixom had misused hospital rations and alcohol. But Stockton was in no hurry to accept Wixom's resignation, perhaps thinking he could, as brigade commander, protect the surgeon. The doctor would probably come to regret, in the months ahead, that the colonel had not simply accepted his resignation and allowed him to return home.[20]

At last on November 17 the 16th Michigan and thousands of other soldiers who were part of their newly organized "grand division" rose before dawn and packed their tents and blankets. They waited in the rain until daylight, when they finally left camp at Warrenton, marching south on the road to Fredericksburg. It was hard traveling with the men turning the muddy roads to muck, and their brigade marched about 15 miles before camping in what Pvt. Apted described as an isolated, poverty-stricken countryside. Their Fifth Corps reached the head of Richland Run, 13 miles from Fredericksburg the next day, and moved a few miles closer on the 19th. The 16th Michigan camped on an open plain of a plantation owned and operated by blacks who had been given their freedom and the property in their dead master's will. "Here we all have the most delightful and pretty location we ever have had," wrote Stockton. "My tent is on a knoll covered with evergreens and overlooks the whole division."[21]

For three days the soldiers camped in the rain and the cold. But while Gen. Burnside did not hurry his army to Fredericksburg, Robert E. Lee did. He brought up his trusted lieutenants, James Longstreet and Stonewall Jackson, and the Confederates dug in on the hills above the town, creating strong, fortified positions. "'Tis said the Rebels have still possession of Fredericksburg and the south shore of the Rappahannock," Stockton wrote on November 20. He added: "[I] have furnished guards today to a number of citizens who are oil vendors, the men of Gen'l [Abner] Doubleday's command are the ones depredating. What a commentary on the North that our men will rob and plunder from helpless women. The next will be violence and rape."

Stockton had written to Maria earlier that month, telling her that he was thinking of resigning and asking her opinion on the matter, and now he received her response. "The mail came tonight," he wrote on November 21. "Two letters from dear wife, giving me, as I asked, her advice and wishes as to my future action." That was all Stockton said about the question of his future with the Union army, but it seems that Maria Stockton advised her husband not to resign. Yes, his beloved McClellan and Porter were gone, and no, as a War Democrat, he was not a supporter of the Emancipation Proclamation; but he was commanding a brigade, and the war was far from over. Perhaps she told him there was still a chance he would get his brigadier general's star. Certainly Stockton disapproved of the Radical Republicans, and he was stuck with Lt. Col. Norval Welch, whom he did not like, nominally in charge of the regiment he had founded. But Maria Stockton may have reminded her husband of the obstacles he had overcome to form his regiment. Whatever argument or opinion she gave, for the moment, Stockton would not resign.[22]

The rain continued as the 16th Michigan's brigade and division got orders to resume the march, the column moving slowly through the mud to camp in a pine thicket near the Aquia-Fredericksburg railroad line about six miles from Fredericksburg and nine miles from the Aquia Creek Landing on the Potomac River. This location was called Stoneman's Switch, or alternatively, Stoneman's Station. "The roads are very bad," wrote John Berry of Company A about the march. "About an hour after dark we give it up for the night, having got our battery stuck in one of the most dismal looking mud-holes in Virginia." Berry had been promoted to sergeant; the next morning, the soldiers "fish the cannon out of the swamp," he said. But while the men suffered in the rain and cold and mud, Lt. Salter insisted that the soldiers were "anxious to meet the enemy and have the war settled as soon as possible."[23]

As the regiment waited in the chilly rain, Lt. Col. Norval Welch returned from recruiting leave, and Lt. Salter explained the new organization of the army to his friends. "Our new commander, Gen. Burnside, is well liked by the entire Army," he said. "There are quite a number of officers as well as soldiers who are dissatisfied McClellan should be removed, but at the same time they like Gen. Burnside. For my part, I am much better pleased with the new commander than with the old one, and I am satisfied that the war will now be pushed ahead with a great deal more vigor." Salter said he was sure that McClellan was "not as good a general as the army always supposed him to be."

He also praised generals Hooker and Butterfield and mentioned Col. Stockton only in passing. He gave glowing comments on Lt. Col. Welch. "We are very glad to have him come back as we have more confidence in him than in any other officer who has ever commanded the regiment," Salter wrote. Sgt. Frank Keeler, on the other hand, expressed gratitude to Stockton. "Col. Stockton, who commands the brigade, never forgets the 16th," he wrote. "We are hoping he will get a star on his shoulder before long; he certainly deserves it."[24]

Salter mentioned that several company officers had tried to resign, but Stockton had refused to accept them, thus keeping them in the service a while longer. Now, because of prior resignations and losses in battle, "we have not one-half of our old officers left," he wrote. Still, promotions were being made to fill vacancies—second lieutenants were becoming first lieutenants, and first lieutenants were being made captains. George Prentiss, Butler Brown, Guy Fuller, Edward Hill, Wallace Jewett, and William Kydd were among those promoted. Old Frederick Forsyth became sergeant major.[25]

The Detroit lieutenant also gave his opinion about the recent off-year elections, which had seen the election of many Democrats; he was sure if the soldiers in the field had been allowed to vote in their home-state elections, as had the troops from Iowa and Wisconsin, "the Democrats would not have carried the few states that they did." Most soldiers, he claimed, were Republicans, and if the war effort was to be broken up by governors, then it should not have been fought at all. Salter ended his letter predicting that there would soon be another major Union offensive. "In a few days, I think you will hear of greater and more decisive battles being fought, than any that have yet taken place during the war," he wrote.[26]

In the meantime, Col. Stockton, suffering from hemorrhoids, wondered why the Union army had not moved. "If we are to attack Fredericksburg, I cannot conceive why we wait to give the Rebels time to prepare," he wrote prophetically on November 26. "If we had done so when our force first arrived I believe it would have saved many lives. But we will soon know the 'why and wherefore.'" The next day was Thanksgiving and Stockton shared dinner with Col. Strong Vincent of the 83rd Pennsylvania and Lt. Col. Robert Richardson of the 12th New York. He was pleased to get a letter from Gen. Dan Butterfield, who said that he and Hooker had recommended Stockton for the post of brigadier general. But a 16th Michigan soldier and correspondent who signed his dispatches to Detroit "H" wrote that the regiment went without a traditional holiday feast. It was a dull day, with soldiers dining on hardtack and salt pork rather than roast turkey and beef.[27]

As the winter season came on and the month wound down, Stockton's brigade supplied 1,000 men for picket duty, perhaps covering the front for their entire corps or "grand division." The colonel wondered if the army was really going anywhere. "This don't look much like 'on to Richmond,'" he wrote, a sarcastic comment on the lack of movement in Burnside's new offensive, using the famous but unfortunate words of aggressive headlines that Northern newspapers used early in war. This fateful observation, made just a few miles from Fredericksburg, would be Col. Stockton's last surviving diary entry of the war.

His men also wondered about the failure of the army to move, since they were aware Confederate forces were waiting for them across the Rappahannock River. "I cannot see what keeps us here so long," Alfred Apted noted, echoing Stockton's concern. Early December was quiet and days of fine weather broke up spells of rain and frosty nights. Picket duty took soldiers down to the Rappahannock River, where both sides filled their canteens but left one another alone, and where Union officers could see Confederate batteries arriving daily. New recruits coming into the 16th Michigan's camp were taught drill, and shipments of badly needed clothing arrived. "The late marches have worn out our shoes and a number of us are almost bare-footed," Sgt. John Berry wrote. "While out drilling the other day, we met an officer who was the next thing to being bare-footed. One of our boys remarked to him, 'Say, Cap, who stole your boots?' His answer was 'Never mind about my boots. It is a free country, and if Uncle Sam don't give us any shoes, why, we will fight bare-footed.'"[28]

Snow fell on the night of December 5 and the men's tents were frosted on the inside when they awoke. "The victuals is froze hard in our haversacks," Berry wrote, "and the water is ice in our canteens, and the blankets are covered with frost and we ourselves turn out half froze to roll call as the drums are beating 'I wish I was in Dixie.' But we think to ourselves as regards the cold weather we might as well be in Lake Superior."[29]

Sgt. William H. Borden of Ionia County was pleased to find out that he had supporters back home and within the regiment who wanted to see him promoted to lieutenant. Capt. Guy Fuller, who was also from Ionia, had been trying to surprise Borden by getting him an officer's commission. But there was a problem: A supporter back home had sent his endorsement of Borden to Lt. Col. Welch, who was theoretically in charge of the 16th Michigan while Col. Stockton commanded the Third Brigade. But because Stockton and Welch did not get along, it was Stockton who decided who was going to be promoted within the regiment, not Welch; thus, it was no boon to have Welch's support.

"I never ask Col. Welch for any favors, nor any other officer in this regiment," wrote Borden, "he [Welch] says he would like to see me a lieutenant in this regiment, but he don't like to appoint me on account of the feeling that exists between him and Stockton. He thinks Stockton will think he is assuming rather too much authority." Despite the bad feelings between Stockton and Welch, Borden eventually got the promotion and became a lieutenant in Company F.[30]

It remained harshly cold at night, and the 16th Michigan stood picket for 48 hours on December 8 and 9, returning from their outposts to camp at noon on the 10th. "We received orders to withdraw the pickets, return to camp and prepare to march," Lt. Salter wrote. "We did so and next morning our entire corps marched down to the river bank opposite Fredericksburg and then awaited further orders."

By moonlight on the early morning of December 11, the men of the 16th Michigan rose and packed their gear. Before they started marching, they could hear artillery firing at Fredericksburg, which lay a few miles away, just across the Rappahannock River. At daylight, their Third Brigade, along with the First Division of the Fifth Corps, got into line and at last marched to a ridge above the town of Falmouth, on the east side of the river. Some accounts say the soldiers got a panoramic view that morning on that plateau—that they could see Fredericksburg nestled on the mist-covered Rappahannock, the open plain behind the town rising gently to the hills where the Confederate guns and crews were in position, waiting.[31]

It had been a bloody and unsuccessful year for the Army of Potomac, yet it was clear to the soldiers filing down toward the river, as the sun rose and the details of the town emerged from the lifting fog, that another terrible battle was about to begin.

9.

DECEMBER 1862–JANUARY 1863

A TERRIBLE AND DESTRUCTIVE FIRE

The fighting began that morning of December 11 before the Fifth Corps reached the Falmouth side of the Rappahannock, as Union engineers attempted to build pontoon bridges over the river to Fredericksburg. A brigade of Confederates, Mississippians hidden in houses and buildings along the town's waterfront, opened fire, killing and wounding them as they worked. Though the 16th Michigan did not arrive with its division until early afternoon, the soldiers heard the firing as they approached and quickly learned what was going on ahead. The Rebels "pick them off so fast they have to fall back," Sgt. John Berry of Company A wrote in his diary about the unfortunate engineers. "Our artillery then play on them [Confederates] with increased vigor and a fight ensues between the Rebels and our sharpshooters." He noted that "the Rebels do not answer our cannonade."

Houses and commercial structures collapsed and burned under the Union bombardment, and by the time the 16th Michigan reached the scene, Union troops were crossing the river by boat and engaging the Confederates in house-to-house fighting as fires raged. The regiment waited with its division on the east side of the river, crouching in the mud at a place called the Philips House, where their commander, Gen. Ambrose Burnside, had his headquarters. Of course, any element of surprise that the general had hoped for was gone, if it ever existed. At some point as the street battle in Fredericksburg raged and smoke rolled into the sky, the Brady Company sharpshooter from Grand Rapids wrote a just-in-case message in his journal: "If anything happens to the owner of this book, Alfred M. Apted, the finder will please write the facts to Francis Apted, Three Rivers, Michigan."[1]

By nightfall, those Confederates who had not been killed, wounded, or captured in Fredericksburg withdrew to their main defensive lines outside of town. More Union troops crossed the two pontoon bridges into the town (two more bridges were also finished further south), but the 16th Michigan remained with its corps bivouacked on the east side of the Rappahannock. The next day, December 12, the sun came up and the weather was fine as thousands of Union troops continued to cross the bridges into Fredericksburg, ransacking what was left in homes and shops that survived the previous day's shelling and fighting. The 16th Michigan did not cross but was shifted closer to the river with its brigade, just across from the southern portion of the town. "There was not much done," Lt. Charles Salter said about that day, "except constant skirmishing by the pickets and occasionally a few shots fired from our heavy batteries for the purpose of feeling the enemy's position." Sgt. Berry agreed. "The troops do not cross fast enough and get into position for us to cross today," he wrote. "We bivouac again in the mud."[2]

Burnside's plan for the Army of the Potomac to quickly cross the river and force Lee's Army of Northern Virginia into open country to fight was in shambles, of course, but he stubbornly pressed on with his attack, even though the Rebels were in an excellent position to stop it. "It was commenced early in the morning of the 13th," Lt. Charles Salter wrote, "by [Gen. Edwin] Sumner's Corps, who were sent up division after division to storm the place." He continued, "The rebels were posted on a range of hills about two miles back the river, they had thrown up a strong line of earth works upon the hills and planted cannon upon them, tier after tier, as thick as they could work them."

In fact, the Confederate artillery was about only half that distance from the river and they had almost unobstructed fields of fire as Union troops emerged from Fredericksburg and advanced up the gentle slope. Only some swales, ditches, and a couple of shallow ridges in the rising plain afforded a soldier any protection, if he was able to keep low enough. Though preparations by Sumner's divisions started early that morning, the attack did not commence until about 11:30 a.m. "Their light artillery [was] upon the first hills and heavy artillery upon higher hills, further back," the Detroit lieutenant continued about the Rebel position. "The ground from these hills towards the river, although undulating, gradually sloped down towards the city, and it was an open plain from the city out to the Rebel works. Of course, the rebels could just sweep our men away by the hundreds.[3]

"In front of the rebel batteries they had a line of infantry posted in rifle pits, and their sharpshooters were concealed in great numbers all over this plain," Salter said. "Under such circumstances, we could expect but one result, which was that when our men advanced they were drove back, every line, with great slaughter." Much of what Salter described as "rifle pits" was really a road cut into the ground along the base of a hill called Marye's Heights. Confederate batteries fired from the top of this hill, while below at the Sunken Road, with a stone-lined wall fronting toward Fredericksburg, hundreds of Rebel soldiers had nearly perfect cover as they fired their rifles over the wall at the approaching Union troops.

"From where our corps were stationed on this (the east) side of the river we could see our troops advance, see them mowed down by the Rebel artillery and although they would charge up bravely again and again, they would only rush upon their own destruction," Salter wrote, in as good a general description of the battle as was recorded by a witness. "The rebels fired their artillery so rapidly that it seemed one continual roar and we could not distinguish the discharge of a single cannon, whilst the musketry kept up such a continual rattling that it seemed more like the popping of immense numbers of firecrackers than anything else." By brigades and divisions, one after the other, the Union soldiers advanced over the open ground, only to be shot down by the score, and ultimately by the thousands. "Our troops had fought all day long until 3 p.m. without gaining any advantage at all," Salter said, "and they had all been engaged except our corps (which was the reserve). And now it came our turn."[4]

One of the soldiers watching this slaughter from the same side of the Rappahannock was a teenage farm boy from Northfield, a few miles from Ann Arbor, named Thomas Trahey. He had joined the Michigan lancers in the fall of 1861 but went home when that regiment was mustered out. Earlier in the fall of 1862 Trahey saw Lt. Col. Norval Welch recruiting for the 16th Michigan from a tent pitched on the lawn of the Ann Arbor court house. "When I went to enlist he asked my age, and I informed him that I was about 18," Trahey wrote later. "He asked if my parents were living, and where? I informed him and he directed a soldier who was sitting in the tent to procure a buggy and take me out to my father and obtain a letter giving his consent." Trahey's father cried as he wrote that letter allowing his boy to go to war. And so young Trahey traveled with thirty-five other recruits with Welch to Virginia, joining the regiment near Aquia Creek. Now in the mid-afternoon of December 13, the lad marched with his regiment and brigade down to the nearby pontoon bridge leading to the southern portion of Fredericksburg.[5]

New colors for the Third Brigade were brought out—a triangular flag called a guidon, with a white field trimmed in blue and emblazoned with a red Maltese cross. Another young soldier, the irrepressible George Sidman of Owosso in Company C, begged Lt. Ziba Graham of Flint to let him carry that brigade flag. The fact Sidman was there in the ranks at all was fairly amazing. After he was wounded in the hip at Gaines' Mill, captured, and subsequently exchanged, the teenager, unable to walk unaided, attempted to rejoin his regiment just before it left the Washington area on the Antietam campaign. But the surgeon had refused to certify young Sidman for service since he could not walk without a crutch. The regiment marched off without him, but Sidman would not be left behind. "He begged a ride across the river to Georgetown and succeeded in reaching his regiment that night, nearly worn out," according to a turn-of-the-century account of Sidman's adventure. "The next morning he found a condemned horse by the road side, and, with a bridle made of knapsack straps, and a pile of blankets to soften the protruding bones of his fiery steed, he rode into camp that night."[6]

After that, Col. Stockton allowed the lad to stay with the regiment. Weeks had passed and Sidman was fully recovered. Now 18, he pleaded to Lt. Graham: Could he carry the new brigade colors? Graham considered Sidman for a moment. It was dangerous business, carrying a flag into battle, and the teenager from Shiawassee County was "a mere boy." Graham said all right but added that the decision was up to the brigade commander. "Col. Stockton in command, admiring his pluck but deprecating his youth, finally gave his consent," Graham wrote years later. So young Sidman got his wish—he would carry the brigade flag into the battle of Fredericksburg.[7]

It took time to move hundreds of men, filing over the narrow pontoon bridge, so it was 4:30 p.m., according to Edward Hill, the former lancer officer, when the Third Brigade of the First Division of the Fifth Corps crossed to the point where it reached a wharf near

Fredericksburg's Princess Elizabeth Street. The soldiers advanced through the town and halted near the outskirts, facing the hills to the west. Thomas Trahey remembered the relief he felt when the regiment's men were ordered to unsling their knapsacks; the straps across his chest caused him discomfort. Still, Trahey decided he should take some things with him into battle. "From my knapsack I took a pair of socks, a shirt, some writing paper and envelopes and rolled them in my blanket, which being new was very bulky," Trahey wrote later. "I tied the ends together and slung it over my left shoulder."

The regiments of their brigade took up a position stretching down Prince Edward Street on the edge of town to a point about 100 yards south at the Richmond, Fredericksburg & Potomac railway station. They watched as their comrades in the First and Second Brigades of their division marched into the fray with another division. Directly ahead a half mile in the distance lay the Confederate defensive line at the base of Marye's Heights. "Here, for one hour and a half, it [the Third Brigade] was subjected to a pelting fire of shot and shell while [Andrew] Humphrey's Division and the First and Second Brigades of [Gen. Charles] Griffin's Division were making a determined but ineffectual assault upon Marye's Heights and the Sunken Road," Hill wrote later. Col. Stockton reported that at least two of the 16th Michigan's men were killed and a number wounded as they awaited the order to advance.[8]

The winter sun set at around 5 p.m., Hill said. Gen. Joseph Hooker, who commanded the grand division of which the Fifth Corps was part, protested to Burnside—first by messenger and then in person: another attack on the Confederate positions was a needless waste of lives. Gen. Dan Butterfield, who now commanded the corps, agreed, Hill wrote. Hill was not present for this meeting, of course, but other generals were, and all but one of them agreed with Hooker—another attack against the Confederate positions could not succeed. But Burnside's mind was made up, so more soldiers of the Fifth Corps would attack as evening fell.

Hill, writing years later, said the bugles sounded for the attack at 6:20 p.m., and that "the plain in front of Marye's Heights was further obscured with clouds of smoke, through which shone the luminous lights of the Federal batteries and musketry, kindling into sheets of flame as it almost united with the enemy's flashing fire from the Sunken Road and Marye's and Willis Hills." Yet Col. Stockton and Lt. Salter indicated shortly after the battle that it was not yet dark. The brigade rose and advanced—the 17th and 12th New York regiments were on the right of their line, the 20th Maine and the 44th New York in the middle, and the 83rd Pennsylvania and the 16th Michigan on the left. Their first obstacle was a mill race, a kind of canal used to power a local mill, and it contained about three feet of water.[9]

The soldiers splashed through the mill race "under a furious fire," Hill wrote, and were ordered to stop beyond it, behind a low crest or hill just outside of town, where the men were realigned. "[Lt.] Col. Welch commanding the 16th Michigan, took occasion to deliver a short and spirited address to his men, as companies came into position with a precision as if forming for dress parade." Other units also halted and formed, though the two New York regiments were hit by artillery; these soldiers, not hearing the commands or bugle calls, did not advance and only rejoined the brigade later. A heavy board fence blocked the 20th Maine and the 44th New York, and these regiments had to move around it. But at last the left and center regiments of the brigade aligned on a small building in the field ahead, up the sloping, undulating ground. The order came and the regiments moved into the field.

Edward Hill wrote that there were nineteen cannon on Marye's Heights and twenty-one on the adjacent Willis Hill, with more nearby. But because their brigade was "veiled in smoke and screened by darkness," the Rebel gunners fired high. "[T]o this cause alone it owed its preservation," he said. Col. Stockton, on the other hand, indicated his line was visible to the Confederates and that it was not completely dark until the regiments of the brigade got out to the second of two "intervening ridges," or rises of ground like low steps or terraces leading up to the Rebel defenses at the base of Marye's Heights. He wrote that they were subjected to "a terrible and destructive fire of shell and musketry on both front and side, and my command was entirely exposed until it reached the second ridge."[10]

Young Tom Trahey, in Company H, said he was in the front rank with his improvised blanket-pack slung across his chest as the 16th Michigan moved forward, only ten feet or so from the regimental colors as the Rebel batteries blasted. A shell exploded in front of him. "A fragment of it struck me on the blanket directly over my heart and knocked me about ten feet, and knocking down the man behind me," he wrote. He lay stunned, his left side temporarily paralyzed as his regiment advanced. The shell fragment had "cut the blanket into strips," he wrote years later, sure that its bulkiness, with the clothing and paper he rolled up in it, had saved him.

Lt. Charles Salter said the Fifth Corps commander, Gen. Dan Butterfield, gave their brigade the order to charge that evening. "[W]e formed on the run, without attempting to fire as the other troops had done, as by doing so we would only have lost time. The rebels sent out shot and shell amongst us, thick and fast, causing great gaps in the ranks, worse on the right, however, than it was on the left." Yet Stockton said his men were firing as they moved briskly forward. Salter indicated that a line of Confederate riflemen was out in front of their defensive works, and that the advancing Union soldiers "drove the Rebel infantry back to their entrenchments."[11]

"We charge through a heavy fire of grape, canister & shell," wrote Sgt. John Berry of Company A. He, too, recorded that their advance drove the Rebels from the crest of the low hill to their works. Again, this seems to have been a Confederate skirmish line in front of the Sunken Road. The Third Brigade swept past the line of Union dead and engaged the Confederates with rifle fire. Hill said later they had been ordered that night to fix bayonets, charge, and break and carry the Rebel line, but this was simply not possible. In his report, Stockton said only that he advanced his brigade to the crest or ridge "some 500 yards this side of the enemy's position." While Hill, writing decades later, claimed the opposing sides were so close that their bayonets were "almost crossing the line of grey in the Sunken Road," the reality was the Third Brigade did not get that close. Lt. Salter, who was usually accurate in his accounts of battle, said at the time that they reached that second ridge, a point that was somewhere between Stockton's and Hill's estimates of their position; he noted the brigade line was about "40 rods" or 660 feet from "the main works of the enemy."

There was nothing more that the soldiers of the Third Brigade could do—they had made the last charge at Fredericksburg that night, and there were no more brigades or divisions coming up the slope behind them. As they reached the top of the incline or low ridge facing the Rebels, "we became entirely exposed to view, and the Rebels opened upon us with one of the most terrific showers of shell and musketry I have every experienced," Stockton wrote in a report to the state adjutant general. "My whole line returned their fire and steadily advanced." But in truth they did not advance far, if at all; the Confederates, as Salter noted, returned to their Sunken Road trench, and the ridge where the Third Brigade halted afforded some cover to the Union soldiers, if they knelt or lay on the ground to fire over the low rise; they did so.[12]

Accompanying Col. Stockton and his staff, Pvt. George Sidman planted the brigade flag. Soon its shaft was broken and the banner pierced with more than ten minié balls. Sidman was grazed by another bullet but not seriously injured. Sgt. Theodore Bullock from Company D, carrying the 16th Michigan's national colors, was shot through the eye and fell mortally wounded, Lt. Col. Welch would write; Edward Hill, who became one of the regiment's unofficial historians, would later say that Sgt. Henry Wigman from Company A was killed as he carried the flag, a statement supported by the diary of Sgt. John Berry of that company. It appears that both Bullock and Wigman died as color bearers that day.

"From this ridge we poured our first fire," Lt. Salter wrote, emphasizing the point that the soldiers did not stop to shoot as they charged over the plain, waiting until they reached the slight ridge before Marye's Heights. "And then, as we knew it would be useless to attempt to storm the enemy's fortifications, we kept ourselves under cover of this ridge, and kept up a lively firing upon the enemy until after dark, and then both sides stopped, as if by mutual agreement." Stockton agreed on that point: "The ridge scarcely afforded us any shelter, except by lay[ing] down." Sgt. Berry also recorded the regiment fought from the depression once they got near the Rebel defenses. "We then form a line of battle under the crest of a hill & then face the music until night when the firing partially ceases," he wrote. Edward Hill wrote that their brigade, "weak from loss and without support . . . reeled, not in retreat, but sinking and holding to the very earth on which it fell." Night at last covered the battlefield and the firing tailed off.[13]

The last attempt to break the Confederate line by the Third Brigade had failed. Many of the Union soldiers who survived that advance undoubtedly believed that they would now be withdrawn from that terrible field under the cover of darkness, since the all-day assault had been an unmitigated disaster for the Army of the Potomac. But they were wrong—Burnside ordered that they stay where they were. The 16th Michigan and the other regiments on the slope outside of Fredericksburg rested under the slight crest of their ridge, hardly more than a depression in the open field. This position afforded them some cover—their real protection was the darkness, and that was temporary. Company A was sent out in the night as advance pickets. "We exchange a few shots and lay on our arms watching each other until morning," Sgt. John Berry wrote.

"All was quiet, except for the groans and the moans of the wounded and dying," Col. Stockton wrote in his report to state authorities. "During the night, we sent in our wounded but the dead were left as they lay, we having no means of burying them *there*. Orders were received during the night that we must hold this position until 10 a.m. next day, when the 9th Army Corps under Gen. [Orlando] Willcox would make a general attack, when we would be either retiring or instructed to 'go in.'"[14]

Some of the men used their bayonets to try to dig earthworks, to try to create better protection for the coming day. Hundreds of Union dead and wounded were sprawled before the Sunken Road and across the field from Fredericksburg; in the darkness wagons arrived with ammunition and took away the wounded. Young Tom Trahey, probably in shock from blow of the shell fragment that struck his chest, rested with his head on the leg of a dead man; a comrade found him early that morning, picked him up and gave him a cup of coffee, eventually sending him to a field hospital to have his wound dressed. Trahey said he ultimately remained with his regiment, although not fit for regular duty for days.

For his comrades on the field in the December night, the cold was now the enemy. These soldiers had splashed through the mill race, charged up the incline for nearly a half-a-mile, and fought until it was too dark to see. Now they were flat on the ground. "The men suffered from exposure on the bare ground," Edward Hill wrote. "The hours passed all too swiftly, for men amid such dire surroundings realize the fleetness of time and precious boon of life."[15]

There was, it seems, a ridiculous moment of levity that gloomy night on the field where the 16th Michigan lay, and it was provided unwittingly by a sleepy Col. Stockton. According to an anonymous anecdote that survived for years before it was written down, "a Michigan regiment lay down on their arms and were soon asleep" after the battle of Fredericksburg ended that night. When the ammunition wagons came up to bring supplies and remove the wounded, some of the mules began braying by the sleeping colonel, who was, according to the story, "much provoked at being thus so unceremoniously disturbed." Thinking army musicians caused the blaring racket, the disoriented colonel called to his adjutant. "Put those damned buglers under arrest and send them to the rear," the colonel demanded. "They will jeopardize the safety of the whole army." Neither the regiment nor the colonel was identified when this tale appeared in a chapter about the 16th Michigan in an 1871 history book, but the inference was clear that the colonel was Stockton. The anecdote was repeated elsewhere in accounts of the 16th Michigan, though the source of the story and the "old colonel" were never formally named.[16]

The pickets of Company A traded a few more rifle shots with the Confederates at daybreak and retired back to their line of battle under the brow of their hillside depression. "As day dawned (on Sunday, December 14), the Rebels opened fire from a gun on our extreme left with shell," Stockton wrote. "It only threw three, when for some reason, they ceased and did not fire another cannon all day." Several men from the 20th Maine were wounded; though the Confederates could have destroyed hundreds more Union soldiers laying on the field, they did not, apparently waiting to see if Burnside's foolish attack would resume. "The enemy's riflemen, however, were now on the watch and if a man showed himself or rose up, they were instantly fired at," the colonel continued. "They had complete range. No one could leave or approach us."

"Our regiment was on the extreme left and my Company B, on the extreme left of the regiment," Lt. Salter wrote. "Where we were, the ridge ended, and beyond it, to the left was a low field, whilst beyond this was another ridge running in the contrary direction from the one that now protected us." The Rebels sent some men around this ridge to get around the end of the 16th Michigan's line, where "they sent a shower of bullets over amongst us," Salter said. "We however turned our fire in that direction and as our regiment were armed with rather the best rifles, we succeeded after about an hour's sharp firing in driving them back and were not troubled by them any more that day."[17]

The sun rose in the sky and the day slowly warmed. For the men, it was a nerve-wracking wait, trapped under the Confederate guns just a few hundred yards away or less. Thoughts of the Judgment Day and a medieval hymn for the dead crossed the mind of Edward Hill as he turned to look at the cross on the spire of St. George's Church below in Fredericksburg—the "prophetic words of the *Dies Irae*—'Seer and sibyl's word confirming, Heaven and earth to ashes turning.'" Stockton described this state of limbo, waiting in the mud for word to attack or for darkness, when they could be withdrawn. But the colonel reported that "our orders were not to fire or bring on an engagement." It was, he said, "the longest, most solemn and anxious Sabbath *I* have ever spent."

Of course, these soldiers had been without food or water for hours. Two men from each company carefully collected canteens from their comrades, first crawling and then leaping to their feet to run back to the water-filled mill canal hundreds of yards behind them, dodging Confederate rifle fire as they went; then they had to make the return trip, racing back to the hillside depression where their comrades waited. One of the runners was young George Sidman, who had been grazed hours before in the advance; he said he made the run for water with Sgt. Milton Miller, a Genesee County man in his twenties, who would be killed in action in 1864 near Spotsylvania Court House. But the day became warmer and men who had nearly frozen overnight slowly dried off on the ground. "Anxiously, the future was awaited from minute to minute and from hour to hour," Hill wrote. Would Burnside resume the attack? Or would he order them to retreat to safety, once night fell?[18]

Slowly the afternoon turned to evening, the sun finally set, and darkness came on. Those who had spent the past twenty-four hours or so laying on the ground under the Rebel guns now understood that they were not going to die here, or be maimed needlessly as had so many thousands of their comrades. "It was, therefore, with buoyant hearts that the sun's low sinking in the west was watched," Edward Hill wrote; the falling darkness brought relief they would survive another day. Stockton was pleased with the conduct of his officers and men during the battle. "I am proud to report I saw no signs of fear in either officers or men," he said in his report to the Union army.

Lt. Heber Woodruff from Saginaw later wrote to relatives in Wayne County about the night of December 13 and 14. "What do you think of lying 36 hours on your back on the ground, not a thing under you and the ground as wet as water can make it, the weather next thing to freezing[?]" he asked. "All a man [had to do] if he wanted a bullet was to raise up, he got it quick enough." But at 10 p.m., the order was passed, whispered from one soldier to the next: "Fall in for the rear." Other Union soldiers came up to relieve them at the hillside depression before Marye's Heights, to stand picket throughout the night; the Third Brigade withdrew down the hill to sleep in the ruins of Fredericksburg on "the cold and uneven brick sidewalks of Caroline Street," Edward Hill wrote. George Sidman bore away what had been the new brigade colors, its cloth torn, and its pole shot and broken.[19]

The battle had been a disaster for the Army of the Potomac, yet Burnside, for the moment, held onto his job. Somewhere between 35,000 and 40,000 Union soldiers, or eighty-five regiments, charged Marye's Heights; they lost over 7,000 men killed wounded, and missing. Total Union casualties, including the portion of the battle that took place just south of town, were more than 12,000. But Fredericksburg, heavily damaged, provided comparative safety for the survivors in the Third Brigade and thousands of other Union soldiers. "The next day, the 15th, everything was generally quiet about the city except the Rebels would occasionally throw a shell over amongst us probably for the purpose of keeping us awake," Lt. Salter wrote. "I had a good opportunity that day to observe the damage to the city by the bombardment. And I saw entire blocks of brick stores on the main street that had been knocked down by our shot . . . both houses and stores had been burned, and those that were left had been ransacked by our troops."

George Ervay, the teen from Grand Ledge, seems to have been so taken with the pillaging of the town that he included more information to his family about that than he did the battle itself. "The city of Fredericksburg is as large as Lansing and there is not a house in it [that doesn't have] two or three cannon ball holes through it, and the town is riddled from one end to the other," he wrote. "You can think for yourself there was about 75,000 troops in it and they done what they was a-mind to, and took whatever they liked." The soldiers found some 2,000 barrels of flour (presumably in warehouses) "and it was all took by the soldiers," he said. "You better believe the pancakes flew, every man was baking wheat pancakes to eat. I had all I could stuff."[20]

But at last Gen. Burnside concluded his Fredericksburg campaign failed, and there was nothing more to be done. The night of December 15 the Army of the Potomac withdrew back across the Rappahannock River. The Fifth Corps acted as rear guard, protecting the retreating soldiers; the 16th Michigan and the Third Brigade of which they were part would be some of the last Union troops to leave. Col. Stockton was sick after being in the battle and on the freezing field, so he left for the brigade's old camp site on the east side of the river near the railroad line. Col. Strong Vincent of the 83rd Pennsylvania took command of the brigade; the men went back out under the cover of darkness to relieve the line of Union troops in the field before the Confederate positions and guns, leaving town on Hanover Street, over a small rise called Federal Hill, and then across a small bridge over the mill race.

They crossed the fields where so many had died, moving back up the gentle slope with its swales. Even in the darkness, the toll of the battle, the sheer number of the dead, was stunning. "In going out there we passed about ½ miles more to the right (north) than we had on Saturday afternoon whilst making our charge, and over the ground where the hardest fighting had taken place," he said, "and nearly all of the dead lay strewn upon the ground yet. In one place we passed where they lay as thick as if a brigade had been ordered to lay down. . . . Supposing it to be the troops we were to relieve, I asked what brigade that was, when someone said they were dead men[. A]nd upon examination, it proved to be so. I thought I had seen some pretty hard sights since I have been in this war, but I never saw anything so horrible as that before."[21]

Lt. Woodruff said the men dropped to the ground when the moon emerged from the clouds as they went over the battlefield, and they quietly cursed the soldier "who rattled his tin pail" or mess kit. A sleeting rain set in as the Third Brigade relieved the soldiers at the front, who withdrew back to town and across the river. "There we lay half the night, watching the dead so thick we could hardly tell the living from the dead," he wrote. Between 3 and 4 a.m., the Third Brigade quietly pulled out, too, following the bed of an unfinished railroad back through the outskirts of Fredericksburg, arriving at the river by 7 a.m.

"We marched down to the bridge and our regiment were the last ones to cross except a few of the engineers who were waiting to take up the bridge," Lt. Salter wrote. Edward Hill claimed that some of the anxious engineers had already cut away the pontoons connected to Fredericksburg's steamboat wharves, but a sharp rebuke from Gen. Butterfield soon had the bridge back in place. It was daylight when the last Union soldiers crossed over to the eastern side of the river, and Col. Stockton was proud that his brigade had helped ensure that all the Union personnel evacuated Fredericksburg before the Confederates realized what had happened.[22]

Incredibly, the 16th Michigan's casualties at this disastrous battle were surprisingly small compared to others. Because their part in the assault took place as darkness fell, only three men were killed in action with thirty-nine men wounded, though about a quarter of the wounded men were severely hurt; the regiment's death toll rose to eleven as several more of these soldiers died in the days after the battle. Their Third Brigade had suffered a combined 200 casualties. The 16th Michigan's wounded included Capt. Theodore Mahan from Adrian and Lt. Thomas F. Hughes of Company H, a Detroit man who had joined the company formed by Capt. Stephen Martin back in the summer of 1861. Another of the wounded was Sgt. Sylvester Ostrander, 26, from Redford, in Company G. After the battle, Ostrander was taken to a large mansion on the Falmouth side of the Rappahannock called the Lacy House—also called Chatham Manor—which served as a Union headquarters and hospital. While there, the wounded Ostrander scribbled his name on the wall of the building's morning room, where it is legible today. Ostrander's name was long covered over but discovered in 1994.[23]

Lt. Charles Salter, who usually showed a clear-eyed view of events and who had not been enamored of Gen. George McClellan, blamed the government and presumably the Lincoln administration—not Gen. Burnside—for the disaster at Fredericksburg. He felt the administration simply had not sent enough troops to the Army of the Potomac, while committing thousands of other Union troops on campaigns that were not as important as taking the Confederate capital. “It seems to me, lately, that our rulers are going mad and are trying to do their best to destroy the army,” he wrote. “But I suppose it seems worse to me, here, than it does to the people of the country North. Yet I cannot help wishing that the people of the North and South could have all seen that horrible massacre, for if they had they would be willing to settle up on the war upon terms without ever fighting another battle.”

Col. Stockton, back in camp after the battle, filed his reports with state and federal authorities and raised with Adjt. Gen. John Robertson the issue of his lack of promotion. “For the past three months, [I] have had command of this brigade,” he wrote. “I feel as I had justly earned and am entitled to promotion. Many others have been, without going through *half* what I have. I ask, therefore, that the Governor will do me justice, by urging my claim for a brigadiership [*sic*].” The colonel included a list of casualties and names of men for promotion, and ended his letter on an old complaint—he needed more soldiers. “My regiment is now very small and I sincerely trust [that] active and immediate measures may be taken to fill it up at once,” he concluded.[24]

Lt. Col. Welch also wrote a letter after the battle, to his friend Benjamin Fisher, the former captain of the Saginaw company who was now the major of the 23rd Michigan Infantry, then camped near Bowling Green, Kentucky. “How are you, you old cuss,” Welch greeted him. “I know you are bully, but are you as mean as ever?” Welch poked fun at Fisher for getting in trouble with the army for failing to file required paperwork, and he told Fisher about the casualties of the 16th Michigan and its corps at Fredericksburg.

“We had a d—d of a fight on last Saturday 13th inst. and as usual got d——dly whipped,” he wrote. “I am all right and safe, as usual, at the head of my regiment, but would have given a heap to have been behind it—a good ways behind it. Fool for luck. Everybody is mad at our unsuccessful enterprise. [Gen. Joe] Hooker is swearing a good deal in your style—not very bad, but still as to be understood.”[25]

Welch’s letter gives a glimpse of his personality, outgoing and personable, joking with his old friend and using self-deprecating humor, but also reflecting his confident leadership. “We are in a pine country and that don’t burn very well, especially when green,” he continued about the 16th Michigan’s camp on the railroad, several miles from Fredericksburg. “I’ll bet if a load of green pine, such as we have, was dumped into h—l, it would put the whole concern out in 15 minutes.” He asked if Fisher still played chess, and he noted that he and Capt. Judd Mott still played occasionally. “All your old friends are well,” he continued. “I often think of you and the days gone by. Now Tom [Stockton] is gone, I have much of my time to myself and my memory groups together old associations and pleasant hours and wreathes them into festoons of remembrances . . . There are a thousand thoughts that please my musing fancy, and to be alone and think of old times is half my pleasure.”[26]

It seems that Welch’s life was easier with Col. Stockton away, and even soldiers in the regiment understood that there was a tension between the two officers; the colonel’s diary entries over the past year showed plainly that he had been at times disapproving and even angry with Welch. In the weeks ahead, their relationship would become even more adversarial, with Stockton and Welch practically at war with each other over the leadership of the 16th Michigan.

Christmas morning was foggy in the camp at Stoneman's Station though the day turned pleasant. "But it is not much like Christmas," Sgt. John Berry regretted. "We have the same hard fare of hard bread, salt pork and coffee, [and] with the exception of drills, the same duties to perform as in other days." It was the second Christmas Berry had spent in the army and neither had been a merry holiday. The next one, he hoped, "will be in old Michigan."[27]

There was action as the year ended, with their entire division called out to march on the afternoon of December 30. This seems to have been start of another ill-fated plan by Gen. Burnside, but one that was stopped before it got too far—a diversionary move or feint while most of the Army of the Potomac would attack again across the Rappahannock. Some soldiers guessed it was an attempt to intercept Jeb Stuart's cavalry on yet another raid, though Lt. Salter heard a wag joke about the Emancipation Proclamation, which was to go into effect on January 1. "As the Negroes would all be free on the 1st, we were going out to drive them in," this soldier joked unsympathetically about slaves. "That is, if the rebels did not drive us in." But Griffin's First Division of the Fifth Corps did march nine miles west, stopped to rest, and continued on to Ellis Ford on the river, bivouacking in the wet and cold that made it impossible for the soldiers to sleep.

In the morning they moved down to the river, their skirmishers finding Rebel cavalry troopers there. Both sides fired and the troopers rode off. "[A] secesh lady living in a house close by was, unfortunately, wounded by a stray shot which was fired at Rebel soldiers near the house," Salter wrote. "Our surgeon attended to her case, but she did not seem to mind it at all but on the contrary said she was used to having bullets whistle and did not mind them at all, but would much rather that she be hit than to see one of the rebel soldiers hit." A historian with the 118th Pennsylvania wrote that the woman was wounded when Confederate sharpshooters fired from her house and Union soldiers returned their fire. The woman was struck in the thigh and survived.[28]

The 16th Michigan and the other regiments of the Third Brigade stayed that day at the ford while other commands made a reconnaissance of the area. The plan to attack Rebel troops at nearby Kelly's Ford was canceled, so their division camped in the woods and marched back to their camp on the morning of January 1, covering fourteen miles in about four hours. "It shows why our brigade is called the 'light brigade,'" Salter wrote. "We were pretty tired after we reached camp and therefore we could not be said to have enjoyed our New Year's very well." Still, he continued, the soldiers had reason to be thankful to God for having survived 1862, "to think that whilst so many of our comrades have fallen in battle, from disease and died from wounds received in the battle, that there are 250 of us left yet to serve and fight for our country when it is needed."[29]

Col. Stockton, meanwhile, had gotten a leave of absence after the battle of Fredericksburg and gone to Washington. Though he was ill, he was not so sick that he could not read the newspapers, and he was angry that Michigan Adjutant General John Robertson had not sent his account about the Third Brigade and the 16th Michigan to the Detroit newspapers. "Did you receive my official report of the battle of Fredericksburg with a list of killed wounded and missing?" Stockton demanded. "I had . . . allowed myself that you must have had the letter, at least, published as has been done, I see by the paper with other Michigan regiments." Stockton resented that the 10th Michigan Infantry, which contained many Flint area soldiers, "blazes forth [in the papers] its every trivial act." No regiment, he charged, had "done or performed its duties better or more faithfully that this same 16th Regiment."[30]

But the colonel's dramatic report of the Fredericksburg never appeared in Michigan newspapers, and he was no closer to getting his brigadier's star. In the coming months, Stockton would finally arrive at the inescapable conclusion that this simply was not his war.

10.

JANUARY–APRIL 1863

THIS CUSSED SOIL OF VIRGINIA

"We occupy the same camps yet and everything goes on in the same old way as before the battle," Lt. Charles Salter wrote after the new year, "and all traces of that affair have disappeared from amongst us, and we are only reminded of it by the decimated ranks of the regiments that were engaged and the numerous graves that have increased so fearfully of late amongst us." Now the soldiers were back to drill, picket, guard duty, and the routine of army life. He said the army had "just received the long expected Emancipation Proclamation of the President," and he supposed the proclamation reflected the government's "plans and policy," meaning its conduct of the war and its aims. "I hope it will change for the better," he wrote.

Salter said he had been plagued with doubts about the war, but a sermon sent by friends in Detroit convinced him to stay in the service and keep up the fight. He told them that he had tried to live the life of Christian and to keep the Ten Commandments "as well as I could here in the army," and he believed this, and prayer, had kept him alive "through all the hardships and dangers I have passed through." There was time to pray before battles, he wrote, "when we are lying down in line of battle behind a ridge or hill waiting for the enemy to charge, or perhaps to charge ourselves."[1]

His brigade's commander, Col. Thomas Stockton, thought about religion somewhat differently. According to George Sidman, sometime during the winter of 1862–1863, the chaplain of the 20th Maine asked if he could address the men of the 16th Michigan on the upcoming Sabbath. The chaplain bragged that he baptized 15 men from his regiment the week before. Stockton, Sidman claimed, turned to his aide. "Adjutant, detail 30 men of the 16th for baptism next Sunday," he said, to the surprise of the Maine chaplain. "I don't propose to let the 20th Maine get ahead of my regiment." Of course, the story may be myth, like the recurring Civil War story of the officer crying in pain with a supposed wound in his foot when it was not there. It could be that other soldiers told the story of the bragging chaplain, inserting their particular colonel and the chaplain of a rival regiment.

But Sidman apparently enjoyed recounting the story for years. Stockton, he declared, "was a blunt old man."[2]

Gen. Burnside held a grand review of the Fifth Corps on January 7, but there were no regimental bands anymore, so "it did not seem as pleasant an affair as when we were received a year ago on Minor's Hill by Gen. McClellan," Lt. Salter said. "The great difference in the numbers of the old regiments makes it seem as if they were only skeletons of what they once were." Of course, many soldiers were also angry and disgusted with Burnside, though Salter did not mention that. There were periodic pleasant days, though almost invariably picket duty was cold and miserable. The day after the review, the 16th Michigan marched four miles to the west to stand picket and the men missed the comfort of the winter camp. On the 9th, a Brady sharpshooter from Kent County named Hiram Gallup, 29, died of illness and Alfred Apted noted his passing. "'Tis hard to leave our numbers on this cussed soil of Virginia, but so it is. God doeth all things well," he wrote.

Inclement weather prevented much from happening when the regiment was back at the large Union encampment near the railroad. "No stir in camp today," wrote Grand Ledge teenager George Ervay on January 10, "on account of its being rainy weather." In his spare time, he carved rings from laurel root for his relatives back home. The next day, the regiment's surgeon, Dr. Isaac Wixom, paid a visit to a volunteer nurse and widow in her mid-forties from Maine named Harriet Eaton, who was staying in a nearby house while she and a colleague from their church visited sick soldiers from Maine regiments, delivering apples and clothing, and making them cocoa, tea, and treats. The women had been at this since October, and Eaton had been under fire from across the river at Fredericksburg. She had witnessed dying men, and what she considered callous treatment of sick soldiers by the army, but she was surprised at Wixom's use of combinations of large doses of powerful drugs on his patients, which she said would "kill or cure them." Wixom agreed this was true. "[T]he way he puts medicine down a man's throat would frighten a Northerner," Eaton wrote. But she liked Wixom, and later that day she took tea and crackers to the sick men in the 16th Michigan's regimental hospital.

Dr. Wixom was more than a little interested in Eaton, an abolitionist, regularly visiting her, advising her and her associate on medicines and treatments, and even carrying pails of tea she made for sick soldiers. The surgeon's periodic social calls continued for weeks, with the doctor telling her late in February that "he is becoming an abolitionist." Soon he apparently raised the subject of marriage with her, but Eaton was committed to her work. "He is a strange man," she recorded in March about Wixom. "He had some *special business* with me today and I think he will understand my answer to his inquiries." Eaton did not encourage Wixom, but apparently respected him.[3]

Plans for marching and fighting for the Army of the Potomac in a new winter offensive were still very much on the mind of Gen. Burnside; by the middle of January, he ordered preparations. The sick were moved to hospitals in Washington, and ammunition and provisions were issued to the regiments. "I do not know what the plan of the attack upon the rebels is to be, but I have confidence in Gen. Burnside to believe that he will not send us into such a trap as we were sent in to last time," Lt. Salter wrote. "I hear a rumor that we are to cross the river both above and below the rebel stronghold [at Fredericksburg] and attempt to outflank them, but of course we cannot tell until the time of the attack arrives what the plan is to be." In the meantime, the 16th Michigan lost more officers, some temporarily, others permanently. Maj. Thomas Barry of Detroit, who had recovered from his wound at the second Bull Run battle, was sick and allowed to go home to recover; Lt. Jonas Titus, an officer in the Brady Sharpshooters, was also sick, and he resigned. So did Lt. Jacob Webber of Company G, from Lansing. "This together with the number of officers who are away sick or wounded leaves us only 17 officers in our regiment," Salter explained.

Col. Thomas Stockton was still on sick leave, so Col. Strong Vincent of the 83rd Pennsylvania continued to command the Third Brigade. Salter said Vincent was "a very good officer . . . liked by the entire brigade." He insisted the army was in "tip top spirits" and ready to fight again, though the men dreaded marching and bivouacking in winter weather. Of course, other accounts say the morale of thousands of soldiers was poor, that there was much desertion and debate over Burnside and his poor leadership, though some gave him the benefit of the doubt, like Salter. These men wondered if Burnside was being pressured by Lincoln and Republican leaders to continue an offensive when the weather made the movement of the army so difficult and dangerous to the men's health. Though the average soldier did not know it, some of the Army of the Potomac's generals were extremely critical of Burnside and actively ensuring President Lincoln knew that they had no confidence in him.[4]

THE "MUD MARCH"

Lt. Salter told his friends he was pursuing a commission in the regular army since he felt that promotions in the volunteer regiments were not made fairly. More significantly, he advised them to watch for news of a great battle in the coming days. But there was no great battle. Burnside's attempt to launch a midwinter offensive turned into the infamous "Mud March." Two days after Lt. Salter wrote his letter, the Fifth Corps' First Division began its part in this ill-fated movement, marching west as rain began to fall on January 20. "We started to reach the river at one of the fords above [upstream from] here," Salter wrote about the campaign's beginning. "The roads were in a bad condition before we started, and on that day the rain commenced again and the storm continued for about 48 hours." The roads quickly clogged as the columns of soldiers and wagons ahead of Salter's regiment bogged down in the thick mud, and they moved only three miles before bivouacking in sodden woods. Because the soldiers left their tents behind in camp, "we received the full benefit of the water," the lieutenant said sarcastically. The next day, the mud was so deep horses and mules could not move the artillery batteries, so "the infantry had to take hold and assist in to drag the cannon and caissons," he continued. Their part of the column took all day to move six miles.

Yet conditions got worse. On January 22, it was impossible to move the artillery at all, nor could the wagons carrying provisions reach the men laboring up the road in the rain. “We had to go to work building a corduroy road to save us from starvation and to get the artillery back to camp,” Salter said, referring to the need to return the guns, once the offensive was canceled. “Our regiment had a certain portion of the road given to them to build. The road ran through a large plantation, and as we had no axes, [we] had to use fence rails to build the road.” As the soldiers quickly took down the fencing and carried it off, the ex-slaves who lived and worked on the plantation laughed uproariously, Salter wrote, using a racist term for blacks common at the time. “[T]he darkies came out of the house and it seemed as if they would go crazy with laughing at the strange sight,” he said. Sometime that day, Burnside decided the offensive was canceled, and the army had to return to its encampments.[5]

Pvt. George Ervay of Company H was with those soldiers detailed to guard their First Division’s wagon train. Drivers attempted to move the wagons to take rations to hungry troops still on the road on January 23, but it did not work. “Very muddy,” he noted “Three wagons tipped over.” The Confederate troops on the other side of the Rappahannock put up their own statement about the unsuccessful Union movement, creating a kind of scarecrow or a figure made of mud, rather than snow. “The soldiers made a man and put it up and then put up a sign and on it said ‘Gen. Burnside stuck in the mud,’” Ervay wrote. After two days of struggling in the muck, and building corduroy roads to get back to their winter camp near Potomac Creek, Burnside’s winter offensive was officially over.

“I think our generals are satisfied also that no active campaign can be carried on in Virginia before the last of March or the first of April,” Lt. Salter wrote. “Marched back to our old camp, mud knee deep,” Pvt. Apted agreed. “Reached camp tired and heavy, and so ends Burnside’s second campaign of ‘stuck in the mud.’” It also marked the end of Burnside’s command of the army, and he was replaced by Gen. Joseph Hooker. Sgt. Frank Keeler of Saginaw could not help joking about the foolish winter campaign. “If no other end has been attained,” he wrote, probably with a grin, “it has at least served to establish a deeper intimacy on part of horses and men with the ‘sacred (sub-) soil of Virginia.’”[6]

Sgt. Keeler could joke about Burnside’s final failure, but thousands of soldiers were ill that winter. One of them was Jacob Craw, a 35-year-old man from Argentine Township in Genesee County. Craw had joined the 16th Michigan’s Company I in October near Antietam, and soon fell ill on the march to Warrenton before the battle of Fredericksburg. “I have found out by sad experience that health is the greatest blessing that anyone can be possessed with,” he wrote to a friend. “No one knows the life of a soldier until they realize it, for when men, if once enlisted and got to the seat of war, they [officers] don’t think any more of them than they would a hog, especially if they are not fit for duty.”

Craw was initially hospitalized for three weeks beginning on November 19 and was then sent to a convalescent camp, probably at Alexandria. It was, he said, “the awfulest place that anyone ever see [*sic*], for anyone that is human to stay at.” He had been put to work on a new hospital camp, probably because authorities decided the existing one had become unhealthy, and he wrote that thousands of men were there. As January ended, Craw wrote again to his friend Agnes Lindley. "I have often thought of you and your folks and of the times I was there last winter, but now I am a good ways from there," he wrote. "I would like to see you very much and I mean to come down there as soon as I get back home, if God should spare my life to get back. I can't see much signs of peace."[7]

Back in camp after the "Mud March," Lt. Ziba Graham of Flint also wrote home, telling of the problems of unpaid soldiers. "The main body of our troops have over six months' pay due them," he wrote. "Consequently, sutlers are a scare commodity, money and tobacco ditto. Old tobacco chewers who have never before known the want of *weed* now go around as if they had lost their best friend; they really command pity." His brigade commander and fellow Flint resident, Col. Stockton, returned to camp briefly from Washington but soon departed again on medical leave before February was over. For the soldiers, bad weather got in the way of a regimental inspection, causing three days of postponement. Sgt. John Berry of the Upper Peninsula sarcastically recorded this. "It snows too much for the general to show himself," he noted on February 6, the second delay in the inspection. The next day was more of the same; "[t]he general finds it very inconvenient to wade through so much mud, so he has the inspection countermanded."[8]

At least the new commander of the Army of the Potomac, Gen. Joseph Hooker, was instituting measures for better food, stoves for baking bread, and more hospitals and better medical care. The men had long since fixed up their winter quarters, using their tents for roofs and building up log walls and fireplaces or using stoves to heat their quarters. William H. Borden of Ionia County had been promoted late in the fall to lieutenant, and now served in Company F; he called their winter home "a very good camp, as good as there is any." The soldiers were getting fresh bread four times a week, and potatoes and onions twice a week. "They have been bringing up ovens and we are a-going to put them up," he explained. "That don't look much as though we were going to move from here right off." Of course, his last remark was one of relief, since bringing up ovens signaled no more offensives in the dead of winter.

Pvt. Marion Munson, from the northeastern corner of Oakland County and in the regiment's Company E, agreed about the improved rations. Though he had complaints about the generals, President Lincoln, and the war itself, he was pleased the soldiers were well fed. "Potatoes, fresh beef, pork, beans, onions, rice, and soft bread and in fact everything a soldier could wish," he wrote.[9]

But sickness exacted a devastating toll. Lt. Salter's company now had thirty-four members present for duty and twenty men reported sick; six men were on detached service (that is, doing assignments outside of regular duty in their regiment) and two men were absent without leave. "When we left Yorktown, we had 103 men," he said, with sixty-five of them present for duty. Salter hoped he could transfer into the regular army and become a professional soldier as a career that would continue for him after the war, but he had little time to work on that. "I feel sometimes as if I was tired of soldiering," he admitted, "and would like to be home rather than endure all the hardships we have to, but then

I feel that whilst the war lasts, it is my duty to do all I can to put down the rebellion."[10] Soon Salter would give up the idea of joining the U.S. Army, finding out that regular army commissions were nearly impossible to get.

Sgt. Berry recorded that one of Company A's respected officers was leaving. "Capt. George Prentiss, having at last got his resignation accepted, bids us goodbye," Berry wrote, giving an incorrect rank for Prentiss, a first lieutenant who had expected to be promoted. "He is the bravest and best officer without exception in this regiment. It is a great loss to Co. A that he has left us in a very dangerous position. [When] he was there, the welfare of the company was his constant study. The reason of his tendering his resignation was caused by a dispute of seniority between him and Capt. [George] Swan." Both Prentiss and Swan were Detroiters and had started out in that company as lieutenants, but their dispute caused Prentiss to end his service.[11]

While soldiers held differing views on abolition and slavery as central issues of the war, they tended be united in their view of conscription, the government's compelling men to serve in the army—something that was in the news as the U.S. Congress moved closer to approving a new bill that aimed to stimulate volunteer enlistments by "the threat of a draft."[12] While some soldiers were empathetic to drafted men's real fear of death or wounds, volunteers in regiments like the 16th Michigan had faced those same dangers for more than a year now; some thought of the men back home as shirkers and cowards. This feeling was illustrated in a story George Ervay heard from a tent mate. According to this soldier, two provost guards, essentially military police, overheard a conversation between three men, civilians, walking down the nearby railroad tracks, with one man telling the others how he had escaped the draft (both the Union and the Confederacy had enacted conscription laws in the summer of 1862). The guards took the men at gunpoint to Col. Stockton, the story continued. "He put them in the guard house and kept them on bread and water for four days and then let them go, telling them if he caught them back there he would tar and feather them," Ervay wrote, capping off the story. Who, exactly, were these men? Virginian civilians? Northern civilians working on the railroad line for the government? The young soldier did not say.

Ervay, who like many men used racist terms for blacks, also wrote of a circulating army rumor that riled him and other soldiers. This story, a false one, was that the federal government was about to impose a tax on Union soldiers to support the ex-slaves declared free under the Emancipation Proclamation. Some soldiers talked of desertion rather than submitting to a tax to support black refugees, to whom the soldiers referred as "contrabands." Ervay did not like idea of such a tax (which did not exist), but said he would not desert. "For if a man stays here, it is death a[nd] if he falls out when they are going into the fight[,] it is instant death [by execution] and if you desert[,] it is sure death [by execution]. So I should prefer living honorable and dying honorable, for as to live in danger of my life as long as I have, and been in as many battles as I have, then to desert is more than I shall do."[13]

The Third Brigade went on picket duty for four days to one of its usual locations a few miles west of camp, near the Rappahannock. While most of the regiments were gone, men left in camp got drunk and rowdy, but the colonel was having none of that. "Old Col. Stockton, who is acting brigade general at headquarters, hears of the spree or smells it, comes over to the camp and hauls over everybody and everything in general," wrote John Berry, who was acting orderly sergeant that day. As officer of the guard, Berry was kept busy arresting intoxicated soldiers the rest of the day and night, per Stockton's instructions.

"We have been kept busy lately in putting our camp in good order," Lt. Salter wrote that month. "We have made a brush fence all around it, and set shade trees out all over the camp, and have trimmed it up about as neatly as a camp could be." Their commander from Ann Arbor oversaw this landscaping. "Some of the officers are inclined to think that our Lt. Col. Welch, who is now in command of the regiment, can superintend such work better than he can a battalion drill, at least since he has had command of the regiment he has avoided battalion drill very carefully." He noted the landscaping certainly impressed visiting civilians from Detroit.[14]

Saginaw's Lt. Heber Woodruff got around to writing to his aunt and uncle in Wayne County, telling them about army life and some of his experiences at Fredericksburg. He also wondered about life back in Michigan and neighborhood characters. "I suppose nothing has been changed and nothing changes except what has been caused by 'Death' & 'Marriages,' the same old houses in the same condition. Old Gentleman Alfred lounges about as usual telling his yarns[.] John Gori will still find things where they are not lost[.] Darkey Green still cracks his whips over 4 yoke of oxen. John Van Riper is still an old 'Bach' and lastly John Miller owns 'Whip Tiger.' Or is it all changed, who is married and who died? I can hard realize that I ever lived there, it seems a dream." Woodruff did not mind being a soldier, at least as long as the war lasted. Though he would not want to be in the army otherwise, he said his health was good and he could deal with its discomforts. But he added that he felt that young men back home should be serving in the army, while older men and family men should remain at home.[15]

The discussion of the draft continued when the new conscription bill passed in early March. "[The legislation] seems to give great satisfaction to our army," Lt. Salter wrote, "the soldiers in general are greatly pleased to think that the government is now bound to bring out men enough to crush the rebellion, whether they are willing to enlist or not. There will not be much pity for the drafted men here in the old regiments."

Artillery and gunboats on the Potomac fired in honor of George Washington's birthday, and the cynical Pvt. Marion Munson could not help but compare the current president, Lincoln, with the Father of his Country. He predicted that Lincoln would be harshly judged by history. "Everyone will begrudge him his time on earth," he wrote, "and when he dies, he will go down like throwing a stone in the water, chug." Munson disapproved of the Emancipation Proclamation and of the removal of George McClellan, and he called Lincoln "the vilest of the vile." He said he was opposed to slavery and thought it should be outlawed "on every foot of soil in the Union." But for white men to shoot each other down over the question, he said, was "a base, mean and barbarous act."[16]

A heavy snow fell on February 22, and it might have been no consequence to the 16th Michigan except for the events it set in motion. Three days after the storm, Lt. Col. Norval Welch ordered his men to build a snow fort. "Yesterday the colonel turned the men out and he laid a plan for a fort and they went to work and put up a snow fort," George Ervay. "The colonel said that today he would put the right wing of the regiment in the fort and the left wing had got to take it from them. He says the left wing is enough for the right wing any time at snow balling . . . and he thinks that we can drive them out of a snow fort with snowballs. The fort was four feet and 8 inches high and [had] a four-foot wall." But another soldier, Pvt. Alfred Apted of the Brady Sharpshooters, was not feeling well and he was not amused by Welch's order for a snow fort and snowball fight. "The colonel ordered all the men out to help build a snow fort. A big thing," he wrote with sarcasm. "But I could not see it, or to work at it, so I was sent to the guard house."[17]

Rain came in and melted the snow, ending Welch's plan for a snowball fight. Still, he wanted Apted punished for insubordination; he ordered the sharpshooter's pay stopped for a month's time on his company payroll. But Apted was not going to accept this punishment without a fight. He appealed to Col. Stockton, explaining that he had been unwell and refused to "carry snow, considering that as this was but for the gratification of Lt. Col. Welch, and not being military duty, it was not necessary for me to do so. For thus refusing," he continued, "I was tied up by the wrists with my hands over my head and placed in the guard house and compelled to stand in the snow and so kept from about 3 o'clock till past 11 o'clock without food or shelter from the inclemency of the weather (the guard house being unfinished at the time)."[18]

Apted pointed out that he had never been in trouble before and faithfully served his regiment for just over a year. He asked that the matter of his severe and arbitrary punishment by Welch be examined; Stockton immediately countermanded Welch's order stopping Apted's pay. But Welch refused and appealed Stockton's order to their First Division headquarters. The months-long feud between Stockton and Welch now came to a head.

Welch had been chafing over the fact that though he was technically in charge of the regiment when Stockton was commanding the entire brigade, the reality was that Stockton ran the regiment, too. That included recommending men for promotion within the regiment, and it meant Stockton's picks, not Welch's, got promotions since the governor and his military advisor generally did not meddle in these, but usually issued officers' commissions in a regiment based on their commander's recommendation. Welch brought the issue up with Stockton's old nemesis, Gov. Austin Blair, stating that the 16th Michigan would have been better served by the promotion of men chosen by him rather than Stockton. Because the colonel was often acting in the role of brigade commander, "he cannot know the most meritorious cases" within the regiment. "He (Stockton) promotes entirely from seniority to the exclusion of as gallant as officers and men as ever goes around," Welch charged.[19] Though Welch was known to be a War Democrat, his complaints about Stockton, a McClellan man, almost certainly got the attention of Gov. Blair.

This feud was bigger than the Apted pay stoppage and the question of who should recommend promotions. Welch initiated an investigation into Stockton's friend, the regimental surgeon, Dr. Isaac Wixom, whom Welch suspected of misusing hospital rations and medicinal liquor. Soon both Welch and Wixom would face formal charges as spring came on; the dispute between Stockton and Welch would also cost the careers of certain officers too closely associated with the colonel.

The weather remained rainy and snowy in early March, an uneventful time except for a skirmish with some Confederate cavalry who, Lt. Salter said, "made a dash at our pickets," apparently hoping to destroy a bridge over the nearby Potomac Creek near this important Union supply center and railroad depot; the Rebels were driven back. A rumor went around the Michigan regiments that some of them would be sent home to enforce the new conscription law, and some thought how lucky it would be to get such duty in Michigan. Salter questioned how "fortunate" it would be to have to "drag men away from their homes to place them amongst the horrors of war. And yet it is no worse for them than it is for us who have volunteered." The lieutenant said he wrestled with such questions, like the morality of fighting and killing while believing that the struggle "is such a holy one." Salter had seen death in all forms now, and realized how "thoughtless and careless" he had been previously, before learning "how frail is human life, and soon we may be called into eternity at any moment." He had also come to understand "what a small consequence, apparently, the life of a human being is." Salter thought it disgraceful, however, when he read about the draft riots in Detroit and how local authorities had not been able to quell them. "If there had been a company from one of the old regiments there," he wrote, "I think they would have scattered the mob in a very few minutes."[20]

With the appointment of Gen. Joe Hooker to the command of the Army of the Potomac came yet another reorganization of the army. Gen. George Meade, a West Pointer and Pennsylvanian who had previously led a brigade and division, now became commander of the Fifth Corps, of which the 16th Michigan was part. While Hooker quickly improved food and medical care, he also had to deal with serious rates of desertion; he instituted a system so that more officers and men could go on leave. But there were victims who got caught in this system, seemingly through no fault of their own or because, perhaps, senior officers used the rules to get rid of rivals or opponents, as in the case of Capt. Judd Mott.

In the 16th Michigan, Mott, Capt. Robert Elliott, and Maj. Thomas Barry had been allowed to go on leaves back to Michigan that winter, but had stayed beyond their deadlines to return to their regiment. They did not do this arbitrarily, but because they were ordered by a U.S. Army colonel in Detroit to wait, to take draftees back with them. But in the Army of the Potomac, generals ruled that Lt. Col. Smith, the federal commander in Michigan, did not have the authority to keep these officers (and other officers from Michigan regiments) on extended leaves. "Gen. Griffin [commander of the First Division of the Fifth Corps] says he will have them tried by a military board to see if their prolonged stay is legal," Lt. Salter wrote about this issue.

Yet it would turn out that Elliott and Barry, who had the support of Lt. Col. Norval Welch, received minimal penalties, while Capt. Judd Mott, who had been friendly with Col. Stockton, was court-martialed and initially ordered dismissed from the army. Barry, it should be noted, had been promoted to major at Welch's recommendation when

Stockton was a prisoner of war, just as Elliott would also soon be promoted at Welch's recommendation.[21]

But the routine of camp life continued, except when Brady Sharpshooter Orrin Hopkins from St. Clair County accidentally injured himself. The private had already been wounded in action at Malvern Hill, but this accident would mean his discharge on disability in the coming summer. Sharpshooter Pvt. Alfred Apted recorded a difference of opinion between their Brady company comrades and Lt. Col. Welch about the weapons the sharpshooters should use; Welch wanted them to use Sharps rifles, but in the slang of the day, Apted said, "we do not see the place."

Pvt. George Ervay told his parents he quit chewing tobacco, though he took up smoking occasionally "for to keep the hanker off." It was an expensive habit, he wrote, with tobacco costing him $11.25 from the time the regiment got paid at Harrison's Landing back in the summer up to the time they drew pay after Fredericksburg. "I made up my mind that the money I would spend for tobacco would do you more good than it did for me," he wrote. Henry "Tip" Aplin from Flint had been thinking about what would become of his mother if he died in the war. "Tip wrote to me some time ago to get a will drawn up and sent to him and he would sign it," Elvira Aplin wrote to another son, "so that what little he owned would fall to me if he should be so unfortunate as to never return."[22]

On St. Patrick's Day, some of the men of the regiment were on picket duty on the Rappahannock, chatting amiably with their Rebel counterparts on the other side. "They told our men that the war would be settled by the first of July," young George Ervay wrote home to Grand Ledge. The soldiers tried trading newspapers, throwing them (unsuccessfully) across the river, he said. Back in camp, the Irish regiments celebrated. "Horse racing, chasing a greased pig and climbing [a] greased pole are the sports most indulged in, and it seem to fit the rollicking nature of the Irish soldier," Sgt. Frank Keeler wrote. Pvt. Apted indicated that soldiers were actually killed while horse racing. More significantly, there was a tremendous clash of Union and Rebel cavalry about 15 miles to the northwest near the Rappahannock that day, and soldiers in their camps near the railroad line heard their batteries firing; some were put on alert. Apted and Keeler were among those who heard the guns, though their regiment was not called out.[23]

The spring weather remained fickle. One of the 16th Michigan's officers, seemingly Robert Elliott, commanding Company E and the regiment's senior captain, held a battalion drill while in a state of intoxication that was obvious to his men. "Captain foolin,' drilling us," George Ervay of Company H noted in his diary. "He was so drunk he had to dismiss us." The soldiers were able to play ball and watch officers hold horse races, with Ervay and diarist Alfred Apted recording respectively that Welch's horse won hundreds, or that he lost $15.[24] Whatever purses Welch's "splendid black horse" won or lost, another contest was playing out between the lieutenant colonel and Col. Thomas Stockton for control of the 16th Michigan. On March 28, at Welch's behest, the regiment's surgeon Dr. Isaac Wixom was placed under arrest to face court-martial.

Wixom had marked his 60th birthday when the proceedings began in a tent near the headquarters of the First Division of the Fifth Corps. The doctor had tried to resign back in November, but Col. Stockton had for some reason refused to send up his papers through the command chain to authorize it. Now Wixom had to defend himself on charges that he had misused hospital rations, that is, taken army food specifically allotted for sick soldiers from October on through December 1862, and that he had also misused medicinal government liquor. Initially, the surgeon was also charged with cursing and questioning the conduct of the war in front of officers and men alike after the battle of Fredericksburg, and also in response to the news of the Emancipation Proclamation.[25]

The judge advocate or prosecutor was a captain from a New York regiment, and the court-martial hearing Wixom's case included Lt. Col. George Lumbard of the 4th Michigan and Lt. Col. Joshua Chamberlain of the 20th Maine. Lt. Col. Welch was also on the panel, but Wixom objected to his presence. "I consider him so prejudiced that he could not impartially try the case," the doctor said. "I am credibly informed and believe he instituted the investigation and caused these charges to be preferred against me."

The panel conceded the point and Welch was excused. But this was only a minor victory for the doctor, who asked for a delay in his trial to prepare his defense; he also argued that only the U.S. Surgeon General had jurisdiction on the issue of government medical supplies. These were rejected. Worse for Wixom were the facts of the case. Surgeons, like other army officers, were responsible for paying for their own food, and most made their "mess" or cooking/eating arrangements by sharing the cost of provisions and wages for a hired cook. But George Bowen of Monroe, a hospital steward recently appointed to be assistant surgeon in the 16th Michigan, testified that Wixom and his son-in-law, James Topping (who had resigned from the regiment after serving briefly), had routinely eaten rations drawn for the regimental hospital.[26]

Bowen explained that rations for those in the regiment's hospital, and for three attendants who worked in it, were drawn from the brigade commissary on orders from the surgeon. But Bowen said Wixom and Topping sometimes joined the hospital attendants at their meals, and he had witnessed the cook deliver food from the hospital mess directly to the surgeon's tent. Not only had Wixom consumed hospital rations, he testified, but also condensed milk and dried fruit from the U.S. Sanitary Commission, which were meant for the soldiers.

What about the doctor's use of liquor, an army medical supply? Bowen replied that during January, Wixom had drawn a dozen quarts of whiskey and a dozen of brandy from the medical stores at Aquia Creek; a month later, Wixom drew four more bottles from the sanitary commission. This alcohol, Bowen testified, was kept in Wixom's tent. Yet the prescription book kept in the regimental hospital showed that only two bottles of liquor were actually dispensed to patients during January. Had Bowen seen Wixom drinking this liquor? Yes, Bowen said, he had seen the doctor and "many" other individuals drinking in the doctor's quarters. Wixom conducted the cross-examination, forcing Bowen to admit that he (Wixom) and Topping had purchased bread, sugar, and potatoes for the hospital mess. But on the matter of the doctor using government liquor, Bowen was firm.[27]

More damning testimony followed. Reuben Crowell, 32, from Ann Arbor, was another former 16th Michigan hospital attendant now working as an army contract physician. He was unequivocal—Wixom and his son-in-law had eaten hospital rations. Soft soda crackers and dried fruit from the Christian commission had also been used by the doctor, and Crowell said he never saw these items go to the sick. The judge advocate elicited more testimony about Wixom's drinking and eating hospital rations, while Wixom tried to minimize this. He did not get far. "What are your feelings toward me personally?" the doctor asked. "Not very good," Crowell answered, "but they are not such as to affect my testimony."

Still another hospital attendant, a former druggist, William H. Larkworthy[28] testified about the drinking that went on in the surgeon's tent, though he admitted that Wixom indeed paid for fresh food for the hospital mess at times. Wixom attempted to point out there were weeks from the fall of 1862 into early 1863 when the 16th Michigan had not set up a regimental hospital at all, again to minimize the charge he improperly consumed hospital food. But the court martial ruled this question irrelevant. The prosecution rested.

Wixom tried to downplay testimony about acquiring so much government liquor; he called to the stand two doctors from other regiments who received bottles from him, and a private who testified that some of the brandy bottles delivered to the doctor in February were broken. His own son-in-law, Topping, testified that three boxes of liquor had recently been stolen from Wixom's tent. Wixom tried to address the charge he had been improperly dining on hospital rations by calling Col. Stockton to testify, asking him about the regiment's hospital fund, a record of the rations drawn to feed the sick and the hospital attendants. Wixom wanted to show that the 16th Michigan used less hospital rations than the other regiments in the Third Brigade. This, he maintained, showed he did not misuse hospital food.

But the prosecutor objected, claiming that the regiment's hospital fund did not reflect whether Wixom misused hospital rations. The court-martial agreed; Stockton could only testify about Wixom's reputation. "His reputation at home and in the service has been first rate," the colonel said. "I know of nothing against it." Had Wixom called the current conflict "a damned abolition war" in front of officers and men? "I have heard Dr. Wixom with other in conversation expression views pro and con in regard to the way the war was carried on," Stockton answered carefully. "These conversations were between officers." Since there was no witness saying Wixom undermined enlisted men's morale or questioned the conduct of the war in front of them, this charge was dropped, though it hardly mattered, given the other testimony against him.[29]

Wixom's defense ground to a halt. He argued that the 16th Michigan had only set up a regimental hospital for a couple of weeks since the battle of Antietam, so the notion that he had eaten hospital rations for months was ridiculous; he pointed out that he and Topping had purchased food for the hospital mess. "The only wrong of it my subsistence has been cooked by the hospital cook, and cooked with the rations of the attendants and patients," he said. "If I eat hard bread or pork drawn for a sick man, and give him in exchange, therefore, soft bread, potatoes and fresh beef, who is wronged thereby?" The fact his regiment had drawn less hospital rations than other regiments "proves conclusively that I purchased supplies and provisions frequently, that Lt. Topping did the same," he argued. But the court-martial was not impressed, and the doctor was quickly convicted on all counts. Wixom was fined $150 "to make good the loss" of the government supplies, and dismissed from the service of the United States with the loss of his back pay. His friend, the volunteer nurse Harriet Eaton, was outraged when she heard about the verdict.[30]

Decades later, Wixom's granddaughter, Helen Topping Miller, wrote a 1949 Michigan historical novel, *Born Strangers,* that romanticized the court-martial and made the doctor out to be a martyred hero. That was fiction; but the war was still going on as spring came in 1863, and there were thousands of sick and wounded men who required care, and thousands more to come. Wixom, though convicted, was nonetheless a trained physician skilled in surgical amputation. Gen. Charles Griffin, commanding the First Division of the Fifth Corps, recommended to his superiors that Wixom should be fined, but not dismissed from the army. His suggestion was ignored. Wixom, a Democrat like Stockton, appealed his case unsuccessfully and returned home in the summer of 1863. "Dr. Wixom is a good surgeon," Saginaw's Frank Keeler had written in 1862 at Harrison's Landing, when the old sawbones had left the regiment after the Seven Days. "But as a physician I have little confidence in him. He doses his patients with spoonfuls of quinine, divers powders and all such powerful remedies as are found in army medical supplies. I regulate the size of my doses when I take any."

A hometown newspaper's sketch of Wixom's life, published decades after he died, perhaps bears on the question of the surgeon and his consumption of government liquor. "'Tis claimed by the old settlers who knew him," the writer noted, "that it was Dr. Wixom's practice when preparing for an operation to imbibe freely of whisky until he could hold the points of two needles together."[31]

Lt. Col. Welch had won the first round in his fight with Stockton with the dismissal of Wixom, but he had personally crossed the colonel by refusing to countermand the stopping of Pvt. Apted's pay in early March. To Stockton, this was Welch refusing to follow a direct order. For more than a year now, Stockton had periodically recorded in his diary disapproving comments about Welch, whom he blamed for the loss of his regiment's flag at Gaines' Mill. And he had complained in an official report of Welch's slighting him in comments to a reporter. Two weeks after Dr. Wixom's court-martial, Stockton's formal complaint against Welch went to trial.

Welch, he charged, had acted illegally and arbitrarily when he stopped Pvt. Apted's pay; Welch had no authority to do this, yet while in command of the 16th Michigan, Welch had done this to other soldiers. The colonel said this was conduct was also prejudicial "to good order and military discipline." Furthermore, Stockton alleged, when Welch refused to follow his order reinstating Apted's pay, he had engaged in "conduct unbecoming an officer." Other allegations outlined in Stockton's complaint charged that Welch deprived Company A's Capt. George Swan of an officer's wall tent by altering an army receipt, a kind of "rain check" entitling Swan to that tent; and that Welch had taken meals with noncommissioned officers and enlisted men—something discouraged, if not prohibited, since generals wanted soldiers to think of their officers as superiors and not co-equals with whom they shared meals.

But the allegation that was probably the most important to Stockton personally dealt with the *New York Herald* article about the Seven Days, published in the previous summer. That article, which was printed in other papers, said that Welch led the 16th Michigan at Gaines' Mill and the rest of the battles. Stockton charged that these statements were "utterly false and without any foundation in truth or fact." By doing this, he alleged, Welch gained credit for himself at Stockton's expense and that of then-Lt. Col. John Ruehle. All told, Welch faced seventeen different charges and specifications.[32]

Welch's court-martial began on April 16 at the headquarters of the First Division of the Fifth Corps. Welch, an attorney by profession, appeared with counsel Lt. Col. Strong Vincent of the 83rd Pennsylvania, a lawyer in civilian life. The prosecutor was a captain from the 83rd Pennsylvania, while the panel hearing the case was made up of eleven officers from their division, including Col. James C. Rice of the 44th New York, Col. Adelbert Ames of the 20th Maine, and again Lt. Col. Lumbard from the 4th Michigan.

Stockton was the first witness. He testified about sending an order to Welch regarding Pvt. Apted's pay on March 6, and that Welch had not obeyed it. He also said he was in command of the 16th Michigan at Gaines' Mill, until the right of the regiment collapsed. Welch conducted his own cross-examination, establishing that he had appealed Stockton's order about Apted's pay; then he turned back to Gaines' Mill. Had not Stockton been ill and deaf from the effect of taking quinine? In response, the colonel admitted he had been sick, but denied he was deaf. Members of the court-martial also asked questions about the collapse of the regiment's right at Gaines' Mill and its position, and then returned to the matter of Apted's pay.[33]

By what authority did Stockton direct Welch to countermand the order in the case of Apted? "By my authority as his superior officer," Stockton replied, "and on the strength of the complaints and the answers he made to these." Stockton admitted he did not investigate the case. Lt. William Burns of the Brady company testified about the Apted matter and the cases of two other sharpshooters whose pay had been stopped. Who was in command when those men had their pay stopped? "Col. Stockton," Burns answered.

Capt. Judd Mott was called next and testified he had been a member of several regimental court-martials in the 16th Michigan called by Welch; some of these men had been fined, some put to hard labor, and some demoted. His testimony prompted questions by panel members about who in a regiment had the authority to convene court-martials. While this was not especially relevant to Apted's case, the discussion reflected that the army gave wide latitude to regimental and brigade commanders in disciplinary matters.

Capt. George Swan of Company A, who had been wounded in the second battle of Bull Run, testified next. Swan told of what must have seemed like a school boys' feud over an officer's wall tent with a fellow officer who had become his rival, Lt. George Prentiss (since resigned). Lt. Col. Welch, Swan said, had warned that he would take that tent himself if the two officers could not resolve their dispute; soon after, Swan had found that Welch indeed changed the quartermaster's receipt for the tent. Though Stockton felt this showed misconduct on Welch's part, Swan admitted on cross-examination that Welch "probably" did this to keep him and Prentiss from squabbling. This matter was probably irrelevant to the court-martial, but for the two last questions. "You say you were assigned to the command of Company A," someone asked. "Who assigned you to that command?"[34]

"Col. Stockton," Swan said.

"Who then commanded the regiment?"

"Lt. Col. Welch."

Stockton's charge that Welch had been improperly sharing meals with enlisted men was even weaker. Lt. Benjamin Partridge, now the regiment's quartermaster, testified that Welch had eaten his meals with himself, Assistant Surgeon George Bowen, Commissary Sgt. Frank Keeler, Pvt. Henry "Tip" Aplin, and two soldiers who worked on supply matters. Military formality frowned on officers and enlisted men sharing meals, since it was assumed the practice would breed familiarity and a lack of respect for the officers. But cross-examination revealed that Welch's dining with these soldiers was strictly temporary, a short-term arrangement when there had not been enough kitchen equipment for all the regiment's cooks and messes. As an offense, the court-martial probably saw this as trivial.

The last witness called by the prosecution was L. A. Hendricks, correspondent for the *New York Herald*. The journalist told of speaking to Welch at Harrison's Landing after the Seven Days' battles. Some of the information in his report came from Welch, he said, and some from others. What had Welch told him? "The statements as to the losses sustained by the regiment I derived from him," Hendricks said. "Also that he led the regiment in all the fights succeeding the Gaines' Mill battle."[35]

"Did or did not the statement that Col. Stockton was taken prisoner in the very beginning of the Gaines' Mill fight come from Col. Welch?" the prosecutor asked. "That was my impression all along," Hendricks answered. "Col. Welch made no mention as to the time." A member of the panel asked if Welch spoke of leading the regiment "to the expense or injury of his superior and absent officers, Col. Stockton and Lt. Col. Ruehle." Again, Hendricks's answer was in Welch's favor. "I think he stated that he led the regiment after Col. Stockton was taken prisoner," the journalist said; that Stockton had been sick, but "nothing affecting the military character" of Stockton or Ruehle.

The prosecution rested. Neither Welch nor his counsel, Strong Vincent, called a witness or made a final statement to the court. On April 18, the tent was cleared for the panel's deliberation, and the officers quickly reached their decision—Welch was not guilty on all charges.[36] Though there is no record of their discussion, it is likely they saw Welch sympathetically and Stockton as an overbearing brigade commander who had not allowed Welch to run the 16th Michigan as he saw fit, and who brought charges against Welch on superficial matters. The changing political nature of the war probably also was a factor. While Welch was likely known as a War Democrat to the officers of their brigade and division, Stockton had worn on his sleeve his esteem for George McClellan and Fitz John Porter—and their time had passed.

There is no record of Stockton's reaction to Welch's acquittal, but one can imagine his mortification—the 16th Michigan had been created by him, yet the regimental commanders on the court-martial had sided with Welch. Stockton's days with the Army of the Potomac were now numbered, by his own choice. Soon two 16th Michigan officers who had been close to Stockton were also court-martialed—Capt. Judd Mott and Capt. Patrick McLaughlin. McLaughlin, a Detroiter who had been with the regiment from the beginning, was accused of striking a soldier in a fight, convicted, and dismissed. Stockton tried to intervene on behalf of McLaughlin with the judge advocate general, the chief prosecutor of the army. Stockton said McLaughlin's punishment was "way too harsh," and he questioned Welch's actions. "What his motives are in this case easy one can judge form himself," Stockton charged, seeming to imply it was Welch's way of striking back at him. But McLaughlin got no re-hearing or appeal. He was able to reenter the service in the fall as a first lieutenant and quartermaster of the 1st Michigan Colored Infantry Regiment in the late fall and was ultimately killed in action at Salkehatchie, South Carolina, on February 8, 1865.[37]

Capt. Mott, who had once played chess with Norval Welch, was the one officer in the 16th Michigan ordered dismissed from the service by a court-martial in March for overstaying his leave at the direct order of the U.S. Army commander in Detroit; the other officers who had done the exact same thing received "the least punishment," Mott wrote. He held Welch responsible for his prosecution; he complained that Welch was an unscrupulous Copperhead, or traitor, who drank with Strong Vincent and who had once referred to Gov. Austin Blair as "a damned abolitionist son of bitch." Though the court-martial ordered him dismissed, Mott was allowed by Welch to stay with the regiment as he appealed his case. Ultimately President Lincoln reviewed Mott's court-martial and ruled that the captain should not be dismissed, but should forfeit two months' pay.[38]

The battle between Stockton and Welch probably had no impact on most men in the regiment or the Third Brigade. On April Fools' Day, officers in the 12th New York had fun at the expense of a slow-witted lieutenant by issuing him a false order. This officer, described as "thick-headed" and target of previous pranks, was told to report to Stockton in the absence of Lt. Wallace Jewett, who had been working as the colonel's aide, wrote Oliver Norton of the 83rd Pennsylvania. Stockton was then observing Dr. Wixom's court-martial and was probably not amused by this joke. The thick-headed lieutenant "was coolly informed that Lieutenant J[ewett] was not absent, and when his services were required, the colonel would send him a mule."[39]

The 16th Michigan's Pvt. Jacob Craw had nothing to smile about—he was still sick and in the convalescent camp miles away. He had only been in the army for six months, but he regretted enlisting. "I was glad to get a few lines from you and to hear . . . that you won't take a foolish notion in your head, as I did, to enlist," he wrote to a friend back in Shiawassee County, "for you are better off at home, or anyone else." Craw was suffering a very bad cough—"the worst," he said, "that I have had in two years . . . I don't look much now as I did last winter." He said he would rather be home, "drawing saw logs than to be here soldiering. It ain't so funny as some folks think."[40]

Late that month, Lt. Charles Salter finally got the furlough he was hoping for and briefly visited Detroit, while Sgt. Keeler and Lt. Jewett also secured leaves and headed home to Saginaw. A local paper said Jewett looked "hale, hearty and cheerful as of yore," and that "no returned soldier has been more cordially welcome here than Frank," who, it reported, had been through every battle the regiment had fought. That, however, was an exaggeration, since Keeler had written home in mid-December that he was with the wagon train "as my duties require" in a wagon park about a mile and a half from Falmouth on the opposite side of the river from Fredericksburg; he had heard about the battles from others.

On his way back from furlough, Lt. Salter traveled by boat to Cleveland and then by rail to Washington. From there he, Lt. Charles Rice of the Brady Sharpshooters, and other returning officers took a Potomac River mail boat to the Aquia Creek Landing. On board were President Lincoln and Secretary of War Edwin Stanton; Gen. Joseph Hooker met them at the landing. "I do not know what they came down here for, unless it was to get some of our good fare (viz., hard bread and salt meat) of which we have such a plenty," Salter joked.[41]

Lincoln was there, of course, to review the troops and meet with Hooker and his generals. He was greeted warmly when he rode by the Fifth Corps on April 7. "We formed in line at half past 11 on the parade ground," Sgt. Berry wrote, "and we are reviewed at 12 o'clock by the President accompanied by Gens. Hooker, Meade, Griffin, Col. Stockton, and others, attended by their respective staffs and an escort of lancers. Each regiment is reviewed in their camps. The President receives a very enthusiastic reception from the troops. Each regiment gives him three tremendous cheers." Capt. Kin Dygert, commander of the Brady Sharpshooters company and back with the army after extended illness, claimed the president singled out the 16th Michigan's site. "President Lincoln, when passing across the parade, pronounced it the finest camp he had visited," Dygert boasted.

Tip Aplin, back with his regiment after capture, illness, parole, and exchange, thought it was Hooker who complimented the 16th Michigan's camp, though in truth, the generals and the president may well have said the same thing about each regiment they visited to buck up the men's morale. "Old Abe looked as natural as ever," he wrote to his sister. "The boys cheered him long and loud as he rode past regiment after regiment . . . Everyone strains their eyes to get a glimpse of him as he passes."[42]

Capt. Dygert praised Lt. Col. Welch, whom he said made his men "models in drill and discipline." Welch had been acquitted in his court-martial days earlier, and Dygert wrote: "Hard and unnecessary as the work seems at time to a few old grumblers (and grumbling and fighting is about the only privilege a soldier has), his officers and men are very much attached to him and cheerfully follow where he leads them. I wish the army had a few more like him." Dygert had been in a struggle of his own with Col. Hiram Berdan, the controversial commander of the U.S. Sharpshooters, regiments of federal marksmen who served in the Army of the Potomac. Berdan wanted the Brady Sharpshooters assigned to him. "From present appearances he is not likely to succeed," Dygert wrote. He said Berdan "is despised by almost every officer and private under his command and by everyone else with whom his official duties bring him in contact with. I won't remain in the service an hour under his command, for he is one of the veriest cowards in the army."[43]

The 16th Michigan had had a U.S. flag since it left Detroit in the fall of 1861, and these colors had been through the regiment's 1862 battles. Now the once-bright silk banner was tattered and faded, its shaft broken. That month, Lt. Col. Welch presented his regiment with a new national flag from the War Department with a patriotic speech, retiring the old banner. "It is for the preservation of this holy thing that we have sacrificed ease and pleasure, and for which we are again willing to imperil our lives," Welch said. Pvt. George Ervay noted that the men "gave three cheers for the old flag." Soon what remained of it would be sent back to Michigan.

By now Lt. Salter gave up on trying to get a commission in the regular army, and he wondered if he might soon be promoted to captain, what with all the resignations and court-martials that occurred. He heard that Capt. Theodore Mahan of Company D had resigned because he had consumption (tuberculosis) and was not expected to live long, and that Capt. McLaughlin of Company C had been dismissed. Yet Lt. Gilbert Chandler, who lost an arm from a crippling wound at Gaines' Mill, was doing fine. Sgt. Keeler said Chandler was "quite well for a man who has had to undergo the surgical operations that he has." Chandler was also promoted to captain that spring.[44]

Pvt. Ervay told his family about going for a walk on a sunny Sunday morning after breakfast. "[I] looked in a great many tents and you cannot imagine how many different things the soldiers has to pass the time," he wrote. "Some was reading novels, some Christian papers and tracts, some playing cards and others checkers and some writing, some one thing and some another." Ervay was interrupted by roll call, an everyday part of camp life. "We have ten drummers in the regiment and they drum us out in the morning and back to bed at night and if a man does not get out to roll call every night and morning he is pricked and put on guard for punishment, or if he is absent from drill or dress parade, he is put on guard." He continued: "So you see that a man has to be on his taps and tend his business else it does not pay."

Col. Stockton was absent with permission when, late that month, after the acquittal of Norval Welch, he dashed to Washington. The rumor was that Stockton was seeking the appointment to be the provost marshal general, or military police chief of Michigan. But more significantly, the Army of the Potomac was expecting orders to march on a new offensive. "But come when or where it will," Capt. Dygert wrote, "we feel confident of success."[45]

11.

APRIL–MAY 1863

ALL THE DEVILS IN HELL

Gen. Joseph Hooker, the boastful commander of the Army of the Potomac, now put into effect his plans for a new spring offensive against the Confederates. On April 13, the men of the 16th Michigan watched as a huge force of cavalry departed into the countryside, though heavy rain that week caused Hooker to change his plan. "We are undoubtedly on the eve of some important movement," wrote Sgt. John Berry of Company A. The regiment underwent a knapsack inspection and it occurred to Pvt. Alfred Apted of the Brady Sharpshooters that it was the second anniversary of the Rebel attack on Ft. Sumter that opened the war. "Two years of fighting has followed," he wrote, "and I can't see that the rebellion is any nearer crushed out than it 'twas one year ago."[1]

Pvt. George Ervay, the teenager from Grand Ledge in Company H, was optimistic. "We have got marching orders," he wrote. "I do not know what moment we shall start off, where we are a-going is more than I can tell. But I expect we are a-going to advance on Richmond but it is hard telling." He said that his comrades "are all as happy as bees" though they "dread the word fight." He continued: "The general talk is that if Fighting Joe starts his men ahead, that he is not a-going to get whipped." But Detroit's Charles Salter wondered if the army was strong enough to go on a long campaign, given that the enlistments of thousands of soldiers who had joined for hitches less than three years would soon be over. "I do not know what we are going to do or what we can do, for even if we drive the rebels back to Richmond, we cannot lay siege to that place at present [for] if we do, we shall be there in May when the time of about one half our army is up," he explained. "And if they leave us, we shall only have an army sufficient to defend Washington."

Pvt. Ervay also sent home to his parents a lithograph or poster, a kind of a landscape portrait of his regiment's camp, published by a Baltimore printing company. The picture was sold to soldiers, who, like Ervay, mailed them home as a souvenir. "I would like to have you get it put in a frame and keep it for my sake," he told his parents. He was sure he was depicted in the lithograph, since he had been working on the side of the guard house (which appeared in the center of the scene) on the day the artist was there, sketching the 16th Michigan's camp.[2]

Also going home was Capt. Stephen Martin, 44, of Detroit, taking with him the tattered U.S. flag the 16th Michigan had carried through the battles of 1862, from Gaines' Mill to Fredericksburg. That flag had been retired two weeks earlier when Lt. Col. Welch brought a new national banner from Washington to the 16th Michigan. Martin had just resigned his commission as captain of Company H for disability and Welch sent a letter back with him, directing him to turn the retired colors over to the state adjutant general. "Ask Genl. Robertson to place it in the most appropriate place for such things in our state, and ask him to take good care of it, for the sake of the men who have died under it, and for those of us who live that have fought under it," Welch wrote.

It would have been one of the regiment's "proudest moments," he continued, to bring that battle-torn flag back to Detroit and carry it along Jefferson Avenue, but this could not be; the regiment had a new flag, and it would take "a place beside the old one some future day—*we mean to place it there.*" Welch said the regiment was happy to send the retired flag with Martin, since he "rescued it at Bull Run, second," and should have the honor of returning it to Michigan.[3]

Three days later, on April 27, the Fifth Corps and others left their winter camp, marching northwest from the Falmouth area toward Kelly's Ford on the Rappahannock. Hooker intended to take this, the main portion of his army, quietly up and around the Confederate stronghold at Fredericksburg, while other Union corps prepared to again cross the river, confronting and engaging the Rebel forces there. Two more corps would wait as a reserve to assist either wing, while a large force of Union cavalry was to cut the Confederate rail lines to Richmond. Hooker envisioned that these two wings of the Army of the Potomac would trap Lee's army between them, forcing the Rebels out of their defensive positions and crushing them in open battle, while cutting off their ability to fall back to the Confederate capital.[4]

The 16th Michigan moved out about 1 p.m. that day, marching on dry roads and getting as far as Hartwood Church, several miles away with their corps and two others. Rain came in and turned the roads to mud the next day, but they moved ten more miles and arrived at Kelly's Ford and again bivouacked. On April 29, the Fifth Corps crossed the Rappahannock on pontoon bridges, marching southeast to the Rapidan, another ten miles. In the meantime, the other Union corps were also crossing the rivers at points east and west, all heading for an obscure country crossroads called Chancellorsville. "Arriving at the Rapidan, we waded across four feet of water and captured a rebel company doing picket duty there," Lt. Salter wrote about the soldiers reaching Ely's Ford. William Borden, from Ionia County, had been promoted to second lieutenant and was now in Company F. "The men had to take off their cartridge boxes to keep their ammunition dry," he said, meaning soldiers slung belts and pouches over their shoulders and around their necks as they forded the river. "A little before dark we pitched our tents on the heights and built large fires and dried our clothes. The next morning we started for Chancellorsville, which was about four miles distant. We went very slow and got there a little before noon."[5]

Chancellorsville was not a town, but a large brick farmhouse and inn, slightly more than ten miles west of Fredericksburg. There were scattered farms and a handful of churches and taverns in the vicinity, but this area, called the Wilderness, was mainly rough country covered by a thick tangle of woods, vine, brush and briars. That night, the men of the 16th Michigan camped in the woods with their division and corps not far from the Chancellor House. But Gen. Robert E. Lee, once realizing what was happening, did not wait in Fredericksburg to be closed in by Union forces. He marched west with a force two-thirds the size of Hooker's to fight; that night, Rebel soldiers moved to within a couple of miles of where 78,000 Union soldiers of Hooker's flanking wing were encamped.

CHANCELLORSVILLE

On the morning of May 1, Union troops moving east from Chancellorsville ran into the Confederates under Gen. Stonewall Jackson, who had come from Fredericksburg at Lee's direction. The 16th Michigan was less than a mile away to the north, marching with its First Division on a route called the River Road when the shooting began. "Our division went on a reconnaissance towards Fredericksburg," Lt. Salter wrote about that day, "when we heard firing in our rear." Their column was near the Rappahannock River, approaching a crossing place called Bank's Ford in the afternoon as the men heard this stiff skirmish widening to the south and southwest; some of this fighting involved part of their Fifth Corps. But what happened next surprised the officers of the Army of the Potomac: A nervous Joe Hooker quickly ordered his troops that afternoon to return to Chancellorsville to take up defensive positions. In doing so, he lost momentum and provided Lee with both opportunity and advantage. "Hooker had relinquished the tactical initiative to Lee, an ominous proposition," wrote historian Jeffry Wert.[6]

Gen. Charles Griffin, commander of the Fifth Corps' First Division of which the 16th Michigan was part, moved back as ordered. "Our corps was given position on the extreme left and formed a line from the river up to near Chancellorsville," Lt. Salter wrote. Their Third Brigade and the rest of their division rested on their arms that night on a country lane called the Mineral Springs Road that led northeast from Chancellorsville. "As soon as daylight [came] each regiment went to work putting up breastworks of logs and earth as we expected the enemy to attack us there," Salter continued about the morning of May 2.

As the 16th Michigan dug trenches and cut down trees that day, Stonewall Jackson took about 26,000 men and moved through the woods, swinging around Union positions south and west of Chancellorsville. It was a daring and dangerous move, but it succeeded. Jackson's force attacked early that evening, coming out of the west with a surprising, hard-hitting attack on inexperienced Union troops a mile or more from where the 16th Michigan was waiting with its corps. "They [Jackson's men] went right up to our right, and attacked the Eleventh Corps first," Salter said. "Their corps is composed mostly of nine-month volunteers who enlisted last summer, and they have not been in any battles before . . . And they did not attempt to hold our position, but broke in confusion and fell back."[7]

In truth, not all those Union soldiers fled before Jackson's surprise attack—some units fought the Rebels desperately. But they were not enough, and the Confederates caved in the right of Hooker's position west of Chancellorsville. The soldiers of the 16th Michigan's division, in defenses just east of the big farm and inn, had no part in this fighting, but they plainly heard the raging gunfire that afternoon and evening; Lt. William Borden of Ionia County said it was the heaviest firing he had ever heard. Thousands of retreating Union soldiers, horses, and wagons came in a rushing tide back to Chancellorsville in the smoke-filled night, and officers struggled to form new lines around it. From about midnight into the early morning hours of May 3, the Fifth Corps, including the 16th Michigan, hurried into defensive positions along Ely's Ford Road, less than a mile north-northwest of the Chancellor House. "Our division moved to the right [west] until we were upon the left of the Second Corps to support them," Lt. Salter wrote about the move. "The battle was kept up all day long [on May 2] and then after sunset the moon shone very brilliant, making it about as bright as day, and the battle raged even more fiercely than it had during the day."[8]

"It was the most terrible battle I have ever yet witnessed," he continued. "The Rebels and our men both fought with much more determination and fierceness than ever before." Though Salter's use of the word "witnessed" indicated the 16th Michigan was not in the fighting that night and early the next morning, Brady Sharpshooter Pvt. Alfred Apted said his company was moved back to the Union right "in time to share in the fight." But the shooting died off and the Rebel assault had become disorganized as their men charged forward, driving the Eleventh Corps back. Reinforcing Union commands helped to blunt their advance that night, and Stonewall Jackson himself was fatally wounded by his own men in the confused fighting. The 16th Michigan came through this first day and night of battle with no fatalities and few wounded.

Those Union regiments and brigades that had been shattered and retreated were sent to occupy the breastworks that had been held by the 16th Michigan's First Division, while Salter's comrades now occupied what some soldiers thought were unfinished Rebel defenses at Ely's Ford Road, facing the Confederates to the west. The 16th Michigan and other regiments of their brigade worked on these defenses, Col. Stockton reported, turning them into rifle pits with abatis—rows of sharpened, projecting wooden spikes that the soldiers positioned to extend out from their earthworks as obstacles to attackers. Apted's diary suggests his company was detached and acted as skirmishers nearer to Chancellorsville as Hooker pulled this main portion of the Army of the Potomac into a contracting loop, with the Fifth Corps protecting his right.[9]

Now it was the morning of May 3. The 16th Michigan, in support of some of their division's batteries, faced southwest, in a line of infantry and guns along the road that stretched north from the Chancellorsville defenses—a line that protected the Union army's route back to the river fords. At about 7 a.m. Stonewall Jackson's troops, now under the command of Jeb Stuart, renewed their attack, again moving from west to east toward

Chancellorsville. Lt. William Borden wrote that the men of his regiment were still working on their defenses when Union skirmishers in the woods in front of them came rushing back to the relative security of their main line as the Confederates reopened their assault. "We had not got them [rifle pits] done when our [skirmish] line in front came back in confusion as soon as the Rebs came out of the woods in sight [of us]," Borden wrote. "Our batteries opened on them and sent them back as fast as they came."

The diary of Pvt. George Ervay, in Company H with Borden, noted this fight in his diary. "Came off picket this morning and went in the breastworks," he wrote. "Hard fighting all day long on [the] lines. The rebs drove us in front, but did not break our lines." Lt. Salter agreed. "They advanced, sometimes out of the wood, and would attempt to break our lines, but would get drove back every time," he said. "When we would in turn pursue them into the wood until we were drove back. At one time the enemy charged out of the wood right in front of our regiment. We waited until they were pretty close and commenced firing, and our artillery fired right over our heads with grapeshot into the rebels, and as soon as they could, they got out of the way."[10]

A Michigan officer witnessing this scene—almost certainly Lt. Salter—drafted a letter the next day to Detroit that was printed in a newspaper, telling how the Union army's commander, Joe Hooker, had visited the 4th and 16th Michigan regiments in line of battle on the morning of May 3. "Whilst the ball was going, Gen. Hooker came where we were and sat down amongst us for about an hour," wrote this officer, who signed his letter "C.H.S."

"He told Gen. Griffin that our position must be held at all hazards; and that everything depended on our being able to hold this place. Gen. Griffin told him he had two of his best regiments here, and could hold it against all the devils in hell, and that the rebels had not men enough in the Southern Confederacy to take it." Brady Sharpshooter Alfred Apted's diary confirmed that Hooker showed up "in person" in the early morning of May 3, visiting his men. Lt. Salter's anecdote about Hooker and Griffin would evolve and get more dramatic as it was retold by veterans over the succeeding years, but it was plain that the Michigan soldiers were proud of their generals' confidence in them.[11]

"C.H.S."—Salter—said he had never seen anything so "terribly grand" as when the Rebel infantry advanced into the open, only to be shattered by the Union guns; these were likely troops who had been under the command of Confederate General A. P. Hill, now wounded. "I saw one officer, ahead of the rest, waving his sword, when a discharge of grape took him and cut him all to pieces; and we could see them destroyed in every possible manner," he said. Then Salter saw the enemy massing about a quarter of a mile away to the southwest. "They came out of the woods, hurrahing and apparently in fine spirits," he wrote. "But as soon as they were fairly out of the woods, 60 pieces of artillery opened fire on them. The rebels paused a moment and then took to their heels, but before they got out of range of our batteries they had left large numbers of lying dead and wounded upon the ground."

The forest in front of the 16th Michigan was soon burning. Lt. Salter and Pvt. Ervay thought the Confederates intentionally set them on fire, but it was likely caused by explosions of shells and burning powder in the dry, brushy woods. "The fire burnt rapidly through the entire length of woods in front of our army," Lt. Salter wrote; he hoped that wounded men in that area had been removed to safety, but he could not say for sure. Ervay was convinced wounded soldiers died in the fire, a fact later confirmed by Union skirmishers who went back into the burned-out forest.[12]

A fraction of a mile from where the 16th Michigan supported those deadly Union batteries, the Brady Sharpshooters Company had been on picket overnight near the Chancellor House, or what Pvt. Apted referred to as "the brick hotel." Whether the sharpshooters became involved in the fighting as the Confederate attack resumed that morning is unclear, though Apted noted that the battle "raged with fearful fury all morning" and that Union troops "fall back a trifle." Nearby, his commanding general, Hooker, was injured when a Rebel cannon ball struck a pillar on the porch of the Chancellor House next to where he had been standing that morning, sending a large section of it crashing into him and knocking him senseless. Hooker was probably in shock, likely with a concussion, for hours that followed, though he had no visible physical injury. In the meantime, around Chancellorsville, relentless Confederate attacks drove his men back, the Union defenses contracting as the artillery battled all afternoon.[13]

But the soldiers of the Fifth Corps, still north of Chancellorsville, did not shift or move from their strong defenses. The next morning, May 4, the Brady Sharpshooters Company rejoined the rest of the 16th Michigan in the lines "a short distance from the brick hotel," Apted wrote. George Ervay recorded there was "heavy skirmishing" that morning and Brady Sharpshooter Sgt. Frederick Smith, 25, from Macomb County was killed in this skirmishing when a bullet struck him in the head. The afternoon fell quiet, however, and their division commander, Gen. Griffin, ordered the Second Brigade to charge into the smoking woods across the road to see if the Rebels had withdrawn.

The soldiers of the 16th Michigan watched from their trenches as their comrades disappeared into the trees, chasing Confederate pickets. Soon came the roar of rifles and artillery, proving that the Rebels were still in strong positions. The Second Brigade, including the 4th Michigan, came running back from the woods, now chased by Rebels, through the Union picket line and back to their defenses on Ely's Ford Road. "I was on picket at the time," Lt. William Borden said of this moment when the soldiers of the Second Brigade retreated. "The Rebs sent them back through the picket line as if the devil had kicked them in end." Four of Borden's pickets were casualties that evening. A member of the 4th Michigan who had charged into the woods only to be driven out again later wrote that the 16th Michigan's commander was distressed his men had not been sent in after the Rebels. "[Lt.] Col. Welch, of the 16th Michigan, felt slighted because his regiment was not selected for the job," O. S. Barrett would say. "I told him I was sorry, as I was willing he should have all the honor that would accrue to me."[14]

The skirmishing went on as darkness fell. "That night I took my company out on picket in front of the regiment," Lt. Charles Salter wrote, "and as it was a bright moonlight night, we could see pretty well and we had a good deal of skirmishing with the enemy . . . At times bullets whistled around us pretty lively." Thomas Trahey, from the Ann Arbor area and who had been wounded at Fredericksburg, later recalled how he spent that day lying in the hot sun in front of the battery, "suffering with a violent headache." Trahey, in Company H, said he was part of the picket line that night as skirmish fire sounded around them and that he took a position behind a pine tree, relieving a soldier who "must have been having a duel with a Rebel who was about 100 feet in front, who kept firing as fast as he could, apparently." Trahey said he "was not in a firing mood or condition, having a severe headache." He lay on the ground, resting his rifle on the root of the tree, making up his mind to "stop the constant firing." Trahey watched the Confederate soldier fire twice more, siting his rifle on his enemy's muzzle flash. "I waited for the flash of his gun and fired simultaneously—which ended his firing," Trahey claimed.[15]

But their fighting there was nearly over. That night, their commander, Gen. Joseph Hooker, told his generals that he intended to retreat back across the river, overruling their votes to attack Lee. It had turned out that the movement of the other wing of the Union army, which, according to Hooker's plan, was to attack the Confederates at Fredericksburg, was plagued with half-hearted, hesitant, and ultimately unsuccessful leadership. Hooker himself had stopped his flanking wing of the Army of the Potomac soon after the fighting started back on May 1, and some of his commanders in this offensive had not led their men boldly. All in all, Hooker had accomplished nothing. The 16th Michigan remained in their defensive position with their comrades through the next day, May 5, until the retreat of the Army of the Potomac from Chancellorsville could begin.

The Confederates made another attack on the Union lines north of Chancellorsville that morning, but were again repulsed by cannon fire. A hard rain set in that afternoon, and Pvt. Ervay was trying to dig a trench around his tent to channel the water away when he broke his bayonet. It hardly mattered, for as night fell, the flanking wing of the Army of the Potomac of which his regiment was part started the retreat to the U.S. Ford on the Rappahannock. The 16th Michigan stood guard with the other regiments of their First Division in the darkness until about 1 a.m. on May 6 as Union commands quietly slogged away in the pouring rain. "And all night long, they were leaving us, and marching down to the river as [we] waited until all the rest were across," Lt. Salter wrote of the muddy retreat. "Then we cross and the 1st Michigan [Infantry] took up the pontoon bridges."

Lt. Borden agreed. "We were in the rear of everything," he wrote. The road to the ford was bad and "dark as a sack of black cats." Dawn was coming up as the 16th Michigan crossed over, but the Rebels did not attack. A few artillery rounds were fired at them, but these fell short of the bridge, Borden said. Once across the river the Union troops headed back for the site of their winter camp near Falmouth, marching in steady rain and "knee deep mud," Pvt. Ervay noted. They arrived back at their former camp site that afternoon.[16]

Salter noted that in the ten days since they had left their old camp for this offensive, they had marched a hundred miles, crossed rivers three times, carried all their supplies, and had a hard fight. But what he did not say was that Hooker's great offensive failed at the cost of more than 17,000 Union soldiers killed, wounded, and captured or missing; Confederate casualties were over 13,000. His own regiment had been lucky not to be have been in the way of Stonewall Jackson's surprise attack, and when the 16th Michigan's position was assaulted later, it was fortunate to be posted with Union batteries that mowed down attackers by the score. Sgt. Frederick Smith of the Brady Sharpshooters was the 16th Michigan's only fatality and several other men had been wounded.

Unlike many Union officers, Salter insisted he was not downhearted about the Chancellorsville campaign. "After all, we were in good spirits and not discouraged as we were after the battle in December last, for we were satisfied we had done everything we could under the circumstances," he wrote; he was defensive about criticism of Hooker. "It is easy enough, after the battle is over, to see where the mistake was," he told friends. But Lt. William Borden got a laugh when his parents wrote that they had just heard the news back in Michigan that 'Richmond had been taken.' "The report is true," Borden joked, "but it was taken by the rebs."[17]

May continued rainy in the aftermath of the Chancellorsville campaign, but moderated into fine and pleasant days. It became warm enough for the men to bathe again in the Potomac Creek. But more importantly, thousands of soldiers whose hitches were up—"two-year men" and "nine-months men"—were leaving for home. "Today we escort the 14th N.Y. to the railroad," Company A's Sgt. John Berry noted. Days later, the 12th and 17th New York regiments followed. With their departure, the Third Brigade was now composed the 16th Michigan, the 83rd Pennsylvania, the 44th New York, and the 20th Maine. Picket duty took the soldiers three or four miles from camp and was probably their most demanding job now. But there was also time, periodically, for fun. Pvt. George Ervay of Company H was part of a detail that escorted a homeward-bound regiment to the rail depot at Stoneman's Switch, but while there, the Michigan soldiers amused themselves with sports and alcohol. "Had a party and ball play," he wrote in his journal. "I got blind drunk."[18]

By this point, Col. Thomas Stockton had reached a turning point in his Civil War career. Surely he understood he was not going to get his brigadier general's star serving in the Army of the Potomac or anywhere else Gov. Austin Blair and the Radical Republicans had influence. Simply put, Stockton was from Michigan, and the Michigan governor and Republican senators were not going to approve his promotion. Even if the governor was somehow not aware of the fact that Stockton had owned a slave three decades earlier, Stockton was a Democrat and he crossed Blair when he was granted federal authority to form his regiment. And Stockton had been a supporter of McClellan and Fitz John Porter, men perceived by Radical Republicans as enemies of a war to end slavery.

Joshua Chamberlain of the 20th Maine, who would soon become a hero of the Civil War, later wrote that "there was a manifest prejudice against the Fifth Corps at Government Headquarters," meaning the War Department. Secretary of War Edwin M. Stanton particularly distrusted the Fifth Corps because of its support for McClellan and Porter, he continued. "This was believed to be reason why no promotion to the rank of General Officers was made by this corps for a long time, unless secured by political influence," he wrote.[19] Chamberlain's explanation fits Stockton's example perfectly. Probably as frustrating to Stockton as his lack of support from powerful Michigan Republicans was that Lt. Col. Norval Welch was succeeding in getting control of the 16th Michigan, the regiment Stockton had created. Welch had managed to cashier Dr. Isaac Wixom and Capt. Patrick McLaughlin; Stockton had been able to do nothing for them, though Capt. Judd Mott, with the intervention of President Lincoln, managed to avoid outright dismissal.

Officers in the regiment were aware for weeks that the colonel was seeking another military commission, with Capt. Kin Dygert of the Brady Sharpshooters noting that Stockton left camp on April 21 to travel to Washington to seek the post of provost marshal general of Michigan. Of course, there was no such appointment for Stockton. But another opportunity presented itself to the colonel, or perhaps it was one that he had been cultivating. Either way, Stockton soon asked for a leave from Gen. Dan Butterfield, his old brigade commander who was now chief of staff of the Army of the Potomac. "I respectfully ask permission to visit Washington for the purpose of attending to the application that you endorsed a few days [ago]—viz., to my being permitted to go on the duty offered me by the Governor of Tennessee," he wrote. "Time is of much importance to enable me to carry out that object."[20]

The governor of Tennessee, or more specifically, the federal military governor of Tennessee, was Andrew Johnson, a former senator and Democrat but a loyal Unionist, appointed to his post by President Lincoln. Johnson and other Unionists from his state had longed for the Union army to invade eastern Tennessee to drive Confederates out, and now, as a federally appointed governor, he had the authority to raise forces for this purpose. As a War Democrat, Stockton appears to have jumped at the idea that he would raise a brigade of troops for Johnson, and thereby get the brigadier general's command that he could not otherwise get with Michigan Gov. Austin Blair standing in his way.

Stockton noted that his brigade was going on picket, so his absence would not be detrimental to his command. Besides, if he got the post offered by Johnson, "it will be far more benefit to my country that if I remain here," the colonel wrote. While the 16th Michigan was on picket in what Pvt. Alfred Apted called a beautiful oak grove in cool and pleasant weather, Stockton went to Washington. It did not take him long to work things out; four days after applying for permission to leave the Third Brigade, Stockton turned in his resignation. It read, in part:

> In taking this step, I deem it proper to state that I do so for the purpose of accepting the position that Gov. Andrew Johnson has given me, to raise three regiments to serve under him in redeeming that state from rebeldom [*sic*], he having full authority from the president to raise troops under the late act of Congress for that purpose.[21]

Stockton asked that his resignation be accepted at once, and it was. On May 22, he left the Third Brigade and the regiment that he had raised in the late summer of 1861. The officers of the 16th Michigan held a meeting when they heard about Stockton's resignation. Lt. Thomas Frank Powers, who had joined the 16th Michigan with the lancers, said they approved a resolution praising the colonel and passed the hat, raising $140 for the purchase of a parting gift. Lt. Charles Salter described it as "a splendid sword and belt." Even enlisted men in the regiment understood Stockton was leaving so he could get the promotion he wanted. "Our old colonel came down to bid us good-bye," Grand Ledge teenager George Ervay noted his diary. "He is to be a general in Tennessee." Sharpshooter Alfred Apted recorded the same in his journal.[22]

Naturally, Lt. Col. Norval Welch could not be expected to say pleasant things about the man who had tried to court-martial him, so the job ironically fell to Maj. Thomas Barry, a man recommended to his post by Welch and who had complained to the Michigan adjutant general about Stockton nearly a year before at Yorktown. Barry, who would in a month's time leave the army on disability, spoke to the assembled regiment of the men's esteem and affection for Stockton, and how he had looked out for the "interest and honor of the regiment" as he turned the volunteers into soldiers. "Unskilled in the practice of arms, ignorant of the duties of camp and the field when we first came under your guidance and direction, for nearly two years we have been under your instruction," Barry said. "And for whatever success we may have attained in military practice we cheerfully and frankly give you the credit."

To Grand Rapids sharpshooter Apted of the Brady company, "the old colonel seemed much affected by their appreciation of his works." Stockton responded feelingly, thanking the officers for their gift and friendship, and he begged them to remain steadfast and true. "Though we had been unsuccessful in some things," he said, referring to the disastrous battles and campaigns they had been through, "victory would yet perch upon their banner, resulting in glorious peace." The men cheered. Stockton said his goodbyes and left, hopeful and confident of his new command. Though he did not know it then, his active participation in the Civil War was over. He planned to recruit new soldiers in Michigan, New York, and Ohio for his Tennessee regiments, but the reality was that volunteers were not rushing to join the army anymore; Stockton would lead no new regiments. Newspaper stories of glorious and heroic battles were no longer accepted as fact, for too many young men had come home from these campaigns maimed or not come home at all, with thousands dead of disease. And eventually Governor Johnson's authority to raise regiments was revoked. As a result, Stockton would never get his brigadier general's star.[23]

"One thing we can say for him," wrote Lt. Powers, "what but few regiments can say of anyone who has commend them so long: that during his command of the 16th, he has never ordered the punishment of a man. Yet with all this, I might say unparalleled leniency, he enforced strict discipline." Lt. Salter's comments exemplified what every man in the regiment understood: "He [Stockton] has been seeking for the position of brigadier general ever since he first assumed command of the brigade," the Detroiter wrote, "but for some reason probably best known to the government, he has been unable to get the promotion." There can be no doubt that Stanton's War Department and Stockton's old nemesis Austin Blair figured in the colonel's disappointed aims. Less than a week after Stockton left, Blair paid a visit to Michigan regiments in the Army of the Potomac and personally inspected the 16th Michigan.

Command of the Third Brigade devolved again to Col. Strong Vincent of the 83rd Pennsylvania, the Harvard-educated lawyer who represented Lt. Col. Welch in his court-martial and was described by Capt. Judd Mott as a friend of Welch. On May 24, a

Sunday, Vincent presided over the brigade's dress parade, and the fact that Stockton was gone was likely the reason for the party that followed. "The officers on a regular drunk," Apted wrote in his diary, "and kept [up] a regular howl all night."[24]

The 16th Michigan had moved its camp the day before Stockton's departure. "It was becoming very dusty in our old camp along the railroad, and, as camps had been very thick around us all winter and spring, it was unhealthy," Lt. Charles Salter wrote. The new camp was located two miles away from the old site, on a large green field on high ground with streams running near, still a few miles from Falmouth but closer to locations where the soldiers did picket duty. Saginaw's Frank Keeler, who had been promoted to second lieutenant in late April and assigned to Company E, agreed that a clean, fresh camp was good, but what the army really needed was a commanding general who could win battles. "If the Army of the Potomac were only as successful as Gen. Grant's forces, the Rebels would soon cry for mercy," he wrote. "We don't accomplish anything. We merely hold our ground and think sometimes we are doing a great deal in that." Like most Union soldiers, Keeler had no sympathy for "Copperheads," as Northern opponents of the war were called. Keeler thought them "double-dyed villains" and "cowardly traitors" who should be hung or bayonetted.[25]

Henry "Tip" Aplin of Flint had his picture taken and sent a print to his mother Elvira, along with money. "He looks dark and sober, as though he did not enjoy himself," Elvira Aplin wrote about her son's portrait. As for the cash he was sending home, she explained to another of her sons that Tip was running a successful side business. "As he is dealing in matches and sutler goods, he makes more money than you do," she told Tip's brother George. Of course, since Tip Aplin had been working with regimental supply officers, it could well be that Aplin's side business was not particularly legal or ethical, but it was tolerated and probably not different from scores if not hundreds of other soldiers throughout the army with access to goods and supplies.

In camp, soldiers knew that the return of good weather meant the resumption of marching and fighting. Grand Ledge's Private Ervay wondered how, with all the thousands of "two-year" and "nine-month" soldiers who had gone home, the Union army could defeat the Confederacy. "I don't believe we will ever whip them, if we fight till our heads is all as gray as rats," he wrote. Lt. Salter was also concerned that the brigade of which they were part now numbered only 1,500 men, and questioned how they could go on another campaign. "I do not think that any more active operations or offensive movements will be undertaken until our army is reinforced sufficiently to bring it up to its old standard in point of numbers," he wrote. That would take two or three months and soldiers thought the Confederates, in the meantime, would attack them or Washington. But that was all right. "We are ready for them at any time they chose to come," he continued, "and in fact we would much prefer that they attack us, than that we should have to attack them, as the party acting on the defensive always has the advantage."[26]

Salter was of course correct. "The Confederate victory at Chancellorsville had given

General Robert E. Lee the strategic opportunity to carry the war in the East beyond the Potomac River for a second time," wrote historian Jeffry Wert; the presence of his army in Virginia had been hard on area farms and food supplies, but another invasion would allow them to raid Northern farms and supplies; a major victory there could force the Union to make peace. Having consulted with Confederate President Jefferson Davis, Lee planned to move his army north, taking the war to the Union.[27]

12.

MAY–JULY 1863

WE SHALL FIGHT BEFORE THE FOURTH OF JULY

The days grew hot and dusty as May went on. "It is so warm here it is fairly suffocating when there is no air," Private George W. Ervay wrote. "The sun comes down as if it wanted to kill somebody, which it will if it keeps on much longer." Sgt. John Berry of Company A noted Gov. Blair's visit to the Michigan regiments in the Army of the Potomac on May 27, and the next day the 16th Michigan struck their tents along with their brigade and marched several miles to bivouac near Ballard's Dam, about two miles from Banks' Ford on the Rappahannock. The river here was so narrow that Sgt. Berry could talk to the Confederate pickets on the other side, and the soldiers bathed and fished without hostility; sometimes Rebels came over for coffee and to trade newspapers. Ervay saw a man from Company I swim out, sit on a log with a Rebel, and shake his hand. "It happened to be one that used to stand guard over him when he was in Richmond, a prisoner," the Grand Ledge soldier explained.[1]

There were rumors a Confederate force crossed the river at Orange Court House and was marching for Warrenton, Ervay wrote as May ended. Men saw this situation just as Lt. Salter told his friends in Detroit—if Lee's army was moving north, it must necessarily attack the Army of the Potomac, or the Army of the Potomac would have to march to the defense of Washington. Hervey D. Stewart, an Ontonagon man in Company A, was sure there would be another battle in the weeks ahead. "I think that we shall soon see another fight before the fourth of July next, if I ain't sadly mistaken," he wrote. Soon after, Sgt. Berry of the same company got a mysterious order to scout the river for what he called "a supposed fording place below the dam." To accomplish this, Berry, when his company went on picket duty, entered the water seemingly to bathe, but he actually checked the depth of the river. To whom he reported his findings, Berry did not say.

But the 16th Michigan was under marching orders as its men walked a two-mile patrol up and down their side of the river. Lt. Salter also spoke with Rebel pickets and was surprised to find that Northern men were serving in the Confederate army. One was from western Michigan; he and others had been working in Virginia when the war broke out, and joined up "for the fun of it," Salter wrote. "But they did not think there was so much fun in it now as they had imagined."[2]

With Thomas Stockton's resignation, Lt. Col. Welch started lobbying for promotion to the rank of full colonel. But there were problems; first, he was a known Democrat, albeit a War Democrat. Second, Capt. Judd Mott, whom Welch tried to cashier, had written a blistering letter to state authorities accusing Welch of being a Copperhead. To men like Austin Blair who saw the war as a holy crusade to end slavery, "Democrat" and "traitor" were practically synonymous. Welch understood that he needed to convince powerful Michigan Republicans that he was worthy of promotion or else he would end up like Stockton, with no influential allies and no commission to a higher command. Welch now wrote letters showing he toed the Radical Republican line, letters with a bloodthirsty, victory-at-all-costs rhetoric. Welch told a friend:

> Give us *vigor, vigor, vigor* in the prosecution of the war. Let us have war to the death, and when it comes to killing we can stand it longer than they can. The [Emancipation] Proclamation has done us more good than any other things during the war. The President struck the right cord [*sic*] when he issued it, and it vibrated tunefully through all loyal hearts and was the death knell of the rebellion.[3]

Welch also turned to Michigan's Sen. Jacob M. Howard, a Republican, for support. Welch admitted he had been a War Democrat, but stressed that he fully supported Republican war aims and policies:

> That so distinguished a man as you and one whose social position is so high should think me a "copperhead" wounds the integrity of my spirit . . . I support President Lincoln in every measure, right or wrong. I uphold him in his Proclamation and in the enlistment of Negroes and would gladly command a colored regiment today . . . There has been no measure, since the war commenced, for its suppression, that I have not bent every energy to carry out, nor have I in deed or word ever stated otherwise . . . And I go this far—if it is necessary to accomplish the ends of this war, I am willing to see and help to aid the utter extinction of the southern race. If it cannot be done otherwise, let every man, woman and child be killed, black or white.

Both of these letters were forwarded to Gov. Blair. "I do not see what further the major could say and be a 'Democrat,'" Sen. Howard noted on the back of Welch's letter, misidentifying his rank. "I think it due him that the governor should see this."[4]

On June 3, elements of the Confederate Army of Northern Virginia began to move out of Fredericksburg, shifting and gathering for the invasion of the North by way of the Shenandoah Valley. Within a day Gen. Joe Hooker was receiving reports that Confederate troops were on the march. The 16th Michigan and the First Division of which it was part also moved on June 4, marching ten miles in the heat toward Kelly's Ford; the next day the regiment went with its Third Brigade by a branch road to the nearby Ellis Ford. Here the men continued picketing along the Rappahannock with the 20th Maine as rain came down that evening. "We sometimes talk with them," Lt. Frank Keeler said about the Rebel pickets, "but our conversation is tinged with blackguard at which the Johnnies are not slow."[5]

The men of the 16th Michigan bivouacked in an oak grove while the rest of their division continued to Kelly's Ford that week. "Our army is on the move for some point," Lt. Keeler wrote on June 8 as his regiment was the reserve picket, "we know not where." Hooker revealed nothing to his men—he did not yet know what Lee was up to—but the rumor, an accurate one, was flying through the ranks that Confederate forces were heading north. Soldiers were cut off from newspapers, which was often the nearest thing they had to authoritative information. Still, it seemed to the men that a fight was in the offing; they were told to be ready to move quickly if the order came.

Pvt. Apted of the Brady Sharpshooters got the terrible news that week that one of his younger brothers, Willy, while serving in the 10th Michigan Infantry, had been killed in action at Antioch, Tennessee, in April, but in his sorrow Apted recorded nothing more about it. It had taken nearly two months for Alfred Apted to get the news of his brother's death. In his company there was still a disagreement, even trouble, over what weapons the Brady Sharpshooters were going to use. The company, angry over what Apted called "the gun matter," refused to go on duty until Lt. Col. Welch came and "made a lot of promises." It should be noted that three months earlier, Apted had written that "Welch wants us to take Sharps rifles, but we do not see the place." Presumably "the gun matter" dealt with this ongoing dispute over weapons. A veteran of the company in later years said that they did end up using Sharps breech-loaders. Clearly the sharpshooters resented that their regimental commander inserted himself into the question of what type of rifles they would use in their deadly work, to the point where they risked charges of insubordination.[6]

The next day, June 9, a tremendous clash between Union and Confederate cavalry erupted several miles up the river at Brandy Station—the men of the 16th Michigan could hear the battle in the distance. In response, the regiment was sent across the river to reconnoiter near Ellis Ford, but the Rebel pickets fell back and no blood was shed there. Though the Union soldiers only heard rumors, a long line of Confederate troops, wagons, and artillery was stretching across Virginia as Lee moved north.

The 16th Michigan remained on picket along the river, but this duty was not always serious business. A week earlier near Falmouth, Pvt. George W. Ervay was charmed by a young lady he had met while on picket there: "I had a pleasant interview with Miss Katie Balard [*sic*]. A fine Virginia flower," he noted. Near Ellis Ford, Sgt. Berry had a similarly pleasant time when he was posted at the estate of an elderly "Miss Maw," who lived on the banks of the river with her adopted 17-year-old daughter; Berry found the young woman "accomplished" and "very social"—unlike earlier acquaintances he had made while on picket in mid-May, where he conversed with several "Virginia belles" whom he said were "very pretty" though "ignorant & uneducated."[7]

But hard marching to the northeast was about to begin in the brutal heat as elements of the Army of the Potomac shifted, gathered, and moved out. The regiments of the First Division of the Fifth Corps, spread out along the river, reunited; the 16th Michigan packed and got underway on the evening of June 13, marching first to a town called Morrisville, then to Cattlet Station the next day, and then to Manassas Junction on June 15. "A number of men drop dead in the ranks, sun struck," Sgt. Berry recorded. "We march today about 15 miles."

As Lee's Army of Northern Virginia marched into the Shenandoah Valley and beyond, the Army of the Potomac also moved, interposed between Washington and the Blue Ridge and other mountains to the west that hid the Rebels' northern advance. The 16th Michigan got a day of rest on June 16 and raided nearby cherry orchards, although some of the men went on picket and scouting duty to watch for "guerillas"—Confederate cavalry guarding passes through the Bull Run Mountains. The regiment's march with its brigade resumed the next day in heat and choking dust, covering eighteen miles. John Berry said that "men never endured hardship with any more will and fortitude than at the present time . . . We pass Centreville and at night reach the village of Gum Springs, close to which we camp."[8]

Again the 16th Michigan's men had a day of relative rest and quiet in the woods on the 18th, though the heat rose and a hard rain fell that night. Still, Pvt. Ervay noted he saw three pretty girls at a nearby farmhouse when he went out foraging near Gum Springs. More significantly, the soldiers again heard cavalry clashing in the distance—Rebel troopers under Jeb Stuart "screening," or blocking the routes by which Union horsemen might get closer to the Army of Northern Virginia as it moved north. The march of the 16th Michigan and its division continued the next day in the afternoon a few miles to the village of Aldie, situated near an important mountain pass.

The women and children of the town looked "sadly frightened" as Union troopers and caissons clattered through, though soldiers continued to forage eggs, chickens, and other foodstuffs from the locals. "The town would have a very quiet and secluded appearance were it not for the large quantity of artillery and cavalry which is constantly passing and re-passing through it," Sgt. Berry wrote. That night, his regiment bivouacked in a nearby field as another shower drenched the landscape.[9]

MIDDLEBURG

"At 1 o'clock a.m. the bugle sounds to arms and up we get on the double quick," Sgt. John Berry wrote of the morning of June 21. "We cook our coffee, pack our knapsacks and leave them in charge of a guard." The regiment, with their brigade under the command of Strong Vincent, was part of a mixed force of infantry, cavalry, and artillery ordered to the nearby town of Middleburg, where Confederate cavalry regiments were posted. "The country through there is very hilly, the road from Aldie to Upperville being nothing but hills and ravines all the way," Detroiter Lt. Charles Salter wrote, "whilst all the fences through there are built of stone, so that it is very easy to get positions for defense." Upperville lay just beyond Middleburg, and these towns were on the road that went through the mountains, a pass called Ashby's Gap.

The gap was still held by the strong Rebel cavalry force with whom Union troopers had been fighting and now Union generals proposed to push the Confederates back with infantry. At about 6 a.m., the 16th Michigan, moving west with their forces, reached Middleburg. Initial reconnoitering showed the Confederates were about a mile beyond it, so the soldiers of the Third Brigade and an artillery battery made a circuitous route of about three miles to reach them through the cover of some woods, Sgt. Berry of Company A wrote. Soon the cannon of both sides were firing.[10]

The Confederates were just off the road—dismounted Rebel troopers positioned behind stone walls, Col. Vincent wrote in his report. Their battery of six guns roared nearby, while other troopers waited on horseback in the adjacent fields, ready to take on the Union cavalry. Gen. Alfred Pleasonton, a cavalry commander, was in charge of the Union forces, and he ordered Vincent to advance a regiment of infantry; he chose the 16th Michigan. According to a correspondent of the *New York Herald,* Vincent's directive to Norval Welch was clear and to the point: "Stop that damn battery from howling," he ordered.

Lt. Col. Welch sent out skirmishers—Company A under Capt. George Swan from the regiment's right and the Brady Sharpshooters under Lt. William H. Burns from the left, and they advanced to the edge of the woods. The Confederate artillery was on a hill, covering the road from about twelve hundred yards to the right, firing at the Union guns and at the blue-clad troopers waiting in the rear. "We were ordered forward and for our skirmishers to pick off the gunners and silence [the guns] if possible," Welch reported.[11]

It seemed to Sgt. Berry that the dismounted Confederate troopers were too well protected behind stone walls for the regiment to dislodge them. But Welch reported that his skirmishers, on the righthand side of this confrontation, reached a house and outbuildings and from this cover opened up on the Rebels, forcing some of them to retreat. In the meantime, the 83rd Pennsylvania, from the Third Brigade's left, also advanced through the woods. They got past the fences and flanked the Confederates from their side of the action. Just as the flanks of this line of dismounted Rebel troopers were being turned, one of their battery's wagons was hit and blew up. "A shot from our artillery exploded a rebel caisson filled with shell," Lt. Salter wrote, "and we charged upon them, driving the rebels from their position."

The butternut-clad troopers fell back. As the 16th Michigan ran forward to gain another stone wall, Capt. Judd Mott fell mortally wounded. According to Dr. William Breakey, the regiment's assistant surgeon, Mott that morning had asked for his sword and permission to lead his company when he learned his regiment was going to fight. Welch agreed, the story went, and so Mott went into battle. This tale was likely a heroic fiction, since Mott's court-martial had ultimately resulted in a fine, and not his dismissal, by the order of President Lincoln some three weeks previously. But Mott was shot through the abdomen as he charged with his men; the former lancer officer lingered for a week. Lt. Col. Welch may have tried to end Mott's career with the 16th Michigan, but he had brief, kind words for the dying officer with whom he had once been friendly. When Mott was hit, Welch wrote, he was "doing his whole duty."[12]

As the Union soldiers advanced, the Rebel gunners hooked up their field pieces to their teams and got away, but one, a Blakely rifled gun, flipped on its side as the crew tried to escape. Lt. Thomas Frank Powers and Sgt. John Kuehn of Company A, part of the regiment's skirmish line, were first at the gun, but then ran on in pursuit of the enemy. Welch stressed that point in his report, since a squadron of Union cavalry rode up after the enemy had fled and claimed they had captured the gun. Kuehn had less than a year to live; the Ontonagon County man was later killed in action on May 8, 1864, near Spotsylvania Court House.

The regiment pressed on after Confederates with the skirmishers in the lead, sometimes supporting the Union battery, sometimes in advance of them. Saginaw's Lt. Frank Keeler thought the Union cavalry detachment present was not taking a very active role in the fight. "Our skirmishers, Company A and 'sharpshooters,' kept driving them with the assistance of artillery and a *show* of cavalry on the flanks," he wrote, "having pushed them from stone wall to stone wall, over hills and through ravines."[13]

The Company A skirmishers ran out of ammunition, so Company B, led by Capt. Guy W. Fuller and Lt. Ziba Graham, took their place. For four miles the Third Brigade, with the Union battery and cavalry, drove the Rebels. At Goose Creek, the dismounted Confederates again took up positions behind stone walls so that Union soldiers crossing the bridge faced heavy fire. Fuller reasoned that troopers could rush the crossing quickly, with covering fire from the skirmishers. "Capt. Fuller sent for a company of cavalry to charge the position, but they were driven back with some loss and much confusion," Welch reported.

Fuller felt he and his men could do better than the cavalry, according to the reporter from the *New York Herald*. "Give me horses to mount 25 men," Fuller said to a cavalry officer, "and I'll take the bridge."

"Can't do it," the officer replied.

"Then I'll take the bridge anyway," Fuller vowed, according to the account. He and his company charged, killing three Rebels and capturing nine. Col. Vincent reported that the 83rd Pennsylvania also charged, and that the Confederates retreated. "We could see them scatter over the walls in front, fire a few wild shots, then turn about and 'light out,'" Lt. Keeler wrote.[14]

But Frank Keeler's assessment about the Union cavalry not participating in the fight that day was not fair or accurate; Union troopers did fight Rebels on horseback in bloody combat, after the initial Confederate defensive positions gave way under the attack of the Third Brigade. The 16th Michigan and its brigade continued their pursuit after taking the bridge at Goose Creek, but by that point their part in the day's action was over as evening came on; the Rebels continued to retreat, through the town of Upperville to Ashby's Gap. The Confederate troopers again held strong defensive positions at the end of the pass, and the Union cavalry was not allowed to see into the Shenandoah Valley, where several Confederate divisions were marching steadily northeast—part of Lee's invading force of 80,000 men.[15]

Gen. Pleasanton's mission to clear away the Confederate screening of the pass had not succeeded, though Union soldiers, including the 16th Michigan's, were proud they pushed the vaunted Rebel cavalry back. Welch gave credit in this report to Capt. Fuller, to the "murderously accurate" rifle fire of the Brady Sharpshooters, and to Adjutant Rufus Jacklin, for his bravery and skill in directing the skirmishers. Capt. Mott was the 16th Michigan's only fatality, having been mortally wounded and dying days later; several others were wounded. One was Corporal George Sidman, the young man from Company C who had been in the regimental color guard that day, wounded through the right foot. The lad had come back from his wounds at Gaines' Mill and Fredericksburg, but now his service with the regiment was at an end. He would soon transfer to the Veteran Reserve Corps, often referred to by soldiers as "the invalid corps," but he would claim later that astonishing Civil War sights and experiences were not over for him.

Pvt. John Steel or Steele of Company K was also severely wounded that day, his right arm mangled by a gunshot. As the 16th Michigan's part in the battle ended, Capt. Edward Hill walked over to where the wounded man lay. Steele, a Detroit man in his mid-twenties, had come into the regiment from the lancers, like Hill. "John," Hill said, "you cannot carry a musket anymore." There were tears in Steele's eyes, according to the story as it was told years later. "No, captain," the wounded soldier replied, "but I can carry the colors, can't I?" Steele's arm was amputated, and he was discharged later than summer.

The regiment bivouacked on the field that night and marched back to its camp near Aldie on the evening of the June 22, "satisfied that we had whipped the rebel Gen. Stuart at last," Lt. Salter wrote. Because their brigade had pushed the enemy back for several miles, Lt. Frank Keeler said, "it was the 'tallest' kind of fighting we have yet seen. It afforded the boys of our regiment more real sport than any former experience we had with the enemy." Even so, the Confederate cavalry had done its job, effectively blocking the pass. "The Rebels are up to something on the other side of the mountains," Keeler wrote as his regiment waited orders to move, "and we must be ready for them."[16]

The Third Brigade of the Fifth Corps' First Division remained camped near Aldie for four days as the commander of the Army of the Potomac, Gen. Joseph Hooker, struggled with the question of how and where to move his army. The Confederates on the other side of the mountains, meanwhile, captured 4,000 badly led Union soldiers at Winchester, crossed the Potomac into Maryland, and then entered Pennsylvania, confiscating food, cattle and hogs, grain, hats, shoes, weapons, saddles, and horses, and capturing free black residents, forcing scores of them South to be sold into slavery. The Union army's intelligence arm was by now gathering and receiving information about Lee's advance, but Hooker and Lincoln's military chief and advisor, Gen. Henry W. Halleck, were feuding about how to respond. In addition, Hooker's subordinate generals lacked confidence in him and told Lincoln so, further undermining his position.

The average soldier knew none of this, however. Back at Aldie, Pvt. George Ervay got in trouble when guards caught him returning to camp after dark from foraging, loaded down with foodstuffs taken from locals. "Had to go on guard for punishment," the Grand Ledge teenager complained. But three days later, on June 26, the march of the Fifth Corps started again as Hooker moved the several corps that made up the Army of the Potomac north by different routes, to stay between the Lee's forces and Washington. The skies opened up with rain, and though the road was muddy and slippery, it was better than parching heat and dust, Sgt. John Berry declared.

"We left Aldie at 6 a.m. on the 26th, marched north through Leesburg, crossed the Potomac at Edwards Ferry upon pontoon bridges and halted at 8 p.m., five miles this side [north] of the river," noted Lt. Charles Salter. "Adieu, Dixie Land," Flint's Lt. Ziba Graham wrote about leaving Virginia and crossing into Maryland. "Again we are on the retrograde movement. Our yearly pilgrimage North has already commenced." Graham noted they bivouacked near Poolesville just before sundown, and Salter said that they covered twenty-three miles.[17]

The soldiers resumed the march in the morning, waded the waist-deep Monocacy River, passed through hamlets called Buck Hill and Boone Hill, and halted in the woods near Frederick. Lt. Graham remembered the anniversary of the Gaines' Mill, while Sgt. Berry remarked on the picturesque Maryland farms and rolling fields of grain. The regiment remained in their camp on Sunday, June 28, and some were allowed to walk to town to buy food better than "U.S. hardtack," noted Pvt. Alfred Apted, the Grand Rapids sharpshooter. A regimental return or report about the 16th Michigan's manpower that day showed that there were 339 enlisted men present and seventeen officers.

But there was big news that Sunday. "Today Gen. Meade, our corps commander, superseded Gen. Hooker in command of the army," wrote Lt. Graham. "He received his appointment about midnight and was as much surprised as the troops were. He thought when awakened to hear it that it was an order for his arrest. So it goes." Hooker had resigned and in his place, the Fifth Corps commander, Gen. George Meade, a Pennsylvanian and West Point graduate who had been recommended by other generals, became Lincoln's choice to lead the Army of the Potomac. Now command of the Fifth Corps went to Gen. George Sykes, a regular army officer who had commanded another division in that corps.[18]

Lt. Graham wrote that soldiers were not happy about these changes on the eve of what they expected to be another major battle. After all, he said, the disasters at Fredericksburg (with Burnside commanding) and Chancellorsville (where Hooker was in charge) had happened when command of the army shifted "at important moments." His statement was a bit of a stretch as regarded Hooker, though it was true that Meade was not known to most of the Union army. Meade was, however, a competent, professional soldier and had the respect of other generals.

Another major development occurred that day, and though Union soldiers knew nothing about it, this would have consequences for thousands of men, North and South: Gen. Robert E. Lee had believed that the Army of the Potomac was still massed in northern Virginia, but that evening at Chambersburg, Pennsylvania, he received a spy's report that his enemy was in Maryland—much closer, threateningly close, since his own

Confederate army was spread out for scores of miles on Pennsylvania roads. He ordered his generals to bring their forces together, and soon chose for this rendezvous the town of Gettysburg.[19]

The march north from Frederick through the countryside resumed for the 16th Michigan in the rain the next morning, June 29, though the Fifth Corps' start was late because another corps ahead of them was delayed. At least Maryland residents were glad to see them. "On the way we are welcomed by the inhabitants," Sgt. Berry noted. That, Lt. Graham wrote, "does us old soldiers good." Pvt. George Ervay, a farmer before enlisting, naturally admired the wheat crop as they marched by, but he was smitten by a girl from Libertytown, where the 16th Michigan camped with its Third Brigade after moving nearly twenty miles that day. "I saw the prettiest girl today that I ever saw," the teenager wrote appreciatively in his diary. If Ervay managed to ask her name or momentarily flirt with her, he did not say.[20]

The rain came again, and the weather stayed cloudy and wet the next day, the end of June. The soldiers were awakened before dawn and marching at 4 a.m., taking roads through Johnsville and Uniontown. "Up again before daylight," Graham wrote. "It does seem as though we were being marched to death." Sgt. Berry said they traveled some of the route by backroads "on the left flank," seemingly west of the main portion of their Fifth Corps' column, watching for Confederate cavalry reported in the area. Gen. Meade had shifted their corps and another corps further east from the main, northbound advance of the Army of the Potomac, in case Lee moved to strike them from that direction. This turned out to be unnecessary, but it required a long march by the 16th Michigan and some of its comrades. Yet Graham and the regiment's young surgeon, Dr. Robert Everett of Hillsdale, who had replaced Dr. Wixom, were able to visit with a civilian doctor and his wife in Uniontown, when the regiment halted for a rest and lunch until the bugle sounded; it was time to march on. The regiment, with its brigade and division, stopped that evening near the Maryland town of Union Mills, on Pipe Creek.

Sgt. Berry wrote that the men were "completely used up," since they had marched nearly 30 miles that day by a circuitous route. But they had been well fed by the farmers and the people of the several small towns they had passed. "Marched through Uniontown and five other villages, the names I forgot," Pvt. Ervay wrote that night, "the people giving the soldiers all they wanted to eat." But Alfred Apted, the Brady Company sharpshooter from Grand Rapids, recorded that day how the men heard that the Rebels were so close that he had expected a fight to erupt before nightfall. He added later, however: "We fail to find the rebs."[21]

Apted was only off by hours. In the coming day, the Union and Confederate armies would indeed find each other some 20 miles to the northwest, and the greatest battle ever fought on the continent would begin as the forces of Lee and Meade collided at the small college and market town and road center called Gettysburg.

The soldiers of the 16th Michigan and their brigade were up before the sun rose July 1 and they were marching by 9 a.m. or later, probably because of the mass of men getting on the road ahead of them; Pvt. Ervay thought it was 10:30 a.m. when his regiment moved out. Lt. Graham wrote that their position in the march was about a mile back from the head of the column. The morning was cloudy, and the men marched proudly with flags flying and bands playing, he said, with residents of villages and farms coming out to cheer their column as they moved into Pennsylvania. The state line was a few miles from their bivouac near Union Mills, Maryland, and Pvt. Apted said they crossed into the Keystone State around 2 p.m., "drums beating and flags flying." "Never did we march in better spirits," Sgt. Berry recorded. "Although footsore & worn out with the late long marches & want of actual rest, we drag along singing and joking as if we were on a pleasure excursion.

"At the head of our regiment marches the remains of our Drum Corps, the majority of whom are from 13 to 15 years old," he continued. "These young soldiers have been inured to hardship in the hard school of war." But the continued march was so arduous that most of the boys eventually fell out, and most of their drums were broken or abandoned. "All the instruments we can muster is 3 drums (2 broken) & one cracked fife," Graham wrote. Yet the musicians did what they could to energize their comrades, "singing patriotic songs as we pass through each village & town." The citizens also helped boost the soldiers' morale, turning out as they marched by, shouting "hurrah for the Union!" and "God bless the Army of the Potomac!" Of course, it was not just drummer boys who fell out on the brutal marches of the past three days—a soldier in the 22nd Massachusetts, in the 16th Michigan's division, wrote that "sunstrokes were numerous," and that by the afternoon of July 1, hundreds of men were dropping, exhausted, by the roadside. Though the cheering and music helped, companies and even whole regiments fell out, he wrote; they would have catch up later as best they could.[22]

By late afternoon the regiment, with its brigade and division, reached Hanover, where dead horses in the streets were evidence of the June 30 clash between Union troopers and Jeb Stuart's cavalry. Lt. Graham said the soldiers "could plainly hear the cannonading in the direction of Gettysburg," to the west, though other 16th Michigan diarists did not mention it and some historians have doubted Fifth Corps soldiers heard the artillery ten miles or more away. But the townspeople put out tables of food for the men and the 16th Michigan rested at a farm adjacent to the town; some men cooked coffee. Their break lasted about two hours, and some may have thought they were going to bivouac there for the night. But orders came for them to keep moving, so the march resumed at 6 p.m. (their commander said at 7 p.m.), with the Fifth Corps turning to the west, for Gettysburg.

Darkness slowly descended over the column, and Sgt. Berry said a full moon rose. But the confidence the soldiers felt during the daylight portion of the march "seemed to have been lost, in our tired condition," Ziba Graham wrote of the night. He noted the soldiers' concern about "experimenting with a new commander" (Meade) as they headed for what was sure to be another battle. "For miles we marched on with ominous silence," the officer from Flint wrote. Robert G. Carter, the Massachusetts soldier in the First Brigade of their division, said soldiers continued to fall out, exhausted, on the night's march, with scores of men resting along the road.[23]

Pvt. Ervay thought they moved six miles beyond Hanover and Sgt. Berry thought it was ten miles, but as they reached a hamlet called McSherrystown, Lt. Graham said the soldiers up ahead at the front of the column began cheering, and the noise spread steadily back as the news was passed along—"McClellan has been reinstated," soldiers shouted. This was not true, but the rumor had the effect of again lifting the spirits of the Fifth Corps soldiers. Now it was early in the morning of July 2 when the 16th Michigan's part of the column turned off the road into the woods to bivouac.

It had been, Lt. Graham wrote, "an almost continuous march of twenty-two hours." The last thing Pvt. Ervay recorded in his diary was the camp story about McClellan's return; Graham said they were three miles from Gettysburg as the soldiers bedded down for what remained of a night's rest, though Pvt. Apted thought they were five miles out; so did Sgt. Berry. He summed up the march from Hanover and their situation before he retired: "We pass through McSherrysville [*sic*] & Brushtown & halt at Oxford, 5 miles from Gettysburg & in close proximity to the enemy."[24]

By the time the 16th Michigan bivouacked outside of Gettysburg with the Fifth Corps, the first day of the battle had long since ended. Many years later 16th Michigan veteran Rufus Jacklin would claim he met former Confederate General Harry Heth when they served together as commissioners tasked with placing monuments at the Antietam battlefield. Heth, Jacklin said, related the story of how he had sent his Rebel division's quartermaster with a brigade to Gettysburg to seize a quantity of shoes, hats, and clothing they had heard was there on the morning of July 1, 1863, and in doing so opened the battle. The Confederates were surprised to find dismounted Union cavalry and artillery on the road west of Gettysburg, blocking their way. "I said to him [the quartermaster], 'We will have the shoes, hats, etc.,'" Heth reportedly told Jacklin. "I immediately ordered my entire division to right about and march on Gettysburg."

So as the Fifth Corps trudged that day into Pennsylvania, the battle opened, intensified, and raged as thousands of men, Union and Confederate, arrived and went into the fight. Heth later told Jacklin that he did indeed get a new soft felt hat, but it was too big; his quartermaster suggested they fold up some paper and place it under the sweat band to properly fit it to the general's head. Not long afterward, a rifle ball hit Heth in the forehead as he rode forward wearing his new hat, knocking him unconscious. "It was found that the folded paper had spared my life," Heth said, according to Jacklin's account.[25]

Hats or no, July 1 had quickly turned into a terrible and bloody day. First, two Union cavalry brigades that morning engaged the oncoming Confederate division that was marching east to Gettysburg, and then a second division also moved in. Soon thousands more Rebels came in from the north as most of Lee's Army of Northern Virginia arrived in the area. Though most of the Army of the Potomac was not yet on hand, the first two Union corps reached the town; they, too, went into battle, were battered, and then were driven back through Gettysburg. But they bought precious time and allowed their artillery batteries and other arriving Union forces to set up defenses that afternoon on high ground south of town called Cemetery Hill, Culp's Hill to its right, and on the ridge that ran south from the town's graveyard, naturally called Cemetery Ridge.

Now on the morning of July 2, the 16th Michigan and the Third Brigade of which it was part, with their division and corps, would soon join the Army of the Potomac, not quite reunited just south of Gettysburg. They had missed the first day of the battle here as they had marched from Maryland, but they would not miss the second.

13.

JULY 2, 1863

THE MOST DESPERATE FIGHTING I EVER SAW

The men of the Fifth Corps got about four hours of sleep that morning of July 2. "The bugle sounds at break of day—'Prepare to march'—and in about an hour (daylight) we march," noted Sgt. John Berry of the 16th Michigan's Company A. Their Third Brigade, in column with the rest of the First Division, marched west on the last three miles to Gettysburg. The Confederates held the town up ahead, so the column turned off the Hanover Road in farm country about two miles east of town. "We soon arrived at the outskirts of the place and were apprised of the fact that our whole army was here," Lt. Ziba Graham of Flint later wrote, though in fact all elements of the Army of the Potomac had not quite arrived. "All had been marching on different roads, and when [Gen. John] Buford's Cavalry and the First and Eleventh Corps became engaged yesterday, it was ascertained the enemy were in force here." The Fifth Corps was positioned near Wolf's Hill, on the right of the Union line, where some soldiers joined in "light skirmishing" with Confederate pickets, though not the 16th Michigan or its brigade.[1]

The defensive position of the Army of the Potomac at Gettysburg on July 2 and 3 has often been described as having the shape of an upside-down fish hook, though on the morning of the 2nd it was more of a horseshoe. Union soldiers and artillery batteries on the two large knolls, Cemetery Hill and Culp's Hill, just south of town, represented the front of this horseshoe. More high ground called Cemetery Ridge extended south from Cemetery Hill, where more Union guns and infantry faced west—the left-hand portion of the horseshoe. This ridge dropped away a mile or so south of town, and then rose again in the form of two rocky hills that would become known as Round Top and Little Round Top; a few hundred yards west of the smaller knob was a strange formation of giant boulders known as Devil's Den.

The 16th Michigan and its brigade were first posted at the tip of right-hand side of the horseshoe. But at 10 a.m., the Fifth Corps was shifted about a mile to the southwest, the soldiers marching to an open rise called Powers Hill. Here they waited in reserve between the Union forces on Cemetery Ridge and those on the hills immediately south of town. Of course, Lee's army confronted the Army of the Potomac along this line. From the location at Powers Hill, the 16th Michigan and its corps could quickly move to wherever the generals needed them. "The morning was quiet and the air calm," recalled Rufus Jacklin, who was the regiment's adjutant then; many soldiers tired from the long marches and short rests lay down in the grass to sleep.[2]

George Ervay, the 18-year-old from Grand Ledge, pulled out some paper and datelined a letter: "Camp of the 16th Michigan, in the field Near Getties burg PA." It had been nearly a month since he had written home. "Dear parents," he began. "I now sit down to wright A few lines to you to let you know that I am well. We have not had any maile since the 14th of June but once. We are here now laying in line of battle. They have been fighting A little this morning but all is still at present. Once in a while there is A cannon fire. We Anticipate a hard battle here now this afternoon or tomorrow."[3]

Ervay did not know when he would be able to mail his letter since his regiment was in the field. "I can not wright much now for we don't know what moment we shall have to fall in," he continued. "The people [here in Pennsylvania] are good union people, they give the soldiers all they want. But M[aryland] is the prettiest State that I ever saw and the best crops in it." The thought of the fine and picturesque farms segued to young women he had seen. "The farmers are harvesting now & there is lots of pretty Girls in MD," he wrote, doubtlessly thinking of the prettiest girl he had seen from Liberty three days earlier. "In P[ennsylvania] there is lots of Girls and young wimmin [*sic*] but they can't come up with the MD girls.[4]

"I was talking with a Girl yesterday in Hanover City, she said that if we let the Grey backs come back there she would Scold all of us for they stole every thing that they could get a hold of," he continued. "They take all of the horses that is good for any thing." While the Rebels were proud of their cavalry, "our men laid them out wright and left down at Hanover," he wrote, referring to the clash between Rebel and Union troopers on June 30. "I don't know as you can read this for I have written it in A hurrey but I shall have to close for this time. Wright soon as you get this. I have got 15 months longer to stay [in the army] or sooner and wright often. Give my best respects to all enquirers. I Remain your Affectionate Son," he wrote. His last word, misspelled, was "Adiew" and he signed, putting the letter away.[5]

Lt. Ziba Graham of Flint, assigned to Company B, said he was allowed to leave the regiment for the moment. "I went to the front to see the line and take a view of the surrounding country," he wrote later. Two of the regiment's medical officers rode north to see Gettysburg—Dr. Robert Everett from Hillsdale, who had served with the 5th Michigan Infantry, and Dr. William Breakey, the assistant surgeon from Salem who had been detached to serve with Battery D of the 5th U.S. Artillery. "Dr. Everett . . . and I rode up the pike to near the picket line at the cemetery," Breakey recounted. "Dismounting and fastening our horses, we walked on towards the ridge partly through the cemetery, to get a view of the field and town in front." The pickets advised them to keep their heads down, no sooner warning them, Breakey said, "when we heard the whistle of bullets from the Confederate pickets." The doctors took cover behind the cemetery gate towers.

Perhaps Graham went with the doctors up the Baltimore Pike, or rode west to Cemetery Ridge, but by 3 p.m. he was back with his regiment. "I had returned to the regiment but a few moments before the Sixth Army Corps came up, and we were moved away toward the left of the Third Corps whilst the Sixth Corp took our place," Graham wrote. In fact, General George Meade, newly appointed commander of the Army of the Potomac, just met with some of his corps commanders and learned that a politically appointed general, Daniel Sickles, who was not present for the meeting, had moved his Third Corps, the Union line's left, out into a vulnerable and dangerous position. Meade was furious, but it was too late for Sickles to withdraw his scattered troops when Confederate artillery began to fire at about 3:30 p.m. Now the division of which the 16th Michigan was part was ordered to march southwest into what was about to become a storm of battle.[6]

By that afternoon, Robert E. Lee had most of the Army of Northern Virginia at Gettysburg and he determined to strike the Union's left on Cemetery Ridge, from the shallow valley north of the hill known since as Little Round Top to Cemetery Hill—a position that was approximately a mile and a quarter in length. The obvious anchor of this Union line was Little Round Top, but Sickles had no force posted here. The summit of this tear-shaped hill or ridge was about 160 feet above the surrounding land, providing a commanding view. Only its neighbor to the south, the larger, tree-covered Round Top (sometimes called Big Round Top), was higher, though it did not have the same military value. The western side of Little Round Top was cleared of trees and there was room on the hill's crest for a handful of artillery pieces.

But Gen. Dan Sickles was *not* a professional soldier. Learning that there were Confederates in the woods ahead of him and dissatisfied with his position, at 2 p.m. Sickles shifted his corps as much as three-quarters of a mile west from Cemetery Ridge to some high ground along a local highway called the Emmitsburg Road. This created an untenable situation for his infantry and artillery—their new defensive line was too long and disjointed to protect.

Events were also unfolding on the Confederate side. As the 16th Michigan had risen that morning of July 2 and marched with the Fifth Corps, Lee sent officers to reconnoiter the Union left south of town, and he was informed (wrongly, at that moment) there were no Yankee troops in the vicinity of the Round Tops. He decided that three divisions—two of them Gen. James Longstreet's—would attack this flank and drive northward, while other Confederate forces simultaneously moved against the Union army's right at Culp's Hill, about two miles away. He hoped this would collapse his enemy's position, wounding if not crippling the Army of the Potomac. Despite objections from Longstreet, Lee ordered the attack to begin as soon as possible.

But delays hampered the movement of Longstreet's men to get into position and his columns marched and countermarched through the afternoon trying to stay out of sight of Union pickets and some signalmen on Little Round Top. It was not until 3 p.m. that the head of this column reached the starting point for the attack. Confederate officers were startled at what they saw before them—Union batteries moving into position in and around the Peach Orchard at the intersection of the Emmitsburg and Wheatfield Roads.

To strike them, Rebel troops would have to cross open farm fields. But from this point at the Peach Orchard, the left of the thin Union line now zigzagged through fields and wood lots southeast toward Little Round Top to Devil's Den. In the vicinity of the Round Tops, Rebel scouts correctly reported, there were no Union troops.

Lee ordered the assault to go forward. As the Fifth Corps was ordered to march to the Union left, the Confederate artillery barrage began. In minutes, their infantry attack would follow.[7]

It was after 3 p.m., in the minutes before the Rebel guns opened fire, when Gen. Meade finally rode with his aides to see what Gen. Sickles had done—messages from Sickles had been arriving at his headquarters throughout the day. Meade sent his chief engineer, Gen. Gouverneur Warren, to Little Round Top to investigate, and Warren was shocked to find there were no Union forces holding this hill—only some signalmen with their flags. Warren saw Rebel troops moving in the trees about a mile away, getting ready to flank Sickles' men and guns and take the ridge on which he stood. Then the Confederate batteries opened up, the prelude to the Rebel infantry assault. Warren sent his aides down the hill, galloping away with urgent messages for Meade: Troops were needed, immediately, to hold Little Round Top. Union artillery fired back in response to the Rebel gunfire, and the "hard battle" George Ervay predicted in his letter to his parents was underway.[8]

As Warren discovered this situation on Little Round Top, the Fifth Corps' First Division was about a mile to the north, marching toward this new battlefield, its Third Brigade commanded by Col. Strong Vincent since the resignation of Thomas Stockton. Oliver Norton of the 83rd Pennsylvania, flag bearer and bugler for Vincent, said that they moved from Powers Hill on a country lane to a main north–south route, the Taneytown Road, turning and crossing into the countryside in a southwesterly direction. Their division halted "a little northeast of the wheatfield," referring to the place known since as "*the* Wheatfield" because of the terrible fighting about to take place there. As nearby cannon roared, the 16th Michigan, 44th New York, 83rd Pennsylvania, and 20th Maine waited with their division comrades on or near the farm of resident John Weikert for the generals to assign their position.

Accounts written by 16th Michigan officers Ziba Graham and Rufus Jacklin, as well as some official battle reports, claimed that General Warren rode down from nearby Little Round Top to meet their brigade, but these were wrong. In truth, one of Warren's aides found the Fifth Corps commander, Gen. George Sykes, telling him that troops were urgently needed to defend the nearby heights. Sykes sent a captain from his staff riding out to find Gen. James Barnes, who commanded the First Division of which the 16th Michigan was part, with orders to send one of his brigades to the rocky hill. Barnes was temporarily in charge of the division while Gen. Charles Griffin was on sick leave, but where Barnes was at that moment no one knew. Soon Sykes's aide rode up to the waiting First Division, looking for Barnes, but he was intercepted by Col. Vincent. Pressed by Vincent, this captain revealed that a brigade was needed to hold Little Round Top.

Though military chain-of-command required Sykes's order to go to Barnes, and through Barnes to a brigade commander, Vincent understood the crisis and ordered his brigade to hurry to the hill. Led by the 44th New York, the regiments turned onto the Millerstown (Wheatfield) Road, that ran east toward Little Round Top. Vincent and his flag bearer galloped ahead.[9]

Lt. Col. Norval Welch and Adjutant Rufus Jacklin were also on horseback. "He (Welch) directed me to give the necessary orders to double-quick," Jacklin wrote, using the army's nineteenth-century term for a jogging-paced run. "We were moving in columns of fours. I rode to the left of the column, precautioning the company commanders to close up their ranks and prepare for a double-quick of at least three-quarters of a mile." Others also spoke of the run to Little Round Top. "Whilst moving to our new position the ball opened and the firing became terrific," Ziba Graham wrote. "We double-quicked over the old stony ground in very short order, whilst shell after shell came bursting amongst us."

The brigade ran "all the while exposed to the fire of the enemy's artillery," agreed Lt. Charles Salter. One shot nearly made a casualty of his fellow Detroiter Jacklin, killing his mount, the impact throwing horse and rider. "A cannon ball took off the top of my horse's head at the moment," Jacklin later wrote. "He was in the air, and fell a mass of quivering flesh, and I partly under him." Men lifted the carcass off Jacklin, who stayed with the regiment though he said his leg was injured. Several men were also wounded in the shelling, Sgt. John Berry noted. He called this fire of grapeshot and canister "very heavy," and it seemed to him that they ran for a mile to reach the knob. The soldiers turned off the road as it passed just north of Little Round Top, and they were temporarily shielded from the Confederate guns as they moved behind the hill.[10]

As the Third Brigade scrambled to Little Round Top, the first two brigades of Confederate infantry, from one of Longstreet's divisions, advanced from the trees at the Emmitsburg Road; it was probably about 4 p.m. More would soon follow, but the first Rebel regiments, already suffering casualties from Union shot and shell, came east across the fields; seven of these regiments, Texans and Alabamans, headed toward Round Top. Almost immediately, skirmishers from Sickles' Third Corps—several small companies from the 2nd U.S. Sharpshooters Regiment—fired on the advancing Rebels from behind a farmer's fences just west of Round Top. Though these were deadly marksmen, the Rebels were too many. The federal sharpshooters retreated and split up, still firing, some of them going up the western slope of Round Top, pursued by the 15th and 47th Alabama regiments. These sharpshooters bought time for Vincent's brigade, allowing it to reach Little Round Top ahead of the Confederates, most of whom turned toward the rocky hill and the nearby Devil's Den, the jumbled collection of giant boulders and the southernmost position of the Third Corps.

About a thousand yards to the northeast, Vincent and his flag carrier reached Little Round Top. They rode part way around the wooded, eastern side of the hill and then up and over to its western face, to an "open" point below the southern crest, but they did not see Gen. Warren, who was probably on the northern crest. They guided their horses out on a rock shelf or ledge, where the 16th Michigan would soon be positioned; "it was in full view of the rebel lines," Oliver Norton wrote. There were no trees here, and in seconds Confederate gunners saw them and fired two exploding shells, bracketing the two Pennsylvanians. "Down with that flag, Norton," Vincent yelled. "Damn it, go behind the rocks with it!" They dismounted, and Vincent scouted the hillside to position his brigade. He had only minutes.[11]

Vincent's brigade arrived and clambered up the eastern slope. "[We] came to a large hill, or a range of hills, which the enemy were at the same time attempting to gain," Lt. Salter said. "We arrived first, formed line and advanced over the hill and as we arrived on top, saw a long line of rebels coming over and down a range of hill opposite us." These were the Confederates advancing across the lower slopes of Round Top, some heading for Devil's Den.

According to Ziba Graham's romanticized account, General Warren stood on a large boulder and pointed out the advancing Confederates to Col. Vincent and Lt. Col. Welch, telling them "to hold this point at all hazards." But this did not happen, Warren wrote; he said that he and Vincent did not meet on Little Round Top. Graham may have heard Col. Vincent telling his regimental commanders to hold their positions at all costs. In any case, Vincent saw the advancing Rebels and positioned the regiments in a line stretching from the hill's south side—the left of the brigade line—to the west side, the brigade's right, facing Devil's Den.

Though the 16th Michigan would be remembered as the regiment on the brigade's right, it was initially but briefly placed on the left. Lt. Col. Norval Welch reported this, and other officers there that day agreed. Benjamin Partridge from Bay City, who had been promoted to captain of Company C, would later explain this first posting was on the low ground at the southern base of the hill, about where the 20th Maine would soon make what turned out to be its famous charge. Ellis Spear, then major of the 20th Maine and in charge of his regiment's left wing, also confirmed this; he later wrote that the 16th Michigan "was at first on the extreme left [of the brigade line] and the 20th Maine next." [12]

Companies from each regiment were now deployed as skirmishers: Company B from the 44th New York; the 20th Maine's Company B; and a third company from the 83rd Pennsylvania. But two companies were sent out from the 16th Michigan—the Brady Sharpshooters and Company A. Why two is unknown, but Vincent had days earlier seen the aggressive performance of these Michigan skirmishers against the dismounted Rebel troopers at Middleburg. These five skirmish companies moved out, disappearing onto the thinly wooded "saddle" between the two Round Tops and the northern slope of the bigger hill, which was slightly more timbered. Oliver Norton, who wrote the first in-depth study of the fight at Little Round Top, thought skirmishers from the 44th New York and the 83rd Pennsylvania moved west while, as indicated by Rufus Jacklin and Capt. Walter Morrill of the 20th Maine, the Maine and Michigan skirmishers moved onto Round Top's northern side. Ellis Spear of the 20th Maine later noted that his regiment's skirmishers did not connect with those further to the right, meaning the companies from New York and Pennsylvania.

Soon after the brigade skirmishers left, Lt. Col. Welch was ordered to quickly take the

16th Michigan up to the brigade's right on the western face of Little Round Top—the exposed ledge Rebel guns just hit when firing at Vincent's flag. "After deploying two of my largest companies as skirmishers—Brady's Sharpshooters from the left, and Company A from my right—I was ordered at double-quick to the right of the brigade," Welch reported. Again, accounts of Ellis Spear and Benjamin Partridge agreed.[13]

This was a last-minute decision by Col. Vincent, hurrying the 16th Michigan, the smallest regiment in the brigade, from the lowest, tree-covered southern part of the hill to the higher position. Amos Judson of the 83rd Pennsylvania, its eventual historian, later claimed Vincent ordered the Michigan men into line with the Pennsylvanians on their left and the 44th New York on their right. But the commander of the New Yorkers, Col. James Rice, reportedly asked that his regiment fight side-by-side with the 83rd Pennsylvania; Vincent agreed, Judson wrote, so the 16th Michigan was placed on the far right of their line.[14]

The regiment's position looked west toward Devil's Den, where a Union battery was firing, and advancing Confederate infantry now opened fire. Below them in the near distance was Plum Run, a narrow creek that flowed in front of the Round Tops to Devil's Den through a shallow, swampy valley choked with boulders; slightly to the north of this valley, the soldiers saw woodlots, scrubby meadows, and farm fields, where more Union cannon fired and rifle volleys spread down the Third Corps' jagged line. The 16th Michigan was not on Little Round Top's crest, but about 50 paces down from the southern summit. Their brigade line descended slightly as it curved around from the western face to the south side of the rocky hill, where the 20th Maine, the largest of the regiments, held the left. All told, the Third Brigade had 1,141 rifles in their line.[15]

How strong was the 16th Michigan? William Fox, a soldier-historian who studied regimental losses after the war, concluded it had "218 engaged" in battle that day (a number that may have included officers), while the historian of the 83rd Pennsylvania, listing the "exact number of rifles for each regiment," stated the 16th Michigan had 188. Joshua Chamberlain, in an 1864 letter, stated the 16th Michigan had 250 riflemen at Little Round Top, but this is too high a number compared to the best contemporaneous account given by Lt. Salter after the battle. He said the regiment went into battle with 200 men, a number in agreement with Welch's report. With his skirmish companies gone, Welch said he had only 150 men in his line. Writing years later, Ziba Graham suggested it was not surprising, given the hard marches they made, that his regiment's number of men "present for duty" dropped from "349" (it was actually 339) in late June to the point where there were only 150 men in the battle line, without Company A and the Brady Sharpshooters—it was "the natural falling out on such a forced march" with the nearly continuous 22-hour trek of July 1 in the heat.[16]

On the left of the 16th Michigan's short line, the position was strong where it connected with the 44th New York, since attackers trying to come up were faced here with a very steep incline. There were also large rocks and boulders on or along their rock shelf, providing some cover though this ledge also jutted forward and was exposed; then it declined away and disappeared into the hillside on the 16th Michigan's right. The approach from the base of the hill from the west-northwest was not as steep, and this approach had plenty of rocks, boulders, and enough trees to provide cover for attackers stopping to pick their targets, fighting, as one Texan called it, "Indian fashion."

The Confederates, having driven off the 2nd U.S. Sharpshooters, approached Little Round Top from the south-southwest. As the 16th Michigan got into its last-minute position, "the firing commenced," Lt. Salter wrote.[17]

THE LEFT: SKIRMISHERS

Rufus Jacklin later claimed that the opening shots in the fight for Little Round Top were fired by his old company, which had moved up the north slope of Round Top with Company A. "The Brady Sharpshooters firing the first shots down upon their advance columns from the Big Round Top was the signal of the attack," Jacklin wrote years later. The evidence of his comrades' diaries indicate that they were on Round Top, though not confirming Jacklin's specific claim. "We get into position into line of battle," Sgt. John Berry of Company A noted. "Our Company with the company of sharpshooters is then sent out & deployed as skirmishers & we advance about half a mile and find the enemy."

The only other available account of a 16th Michigan skirmisher, the diary of Brady Sharpshooter Alfred Apted of Grand Rapids, transcribed by his great-grandson, was less specific as it began. "The enemy are now fighting over (obstacles? illegible) near Gettysburg. Started about 4:00 and came around the west (?) of our lines and took position on the next extreme left of our lines," Apted wrote. This was the sharpshooter summing up what he first saw and experienced that day—attacking Confederates, coming over Round Top, flanking their position.[18]

Col. Joshua Chamberlain of the 20th Maine later reported that he had sent Capt. Morrill's Company B forward as skirmishers, to "extend my left flank across this hollow"—the valley or saddle between the south side of Little Round Top and the northern slope of Round Top—"with directions to act as occasion might dictate, to prevent a surprise on my exposed flank and rear." Yet Morrill was also acting, at least initially, in concert with Welch's Company A and Brady Sharpshooters; he ordered his men "to connect on the right with the 16 Mich. Regt. skirmishers." Ellis Spear of the 20th Maine later wrote that Morrill's company "disappeared in the woods on the front and left [of the regiment's line], but did not connect with the skirmishers on the right." In other words, the Maine company started up the northeast side Round Top, with Morrill indicating his men were to link with the Michigan skirmishers.

In the meantime, the other brigade skirmishers moved briefly west down the slope onto the lower, northwestern portion of Round Top and met the Rebels, who quickly pushed them back. The soldier-historian of the 83rd Pennsylvania wrote that soon after moving out, "our skirmishers were driven in, the enemy following closely." The history of the 44th New York, written by one of its veteran officers, said that its skirmishers, Company B under Capt. Lucius Larabee, moved about 200 yards or less before running into the enemy. Larabee saw Rebels coming in "at least two lines of battle" and ordered his men to retreat. As he directed them back, he was shot and killed.[19]

Confederate officers also reported this—a short but intense clash before they reached Little Round Top. Major John Bane of the 4th Texas wrote of pushing a line of Union soldiers from the rocks and trees back to their main line on the next hill—Little Round Top—that his men met them "full force" in "a sharp contest." This action is echoed in other Confederate reports and accounts; Lt. Col. L. H. Scruggs of the 4th Alabama, adjacent to the 4th Texas, said his men "advanced up the mountain under a galling fire, driving the enemy before us" to another "stone fence." This meant the Rebels drove off Third Brigade's skirmishers before reaching the brigade's main line along the rocks and ledges, since there was no "stone fence" there. Oliver Norton was convinced that Bane here referred to driving back Vincent's skirmishers, who, he wrote, retreated to their brigade line.[20]

But not all the Third Brigade skirmish companies went back to their regiments, and at least one did not fire a shot in this preliminary clash—the 20th Maine's Company B. Morrill's men were starting up Round Top's northeastern slope when the captain heard "heavy volleys of musketry in our rear." Morrill wrote nothing more about connecting with the 16th Michigan skirmishers, but turned his men back through the woods until they came to a field that was almost behind Little Round Top.

Along the way, Morrill found "twelve or fifteen U.S. Sharpshooters," some of the men from the Third Corps who had minutes earlier skirmished with the Confederates and retreated over Round Top. The Maine company and these sharpshooters took cover behind a stone wall, and waited while the fighting spread along the Third Brigade's line. The Alabama regiments that pursued these 2nd U.S. Sharpshooters up Round Top came down the north side and ran headlong into the 20th Maine, but cut off Morill's men and the federal sharpshooters who had joined them.[21]

This situation on the south side of Little Round Top provides the context for understanding the diaries of 16th Michigan skirmishers John Berry and Alfred Apted. First, in the course of the next hour or so, Morrill's company and the dozen U.S. sharpshooters became part of the heroic story of the 20th Maine's struggle at Little Round Top. At the battle's climax on the southern hillside, Chamberlain's regiment, low on ammunition, charged down from its position on the hill, chasing the Alabamans up Round Top; Morrill's men and the U.S. sharpshooters joined them. For the record, Chamberlain maintained the Rebels were gathering for yet another attack, while the Alabamans' commander said he already ordered his men to withdraw. But scores of Rebels surrendered or were captured, while others ran and escaped. Ellis Spear wrote that after the Maine regiment charged, he learned that their Company B and that squad of U.S. sharpshooters, from the stone wall, "had been keeping up a fire on the enemy, from the rear, during the fight & when we charged and the enemy fell back."[22]

But this charge was the *end* of the 20th Maine's struggle on Little Round Top. Historically, other Third Brigade skirmishers received little acknowledgment that they also played a role in this fighting. Yet the diary of 16th Michigan skirmisher Sgt. Berry shows that his Company A did *not* return to his regiment's line on the face of Little Round Top, but remained on the left, or the brigade's southern flank, in proximity to the 20th Maine. "About 3 o'clock the battle commences in earnest along the whole line which lasts until dark," Berry wrote. "In the afternoon a rebel Regiment makes a desperate charge cutting off the skirmishers and we retreat by the left flank."[23]

This short sentence is significant in the story of the 16th Michigan skirmishers. After the 4th and 5th Texas and 4th Alabama regiments first struck the center of Third Brigade's line on Little Round Top—and made no headway against Vincent's strongly posted soldiers—they were joined by the 47th and 15th Alabama regiments, which had pursued those U.S. sharpshooters up Round Top. These two Rebel regiments came down the big hill and joined in the attack on the 20th Maine and the 83rd Pennsylvania. As noted, the Alabamans cut off the 20th Maine's skirmishers and federal sharpshooters, hidden a couple hundred yards away. As the Rebels tried to flank the 20th Maine's position, they opened themselves to rifle fire by the concealed soldiers, making the Alabamans think they were being flanked and surrounded.

Sgt. Berry noted that the 16th Michigan skirmishers were *also* cut off by charging Rebels, and sharpshooter Apted would write that "much ammunition [was] expended" by the close of the fight. The phrase or comment "much ammunition [was] expended" seems to have been sometimes used by soldiers sarcastically, meaning that though there had been much shooting and fighting in a given clash, nothing was gained or accomplished. It may have been in that sense that Apted used the phrase about the struggle on the south side of Little Round Top—that the Confederates made a desperate attack that did not succeed. But whether or not Apted's words were meant to be sardonic, they indicated the Michigan skirmishers' involvement in this struggle. And they were not alone.[24]

A letter written that summer by Peter Schaffer of the 44th New York's Company B, who was also a skirmisher, shows his company did not return to the brigade line, either, and was itself flanked in this combat. "We went into the fight," Schaffer wrote. "This was about four o'clock and I was taken prisoner about half past five. Company B was out skirmishing and when I was taken, the Rebels flanked us and got in the rear of us." So even though his captain, Larabee, ordered the company to retreat in the opening of the battle for Little Round Top, Schaffer's letter shows that they also remained detached from his regiment and were flanked by Rebels ninety minutes later—more evidence of continued action by Third Brigade skirmishers on the south side of the hill. Schaffer was captured, as was Capt. Kin Dygert of the Brady Sharpshooters, though Dygert, in time, escaped. Newspaper articles about the 44th New York that summer state that eleven or twelve of Schaffer's skirmishing comrades were killed, wounded, and missing.[25]

Though this picture is not clear about where the Michigan and New York skirmishers specifically were and what they did, Berry's and Apted's diaries and Schaffer's letter show they did not "fall back" to their respective regiments. Consider that the 16th Michigan diarist John Berry, after telling of the Michigan skirmishers being cut off and retreating "by the left flank," continued: "& finally, by maneuvering we (the skirmishers) capture about 200 rebels." The parenthetical part of this quotation, "the skirmishers," was Berry's emphasis. There is no question as to whom he was giving credit—he and his comrades also took Rebel prisoners.

Berry went on: "We skirmish until dark when we are relieved but we are not able to find our Regiment." That was because the 16th Michigan was no longer where the skirmishers left it on the south side of Little Round Top. Their regiment had been moved, and in the nighttime, with new reinforcements holding Little Round Top, Berry and his comrades were not able to find their comrades. Berry's diary is proof of the 16th Michigan's role as skirmishers in the struggle on the southern side of Little Round Top.[26]

The diary of Brady Sharpshooter Alfred Apted confirms and complements Berry's. Again, from the beginning, Apted wrote: "The enemy are now fighting over (obstacles?) near Gettysburg. Started about 4:00 and came around the west (?) of our lines. And in the short space of 5 minutes lost a great number of men and officers. Col. Vincent wounded. The regiment took a large number of prisoners." The first three sentences of this diary entry are a typical, compressed account of battle; Apted spoke specifically of "the enemy" who attacked and flanked his brigade, and who, within a matter of minutes, suffered a large number of casualties. The battle for Little Round Top went on for about two hours, so the losses to which Apted referred—"a great number of men and officers" within five minutes' time—are not to his own company or regiment or brigade, but to scores of Confederates who were shot, wounded, and captured on the south side of the hill with the charge of the 20th Maine, aided by Third Brigade skirmishers.

After noting that his brigade commander had been wounded, Apted continued, "the regiment took a large number of prisoners." Apted was a skirmisher that day, and not with the 16th Michigan, up the hill in the battle line; his regiment, in fact, did *not* take a large number of prisoners. Then was Apted referring to his own Brady Sharpshooters, Company A, and other brigade skirmishers? Probably, since his comrade, Sgt. Berry, noted, "we (the skirmishers) captured about 200 rebels." Though Pvt. Apted's great-grandson admitted he was "approximate" in his transcription of this last sentence of the sharpshooter's diary entry for July 2, he felt that Apted concluded: "we (?) stopped the battle. Much ammunition expended, and then stopped the battle for the night." It is more evidence of the involvement of the 16th Michigan skirmishers on the brigade's left.

It is usually noted in accounts of Little Round Top that Col. William Oates, the commander of the Alabama troops who had attacked the 20th Maine, ordered his men to retreat when he felt he was being flanked on his right. He wrote that "two [Union] regiments were advancing rapidly upon my rear." Of course, there were *not* two regiments attacking Oates, who saw his men cut down by shots striking them from behind. His description of this, the end of his fight for Little Round Top, begs the question: Did one Maine skirmish company and a dozen federal sharpshooters cause this mayhem, causing Oates to believe he was being surrounded? Or did other Third Brigade skirmishers, "maneuvering on the left" and expending "much ammunition," have a role, as Sgt. Berry's diary and Pvt. Apted's diary state?[27]

Admittedly, the casualties suffered by the 16th Michigan skirmishers at Gettysburg, like the 20th Maine's Company B, were light. Records show the Brady Sharpshooters' Capt. Dygert was captured and indicate that two others were wounded. In Company A, Corporal John M. Nestor of Detroit was killed and eight men were wounded.[28] How did these companies escape worse losses? The 20th Maine fought in a spot where large boulders and the rocky shelf on the south side of Little Round Top gave way first to "smooth" thinly wooded ground of the saddle, immediately adjacent to the "broken ground" of Round Top, with its scattered boulders and rocks, brush, and thicker woods—a good place for soldiers like the 16th Michigan skirmishers to conceal themselves after opening fire on the advancing Rebels, as Rufus Jacklin claimed. And there were known instances where this happened that day.

For example, when 22 men from the 15th Alabama Regiment were bringing canteens of badly needed water to their comrades who advanced over Round Top late that afternoon, they were captured by some of the very federal sharpshooters their regiment pursued; those sharpshooters hid in a wooded ravine to ambush their Rebel pursuers. Col. Oates, commander of these Alabamans, claimed that he sent an entire company down behind Round Top to capture parked Union supply wagons, but these men were fired upon by Union soldiers hidden in the woods. This Confederate company quickly retreated and sat out the rest of the battle, loitering unnoticed nearby.

Oates thought the Union troops who fired on this company were more of the federal sharpshooters and 20th Maine skirmishers, but they could have been others from the Third Brigade, like those of the 16th Michigan. Ellis Spear later noted that as the battle on Little Round Top was starting, advancing Rebels came down Round Top, while at nearly the same time the 20th Maine skirmishers went up and then down the same ridge—yet these soldiers missed each other, seeming to prove that the rugged, wooded hillside, with its brush and boulders, effectively hid them.[29]

In one of the earliest regimental histories from the Third Brigade, published the same year the Civil War ended, the officer-author of the book on the 83rd Pennsylvania acknowledged that other brigade skirmish companies "followed and supported" the 20th Maine as it charged and pursued the Rebels, though specifically mentioning only his regiment's. The diaries of Apted and Berry show the 16th Michigan skirmishers were part of this fight—cut off from their battle line, "maneuvering" on the left, "expending ammunition," and helping to capture scores of Confederates. The 16th Michigan's Brady Sharpshooters and Company A could only have contributed here to the repulse of the Rebel attack on the south side of Little Round Top.[30]

THE RIGHT

Shortly after Company A and the Brady Sharpshooters went out from the south side of the hill, the 16th Michigan was ordered to move up to the western face, the right of their brigade's line. Lt. Col. Welch reported his men were under "heavy fire" as they reached their position and "succeeded, however, in securing our places after some loss." Benjamin Partridge agreed Rebels immediately hit the regiment with rifle fire. "At the moment when we halted the fire opened upon us, and we returned with vigor and precision behind, now and then, a large rock where we maintained our position," he wrote. Another veteran of the battle, William W. Colestock, from Calhoun County, in Company K, claimed the regiment did not have a "proper" position. "We could not form a line, so had to go to work without any formation behind the rocks and trees," he wrote decades later. Colestock was correct in that it was not a typical defensive line, though the boulders obviously offered some cover. He claimed that Company K was responsible for the regimental colors, which would have placed its men at the center of the regiment on the rock shelf.[31]

Lt. Charles Salter agreed the firing began as they advanced over the hill to their position, perhaps hearing the clash of the brigade skirmishers below. Oliver Norton believed the initial Confederate assault struck the center of the brigade's position (the 83rd Pennsylvania and 44th New York), which suggests the fire against the 16th Michigan initially may not have been "heavy" as the Rebels felt out their enemy's position, determining how far their line extended. In any event, the 4th and 5th Texas regiments emerged from the trees at the foot of Round Top as the rest of the Confederate line approached the 83rd Pennsylvania and the 20th Maine on Little Round Top's southern, wooded hillside. But whether approaching through the woods or over open ground, the Rebel advance was hit by rifle fire as it came into view of Vincent's men. It is likely the 4th Texas partially fronted on the 16th Michigan's line as they started up the rocky hill, with the 5th Texas on their right.

"Many of our officers and men [were] falling in passing the open space between the heights," the lieutenant colonel of the 5th Texas wrote, referring to the area between the Round Tops that was largely clear of trees on the lower, western slopes. In addition, huge rocks broke up their line of battle. The top two officers of the 4th Texas were wounded in the advance to Little Round Top, but still the men climbed the hill in the assault. "I had gone a considerable distance up the mountain when one of the rascals put me to a standstill," 4th Texas Pvt. Zack Landrum wrote his mother, "by the means of a Minnie ball through the thigh just above the knee." Pvt. William Fletcher of the 5th Texas said the men going up "were falling rapidly," and he and comrades took cover behind a rock, as did others. Texan John Stevens said their attack got within 25 or 30 steps of the troops "posted behind the rocks on the crest," but the first Union volley "was most destructive to our line."[32]

The Texans fired from cover of the boulders on the slope, with one soldier remembering a lieutenant urging them: "Boys, aim well." Fletcher described the Yankees above as "leaning over their protection to shoot to hit our position," while Pvt. J. Mark Smither, in the 5th Texas, said his comrades "took shelter, Indian fashion, behind rocks & trees and commenced popping away at the Yankees whenever they showed their heads." His major reported they did so "with accuracy and deadly effect," and their lieutenant colonel agreed, though he was soon wounded.

One of the first 16th Michigan casualties may have been Pvt. George Ervay of Grand Ledge, in Company H. "Soon after the enemy opened fire on us, your son was shot," wrote Corporal Reuben Turrell to Ervay's father. The young man was mortally wounded, struck in the head as he stood in the firing line on the hill next to his friend Allen Young.[33]

Ziba Graham claimed years later that this first Confederate attack came up from the low ground along the Plum Run in front of the 16th Michigan and that "an almost hand-to-hand conflict raged for fully half an hour" before the Texans retreated. While this was dramatic, more dependable Confederate reports said they came out of the woods of Round Top, referred to as "the skirt of timber," by Maj. Bane of the 4th Texas. But Pvt. Smither agreed that the Confederates got "within 25 steps of the [Union] works" (meaning the rocks and ledges up Little Round Top)—incredibly close for rifle combat. Their attack stalled in the torrent of bullets and the Texans fell back to these trees, where they reformed for another assault.[34]

Though the 16th Michigan probably came through this first assault with light casualties compared to the Rebels, battlefield conditions were changing. In front of Little Round Top, other Confederates, including the 44th and 48th Alabama regiments, were attacking Third Corps soldiers and guns at Devil's Den and vicinity. Beyond Devil's Den, fighting was raging in the woods and fields stretching toward the Peach Orchard. "We could see line after line of Longstreet's men forming and advancing," Graham wrote of this fighting. "Also the close contact, the repulses, the fierce havoc of artillery, the close range of musketry."

What the Michigan soldiers could *not* see was the south side of their hill, where the 47th and 15th Alabama came down Round Top and threw their weight against the 20th Maine, allowing the Texans and the 4th Alabama to concentrate their next attack on the Third Brigade's center and right. It was not long in coming.[35]

As the fight for Little Round Top raged, six guns from Battery D of the 5th U.S. Artillery under Lt. Charles Hazlett arrived on the northeast side of the hill. This was the outfit to which Dr. William Breakey of the 16th Michigan was temporarily assigned as surgeon. It was a nearly impossible task, but these heavy Parrott Rifles were dragged, pulled, pushed, and at times lifted over the rocks to the hilltop, to a point above and behind the 16th Michigan, by teams of horses, gun crews, teamsters, Third Corps stragglers, and Gen. Gouverneur Warren himself. Edward Hill of the 16th Michigan later indicated that members of his regiment helped manhandle the guns into place. Indeed, a regimental record showed a private in Company D, the Saginaw company, was killed in action that day after being detached to help the gunners. These cannon inflicted many casualties on Rebels who were further away, but their barrels could not be depressed enough to shoot down Little Round Top's slopes at the attackers there.[36]

That was left to Vincent's men, who faced the second assault by Confederates. The Texans moved against the center and right side of the Third Brigade's line. "Being joined by the 5th Texas on my right, I again attempted to drive the enemy from the heights by assaults," reported Major Bane of the 4th Texas. Bane's counterpart in the 5th Texas, Maj. J. C. Rogers, said that the second attack on Little Round Top was made "in connection with the other regiments," clearly indicating coordination between the Confederate battalions. Again, their section of the battle line went forward from the trees and rocks of Round Top. A 5th Texas veteran, Pvt. Fletcher, years later insisted he and his comrades knew what a terrible situation awaited them on Little Round Top, and they only advanced until they reached "the danger point" and quickly turned away. But his account was contradicted by J. Mark Smither, who wrote that July that they made the attack three times, while their 4th Texas comrade John West wrote they "renewed the charge several times."[37]

Though it is impossible to know in which assault the 16th Michigan lost specific officers and men, the second and third attacks on Little Round Top inflicted most of their casualties. Soldiers who had cover behind rocks had to rise to shoot at the Texans, and some on the right of the regiment's line had little if any cover. Officers, of course, had to lead, standing and directing their men, but in doing so became conspicuous targets. Lt. Wallace Jewett of Saginaw, a former lancer in Company K, was shot in the forehead as he stood with sword in hand; Lt. Butler Brown of Hillsdale, in Company E, was also killed instantly by a rifle shot.

"Lt. Jewett and Lt. Brown were both killed within three feet of me," Lt. Salter said. Now assigned to Company H, Salter was hit by a piece of rock, blasted up by flying lead, that struck him in the face. A wounded officer, Detroit's Lt. Martin Borgman, heading back over the hill to get medical attention, saw Salter hit and bloodied, but the story turned into the claim he had been killed. Soon after, his misspelled name appeared in a Detroit newspaper listing those killed. "They did not get rid of me quite so easily as that after all," Salter wrote.[38]

Bay City's Benjamin Partridge, then a captain, said he was hit twice in the leg, by a bullet and a piece of shell, indicating Confederate batteries at times still fired at the 16th Michigan's ledge. He said these were "slight wounds" and stayed with the regiment. Lt. Borgman, from Company F, was wounded in the left arm, while his brother-in-law, Sgt. James Beckett in Company I, was killed. Their wives' brother, Cpl. Henry Welbon, also serving in Company F with Borgman, was lightly wounded in the arm, while a comrade from Borgman's and Beckett's days in the lancers, Pvt. James Bogart from Pinckney, was killed.

As the Texans brought the second attack against the 16th Michigan's and the 44th New York's part of the line, Union soldiers continued to pour down deadly rifle fire, preventing the Rebels from getting close enough to break through their position. The 5th Texas's John Stevens's description would become a favorite of writers and historians: "The balls are whizzing so thick around us that it looks like a man could hold out a hat and catch it full." Maj. Bane said the second attack had "like results" as the first—they couldn't overwhelm the Union soldiers on the hill. "A farther advance being impracticable," wrote Maj. Rogers, his men again retreated "to an open space about 50 yards in [the] rear," probably meaning large rocks at the edge of the trees near the base of Round Top.[39]

The Confederate attacks on the Third Brigade's line had twice been beaten back as evening slowly came on, but soon the Texans and Alabamans were joined by two more regiments that had come from Devil's Den, according to Maj. Bane of the 4th Texas. These were the 44th and the 48th Alabama, coming to help the Texans strike and flank the Union right on Little Round Top—the 16th Michigan's position. "Again, being reinforced by the 48th Alabama, commanded by the gallant Colonel [James] Sheffield, and the 44th Alabama, whose commander I did not learn, we again charged their works," Bane reported. His 5th Texas counterpart did not specify coordination with other regiments in that last attack, but he had done so previously. About the third assault, he said that, "in obedience to orders, I again moved the regiment forward to attack the enemy in their impregnable position." These four Confederate regiments had suffered severe casualties by the time this last assault was made on Little Round Top, but they still outnumbered the 16th Michigan. Though these officers' reports give no details about the coordination of this assault, 5th Texas Pvt. Smither said their new division commander, Gen. Evander Law, came up and "gave orders to advance on the place." It is hardly conceivable the attack was ordered by Law without coordination of these four regiments, just as Bane indicated.

For these Rebels, "the place" was the 16th Michigan's part of the line, its right flank open and vulnerable on the western hillside. Ziba Graham said it was about 7 p.m. Above and to the right of the regiment, Hazlett's battery was firing steadily, but these gunners could not assist the Michigan men. Oliver Norton thought the Rebels attacked by moving through the valley of Plum Run, which was sheltered from Little Round Top by rocks, and then turning and charging up the western slope to overlap the 16th Michigan's right. Some of the 44th New York, on the left of the 16th Michigan, tried to help by turning their fire to the right to shoot down the charging Confederates, but it was not enough.

Though no Michigan soldier described this flank attack, other witnesses apparently did. Norton said the Rebels "came up in a mass with great courage, without stopping to fire until they reached the Union line; here they engaged in a hand-to-hand conflict with the Michigan men, firing and using the bayonet." The three Michigan companies furthest to the right "refused" or bent back their part of the line to meet the Rebel flank attack, Norton claimed, but the fury of the Confederate attack and their increasing numbers caused them to "fall back in disorder."[40]

The 44th and 48th Alabama regiments and 4th and 5th Texas regiments were at last succeeding, overwhelming the Michigan soldiers, though again, the few Rebel accounts available said nothing of this—only of the difficulty of going up Little Round Top and the closeness of their lines of battle. A soldier of the 44th Alabama wrote that they "charged on top of a mountain to the enemy's breastworks," referring to the stones and boulders on Little Round Top. His commander, though wounded back in the rocks of Devil's Den, agreed his regiment moved on and took part in the attack on the hill. Lt. Henry L. Figures of the 48th Alabama told of the steepness of the "mountain," the bravery of his commander, Col. Sheffield, and of four attempts to "take the heights."[41]

Lt. Salter wrote hand-to-hand fighting took place but did not mention that part of his regiment broke. "But, it was the hardest work we ever done to drive them back, and the most desperate fighting I ever saw," he wrote, "for where we were there was scarcely any artillery engaged on that day, the fighting was all done by infantry, although we have been engaged in other battles where we have had more men cut down by artillery, but we never had such a terrible, close bayonet fight before. It seemed as if every man on both sides was actuated by the intensest [*sic*] hate, and determined to kill as many of the enemy as possible, and excited up in an enthusiasm far exceeding that on any battlefield before that we have been engaged in. I know I felt so myself although I never did before." Edward Hill, who had come with the lancers into Stockton's regiment, was the captain of Company H at Gettysburg; he would write later in a dramatic speech of the "desperate onset of a hand-to-hand struggle that only ceased with life," with "sabers clashed, bayonets crossed, guns clubbed, stones hurled." Yet it should bc noted that there was no mention of bayonet wounds suffered by 16th Michigan soldiers in the regiment's casualty report, newspaper reports about the Gettysburg wounded, or postwar rosters.[42]

Nearly a year earlier, Company B's Sgt. Hubbard Barrett, from Ionia County, had come through the Seven Days battles and wrote of the bodies of friends left behind on the Gaines' Mill battlefield, and how he might have to follow them in death in the next battle. Now at Little Round Top, Barrett, 28, did so, killed in action. Also dying on the rocks was his comrade from Ionia County, 22-year-old Lt. William H. Borden in Company F, who had once thought the war would be a short one back in the winter of 1861, and told his parents not to lend out his ice skates. Lansing's Lt. Alexander Cameron of Company G, wounded in 1862 and just promoted, was struck in the right side of his chest by a bullet that grazed his lung and shattered his right arm, requiring its amputation.[43]

Again, the ledge on which much of the regiment stood disappeared on the right of their line, where the Texans and Alabamans flanked them, so the three 16th Michigan companies here had no cover from the attack coming up the west slope. Oliver Norton wrote that most of these men were "seized with panic and ran for shelter behind the rocks" at the top of the hill; he blamed this on "the misconduct of Lt. Col. Welch" and "a large portion of the three companies on the right," more than forty men, for not holding their ground as they did in previous battles.[44]

Benjamin Partridge, who would later go to lead the regiment, gave two very incomplete accounts of what happened. First, he told a Gettysburg historian that "Welch stood with the regt. colors on a flat rock near the centre of the regt. till it was not possible to remain longer in that place. The flag had several holes through it." Partridge said he was directly in front of Welch "and several shells burst near us, throwing rocks everywhere." Yet other witnesses said nothing about artillery fire causing the regiment to break. In a statement given two years after his first one, Partridge was not sympathetic to Welch. "During the hottest part of the battle in the p.m. towards *night,* the colonel *left with the colors* for some reason," he wrote in a not-for-publication letter to Michigan's adjutant general.[45]

Welch, in his battle report, blamed whatever happened that day on a young officer from Detroit, Lt. William Kydd, now in Company C. Welch claimed Kydd ordered the colors withdrawn when the commander of the Fifth Corps or perhaps a different brigade leader—he was not sure which—supposedly shouted down from the crest of Little Round Top for them to fall back. In fact, neither of those generals was on the hill. Oliver Norton dismissed this explanation as one of Welch's "misstatements which were not accepted by the brigade commander nor the commanders of the other regiments."[46]

Yet even if Welch lied about the circumstances by which his regimental flag was withdrawn, later accounts about the colors indicated there truly may have been confusion. Edward Hill, who wrote romanticized, patriotic speeches and articles after the war, spoke of all but one of the 16th Michigan's color guard being killed, and that the flag was "shot from the staff," falling on its brave defenders. Yet in the postwar accounting by Hill himself, who researched a "Roll of Honor" of the 16th Michigan's casualties, it was reported that the color bearer, Sgt. Eldridge Potter of Company I, fell wounded in the right leg, and reluctantly released the flag to another soldier (perhaps Sgt. Tommy Morton of Detroit, in Company K?). Potter survived, as did William Colestock, who said he was the color corporal, and Morton, reportedly the color sergeant. Colestock wrote nothing of the flag being shot from the staff, but claimed Morton struggled to keep the flag upright as he lay on the ground. That brought a visit from Lt. Kydd, "to see about it," Colestock said, and he urged Kydd to leave Morton alone—that "it was all right."

But it was not all right, and Norton and Benjamin Partridge made plain that the 16th Michigan's flag was withdrawn in "the hottest part" of the fight. If Morton was holding the flag at that moment, presumably he left with the colors along with Welch and more than forty men from the regiment's right wing. They ran up the hill for cover behind the rocks, Norton wrote.[47]

No member of the regiment seems to have acknowledged this break. Colestock, who said he was with the flag, claimed decades later that he remained and fired his rifle until it fouled and then used a dead comrade's rifle until he heard "the bugle sound truce that evening"—something no one else reported. Another member of the regiment, who used the pen name "Erin" writing to the Republican newspaper in Flint later that summer in 1863, claimed that the men of the regiment "rallied around" their flag, saving it from the Rebels who were trying to seize it, though not saying that the colors were borne away when the regiment's line broke. Of course, if Welch and a number of men fled to keep the flag from being captured, that certainly would have caused confusion among the Michigan troops. Yet most of the 16th Michigan's line did not retreat, as Oliver Norton acknowledged.[48]

An ex-soldier who said he witnessed the collapse of the 16th Michigan's right was Charles E. Sprague, then a sergeant in the 44th New York. Wounded in the left shoulder, he was told by his lieutenant to seek medical attention back over the hill. He was cutting behind the left of the 16th Michigan's line, Sprague wrote forty-five years later, when he saw men falling back. "The 16th seemed to be retiring in some confusion," he wrote. Sprague said he shouted at the Michigan men to stand firm, and then realized some of the soldiers were "staring at me curiously." Actually, it was not Sprague they were looking at, but their brigade commander, Col. Strong Vincent, who, clenching his wife's riding crop, was striding up to the Michigan regiment. "That will do, Sgt. Sprague," Vincent told him, in those words or very close to them. "I'll take hold of this."

"Vincent went to driving the men of the 16th back into line with the little whip, and that was the last attitude in which I saw him," Sprague continued.[49] The scene must have been chaotic as the 16th Michigan's line broke, with the soldiers on the left and center turning in shock and surprise to see they were "almost enveloped" by the Confederates; Vincent was hit, a bullet striking him in the groin and fatally wounding him. But then help arrived in the nick of time.

Before the Texans and Alabamans made their last attack on Little Round Top, Union reinforcements were arriving and being marched by the hill on their way into battle. Gen.

Warren, the engineering chief who was grazed by a bullet as he helped position Hazlett's guns on the crest, rode down from the hill to the Wheatfield Road. Here he intercepted a brigade of Fifth Corps soldiers he had once commanded, including the 140th New York. Warren told its commander, Col. Patrick O'Rorke, that he was taking responsibility for detaching the regiment and quickly ordered it up the northeast slope of Little Round Top. The men of the 140th New York had not even loaded their rifles when they came out on the southern crest of the hill and saw the fight raging down the slope as the 16th Michigan was flanked and breaking; some Rebel fire began hitting the New Yorkers, too. O'Rorke shouted, "Down this way, boys!" Some of the Confederates on the hillside must have been stunned to see a mass of fresh Union soldiers rushing down from the top, coming into line with the Third Brigade, some of them dropping behind the rocks to load and fire. More Rebels turned and fired into these newly arrived Yankees—dozens were killed and wounded—but soon they began to give way. A soldier in the 48th Alabama remembered his commander, Col. Sheffield, standing among the Texans, urging them "to advance once more" and "never to yield." But they had been stopped. "In less time than it takes to write it the onslaught of the rebels was fairly checked," Porter Farley of the 140th New York wrote of this moment.[50]

Col. O'Rorke was shot and killed in this brief but intense fight, but the Confederates who had just outflanked the 16th Michigan now found themselves flanked. Capt. D. U. Barziza of the 4th Texas said his men were again "not more than 20 or 30 paces apart," probably firing at the Michigan troops when it happened. "Our left flank was turned & we were compelled to fall back," he wrote. He was captured; so was John Stevens of the 5th Texas. He and his comrades "had fired some 10 or 12 rounds" in that last assault, but he did not realize that fellow Rebels to his left were retreating. Stevens felt a slap on his back as a Union officer stood over him, striking him with the flat of his sword; Stevens dropped his rifle and surrendered.

Men like him who did not retreat in time were cut off and captured. Maj. Bane of the 4th Texas reported only that his men, reinforced with the 44th and 48th Alabama, had charged but were repulsed, and were ordered by their division commander, Gen. Law, to retreat. Their regiments had suffered terrible casualties and they did not have the men to make another attack; scores of their dead and wounded lay on the slope and down to Plum Run. One was Capt. William Dunklin of the 44th Alabama, dead at the base of the hill near the bodies of thirty-seven other Confederate soldiers. Now it was evening, and though skirmish fire would go on until darkness, the Confederate attack on Little Round Top was over. Over the course of the next hour or so, along Cemetery Ridge to the Round Tops, the Confederate attack on the Union left waned, stopped, or was repulsed, at the cost of thousands of soldiers killed, wounded, and missing.[51]

In the 16th Michigan, twenty-one men and officers died in action on Little Round Top, though six other soldiers, one of them George Ervay, died from wounds in the days and weeks ahead. A respected tabulator of Union casualties would put the number of the regiment's killed and mortally wounded at twenty-nine, while a member of the regiment wrote that summer they lost thirty officers and men killed or mortally wounded. Forty or more others survived their wounds, some who had been grazed, but almost half suffering severe wounds; two men were missing. "We who had survived the battle thanked God that we had been spared," wrote Lt. Graham, "whilst so many of our comrades had fallen, and as we groped around in the darkness for our wounded on the rock-bound mountainside, friend grasped the hand of friend and congratulated each other that they had been spared.

"When the task of caring for the wounded had been finished it was nearly midnight; we sank down upon that [Little] Round Top weary and exhausted, but with the proud feeling that we still held the important position entrusted to us." Graham's comrade, Lt. Salter, writing ten days later, also stressed that Michigan soldiers remained there, without mentioning the forty-plus men who left with Welch and the flag. "That night," he wrote, "we slept upon the hill."[52]

As evening fell on July 2, Oliver Norton, the bugler and flag carrier for the Third Brigade, now commanded by Col. James Rice of the 44th New York, was sent to find ambulances and stretcher bearers for the wounded. He rode off the hill, and at the nearby house of farmer Lewis Bushman, he was surprised to see Lt. Col. Welch with his regimental colors "and near him some forty or fifty" men. "I asked him where the brigade was," Norton said. "He replied that he did not know; that they had been driven from their position and he had followed my brigade flag, thinking they had gone in that direction." Norton thought Welch was lying, attempting to explain and justify what he and his men were doing away from their brigade, which of course had *not* been driven off the hill. Norton dismounted to go in the house to see the dying Vincent, leaving his flag and horse with one of the Michigan soldiers. "This man told me that he did not believe the brigade had left its position; neither did I," Norton wrote. Though he did not assert that he thought Welch lost his nerve on Little Round Top, the inference was clear.[53]

Thousands of words would be written and spoken about the struggle for Little Round Top in the years that followed, though in truth it was a very localized and comparatively small fight in one corner of a very large battlefield, involving what amounted to two brigades, North and South. The hill had been important high ground for the Army of the Potomac, but from then on through the next 150 years it was emphasized to the point of exaggeration as the key turning point of the Civil War, with the notion very much accepted, advanced and promoted by veterans, journalists, and historians, that if the Confederates had taken Little Round Top, the Union line would have collapsed, the Army of the Potomac would have been destroyed, and the Civil War lost to the North.[54]

Of course, all wars need heroes, and Col. Chamberlain of the 20th Maine was instantly hailed by Northern newspapers as the epitome of the volunteer soldier-officer fighting for his country and triumphing "against the odds" at Little Round Top. Chamberlain, a good soldier who would become governor of Maine after the war, wrote dramatic articles and books that only helped his political career, though riling his former comrade Ellis Spear, who later in his life called Chamberlain's popular Civil War memoir "a tissue of lies," and who wrote that the famous 20th Maine charge was started by the soldiers themselves as some started down the hill to reach wounded comrades. But the mythic tale of Little Round Top, "saved" by Joshua Chamberlain and the 20th Maine, prevailed and continues to be a popular and accepted piece of Civil War lore.[55]

In truth, even if the Confederates had managed to drive the Third Brigade off Little Round Top, they simply did not have enough men and ammunition to hold it. Thousands of additional Union troops from the Army of the Potomac's Fifth and Sixth Corps were arriving at Little Round Top and its vicinity as the Texans and Alabamans waged their attack on the right of the Third Brigade's line. Even if the Rebels had driven the brigade off the hill, entire fresh Union divisions almost certainly would have taken it back. Lt. Charles Salter of Detroit summed this up succinctly and correctly: "If we had been 5 minutes late, the enemy would have gained the ridge we were on and turned our left flank, and it would have been very hard to drive them from it." Note that he did not say it would be impossible, or that the battle would have then been lost—only that it would have been "hard" to take the hill back.[56]

Accounts written by veterans of the 16th Michigan show they did not publicly discuss the break of their right companies. Welch, who reported that only "three of color guard" had left the regiment's line when Lt. Kydd allegedly gave his unauthorized order to withdraw the flag and fall back, still acknowledged that forty-five of his men also left "during or after the fight." Of course, so did he; he gave no explanation as to how or why. Lt. Salter, writing to friends in Detroit about the battle, said nothing about the break. "Erin," who wrote to a Flint newspaper, said only that the men saved the colors from the Rebels, but did not mention it was saved by a retreat up the hill. Ziba Graham, Rufus Jacklin, and Dr. Breakey would all later mention the 16th Michigan's presence on Little Round Top, but with no real explanation of what happened.

When Partridge described the regiment's position to a historian, he said that Welch stood with the regiment's flag "till it was not possible to remain longer in that place." To his state adjutant general, he said only that Welch left with the flag "for some reason." William Colestock, writing about Little Round Top decades later, said "We stayed there as long as required"—perhaps a rationalization that, if part of his regiment broke and fled, what did it matter since reinforcements arrived in time?[57]

Of course, there was nothing uncommon in the Civil War about troops fleeing, retreating, or falling back, when they were flanked—that is, when hit by fire from front and side. This was an untenable situation for soldiers, and when men found themselves in such a position, they got out of it by leaving, though ideally, they would stop and reform their line. Histories by Union soldiers who were present that day were sympathetic to the men of the 16th Michigan who broke and ran; the regimental historians of the 83rd Pennsylvania and the 44th New York acknowledged that a portion of the Michigan regiment had been "somewhat thrown into confusion" by the attack on their exposed position and "temporarily forced back." These were not criticisms, but statements of fact. A soldier of the 83rd Pennsylvania would later defend the 16th Michigan as an outfit that had done its job. "At the close of the engagement," he graciously wrote, "every regiment of that brigade was just where it took its position at the beginning."[58]

Unfortunately for the 16th Michigan, this break on the right happened to them at Little Round Top, surely an important victory but one to which the surviving participants, commanders, writers, and historians ascribed such significance that it became the stuff of legend. Consider that in the terrible toll of individuals killed and wounded, for example, the regiment had suffered worse casualties at Gaines' Mill—seventy-eight men and officers killed and mortally wounded; the regiment was one of many that had broken during that fight as they were flanked. But the struggle for Little Round Top took on mythic importance over the decades, and here the regiment would be remembered, with the publication of Oliver Norton's 1913 book on the battle, as the one that broke, even though it was the smallest regiment in the most exposed position, overwhelmed in part by elements of four Rebel regiments.[59]

Norton would dedicate part of the rest of his life to preserving the memory of Strong Vincent, correcting inaccurate accounts and histories of the battle, and emphasizing in articles and then a book that it was Vincent who brought the Third Brigade to Little Round Top and who placed his regiments to save the position. Norton was critical of Norval Welch, whom he accused of lying in his Gettysburg report, and not properly leading his men. His view of the circumstances of Vincent's fatal wounding seems to have changed over the years; writing in 1888, he stated that his colonel was shot as he exhorted reluctant men of the 140th New York to charge into the fray where the 16th Michigan's right was breaking. But in his later writings, Norton maintained Vincent was hit as he tried to staunch the collapse of the 16th Michigan's right. It hardly mattered, since the events were so intertwined; in one letter, written late in his life, he admitted: "No living man can point out the exact spot where Vincent stood when he was shot."[60]

But when Norton published his detailed and comprehensive study of the fight, *The Attack and Defense of Little Round Top,* he made major factual errors in his criticism of Welch and the 16th Michigan that minimized their dangerous and vulnerable circumstances, and undermined their contribution and their reputation, in a historical sense. Norton charged that two skirmish companies had not been sent out from the regiment. Of course, he was wrong; the 16th Michigan detached two companies, and they fought to the left of their brigade line, helping the 20th Maine's part of the struggle. Norton said there was no loss in the 16th Michigan before it reached its place in the line on the hill. Again, he was wrong; several men were wounded by artillery while running to Little Round Top, as noted in John Berry's diary. And he claimed that Welch was not telling the truth about the 16th Michigan being moved at the last second from the brigade's left to the brigade's right. Again, Norton was wrong; it happened just as Welch indicated. But Welch had been forced to retreat there on Little Round Top, and he had not come close to telling the truth about what happened.

Welch, in time, would win back his good reputation as a brave commander at the cost of his life. But when the new brigade commander, Col. Rice of the 44th New York, wrote his Gettysburg report, he praised only Capt. Robert Elliott and Adjt. Rufus Jacklin in the 16th Michigan for their brave and gallant conduct, and said nothing of Welch. For the officers and men of the regiment who survived the fight, the topic of the breaking of the 16th Michigan's line on Little Round Top was not discussed publicly. Decades later, Edward Hill would memorialize the 16th Michigan's sacrifice, and touch on the survivors' ambivalence over the regiment's role in the fighting, without using the term "break" or "retreat"; he did not have to, as he addressed a small group of veterans on the hill that day in 1889. "There can be no invidious distinction made in favor of one body of men over another who fought at Gettysburg," Hill said. "The record of one regiment is the history of all; they were a tired army of veterans . . . The ranks broken by casualties were voluntarily closed to the right." The veterans understood what he was saying.[61]

But Hill's speech lay far off in a distant future. As the sun went down behind the hills to the west that night of July 2, 1863, and the soldiers carried the wounded back to field hospitals and surgeons set up in farm houses and barns, the battle at Gettysburg was not yet over.

14.

JULY–NOVEMBER 1863

WE ARE NOT FIGHTING FOR GENERALS, BUT OUR COUNTRY

As darkness fell over Gettysburg on July 2, the regiments of the Third Brigade, excepting the 16th Michigan, were sent up Round Top to better secure the left of the Union line, leaving less than a hundred Michigan men and officers on Little Round Top, along with the reinforcements that arrived that evening. Though the personnel of the 16th Michigan did not have specifics, it was clear that more than fifty of their comrades in the regiment had been killed and wounded in the fighting. Missing were Lt. Col. Norval Welch and the forty-some men who had broken on the right of the regiment's line. Also missing were the regiment's skirmishers, Company A and the Brady Sharpshooters, who had been deployed from the south side of Little Round Top and had not found what was left of the regiment on the hill that night after the battle. It is likely that the skirmishers and the missing men with Welch bivouacked in different places south and east of the hill.[1]

The regiment's soldiers on Little Round Top continued working in the darkness, carrying their wounded from the battlefield. Allen Young, 23, from Hubbardston, a small town in the center of lower Michigan, had not been able to remove George Ervay from the battle line as the fighting raged. But once darkness was falling, Young and comrades carried him and other wounded men from the hill, to a point where ambulance crews and stretcher bearers were carrying them to hospitals set up at local farms. Of course, a system of triage was being practiced, as Ervay's friends would learn in the morning.

The surgeons and hospital attendants were busy at their bloody work since the previous afternoon, trying to save the wounded. Dr. William Breakey, the regiment's assistant surgeon detached to serve with the Battery D of the U.S. Fifth Artillery (whose Capt. Hazlett had been killed on Little Round Top), labored long into the morning of July 3, operating on scores of the battle's victims. Since the previous afternoon, he had been with the Fifth Corps' First Division hospital set up near Rock Creek. "The wounded came back from the front thick and fast," he wrote. "The operating tables were put up and the work of caring for the wounded went on far into the night. Actual heaps of amputated limbs accumulated at these tables. The wounded brought to these tables were of the gravest character and that needed the promptest care."

Breakey remembered only two or three operating tables there, though they were used constantly through the afternoon of July 2 on into the night. "I kept records, administered chloroform, made operations and dressed wounds in turn," the doctor wrote. "No grave or capital operation was undertaken without a full consultation and concurrence of the most prominent surgeons present." Surgeons would stay busy at Gettysburg for weeks to come. But there was nothing they could do for a victim like young Ervay, who suffered terrible brain trauma, but wait for death to take him. When Corporal Reuben Turrell came off the hill on the morning of July 3, he found that the ambulance crews and stretcher bearers had left Ervay where he lay overnight with several other wounded men, probably judged to be hopeless cases. Turrell, also from Hubbardston, was allowed to walk to a hospital more than a mile away, to get help to take Ervay in. Adjt. Rufus Jacklin believed Ervay died two days later, on or about July 5, though other records said he died on the 6th at the division hospital. It hardly mattered; Turrell assured George's parents he had not spoken a word after he was shot, trying to comfort them that George was unconscious and felt no pain as he died.[2]

It was a cloudy morning as daylight came up on July 3. The 16th Michigan's skirmishers rejoined the regiment—Sgt. John Berry of Company A noted that they found their comrades, though Alfred Apted of the Brady Sharpshooters did not mention it. Berry learned that Lieutenants Brown, Jewett, and Borden had been killed, and Lieutenants Borgman and Cameron were among the wounded. The generals decided the brigades of their division should reunite at a position slightly north of Little Round Top, in the defenses near Cemetery Ridge.

With Welch having left the hill during the fight of July 2, command of the 16th Michigan devolved to Capt. Robert Elliott of Detroit, the senior captain; Elliott had just been commissioned major of the regiment, though it seems neither he nor the army knew that yet. Col. James Rice, the Third Brigade's new commander, ordered the regiment to move out. But in one of the strangest aspects of the 16th Michigan's terrible experience at Gettysburg, Elliott, supported by Adjt. Jacklin, Capt. Benjamin Partridge, and other officers who had stayed with the regiment through the fight, refused to leave Little Round Top until their colors were returned, Partridge wrote. It was their way of saying that the flag should not have been withdrawn and must return to the place it belonged, with the regiment, before they moved out. Rice seems to have understood this was not insubordination, but a point of honor for those in the regiment who had not left the hillside.

"Col. Rice ordered Welch with the colors returned, and we took our place and moved out," Partridge later told Michigan Adjutant General John Robertson. This must have been an embarrassing moment for Welch, who had previously had a good reputation as a brave officer. When Partridge wrote this in 1868, Robertson was gathering information about his state's contribution in the Civil War. But Partridge preferred that he not share this information. "This need not be put into your history, I imagine," he wrote.[3] It's possible Robertson already knew that Welch had retreated from the fight, since one of the regiment's captains wrote a letter back to Michigan in the days after the battle that was critical of Welch's conduct. Either way, Robertson did not put the anecdote of Welch at Little Round Top in his history.

The battle of Gettysburg continued. Brady Sharpshooter Alfred Apted noted the cannon fire echoing over the landscape early that July 3 morning—this was fighting raging two miles to the northeast at Culp's Hill, where Union forces would soon prevail. At 10 a.m., Lt. Ziba Graham later wrote, his reunited regiment moved off Little Round Top, marching to the farm property of one of the Weikert families slightly north of the Wheatfield Road. This was just left of the center of the Union line on Cemetery Ridge. Their brigade and other troops were in reserve just west of the Taneytown Road, with powerful batteries to their left and right pointing across the fields toward the Confederates. "We build breastworks of stone, this being a very rocky and broken part of Pennsylvania," said Sgt. Berry. Graham would write that the building of walls was something "we had not time to do in our hurried engagement of yesterday."[4]

Graham had been suffering from a toothache since the previous night, and while it was still quiet in their part of the line, he got permission to seek attention for it. He found Dr. Robert Everett, the regimental surgeon from Hillsdale, who had been working at the amputating table all night. Everett was in no mood to fuss over Graham's troublesome tooth and "made short work" of it. "He laid me on the ground, straddled me and with a formidable of nippers pulled and yanked me around until either the tooth had to come out or my head off," Graham remembered. "I then made up my mind never to go to a surgeon for a tooth-pulling matinee the day after a fight." Worse was the terrible scene of dying, maimed, and wounded men all around the hospital. "It unmans [*sic*, breaks the heart of] one for the bloody work before him to witness the sufferings of the field hospital," the officer wrote. "No soldier but of iron nerves should ever leave the front to see the sufferers."[5]

The day grew hot. As Graham went back to his regiment, the Confederate artillery bombardment opened just after 1 p.m., preceding the massive July 3 infantry attack that became known as Pickett's Charge. He called it "the most terrific artillery firing that was ever heard upon this continent," and other Union soldiers who recorded their memories of it had similar reactions. Shells dropped in and burst over them, but no members of the 16th Michigan appear to have been wounded in the barrage. Graham said he stopped at a farm for a drink of water as he made his way back, finding fifty wounded Confederate prisoners and some wounded Union soldiers in the yard. The captain of the prisoners asked Graham if he could get them water, since the farmer, one of the Weikerts, had just removed the well crank, stating that he was not going to have his water wasted on Rebels.

Graham said he went into the farm house and "found this man, a mean Dutchman, buried in the bosom of his family and his family buried in the bowels of the cellar, they having taken safe refuge from the hail of iron." Graham said he demanded the well crank, but the farmer refused. At that moment a projectile hit the chimney, sending bricks flying and clattering down, scaring the family. Graham threatened to shoot the man, who turned over the well crank, and the wounded men got water. Graham noted that he visited Little

Round Top after the war, after the farmer had died; each time he saw "old Wikerts' son," the man told visitors of his father's "wonderful acts of heroism" in caring for the wounded in their yard.[6]

The Rebel guns ceased. "Pickett's charge was on," stated Rufus Jacklin, writing later. Some 13,000 Confederate troops advanced from the west across the rolling fields toward Cemetery Ridge. Their attack aimed for roughly the center of the Union line. "It was one of the most magnificent sights that human eyes ever beheld," Jacklin wrote. The Confederates' lines of battle stretched for more than a mile, and as they moved over the three-quarters-of-a-mile course, they funneled down toward a point on Cemetery Ridge, north of where the 16th Michigan was posted. As the Rebels advanced, Union guns fired shot and shell of every type. They were, Jacklin said, "mowed down with terrible slaughter." Those soldiers who survived the cannon fire were met by volleys of rifle fire as they came within range, and Union reinforcements rushed to the point where attacking Confederates threatened their line. Pickett's charge was over, and its survivors ran, limped, walked, or crawled west back to the woods of the Rebel-held Seminary Ridge. Some 1,200 Confederates had been killed in the charge, and more than 3,300 were captured, many of them wounded.[7]

The southernmost portion of the Confederate infantry assault probably passed about a thousand yards or more northwest of where the 16th Michigan and their Third Brigade waited near the Weikert farm, and it may be that most of the men could only hear, and not see, the repulse of the Rebels. They would not have to fight this day, though they heard that others did. "Terrible fighting again takes place today," Sgt. Berry noted. "We take an enormous pile of prisoners." He was in this case probably using the editorial "we," meaning his Union comrades, since there is no mention of the 16th Michigan taking part in this in the reports filed after the battle. Alfred Apted gave more detail, recording that "our line advanced on the left and wheeled around and captured a large number of prisoners." This was, essentially, a mopping-up operation, gathering up the survivors of the disastrous Rebel infantry attack.

Apted also noted that he witnessed "our cavalry make a charge on our extreme left"—a foolish and unnecessary action ordered that late afternoon on the extreme southern end of the battlefield by a glory-hungry Union cavalry division general named Judson Kilpatrick, who was sarcastically called "Kill-cavalry" by his men. "Kill-cavalry" indeed got scores of Union troopers needlessly killed, wounded, and captured that day, though Apted could not see this when they were trapped behind Confederate lines. The Grand Rapids sharpshooter wrote that these cavalry men captured "a large number of prisoners," though it was about a hundred Rebels, and at an awful cost. But Apted recorded that Gen. Meade rode down the Union line that day, telling his men they had taken 2,000 prisoners after stopping the Rebel infantry attack and, wrongly, "that reb General Longstreet was today captured."[8]

It rained that night and continued the next day. Those soldiers who still had their poncho tents pitched them "behind their breastworks," Graham remembered, but there was skirmish fire up and down the line. Eventually both the rain and firing let up. Sgt. Berry, like Graham, ventured out onto the battlefield. "Thousands of men, poor fellows, lay upon the ground, many of them in a condition unrecognizable," Graham wrote, choosing not to describe the awful horror of the sight and smell of the mangled dead. He said he walked back "where our regiment was engaged"—Little Round Top—and counted 150 bodies of Confederates, and in another nearby place, seventy more. "Truly a valley of death!" he wrote, probably referring to area before the rocky hill. But that was just a fraction of the fatal toll across the battlefield. Apted noted that the men started burying the dead that afternoon, probably their own regiment's, and they heard the rumor that "the enemy is supposed to be retreating."[9]

His comrade, Lt. Charles Salter of Detroit, also heard that Lee's retreat had begun. On July 5, their regiment and others advanced over the field, "and over all that space the dead bodies of both men and horses were strewn very thickly, both our own and the rebels, although the rebels had many more dead than we," he wrote. It was awful to see, "with the dead lying in all places, mangled and mutilated in every manner. We buried all of our own dead," [Apted said they had done this on the 4th] "and marked the graves in such a manner as to designate who they were," he continued; the Rebel dead went into mass graves.

Dr. Breakey later wrote that when he returned to Gettysburg weeks afterward, he found "a large shallow grave at the foot of the left of the rock front of the ledge" where his regiment had fought on Little Round Top, with a board marker that read "20 Men of the 16th Michigan buried here." His description of this grave roughly corresponded with contemporaneous accounts. A correspondent who signed his dispatch "Michigan" wrote later in the summer that "at the foot of Round Top mountain I found the graves of fourteen Michigan heroes, all members of the 16th Regiment and all buried in one grave, with the name of each written on a rough pine board, and placed over the grave."[10] Why the number of men buried there would have changed is unclear, but the bodies of these men were later removed and reburied with others in what would soon become the National Cemetery, though it seems two of the 16th Michigan's dead may have been sent home by the arrangement of families.

Apted wrote that some straggling Rebels were taken prisoner that rainy morning of the 5th, and they told their captors that Lee had begun their retreat at 10 p.m. the previous night. The Michigan soldiers picked up scores of abandoned rifles, and of course they came across more and more of the dead. Though none of the regiment's diarists or letter writers wrote of it as graphically as others did, the bodies had swollen and blackened in the summer heat, and the stench of the corpses and carcasses of the horses caused men to retch. Adjt. Rufus Jacklin said he was ordered out with a party of ten men to bury Confederate dead near the Emmitsburg Road near the Peach Orchard, which had become another famous Gettysburg landmark. "I took up my work near the Sherfy house," Jacklin would write. "I ordered the men to dig a trench in the garden to the left and in front of the house, near the road." He told a sad and tragic tale of burying the disowned Rebel son of the family in the very yard where the young man had grown up, but the story was simply not true. It was another example of how soldiers told and repeated rumors and tall tales as fact.

Graham, who said he led the regiment's skirmish line that went out toward the positions previously held by the Rebels, recorded a veritable catalog of items taken by them, but left on the battlefield—bits of food, "crocks of butter, lard, preserves, baskets containing delicacies from the cellars of the wealthy farmers in the vicinity . . . Dressing apparel which could do them no earthly good, such as old bonnets . . . babies' shoes, young misses' gaiters, feather beds, in fact everything stealable could be found here in profusion." Sgt. Berry's detail, meanwhile, continued to "bury a large number of our dead."[11]

That afternoon the regiment's skirmishers were relieved, returning to their comrades with just enough time to cook some coffee before preparing to move out. That night, they joined the long lines of Union soldiers moving after the Confederate army. "A portion of our army was already in pursuit of the rebels and we had to go also," wrote Lt. Salter. But the road ahead was jammed. "Towards night we march," Sgt. Berry wrote. "We travel about 7 miles which takes us until about midnight. The roads being very rocky & the mud over our shoes, & the night so dark, we stumble every few rods. We are marching in the direction of Emmitsburg. We bivouac at Marsh Creek."

Wagons and guns got stuck in the mud that night, but a cautious sort of chase had begun as the men marched away from Gettysburg. The Union army had suffered more than 3,100 dead there, and many thousands more were wounded. The Confederates had lost more than 22,000 killed, wounded, and captured; their dead alone amounted to more than 4,500 men. Though President Lincoln wanted an aggressive pursuit to destroy Lee's army, his generals were urging restraint, so as not to allow the Confederates to do to the Army of the Potomac what it had just done to them.[12]

The rain kept falling. With the road jammed with traffic, the regiment moved only two miles the next day, yet experienced what Sgt. Berry called one of their hardest dawn-till-dark marches yet. "Added to this we are short of rations and march hungry," he complained. Their corps at last passed through the town of Emmitsburg, crossed into Maryland, and halted a few miles from Frederick. They moved west on July 8 over the Catoctin Mountains to Middletown and the next day to Boonsboro in marches that took them over fences and ditches, into the hills, and across brooks and through woods, their commanders hopeful that the Army of the Potomac could intercept Lee's army. Of course, they were "tired, wet & hungry," Berry wrote.

"On the 10th we marched up on South Mountain and bivouacked in the mountains," Salter said. Squads from the regiment were sent out as skirmishers when Union forces came upon retreating Confederates at a place called Jones' Crossroads on the Sharpsburg Pike. "We have a brisk skirmish fight the whole day," Sgt. Berry wrote. "The rebels offer a stubborn resistance but we succeed in driving them towards night." Two of the 16th Michigan's men were wounded.[13]

The clashes continued in the summer heat as the Army of the Potomac caught up with the Confederates, who dug trenches and built fortifications in an area stretching nearly ten miles from Hagerstown, Maryland, south to the rain-swollen Potomac River near Williamsport. Fords where men could usually cross the river safely were now deeper under water, so Confederate engineers and their men rushed to build a pontoon bridge at a point near Falling Waters, Virginia, as Union troops pushed closer. The 16th Michigan marched on the Williamsport Road with its division on the 11th, crossed Antietam Creek, and became involved in heavy skirmishing at a place called Fairfield. They advanced in a line of battle that evening as the Confederate defensive line contracted, but no massive assault was made. Pvt. Apted noted that he had some "close calls," but "gave back better than received."

There was more of the same the next day—the men in good spirits despite the rain, pushing closer. "From what I see I should judge we are trying to surround and destroy their army if possible," Lt. Salter wrote. But soon it was too late for the Union army to do so. It was rainy and quiet on July 13, and the Union troops with the 16th Michigan built their own defenses while other forces probed and pushed. "Can't see the reason why General Meade don't attack the rebs," Apted complained. That night, a detail from the 16th Michigan went out under Lieutenant Frank Eddy of Flint, in Company G, and there was "considerable skirmishing." But it was the Confederate rearguard keeping Union soldiers busy and distracted. The Army of Northern Virginia crossed back over the Potomac, into Virginia.[14]

By now the soldiers had seen the press reports on Gettysburg and some of the men of the 16th Michigan were disturbed and perhaps resentful about the attention received by the 24th Michigan for its role on the first day of the fighting. The brother of Lt. Salter's stepmother, Lt. Reuben Humphreyville of Livonia, had been killed serving with the 24th Michigan. Humphreyville was only a few years older than he was, and Salter had considered him a good friend; still, Salter said he was not that impressed by that regiment's sacrifice. "The 24th Michigan are reported as losing 378 men, but out of that there is only 30 killed, both officers and men," he wrote. "They had very much the same sort of fight as the 4th Michigan had, and the 4th had more men killed and full as many wounded and hardly any prisoners, as they are too old soldiers to *allow themselves* to be taken prisoner."[15]

Though Salter's criticism was not particularly accurate or fair, he went on to take issue with the fact that newspapers were giving Gen. Meade credit for the Gettysburg victory:

> I contend it was the Army of the Potomac that won the battle, and not Gen. Meade, and that we would have done just as well or better under McClellan, Hooker or any other general. We are not fighting for generals, but for our country and I hope the northern people someday will give the credit of our fighting to the soldiers, and not make such gods of the generals, past or present, as they do.[16]

Back in Michigan, George Prentiss of Detroit, a former lieutenant in the 16th Michigan, read the news about the death of Lt. Butler Brown, 27, of Company E, at Gettysburg, and wrote letters to Brown's parents and the newspaper in their hometown of Hillsdale, telling them what a fine soldier he had been. "Too modest and with too much self-respect to clamor for promotion as some do, while his worth and bravery have never been questioned, he has not received the promotion he deserves," wrote Prentiss. He had loved Brown as a comrade and recalled the part they played in rallying the regiment in the previous summer near Richmond. "I cannot forget his coolness and bravery at Gaines' Mill in June 1862," he wrote of the former store clerk.[17]

The day after Lee's army went back into Virginia, Union soldiers and troopers near Williamsport moved forward in the rain and captured the last of the rearguard and stragglers who had waited too long to get over their pontoon bridge. Pvt. Apted recorded that he heard the news that Gen. Ulysses Grant had taken Vicksburg on July 4—an important strategic victory for the Union, cutting the South in two. Apted examined the Rebel defenses near Williamsport, where they had held the Union soldiers off for the past few days; he had to admit the position was strong, "though I believe we could have took it," he noted. Sgt. Berry thought the Union pursuing forces had that morning captured or drowned "a few hundred," referring to Rebels who tried to swim the river after their pontoon bridge was cut loose.

From Williamsport, the Union army's march to the southeast began in mid-July in a renewed pursuit of Lee. The diarists and letter writers of the 16th Michigan noted that they marched over the old Antietam battleground at Sharpsburg and moved the next two days to the small Potomac River town of Berlin, where Union engineers had built a pontoon bridge. The Brady Sharpshooters company, which seems to have been detached from the regiment during the skirmishing near Williamsport, rejoined the 16th Michigan at their bivouac here, and the next day, July 17, crossed into Virginia. But their commander was not with them: Lt. Col. Norval Welch left on sick leave. Lt. Frank Keeler, the Saginaw man in Company E, noted this, too, but almost doubtfully: "Col. Welch left for Michigan the other day," Keeler wrote home three days later. "—was sick, I guess."[18]

Welch's return to Michigan seems to have gone largely unnoticed or perhaps unpublicized, unlike the return of the colonel of the 24th Michigan. Perhaps Welch did not seek out any publicity; but he wrote to Gov. Blair when he returned to his regiment several weeks later, stating that one of his officers had signed a letter, sent to Michigan, that was "critical" of his "conduct at Gettysburg." It is not clear which officer sent this letter, or who received it, but eventually someone showed it to Welch. Whether this critical letter was shared with anyone else is not known, but Welch was clearly defensive about it and worried that it could affect his military career.[19]

When Frank Keeler got the chance to write home, he said nothing about the battle of Gettysburg. "It has been impossible to write for the past two weeks as we have been constantly on the march, and all our baggage, writing materials, etc. have been packed and in the wagons," he said. Since Butler Brown's death on Little Round Top, the paperwork for Company E fell to him. "Lt. Salter of Company H has charge of two companies, H and E, but I have to run Company E about the same as though I commanded it," he complained.[20]

Lee's army headed into the Shenandoah Valley on the retreat south, while the Union army marched on the east side of the Blue Ridge Mountains. For the next several days, the 16th Michigan marched in the mornings and camped in the afternoons, traveling from Lovettsville and Wheaton (foraging bread, honey, butter, and blackberries as they went) to Purcellville and on toward Middleburg, Ashby's Gap, and beyond, covering several miles a day in clearing weather. They halted on July 21, and the next day Sgt. John Berry was assigned to herd forward those men who fell behind while their brigade and division marched on several more miles. "I am detailed and left behind to bring up the stragglers, which I do to perfection," he proudly noted.[21]

The Army of the Potomac had nearly caught up with Lee, but it would have to force its way through the Manassas Gap in the mountains to intercept him. But by the time it did so on July 23 it was too late. Elements of the Third Corps and the 16th Michigan's Fifth Corps advanced into the pass, where Rebels were holding the western end, Lt. Salter wrote of this fight. He and his Company H went out as skirmishers with others from the Third Brigade on the extreme right of their line that day, "and we had to climb up over some of the largest and steepest hills I ever saw," he wrote. Confederate skirmishers fell back as the Union soldiers advanced—Pvt. Apted said they "had quite a skirmish" and Salter said they took 200 of them prisoners, while none of his men were wounded. As darkness was falling, Salter wrote, they saw their main battle line advancing below the heights on which the skirmishers stood, driving the Rebel rearguard out of the pass. Though they had a stunning view of the surrounding countryside from this peak at the western end of the gap, Lee had successfully continued on his way south. Historian Stephen Sears wrote that the Third Corps commander William French had "crept ahead" that day, engaged in light skirmishing, but failed to force his way through to engage the trailing Rebel corps. In the morning, the Union soldiers realized that "the entire rebel army had gone so far south, that we had to give up all hopes of cutting them off," Salter wrote.[22]

Another division of Union soldiers pressed on the next morning to the town of Front Royal, but the Rebels were gone, except for stragglers and badly wounded men who had been left behind. But on the way back through the Manassas Gap, Salter recorded a shocking sight: He said he and his men "found over 100 bodies of rebels who had been killed or wounded and afterward bayonetted by our men, who have not forgiven their atrocities at Gettysburg and other places, and, I am afraid they never will, as the majority of the 3rd & 5th Corps declare they will bayonet every rebel they can get at, on the battlefield." These atrocities, if they were indeed committed on wounded Confederate soldiers, had taken place in the previous day's fighting in the pass, though it seems that no one else made note of it.

For the next three days, most of the Army of the Potomac marched southeast for more than twenty miles, back to the area around Warrenton, with the 16th Michigan setting up camp about four miles southeast of the town on the Bealton Road. The men were ragged and tired, but new clothing came and washing, inspection, fatigue duty, and typical camp responsibilities were the order of business for a few days. Salter wrote that he was grateful to God for having been spared while so many friends had been killed at Gettysburg. "But I try my best to do my duty faithfully to my country and to the men under my charge, and have kept up and had charge of my company, many times on the march when really sick," he wrote. "And I would have dropped out of the regiment, but for the bad example it would set." Brady Sharpshooter Alfred Apted noted the ironic fact that Lee's men were reoccupying the same places, some twenty miles and more away, that they did before the Gettysburg campaign started nearly two months earlier. "The rebel army [are] all back in their old position at Culpeper, [and] Gordonsville," he wrote, "having passed through Chester Gap [in the Blue Ridge Mountains]."[23]

The momentary end to the marching and skirmishing gave George Ervay's friend the chance to write to his parents. "My name is Allen A. Young," the soldier wrote, "the fellow that went from Grand Ledge with your son George W. Ervay." They had come through the regiment's battles together, until Gettysburg. "I am so lonesome since that he is gone that I don't know what to do," Young wrote. "George was a good and faithful soldier and tended his duty well. But we had to part with him." Young would decide, in the coming year, that he had enough of soldiering. Early in 1864, when the regiment came back to Michigan on furlough, Young would desert.

Corporal Reuben Turrell also wrote to Ervay's father, sending home George's diary, a silver badge, a gold pen, and the letter George had written shortly before he was mortally wounded. "I know that it is hard to lose friends so far away from home," Turrell wrote. "I have had the trial of it by the loss of a dear brother here in the army. But the good Lord has been my helper and deliverer from all my troubles and I must stand by the good government which he has given us."[24]

In the meantime, Robert E. Lee positioned his battered army along the Rapidan River, so there were days of relative quiet from a military standpoint, though the soldiers of the 16th Michigan and others in their brigade and division were soon put to work. On the morning of August 3, officers woke up 100 men from the 16th Michigan, along with soldiers from the rest of the Third Brigade, for a fatigue detail that included Company A and the Brady Sharpshooters. "We start with three days provisions, arms and all our traps," Sgt. John Berry wrote of that work detail. "We march about nine miles within half a mile of Warrenton Junction." It was a hard march in the hot weather, but the men "cooked and demolished" their coffee and set to work, building a bridge, fixing roads, and chopping logs. Periodic thunderstorms did nothing to lessen the oppressive heat but only made the atmosphere more humid; the men worked, though they were allowed a Sunday off. "It is two years ago today since I was sworn into Uncle Sam's service," Berry noted on August 8. "I have yet one year of the soldier's life."[25]

The rest of the regiment moved out with the Fifth Corps to a new camp site on the Rappahannock River about eight miles away from Warrenton at the Beverly Ford, where the men dug emplacements for artillery batteries, trenches, worked on roads, and stood picket. "These preparations are all for defense," wrote Lt. Salter, "and now we are every day expecting to have use for them, as the rebels have found out that our army is not as large as they thought it was at Gettysburg." The losses suffered there by their Fifth Corps, and the detachment of brigades to keep order after draft riots had rocked New York in July, meant "that it would be madness for us to attempt to act on the offensive," Salter wrote.

He praised the Veterans Reserve Corps, the military body that kept wounded and incapacitated soldiers in the service by having them perform light duty—an excellent way, he felt, for sick and lightly wounded officers to continue to serve. "Four officers from our regiment have entered that corps," Salter continued. "Capt. Meyers and Martin and Lieuts. Chandler and Hough. And more that are wounded will also join."[26]

There were also changes in their brigade. Col. James Rice of the 44th New York, commanding the Third Brigade since Strong Vincent was fatally wounded, was promoted to brigadier general and transferred to a new command. Col. Joshua Chamberlain of the 20th Maine, a hero after the battle of Gettysburg, was the new brigade commander. With Welch on sick leave, Robert Elliott of Detroit, promoted to major, commanded the 16th Michigan. Elliott, who had gotten a reputation as an officer who sometimes drank too much, was acknowledged by Rice for his actions on Little Round Top. Apted would record a pointed observation that month after a regimental inspection by the major. "Inspection at 8:00 a.m.," the sharpshooter wrote. "Bob Elliott in a glorious state of intoxication."[27]

The soldiers had not been paid in months, so it was a happy day when the paymaster came. "We get paid today for the first four months ending June 30th," Sgt. Berry wrote. "The reinforcement of greenbacks come very acceptable as we are all hard up." For the most part, August was drill, fatigue, inspection, and picket; they worked on the local railroad and in their spare time the men could swim in the river or perhaps attend a temperance lecture. But the heat did not let up, and the rain sometimes flooded their camp and bivouacs where details were out to work or picket. Some new recruits were arriving, and they learned the elements of drill and maneuvers of the company and the battalion under the Virginia sun. When picket duty required the soldiers to march half a mile to a nearby creek, Berry noted that "[we] see nothing of the rebs, but we fight mosquitoes all night."[28]

A stunning exception to the men's routine was being assembled to watch a firing squad execute deserters as the month ended. Berry noted:

> Today about 3 o'clock five deserters were of the 118th Pennsylvania are shot. The whole division have to turn out under arms to see the execution. They have enlisted or gone as substitutes for drafted men several times and then deserted. They played this game once too often. They will never desert again. They were all foreigners by birth, two of them were Protestant, two Catholics and one Jew. They were said to be very intelligent, smart men and it is also said this is not the first roguery they had done.[29]

Apted described the execution as "a fearful scene."[30]

September weather was more pleasant, with some fine days and dewy nights. On the 3rd, Lieutenant Colonel Norval Welch returned to their camp. While he was in Michigan, he had been shown the letter that was critical of his conduct at Gettysburg, sent by one of the captains in the regiment, and it seems as if Welch was not in the best of moods when he got back to his command. "Welch came back to the regiment today," Alfred Apted noted. "Told it would be a good thing if [we] were to stay away." Welch, in turn, immediately wrote to Gov. Blair, concerned that the critical letter might affect his desired promotion to the full rank of colonel. He denounced this letter as a fraud. "Before I left Detroit I saw a letter purporting to have been written by a captain in my regiment, disparaging my conduct at Gettysburg," Welch wrote. "The letter was concocted in Detroit, sent on here for signature, and returned to parties using it to injure me. I hope my promotion may meet your approbation."[31] Which captain sent this critical letter and to whom is unknown, but Welch was eventually promoted to colonel.

Welch did not remain long in camp, though it is not clear whether he returned to Michigan or Washington. It appears that Capt. George Swan of Company A was left in charge, since Major Elliott was also absent then, sick and injured accidentally by falling timber. Alfred Apted, who just turned twenty-six, was bored with camp life and declared he would just as soon fight. "I wish the rebs would come around to the camp so that we could have some stirring times," he wrote. "Anything for a change." About his new brigade commander, he said: "Brigade drill by Chamberlain. He does not know much about military movements, although he handles a brigade tolerably well."

Lt. Frank Keeler of Saginaw wrote home complaining about the fact that new cavalry regiments were being created back in Michigan, while the "old regiments"—regiments formed back in 1861—were in such bad shape. "And here we are our old regiments, suffering for recruits! Why in the name of common sense doesn't the governor fill up the old regiments?" he demanded. Of course, Keeler seemed not to recognize that it was more politically profitable for the governor to create new regiments and hand out new commissions for officers, rather than merely send men to fill up existing outfits.[32]

The local Orange & Alexandria railroad line had been repaired by now, and trains were running to the area where the Fifth Corps encamped, bringing supplies to its soldiers and other elements of the Army of the Potomac. In the meantime, Union cavalry crossed the river and clashed with Rebel troopers. On September 13, the men of the 16th Michigan, under marching orders for an advance across the Rappahannock, heard cannonading as the cavalry battled on the opposite side of the river, but their brigade did not move for three more days. Gen. Meade had by now learned that Gen. James Longstreet's corps (most of his corps, but not all) had been sent by the Confederate government to Tennessee. Naturally, President Lincoln wanted his commander to attack Lee's weakened army. The 16th Michigan broke camp on the morning of September 16 and with other troops crossed the river on pontoon bridges, advancing in the heat by Brandy Station and toward Culpeper Court House and the Confederate lines at the Rapidan River. "A continual cannonading heard in the advance," Sgt. Berry wrote.[33]

Yet to the disappointment of the Lincoln administration, Meade did not attack. For the next three weeks the Union army was stalled in this area between the Rappahannock and Rapidan rivers; the 16th Michigan bivouacked near Culpeper Court House, which had been shot up in the previous fighting there. The men observed another execution of a deserter from the 12th New York; they got paid and tried to stay warm and dry when the nights were frosty and the rain came in; they underwent inspection, stood picket, and saw new conscripts for the 83rd Pennsylvania arrive. Lt. Keeler thought many of these drafted men were ruffians and criminals who had to be watched closely. Still, he believed the Union army was becoming stronger. "We will soon be able to sweep down on Richmond with overwhelming force," he predicted.[34]

But Keeler was wrong. Since Meade launched no campaign against the Army of Northern Virginia, two corps from the Army of the Potomac were removed by the War Department and sent west to Tennessee, where Union forces had suffered a serious defeat. The removal of these troops left Meade with 76,000 men, far outnumbering Lee's 50,000. But when Lee learned that two Union corps had been transferred from northern Virginia, he struck.

In the days before Lee pushed back against the Army of the Potomac, as a cold and rainy October began, soldiers like Pvt. Apted hoped they would soon be going into winter camp, and some started fixing up their tents. Sgt. John Berry decided it was time to try to get an officer's commission and he began studying tactics in his spare time; he also turned in an application to appear before an examining board seeking candidates for officers to lead "colored" (African-American) regiments.[35] But for most soldiers the talk was probably about an offer the War Department was making to them about extending their service beyond 1864. Lt. Keeler described it:

> An order has just been issued by the War Department offering to men of the old regiments an opportunity to reenlist. Regiments whose terms of service expire next spring or summer can re-enlist for another term and receive $402 bounty (to be paid by installments), 60 days furlough and the regiment so enlisting to be sent home to reorganize and recruit. A great many of our men are in favor of the plan and would take up the offer readily.[36]

But talk of the reenlistment offer was interrupted by a long and tiring game of cat-and-mouse between Lee's Army of Northern Virginia and Meade's Army of the Potomac. It jumped off to a surprising start on October 9 with the Confederates crossing the Rapidan River and moving in a sweeping curve around the right of the Union line. The 16th Michigan, bivouacked with thousands of other Unions soldiers at Culpeper, were awoken between 1 and 2 a.m. the next morning. Their orders were to push forward to form a new line to confront the Confederate army, though the regiment would see no Rebels this day.

"Out we tumble from our shelter tents, and commence to prepare in double-quick time for the march," Sgt. John Berry wrote. Then men struck their tents, throwing the logs on which they had built them into the campfires. "Eight days rations are then issued to each man and packed away in knapsack and haversack," Berry continued. "Coffee is then cooked and breakfast eat [*sic*] and camp being completely broke up, the bugles sound the Brigade Call (Dan Butterfield) and then we fall in." The call, of course, was that rhythmic, musical recitation of their old commander's name—*Dan-Dan-Dan But-ter-field! But-ter-field!*

The regiment marched forward with its brigade about four miles or more south in the direction of the Rapidan, and formed a line of battle as the army received reports of enemy troop movements. Though they expected all day that a battle would begin, they were surprised when they were marched back to their former camping grounds for the night. But it was two more days of back-and-forth marches for the 16th Michigan in that area, advancing and retreating and waiting as sick soldiers were put on the last train and ambulance wagons leaving Culpeper, back over the Rappahannock. "One lady poked her head out of the window and snarled out to us, 'I am glad you are going, Yanks!'" Berry wrote about leaving Culpeper Court House. "'Go to Bull Run and dig your graves there.'" In response, one of the 16th Michigan lads removed his cap, gave her a bow and a humorous reply. Some of Lee's force drew close as the Union soldiers withdrew, looking for an opportunity to attack near Brandy Station; in response the 16th Michigan went out as skirmishers and drove the probing Confederates back with the help of Union cavalry. At last, on the night of October 12, the men built huge bonfires on the hills above Brandy Station, on the railroad line between Culpeper and the Rappahannock, to give the appearance that a large Union force was encamped there, but then they marched away to the east.[37]

Lee was hoping to catch the Army of the Potomac while it was strung out on the march, while Meade had to protect his long supply line going back and prevent Lee from getting around his force to strike at Washington. Lee did not succeed, and Meade did not seek a major confrontation with the Confederates. So the routine of tiring marches continued for two more days in sometimes bad weather, when part of the Confederate force attacked and was defeated at Bristow Station on the Orange & Alexandria Railroad line on October 14. The 16th Michigan and other Fifth Corps soldiers were sent running back to help in this fight, but they were not needed. A driving rain fell on the tired men, who kept moving and bivouacking in the wet and cold. At last they reached the eastern-most point of this miserable campaign at Fairfax. The Union soldiers hoped Lee would attack their strong defenses there, but he did not. Instead, after his men destroyed as much railroad as possible, Lee began his retreat with Meade's soldiers now following the Confederate army back the way they came.[38]

It was a wet and muddy journey back to the front, though there was an immediate counter-march one day that angered the soldiers of the 16th Michigan and their brigade. "Oh, how I do hate this changing around," complained Pvt. Apted about the back-and-forth. "I would rather go into battle." But Lee's army continued moving to the southwest; the 16th Michigan marched with its brigade on October 19 across Bull Run on bridges and camped near their old position at the battle that had taken place here just over a year before—the second battle of Bull Run. The rain, falling on the shallow battlefield graves dug here, revealed a grisly sight: the remains of comrades "mostly unburied where they fell," noted Sgt. John Berry of Company A.[39]

"I went over the ground that our brigade had fought over, and found it pretty well covered with human bones and many skeletons entire," Lt. Salter wrote. "Also found the remains of Capt. Ransom and Lt. Chittick and the color bearer, a young man named——of our regiment. They were recognized by the clothing which still remained upon them." Salter was not sure of the identity of this particular man and made a series of dashes in place of a name. But at daylight their brigade marched to the Warrenton turnpike; the road was bad but the weather was good for a change, and they marched 14 miles west and stopped a few miles north of Warrenton. "Our corps is now in reserve, all the other corps are in advance of us," Salter wrote while the men rested and washed. "We expect that we are now to hold the line of the Rappahannock, the same as we had last August and September before advancing."[40]

Lee's campaign had cost him about the same number of casualties that he had inflicted on Meade, and he had again destroyed the railroad stretching back to Washington and Alexandria, though the Union army would repair it in short order. Salter believed that the fact the Lincoln administration sent so many soldiers from the Army of the Potomac to fight on the Tennessee–Georgia line under Union Gen. William Rosencrans had made their position too difficult to safely hold when Lee had started the fifty-mile chase-and-dodge campaign of early October. "I would prefer to see Gen. [Ulysses] Grant in command of the Army, as I believe he is the best general, but we must wait and see what Gen. Rosencrans will do," Salter said about the Union command in the west.[41]

It turned out that President Lincoln saw the army's leadership in the same manner. That month, he made Grant commander of the armies of the Tennessee, Ohio, and the Cumberland, and Grant promptly replaced Rosencrans. The time was not far off when the Army of the Potomac would also fall under Grant's command.

Norval Welch at last got his promotion to colonel, retroactive to May, when Thomas Stockton had resigned. But he continued to be away from the 16th Michigan. Major Robert Elliott had also been sick for several weeks, "so that we have not, in reality, anyone to command us, and the interests of both the men and officers of our regiment have been sadly neglected," Lt. Salter complained. He had been expecting to finally be promoted to captain after all the resignations, deaths, and wounds that took so many officers from the regiment.[42]

The camps of the Third Brigade and its Fifth Corps shifted late in October and settled briefly near Warrenton Junction, where the men fixed their tents and hoped this was their winter home. "Policing and fixing up camp, which is a sure sign of our moving soon," Pvt. Apted noted with sarcasm. He was right, since there would be more marching by Army of the Potomac before the year was over. But as the month ended, Sgt. John Berry got permission to travel to Washington with orderly Sgt. James Maguire, who was also in Company A and had joined it from Ontonagon, to appear before a board of examination. Berry, who had expressed interest in becoming an officer in a U.S. Colored Regiment, journeyed by foot, wagon, train, and steamboat back to the city, where he enjoyed going to the theater and the Smithsonian, visiting friends in the hospital, and shopping; he even found some time to study for his exam. "Have a gay time generally with Lt. Cameron and Sgt. Maguire," he wrote. That happy line was the last surviving note Berry made of his Civil War experience. Whether or not he continued to keep a journal, he was not assigned to be an officer in a black regiment, and remained with the 16th Michigan for the rest of the war. Not long after his visit to Washington, Berry reenlisted and eventually was commissioned a lieutenant after the Civil War in Virginia came to a close.[43]

RAPPAHANNOCK STATION

While Sgt. Berry traveled to Washington, the 16th Michigan moved out with its brigade in the rain, bivouacking in the mud and cold at a point closer to Warrenton Junction. "At such times I get sick and tired of a soldier's life," Apted lamented. But Gen. Meade had more for his men to do as November arrived. Lee had pulled his Army of Northern Virginia back to the Rappahannock, and held a point near Kelly's Ford where the railroad once crossed the river on a trestle. It was called Rappahannock Station, and here the Confederates built strong fortifications on a hill on the northeastern side of the river. Less than twenty miles away to the northeast, loads of supplies were reaching the Army of the Potomac on the rebuilt railroad, and now the Fifth and Sixth Corps were put under marching orders. On November 7, the men of the 16th Michigan packed before daylight and marched south with their corps, past the ruins of Bealton and portions of the rail line that were still torn up. It was a cool, windy day and their brigade and division proceeded to within two miles of Rappahannock Station, where the Fifth and Sixth Corps met and formed line of battle in the woods; then they advanced on the Rebel trenches and fortifications near the river.

Other Union forces were also moving against nearby Confederate defenses down the Rappahannock, but on the Fifth Corps' side of the battle line was a wide plain through which the railroad ran. A belt of trees along the tracks partially blocked the view of the Confederates, who were about a mile back in their defenses near the river. All morning Union officers reconnoitered and put their men into position. The battle began in the afternoon.[44]

"The Sixth [Corps] upon the right of the railroad, and our corps on the left, skirmishers were sent out on ahead, and forward we went," Lt. Salter wrote. The 900 skirmishers included those from the 16th Michigan and other regiments of their brigade and corps, and they commenced the attack, advancing into a brisk wind toward the Rebel pickets. Then the brigades of their First Division joined in; the Third Brigade was on the left of their division's part of the line, while the 16th Michigan was in the right-center of the brigade.

The Confederate pickets saw a veritable wall of blue-clad soldiers coming at them over the field, and they fell back. Their guns in the fortifications cut loose on the advancing Union soldiers, but remarkably did not inflict large numbers of casualties. "The rebel artillery kept up a lively fire upon us, but our artillery, coming up, engaged them," Salter said. "Our skirmish line drove back that of the rebels until they took refuge in the forts near the railroad bridge." Elements of the Sixth Corps pressed closer to the enemy defenses on their side of the battle line, with its soldiers gaining some high ground. Then six artillery batteries moved into position and hammered at the Rebel defenses. But as the lengthening afternoon turned toward evening, Union commanders understood that these guns were not going to drive the Confederates out of their stronghold.[45]

A Maine regiment in the Sixth Corps was ordered to charge the Confederate works, but as these men advanced, the skirmishers from the 20th Maine went forward with them; so did the other skirmishers from the Third Brigade, of which the 16th Michigan was part. These brigade skirmishers, led by Capt. Edward Hill of the 16th Michigan, entered the

Rebel fortifications. "And then our skirmishers charged upon the forts and took them by storm," Salter said, "and they had a desperate conflict with the Rebels in the ditches and in the forts, but captured them all and that, too, before the main body of our troops could get up."

One correspondent's report said that Hill had no orders to attack, and that his men were running low on ammunition. Shouting, these men rushed forward and fought the Rebels in a "purely hand-to-hand fight." The Confederate gunners stopped firing and began to flee the fort, but scores of other Rebels surrendered. "After that, they captured many more on the river bank." Lt. Salter wrote about the skirmishers, "and charged upon a pontoon bridge, and captured the bridge and prevented many more rebels from crossing so that all of them on the north side of the river were captured."[46]

Three of the 16th Michigan's skirmishers were wounded in the fight. Pvt. Apted described it as "quite a smart skirmish," while Salter called it "the most perfect and glorious little victory." Prisoners came from ten different Confederate regiments, and out of two enemy brigades, only 600 soldiers had escaped, he boasted. The 16th Michigan bivouacked with its corps there that night. Meade's men had pushed Lee's forces back across the river.[47]

Lee withdrew his army south to the Rapidan as the Army of the Potomac once again advanced to Culpeper Court House. Though soldiers hoped the season for fighting and marching was finally over as winter approached, their generals were not yet convinced.

15.

NOVEMBER 1863–MAY 1864

OLD LEE IS A TOUGH CUSS

The 16th Michigan bivouacked at the scene of the Rappahannock Station victory with its corps, and in the morning crossed the river at Kelly's Ford and marched three miles toward Culpeper. Here they bivouacked for the night as the Army of the Potomac again began to occupy the area, south to the Rapidan. On November 9, their First Division was detached from the Fifth Corps and sent back across the Rappahannock for picket duty between Bealton and the river, not far from the ford. The soldiers felt they had not been provided with adequate rations during this November mission, and they let their new temporary division commander know about it when he watched them march by.

"General [Joseph] Bartlett in command," recorded Pvt. Alfred Apted of the Brady Sharpshooters, "and as our division rode through, the boys commenced to call out 'hardtack' to him. It made him mad and he ordered the division out to drill." Shouting at generals is rarely a good idea for soldiers, and members of the 118th Pennsylvania later claimed that this incident was a simple misunderstanding. It was common practice, they explained, for dissatisfied men to shout at their supply officers: "Hardtack! Fresh beef! Coffee!" They were not being disrespectful to their division commander—they had just mistaken him for the commissary.[1]

Apted, from Grand Rapids, continued to be exasperated that the generals kept shifting them from one spot to another, without any purpose that the men could see—just as they had been told it was all right to fix up their camp, they had been moved, and then moved again. "I am getting tired of this marching and counter-marching," he grumbled. "I wish we could have a decisive battle and then we should have some rest." He also received a letter from his brother Henry, who had joined the 1st Michigan Sharpshooters Regiment, and was guarding Confederate prisoners in Illinois. "[I] am sorry that the foolish boy has enlisted, although now he must take his lessons in trial and hardships," he wrote. The weather was alternately rainy and fine and the division of which the 16th Michigan was part rejoined the Fifth Corps, three miles south of Kelly's Ford on November 19. It struck Lt. Charles Salter of Detroit as ironic that Union forces were on the north bank of the Rapidan, with Confederate forces on the south side—"same as before we fell back last month," he noted. The 16th Michigan camped in woods by a stream called Mountain Run, and Col. Norval Welch at last returned to his regiment.[2]

But again, Gen. George Meade was not done with offensive operations as November was ending. Lee's army was building a long line of defenses along the Rapidan to the point where a creek called the Mine Run flowed north into the river. Meade now planned an offensive where the Army of the Potomac would cross the Rapidan at fords east of Mine Run, and seize the main east–west roads of the wooded Wilderness. Here Meade wanted his army to drive west, to strike Lee before he could prepare an adequate defense. On November 24, the men of the 16th Michigan, with thousands of other soldiers, were awoken before dawn and moved out at 6 a.m. But the weather did not cooperate. "It rained very hard that morning," wrote Lt. Salter, "and the ground was becoming unfit for marching, so after we had gone 3 miles, Gen. Meade sent us orders to return to camp and remain 2 days longer."[3]

THE MINE RUN CAMPAIGN

After waiting for the roads to dry, the general ordered his men to move out again on Thanksgiving Day, November 26. The Fifth Corps marched to the Gold Mine Ford on the Rapidan, but then most of the men waited as pontoon bridges were built, Apted and Salter noted; then they marched toward Chancellorsville and bivouacked, and were moving the next morning when Confederate cavalry (again called "guerillas" by some of Union diarists) attacked the unguarded wagon train following behind their corps. The rebel troopers captured drivers, horses, and mules, seizing and destroying wagons; Lt. Frank Keeler called this an ordnance train, meaning it was hauling ammunition, but Salter and others indicated there were also ambulances in the column. One of the teamsters, Pvt. Martin Henderson of Company A, shot the Rebel officer who demanded he surrender his wagon and mules. John Berry would later say that the Confederate troopers hung Henderson right then and there with the lines taken off his team; another wagoner from the regiment, Francis Vanakin, was among those taken prisoner. He would die at Andersonville within less than a year. Salter said the Rebels shot down the horses and mules of drivers who tried to escape, and captured about fifteen ammunition wagons and ambulances, setting fire to what their commander claimed was at least thirty-five others.[4]

On the road ahead, the Union soldiers heard the gunfire as the enemy raiders struck the ammunition train, and the 16th Michigan was sent running back with part of the 62nd Pennsylvania to fight them. But it was too late. The men shot down one Rebel officer who tarried too long, trying to set one more wagon ablaze, but that was all the damage they did to the raiders. The attacking cavalry, under Confederate Gen. Thomas Rosser, departed otherwise unscathed with the ammunition and wagons his men managed to steal, leaving other wagons burning, shells and powder exploding. After this embarrassing attack on the wagon train, the 16th Michigan was detailed to guard it, so the regiment spent the next three days accompanying their corps' supply column as they moved from a river ford to the front. Of course, they bivouacked, as all the soldiers did, in the cold rain.

The new offensive was already off to a bad start when the Union army's Third Corps, which was to lead this movement, was delayed and then got lost, making a mess of Meade's plan, and giving Lee's Confederates plenty of warning that Union attackers in the thick forest were coming their way. Rebels then attacked the Third Corps and fell back as Meade changed his plans. Fortunately for the soldiers of the Fifth Corps, of which the 16th Michigan was part, they would now be in reserve.[5]

Apted's Brady Sharpshooters Company and Company I were detached from the regiment on November 29, and they stayed at the front near Mine Run in the woods and fields, while the rest of the 16th Michigan went back to the ford. Apted heard the cannonading the next day as the soldiers awaited the order to attack the Confederate defenses across the creek. "The rebs have strong works and 'twill be very difficult to take them," he noted. It was bitterly cold; the attack was supposed to go forward that morning and thousands of Union soldiers were sure that this could well be end of their lives as they attacked the Confederate defenses—almost everyone had by now seen what happened when infantry attacked entrenched positions and artillery, at Malvern Hill, Fredericksburg, and Gettysburg. But the 30th came and went without an order for the assault. An examination of the Rebel works across the creek to the west had surprised the same generals who had previously believed they could be taken: Lee's men, they saw, had strengthened and extended their defensive positions along the creek. At this, Gen. Meade had to agree with his generals who said an attack here could not succeed, deciding his soldiers would not be sacrificed.[6]

Apted's company and Company I were still detached from the regiment, seemingly with soldiers who would have made the assault. It must have been an incredible relief to see what was happening on the morning of December 1: "Our forces are moving off to the left," he wrote, indicating the turn the soldiers made to march back to the river. "Wagons are going to the rear, and at about 9:00, the whole army is marching for Germanna Ford. The rebs had such a strong position that Meade determined not to attack." With that, Apted succinctly and accurately summed up what had happened. Lt. Salter read in some newspapers soon after that Meade was going to be removed by Lincoln for not attacking Lee's position, but he did not believe it; certainly the soldiers knew it would have been a foolish and useless assault. "Lee's army was in such good position, our loss would have been very heavy if we attempted to drive him from it, and our wounded would suffer terribly with cold before they could be got to Washington," he wrote. "As it was, some of our men on picket, out in front, froze to death on account of getting wet and not having any fires to warm by." He said Meade's decision not to attack was "a measure of humanity, and our entire army thinks he done just right, and we thank him for it."[7]

The army went back to the Rapidan fords, where Apted and those detached from the 16th Michigan bivouacked early on the morning of December 2. Moving back to the Rappahannock River the next day, they found the rest of their Third Brigade. The brigade had been ordered back to the forts and defenses they had taken from the Confederates on November 7 at Rappahannock Station; they named the place Ft. Vincent in honor of Strong Vincent, their brigade commander fatally wounded at Little Round Top. But more importantly for the soldiers, the generals decided it was truly the season of winter camp, though Lt. Frank Keeler warned that until the mud was two or three feet deep, one could not be certain. There were plenty of stones at the river, so soldiers built foundations and fireplaces for their winter quarters, while the homes and barns of local residents who had abandoned the area were torn down for building materials. Some soldiers went up the river to cut down trees and raft timber back to the fort, though Apted cut his knee as he chopped wood and was stitched up by the doctor. His comrades shot a hog a few days later and the friends "had a good dinner of pork steak."[8]

Charles Salter, running Company H, finally got word that Col. Welch was recommending his promotion to captain; he would soon be in formal command of Company E, his old company. Though the weather was cold and at times rainy in that bleak countryside, he insisted the regiment "is all in fine spirits," thinking of the prospect of going home on furlough. "We have concluded to accept the offer of the Government to reenlist for *another three years* and go home to reorganize and recruit," Salter wrote. "This offer applies to all soldiers that have been in the service 2 years, and are willing to reenlist. They [will] receive $402 U.S. bounty, and the bounties now offered by the state and counties." Of thirty-two men in Company H who were eligible to sign up for the offer, all of them eventually did so, he wrote proudly. Lt. Frank Keeler echoed Salter. "My company (E) has reenlisted, every man that can, under the orders," he noted.

One reenlisting veteran was Henry "Tip" Aplin of Flint, much to the surprise of his younger brother, Tommy, who was serving in the 35th Illinois Infantry. "I thought he would be the last one to do that," Tommy Aplin wrote to their brother George in the 10th Michigan. Tommy wrote that he wondered if Tip would regret his decision to commit to three years more in the service, but it was he, the youngest Aplin brother, fated to die of illness in the coming summer. The Brady Sharpshooters' Pvt. Apted noted that within the regiment, two-thirds of those who qualified for the reenlistment offer did so by December 21, though there was not strong sentiment for it in his own company. By the end of December, 25 of the sharpshooters signed up, which Apted called "a large number" of the company.

In the meantime, the men enjoyed a routine of relative quiet, sometimes unloading railroad cars, working on roads and going on patrols, while officers did the paperwork required for the reenlistment extension. Historian Jeffry Wert wrote that some 28,000 veterans took the offer, extending the terms of their service with the army for three years.[9]

As the year wound down, Col. Welch submitted to the Michigan Adjutant General his yearly report of the regiment's service since November 1, 1862, the period that took in Fredericksburg, the "Mud March," Chancellorsville, Gettysburg, and the subsequent movements of the 16th Michigan on through October 1863. Not counting picket marches and minor reconnaissance, the regiment had marched eight hundred miles in that time, he wrote; forty men and four officers had been killed in battle or mortally wounded, and five officers and seventy-seven men had been wounded and survived. Another seventeen men had died of disease; in addition, twelve officers and 171 men had been discharged for disability.

Eight officers and seventeen men had been discharged "by order, etc." (generally meaning court-martials). One officer, Capt. Kin Dygert of the Brady Sharpshooters, had been captured at Little Round Top, and so too had ten soldiers over the course of the year. Lastly, seventy-nine men had deserted, Welch wrote. For all those losses, only two new officers and 102 men had joined the regiment. Of course, that meant the 16th Michigan was very much under strength.[10]

Welch also sent back to Michigan that month the tattered U.S. flag that had accompanied the regiment on the campaigns since the spring, and that had been hit by shot and shell at Gettysburg. "There is a shell hole through the field," Welch wrote, "and some 35 bullet holes in it." How the regiment replaced the flag, which had been described as a gift of the War Department before the Chancellorsville campaign, he did not say, though a newspaper report reflected they had another "battle flag" when they returned home on leave. This would suggest that the banner replacing the 1863 flag was likely another standard, War Department-issued U.S. flag.

The excitement of going home on thirty-day furlough for the reenlisting veterans, and those men with less than two years' service, was palpable. Though they did not know exactly when they would be leaving, they understood it was going to be soon, so the chores, inspections, and routine of camp life continued through Christmas and New Year's. "But we do not mind now," Lt. Salter wrote, since the prospect of visiting home made it worth the wait. As 1863 ended, Welch filed a report on the reenlistment in the 16th Michigan. First, he wrote, the regiment numbered 340 men, and of that number sixty were ineligible for the reenlistment offer because they had not enough time in the service, although these men were going to be allowed to go on leave with the veterans who signed up for the government's deal. Of the 280 soldiers who were eligible for the offer, at least 260 of them did so by the time Welch made his report.[11]

There was red tape in the processing of the reenlistments of the veterans, and it took time. Officers scrambled to get this done before they went on furlough and then learned some of their rolls were incorrectly completed. "We are busy day and night," wrote Lt. Keeler, "preparing the rolls and other papers necessary for the reenlisting of a regiment. It requires a vast amount of work for the process. My papers are finishing today and tomorrow we are to be paid, and soon will be on the road home."

"Gen. Meade told me we could leave before the 1st [of] January," Welch wrote in that last week of 1863. "I think we will be able to get started by Friday or Saturday, the 1st or 2nd." Most of the men wanted to return to Detroit, Welch continued, and he hoped the regiment would be greeted as heroes. "Please tell the governor and have him there," he said. "We wish to meet him. Can't we be received with a little *eclat* in Detroit? The officers and men all would be glad of some little notice of this sort. We mean to be the first regiment from the state to respond to the call for 'veterans.'" It would be necessary for the men to stay in a barracks for two or three days in Detroit before they could start their furloughs, so Welch asked if Adjutant General Robertson could have a place ready for them.

The weather was cold and rainy as December ended, but on January 2 of 1864, 289 veteran soldiers and officers of the 16th Michigan, along with scores of their comrades who had been in the service less than two years, boarded cars at Rappahannock Station for the long road home. Those soldiers who had chosen not to take the reenlistment offer, whose hitches in the army would end in the coming September, had to remain in camp at Fort Vincent.[12]

Though the regiment did not leave northern Virginia until just after the New Year, its assistant surgeon, Dr. William F. Breakey, who had been detached from the 16th Michigan for months, was joining them for the trip home. He later wrote that he was already in Washington on January 1, apparently awaiting the arrival of the rest of the returning regiment. He and some unnamed officers decided to try to pay a visit to the President of the United States. It was a tradition that the American president on New Year's Day received well-wishers, ranking political figures, and ambassadors, so with hours to wait before he was to leave, Breakey got in line with hundreds of others. Though diarist Alfred Apted wrote that it had been cold and rainy as 1863 ended, the weather that first day of 1864 was surprisingly mild, the doctor wrote.

"The morning was so warm we started out without overcoats," Breakey said. He himself had just recovered from a lingering illness and an injury from a bad fall, suffered after the battle of Gettysburg, that had confined him to bed for weeks. But as the doctor waited with others in the long receiving line, the temperature plunged, and he realized that VIPs were getting in to see Lincoln while soldiers stood in line. "After standing an hour or more to see the distinguished gentleman of our own country, and the decorated ministers of foreign countries arrive and depart, the rapidly growing cold drove us to the shelter of our hotels." Incredibly, a large portion of the country experienced what he said was a sixty-degree drop in temperature.[13]

Breakey said that his regiment boarded the train on the B & O Railroad for the trip from Washington that night, though it must have been the night of January 2nd, given that the 16th Michigan had not left Rappahannock Station until that day; the troopers of the 1st Michigan Cavalry were traveling with them. Some of the cars had no heat, he wrote, but some had stoves, though enough not wood. "While the train was standing on a siding we went out and broke off the boards from fences for fuel and managed to get the cars in which there were stoves tolerably heated," he wrote.

The weather remained cold and the return of the two regiments was plagued by delays—one car jumped the track before they got out of Virginia, and their train was often "sidetracked" and had to wait when railroad operators let other trains go by them. Officers and men alike suffered bad colds, the doctor wrote, and the hours dragged into days and nights as their train crept through Pennsylvania and into Ohio. At one stop, Breakey claimed, the men actually carried a stove, with a fire burning inside it, out of a train station and into an unheated car—they had proverbially "stolen a hot stove," probably using poles. At another stop, within about forty miles of Cleveland, portions of their train separated, so that the men were sent on ahead, while the cars containing the officers of the 1st Michigan Cavalry and the 16th Michigan were left behind.[14]

The angry officers had reached their breaking point. "On the fifth day out . . . we were again stopped on a sidetrack for the regular train and some freights to pass on," Breakey wrote; the officers declared a martial law of their own. "For nearly a week we had respected civil authority and had been snubbed and treated with no more regard than if we had been so much freight," he continued, "—and not forward with as much dispatch as is given to perishable freight." The Michigan officers somehow placed two railcar axles and wheels on the track, blocking an approaching train, and posted guards at the station. They found an engineer and "drafted" him at the point of bayonets in the event they would need their own driver, the doctor wrote.

The personnel of the incoming train were surprised but understanding when they found the 16th Michigan and 1st Michigan cavalry officers taking over their engine and train. A sympathetic director of the railroad, who happened to be on the arriving train, ordered the conductor to immediately take the officers on to Cleveland, where they caught up with their regiments "in time to prevent the scattering of 700 men without officers," Breakey wrote. Seeing the results they achieved by getting tough with the railroad made them wish they had taken these measures much earlier, and the remainder of the trip was uneventful.[15]

In the meantime, officials in Detroit and Saginaw made ready to receive the 16th Michigan. The regiment was to rendezvous in Saginaw once the leave was over, so civic leaders prepared quarters that could house up to 400 men and supply them with food, water and cooking and eating space. "We have made the necessary arrangements this day and given you notice by telegraph," wrote David H. Jerome, a prominent businessman and Republican politician, to the state adjutant general. Jerome was serving as a military aide to Gov. Blair, and he promised anything would be done for the comfort of the soldiers. Their quarters, he said in early January, would be finished in a few days.[16]

The 16th Michigan's trip home took an entire week. A press report said they had lost nearly an entire day when a loose rail between Wellsville, Ohio, and Cleveland delayed their train and caused some of the men bumps and bruises. There was no mention, however, of the train station takeover described by Dr. Breakey. "Their impatience to reach home was appeased only by the knowledge that the length of time they were upon the road was not to be deducted from their furloughs," a *Detroit Free Press* correspondent wrote. Shortly before 1 p.m. on Saturday, January 9, their train pulled into Detroit to a crowd that had waited in freezing weather for nearly two hours.

> When the train came into the depot, the returning heroes were greeted with cheer upon cheer from the crowd, whose enthusiasm was not lessened by impatient waiting, nor frozen out by the coldest winter atmosphere. The band struck up a national air as the boys disembarked from the cars, the music, cheering, and hearty hand shakings and greetings and exclamations of joy at meeting made the scene altogether pleasant and exhilarating.[17]

The crowd and the soldiers and the troopers, led by the Detroit Light Guard's band, marched in a procession from the train station to the Fireman's Hall, and listened to a speech by a local Republican politician, Detroit Postmaster William A. Howard. He said he came before them with feelings of admiration for their deeds, and sympathy for their suffering; pride in their endurance and sorrow for their losses. But Howard kept his remarks short, and let them get on with dinner rather than go into a long review of their battles. The soldiers were variously taken to the Cass Hotel, the Garrison House, the Franklin Hotel, the Railroad Hotel, and the Merchants Exchange Hotel, while the officers were taken to the Michigan Exchange.

After dinner, the men returned to the Firemen's Hall, where their 30-day furloughs were formally issued. Then both regiments paraded through the streets, led by the old band of the 16th Michigan, the Steuben Guards band that had joined Stockton's Regiment back in its early formation in 1861, but that had been mustered out of service a year later. The men carried three of their battle flags—two of them the U.S. flags that had been carried in the campaigns of 1862 and 1863, and presumably, the new banner that replaced the 1863 flag. "The boys were repeatedly cheered by the crowds of citizens which assembled to look upon them," the paper reported, "and the demonstrations everywhere must have served to convince them that Detroit and Michigan is [*sic*] proud of their glorious deeds, and bids them a hearty welcome home."[18]

Some of the veterans of the 16th Michigan seemed to have spent a relaxing Sunday in Detroit, before starting for home. On Monday, Sarah Cushman Miles Case, a widowed housewife in Flint, noted the arrival of the volunteers from the area. "A good many furloughed soldiers come in the stages this p.m.," she wrote in her journal. "Most of them belonging to the 'Veteran 16th' or Stockton's Regiment, which arrived in Detroit on Saturday and were so handsomely received."[19]

A letter by Elvira Aplin of Flint to her son George, then in Nashville with the 10th Michigan Infantry, gave a glimpse of the experiences of her son Tip, who seems to have spent a couple of days in Detroit before heading back to his hometown. "Tip arrived in Flint on the 12th of January after a tedious journey of 8 days," she wrote. "The regiment suffered severely from the cold. They broke camp on the 2nd of January and arrived in Detroit on the 8th [the 9th] and came to Flint on the 12th. Tip looks just as he did when you saw him last. I do not see as he changed at all . . . It seemed good to see him once more."[20]

There is little else in the record that describes the experiences of other soldiers on furlough, though one can imagine the reunions of sons with their parents, of husbands with their wives and children, and of sad and bittersweet scenes where returning men visited the families of dead comrades in towns like Adrian and Flushing, Ionia or Hillsdale. Detroit's Charles Salter, now captain of Company E, was kept busy on recruiting service, trying three times to see his friends the Duffield family, but missing them. "I did not have much time to visit my friends," he apologized later. But he and other officers apparently did a good job at convincing men to enlist, as the 16th Michigan would leave the state back to the war with nearly 150 new recruits.

Dr. Breakey, the regiment's assistant surgeon, would later write that he was home with his wife, seemingly in Washtenaw County's Salem Township, for only a few days when he received orders to go to Saginaw to examine the new recruits coming into the 16th Michigan. "We were very hospitably treated in Saginaw," he wrote of the rendezvous of the regiment before the trip back to Virginia. Tip Aplin, who had spent much of his leave "a-visiting with family," headed to the rendezvous on February 3, said his sister, schoolteacher Sarah Aplin. "Yesterday [I] bid goodbye to Tip, perhaps for the last time," she wrote. "His furlough has expired and he had to report at Saginaw yesterday." Before he left, Tip presented miniature pins with his likeness inside to his mother, sister, and aunt.[21]

Capt. Salter left Detroit for Saginaw on February 9, and a week later, as their furlough was coming to an end, a ball was held to honor the regiment on the evening of the 16th at the town's Webster Hotel. Capt. Edward Hill of Company K noted that his dance partner was a beautiful woman named Elvira Ward of Cincinnati, and that "everything passed off agreeably." But in the morning, officers and men boarded the cars for Detroit and stayed for the night. In the morning of February 18, before again boarding the train for Toledo, the officers of the regiment presented Col. Norval Welch with what one of the newspapers called "a magnificent gold watch" of "the best American make, with fine heavy gold cases." On the front exterior of the case was engraved the Maltese Cross, the badge of the Fifth Corps, with Welch's name and regiment inscribed; on the back was an eagle and shield. On the inside of the front case were the names of all the regiment's battles, while the interior side of the back of the case bore the names of those who presented it. With a heavy gold chain and a keystone of white onyx bearing Masonic symbols, the watch, manufactured by Charles H. Dunks of Detroit, cost $350, the paper said.[22]

Yet Welch was in no hurry to return to Virginia. The day before the 16th Michigan left, state Adjutant General John Robertson was trying to arrange permission for Welch and other unspecified officers to be detailed as recruiters. The War Department, however, said no. "I am directed to inform you that it is not conducive to the interests of the service to accede to the request at the present time," wrote Thomas M. Vincent, assistant adjutant general.[23] Despite Vincent's denial of the request, Welch, although returning to the front for a while, would indeed spend weeks away from his regiment. It seemed that Welch had cultivated powerful allies in Governor Blair and other Radical Republicans, though his officers and men would come to resent his continued absence in the weeks ahead.

In the meantime, the train carrying the 16th Michigan rolled on from Toledo in the bitter cold, to Dunkirk, Pennsylvania; then to Elmira, then Harrisburg and Baltimore, each part of this journey taking almost all day. "We stayed in Washington on the night of the 22nd," said Lt. Frank Keeler of Saginaw, "and on the night of the 23rd stopped in our old camp at Fort Vincent."[24]

Salter got a pleasant surprise from his men as they paused in the nation's capital before continuing to their old post in Virginia. "I was presented with a splendid sword by the members of the company as a token of esteem, etc.," he proudly wrote. "The sword is the best one in our regiment and is very neatly inscribed, as presented to 'Capt. Charles H. Salter by the members of Co. E 16th Mich. Vet. Vol's, as a token of esteem, Feb. 22nd, 1864.' Coming as it does from the men who have served with me nearly three years, I appreciate it very highly."

But as the regiment came back to northern Virginia, the matter of weapons was back on the minds of Pvt. Apted's Brady Sharpshooters. When the company formed in the fall of 1861, these marksmen brought their own rifles into the service, while their captain, Kin Dygert, was reported to have let at least one contract for arms as the company joined the 16th Michigan early in 1862. Now, however, they were issued the same standard rifle that most of the rest of the Union army used. "Returned to duty," Apted noted. "Took Springfield muskets with the assurance of Colonel Hayes that as soon as possible to get them, we shall have Sharps rifles."[25] The identity and position of Hayes was not given, but he obviously had responsibility for issuing arms in the 16th Michigan's brigade or division.

When the regiment got back to their old quarters at Fort Vincent near Rappahannock Station, the men found the cabins and walls and foundations they put up in December had been torn down, turned into firewood or otherwise stripped by other soldiers in need of building materials. Fortunately, the bitter cold of the past weeks gave over to dry and mild weather. "We had to sleep out of doors for that night," Salter wrote. The 16th Michigan was being shifted from the forts on the river a bit further south and west along the railroad to their First Division headquarters, about two miles from Bealton, "and we set to work right away building up log cabins again for quarters," he said. The regiment had become so skilled at erecting such buildings, he added, they quickly put up their new camp; Pvt. Marion Munson said it was a busy time. "I am working like a nailer," the Oakland County man wrote, "and packing logs and chopping them for our winter quarters." Lt. Keeler, now acting regimental quartermaster, was invited with a couple of friends to share quarters with the division's commissary captain. "We are as comfortably quartered as we would be at the National Hotel in Washington," he boasted.[26]

While the regiment reestablished its camp, Capt. Edward Hill was allowed a leave for medical treatment of an illness he did not specify, traveling from Washington to Baltimore, where he visited doctors and enjoyed socializing and attending the theater with friends, not returning to the 16th Michigan until April 17. Near Bealton, camp life in the 16th Michigan was routine, with the exception of an alarm late in February; the men were called out early one morning and ordered to be ready to march. The rumor was that Lee was about to attack, but the marching order was countermanded twenty-four hours later, and everyone was glad of it. Pvt. Munson, who often expressed sardonic comments on the army and the war, wondered if there was a chance there would be a cessation of hostilities, and the war would not resume with the spring. "Let us hope that the rebellion is near played out," Munson wrote, "and hope that there need not be a gun fired on either side."[27]

By mid-March, the men of the 16th Michigan had graded their camp roads, put up a brush fence, and built cabins. They performed picket duty, of course, guarded the railroad line, and drilled the new recruits, who had to learn the maneuvers of their platoon, company, battalion, and brigade. They were fortunate to have good weather, but danger lurked in the countryside. "Today was a warm day," Tip Aplin wrote. "I took a short walk into the country today, not daring to go far for fear of the guerillas. They are very thick in this region of country, five or six men have been murdered by them within the week."

Despite the War Department's earlier denial of Michigan Adjt. Gen. Robertson's request to allow Welch to recruit in Michigan past the end of the furlough, the colonel and one of the lieutenants left the regiment to go back to do just that. On March 16, Gen. Joseph Bartlett, then in command of the division of which the 16th Michigan was part, threw a ball at the brick house where he stayed. Lt. Frank Keeler, who was now assigned to Company F, said Bartlett made "extensive preparations" for the occasion, including the construction of a "palace of evergreens"—a temporary hall for dancing—as well as having the house and grounds decorated with banners and flags. Scores of civilians, including sixty women, were brought by train from Washington. "Our camp is only a dozen rods from this gorgeous place, and when he [the general] formed for dress parade, the ladies and their escorts formed in an irregular line facing us, anxious to witness our daily ceremony," the Saginaw man wrote. "Altogether it was a very pleasing affair."[28]

Captain Salter, who was a promoter of Christian tracts and Sunday prayer meetings, did not like the idea of a dance in the middle of the camps. "I suppose they had a very pleasant time there, but cannot say, for as I did not approve of having balls here in the army, I did not go to it," he wrote. But Salter may not have had a choice; according Lt. Keeler, only the regiment's major, Robert Elliott, and the officer of the day were invited to the dance. That weighed on the mind of Tip Aplin, who, as an enlisted man, was not invited to the general's ball, either. "Do you go to many dances?" he asked his sister that week. "I like dancing better than anything else that I know of for an evenings [*sic*] enjoyment. The Boys have dances here almost every night but there is a lack of young ladies to make it go off as it ought to. Our ballroom is out doors on the grass which is good enough for a Soldier."

Dr. Breakey would later write that certain small details stood out in his memory of the war, and for him it was the food served in his mess that season. The assistant surgeon had joined the regiment's headquarters staff mess, or cooking and kitchen arrangements, and he fondly remembered their cook and his dinners. That cook "always made the same puddings for dessert, and always flavored them with orange peel," Breakey recalled.[29]

On St. Patrick's Day, the soldiers got the chance to have some fun. Lt. Keeler said that the 9th Massachusetts, considered an "Irish" regiment, was "the center of excitement" for the First Division of the Fifth Corps; there were horse races, cock fights, greased pig chases, greased pole climbing contents, and of course, drinking and fighting. "Last year two men were killed and several others seriously injured in these 'harmless' sports," he noted. "It is a pleasant day, and the memory of the beloved saint will be celebrated with a zest and spirit characteristic of Irish jollifications."

The more religiously minded Capt. Salter told of passing out books, Bibles and tracts from the Christian Commission, a volunteer organization that provided these to the soldiers, along with Sgt. Reuben Turrell, from Hubbardston, who had written to the father of Pvt. George Ervay after he died at Gettysburg. "We distributed 50 testaments in our regiment today furnished by them," Salter wrote on a Sunday about the U.S. Christian Commission, "and I believe they are doing a great deal of good." He had to admit that his fellow officers did not take much part in regimental prayer meetings, and the veterans were not as interested in the sessions as were the new recruits.[30]

Two of the new recruits in Salter's Company E—friends of young Marion Munson—were a father and son from Rochester, a small town in northern Oakland County. These were 50-year-old Oramill Gibbs and Josiah H. Gibbs, 18. The elder Gibbs fell ill once they reached the army in Virginia. "Father, he is in the hospital now," Josiah Gibbs wrote home. "He has been very sick with the measles, but is able for duty now, that is [light] duty." Oramill Gibbs would spend weeks in Washington before he was sent to McClellan Hospital in Pennsylvania. His son, however, liked that the army fed him well. "I [weigh] the most now that I ever [weighed] in my life," Josiah wrote. "I [weigh] 178 pounds. I have an appetite like the devil. I eat double rations. Now and then I don't have enough. . . . We have soft bread and pork, beef and potatoes, dried apples, sugar, coffee and beans."[31]

But there was serious business ahead and the soldiers knew it. Gen. Ulysses S. Grant had been brought from the western theater of the war; after his victories at Vicksburg and Chattanooga, Lincoln appointed him to command all Union forces. "Gen. Grant is expected here soon to take command of our army in person," Salter wrote, "and we expect to have an active campaign and a desperate one too, very soon. Gen. Grant has now a more difficult task before him than any he has every before undertaken." Here, in the eastern theater of the war, he would face Gen. Robert E. Lee and the Army of Northern Virginia, the captain wrote, and in a terrible country for campaigning. "Yet we have great confidence in Gen. Grant and hope he will be successful here," he said.

Of course, there was also a conspiracy theory making the rounds, Salter noted. Northern politicians, this rumor went, were fearful that Grant's success out west had made him too popular, so he was being put against Lee, against whom Grant would fail and thus damage his reputation. Salter did not discount the theory, but said only that the war would go on: "One thing is certain," he wrote, "that the Army of the Potomac has got to suffer and struggle on in the same manner we have been doing for the last three years."[32]

So the soldiers drilled, preparing for the spring campaign. Union generals had found that many soldiers had not handled their rifles very well at Gettysburg, and ordered more firing exercises (though some veterans maintained these were aimed at the new recruits and not at themselves). "We are to have target practice from now on three days a week," said Lt. Keeler. "The recruits must be taught to shoot and be able to hit something."

On April's Fool Day, Frederick Wellington, 19, a new enlistee from Saginaw, turned the tables on Detroit's Capt. George Swan when the officer tried to trick the rookie soldier into applying for the job of "ordnance sergeant" and thereby embarrassing himself at division headquarters. Wellington knew that he did not have the rank or experience to apply for such a job, but played along with Swan and, in turn, tricked the captain into believing that there truly was such an opening—and that Lt. William Kydd from Detroit was applying for it. The officer who got that position in the First Division would be taken out of the battle line, of course; Swan, who longed for such an assignment, quickly borrowed a horse and hurried to division headquarters to apply for the post, only to find that there really was no such opening—he had been fooled by the rookie soldier. By the time Swan got back to the 16th Michigan, everyone knew Wellington's story of his trick; Swan was given a new nickname by his comrades—"Ordnance Sergeant." "For a little while he was so mad that he could have shot me," Wellington wrote of Swan, "but that made [it] all the more fun."[33]

Pranks aside, the Army of the Potomac was again reorganized. Two entire army corps were split up, with their various divisions reassigned to the three remaining corps, including the Fifth Corps of which the 16th Michigan was part. The Fifth Corps' commander since Gettysburg, Gen. George Sykes, was replaced with Gen. Gouverneur Warren. There were other consolidations and replacements of commanders, but the most important change to Salter (and, he said, to other soldiers) was that, with Grant's promotion, the previous general-in-chief, Henry W. Halleck, considered an intriguer who interfered with Union commanders, would not have the power and influence as he had previously. Halleck now became the army's chief of staff, answerable to Grant. "We feel that the dark days of the 'Army of the Potomac' are about over now," Salter wrote of the change. Within his regiment, though, there was still the basic routine of inspection, young Fred Wellington wrote. "[A]nd woe! to the poor fellow that 'shows shit,' either on his person or about his quarters," he told his parents. "one poor chap got bad off this morning for having a dirty shirt on, another because his feet smelled."[34]

Cold, snow, and rain continued well into April, but there were obvious signs that the army would be on the march soon. "We have been making preparations for marching, and last week the sutlers and all the citizens were ordered to leave the army, and all of our extra baggage was sent to Alexandria to be stored so as to leave us in light marching order," Salter wrote. Grant reviewed the Army of the Potomac, one corps at a time, but the Fifth Corps was spread out over the countryside for about twenty miles, so they were not able to see their new commander.

Col. William A. Throop of the 1st Michigan Infantry, returning from furlough, stopped at the 16th Michigan's camp and complained how difficult it had been to get new recruits. In the reorganization of the Fifth Corps, his regiment was now assigned to the First Division's Third Brigade, as were the 18th Massachusetts and the 118th Pennsylvania. Capt. Salter wrote that Throop said returning to the camp "seemed like getting back home again. And so it is with most all of us, unless we have some extraordinary strong tie to bind us at home, we cannot stay away from the army."[35]

Marion Munson echoed his captain's sentiments, but with wry humor. "Be it ever so humble, there is no place like home, even if it is an old tent sleeping on the ground," he joked early in April when he had been assigned to "safeguard" duty, watching the house of Rebel sympathizer. He compared the job to that of "a watch dog"—his latest assignment since he bound himself to Uncle Sam for three more years as a "mud crusher and rebellion smasher." His usual cynicism showed through when he discussed the political situation and disapproval of the war as the instrument of abolition. He was hoping Gov. Andrew Curtin of Pennsylvania would be a candidate for president in the fall, but he doubted it mattered. "I suppose there is no use of talking, old Abe is [the] devil that will be elected," he predicted. Heavy rain meant there was still plenty of mud and swollen rivers and creeks to cross while coming and going from picket, and it was miserable. "I was gone three days and nights from camp." Munson complained, "During that time my closes [clothes] were not dry and I had wet feet all the time."[36]

Knowing the season of battle was coming, officers wanted to see Col. Welch successful in recruiting. "It may be we shall be on the road within a week," wrote Lt. Frank Keeler. "Col. Welch has not returned, perhaps he is in Saginaw now. We hope he will get his new companies full soon and return as recruits will need drill before they can do service." By April 30, the regiment was breaking camp for a general move. "Probably hot work will come soon," he wrote in the hours before the soldiers struck their tents."[37]

The start of Grant's new offensive marked the end of the service of the regiment's assistant surgeon, Dr. William Breakey. He had injured his left leg in what must have been a bad fall at Gettysburg while taking care of wounded men after the battle, but the cold and wet of winter camp had aggravated his condition, and he knew he would be unable to handle the physical demands on a surgeon in the field, now that the Army of the Potomac was about to go on the offensive. He resigned on April 18, and before his regiment moved out, said his goodbyes and walked up to the railroad line to get on the train back to Washington. "There was no platform and the train hardly stopped," Dr. Breakey wrote of his departure. The soldiers helping him threw his luggage into one of the open freight cars, but the doctor had a more difficult and nearly deadly exit. Breakey leaned in and "caught the floor of the moving car, my feet and legs dangling, unable to pull myself up and afraid to let go, for fear that if I did not drop under the wheels, I would fall twenty feet into the Rappahannock, over which the train was by that time passing." But someone inside the car, perhaps a soldier who was too ill go into the field or a sutler or civilian being sent away, grabbed the doctor's arms and pulled him in. If Breakey managed to turn and look out the open door, he likely got a last glimpse of his army's camps and forts at the Rappahannock as the train clattered on toward Washington.[38]

The 16th Michigan moved on May 1 to a point near Brandy Station, and camped in the mud as the Fifth Corps commands gathered for the new offensive. Pvt. Munson scrawled a quick note home, warning his friends not to be overly optimistic. "Don't set your mark too high on our success as old Lee is a tough cuss and old Grant will have to git up and go if he is to [be] successful out there," he said. Pvt. Alfred Apted, ordered to stay behind temporarily to make sure that those soldiers out on picket got the supplies they would need, had the chance to look for his brother Henry, whose regiment had been sent to the Army of the Potomac, but was unsuccessful. He and the 16th Michigan's pickets, under Capt. Salter, rejoined the regiment near Brandy Station on May 2, where rain had prevented the generals from holding a dress parade.

Captain Hill, back with his regiment after a medical leave during which he enjoyed going to theaters and socializing in Baltimore with a woman he identified as Kate Adelina, noted that the 16th Michigan "badly" lost a ballgame to the 44th New York the next day.

More importantly, the advance now began, and they moved out late that night, marching south through the early morning hours of May 4 toward the Rapidan River fords.[39]

Their march was just one part of Grant's offensive against the Confederacy on various fronts that day. In the western theater of the war, Gen. William T. Sherman was beginning an advance from Tennessee into Georgia; elsewhere in Virginia, Union forces were to move into the Shenandoah Valley (the "breadbasket," or main source of crops for food, for Lee's army), and up the James River to menace Richmond. But in northern Virginia, the 16th Michigan and its corps trooped through what Apted called "the dilapidated town of Stevensburg" to the Germanna Ford. Their generals intended for them to pass around the right of Lee's Army of Northern Virginia into open country, going through the western side of rough, brushy forest around Chancellorsville called the Wilderness, where the two armies had clashed in the spring of 1863.

The Fifth Corps, to which the 16th Michigan belonged, and another corps, accompanied by cavalry, crossed the Rapidan that day. The 16th Michigan went over the river on a pontoon bridge at about 10 a.m., and Pvt. Apted noticed his new corps commander, apparently looking at maps and issuing orders. "Here we passed Gen. Warren who was quietly seated on the grass, busily engaged and planning this, I hope the last campaign of the Army of the Potomac," he noted. Capt. Hill realized that just one year ago, "we were getting out of Chancellorsville."

Apted recorded that the men "struck a dog trot," jogging by a quartz mill. About five miles from the ford, the men "turned off to the right on the Gordonsville Road [the Orange Turnpike] and after much marching around through the thick woods, finally bivouacked that afternoon in line of battle and made such preparations as the case needed to guard against a surprise." Other than a few farms carved out of this forest, the nearest landmark to them was a log structure called the Wilderness Tavern, at the intersection of the ford road and the Orange Turnpike. The turnpike ran roughly east and west, and the ford road to the southeast, where it intersected with a major route to Richmond called the Brock Road. The 16th Michigan's bivouac was just four miles or so west of where they had fought a year ago, noted Company I veteran Pvt. Dewitt Clinton Smith, a short fellow, about 20, from Tuscola County. The land here was uneven with hills and ravines, mostly covered with trees.

Pvt. Apted noted that the men had not even bedded down for the night—at a point west of the turnpike–ford road intersection—when rumors circulated. "Reports in bivouac that the Confeds have fell back to Gordonsville," Apted recorded. "I hope not, for I would rather fight them here than run them down to Richmond [and] then fight them there."[40] His comment was, perhaps, an example of the warning adage, "be careful what you wish for." In the morning would begin some of the bloodiest fighting the Army of the Potomac had yet experienced, in the woods and fields of the Wilderness.

16.

MAY–JUNE 1864

BATTLES WITHOUT GAINING GROUND

Despite Pvt. Alfred Apted's desire to fight Lee's army "here" rather than at Richmond, his commanding generals did not intend to begin the battle in the tangled woods, briars, and brush of the Wilderness. Their plan was to move the Army of the Potomac through this forest into the countryside before Robert E. Lee could react, to fight the Confederates in a battle where Grant would have the advantage of his superior numbers and guns. But that did not happen.

The rumor that the Grand Rapids soldier heard on the night of May 4—that the Rebels were falling back—was not true. Lee was quickly informed that Union forces were crossing the Rapidan, and he was not waiting for them to march out of the Wilderness. Confederate troops were actually moving toward the Army of the Potomac, not away from it, to strike as quickly as possible, where the forest thickets would diminish the Union's larger manpower and artillery. Lee correctly guessed that when the Army of Northern Virginia attacked, the advance of the Union army would halt in the forest. There, his army, bolstered by the return of Gen. James Longstreet and his men, would try to destroy those elements of Grant's army.[1]

THE WILDERNESS

Yet May 5 was a reasonably lucky day for the 16th Michigan, though not for thousands of other soldiers, for the simple reason that the regiment was not sent into battle. With Col. Welch back in Michigan, the regiment was now under the command of Major Robert Elliott of Detroit. Apted of the Brady Sharpshooters noted the regiment was initially ordered to go back to the fords that morning to guard the army's supply train. The order was changed, temporarily, when other troops reported that Rebels were advancing, coming east up the Orange Turnpike that morning. Instead of being sent out to confront the enemy, the regiment was put to work. "Returned," Apted said about being brought back to a spot along the turnpike, slightly more than a mile from the Germanna Ford Road, "and commenced to build breastworks. We almost finished them when we received orders to report to Culpeper Ford to guard [the] corps supply train."

As the regiment marched back to the river that afternoon, the battle of the Wilderness was igniting. Their comrades in the Third Brigade of their division became involved in the opening of the fight; Capt. Salter heard that the 1st Michigan Infantry was out in front when the Rebels hit them and drove them back. "They came into the division with the rebels on their heels, but we met them and drove them back about 1 ½ miles or so," Salter wrote, using the editorial "we" for the soldiers of his brigade and division, since the 16th Michigan was not present. "And then they became too many for us and drove us back a short distance." But the rest of the Fifth and Sixth Corps advanced into the fight, some of it taking place in forest underbrush, and "a battle was fought lasting all day long without either side being able to gain any ground."[2]

Though the 16th Michigan was at the ford a few miles northeast of this fighting on the Orange Turnpike, the men could hear the heavy firing that afternoon and evening. The regiment bivouacked with the supply trains, and was spared the horror those soldiers further south experienced as fires burned through the brush, killing wounded soldiers from both sides who were unable to get away. The men of the 16th Michigan were awakened in the early morning hours of May 6 and marched back to their brigade. Pvt. Apted noted that the quartz mill they had passed by previously was now filled with wounded Union troops.

The front with Lee's army soon stretched about four miles through the woods, northwest to southeast. The regiment moved past the line of breastworks they had built the previous day near the turnpike, and formed up behind two other lines of battle stretching across the road, supporting part of their brigade, seemingly at the edge of an opening in the woods called Saunders' Field. Apted wrote that the skirmishers up ahead "are busily engaged firing at each other." Across the clearing were Confederate breastworks—"a very difficult place to take," the sharpshooter continued. Heavy firing could be heard to their left, or south.

The 16th Michigan's officers and men heard from their comrades about the previous day's fighting. "Our brigade lost heavily yesterday," noted Capt. Edward Hill of Company K. On this day, however, Gen. Grant wanted his forces to again aggressively attack the Confederates, but the commanders in the Fifth Corps proceeded more cautiously. The historian of the 44th New York wrote later that their brigade received orders to prepare to attack the Confederate defenses that morning of the 6th, but they were soon countermanded. Instead, a strong skirmish line was sent out to suppress enemy fire. "The 6th [of May] our regiment had to go in on the front and fight, we went in like good fellers," wrote Josiah Gibbs of Company E. "My orderly sergeant was wounded and 4 others in [the] company." Corporal Joseph Putnam, a Wayne County man about 20 years old in Company F, was struck in the head and killed instantly.[3]

But this skirmishing and these casualties were minor compared to what was happening around them—terrible and sometimes blind fighting on either side, some of it involving elements from their corps and thousands of other troops as attacks and counterattacks raged in the woods. "Heavy fighting on our left," Apted wrote that morning when another corps struck Confederate positions to the south. "Don't know, but guess all goes well. At 8:00 with a yell, our men charged the rebs and now there is probably going on one of the heaviest musket fights of the war." But all did not go well for the Army of the Potomac. Though a large Union assault was launched on Confederates south of where the 16th Michigan was with its division, Gen. James Longstreet, who arrived that morning with his reunified corps of Rebel veterans, stopped it with a punishing counterattack.

Later that afternoon, another Confederate assault struck hard on the Union right, just north of where the 16th Michigan was posted with its brigade. Though the Union line was battered, it did not break. Longstreet, an important Confederate corps commander, was critically wounded that day when he was mistakenly fired on by Rebel troops. One of his trusted lieutenants, Brig. Gen. Micah Jenkins, who led the South Carolina troops who captured Stockton's blue regimental flag at Gaines' Mill, was killed. Incredibly, nearly 18,000 Union troops and 11,000 Confederate troops had been killed, wounded, or were missing in the fighting of May 5 and 6.[4]

By comparison, the 16th Michigan, in a position between these two scenes of terrible fighting, suffered a relative handful of casualties. They hadn't been present for the first day of the battle, and were in skirmishing on the second day; they had not been involved in the massive attacks and counterattacks. That evening, a detachment from the regiment, including Pvt. Dewitt C. Smith of Company I, was sent to carry logs and timbers out to make breastworks in their front—something Pvt. Apted felt should have been done that morning. The 16th Michigan was withdrawn to defenses closer to the intersection of the Orange Turnpike and Germanna Ford Road, though the Brady Sharpshooters company was sent out to the front line. "And we could hear the rebs at work defending their line by cutting timber and digging earthworks," he wrote that night. Scattered skirmish fire kept him and his comrades alert that night.[5]

The 16th Michigan remained in the section of the line near the turnpike on May 7, and Union artillery there opened fire that morning when Confederates charged their breastworks. "Old 'Grif' was there and he allowed them to come on until they were at close quarters," Apted wrote of his division commander, Charles Griffin, a veteran artillerist, "when he ordered several batteries with double-shotted canister [to fire], and they did not relish this little joke." In turn, Apted's brigade commander, Joseph Bartlett, sent his men forward; at noon, the Brady Sharpshooters were on the skirmish line with the 16th Michigan, led by Capt. George Swan, with the 20th Maine, the 118th Pennsylvania, and soldiers from other units. They pushed the Rebels out of "an advanced line of rifle pits," reported Capt. Guy Fuller. Pvt. Apted said as they charged, the enemy skirmishers quickly fell back—probably getting out of the way fast, so the Confederate batteries could fire on the advancing soldiers. This artillery prevented supporting Union troops from coming up, and the Third Brigade skirmishers retreated, first to the crest of a hill and eventually to their own line. The 16th Michigan lost seven men killed or mortally wounded in this last day in the Wilderness, with another 30 or more men suffering nonfatal wounds. Again, these were small numbers compared to the casualties of those regiments that had been in the thick of the terrible combat of May 5 and 6.

The Union army's attacks on the strong Confederate positions were failing at a terrible cost. That day, the 7th, Grant decided to shift his army ten miles south during the night, to get around the Rebel army and threaten Richmond. This, he hoped, would force Lee to move to intercept him. The soldiers continued to skirmish and probe each other's strength in the Wilderness as their armies prepared to march through the night.[6]

The fighting in these woods ended, said Capt. Charles Salter, "without being able to accomplish much (except to get immense numbers of men killed and wounded)." The regiment stayed on picket or watching from their works with the 20th Maine until about 2 or 3 a.m. on May 8. As they stood guard in the darkness, their Fifth Corps and most of the rest of the Army of the Potomac was moving down dark country roads to the southeast, toward a small town and road center called Spotsylvania Court House. But Lee, anticipating Grant's move, got his men there first and blocked the way.[7]

SPOTSYLVANIA COURT HOUSE

It was long before dawn when the 16th Michigan and the 20th Maine got on the road, marching south to rejoin their brigade, division and corps, which were miles ahead of them. By noon, it was brutally hot and several men in the column were sun struck, but the two regiments, along with the 118th Pennsylvania, reached the rest of the Fifth Corps about two miles northwest of Spotsylvania Court House. Here they learned that tired comrades in their brigade and division had been bloodied that morning when Lee's men managed to cut across the Union army's path on the Brock Road. This fight escalated as more soldiers arrived, North and South, but the Confederates held the all-important high ground and dug in. "[The] 44th NY and the 83rd Pennsylvania made a charge on a battery," Apted heard about that morning's fighting, "and got badly cut to pieces." Other Union troops also attacked up the wooded rise—they called it Laurel Hill—but were driven back. By the time the 16th Michigan arrived on the scene hours later, the two sides were digging in, establishing a line of trenches that would soon spread for miles around Spotsylvania Court House.[8]

The 16th Michigan, the 20th Maine, and the 118th Pennsylvania, ordinarily part of the Third Brigade of the Fifth Corps' First Division, were now temporarily assigned to the Third Division, under Brig. Gen. Samuel Crawford, "much to our discontent," later wrote Ellis Spear, who was major of the Maine regiment at that time. The men did not like Crawford, and "detachment" usually meant an "unpleasant" assignment, Spear said. Grant wanted yet another assault made on the Rebel position late that afternoon of the 8th, so elements of the Fifth and Sixth Corps were ordered to attack. But it was evening before they moved into position. Spear said that their detachment waited in an oak forest as heavy Confederate shelling blasted at them at dusk. It was too late to make an attack, the soldiers felt, but the decision was not up to them; at last they were ordered forward.

The 16th Michigan's Capt. Guy W. Fuller, from Ionia, reported that as darkness fell, his regiment advanced with the 118th Pennsylvania, supporting the left of Crawford's line of battle in the dense woods. Unfortunately, their advance took them through "an almost impassable swamp," Fuller reported, and most of his regiment became separated from the Pennsylvanians as night enveloped the woods. Then Crawford's troops, who had led the advance, were blasted by the Rebels; they retreated, adding to the confusion. Fuller gathered as much of the 16th Michigan as he could and formed his men at the edge of the swamp as Confederates from two regiments approached in the darkness, coming through a ravine on the regiment's left. "But the regiment opened upon them a destructive fire, throwing them into confusion, and many of our men advancing, a hand-to-hand conflict ensued," Fuller reported.[9]

Apted said the opening of this clash "commenced the heaviest rain of bullets that I ever experienced." Since the regiment divided while attempting to cross the swamp, and since Apted wrote nothing about the hand-to-hand fight, it may be his part of the regiment remained in a battle line that, while firing at close range, did not become involved in the personal combat that Fuller and Salter described. The soldiers of the 20th Maine and the 118th Pennsylvania also fought Confederates, clubbing their muskets and stabbing with bayonets; Major Spear said it was almost impossible to tell one side from the other in the darkness, but that the Confederates wore short jackets. "Suddenly *we found ourselves mixed up with the rebel lines* and a terrible scene of carnage and horror ensued," wrote Capt. Salter. "We captured a number of the enemy, and held our ground." Capt. Hill called this "an awful struggle." A Rebel colonel was captured in the fight, who Apted said was from the 10th Georgia Infantry Regiment. "It was pandemonium for a while," wrote Ellis Spear, "but it suddenly ceased." The Rebels retreated, and the Michigan, Maine, and Pennsylvania regiments were alone in the dark woods.[10]

The division under Gen. Crawford that made the initial attack that evening had disappeared back to the main Union line, leaving the detachment from the Third Brigade on its own. Was it safe for their detachment to withdraw? Had they been surrounded in the darkness? They had heard nothing from Crawford or his staff, Spear said; it was as if they had been forgotten. Officers of the 16th Michigan, the 20th Maine, and the 118th Pennsylvania conferred; Rufus W. Jacklin, the diminutive adjutant of the 16th Michigan, volunteered to go back to through the woods to Union lines and get orders, but hours passed and he failed to return—he had been captured by the Rebels, though none of his comrades knew what happened. Spear and other soldiers managed to find their main line, and brought the regiments back from the front at 3 a.m. on May 9. "In our regt., one of my best and closest friends is missed," wrote Capt. Salter, "—that is R. W. Jacklin, our Adjt., who is either killed or a prisoner, we do not know which." Capt. Fuller wrote that the regiment's losses in that nighttime clash were "small"—Apted said several men were killed and wounded—and both he and Capt. Hill also noted that Jacklin was missing.[11]

The 16th Michigan and the other detached regiments rejoined their First Division's Third Brigade at noon and remained in line—relative quiet for most of the exhausted soldiers, though skirmish fire and cannonading sounded to their left and right as thousands more Union soldiers arrived. Apted said they got orders to fall in without their knapsacks at 4 p.m., and the soldiers expected they were once again going into battle or skirmish, but instead they marched "about four miles to the rear" and "commenced the grand drive of stragglers to the front." Though they did not net as many wayward soldiers as the sharpshooter would have liked, they returned to the front that night, their sleep interrupted by occasional skirmish fire that required them to fall in at the ready. They would soon learn their adjutant, Rufus Jacklin of Detroit, was with hundreds of other captured Union soldiers rescued that evening by the cavalry miles to the south as the Confederates herded them to a railroad line that would have taken them to prison camps, where many would have died of illness and starvation. In the days ahead, Jacklin rejoined his regiment.[12]

The next day, May 10, Grant wanted attacks all along the Confederate line as the remainder of his force arrived. The brigades in the First Division of the Fifth Corps, part of the Union right, continued to engage the Rebels before them, but not in a full-fledged assault. The 16th Michigan was sent with the 18th Massachusetts and the 1st Michigan to the trenches at noon to relieve their comrades in the Second Brigade of their division, who had taken an advanced line of Rebel rifle pits in the open ground before them. "The rebs fired at us pretty brisk going up to the rifle pits," Apted reported, "but as soon as [we got] there, we were tolerably well protected." Again, it was "heavy skirmishing" for these men. Lt. Col. William Throop of the 1st Michigan called the rifle fire "terribly severe." The major of the 20th Maine wrote that his regiment and the 16th Michigan later moved out in a skirmish line to a shallow ravine at the edge of this field, with Union guns behind them firing over their heads into the pine woods that hid the Rebels. But they never were ordered to charge. Gen. Warren reported that part of his Fifth Corps did make unsuccessful attacks with other elements of the army in the major assault of that day, but not his First Division's Third Brigade, which included the 16th Michigan.

For thousands of other Union troops, there was no protection that day—they were ordered to attack the strong Confederate works that formed a bulging line, or salient, to the left, east of the Fifth Corps' position. Charging out of the woods into fields in front of the Rebels, a few thousand men from the Sixth Corps smashed through the Confederate line, but were ultimately driven back with an estimated 4,000 killed, wounded and missing. One of the officers fatally wounded that day was the former commander of the Third Brigade of which the 16th Michigan was part, Brig. Gen. James Rice. Rice had been promoted after Gettysburg and moved from his old regiment, the 44th New York, to command another brigade in their corps.[13]

The 16th Michigan was relieved "under a heavy fire of musketry" at about 9 p.m., and spent the night in their works. For them, May 11 was more of the same—they were sent out to the advanced line of rifle pits to relieve other brigade skirmishers, and were involved in steady and even heavy exchanges of fire. Soon after they got to this position, Nathan Barton from Company I, who was about 24 years old and from Argentine Township in Genesee County, was killed; veteran Sgt. James Cowan of the Brady Sharpshooters, about 30 and from Bostwick Lake, fell mortally wounded as he took aim at a Rebel. He died three hours later, and was buried that evening at the spot where he fell. Several other men were wounded. Whether he was referring to himself or his men on this day of fighting, Capt. Edward Hill wrote in his diary: "suffered a thousand narrow escapes." Grant, however, ordered no major attacks this day. Rain showers set in that night, turning trenches and rifle pits into miserable, mud-filled holes.[14]

This was considered comparatively quiet for the army, but there were more terrible events in store. Grant wanted an even more massive attack on the bulging Confederate salient north of Spotsylvania Court House that had become known as "the Mule shoe"; early on the morning of May 12, the entire Second Corps, commanded by Gen. Winfield S. Hancock, smashed into the northern curve of the "shoe" while another corps hit its east side. Warren's Fifth Corps shifted to cover the Second Corps' previous position on the Union right, and two of its divisions were ordered to support the assault. Apted said the men were awakened at 2 a.m. and marched; Capt. Fuller reported they moved further to the Union right, stretching their line west. This would be the bloodiest day of the fighting near Spotsylvania Court House for the Army of the Potomac, with nearly 20,000 men charging the Confederate defenses of the "Mule Shoe" at 4:30 that rainy morning. Word quickly spread long the rest of the Union line that the Second Corps had broken through. Thousands of men on both sides were killed and wounded, the combatants shooting each other at close range and clubbing each other with their rifle butts in the driving rain.

"At 9:00 [a.m.] news came from him [Hancock] that we had turned the rebel right," Apted noted, with the capture of Confederate generals, thousands of soldiers and fifteen artillery pieces. "Everything was going on well!" Yet this massive Union thrust failed as Confederates rushed reinforcements to stop it, forming a new defensive line. The 16th Michigan, now near the Po River–Laurel Hill area west of Spotsylvania Court House, waited with its brigade while another division from their Fifth Corps was sent in to attack the Rebel positions before them; they were driven back. According to the sharpshooter from Grand Rapids, their First Division was then sent in a brigade at a time, but the result was the same. "The first and second [brigades] charged to the Rebel breastworks," Apted wrote in his diary, "but were driven back with severe loss." He knew his Third Brigade would be next to go in.[15]

As they waited, Capt. Hill also heard about the initial success of the massive Union charge to the left, but he noted: "Still the battle terrifically rages. When will the end come[?]" The battle continued through the morning. Though the 16th Michigan's sector was not the worst scene of the fighting, Confederates here were obligated to tie up the Yankees before them, so that they could not help Hancock's men; the Rebel rifle and cannon fire was fierce around noon that day when the regiment and their Third Brigade went into their advanced line of breastworks. Soon these Union soldiers received word to prepare to charge across the ground in view of Rebel gunners and infantry. It must have been a grim and anxious time, waiting for the order; their comrades had tried and failed, and now it was their turn. "But the order, I am glad to hear, has been countermanded, and for 'tis just about like taking men to a slaughter pen," Apted wrote that day. The relief of the Michigan soldiers must have been palpable. While thousands of men perished in the fighting that day, mostly at the "Mule Shoe" further down the line, the 16th Michigan and its comrades in their brigade had again been fortunate. More than 17,000 men, Union and Confederate, were killed, wounded, or captured or missing that day.

Incredibly, the 16th Michigan's Third Brigade suffered a handful of casualties after they were shifted out of their breastworks and marched more to the left late that afternoon and early that evening, when nearly spent bullets fired by soldiers they probably could not see fell into their ranks. Historians said that by this point in the campaign, Generals Meade and Grant were increasingly unhappy with the Fifth Corps commander, Gen. Gouverneur Warren, for his caution and reluctance to send his men on aggressive attacks when he was ordered to do so. Warren was personally brave, but hated to send his men on what he thought were useless and costly charges.[16]

The average soldier probably knew nothing of this. Capt. Salter, the Detroiter and commander of Company E, usually wrote detailed letters to his friends about his regiment's travels and fights, but not this time—there had been too many shifting positions, marches, skirmishes, and clashes to explain. Though he gave them a general idea of the army's movement, he was only specific about the terrible night fighting his regiment was in on May 8–9; the overall scale of the campaign's casualties was stunning, he wrote. "It is estimated by an officer high in command we have left enough dead on the route to make a continuous road of dead back to where we started from," he wrote. "This may sound perhaps wicked, at least shocking, but *it is true* nevertheless, and the men composing our army have all suffered terribly. It has been a harder campaign than any we ever had before or imagined, and the terrible used-up expression on every man's face seems to say, 'My God! How long must we suffer?'"[17]

> Many great events have occurred, many great battles have been fought all inside one great battle, and a writer fond of noting the movements, scenes and all the various details of it might fill up a large notebook about it. But I am sick and weary of all this carnage and bloodshed, and [I] only thank God that he has in mercy spared my life, whilst I have lost many dear and valued friends.

Salter estimated that about 90 men from the 16th Michigan had been killed, wounded, or captured in the fighting since the spring campaign began. "This is very light compared to the loss in most of the regiments of our army," he stressed. Ultimately it would be determined that his regiment had lost fourteen men killed and mortally wounded outside of Spotsylvania Court House, for a total of twenty-one fatalities since Grant's offensive was launched. Other reports and records indicate that more than fifty other soldiers in the 16th Michigan had been wounded, with several men missing.[18]

The regiment's men were awakened in their bivouac with their brigade and shifted early on the morning of May 13, "back to the old place where we had been for the past few days," Apted noted about their previous position, seemingly in front of the ridge they called Laurel Hill. The men worked on their defenses, but at some point struck their camp and at 10 p.m. started on a long, difficult, and exhausting march with their corps around from the right of the line, west of Spotsylvania Court House, to the opposite side, east of town. They forded the Ni River and struggled through woods and farm fields on roads and paths turned into thick muck by the continuing rain and trudging comrades. "The roads were horribly muddy and 'twas as much as a man could do to stagger through it," the sharpshooter recorded the next morning.

Grant wanted another massive attack on the Confederate line from points east of Spotsylvania Court House early that morning of May 14, but it had not been possible for the generals to move the Fifth and Sixth Corps through the darkness and mud to get in position in time. The men of the 16th Michigan, like all soldiers, were tired, soaking wet, and uncomfortable, and generally short of rations, but they had been spared from making another attack in which thousands of men would have been killed and maimed. Now positioned near the road to Fredericksburg on a farm owned by a family named Beverly, they remained under periodic artillery fire—a constant reminder about the fate that awaited men sent to charge the still-strong Confederate positions.[19]

Once the regiment reached this new place in line east of Spotsylvania Court House, Pvt. Apted got terrible news when he was allowed to visit another state command, the 1st Michigan Sharpshooters Regiment; his younger brother Henry had been fatally wounded on May 6. "I found his regiment, and there learned from Sgt. Danson of Company H that poor Henry was killed at the battle of the Wilderness," Apted wrote.

> They said he was shot through the side but he lived some 20 minutes after being shot, and his money and papers were given to Lt. Fowler, who was wounded since the 6th, and has gone to the hospital, so I did not see him. Alas, poor boy. He would not take my advice and keep out of the army. This makes two of us killed and I suppose I shall be the next victim.[20]

There were clashes up and down the line, and some artillery and skirmish fire in the 16th Michigan's new position. That night, two Detroiters who had known each other from their civilian days—Major Elliott, commanding the regiment, and George Hopper, the major of the 1st Michigan Infantry—happened to meet in the darkness outside of Spotsylvania Court House as their men stood picket in newly dug breastworks. Hopper had walked to the end of his regiment's line and asked, "Who is guarding our right?" "I am," Elliott replied. "Is that you, Hopper?" The two officers walked the new line together and Elliott mentioned that the Confederate pickets, who were on a more elevated ridge, could be seen against the skyline. "My men could easily pick them off," Elliott continued, "but I would not let them do it." What else the officers may have talked about, Hopper did not say, but it was his last conversation with the 16th Michigan's major.

The next day, a Sunday, there was comparative quiet as the soldiers bivouacked and continued picketing. The 16th Michigan's luck held, and they were not ordered to attack or even to test the strong Confederate defenses that lay in their new front; the rain finally stopped, and rations were issued. "Oh what a different Sunday to what one would spend in a civilized country with the blessing of peace," Apted wrote. He was sent back to the regiment's place in line to get rations for the men on picket out in the breastworks, "and saw Grant taking a survey of the Confederacy. I should not be much surprised if we make an advance on them tomorrow."

Col. Joshua Chamberlain of the 20th Maine, who had just returned to duty after extended illness, was now in command of the Third Brigade, since Joseph Bartlett was sick and incapacitated. There was talk of new orders to attack Rebel lines, but the 16th Michigan remained behind their breastworks or were otherwise in picket posts near the Fredericksburg Road. Life in the trenches continued wet and muddy and the roads were impassable for moving artillery, the rain having caused delays in Grant's plans for relentless attacks.[21]

The quiet continued along the lines, which now ran about four miles, roughly northwest to southeast, as the Union army shifted east. Pvt. Apted wrote letters, telling his family back home of the death of his younger brother. But that night of May 17, the regiment moved out with the 118th Pennsylvania and the 11th Massachusetts, beyond their own pickets to within a fraction of a mile from the Confederate line, Salter said. Edward Hill wrote that the soldiers "noiselessly" dug and worked, creating a new line of trenches; this extended their position and allowed thousands of other troops to again attack the Rebel defenses in the morning, to strike them at points to the right of the 16th Michigan's division and corps. Batteries were brought up to the point where the soldiers in the Third Brigade dug these new works, and all of this was accomplished without the Confederates realizing what was happening. "When daylight revealed to the astonished gaze of the rebels, what the Yankees had done during the night, they opened upon us a heavy fire from 24 pieces of artillery, thinking to shell us out of our position," Salter wrote. The Union batteries responded, firing over the heads of the soldiers on their new front line.

Yet this was almost inconsequential compared to the action to their right, the location of what had been called "the Mule Shoe." Fighting raged that morning as Grant's latest attack moved forward with roughly half of the army. But just as the other Union frontal assaults failed, so did the attack of May 18, which in places was a veritable slaughter when the attackers charged the still-strong Confederate positions. More than 1,500 Union soldiers were casualties. As historian Gordon Rhea wrote, Grant should have known that the Confederates had spent days strengthening their defenses "before sending thousands of men to be killed or wounded." Again, the men of the 16th Michigan had been fortunate not to be a part of the disastrous attack, but this was largely because Grant had come to distrust their cautious corps commander, Gen. Warren.[22]

The artillery fire tailed off about noon, though picket firing continued in the regiment's part of the line with their brigade and division. But by the next day, soldiers North and South ventured out to meet each other halfway between the lines to trade newspapers, wrote Oakland County's Josiah Gibbs of Company E, though their division commander, Gen. Charles Griffin, was outraged by this fraternization. So the soldiers went back to their lines, where "both parties were ready to shoot each other the next minute," noted Gibbs's captain, Charles Salter. But the quiet continued, and Salter said that the band of the 18th Massachusetts played as he wrote to his friends in Detroit on May 19.

The soldiers received their first mail in about two weeks, and read news reports of

Confederate victories over the forces of Gen. Benjamin Butler, who had tried to advance up the James River, and Gen. Franz Sigel, who had tried to drive south in the Shenandoah Valley, the important food-producing region for the Confederates. A story in a Southern newspaper, which Salter dismissed as blatantly false, claimed Union soldiers were provided alcohol before they attacked. "They also claim that Gen. Grant gives his troops whiskey to make them drunk before going into battle, and that is not true in any sense," the captain objected, "for we have only had whiskey issued twice to the men whilst on this move, and then when they were exposed to bad weather." Lt. George Kilets of Company E also wrote to a Detroit newspaper, saying the 16th Michigan had lost slightly in comparison to others; the loss of Adjt. Rufus Jacklin "has spread gloom over the whole regiment. He was brave and good, and won hosts of friends by the untiring manner in which he discharged his duty."

With Grant's attacks on the Rebels' strong positions having failed, he continued to shift his line east and southeast of Spotsylvania Court House, preparing to carefully withdraw and march south into countryside in another attempt to outmaneuver Lee. The temporary calm, which Capt. Salter called "the sunny side of war," ended later that hot day when Confederate soldiers under Gen. Richard Ewell left their trenches and made an attack about a mile to the right of the 16th Michigan. The surprise Rebel assault struck what was now the far right of the Union line as Grant prepared to leave the area. Much of this battle took place on or near the farm of a family named Harris; the 16th Michigan had no role in the fight, but parts of the Fifth Corps, including many rookie soldiers, helped to slow and stop the Rebel assault. "We were prepared for them, but they did not come," said Pvt. Apted of the enemy. This was the last battle at Spotsylvania Court House.[23]

The next morning Apted saw the signs, and realized that Grant's next step was underway: "I think that our whole army is swinging around to the left and [I] should not be surprised if we leave soon." He was correct, and that evening, parts of both armies began moving out. Historian Jeffry Wert noted that from May 5 to this point, Grant's campaign against Lee had resulted in 60,000 men on both sides killed, wounded, or missing, and 36,000 of those were Union soldiers. Sharpshooter Apted was sure when the two sides fought each other again, as was inevitable, "it will be with fearful fury."

The soldiers heard skirmish fire in the distance the next morning, May 21, but at 1 p.m. the 16th Michigan moved out with the Fifth Corps, following the route of another corps. "Marching east to the [Richmond & Fredericksburg] railroad at Guinea Station, we then moved south[east] to Bowling Green, where we stayed that night," Capt. Salter wrote of the march. Pvt. Apted said the men crossed the Mattaponi River on a rickety bridge, "which trembled and shook at every step. But it carried us safely over." Capt. Fuller thought it was a march of twelve miles when they stopped to bivouac in the countryside that night. For the officers who were friends of the regimental adjutant, and for the soldiers who respected him, it was also a day of some good news—they learned Rufus Jacklin, captured back on the night of May 8–9, had been freed by raiding Union cavalry under command of Generals Phil Sheridan and George Custer. That night, pickets from the 16th Michigan captured three Rebel cavalry troopers, who Apted said were surprised—"they state that they were not expecting any Yanks so near them."[24]

Before dawn, the soldiers were awakened and soon moved out, with the 16th Michigan and the Third Brigade leading the Fifth Corps, first marching west on a country road and then south on a highway called the Telegraph Road. Union soldiers had been foraging in the countryside as the army went by prosperous farms, so much so that Apted was ordered to stay behind when the regiment moved out, to gather up and push forward men who had gone missing to take food from nearby farms during the night. In the meantime, their comrades marched south that afternoon until they ran into a contingent of Confederate cavalry in a belt of woods at a run that Capt. Fuller and other brigade officers thought was called Pole Cat Creek. Just beyond the woods was a Rebel battery on a nearby hill. These Confederates tried to delay the Union column as Robert E. Lee also moved his army south. Gunfire quickly erupted.

"Four companies of this regiment were at once deployed as skirmishers," reported Fuller of his regiment's role in this fracas, "and advancing, drove the enemy from their position, capturing a number of prisoners." Some thought the Rebel troopers initially advanced aggressively toward the Michigan skirmishers, but it could not have been far, as other regiments from the Third Brigade quickly formed in a line of battle and advanced down the road to the fight. Fuller said his skirmishers pushed the enemy troopers out of the woods; one of his men, Corporal William Nahorn of Dearborn, about 20 years old and one of the Brady Sharpshooters, was killed. But men from other regiments of their brigade ripped down a fence and threw it over the creek to make an impromptu bridge, and artillery was brought up to bear on the Rebel battery; the Union soldiers flanked these gunners and forced them to retreat. The historian of the 44th New York said their division commander, Gen. Charles Griffin, personally supervised the Union batteries, shouting, "Give them hell!"

"We had considerable firing with them, but drove them back and marched 10 miles that day," Capt. Salter said of the skirmish. The historian of the 83rd Pennsylvania described this clash as taking place in two phases, a mile apart, but the result was the same—the Rebels retreated. The Union soldiers took a number of prisoners, but several Third Brigade soldiers were killed and wounded. That night was quiet and the men from the 16th Michigan were on duty as picket supports near a homestead, three or four miles from the scene of the skirmish.[25]

NORTH ANNA RIVER OR JERICHO MILLS

The dusty march of the Fifth Corps continued the next morning, May 23, and about noon reached the North Anna River, which was about four feet deep and 150 feet across. Both the Union and Confederate armies had been strung out over the roads on routes south over the past two days, and there had been minor clashes between scouting parties and rearguard forces. Now both armies had reached the vicinity of the river—a natural obstacle for Grant's men. The Union commander realized that Lee's army had won on the race to get here, a point within twenty-five miles of Richmond, but Grant nonetheless wanted his army to find and attack the Confederates on the south side of the river. The Army of Northern Virginia was indeed there, though not dug in, since the Confederate commander was not yet sure of how and where Grant intended to cross and proceed; Lee was then allowing many of his men to rest.[26]

Though Union generals were plagued by inaccurate maps, the Fifth Corps, the right wing of the Grant's army, reached the river at a place called Jericho Mills, alerting Rebel lookouts as they did so. Other Union corps reached the river at points about three miles further east. It was already another brutally hot day when the 16th Michigan's comrades in their division's Second Brigade waded across and made their way up the high river bank and bluff into the woods south of the river; beyond these woods were a railroad, fields, and more woods. Soldiers rested, but some were ordered to set up defensive positions as more of their comrades joined them. Next came the 16th Michigan's Third Brigade, wading over at about 3 p.m. and making the climb up the Ford Road into the hills. Again, these soldiers got a chance to rest and dry out, while behind them, engineers laid pontoons for bridging the river, allowing other Fifth Corps troops to stay dry crossing. By the mid to late afternoon, a regiment from the 16th Michigan's division, sent out as skirmishers and moving southeast, saw Confederate pickets ahead in the woods. Rifle fire soon broke the quiet. Reinforcements for both sides hurried to the fight, which grew in intensity.

Warren, the Fifth Corps commander, passed word back that the Rebels were not there in force at the North Anna, but he was wrong. The Confederate Third Corps under Gen. A. P. Hill had been resting in camps set up in the area about a mile south of the river. One of its divisions, under Gen. Cadmus Wilcox, hurried to attack what their commanders had been wrongly told was a small Union force. Soon Rebel guns were blasting at the troops—nearly two full divisions of the Fifth Corps, which formed in a mile-long line, facing south. The corps' batteries answered, but as evening came on, Wilcox's men charged through the woods, surprising, flanking, and driving back Warren's soldiers, who actually outnumbered the attacking Confederates. Capt. Hill of the 16th Michigan, who was guarding a crossroads with Company K on the north side of the river, heard that his corps was "furiously attacked." It was true; the famous Iron Brigade, which contained the 24th Michigan and had been assigned to the Fifth Corps, broke, allowing the Rebels to flank Griffin's division's First and Second Brigades. The 4th Michigan Infantry was among the regiments that broke and retreated.[27]

Like other Fifth Corps regiments resting that afternoon, the 16th Michigan and the others in the Third Brigade were ordered to prepare for battle when the shooting began, but then were held back as a reserve. They were under the command of Gen. Joseph Bartlett, who had returned after recovering from illness. Capt. Guy Fuller reported that the 16th Michigan had just been ordered into a second line of battle when Confederates "opened a heavy fire of artillery and charged the right of the line, causing a portion of it to retire." This was the western end of the first Union battle line, its men running and giving advancing Confederates the chance to drive the Fifth Corps back to the river. The 16th Michigan, along with the 83rd Pennsylvania and the 1st Michigan, were sent to stop them.

"This regiment, with the Eighty-third Pennsylvania, was ordered to regain possession of the ground, and moving by a flank to the spot, formed a line of battle under a heavy fire of musketry," Fuller reported. So did the 1st Michigan; Amos Judson of the 83rd Pennsylvania wrote that their brigade went forward "on the run" through the woods, and that his regiment and the 16th Michigan stopped the Rebels in a fierce rifle battle. Capt. Salter said the regiment held its ground while other parts of their corps came up, and so did artillery batteries. "The balls flying in all directions, [we] have succeeded in repulsing the rebel charge," Pvt. Apted agreed. Salter bragged that his corps "drove the enemy 2 miles."

Records show that three of the 16th Michigan's men were killed that evening. Apted thought that the enemy had attempted to spring a trap, to cut off the Fifth Corps and push its men back into the river, but it had not succeeded. He realized later that he had come close to death or serious injury when he discovered that two bullets had passed through his haversack and a small tin pail/coffee pot inside it, also ruining his stationery. By Salter's count, their corps had killed 260 Rebels and captured hundreds more in the battle. "We should have done much better than this," he admitted, "but night came upon us and we had to hold up till the next morning." The attacking Confederate division suffered some 730 casualties that day.[28]

The other Union corps down river from Jericho Mills had also clashed with Lee's army on May 23 and 24, but made no headway. On the night of the 23rd, the Confederates dug in, building strong defensive positions in what was called an "inverted V" formation, with the point of the V resting at the North Anna more than two miles from Jericho Mills. Though Grant thought Lee and his army were retreating from the river, Union generals found that the Army of Northern Virginia was there in force, in a battle line that the Army of the Potomac could not break without huge casualties and great risk to itself. The eastern-most arm of the Confederates' inverted V also protected the next road-and-railroad center that Grant had hoped to reach, a town called Hanover Junction. Simply put, the North Anna was another stalemate—just like the Wilderness and Spotsylvania Court House.[29]

The Fifth Corps, linked with half of the Army of the Potomac on the Union right at the North Anna, moved forward on May 24, and found that the Confederates were in strong defenses. Like other Union troops, the 16th Michigan was shifted from place to place in the area that day and the next, destroying ten miles of the Virginia Central Railroad, burning ties and bending rails, but also having to skirmish with the Confederates who hoped to stop them. The weather was very hot and at times rainy as they moved with their brigade to a point near the Little River, facing the entrenched Confederate corps of A. P. Hill. But there was also good news for the 16th Michigan: Adjt. Rufus Jacklin, the Detroiter who had been recognized as a brave and respected officer, returned to the regiment with five men after having been captured by the Rebels after the night fighting of May 8 near Spotsylvania Court House.

Jacklin was one of hundreds of Union soldiers rescued by Michigan cavalry troopers under Brig. Gen. George Custer. Jacklin told his friends about what he had heard and seen while a prisoner for a day—that "matters are rather dubious in the Confederacy," Apted wrote. For years to come, Jacklin would tell how he had been captured by the 8th Alabama Infantry, and that he and fellow prisoners were marched to Lee's headquarters, and from there taken to a stop on the railroad going south called Beaver Dam. There, he and hundreds of others were freed in what he said was the exciting raid by the Michigan troopers.[30]

There was more skirmishing in the trenches in the morning of May 26 after their Third Brigade took positions in the front line—Tuscola County's Pvt. Dewitt C. Smith, from the small town of Watrousville, called it "brisk fireing" (sic), though Pvt. Apted said they "got some good shots at the johnnies." But Pvt. George W. Raynor, about 20, who was serving in Company G and came from the town of Osseo, was shot in the head and died soon after; he was one of the reenlisting veterans, having first volunteered at the age of 17 in the summer of 1861 in Stockton's Independent Regiment. A Brady Sharpshooter from Kent County, Lorenzo Thompson, in his early 40s, was wounded. Heavy rain fell and in the afternoon the soldiers were put to work destroying more of the railroad. There was continued skirmish firing as Confederates harassed them and the rain turned their rifle pits into muddy holes.

Grant decided it was again time to move his army to try to bypass Lee's strong defenses, by having his men carefully re-cross the North Anna and march east around the Army of Northern Virginia. When darkness fell on the night of the 26th, the men of the 16th Michigan were brought in from the skirmish line and made their suppers; then they moved out in the rain, crossing to the north side of the river and marching a few miles on the road from Jericho Mills in thick mud, stopping to draw rations from the supply wagons, and then pressing on along country roads to the southeast. Eventually, the exhausted men were allowed to rest, though some dropped out to make their own temporary bivouac. Either way, the respite was short and the march resumed long before the sun came up on May 27. Capt. Guy Fuller called this "the forced march," and Capt. Hill said it was "a terrible march indeed" after having had "excessive duty for days previously." Yet Pvt. Apted noted it was "a dandy, hill country with some few fine plantations." They covered some twenty-five miles before halting that evening with another corps to bivouac in the woods near a creek, a mile from a meeting hall called Mangohick Church. Hill indicated that their division was exhausted and there was much straggling.[31]

In the morning, the regiment took up the march with its corps and crossed the Pamunkey River around 9 a.m. on pontoon bridges that had just been built by Union engineers, not far from Hanover or Hanover Town, at a point called Dabney Ferry. The weather was hot and dry, and though the roads were in good condition, it was a dusty march. "We are now where McClellan was two years ago, and if we had been promptly reinforced there, there would have been no cause for our being here now," Pvt. Apted groused, invoking the former Union commander's argument about the failure of his 1862 offensive. But it was true that Gaines' Mill, where the 16th Michigan had fought its costliest battle, was only several miles away to the southwest. The regiment moved with its corps a short distance south of the river, while a few miles away, Union cavalry fought their Rebel counterparts. Pvt. Dewitt Clinton Smith said the men started to build breastworks when they halted; men noted that they were within fifteen miles of Richmond. After digging in on high ground on a local farm—they would almost always do this now—the soldiers bivouacked. Their Fifth Corps' left rested on another stream through this countryside called Totopotomoy Creek. The soldiers would soon find that Lee's army was again nearby, ready to block their way.[32]

TOTOPOTOMOY CREEK—BETHESDA CHURCH

A new round of skirmishes and battles now began as Grant's campaign continued in the area northeast of the Confederate capital. Apted said reveille sounded at 4 a.m. on May 29. The men had breakfast, and his friend Davis Richards, who had been left behind to guard a household from the passing Union soldiers, caught up with his regiment. "He says that the whole army is now here, and I do wish that the rebs would come and attack us instead of our having to go to them," the sharpshooter wrote. It was clear that their corps and the entire army had "made a grand flank move. . . . I think we shall flank again today." The regiment moved out with its brigade toward the Totopotomoy, which ran roughly west to east and eventually joined the Pamunkey River.

Their First Division under Gen. Charles Griffin, on one of the Union army's reconnaissance missions to locate the Confederates, waded into the swamp and crossed to the south side of the Totopotomoy, emerging onto a farm. Apted said the advancing soldiers "found a nest" of Confederate pickets at 3 p.m. The skirmishing quickly began in this area of woods, swamps and farm fields, and one of their division's other brigades pushed the Rebels south about a mile to an east–west lane through the country called Shady Grove Road. In the meantime, the 16th Michigan's Third Brigade and the Second Brigade quickly dug defensive positions across farm property south of the creek. Pvt. Smith noted his Company I was detailed as "flankers," presumably to help cover the skirmish line advance of their First Brigade comrades.

But these men from the 16th Michigan were relieved and returned to their regiment. As afternoon turned to evening, more Confederate troops, a brigade from Gen. Jubal Early's Second Corps, arrived and pressed the Union skirmishers—Capt. Edward Hill said they could hear this fighting in the near distance. The First Brigade dropped back to the farm, where Gen. Griffin formed his division in a defensive line. The skirmishing continued till darkness, Apted wrote, though he was sure both sides had suffered small numbers of casualties. He and his comrades rested behind works of earth and fence rails that night. This fight, and other battles and skirmishes in the area that day and in the days that followed, would be named for the creek or for a local landmark and meeting house, the Bethesda Church, about two miles away from where the 16th Michigan rested.[33]

Neither side had known exactly where their enemy was before the events of May 29, but a more complete picture had emerged as the two armies found each other and clashed, in forming lines that stretched from the northwest to southeast. Grant thought Lee's Army of Northern Virginia was by now seriously weakened, and he wanted his army, reunited and with reinforcements coming, to attack in the morning. On the other side, Lee, who had been ill for days, wanted his generals on May 30 to strike the Fifth Corps—now the Union army's left—in an assault by three Confederate divisions that would first hit its southern flank and then head on, attacking from west to east. He hoped these attacks would collapse Gen. Warren's position, still somewhat isolated from the rest of the Union army.

The next morning was warm and clear when the 16th Michigan moved out with its division to the Shady Grove Road, the Second Brigade driving west and pushing Rebel skirmishers. Sharpshooter Alfred Apted correctly noted in his diary that morning he expected "a heavy battle" and now it took shape. The rest of the Fifth Corps crossed the Totopotomoy, one of its divisions marching to another east–west lane called the Old Church Road, about a mile to the left, or southeast from where Griffin's division, including the 16th Michigan, was advancing. This was a two-pronged assault along these roughly parallel roads by the Fifth Corps; Griffin's men heard skirmish fire coming from this area, but the sound of battle intensified that afternoon when the first of the Confederate divisions struck the southern wing of the Fifth Corps. The Rebels drove these Union soldiers back from Bethesda Church, about a mile east of Griffin's division. But other Fifth Corps reinforcements and artillery hurried to form a defensive line, halting this part of the Confederate assault late in the afternoon.[34]

The 16th Michigan's wing of their corps' advance, meanwhile, skirmished further west along the Shady Grove Road; its First Division reached open ground and found Rebels in trenches in their front and to their left. The regiment's comrades in the Second Brigade led this advance, but they were hit with an effective crossfire. Gen. Griffin extended the brigade's line to counter this with more of his forces; Capt. Guy Fuller reported that at about 1 p.m., the 16th Michigan was ordered into the fight, along with the 83rd Pennsylvania.

They formed their line "under a heavy fire and threw out skirmishers," Fuller continued. "Exposed on an open field to a raking fire, the men stood their ground with great pertinacity, and protected themselves by heaping up earth with their hands, bayonets and [tin] plates." Major Robert T. Elliott of Detroit was commanding the 16th Michigan that day. Pvt. Apted said the Brady Sharpshooters were the regiment's skirmishers, though Capt. Edward Hill recorded that the entire regiment was eventually on the skirmish line. One of Apted's officers, Lt. William H. Byrns or Burns, from Dearborn and about 24 years old, was wounded in the left arm.[35]

Amos Judson of the 83rd Pennsylvania wrote that his regiment and the 16th Michigan were "lying in a dangerous position, exposed to a cross fire of the enemy's sharpshooters," when the Michigan regiment's major was mortally wounded. Capt. Fuller reported that "Elliott was struck down while engaged in disposing his men for greater safety." A soldier who claimed he witnessed Elliott's fatal wounding was Thomas R. Lackie, a soldier in Company E and Detroiter who had enlisted in the summer of 1861. "We were lying down in an open field making ourselves as safe as bayonets, tin plates, earth and sand would permit," Lackie wrote years later. "Rebel sharpshooters were strung along a piece of woods on the opposite side of the opening. Major Elliott did not take to cover, but walked about as coolly as if in camp."[36]

Lackie, who had known Elliott before the war, claimed that the major walked over to him, sword tucked under his arm, and asked for a match to light his pipe. "I had none, but entreated him to lie down or he would get hit," Lackie wrote. "He replied, 'They will not get the range.'" A moment later a bullet ripped through Elliott's body. The major exclaimed, "My God," dropped his pipe and sword, and slumped to one knee. Lackie said Elliott bowed his head, raised his hands as if to pray and dropped to the ground, quivering. But the Union skirmishers, including the Brady Sharpshooters, struck back; the 16th Michigan, now commanded by Capt. George Swan, and others from the Third Brigade, pushed the Confederates to their main line, though Pvt. Apted said Rebel artillery "commenced to shell us." Meanwhile, stretcher bearers carried Elliott off the battlefield, but his wound was fatal. The major died about 6 p.m.

By now, the generals of the Fifth Corps had reformed their divisions along the Shady Grove Road behind Griffin's division, men and batteries facing south to confront the flank attack of the Confederates. Another Rebel division, under Gen. Stephen Ramseur, then attacked from Bethesda Church; Griffin's men held the right, or western-most, portion of the Union line, and Pvt. Dewitt Smith noted the 16th Michigan dug in on a hill by an old mill. When the next part of the Confederate assault struck, aiming at the Fifth Corps' line to the left of the 16th Michigan, it was stopped and driven back with heavy rifle and artillery fire. Brady Sharpshooter Apted summed this up, noting that "the rebs advanced about a few miles and we soon sent them back completely demoralized." Capt. Salter said that in addition to Maj. Elliott and Lt. Burns, ten other men of the 16th Michigan were killed or wounded. Years later, ex-Civil War soldier and historian William Fox would write that the regiment suffered three killed or mortally wounded that day. The 16th Michigan had been involved in sometimes heavy skirmishing, but they had not come under a strong Confederate attack as had their corps' left wing.[37]

The assault by Gen. Jubal Early on the Fifth Corps this day was a costly failure for the Rebels, but Lee continued to move forces southeast to block Grant. Skirmish fire continued into the night, and the Brady Sharpshooters stayed on the picket line while the rest of the regiment was moved into breastworks built by men of another Union corps. On this last day of May, the sharpshooters were relieved and rejoined their regiment, though they all returned to the picket line that afternoon.

The weather was very hot, and Capt. Salter wrote they fought all day on the skirmish line. Pvt. Smith that day noted "heavy fighting on the left and heavy [cannonading] on the right," and Pvt. Apted agreed. The soldiers got mail that day, with Apted hearing that his parents were well, though "terribly grieved" about the loss of their son Henry. Capt. Hill recorded that "the gallant Elliott" had died the previous evening. "Peace be to his ashes," he wrote.[38]

With a break for their supper, the 16th Michigan remained in their advanced position through the night. Other parts of the Army of the Potomac, and another corps that was arriving to reinforce it, would soon shift further south to a new objective—a crossroads town whose name was familiar to those Fifth Corps veterans who had survived since the terrible Seven Days battles of 1862—Cold Harbor. On June 1, the careful movement of Union and Confederate soldiers was underway, though the Fifth Corps remained in a thin line stretching south from the Bethesda Church area, short of Cold Harbor. With Col. Norval Welch still away from the 16th Michigan and Major Elliott dead, Capt. Guy Fuller was appointed to the post of acting lieutenant colonel by the Third Brigade commander, Gen. Joseph Bartlett; Capt. Benjamin Partridge was made the acting major.

That morning, Fuller was ordered to advance his regiment as skirmishers, and they moved forward through the woods to what Pvt. Apted called the Richmond Pike. This probably meant that they went with their brigade west along the Old Church Road, driving the Confederate pickets from their rifle pits. Capt. Salter thought they moved about a mile; the Rebels again fell back to their main line, and the 16th Michigan took a position on a hill with their brigade above marshy ground that officers would later say was called Magnolia Swamp. The two sides were within rifle range, and the Confederates kept up what Fuller called "an annoying fire of musketry." "The first day of summer," Apted noted in his journal, referring to June 1, incorrectly, as the start of the season, "and here we busily striving to kill each other. Oh, how I wish that this war could end, but these rebs must be annihilated first."[39]

The enemy's fire was more than just "annoying." As the regiment reached the top of the hill, Capt. Edward Hill, 30, the former lancer officer who had helped bring two companies of volunteers to the 16th Michigan in early 1862, was hit in what he initially thought was his right thigh, but in fact the bullet struck his hip and, deflecting, lodged in his gut. He probably collapsed from the shock and pain, and a soldier serving as his orderly, Pvt. John "Jack" Wood of Company G, later said Hill was placed on a stretcher and taken to a field hospital. It must have been apparent to the doctors that the captain had an intestinal wound, which they figured was fatal, since Wood said that Hill was initially "left to die." This was probably a harsh triage decision by army surgeons, who thought there was nothing they could do for him. Wood was sent to gather Hill's personal effects so that they could be returned to his family.

But Hill did not die and, at some point, picked up his diary to write. Though it is impossible to know exactly what Hill was told about his wound, it seems he knew it was dangerous if not fatal. "Alas poor Yorick," read Hill's last notation that day, citing *Hamlet* before he underwent surgery behind the battlefield. Though he alluded to himself as a man who would soon be dead, doctors eventually realized the bullet had not torn or penetrated his gut. To everyone's surprise, Hill, taken back to Washington, survived even though surgeons could not remove the bullet. But it was the end of his active service with his regiment, though his friend Benjamin Partridge would recommend Hill's promotion in the months ahead, despite the fact he could no longer handle the rigors of marching and fighting.[40]

In the meantime, most of the 16th Michigan's First Division dug in; soldiers like Pvt. Dewitt Smith saw Confederates marching to the southeast; Apted thought it was an entire Rebel division. Though some felt Confederate troops were being shifted away (which suggested to Union generals the positions before them had been significantly weakened), the soldiers here thought the Rebel position remained strong. Artillery from both sides opened fire, though the sharpshooter from Grand Rapids bragged he and his comrades silenced or forced back the Rebel batteries. "We soon dried them up," he wrote with satisfaction on June 1.[41]

Again, Grant wanted the Fifth Corps commander to launch a strong attack on the enemy before the 16th Michigan that day, but the officers said that swampy ground ahead would be difficult to cross. Nor did they have enough manpower, soldiers and officers agreed. But the skirmishing was heavy that morning, and by noon the 16th Michigan burned through plenty of ammunition and the Brady Sharpshooters had expended theirs. Capt. Salter said the entire regiment was relieved at the front to return to their main line, where Apted said they replenished their cartridges. The men could hear the roar of battle coming from more than two miles to their left, or south, where Grant ordered two of his other corps to attack Confederate defenses at Cold Harbor. This soon resulted in another terrible Union defeat.

In the meantime, the soldiers of the 16th Michigan finished collecting their ammunition when Confederates assaulted the position they had just left. "We had just got back to our main line when the rebels advanced in three lines of battle to attack us," Capt. Salter wrote. "We laid low until they came within a short distance of us, when we opened fire on them and for 2 hours a desperate battle ensued. But we finally drove them back to their breastworks before dark, and so gained another victory." Pvt. Apted said though they had driven "the rebs like so many sheep" his comrades in their brigade and division just did not have enough manpower to break the Confederates' main line to the west. In addition to Capt. Hill of the 16th Michigan's Company K, Lt. Menzo Swartz, 24, of Flushing, was wounded that day, and so were ten men.[42]

Capt. Salter's use of the word "victory" for this day's fighting was somewhat misleading. In truth, his regiment, brigade, and division had been in a localized, back-and-forth struggle covering about a mile of ground—an insignificant clash compared to the larger defeat of the Union forces to the south, outside of Cold Harbor, where more than 2,000 of them were killed, wounded, or captured. But in this portion of the Union line some three miles north of the failed assault, the 16th Michigan remained in the trenches until evening. Capt. Fuller reported that they had been on their feet for 36 hours of picket duty and skirmishing. Pvt. Apted wrote that after they were relieved and moving away from the front as darkness came on, a rifle shot struck his friend Davis Richards, from Wayne County, in the head, killing him instantly. "Poor fellow, he was one of the best friends I ever had, I mourn him as a brother," the sharpshooter wrote.

Even then, the men of his regiment, sent back to the rear of their brigade, got only a brief break and apparently not enough of a pause for soldiers to get their suppers, Pvt.

Smith complained. At dark, another Confederate attack on their division's position again required the 16th Michigan to march out to support part of their brigade's line. Seemingly a probing action by Confederate elements under Jubal Early, it was repulsed. The regiment remained in the trenches at the front throughout the night with their brigade and into the morning and afternoon of June 2. At last the men left the front, moving east toward Bethesda Church and, they hoped, rest.[43]

But it was not to be. Grant wanted another major attack that day on Lee's Cold Harbor defenses and again both he and Lee moved more troops to the southeast. Most of the Fifth Corps was ordered to also shift in that direction, though for Griffin's division, this was not very far. At 2 p.m., it was pulled back to a point about a mile west of Bethesda Church, and Joseph Bartlett's Third Brigade, of which the 16th Michigan was part, was posted as pickets on another hill near the wooded swamp. Their division was now the right of the Union line, supported by another Union corps, the Ninth, which was ordered also to move away from the front and to mass behind Griffin's men.

But Confederate General Early recognized that the Union troops in his front were withdrawing, leaving their northern flank vulnerable. He ordered his division commanders to hit the Union forces remaining here with a massive head-on attack while also flanking them, coming around their right. This position was held in part by the 16th Michigan and other regiments of Bartlett's Third Brigade, and skirmishers from brigades in the Ninth Corps, who faced north. But these units were separated by those tree-covered swamps; the Union soldiers from the two corps could not see each other's position.[44]

There was routine skirmish fire that morning before the Rebel attack began. Capt. Charles Salter and Pvt. Apted were among those convinced that the Confederates witnessed the 16th Michigan and troops from the Ninth Corps moving back from the front, and saw they were vulnerable. Yet before this Rebel attack materialized in force that afternoon, historians of the 83rd Pennsylvania and the Fifth Corps wrote, a heavy thunderstorm opened up, causing an hour delay in the fight. But as the storm passed, the Confederates assault came on. "The rebels discovered the movement and pressed us, driving in our skirmishers," Salter wrote. The attackers pushed back the Ninth Corps skirmishers and caught the Third Brigade's skirmishers by surprise, capturing a portion of their line. Capt. Fuller, commanding the 16th Michigan, said they were withdrawing back toward Bethesda Church when the Confederates made "great efforts to harass our movements." Apted and others thought it more than harassment, describing it as a full-on Rebel charge. The soldiers of the 16th Michigan and their brigade scrambled into position, probably into empty trenches dug previously by Ninth Corps soldiers.[45]

Some of Union troops present that day were said to have panicked and fled as the Rebels pressed them from the north and west. A member of the 16th Michigan, probably Benjamin Partridge, later recounted the story of a Maryland regiment that fell back in disorder as it came under heavy rifle fire, despite the attempts of its colonel to rally his men. According to this story, it was the 16th Michigan that checked the retreating Maryland soldiers, and held the line. The embarrassed colonel of these Maryland troops, according to the story, turned to Partridge with tears in his eyes. "Would to God that I commanded a Michigan regiment," the colonel allegedly said. A moment later he was killed by rifle shot. It is likely that Partridge, then a captain, was the source of the story; he would soon become the 16th Michigan's major, his promotion dating from June 1, the day after Robert Elliott's death. Some accounts of this battle claimed that as the Confederates came into the open where Griffin's men could see them, the First Division left their trenches and stood in brigade lines, one next to the other, to fight.

Capt. Fuller reported that the rifle fire of the 16th Michigan and its brigade "completely repulsed" the Confederate attack, though again, their entire division formed that battle line. Capt. Salter described this as a desperate fight that lasted more than two hours; Pvt. Dewitt Smith, who had been wounded himself nearly two years previously at the battle of Gaines' Mill, called it "hard fighting" that went on till dark. Yet only three of the 16th Michigan's soldiers were wounded or killed, with Pvt. Marion Munson of Oakland County suffering a severe wound to his left hand. For the Fifth and Ninth Corps overall, the losses were much higher, with nearly 1,500 casualties, half or more of these men captured. The soldiers spent another rainy, miserable night in the trenches. Yet this discomfort was nothing compared to what their comrades just outside of Cold Harbor would face.[46]

The next morning, June 3, south of the Fifth Corps' position, Grant ordered troops, along more than two miles of the front near Cold Harbor, to break through the Confederate defenses. Thousands of Union soldiers fell dead and wounded in this last, failed attempt, which Grant later wrote he "always regretted" ordering. Near the far right of the long Union line, just west of Bethesda Church, the 16th Michigan and their brigade comrades skirmished, came under artillery fire, captured a few prisoners, and held a hillside, acting in support of an attack by comrades in their division and elements of the Ninth Corps on Confederate positions. But it was merely the seizure of a few hundred yards of farmland and woods, insignificant compared to the big assault at Cold Harbor.

Here the regiment remained for two more days, periodically skirmishing and suffering three more soldiers wounded. Once again, in the last battle of Grant's Overland Campaign at Cold Harbor, the 16th Michigan was fortunate to not have been part of the three corps that attacked on June 3, where historians believe between 3,500 and 4,500 Union soldiers and officers became casualties in another unsuccessful attempt to break through Lee's defenses. Since the campaign began a month earlier, the 16th Michigan had lost thirty-two men killed or mortally wounded, according to the tabulations of one Civil War historian. Capt. Salter thought his regiment's total casualties for the campaign were 120, a number that indicates nearly ninety men had been wounded. Salter expected that half of these wounded soldiers would recover and be back on duty in the 16th Michigan within three months. But overall, the Union army had lost more than 55,000 killed, wounded, and missing since Grant's campaign began. Lee's forces, though weakened and lacking supplies, had mainly fought from entrenched positions and breastworks, stopping the Union attacks time after time.[47]

Perhaps Capt. Salter had been asked by friends at home about the morale of the troops, and their feelings about Grant and the conduct of the bloody campaign, with the stunning Union losses. But Salter insisted they were ready to fight on. "Our army are all feeling in very good spirits now," he wrote four days after the Cold Harbor defeat, "and after the few days rest we have had are all willing to go ahead and do whatever may be required of us." The fact that the Union army had stood the terrible losses of May and early June, and was ready to continue, was proof of its strength and commitment. He continued: "We have the proud satisfaction of knowing that at last the world acknowledges that the Army of the Potomac is the best and greatest army of our country." Grant, he wrote, had learned what the soldiers already knew—that he was facing the Confederacy's most skilled generals and most disciplined soldiers.

By the time Salter finished his letter, the commanding general had already decided on a new course of action.[48]

Henry H. Aplin

WILLIAM L. CLEMENTS LIBRARY

Alfred M. Apted

GRAND RAPIDS PRESS/GRAND RAPIDS PUBLIC MUSEUM

Lewis B. Barber

PAUL MEHNEY

George Beard *or* **Beaird**

PAUL MEHNEY

Irving Belcher

DAVE PARKS

John G. Berry

DALE NIESEN

George Bowen

PAUL MEHNEY

Martin Borgman

DONALD M. D. THURBER

Doctor Bradley

DAVE PARKS

Dr. William F. Breakey

PAUL MEHNEY

Solomon Brockway

ALBION HISTORICAL SOCIETY COLLECTION, USAHEC, CARLISLE, PA.

William H. Brockway

COLLEGE HISTORICAL PHOTOGRAPH FILES, ALBION COLLEGE ARCHIVES AND SPECIAL COLLECTIONS

William Burns

DALE NIESEN

George Cook

PAUL MEHNEY

Bradley Crippen

MIKE WASKUL

Gilbert Chandler

DALE NIESEN

James Dafoe

DALE NIESEN

Frank Eddy

COURTESY ARCHIVES OF MICHIGAN

Robert T. Elliott

MONROE COUNTY MUSEUM

Dr. Robert Everett

JEFF KOWALIS

Hiram Felton

COURTESY ARCHIVES OF MICHIGAN

Benjamin F. Fisher

PAUL MEHNEY

George Gibbs

PAUL MEHNEY

Thomas Gilbey

SLOAN MUSEUM, PERRY ARCHIVES

Ziba Graham

PROCEEDINGS OF THE THIRD BRIGADE ASSOCIATION

Mathew Goodhoe

PAUL MEHNEY

William Hardick

COURTESY ARCHIVES OF MICHIGAN

Martin Heath

BOB COCH

Edward Hill

MIKE WASKUL

Theodore Hoeninghausen

STOCKTON CENTER MUSEUM

Rufus W. Jacklin

OSBORN PHOTO ALBUM, BENTLEY HISTORICAL LIBRARY, UNIVERSITY OF MICHIGAN

George Jardine

PAUL MEHNEY

Gustav Kast

OSBORN PHOTO ALBUM, BENTLEY HISTORICAL LIBRARY, UNIVERSITY OF MICHIGAN

Frank Keeler

PAUL MEHNEY

William Kydd

MIKE WASKUL

Carlos King

PAUL MEHNEY

Guy Kingsley

DAVE FINNEY

James Laird

PAUL MEHNEY

Thomas Lackie

COURTESY ARCHIVES OF MICHIGAN

William Larkworthy

DAVE PARKS

Theodore Mahan

COURTESY ARCHIVES OF MICHIGAN

Charles Meyers

STOCKTON CENTER MUSEUM

Judd Mott

PAUL MEHNEY

Thomas Morris

PROCEEDINGS OF THE THIRD BRIGADE ASSOCIATION

Allen B. Morse

COURTESY ARCHIVES OF MICHIGAN

Charles Northrop

PAUL MEHNEY

Marion Munson

PAUL MEHNEY

John Northwood

MICHAEL A. LEESON, *HISTORY OF SAGINAW COUNTY* (CHICAGO: CHAS. C. CHAPMAN, 1881).

John F. Parker and wife

JOHN PARKER AND ED PARKER

Alonzo Palmer and James McKnight

COURTESY ARCHIVES OF MICHIGAN

Benjamin Partridge

ROGER D. HUNT COLLECTION, USAHEC, CARLISLE, PA.

Thomas Frank Powers

DAVE FINNEY

James B. Rolls

COURTESY ARCHIVES OF MICHIGAN

George Prentiss

JOHN PARKER AND ED PARKER

William Rolfe and wife

RG98S CIVIL WAR PHOTOGRAPH COLLECTION, USAHEC, CARLISLE, PA.

John V. Ruehle

DAVE FINNEY

Charles Rice

DALE NIESEN

Charles H. Salter

MIKE WASKUL

Dr. Thomas Seeley

PAUL MEHNEY

Henry Sibley

COURTESY ARCHIVES OF MICHIGAN

George D. Sidman

COURTESY ARCHIVES OF MICHIGAN

Joseph Slack

DAVE FINNEY

Edward Strong

MIKE WASKUL

Thomas B. W. Stockton

HARRISBURG CIVIL WAR ROUND TABLE, U.S. ARMY HERITAGE AND EDUCATION CENTER

George Swan

DALE NIESEN

Eugene Thompson

MIKE WASKUL

Menzo Swartz

MIKE WASKUL

Lafayette Trask

PAUL MEHNEY

Horace Truesdell

COURTESY ARCHIVES OF MICHIGAN

Morris W. Tucker

DALE NIESEN

William Visscher

JOINT ARCHIVES OF HOLLAND, HOPE COLLEGE

Isaac Welbon

CHARLES VERHOVEN

Norval Welch

MIKE WASKUL

John Weller

JAMES COOKE MILLS, *HISTORY OF SAGINAW COUNTY*

Morris Wells

DALE NIESEN

William Welsh

DAVE FINNEY

Nathan Whitfield

PAUL MEHNEY

William S. Williams

DAVE FINNEY

Thomas Whitfield

PAUL MEHNEY

John Williamson

COURTESY ARCHIVES OF MICHIGAN

Dr. Isaac Wixom

AMERICAN BIOGRAPHICAL HISTORY, MICHIGAN, VOL. 2

John Wood

PAUL MEHNEY

Heber Woodruff

MIKE WASKUL

This illustration of the Michigan Lancers in camp in Detroit appeared in *Harper's Weekly* on December 21, 1861. Though this controversial regiment, formed by a Canadian military man, was soon disbanded, about 200 recruits from the lancers volunteered to join the 16th Michigan, including officers Edward Hill, Benjamin Partridge, and Judd Mott.

DETROIT PUBLIC LIBRARY, BURTON HISTORICAL COLLECTION

A lithograph of the camp of the 16th Michigan in the winter of 1862–1863 was a popular souvenir that soldiers purchased and sent home. The camp was a few miles from Fredericksburg and Falmouth, Va., near a place on the local railroad called Stoneman's Station and creeks that flowed to the Potomac. The poster, printed by A. Hoen & Co. of Baltimore, also listed the regiment's battles up to that point. Pvt. George Ervay of Grand Ledge thought he was depicted in the scene, since he was working on the guard house (the log structure near the center of camp) when the artist sketched it.

A. HOEN & CO., BENTLEY HISTORICAL LIBRARY, UNIVERSITY OF MICHIGAN

Theodore Hoeninghausen, who joined the regiment as a teenaged bugler in Detroit early in 1864, made these pictures in his sketchbook of the deteriorating condition of the 16th Michigan's colors as it progressed through the battles of the last year of the Civil War. The young bugler sounded the brigade's assembly call, "Dan-Dan-Dan Butterfield," for the last time on the field at Appomattox Court House.

DAVE PARKS

Col. Norval Welch falls near his regiment's flag, instantly killed by a gunshot as he and his men storm the Confederate earthworks at Peeble's Farm, also sometimes called the battle of Poplar Grove (or Spring) Church, on the afternoon of September 30, 1864. Part of Grant's campaign to take Petersburg, the scene was recorded by artist Joseph Becker for *Frank Leslie's Illustrated Newspaper*, October 22, 1864. Moments before Welch was killed, diarist and sharpshooter Alfred Apted was wounded in the charge, causing him to lose the use of his left arm and ending his service in the 16th Michigan.

UNIVERSITY OF MICHIGAN

Veterans of the 16th Michigan stood on the steps of the state capitol in Lansing for this photograph of their regimental reunion.

WESTERN MICHIGAN UNIVERSITY ARCHIVES AND REGIONAL HISTORY COLLECTION

17.

JUNE–SEPTEMBER 1864

I AM NOT MUCH MORE THAN A SHADOW

The day after the disastrous assault on the Confederate defenses at Cold Harbor, the 16th Michigan remained in position near Bethesda Church with its brigade, in and near breastworks, as rain fell that afternoon and continued all night. Though many narratives of the Civil War note that the Union soldiers were angry and depressed about what they considered foolish orders for suicidal attacks on strong Confederate lines over the preceding weeks, such sentiment was not recorded in the diaries and letters available for the 16th Michigan. Of course, soldiers in the Fifth Corps had been spared from making many of these attacks due to the reluctance of their commander, Gen. Gouverneur Warren, to order them in.

Now the men of the 16th Michigan shared the misery of the rain and existence in the trenches with a newly arrived company of sixty-four men under the command of their captain, George Jardine of Saginaw. The company, which may have ultimately totaled some eighty men, was officially recorded as "the second independent company of sharpshooters"—the Brady Sharpshooters being the first—but these soldiers would always be known in the regiment as "Jardine's Sharpshooters." Jardine was another alumnus of the ill-fated lancer regiment that Canadian Col. Arthur Rankin tried to organize in the fall of 1861. Then 37, Jardine, a Scotland-born merchant, had been, or was supposed to have been, a captain in the lancers, but was mustered out in Detroit early in 1862 when the War Department ruled what was left of the regiment must disband. Col. Norval Welch, in Michigan for much of spring of 1864, was involved in the organizing of Jardine's next company, writing in mid-May to Governor Austin Blair and asking him to commission Jardine and his lieutenants, Arnold J. West of Saginaw and Cyrus Wellman of Spaulding. Pvt. Alfred Apted, a Brady Company sharpshooter, figured the new company "will be broke up"—that is, its men divided up and placed in other companies—and its officers sent home. But he was wrong; the second company of sharpshooters was left intact, and Jardine's military career would last nearly a year before he was "discharged at [the] recommendation of a board for incompetency."[1]

Though Grant's spring offensive was at a halt after the Cold Harbor disaster, the soldiers of the 16th Michigan heard cannonading in the distance and were on alert for an attack on their position on the night of June 5—some felt this was another probing action, but others thought it was a false alarm. Pvt. Apted was on the skirmish line. "Soon after dark we withdrew from our position and traveled all night a few steps at a time," he recorded. The regiment moved about five miles on a narrow country track to a point near Cold Harbor, and his Fifth Corps commander, Gen. Warren, said they were "on the road all night." The next day, Capt. Charles H. Salter of Detroit said they "heard of cavalry in their rear"—Confederate troopers following the soldiers as they withdrew from what had been their main line. The 16th Michigan and the 1st Michigan were briefly consolidated into one command, since that regiment was now reduced to about 100 men, while the 16th Michigan's troop strength stood at 300. But the regiment went out to confront the Rebels who were following them at a location called Allen's Mills, Salter wrote. He led sixty skirmishers to clash with the Rebel cavalry and drove them back a half mile. Pvt. Apted said they traded shots until night when they were relieved, and returned to bivouac with their division near Cold Harbor. Before dawn on June 7, the regiment's First Division, along with another of their corps' divisions, was shifted five miles east to the Chickahominy River to a place called Kidd's Mill, or alternately, Summit, where the veterans of 1862 like Apted and Salter had briefly camped and worked before the Seven Days battles.[2]

It was cool and pleasant as the soldiers were told to put up their tents in a pine grove. Lt. Frank Keeler of Saginaw was now back with the regiment after having spent much of May with an injured foot at Fredericksburg, missing most if not all of the spring campaign. The local orchards were filled with all the cherries a man could want, he wrote, and good sweet potatoes were available. Pvt. Apted, who had come through the fighting without a scratch, cut his foot as he was fixing his tent. His injury was attended by the former hospital steward and now assistant surgeon, William Larkworthy. Still, Apted was sent to the First Division's hospital where his cut was stitched up. "It pained like a fiend," the sharpshooter complained. The next day, on the afternoon of June 8, Apted was carried in a wagon with four other sick and wounded soldiers to the Union hospital and supply base at White House Landing on the Pamunkey River, where three days later he was put on a boat to Washington. But at White House Landing he heard that the entire army was about to make another big move. "The reports are that our forces are going to evacuate this place and swing around to the James River, and then receive supplies by a much shorter route," he wrote. Apted witnessed blacks, former slaves now working for the army, tearing up nearby railroad track so it could not be used by the Confederates, once the Union forces had moved away.

Of course, it was not primarily the Union supply route that prompted Grant to plan this move. Unable to maneuver the Army of Northern Virginia into the open, and incurring terrible losses in the attempt, Grant now planned to quickly shift his army south across the James at Charles City Court House to strike at Petersburg, about twenty miles south of

Richmond, and surprise the small garrison there. Once Petersburg was in Union hands, Richmond could truly be cut off from further supply by the destruction of still-open rail lines and roads. Then Grant could besiege the Confederate capital and trap Lee, assuming the Rebel army would fall back to it.[3]

In the meantime the 16th Michigan, with its brigade and division, had a few days of relative quiet along the Chickahominy, though regimental casualties published later suggested there was still skirmishing going on before the march to Petersburg began. "[We] have been resting most of the time . . . and now feel much better than when we first arrived here," Capt. Salter wrote. They had religious service that day—the chaplain of the 21st Maine conducted it—the first in a long time, he continued. Union and Confederate soldiers were on patrol along the river; "by mutual agreement, they have ceased the mischievous plan of picket firing," he wrote. But the regiment, and all of Grant's troops, were warned that they needed to be ready to move out at a moment's notice.

The regiment's consolidation with the 1st Michigan had lasted only a week, Salter wrote. But he revealed that Col. Norval Welch's continued absence from the 16th Michigan had become an embarrassment. "Our Colonel (Welch) has not come back yet, and our generals somehow do not seem to like the idea of his being away from his regt., and I am much mistaken if he does not get himself into serious trouble about it," Salter wrote.

> Our brigade commander, Gen. Bartlett, and division commander, Gen. Griffin, are apparently determined not to let the matter go unnoticed, and what makes it worse for the Col., is that whilst Major Elliott was lying dead in his grave (having been killed whilst leading his regt. to meet the enemy), Col. Welch was casting reflections [sic, aspersions] on his character in Detroit, and saying he was not fit to command the regt., etc., whilst every man in our regt., and every soldier in our army that knew Major Elliott, knew that no braver man ever lived than the Major was, and that he had done his duty in ten battles where Col. W. had in one.
>
> This is the simple truth, and although I suppose I have no business to cast reflections upon a superior officer, I cannot help it. I know that his conduct has disgraced our entire regt., and that had he been here leading his regt., as other Michigan colonels were, our regt. would have had a better name, and more notice taken of it, during the campaign than we had. As it was, what Detroit paper would notice a regt. whose Col. was in Detroit pleasure seeking whilst his officers and men were battling for the country, and giving up their lives on every battle field. But I believe God is just and will surely bring such men to punishment, in his own good time and way.[4]

As night fell on June 12, the four corps of the Army of the Potomac, and one from the Army of the James that had joined them at Cold Harbor, quietly marched away on different roads and routes; some went to the Pamunkey River to board transports. While 100 men from the 16th Michigan stood picket, the rest of the regiment moved with its brigade and division through the wooded countryside, eventually joining the rest of the Fifth Corps and marching ten miles into the next morning to a place on the Chickahominy River called Long Bridge. Union cavalry drove off Rebels guarding this place—the bridge had been destroyed—but engineers put up a pontoon bridge that Gen. Charles Griffin's First Division crossed that morning. Salter wrote that his division "went up 2 miles toward Richmond, formed [a] line, and protected the crossing of our army that day," though in truth about half the army went over the Chickahominy at that point. Another division of the Fifth Corps and Union cavalry clashed with the Confederates nearby that afternoon, causing Rebel commanders to believe that a new attack by Grant was in the offing here. This fight involving the 16th Michigan's comrades allowed Grant's entire force to leave the area unhindered, literally slipping away from Robert E. Lee's scouts.[5]

"Then at 10 p.m. we fell in," Salter continued. The 16th Michigan marched south with its division and corps toward the James River, covering about ten miles and briefly halting to rest, and then resuming the march at 5 a.m. on the morning of June 14 for the last several miles to the area of Charles City Court House. Pvt. Dewitt Clinton Smith of Company I, from a small town in Tuscola County, said they marched to the river and "layed in line all day" until they moved into some breastworks as darkness fell, and bivouacked at a point that Capt. Salter said was a mile from the James. As thousands of other nearby soldiers walked across a new pontoon bridge over the river, or were transported by boats and barges to the south side, the 16th Michigan's brigade and division had a day of rest, drawing rations and swimming and bathing in the James. Early on the morning of June 16, the 16th Michigan and other regiments of the Fifth Corps' First and Fourth Divisions were awakened and filed down to the river, where transports ferried soldiers to the other side. The regiment, now under Capt. Guy Fuller from Ionia, with its division, then took up the line of a twenty-five-mile march on the long, hot and dusty road to Petersburg; Salter called it "very fatiguing" and wrote that the march halted early on the morning of June 17 outside of the town; Capt. Fuller said they went into position at a local residence he called "Barton's house." The men could hear the thunder of battle ahead.[6]

PETERSBURG

The Union army's attack on Petersburg's defenders had begun two days earlier as the first of their corps arrived east of town. Confederate General Pierre G. T. Beauregard called on Lee for more reinforcements as his small force—initially about 2,500 men—held off superior Union numbers from their fortifications, lines of trenches outside the city. The Confederates hurried more troops into the defenses over the course of the first three days of fighting, vastly outnumbered by the three Union corps that reached Petersburg during that time. Unfortunately for Grant and his men, these corps struck the Rebel lines in uncoordinated, piecemeal, and poorly led attacks. At times during the first two days there were examples of Union soldiers who saw that the way was clear to take Petersburg, if their officers would only give the order to attack. But by the third day, when Lee's veterans arrived, there were Union troops who simply refused to assault the now-strong Confederate positions, thinking these charges suicidal and hopeless.

"The 2nd, 9th and 18th (corps) had already taken these lines of rebel earthworks, and some dozen or so small forts, and were pushing on as close to the city as possible," Capt. Salter wrote. It was not enough; the Confederate defenders fought the Union forces to a standstill, digging more trenches and building more breastworks, filling these with soldiers adequate to hold them. The First Division of the Fifth Corps, arriving at Petersburg early in the morning of June 17, went into position to the left, or south, of the Ninth Corps, and was held as a reserve, while other divisions were sent in. "That night there was some terrible fighting out in the front," Salter wrote. In the morning of June 18, the division of which the 16th Michigan was part went out to relieve elements of the Ninth Corps that had been in the fighting. Capt. Fuller reported his regiment "moved forward to the left, taking up position in the second line." Here they held ground taken by their comrades hours earlier in the hills and fields southeast of Petersburg.[7]

The advancing soldiers of the 16th Michigan saw the result of the desperate battle that had raged hours before. "Coming up to a line of breastworks that had been repeatedly charged by both sides the previous night [June 17], a terrible sight met our gaze," Salter wrote. "Our men lay piled up on the outside and the rebels on the inside, most of them on both sides having been killed with the bayonet." The Union dead there included members of the 1st Michigan Sharpshooters. "I do not think I have seen such terrible fighting since Gettysburg," Salter continued. "Over 200 dead on each side lay piled up about a line of breastworks, not 100 yards long."

In fact, attacks had been ordered all along the Union line early that morning, but these ended up uncoordinated or delayed, and a frustrated Gen. George Meade ordered assaults again in the afternoon. In the Fifth Corps, the brunt of this deadly work fell to the 16th Michigan's comrades in the First and Second Brigades of their First Division. Pvt. Dewitt Clinton Smith said it was "hard fighting in the afternoon," though Capt. Fuller reported the 16th Michigan moved forward at dusk (with other regiments) to support the First Brigade. This brigade had been briefly under the command of Col. Joshua Chamberlain, who was critically wounded in the thigh, hip, and groin that day. "We advanced a short distance further & passing the 9th Corps," Salter continued, "we became engaged and drove the rebels back ½ mile, gained possession of the Norfolk Railroad and, that night, crept up to within 300 yards of the rebel earthworks and threw up a line of breastworks and established our line within 150 yards of them." But the Confederate line held. Pvt. Smith wrote that he was detailed, probably with his company and others, to go on picket.[8]

In three days of fierce but largely uncoordinated fighting at Petersburg, the Union army lost nearly 10,000 men killed, wounded, or captured and missing. The first elements of the Army of Northern Virginia arrived at Petersburg that morning of the 18th, joining its defenders—Lee had not believed that the entire Union army slipped away from Cold Harbor to strike here until it was nearly too late. But the Confederates blocked the attacks and extended their defenses. For the moment, the Union generals halted their costly attacks; Grant's chance to quickly take Petersburg and force Lee to withdraw to Richmond was over.

"And next day [June 19] not a man could show his head about our works, or theirs but that a dozen balls would whistle around their head and every little while a man would get hit," Salter wrote. Between the advance the 16th Michigan made on the evening of the 18th and the skirmish-and-picket fire of June 19 and 20, some thirty men were killed or wounded, Salter noted, "most of them killed on account of the fighting being on open ground and over the breastworks."

The Union soldiers continued to move out under the cover of darkness to dig new positions closer to the Rebel lines, or to extend their own lines. Though they probably could not have understood it then, this was how they would spend much the next year, in trenches or moving and advancing to dig more earthworks as Grant's force besieged Petersburg. There would be periodic battles as they maneuvered to cut remaining supply routes and railroads into town, but in general, duty at the front meant life, and often death, in breastworks.[9]

Now the regiment experienced what Pvt. Dewitt C. Smith called "sharp picket firing" as Rebel sharpshooters watched for soldiers to show themselves, however briefly, in their earthworks. Company I's Corporal William H. McRoberts from the town of Milford in Oakland County was one of three men killed on June 20. His lieutenant, William Kydd, told McRoberts's family that the young soldier, who had not been feeling well, was napping in their breastworks—at that point, nothing more than a shallow trench—when he sat up and was struck by "random" fire, though the circumstances surely indicate he had been spotted by a Confederate rifleman on higher ground. "He got up on one knee and one hand on the ground when the ball struck him in the right shoulder and passed down through his body," Kydd wrote. "All he said before he died was, 'give me a drink of water and put me in the shade,' which was done."

McRoberts died minutes later. Since there was no way to send his body home, Lt. Kydd had the young man buried, as probably were others killed that day, on the grounds of a plantation behind their line. The lieutenant sent McRoberts's rings home and submitted army paperwork so his family would receive his back pay and whatever bounty payment was due him. "William was a good soldier and was loved and esteemed by his comrades," Kydd wrote. "For his good conduct I promoted him to corporal May 1, '63. I always found him ready for duty and always at his post when duty called him. His loss is felt in the company very much." Also killed were John Owen of Company H and Martin Watts of Company A; at least two other men were wounded, wrote Company I's Pvt. Smith.[10]

That night the 16th Michigan was relieved from its position at the front and rejoined its Third Brigade in reserve, where officers and men learned that Col. Norval Welch had returned and was once again in charge of the regiment. Salter, who had been so critical of Welch's long absence from the regiment, made no comment on his reappearance. The regiment bivouacked in woods south of the front and drew rations, but returned to the trenches the next morning, June 21, extending the Fifth Corps line to the Jerusalem Plank Road, a main route to Petersburg. That night, the men dug and built breastworks about a mile from their previous position. "It was a hard task and it took us all night long, as the ground was full of stumps and roots, and we finished just at daylight, completely tired out," Salter wrote. The soldiers had to "hug the earthworks close" as firing erupted along the lines on the morning of the 22nd, and there were battles nearby that day to the west when the Confederates successfully attacked a gap in a Union advance as two other corps attempted to extend their line west to cut the Weldon Railroad. But the 16th Michigan and its brigade and division were not involved in this embarrassing defeat, which cost the Union army 2,500 casualties.[11]

A fatigue detail from their Third Brigade was sent out in front that night to dig trenches even closer to the Rebel defenses. "I had 100 men with me and advanced under cover of the darkness to about halfway to the enemy's lines and then commenced to throw up rifle pits to protect the skirmish line," Capt. Salter wrote. The Rebels heard them and opened fire but could not see their targets in the darkness. By morning the soldiers of the detail were in their new trench. "That day was an *extremely warm one* in more senses than one," the captain continued. When the Confederate battery crews in front of them tried to man their guns, the 16th Michigan's skirmishers shot them down. "We were so close to them we could with perfect ease pick off their gunners in case they attempted to use their artillery, or in fact anyone that showed their heads above the works," Salter continued. Pvt. Smith noted that at least one soldier was killed and two wounded that day as the rifle fire sounded and nearby cannon roared. Salter's men were relieved that night, and went back to their main line of breastworks.[12]

Here, from late June into July, the soldiers worked in hot, muggy nights, digging new gun emplacements and trenches, strengthening and improving their brigade line, and adding long lines of sharpened stakes in front of their trenches that projected toward the enemy, to impede Confederates, should they attack. Now the line held by the 16th Michigan and their comrades was "favored with comparatively quiet times," wrote Saginaw's Lt. Frank Keeler shortly before June ended. Though not yet a true siege of Petersburg, the miles of trenches meant that neither side could mount a major assault on the other with any chance of success. To the Fifth Corps' soldiers, this raised a serious question: Why risk getting killed in meaningless exchanges of picket firing when, for the moment, the two sides were not realistically able to attack each other? Capt. Salter noted that "the pickets of both parties in front of us came to an understanding between themselves not to fire anymore unless in case of a fight and now all along the line of our corps the pickets pace up and down along this line, without ever thinking of firing at each other, and they are so close together that they can easily converse across the line." Occasionally the pickets met halfway between the lines to trade newspapers and articles like tobacco or knives, he continued; soldiers not on picket could climb to the top of their earthworks, without fear of getting shot, to look at the other side. Yet other army corps did not enjoy such quiet, and kept up aggressive picket fire, said Lt. Keeler.

The neighborly state of relations the Fifth Corps pickets had with their counterparts did not extend to the Union artillery. The gunners sometimes "bang away at each other," Salter wrote, "especially if they see a wagon train, or any wagons across in the enemy's line. On the morning of July 4, he continued, Union officers spotted wagons in the rear of the Rebel works; the battery assigned to the Third Brigade "scattered them in pretty quick time." Also firing at times were Union batteries of mortars—simple, large guns that blasted explosive shells high into the air so they would drop on their targets from above, avoiding protective earthen walls and embankments. "Our mortars fire a few shells over into the rebel fort occasionally, just to annoy them," Keeler wrote. "In the daytime we can see where the shells strike the forts, and at night we can see the shells travel high in the air. There is a fuse fixed to the shell which burns like a string of firecrackers until the shell arrives near the rebel works, where it explodes, scattering fragments in all directions."[13]

There were developments within the regiment involving veteran officers. First, one of the lieutenants filed a complaint against Capt. George Swan of Detroit, for "misbehavior on the field" and "false muster," or fraudulent record keeping regarding his pay. Swan was placed in arrest in June, seemingly around the time Col. Welch had returned to the regiment. The days of Swan's military service were now numbered, and he was soon dismissed by a general court-martial, with Welch siding against him.

Welch also wrote to Gov. Blair about commissions for his choices to take the posts of his top two officers: For lieutenant colonel, he wanted Capt. Guy Fuller of Ionia, who had led the regiment since the death of Major Robert Elliott; for major, he wanted Capt. Benjamin Partridge of Bay City. By seniority, George Swan would have been a candidate for major, but he was facing court-martial. "These officers [Fuller and Partridge] have won their promotion by conspicuous and meritorious conduct on the field during the late campaign," Welch explained. "The generals of the brigade and division speak in strong terms of their gallantry and good conduct and fitness for higher rank."

But Fuller had a problem back in Michigan—someone had written to the authorities, accusing him of being a Copperhead, or traitor to the United States and sympathizer to the Confederacy. Michigan Adjutant General John Robertson scrawled directions to his staff on Welch's letter. "Commission Partridge," he noted. "Wrote to ask Col. Welch why Capt. Swan is jumped [passed over for promotion] and state that Capt. Fuller is charged with being a Copperhead. *Hold on.*"

It would take a nearly two weeks for Welch to answer these questions:

> When I returned to the regiment, I found Capt. Swan in arrest with charges preferred against him for misbehavior on the field and for false muster, upon which he has been dismissed. The evidence placed before me as to his conduct in action was such as to preclude the idea of recommending him for promotion. The sense of the whole regiment was against it.[14]

Captains Fuller and Partridge had been serving in the respective roles of acting lieutenant colonel and major at the direction of Gen. Joseph Bartlett, the Third Brigade commander, in recognition of their service during the campaign, Welch continued; he agreed with their promotions, and so did most of the regiment's officers. "As for Capt. Fuller being a Copperhead and hostile to the government, I do not know of ground for such an accusation," he wrote. "On the contrary, I have heard him express himself in the strongest terms in support of the administration, and no longer ago than yesterday heard him say that he would not vote for any other candidate than Mr. Lincoln under any circumstances."[15]

But even with Welch vouching for him, Fuller did not get the promotion to lieutenant colonel. In less than two months, Fuller would leave the regiment on the completion of his original three-year hitch, though he could have resigned at any time, especially given that many officers of his rank and experience would likely have left at being denied this promotion by the governor. Ironically, after surviving three years of battles, skirmishes, and exposure, Fuller would be killed by Confederate guerillas or raiders as he worked as a civilian employee on an army-run railroad.

July weather continued hot, dry and dusty—it had not rained since June 2—and Lt. Keeler said the men erected an arbor over trenches where they pitched their tents, though Salter wrote the "arbor" was nothing but a few bushes and branches soldiers placed overhead. "In the daytime we have nothing to do but sit in the shade, read, write letters or play whist," Keeler said. "The rebs have not fired a shot at us for some days; we hardly realize we are so near them." Yet as the soldiers dug trenches closer and closer to the Confederate lines, Rebel guns did regularly fire at them, "to prevent us from working," Capt. Salter wrote. He described the Fifth Corps' position as near the center of a long line of fortifications stretching south from the James River, to the Appomattox River, and continuing just east of Petersburg to a point south of town. This line was held by six Union army corps. From the neighboring Ninth Corps position "the city is plainly seen," he wrote, though a big rise of ground called Reservoir Hill stood between the town and the Fifth Corps.

Salter learned that Union engineers and soldiers from the Ninth Corps, to his right, were "mining" Rebel defenses—that is, digging a tunnel a few hundred feet in length to reach under the Confederate line. The goal of this operation was to undermine, or to place and detonate explosives in an underground chamber, to blow up a section of the Rebel works, allowing Union troops to charge through the gap. The tunneling was conducted by a regiment from Pennsylvania that contained men who had been coal miners and engineers. It was probably not wise for Salter to tell his friends in Detroit about this operation for security's sake, but then he gave no specific details. "You may expect to hear of our blowing up some of these rebel forts, together with the force that may be in them," he explained. "It is a terrible mode of warfare, but it is the only way we can make a break in the enemy's walls." Lt. Keeler's letter home hinted that he perhaps knew this operation was underway. "We are quiet on quiet on this line," he wrote, "no movement on either side. In fact, an advance would be impossible unless it were made underground. It would be perfectly useless to charge from either side."[16]

And so the 16th Michigan and other Union troops dug new trenches nightly; when they finished their own work, they then dug gun emplacements for batteries, which were positioned in the middle of their regimental line, Salter wrote. By mid-July the trenches of the Fifth Corps were six feet deep, so that the men had to stand on a two-foot step to fire over the top; the front of this embankment was steep, making it difficult for any attackers to climb it. Officers and men alike also dug and built bomb shelters they called "bomb proofs"—subterranean wooden structures with roofs of logs or beams, covered with earth, where they were protected from Confederate artillery shells (though Salter said he only topped his more skeletal shelter with some branches, "trusting my life in the hands of the Lord"). Though it was uncomfortable in the trenches, the men were regularly receiving mail and newspapers, and they were periodically supplied with shipments from the U.S. Sanitary Commission of canned meat, fruit, and vegetables; Union supply officers had for days been issuing soldiers some "soft bread," according to Pvt. Dewitt C. Smith, meaning that ovens had also been brought up.[17]

The nutritious additions to the soldiers' diet could not help Jacob Craw, a soldier from rural Genesee County in Company I, who had joined the regiment in the fall of 1862 and who was again sick. He had spent most of his first year as a soldier in hospitals or convalescent camps, but he recovered his health to the point where he rejoined the 16th Michigan in April 1864 and took part in the fighting that spring and summer. "I have at least seen the elephant," Craw wrote his friends, using the soldiers' term for experiencing battle for the first time. "I have seen all that I want, for it is an awful thing to stand and see men shot down by your side, although I stood it better than I thought that I should. I was in all the battles from the time we crossed the Rapidan on the third of May until now, and I have come out with a whole hide. I have had some very narrow escapes both with minny [*sic*] balls and shells. I don't like their music much."

Though he had been suffering with diarrhea, it seems Craw was not excused from duty until July 1. "It is not here as it is there [at home]," Craw told friends. "If anyone is a little sick they can't give up work when they are a mind to. They have to keep going as long as they can." He figured he would be sent to a hospital if his health did not improve. "Oh, how glad I will be when this awful war comes to a close so that us poor boys can come home and enjoy themselves once more," he wrote. Yet there was no sign of the war ending. "I am the poorer now, I think, than I ever was," he said of his physical state. "If I get much poorer I shan't make more than half a shadow." Jacob Craw was eventually so sick that he was sent north, but he never made it home. He died of illness at Germantown, Pennsylvania on November 20, and was buried in the National Cemetery in Philadelphia.[18]

Capt. Salter echoed Craw's comment when describing his own health and physical condition in hot, insect-plagued conditions in the trenches in mid-July. The nightly entrenching was exhausting, and rest was nearly impossible. "It is so warm in the day time we cannot sleep and the flies are more numerous here than I have ever seen. . . . They keep us awake even if we [have] cooler weather, and in consequence of so much night work, we are all becoming pretty well worn out. I am for one, and [I] am not much more than a shadow of what I was last spring."

He and others had heard about the raid into Maryland by troops under Confederate Gen. Jubal Early—the Union army's Sixth Corps had been withdrawn earlier that month to protect Washington from them. Though the men were sorry to see their comrades temporarily taken from the front to protect the federal capital, Salter hoped it was a lesson for Northern residents. "It will serve to rouse up the people of the north to renewed action, and to the great fact that the Army of the Potomac must have more men if they expect us to take Richmond and protect Washington at the same time," he wrote.[19]

Though the Union army was not conducting a true siege that surrounded Petersburg entirely, the operation, less than a month old, was having its effect, tightening Confederate supplies; the defenders were placed on short rations. "Some of them desert and come over to us every day," Salter wrote on July 14. "Last night 2 men came over in front of our regt. and they looked pretty hard, dirty and ragged & poor." Two days later, Pvt. Dewitt C. Smith recorded, seven more Rebels deserted, coming into the regiment's line. It was also dangerous for the Rebels to try to place a battery within view of the Union gunners, Lt. Keeler wrote; the next day, a mortar battery opened fire and struck Confederate munitions. "A rebel magazine was blown up the day before yesterday by one of our mortar shells," Lt. Keeler wrote that week. "The explosion was terrific. An immense cloud of smoke arose and floated along the rebel line of battle for two hours." Salter said Union soldiers broke into cheers all along the line, and they heard that seventy-three Confederate soldiers had been killed and wounded in the blast.[20]

The result of the Union army's engineering, digging, and building that took place outside Petersburg in these several weeks was nothing short of incredible—there were covered roads that ran four feet below ground level, enabling troops and even wagons to come up to the front unobserved by the Rebels. "It would be perfectly astonishing to any citizen, or any person, outside of our army, to come here and see the immense amount of earth we have dug up since we have been here," Salter wrote that month. "We thought we had done a great deal of such work at Yorktown, but it was very small compared with our immense work here." Keeler said their lines "are approaching the city continuously, by zigzags and parallels."

At last a welcome rainstorm blew in, and the Union soldiers heard that the Confederate raid to attack Washington was ended; they were hoping and waiting for the news that, in the western theater of the war, Gen. William T. Sherman had taken Atlanta, a major Rebel manufacturing and rail center. Capt. Salter again stressed the need for more soldiers. "Our army are all pleased to hear the proclamation of the President calling for another 500,000 men (out of which he will probably get 100,000)," he wrote to friends, referring to the actual rates of previous efforts to recruit and draft men for service, "and hope the draft will proceed at the time appointed and that the men will be promptly furnished. It makes us old soldiers pleased to think how the clerks and all the nice young men at home are trembling in their shoes at view of the approaching draft. Well, we can afford to laugh, I suppose."[21]

Gen. George G. Meade issued orders in mid-July from the headquarters of the Army of the Potomac for a new battalion of sharpshooters to be created within the Fifth Corps' First Division. This command, to be raised within the division, would be under the 16th Michigan's adjutant, Rufus W. Jacklin, who had joined the regiment early in 1862 with the Brady Sharpshooters. His marksmen would be drawn from each regiment in the division, and they would serve as an independent command. For Jacklin, his friend Capt. Salter said, this duty "is much pleasanter than being in our regiment"—an apparent swipe at Col. Welch. An article that appeared in Detroit signed by "GIBLEM" (an apparent anagram/pseudonym) said that Jacklin's sharpshooters "are to be armed with telescopic, target and Sharp's breech-loading rifles."[22]

Frank Keeler was chafing at the fact the army had not been paid in four months. The paymaster had written to Capt. Salter, assuring him that their pay was coming, but this did little to calm Keeler, who was concerned about his men and their families. "It is awful to let the soldier's pay run so far behind," he complained. "Some men here say their families are actually suffering at home for food. Scarcely anyone here has money." But Keeler had bigger news for his parents—he would soon be coming home.

> There is nothing to prevent my going out of the service now. An order issued yesterday by our division mustering officers provides that all officers mustered previous to January 1st, 1864, may be mustered out on the expiration of three years from their first muster in. So there can be no difficulty now. Only 20 days more, when I can go to Washington, settle with the ordnance and quartermaster's offices, draw my final pay and journey homeward.[23]

Those seem to have been the last words Second Lieutenant Frank Keeler wrote while serving in the 16th Michigan. In September, he was discharged and went home to Saginaw.

A heavy rain fell late in July, flooding some soldiers out of their tents, but Capt. Salter said the 16th Michigan's men avoided this by creating drains to channel water away from them. Col. Welch, for a period, commanded the Third Brigade while Gen. Joseph Bartlett was incapacitated as the wearying stalemate continued into midsummer. But more action was in the offing. "Last Friday Gens. Grant and Meade passed along the front line of our works to inspect them, stopping in our earthwork some time to view the rebel fort opposite us," Capt. Salter wrote in late July, "and passed some time in our regimental headquarters, where quite a crowd of officers collected, all anxious to hear what the commander-in-chief had to say of the situation, and were gratified in as much as he told us that Petersburg would be ours in two weeks' time at the farthest [latest] and I believe he meant just what he said. Both of the generals looked anxious and careworn, more so than I have ever seen before."

More guns were brought up to their division's line, and a fort was built to the 16th Michigan's left that would have eighteen heavy artillery pieces, he continued; the Rebel pickets continued their policy of not firing at the Union's, but their gunners fired every day, trying to hit work parties and periodically wounding men. Salter said they were "under orders to be ready to move at a moment's notice." This was undoubtedly because the generals were aware that the mining operation in the Ninth Corps' front, going on a mile or more from where the 16th Michigan's Third Brigade was posted, was nearly finished. On July 29, Salter was ordered to take a 100-man detail to help gun crews position the mortars behind the 16th Michigan. Knowing that a major offensive operation was coming, and that the mortars could attract Confederate artillery fire, Salter hurried to finish a proper bomb-proof with heavy wooden beams over the top.[24]

The next morning after 4 a.m., Union officers lit the fuse to set off four tons of gunpowder packed in the underground chamber that those Pennsylvanian miners tunneled beneath part of the Confederate line east of Petersburg. Capt. Salter was one of thousands of Union soldiers and officers who witnessed it blow up later that morning. "With a terrific explosion and rumbling noise that seemed more like an earthquake than anything else, huge masses of earth, timber, &c. went high up in the air, and of the 3 regiments in the fort, but 4 men escaped to live of all of them," Salter wrote. As bodies of Rebels, pieces of shattered guns and beams, and huge plumes of dirt and sand fell back through the smoke to the scorched earth, Union artillery opened fire.

In the Fifth Corps, in the rear of the First Division's Third Brigade, eighteen mortars began to fire 32- and 64-lb. shells. Another twenty-six heavy artillery pieces to their left pounded the Confederate line, as did twelve field guns to their right. "These all concentrated their fire upon the fort just opposite us, knocking down the walls, tearing the embrasures all out of shape," Capt. Salter wrote. Not one Rebel soldier could be seen raising his head during this storm of shells; then the infantry opened fire, too. "The roar of the musketry and artillery combined was greater that any I have heard since Gettysburg," Salter continued. Pvt. Dewitt C. Smith, the short, fair-haired soldier from Tuscola County, was among the soldiers detailed to carry ammunition to the guns that morning, and if he did not see the mine explosion he certainly heard it. In total, more than 160 Union guns pounded the Petersburg defenses following the blast.[25]

Yet even with this bombardment and fusillade raining lead and iron on them, Confederate troops rushed toward the smoking hole blown in their line. A division of African-American soldiers, called United States Colored Troops, had trained to attack the Rebels after the explosion, but at nearly the last moment Gen. Meade ordered they be replaced by a white division on the grounds the black troops would be blamed if the assault failed. But the replacement troops were badly led and many hesitated and milled around, confused, after the mine blew up. These men were not trained for the operation and many failed to bypass the huge hole, known since that day as "the Crater." The Union attack stalled as hundreds of men went into the Crater instead of charging around it.

The Rebels quickly recovered, their reinforcements fiercely engaging the attackers, including the U.S. Colored Troops sent in after the first Union soldiers made their tentative advance. Confederates drove them back, but many black soldiers were not allowed to surrender; they were killed on the spot. The fighting raged into the mid-morning, but the Union assault at the Crater failed, with more than 3,800 casualties, while the Confederates lost about 1,500 men. The Rebels reformed their shattered line and covered the gap the exploding mine made in their defenses. Of course, as was typical of the time, the failure of the attack *was* blamed by some white soldiers on the black troops, rather than on the incompetence of Union generals and their lack of preparation and leadership. On the morning of August 1, Salter wrote, a party went out from the Fifth Corps line to bring in wounded Confederates and bury the dead who lay in front of the Rebel fort that had been shattered by Union artillery.[26]

> We had tried to get permission from the rebels to do this before, but Lee, with his usual inhumanity, refused to allow it to be done until this morning, 48 hours after the fighting was over, and the wounded lay between the two lines, exposed to the hot rays of the sun, and

> no one to even so much as give them a drink of water, for it would have been certain death for any of our men to attempt to go to their assistance.[27]

The siege dragged on into August in a routine, even tedious fashion for the 16th Michigan and other soldiers, punctuated periodically by cannonading and explosions, according to the diary of Pvt. Dewitt C. Smith. One of the odder moments in the history of weapons in the Civil War took place on August 10, when the commander of the Third Brigade of the First Division, Joseph Bartlett, sent for Ellis Spear, commanding the 20th Maine. Bartlett had a new rifled musket he wanted Spear's men to try, nameless in Spear's account but that was called the Lindsay rifle—a two-hammered, two-barreled weapon that was supposed to allow a soldier to fire two separate shots before reloading it. Although this strange rifle worked in theory, Spear claimed he had seen these weapons tried previously by other Union troops—and the results were not good. Soldiers were supposed to fire the cartridge in the top barrel first, but "such nice calculations could not be depended upon in the heat of battle," he recalled; it was a "worthless" weapon and Spear declined to take it—but Col. Norval Welch said he would. Thus, when the 16th Michigan went into battle a month later, at least some of the men—it is not known how many—would carry this Lindsay rifle.[28]

Pvt. Alfred M. Apted of the Brady Sharpshooters returned to his regiment on August 13. The young soldier had cut his foot back at the Chickahominy River, and was eventually loaded onto a boat with other sick and wounded men that took them to Washington. From there, Apted was transferred to Lincoln Hospital, where he worried about his regiment and wrote letters. During this time away from his comrades, he had witnessed wounded men die, and he replied to a letter from the sister of his good friend, Davis M. Richards, who had been killed near Bethesda Church. He had seen another soldier killed accidentally, playing with another man's rifle. "How foolish many of the soldiers are with loaded guns, and then fooling around with them," Apted lamented.[29]

In July, when Gen. Jubal Early threatened Washington with his small force of invaders, Apted and other hospitalized soldiers had been pressed into militia service to defend the city. He was posted in breastworks near Fort Stevens at the edge of the city, where he found two other Kent County men from his company, John Wade and Leroy Lobdell, who had been wounded as the Petersburg siege began, also carrying rifles. But they had not been needed, as soldiers from the Army of the Potomac arrived in the nick of time, causing the Rebels to retreat. But at last in the second week of August, medical personnel cleared the bored and anxious Apted to return to his regiment. He arrived at Petersburg on the 13th. "The boys [are] all well and I was very glad to see them," he wrote of his return. He got back in time to repack and leave the next day as Grant ordered new offensive moves, taking the 16th Michigan out of the trenches. A later reckoning would show that twenty-two men in the regiment had been killed and mortally wounded in the initial fighting and siege of the town.[30]

On August 14, the two Union army corps to the right of the 16th Michigan stretched their lines to cover the Fifth Corps' place, relieving it from the front. Capt. Salter said that his regiment and the others of their corps moved back into some woods near the Weldon Railroad in preparation for a new offensive to cut other important roads into Petersburg. But the ground where they camped flooded in a hard rain and hot, humid weather, and the men remained under orders to move out at a moment's notice for the next few days.[31]

THE WELDON RAILROAD

While another part of the Army of the Potomac made a threatening move up the James River toward Richmond, the commander of the Fifth Corps, Gen. Warren, received orders to move in a reconnaissance in force against the Weldon Railroad, the line that ran from North Carolina to Petersburg at a point west of the Union's siege line. "Our entire corps fell in at daylight on the 18th [of August]," wrote Capt. Salter, "and moved off to the left of our army, our First Division in the advance." The soldiers moved a few miles southwest through scrubby woods and muddy fields, and the brigades formed in battle lines when they saw Confederate cavalry pickets ahead, trying to protect the railroad. But those troopers fell back as the Union soldiers approached, and at about 10 a.m. the 16th Michigan's division, under Gen. Charles Griffin, reached the track. Cutting the line would further reduce the supplies and troops the shrinking Confederacy could send to Gen. Lee, and he could not allow this happen without a fight.

Col. Welch of the 16th Michigan reported his regiment went into the line of battle on the right of an inn he and others referred to as the Yellow House (also known as the Globe Tavern), while other Fifth Corps elements advanced into dense woods to the north and became involved in fighting with Confederates under Gen. Harry Heth. The Rebels tried to push them away from the railroad, but could not. The 16th Michigan had no role in this fighting, but built breastworks alongside the rail line once the battle ended that hot afternoon. Some of the Union troops went to work tearing up the tracks.[32]

"That night I was detailed in command of 250 men of our brigade to establish a picket line out in front of our line," Capt. Salter wrote; it was a difficult business in the rain and darkness. But the next day Gen. Griffin ordered an advance by his men to cut a road, called the Vaughan Road, which at that point was running parallel to the railroad tracks, about a mile away to the west. Salter's pickets were part of a skirmish line that was a half mile long; it was raining heavily, but the Union soldiers drove back the Confederate cavalry troopers who were trying to protect the road. At 2 p.m., though, Rebel infantry of Gen. A. P. Hill attacked. Again the 16th Michigan was not involved in the fighting that day, though Salter and his skirmishers were. Yet the heaviest fighting and most important part of the action that day took place less than a mile away to the north, where Confederates battered and broke the Union line and captured hundreds of soldiers. (In this fighting Capt. Horatio Belcher of the 8th Michigan, father of the 16th Michigan's Lt. Irving Belcher, was killed. After the battle, the son escorted his father's body back to Flint, where Col. Thomas Stockton, home from the war and his thwarted hope to raise a brigade for Tennessee, led Horatio Belcher's funeral procession.)

But reinforcements arrived and prevented a complete disaster for the Union soldiers here, and they kept their hold on the railroad. Salter and his pickets were involved in more skirmishing that night of the 19th when Rebel troopers attacked them on the road, but the pickets repelled them in a lively fifteen-minute fracas. A trooper was captured, and Salter took possession of the man's horse; the captain was proud that he and his pickets had been on duty or skirmishing in bad weather for thirty-six hours before they were relieved and returned to their Third Brigade line in the morning.[33]

Convinced the Confederates would again try to break the Union hold on these important supply routes, Gen. Warren pulled his Fifth Corps back slightly into more consolidated positions, and his officers put the men to work digging trenches, building breastworks and placing batteries in preparation for an attack. It came from the north and west on the foggy morning of August 21 with a combined assault by Confederate artillery, cavalry, and infantry under Gen. A. P. Hill. The 16th Michigan's First Division faced west; the major of the 1st Michigan was with the pickets of the Third Brigade in the woods when he saw Confederates hurriedly crossing the Vaughan Road to reach some high ground that would partly shield them when they launched their flank attack on the Fifth Corps. The brigade skirmishers opened fire and the reserve pickets from the 16th Michigan, under Salter, quickly reinforced them. "Captain Salter had brought up his men and we made a stiff fight and did not move from our line until their lines of battle were well developed in our front," the 1st Michigan's Major Hopper reported.[34]

"They suddenly made their appearance in large force, [and] drove in our picket line, capturing some 15 or 16 of them, amongst whom were two men of my company," wrote Salter. Although these woods had hidden the Confederate infantry attackers, it also obscured the Rebels' view of the Fifth Corps trenches. They boldly marched forward, believing they were about to strike the left flank of the Union position. Unfortunately for these South Carolina troops, they could not see that the 16th Michigan and the rest of the Third Brigade were behind and to the left of that line, a few hundred yards. These trenches "could not be seen by the enemy until they were right upon it," Salter said.

> And on they came over an open field on our right, waving their banners and keeping perfect line, whilst our artillery was making fearful havoc in their ranks[.] But confident of outflanking us, they pressed right on through the gap with one brigade, when our brigade jumped up on our works, and with loud cheers, closed in up to the Fourth Division, they coming down to meet us.[35]

The attacking Confederates were trapped—scores were shot down and more surrendered. Seven hundred men, four regimental stands of colors, and a brigadier general were captured, Salter claimed. "The loss on our side was very small, owing to our fighting behind the breastworks we had put up," the captain continued. The 16th Michigan suffered five men wounded and a few taken prisoner out on the picket line that morning. "They [the Rebels] were using this road, before we gained it, to bring up most all of their supplies—so I was informed by the reb cavalry man I captured, who said Lee was bound to have the road back again at any cost," Salter said. "I told him Lee would probably change his mind after he knew the Fifth Corps, the best part of our army, held it." Gen. Warren was proud of his corps' defensive victory here at the railroad, but Gen. Grant was not impressed since Warren did not order his men to pursue and destroy the retreating Confederates that day.[36]

While this was a proud moment for the 16th Michigan, it was the beginning of a long and awful imprisonment for Pvt. Dewitt C. Smith of Company I, one of the men captured that day on the brigade skirmish line early in the battle. The captured men were soon taken to Libby Prison in Richmond, and then marched to Belle Isle, the prison in the James River on August 24. "Drawed [a] chunk of corn Bread and a little Stinking Bacon and Some slop," Smith recorded of that day's meal.

Smith, a short, fair-haired man from Watrousville in Michigan's Thumb, was probably about 21 years old when he was captured. His diary survived the war, though whether he did is an open question. Smith saw the Rebel guards punish a man who had tried unsuccessfully to escape—the Union soldier was forced to "ride" a wooden horse—that is, made to sit on a pole for five hours with his hands tied behind his back. Smith and others read hopeful reports of possible prisoner exchanges in newspapers they sometimes saw, and they read that Union forces had captured Atlanta. He witnessed or heard of Union soldiers, including a man from his regiment, taking an "oath of allegiance" to the Confederacy, whereby those prisoners were allowed out of prison, though it obligated them to work for the Rebels in some fashion.

On other occasions, he witnessed the prison's sick men being released on parole. On October 7, Smith was with a number of men sent to Salisbury, North Carolina; within days he was recording a daily toll of men who died overnight—a terrible, rising toll he listed matter-of-factly into November. Smith stopped making entries in his journal that month, though he made a final entry on March 2 in 1865 when he seemed to be in Wilmington. But what became of him after that is unknown. The army had "no further record" of Smith after his capture at the Weldon Railroad, nor did his fellow soldiers who survived the war know what became of him.[37]

Colonel Welch would report that during their skirmishing near the rail line that took place over those several days in August, the 16th Michigan lost six men wounded and thirteen men missing. It would ultimately be determined that five of them were killed or mortally wounded. The men of the 16th Michigan and thousands of other soldiers spent the remainder of August on picket or working on two large forts near the railroad, and digging and improving more trenches in rainy weather. The work was exhausting, but Capt. Salter noted that it meant the Confederates would also have to extend their defenses, spreading their limited manpower further around Petersburg. No comment seems to have been made about the odd two-hammered, double-barreled Lindsay rifle, though it almost certainly would have been used in this skirmishing.

But Union lines in front of Petersburg were strong enough to stand up to a severe attack. The army's engineers had also built their own railroad—one that ran right up to the Fifth Corps headquarters at the Globe Tavern, an extension of the line that ran from the huge Union supply depot at City Point, Virginia, several miles east of Petersburg, to the front.

The soldiers also received good news from another theater of the war—Atlanta had fallen at last. The men cheered, and General Grant ordered a salute be fired from every battery that bore on the enemy. When the guns were fired at midnight, the Rebels thought an attack was being launched and responded in kind. "For a couple of hours we had a very lively cannonade, but as usual, nobody was hurt," Capt. Salter noted.[38]

There was a lull in the fighting in September. The weather cooled, and there was time for those soldiers and officers who wanted religious services "to put up a large shade of pine boughs for the purpose of holding meetings in," he wrote. Between fifty and 100 men of the regiment attended these—Sunday sermons given by representatives of the Christian commission and evening meetings, weather permitting, Salter explained. Soon the men had improved this shelter with side walls of brush and branches. "Most all of the regts. in our division hold meetings also nearly every night," the captain continued, "and I think there is more interest manifested in them by the men than I have ever before seen in the army." Salter was happy to find that the colonel of the 118th Pennsylvania, James Gwynn, encouraged "the cause of religion" while temporarily in charge of their brigade.[39]

There was a bittersweet moment in the 16th Michigan when forty soldiers and six veteran officers, including Frank Keeler and Guy Fuller, mustered out of the service as their original three-year enlistment expired. These were men who volunteered in the summer of 1861, and though they had not signed up for the reenlistment offer, they were true veterans who had been through the battles and privations of the past three years—from Gaines' Mill to Gettysburg to the fights there at Petersburg. On September 7, they left their regiment at the front and started for home. "Yesterday we had a somewhat sad duty to perform—parting with old comrades, men with whom we fought side by side for the honor of the old flag, on many a bloody field," wrote Capt. Thomas Frank Powers of Flint, who signed his letter to a Detroit newspaper "Veritas." Salter, who was staying on, agreed. "It made us old veterans feel homesick for a while when we see them going, yet we hope that the war will end in the course of a few months, or a year at the most, and then we shall go home also," he wrote, "at best, what is left of us."[40]

Within days, the Union offensive operations around Petersburg would indeed resume into the fall.

18.

SEPTEMBER–DECEMBER 1864

THE WORST FIRE A MORTAL EVER ENDURED

The soldiers of the 16th Michigan and scores of other regiments in the Army of the Potomac had practically idolized General George McClellan as their commander in 1861 and 1862, but there was a different feeling about him as they enjoyed some calm outside of Petersburg in the early days of September. McClellan now became the Democratic Party's nominee for president, running against Abraham Lincoln in the November election. The soldiers' concern was that a major wing of the party stood for an immediate end to the war—Democrats had placed a plank to this effect in their party platform and nominated a man who stood for this as their vice-presidential nominee. It was not that Union soldiers did not want an end to the war—obviously, they did. But they wanted victory, not just an armistice. As a result, Capt. Charles Salter told his friends in Detroit, most Union soldiers would support Lincoln when the election came:

> The presidential election does not cause but very little excitement or attention here, yet when the time comes to vote the Army will be found to vote on the side of the Union by a tremendous majority. Gen. McClellan had an immense number of friends in our army before he allowed his name to be used by the "peace at any price party." But although they like him, they do not like the Chicago platform, nor the southern sympathizer, [Ohio Congressman George] Pendleton, candidate for vice president.
>
> As an illustration, Gen. [Charles] Griffin, commanding our division, has always been a strong McClellan man (as are in fact most generals of our army), and he has been looking for a long time to see him set up by the war democrats as their candidate. But when he read the proceedings of the Chicago convention, their platform, and saw Pendleton on the same ticket with McClellan, he said he was sorry to see George in bad company.[1]

Pendleton had opposed the war from the start. He sympathized with the South and slave owners, and was close to the leaders and aims of the "Copperheads," Northern men who actively opposed the Lincoln administration and the war effort. Though McClellan eventually declared he would not seek an immediate halt to the war if elected, many Union soldiers were not impressed. What would happen, Salter asked, if McClellan should win the election, but then die in office? The captain said the soldiers knew the answer—the war would end quickly, the Confederacy would live on, and the sacrifice of the lives of thousands of Union troops would have been in vain.

An officer from the 16th Michigan, writing to the Republican newspaper in Flint, agreed with Salter: Most troops would not support the Democratic ticket. "Our soldiers talk not of 'peace on any terms'—of an armistice to enable the Rebels to recruit exhausted resources," this officer wrote. "But they talk of peace, honorable to our name and history, *secured by total overthrow of armed traitors.* This being their sentiment, many friends of the 'Young Napoleon' have dropped him since the Chicago convention." Soldier Henry "Tip" Aplin of Flint thought so. Now 23, he had been sick and out of the ranks for most of the summer, but he told his sister he was not supporting the Democratic ticket. "Tip says he is voting for Lincoln," Sarah Aplin wrote, passing word to their brother George.[2]

Capt. Salter was assigned to the post of acting inspector general for the Third Brigade and that kept him busy in what were generally quiet times marked by two major events. First, the Confederate cavalry conducted a raid behind Union lines there at Petersburg a few days earlier, rustling what he said were 4,200 head of cattle, though it was actually about 2,500. Either way, it was an embarrassment for the army. Second, the men received welcome news that Union cavalry commander Gen. Phil Sheridan had won a major (but not final) victory over Gen. Jubal Early's troublesome force in the Shenandoah Valley, where Union troopers were about to begin a systematic but terrible campaign of destruction of thousands of productive farms, fields, and livestock that had helped feed the Confederacy. It would prove devastating.[3]

POPLAR GROVE CHURCH OR PEEBLE'S FARM

The 16th Michigan and their brigade and division, in the meantime, were back on the offensive on September 30, rising at 4 a.m. but not moving out for four hours. "We all thought that there was to be no move but soon saw Warren and Griffin come along," Brady Company sharpshooter Alfred Apted noted. "And then we made up our minds that somebody would be hurt." Capt. Salter, who had been assigned to work on the brigade staff, reported back to his regiment, where he was acting in the capacity of major. With their brigade leading the march, their division moved west with their corps' Second Division; marching with them were two divisions of the Ninth Corps. Once away from the Union breastworks, the soldiers marched through scrubby woods and brush on a route through the country south of Petersburg. It led to a church at the intersection of an oddly named road going south, the Squirrel Level Road.

The Union objective was another rail line, still intact and several miles away, that ran from the west into Petersburg. This was the Southside Railroad, and of course Confederate forces were trying to protect it and other main roads with lines of earthworks and forts. Salter thought his men moved three miles when the skirmishing began—Pvt. Apted thought it was a mile and a half. Their division commander was said to have ordered the 20th Maine into the advance as skirmishers, with the 16th Michigan to its left. As the Maine regiment moved into position to begin the attack, Lt. Col. Ellis Spear passed Col. Norval Welch. "Goodbye," Welch said to him. "I will meet you on the other side of the water." The regiments moved forward and rifle fire "announced we had found the pups," Apted wrote. "There we had a skirmish and [they] were quickly driven in with small loss to either side."[4]

From the intersection at the Poplar Grove Church (sometimes given as Poplar Spring Church), the Confederate skirmishers left their rifle pits and dropped back as the 16th Michigan and other regiments of their brigade came on, pursuing the Rebels into more woods. The position ahead, called Fort McRae (also given as Fort Archer), was built on a farm owned by a man named Peeble, with another fortification on the property of a family named Pegram, on a ridge about a half mile away. This ground was open, and the position was defended by more than a brigade of dismounted Confederate cavalry troopers and infantry; on either side of the fort were strong trenches, and it was protected by a wall of sharp wooden stakes. Here the Union troops were no longer advancing as skirmishers—now they would make a full-fledged attack in line of battle. "[We] soon came in sight of a long line of the enemy's earthworks with a strong fort in the center," Salter wrote. "We formed in line, our brigade on the right, the Second Brigade on the left of the division line, and Gen. Griffin ordered us to charge their works."

It was around noon when the order came. Griffin's division emerged from the woods and Confederate fire immediately erupted. As sharpshooter Apted stood in the battle line in the moments before the charge began, a spent minié ball struck him on the right shoulder "but did no damage." The 16th Michigan was on the right of their brigade line and the 118th Pennsylvania on the left as they led the charge. A Confederate battery in the fortifications, four guns, blasted at them as they ran the few hundred yards to the abatis. The soldiers cut and smashed a passage through this barricade of stakes wide enough for eight men, and the Pennsylvanian and Michigan troops went through by fours, side by side.[5]

"We went forward on the double-quick over a field ½ mile wide," Salter wrote. "The rebels poured a heavy fire of musketry, grape shot and canister into us, yet the line never wavered nor halted, but pushed on until we arrived at the enemy's works." Pvt. Apted called it "the cussedest [sic, damndest] fire of musketry and cannon ever! It was the worst fire that a mortal ever endured. But still the line moved forward in good stride and when within about four rods [just under 70 feet] of the rebel fort, a minie struck me, going through my left arm and side and lodging in my knapsack." Though Apted undoubtedly reeled and fell, he eventually got to his feet and, able to walk, headed to the rear as his comrades rushed the fort. His corps' commander, Gen. Gouverneur Warren, called the charge "one of the boldest I ever saw."

The charging soldiers reached the trench outside of the fort, and Welch, ahead of his regiment, jumped it, shouting to his men, "come on," according to the regiment's acting quartermaster, Capt. Thomas Frank Powers. Powers was not with the regiment, but probably witnessed the attack. The men scrambled up the embanked walls with Welch in the lead. A *New York Herald* journalist wrote that the colonel waved his sword as he climbed, and shouted: "A commission to him who first mounts the parapet of that redoubt! Follow me!" This dialogue was likely created by the newspaper, yet it was truly a dramatic moment as Welch climbed to the top of the wall. "A private named Scott was the first over and myself the second," Salter said. "Our colonel stood on top of the works, urging the men to get over." Scott was Walter Scott, a member of the Brady Sharpshooters who had joined the company in Detroit as a teenager in the fall of 1861. He was immediately wounded.[6]

But it was in that instant that a dismounted Rebel trooper with a carbine drew a bead on Col. Norval Welch, according to members of the 118th Pennsylvania. "He was shot through the head and fell dead," Salter wrote. The captain thought that Welch had been hit with two rifle bullets, though the Pennsylvanians later wrote it was a single shot. One shot or two—it did not matter. Salter was immediately at Welch's side and it was clear he had been instantly killed. Thomas Lackie, the Detroit soldier who decades later wrote that Major Robert Elliott was fatally shot while asking him for a match, also said that he was behind Welch when he was killed. Lackie claimed it was a Rebel artillery officer who shot the colonel, though he probably based this on a contemporaneous illustration of the colonel's death in *Harper's Weekly* that Salter said "was not correct at all." But Lackie wrote that Welch tumbled back, knocking him over.[7]

"Yet the men got over and the rebels left the breastworks," Salter continued. His brief mention that the Confederates "left" their fort was modest, if not understated. Capt. Powers, who quickly sent an account back to Detroit, said there was hand-to-hand fighting; Major Benjamin Partridge of the 16th Michigan, who was commanding the 83rd Pennsylvania that day and fighting nearby, also said that the Michigan soldiers engaged "in a hand-to-hand fight for some time," calling it "desperate in the extreme." Partridge himself barely escaped death when a shot tore across his lower jaw and went through his neck and shoulder, exiting near his spine "under the collar button on the back" of his uniform. He later said this bullet nicked the jugular, yet luck was with him and he did not bleed to death, though officers who saw him wounded and fall were convinced he he'd been killed.[8]

With Union soldiers pouring over the fort's walls and engaging Confederates in a close-quarters fight, the Rebel gun crews hauled off their battery and retreated with some of their soldiers. Salter, now the senior officer of the 16th Michigan present, said he captured one gun at the gateway. "We had a short struggle there and captured 47 prisoners whom I sent back to the rear. . . . We did not stop here but pushed right on and gained another slight work about ¼ mile farther on," he wrote. In the meantime, about a half mile away, the 1st Michigan Infantry and the 18th Massachusetts took another fort. The victorious soldiers of the Fifth Corps' First Division cheered as Gen. Griffin rode proudly along their line of captured forts and works.

It was likely during this break in the fighting that soldiers of the 16th Michigan who were carrying the unusual two-hammered, two-barreled Lindsay rifle, given to some if not all of them, ditched this complicated and undependable weapon. Ellis Spear, who had declined to take the rifles for the 20th Maine, later wrote that "[Welch's] men threw all of them away & replaced them from arms left by the killed and wounded."[9]

The men rested for a moment as the Ninth Corps' divisions, "coming up, passed us and going on to the front, engaged the enemy," Salter wrote. The Confederates who retreated from the Ft. McRae line had fallen back, but now their reinforcements arrived. "And soon [A. P.] Hill's corps came up and charged the Ninth, who to our surprise, broke and ran, and we were ordered to advance to meet the enemy," he continued. It was early evening when part of this corps collapsed, Salter said, and Griffin's First Division went to meet the Rebel counterattack.

> Our brigade, yet in front, moved out by the right flank, every man in his place as if going on parade, officers mounted. . . . My regiment being the last in the brigade was thus placed on the extreme left and most exposed. We were just in line when the enemy opened fire with a battery and the solid shot plowed through the ranks, piling up 7 or 8 dead and wounding many more, and the column reeled like a drunken man.
>
> Yet none of them ran to the rear, and fortunately at that time, we were ordered to move off the field a short distance to the right, where we got position on the brow of a small hill, the 9th Corps rushing past us to the rear, and our brigade, standing like a stone wall, pouring our fire into friend and foe alike. It was a fearful struggle, and a terrible alternative, but we had to do it or our own ranks would be broken. Soon the rebels were within 10 feet of us, pouring a withering fire into our ranks, but we checked them.
>
> And our 2nd Brigade just then came up and, strengthening our line, poured such a fire into the enemy that they fell back, and our batteries just getting into position opened fire on them, and assisted their retreat.[10]

The fighting ceased at dusk, and the regiment remained with its brigade and division in line of battle that night. The victory here "was gained not by our army, but by our brigade," Salter wrote with pride. "For if it had not been for the desperate stand taken by our brigade, the entire 9th Corps would have been driven back in confusion. . . . Their generals seem to be the most utterly incapable men, and their troops the most cowardly of any in our army." Salter was proud that the division commander, Gen. Griffin, personally thanked him after the battle.

Meanwhile, Brady Sharpshooter Pvt. Apted made it to the rear, probably to a temporary field hospital, where his wounds were dressed by a surgeon from the Ninth Corps. He had not been there long before the wounded Maj. Partridge was also brought in. Apted learned that their brigade and division had carried the Confederate works. By that evening, he was moved back to the Union railroad line and placed on a car that took him and other wounded men to City Point, the great Union army depot on the James River east of Petersburg. There he was cared for overnight by U.S. Christian Commission staff, and in the morning went to the Fifth Corps hospital. "Wound very painful," Apted wrote, "though thank God no bones were broken. I will soon get well." In fact, a surgeon eventually removed a fragment of bone from his arm, and then advised Apted that the arm should be amputated; Apted refused. But he lost the use of his left arm, and his active service in the army was over. He mustered out in March 1865, and went home to Grand Rapids.

But Apted soon found wounded comrades there in the Fifth Corps hospital on October 1, including Walter Scott, and he learned that Welch was dead; he made no comment on his commanding officer. "The regiment suffered severely though but few killed—many wounded," he noted. Capt. Salter, now in command of the regiment, wrote that the 16th Michigan went into the battle at Peeble's Farm with only 175 men, losing their colonel and nine men killed and their major and thirty-seven men wounded, though the regiment's death toll rose to eighteen as wounded soldiers died in the aftermath.[11]

Salter, who in June angrily predicted that God would mete punishment to men such as Welch, also made no further comment about the colonel. At the time Salter wrote those harsh words, he had been angry that Welch, while in Detroit, said unkind things about Major Robert Elliott, a brave officer who sometimes drank to excess and who was fatally wounded soon after near Bethesda Church. Salter had known that Welch stayed away from the regiment during the spring campaign, and resented it. Like many officers, Welch had curried political favor for his advancement. And though Welch boldly led the men at Gaines' Mill, at least one of his captains, in a letter to Detroit, criticized his conduct at Gettysburg; Benjamin Partridge, after the war, also questioned Welch's actions there.

In terms of military history, Welch's death as he bravely led the 16th Michigan's charge at Peeble's Farm would be overshadowed by the remembrance of him as the regimental commander who fled the fighting on Little Round Top as his regiment was overwhelmed, making him, perhaps, one of the tragic figures of the Civil War. From that perspective, Charles Salter's terrible prediction indeed came to pass. Part of a letter by Henry "Tip" Aplin, thought to have been written that October, seems to refer to Welch in terms of a surprising familiarity and friendship—somewhat atypical for a soldier and his commanding officer. Welch's name does not appear in the surviving portion of Aplin's letter, but it tells of an officer killed in battle, who had the authority to take Aplin out of the battle line that day—indications that he was writing about Col. Welch. Aplin had suffered diarrhea that summer and he was often weak, "just the same as the rest of the boys," he wrote. But this unnamed officer made quite an exception for Aplin. "He was a good friend to me," Aplin told his sister. "I never yet asked him for anything but what I got it. This summer when I have not felt well he always got another man to take my place and told me to go to the wagon train or hospital or anywhere I wanted to.

"The day he was killed," Aplin continued, "he got another man to take my place and told me to go to the wagon train and stay until I got well." This unnamed officer had done Aplin a tremendous favor, excusing him from the battle line. If this officer was not Welch, then to whom did Aplin refer? No other officer from the 16th Michigan was killed at Pebble's Farm. Was it a coincidence that Aplin had been listed as a potential witness in Welch's court-martial, when early in 1863, Col. Stockton accused Welch of improperly dining with Aplin and three other enlisted men assigned to work with supply officers?

Rufus Jacklin, who was a friend of Capt. Salter's, undoubtedly knew of Welch's shortcomings, but also witnessed his bravery. When it came to the colonel's death at Peeble's Farm, Jacklin remembered him with reverence. "Honor to his sacred memory," Jacklin wrote of Welch, "for his gallant and dashing conduct on this field." After the battle the body of Norval Welch was embalmed, probably at City Point, and sent home to Michigan in the care of one "Capt. Finely," who was described as a commissary, classmate, and fellow townsman, for burial in Ann Arbor. Welch's remains were interred in Forest Hill cemetery after a military and Masonic funeral.[12]

Union generals had hoped the attack on the Confederates forts would break through to the targeted rail line, but that had not happened. The soldiers had lengthened the Union line stretching around Petersburg and pushed the Rebels back, but that was all. "Had the Second Corps been with us instead of the Ninth, we could have gained the Southside Railroad," Capt. Salter wrote. "I cannot say I am very anxious to push ahead with such men as the Ninth Corps with us. Our men hate them about as much as the rebels." The 16th Michigan remained in the line of battle near Peeble's Farm on October 2, and a heavy thunderstorm blew in, but they buried their dead and dug new lines of breastworks. Now the place was called Fort Welch. The Confederates periodically shelled the Union positions in the days after the battle, but eventually stopped.[13]

Though the 16th Michigan was just a fraction of its original strength, there was still much to do, since Salter and four lieutenants were the remaining officers at that moment, though promotions would soon create several new captains to command companies; one vacancy had been created when Capt. Frank Eddy of Flint left to become the lieutenant colonel of a new regiment, the 29th Michigan Infantry. Now it was Salter's job to run the 16th Michigan, assisted by the acting quartermaster, Captain Powers. Salter soon knew that Major Benjamin Partridge was recovering from his wound, and that when he returned, Partridge would probably be commissioned lieutenant colonel. But what would that mean for Salter? Would he formally become the regiment's major? "There is another captain absent wounded who outranks me," Salter wrote about Edward Hill, who had been seriously wounded in the fighting near Bethesda Church, "and so if I do not yet get promoted to major right away I shall not complain. Yet if another than that one should be promoted over me, it would take me only about 30 minutes to make out my muster-out papers, take them to the division mustering officer, and be made a citizen." After all, he had served just over three years and he could resign his commission at any time. Yet he did not want to do that. "I feel it is my duty to remain," he wrote, "and take care of it as long as it has so few officers."[14]

On October 14, the men of the 16th Michigan learned from the newspapers that Guy Fuller, the former captain from Ionia, had been killed—"murdered by guerillas"—as he worked as conductor on a military railroad operated by the army near Manassas. Though Fuller should have been promoted earlier in the summer to the post of lieutenant colonel, Michigan's governor had not given him the commission. Fuller, who had been the senior captain, had led the regiment after the death of Major Robert Elliott, while Welch was away from the regiment. Fuller probably saw the refusal of the governor to commission him to lieutenant colonel as an insult, but he remained with the regiment until mustering out on September 7 with the men who had served out their original three-year hitches. The train on which he was working when he was killed, on the old Orange & Alexandria line, may have been raided by Confederate cavalry under Col. John S. Mosby. "The old officers of the 16th seem to be unlucky, and to be stepping off every few days," Salter continued. "The Major [Partridge], Captain [Edward] Hill (absent wounded), and myself are the only old officers now with the regt., either present or absent."

Salter said the men in the field were amused to read about the draft in Michigan, and he had been surprised to read an article that mentioned him in the Peeble's Farm battle in the *Detroit Advertiser and Tribune*. "I was considerably surprised, as I have always avoided newspaper notoriety, when I could. But, come to find out it was Captain [Thomas Frank] Powers of our regt. who wrote it. He was, at the time, acting quartermaster, and so not with the regt., therefore, did not do full justice to our last engagement that day, when we repulsed [A. P.] Hill's Corp. But he gave me more praise than I deserve, for I did nothing but my duty."[15]

October went on in a relatively quiet vein for the 16th Michigan, though Salter expected that another attack on the Confederate positions could be ordered at any time. He played a small part of media critic for his friends back home when he told that *Frank Leslie's* newspaper, and not *Harper's,* had the most accurate illustration of the death of Norval Welch. "Speaking of that picture in Harper's of Col. Welch jumping over the works, it is not correct at all as he never got over the works, but was shot whilst on top of them. You would have seen in Frank Leslie's of that same date a picture of our charge as correct as anything possibly could be, where Col. Welch being shot, is falling over backward and Capt. S. [Salter] is by his side, the men rapidly getting over."

Salter had heard from one of the sergeants that one of the regiment's officers, recently promoted Capt. George F. Kilets of Lexington, back in Michigan, was lobbying influential people to try to get promoted to the major's post. This worried Salter, and he vowed he would resign and go home if Kilets was promoted over Capt. Edward Hill and himself. But Salter had nothing to worry about. That same day, Major Benjamin Partridge, back in Bay City recovering from his wounding at Peeble's Farm, wrote to Michigan's adjutant general. In his letter, he recommended that he (Partridge) should be commissioned lieutenant colonel, and that Capt. Hill, who had also survived what soldiers thought was a fatal wound, become major. These recommendations were accepted by Gov. Blair, so Salter remained the regiment's senior captain, for the time being.[16]

The next day their commander, Gen. Grant, ordered Gen. Meade to prepare to make a three-pronged attack, with cavalry, to cut the Southside Railroad into Petersburg. The generals received information that the Confederate trenches were being extended west to a point where a creek through the woods called Hatcher's Run crossed under the Vaughan Road; these defenses were not finished, and presumably vulnerable. The plan was to send a force of at least 30,000 soldiers from three different corps, plus batteries and a division of troopers, to strike, flank, and crush this end of the Confederate line. The targeted railroad was just north of these positions, so destroying them would allow the Union army to stop trains from bringing supplies to the Rebels by this route.

HATCHER'S RUN OR BOYDTON PLANK ROAD

But moving these three wings for coordinated attacks in a predawn darkness, through an unfamiliar wooded countryside, was easier said than done. On October 27, the men of the Fifth Corps, in the middle section of this movement, were moving at 4 a.m.—a full ninety minutes earlier than Gen. Warren wanted, but he was overruled by Meade. The corps' First Division, which included the 16th Michigan, left their camp near the forts and trenches built since the battle at Peeble's Farm, leading their corps in what would be a three-mile march to the west. The early start in the darkness, however, did not go well. The various brigades became separated and mixed, and only when there was sufficient light in the sky did the lead regiments move into the woods out beyond their trenches as a light rain fell. Then the Fifth Corps' column moved too far to the southwest as they tried to stay in position with other advancing Union troops. Warren soon put his men to work cutting a road west through the woods to a road that brought the 16th Michigan's First Division into contact with Rebel skirmishers at 9 a.m. A brigade from their division advanced and drove these Confederates back through the woods near Hatcher's Run—and found them in strong defenses ahead.

So to, in the meantime, did Union soldiers in the two corps to their left (west) and right (east), striking Rebels along a main route into Petersburg called the Boydton Plank Road. These were not weak, unfinished trenches, but solid breastworks with plenty of defenders. Warren was ordered to send one of his divisions across Hatcher's Run to help the Second Corps, to the Fifth Corps' left, but the brigade and division of which the 16th Michigan were part remained on the other side of the creek and engaged the Rebels there in skirmish fire early in the afternoon. "We skirmished with the enemy all day long, and took up our position quite close to their works there that guard the Southside railroad, until towards night," Capt. Salter wrote.[17]

But almost nothing went right with the Union advance that afternoon; there were problems as the Union generals were unable to coordinate their moves in thick woods, confusing branches of the creek, and heavy rain. Meanwhile, the Confederate commander here, Gen. Heth, ordered his lieutenants to attack this flanking move with all available forces. Troops from both sides became lost and confused as they maneuvered and clashed in this area of forest along Hatcher's Run, south of the plank road. The Union troops furthest to the west, from the Second Corps, were attacked and some nearly surrounded by the Confederates. Union losses there were heavy, yet soldiers also took hundreds of Rebels prisoner in the confusion. Late that day, these Union troops retreated. The Fifth Corps' men remained in their positions that night, with the 16th Michigan on the east side of Hatcher's Run with its division. "Our corps remained there until [the] next morning, when we also received orders to fall back," Salter wrote. "But our brigade was to cover the retreat, and was deployed as skirmishers on the front line and remained there until noon, when as all of our corps had gone back, we fell back slowly."

Salter said nothing about the 16th Michigan suffering casualties that day, and the regiment's roster published later by Michigan's adjutant general's office, as well as a "Roll of Honor" also produced decades later, suggest none of the regiment's men were killed in their division's skirmishing near Hatcher's Run. But the assault that Grant envisioned would crush the western end of the Rebel defenses and cut the Southside Railroad had failed. Salter said the Rebel cavalry closely followed the retreating Union soldiers, but did not engage them. By 4 p.m. on October 28, "we arrived back in our old camp," Salter wrote. "And so ended the greatest reconnaissance our army ever saw." With the rail line from the west remaining intact, supplies would continue to reach Lee's Petersburg defenders. The war would go on, but for now, at least, the soldiers went into winter quarters.[18]

Election commissioners arrived from Michigan to conduct the polling of troops in the 16th and 1st Michigan for the presidential election, and they stayed with Capt. Salter. Although the 16th Michigan had been formed by Flint Democrat Thomas B. W. Stockton, and many of the original officers had also been Democrats, most soldiers would vote for President Lincoln's reelection, Salter predicted. "Our regiment, as you are probably aware, came out as a Democratic regiment, so-called, but I am morally certain that in this election, we will cast a big majority for Lincoln and [Andrew] Johnson," he told friends. "All the officers in the regiment but two go in for the Union side, and one of them has already sent in his resignation on the ground of incompetency. I forwarded it, approved and recommended for the good of the service."[19]

Though the Army of the Potomac did indeed vote overwhelmingly for Lincoln, giving him 13,500 votes to McClellan's 5,500, the 16th Michigan voted for its former general by a slim majority, eighty-one to seventy-eight. This was embarrassing to Salter, who claimed that two of the regiment's officers had "worked as hard as they could to get the men to vote for McClellan and did influence a great many of them that way." He contemptuously dismissed these officers, whom he did not name, as "not our fighting officers, but . . . a captain on the brigade staff and our quartermaster, men who never go near the field of battle." Salter was proud that this was his second time voting for Lincoln.

By now Salter had learned that Capt. Edward Hill, whom the soldiers thought was mortally wounded back near Bethesda Church on June 1, was being commissioned as the 16th Michigan's new major. Hill was the one captain in the regiment who had more seniority than Salter, and Salter considered him a good officer. But Salter wondered if Hill could fulfill the duties of the regiment's major. After all, Hill was carrying a bullet in his abdomen and it was considered a miracle that he survived. If it turned out that Hill could not physically handle the job, then Salter expected to become major. Because of this uncertain situation, Salter decided to remain with the regiment.[20]

The weather turned rainy as the soldiers completed their winter tents. Salter said his had log walls six feet high, a fire place, a canvas roof, and a plank floor, with boards removed "from the house of Col. Pegram of the rebel army for tables, chairs and shelves." He had heard that a friend from Detroit had mustered out of the army and was settling down to study law, and he wondered about his own future once the war was over. "It sometimes seems to me that I never could settle down into civil life again after the exciting life I had led for the last three years," he wrote.[21]

One soldier from the 16th Michigan who had the adventure of a lifetime that month was a 20-year-old from Detroit named Edward Kelly, a member of the Brady Sharpshooters. On the night of November 17, Kelly volunteered to take handbills to the front and deliver them to the pickets, who were to post them where the Confederates would find them. These handbills invited the Rebel soldiers to surrender—if they came into the Union lines, the poster said, they would be treated well and not forced to fight against the Confederacy. Unfortunately for Kelly, in the darkness he walked by the Union picket line and was made prisoner by the Rebels.

According to an account written by a member of the 16th Michigan who signed his dispatch with the initials "J.F.W."—probably Jacob F. Wagar of the Brady Sharpshooters—Kelly was interrogated and sent to Libby prison in Richmond. Confederates took his $60 and watch, though Kelly was able to get $100 in Rebel currency for his gold ring. Over the next four weeks, the extra cornbread and meat he was able to buy kept him from starving, J.F.W. wrote. The Confederates took Kelly's clothing and provided him with Rebel rags; other prisoners also were wearing these, and many had their shoes and boots taken away.[22]

"It was a pitiable sight to see perhaps 80 or 100 men, almost naked, shivering with cold, huddled up on the floor to keep from freezing," J.F.W. continued, "yet they dare not complain and with patient submission permitted those who were barefooted a place nearest the stove. They were allowed three armfuls of wood for every 24 hours to warm a room about 100 feet by 36 feet wide and even this allowance was denied them when they sing Union songs."

Kelly befriended a prisoner named Ambrose Burdick and together they planned to escape. According to J.F.W.'s lively account, there was a crack in one of the prison walls large enough that Rebels could reach through to sell food to the prisoners. The two men drew lots to crawl through this crack to see if there was a way out. Burdick lost, and went through the gap, presumably at night. He returned to tell Kelly that on the other side of the crack was another room, wet and slimy, but without a floor. There was a grate covering a kind of passage, or opening, the story continued, and in turn led out onto a roof top. Of course, J.F.W.'s description of cracks in prison walls and dank passageways leading to the roof sounds like a romantic drama, and it was perhaps meant to confuse any Confederate authority who might read the account. But the men "laid flat on the roof, in the gutter, until the guard had passed, when they arose and walked boldly forth." Since they were wearing Confederate clothing, they passed guards but were not stopped, and walked from Richmond to within a few miles of Union lines, J.F.W. wrote.[23]

Cold and hungry, Kelly proposed the two of them stop at a house to ask for something to eat. But at that moment, some Confederate troopers rode up and, suspecting they were deserters, put them under guard. The two of them insisted they were from a North Carolina regiment to try to put their guard at ease, and they bolted away into some nearby woods when they had a chance. The troopers pursued, firing, but the pair avoided recapture and headed toward Union lines. "They went directly east and finally passed the Rebel pickets, ran up to a Rebel vidette, who halted them and fired. They fled and again hid until about 3 o'clock in the morning, and made their way east, when they crawled forth upon hands and knees towards our campfires."

The two escapees made it to Union lines, where they were warmed and fed and sent, according to J.F.W., to see Gen. Benjamin Butler, though this seems unlikely since that general had been on leave for months and then placed in charge of a Union attack on a coastal North Carolina fort. Whether or not Kelly met the controversial general, he was back with the 16th Michigan by the second week in December. "The above is a simple, unvarnished tale," J.F.W. insisted to a newspaper editor, "and we trust may beguile a few short moments of your readers." A summary of Kelly's service record published by the Michigan Adjutant General's office decades after the war indeed shows that Kelly was taken prisoner while on picket duty on November 17, 1864, and returned to his regiment on December 10. Kelly survived the war and presumably had a fine story to tell in later years.[24]

By early December, the regiment's winter quarters were done—"good enough to live in all winter, if we are allowed to remain," Capt. Salter wrote. He was proud that the army's inspector general had come through to examine the Second, Ninth, and Fifth corps and chose the 16th Michigan's as "the best arranged camp in the army, and our quarters as the best of any in all the camps he had inspected." That was especially important to Salter, since other regiments were commanded by majors, lieutenant colonels, and colonels. The 16th Michigan's streets were graded, and their tents, which housed three or four soldiers each, had log walls and good fireplaces. Unfortunately for the soldiers, they only had days to enjoy their newly constructed winter quarters.

Grant's campaign that started in the spring and continued to Petersburg had been hard on their brigade. Each of its eight regiments, which had come into the Union army with about 1,000 soldiers, now contained between 150 to 400 men, the captain continued. Though he did not say how many new soldiers had come into the 16th Michigan because of the draft, it would soon be scores and even hundreds of men. Salter said he was "busy putting my regiment through a regular course of drill, all the old officers having nearly all left the regiment and the present officers being nearly all new ones." This made his life a bit more difficult, "but we are getting along very well," he added. Salter was having a chapel built for this regiment, and each Sunday, at his request, a member of the U.S. Christian Commission came to address the regiment. "And I try to do everything I can to induce the men to keep a proper observance of the Sabbath, which is something new to our regt."[25]

But just as the coming of winter did not end drill, it also had not yet brought an end to offensive operations. Though the Union army had long since cut the Weldon Railroad that ran up from North Carolina, Confederates continued to utilize the undamaged, southern portion of the line by bringing food and supplies on trains to a point about 30 miles south of Petersburg, beyond the immediate reach of the Union forces. There, the cars were unloaded, and Rebel supplies were placed on wagon trains. By driving miles to the west, these wagons avoided interception by Union soldiers and eventually turned east, reaching Petersburg. But if Union troops destroyed the Weldon Railroad farther south, down to the vicinity of the North Carolina border, that supply route would be rendered unworkable.

Two days after Salter wrote his December 4 letter, the 16th Michigan, along with its brigade and division, left its camp near Poplar Grove Church and moved with the Fifth Corps about five miles east, back to the Weldon Railroad, and there they bivouacked in a field. With another division from the Second Corps and a division of cavalry, the Fifth Corps started the next morning on an initial march of twenty miles almost directly south on the Jerusalem Plank Road. A cold rain began falling on the soldiers as they trudged away from Petersburg.[26]

RAID ON THE WELDON RAILROAD

The First Division of which the 16th Michigan was part followed another division from their corps in an all-day march, and they halted that night in clearing weather, about two miles from the Nottaway River, Salter said. Engineers bridged the river and the leading division moved on; after a short rest, the march resumed for the 16th Michigan and its division at 2 a.m. on December 8, with the soldiers going through Sussex Court House to a point on the railroad called Jarrett's Station. "We then worked until 12 o'clock, tearing up and destroying the railroad track," the captain said. "And our division alone destroyed about 5 miles that evening, then the next day, we marched to within 2 miles of Hick[s] ford, a village near the North Carolina line, destroying the track as we went along and bivouacked overnight." Ellis Spear, commanding the 20th Maine, said the soldiers pried up the rails and ties and piled them in stacks a few feet tall, then set the ties on fire with whatever other wood and fence rails they could find. With a strong wind blowing, these fires blazed and turned the middle of these rails red hot and pliable, allowing the men to twist them around nearby trees.

The Union force was now some forty miles south of Petersburg; between the cavalry and the infantry on the raid, some seventeen or eighteen miles of track were destroyed. There was some skirmishing that did not involve the brigade of which the 16th Michigan was part; but there were strong Rebel positions ahead, and Gen. Warren, the Fifth Corps commander, felt his men had accomplished their mission. A seemingly endless storm of hail, mist, and snow began on that evening of December 9, and Salter said they suffered for some thirty-six hours. "The next morning, the 10th, we started back," he wrote. "The roads were very muddy, and the weather cold and disagreeable." The soldiers had been issued four days' rations before they had started on this mission—there was another two days of food carried on their wagons—so by this point many men had eaten what they had. Of course, hungry soldiers almost always foraged from nearby farms, taking whatever they could carry off from Rebel civilians, and the Fifth Corps men on this raid were no exception.[27]

Sometime before the soldiers began the march back to their Petersburg encampments, some of the foragers discovered barrels of applejack and peach brandy hidden by local residents, and scores of Union troops were drunk as officers were trying to move them out on the morning of the 10th. Captain Salter wrote nothing of this, but other officers and soldiers from the Maine, Massachusetts, and Pennsylvania regiments did. This aspect of the raid—later called "the Applejack Raid" by Union soldiers—might have gone down as a somewhat humorous escapade of soldiers' illicit drinking, were it not for the terrible consequences and aftermath. Word soon spread among the men of the Fifth Corps that the bodies of a few of the soldiers were found along the roadside, murdered by Rebel guerillas. Postwar records say two of these were 16th Michigan soldiers, Michael Shea or Shay, and Daniel Byrman or Dryman, both of Company A.

The soldiers of the Fifth Corps were enraged. It was obvious that there were no men among the civilian residents of the vicinity, only women and children; Gen. Warren reported that his soldiers were aware of evidence that the local men were hiding nearby, "lurking about in the woods." Marion Munson, an Oakland County man who had returned to Company E after being wounded in the left hand near Bethesda Church–Cold Harbor, wrote that "the men [Rebel sympathizers or guerillas] shot some of our men and cut their throats and otherwise mutilated them, those that had squandered [sic, wandered] away from the regiment." His general did not know if these reports were true, but the soldiers on the raid insisted they were—that six or seven soldiers were indeed found murdered in woods just off the road.

Apart from the two Michigan men allegedly murdered, other stragglers from the 16th Michigan who were captured on the march of the 10th were lucky by comparison. Summaries of the records of others in the regiment, published after the war, show five of them were taken prisoner by Confederates—presumably cavalry. These were Michael Brown and Henry Davenport of Company A, William O'Keif and John Farul or Faviel of Jardine's Sharpshooters, and John Hardwick of Company F.[28]

But the report of the murders brought angry reprisals that fell heavily on nearby residents, whose homes and outbuildings were destroyed by outraged Union troops. "We . . . left a track of fire on our return march by burning nearly every house and barn on the route," Salter wrote of the destruction, without explaining what had happened. "In fact, we destroyed everything on our route through the country that could be of use to the rebels in any way, shape or manner." Marion Munson of Company E, knowing that the soldiers wanted vengeance for the murders, felt awful about the destruction of the civilian homes. "I was on a raid this fall [winter], may God forbid of the enemy making the like through Michigan or any northern state," he wrote. "We burnt the houses over the peoples' heads and destroyed everything that came in our way," he wrote. "It looked hard to see the women crying, no shelter from the storm."

Munson thought the war was coming to a close, but was troubled by the harm done to these civilians. "Everything is lawful in war time, but let us hope that the so-longed look for [i.e., Union victory] is near at hand," he told a friend, "and when that does come, may it be in such a manner that is right and just. I think that we have some rights, and we should stand by those rights . . . but not because we [who] are strong play the part of the tyrant."[29]

The march back to the Petersburg front, in miserable weather and over muddy roads, took two days. The 16th Michigan, with their corps, arrived on the night of December 12 and bivouacked in woods about four miles south of the works and winterized quarters they had left on the 6th. Now the soldiers had to again rebuild their winter camps. The cold, stormy weather continued, just as bad as a typical Michigan winter. "It seems as if we were not to be allowed to go into winter quarters at all, but to keep up the campaign all winter," Capt. Salter wrote. "It seems hard but I suppose we shall have to stand it as long as we can."[30]

But in fact, Salter, in charge of the regiment since the death of Col. Welch, did not have to stand it at all anymore. He had been in the original ninety-day 1st Michigan before he had been made a second lieutenant with Stockton's Independent Regiment in the summer of 1861, and it appears that every other officer with whom he had originally served was gone; he had been a conscientious soldier, and awarded the brevet (honorary) rank of major for his bravery all through the 1864 battles and skirmishes. Now Benjamin Partridge, who had come into the regiment early in 1862 from the Michigan lancers, was returning to the regiment as lieutenant colonel, having recovered from his wound at Peeble's Farm. Perhaps Salter reasoned that the regiment was in capable hands and he could go home at last.

But it is also possible that Salter was dissatisfied about the position of major in the 16th Michigan. It was being filled, at least on paper, by Edward Hill, the senior captain and Partridge's choice; they had been in the lancers together. Though Salter felt Hill was a good officer, he almost certainly learned that Hill was not physically able to rejoin the 16th Michigan at the front because of his wound—in other words, Hill was being promoted to major in spite of the fact that he could not and would not be able to do the job. Regimental records show that Hill was in Michigan during the last months of the war in 1865, assigned to a camp for drafted men in Jackson. If Salter was aggrieved at this, feeling that he should have the post of major since Hill could not serve with the regiment, it may have been the deciding factor for him to resign at last.

Within about a month of writing that last letter to his friends in Detroit, Charles H. Salter mustered out of the army in January 1865 and left the 16th Michigan. But those soldiers he left behind at Petersburg were sure that the final curtain would soon be falling on the Confederacy and the conflict. "The end of this war is drawing to a close," Marion Munson wrote as 1864 ended. "I think that we will be able to settle on old Abe's terms soon if we keep on as we have of late. If we can get the main spring of the Confederacy broke, then we will have the thing our own way."[31]

19.

DECEMBER 1864–APRIL 1865

A BLUE WHIPLASH ENCIRCLING LEE

Back at the Petersburg front after the raid on the Weldon Railroad, the 16th Michigan and the Third Brigade built their new winter camps in mid-December with their division and corps in the country south of town, in the area between the Halifax Road to the west and the Jerusalem Plank Road on the east. The soldiers enjoyed gifts of foodstuffs and treats from the national sanitary and Christian commissions around Christmas, while the winter weather continued bitterly cold into the New Year. But the men were well supplied, and the news for the Union cause was good: Gen. William T. Sherman's men were cutting a swath of destruction through the South and the Confederates suffered serious defeats in Tennessee. There were Rebel civilian refugees on the road, food shortages, and rampant inflation; the Confederacy was not just shrinking, but coming apart. Hungry soldiers continued to desert the Petersburg defenses, even as new men entered the Union army by conscription and for bounties offered Northern enlistees.[1]

The brigade of which the 16th Michigan was part now included the 20th Maine, the 83rd Pennsylvania, the 1st Michigan, the 32nd Massachusetts, and the 118th and 155th Pennsylvania regiments, and soon the 1st Maine Sharpshooters would join them. The regiment itself was under the command of Col. Benjamin F. Partridge of Bay City, who had begun his military service in the fall of 1861 as a second lieutenant in the ill-fated Michigan lancer regiment, and who had just returned to the Petersburg front after recovering from what some had thought was a fatal wound while leading the 83rd Pennsylvania at Peeble's Farm.

Partridge, 42, a Michigan native, was a former sheriff, surveyor, and businessman who had taught school and studied law as a young man, and it was said he had provided for his widowed mother and siblings since he was 14. A Mason and a Baptist, he abstained from alcohol (at least later in his life, if not also during the war). He turned 39 as the conflict began, leaving his wife and children that fall to join the lancers as an officer, and then following Capt. Judd Mott, and then-Lt. Edward Hill, with the two companies who joined Stockton's regiment early in 1862; he was subsequently wounded at Malvern Hill and, lightly, at Gettysburg, where, having been promoted to captain that spring of 1863, he led Company C. Since then, Partridge had been back leading ex-lancers in Company I; was promoted to major after the death of Robert Elliott near Bethesda Church; and had just been commissioned to the position of full colonel in mid-December. Thomas Lackie, a Detroit private who would survive the war, later claimed that the men gave Partridge a nickname—"Old Pheasant"—playing off his last name, and perhaps his personality.[2]

The soldiers enjoyed a few weeks of quiet in January, but that changed as Grant and Meade learned that the Confederates were moving supplies on wagon trains that came from the southwest to Petersburg on the Boydton Plank Road, which Confederates continued protecting with lines of trenches as it neared town by Hatcher's Run. This was the area where, in late October, the Union generals tried unsuccessfully to smash the Rebels' western positions. This time, they wanted their attacking force to move miles further to the southwest, where the plank road left a small hamlet called Dinwiddie Court House on its way to Petersburg. To defeat Confederate defenders here and disrupt this supply route, Union infantry and cavalry would have to cross flooded creeks in a region of generally open country but with hills and ravines and swamps, some of it covered with scrubby brush; where there were woods in this area, they could be nearly impenetrable for soldiers in battle formation.

The 16th Michigan's Fifth Corps and other Union corps were to support a cavalry division on this attack. The regiment, with their Third Brigade, now under the command of Brig. Gen. Alfred Pearson of the 155th Pennsylvania, moved at 6:30 a.m. on February 5, going south several miles along the Weldon Railroad and Halifax Road with their corps; then they turned on roads to the southwest. Late in the morning, their columns reached the point where two winding streams, Hatcher's Run and Gravelly Run, met to form Rowanty Creek. The soldiers ahead of their brigade engaged and drove off some dismounted Rebel troopers at the creek; then they waded the freezing water—some reportedly crossed on ice—while others cut down trees to make an impromptu bridge. Still others built a proper bridge that wagons and batteries could cross. The First Division of the Fifth Corps followed next, and crossed the creek at about 2:30 p.m. The head of their column reached the Vaughan Road, which, at this point, led west to the hamlet of Dinwiddie Court House. The soldiers marched on, stopping east of the village, where their generals wanted them to link with Union cavalry. These troopers captured eighteen Confederate wagons and fifty prisoners—not the big haul they anticipated. Gen. Pearson reported that his brigade was about three miles from the court house when they halted with their division and formed a line of battle in the countryside. They also set up a bivouac, expecting to rest there that night.[3]

But then the Union commanders' plan changed dramatically. A few miles to the northeast, elements of their Second Corps, whose job it was to protect the Fifth Corps' flank, had run into Confederates that day, blocking their way on the Vaughan Road where it crossed Hatcher's Run. Though the Union troops drove these Rebels off, their advance along the creek again brought them to the strong Confederate fortifications guarding the Boydton Plank Road. Confederate generals decided to counterattack this advance that afternoon near Hatcher's Run at a place called Armstrong's Mill, but the Union soldiers fought this assault to a standstill.

It was because of this fighting that Warren, the Fifth Corps commander, was ordered by Gen. Meade to move back to the northeast, to concentrate Union forces at the Hatcher's Run–Vaughan Road intersection, since generals learned that a larger Rebel attack was coming. The 16th Michigan and their comrades in the Third Brigade were in their division picket line outside of Dinwiddie Court House when the order to withdraw reached them at 11:30 p.m. Their brigade covered the others as they pulled back, since it was known Rebel cavalry had been in the vicinity.[4]

DABNEY'S MILL

Though it was only a few miles from their location outside of Dinwiddie Court House to the intersection of the Vaughan Road and Hatcher's Run, it took all night for officers to carefully bring in the pickets, break their bivouac, and move through the darkness in the biting cold. The soldiers of the 16th Michigan and their brigade got a brief rest once there, and were sent at 10 a.m. on February 6 into unfinished breastworks near Armstrong's Mill, where they relieved soldiers from the Second Corps. The men completed these trenches, which stretched from the creek into the sandy, brush-covered country to the Vaughan Road. The Michigan soldiers waited in reserve with their division, while other Union troops and cavalry moved out in force that afternoon, searching south and west for the Confederates they knew had to be nearby.[5]

Their Fifth Corps comrades in another division found the Rebels about a mile to the west, at a lumber cutting site called Dabney's Mill on a creek. The fighting began, and then more fighting ignited nearby on the Vaughan Road to the south. The soldiers of the 16th Michigan and their brigade could only hear this fighting, but the firing grew in intensity as more troops were sent in, and the battle at the mill seesawed back and forth. Then Confederate reinforcements arrived. Gen. Warren said he had been "reserving for myself General Griffin's Third Brigade (his largest and best)," but decided it was now needed to help hold the Union line. At about 4 p.m. the 16th Michigan and the regiments of the brigade moved out of their trenches to support their comrades, and advanced into a marshy strip of woods near the scene of the fighting at the sawmill. A Rebel battery of three-inch guns opened fire, "killing and wounding a few of my men," Gen. Pearson reported. Some shells ripped through the branches above the soldiers' heads as they waited to be sent in.[6]

It was not long. The Third Brigade formed in a line of battle and moved into the open, in close support behind the Union troops fighting near the mill. Then orders came that sent the regiments of their brigade running to different critical hot spots in the fight; Gen. Romeyn Ayres, one of the Fifth Corps' division commanders who had his hands full as his men were hard pressed, ordered Pearson to send another regiment to help his men, so the 16th Michigan went in "with orders to the commanding officer (Colonel Partridge) to hold the position as long as possible." The Michigan troops hurried forward over the mucky ground, seemingly to the skirmish line. The historians of the 118th Pennsylvania wrote that "the Michigan skirmishers, with the 32nd Massachusetts and the 155th Pennsylvania, were the first of the brigade to come in contact with the enemy." Partridge later said he was struck on the right leg by a spent shell fragment, but did not go to a hospital. "Both officers and men of the old 16th went bravely at work to accomplish the task before them," wrote a proud 16th Michigan officer, probably Lt. James N. Nellis.[7]

But what happened next was embarrassing and tragic for some of the Union soldiers. Gen. Pearson and various soldiers claimed that as this fight raged, other troops from the Fifth Corps or the Sixth Corps, or both, mistakenly fired into their comrades in the Third Brigade, causing them to break and run. Some Union men blamed their own generals for the collapse, saying that their troops had been extended too far, too fast, and that their reserves had been poorly placed. But there were hundreds of inexperienced recruits present who had never been in battle and who probably did not know whether the troops in front of them were friend or foe. Some fired into their comrades, and the Union line crumbled as soldiers fled from Dabney's Mill.

An officer from the 16th Michigan who signed his letter "Lt. A.J.W."—Lt. Arnold J. West of Jardine's Sharpshooters company—said his regiment "took a brave and active part" in the fight, and witnessed this. "We held the ground within five rods of the enemy until the Sixth Corp, thinking they were attacking the enemy, fired on us from the right flank while the enemy was firing on the left flank and front. Under these circumstances, we were forced to retreat to the line of works we had left in the former part of the day." Other soldiers in the brigade agreed. "It became impossible for the regiments of the Third Brigade to maintain their order and utter confusion resulted," wrote the historians of the 155th Pennsylvania.[8]

Gen. Pearson reported that he struggled to reform the regiments of his broken brigade. The buglers for these regiments and the Third Brigade sounded their assembly call, and the men reformed behind the relative safety of Union batteries on a nearby ridge, which checked the Rebels. One of the 16th Michigan's officers who wrote home about the fighting at Dabney's Mill did not go into the embarrassing particulars. This man signed his letter with the initials "J.J.N."—almost certainly Lt. Nellis, an ex-lancer in Company I. "[Our regiment] stood to their ground as veterans only can," he claimed. Of course, his implication was other regiments panicked and fled. Yet it was certainly true the 16th Michigan and their brigade had no choice but to retreat.

The Third Brigade withdrew to the trenches near Hatcher's Run, and for them the battle was over, though other parts of their corps would continue to fight the next day. Gen. Warren, for the record, denied that Union troops fired into their comrades at Dabney's Mill, despite Pearson's report and a news report of the battle that said this happened. Warren privately admitted that new Union recruits were "such poor soldiers that we have to lead them everywhere, and even then they run away from us."[9]

The Union commands that fought on February 5, 6, and 7 near Dabney's Mill and the nearby roads lost a total of more than 1,500 men killed, wounded and captured, while the three Confederate divisions that engaged them were estimated to have lost about 1,000 men or more. Though the battle felt like a defeat to the men of the Third Brigade as they trudged back to their former position in the rain, the truth was that Confederates could not drive the Union commands away, nor could they replace their men lost in battle.

The 16th Michigan's brigade lost 178 men killed, wounded, or missing. Within the regiment, two men were killed and twenty-two were wounded—several of whom would not survive—for a total of nine men killed and mortally wounded; another six were missing. One soldier who experienced a close call was young Fred Wellington of the Brady Sharpshooters, who had victimized Capt. George Swan a year earlier on April Fool's Day; a bullet grazed Wellington's head, injuring him slightly. Corporal Marion Munson of Company E, the Oakland County man who bemoaned the destruction of civilian homes by his comrades back in December, and who had been wounded in the hand near Bethesda Church, was this time wounded in the left arm. It was characterized as severe, and his active military service was over; he would be discharged in the coming summer.

Col. Partridge was one of several regimental commanders credited by Pearson with keeping order in the confusion of the battle that day, and so was his adjutant, whom the general identified as Lt. James Laird of Hillsdale. Pearson gave special credit to Pvt. John Gottlieb Heydlauff of the 16th Michigan, who served as the general's color bearer and bugler. Heydlauff, from Ionia County, had "placed himself on the front line, and by constantly sounding the brigade call did much help to reorganize the troops of the brigade," Pearson wrote. "I would earnestly recommend that a gold medal be granted him for meritorious conduct."[10]

The soldiers of the Third Brigade and their comrades spent a cold, miserable week bivouacked in trenches near Hatcher's Run without the gear and equipment they needed to shelter themselves, but the bad weather eventually lifted. Again, the soldiers of their corps were put to work digging and extending their defensive works. Not long afterward, they were relieved in these trenches and built brigade camps in the pine woods in a line stretching from the creek, and not far from their breastworks. The historian of the 32nd Massachusetts, a regiment that served with the 16th Michigan, would write that "we soon had a camp more comfortable than that we had left on the Jerusalem road."[11]

By now the 16th Michigan had a total of only 214 men and officers fit for duty, Col. Partridge complained, and he wanted more troops for his depleted regiment. Hundreds of newly drafted men were coming into the Union army, and soon new recruits began to arrive from Michigan. One was a Dutch-born student who had come to the state as a baby with his family from the village Geneminden on Zuider Zee in the Netherlands. Now he was a six-foot, blue-eyed, blond-haired, 19-year-old recruit for the 16th Michigan. His name was Willem (William) Visscher. Visscher's family had settled on the shores of Macatawa Bay on Michigan's western coast, living on a government homestead in a settlement with other Dutch families that naturally became known as Holland. As a child, his relatives would write, William romped with Indian children, cut wood, and fished, but also studied hard in his community's schools.

When the Civil War broke out, both an enthusiastic William Visscher and his father enlisted, but William's mother had begged her husband not to take the boy and leave their large family. He relented, and ruled that William, who was then only 15, could not go, either. But when William's uncle was drafted four years later, William, devout and patriotic, was now a young man, and his parents' objections to him going into the army were not so strong. They decided he could join as a substitute for his uncle, who also had a large family. On February 20, 1865, the Visscher family hooked up their sleigh and drove William to Grand Rapids, where recruits and drafted men were gathering. William had his picture taken and the next day rode the train to Jackson, where Camp Blair, a central rendezvous point, was located to send Michigan recruits off to war. Before he left western Michigan, William wrote a note to his mother, assuring her that he was cheerful and satisfied with his decision, and certain that he would not give in to negative behaviors like gambling, cursing, smoking, and drinking. "Sometimes the future seems dark for a moment but I have completely given myself to God and his service and then the dangers of the camp and its evil influence cannot hurt me," Visscher wrote.[12]

Camp Blair surprised the young Dutchman, what with the recruits' rough language and card playing. "Here I am in a queer place, I declare—in a bunk or bed on the third floor of our room, surrounded by men of every color and language and nationality." He and other Hollanders got together on their first Sunday in the camp and sang hymns and read the Bible. Again, Visscher stressed he was unafraid. "If I live, I live unto the Lord," he wrote his sister. "If I die, I die unto the Lord."[13]

His time at the camp was brief, and he and a batch of recruits left Michigan on March 8, traveling the rails across Ohio and Pennsylvania to Baltimore. There they were placed on a steamer that took them to City Point, where they rode the military train to Petersburg and joined the Army of the Potomac's Fifth Corps in the camps and trenches near Hatcher's Run. "We sat on the tops of the cars, and I can tell you it was a fine view we had looking down twenty or thirty feet," he said of the ride to the front. Visscher was assigned to the 16th Michigan's Company K. Some good weather finally arrived in Virginia, so drills and reviews were among the new recruits' first experiences as soldiers. Visscher was dazzled by the marching columns of thousands of men and was surprised the next day when he and the other rookie soldiers were put in the review of the Fifth Corps, even though they hardly knew the drill. "We are still so green at it and have no rifles," Visscher said to his sergeant. "Oh, you can get my gun," the sergeant assured him. The fresh recruits participated with grizzled veterans, marching to their headquarters where Generals Warren and Griffin reviewed the troops. "When the generals rode past we took off our hats and would greet them," he wrote. "The boys enjoyed it still more when the wife of Gen. Griffin rode with him, for ladies seem more popular than men."

His regiment's quarters were impressive and the soldiers well supplied. Two-story tents, beds covered with pine boughs, food and coffee in abundance—the young soldier was shocked at how comfortable it was. "We must be our own cooks, which is pretty hard at first, but are already getting the hang of it," he wrote. "I like things first rate here. I did not think it would be as nice as it is." Another soldier who was having a comparatively easy if not also profitable time of it was Tip Aplin, who had become the regiment's quartermaster sergeant. Aplin had been running a side business, selling food, matches, and various sutler-type items for months, and it seems he was thinking he should give this up, though reluctant to do so. "He said he should quit trading now that he had an office," wrote his mother, Elvira Aplin, to Tip's brother George, "although his office was not worth as much to him as the trade." Tip had been refusing promotion to lieutenant for that very reason, she wrote.[14]

The last battles for the Army of the Potomac and other Union forces were in the offing. Grant, now with more than 120,000 men, planned for massive attacks on the Petersburg defenses, but he was concerned Lee could lead his shrinking army in an escape into the countryside, to link with the nearly defeated Rebel force in North Carolina led by Gen. Joseph Johnston in an attempt to keep the Confederate army alive. His worry was not misplaced; Lee, with about 55,000 men, now allowed Gen. John Gordon to execute a desperate plan to quietly infiltrate the Union line at Petersburg, spring a surprise attack, and make a major breakthrough, knocking the Yankees back and destroying their lines of communication and supply.

With nearly half of the Confederate soldiers at Petersburg ready to make this attack, Gordon's initial infiltration force, led by some men pretending to desert, did indeed deceive Union pickets in the line east of town at a place called Ft. Stedman, early in the morning of March 25, seizing the fort and three nearby batteries. But the alarm was raised, and nearby Union gunners began pounding the Rebel infiltrators; then Ninth Corps soldiers counterattacked the fort, eventually driving the Confederates out.[15]

Most of the soldiers in the Fifth Corps, a few miles away to the west, would have no role in the fighting this day, but the two Union army corps between the 16th Michigan and Ft. Stedman were ordered to push forward to engage the Confederates, probe the strength of their defenses, and seize what portions of the Rebel front line trenches they could. Gen. Charles Griffin's First Division of the Fifth Corps was also ordered to move out that afternoon, to support the advancing troops of the Second Corps, to their right.[16]

SECOND HATCHER'S RUN

It was foggy that morning when the Confederates began their surprise attack at Ft. Stedman, and a few miles to the west, the soldiers of the 16th Michigan had finished an early breakfast when the regiments of their Third Brigade of Griffin's division were summoned to their headquarters; soon they were marched to an assembly point near the creek about two miles away as the sun came out. The men waited in reserve as the sound of musketry rose in intensity—some said the wait was two or three hours, some thought it was longer. Pvt. Visscher, of course, was with the 16th Michigan and would soon go into action. "The Rebels began to attack about 2 o'clock," Visscher said of his first fight (though in fact Union troops there had started the engagement, with their advance against Rebel positions). "We could distinctly see our men shooting. The rebels tried repeatedly to drive them back." His reference to "our men" meant soldiers from the Second Corps, and now the 16th Michigan and some of its comrades moved up to take their place that afternoon. "When this [fighting] had lasted a few hours, our division was ordered thither," Visscher wrote of this moment.

Col. Partridge was not with his regiment that day, so the 16th Michigan was led by Maj. William O. Colt of the 83rd Pennsylvania. They moved forward on the left of the 155th Pennsylvania in this hilly terrain, and Colt reported the Michigan soldiers encountered "a sharp musketry fire" from their front and right. "With a yell and hurrah we rushed in," Visscher said about the regiment's advance. "The bullets whistled over our heads. We stood and looked where we were most needed. With a yell we went forward to the fight, forward again into the edge of the woods where the devils were located."[17]

This was not a major battle for the 16th Michigan and its fellow regiments, and some from their Third Brigade comrades did not fire a shot that afternoon. Colt reported that the 16th Michigan's part in the fighting lasted only about ten minutes, though it was a thrilling experience for young Visscher. "Now we could shoot as much as we wanted to," he said. "We three Hollanders (B. is in the hospital) laid our guns over a pile of sand to be able to take better aim, and it served as a shelter, too. When the rebels heard the cheering, they recognized that we were fresh troops and at once their courage sank into their shoes." Of course, the truth of Visscher's last comment was doubtful; it is unlikely that veteran Rebel fighters were intimidated by mere cheers from Union soldiers, though they probably realized they were facing far superior numbers. Of course, there was no Confederate breakout.

But the firing soon ceased on that portion of their line, and the fighting ended. The earlier battle to the east at Fort Stedman, where the Rebels lost over 2,000 men, was obviously the best-remembered clash that day because of the initial surprise takeover of the fort by Gordon's men, and the terrible casualties they suffered. The Union troops who fought in the countryside to the west, like the 16th Michigan, would call their fight the "second battle of Hatcher's Run." Colt reported the officers and men in the 16th Michigan "behaved well," and that the casualties in the regiment were slight in their brief part in the fracas. Only 19-year-old Truman Davis (whose first name was also given as Freeman) was killed in action. Davis, from Midland, had joined the regiment a year earlier and had been wounded in June of that year. Lt. James Nellis of Company I was slightly wounded. The other regiment from their brigade in the fighting, the 155th Pennsylvania, suffered more men wounded.[18]

Relief came to the front that night, and the 16th Michigan and its brigade were sent back to their camp. "Though our stomachs were clamoring loudly for food, we were full of rejoicing when we went into camp again," Visscher told his family. He could not have been prouder or more satisfied, and he was sure he had done the right thing for God and country by joining the 16th Michigan. "I like my regiment very much," he said, "and am contented as I could be at home."[19]

There were a few quiet days late in March as Grant planned what would prove to be the last Union assaults on the Petersburg defenses. The aggressive Union cavalry commander, Gen. Phil Sheridan, rejoined the massive armies there after destroying what remained of the Confederate force in the Shenandoah Valley, and Grant placed him in charge of the Fifth and Second Corps. Their mission was to now flank and destroy the linchpin of the Confederate defenses west of Petersburg and a few miles north of the village called Dinwiddie Court House. Getting around or breaking through the western Rebel trenches here would allow Grant's men to finally cut the Southside railroad line into Petersburg, and perhaps force the Confederates out of their fortifications. Again, the plan called for the Fifth Corps to support both the Second Corps on its right and Sheridan's cavalry on its left, furthest west.[20]

For the 16th Michigan and the Fifth Corps, the new move began on the morning of March 29 at the order of General Meade. The regiment was under Col. Partridge as they left camp near Hatcher's Run and the Vaughan Road with the First Division at 5 a.m.; one of the other divisions preceded them, once more moving on roads south and then west toward Dinwiddie Court House, where Sheridan's cavalry was in motion. The soldiers encountered little opposition from the Rebels and moved on toward the court house hamlet. But at noon, just as the previous advances to that place had been halted, Meade ordered Warren to send his troops back to the north—this time on the Quaker Road to the creek called Gravelly Run—to link with the Second Corps. Those soldiers again found Confederates blocking their way north, so Meade wanted Warren's men to move against the Rebels here. Warren sent his First Division; its First Brigade, led by Gen. Joshua Chamberlain, who had survived a dangerous wound back in June of 1864, soon met Confederate skirmishers along the Quaker Road, forcing them back from rifle pits near the damaged bridge over the creek. But there were thick woods here, and it was impossible for the Union soldiers of these two corps to stay in an unbroken battle line as they pushed forward. Chamberlain's men advanced past the Second Corps troops, pressing on to the farm property of a family named Lewis.[21]

QUAKER ROAD–WHITE OAK ROAD

But the further the Confederates were pushed back toward their main line near the Quaker Road intersection with the Boydton Plank Road, the more stubborn their resistance became. The fighting intensified in the afternoon, with the pace of the rifle volleys and the forces involved increasing to the point where this was no longer a mere skirmish, but a battle. Gen. Warren sent more guns and troops into the fight, but the First Brigade was hard pressed; after two hours of this fighting, its men were running out of ammunition and their line began to break.

Chamberlain was trying to reform it when reinforcements, including the 16th Michigan, advanced into the fight with the 1st Michigan and the 155th Pennsylvania. Chamberlain reported these regiments from the Third Brigade "came on in the most handsome manner, passing to my front," with their commander, brevet Brigadier General Alfred Pearson, leading his men in a charge straight against the Confederate line. With Union guns now also pounding them, the Rebels retreated to their main defensive line.

Col. Partridge filed no specific report about his regiment's part in the fighting at the Quaker Road. A later compilation of Civil War casualties states that three of his men were killed or mortally wounded in what was referred to as "Gravelly Run," but this could also refer to another fight at a branch of the creek two days later. Either way, Griffin's entire First Division, of which the 16th Michigan was part, lost 367 men killed, wounded, or missing that day. The general reported that his division took 200 prisoners and that they buried 130 Confederate dead. His men moved forward before dark and dug trenches just south of the Boydton Road with open ground in front of them. The weather was wet and stormy that night.[22]

Warren, the Fifth Corps commander, was ordered to attack the Confederate defenses in the morning of March 30, but the rain continued and the soldiers covering his right could not get into position in time. The 16th Michigan's Third Brigade was sent out in a skirmish line when the fog lifted, to locate and test the new Confederate defenses, but Gen. Joseph Bartlett, who was again in charge of the brigade, was not optimistic; an attack on the enemy rifle pits would be "hotly contested," he thought. Reports arrived that the Confederates had fallen back a short distance to the north and were digging in along a main east–west highway called the White Oak Road. Later that day, a part of Griffin's division, including the 16th Michigan, advanced over a field and the Boydton Plank Road to what had been a line of Confederate rifle pits, now abandoned; the new Rebel line was now only a short distance to the north. But the rain continued and "little was done," Griffin reported. Confederates "made a demonstration" against his positions in the afternoon, and also skirmished with troops to Griffin's right, or east, but these were not major fights. Still, Gen. Lee was sending his remaining reinforcements that rainy day from the Petersburg area to the White Oak Road, to counter this new Union threat west of Petersburg.[23]

It was another cold, uncomfortable night in the Fifth Corps' wet, muddy trenches and bivouacs south of the road, but before dawn on March 31, a division from another corps came up and relieved Griffin's First Division, which included the 16th Michigan's Third Brigade. Warren had proposed an attack to cut the White Oak Road that morning, to isolate the Confederate forces and break their line of communications back to Lee in Petersburg, but Grant ordered that, because the road conditions were so bad, offensive operations were suspended for the day. Griffin's men were pulled back from the front line; believing they would not go into action, they waited near a branch of the Gravelly Run, hoping to dry their blankets and cook their coffee and breakfast, while the other two divisions of their corps were a short distance away to the north, some of them waiting and some preparing to go out on a skirmish line.

But at 10:30 that morning—Griffin thought it was 11—the Confederate reinforcements sent the previous day attacked the Fifth Corps across the White Oak Road, coming through a thick patch of forest, in "heavy force" from the north and west, Warren reported. These were two Rebel brigades and elements of two others; they surprised and forced back his

Second and Third divisions, sending these Union troops running. The men of Griffin's First Division, who could not see this attack from their position a few hundred yard to the south, undoubtedly looked up toward the sound of this rifle fire. It was obviously an attack on their position, and officers in the brigades of their division shouted at their men: "Fall in! Fall in!"[24]

Quickly formed in line of battle to meet the attack, the regiments and brigades of Griffin's division, including the 16th Michigan, marched north to a rise of ground overlooking the stream. Ahead of them, they could see their comrades from the other Fifth Corps divisions running toward them to escape the Rebel attack. "For God's sake, let them through," Griffin shouted at his men, "or they will break our line!" Two Union batteries were also dragged into position at that moment. As these retreating Union soldiers splashed across the stream, the soldiers of the First Division saw the Confederate battle line coming over a low hill on the other side; once the fleeing troops were clear, the guns opened up and Griffin's soldiers let loose with rifle fire that halted the Rebels. Then the First Brigade under Chamberlain charged north across the stream to engage them, and so did 16th Michigan's Third Brigade, as skirmishers under Gen. Alfred Pearson. Fifth Corps soldiers who had retreated that morning also reformed and advanced with this counterattack, joined by part of another Union army corps to their right, driving the Rebels back.

Col. Benjamin Partridge led the 16th Michigan into the fight, but was struck on the forehead by a bullet that, by almost any expectation, should have killed him; those who saw him fall thought he was dead by a gunshot through his head. Incredibly, luck was again with Partridge, who had already survived a wound through the neck back at Peeble's Farm. This bullet struck the left side of his forehead but did not penetrate his skull; it grazed a bloody path around part of his scalp, "and caused insensibility for a time," he later explained. Major Ellis Spear, the 20th Maine officer then serving on the First Division staff, was told soon after by Gen. Bartlett that he had seen Partridge on the ground with a bloody head wound and, like everyone else, assumed the Michigan colonel had been killed. No one, it seems, examined him.[25]

The Fifth Corps' counterattack, pressing on, regained the ground they had lost that morning, and more. The Rebel soldiers retreated, and the Fifth Corps pushed across the White Oak Road, suffering 1,400 casualties that day. The important consequence of this battle was that Gen. Warren's men and those of the Second Corps had cut communication (that is, the ability for the Confederates to easily move troops and messages) between Dinwiddie Court House and Petersburg. Once the firing was over that afternoon, the 16th Michigan and their Third Brigade were pulled from the front and held in reserve south of the road.

In the meantime, about a half hour after being grazed by that bullet, Partridge regained consciousness; he had been stunned, bruised, and cut, but was very much alive. It must have been an astounding and grisly sight for whoever was nearby when the 16th Michigan's colonel sat up, looked around, and got to his feet. Partridge (or perhaps someone else) tied a handkerchief around his wounded head, put his hat back on, and found his horse. Then he rode north to where the division officers were placing their men in a new line.

Ellis Spear said he was resting on the ground after the battle when he noticed an officer on Partridge's horse approaching. "It was undoubtedly Partridge, and as one rising from the dead," Spear later wrote.[26]

It is unlikely Partridge remained in charge of the 16th Michigan that afternoon of March 31—he was likely suffering a concussion. But there was little or no rest for his men, nor any of the other soldiers in their Fifth Corps. Since this new advance began on the 29th, Gen. Phil Sheridan's powerful cavalry divisions had moved a few miles further to the southwest to Dinwiddie Court House. There the troopers clashed with Confederates without any assistance from Union infantry, which was tied up in fighting near the Quaker and White Oak roads. But just as Lee sent some of his last available men to this point to hold back the Fifth Corps, the rest of the Rebel reinforcements, under Gen. George Pickett, were sent farther west to block and attack Sheridan's troopers near Dinwiddie Court House. Lee ordered Pickett to "hold Five Forks at all hazards," and he had about 10,000 men, infantry and cavalry, to do so.[27]

What was Five Forks and why was it important? A few miles north-northwest of Dinwiddie Court House, and about the same distance west of the Fifth Corps' position, lay this junction of several roads called Five Forks. The main east–west road through this intersection was the White Oak Road—the same White Oak Road where, a short distance to the east, the Fifth and Second Corps had clashed with Rebels (and where Ben Partridge had narrowly missed being killed leading the 16th Michigan). The long-targeted Southside Railroad lay just north of this road on its way into Petersburg. Five Forks was, essentially, the last place where Lee could try to defeat Union forces flanking his western defenses. If Grant could destroy or drive off the Rebels here, Petersburg would practically be isolated from the rest of the shrinking Confederacy; the town would almost certainly fall to the Union army, and Richmond would be next. But to reach Five Forks, Sheridan's cavalry needed infantry support to break through Rebel forces blocking their way north from Dinwiddie Court House.

Since the new Union offensive started, Sheridan's cavalry had ridden to this village, carried out reconnaissance at Five Forks, and clashed with the Rebels from two cavalry divisions. But when Pickett's reinforcements arrived, the Rebels attacked the Union cavalry on March 31, pushing the troopers back to the court house village. Sheridan's men held on as evening fell, but it was clear that if they did not get reinforcements, they would have to withdraw. In the meantime, Gen. Warren, commander of the Fifth Corps, heard this fighting that afternoon from a few miles away to the northeast once his own battle was over, and he recognized that the Union troopers at Dinwiddie Court House probably needed help.

This was almost certainly the reason Warren pulled the 16th Michigan's brigade—his "largest and best"—back into reserve once his corps' battle was over that afternoon; Gen. Joseph Bartlett was in charge of the brigade, and at about 5 p.m. Warren directed Gen. Griffin to send it across country to the southwest, to strike Pickett's men as they confronted Sheridan's troopers. The entire brigade was not sent on this mission, however—just three of its regiments in a detachment under Bartlett—and here the movement of the 16th Michigan becomes hard to discern.

These three unidentified regiments moved over open land, crossed streams, and found a narrow road that took them south about three miles through the woods toward Dinwiddie Court House. When Bartlett's men came out of the trees just before darkness, they met Confederate skirmishers and clashed, driving them down the slope to the creek called Gravelly Run. Although these Rebels withdrew after "considerable skirmishing," Bartlett's soldiers were on their guard, for across the run to the south were campfires that one officer said "seemed to stretch for miles." This large Confederate force, Pickett's, would soon fall back, retreating north to Five Forks, since their commanders feared that they were going to be attacked by the Fifth Corps on their eastern flank.[28]

Meanwhile, the rest of the Third Brigade was also put in motion. Less than two hours after Bartlett and his detachment left on their mission to help Sheridan's troopers, the rest of the Third Brigade, under Brig. Gen. Pearson, was sent south on the plank road, again to reach Dinwiddie Court House. Union generals had by now learned Sheridan's force had been in a tough battle, and they wanted an entire division, and not just a brigade, to reinforce his cavalry as soon as possible. Thinking that these regiments of the Third Brigade could get there faster than Bartlett's detachment, Warren dispatched Pearson's remaining regiments about 7 p.m. But Confederates had heavily damaged the plank road bridge over Gravelly Run; the creek was overflowing with the heavy rains of the past three days, and could not be forded. Later that night, Warren's men tore down a nearby house for the lumber they needed to repair the bridge, so their First Division could get to Dinwiddie Court House. In the meantime, Pearson's detachment went back to the Fifth Corps' position that night, just as Bartlett's detachment was also ordered back. Which one of these two parts of the brigade the 16th Michigan accompanied that night was not revealed in the army's reports, nor was it outlined in any subsequent soldier's letter or memoir.[29]

Either way, nothing was simple or easy that night for Gen. Warren and his men. He continued to receive confusing and sometimes contradictory orders throughout the night, from his superiors, Meade and Grant, and their intermediaries, who did not have a clear picture of the Fifth Corps' situation. These orders required Warren to quickly go to Sheridan's aid, yet Warren had to quietly and carefully pull his entire corps out from under the noses of strong Confederate positions on the White Oak Road without inviting attack. His engineers had to repair the bridge over Gravelly Run to get thousands of his tired soldiers marching to Dinwiddie Court House. These were risky and complicated moves, executed during a stormy night in complete darkness, yet the Union commanders were promising Sheridan, unrealistically, that he would soon have reinforcements. As a result, the generals expected that the Fifth Corps would be in position to attack the Rebels there by dawn on April 1.[30]

Whether the 16th Michigan was in Bartlett's detachment or with Pearson's on the night of March 31, it had been an exhausting day and night of fighting, marching, and skirmishing with little rest, and it continued into the cold, clear morning of April 1. The two parts of the Third Brigade reunited near the Union line at the White Oak Road about midnight; the tired soldiers were angry and cursed expressively about this night of moving for miles back and forth through the dangerous countryside, with half of them also skirmishing with Confederate veterans. They now got a brief rest, but at about 5 a.m. on the 1st, they were relieved by other soldiers and began the march with their division southwest, once more toward Dinwiddie Court House. These men, one soldier-historian in the Third Brigade wrote, were "fatigued to the limit of endurance."[31]

Three of the 16th Michigan's men, now assigned to Maj. Rufus Jacklin's division sharpshooters, had been moving in the predawn darkness to rejoin their First Division after all the nighttime marching when they stumbled upon—and captured—over a dozen Confederate troopers. These soldiers were William H. Streeter of Ionia, Walter Cronkite of Saginaw, and Achlind McCrory of Ottawa County. An officer's report said that the three crossed a Union picket line established by the corps next to them, walking back to their own division, when they found and surprised a Capt. B. C. Clement of the 16th North Carolina Cavalry and fourteen of his men in two different squads—troopers unaware they had ridden behind Union pickets.

"Halt and surrender," ordered Streeter, according to a version of the story that appeared in newspapers. A disbelieving Clement turned and demanded, "Surrender to whom?" "You are in rear of our battle line," Streeter bluffed, "and it is surrender or death to you." Fortunately for the Michigan soldiers, the Rebel captain and his men, who clearly outgunned the three sharpshooters, dropped their weapons and surrendered. General Warren later said the incident was "indicative of the sinking spirits of the Confederates."[32]

But his corps' First Division quietly moved out that morning of the 1st, eventually heading south on a road that intersected the Dinwiddie Road between the court house village and Five Forks. Between 7 and 8 a.m., their column met Sheridan at this intersection after the wearying, all-night move. Sheridan was impatient and angry at how long it had taken for the Fifth Corps to reach him since, based on unrealistic promises made by the commanding generals, he had expected the infantry hours earlier. But the Rebels had fallen back from Dinwiddie Court House, going north to Five Forks; now Sheridan wanted to strike them there.[33]

For the moment, once the 16th Michigan arrived with its division southeast of this intersection, the soldiers were allowed a rest as Sheridan made his plans to attack. At 1 p.m., Warren was ordered to march the Fifth Corps north into position for the assault, a point several hundred yards south of the White Oak Road. This location, near the Gravelly Run Church, was about an hour's march away, but it took time to move the thousands of soldiers north in the formations Sheridan wanted, through the woods and along a country lane to the church. The 16th Michigan's First Division marched at about 2 p.m. and it was forty-five minutes more once they arrived for their corps to be aligned for battle. In the meantime, Sheridan was impatient for the attack to begin; he had already been given the authority by Grant to remove Warren from command of the Fifth Corps, since the generals had come to think Warren was too cautious and slow in following their orders.[34]

FIVE FORKS

The Confederate defenses ran roughly east and west for just under two miles through the Five Forks junction, manned by both mounted and dismounted cavalry and five brigades of infantry. This force was mainly in trenches in a line in the woods along the White Oak Road, but then the line jutted to the northeast at an angle. Sheridan wanted his cavalry to engage the Rebels in the western portion, or the left of the line; then the Fifth Corps would attack from the east, striking the right, to turn and crush that end of the enemy defenses. Sheridan had met and explained this to Warren, who made a sketch of Sheridan's plan of attack for maps for his division commanders. But there was a problem: The map and information Warren used for his maps did not accurately reflect the Confederate line's location. As a result, the Fifth Corps, as it got into position, was hundreds of yards too far east of the Rebel breastworks at Five Forks.[35]

Now the 16th Michigan formed at the edge of the woods on the right of the Gravelly Run Church Road with thousands of other Union soldiers. With Col. Partridge wounded, Major William Colt of the 83rd Pennsylvania was again in charge of the regiment. Though they were part of their corps' First Division, the Michigan soldiers and the 91st Pennsylvania were to remain on the right end of their division's line, just behind the left of their corps' Third Division, commanded by Gen. Samuel Crawford. In other words, the 16th Michigan and the Pennsylvanians would link the two divisions in what was supposed to be a sweeping attack along the White Oak Road, from east to west.

The attack began at 4 p.m. as the troops ahead of the 16th Michigan marched first, immediately followed by Griffin's First Division. The soldiers broke into a run, charging north and crossing the road, and so did the 16th Michigan with the 91st Pennsylvania alongside. As far as their commanders knew, the Confederate positions were straight ahead—but they were wrong. The charging Union troops soon engaged Rebel cavalry pickets, who quickly retreated north. But when then Third and First Divisions advanced over the road, chasing the pickets, they completely missed the Confederate trenches, off to their left. Helping to confuse this situation further was the fact that the countryside was rough, with forested gullies and hills, so it was difficult for the different commands to keep in sight of one another.[36]

Just to the 16th Michigan's left, other Fifth Corps officers realized, by the sound of rifle fire, that they had bypassed the enemy trenches, and turned their men accordingly, attacking the eastern portion of the Rebel line in the woods. Gen. Charles Griffin, the First Division's commander, and Gen. Joseph Bartlett, the commander of the Third Brigade, also figured out what had happened, and shifted their troops so their assault smashed into the Confederates along the road. But the Fifth Corps' Third Division charged on to the north, chasing Rebel skirmishers, and the 16th Michigan and the 91st Pennsylvania went with them.[37]

Soon officers caught up with the errant Third Division, and turned them around so that they were heading south through the woods, into the rear of the enemy positions on the White Oak Road—a devastating situation for the Rebels there. The 16th Michigan and other regiments had forded a stream on the charge that missed the breastworks, but now they reformed their line with the Third Division, driving away enemy cavalry and taking prisoners in the woods as they went south. “The line again moved forward, the firing from the enemy becoming more rapid,” reported Lt. Col. Eli Sellers, commander of the 91st Pennsylvania, about his men and the Michigan soldiers. “The men moved forward in good order, capturing many of the enemy who were straggling through the woods.”[38]

The Confederate positions collapsed as they were hit and overwhelmed from different directions, and soon the Five Forks crossroads were in Union hands. But the troops of the Fifth Corps had become badly disorganized during this confused attack, and some officers claimed the remaining Rebels made a last stand, just west of the junction, as the Third Division’s wing of the assault stalled; the Union soldiers continued to fire, but their charge had halted. Some said Gen. Warren saw what was happening—he rode forward with his officers, shouting for his men to follow. “The effect was electrical,” later wrote the historians of the 155th Pennsylvania. “There was a wild rush, irrespective of organization, and a large part of the enemy that remained were captured.” Warren was nearly killed in this charge, while an officer, an orderly, and even the general’s own horse were shot dead.[39]

Those Confederates who could escape did so, but their army lost more than 2,000 men that day. The 16th Michigan had covered a few miles that afternoon and evening, charging in a great semicircle. Though they and their comrades initially missed their target, they had come back into the battle and fought well. In their regiment, two men were killed that day and several others wounded. A young officer of the 16th Michigan, Capt. Irving Belcher of Flint, serving on the staff of Gen. Bartlett, was one of several officers the general credited for the “efficiency and bravery” during the attack. The regiment halted at dark with the Third Division now back on the White Oak Road. Union soldiers knew they had won a major victory, and they were jubilant. Gen. Warren would later write that the battle at Five Forks was the Fifth Corps’ last serious battle.

But for Warren, the war was over. An angry General Sheridan felt Warren had taken too long getting his men where they were supposed to be over the course of the last two days, and he relieved Warren of command of the Fifth Corps on the spot that evening. The action was harsh and unfair, but Sheridan was brash and aggressive, while Warren, though personally brave, had long since created for himself a reputation with his superiors for being argumentative, critical, and nearly insubordinate. Of course, his men’s view was that he was a thoughtful, careful, and decent commander who had been reluctant and even unwilling to send them on suicidal attacks that could not succeed; ultimately, he would be cleared of Sheridan’s accusations. Though no member of the 16th Michigan appears to have left his thoughts or feelings about Warren’s removal, other accounts of Fifth Corps soldiers show they were unhappy and even indignant. But they knew the end of Lee’s army was at hand, and it was their job to finish it. Sheridan placed the 16th Michigan’s respected division commander, Charles Griffin, in charge of their corps, and made Joseph Bartlett commander of the First Division; Gen. Alfred Pearson again commanded their Third Brigade.[40]

With the Confederates’ western-most defenses now crushed, Grant ordered attacks on the Petersburg lines on the next morning; early on April 2, more than a hundred Union guns pounded the defenders. Soldiers at Five Forks said the glow of the artillery fire in the sky to the east was like an aurora, and then thousands of soldiers from three Union army corps attacked, some of them overrunning Lee's outer fortifications. Another corps smashed through the Rebel defenses of the Southside Railroad at a point between Petersburg and Five Forks; the rail line was cut and Confederate troops there fled north and west along the Appomattox River. Lee warned his president, Jefferson Davis, that the Confederate government must evacuate its capital, since he and his army were retreating late that night, west from Richmond and Petersburg, to escape being cut off and surrounded. His army headed toward the town of Amelia Court House, about forty miles west, where there was a still-intact railroad line going south.

Back at Five Forks on the morning of the 2nd, the 16th Michigan and other Fifth Corps soldiers destroyed Confederate weapons and munitions, buried the dead, and took care of the wounded. Then their corps was ordered to move back toward Petersburg, and that afternoon the 16th Michigan marched with its division, first going north to the railroad line, now in Union hands, and then a few miles east to a point called Sutherland Station, where their comrades had defeated the Confederates protecting the railroad. The Fifth Corps stayed here for the night, but as the men rested, the last of the Rebel defenders withdrew from Petersburg, blowing up munitions that could not be carried, and destroying the bridges over the Appomattox River. Early on April 3, Union troops found Petersburg empty of Confederate soldiers.[41]

There are almost no reports or accounts of the experiences of the soldiers of the 16th Michigan for the next few days, and for good reason: Nearly the entire Union army now started in pursuit of Lee—a time of hard marches, long days, and no mail service. But there is a record of some of their comrades who marched with them, and these accounts from their division and brigade say the men cheered as the news spread that the Confederate army had abandoned Petersburg. Union cavalry moved out first, and then the Fifth Corps. One soldier-historian from the Third Brigade wrote they initially were started marching north toward Richmond, but were stopped when word arrived that the Rebel capital had also been evacuated by Lee's men.

It was about 10 a.m. when the 16th Michigan's brigade, about ten miles outside of Petersburg, headed west on the River Road into the countryside, in their First Division column, with the entire Fifth Corps, eventually fording the Namozine Creek that flowed into the Appomattox River. They pressed on; the road was difficult for the men and nearly impossible for the wagons following them. Some soldiers were put to work to make the road passable, but eventually their corps bivouacked that night near another river called Deep Creek, having covered twenty miles. The pursuit of Lee's army, often slow-moving and tiring in the dust and heat, was underway.[42]

When Jefferson Davis and the Confederate government fled Richmond to the southwest, they did so on trains on the Danville Railroad. Union commanders were concerned that Lee, too, would use this route to escape to North Carolina, where his army could join

Rebel forces there to keep their fight going. On April 4, the Fifth Corps moved out from its bivouac between 5 and 7 a.m. "We pushed on rapidly," Maine's Ellis Spear would later write. "It was understood that we were making for Jetersville . . . to obstruct the passage of Lee's Army." Again, marching all day, the Third Brigade crossed the railroad at 6 p.m. and moved northeast toward the town, forming lines of battle with their division since it seemed certain that Lee's army was coming their way. The soldiers covered thirty miles that day, and the 16th Michigan, like other regiments, dug trenches and took a position with the expectation of a fight that evening. There was none, however, and the soldiers eventually bivouacked that chilly night, remaining there the next day. They had indeed managed to block Lee's intended route to the southwest.

On the afternoon of the 5th, part of their corps moved northeast, again expecting to clash with the Confederates, who had had to stop to gather supplies near Amelia Court House. But there was no fight. With the Danville Railroad now cut and that way blocked, Lee pressed west, marching through the night of April 5–6. But he had lost precious time. Officers of the Fifth Corps would later express pride that their infantry, alone with some cavalry support, had faced the gathering of the Confederate army there at Amelia Court House between April 4 and 5, since other Union infantry had not yet arrived.[43]

The Fifth Corps, which had been under the control of Gen. Sheridan, was now transferred back to Gen. George Meade, the commander of the Army of the Potomac, though that probably did not matter to the soldiers. They moved out with two other army corps from the town of Jetersville on April 6, with their First Division in the lead, their commanders still expecting to find and fight the Confederates. They first moved toward Amelia Court House, and then further north toward a village called Paineville. But the Rebel army was gone, and the Fifth Corps made a turn back to the southwest, ultimately halting at a place called Ligontown Ferry—a long, semicircular march of thirty miles that day to the Appomattox River; here they bivouacked for the night. Throughout the day, their column passed broken and abandoned Confederate caissons and wagons, some burning. Lee's army had stayed ahead of them, with Union commanders learning that he was hoping to meet with a shipment of badly needed rations on rail cars.

But while the Confederates had evaded the 16th Michigan's Fifth Corps, other Union forces, making a more direct route west, struck the rear of the Rebel army late that afternoon, attacking nearby at a mill on a stream called Sailor's Creek that flowed into the Appomattox. In fighting at different points there with Union infantry and cavalry, the Rebels lost several thousand men, mostly captured—a devastating loss that astounded Lee and his generals. But the Confederates, concentrating their remaining forces, kept going. Lee's goal was Appomattox Station, thirty miles away, where he expected to feed and resupply his hungry men.[44]

On the morning of April 7, the Fifth Corps followed Sheridan's cavalry southwest from the river in the rain as the Rebel rearguard tried to try to hold off Union forces at High Bridge across the Appomattox, where Lee had his army cross to the north side of the river. While parts of two Union army corps were now directly behind the Confederates, Grant needed infantry to get in front of Lee, to stop his army. South of the river, the

16th Michigan's corps first marched past this fighting and, with other large infantry commands, went by the hamlet of Rice's Station and west through a town called Prince Edward Court House on the railroad line—a distance of about twenty miles when they halted that evening.[45]

Like all soldiers, those from the Fifth Corps were tired; they were far ahead of their supply train and foraged from local farms, which had not been previously affected by the war, as had other parts of Virginia. But accounts say their morale was high, for they knew that the end of the war could truly be around the next corner. When they bivouacked that night, along with thousands of comrades nearby, Lee's soldiers, who marched through the night of April 7–8, came to rest just ten miles away to the northwest.[46]

"On the morning of April 8, the Fifth Corps started from Prince Edward and marched to Prospect Station, thence along the Prospect Road, preceded by the Twenty-fourth Corps," Thomas Lackie of the 16th Michigan wrote years later. It was not just these commands, but also thousands of other Union soldiers on the road that morning. Though Lackie, a sergeant, did not describe this day, Gen. Griffin reported it was a "very slow and tedious march" that began at 5 a.m., with the soldiers having to stop and start repeatedly on this road, jammed with soldiers and wagons. Maine's Col. Ellis Spear, who now commanded a new regiment of his own, called it a severe and even painful march—the men were hungry and many were angry, with fights breaking out with wagoners as they jostled forward a few steps, halted, waited, and then trudged forward again on the muddy road; soldiers cursed their officers as the slow trek dragged on, and after darkness the column turned onto a narrow lane winding through deep woods, a road that would lead to a village called Appomattox Court House. It was 2 or 2:30 in the morning of April 9, Palm Sunday, when the 16th Michigan's Third Brigade at last halted. Spear saw soldiers step out of the column and collapse at the side of the road, exhausted. Though none of them yet knew it, the last battlefield in Virginia lay only a few miles away.[47]

APPOMATTOX

The weary Fifth Corps soldiers dropped to the ground to sleep in the woods, but the rest was only two hours. Riding ahead of them, the Union cavalry division under Gen. George Custer had captured or destroyed the trainloads of badly needed supplies meant for the Confederate army on the evening of April 8, on the railroad line at a point called Appomattox Station. In short, the Union troopers had got ahead of Lee, who was resting with his army a few miles north, just beyond the village called Appomattox Court House.

But it would take infantry to truly trap and defeat the Rebels, and now the Fifth Corps and those commands moving on the same route moved quickly. The 16th Michigan and comrades in their Third Brigade of the Fifth Corps' First Division were awakened by their familiar bugle call: *Dan, Dan, Dan, But-ter-field!* Gen. Alfred Pearson, the brigade commander, remembered that some of the tired soldiers rose from the damp ground and answered, singing out "Damn, damn, damn Dan Butterfield," as others laughed, though doubtless there was groaning and grumbling, too.[48]

The men of the Fifth Corps started the march at 4:30 a.m. on the 9th, and Gen. Joshua Chamberlain later said that their division's Third Brigade led their column as the soldiers filed onto the road. Soon word spread among the soldiers that Sheridan's cavalry had cut across Lee's path, and they, the infantry, could now prevent the Confederates from escaping. Pearson said the soldiers acted accordingly in what, decades later, he described in heroic terms: "Each man felt that the last battle for the Union was to be fought," he said to the veterans of the brigade. "On you moved, each man striving to keep close to his command, and be ready to do his part in the final scene of the great drama." In fact, many unhappy hungry soldiers quickly got to their feet because they were told that there were captured Confederate rations and supplies—breakfast—waiting for them ahead at Appomattox Station.[49]

The 16th Michigan and its brigade reached that final scene between two and three hours later, between 6 and 7 a.m., on the road that had led them from Prince Edward Court House. The day was dawning clear and they could hear guns, Rebel field artillery, in the distance. The Confederates, now numbering about 30,000 men, of course knew there was a Union force behind them, northeast of Appomattox Court House, but that morning they found Sheridan's cavalry was in their front, trying to block the way west and south—their only way out. Soldiers of Gen. John Gordon's infantry, Gen. Fitzhugh Lee's cavalry, and the Rebel artillery engaged them, trying to open an escape route for the rest of what remained of the Confederate Army of Northern Virginia.

The 16th Michigan's Tom Lackie, a Detroiter, said their corps halted a mile or so from Appomattox Court House near a farm that was owned by a family named Inge, and ahead of them Union cavalry skirmishers were being pushed back by the Rebels. The Third Brigade, and others from their division, filed into a field just north what he called "the old turnpike," to Appomattox Court House; Pvt. Theodore Hoeninghausen, a youth from Detroit, sounded the Third Brigade's assembly call on his bugle. Though the veterans had heard it many times before, this was the last time they would hear the "Dan Butterfield" call on the field of battle.[50]

Gen. Pearson gathered his men around him and gave a two-minute speech as the Union infantry who had marched ahead of them, to their left, or west, moved up, drawing closer to Lee's army. The order to advance was given, and Third Brigade marched north with its First Division on what Lackie described as "a narrow road which branched off from the turnpike" to Appomattox Court House. He said that they passed a wrecked Confederate wagon train that morning, one that had been destroyed by Union cavalry the evening before. "It must have carried at least part of the Treasury Department stores, as I picked up a package of Confederate $100 Missouri bonds," he wrote later. Lackie put the worthless bonds into his empty haversack. The soldiers splashed across a stream called Plain Run, "passed through some woods and entered the open field of Appomattox and formed line of battle one hundred and fifty yards southeast of the Wright House." This home was about a half mile southwest of the village. The land here was open and sloped on a northerly incline, and Confederate pickets were posted up this hill and around the house; beyond this were more woods, and Appomattox Court House.

The 16th Michigan was on the left of the brigade as they advanced, northeasterly, up the hill with their division in two lines of battle. To their left was another division from their own corps, and then two more divisions from the Twenty-fourth Corps, advancing from west to east, hemming the Confederates in. Sgt. Lackie did not know the identity of these troops coming eastward before they disappeared from his view into the woods, but he remarked that they looked like "a blue whip-lash encircling Bobbie Lee."[51]

The Rebel pickets ahead on the ridge opened fire, and Lackie would later wrongly claim that the Third Brigade did not return it; Gen. Joshua Chamberlain, commanding the First Brigade agreed, to a point. "No man wantonly or in excitement struck at the life of his antagonist," he wrote later. Yet his battle report and that of his corps' commander state clearly that their skirmishers were engaged and fighting. His comrade Ellis Spear, who was often highly critical of Chamberlain's later accounts, agreed with him in his own memoir. "I rode on with the skirmish line and could see the whole line advancing steadily, in good order, and without firing a shot on the level field." Possibly Spear meant that his brigade's skirmishers did not open fire until they moved up the hill.

These statements about Union troops not firing back, written years after the war, reflect an unlikely romantic heroism after the fact. Though Spear said "we did not fire a shot," his and other such statements were contradicted by official reports. Brevet Major Rufus Jacklin of the 16th Michigan, who was on the firing line and probably directing the division's sharpshooters battalion, as well as men of the 118th and 155th Pennsylvania (also on the Third Brigade skirmish line) all described their skirmishers firing as their line moved forward, forcing the Rebel pickets and guns back toward the woods and the village. This last Union advance was a grand sight, and one that would not be seen again. "Not since Gettysburg had we seen, in the open, such an extended line of battle," Spear wrote.[52]

Up on the ridge, the Rebels saw this tide of Union soldiers coming toward them; Sheridan's troopers, whom they had pushed back that morning, were gone, replaced by a wall of thousands of blue-clad infantrymen who were not going to be turned aside. "As we advanced," Lackie said, "the enemy's pickets retreated into this wood, the Third Brigade taking ground to the right as we passed the Wright House, and then broke into a double-quick." They passed over the top of the hill, he said, expecting to see the Confederate battle line emerge from the trees. There was a rail fence ahead, running along the edge of the woods that hid the Rebels. "Capt. [Warren T.] Angevine and I ran a little ahead of the line to make an opening in the fence," he continued. Angevine, from Adrian, was a veteran of Company E who had been wounded in the side in the skirmishing near Cold Harbor after the disastrous attack there; he had just been commissioned captain of Jardine's Sharpshooters company, though whether he knew that at that moment is not known. But as the two men reached the fence, Lackie said he noticed "something white coming up the incline beyond the road." It was a Confederate officer on a bay horse, and in his upraised hand he held a sword with a white towel tied to its point.[53]

"At the terrific speed in which he was coming he was unable to stop the horse before he had approached within thirty feet of where I stood," Lackie said. "In the meantime he shouted 'Halt!'" Lackie was sure in later years that this was Confederate Capt. Robert M. Sims who galloped up and stopped in front of Companies E and H of the 16th

Michigan—Company H was the regiment's color company that day. "Where is the officer commanding these troops?" the officer asked, according to Lackie's account. "Tell him to halt them. Gen. Lee desires hostilities suspended; he is going to surrender."[54]

Sims wrote in an 1886 letter that he indeed carried a white flag of truce that morning, looking for Gen. Sheridan, to ask for a suspension of hostilities. But there are also accounts that other Confederate officers carried white flags into the Union lines on the front where the 16th Michigan halted with its brigade. Lackie claimed Gen. Bartlett, his division commander, rode quickly down to where he and Angevine stood, and spoke to the Confederate officer briefly; then they turned their horses to Appomattox. "I noticed the Confederate officer take the truce [white flag] from his sword and place the sword back in its scabbard," he wrote.[55]

Claims and different accounts of various Confederate white flags and who received them would go on for decades, and in the Third Brigade alone men from at least three regiments claimed that theirs was the one approached by the truce-bearing Rebel officer. Even Detroiter Jacklin claimed to have a hand in the matter. "I was directing part of the skirmish line when the flag of truce from Gen. Lee's headquarters appeared," he wrote later. "I at once ordered the line to halt, firing to cease, and directed the flag to headquarters, Fifth Army Corps."

In truth, Confederate generals sent various officers out that morning with white flags, asking for the cessation of hostilities, but outbursts of rifle and artillery continued at points along the battle line nonetheless. One Third Brigade historian said a young Pennsylvanian was mortally wounded by Rebel artillery, firing in violation of their own flag of truce, and that Gen. Griffin ordered his corps' skirmishers to resume firing. It took some time for Rebel officers to finally stop all their men from firing, and Griffin reported he was notified by Gen. Sheridan of the cease-fire. Though a number of soldiers on both sides had been killed or wounded that morning, Lackie felt that white flag carried by the Rebel officer to their brigade line averted a bloodbath for the Confederates. "Had that truce delayed two minutes longer, there would have been no use for one," he wrote later, "as Gordon's and Longstreet's muster would have been wiped out."

At last a silence fell over the field, and word spread across the ranks that Grant and Lee were to meet in the hamlet down beyond the hillside on which the soldiers now stood, waiting and watching, as did the Confederates, less than a rifle shot away.[56]

20.

APRIL–JULY 1865

THINK OF THE NOBLE SPIRITS WE LOST

Decades later, Detroit's Thomas Lackie would claim it was announced at 8:45 that morning to the 16th Michigan's Third Brigade that Lee had surrendered, but this was incorrect. It was still nearly five hours before Grant and the Confederate commander met at the McLean House in Appomattox Court House. That Rebel officer who rode up with the white flag, seen by hundreds if not thousands of soldiers, was bringing a request for a cease-fire so the generals could discuss the terms of Lee's surrender; that flag did not represent the surrender itself. Still, Maine's Ellis Spear, in his memoir, said he saw the soldiers react as Lackie described; as the officer with the flag of truce rode along the line, shouting followed him—Union soldiers yelling "Lee surrenders!" The news, though premature, swept through the ranks. "I cannot describe the cheering, yelling and hat-tossing that followed," Lackie said of the moment.

Yet other soldiers in the brigade did not agree that all men broke out cheering, saying that they regarded the quiet that followed the cease-fire with more skepticism. There were hundreds of new and inexperienced men present as a result of the draft, but even veterans had never seen anything like this. Some soldiers cautioned others—maybe it was a Rebel trick, and the flag of truce was only stalling them as Lee's army attempted to sneak off toward Lynchburg. After all, it was an amazing thing to comprehend: Could the war really be over?[1]

But the war *was* over for these soldiers. Early that afternoon, Grant and Lee met in Appomattox Court House to work out the surrender of the Army of Northern Virginia. Before they got down to business, Grant spoke briefly of having met Lee in the Mexican War, when Lee visited the brigade of John Garland—the veteran soldier and Virginia native who had been brother-in-law to Col. Thomas Stockton of Flint and father-in-law to Gen. James Longstreet, one of Lee's top lieutenants. Then they got on with the overall terms of the Confederate army's surrender, while the details were left to the commanding generals' subordinates.[2]

Brig. Gen. Joshua Chamberlain, who had once commanded the 16th Michigan's brigade and still served in their corps' First Division, wrote it was about 4 p.m. that "the thrilling message" swept along the line—Lee surrenders! "Even the rebels were loud in their joyous demonstration when they heard it," wrote young William Visscher, the Dutch-born soldier, to his family; it could be the cheering, cap-tossing scene Thomas Lackie later described took place in the afternoon with the formal announcement of the surrender. The next day, Grant would issue orders for the Twenty-fourth Corps and the Fifth Corps to handle the paroling of Confederate soldiers and receive their surrendered weapons and flags, and as a result, Lackie and his comrades would witness their old foe marching into Appomattox Court House to lay down their arms. Most of the rest of the Union army there was ordered to start the march back to the east.[3]

Now that their part in the war was over, soldiers went wild for mementos of the surrender of the Army of Northern Virginia. Lee, while waiting for Grant's representative on the 9th to arrange a suitable place for their meeting, had rested under an apple tree in a small orchard on a hill north of the village near the Appomattox River; he returned to this spot for a time after the surrender meeting. Before the day was over, Lee's soldiers began to cut and break the tree's branches and limbs for keepsakes, to the point that Confederate officers posted guards around it until the general and his staff left the orchard. "This was done by the Confederate soldiers," wrote Porter Alexander, a Rebel brigadier general, about the disappearing tree, "and finished by the Federals." Why? While some Confederates looked at this tree as a place of the last moments of their army with Lee as their commander, the rumor swept through the ranks that Lee and Grant signed the surrender under its boughs. The myth of the apple tree was born, and it would linger for years. By the next day, the tree was gone, dug up and chopped to pieces by souvenir-hunting soldiers.

One of the men who brought home a piece of the tree from Appomattox was the 16th Michigan's Cpl. John F. Parker in Company A, a farm laborer from Argentine Township in Genesee County. Parker, who enlisted in the summer of 1862 at age 20 and had been wounded in the shoulder in an attack on Rebel rifle pits at the Wilderness, was a veteran; he lost his younger brother, Hollis, who had also joined the regiment, to typhoid fever in December 1862. Parker got a piece of the tree about the size of his hand, and later cut it into four blocks for each of his sons.[4]

The laying down of arms by Confederate forces started the day after Lee signed the surrender, beginning with the Rebel cavalry on April 10, and then the artillery the next day. Union soldiers were not supposed to leave their bivouacs, though men who two days earlier had been trying to kill each other in battle now traded mementos and shared meals, while officers had time to ride into Appomattox Court House and see where the surrender was signed in the house of Wilmer McLean—the man whose previous home had been damaged in the first major battle of the Civil War, Bull Run, in the summer of 1861.[5]

It was on the evening of April 10 that a Texan named A. S. Drewry, who served in the Confederate Third Corps artillery, perhaps had one of the most bitter experiences of the surrendered Rebels: He suffered the loss of his horse to Col. Benjamin Partridge of the

16th Michigan. Ironically, the Texan's story of the theft of his horse started on a note of reconciliation and respect. "A party of us went over toward the [U]nion army to see the cavalry surrender their arms," wrote Drewry, of Galveston, nearly thirty-five years later. "We were in front of the Fifth Corps, and here I came in contact with the 16th Michigan." It was nearly dark when the Rebel troopers finished surrendering their arms. "Have you chaps anything to eat?" a Yankee soldier from Michigan asked Drewry and his comrades. "Very little," one of the Rebels replied. "Come over to our camp and take supper with us," the man said.[6]

"For my part I was willing to begin to close the 'bloody chasm' right there," Drewry wrote. Drewry owned a fine brown mare, and because she was his personal property, he was being allowed to keep the horse when the Rebel artillery surrendered. He tied her while he enjoyed what he considered a hearty meal with coffee and condensed milk with the Yankees. Then a soldier he took to be an orderly walked up and offered to trade horses; Drewry had already turned down a Union officer who offered him $175 for the horse, so again he said no. But then the orderly told Drewry that he could not take the horse out of camp. "Who said so?" demanded the Texan. "The colonel," the orderly replied. Drewry immediately found the officers' tent and asked to speak to the colonel, whose name he did not know, and was presented to the commander of the 16th Michigan. Drewry complained that his horse was wrongly taken from him.[7]

What business did he have with a horse, the colonel demanded, noting that Drewry was a sergeant, not a commissioned officer. "No, only a non-commissioned," Drewry answered. "But in our army we have to furnish our own horses, or walk, as our government is too poor to furnish them." Because the mare was his personal property, he was allowed to keep it, under the surrender terms, when his battery turned in its guns and Confederate-issued teams of horses and mules. But the Yankee colonel ended the meeting abruptly, cursing Drewry and flatly stating that he could not have the mare. When the outraged Confederate stepped outside, his horse, bridle, saddle, and what clothes he had packed on it were gone. It was, he said, "a dastardly act," and the "only unkind, ungenerous act that I heard of at Appomattox."

Drewry told a Union cavalry officer on Gen. Sheridan's staff the next day about how his horse was stolen, and the officer said if Drewry would point out the offending officer, he would get it back. "But I was mad with all the Yankees then, and felt that my word would not stand against a colonel in the Union army," Drewry wrote. Years later, he learned from a friend the identity of the colonel of the 16th Michigan—Benjamin F. Partridge. His friend asked Partridge about Drewry's horse; "He [Partridge] admitted taking a horse from an artillery sergeant, but thinks he turned it over to the quartermaster," Drewry wrote of the explanation that was passed along to him.

The 16th Michigan's Thomas Lackie added a postscript to this after Drewry told him the story at the turn of the century. "I met him [Partridge] several years ago before he died [in 1892], and he told me that he was prosecuting a claim against the government for the loss of a horse," Lackie wrote. "This was an old gray nag, which died one rainy night at Appomattox Court House. I remember he got another horse exactly answering the description of the animal owned by Mr. Drewry, and for which he informed me . . . he paid $170." Of course, according to Drewry, Partridge had paid him nothing for the horse.[8]

The Texan probably never knew that Partridge received a kind of ironic and painful justice in the weeks that followed the surrender and his taking Drewry's mare. On the 16th Michigan's march back to Washington, on April 27, Partridge later reported that "my horse mired and fell onto me, breaking the second and third ribs, causing me much suffering for a long time." Though Partridge had been a brave officer wounded multiple times, Lackie told Drewry that Partridge, nicknamed "Old Pheasant" by his men, was not popular with them.[9]

Following the surrender of flags and arms by the Rebel cavalry and artillery, it was the turn of the infantry. Joshua Chamberlain, then a brigadier general, later wrote that he was called on the evening of April 10 to their Fifth Corps headquarters and was told he was in charge of "the parade" of Union soldiers who would receive surrendered weapons and banners "of the rebel army the next morning." In turn, Chamberlain said he asked if he could command his old Third Brigade, which included his old regiment, the 20th Maine, and the 16th Michigan. Though his one-time comrade Ellis Spear would later dispute many of Chamberlain's accounts, records show that on April 10, Gen. Joseph Bartlett, their First Division commander, indeed ordered Chamberlain to command the Third Brigade, and that their corps commander, Gen. Griffin, ordered the First Division to move into town at noon on April 11 to relieve other Union troops who had been receiving Confederate weapons. Then-Col. Spear himself recorded in his diary that their brigade moved into town that foggy morning of the 11th, waiting for their old enemy "to turn over their arms."

Their part in receiving the surrender of Lee's infantry began the next day. The Third Brigade, with their entire division, formed along the main road through Appomattox Court House—the stage road that stretched between Lynchburg and Richmond. The 16th Michigan stood near the center of their brigade line on the south side of the road, with the 20th Maine to their right and others to their left, just east of the court house. More regiments from their First Division lined the north side of the road or stood in a second line behind the Michigan and Pennsylvania troops. Confederate infantry had been encamped just east of town, so they made their last march westward into town. Chamberlain said it was "a thrilling sight."[10]

Chamberlain prepared his men to acknowledge their old foe, the Army of Northern Virginia, ordering them to be ready for a bugle call at which the Union troops would shift their rifles from an "attention" position called "order arms" to "shoulder arms," where the men quickly shifted the position of their rifles, holding them in the right hand to the right side, perpendicular to the shoulder. They did so as the first of 21,000 or more Rebel soldiers came by their line—"a mark of respect," wrote the historians of the 118th Pennsylvania. The Confederates returned this marching salute, and regiment by regiment they stacked their arms, unslung their cartridge boxes, and turned over their colors. Yet Ellis Spear later rejected this claim that the Union soldiers saluted the Rebel infantry. "The whole business was without ceremony and the mere matter of detail consequent upon the surrender of two days before," he wrote dismissively. "There was no such 'gush.'"[11]

But both men, writing years later, agreed that it was a somber, quiet occasion. The 16th Michigan's Lackie said there was conversation during this process when soldiers from either side would ask: "What regiment is that?"

"Palmetto Sharpshooters," replied a South Carolinian. "16th Michigan," someone answered. Lackie said a Capt. W. B. Smith of the Rebel regiment turned to his veterans. "Boys, do you remember the 27th of June, 1862?" he asked. "This is the regiment that fired on us in the hollow and we captured their banner." Lackie said Smith looked at him as the South Carolinians began to march away, now without their rifles and flags. "Good bye," Smith said. "It is not over yet. We hope to meet you again." Lackie said "Capt. McGuire" of the 16th Michigan—meaning then-Lt. James Maguire of Ontonagon—pointed out to Smith his Rebels' "current condition"—that they had just surrendered, and they were not prisoners of war because they had agreed to put down their weapons and end the war. Go home, Maguire said, and live peacefully as citizens.[12]

Most of the paroled Confederates, having surrendered, immediately left for home; thousands already had. Though the surrender was a solemn occasion, once it was over Union soldiers again took souvenirs, cutting pieces from the Confederate flags. "Our regiment alone took thirteen flags," wrote William Visscher to his younger brother. "Lee's army gave their flags to our brigade. I send a small piece of two to you. Give a piece of one to A. and L." But the surrender was over on April 13, with more than 28,000 Confederate troops having signed paroles and turned in their weapons. Now the primary concern for the soldiers of the 16th Michigan and their comrades was a simple one—finding enough to eat by scavenging and taking food and cattle from local farms. With the bridges and railroads from the east destroyed during the campaign, and few supplies of provisions arriving at Appomattox Court House in the days after Lee's surrender, soldiers said they had no other choice.

"We have had some hardships here at times," Visscher wrote, "because the wagons cannot come up in time. At one time we had nothing but fresh beef to eat for two days, though I had a little corn which I roasted." When soldiers did not have rations, he told his family, they "generally go out to forage. That is, we go from camp and kill the first thing of the farmers we find, such as geese, turkeys, hens or cattle." Visscher gave as an example how he and his comrades went out, shot a fat heifer, and after cleaning and skinning the carcass, carried it back to camp with their rifles.

Visscher had learned his little brother was collecting funds for sick and wounded soldiers. "I am very glad of that," he wrote. "Poor boys, they suffer enough! I have seen them shot right near me, and I know it is bad." He committed a dollar to his brother's effort, but noted he would match whatever amount their father contributed.[13]

The shooting war was at last over for these soldiers. Yet the tragedy played on.

One of the officers of the 16th Michigan who spent much of his time in Washington in 1864 and 1865—and not by his choice—was Capt. William B. Roe of Plymouth, who had joined Stockton's Independent Regiment back in the summer of 1861 as first lieutenant in Company F. In December of that year, Lt. Roe was detailed for signal duty—the job of sending and receiving visual messages from station to station by signal flag, or torch, when the telegraph could not be used. Both Stockton and Roe thought this assignment, which had come down from their commanders, would take place within the regiment. But they were wrong. Roe was detached from the regiment, and reported to then-Maj. Albert G. Myer, chief of the army's signal officers.

Initially, Roe served on this duty with the Army of the Potomac in 1862. He was one of many signal officers to come under fire at the Yorktown siege as he kept McClellan's headquarters in communication with the navy squadron on the York River; he was part of the Union army's network of watchers and signal men who, from hilltops, monitored the Confederate invasion of Maryland in the Antietam campaign; and he was nearly captured by Rebel cavalry during Jeb Stuart's raid there a month later.[14]

Promoted to captain in 1863, Roe was sent to the Union army's Department of the Gulf of Mexico, where he soon was placed in command of signal officers who provided communications between navy gunboats and Union infantry in the campaign that captured Port Hudson, Louisiana, on the Mississippi, and also in later unsuccessful Union campaigns in Louisiana and Texas. He probably traveled more miles than any other member of the 16th Michigan. But ultimately he was sent back east to serve early in 1864 as the chief signal officer of the Department of Washington, where he was credited with his superiors for his important work when Jubal Early's men threatened the capital that summer.[15]

Though Capt. Roe's superiors routinely complimented his hard work and energy, he longed to return to the 16th Michigan and to have the chance for promotion that he seemed unable to get on detached service, though certainly his job in Washington was probably more routine once Lee surrendered. He had not been completely satisfied with his assignment, but his young wife, Ella, was absolutely delighted to be with him in the nation's capital.

She and Roe were engaged when the war had started, so Roe, then 30, and Ella, 18, married before Stockton's regiment left Michigan that fall in 1861. "I was a war bride," Ella Roe Nichols explained more than a half-century later. "We were married all in a flurry of hurry and excitement, the way war brides always are, I guess."[16]

Ella went with her husband to Washington—and had a ball during what she recalled as a busy, gay existence in the capital. "What a grand time I had there," she said about its social life. "Of course, there was much sorrow all around us and there was worry and responsibility for those in charge of affairs . . . I never saw any of that." She and other officers' wives organized parties and picnics; once her husband was back in Washington, they could ride out to the Georgetown signal camp together—"one of my favorite jaunts," she said.

Ella Roe had watched Lincoln's second inauguration from her window, across the street from the newly finished Capitol Building. By that time, she and her husband were a popular couple, well known enough in Washington social circles to be invited to the inaugural ball and dinner held in the Patent Building. Ella wore a brown silk dress with a white bodice, and had her hair done in what was then a fashionable "waterfall" style. "Eight of us went together, and we formed our own group for the cotillion and lancers that were the order for the evening," she remembered. "The president and Mrs. Lincoln sat in a flag-draped box and looked on. No, he didn't dance or mingle with the crowd and I didn't meet him that evening.

"But I did at other times, at receptions at the White House. He looked serious and careworn that night, as though he felt he did not feel in the mood for dancing." Everyone was certain the war was coming to an end as April began, she said, and by the time of Lee's surrender, U.S. flags hung in abundance from public buildings and houses. Though Ella Roe did not discuss what her husband's work was like as the war in Virginia came to an end, it is clear Capt. Roe "commuted" to his job a few miles away while they resided in Washington.[17]

Another 16th Michigan alumnus, who said he was in Washington in mid-April, was veteran George D. Sidman, then 20. After being wounded in the foot in the clash with Rebel cavalry as his corps was on the march in June 1863, Sidman was eventually assigned to the Veteran Reserve Corps, the service where sick and wounded soldiers who could still carry out light duty were assigned work as clerks, messengers, and guards in government offices; he was put in the reserves' 12th Regiment, Company D.

Sidman would later claim he was on his way to his quarters on the night of Good Friday, April 14, 1865, but stopped to lounge against a fence at the corner of Washington's 15th Street and Pennsylvania Avenue; he said he heard a gunshot and witnessed a large man run from a house on 15th and disappear into an alley, followed by the sound of screams. Sidman wrote that he ran into the house—the home of Secretary of State William Seward (which for the record was near, but not on, 15th Street)—and up its stairs, past a maid who was screaming, "the secretary has been killed." As he reached the secretary's bedroom, he continued, a man shouted, "Get a doctor! The secretary has been stabbed!" In response, Sidman claimed he ran to the surgeon general's office to get medical help, and gave the alarm to others. Later that night, as he gave a statement to officers about what he had seen, he said he learned that President Lincoln had been assassinated.[18]

Sidman's story as he told it years later was dramatic, but must be taken with a grain of salt; it simply does not correspond with the facts as they were recorded by other witnesses to the attempt on Seward's life by would-be assassin and Confederate veteran Lewis Payne, alias Powell, after 10 p.m. on the night of the 14th. Though Sidman claimed in a memoir that he saw the suspect run from Seward's house (which was on Madison Place), he also said he was not able to identify that man was Powell. Sidman also claimed he "was the first man in Seward's room after the assassination [attempt]," but there is simply no record of this, and it is evident that his story got taller with the telling; other details he gave were blatantly wrong. In truth, Sidman was probably a witness to the chaos that followed the assassination attempt on the secretary of state, sent to the scene with the reserves to keep order and protect the Sewards, after the fact.[19]

Within minutes of the attack on Seward, of course, actor and Confederate sympathizer John Wilkes Booth fatally shot the president at Ford's Theater. Capt. Roe and his wife were asleep as all hell broke loose, and within the hour they were awakened. "About 11:30 my husband's orderly knocked on our door and cried out, 'The president has been shot and Secretary Seward's throat cut!'" Ella remembered. The orderly continued, shouting, "'The city is in an uproar! Get up, sir!'" Orders were quickly given that no one could leave the city. "My husband went out to see that the directions were signaled to the outposts," she said.

Roe spent the rest of the night and morning of the 15th sending instructions to the signalmen to pass to the authorities. Of course, Booth escaped Washington, only to be killed eleven days later. Within a month's time, Roe, then 34, was discharged from the army for disability. He had spent most of his army service in the field, and his wife claimed it was this exposure that damaged his health. Roe died in 1867.[20]

George Sidman said decades later that he was held as a witness (though not able to identify Lewis Powell) or alternately, that he served as an orderly at the military tribunal that tried and convicted Booth's conspirators Powell, George Atzerodt, David Herold, and Mary Surratt. He said he saw them hanged on July 7, 1865, at the Old Penitentiary Building on the grounds of the Arsenal. Two years later, in recognition of his service during the trial, Sidman said he was briefly appointed U.S. consul to Mecklenburg, Germany. For some years afterward, Sidman worked as a clerk and pension examiner for the federal government.[21]

As Roe and Sidman were about to witness the terrible drama in Washington, the skies opened on their old 16th Michigan comrades on April 14. Their victory at Appomattox meant nothing to the forces of nature, nor could it get them rations. They were muddy, wet, and hungry, and many soldiers had no tents; they passed a miserable day. Around noon the next day their corps began a bedraggled, hungry march from Appomattox Court House. On the 16th they crossed the Appomattox River around noon, and near the town of Farmville, as the rain stopped, the soldiers were given the news that Lincoln had been assassinated. The president murdered? It had to be a camp story, some said; but a pall fell over them. Ellis Spear said the news was "a stunning blow which marred all our rejoicing, and filled us with pain and resentment."

The soldiers marched on to Burkeville, where the 16th Michigan camped with their comrades until April 20. Next came a stop-and-go and turn-around-again march along the Southside Railroad back to Sutherland Station that took three days. By the time their Fifth Corps camped there, William Visscher had to admit that the news of Lincoln's assassination was true.[22]

"I have written nothing about Lincoln's death as the soldiers did not believe the rumor," he wrote back to Holland, "but however sad, the report is true. Lincoln, Abraham Lincoln, the second Washington, has fallen through the bullet of a child of Satan, Booth. The Savior of his Country ended his earthly career just when the cannons announced the surrender of Lee." The chaplain of the 91st Pennsylvania gave an address to the soldiers, comparing the martyred president to John the Baptist—that Lincoln was a man sent of God, who in death was with Jesus. "I hope so," Visscher wrote about the sermon. "The event causes much grief in the army."[23]

Another recent recruit from western Michigan in the 16th Michigan, 26-year-old Herschel Foster from Brady Township in Kalamazoo County, heard from his wife Ellen about the reaction back home. "The greatest excitement prevails here on the account of the death of our nation's best friend, Abraham Lincoln," Ellen Foster wrote. "Saturday [April 15] every business place in Kalamazoo was closed and groups of men were to be seen in every part of the street, talking about it, while tears of sorrow ran down their cheeks." A man in Battle Creek who had gladly hailed the news was shot and dragged through the streets, she wrote, and a Kalamazoo man had been jailed for expressing the same thought. Those who hated Lincoln and rejoiced in the news, however, "had not better be heard saying" that, Ellen wrote; most of the local residents "are so enraged they will not stand a word from these fools."[24]

The man who received this letter was a new recruit in the 16th Michigan, yet no stranger to army life. Herschel Foster had joined the 13th Michigan Infantry back in the fall of 1861 and served in the west until being discharged for disability early in 1862. His family had already paid a heavy price in the war, with other members of their clan in the service dying of illness. Foster, probably figuring his army days were over, came home and married Ellen Hawkins, a 22-year-old schoolteacher. But Foster was drafted late in 1864 and reported to Camp Blair in Jackson, where he was assigned to the 16th Michigan that spring. Now that the war was over in Virginia, Ellen was hoping he would be sent home right away. "My dear husband," she wrote after telling of the reaction to the assassination, "I heard some good news yesterday. I heard the drafted men were to be discharged soon and come home. Oh! That it may be so. We know that they have discharged some and I should think if anyone of the drafted men are discharged, they all might."[25]

There was an ugly and dangerous moment at Sutherland Station when hungry (and angry) soldiers of the Third Brigade brawled with black troops assigned to guard a sutler's store, which was pillaged by men from the brigade. It led to an armed face-off between the soldiers and Union cavalry troopers, but the troopers backed down. "The brigade commander advised the cavalry commander to move his regiment away or some of them might get killed," wrote a historian of the 118th Pennsylvania. Of course, it was wrong for the soldiers to rob the sutler of his goods and threaten other Union troops, but these veterans were not going to be denied food while their own army was unable to supply them.[26]

For several days the 16th Michigan camped with their corps at or near this place, at last moving slowly in the direction of Petersburg, which they reached on May 5. This part of their march was a strange and moving experience for the veterans—passing through the country and battlefields where they had lost comrades over the past months. But they paraded through Petersburg, cheering their popular but wronged former commander of the Fifth Corps, Gen. Warren, and continued on their way toward Richmond and the James River. The marching and bivouacking went on for the next several days—over the

Chickahominy River, past Hanover Court House, across the Pamunkey, through Bowling Green to near Fredericksburg, and then across the Rappahannock.[27]

On May 11, as their marching column neared Washington, a thunderstorm blew in and lightning killed a headquarters wagon driver and two mules, Visscher wrote. "The boys swore as bad as ever because it rained and they wanted to stop," he wrote his family. Then, deciding he had to explain to them the shocking tendency for soldiers to curse and swear, he added: "In the field, one has rough associations." It was a hard march, he wrote, and it was nearly over. "The common report is that we shall be mustered out in the course of a few weeks, but I do not know," he said.

The regiment bivouacked with its corps near Fairfax Station on the Alexandria Railroad, and the next day reached Arlington Heights, just across the river from Washington. The men cheered as the dome of the Capitol came into view; good weather finally arrived but Visscher complained that he had no money, and that mail delivery was irregular. Nor were the men allowed to leave camp. "Here I am near the capital, U.S.A.," Visscher wrote. "I hope to see it [the Capitol] next week, for the report is that we will have a general review and then we may march all through Washington. It will be a nice thing if it is a cool day." Edward Hill, the veteran officer wounded in the gut as a captain nearly a year earlier, at last returned to the 16th Michigan, now promoted to lieutenant colonel. The soldier who helped Hill in his recovery, Pvt. John "Jack" Wood, later explained that Hill's wound had left him incapable of field duty.[28]

Though the shooting was over, disease continued to take its toll. Capt. Irving Belcher, a young officer from Flint whose father, Horatio Belcher of the 8th Michigan, had been killed in battle, was discharged for illness that week. For some reason, Belcher, who had survived the fighting, did not remain in the hospital, perhaps so he could accompany his regiment in the great review of the Union army that Visscher mentioned to his family. In the meantime, his regiment, with thousands of other soldiers, went into camp near Fall's Station, with thousands more men arriving over the course of the next several days for the review.

"Sherman's army arrived here last night," Herschel Foster wrote his wife about the Union soldiers who had closed out the war in the Carolinas. "You can walk all day as hard as you can and [still] be in camp all the time." But the weather began to turn hot, and Foster pleaded with his wife to send more letters, since life in camp was so boring and he had no news yet about when their discharge was coming. "We do not get any papers that have any news in them about the army," he wrote her. "You know more about what is to be with us than I do."[29]

At last, the 16th Michigan participated with its brigade, division, and corps in the grand review of the Union armies on May 23 and 24, rising before dawn on the 23rd to line up with the Army of the Potomac for the great parade. The day dawned clear and warm, and the Third Brigade of which the regiment was part was said to have led its division as the men of the Army of the Potomac crossed the Long Bridge and marched by the reviewing stand for President Andrew Johnson, the commanding generals, and dignitaries. The 16th Michigan was in the last half of their brigade's columns, marching down Pennsylvania

Avenue with the 1st Michigan Infantry and the remnants of the old 4th Michigan that had been assigned to that regiment. Riding with the regiment was Irving Belcher, who, though discharged and ill, nonetheless participated with the 16th Michigan as the parade tramped through. Within three months' time, however, Belcher would be gone, dying at Ithaca, New York, on August 11, 1865, a month short of his 23rd birthday while reportedly on his way home.

But the grand review was a joyous event. Though no accounts or commentaries of this moment by any member of the 16th Michigan seem to exist, others in their brigade described it as a glorious day, with cheering crowds and stirring music. "Pennsylvania Avenue was a mass of men, women and children to limit of the pavements," wrote a historian of the 155th Pennsylvania. "Housetops, balconies, porches, doors, windows, platforms, everywhere, a roaring, cheering mass of humanity." Maine's Ellis Spear said the march of the Union army was "such as none now living may ever see again."[30]

The soldiers went back to their giant encampments, and soon young Visscher was sick with diarrhea and fever. "I went to the doctor and got some medicine, I do so every morning," he wrote his family. "I am recovering now." Being ill was an expensive proposition, for sutlers' food prices were high, and he had to ask his parents to send him money. "Everything here is shamefully expensive," he complained. "Butter, 30 [cents], cheese 20 cents a pound, and eggs 50 cents a dozen." Herschel Foster, writing to his wife that same night, told of a spontaneous and beautiful candlelight parade put on by the soldiers themselves. "Night before last about 75 or 80 thousand of our men all lit a candle and put it in their bayonet and fell in and marched all over camp," Foster said, overestimating the number of participants in the event. "It made a very nice sight." Others thought it was moving and spectacular. Some men had been singing as darkness fell, and others took out candles they had been issued that evening and fell into line with the singers, starting an informal march through the camps. The parade took on a life of its own as several thousand soldiers formed a procession with their bayonet-mounted candles "out of pure joy," a veteran of the Third Brigade wrote." It went on until their candles went out, the last march the men of the 16th Michigan's brigade, division, and corps would experience together. In the days ahead, scores of these regiments mustered out of the army and the men went home, their service done.[31]

The weather was warm and periodically rainy though the end of May and into June; the soldiers' duty was dull and tedious, the men restless and impatient to go back to Michigan. The war was ended, yet soldiers of the 16th Michigan were not being sent home, probably because the government could not just muster out scores of thousands of Union troops at the same time; historian Jeffry Wert noted that the disbandment of the armies took weeks. On June 5, General George Meade issued orders that ten regiments from the Fifth Corps, including the 16th Michigan, were to be moved to Louisville, Kentucky. Doubtless there was much complaining and grousing, since regiments that had not served as long as the veterans of the 16th Michigan were already being sent home. Thomas Lackie later blamed his regiment's continued service on Col. Partridge, "Old Pheasant," who he claimed had "endeavored to have the government make us serve the balance of our enlistment." How or why Partridge could have possibly done this Lackie did not explain—in truth, the dispersing of Union regiments in this way probably helped the mustering-out process. But he claimed Partridge received threats as a result, and that the colonel of the 16th Michigan had to hide, eventually leaving the regiment while the governor of Michigan promised a speedy muster out. "We never saw him again until the day we were paid off in the city of Detroit," Lackie later wrote of the colonel.[32]

Days after Meade's order, on the morning of June 16, the soldiers of the 16th Michigan broke camp, marched into Washington, and boarded a westbound train. "We passed through Harper's Ferry in the evening and went through a range of the Alleghenys [sic, Appalachians] where we had glorious views," William Visscher wrote of the trip. It was amazing for the young man to experience rocky tunnel walls and mountainsides passing within a few feet of the rolling cars.[33]

The train stopped at Parkersburg, West Virginia, on the evening of June 18 and the men camped for night. In the morning, they boarded a steamer for the trip down the Ohio River to Louisville—a trip Herschel Foster said took three days and two nights. They arrived on June 21 and afterward moved across the river to Jefferson, Indiana. "We camped in a very good place," Foster wrote as the month ended. "Plenty of good water." But his comrade Visscher landed in the hospital not far from the camp within a few days; he urged his family not to be alarmed. "Nothing is ailing me other than some swelling of the feet," Visscher wrote. "I have an excellent place here—the best of bed and board and everything I need." His comrades could visit him, since their camp was so close.[34]

As June ended, soldiers at last got the word they had been waiting for. "Now, dear wife," wrote Foster, "I have some good news to tell you. Our lieutenant colonel told me yesterday that we should be home in ten days and perhaps before, so you see if that is true I shall be with my darling wife before long." The regiment would have to go to Detroit first, he wrote, so that they could get their pay, but he hoped he would have a chance to see her if their train ride home took them through Kalamazoo. If the men had to stay in Detroit for a period in order to get their pay, well, there was nothing to be done about it. "I shall have all the more to tell you when I get home," he wrote.[35]

The 16th Michigan's last days in Jefferson were hot and rainy, and Visscher spent the Fourth of July in the hospital. The day there was notable for its "first rate dinner," he said, topped off by a bottle of sweetened, slightly diluted wine, compliments of the ward doctor. "I expect to be mustered out any day, with my regiment," Visscher continued. "I would like to be in perfect health before I leave, but if the regiment goes, I intend to go along."[36]

Three days later, on July 8, the 16th Michigan was formally mustered out of the service of the United States. On the 10th, 555 soldiers and officers of the regiment boarded a train and left for home, arriving first in Jackson and then in Detroit on July 12. Visscher, as promised, was with them. "We arrived in the evening and had a splendid reception and supper," he wrote home. "The 16th received a hearty welcome," the *Detroit Free Press* agreed, "and the gladly fluttering display of white handkerchiefs along the line of First

Street, Woodward and Jefferson Avenue, as they marched to the barracks, escorted by a detachment of Metropolitans [Detroit police officers] in full uniform, cheered the weary soldiers only less than the smiles that were likewise liberally bestowed."[37]

Now it was a matter of waiting for their final pay, which came less than two weeks later on July 25. Col. Partridge said their conduct during that time was excellent, and that they acted as gentlemen and citizens; he issued each man a certificate of their service, listing the battles in which each soldier had taken part. Finally, he gave them a last address—that it was now the moment they were going home, the time they had so long anticipated. "This is the hour which has served as talisman to each of you during the last four years," he said. "The rebellion crushed out of existence, the Union one and inseparable, and yourselves enabled to return to your homes, to follow the pursuits of life. May your career in civil life be as successful as your military has been."

He praised them as patriots and soldiers and called on them not to forget the loved ones of those who had not come back. "When I look around me and see the heroes of such battles as Gaines' Mill, Malvern Hill, Chancellorsville, Gettysburg and the tremendous Wilderness fights, and then think of the noble spirits we lost at those places," Partridge continued, "it would seem that we were cemented to each other by something stronger than common ties of friendship . . . Let us cherish with reverence the memory of our fallen braves; and let us ever be ready to the extent of our power, to aid a dependent relative of any of those who fell in the cause of liberty, and in the ranks of our glorious organization."

Partridge invoked the memory of Major Robert Elliott, the Detroiter and commander who had been fatally wounded in action near Bethesda Church, and Norval Welch, the young Ann Arbor attorney and colonel killed at Peeble's Farm. "He fell with sword uplifted in the air, his foot upon the enemy's works, and the shout of victory upon his lips," the colonel said. "May their names and their gallant deeds never be forgotten." He again praised the men's patriotism and wished them well, and closing, called them the "bravest of soldiers, kindest of comrades. God bless you. Farewell."[38]

Home beckoned, but the war's toll had not yet ceased. Frank McGinness, 29, had joined the Saginaw company, D, on a late summer's day nearly four years earlier, and was later a corporal and sergeant in Company E; but he had taken a bullet that passed through both lungs while a member of the color guard at Second Bull Run in August 1862. Left for dead, he was recognized the next day by the burial detail. McGinness spent six months in the hospital before rejoining the 16th Michigan, serving for the rest of the war "without reprimand." Now, two weeks after his honorable discharge and return with his regiment, McGinness died in Detroit's Harper Hospital from the effects of his wounds.

Sixty-five miles north in Genesee County, schoolteacher Sarah Aplin, the sister of Lt. Henry "Tip" Aplin, was waiting expectantly for more than a week in mid-July for the arrival of her brother. Sarah had been spending the summer in the country at the family's property outside of Flint. But hearing that the 16th Michigan was now back in the state, she decided to leave the farm in Thetford Township and go into town, to keep a vigil at the train depot. Their family had lost Sarah's youngest brother Tommy in the war, and their older brother George, in the 10th Michigan, was also mustering out. But now it was just a matter of days, perhaps hours, that her brother Tip—who had loved to dance more than anything else, who had been captured taking care of sick and wounded men, who had been under fire, dangerously sick, and successful at selling matches and goods—returned home.

"I think I shall go to Flint tomorrow," she wrote, "and watch the cars till Tip comes."[39]

EPILOGUE

YOUR NAMES ARE AN ETERNAL BENEDICTION

William Visscher went home to Holland, Michigan, sick and thin after his five-month stint with the 16th Michigan. He recovered his health and helped build a fine new three-story brick home for his family with the bounty he had been paid. According to a sketch of his life, based on his letters and those of his relatives, he studied theology and earned degrees at Hope College near his home, eventually heading to New York City, where he studied medicine and taught Sunday school across the Hudson River at Guttenberg, New Jersey.

Early in February 1872, Visscher came down with what he and his associates there thought was a cold, but it soon proved to be smallpox. Either he had not been vaccinated against the disease in the war, as had so many thousands of his former comrades, or his vaccination was ineffective. His family in Michigan was stunned to learn that he died several days later; he was only 26. Visscher was buried in the Lutheran Cemetery in Brooklyn. The story of his service with the 16th Michigan survived in a collection of letters, written in Dutch, found decades later by his American relatives in a box in his parents' original hometown of Geneminden, in the house where he had been born in 1845.[1]

Lt. Henry "Tip" Aplin returned to Flint, but eventually settled in Bay City and married. Perhaps his experiences selling matches and other commodities to soldiers, and then serving as quartermaster sergeant, shaped his future, for he ran a news and stationery business there; he also went into public service and politics, serving as postmaster, township clerk, and chairman of the local Republican congressional district committee. Later he was elected state auditor general and state representative, and served as a U.S. congressman, sent to the House of Representatives in 1901 to fill a vacancy after the sitting member from his district died in office, though Aplin was not renominated to run for that post.

Aplin was active in the Union veterans' organization called the Grand Army of the

Republic (G.A.R.), as well as his regiment's association. He was a partner in a local ice company; in a venture that brought electric street cars to his town; and even in a popular amusement park. Yet it was said he was never truly rid of the intestinal ailment that had plagued him when he had fallen ill in the summer of 1862, staying behind at Savage's Station with sick and wounded Union soldiers as McClellan's Army of the Potomac retreated from Richmond; in the last years of Aplin's life, he was extremely sick several times. His heart probably weakened by chronic illness, he died in Bay City at the age of 69.[2]

Another veteran of the 16th Michigan from the Saginaw Valley who became known for his public service was John Northwood, a London-born lad who had come to Ohio and then Michigan with his family as pioneers in Saginaw County's Maple Grove Township, and who had worked as a sailor on the Great Lakes. Northwood was 23 when he joined Stockton's regiment in the summer of 1861 and a year later was wounded in both arms as he served with Company C; his right arm was amputated, and his army service was over.

Returning to Michigan, Northwood moved to a nearby community where he served as township clerk, supervisor, justice of the peace, school inspector, and Republican state legislator. He was a proponent for a state home for disabled Michigan veterans and served as paymaster general on the military staff of the governor's office; he also served as the commander of the Michigan department of the G.A.R. Northwood died in New Lothrop at the age of 84.[3]

Dr. William F. Breakey, the surgeon who resigned his commission because of disability in April 1864, went back to Ann Arbor. In 1868 he was appointed assistant demonstrator of anatomy and prosecutor of surgery at the University of Michigan, and he remained associated with the school until 1912. There he established the department of dermatology and syphilology in 1905, and wrote articles on medical and scientific subjects; he also examined veterans who applied for government pensions and served as Ann Arbor's health officer. "He never harshly criticized others," wrote the author of the *Medical History of Michigan,* "but had a kind word for everybody. He was an able physician, a high-minded gentleman, a loyal friend and an esteemed colleague." The injury to his left leg, incurred accidentally in a collision or fall as he tended the wounded of Gettysburg, was increasingly troublesome and painful as the years progressed, but the doctor was said to have borne it without complaint. Dr. Breakey died in 1915 at 79.[4]

Benjamin F. Partridge returned to Bay City after the war with the brevet rank of brigadier general for his gallant conduct at the White Oak Road on March 29, 1865. He complained it was a struggle to return his farm to prosperity and he became an employee in the U.S. Internal Revenue Department for the Michigan district that took in Bay City from 1867 to 1871; he also served as township supervisor and was elected to the post of commissioner of the state land office in 1877.

Partridge sent letters about the 16th Michigan at Gettysburg to historian John Bachelder and Michigan Adjutant General John Robertson, who was preparing a book on Michigan's contribution in the war, in response to their queries for information. His letter to Robertson contains the only known statement made by a member of the regiment about the actions of Col. Norval Welch at the battle for Little Round Top. In the spring of 1889, he was chosen to serve on a legislative committee with two other Michigan veterans as the state prepared to memorialize its soldiers who fought at Gettysburg. Monuments were then being built, and it was the job of Partridge and his fellow committee members to enlist the Michigan Legislature for financial support for the dedication of these monuments. They succeeded; state lawmakers approved $2,000 for ceremonies at Gettysburg and another $5,000 so that surviving Michigan soldiers who had participated in the battle could attend.

Partridge said his war wounds—and he had several—continued to bother him. He died on October 19, 1892, at his home in Portsmouth Township and was buried in Bay City's Elm Lawn Cemetery.[5]

John G. Berry, the volunteer from Ontonagon in Company A who kept a diary for at least part of his service with the 16th Michigan, got his lieutenant's commission about a month after the war ended in Virginia. In Detroit after the war, Berry was successful in business and real estate and led a group of veterans in the founding of his own town, Berryville, in what became Michigan's Otsego County, in 1877. Unfortunately for residents, a fire burned it to the ground in 1910 and it was never rebuilt. In the meantime, Berry served in Lansing as a state senator, and was elected to the post of commissioner of the state land office, like other former 16th Michigan officers. But unlike other land office commissioners, he was removed from the position in 1894 by the governor when it was determined that Berry, along with the state treasurer, and the secretary of state, as members of the state board of canvassers, had conducted a grossly negligent vote count for a measure to increase the pay of certain Michigan officials. Why? The board had reported this measure was approved by voters, when in fact it had been defeated.

But Berry remained active in veterans' organizations and their activities and traveled extensively around the country and the world, visiting Hawaii and New Zealand, and reportedly was in San Francisco when the great earthquake struck, but he was unhurt. Berry died in Otsego County at the age of 85 in August 1923.[6]

Alfred M. Apted, the Brady Sharpshooter wounded in the left arm at Peeble's Farm, mustered out of the army in March 1865. He returned to Grand Rapids, married, and was eventually made a superintendent of the mills of the Grand Rapids Plaster and the Grand Rapids Gypsum companies. Army surgeons had wanted to amputate his arm back in 1864, but Apted said no; his left arm was useless, and at some point doctors removed four inches of bone. Whenever this surgery took place, whether during or after the war, it would have been a painful and probably risky procedure.

On August 4, 1877, Apted became the first person in Grand Rapids to speak on the newly invented telephone, created just a year earlier. Alexander Graham Bell had given a set of the devices to the president of the plaster company, a close friend. The proud owner of these examples of new technology decided to have a demonstration for some visiting dignitaries, so the telephones were hooked up to a telegraph line running between his company's downtown office and the mill that Apted ran, two miles away.

Speaking on the device from the office, Apted told the man on the other end of the line, a mill employee, to sing into the telephone. "There is a party visiting you here and would like to hear you sing 'John Brown's Body,'" directed Apted, who was known to enjoy singing Civil War songs. The employee at the other end of the line dutifully sang "Glory, glory, hallelujah" several times over while, two miles away, the astonished crowd around Apted listened in awe.

A few pages of notes, accounts of the experiences of 16th Michigan soldiers and transcriptions of official reports from the war, found with Apted's diary, indicate that Apted and Benjamin Partridge were gathering information for a regimental history, but nothing came of it. According to Apted's obituary, complications from his disabling wound to his arm caused his death at age 62 in February 1900.[7]

Edward Hill, who left the army as lieutenant colonel of the 16th Michigan (and the brevet rank of colonel), carried a minié ball in his abdomen for the rest of his life. He periodically wrote or spoke about his regiment and their Third Brigade. But the wound increasingly troubled him, requiring him to have help getting dressed, and worse, leaving him without control of his bowels—"and in consequence [I] am compelled to lead a life of seclusion," he wrote in 1890. Yet he married and traveled, seeking medical help, residing for periods in New York, Fredericksburg, St. Louis, Michigan, and Green Bay, Wisconsin. Hill, wrote a Michigan newspaper in 1897, "is a sufferer from the war and at present is at Alma Sanitarium."

Hill made it a goal to tabulate the 16th Michigan's sacrifice in the Civil War by going through transcripts and muster rolls of the War Department, the state of Michigan, and other official sources. He used unofficial sources as well, conferring by letter with the regiment's veterans to ensure that men who had been listed as missing in action had not really deserted. The project took him and his helpers two years and many revisions. Hill said that his list, completed in 1899 and published the next year, showed that 168 men and officers of the regiment had been killed in action, and that another 98 died of their wounds or perished in Confederate prisons (a number that breaks down to more than seventy mortally wounded, with more than twenty others dying in Rebel prison, some of whom were wounded when they were captured). At least ten men had gone missing in action and were never heard from again. All told, 632 men from the regiment had been wounded, Hill found, and another 106 men died of disease.

Put another way, Hill's research showed that about 250 members of the 16th Michigan died in battle or as a result of wounds—a number that rises if one includes those who went missing in action and those who died of starvation and disease at Andersonville, or

Salisbury, or other Confederate prisons. Naturally, he spoke of the regiment's sacrifice in dramatic, heroic terms. "This fact stands as an undisputed proof in the history of the war," he wrote in 1888, "that where the black smoke of battle rolled heaviest, there the 16th could be found."[8]

Several years before his death, Hill decided that George Sidman, the teen who had been one of the youngest volunteers in the 16th Michigan, should be nominated for the Medal of Honor for gallantry in battle. In the spring of 1892, Hill wrote to General Daniel Butterfield, then living in New York, outlining Sidman's war record. His petition told of Sidman's decision to carry a rifle and give up his drum; of the teen's wounding and capture at Gaines' Mill, and his time in Confederate prisons; of Sidman's refusal to stay in the hospital, and how he had rejoined his regiment on the march to Antietam. And it told how Sidman carried the brigade flag at Fredericksburg, and risked his life the next day to bring water to his comrades while they were trapped under the guns on Marye's Heights. Butterfield endorsed the nomination and sent it on to the secretary of war. Sidman, then a clerk in the U.S. Department of the Interior, was issued the Medal of Honor on April 6, 1892. Sidman's medal has routinely been on display in the Civil War exhibit of the Michigan Historical Museum in Lansing.[9]

Sidman himself had initially gone home to live in Shiawassee County and other places in Michigan after the war but eventually traveled to South Africa, where he edited a newspaper, mined diamonds, and made safari-type expeditions before returning to the United States in 1879 and working as an examiner of the government's pension bureau. He outlived two wives and married a third, residing in Rochester, New York, and then near Washington before he died at 55 of chronic nephritis early in 1900. Sidman was buried in Arlington National Cemetery. When a member of his clan took on the family's genealogy in the 20th century, she wrote that George Sidman was "far and away the most colorful figure encountered" in her research.[10]

In 1893, the year of the 16th Michigan's reunion in Sidman's old hometown of Owosso, thirty-five members of the regiment signed a petition requesting that Edward Hill be granted a Medal of Honor, for gallantry in the skirmish line attack on Rebel positions on June 1, 1864, near Bethesda Church—an attack, the veterans maintained, that was to reveal the placements of hidden Confederate batteries. It was in that skirmishing that Hill was severely wounded. Again, Dan Butterfield made the formal nomination to the secretary of war, and on December 4, 1893, Hill, then living in St. Louis, Michigan, was issued the Medal of Honor.[11]

On May 25, 1900, Hill gave a speech during the ceremonies at the laying of a cornerstone for a monument to the Fifth Corps at Fredericksburg, and that fall he attended the reunion of the 16th Michigan in Flint, "where his patriotism and love of comrades impelled to overdo, perhaps, and thereby hastened his death," a newspaper reported. The effects of his 1864 wound finally took his life, and Hill died of a bowel obstruction on October 26 that year in Green Bay; he was buried in the Fredericksburg National Cemetery.[12]

Charles H. Salter, the modest and conscientious volunteer from Detroit who started the Civil War as a private in the ninety-day 1st Michigan and ended his service as brevet major with the 16th Michigan for his conspicuous bravery throughout the 1864 campaign in Virginia, went back home into the grocery business. In 1865, he opened his own store on West Fort Street, and eventually married and had a family. David Lee Poremba, a veteran writer and editor of books on Detroit history, would note that Salter eventually applied for an invalid pension—that the young officer had suffered a severe hernia while on the march during the Second Bull Run campaign in the fall of 1862. Though Salter told his friends he became sick with fever and was hospitalized, he said nothing of this ailment and carried on into 1865.

Salter continued in his postwar life the practice he had maintained during the war: He sought no attention about his army experience, published no accounts, and gave no speeches as did his old comrades Frank Keeler, Ziba Graham, Edward Hill, and Rufus Jacklin. But his letters to Isabella Duffield stand as the most comprehensive account of the 16th Michigan in the Civil War up to its final weeks. Salter died of a stroke at the age of 52 in March 1892 and was buried in Woodmere Cemetery, his passing unnoted in Detroit newspapers, though he had commanded the 16th Michigan from the death of Norval Welch at Peeble's Farm in the fall of 1864, to the Applejack Raid that winter.[13]

Marion H. Munson, the young volunteer in the 16th Michigan's Company E who made sometimes biting comments about the war, Lincoln, and his own officers, but who served his regiment loyally, returned to Oakland County after the war, married, and became a farmer in Orion Township. He moved in and out of the state until settling in Fenton, where he had relatives. The fact that Munson had two wounds to his left hand and arm, suffered in 1864 and 1865, undoubtedly made farming very difficult; by the turn of the century, he was listed as a pensioner. Munson had a long life and a seemingly quiet one, dying in June 1933. He was buried in Fenton's Oakwood Cemetery.[14]

Perhaps the most successful former member of the regiment in postwar politics had probably also been the 16th Michigan's youngest volunteer. This was James S. Laird, a soldier from Company G, reportedly 13 at the time he joined Stockton's regiment in the summer of 1861. Laird was wounded and captured at Gaines' Mill and later exchanged, but he returned to the regiment that fall. He rose through the ranks, mustering out as a captain, having been promoted a month after the war ended in Virginia. Laird attended Adrian College and graduated from the University of Michigan's law school in 1871. He went into Republican politics in Nebraska and served in the U.S. House of Representatives from 1883 to 1889. He was said to be a popular figure, but reportedly drank heavily and suffered a nervous breakdown in his last campaign. Laird died that year at the age of 40 and was buried in Hastings, Nebraska.[15]

These brief biographies are indicative as to how, when the ex-soldiers went into public service, they were almost always conservative Republicans; one who was a Democrat, Pontiac's Charles Nisbett, who served briefly in the 16th Michigan during the last weeks of the war and published a newspaper in Big Rapids afterward, was noted for that singularity. Like thousands of veterans, many of these men participated in civic and political activities in their communities and in the Grand Army of the Republic, and of course they honored those who had not come home. In Ionia, the local G.A.R. chapter was called the Borden Post in memory of the young lieutenant William Borden, killed at Gettysburg. In Ann Arbor, the local chapter was named the Welch Post for Col. Norval E. Welch. "Those who were once his comrades will never lack a welcome in our midst," an Ann Arbor editor wrote in 1894.[16]

Two decades or so after the Civil War, the surviving veterans of the 16th Michigan tracked each other down and organized yearly reunions, held at locations around the state. The comradery and fellowship of these reunions, as reflected in news accounts, made them warm and moving events, with humorous speakers, patriotic toasts, and touching memorials almost always part of the programs. In 1893, for example, Ellis Spear, a former commander of the 20th Maine, sent a letter to the 16th Michigan's association to be read to the assembled veterans in Owosso, saying that he had hoped to get back the axe stolen from him thirty years previously. He also wanted to know what had become of the hot stove they had carried away, a reference to the one the regiment had stolen on their train trip back to Michigan early in 1864. But there were also serious and reflective moments, such as in the fall of the next year when the 16th Michigan veterans held their reunion in Ann Arbor. On that afternoon after their business meeting, they boarded electric trolley cars and journeyed to Forest Hill Cemetery to visit the grave of Col. Norval Welch.[17]

Ziba Graham presented his paper, "On to Gettysburg," loosely based on his diary at the regiment's business meeting that afternoon, and that evening Dr. Breakey served as toastmaster at their dinner. The now-reverend Reuben Turrell gave the invocation, Theodore Hoeninghausen sounded the "Dan Butterfield" brigade call on his old bugle, and Rufus Jacklin read his paper, "The Famous Old Third Brigade." Alfred M. Apted, secretary of the 16th Michigan's association, read the letters and telegrams of those who could not attend. But Dr. Robert Everett also spoke, and so did George Prentiss from Detroit, who had resigned from the regiment back in early February 1863, and who talked about "our comrades mustered out." Tip Aplin spoke on the women left behind when the volunteers had gone to war, and perhaps he told of his own mother Elvira and his sister Sarah. Aplin, Saginaw's Frank Keeler, and Detroit's Thomas Lackie were among several men who vied for a haversack of mixed rations of hardtack, coffee, and tobacco "for the best three-minute story of life in the old 16th."

When the evening was over, Hoeninghausen played another composition by their old Third Brigade commander that was now known through the U.S. Army and beyond—the plaintive "Taps" that Dan Butterfield had adapted in 1862 after the Seven Days. The "day is done" bugle lullaby, wrote historian John Pullen, is "the one expression of tenderness the army ever allows itself."[18]

The man who had formed the 16th Michigan as his own regiment, Col. Thomas B. W. Stockton, went back to Flint after being unable to raise regiments for the state of Tennessee, and tended his business as a "forwarding and commission agent" from his warehouse near the city's downtown. He remained a Democrat in what was a Republican state for the rest of his life and was a delegate to the national convention that nominated Horace Greeley in his bid for the presidency in 1872 against incumbent President Ulysses Grant. Politics makes strange bedfellows, and one can only wonder whether Greeley's candidacy as an "independent" or "liberal" Republican, with the backing of the Democratic Party, brought Stockton into some sort of agreement with his old antagonist, former governor Austin Blair. Blair ran again for governor that year as a Liberal Republican but, like Greeley, was badly defeated.

But Stockton was successful in business and built a gracious Italianate home for his wife Maria. Along with their son Bayliss, they joined the Roman Catholic Church in 1868. The husband of their niece Louise, James Longstreet, was a regular visitor to their home for many years after the war. Did the two old soldiers refight battles or argue politics, since Longstreet was now a Republican who supported his old army friend, Grant? One can only imagine.

Perhaps even more ironic was the fate of the Stockton's other former Confederate nephew, George Deas, Longstreet's brother-in-law, who also settled with his wife's relatives in Michigan. As a colonel in the rebel army, Deas had snubbed Stockton personally when, as a prisoner in Richmond, Stockton had asked him for help. Yet after the war Deas and his wife Bessie, another member of the John Garland clan, moved to Flint. Deas died in May 1870 of "a broken rebel heart," his friends said. Once an important Confederate military official, he remains in death with his Yankee relatives, buried with his wife, the Stocktons, and other relatives of the Garlands nearby in Flint's Glenwood Cemetery.

Stockton's health began to decline in the 1880s, and when the regiment held its reunion in Flint in 1888, the veterans marched to Stockton's house to visit so that the old colonel would not have to stand the strain of their afternoon business meeting, though he attended their dinner at the Bryant Hotel that evening. Increasingly frail, he attended his regiment's next reunion at Saginaw's McCormick Hall the next fall. "The venerable Col. Stockton . . . was too weak to take part in all the exercises yesterday, but last evening he occupied the place of honor at the banquet," a news account said. At the closing of the event, Rufus Jacklin presented a silver water service to Stockton, then 84, and his wife.

Stockton rose from his chair. "God bless you all," the old soldier said, and sank back into his seat. It was his last appearance in public; for the last year of his life, he was not able to leave his home. He did at 85 on the morning of December 13, 1890. The fact that Stockton had, as a young army officer and husband, owned a slave in the 1830s had been forgotten in his time, with perhaps the last word published on the matter being the infamous Dred Scott decision itself. What was remembered in the local history books was that Stockton virtually fought his way into serving his country during the Civil War, despite his dislike for Republicans, abolition, and the fact that Governor Blair tried to block his way.[19]

By 1910 nearly 200 members of the 16th Michigan were still living, and between sixty and seventy-five of these veterans were said to be attending the yearly reunions. Frank Keeler was nearly 70 but he was left little choice about his continued involvement in the reunion. "There is general consent that Frank Keeler will have to keep the secretary-treasurership [*sic*], unless he wants to prompt a small rebellion in the ranks," a Saginaw paper wrote.[20]

The regimental association brought together Oakland County brothers James A. Clark and Robert B. Clark, who had first joined the lancers and then entered the 16th Michigan. Both had been wounded at Gaines' Mill, and James, the younger of the two, had been held for a while by the Confederates. But James had served until the close of the war, while Robert was mustered out in the late fall of 1862, and they lost track of each other over the decades. "One very delightful effect of the reunion was the bringing together of two brothers who had not met before for forty years," reported the Owosso paper at the regiment's 1912 gathering. George Sidman, who was then working as a clerk in Washington, had used pension records to invite both men to the reunion, not knowing they were brothers. Robert, 72, was living in St. Cloud, Florida, while James, 71, lived at the Michigan Soldiers' Home in Grand Rapids. They recognized each other immediately. "To say they were overjoyed would be putting it mildly," the paper reported.[21]

A newspaper report about the 16th Michigan's reunion states that nineteen surviving veterans and their spouses and family members met in Plymouth in 1919, and that they made plans for a 1920 gathering at Grass Lake, a small town near Jackson. John Berry and Frank Keeler were still in attendance. Saginaw's Keeler was likely one of the last survivors of the 16th Michigan. For more than fifty years he worked for the Flint & Pere Marquette Railway, starting as a freight clerk and retiring as paymaster. He served on the school board and was secretary to the city's water board, and he enjoyed telling local high school students about his experiences in the Civil War.

One of Keeler's sons came into possession of a printing press and for a lark he transcribed and edited the surviving letters his father had written during the war, using the hand-powered press to print one page at a time and bind the pages into a small book. The resulting *War Letters Written During the Rebellion* was the only book published about the 16th Michigan, but the number printed was quite small. It is a rare book, and an important source of non-official information about the regiment's experiences.[22]

Keeler was active in veterans' affairs for decades after the war, and by the mid-1930s he was one of a handful of Michigan men alive who had served in the Civil War. He died on June 4, 1937, just short of his 96th birthday, and was buried in Saginaw's Forest Lawn Cemetery. At 92, Keeler had been elected state commander of the Grand Army of the Republic, and there had been talk of merging the GAR with their Confederate counterparts, but it was a controversial issue. Keeler's position was clear. "The time is not yet ripe," he declared. "I do not believe joint conventions of the two organizations would be advisable at this time."[23]

In 1887, the state of Michigan appointed three veteran officers to a Gettysburg Battlefield Commission, to seek proposals and designs for monuments to be located at or near the scenes where state soldiers fought on July 1, 2, and 3, 1863. The Legislature decided that Michigan would have nine monuments; the 16th Michigan's, like those of the other commands at the battle, was allocated $1,350. The Smith Granite Company of Rhode Island got the contract for the 16th Michigan monument, and four others as well. Bronze work for these monuments was awarded to the American Bronze Company of Chicago.[24]

The 16th Michigan monument on Little Round Top was modest compared to the 44th New York's tower, which rises dramatically from the hill's southern crest. Block-like, solid, and plain, the regiment's marker stands on the first shelf below the hilltop; five and a half feet tall, it rests on a base just over seven feet long and three-and-a-half feet wide. Carved just below the peak of the monument is the Maltese cross, the symbol of the Fifth Corps of the Army of the Potomac, wreathed in laurels. Directly below the emblem, in similar bas-relief, is a rifle.

The words "SIXTEENTH MICH. INF'TY" are carved on the monument's face, just over a bronze State of Michigan seal, and on either side of this appear the regiment's brigade, division, and corps designations; there is an outline of the regiment's record on the western face of the monument, with the dates of its enrollment and muster-in and muster-out, and the numbers of men and officers killed in action. Also included are the number of men who died of wounds and disease, although the number, based on state and federal figures, was less than those reflected in the casualty study complied by Edward Hill.

A brief and incomplete history on the monument reads: "Regiment held this position during the afternoon and night of July 2, 1863, and assisted in defeating the desperate attempts of the enemy to capture Little Round Top. Present for duty, 17 officers, 349 men—total 365. Casualties: Killed, 3 officers, 20 men; wounded, 2 officers, 32 men; missing, three men—total 60." Again, these numbers do not reflect the smaller number of men of the 16th Michigan—about 200—who actually fought that afternoon, nor the larger number of casualties they suffered, but this was the information used for the monument.[25]

On the afternoon of June 12, 1889, about thirty veterans of the 16th Michigan gathered on Little Round Top for the dedication of their monument on the southwest face of the hill. John Weller, a Saginaw County veteran who had been a sergeant at Gettysburg, called the gathering to order, and the regiment's former chaplain, William Brockway, offered the invocation. Then Col. Edward Hill stepped forward to address them in the heroic language of his time, on the notion that was accepted as fact then by most veterans and students of history: that Little Round Top was the turning point of the Civil War.[26]

"Comrades," Hill began. "To the casual wanderer, the contemplation of a field made historic by a great battle naturally inspires solemn reflection, deep emotion and high resolve. What then must be the feelings of a comrade, who stood on Little Round Top, his feet upon this battle line, his face toward the foe, as he looks back through the vista of more than a quarter of a century, to the day when the sun, obscured by sulphurous smoke, sank behind Little Round Top, and mercifully closed the sight from the appalling carnage of Gettysburg?"

Hill addressed the dramatic memories the survivors would recall—the signal service men waving their flags on the crest, and their generals and staff officers, galloping on the field below, and watching other soldiers move in lines of battle in the Wheatfield and Peach Orchard. "Will he not again feel the muscles of his body yield, as he places his shoulder to Hazlett's Battery wheels, lifting its guns in position on rocky eyries where eagles built their nests?" he asked.

> Will he not again listen for the voices of our own beloved dead, Welch, Elliott, Brown, Jewett and Borden, cheering on the Sixteenth, leading brave Vincent's Brigade as it swept forward in its grand charge, securing the Round Tops, thus saving the Army of the Potomac from disaster and assuring victory to the Union arms? Will he not, in imagination, as line of battle is formed at a double-quick, across the crest of this scarred mountain top, realize that the air is filled with bursting shell, and that Hood's Brigade of Robertson's and Law's are rallying on this objective point, deploying from Devil's Den their deadly sharpshooters behind every rock along this slope, their battle line scarcely ten paces away?

Hill spoke of the "desperate onset of a hand-to-hand struggle," men clubbing muskets, stabbing with bayonets and even throwing stones, of "every man of the color guard save one" being killed and the regiment's flag falling, shot from its staff. He invoked the mortal wounding of Col. Vincent, and that his men were fighting "for victory or to die in the attempt." Hill's description of the color guard's casualties did not tally with other records, including his own, but he spoke of the victory that the regiments of Vincent's brigade had won—a victory that they could not then proclaim.

"All around lay the sacred dead and wounded comrades on many a weary march and hard-fought field," he continued. "Neither the pen of the writer, the pencil of the artist, the rhetoric of the orator, can describe the horrors of the scene. Nor can the enactments of legislatures add glory to the renown of those who died here that the Nation might live. Comrades of the gallant Sixteenth, these memories are the ghastly legacies bequeathed the veteran, who in retrospective silken recalls the close of that dreadful day."

In what was the nearest Hill came to addressing the regiment's break under the flanking assault by the Rebels, he said: "There can be no invidious distinction made in favor of one body of men over another who fought at Gettysburg. The record of one regiment is the history of all, and they were a tired army of veterans." Together, Union soldiers had stopped the Confederate invasion. "The graves of this battlefield mark the place where secession received its fatal thrust, where victory at last and finally proclaimed, 'the Union Now and Forever,'" he said; the battlefield was for all time "a hallowed place."

> Consecrating it apart, the martyred Lincoln here pled to the living, "that from these honored dead we take increased ardor to the cause for which they gave the last full measure of devotion." Let the nation never forget that the decisive victory of Gettysburg as won by the subline valor of its fighting men. . . .
>
> So may a grateful people ever hold in reverential trust the remembrance of our blessed dead, slain at Gettysburg. On this holy ground, sanctified by the blood of heroes, we dedicate

this shaft to you, our fallen comrades, a mute testimonial to your fidelity and devotion, and that you died "upon the field of honor."

As the early light of morning gilds it, and parting day lingers and plays upon its summit, may it ever be a beacon to guide the loyal wayfarer in the paths of patriotism, where you trod. Your names are to us an eternal benediction, and to Thee, O God of battles, we command your immortal souls.[27]

APPENDIX

ROSTER OF THE 16TH MICHIGAN INFANTRY REGIMENT

This roster is based on the Michigan Adjutant-General's Dept. *Record of Service*, vol. 16 (1905); the regiment's "Roll of Honor" of men killed, wounded, and who died of disease in *Proceedings of the Third Brigade Association, First Division, Fifth Army Corps, Army of the Potomac, Held at the National Encampment of the G.A.R., Washington, D.C.*, vol. 3 (1900); and the author's files, including copies of regimental records, reports, and newspaper articles. All enlistments and assignments for drafted men are for the 16th Michigan unless otherwise noted. Volunteers between August 1861 and early 1862 of course entered Stockton's Independent Regiment, and after that joined the 16th Michigan. References to "First Company Sharpshooters" are to the Brady Sharpshooters Company, also known as Dygert's Sharpshooters, while "Second Company Sharpshooters" refers to Jardine's Sharpshooters.

Abbey, Charles H. Enlisted in Company D, Feb. 3, 1864, at Saginaw, for 3 years, age 18. Corporal, May 1, 1865. Mustered out at Jeffersonville, Ind., July 8, 1865.

Abbott, Franklin B. (Veteran), Howell. Enlisted in Company B, Lancers, Dec. 24, 1861, at Howell, for 3 years, age 18. Transferred to Company I, 16th Michigan, Feb. 28, 1862. Reenlisted Dec. 22, 1863, at Rappahannock Station, Va. Corporal, May 1, 1865. Mustered out at Jeffersonville, Ind., July 8, 1865. Resided Fowlerville, Mich.

Abbott, John, Albion. Enlisted in Company K, March 1, 1862, at Detroit, for 3 years, age 44. Discharged for disability at Yorktown, Va., May 4, 1862.

Abel, William A. Enlisted in Company E, March 24, 1865, at Stockbridge, Ingham County, for 1 year, age 19. Substitute for Wheeler Gaylord, drafted from Stockbridge. Discharged at Washington, D.C., June 16, 1865. Resided Bath, Mich.

Abelie, Charles, Ontonagon County. Enlisted in Company A, Aug. 3, 1861, at Ontonagon, for 3 years, age 25. Deserted at Hall's Hill, Va., Dec. 1, 1862.

Abity, Lewis. Enlisted in Company G, Aug. 28, 1861, at Detroit, for 3 years, age 40. Deserted at Detroit, Sept. 16, 1861.

Acton, Alfred. Enlisted in Company C, March 28, 1865, at Convis, Calhoun County, for 1 year, age 28. Substitute for Daniel H. Way, drafted from Convis. Mustered out at Jeffersonville, Ind., July 8, 1865. Resided Ann Arbor, Mich.

Adams, Hiram. Enlisted in Company E, Lancers, Nov. 18, 1861, at Pigeon River, for 3 years, age 34. Transferred to Company I or K, 16th Michigan, Feb. 28, 1862. Killed in action at Gaines' Mill, June 27, 1862.

Adams, James. Enlisted in Company E, Feb. 6, 1864, at Romulus, for 3 years, age 19. Mustered out at Jeffersonville, Ind., July 8, 1865. Died March 1890.

Adams, James H., Detroit. Enlisted in Company G, July 26, 1862, at Detroit, for 3 years, age 34. Joined regiment at Sharpsburg, Md., Oct. 30, 1862. Discharged at Washington, D.C., May 30, 1865.

Adams, Samuel B. (Veteran). Enlisted in Company G, as Corporal, Aug. 15, 1861, age 30. Wounded in action at Gaines' Mill, June 27, 1862. Wounded in action at Malvern Hill, July 1, 1862. Reenlisted Dec. 21, 1863, at Rappahannock Station, Va. Corporal. Killed in action at Laurel Hill–Spotsylvania Court House, May 8, 1864.

Aikin, Earl N., or M., Tekonsha, Calhoun County. Enlisted in Company E, March 27, 1865, at Girard, for 1 year, age 19. Substitute for James M. Aikin, drafted from Girard, Branch County. Died of disease at Washington, D.C., June 14, 1865.

Airheart, Ira, St. Clair County. Enlisted in First Company Sharpshooters, Aug. 10, at Detroit, for 3 years, age 20. Joined regiment at Hall's Hill, Va., Feb. 14, 1862. Discharged on Surgeon's certificate of disability at Fortress Monroe, Va., Feb. 11, 1863.

Alberts, Frank B., Albion. Enlisted in Company F, Aug. 4, 1861, at Plymouth, for 3 years, age 28. Discharged for disability at Detroit, July 5, 1862.

Albro, Henry (Veteran), Greenfield. Enlisted in Company K, March 17, 1862, at Detroit, for 3 years, age 26. Wounded accidentally July 1862 with wagon train and taken prisoner. Exchanged. Reenlisted March 1, 1864, at Bealton, Va. Corporal. Sergeant, May 14, 1865. Mustered out at Jeffersonville, Ind., July 8, 1865. Resided Woodville, Mich.

Aldrich, Charles A., Hillsdale County. Enlisted in Company C, Aug. 15, 1861. Discharged for disability Dec. 29, 1861.

Aldrich or **Aldridge, Martin**. Enlisted in Company F, Lancers, as Corporal, Oct. 5, 1861, at Wellsville, for 3 years, age 18. Transferred to Company I, 16th Michigan, Feb. 28, 1862. No further record.

Alger, Benjamin. Enlisted in Company B, Feb. 9, 1864, at Saginaw, for 3 years, age 19. Mustered out at Jeffersonville, Ind., July 8, 1865.

Allan, Robert. Enlisted in Second Company Sharpshooters, attached to 16th Michigan, March 31, 1864, at Taymouth, Saginaw County, for 3 years, age 29. Deserted at Jeffersonville, Ind., July 10, 1865.

Allen, Frank. Enlisted in Company I, March 24, 1865, at Dover, Lenawee County, for 1 year, age 21. Substitute for John M. Payne, drafted from Dover. Mustered out at Jeffersonville, Ind., July 8, 1865.

Allen, Henry E. Enlisted in Company B, March 31, 1865, at Converse, for 1 year, age 21.

Substitute for Arnold Phillips, drafted from Convis, Calhoun County. Deserted near Washington, D.C., June 13, 1865.

Allen, Joseph, Milford. Enlisted in Company B, Lancers, Oct. 19, 1861, at Milford, for 3 years, age 20. Transferred to Company I, 16th Michigan, Feb. 28, 1862. Discharged at Washington, D.C., Nov. 12, 1862. Resided Milford.

Allen, Joseph, Detroit. Enlisted in Company D, Dec. 12, 1861, at Detroit, for 3 years, age 39. Dropped from rolls April 30, 1864.

Allen, Thomas. Enlisted in Second Company Sharpshooters, attached to 16th Michigan, March 30, 1864, at Taymouth, Saginaw County, for 3 years, age 32. Mustered out at Jeffersonville, Ind., July 8, 1865.

Almy, Daniel E., or **David**. Enlisted in Company G, March 25, 1865, at Grattan, Kent County, for 1 year, age 18. Substitute for Francis M. Slayton, drafted from Grattan. Discharged at Washington, D.C., May 30, 1865.

Ameigh, or **Nichols, George D.** Enlisted in Company G, March 22, 1865, at Liberty, Jackson County, for 1 year, age 19. Substitute for George L. Loomis, drafted from Liberty. Mustered out at Jeffersonville, Ind., July 8, 1865.

Ameigh, or **Nichols, James H.** Enlisted in Company G, March 22, 1865, at Liberty, for 1 year, age 19. Substitute for Stacy Choate, drafted from Liberty. Mustered out at Jeffersonville, Ind., July 8, 1865.

Amos, Jacob. Enlisted in Company D, March 28, 1865, at Pontiac, for 1 year, age 18. Mustered out at Jeffersonville, Ind., July 8, 1865.

Anderson, Andrew J. Enlisted in Company D, Feb. 12, 1864, at Saginaw, for 3 years, age 18. Mustered out at Jeffersonville, Ind., July 8, 1865.

Anderson, Charles W. Enlisted in Company C, March 12, 1865, at Jackson, for 3 years, age 20. Substitute for Luther Hurd, drafted from Newton, Calhoun County. Mustered out at Jeffersonville, Ind., July 8, 1865.

Anderson, Edward. Enlisted in Company E, March 24, 1865, at Comstock, Kalamazoo, for 1 year, age 22. Substitute for Curtis Gates, drafted from Comstock. Mustered out at Jeffersonville, Ind., July 8, 1865.

Anderson, John, Milford. Enlisted in Company B, Lancers, Oct. 19, 1861, at Milford, for 3 years, age 25. Transferred to Company I, 16th Michigan, Feb. 28, 1862. Deserted at Detroit, March 24, 1862.

Anderson, Nathaniel N. Drafted for 1 year, from Flint, age 31. Mustered Dec. 20, 1864. Assigned to Company I. Mortally wounded in action at Quaker Road, March 29, 1865. Died March 31, 1865.

Andrews, Albert E. Enlisted in Company I, March 30, 1865, at Meridian, Ingham County for 1 year, age 23. Substitute for James G. Smith, drafted. Mustered out at Jeffersonville, Ind., July 8, 1865. Resided Williamston, Mich.

Andrews, Joseph. Enlisted April 26, 1864, at Casco, for 3 years, age 18. Died Oct. 2, 1864.

Andrews, Peter. Enlisted in Second Company Sharpshooters, April 30, 1864, at Birch Run, for 3 years, age 18. Mustered out at Jeffersonville, Ind., July 8, 1865.

Andrews, Phillip. Enlisted in Company F, March 31, 1865, at Alaiedon, Ingham County, for 1 year, age 21. Substitute for Charles Foles, or Foler, drafted from Alaiedon. Deserted May 17, 1865.

Andrews, William B. Drafted March 15, 1865, for 1 year, from Bowne, Kent County, age 42. Assigned to Company E. Discharged at Washington, D.C., June 27, 1865.

Angevine, Warren T. (Veteran), Adrian. Enlisted in Company E, as Corporal, Sept. 6, 1861. Wounded in action, arm, Gaines' Mill, June 27, 1862. Listed among the Gettysburg wounded in Philadelphia and Washington hospitals in newspapers, July–Aug. 1863, but no specific wound given. Reenlisted as 1st Sergeant, Dec. 21, 1863, at Rappahannock Station, Va., age 19. Wounded in action July 7, 1864, Petersburg, Va. Commissioned 1st Lieutenant, July 20, 1864. Commanding Company E from Dec. 31, 1864, to July 8, 1865. Commissioned Captain, Second Company Sharpshooters, April 4, 1865. Mustered out at Jeffersonville, Ind., July 8, 1865.

Ankle, George. Ontonagon County. Enlisted in Company A, Aug. 3, 1861, at Ontonagon, for 3 years, age 22. Discharged for disability Feb. 22, 1862.

Aplin, Henry H. (Veteran), Flint. Enlisted in Company C, July 31, 1861, at Flint, for 3 years, age 20. Mustered Sept. 7, 1861. Taken prisoner at Savage's Station, June 27, 1862. Paroled Sept. 1862. Reenlisted Dec. 24, 1863, at Rappahannock Station, Va. Quartermaster Sergeant, Jan. 1, 1865. Commissioned 2nd Lieutenant, July 7, 1865. Discharged at Jeffersonville, Ind., July 1, 1865.

Applebee, James (Veteran), Genesee County. Enlisted in Company C, July 30, 1861, at Flint, for 3 years, age 22. Wounded and missing in action at Gaines' Mill, June 27, 1862. Reenlisted Dec. 24, 1863, at Rappahannock Station, Va. Mustered out at Jeffersonville, Ind., July 8, 1865.

Apted, Alfred M., Grand Rapids. Enlisted in First Company Sharpshooters attached to 16th Michigan, Jan. 27, 1862, for 3 years, age 25. Joined regiment at Hall's Hill, Va., Feb. 14, 1862. Wounded in action, left arm and side, at Peeble's Farm, Sept. 30, 1864. Discharged at expiration of term of service, March 11, 1865. Died Feb. 20, 1900.

Armon, or **Armond, Alfred**. Enlisted in Company D, Feb. 15, 1864, at Saginaw, for 3 years, age 26. Corporal May 1, 1865. Mustered out at Jeffersonville, Ind., July 8, 1865.

Armstrong, Edward, St. Clair County. Enlisted in Company D. Mustered Feb. 11, 1862. Joined regiment at Hall's Hill, Va., Feb. 14, 1862. Wounded and missing in action at Gaines' Mill, June 27, 1862. Discharged at Philadelphia, Jan. 12, 1863.

Armstrong, James, Tyrone, Livingston County. Entered service as substitute for David, or Daniel, Betts. Drafted Feb. 24, 1863, for 9 months, from Tyrone. No further record.

Armstrong, John W. Drafted Sept. 20, 1864, for 1 year, from Kalamo, Eaton County, age 32. Assigned to Company I. Discharged near Washington, D.C., May 29, 1865.

Arndt, William, Wayne County. Enlisted in Company F, Aug. 4, 1861, at Plymouth, for 3 years, age 26. Corporal. Discharged for disability at Warrenton, Va., Nov. 12, 1862.

Arnet, George. Enlisted in Company H, Sept. 26, 1861, at Detroit, for 3 years, age 22. Deserted Sept. 28, 1861.

Arrance, James. Enlisted in Company D, Jan. 25, 1864, at Midland, for 3 years, age 19. Corporal May 1, 1865. Mustered out at Jeffersonville, Ind., July 8, 1865.

Arrance, William (Veteran), Midland County. Enlisted in Company D, Sept. 14, 1861, at

Detroit, age 20. Reenlisted as Corporal, Dec. 21, 1863, at Rappahannock Station, Va. Left arm amputated and died at Alexandria, Va., July 10, 1864, of wounds received in action at Bethesda Church, June 3, 1864.

Aseltein, Darrius O. G. Enlisted in Company G, March 24, 1865, at Ash, Monroe County, for 1 year, age 18. Substitute for Michael Tares, drafted from Ash. Admitted to Harper Hospital July 8, 1865. Discharged at Detroit, Aug. 12, 1865. Resided Marlette, Mich.

Ashley, Chester, Wayne County. Enlisted in First Company Sharpshooters, attached to 16th Michigan, Sept. 16, 1861, at Detroit, for 3 years, age 40. Joined regiment at Hall's Hill, Va., Feb. 14, 1862. Discharged at Antietam, Md., Oct. 26, 1862.

Aspel, James, Wayne County. Enlisted in Company A, Aug. 3, 1861, at Ontonagon, for 3 years, age 19. Mustered Sept. 9, 1861. Killed in action at Gaines' Mill, June 27, 1862.

Aspel, Patrick (Veteran), Ontonagon. Enlisted in Company A, Aug. 3, 1861, at Ontonagon, for 3 years, age 25. Reenlisted Dec. 21, 1863, at Rappahannock Station, Va. Mustered out at Jeffersonville, Ind., July 8, 1865.

Atherton, Samuel H. (Veteran), Argentine. Enlisted in Company A, as Corporal, Aug. 13, 1862, at Argentine, age 22. Joined regiment at Antietam, Md., Oct. 12, 1862. Wounded at Middleburg, Va., June 21, 1863. Reenlisted Dec. 21, 1863, at Rappahannock Station, Va. Wounded in action May 6 or May 8, 1864, at Wilderness, or Laurel Hill–Spotsylvania Court House. Wounded in action at Petersburg, Va., June 24, 1864. Sergeant. Mustered out at Jeffersonville, Ind., July 8, 1865.

Atherton, William, Argentine. Enlisted in Company I, Aug. 30, 1862, at Argentine, for 3 years, age 22. Joined regiment at Antietam, Md., Oct. 12, 1862, but listed as absent wounded that month. Transferred to Veteran Reserve Corps. Regiment's "Roll of Honor" states he was discharged on Sept. 6, 1864, though the roster states he was discharged at Augur's Hospital, Alexandria, Va., July 10, 1865, from Company E, 14th Regiment, Veteran Reserve Corps.

Atkinson, William. Enlisted in Company B, Lancers, Oct. 21, 1861, at Milford, for 3 years, age 20. Transferred to Company I, 16th Michigan, Feb. 28, 1862. Deserted at Detroit, March 24, 1862.

Aufska or **Ausske, Joseph**, Saginaw County. Enlisted in Company A, Feb. 11, 1864, at Saginaw, age 33. Wounded in action May 10, 1864, at Spotsylvania Court House. Killed in action before Petersburg, Va., June 23, 1865.

Austin, Henry S. Drafted Dec. 29, 1864, for 1 year, from Hamlin, Mason County, age 36. Assigned to Company I. Mustered out at Jeffersonville, Ind., July 8, 1865.

Austin, Nathaniel, Argentine. Enlisted in Company K, Aug. 1, 1862, at Argentine, for 3 years, age 25. Joined regiment at Antietam, Md., Oct. 3, 1862. Discharged at Washington, D.C., May 29, 1865. Resided Harbor Beach, Mich.

Averill, Lafayette. Enlisted in Company C, Feb. 16, 1864, at Saginaw, for 3 years, age 25. Mustered out at Jeffersonville, Ind., July 8, 1865.

Avery, Merrit J., Genesee County. Enlisted in Company C, July 30, 1861, at Flint, for 3 years, age 18. Discharged for disability at Detroit, March 28, 1863.

Axtell, Alfred R., Flint. Enlisted in Company D, Dec. 22, 1862, at Flint, age 33. Joined regiment near Falmouth, Va., Jan. 8, 1863. Corporal. Killed in action before Petersburg, Va., June

23, 1864.

Babcock, Nelson A. Enlisted in Company E, First Lancers, as Sergeant, Oct. 7, 1861, at Saginaw, for 3 years, age 22. Transferred to Company K, 16th Michigan, Feb. 28, 1862. Discharged to accept promotion when commissioned 2nd Lieutenant, Company E, 23rd Michigan, Nov. 7, 1862.

Bachaunan, Murdock. Enlisted in Second Company Sharpshooters, attached to 16th Michigan, April 15, 1864, for 3 years, age 25. Deserted May 3, 1864.

Bacon or **Badion** or **Badison,** John. Enlisted in Company A, Feb. 2, 1864, at Ann Arbor, for 3 years, age 29. Wounded and missing in action at Dabney's Mill, Feb. 6, 1865. No further record.

Badger, William, Saginaw. Enlisted in Company D, Sept. 10, 1861, at East Saginaw, age 19. Mustered Sept. 14, 1861. Killed in action at Gaines' Mill, June 27, 1862.

Bagg, William H., Genesee County. Enlisted in Company C, Sept. 7, 1861, at Detroit, for 3 years, age 29. Wounded during 1862, probably at Gaines' Mill or Malvern Hill. Discharged at expiration of term of service at Weldon Railroad, Petersburg, Va., Sept. 16, 1864.

Bailey, George S., Fenton. Enlisted in Company D, Jan. 25, 1864, at Fenton, for 3 years, age 39. Died of disease at City Point, Va., July 28, 1864.

Bailey, Lorenzo or **Louis** (Veteran), Lapeer County. Enlisted in Company C, Sept. 4, 1861. Reenlisted Dec. 24, 1863, at Rappahannock Station, Va. Mustered out at Jeffersonville, Ind., July 8, 1865. Resided later at the Michigan Soldiers' Home.

Bailey, Melvin L. (Veteran), Eaton Rapids. Enlisted in Company G, Aug. 24, 1861, at White Pigeon, for 3 years, age 21. Wounded in action and captured, second Manassas, Aug. 30, 1864, bullet passing through his body. Paroled Sept. 5, 1862. Reenlisted Dec. 21, 1863, at Rappahannock Station, Va. Wounded in action at Wilderness, May 7, 1864, bullet passing through his torso from back of right hip joint to above the front of left hip joint. Discharged for disability at Washington, D.C., Dec. 21, 1864. Resided Eaton Rapids, Mich.

Bailey, Virgil A. Enlisted in Company C, at Pontiac, for 3 years, age 18, and mustered Aug. 8, 1864. Substitute for Ashley Potter, or Thomas, drafted from Cascade, Kent County. Corporal April 1, 1865. Mustered out at Jeffersonville, Ind., July 8, 1865. Resided Hadley, Lapeer County.

Bairwird, Ferdinand, Detroit. Enlisted in Company I, March 18, 1862, at Detroit, for 3 years, age 32. Discharged for disability.

Baker, Jacob. Enlisted in Company F, Jan. 25, 1864, at Detroit, for 3 years, age 17. Wounded in action, thigh, at Laurel Hill–Spotsylvania Court House, May 8, 1864. Discharged on Surgeon's certificate of disability Aug. 3, 1865.

Baker, John. Enlisted in Second Company Sharpshooters, March 18, 1864, at Saginaw, for 3 years, age 32. Deserted at Saginaw, May 3, 1864.

Baker, Joseph (Veteran), Wayne. Enlisted in First Company Sharpshooters, Sept. 25, 1861, at Detroit, for 3 years, age 22, attached to 16th Michigan. Mustered Jan. 23, 1862. Joined regiment at Hall's Hill, Va., Feb. 14, 1862. Reenlisted Dec. 22, 1863, at Rappahannock Station, Va. Corporal May 1, 1865. Mustered out at Jeffersonville, Ind., July 8, 1865.

Baker, Nelson, Saginaw County. Enlisted in Company D, Aug. 1, 1861, at East Saginaw, for 3 years, age 28. Discharged at expiration of term of service before Petersburg, Va., Sept. 17, 1864.

Baladieu, George, Detroit. Enlisted in Company C, Lancers, Jan. 13, 1862, at Detroit, for 3 years, age 36. Transferred to Company I, 16th Michigan, Feb. 28, 1862. Deserted at Detroit, March 24, 1862.

Balcom, Dennis. Enlisted in Company B, Aug. 5, 1861, at Ionia, for 3 years, age 39. Transferred to Company F, May 1862. Died of disease in hospital, 1862.

Bancroft, Charles H. (Veteran), Romeo. Enlisted in First Company Sharpshooters, Nov. 27, 1861, at Detroit, for 3 years, age 23. Joined regiment at Hall's Hill, Va., Feb. 14, 1862. Reenlisted Dec. 22, 1863, at Rappahannock Station, Va. Corporal. Died of disease at City Point, Va., Sept. 21, 1864.

Banister, Newall. Drafted for 1 year, from Fulton, age 24. Mustered March 17, 1865. Assigned to Company K. Discharged at Washington, D.C., May 30, 1865.

Banks, William H., Walled Lake. Enlisted in Company B, Lancers, as Bugler, Nov. 20, 1861, at Walled Lake, for 3 years, age 23. Transferred to Company I, 16th Michigan, Feb. 28, 1862. Discharged at expiration of term of service, Nov. 23, 1864.

Barber, Lewis B. Drafted Nov. 29, 1864, for 1 year, from Carlton, Barry County, age 39. Assigned to Company K. Mustered out at Jeffersonville, Ind., July 8, 1865.

Barber, Luther J., Kent County. Enlisted in First Company Sharpshooters at Detroit for 3 years, Oct. 21, 1861, age 24. Joined regiment at Hall's Hill, Va., Feb. 14, 1862. Discharged at David's Island, N.Y., Oct. 4, 1862.

Barber, Philetus (Veteran), Saginaw County. Enlisted in Company D, Aug. 1, 1861, at East Saginaw, for 3 years, age 22. Reenlisted Dec. 21, 1863, at Rappahannock Station, Va. Mustered out at Jeffersonville, Ind., July 8, 1865.

Barclay, Marcus H., Lowell. Enlisted in Company C, Lancers, Oct. 23, 1861, at Lowell, for 3 years, age 19. Transferred to Company I, 16th Michigan, Feb. 28, 1862. Died of fever at Harrison's Landing, Va., Aug. 6, 1862.

Bardie or **Bardy, Lewis** (Veteran), Ontonagon County. Enlisted in Company E, Aug. 14, 1861, at Detroit, for 3 years, age 38. Transferred to Company A. Wounded in action at Gaines' Mill, June 27, 1862. Reenlisted Dec. 21, 1863, at Rappahannock Station, Va. Mustered out at Jeffersonville, Ind., July 8, 1865.

Barker, Joseph H. Enlisted in Company G, Lancers, Nov. 22, 1861, at North Shade, for 3 years, age 27. Transferred to Company K, 16th Michigan, Feb. 28, 1862. Discharged at Petersburg, Va., March 1, 1865.

Barker, Joseph H., Detroit. Enlisted in Company K, March 1, 1862, at Detroit, for 3 years, age 27. Discharged at expiration of term of service, March 4, 1865.

Barlow, Edwin, or **Edward**, Genesee County. Enlisted in Company C, July 31, 1861, at Flint, for 3 years, age 18. Wounded in action at Gaines' Mill, June 27, 1862. Discharged at Warrenton, Va., Nov. 13, 1862.

Barnes, Allen L. or **Almond.** Enlisted in Company D, Jan. 19, 1864, at Thomastown, Saginaw County for 3 years, age 17. Wounded in action Nov. (?) 1864; listed as absent, wounded in casualties for 1864–65. Mustered out at Jeffersonville, Ind., July 8, 1865.

Barney, James. Enlisted in Company E, March 29, 1865, at Howell, for 3 years, age 19. Substitute for Solomon Hilderbrant, drafted from Howell, Livingston County. Mustered out at Jeffersonville, Ind., July 8, 1865.

Barnhart, Levinius or **Bernard, Jervenus**. Enlisted in Company G, Feb. 2, 1865, at Detroit, for 1 year, age 18. Substitute for L. Freeman, drafted. Mustered out at Jeffersonville, Ind., July 8, 1865.

Barns, George. Enlisted in Company F, Aug. 2, 1861, at Plymouth, for 3 years, age 32. Mustered Sept. 7, 1861. No further record.

Barorast, Sao or **Bunorant, Levi**. Enlisted in Company F, March 27, 1865, at Kalamazoo, for 1 year, age 20. Substitute for Levi A. Churchill, drafted from Volinia, Cass County. No further record.

Barr, Jordan, Detroit. Enlisted in Company K, Feb. 25, 1862, at Detroit, for 3 years. Wounded in action at Malvern Hill, July 1, 1862. Discharged for disability Sept. 1862.

Barren, George. Enlisted in Company C, March 13, 1865, at Groveland, Oakland County, age 18. Substitute for Israel S. Bird, drafted from Groveland. Mustered out at Jeffersonville, Ind., July 8, 1865.

Barrett, Cornelius S., Walled Lake. Enlisted in Company I, March 3, 1862, at Walled Lake, for 3 years, age 21. Discharged for disability Dec. 23, 1862.

Barrett, Hubbard H., Ionia County. Enlisted in Company B, as Corporal, Aug. 5, 1861, at Ionia, for 3 years, age 26. 1st Sergeant. Killed in action at Gettysburg, July 2, 1863.

Barrett, Oliver (Veteran), Ionia County. Enlisted in Company B, as Corporal, Aug. 8, 1861, at Ionia, for 3 years, age 19. Reenlisted Dec. 24, 1863, at Rappahannock Station, Va. Wounded in action, July 1864. Sergeant May 17, 1865. Mustered out at Jeffersonville, Ind., July 8, 1865.

Barrett, Sylvester. Saginaw County. Enlisted in Company B, Jan. 26, 1864, at Grand Rapids, for 3 years, age 35. Killed in action before Petersburg, Va., June 19, 1864.

Barrie or **Barrey, George**, Houghton County. Enlisted in Company E, Aug. 21, 1861, at Hancock, for 3 years, age 45. Wounded in action at Gaines' Mill, June 27, 1862. Discharged at David's Island, N.Y., Dec. 9, 1862.

Barry, Thomas J., Detroit. Entered service in Company A, at organization, as Captain, Aug. 1, 1861, at Ontonagon, for 3 years, age 35. Commissioned Aug. 9, 1861. Wounded in action at second Manassas, Aug. 30, 1862. Commissioned Major July 6, 1862. Resigned on account of disability at Aldie, Va., June 20, 1863.

Barry or **Barz, Joseph**, Detroit. Enlisted in Company F, Sept. 19, 1862, at Detroit, age 26. Joined regiment at Antietam, Md., Oct. 30, 1862. Deserted at Fredericksburg, Va., Dec. 23, 1862.

Bartleson, Edwin A. Enlisted in Company C, Aug. 4, 1861, at Flint, for 3 years, age 20. Transferred to Company F. Listed in newspaper report with Gettysburg wounded in Philadelphia and Washington hospitals, July 1863. Transferred to Invalid Corps Jan. 15, 1864. Discharged from 129th Company, Veteran Reserve Corps, July 21, 1864.

Barton, Nathan, Argentine, Genesee County. Enlisted in Company I, Aug. 13, 1862, at Argentine, age 23. Joined regiment at Antietam, Md., Oct. 12, 1862. Killed in action near Spotsylvania Court House, May 10, 1864.

Bartram, Horace. Enlisted in Company G, Aug. 17, 1861, at White Pigeon, for 3 years, age 23.

Wounded in action at Gaines' Mill, June 27, 1862. Enlisted in Battery B, 2nd U.S. Artillery, Sept. 1862.

Barward or **Barnard, William**. Enlisted in Company E, Jan. 28, 1864, at Detroit, for 3 years, age 18. Discharged at Washington, D.C., June 13, 1865.

Bashford, Solomon A. Enlisted in Second Company Sharpshooters attached to the 16th Michigan on April 22, 1864, at Spaulding, for 3 years, age 27. Deserted at Saginaw, May 3, 1864.

Bates, Dewitt C. Enlisted in Company B, Aug. 6, 1861, at Ionia, for 3 years, age 44. Transferred to Company C, May 1862. Discharged for disability at Washington, D.C., May 11, 1862.

Baxter, Alonzo. Enlisted in Company B, Feb. 2, 1864, at Bridgeport, for 3 years, age 33. Discharged at Washington, D.C., May 27, 1865.

Baxter, James, Wayne County. Enlisted in Company C, Nov. 22, 1861, at Detroit, for 3 years, age 30. Reported as wounded in action at second Manassas, Aug. 30, 1862 or missing in action Sept. 12, 1862. Alternately reported as having died from wounds, Sept. 22, 1862, or that he was discharged for disability at Washington, D.C., Dec. 22, 1862, for wounds received in action.

Beagle, John R. Enlisted in Company G, Aug. 15, 1861. Killed in action at Gettysburg, July 2, 1863.

Beaird or **Beard, George**, Detroit. Enlisted in Company H, Lancers, Dec. 31, 1861, at Detroit, for 3 years, age 22. Transferred to Company I, 16th Michigan, Feb. 28, 1862. Corporal. Wounded in action, side and arm, at Gaines' Mill, June 27, 1862. Sergeant. Commissioned 2nd Lieutenant, April 25, 1863. Commissioned 1st Lieutenant, July 16, 1864. Wounded in action at Peeble's Farm, Sept. 30, 1864. Commissioned Captain, Company A, Sept. 7, 1864. Mustered out at Jeffersonville, Ind., July 8, 1865.

Beard, Henry, Lansing. Enlisted in Company C, Jan. 10 1863, at Lansing, for 3 years, age 18. Deserted at Chancellorsville, Va., May 2, 1863.

Beardsley or **Bradley, Ebenezer**. Enlisted in Company H, Feb. 1865, at Elba, Lapeer County, for 1 year, age 44. Substitute for Charles B. Pitcher, drafted from Elba. Accidentally wounded March 12, 1865. No further record.

Beardsley, Joseph. Enlisted in Company F, Aug. 2, 1861, at Plymouth, for 3 years, age 21. No further record.

Bechaud, Armand. Enlisted in Company A, Aug. 2, 1861, at Ontonagon, for 3 years, age 19. Wounded in action, arm, at Gaines' Mill, June 27, or Malvern Hill, July 1, 1862. Discharged at expiration of term of service, Sept. 6, 1864.

Beckett, James. Enlisted in Company A, Lancers, as Sergeant, Oct. 11, 1861, at Detroit, for 3 years, age 24. Transferred to Company I, 16th Michigan, Feb. 28, 1862. Discharged Sept. 11, 1862. Reentered service in Company I, Sept. 29, 1862, at Detroit. Joined regiment near Falmouth, Va., Nov. 27, 1862. Corporal. 1st Sergeant. Killed in action at Gettysburg, July 2, 1863.

Beecher, Levi. Enlisted in Company E, Feb. 2, 1865, at California, Branch County, for 3 years, age 34. Substitute for Daniel Sharon, drafted from California. Mustered out at Jeffersonville, Ind., July 8, 1865.

Beiber, George W., Van Buren County. Enlisted in First Company Sharpshooters, later attached to 16th Michigan, Oct. 16, 1861, at Detroit, for 3 years, age 23. Joined regiment at Hall's Hill, Va., Feb. 14, 1862. Corporal. Discharged at expiration of term of service, Oct. 15, 1864.

Belanger, James, or **Bellinger, Jean**. Enlisted in Company A, March 21, 1864, at Houghton, for 3 years, age 21. Wounded at Peeble's Farm, Sept. 30, 1864. On furlough from Lincoln Hospital, Washington, D.C., Oct. 25, 1864. No further record.

Belcher, Irving M., Flint. Enlisted in Company C, as 1st Sergeant, July 31, 1861, at Flint, for 3 years, age 20. Commissary Sergeant Sept. 22, 1861. Commissioned 2nd Lieutenant, Company B, Aug. 30, 1862. Acting Quartermaster, Dec. 1862. Commissioned 1st Lieutenant, Company K, April 17, 1863. Acting Aide-de-Camp on staff of General Bartlett, commanding Third Brigade, First Division, Fifth Army Corps, May 1, 1864. Commissioned Captain, Company C, July 16, 1864. Brigade Inspector, Third Brigade, First Division, Fifth Army Corps, Dec. 1864. Discharged on account of physical disability May 15, 1865; died of disease Aug. 11, 1865 at Ithaca, N.Y.

Belden, Thomas (Veteran), Genesee County. Enlisted in Company C, as Teamster, Aug. 2, 1861, at Flint, for 3 years, age 25. Reenlisted Dec. 24, 1863, at Rappahannock Station, Va. Corporal. Mustered out at Jeffersonville, Ind., July 8, 1865.

Belding, Edward E., Orleans. Enlisted in Company B, Aug. 9, 1861, at Ionia, for 3 years, age 28. Died at Harrison's Landing, Va., July 18, 1862.

Belisle, Charles. Enlisted in Second Company Sharpshooters, March 29, 1864, at Albee, for 3 years, age 45. Mustered out at Jeffersonville, Ind., July 8, 1865.

Bell, Chester L., Albion. Enlisted in Company K, March 1, 1862, at Detroit, for 3 years. Corporal. Reported Aug. 1864 as absent, wounded. Discharged at expiration of term of service at Washington, D.C., May 3, 1865.

Belliner, Dennis. Enlisted in Company B, March 31, 1865, at Tompkins, Jackson County for 1 year, age 18. Substitute for Ira Martin, drafted from Tompkins. Mustered out at Jeffersonville, Ind., July 8, 1865.

Bellington, David, Pittsford, Hillsdale County. Enlisted in Company C, Aug. 16, 1861, at White Pigeon, age 19. Killed in action at Malvern Hill, July 1, 1862.

Bellows, Carlos R. (Veteran), St. Johns. Enlisted in Company E, Aug. 13, 1861, at Detroit, for 3 years, age 19. Transferred to Company H. Reenlisted Dec. 24, 1863, at Rappahannock Station, Va. Sergeant, May 1865. Mustered out at Jeffersonville, Ind., July 8, 1865. Resided Stanton, Mich.

Benedict, William H. Enlisted in Company C, March 28, 1865, at Seneca, Lenawee County, for 1 year, age 44. Substitute for J. Camburn, drafted from Seneca. Mustered out at Jeffersonville, Ind., July 8, 1865.

Benhardt, Edward. Enlisted in First Company Sharpshooters, attached to 16th Michigan, Feb. 8, 1864, at Niles, for 3 years, age 29. Wounded in action at Magnolia Swamp–Bethesda Church, June 1, 1864. Discharged for disability at Detroit, Feb. 7, 1865. Resided Berrien Springs, Mich.

Benjamin, James, Osseo. Enlisted in Company C, Aug. 24, 1861, at White Pigeon, for 3 years, age 28. Died in Columbia Hospital, Washington, D.C., Dec. 4, 1862, of wounds received in action at second Manassas, Aug. 30, 1862.

Benneman, Henry. Enlisted in Company C, March 7, 1865, at Orangeville, for 1 year, age 37. Substitute for James Stewart, drafted from Orangeville, Barry County. Deserted at Jeffersonville, Ind., June 27, 1865.

Bennett, George R., St. Joseph County. Enlisted in Company C, Aug. 23, 1861. Discharged for disability Dec. 29, 1861.

Bennett, John. Enlisted in Company G, March 24, 1865, at Van Buren, for 1 year, age 30. Substitute for William A. Chamberlain, drafted from Van Buren, Wayne County. No further record.

Benson, John M. (Veteran), Midland County. Enlisted in Company D. Mustered Sept. 14, 1861. Wounded and missing in action at Gaines' Mill, June 27, 1862. Reenlisted as Sergeant Dec. 21, 1863, at Rappahannock Station, Va. Promoted to 2nd Lieutenant, May 17, 1865. Mustered out at Jeffersonville, Ind., July 8, 1865.

Benton, Eli (Veteran), Ionia County. Enlisted in Company B, Aug. 6, 1861, at Ionia, for 3 years, age 34. Reenlisted Dec. 24, 1863, at Rappahannock Station, Va. Taken prisoner at Weldon Railroad, Petersburg, Va., Aug. 24, 1864. No further record.

Berry, Abel, Genesee County. Enlisted in Company C, Feb. 18, 1862. No further record.

Berry, George. Enlisted in Company F, Jan. 28, 1865, at Park, St. Joseph County, for 3 years, age 18. Substitute for John L. Horton, or Norton, drafted from Park. Taken prisoner March 27, 1865. Paroled April 10, 1865. Discharged at Camp Chase, Ohio, June 27, 1865.

Berry or **Bovie, Gilbert**, Detroit. Enlisted in Company E, Sept. 11, 1861, at Detroit, for 3 years, age 22. Killed in action at Malvern Hill, July 1, 1862.

Berry, Hugh, Detroit. Enlisted in Company E, Lancers, Oct. 16, 1861, at Kenosha, Wis., for 3 years, age 19. Transferred to Company K, 16th Michigan, Feb. 28, 1862. Corporal. Taken prisoner at Hanover Court House, Va., May 27, 1862. Died in prison at Salisbury, N.C., July 10, 1862.

Berry, John (Veteran), Ontonagon County. Enlisted in Company A, Aug. 2, 1861, at Ontonagon, for 3 years, age 24. Reenlisted as Sergeant Dec. 21, 1863, at Rappahannock Station, Va. Sergeant. Commissioned 1st Lieutenant, Company G, May 8, 1865. Mustered out at Jeffersonville, Ind., July 8, 1865.

Berry, William L. See **Larkworthy, William.**

Bertman, Martin (Veteran), Wayne County. Enlisted in Company E, Aug. 14, 1861, at Detroit, for 3 years, age 19. Reenlisted Dec. 21, 1863, at Rappahannock Station, Va. Mustered out at Jeffersonville, Ind., July 8, 1865.

Bertram, John. Enlisted in Company G, Sept. 25, 1861, at Detroit, for 3 years, age 45. Deserted at Detroit, Sept. 16, 1861.

Besner, Joseph or **John**. Enlisted in Second Company Sharpshooters, March 29, 1864, at Birch Run, for 3 years, age 21. Deserted at Saginaw May 3, 1864.

Bester, Charles, Ontonagon County. Enlisted in Company A, Aug. 2, 1861, at Ontonagon, for 3 years, age 40. Killed in action at Gaines' Mill, June 27, 1862.

Betwee, William. Enlisted in Company F, Jan. 26, 1865, at Berlin, St. Clair County for 3 years, age 19. Substitute for Wallace Stoddard, drafted from Berlin. Discharged July 8, 1865. Resided New Haven, Mich.

Bigelow, James W., Ionia County. Enlisted in Company B, as Corporal, July 30, 1861, at Ionia, for 3 years, age 20. Discharged at expiration of term of service at Petersburg, Va., Sept. 6, 1864.

Bigelow, Jonathan, Ionia County. Enlisted in Company B, Aug. 6, 1861, at Ionia, for 3 years, age 18. Discharged for disability Feb. 24, 1863.

Bigg, Edward C., Genesee County. Enlisted in Company C, Aug. 3, 1861, at Flint, for 3 years, age 18. Wounded in foot and missing in action at Gaines' Mill, June 27, 1862. Discharged for disability at Philadelphia for wounds, Nov. 28, 1862.

Biglow, Abram. Enlisted in Company E, Aug. 15, 1861, at Detroit, for 3 years, age 22. Discharged at Hall's Hill, Va., Feb. 25, 1862.

Biglow, Abram, St. Johns. Enlisted in Company H, Aug. 20, 1861, at Detroit, for 3 years. Discharged for disability at Hall's Hill, Va., Feb. 21, 1862.

Birch or **Burch, Rice W.** (Veteran). Enlisted in Company A, Aug. 2, 1861, at Ontonagon, for 3 years, age 21. Transferred to Company F. Wounded in action at Gaines' Mill, June 27, 1862. Reenlisted Dec. 21, 1863, at Rappahannock Station, Va. Sergeant May 1, 1865. Mustered out at Jeffersonville, Ind., July 8, 1865.

Bird, John W. Enlisted in Company K, March 28, 1865, at Berlin, Ionia County, for 1 year, age 24. Substitute for John A. Sessions, drafted from Berlin. Died of disease June 11, 1865.

Bischoff, Gottlieb. Enlisted in Company A, March 27, 1865, at Ann Arbor, for 1 year, age 20. Mustered out at Jeffersonville, Ind., July 8, 1865.

Bishop, Richard. Enlisted in Company E, Aug. 13, 1861, at Detroit, for 3 years, age 21. Transferred to Company B. Wounded in leg in action at Gettysburg, July 1, 1863. Corporal. Discharged at Baltimore, April 16, 1864.

Black or **Block, John**. Enlisted in Company A, Jan. 24, 1864, at Taymouth, Saginaw County for 3 years, age 44. Wounded in action, right breast, at Wilderness, May 7, 1864. Mustered out at Jeffersonville, Ind., July 8, 1865. Died Jan. 2, 1886. Buried in Forest Lawn Cemetery at Saginaw.

Black, William. Enlisted in Company D, Feb. 17, 1864, at Monguagon, Wayne County, for 3 years, age 34. Missing in action at Laurel Hill–Spotsylvania Court House, May 8, 1864. He was never heard from after; no further record.

Blair, Oliver. Drafted Feb. 10, 1863, for 9 months, from Amboy, Hillsdale County, age 36. Assigned to Company D. Joined regiment near Falmouth, Va., March 18, 1863. Transferred to Invalid Corps July 1, 1863.

Blanchard, Curtis, Hillsdale County. Enlisted in Company C, Aug. 24, 1861, at White Pigeon, for 3 years, age 23. Missing in action Aug. 29, 1862. Transferred to Invalid Corps July 1, 1863. Reenlisted in Company C, 14th Regiment, Veteran Reserve Corps, April 12, 1864. Discharged at Washington, D.C., Nov. 14, 1865.

Bliss, Alonzo C., Ann Arbor. Enlisted in Company D, Aug. 9, 1862, at Ann Arbor. Joined regiment near Falmouth, Va., Nov. 26, 1862. Discharged near Falmouth, Va., March 12, 1863.

Blodgett, Cyrus E. (Veteran). Enlisted in Company G, Aug. 15, 1861. Wounded in action at Gaines' Mill, June 27, 1862. Reenlisted Dec. 21, 1863, at Rappahannock Station, Va. Corporal, May 1, 1865. Mustered out at Jeffersonville, Ind., July 8, 1865.

Blood, Alvah G., Wayne County. Enlisted in Company C, Sept. 9, 1861, at Detroit, for 3 years, age 20. Transferred to U.S. Signal Corps Aug. 12, 1863. Discharged at expiration of term of service at Detroit, Sept. 12, 1864. Resided at Burt, Saginaw County.

Blood or **Blover, William**. Enlisted in Company D, Feb. 5, 1864, at Saginaw, for 3 years, age 45. Wounded in action, thigh, June 6, 1864, withdrawal from Cold Harbor. Discharged at Philadelphia, July 7, 1865.

Bodinus, Ernest, Ontonagon. Enlisted in Company A, Aug. 2, 1861, at Ontonagon, for 3 years, age 23. Discharged for disability Sept. 4, 1862.

Bodinus, William, Ontonagon County. Enlisted in Company A, Aug. 3, 1861, at Ontonagon, for 3 years, age 29. Wounded and missing in action at Gaines' Mill, June 27, 1862. Discharged for disability at Fortress Monroe, Va., Feb. 16, 1863.

Bogart, James P., Pinckney. Enlisted in Company E, Lancers, Dec. 10, 1861, at Pinckney, for 3 years, age 22. Transferred to Company I, 16th Michigan, Feb. 28, 1862. Killed in action at Gettysburg, July 2, 1863.

Bogue, Almon or **Almos P.**, Kent County. Enlisted in First Company Sharpshooters attached to 16th Michigan, Dec. 16, 1861, at Grand Rapids, for 3 years, age 34. Mustered Jan. 23, 1862. Joined regiment at Hall's Hill, Va., Feb. 16, 1862. Wounded in action at Gaines' Mill, June 27, 1862. Transferred to Veteran Reserve Corps, Aug. 1, 1863. Discharged Nov. 20, 1865. Commissary Sergeant, 12th Regiment, Veteran Reserve Corps.

Bogue, Ezra, Kent County. Enlisted in First Company Sharpshooters, attached to 16th Michigan, Dec. 9, 1861, at Grand Rapids, for 3 years, age 21. Joined regiment at Hall's Hill, Va., Feb. 14, 1862. Discharged at David's Island, N.Y., Oct. 4, 1862.

Bolton, Edward B., Saginaw. Enlisted in Second Company Sharpshooters, March 28, 1864, at Tittabawassee, for 3 years, age 27. 1st Sergeant May 17, 1865. Commissioned 2nd Lieutenant, July 7, 1865. Mustered out at Jeffersonville, Ind., July 8, 1865.

Bond, Franklin. Enlisted in Company C, Aug. 1, 1861, at Flint, for 3 years, age 21. Transferred to Company F. Sergeant. Discharged for disability Aug. 20, 1862.

Bond, Josiah G. Enlisted in Company C, Aug. 3, 1861, at Flint, for 3 years, age 27. Transferred to Company F. Corporal. Sergeant. Killed in action at Gettysburg, July 2, 1863.

Bone or **Bohn, Henry**, Ontonagon County. Enlisted in Company A, Aug. 3, 1861, at Ontonagon, for 3 years, age 19. Killed in action at Gaines' Mill, June 27, 1862.

Bongarts, Ralph. Enlisted in Company K, Feb. 20, 1865, at Holland, for 1 year, age 27. Substitute for Peter Pfanstahl, drafted from Holland, Ottawa County. Mustered out at Jeffersonville, Ind., July 8, 1865.

Bonnell, George W., Saginaw County. Enlisted in Company C, Lancers, Oct. 28, 1861, at Saginaw, for 3 years, age 18. Dec. 9, 1861. Transferred to Company I, 16th Michigan, Feb. 28, 1862. Wounded in action at Chancellorsville, Va., May 3, 1863. Discharged for disability at Washington, D.C., Sept. 6, 1864.

Boonstra, Sake. Enlisted in Company K, Feb. 20, 1865, at Holland, Ottawa County, for 1 year, age 19. Substitute for John Hilder, drafted from Holland. Joined regiment March 14, 1865. Mustered out at Jeffersonville, Ind., July 8, 1865.

Borden, William H., Ionia County. Enlisted in Company B as Sergeant, Aug. 10, 1861, at Ionia, for 3 years, age 20. Commissioned 2nd Lieutenant, Company F, Nov. 8, 1862. Killed in action at Gettysburg, July 2, 1863.

Borgman, Martin V., Detroit. Enlisted in Company A, Lancers, as 1st Sergeant, Oct. 1, 1861, at Detroit, for 3 years, age 23. Mustered out at Detroit, March 20, 1862. Reentered service in Company F, 16th Michigan, as 2nd Lieutenant, commissioned July 16, 1862. Commissioned 1st Lieutenant, Nov. 8, 1862. Wounded in action, left arm, at Gettysburg, July 2, 1863. Acting Adjutant Dec. 22, 1863. Discharged on Surgeon's certificate of disability June 21, 1864.

Bosford, Edgar. Enlisted in Company E, Aug. 15, 1861, at Detroit, for 3 years, age 24. No further record.

Bostwick, John T., Argentine, Genesee County. Enlisted in Company K, Aug. 9, 1862, at Argentine, for 3 years, age 36. Joined regiment at Antietam, Md., Oct. 3, 1862. Died of disease near Falmouth, Va., Nov. 26, 1862.

Bostwick, Samuel D., Argentine. Enlisted in Company K, Aug. 9, 1862, at Argentine, for 3 years, age 18. Mustered Sept. 5, 1862. Joined regiment at Antietam, Md., Oct. 3, 1862. Died of disease near Falmouth, Va., Dec. 8, 1862.

Bothwell, James. Enlisted in Company E, Feb. 13, 1864, at Saginaw, for 3 years, age 26. Wounded in action, head, at Magnolia Swamp–Bethesda Church June 1, 1864. Mustered out at Jeffersonville, Ind., July 8, 1865.

Botsford, Robert G., Van Buren County. Enlisted in First Company Sharpshooters attached to 16th Michigan, March 18, 1862, at Detroit, for 3 years, age 42. Wounded in action at second Manassas, Aug. 30, 1862. Discharged at Washington, D.C., Oct. 22, 1862.

Bounting, Richard A., Saginaw. Enlisted in Company E, Lancers, Oct. 18, 1861, at Saginaw, for 3 years, age 26. Transferred to Company K, 16th Michigan, Feb. 28, 1862. Corporal. Missing in action June 30, 1862, after the Gaines' Mill battle. Discharged for disability near Falmouth, Va., Nov. 18, 1862. Reenlisted in Company B, March 11, 1865 at Saginaw, for 1 year. Mustered out at Jeffersonville, Ind., July 8, 1865. Resided Barryton, Mecosta County.

Bovee, Andrew A., or I. (Veteran), Ionia County. Enlisted in Company D, Lancers, Nov. 15, 1861, at Fulton, for 3 years, age 24. Transferred to Company K, 16th Michigan, Feb. 28, 1862. Wounded in action, at Gettysburg, July 2, 1863. Reenlisted as Sergeant Feb. 26, 1864, at Bealton, Va. Commissioned 2nd Lieutenant July 7, 1865. Mustered out at Jeffersonville, Ind., July 8, 1865.

Bovee, Holsey, Wayne County. Enlisted in Company F, as Wagoner, Aug. 4, 1861, at Plymouth, for 3 years, age 21. Discharged for disability Dec. 13, 1862. Resided at Soldiers' Home, Milwaukee, Wis.

Bovee, Philip V. Enlisted in Company C, Lancers, as 1st Sergeant, Oct. 31, 1861, at Milwaukee, Wis., for 3 years, age 45. Transferred to Company I, 16th Michigan, Feb. 28, 1862. Commissioned 2nd Lieutenant? Reportedly wounded in action at Gaines' Mill, June 27, 1862. Discharged at Fortress Monroe, Va., Oct. 8, 1862.

Bowen, Charles E. Wayne County. Enlisted in Company F, Aug. 25, 1861, at Plymouth, for 3 years, age 21. Listed as absent, wounded from Dec. 1862 to July 1863. Sergeant. Transferred to Invalid Corps Nov. 15, 1863. Discharged Aug. 26, 1864, from Company D, 16th Regiment, Veteran Reserve Corps.

Bowen or **Brown, David**, Detroit. Enlisted in Company F, Sept. 9, 1862, at Detroit, for 3 years, age 44. Joined regiment at Antietam, Md., Oct. 15, 1862. Transferred to Invalid Corps Aug. 1, 1863.

Bowen, George W., Monroe. Enlisted in 4th Michigan Infantry as Hospital Steward, June 20, 1861, at Adrian, for 3 years. Transferred to 16th Michigan and commissioned 2nd Assistant Surgeon Dec. 1, 1862. Discharged May 6, 1863 and recommissioned June 9, 1863, serving with two different U.S. Colored Troop regiments. Reportedly later resided Groveland, Oakland County.

Bower, Michael (Veteran), Redford. Enlisted in Company G, as Corporal, Aug. 24, 1861. Reenlisted as Sergeant, Dec. 21, 1863, at Rappahannock Station, Va. Killed in action at Laurel Hill, Va., May 8, 1864.

Bowlby, William, Oakland County. Enlisted in Company C, Aug. 9, 1861, at Detroit, for 3 years, age 41. Discharged on Surgeon's certificate of disability at Alexandria, Va., April 14, 1863.

Boyer, Daniel. Enlisted in Company K, March 29, 1865, at Seville, Gratiot County, for 1 year, age 17. Substitute for Jacob Bayer, or Boyer, drafted from Seville. Mustered out at Jeffersonville, Ind., July 8, 1865.

Boyers, Horace. Enlisted in Company E, Aug. 13, 1861, at Detroit, for 3 years, age 23. Transferred to Company F. Deserted Sept. 12, 1861.

Boylan, Frank, Wayne County. Enlisted in Company E, Sept. 3, 1861, at Detroit, for 3 years, age 33. Wounded in action at Gaines' Mill, June 27, 1862. Severely wounded in action, right leg, Gettysburg, July 2, 1863. Discharged at expiration of term of service at Detroit, Sept. 19, 1864.

Brackett, Robert J. or **Albert J.** Drafted for 1 year, from Sparta, Kent County, age 26. Mustered March 28, 1865. Assigned to Company E. Mustered out at Jeffersonville, Ind., July 8, 1865.

Bradford, James W. or **M.** (Veteran). Enlisted in Company B, Aug. 6, 1861, at Ionia, for 3 years, age 26. Wounded in action at Gaines' Mill, June 27, 1862. Reenlisted Dec. 24, 1863, at Rappahannock Station, Va. Fatally wounded in action at Dabney's Mill, Feb. 6, 1865 and died at Point Lookout, Md., Feb. 17, 1865.

Bradford, John, Detroit. Enlisted in Company A, Lancers, Nov. 25, 1861, at Detroit, for 3 years, age 19. Transferred to Company I, 16th Michigan, Feb. 28, 1862. Wounded in action at Gaines' Mill, June 27, 1862. Transferred to Veteran Reserve Corps Sept. 30, 1863.

Bradish, Reuben (Veteran), Ionia County. Enlisted in Company C, Dec. 11, 1861, at Ionia, for 3 years, age 23. Joined regiment at Hall's Hill, Va., Jan. 11, 1862. Missing Sept. 12, 1862, but returned. Reenlisted Dec. 24, 1863, at Rappahannock Station, Va. Corporal April 1, 1865. Mustered out at Jeffersonville, Ind., July 8, 1865. Resided Otisco, Mich.

Bradish, William L., Ionia. Enlisted in Company C, Dec. 11, 1861, at Ionia, for 3 years, age 21. Joined regiment at Hall's Hill, Va., Jan. 11, 1862. Wounded in action, hip, at Gaines' Mill, June 27, 1862. Corporal. Died of disease at Beverly Ford, Va., Sept. 16, 1863.

Bradley, Doctor B., Ionia County. Enlisted in Company B, Aug. 7, 1861, at Ionia, for 3 years, age 29. Corporal. Killed in action at second Manassas, Aug. 30, 1862.

Bradley, Frank (Veteran), Saginaw County. Enlisted in Company D, Aug. 1, 1861, at East Saginaw, for 3 years, age 23. Musician, July 1862. Reenlisted Dec. 21, 1863, at Rappahannock

Station, Va. Mustered out at Jeffersonville, Ind., July 8, 1865.

Bradley, Patrick (Veteran), Flint. Enlisted in Company C, as Corporal, Aug. 31, 1861, at Detroit, for 3 years, age 23. Reenlisted Dec. 24, 1863, at Rappahannock Station, Va. 1st Sergeant. Wounded in action at Weldon Railroad, Petersburg, Va., Aug. 21, 1864. Both legs amputated. Died at City Point, Va., Sept. 16, 1864.

Bradley, Russell. Enlisted in Company I, Sept. 4, 1862, at Argentine, for 3 years, age 19. Sergeant. Mustered out at Jeffersonville, Ind., July 8, 1865.

Bradmire, George. Enlisted in regimental Band, Sept. 13, 1861, at Detroit, for 3 years, age 22. Mustered out Aug. 11, 1862.

Bradshaw, Joseph. Enlisted in Second Company Sharpshooters, March 23, 1864 at Kochville, Saginaw County, for 3 years, age 24. Corporal May 1, 1865. Mustered out at Jeffersonville, Ind., July 8, 1865.

Brady, James W. or **M**. Enlisted in Company A, March 11, 1865, at Argentine, for 1 year, age 27. Mustered out at Jeffersonville, Ind., July 8, 1865.

Braford, Edmond. Enlisted in Company B, Lancers, Oct. 22, 1861, at Cohoctah, Livingston County, for 3 years, age 20. Transferred to Company I, 16th Michigan, Feb. 28, 1862. Discharged for disability Jan. 20, 1863.

Bramhall, Joseph, Detroit. Enlisted in Company E, Lancers, Oct. 2, 1861, at Milwaukee, for 3 years, age 29. Transferred to Company K, 16th Michigan, Feb. 28, 1862. Corporal. Sergeant. Discharged at Falmouth, Va., Dec. 24, 1862.

Bramin, Dennis, Genesee County. Enlisted in Company C, Aug. 4, 1861, at Detroit, for 3 years, age 18. Mustered Aug. 14, 1861. Wounded in action and taken prisoner at Savage's Station, June 30, 1862. Paroled Sept. 1862. Alternately listed as having died a Rebel prisoner or that he deserted April 30, 1863.

Brandon, Albert J., or I. Enlisted in Company D, March 23, 1865, at Fredonia, Calhoun County, for 3 years, age 28. Substitute for David Annis, drafted from Fredonia. Mustered out at Jeffersonville, Ind., July 8, 1865.

Breakey, Dr. William F., Ann Arbor. Entered service in 16th Michigan as Assistant Surgeon. Commissioned June 18, 1862. Resigned on account of disability April 18, 1864. Resided Ann Arbor, Mich.

Breen, Michael, Detroit. Enlisted in Company B, March 28, 1865, at Detroit, for 1 year, age 22. Substitute for W. H. C. Subkent, or Lubkent, drafted from Detroit. Deserted near Louisville, Ky., June 25, 1865.

Breen, Peter (Veteran). Detroit. Enlisted in Company H, Nov. 4, 1861, at Detroit, for 3 years, age 18. Wounded in action at Gaines' Mill, June 27, 1862. Wounded in action, face, at Gettysburg, July 2, 1863. Reenlisted Dec. 24, 1863, at Rappahannock Station, Va. Wounded in action, hand and leg, at Laurel Hill–Spotsylvania Court House, May 8, 1864. No report of muster out.

Bremer, John. Enlisted in Company K, Jan. 19, 1864, at Detroit, for 3 years, age 31. Wounded in action at Malvern Hill, July 1, 1862. Wounded in action, left side, at Petersburg, Va., June 24, 1864. Transferred to Veteran Reserve Corps. Discharged at Alexandria, Va., Aug. 10, 1865, from 100th Company, 2nd Battalion, Veteran Reserve Corps.

Brennen, William. Enlisted in Company D, March 22, 1865, at Port Huron, for 3 years, age 19. Substitute for James T. Howard, drafted from Port Huron. Mustered out at Jeffersonville, Ind., July 8, 1865.

Brennan, John. Enlisted in Company G, Aug. 21, 1861, at Detroit, for 3 years, age 25. Wounded in action, at Chancellorsville, Va., May 3, 1863. Discharged at expiration of term of service near Petersburg, Va., Sept. 7, 1864.

Brennan, Peter. Enlisted in Second Company Sharpshooters, April 5, 1864, at Frankenmuth, for 3 years, age 22. Deserted at Saginaw, May 3, 1864.

Bretz, Charles E. Drafted March 15, 1865, for 1 year, from Odessa, Ionia County, age 36. Assigned to Company D. Mustered out at Jeffersonville, Ind., July 8, 1865.

Bridge, Henry, Plymouth. Enlisted in Company F, July 31, 1861, at Plymouth, for 3 years, age 21. Died of disease at Hall's Hill, Va., Dec. 14, 1861.

Briggs, Francis M., Birch Run. Enlisted in Company D, Aug. 1, 1861, at East Saginaw, for 3 years, age 24. Died of disease at Hall's Hill. Va., Dec. 18, 1861.

Briggs, Hiram A., Wayne County. Enlisted in Company H, Sept. 30, 1861, at Detroit, for 3 years, age 43. Missing in action at Garlick's Landing June 13, 1862. Prisoner of war. Discharged at expiration of term of service at Detroit, Jan. 9, 1865. Died March 18, 1890.

Briggs, Hiram A. Enlisted in Company H, Feb. 6, 1865, at Madison, for 1 year, age 40. Mustered out at Jeffersonville, Ind., July 8, 1865. (Editor's note: It is not clear if these listings for Hiram A. Briggs refer to the same man, who may have enlisted a second time.)

Briggs, Silas M. Drafted March 15, 1865, for 1 year, from Algoma, Kent County, age 31. Assigned to Company I. Mustered out at Jeffersonville, Ind., July 8, 1865.

Britt, John. Enlisted in Company A, Feb. 2, 1864, at Ann Arbor, for 3 years, age 27. Deserted at Ann Arbor, Feb. 12, 1864.

Britton, Andrew, Argentine, Genesee County. Enlisted in Company I, Aug. 18, 1862, at Argentine, for 3 years, age 29. Sergeant. Reportedly wounded in action, Petersburg, Va., in summer 1864. Died of wounds at David's Island, New York Harbor, Aug. 25, 1864. Buried in National Cemetery at Brooklyn, N.Y., Grave No. 1737.

Britton, Edward, Flushing. Enlisted in Company C, July 30, 1861, at Flint, for 3 years, age 26. Discharged for disability at Detroit, Sept. 24, 1862.

Brockway, Solomon P., Albion. Appointed 2nd Lieutenant of Company F at its organization, Aug. 9, 1861. Resigned in the fall of 1862, and commissioned Major, 9th Michigan Cavalry, Nov. 3, 1862. Mustered out, with brevet promotions for gallantry, July 25, 1865.

Brockway, Theodore A. Enlisted in Company G, Aug. 17, 1861, at White Pigeon, for 3 years, age 18. Paroled prisoner, Oct. 1862. Died Feb. 12, 1863, of wounds received in action at Malvern Hill, July 1, 1862.

Brockway, William H., Albion. Entered service in the regiment at organization, as Chaplain, Aug. 19, 1861, at Detroit, for 3 years, age 48. Resigned on account of disability Nov. 23, 1862. Died at Albion, Mich., Oct. 21, 1891.

Brookins, George R. Enlisted in Company E, Aug. 13, 1861, at Detroit, for 3 years, age 21. Transferred to Company D. Wounded in action at Gaines' Mill, June 27, 1862. Discharged at Baltimore, Feb. 22, 1863. Died June 5, 1903, and buried in Brady Hill Cemetery, Saginaw.

Brookman, John, Plymouth. Enlisted in Company C, Aug. 3, 1861, at Flint, for 3 years, age 18. Transferred to Company F. Died of disease July 7, 1862.

Brooks, Jessie N. Enlisted in Company E, March 27, 1865, at Kalamazoo, for 1 year, age 26. Substitute for Barnabas Cotton, drafted from White Pigeon, St. Joseph County. Discharged at Washington, D.C., May 30, 1865.

Broulette, Edward. Enlisted in First Company Sharpshooters attached to 16th Michigan, Feb. 12, 1864, at Bridgeport, for 3 years, age 31. Wounded in action at Peeble's Farm, Sept. 30, 1864. Mustered out at Jeffersonville, Ind., July 8, 1865.

Brower or **Brown** or **Burns, John W**. Enlisted in Company B, Jan. 28, 1865, at Monterey, Allegan County, for 1 year, age 27. Substitute for Ledra Hazlit, drafted from Monterey. Joined regiment Feb. 21, 1865. Mustered out at Jeffersonville, Ind., July 8, 1865.

Brown, Amos or **Aaron** (Veteran). Enlisted in Company F, July 30, 1861, at Plymouth, for 3 years, age 21. Transferred to Company G. Reenlisted Dec. 21, 1863 at Rappahannock Station, Va. Mustered out at Jeffersonville, Ind., July 8, 1865.

Brown, Butler. Adrian. Entered service in Company F, as 2nd Lieutenant, Aug. 9, 1861. Commissioned 1st Lieutenant, Company C, Sept. 28, 1862. Transferred to Company E, April 1, 1863. Killed in action at Gettysburg, July 2, 1863.

Brown, Gehiel or **Gent**, Plymouth. Enlisted in Company F, Sept. 16, 1861, at Plymouth, for 3 years, age 18. Killed in action at Malvern Hill, June 30, 1862.

Brown, George No. 1 (Veteran). Enlisted in Company E, Aug. 15, 1861, at Detroit, for 3 years, age 22. Transferred to Company H. Wounded in action at Fredericksburg, Va., Dec. 13, 1862. Reenlisted Dec. 24, 1863, at Rappahannock Station, Va. Discharged March 1, 1865, at Washington, D.C., for wounds received in action, Petersburg, Va., June 30, 1864.

Brown, George No. 2 or Senior, Grand Traverse. Enlisted in Company H, Sept. 1861, at Grand Traverse Bay, for 3 years, age 31. Discharged for disability at Detroit, Dec. 16, 1862, for wounds received in action, shoulder and foot, at second Manassas, Aug. 30, 1862.

Brown, George W., Pine Grove, Van Buren County. Enlisted in Company K, Feb. 26, 1863, at Otsego, Allegan County, for 9 months, age 20. Substitute for Nier Nies, drafted Feb. 11, 1863, from Otsego. Joined regiment near Falmouth, Va., March 19, 1863. Discharged at expiration of term of service at Kelly's Ford, Va., Nov. 21, 1863.

Brown or **Bunn, Henry**. Enlisted and mustered in Company F, March 17, 1865, at Climax, Kalamazoo County, for 1 year, age 28. Substitute for Oscar F. Seeley, drafted from Climax. No further record.

Brown, John. Enlisted in Company E, March 28, 1865, at Evergreen, Montcalm County, for 1 year, age 33. Substitute for Legrand D. Abbey, drafted from Evergreen. Mustered out at Jeffersonville, Ind., July 8, 1865.

Brown, Mathew. Enlisted March 31, 1864, at Ovid, for 3 years, age 30. No further record.

Brown, Michael. Enlisted in Company A, March 1, 1864, at Houghton, for 3 years, age 24. Taken prisoner Dec. 10, 1864, at raid on the Weldon Railroad, Petersburg, Va. Discharged at Camp Chase, Ohio, June 10, 1865.

Brown, Michael. In regiment's "Roll of Honor," reportedly a corporal in Company G who was killed in action, Laurel Hill–Spotsylvania Court House, May 8, 1864. No age or hometown or enlistment date given.

Brown, Nelson. Enlisted in Company E, March 15, 1865, at Dryden, Lapeer County, for 3 years, age 22. Substitute for Brazillian R. Emmons. Discharged at Washington, D.C., May 30, 1865.

Brown, Oliver. Enlisted in Company C, Jan. 13, 1864, at Ecorse, for 3 years, age 19. Wounded in action at Magnolia Swamp–Bethesda Church, May 31, 1864. Discharged on Surgeon's certificate of disability at Washington, D.C., Nov. 16, 1864.

Brown, Robert. Enlisted in Company F, Aug. 2, 1861, at Plymouth, for 3 years, age 25. Transferred to Company E, May 1862. Discharged for disability at Georgetown, May 15, 1862. Died Aug. 19, 1897.

Brown, William D., Ionia County. Enlisted in Company B, Aug. 7, 1861, at Ionia, for 3 years, age 19. Discharged for disability at Hall's Hill, Va., Feb. 25, 1862.

Bruce, Alma L., Delhi. Enlisted in Company E, Dec. 30, 1862, at Delhi, for 3 years, age 18. Joined regiment at Falmouth, Va., Jan. 2, 1863. Transferred to Invalid Corps July 1, 1863.

Brust, James or **John**, Detroit. Enlisted in Company K, Jan. 15, 1864, at Detroit, for 3 years, age 28. Taken prisoner during the Overland Campaign and died of disease in prison at Andersonville, Ga., July 18, 1864. Buried in National Cemetery at Andersonville. Grave No. 3517.

Bryan, James. Enlisted in Company A, March 27, 1865, at Fabius, St. Joseph County, for 1 year, age 21. Substitute for Valentine Beadle. Mustered out at Jeffersonville, Ind., July 8, 1865.

Buckfink, Jacob (Veteran), Ontonagon County. Enlisted in Company A, Aug. 2, 1861, at Ontonagon, for 3 years, age 23. Missing in action at Gaines' Mill, June 27, 1862. Wounded in action, arm, at Gettysburg, July 2, 1863. Reenlisted Dec. 21, 1863, at Rappahannock Station, Va. Died Jan. 26, 1865, at Harwood Hospital, Washington, D.C., of wounds received in action at Peeble's Farm, Sept. 30, 1864.

Buckley, Daniel (Veteran). Enlisted in Company E, Aug. 13, 1861, at Detroit, for 3 years, age 21. Transferred to Company F. Slightly wounded in head in action at Gettysburg, July 2, 1863. Reenlisted Dec. 21, 1863, at Rappahannock Station, Va. Mustered out at Jeffersonville, Ind., July 8, 1865.

Buckley, John. Enlisted in Company C, Aug. 2, 1861, at Flint, for 3 years, age 32. No further record.

Buckshicker or **Booksheker, Henry**, Ontonagon County. Enlisted in Company A, Aug. 2, 1861, at Ontonagon, for 3 years, age 29. Wounded and missing in action at Gaines' Mill, Ga., June 27, 1862. Discharged at expiration of term of service at Petersburg, Va., Sept. 7, 1864. Resided Michigan Soldiers' Home.

Bull, George E. Enlisted in Company C, March 27, 1865, at Concord, Jackson County, for 1 year, age 25. Substitute for Samuel P. Baker, drafted from Concord. Mustered out at Jeffersonville, Ind., July 8, 1865.

Bullfinch, Oscar F. Enlisted in Company D, May 9, 1864, at Saginaw, for 3 years, age 35. Missing in action at Dabney's Mill, Feb. 6, 1865. No further record.

Bullock, Nelson, Gratiot County. Enlisted in Company B, Aug. 6, 1861, at Ionia, for 3 years, age 28. Wounded in action at Gaines' Mill, June 27, 1862. Discharged Feb. 9, 1863.

Bullock, Thomas, Detroit. Enlisted in Company D, Dec. 1, 1861, at Detroit, for 3 years, age 32.

Killed in action at Fredericksburg, Va., Dec. 13, 1862.

Bunyea, Chauncey (Veteran), Jackson. Enlisted in Company K, March 4, 1862, age 21. Wounded in action at Chancellorsville, Va., right arm and side, May 3, 1863. Reenlisted March 4, 1864, at Bealton, Va. Corporal. Discharged at Camp Chase, Ohio, June 16, 1865. Resided Plymouth, Mich.

Bunyea, George. Enlisted in Company K, Dec. 21, 1863, at Rappahannock Station, Va., for 3 years, age 21. Mustered out at Jeffersonville, Ind., July 8, 1865. Resided Wayne, Mich.

Burch, James. Blissfield. Enlisted in Company F, Lancers, as Sergeant. Oct. 13, 1861, at Blissfield, for 3 years, age 30. Transferred to Company I, 16th Michigan, Feb. 28, 1862. Deserted at Detroit, March 24, 1862.

Burey or **Burns, John**. Enlisted in Second Company Sharpshooters, May 2, 1864, at Bloomfield, for 3 years, age 19. Sergeant. Mustered out at Jeffersonville, Ind., July 8, 1865.

Burg, Charles. Enlisted in Company C, March 28, 1865, at Blissfield, Lenawee County, for 1 year, age 19. Substitute for R. S. Ingersoll. Mustered out at Jeffersonville, Ind., July 8, 1865. Resided in Ida, Mich.

Burke, John. Enlisted in Company A, March 28, 1865, at Ash, Monroe County, for 1 year, age 40. Substitute for Julius Beaumice, drafted from Ash. Mustered out at Jeffersonville, Ind., July 8, 1865.

Burke, Thomas H. Enlisted in Company F, Aug. 2, 1861, at Plymouth, for 3 years, age 31. Mustered Sept. 7, 1861. Transferred to Company E. Discharged Dec. 1863.

Burkhead, Thomas, East Saginaw. Enlisted in Company D, Jan. 25, 1864, at Saginaw, for 3 years, age 44. Killed in action at Peeble's Farm, Sept. 30, 1864.

Burkhouse, Edward, Detroit. Enlisted in Company I, Feb. 26, 1862. Discharged for disability at Gaines' Mill, June 29, 1862.

Burlingame, Charles L. Enlisted in Company G, March 24, 1865, at Carmel, Eaton County, for 1 year, age 16. Substitute for Horace Johnson. Mustered out at Jeffersonville, Ind., July 8, 1865.

Burlison, Eli. Enlisted in Company A, March 14, 1865, at Garden, Delta County, for 1 year, age 19. Substitute for Edward Ansel, drafted from Garden. Mustered out at Jeffersonville, Ind., July 8, 1865.

Burnham, Daniel. Enlisted in Company D, Feb. 29, 1864, at Midland, for 3 years, age 22. Mustered out at Jeffersonville, Ind., July 8, 1865.

Burnham, Henry or **John H**. Enlisted in Company D, Feb. 6, 1864, at Saginaw, for 3 years, age 18. Joined regiment Feb. 23, 1864. Wounded in action Nov. 1864. Mustered out at Jeffersonville, Ind., July 8, 1865.

Burnham, George. There is no official state roster or regimental casualty listing for this soldier, reportedly in Company I, but Burnham was listed among the Gettysburg wounded in Washington and Philadelphia in newspaper reports, July–Aug. 1863, as wounded in the leg, Chestnut Hill hospital.

Burns, James (Veteran), Detroit. Enlisted in Company H, as Musician, Aug. 8, 1861, age 18. Reenlisted Dec. 24, 1863, at Rappahannock Station, Va. Corporal May 1, 1865. Mustered out at Jeffersonville, Ind., July 8, 1865. Resided Detroit.

Burns, James, Detroit. Enlisted in Company H, Oct. 4, 1861, at Detroit, for 3 years, age 40. Discharged for disability at Washington, D.C., April 7, 1862.

Burns, Michael. Drafted March 15, 1865, for 1 year, from Cascade, Kent County, age 30. Assigned to Company B. Discharged at Washington, D.C., June 8, 1865.

Burns or **Barnes, William**. Enlisted Feb. 5, 1865, at Washington, Sanilac County, for 3 years, age 19. Substitute for J. M. Cole, drafted from Washington. No further record.

Burns or **Byrns, William H.**, Dearborn. Enlisted in First Company Sharpshooters attached to 16th Michigan as Corporal, Nov. 1, 1861, at Detroit, for 3 years, age 21. Joined regiment at Hall's Hill, Va., Feb. 14, 1862. 1st Sergeant. Commissioned 2nd Lieutenant Jan. 15, 1863. Commissioned 1st Lieutenant Jan. 20, 1864. Wounded in action, left arm, at Totopotomoy–Bethesda Church, May 30, 1864. Discharged at expiration of term of service, Dec. 1, 1864.

Burrett or **Barrett, Daniel**. Enlisted in Company I, March 3, 1862, at Walled Lake, for 3 years, age 19. Dropped from rolls Oct. 7, 1862.

Burroughs, William, St. Joseph County. Enlisted in Company C, Aug. 15, 1861, at Hillsdale, for 3 years, age 22. Discharged at expiration of term of service, Sept. 7, 1864.

Burton, Edward or **Edwin**, Midland County. Enlisted in Company D, Aug. 1, 1861, at East Saginaw, for 3 years, age 23. Discharged at New York Oct. 2, 1862.

Burton, Edward, Sheridan. Enlisted in Company K, March 1, 1862, at Detroit, for 3 years, age 37. Killed in action at Gettysburg, July 2, 1863. Buried in National Cemetery at Gettysburg.

Burton, Melzar, Almont. Enlisted in First Company Sharpshooters attached 16th Michigan, Nov. 14, 1861, at Detroit, for 3 years, age 20. Joined regiment at Hall's Hill, Va., Feb. 14, 1862. Killed in action at Gaines' Mill, June 27, 1862.

Burzalles, Edward, Detroit. Enlisted in Company E, Dec. 16, 1862, at Detroit, for 3 years, age 17. Joined regiment at Falmouth, Va., Jan. 2, 1863. Missing or deserted July 2, 1863.

Busha, Camel or **Carmon**. Enlisted in Second Company Sharpshooters, April 26, 1864, at Saginaw, for 3 years, age 18. Corporal, May 1, 1865. Mustered out at Jeffersonville, Ind., July 8, 1865.

Butler, Eli. Enlisted in Company G, March 30, 1865, at Leroy, Calhoun County, for 1 year, age 19. Substitute for Charles M. Fish, drafted from Leroy. Mustered out at Jeffersonville, Ind., July 8, 1865.

Butler, Phineas, Cohoctah, Livingston County. Enlisted in Company B, Lancers, as Corporal, Dec. 9, 1861, at Cohoctah, for 3 years, age 33. Transferred to Company I, 16th Michigan, Feb. 28, 1862. Killed in action at Gaines' Mill, June 27, 1862.

Butler, Dr. William H., Buffalo, N. Y. Entered service in the regiment at organization, as Assistant Surgeon, Aug. 19, 1861, at Detroit, for 3 years, age 36. Resigned June 17, 1862.

Button, William. Enlisted in Company E, March. 29, 1865, at Port Huron, for 1 year, age 22. Substitute for Bethel C. Farrand, drafted from Port Huron. Mustered out at Jeffersonville, Ind., July 8, 1865.

Buttrick, Charles R. Drafted March 15, 1865, for 1 year, from Ada, Kent County, age 25. Assigned to Company I. Mustered out at Jeffersonville, Ind., July 8, 1865.

Byrman or **Dryman, Daniel**. Enlisted in Company A, Aug. 6, 1864, at Jackson, for 3 years, age 40. Substitute for Gotlieb H. Brindle, or Brinder, from Ann Arbor. Listed as deserted

Dec. 13, 1864, but was likely captured and shot by guerillas while on the raid on Weldon Railroad, Petersburg, Va.

Bythel, John. Enlisted in Second Company Sharpshooters, March 30, 1864, at Spaulding, for 3 years, age 31. Supposed to have died Oct. 1864. No further record.

Caldwell, John M., Deerfield, Livingston County. Drafted March 10, 1863, for 9 months, from Deerfield. Assigned to Company G. Joined regiment at Falmouth, Va., March 1863. Discharged at expiration of term of service at Kelly's Ford, Va., Nov. 22, 1863.

Camer or **Carner, Jerome**, Saginaw County. Enlisted in Company D, Aug. 2, 1861, at East Saginaw, for 3 years, age 23. Discharged on Surgeon's certificate of disability April 27, 1862.

Cameron, Alexander, Lansing. Enlisted in Company F, Aug. 4, 1861, at Plymouth, for 3 years, age 30. Reported in Company G, June 1862. Wounded in action at Gaines' Mill, June 27, 1862. Promoted 1st Sergeant. Commissioned 2nd Lieutenant, April 17, 1863. Wounded in action at Gettysburg, July 2, 1863, loss of right arm. Resigned to accept appointment in Veteran Reserve Corps, Oct. 28, 1863. Was placed in command of Lodies Island, S.C.; in the summer of 1864 he was appointed Chief of Ambulance Department of the South, with rank and pay of Captain. Resided in Lansing.

Cameron, Angus. Enlisted in Second Company Sharpshooters, March 31, 1864, at Ingersoll, for 3 years, age 35. Discharged for disability at Washington, D.C., June 5, 1865.

Cameron, Hugh. Enlisted in Second Company Sharpshooters, March 21, 1864, at Bloomfield, for 3 years, age 22. Absent sick Sept. 6, 1864. No further record.

Cameron, Hugh. Enlisted in First Company Sharpshooters attached to 16th Michigan, Feb. 18, 1864, at Detroit, for 3 years, age 20. Corporal, May 1, 1865. Mustered out at Jeffersonville, Ind., July 8, 1865.

Cameron, John J. Enlisted in Company D, Feb. 5, 1863, at Thomastown, Saginaw County, for 3 years, age 24. Joined regiment near Falmouth, Va., March 26, 1863. Wounded in action June 7, 1864, withdrawal from Cold Harbor, Va., Corporal, May 1, 1865. Mustered out at Jeffersonville, Ind., July 8, 1865.

Camp or **Cramp, Henry**. Drafted March 15, 1865, for 1 year, from Cascade, Kent County, age 36. Assigned to Company B. Died of disease at Washington, D.C., May 12, 1865.

Campbell, Angus. Enlisted in Company K, Feb. 23, 1865, at Pontiac, for 3 years, age 19. Substitute for Jerome Paddock. Joined regiment March 14, 1865. Mustered out at Jeffersonville, Ind., July 8, 1865.

Campbell, Harmon. Drafted for 1 year, from Dorr, Allegan County, age 33. Mustered March 17, 1865. Assigned to Company H. Discharged at Washington, D.C., June 14, 1865.

Cann or **Case, John A.** Enlisted in Company G, Jan. 24, 1865, at Carmel, for 3 years, age 36. Substitute for Francis H. Higby, drafted. Mustered out at Jeffersonville, Ind., July 8, 1865.

Cantine, Thelesphe. Enlisted in Company D, March 1, 1864, at Houghton, for 3 years, age 21. Prisoner of war Aug. 1864. Discharged at Weldon Railroad near Petersburg, Va., Aug. 20, 1864.

Cape, Henry. Enlisted in Company E, Aug. 16, 1861, at Detroit, for 3 years, age 39. Transferred to Company H. Discharged for disability at Gaines' Mill, June 27, 1862.

Carew or **Carrew, John**. Enlisted in Second Company Sharpshooters, April 24, 1864, at Saginaw, for 3 years, age 26. Wounded in action and taken prisoner June 9, 1864, withdrawal from Cold Harbor, Va. Paroled June 18, 1864. Discharged at Camp Chase, Ohio, June 16, 1865.

Carill or **Carroll, Stephen**, Calhoun County. Enlisted in Company F, Aug. 3, 1861, at Plymouth, for 3 years, age 20. Discharged for disability Dec. 26, 1861.

Carl, Henry E., or **Caul, Edwin H.** (Veteran), Nankin, Wayne County. Enlisted in Company K, March 4, 1862, at Detroit, for 3 years, age 22. Taken prisoner at second Manassas, Aug. 30, 1862. Paroled September 1862. Reenlisted March 26, 1864, at Bealton, Va. Deserted.

Carleton, Nelson, Macomb County. Enlisted in First Company Sharpshooters attached to 16th Michigan, Dec. 3, 1861, at Detroit, for 3 years, age 18. Joined regiment at Hall's Hill, Va., Feb. 14, 1862. Discharged at a hospital Dec. 1862.

Carmody, John (Veteran), Detroit. Enlisted in Company H, Oct. 15, 1861, at Detroit, for 3 years, age 19. Missing in action at Gaines' Mill, June 27, 1862. Reenlisted Dec. 24, 1863, at Rappahannock Station, Va. Died June 15, 1864, of wounds received in action at Magnolia Swamp–Bethesda Church, June 1, 1864.

Carmody, Mathew. Enlisted Jan. 13, 1864, at Canton, for 3 years, age 26. No further record.

Carmody, Thomas, Detroit. Enlisted Company H, Nov. 11, 1861. Discharged (possibly he was underage?) but apparently enlisted again in First Company Sharpshooters attached to 16th Michigan, Oct. 28, 1864, at Whiteford, Monroe County, for 1 year, age 19. Mustered out at Jeffersonville, Ind., July 8, 1865. Died Sept. 21, 1895.

Carney or **Kearney, John**. Enlisted in Company B, Lancers, Jan. 2, 1862, at Howell, for 3 years, age 40. Transferred to Company I, 16th Michigan, Feb. 28, 1862. Discharged for disability Aug. 24, 1863.

Carney, Samuel. An enlistee in the Second Company Sharpshooters, according to regiment's "Roll of Honor," who died of disease, July 27, 1864, at City Point, Va.

Carpenter, Augustus C., Detroit. Enlisted in Company D, Dec. 20, 1862, at Detroit, for 3 years, age 18. Joined regiment near Falmouth, Va., Jan. 8, 1863. Sergeant. Wounded in action Sept. 1864, probably Peeble's Farm. Mustered out at Jeffersonville, Ind., July 8, 1865.

Carpenter, George (Veteran), Ionia County. Enlisted in Company B, Aug. 8, 1861, at Ionia, for 3 years, age 18. Reenlisted Dec. 24, 1863, at Rappahannock Station, Va. Transferred to Veteran Reserve Corps April 30, 1864. Discharged at Washington, D.C., July 20, 1865, from Company A, 24th Regiment, Veteran Reserve Corps.

Carr, James. Enlisted in Company I, Feb. 9, 1864, at Bangor, for 3 years, age 24. Listed as absent, wounded from Aug. 1864 to Feb. 1865. Corporal May 1, 1865. Mustered out at Jeffersonville, Ind., July 8, 1865.

Carr, James H. Enlisted in Company E, March 31, 1865, at Fredonia, Calhoun County, for 3 years, age 18. Substitute for Vinder Arnold. Mustered out at Jeffersonville, Ind., July 8, 1865.

Carr, Thomas C., Flint. Entered service in Company C, at regiment's organization, as Captain, July 30, 1861, at Flint, for 3 years, age 34. Commissioned Aug. 9, 1861. Killed in action at Gaines' Mill, June 27, 1862.

Carroll, John, Kochville. Enlisted in Company D, Feb. 11, 1863 at Detroit. Joined regiment near Falmouth, Va., March 18, 1863. Transferred to Invalid Corps Nov. 15, 1861.

Carter, Lysander, Pittsford, Hillsdale County. Enlisted in Company C, Aug. 24, 1861, at White

Pigeon for 3 years, age 20. Died at Harrison's Landing, Va., July 20, 1862, of wounds received in action at Gaines' Mill, June 27, 1862.

Cartwright, Amos. Drafted for 1 year, from Dayton, Tuscola County, age 37. Mustered March 17, 1865. Assigned to Company F. Discharged for disability at Chester, Pa., June 3, 1865.

Carver, William R., Battle Creek. Enlisted in Company G, Aug. 24, 1861, at White Pigeon, for 3 years, age 20. Wounded in action and taken prisoner at Gaines' Mill, June 27, 1862. Died in prison.

Carwell or **Castle, Luke D.**, or B. Enlisted in Company B, Jan. 30, 1865, at Berlin, Ionia County, for 1 year, age 21. Substitute for William Goldthroatt, drafted. Mustered out at Jeffersonville, Ind., July 8, 1865.

Case, Jerome. Enlisted in Company F, Aug. 3, 1861, at Plymouth, for 3 years, age 19. No further record.

Case, Lewis (Veteran), Argentine, Genesee County. Enlisted in Company A, Aug. 1, 1862, at Argentine, age 28. Joined regiment at Antietam, Md., Oct. 12, 1862. Reportedly wounded at Chancellorsville, Va., [May 2 or 3?], 1863. Reenlisted Dec. 21, 1863, at Rappahannock Station, Va. Mustered out at Jeffersonville, Ind., July 8, 1865.

Casner or **Casmer, Noah**. Drafted March 15, 1865, for 1 year, from Grattan, Kent County, age 44. Assigned to Company G. Died of disease at Washington, D.C., June 6, 1865.

Cassimere, Martin. Enlisted in Company C, Aug. 7, 1861, at Flint, for 3 years, age 31. Mustered Sept. 7, 1861. Transferred to Company G. Wounded in action at Gaines' Mill, June 27, or Malvern Hill, July 1, 1862. Corporal. Discharged for disability at Washington, D.C., Sept. 8, 1863. Died at Lansing, May 7, 1896.

Catlin, George W., reported enlistee in Company C, no age or hometown given, died of typhoid fever Oct. 26, 1862, near Sharpsburg, Va.

Catlind, Thomas W. Drafted for 1 year, from New Haven, Shiawassee County, age 30, March 1865. Assigned to Company F. Discharged at Washington, D.C., July 6, 1865.

Caukin, Henry M., Montcalm County. Enlisted in Company B, as Fifer, Aug. 7, 1861, at Ionia, for 3 years, age 30. Mustered Sept. 7, 1861. Discharged for disability at Georgetown, March 13, 1863.

Caul, Joseph. Drafted for 1 year, from Lockport, St. Joseph County, age 28. Mustered March 16, 1865. Assigned to Company K. Deserted at Jeffersonville, Ind., July 2, 1865.

Cavanaugh, John. Enlisted in Second Company Sharpshooters, March 24, 1864, at Bridgeport, for 3 years, age 16. Mustered out at Jeffersonville, Ind., July 8, 1865.

Cedar, Cater or **Kator, Calvin**, Almont. Enlisted in Company K, Feb. 5, 1862, at Almont, for 3 years, age 23. Reported in Company H. Dropped from rolls Aug. 7, 1863.

Cerat, Rolland or **Ronald**, Wayne County. Enlisted in Company E, Sept. 5, 1861, at Detroit, for 3 years, age 21. Wounded in action at Gaines' Mill, June 27, 1862. Discharged on Surgeon's certificate of disability at Washington, D.C., Nov. 27, 1862. Died at Dayton, Ohio.

Chamberlain, James A. Enlisted in Company D, Jan. 19, 1864, at Thomastown, for 3 years, age 19. Wounded in action, hand, June 7, 1864, withdrawal from Cold Harbor. Discharged at Washington, D.C., May 2, 1865.

Chamberlain, Levi B., Saginaw County. Enlisted in Company D, Aug. 1, 1861, at East Saginaw, for 3 years, age 18. Wounded in action at Gaines' Mill, June 27, 1862. Sergeant. Transferred to Veterans Reserve Corps July 1, 1863, and reenlisted April 11, 1864.

Chamberlain, Urial or **Erial**. Enlisted in Company D, Feb. 15, 1864, at Saginaw, for 3 years, age 44. Died of disease in field hospital, Nov. 27, 1864.

Chamberlain, William A. Enlisted in Company F, Jan. 18, 1865, at Arcada, Gratiot County, for 1 year, age 18. Substitute for William S. Hall, drafted from Arcada. Discharged for disability at Washington, D.C., June 15, 1865.

Champing, Louis. Enlisted in Company D, May 11, 1864, at Detroit, for 3 years. Mustered out at Jeffersonville, Ind., July 8, 1865.

Chance, Louis. Enlisted in Company H, Lancers, Nov. 23, 1861, at Bay City, for 3 years, age 20. Transferred to Company K, 16th Michigan, March 1, 1862. Deserted at Detroit, March 15, 1862.

Chandler, Gilbert R., East Saginaw. Entered service in Company D at organization of regiment 2nd Lieutenant, July 30, 1861, at East Saginaw, age 28. Wounded in action at Gaines' Mill, June 27, 1862. Arm amputated. Commissioned 1st Lieutenant Aug. 23, 1862. Commissioned Captain April 22, 1863. Accepted appointment in Invalid Corps, Aug. 11, 1863.

Chandler, William, Detroit. Enlisted in Company C, Lancers, Dec. 1, 1861, at Detroit, for 3 years, age 24. Transferred to Company I, 16th Michigan, Feb. 28, 1862. Discharged on Surgeon's certificate of disability, Sept. 13, 1862.

Chandler, William P., Ontonagon County. Enlisted in Company A, Infantry, Aug. 2, 1861, at Ontonagon, for 3 years, age 26. Wounded and missing in action at Gaines' Mill, June 27, 1862. Discharged at expiration of term of service, Sept. 6, 1864.

Chapell, Augustus, Genesee County. Enlisted in Company C, Aug. 3, 1861, at Flint, for 3 years, age 35. Discharged for disability at Yorktown, Va., May 8, 1862. Deceased and buried at Quincy, Mich.

Chapman, Lorenzo. Drafted for 1 year, from Sparta, Kent County, age 27. Mustered March 28, 1865. Assigned to Company K. Mustered out at Jeffersonville, Ind., July 8, 1865.

Chapman, William. Drafted March 15, 1865 for 1 year, from Sparta, Kent County, age 37. Assigned to Company E. Mustered out at Jeffersonville, Ind., July 8, 1865.

Chase, George W. Enlisted in Company A, March 11, 1865, at Argentine, for 1 year, age 30. Mustered out at Jeffersonville, Ind., July 8, 1865.

Chatfield, David S. Enlisted in Company K, March 29, 1865, at Tompkins, Jackson County, for 1 year, age 18. Substitute for Jasper King, drafted from Tompkins. Mustered out at Jeffersonville, Ind., July 8, 1865.

Cheyne, James. Enlisted in Company D, March 25, 1865, at Ada, Kent County, for 1 year, age 19. Substitute for Cornelius Courtright, drafted from Ada. Mustered out at Jeffersonville, Ind., July 8, 1865. Resided Big Rapids, Mich.

Cheyne, Robert. Enlisted in Company D, March 25, 1865, at Ada, for 1 year, age 19. Substitute for Charles J. Robinson, drafted from Ada. Mustered out at Jeffersonville, Ind., July 8, 1865.

Chilson, Gilbert, Ionia County. Enlisted in Company B, as Corporal, Aug. 5, 1861, at Ionia, for 3 years, age 24. Discharged for disability at Fortress Monroe, Va., Dec. 19, 1862.

Chittick, Michael, Greenville. Enlisted in Company B, as 1st Sergeant, Aug. 5, 1861, at Ionia, for 3 years, age 21. Commissioned 2nd Lieutenant June 27, 1862. Killed in action at second Manassas, Aug. 30, 1862.

Chittick or **Chittock, William** (Veteran), Wayne County. Enlisted in Company H, as Sergeant, July 25, 1861, age 38. Wounded in action at Malvern Hill, July 1, 1862. Reenlisted Dec. 24, 1863, at Rappahannock Station, Va., 1st Sergeant, May 1, 1865. Mustered out at Jeffersonville, Ind., July 8, 1865.

Chosaro or **Chesaro, Joseph**. Enlisted in Second Company Sharpshooters, April 26, 1864, at Spaulding, for 3 years, age 46. Absent sick May 7, 1865. No further record.

Cilliway, Joseph (Veteran), Hillsdale County. Enlisted in Company C, Aug. 15, 1861, at Flint, age 24. Reenlisted Dec. 24, 1863, at Rappahannock Station, Va. Killed in action, by bayonet, at Laurel Hill–Spotsylvania Court House, May 8, 1864.

Cilliway, Thomas, Hillsdale County. Enlisted in Company C, Aug. 15, 1861. Discharged on Surgeon's certificate of disability at Hall's Hill, Va., Feb. 28, 1862.

Cisco, Lorenzo F. Enlisted in Company H, Oct. 20, 1861, at Detroit, for 3 years, age 20. Deserted June 8, 1865.

Clark, Burnet C. Enlisted in Company D, March 29, 1865, at Seneca, Lenawee County, for 3 years, age 28. Substitute for George W. Kinney, drafted from Seneca. Mustered out at Jeffersonville, Ind., July 8, 1865.

Clark, Charles, Orleans. Enlisted in Company B, Aug. 9, 1861, at Ionia, for 3 years, age 30. Died of disease at Camp Backus, Detroit, Aug. 29, 1861.

Clark, Charles. Entered service in 16th Michigan as substitute. Sent to regiment March 11, 1863. No further record.

Clark, David. Drafted for 1 year, from Dallas, Clinton County, age 34. Mustered Sept. 24, 1864. Assigned to Company G. Discharged at Washington, D.C., May 29, 1865.

Clark, Jacob A. Enlisted in Company A, Aug. 11, 1862, at Argentine, for 3 years, age 23. Joined regiment at Antietam, Md., Oct. 12, 1862. Listed as hospitalized Jan. 1863, at Washington, D.C., seemingly for wounds at Fredericksburg, Va., Dec. 13, 1862. Discharged for disability. Died March 1891 and buried at Sherman, Mich.

Clark, James A. Enlisted in Company B, Lancers, Nov. 26, 1861, at Detroit, for 3 years, age 20. Transferred to Company I, 16th Michigan, Feb. 28, 1862. Wounded and taken prisoner at Gaines' Mill, June 27, 1862. Wounded in action at Chancellorsville, Va., May 3, 1863. Discharged at expiration of term of service at Detroit, Jan. 16, 1865 (1864 also given).

Clark, John, Ionia County. Enlisted in Company B, Aug. 7, 1861, at Ionia, for 3 years, age 18. Deserted.

Clark, John Charles. Enlisted in Company D, Feb. 1, 1863, for 9 months, age 23. Joined regiment near Falmouth, Va., March 18, 1863. Discharged at expiration of term of service, Nov. 11, 1863.

Clark, Judson, Ionia County. Enlisted in Company B, Aug. 23, 1861, for 3 years. Discharged by civil authority at Detroit, Sept. 2, 1861.

Clark, Leonard. Enlisted in Company B, March 28, 1865, at Detroit, for 1 year, age 20. Substitute for Stephen R. Stanton, drafted from Detroit. Mustered out at Jeffersonville, Ind., July 8, 1865.

Clark, Peter, Ionia County. Enlisted in Company B, Aug. 7, 1861, at Ionia, for 3 years, age 27.

Discharged at Philadelphia, Jan. 12, 1863, for wounds received in action at Gaines' Mill, June 27, 1862.

Clark, Robert (Veteran), Saginaw County. Enlisted in Company D, as Corporal, Aug. 1, 1861, at East Saginaw, for 3 years, age 30. Reenlisted Dec. 21, 1863, at Rappahannock Station, Va. Discharged at Detroit, Aug. 2, 1865.

Clark, Robert B., Milford. Enlisted in Company B, Lancers, Oct. 22, 1861, at Milford, for 3 years, age 21. Transferred to Company I, 16th Michigan, Feb. 28, 1862. Wounded in action Gaines' Mill, June 27, 1862. Discharged for disability Nov. 30, 1862.

Clark, Thomas D., Saginaw County. Enlisted in Company D, Dec. 19, 1861, at Ionia, for 3 years, age 34. Joined regiment at Hall's Hill, Va., Jan. 11, 1862. Discharged March 18, 1863.

Clawatha, John. Enlisted in Company A, Aug. 2, 1861, at Ontonagon, for 3 years, age 35. Transferred to Company H. Deserted at Frederick, Md., June 29, 1863.

Clepful or **Clipfell, Evelyn**. Enlisted in Company G, Aug. 24, 1861, at White Pigeon, for 3 years, age 19. Wounded in action and taken prisoner at Gaines' Mill, June 27, 1862. Died at Richmond.

Cloney, William B. Enlisted in Company E, Aug. 14, 1861, at Detroit, for 3 years, age 45. Mustered Sept. 7, 1861. Transferred to Company G. Discharged for disability Oct. 1, 1862.

Coffin, Elijah B., Utica. Enlisted in Company D, Aug. 2, 1861, at East Saginaw, for 3 years, age 22. Transferred to Company E. Corporal. Killed in action at second Manassas, Aug. 30, 1862, reportedly one of the color bearers.

Coit, Anthony. Enlisted in Company A, Aug. 2, 1861, at Ontonagon, for 3 years, age 35. No further record.

Cole, Adoniram J., Ionia County. Enlisted in Company B, as Corporal, Aug. 3, 1861, at Ionia, for 3 years, age 22. Wounded in action at Gaines' Mill, June 27, 1862. Discharged for disability at Philadelphia, Jan. 27, 1863.

Cole, Albert. Drafted March 15, 1865, for 1 year, from Sparta, Kent County, age 39. Assigned to Company D. Mustered out at Jeffersonville, Ind., July 8, 1865.

Cole, Bradley. Drafted March 15, 1865, for 1 year, from Sparta, Kent County, age 26. Assigned to Company D. Discharged at Philadelphia, June 9, 1865.

Cole, Ezam or **Egan**. Enlisted in Second Company Sharpshooters, March 28, 1864, at Spaulding, for 3 years, age 20. Corporal. Sergeant May 1, 1865. Mustered out at Jeffersonville, Ind., July 8, 1865.

Cole, John (Veteran). Ontonagon County. Enlisted in Company A, Aug. 2, 1861, at Ontonagon, for 3 years, age 22. Wounded in action in 1862; wounded in action, hand, Gettysburg, July 2, 1863. Reenlisted Dec. 21, 1863, at Rappahannock Station, Va. Wounded in action, Spotsylvania Court House, May 18, 1864; Corporal, May 1, 1865. Mustered out at Jeffersonville, Ind., July 8, 1865.

Cole, Levi. Enlisted in Company G, March 23, 1865, at Pine Grove, Van Buren County, for 1 year, age 26. Substitute for Charles Goodwin, drafted. Mustered out at Jeffersonville, Ind., July 8, 1865. Buried at Mayville, Mich.

Cole, Nelson H. Enlisted in Company G, March 23, 1865, at Pine Grove, for 1 year, age 21. Substitute for Chauncey Wise, drafted from Pine Grove. Mustered out at Jeffersonville,

Ind., July 8, 1865.

Coleman, Dowd J. Enlisted in Company G, Nov. 15, 1862, at Detroit, for 3 years, age 19. Joined regiment at Falmouth, Va., Nov. 26, 1862. Reported as absent, wounded from Aug. 1863 to Jan. 1864. Taken prisoner at Weldon Railroad, Petersburg, Va., Aug. 21, 1864, parole or release date unknown. Corporal. Mustered out at Jeffersonville, Ind., July 8, 1865.

Coles, John, Argentine. Enlisted in Company I, Aug. 10, 1862, at Argentine, Genesee County, for 3 years, age 26. Joined regiment at Antietam, Md., Oct. 12, 1862. Discharged at Detroit, May 30, 1865.

Colestock, William W., Calhoun County. Enlisted in Company K, March 1, 1862, at Detroit, for 3 years, age 23. Wounded in action at Laurel Hill–Spotsylvania Court House, May 8, 1864. Discharged for disability at Washington, D.C., Dec. 9, 1864.

Collar, Joseph. Drafted March 16, 1865, for 1 year, from Ensley, Newaygo County, age 35. Assigned to Company D. Mustered out at Jeffersonville, Ind., July 8, 1865.

Collins, Dennis. Enlisted in Company A, Aug. 2, 1861, at Ontonagon, for 3 years, age 36. No further record.

Collins, James. Enlisted in Company D, Jan. 8, 1864, at Saginaw, for 3 years, age 34. Mustered out at Jeffersonville, Ind., July 8, 1865.

Colsher, William E., Ionia County. Enlisted in Company F, Dec. 20, 1861, at Ionia, for 3 years, age 22. Joined regiment at Hall's Hill, Va., Jan. 11, 1862. Wounded in action at Chancellorsville, Va., May 8, 1863. Deserted Sept. 1, 1864.

Comfort, Samuel, Zilwaukee. Enlisted in Company E, Aug. 16, 1861, at Detroit, for 3 years, age 27. Transferred to Company D. Killed in action at Gaines' Mill, June 27, 1862.

Comstock, Benjamin, Ionia County. Enlisted in Company B, Aug. 9, 1861, at Ionia, for 3 years, age 19. Discharged for disability June 30, 1863. Resided Ronald, Mich.

Comstock, James H. Drafted for 1 year, from Algansee, Branch County, age 30. Mustered March 17, 1865. Assigned to Company C. Recorded as absent with wounds, June 25, 1865. Died Aug. 2, 1865. Buried in National Cemetery at New Albany, Ind., Grave No. 797.

Comstock, Rowland S., Ionia County. Enlisted in Company B, Aug. 9, 1861, at Ionia, for 3 years, age 24. Transferred to Invalid Corps Oct. 30, 1863.

Condon, George R., Wayne County. Enlisted in Company A, as Corporal, Sept. 10, 1861, at Detroit, for 3 years, age 25. Wounded in action at second Manassas, Aug. 30, 1862. Discharged for disability at Detroit, March 6, 1863, on account of wounds received in action.

Conklin, Alfred G. Drafted for 1 year, from Pipestone, Berrien County, age 29, March 1865. Assigned to Company K. Mustered out at Jeffersonville, Ind., July 8, 1865.

Conkling, John, Onondaga, Ingham County. Drafted Feb. 10, 1863, for 9 months, from Onondaga, age 20. Assigned to Company K, Joined regiment near Falmouth, Va., March 19, 1863. Discharged at expiration of term of service at Kelly's Ford, Va., Nov. 21, 1863.

Connaly, Thomas. Enlisted in Company D, March 25, 1865, at Climax, Kalamazoo County, for 1 year, age 24. Substitute for Joseph Moulton, drafted. Mustered out at Jeffersonville, Ind., July 8, 1865.

Connors, William. Drafted for 1 year, from Dexter, age 28. Mustered March 17, 1865. Assigned to Company B. Mustered out at Jeffersonville, Ind., July 8, 1865.

Conover, William S., or J. Enlisted in Company G, as Corporal, Aug. 19, 1861, at White Pigeon, for 3 years, age 24. Wounded in action at Gaines' Mill, June 27, 1862. Discharged at Sharpsburg, Md., Sept. 26, 1862.

Conquest, John, Genesee County. Enlisted in Company C, Aug. 6, 1861, at Flint, for 3 years, age 24. Discharged Nov. 28, 1862, for wounds received in action at Gaines' Mill, and second Manassas. Reported to have been murdered with his wife and child on Oct. 10, 1878, in Vienna Township, Genesee County.

Conrad, Charles. Enlisted in Company B, March 28, 1865, at Dover, Lenawee County, for 1 year, age 20. Substitute for Elon Abbott, drafted. Mustered out at Jeffersonville, Ind., July 8, 1865.

Conway, William. Enlisted in Company I, Feb. 4, 1865, at Detroit, for 3 years, age 19. Substitute for Stillman W. Robinson, drafted. Wounded in action at White Oak Road, Va., March 31, 1865. No further record.

Cook, Arthur or **Arisha**. Enlisted in Company B, Feb. 7, 1865, at Flowerfield, St. Joseph County, for 1 year, age 26. Substitute for Henry Bowe, drafted. Deserted near Louisville, Ky., June 25, 1865.

Cook, Benjamin L. Enlisted in Company D, March 30, 1865, at Hartland, Livingston County, for 1 year, age 21. Substitute for George H. Cook, drafted. Discharged at Washington, D.C., June 22, 1865.

Cook, Casper L. Enlisted in Company H, Sept. 11, 1861, at Detroit, for 3 years, age 41. Discharged for disability at Alexandria, Va., March 30, 1863.

Cook, Dewillions or **David**. Enlisted in Company D, Jan. 18, 1864, at Richland, for 3 years, age 18. Wounded in action Nov. 1864. In hospital at Detroit, Sept. 3, 1864. No further record.

Cook, George W., Ann Arbor. Enlisted in Company A as 1st Sergeant, July 9, 1861. Wounded in action at Gaines' Mill, June 27, 1862. Commissioned 2nd Lieutenant. Commissioned 1st Lieutenant Nov. 3, 1862. Commissioned Captain, Company H, Dec. 16, 1863. Transferred to Company A, Aug. 9, 1864. Discharged at end of term of service, Sept. 26, 1864.

Cook, Luke. Enlisted March 15, 1864, at Houghton for 3 years, age 22. No further record.

Cooley, Alfred. Enlisted in Company D, Feb. 8, 1864, at Saginaw, for 3 years, age 18. Reported Sept. 1864 as absent wounded. Mustered out at Jeffersonville, Ind., July 8, 1865.

Cooper, Solomon W. Drafted March 15, 1865, for 1 year, from Grattan, Kent County, age 28. Assigned to Company I. Mustered out at Jeffersonville, Ind., July 8, 1865.

Cooper, William W., Berlin, Ionia County. Enlisted in Company B, Aug. 6, 1861, at Ionia, for 3 years, age 23. Killed in action at Gaines' Mill, June 27, 1862.

Cope, Hiram. Enlisted in Company G, Aug. 24, 1861, at White Pigeon, for 3 years, age 18. Discharged.

Copley, Hiram, Saginaw. Enlisted in Company D, Aug. 2, 1861, at East Saginaw, for 3 years, age 24. Deserted at Detroit.

Copp, John S., Genesee County. Enlisted in Company C, Aug. 1, 1861, at Flint, for 3 years, age 18. Wounded in action at second Manassas, Aug. 30, 1862. Discharged on Surgeon's certificate of disability at Washington, D.C., Nov. 21, 1862.

Corbett, Austin. Drafted for 1 year, from Allegan, age 40. Mustered March 17, 1865. Assigned to Company B. Admitted to Harper Hospital July 21, 1865. Discharged at Detroit, Aug. 26,

1865. Resided Harbor Beach.

Corbett, James, Wayne County. Enlisted in Company H, Sept. 21, 1861, at Detroit, for 3 years, age 32. Missing in action at Gaines' Mill, June 27, 1862. Discharged at Antietam, Md., Oct. 25, 1862. Died Nov. 28, 1862. Buried in Military Asylum Cemetery at Washington, D.C.

Cordy, Manuel. Enlisted in First Company Sharpshooters attached to 16th Michigan, Feb. 18, 1864, at Dearborn, for 3 years, age 18. Mustered out at Jeffersonville, Ind., July 8, 1865.

Coree or **Corse, Hiram** (Veteran). Enlisted in Company G, Aug. 23, 1861, age 17. Reenlisted Dec. 21, 1863, at Rappahannock Station, Va. Sergeant Nov. 1, 1864. Reported in Feb. 1865 as absent, wounded. Mustered out at Jeffersonville, Ind., July 8, 1865.

Corey or **Cory, Andrew**, Wayne County. Enlisted in Company F, Sept. 12, 1861, at Plymouth, for 3 years, age 22. Deserted.

Corey, Egbert, Wayne County. Enlisted in First Company Sharpshooters attached to 16th Michigan, Nov. 26, 1861, at Detroit, for 3 years, age 22. Joined regiment at Hall's Hill, Va., Feb. 14, 1862. Taken prisoner at Gaines' Mill, June 27, 1862. Corporal. Wounded in action at Petersburg, Va., June 20, 1864. Discharged at expiration of term of service, July 10, 1865.

Corey, Gilbert F. (Veteran), Wayne County. Enlisted in First Company Sharpshooters attached to 16th Michigan, Dec. 10, 1861, at Detroit, for 3 years, age 20. Joined regiment at Hall's Hill, Va., Feb. 14, 1862. Taken prisoner at Gaines' Mill, June 27, 1862. Reenlisted Dec. 22, 1863, at Rappahannock Station, Va. Died of disease at Washington, D.C., Dec. 6, 1864.

Corkins, Daniel A. (Veteran), Ionia County. Enlisted in Company B, Aug. 7, 1861, at Ionia, for 3 years, age 27. Reenlisted Dec. 24, 1863, at Rappahannock Station, Va. Mustered out at Jeffersonville, Ind., July 8, 1865.

Cornell, Albert. Enlisted in Company A, March 14, 1865, at Orange County, for 1 year, age 21. Substitute for Philander R. Riker, drafted. Mustered out at Jeffersonville, Ind., July 8, 1865.

Cornell, Lewellyn, Wayne County. Enlisted in Company F. Aug. 4, 1861, at Plymouth, for 3 years, age 19. Discharged for disability at Washington, D.C., May 2, 1862.

Cory or **Cary, James B.**, Ontonagon County. Enlisted in Company A, Aug. 2, 1861, at Ontonagon, for 3 years, age 23. Deserted at Banks Ford, Rappahannock Station, Va., June 7, 1863.

Cotter, James, Wayne County. Enlisted in First Company Sharpshooters attached to 16th Michigan, Dec. 19, 1861, at Detroit, for 3 years, age 19. Joined regiment at Hall's Hill, Va., Feb. 14, 1862. Wounded in action at Fredericksburg, Va., Dec. 13, 1862. In hospital at Chester, Pa., Jan. 1863. No further record.

Cowan, James (Veteran), Bostwick Lake. Enlisted in First Company Sharpshooters attached to 16th Michigan as Sergeant, Dec. 30, 1861, at Grand Rapids, for 3 years, age 28. Joined regiment at Halls' Hill, Va., Feb. 14, 1862. Reenlisted Dec. 22, 1863, at Rappahannock Station, Va. Killed in action near Spotsylvania Court House, May 11, 1864.

Cowan, William S., Kent County. Enlisted in First Company Sharpshooters attached to the 16th Michigan, Dec. 30, 1861, at Grand Rapids, for 3 years, age 23. Joined regiment at Hall's Hill, Va., Feb. 14, 1862. Discharged.

Cowden, Abel F. or **Albert F.** Enlisted in Company D, March 21, 1865, at Eureka, Montcalm County, for 1 year, age 19. Substitute for John Lewis, drafted. Mustered out at Jeffersonville, Ind., July 8, 1865.

Cowen, John, Wayne County. Enlisted in Company H, Sept. 23, 1861, at Detroit, for 3 years, age 33. Killed in action at Gaines' Mill, June 27, 1862.

Cowles, Elias, Jr. Enlisted in Company H, Feb. 20, 1865, at Highland, Oakland County, for 3 years, age 19. Substitute for Anson W. Baker, drafted. Mustered out at Jeffersonville, Ind., July 8, 1865.

Cowper, Major. Enlisted in Company G, Feb. 3, 1865, at White Rock, Huron County, for 1 year, age 19. Substitute for Michael Henlsteman, drafted. Discharged at Philadelphia, June 13, 1865. Resided Verona Mills, Mich.

Coykendall, Jerry W. (Veteran), Macomb County. Enlisted in First Company Sharpshooters attached to 16th Michigan, Nov. 27, 1861, at Detroit, for 3 years, age 30. Joined regiment at Hall's Hill, Va., Feb. 14, 1862. Reenlisted Dec. 22, 1863, at Rappahannock Station, Va. Corporal May 1, 1865. Mustered out at Jeffersonville, Ind., July 8, 1865.

Coykindale, Alfred. Enlisted in Company C, Aug. 5, 1861, at Flint, for 3 years, age 18. Transferred to Company F. Discharged for disability.

Craft, John W. Drafted for 1 year, from Algansee, Branch County, age 38. Mustered March 17, 1865. Assigned to Company I. Discharged at Washington, D.C., June 16, 1865.

Crampton, Charles. Enlisted in Second Company Sharpshooters, April 15, 1864, at Saginaw, for 3 years, age 18. Deserted at Saginaw, May 1864.

Crandall, Abner. Enlisted in Company C, March 1, 1865, at Marion, Livingston County, for 3 years, age 20. Substitute for Thomas Gibbs, or Gibson, drafted. Reported as absent wounded and ordered discharged at Washington, D.C., June 13, 1865.

Crandall or **Crandle, Mathias** or **Mathew L.** Enlisted in Company A, March 25, 1865, at Homer, Calhoun County, for 1 year, age 19. Substitute for Philo Gibbs, drafted from Homer. Mustered out at Jeffersonville, Ind., July 8, 1865.

Crandall, Theodore F. Enlisted in Company C, Aug. 5, 1861, at Flint, for 3 years, age 18. Transferred to Company F. Reported in hospital in July 1862 "for wound of left hip." Discharged on account of wounds Dec. 22, 1862, at Detroit. Resided in Detroit.

Crane, James, Genesee County. Enlisted in Company C, Aug. 1, 1861, at Flint, for 3 years, age 19. Deserted at Detroit, Sept. 1863.

Cranmer or **Cramer, Jeremiah,** or **Creamer, Joseph**, Wayne County. Enlisted in Company F, as Corporal, Sept. 12, 1861. Wounded in action July 1862. Discharged for disability at Detroit, Dec. 23, 1862.

Cranson, Asa F. (Veteran), Ionia County. Enlisted in Company B, Aug. 5, 1861, at Ionia, for 3 years, age 30. Reenlisted Dec. 24, 1863, at Rappahannock Station, Va. Corporal June 20, 1865. Mustered out at Jeffersonville, Ind., July 8, 1865.

Craw, Jacob W. Enlisted in Company I, Aug. 30, 1862, at Argentine, for 3 years, age 35. Joined regiment at Antietam, Md., Oct. 12, 1862. Died of disease at Germantown, Pa., Nov. 20, 1864. Buried in National Cemetery at Philadelphia, Grave No. 269.

Craw, Marcirnus, Osceola, Livingston County. Enlisted in Company K, March 10, 1863, at Osceola, for 9 months, age 25. Substitute for Martin P. Van Camp, drafted for 9 months. Joined regiment near Falmouth, Va., March 19, 1863. Discharged at expiration of term of service at Kelley's Ford, Va., Nov. 21, 1863.

Crawford, George. Enlisted in Company C, Feb. 21, 1865, at Port Huron, for 3 years, age 18. Substitute for George N. P. Carlton, drafted. Discharged on Surgeon's certificate of disability at Washington, D.C., May 30, 1865.

Crawford, James. Enlisted in Company C, Jan. 4, 1864, at Flint, for 3 years, age 20. Died June 4, 1864, at West Philadelphia of wounds received in action. Buried in National Cemetery at Philadelphia, Grave No. 349.

Cresswell, William. Enlisted in Second Company Sharpshooters, April 30, 1864, at Kochville, Saginaw County, for 3 years, age 46. Discharged for disability Aug. 10, 1864.

Cribbs, Eugene W. Enlisted in Company G, March 28, 1865, at Lockport, St. Joseph County, for 1 year, age 19. Substitute for John H. Waltz, drafted. Mustered out at Jeffersonville, Ind., July 8, 1865.

Cronach or **Cronouge, William**, Wayne County. Enlisted in Company E, Aug. 31, 1861. Wounded in action at Gaines' Mill, June 27, 1862. Transferred to Invalid Corps July 1, 1863. Discharged at Washington, D.C., Sept. 6, 1864.

Cronkite, John G. Enlisted in Company E, Aug. 13, 1861, at Detroit, for 3 years, age 20. Reported in Company F. Discharged for disability Dec. 26, 1861.

Cronkite, Josiah, Plymouth. Enlisted in Company F, Aug. 4, 1861, at Plymouth, for 3 years, age 20. Corporal. Killed in action at Gaines' Mill, June 27, 1862.

Cronkite, Walter M. (Veteran). Enlisted in Company D, Aug. 2, 1861, at East Saginaw, for 3 years, age 18. Transferred to Company F. Reenlisted Dec. 21, 1863, at Rappahannock Station, Va. Listed as absent, wounded from Sept. to Nov. 1864. Sergeant May 1, 1865. Mustered out at Jeffersonville, Ind., July 8, 1865.

Cross, Charles M., or A. Drafted Dec. 23, 1864, for 1 year, from Trowbridge, Allegan County, age 40. Assigned to Company C. Deserted.

Cross, Joseph, Ionia County. Enlisted in Company B, Aug. 9, 1861, at Ionia, for 3 years, age 45. Discharged for disability for wound suffered at Gaines' Mill, June 27, 1862.

Cross, Joseph B., Ionia County. Enlisted in Company B, Aug. 10, 1861, at Ionia, for 3 years, age 19. Discharged for disability at Georgetown, July 28, 1862, for wounds received in action at Gaines' Mill, June 27, 1862.

Crossey, Allan. Enlisted in Second Company Sharpshooters May 2, 1864, at Bloomfield, for 3 years, age 18. Mustered out at Jeffersonville, Ind., July 8, 1865.

Crouch, William. Substitute for George E. Gee, drafted. Assigned to Company B. Discharged at Detroit, June 8, 1865.

Crouch, William (Veteran), Wayne County. Enlisted in First Company Sharpshooters attached to 16th Michigan, Oct. 28, 1861, at Detroit, for 3 years, age 19. Joined regiment at Hall's Hill, Va., Feb. 14, 1862. Reenlisted Dec. 22, 1863, at Rappahannock Station, Va. Reported as absent, wounded Sept. 1864 and May 1865. Discharged at Detroit, June 8, 1865.

Crowell, Reuben, Ann Arbor. Enlisted in Company A, Oct. 10, 1862, at Ann Arbor, for 3 years, age 32. Joined regiment near Falmouth, Va., Nov. 26, 1862. Discharged for disability at Falmouth, Va., Feb. 20, 1863.

Crowley, Patrick, Detroit. Enlisted in Company H, Sept. 11, 1861, at Detroit, for 3 years. Missing in action at Gaines' Mill, June 27, 1862. Discharged for disability at Detroit, Sept. 6, 1862.

Crowter or **Crowther, Mathew** (Veteran). Enlisted in Company E, Aug. 14, 1861, at Detroit, for 3 years, age 22. Transferred to Company H. Reenlisted Dec. 24, 1863, at Rappahannock Station, Va. Died June 21, 1864, near Petersburg, Va., of wounds received in action June 19, 1864.

Croy, Jacob. Enlisted in Company D, Aug. 2, 1861, at East Saginaw, for 3 years, age 43. Transferred to Company G. Discharged for disability at Hall's Hill, Va.

Cuddy, Thomas, Detroit. Enlisted in Company I, March 24, 1862, at Detroit, for 3 years, age 30. Discharged at expiration of term of service, April 27, 1865.

Cudney, Robert. Enlisted in Company K. Feb. 9, 1865, at Fulton, Gratiot County, for 1 year, age 17. Substitute for Richard O. Jenney, drafted. Mustered out at Jeffersonville, Ind., July 8, 1865.

Culver, Boyd, Genesee County. Enlisted in Company C, Aug. 1, 1861, at Flint, for 3 years, age 18. Discharged on Surgeon's certificate of disability at Washington, D.C., Dec. 22, 1862.

Cummings, Alfred C. Enlisted in Company G, Aug. 20, 1861, at Detroit, for 3 years, age 23. Discharged at expiration of term of service near Petersburg, Va., Sept. 7, 1864.

Curry, John. Enlisted in Company H, Sept. 7, 1861, at Detroit, for 3 years, age 28. Discharged for disability at Philadelphia, Sept. 11, 1862.

Curry, Samuel. Enlisted in Second Company Sharpshooters, April 26, 1864, at Spaulding, for 3 years, age 20. Died of disease at City Point, Va., July 27, 1864.

Curtis, Henry, Wayne County. Enlisted in Company E, Sept. 6, 1861. Wounded in action at Malvern Hill, July 1, 1862. Deserted at Detroit, Sept. 1862.

Cushway, Magloire, Mt. Clemens. Enlisted in Company C, Lancers, Dec. 24, 1861, at Mt. Clemens, for 3 years, age 40. Transferred to Company I, 16th Michigan, Feb. 28, 1862. Missing in action Gaines' Mill, June 27, 1862. Discharged for disability Jan. 12, 1863. Died April 16, 1897.

Cuthina or **Culhina, Patrick**. Enlisted in Jan. 13, 1864, at Canton, for 3 years, age 32. No further record.

Cyr, Joseph. Enlisted in Second Company Sharpshooters, April 22, 1864, at Spaulding, for 3 years, age 19. Deserted at Saginaw, May 3, 1864.

Daily, Hugh. Enlisted in Company B, March 15, 1865, at Flint, for 1 year, age 18. Substitute for Jeremiah Shaver, drafted from Emerson, Gratiot County. Mustered out at Jeffersonville, Ind., July 8, 1865.

Dafoe, James, Greenfield, Wayne County. Enlisted as Captain of Company F at organization. Resigned April 15, 1862, citing health but disapproved of Col. Stockton's criticism of Republican leaders and policies. Commissioned Captain of Company D, 27th Michigan, Oct. 10, 1862. Discharged Dec. 10, 1864.

Dake, John G., Lansing. Enlisted in Company C, July 30, 1861, at Flint, for 3 years, age 19. Transferred to Company G. Died of disease at Hall's Hill, Va., Oct. 21, 1861.

Daley or **Daly, John** (Veteran), Detroit. Enlisted in Company H, as Sergeant, Oct. 29, 1861, at Detroit, for 3 years, age 18. Wounded in action at Gaines' Mill, June 27, 1862. Wounded in action at second Manassas, Aug. 30, 1862. Reenlisted Dec. 24, 1863, at Rappahannock Station, Va. Sergeant. Mustered out at Jeffersonville, Ind., July 8, 1865. Resided Detroit.

Daly, John. Drafted for 1 year, from Climax, Kalamazoo County, age 35. Mustered March 15, 1865. Assigned to Company C. Mustered out at Jeffersonville, Ind., July 8, 1865.

Daly, John S. Enlisted in Company E, Aug. 16, 1861, at Detroit, for 3 years, age 18. No further record.

Damon, William R. Drafted for 1 year, from Leonidas, St. Joseph County, age 31. Mustered March 16, 1865. Assigned to Company K. Deserted at Jeffersonville, Ind., July 2, 1865.

Damen or **Damon, Orrin W**., Saginaw County. Enlisted in Company D, Aug. 2, 1861, at East Saginaw, for 3 years, age 18. Discharged at expiration of term of service near Petersburg, Va., Sept. 17, 1864. Resided Chesaning, Mich.

Daniels, Charles A. M., Cheshire. Enlisted in Company D, Aug. 25, 1863, for 9 months. Substitute for Zenus C. Howard, drafted Feb. 10, 1863, from Van Buren County. Discharged at expiration of term of service near Petersburg, Va., July 6, 1864.

Darling, Hiram G. or **Herman**, Flushing. Enlisted in Company C, Feb. 26, 1864, at Corunna, for 3 years, age 34. Wounded in action July 1864, Petersburg, Va. Died Aug. 22, 1864, at New York Harbor of wounds. Buried in National Cemetery at Brooklyn, N.Y. Grave No. 1698.

Davenport, Henry L. (Veteran), Ontonagon County. Enlisted in Company A, Aug. 2, 1861, at Ontonagon, for 3 years, age 27. Reenlisted Dec. 21, 1863, at Rappahannock Station, Va. Wounded and taken prisoner, at raid on Weldon Railroad, Petersburg, Va., Dec. 10, 1864. Returned to regiment Feb. 28, 1865. Corporal May 1, 1865. Mustered out at Jeffersonville, Ind., July 8, 1865.

Davidson, James. Enlisted in Company G, March 27, 1865, at Grattan, Kent County, for 1 year, age 19. Substitute for Marshall King, drafted. Mustered out at Jeffersonville, Ind., July 8, 1865.

Davie, Henry, Genesee County. Enlisted in Company C, as Fifer, Aug. 2, 1861, at Flint, for 3 years, age 45. Discharged at Sharpsburg, Md., Oct. 25, 1862.

Davis, Barlow, Macomb County. Enlisted in First Company Sharpshooters attached to 16th Michigan as Corporal, Oct. 15, 1861, at Detroit, for 3 years, age 37. Joined regiment at Hall's Hill, Va., Feb. 14, 1862. Sergeant. Discharged at Fortress Monroe, Va., Oct. 6, 1862.

Davis, Edward (Veteran), Genesee County. Enlisted in Company C, Aug. 2, 1861, at Flint, for 3 years, age 24. Reenlisted Dec. 24, 1863, at Rappahannock Station, Va. Corporal May 31, 1865. Mustered out at Jeffersonville, Ind., July 8, 1865.

Davis, Freeman. See **Davis, Truman**.

Davis, Jefferson W., Genesee County. Enlisted in Company C, Aug. 3, 1861, at Flint, for 3 years, age 18. Wounded in action at Hanover Court House, Va., May 27, 1862. Discharged to date May 20, 1863, with no report of muster out.

Davis, Lorenzo (Veteran), Midland County. Enlisted in Company D, Aug. 2, 1861, at East Saginaw, for 3 years, age 18. Wounded in action at Middleburg, June 21, 1863. Reenlisted as Corporal Dec. 21, 1863, at Rappahannock Station, Va. Sergeant. Mustered out at Jeffersonville, Ind., July 8, 1865. Resided at Auburn, Mich.

Davis, Miles, Ionia County. Enlisted in Company B, Aug. 6, 1861, at Ionia, for 3 years, age 26. Taken prisoner at Weldon Railroad, Petersburg, Va., Aug. 21, 1864. Discharged at expiration of term of service near Petersburg, Va., Sept. 7, 1864.

Davis, Truman, or **Freeman**, Midland. Enlisted in Company D, Feb. 29, 1864, at Midland, for 3 years, age 18. Wounded in action June 1864 near Bethesda Church–Cold Harbor. Killed in action March 25, 1865, at second Hatcher's Run, Va.

Davis, William, Bushnell. Enlisted in Company I, Aug. 20, 1862, at Ionia, for 3 years, age 18. Joined regiment at Antietam, Md., Oct. 12, 1862. Wounded in action at Laurel Hill–Spotsylvania Court House, May 8, 1864. Discharged near Washington, D.C., May 29, 1865.

Davy, Thomas, Houghton. Enlisted in Company D, March 3, 1864, at Houghton, for 3 years, age 21. Reported as absent wounded in returns, Nov. 1864–Jan. 1865. Discharged at Philadelphia, May 31, 1865. Resided at Stark, Mich.

Dawson, Walter (Veteran), Wayne County. Enlisted in Company H, Oct. 10, 1861, at Detroit, for 3 years, age 42. Listed as wounded in action, leg, in 1862, no date given. Reenlisted Dec. 24, 1863, at Rappahannock Station, Va. Transferred to U.S. Navy at Brandy Station, Va., May 2, 1864.

Dean, Jacob. Drafted for 1 year, from Burr Oak, St. Joseph County, age 27. Mustered March 17, 1865. Assigned to Company C. Reported as absent, wounded, June 1865. Mustered out at Jeffersonville, Ind., July 8, 1865.

Dean, Leonard, Girard, Branch County. Enlisted in Company E, March 30, 1865, at Girard for 1 year, age 19. Substitute for Dudley Smith, drafted. Mustered out at Jeffersonville, Ind., July 8, 1865.

Dean, Nelson J. B., or **V.** Enlisted in Company C, Feb. 8, 1865, at Hart, Oceana County, for 1 year, age 18. Substitute for William H. Chany, or Cheney, drafted. Apparently reported as absent, wounded in action June 1865. No further record.

De Bolt, Henry S., Van Buren County. Enlisted in First Company Sharpshooters attached to 16th Michigan, March 18, 1862, at Detroit, for 3 years, age 32. Listed in a newspaper among the 16th Michigan wounded after Gettysburg in a West Philadelphia hospital, July 1863, but not listed in regiment's "Roll of Honor." Transferred to Invalid Corps Nov. 15, 1863.

Decker or **Deeker, Andrew**, Ionia. Enlisted in Company B, Aug. 5, 1861, at Ionia, for 3 years, age 33. Transferred to Company A. The regiment's "Roll of Honor" states he was wounded in action at Gettysburg, July 2, 1863, while Michigan Adjutant-General's Dept. *Record of Service,* vol. 16 (1905), states he was discharged for disability at Fortress Monroe, Va., Jan. 21, 1863. Resided in Detroit.

Decker, Henry S., Albion. Enlisted in Company E, Aug. 16, 1861, at Detroit, for 3 years, age 21. Transferred to Company F. Died of disease at Washington, D.C., March 14, 1862.

De Claire, Theodore (Veteran). Enlisted in Company F, Aug. 4, 1861, at Plymouth, for 3 years, age 18. Transferred to Company E. Paroled prisoner in 1862. Reenlisted Feb. 26, 1864, at Bealton, Va. Seemingly wounded at Petersburg, Va., and listed as absent, wounded Sept. 1864-Jan. 1865. Corporal, March 1, 1865. Mustered out at Jeffersonville, Ind., July 8, 1865. Resided Detroit.

De Forest, William. An enlistee in the Second Company Sharpshooters, wounded in action, according to regiment's "Roll of Honor," at Peeble's Farm, Sept. 30, 1864. Discharged June 28, 1865.

De Kraker, Louis. Enlisted in Company K, Feb. 20, 1865, at Holland, for 1 year, age 24.

Substitute for Peter Vandebosh, drafted. Mustered out at Jeffersonville, Ind., July 8, 1865.

De Kruif, John P. or **Johannes**, Holland. Enlisted in First Company Sharpshooters attached to 16th Michigan, Dec. 14, 1861, at Grand Rapids, for 3 years, age 25. Joined regiment at Hall's Hill, Va., Feb. 14, 1862. Died at Alexandria, Va., June 29, 1864, of wounds received in action at Po River–Spotsylvania Court House, May 10, 1864.

Delavergnet Tunis, Saginaw County. Enlisted in Company D, Aug. 2, 1861, at East Saginaw, for 3 years, age 18. Deserted July 8, 1863.

Delevan, Lewis, Saginaw County. Enlisted in Company C, Lancers, Nov. 25, 1861, at Saginaw, for 3 years, age 18. Transferred to Company I, 16th Michigan, Feb. 28, 1862. Deserted at Detroit, March 24, 1862.

De Maes, Nicholas, Ontonagon County. Enlisted in Company A, as Corporal. Aug. 2, 1861, at Ontonagon, for 3 years. Killed in action at Gaines' Mill, June 27, 1862.

Dennison, Allen (Veteran), Calhoun County. Enlisted in Company K, March 1, 1862, at Detroit, for 3 years, age 21. Wounded in action July 1, 1862, at Malvern Hill. Reenlisted March 1, 1864, at Bealton, Va. Sergeant. Mustered out at Jeffersonville, Ind., July 8, 1865.

Dennison, Newton (Veteran), Calhoun County. Enlisted in Company K, March 1, 1862, at Detroit, for 3 years, age 27. Listed as absent, wounded in leg, in 1862, no date given. Reenlisted as Corporal March 1, 1864, at Bealton, Va. Wounded in action, arm, at Po River–Spotsylvania Court House, May 10, 1864. Mustered out at Jeffersonville, Ind., July 8, 1865.

Denny, William or **James**. Enlisted in Company C, Feb. 21, 1865, at Pontiac, for 3 years, age 18. Substitute for Hiram Paddock, drafted from Pontiac. Deserted at Jeffersonville, Ind., June 26, 1865.

Depuy, Reuben. Enlisted in Company E, Aug. 17, 1861, at Detroit, for 3 years, age 36. Transferred to Company H. Discharged for disability Sept. 27, 1861.

Desotelle, James, Wayne County. Enlisted in Company A, Aug. 28, 1861. Deserted at Detroit, Sept. 4, 1861.

De Spelder, Peter (Veteran), Eagle Harbor. Enlisted in Company F, Lancers, as Corporal. Oct. 3, 1861, at Eagle Harbor, for 3 years, age 22. Transferred to Company I, 16th Michigan, Feb. 28, 1862. Missing in action at Gaines' Mill, June 27, 1862. Reenlisted Dec. 22, 1863, at Rappahannock Station, Va. 1st Sergeant, May, 1865. Commissioned 2nd Lieutenant May 8, 1865. Commissioned 1st Lieutenant July 7, 1865. Mustered out at Jeffersonville, Ind., July 8, 1865.

Devoe, Eli, Genesee County. Enlisted in Company C, July 30, 1861, at Flint, for 3 years, age 37. Discharged at Warrenton, Va., Nov. 13, 1862.

Dewald, Frank (Veteran). Ontonagon County. Enlisted in Company A as Sergeant, Aug. 2, 1861, at Ontonagon, for 3 years, age 30. Reenlisted Dec. 21, 1863, at Rappahannock Station, Va. Died of disease at City Point, Va., Dec. 19, 1864.

Dexter, James L. Drafted March 15, 1865, for 1 year, from Wyoming, Kent County, age 43. Assigned to Company I. Mustered out at Jeffersonville, Ind., July 8, 1865.

Dicey, Levi. Enlisted in Company E, March 27, 1865, at California, Branch County, for 1 year, age 18. Substitute for Russell Jameson, drafted from California. Mustered out at Jeffersonville, Ind., July 8, 1865.

Dick, Frank J. (Veteran), Van Buren County. Enlisted in First Company Sharpshooters attached to 16th Michigan, Oct. 16, 1861, at Detroit, for 3 years, age 24. Joined regiment at Hall's Hill, Va., Feb. 14, 1862. Reenlisted Dec. 22, 1863, at Rappahannock Station, Va. Sergeant. Commissioned 2nd Lieutenant July 7, 1865. Mustered out at Jeffersonville, Ind., July 8, 1865.

Dickenson or **Dickinson, Cyrus W.** (Veteran), Montcalm County. Enlisted in Company B, as Corporal, Aug. 8, 1861, at Ionia, for 3 years, age 24. Reenlisted Dec. 24, 1863, at Rappahannock Station, Va. Mustered out at Jeffersonville, Ind., July 8, 1865.

Dickinson, Charles. Enlisted in Company D, Jan. 15, 1864, at East Saginaw, for 3 years, age 18. Corporal, May 1, 1865. Mustered out at Jeffersonville, Ind., July 8, 1865. Resided Saginaw, Mich.

Diehl, William (Veteran). Enlisted in Company A, Oct. 4, 1862, at Ann Arbor, age 19. Joined regiment at Falmouth, Va., Nov. 26, 1862. Reenlisted Dec. 21, 1863, at Rappahannock Station, Va. Wounded in both legs, in action at Po River–Spotsylvania Court House, May 10, 1864. Corporal, May 1, 1865. Mustered out at Jeffersonville, Ind., July 8, 1865.

Dillen, William. Enlisted in Company A, March 27, 1865, at Coldwater, for 1 year, age 20. Substitute for J. D. Crippen, drafted. Mustered out at Jeffersonville, Ind., July 8, 1865.

Dillon, John. Enlisted in Company I, Feb. 17, 1865, at Shelby, Macomb County, for 3 years, age 18. Substitute for George H. Canon, drafted. Joined regiment March 14, 1865. Mustered out at Jeffersonville, Ind., July 8, 1865.

Disbrow, Israel (Veteran), Detroit. Enlisted in Company D, Aug. 24, 1861. Wounded in action at Malvern Hill, July 1, 1862. Sergeant. Reenlisted Dec. 21, 1863, at Rappahannock Station, Va. Mustered out at Jeffersonville, Ind., July 8, 1865.

Dixon, John. Enlisted in Company C, Jan. 25, 1865, at Park, St. Joseph County, for 3 years, age 32. Substitute for David W. Miller, drafted. Discharged at Detroit, Aug. 8, 1865.

Doan, Albert, Genesee County. Enlisted in Company C, Aug. 1, 1861, at Flint, for 3 years, age 19. Wounded in action, Fredericksburg, Va., Dec. 1862, and reportedly died in a hospital in 1863.

Doan, John, Canada West. Enlisted June 1, 1863, at Casco, St. Clair County, for 3 years, age 22. Substitute for Cornelius Berget, drafted for 9 months, from Casco. No further record.

Doan, William H. Drafted for 1 year, from Pipestone, Berrien County, age 40. Mustered March 18, 1865. Assigned to Company K. Mustered out at Jeffersonville, Ind., July 8, 1865.

Dobsen or **Dobson, Charles F.**, East Saginaw. Enlisted in Company D, as Sergeant, Aug. 1, 1861, at East Saginaw, for 3 years, age 29. 1st Sergeant. Killed in action at Gaines' Mill, June 27, 1862.

Dodds, John. Enlisted in First Company Sharpshooters attached to 16th Michigan, Feb. 18, 1864, at Detroit, for 3 years, age 26. Mustered out at Jeffersonville, Ind., July 8, 1865.

Dodge, Isaac, Brooklyn. Enlisted in Company F, Aug. 5, 1861, at Plymouth, for 3 years, age 19. Wounded in action, right leg, and captured, at second Manassas, Aug. 30, 1862. Discharged for disability, Dec. 29, 1862.

Dodge, Joshua or **Josiah**, Detroit. Enlisted in Company K, March 17, 1862, at Detroit, for 3 years, age 18. Discharged for disability at Yorktown, Va., April 30, 1862.

Doherty, Michael, Detroit. Enlisted in Company H, Oct. 11, 1861, at Detroit, for 3 years. Discharged for disability at Detroit.

Doller, Andrew. Enlisted in Second Company Sharpshooters, March 30, 1864, at Saginaw, for 3 years, age 19. Deserted at Saginaw, May 3, 1864.

Donahue, John T. (Veteran). Enlisted in Company G, Aug. 20, 1861, age 17. Wounded in action and taken prisoner at Gaines' Mill, June 27, 1862. Paroled Sept. 1862. Reenlisted Dec. 21, 1863, at Rappahannock Station, Va. Corporal. Sergeant, April 1, 1865. Mustered out at Jeffersonville, Ind., July 8, 1865.

Donahue, Michael, Detroit. Enlisted in Company I, Aug. 5, 1862, at Ann Arbor, for 3 years, age 35. Joined regiment at Antietam, Md., Oct. 12, 1862. Wounded in action, shoulder, at Laurel Hill–Spotsylvania Court House, May 8 or 9, 1864. Discharged near Washington, D.C., May 29, 1865. Resided Ann Arbor.

Donoghue, Stephen. Enlisted Feb. 2, 1864, at Detroit for 3 years, age 31. Deserted at Detroit, Feb. 8, 1864.

Doolittle, John, Ottawa County. Enlisted in First Company Sharpshooters attached to 16th Michigan, Nov. 12, 1861, at Grand Rapids, for 3 years, age 34. Joined regiment at Hall's Hill, Va., Feb. 14, 1862. Discharged for disability near Falmouth, Va., April 7, 1863.

Doran, Dennis M. (Veteran), Ionia County. Enlisted in Company F, Aug. 5, 1861, at Plymouth, for 3 years, age 22. Transferred to Company B. Reenlisted as Corporal Dec. 24, 1863, at Rappahannock Station, Va. 1st Sergeant, March 14, 1865. Discharged at Washington, D.C., July 7, 1865, for wounds to his face received in action at Bethesda Church, June 2, 1864. Resided Harrison, Mich.

Doran, William. Enlisted in Second Company Sharpshooters, March 31, 1864, at Tittabawassee, for 3 years, age 24. Mustered out at Jeffersonville, Ind., July 8, 1865.

Doty, Nelson W. (Veteran), Lowell. Enlisted in Company C, Lancers, Oct. 6, 1861, at Lowell, for 3 years, age 24. Transferred to Company I, 16th Michigan, Feb. 28, 1862. Wounded in action at Gaines' Mill, June 27, 1862. Reenlisted Feb. 26, 1864, at Bealton, Va. Corporal. Wounded in action at Wilderness, May 7, 1864. 1st Sergeant May 16, 1865. Mustered out at Jeffersonville, Ind., July 8, 1865. Resided Central Lake, Mich.

Douglas, George. Enlisted in Company A, Feb. 15, 1864, at Bridgeport, for 3 years, age 36. Corporal. Wounded in action at Wilderness, May 7, 1864. Discharged at General Hospital, Chester, Pa., June 21, 1865.

Dowger, John. Enlisted in Company F, Aug. 4, 1861, at Plymouth, for 3 years, age 25. Discharged on Surgeon's certificate of disability Feb. 20, 1865.

Dowin or **Dowier, John**. Enlisted in Company A, Aug. 8, 1861, at Ontonagon, for 3 years, age 25. No further record.

Dowling, Charles. Enlisted in Company G, Jan. 4, 1864, at Detroit, for 3 years, age 20. Mustered out at Jeffersonville, Ind., July 8, 1865.

Dowling, Morgan, Detroit. Enlisted in Company H, Oct. 18, 1861, at Detroit, for 3 years, age 18. Discharged for disability at Georgetown, April 24, 1862.

Dowling, Patrick. Reportedly enlisted and mustered in Company K, Feb. 15, 1865, at Port Huron, for 3 years, age 35 as a substitute for Abram L. Stebbens, drafted. But this date is not correct, since Dowling was reported wounded in action at Dabney's Mill, Feb. 6, 1865, obviously meaning he enlisted earlier. Dowling died April 16, 1865, at Washington, D.C., of wounds received in action.

Downer, William. Enlisted in Company B, Jan. 2, 1864, at Harrisville, for 3 years, age 40. Wounded in action May 1864 during the Overland Campaign. Discharged at Detroit, May 23, 1865.

Drake, John G. Enlisted in Company G, date unknown, and died Oct. 21, 1861, in the field at Hall's Hill, Va., according to regiment's "Roll of Honor," no cause given but likely from illness.

Drake, Oscar F. Enlisted in Company D, Aug. 2, 1861, at East Saginaw, for 3 years, age 22. Killed in action at Gettysburg, July 2, 1863.

Drake, Theodore A. Enlisted in Company A, Aug. 2, 1861, at Ontonagon, for 3 years, age 19. Transferred to Company G. Deserted at Antietam, Md., Sept. 12, 1862.

Drew, Walter. Enlisted in Company B, March 27, 1865, at Stockbridge, Ingham County, for 1 year, age 18. Substitute for John Douglass, drafted. Deserted at Louisville, Ky., June 24, 1865.

Driskell or **Drescoll, Henry**, Wayne County. Enlisted in Company H, Oct. 21, 1861, at Detroit, for 3 years, age 34. Missing in action at Gaines' Mill, June 27, 1862. Discharged for disability at Washington, D.C., Nov. 9, 1862.

Drouger, Moses. Enlisted in Second Company Sharpshooters, March 29, 1864, at Saginaw, for 3 years, age 44. Deserted at Saginaw, May 3, 1864.

Drueyer or **Dwyers, James**. Enlisted in Company H, Oct. 7, 1861, at Detroit, for 3 years, age 44. Deserted Nov. 13, 1861.

Drury, Samuel. Drafted for 1 year, from Cheshire, Allegan County, age 21, March 17, 1865. Discharged at Washington, D.C., June 30, 1865.

Duben, Gregoire. Enlisted in Second Company Sharpshooters, April 25, 1864, at Spaulding, Saginaw County, for 3 years, age 25. Mustered out at Jeffersonville, Ind., July 8, 1865.

Ducharme, Joseph. Enlisted in Second Company Sharpshooters, March 29, 1864, at Kochville, Saginaw County, for 3 years, age 28. Wounded in action at Peeble's Farm, Sept. 30, 1864. No further record.

Dufrene or **Duphrene, George W.**, Wayne County. Enlisted in Company E, Aug. 12, 1861, at Detroit, for 3 years, age 22. Discharged on Surgeon's certificate of disability at Washington, D.C., Dec. 31, 1862.

Duggan, James. Enlisted in Company E, as Sergeant, Aug. 16, 1861, at Detroit, for 3 years, age 23. Transferred to Company H, July 1862. Wounded in action at Gaines' Mill, June 27, 1862. Discharged for disability at New York City Dec. 1862, for wounds.

Duggan, John (Veteran), Wayne County. Enlisted in Company H, as Drummer, Sept. 28, 1861, at Detroit, for 3 years, age 16. Reenlisted Dec. 24, 1863, at Rappahannock Station, Va. Corporal, May 1, 1865. Mustered out at Jeffersonville, Ind., July 8, 1865.

Dumars or **Dumas, John**, Ontonagon County. Enlisted in Company A, as Corporal, Aug. 5, 1861, at Ontonagon, for 3 years, age 25. Died of disease at Georgetown, Feb. 5, 1862.

Dumphry, William. Enlisted March 31, 1864, at Ovid, for 3 years, age 22. Mustered April 9, 1864. No further record.

Duncan, William. Enlisted in Second Company Sharpshooters, March 31, 1864, at Thomastown, for 3 years, age 26. Deserted Aug. 4, 1864.

Dundass, John M. Enlisted in Company G, Feb. 2, 1865, at Adrian, for 3 years, age 18. Substitute for Lewis C. Baker, drafted. Discharged at Philadelphia, June 24, 1865.

Dunkin, William I., or J. Enlisted in Company C, March 29, 1865, at Dover, Lenawee County, for 3 years, age 19. Substitute for Wallace Bryant, drafted. Mustered out at Jeffersonville, Ind., July 8, 1865.

Dunn, James. Enlisted in Company F, Jan. 8, 1864, at Saginaw, for 3 years, age 18. Mustered out at Jeffersonville, Ind., July 8, 1865.

Dunn, Jeremiah. Enlisted in Second Company Sharpshooters, March 28, 1864, at Frankenmuth, for 3 years, age 44. Discharged at Summit House Hospital at Philadelphia, June 16, 1865.

Dunn, Sylvester. Enlisted in Company H, Sept. 20, 1861, at Detroit, for 3 years, age 26. Deserted Oct. 10, 1861.

Dunnagan, John. Enlisted in Company F, March 25, 1865, at Flowerfield, St. Joseph County, for 1 year, age 21. Substitute for Joseph W. Kirby, drafted. No further record.

Dunovan, George (Veteran). Enlisted in Company G, Aug. 24, 1861, age 17. Reenlisted Dec. 21, 1863, at Rappahannock Station, Va. Mustered out at Jeffersonville, Ind., July 8, 1865.

Dunton, Francis, Saginaw County. Enlisted in Company D, Aug. 2, 1861, at East Saginaw, for 3 years, age 19. Deserted at Detroit.

DuPree, Antoine. Enlisted in Company A, March 31, 1865, at Brookfield, Eaton County, for 1 year, age 31. Substitute for Martin Fox, drafted. Mustered out at Jeffersonville, Ind., July 8, 1865.

Durham, Hiram. Reported enlistee in Company C, died of disease Sept. 16, 1864 at City Point, Va.

Durham, Silas E. (Veteran). Enlisted in Company E, Aug. 13, 1861, at Detroit, for 3 years, age 21. Transferred to Company G, July 1862. Paroled prisoner Oct. 1862. Reenlisted Dec. 21, 1863, at Rappahannock Station, Va. Corporal, April 1, 1865. Mustered out at Jeffersonville, Ind., July 8, 1865. Resided Howard City, Mich.

Durland, Charles P. Enlisted in Company H, Feb. 16, 1865, at Bushnell, Montcalm County, for 1 year, age 17. Substitute for George W. Comstock, drafted from Bushnell. Mustered out at Jeffersonville, Ind., July 8, 1865.

Dusenburg or **Dusenberry, George N.**, or W. Enlisted in Company B, Feb. 7, 1865, at Prairie Ronde, Kalamazoo County, for 3 years, age 22. Substitute for Samuel S. McCreary, drafted. Discharged at Washington, D.C., June 7, 1865.

Dwyer, John (Veteran), Wayne County. Enlisted in Company E, Aug. 28, 1861. Reenlisted Feb. 26, 1864, at Bealton, Va. Injured while on picket by a falling tree, Sept. 15, 1864. Discharged for disability at Washington, D.C., Feb. 20, 1865.

Dwyer, Michael. Enlisted in Company I, Oct. 3, 1862, at Detroit, for 3 years, age 23. Joined regiment near Falmouth, Va., Nov. 27, 1862. Corporal May 1, 1865. Mustered out at Jeffersonville, Ind., July 8, 1865.

Dygert, Henry, Almont. Enlisted in Company K, Feb. 5, 1862, at Almont, for 3 years, age 24. Transferred to Company B. No further record.

Dygert, Kin S., Wayne County. Entered service in First Company Sharpshooters at its organization, Sept. 3, 1861, age 38, eventually attached to 16th Michigan early in 1862. Taken prisoner at Gettysburg, July 2, 1863. Escaped and joined regiment Jan. 28, 1865, though no details given. Discharged at expiration of term of service, Feb. 4, 1865.

Eames, Charles F., Wayne County. Enlisted in Company H, Oct. 10, 1861, at Detroit, for 3 years, age 37. Killed in action at second Manassas, Aug. 30, 1862.

Earl, Evelin or **Elvin**. Enlisted in Company E, March 31, 1865, at Matteson, Branch County, for 1 year, age 19. Substitute for Alexander Baxter, drafted. Mustered out at Jeffersonville, Ind., July 8, 1865.

Earle, James. Enlisted in Company A, Feb. 2, 1864, at Saginaw, for 3 years, age 38. Absent sick or wounded Dec. 1864. No further record.

Eastman, Adoniram F. J. Drafted for 1 year, from Climax, Kalamazoo County, age 25. Mustered March 15, 1865. Assigned to Company C. Mustered out at Jeffersonville, Ind., July 8, 1865.

Eddy, E. Frank, Flint. Entered service in Company G, at organization, as 2nd Lieutenant, July 21, 1861, age 21. Commissioned Aug. 9, 1861. Wounded in action, back, leg, and arm, at Gaines' Mill, June 27, 1862. Commissioned 1st Lieutenant, Nov. 3, 1862. Commissioned Captain Aug. 11, 1863. Commissioned Lieutenant Colonel, 29th Michigan Infantry at organization, July 29, 1864. Mustered out at Murfreesboro, Tenn., Sept. 6, 1865.

Eddy, Malcolm. Enlisted in Company K, March 27, 1865, at Grattan, Kent County, for 1 year, age 18. Substitute for Abram Smith, drafted. Absent sick May 1865. No further record.

Edwards, William H. (Veteran). Enlisted in Company G, Jan. 18, 1862, age 17. Joined regiment at Hall's Hill, Va., Feb. 14, 1862. Wounded in action at Fredericksburg, Va., Dec. 13, 1862. Reenlisted Dec. 21, 1863, at Rappahannock Station, Va. Severely wounded in action May 26, 1864, at Noel's Turn–Jericho Mills, Va. Corporal. Sergeant, May 1, 1865. Mustered out at Jeffersonville, Ind., July 8, 1865.

Effinger, Martin, Eagle River. Enlisted in Company A, Aug. 2, 1861, at Ontonagon, for 3 years, age 26. Transferred to Company H, June 1862. Died July 8, 1862, on board steamer on James River, Va., of wounds received in action at Malvern Hill, July 1, 1862.

Eggleston, James W. Enlisted in Company G and mustered Jan. 10, 1863, at Lansing, for 3 years, age 18. Deserted July 10, 1863.

Eichenburg, John. Enlisted in Company A as Corporal, Aug. 5, 1861, at Ontonagon, for 3 years, age 34. No further record.

Eichenburg, Bernard, Ontonagon County. Enlisted in Company A, Aug. 3, 1861, at Ontonagon, for 3 years, age 24. Taken prisoner at Gaines' Mill, June 27, 1862. Reportedly deserted at Fredericksburg, Va., Dec. 13, 1862.

Eitelbuss, George (Veteran), Montcalm County. Enlisted in Company B, Aug. 5, 1861, at Ionia, for 3 years, age 25. Reenlisted as Sergeant Dec. 24, 1863, at Rappahannock Station, Va. Commissioned 1st Lieutenant, Company K, May 8, 1865. Mustered out near Jeffersonville, Ind., July 8, 1865. Resided Bushnell, Mich.

Elbert or **Albert, John**, Ontonagon County. Enlisted in Company A, Aug. 2, 1861, at Ontonagon, for 3 years, age 32. Prisoner of war Jan. 1863. No further record.

Eldred, Horace H. Enlisted in Company G, Aug. 16, 1861, at White Pigeon, for 3 years, age 21. Wounded in action at Rappahannock Station, Nov. 7, 1863. Discharged at Washington, D.C., May 8, 1864, on account of wounds received in action.

Ellard, Joseph, Detroit. Enlisted in Company D, Lancers, Oct. 6, 1861, at Detroit, for 3 years, age 31. Transferred to Company K, 16th Michigan, Feb. 28, 1862. Deserted at Detroit, March 16, 1862.

Elliot, Charles. Enlisted in Company H, Lancers, Nov. 10, 1861, at Detroit, for 3 years, age 26. Transferred to Company K, March 1, 1862. Deserted March 24, 1862.

Elliott, Robert T., Detroit. Entered service in Company E at organization as Captain, Aug. 13, 1861, at Detroit, for 3 years, age 38. Wounded in action at second Manassas, Aug. 30, 1862. Commissioned Major June 20, 1863. Mortally wounded in action and died at Totopotomy–Bethesda Church, May 30, 1864.

Ellis, Andrew. Enlisted in Company F, March 24, 1865, at Stockbridge, Ingham County, for 1 year, age 37. Substitute for Peter McKenzie, drafted. No further record.

Ellison, Benjamin W. Drafted for 1 year, from Courtland, Kent County, age 23. Mustered March 28, 1865. Assigned to Company G. Mustered out at Jeffersonville, Ind., July 8, 1865.

Ellsworth, David or **Daniel**. Enlisted in Company G, Feb. 1, 1865, at Charleston, Kalamazoo County, for 3 years, age 20. Substitute for Walter L. Smith, drafted. Mustered out at Jeffersonville, Ind., July 8, 1865.

Elmer, Lewis. Enlisted in Company E, Aug. 13, 1861, at Detroit, for 3 years, age 18. No further record.

Elseffer, George, Saginaw County. Enlisted in Company D, Aug. 3, 1861, at East Saginaw, for 3 years, age 21. Discharged Nov. 28, 1862, to enlist in U.S. Army. Died Dec. 7, 1870, and buried at Saginaw.

Emery, William. Enlisted in Second Company Sharpshooters, April 28, 1864, at Frankenmuth, for 3 years, age 32. Reported ill Sept. 9, 1864. No further record.

Engle, John, Ontonagon County. Enlisted in Company A, Aug. 2, 1861, at Ontonagon, for 3 years, age 32. Corporal. Wounded in action, Fredericksburg, Va., Dec. 13, 1862. Transferred to Invalid Corps Jan. 11, 1864.

Engleckee, August, Saginaw County. Enlisted in Company E, Lancers, Oct. 18, 1861, at Linden, Wis., for 3 years, age 25. Transferred to Company K, 16th Michigan, Feb. 28, 1862. Discharged on Surgeon's certificate of disability at Philadelphia, Sept. 4, 1862.

Ensban or **Enslan, James H.** (Veteran), Lansing. Enlisted in Company G, in 1862. Reenlisted Feb. 24, 1864, at Bealton Station, Va. Entered Satterlee Hospital, Philadelphia, Aug. 10, 1864. Reported as absent, wounded, Feb. 1865. No further record.

Enslen, Hiram. Enlisted in Company E, Aug. 14, 1861, at Detroit, for 3 years, age 32. Transferred to Company G, July 1862. Deserted May 31, 1865.

Ernhuff, Charles J., Detroit. Enlisted in Company D. Mustered Aug. 24, 1861. Discharged for disability at Yorktown, Va., May 6, 1862.

Ervay, George W., Grand Ledge. Enlisted in Company E, Aug. 18, 1861, at Detroit, for 3 years, claiming to be 18 (he was 16). Transferred to Company H. Wounded in action, struck on the side by spent shell piece, at second Manassas, Aug. 30, 1862. Fatally wounded in head in action at Gettysburg, July 2, 1863, dying July 5 or 6. Buried in National Cemetery at Gettysburg.

Esser, William. Enlisted in Company F, Jan. 31, 1864, at Detroit, for 3 years, age 23. Corporal

May 1, 1865. Discharged at Louisville, Ky., July 22, 1865.

Eufer or **Enfer, John**. Enlisted in Company F, Aug. 5, 1861, at Plymouth, for 3 years, age 35. Reported as of Company E. Died of disease at Hall's Hill, Va., Dec. 21, 1861.

Evans, Joseph M., or **Merritt J**. Enlisted in Company E, Aug. 13, 1861, at Detroit, for 3 years, age 19. Transferred to Company B. Wounded, right hand, in action at Gettysburg, July 2, 1863. Transferred to Company G, 19th Regiment, Veteran Reserve Corps, Dec. 22, 1863. Discharged at expiration of term of service at Petersburg, Va., Sept. 6, 1864.

Evans, Mathew. Enlisted in Company E, Aug. 16, 1861, at Detroit, for 3 years, age 24. Transferred to Company B. Transferred to Invalid Corps Feb. 15, 1864.

Evans, Myron B., Ionia County. Enlisted in Company B, Aug. 7, 1861, at Ionia, for 3 years, age 24. Corporal. Wounded in action at Malvern Hill, July 1, 1862. Discharged at expiration of term of service near Petersburg, Va., Sept. 6, 1864.

Evans, Oscar E., Saginaw. Enlisted in Second Company Sharpshooters, March 23, 1864, at Frankenmuth, for 3 years, age 19. 1st Sergeant. Commissioned 2nd Lieutenant, Company C, May 8, 1865. Commissioned 1st Lieutenant July 7, 1865. Mustered out at Jeffersonville, Ind., July 8, 1865.

Evans, Selby. Enlisted in Second Company Sharpshooters, April 27, 1864, at Spaulding, for 3 years, age 20. Sergeant Feb. 1865. Taken prisoner Feb. 25, 1865. Paroled. Discharged at Columbus, Ohio, June 9, 1865.

Evans, Silah or **Seleah J.** Enlisted in Company K, March 17, 1865, at Waterloo, Jackson County, for 1 year, age 19. Substitute for Tobias Lanbinguire, drafted. No further record.

Evans, Jacob H. Enlisted in Company F, March 16, 1865, at Waterloo, for 1 year, age 18. Substitute for Zopher Scidmore, drafted from Waterloo, Jackson County. Died of disease at Washington, D.C., June 5, 1865.

Everest, Stephen E. Enlisted in Company F, Aug. 5, 1861, at Plymouth, for 3 years, age 25. Transferred to Company B. Discharged for disability at Yorktown, Va., April 30, 1862.

Everest, Theodore L. Enlisted in Company E, Aug. 16, 1861, at Detroit, for 3 years, age 44. Transferred to Company H. Musician. Discharged at Philadelphia, Sept. 17, 1862. Resided Sethton, Mich.

Everett, Dr. Robert A., Hillsdale. Entered service in 5th Michigan Infantry at organization as Assistant Surgeon, July 3, 1861, at Fort Wayne, age 21. Commissioned July 31, 1861. Commissioned Surgeon, 16th Michigan, April 18, 1863. Discharged at expiration of term of service, Oct. 11, 1864.

Everington, Henry, Eagle River. Enlisted, in Company H, as Corporal, Aug. 6, 1861, at Eagle River, for 3 years, age 20. Killed in action at second Manassas, Aug. 30, 1862.

Evers, Barney. Enlisted in Company G, Jan. 4, 1864, at Saline, for 3 years, age 19. Wounded in action at Spotsylvania Court House, May 18, 1864, right leg amputated. Discharged June 19, 1865, at Harper Hospital, Detroit. Resided Pentwater, Mich.

Evlyn, Herbert C. (Veteran), Detroit. Enlisted in Company K, as Sergeant, March 22, 1861, at Detroit, for 3 years, age 22. Reenlisted Dec. 21, 1863, at Rappahannock Station, Va. Dropped from rolls June 30, 1864.

Ewing, Robert L. Enlisted in Company F, Feb. 10, 1864, at Pontiac, for 3 years, age 19. Corporal,

May 1, 1865. Mustered out at Jeffersonville, Ind., July 8, 1865.

Fairbanks, Francis A. Enlisted in Company G, Aug. 19, 1861, at Coldwater, for 3 years, age 21. Sergeant. Wounded in action, right knee, at Wilderness, May 7, 1864. Discharged at expiration of term of service at Petersburg, Va., Sept. 6, 1864.

Fairbrother, Alonzo C., Detroit. Enlisted in Company I, March 4, 1862, at Detroit, for 3 years, age 20. Corporal. Regiment's "Roll of Honor" listed him among officers and men absent, wounded, but no date given. Discharged at expiration of term of service, April 27, 1865. Resided Capac, Mich.

Falby, Dennis, Flushing. Enlisted in Company C, July 31, 1861, at Flint, for 3 years, age 18. Discharged on Surgeon's certificate of disability at Hall's Hill, Va., Feb. 3, 1862. Reentered service in Company G, Feb. 10, 1863, for 9 months, as substitute for Orion Hart, drafted from Flushing. Joined regiment at Falmouth, Va., March 18, 1863. Discharged at expiration of term of service at Kelly's Ford, Va., Nov. 21, 1863. Reentered service in Company K, 4th Michigan Cavalry, Jan. 5, 1864, at Flushing, for 3 years, Joined regiment at Nashville, Tenn., April 3, 1864. Accidentally wounded July 16, 1864, and discharged at Edgefield, Tenn., Aug. 15, 1865. Resided at Michigan Soldiers' Home.

Falvey, Daniel J. (Veteran), Wayne County. Enlisted in Company E, Aug. 16, 1861, at Detroit, for 3 years, age 19. Reenlisted Dec. 21, 1863, at Rappahannock Station, Va. Sergeant. Mustered out at Jeffersonville, Ind., July 8, 1865.

Fanthorpe, George H., Detroit. Enlisted in Company D, Lancers, as Corporal, Nov. 21, 1861, at Detroit, for 3 years, age 28. Transferred to Company K, 16th Michigan, Feb. 28, 1862. Deserted at Detroit, March 24, 1862.

Farman, Myron. Drafted for 1 year, from Climax, Kalamazoo County, age 37. Mustered March 15, 1865. Assigned to Company C. Mustered out at Jeffersonville, Ind., July 8, 1865. Died June 12, 1903. Buried at Athens, Mich.

Farmer, Edwin R., Van Buren County. Enlisted in First Company Sharpshooters attached to 16th Michigan, as Sergeant, Oct. 14, 1861, at Detroit, for 3 years, age 31. Joined regiment at Hall's Hill, Va., Feb. 14, 1862. Wounded in action at second Manassas, Aug. 30, 1862. Discharged for disability at Washington, D.C., Oct. 28, 1862.

Farr, George. Enlisted in Company F, Lancers, as Corporal, Nov. 6, 1861, at Blissfield, for 3 years, age 19. Transferred to Company I, 16th Michigan, Feb. 28, 1862. No further record.

Farrell, Barzilla F. (Veteran), Hillsdale. Enlisted in Company G, as Corporal, Aug. 12, 1861. Missing in action at second Manassas, Aug. 30, 1862. Reenlisted Dec. 21, 1863, at Rappahannock Station, Va. Wounded in action, left leg, at Wilderness, May 7, 1864. Sergeant. Commissioned 2nd Lieutenant, July 7, 1865. Resided Amboy, Mich.

Fauth, George. Enlisted in regimental Band, Sept. 13, 1861, at Detroit, for 3 years, age 24. Mustered out Aug. 11, 1862. Died Dec. 5, 1886. Buried at Owosso, Mich.

Fauth, William. Enlisted in Band, Sept. 13, 1861, at Detroit, for 3 years, age 21. Mustered out Aug. 11, 1862.

Faviel or **Farul, John**. Enlisted in Second Company Sharpshooters, April 27, 1864, at Spaulding, for 3 years, age 22. Taken prisoner in the raid on Weldon Railroad, Petersburg, Va., Dec. 10, 1864. Mustered out at Jeffersonville, Ind., July 8, 1865.

Fawcett, John. Enlisted in Second Company Sharpshooters, March 31, 1864, at Taymouth, Saginaw County, for 3 years, age 25. Corporal. Mustered out at Jeffersonville, Ind., July 8, 1865.

Felton, Hiram D., Nankin, Wayne County. Enlisted in Company F, Aug. 5, 1861, at Plymouth, for 3 years, age 18. Corporal. Reported Nov. and Dec. 1862 as in the hospital, wounded. Discharged for disability at Detroit, Dec. 30, 1862, for wounds received in action. Resided in Flint.

Fennick or **Fenwick, John**. Drafted for 1 year, from Climax, Kalamazoo County, age 32. Mustered March 15, 1865. Assigned to Company C. Mustered out at Jeffersonville, Ind., July 8, 1865.

Ferrigan or **Fenigan, John** (Veteran), Milford. Enlisted in Company B, Lancers, Oct. 22, 1861, at Milford, for 3 years, age 22. Transferred to Company I, 16th Michigan, Feb. 28, 1862. Wounded in action, head, at Gaines' Mill, June 27, 1862. Reenlisted Dec. 22, 1863, at Rappahannock Station, Va. Sergeant. Wounded in action in the shoulder, at Wilderness, May 7, 1864. Commissioned 2nd Lieutenant July 7, 1865. Mustered out at Jeffersonville, Ind., July 8, 1865.

Ferris, Orris S. Drafted for 1 year, from Leonidas, St. Joseph County, age 32, March 1865. Assigned to Company K. Mustered out at Washington, D.C., June 20, 1865.

Field, Frederick W. (Veteran), Saginaw County. Enlisted in Company D, Aug. 3, 1861, at East Saginaw, for 3 years, age 24. Discharged at Washington, D.C., March 19, 1864, to enlist as Hospital Steward in U.S. Army.

Fields, Myron A. Enlisted in Company A, March 24, 1865, at Nottawa, St. Joseph County, for 1 year, age 22. Substitute for John C Murin, drafted. Absent without leave. No further record.

Finely, John S., Wayne County. Enlisted in Company C, Aug. 1, 1861, at Flint, for 3 years, age 48. Deserted at Detroit, Sept. 14, 1861.

Finley, John B., Detroit. Enlisted in Company H, Lancers, Dec. 10, 1861, at Detroit, for 3 years, age 35. Transferred to Company I, 16th Michigan, Feb. 28, 1862. Wounded in action and taken prisoner June 27, 1862, at Gaines' Mill. Paroled at Annapolis, Md., Oct. 1862. Discharged for disability.

Finnegan, John, Eagle River. Enlisted in Company D, Aug. 3, 1861, at East Saginaw, for 3 years, age 30. Transferred to Company H. Killed in action at Gaines' Mill, June 27, 1862.

Finton, James, Wayne County. Enlisted in Company F, Aug. 12, 1861, at Plymouth, for 3 years, age 19. Discharged at expiration of term of service at Petersburg, Va., Sept. 7, 1864.

Fisette, George. Enlisted in Second Company Sharpshooters, April 28, 1864, at Frankenmuth, for 3 years, age 32. Deserted at Saginaw, May 14, 1864.

Fisette, George S., Wayne County. Enlisted in Company E, Sept. 6, 1861, at Detroit, for 3 years, age 27. Wounded in action at Gaines' Mill, June 27, 1862. Discharged at Annapolis, Md., Sept. 16, 1862. Resided Petersburg, Monroe County.

Fish, George B., Ionia County. Enlisted in Company B, Aug. 3, 1861, at Ionia, for 3 years, age 19. Wounded in action at Gaines' Mill, June 27, or at Malvern Hill, July 1, 1862. Discharged for disability at Philadelphia, Dec. 27, 1862.

Fish, Robert, Wayne County. Enlisted in Company E as Wagoner, Sept. 5, 1861, at Detroit, for

3 years, age 38. Discharged on Surgeon's certificate of disability, Nov. 17, 1862.

Fisher, Alexander. Enlisted in Company G, March 29, 1865, at Deerfield, Livingston County, for 1 year, age 28. Substitute for John F. Topping, drafted. Mustered out at Jeffersonville, Ind., July 8, 1865.

Fisher, Anson B., Commerce, Oakland County. Enlisted in Company B, Lancers, as Sergeant, Oct. 29, 1861, at Commerce, for 3 years, age 21. Transferred to Company I, 16th Michigan, Feb. 28, 1862. Discharged Dec. 18, 1862.

Fisher, Benjamin F., East Saginaw. Entered service in Company D at organization, as Captain, July 30, 1861, at East Saginaw, for 3 years, age 39. Taken prisoner at Gaines' Mill, June 27, 1862. Released Aug. 12, 1862. Commissioned Major in 23rd Michigan Infantry at organization, Aug. 23, 1862. Resigned Feb. 13, 1863.

Fisher, George E., Plymouth. Enlisted in Company C, Aug. 3, 1861, at Flint, for 3 years, age 28. Transferred to Company F. Reported to have transferred to Gunboat service April 20, 1862, and killed in action April 22, 1863, in Michigan Adjutant-General's Dept. *Record of Service,* vol. 16 (1905). This is probably accurate; he was also reported as killed in action at Gettysburg, July 2, 1863, in regimental "Roll of Honor," but this is not supported by the regiment's contemporaneous record.

Fisher, Samuel. Enlisted in Company E, March 31, 1865, at Cohoctah, Livingston County, for 1 year, age 27. Substitute for Hiram Boyd, drafted. Mustered out at Jeffersonville, Ind., July 8, 1865.

Fisher, William F., or **S.**, Kent County. Enlisted in First Company Sharpshooters attached to Dec. 17, 1861, at Grand Rapids, for 3 years, age 21. Deserted at Detroit, Feb. 3, 1862.

Fitchworth, Casper. Reportedly an enlistee in Company F, wounded in action at Gaines' Mill, June 27, 1862. Discharged for wounds on Nov. 28, 1862.

Fitzgerald, Patrick. Enlisted in Second Company Sharpshooters, March 31, 1864, at Saginaw, for 3 years, age 26. Corporal May 1, 1865. Mustered out at Jeffersonville, Ind., July 8, 1865.

Fitzpatrick, Nicholas, St. Johns. Enlisted in Company E, Aug. 13, 1861, at Detroit, for 3 years, age 30. Transferred to Company H. Died of disease at Hall's Hill, Va., Nov. 14, 1861.

Fitzrobert, Robert. Enlisted in Company I, March 24, 1865, at Detroit, for 1 year, age 22. Substitute for August Rasch, drafted. Mustered out at Jeffersonville, Ind., July 8, 1865.

Fitzsimons, Thomas R., Detroit. Enlisted in Company I, as Drummer, Aug. 15, 1862, at Detroit, for 3 years, age 18. Discharged near Washington, D.C., May 29, 1865.

Flannery, John. Enlisted in Second Company Sharpshooters, March 27, 1864, at Bloomfield, for 3 years, age 45. Deserted June 27, 1864.

Flannigan, James. Enlisted in Company D, March 1, 1865, at Kalamazoo, for 3 years, age 25. Substitute for Daniel Kimble, drafted. Mustered out at Jeffersonville, Ind., July 8, 1865.

Flansburgh, James (Veteran), Sheridan. Enlisted in Company K, March 1, 1862, at Detroit, for 3 years, age 24. Reenlisted March 1, 1864, at Bealton, Va. Corporal. Mustered out at Jeffersonville, Ind., July 8, 1865.

Flesser, Daniel (Veteran), Ontonagon County. Enlisted in Company A, Aug. 2, 1861, at Ontonagon, for 3 years, age 22. Wounded in action at Malvern Hill, July 1, 1862. Reenlisted Dec. 21, 1863, at Rappahannock Station, Va. Mustered out at Jeffersonville, Ind., July 8,

1865. Died Aug. 1890.

Foote, Horace G. (Veteran), Utica. Enlisted in Company H, Lancers, Dec. 10, 1861, at Utica, for 3 years, age 20. Transferred to Company I, 16th Michigan, Feb. 28, 1862. Reenlisted Feb. 26, 1864, at Bealton, Va. Sergeant, May 1, 1865. Mustered out at Jeffersonville, Ind., July 8, 1865.

Forbes, Joseph H. Enlisted in Company G, Feb. 7, 1865, at Port Huron, for 3 years, age 20. Substitute for Edward Insli, drafted from Port Huron. Mustered out at Jeffersonville, Ind., July 8, 1865.

Ford, James. Enlisted in Company G, Feb. 17, 1865, at Bloomfield, Oakland County, for 3 years, age 19. Substitute for Spencer B. Gray, drafted. Deserted at Jeffersonville, Ind., June 27, 1865.

Ford, John H. Enlisted in Company C, Lancers, Oct. 24, 1861, at Saginaw for 3 years, age 18. Transferred to Company I, 16th Michigan, Feb. 28, 1862. Transferred to Company K. Discharged for disability Feb. 9, 1863.

Forn, William, Wayne County. Enlisted in Company A, Sept. 4, 1861, at Detroit, for 3 years, age 24. Discharged for disability at Yorktown, Va., May 1, 1862.

Forsyth, Frederick J. Enlisted in Company E, Lancers, Nov. 18, 1861, at Bay City, for 3 years, age 44. Transferred to Company K, 16th Michigan, Feb. 28, 1862. Sergeant. Sergeant Major. Commissioned 2nd Lieutenant, Nov. 3, 1862. Discharged for disability near Auburn, Va., Oct. 27, 1863.

Forsyth, Smith, Genesee County. Enlisted in Company C, Aug. 1, 1861, at Flint, for 3 years, age 23. Discharged on Surgeon's certificate of disability at Hall's Hill, Va., Feb. 25, 1862. Resided Dayton, Ohio.

Fosciaiac or **Focie, John**. Enlisted in Company F, Jan. 24, 1865, at Dexter, for 3 years, age 35. Substitute for William E. Stevens, drafted. Deserted at Washington, D.C., June 12, 1865.

Foster, Charles. Enlisted in Company B, Feb. 27, 1865, at Algoma, Kent County, for 1 year, age 24. Substitute for Oscar House, drafted. Discharged at Jeffersonville, Ind., June 29, 1865.

Foster, Herschel A. Drafted for 1 year, from Brady, Kalamazoo County, age 26. Mustered March 15, 1865. Assigned to Company I. Mustered out at Jeffersonville, Ind., July 8, 1865.

Foster, James (Veteran), Detroit. Enlisted in Company K, Jan. 23, 1862. Wounded in action at Gettysburg, July 2, 1863. Reenlisted Dec. 21, 1863, at Rappahannock Station, Va. Corporal. Mustered out at Jeffersonville, Ind., July 8, 1865.

Foster, John. Drafted Sept. 20, 1864, for 1 year, from Escanaba, age 37. Assigned to Company K. Discharged at Washington, D.C., April 30, 1865.

Foster, Joseph. Enlisted in Company F, Aug. 5, 1861, at Plymouth, for 3 years, age 35. Transferred to Company E, May 1862. Discharged for disability at Georgetown, April 24, 1862.

Foster, Lambert L., or S. Enlisted in Company B, Feb. 11, 1864, at Gaines, for 3 years, age 28. Mustered out at Jeffersonville, Ind., July 8, 1865.

Fountain, Florvane, Wayne County. Enlisted in Company F, as Sergeant, Sept. 13, 1861. Discharged at Gaines' Mill, June 1862.

Fowler, James. Enlisted in Company I, March 21, 1865, at Waterloo, Jackson, for 3 years, age 25. Substitute for Edmund Hawley, drafted. Discharged at Washington, D.C., May 30, 1865.

Fox, John. Enlisted in Company D, March 25, 1865, at Detroit, for 1 year, age 24. Substitute for

Lafayette Holmes, drafted. Reported on May 1865 rolls as absent, wounded. Discharged for disability Aug. 4, 1865.

Fox, Joseph S., Bay City. Enlisted in Company H, Lancers, as Wagoner, Oct. 15, 1861, at Bay City, for 3 years, age 32. Transferred to Company I, 16th Michigan, Feb. 28, 1862. Wounded in action at Gaines' Mill, June 27, 1862. Discharged for disability, no date.

Frank, Francis. Enlisted in Company H, Oct. 24, 1864, at Detroit, for 1 year, age 34. Substitute for James Armstrong, drafted. Discharged at Jackson, May 6, 1865.

Frazer, Alfred R. Enlisted in Company E, Aug. 21, 1861, at Detroit, for 3 years, age 45. Transferred to Company H. Wagoner. Discharged for disability at Hall's Hill, Va., Dec. 13, 1861.

Frazer, Thomas, Saginaw County. Enlisted in Company D, as Corporal, Aug. 1, 1861, at East Saginaw, for 3 years, age 23. Discharged at Yorktown, Va., May 6, 1862.

Freehouse, Samuel, Sebewa, Ionia County. Enlisted in Company B, Aug. 5, 1861, at Ionia, for 3 years, age 30. Died of disease at Georgetown, Oct. 18, 1862.

Freeman, Erastus H., Newaygo County. Enlisted in First Company Sharpshooters attached to 16th Michigan, Oct. 24, 1861, at Detroit, for 3 years, age 38. Joined regiment at Hall's Hill, Va., Feb. 14, 1862. Discharged for disability April 12, 1862.

Frey or **Fry, Charles**, Detroit. Enlisted in Company H, Oct. 1, 1861, at Detroit, for 3 years, age 42. Missing in action at second Manassas, Aug. 30, 1862. Deserted near Antietam, Md., Oct. 9, 1862.

Frey, John Alden. Enlisted in Company A, Aug. 25, 1864, at Jackson, for 3 years, age 23. Substitute for Frederick Hutzel, from Fredonia, Jackson County. Mustered out at Jeffersonville, Ind., July 8, 1865. Resided Ann Arbor, Mich.

Fripp or **Kripps, Ferdinand**. Enlisted in Company A, Sept. 6, 1861, at Detroit, for 3 years, age 30. Wounded and missing in action and taken prisoner at Gaines' Mill, June 27, 1862. Discharged for disability Oct. 15, 1862.

Frissinger, Thomas. Enlisted in Company A, March 15, 1865, at Greenwood, St. Clair County, for 3 years, age 20. Substitute for Lincoln Small, drafted. Mustered out at Jeffersonville, Ind., July 8, 1865.

Frost, Origin. Enlisted in Company E, Aug. 20, 1861, at Detroit, for 3 years, age 20. Transferred as Corporal to Company F. Sergeant. Discharged at Philadelphia, Nov. 20, 1862.

Frost, Pulaski. Drafted March 16, 1865, for 1 year, from Crystal, Montcalm County, age 24. Assigned to Company E. Died of disease near Washington, D.C., June 10, 1865.

Fuller, Guy W., Ionia. Entered service in Company B at organization, as 1st Lieutenant, July 30, 1861, at Ionia, for 3 years, age 27. Commissioned Captain Sept. 28, 1862. Acting Lieutenant Colonel, May 1, 1864. Discharged at expiration of term of service, Sept. 7, 1864. Murdered by Confederate guerillas while working as a civilian employee for U.S. government railroad.

Fullery, Patrick, Ontonagon County. Enlisted in Company A, Aug. 3, 1861. Deserted at Detroit, Aug. 10, 1861.

Gabriel, James, Wayne County. Enlisted in Company F, Sept. 16, 1861, at Plymouth, for 3 years, age 22. Discharged for disability at Hall's Hill, Va., Feb. 25, 1862.

Gager, Frank (Veteran). Enlisted in Company F, Aug. 5, 1861, at Plymouth, for 3 years, age 22. Reported in Company E. Sergeant. Wounded in action, arm, at Gaines' Mill, June 27, 1862.

1st Sergeant. Sergeant Major, March 1, 1863. Reenlisted Dec. 24, 1863, at Rappahannock Station, Va. Commissioned 2nd Lieutenant, Company A, June 28, 1864. Transferred to Company G, Aug. 19, 1864. Commissioned 1st Lieutenant, Company B, Sept. 20, 1864. Commissioned Captain, Company I, May 8, 1865. Brevet Captain, U.S. Volunteers, Sept. 30, 1864, for gallant services at the battle of Peeble's Farm. Mustered out at Jeffersonville, Ind., July 8, 1865.

Galamine or **Galerneau, George**. Enlisted in Company A, March 14, 1864, at Houghton, for 3 years, age 21. Wounded in action at Peeble's Farm. Sept. 30, 1864. No further record.

Gallagher, Michael, Seymour, Md. Enlisted June 25, 1863, at St. Clair, for 3 years, age 22. Substitute for Henry Byrne, drafted for 9 months. No further record.

Gallinger, Benjamin. Enlisted in Company G, March 22, 1865, at Port Huron, for 3 years, age 24. Substitute for Robert Walsh, drafted. Deserted June 28, 1865.

Gallup, Hiram, Kent County. Enlisted in First Company Sharpshooters attached to 16th Michigan, Jan. 31, 1862, at Grand Rapids, for 3 years, age 28. Joined regiment at Hall's Hill, Va., Feb. 14, 1862. Died of disease Dec. 22, 1862 or Jan. 9, 1863.

Ganey, Thomas, Detroit. Enlisted in Company H, as Corporal, July 25, 1861, at Detroit, for 3 years, age 20. Sergeant April 22, 1862. Discharged at expiration of term of service near Petersburg, Va., Sept. 7, 1864.

Ganson, Alfred, Genesee County. Enlisted in Company C, Aug. 15, 1861. Discharged at Yorktown, Va., May 8, 1862. Resided Fenton, Mich.

Gantz, George H. Drafted for 1 year, from North Star, Gratiot County, age 40, and mustered Sept. 24, 1864. Assigned to Company H. Discharged near Washington, D.C., May 30, 1865. Resided Alma, Mich.

Gardner, Charles (Veteran). Enlisted in Company A, Feb. 9, 1864, at Ann Arbor, for 3 years, age 31. Sick at Detroit at muster out of regiment. No further record.

Gardner, John. Enlisted in Company F, Aug. 7, 1861, at Plymouth, for 3 years, age 20. No further record.

Gardner, John S., Lansing. Enlisted in Company G. Aug. 15, 1861, at Lansing, age 20. Killed in action at Gaines' Mill, June 27, 1862.

Garner, George. Enlisted in Company B, Jan. 25, 1864, at Fenton, for 3 years, age 17. Mustered out at Jeffersonville, Ind., July 8, 1865.

Garner, James. Enlisted in Company F, Aug. 7, 1861, at Plymouth, for 3 years, age 28. No further record.

Garrison, Horatio. Drafted for 1 year, from Pipestone, Berrien County, age 20. Mustered March 18, 1865. Assigned to Company H. Discharged at Washington, D.C., July 17, 1865.

Garrison, William. Enlisted in Company F, Aug. 7, 1861, at Plymouth, for 3 years, age 27. No further record.

Gashal, Andrew. Enlisted in Company F, March 21,1865, at Lockport, St. Joseph County, for 1 year, age 23. Substitute for Robert Hill, drafted from Lockport. Discharged at Washington, D.C., Aug. 4, 1865. Resided Whitehall, Mich.

Gates, Peter. Enlisted in Company F, Aug. 7, 1861, at Plymouth, for 3 years, age 24. Transferred to Company E, May 1862. Corporal. Discharged for disability at Georgetown, May 3, 1862.

Gates, Walter, Delhi. Enlisted in Company E, Dec. 30, 1862, at Delhi, Ingham County, for 3 years, age 18. Joined regiment near Falmouth, Va., Jan. 2, 1863. Died of disease near Falmouth, Va., Feb. 28, 1863.

Gattis, Hiram. Enlisted in Company I, March 1, 1865, at Grand Rapids, for 1 year, age 19. Substitute for Truman Gilbert, drafted from Grand Rapids. Mustered out at Jeffersonville, Ind., July 8, 1865.

Geddis, George. Enlisted in Company B, Lancers, Nov. 26, 1861, at Detroit, for 3 years, age 21. Transferred to Company I, 16th Michigan, Feb. 28, 1862. No further record.

Geedy, John H. Enlisted in Company E, Feb. 9, 1865, at Algansee, Branch County, for 1 year, age 18. Substitute for Hiram Fiero, drafted. Mustered out at Jeffersonville, Ind., July 8, 1865.

Geisenhoefer or **Giesenhoffer, Jacob**. Enlisted in Company A, Aug. 3, 1861, at Ontonagon, for 3 years, age 31. Transferred to Company G. Discharged for disability at Washington, D.C., July 14, 1863. Resided DeWitt, Mich. See also, **Giesenhoffer, Anthony.**

Gelenaw, William. Enlisted in Second Company Sharpshooters, March 31, 1864, at Bridgeport, for 3 years, age 19. Mustered out at Jeffersonville, Ind., July 8, 1865.

Gelick, Master F. or **Martin T.**, Ionia County. Enlisted in Company B, Aug. 2, 1861, at Ionia, for 3 years, age 26. Paroled prisoner at Annapolis, Md., Aug. 1862. Transferred to Invalid Corps Aug. 19, 1863.

Genereau, Abraham, Ontonagon County. Enlisted in Company A, Aug. 2, 1861, at Ontonagon, for 3 years, age 45. Killed in action at Gaines' Mill, June 27, 1862.

Genner, Jacob. Enlisted in Company G, Sept. 10, 1861, at Detroit, for 3 years, age 32. Died July 14, 1863, at Gettysburg, of wounds received in action, shot in the chest, on July 2, 1863. Buried in National Cemetery at Gettysburg.

George, John. Enlisted in Company B, March 23, 1865, at Stockbridge, Ingham County, for 1 year, age 36. Substitute for William C Nichols, drafted. Discharged at Louisville, Ky., Sept. 27, 1865.

Gibbs, Charles F. Enlisted in Company E, March 7, 1865, at Grosse Pointe, for 3 years, age 18. Mustered out at Jeffersonville, Ind., July 8, 1865.

Gibbs, George G., Avon, Oakland County. Enlisted in Company E, Feb. 11, 1864, at Avon, for 3 years, age 18. Severely wounded in action at Magnolia Swamp–Bethesda Church, June 1, 1864. Discharged for disability at Washington, D.C., June 3, 1865.

Gibbs, Josiah, Rochester. Enlisted in Company E, Feb. 17, 1864, at Pontiac, for 3 years, age 18. Corporal May 17, 1865. Mustered out at Jeffersonville, Ind., July 8, 1865.

Gibbs, Oramill, Rochester. Enlisted in Company E, Feb. 13, 1864, at Pontiac, for 3 years, age 50. Mustered out at Jeffersonville, Ind., July 8, 1865.

Giesenhoffer or **Greishafer, Anthony**, Jackson. Enlisted in Company G, Feb. 10, 1864, at Northfield, for 3 years, age 21. Taken prisoner at Weldon Railroad, Petersburg, Va., Aug. 21, 1864. Died in prison at Salisbury, N.C., Nov. 14, 1864.

Gilbert, George B., Almont. Enlisted in Company K, Feb. 5, 1862, at Almont, for 3 years, age 38. Transferred to Company D. Discharged at Fortress Monroe, Va., Sept. 21, 1862.

Gilbey, Thomas W. (Veteran), Detroit. Enlisted in Company H, Oct. 29, 1861, at Detroit, for 3 years, age 18. Reenlisted Dec. 24, 1863, at Rappahannock Station, Va. Corporal, May 1,

1865. Mustered out at Jeffersonville, Ind., July 8, 1865. Resided Flint, Mich.

Gilfillin, Joseph. Enlisted in Company E, Feb. 16, 1865, at Algoma, Kent County, for 1 year, age 24. Substitute for Dennis Porter, drafted. Mustered out at Jeffersonville, Ind., July 8, 1865.

Gilg, Frank, Ontonagon County. Enlisted in Company A, Aug. 2, 1861, at Ontonagon, for 3 years, age 22. Wounded in action at Gaines' Mill, June 27, 1862. Killed in action at second Manassas, Aug. 30, 1862.

Gill, Franklin, Detroit. Enlisted in Company E, Oct. 3, 1862, at Detroit, for 3 years, age 18. Joined regiment at Antietam, Md., Oct. 30, 1862. Mustered out at Jeffersonville, Ind., July 8, 1865.

Gill, Patrick (Veteran), Detroit. Enlisted in Company D, Lancers, Oct. 5, 1861, at Detroit, for 3 years, age 24. Transferred to Company K, 16th Michigan, Feb. 28, 1862. Listed among 1862 casualties, wounded in the arm, but no date given. Reenlisted Dec. 21, 1863, at Rappahannock Station, Va. Taken prisoner Weldon Railroad, Petersburg, Va., Aug. 25, 1864. No further record.

Gill, William. Enlisted in Company F, Aug. 7, 1861, at Plymouth, for 3 years, age 18. Transferred to Company E. Deserted Sept. 12, 1862.

Gilland, William H., or **Henry W.**, Washtenaw County. Enlisted in Company A, Sept. 6, 1861, at Detroit, for 3 years, age 21. Corporal. Died of disease at Yorktown, Va., May 6, 1862.

Gillean, Hillaird. Enlisted in Second Company Sharpshooters, March 21, 1864, at Saginaw, for 3 years, age 21. Deserted at Saginaw, May 3, 1864.

Gillett, George H. Enlisted in Company A, March 28, 1865, at Algoma, Kent County, for 1 year, age 18. Substitute for William H. Long, drafted. Mustered out at Jeffersonville, Ind., July 8, 1865.

Gillson, William A. D., Three Rivers. Enlisted in Company G, Aug. 5, 1861, at Three Rivers, age 19. Wounded in action Dec. 1862 (probably Fredericksburg, Va.) Reported absent, wounded, Jan. 1863. Died March 10, 1863, of wounds.

Girodot, John. Enlisted in Company F, Aug. 7, 1861, at Plymouth, for 3 years, age 35. Transferred to Company E. Sergeant. Died Nov. 21, 1863, at Washington, D.C., of wounds received in action at Rappahannock Station, Va., Nov. 7, 1863.

Glasier or **Glazier, Gottlieb** (Veteran), Detroit. Enlisted in Company A, July 24, 1862, at Detroit, age 23. Joined regiment at Antietam, Md., Oct. 12, 1862. Wounded in action at Bristow Station, Va., Oct. 14, 1863. Reenlisted Dec. 21, 1863, at Rappahannock Station, Va. Mustered out at Jeffersonville, Ind., July 8, 1865. Died March 12, 1894.

Glass, Milton C. (Veteran), Wayne County. Enlisted in Company F, as Corporal, Aug. 2, 1861, at Plymouth, for 3 years, age 21. Reenlisted as Sergeant Dec. 21, 1863, at Rappahannock Station, Va. Sergeant. Died at Baltimore, March 1, 1865, of wounds received in action at Dabney's Mill, on Feb. 6, 1865.

Gloid, Nelson H. Enlisted in Company D, Jan. 28, 1864, at Midland, for 3 years, age 24. Mustered out at Jeffersonville, Ind., July 8, 1865.

Glover, Henry B. Enlisted in Company A, Aug. 3, 1861, at Ontonagon, for 3 years, age 43. No further record.

Glover, William (Veteran), Saginaw County. Enlisted in Company D, Aug. 3, 1861, at East Saginaw, for 3 years, age 19. Reenlisted as Corporal Dec. 21, 1863, at Rappahannock Station,

Va. Severely wounded in action June 6, 1864, left shoulder, at Bethesda Church–Cold Harbor. No further record.

Gloverfield or **Glerfield, Peter**. Enlisted in Company F, Lancers, Nov. 5, 1861, at Portage Lake, for 3 years, age 24. Transferred to Company K, 16th Michigan, Feb. 28, 1862. Discharged for disability Nov. 2, 1862.

Goddard, Rufus. Enlisted in Company B, Aug. 3, 1861, at Ionia, for 3 years, age 28. Discharged for disability at Detroit, June 21, 1862.

Goetz, Joseph (Veteran), Barton, Wis. Enlisted in Company E, Lancers, Nov. 26, 1861, at West Bend, Wis., for 3 years, age 27. Transferred to Company K, 16th Michigan, Feb. 28, 1862. Reenlisted Dec. 21, 1863, at Rappahannock Station, Va. Wounded in action at Petersburg, Va., July 9, 1864. 1st Sergeant 1864. Discharged to date March 8, 1865.

Gognion, John. Enlisted in Company H, Nov. 5, 1861, at Detroit, for 3 years, age 38. Discharged Nov. 9, 1861.

Golden, Henry. Enlisted in Company E, Lancers, Dec. 21, 1861, at Midland, for 3 years, age 22. Transferred to Company K, 16th Michigan, Feb. 28, 1862. Deserted at Detroit, March 20, 1862.

Goodall, Edwin or **Edward**, Birmingham. Enlisted in Company C, Aug. 17, 1861, at Detroit, age 21. Died of disease at Hall's Hill, Va., Jan. 2, 1862.

Goodrich, James H. (Veteran), Wayne County. Enlisted in Company F, Sept. 12, 1861. Wounded in action at Gaines' Mill, June 27, 1862. Reenlisted Dec. 21, 1863, at Rappahannock Station, Va. Discharged for disability at Washington, D.C., April or May 1865.

Goodwin, Thomas. Enlisted in Company C, March 21, 1865, at Detroit, for 1 year, age 25. Substitute for John H. Carew, drafted. Mustered out at Jeffersonville, Ind., July 8, 1865.

Gordee, Casper. Enlisted in Company A, Aug. 2, 1861, at Ontonagon, for 3 years, age 27. Killed in action at Gaines' Mill, June 27, 1862.

Gordon, Omazin or **Oniagan** (Veteran), Ontonagon County. Enlisted in Company A, Aug. 2, 1861, at Ontonagon, for 3 years, age 31. Wounded at Bristow Station, Oct. 14, 1863. Reenlisted Dec. 21, 1863, at Rappahannock Station, Va. Mustered out at Jeffersonville, Ind., July 8, 1865. Resided in Bear Lake, Mich.

Gordon, David. Drafted for 1 year, from Middlebury, Shiawassee County, age 39. Mustered Sept. 21, 1864. Assigned to Company H. Discharged at Washington, D.C., May 30, 1865.

Gordon, Harvey. Enlisted in Company E, Aug. 18, 1861, at Detroit, for 3 years, age 20. Transferred to Company G. Reported at some point as absent, wounded; was listed with Gettysburg wounded in Washington, D.C., and Philadelphia hospitals, July 1863 (possibly also wrongly listed as "Michael Gordon," wounded in thigh). Transferred to Veteran Reserve Corps, Sept. 30, 1863.

Gordon, James S., Ionia County. Enlisted in Company B, Aug. 5, 1861, at Ionia, for 3 years, age 43. Discharged for disability at Washington, D.C., Nov. 20, 1862.

Gordon, Jasper. Enlisted in Company A, Aug. 3, 1861, at Ontonagon, for 3 years, age 18. Transferred to Company G. Died Sept. 30, 1862, at Georgetown of wounds to skull received in action at second Manassas, Aug. 30, 1862.

Gornis or **Grimus, Joseph**. Enlisted in Second Company Sharpshooters, April 25, 1864, at

Bridgeport, for 3 years, age 19. Mustered May 3, 1864. Mustered out at Jeffersonville, Ind., July 8, 1865.

Goshman or **Behmann, Frederick**, Wayne County. Enlisted in Company C, Nov. 25, 1861, at Detroit, for 3 years, age 27. Discharged for disability at Alexandria, Va., Dec. 28, 1862.

Gould, Jacob. Enlisted in First Company Sharpshooters attached to 16th Michigan, Feb. 15, 1864, at Bridgeport, for 3 years, age 21. Wounded in action, head, at Petersburg, Va., June 20, 1864. Corporal July 1, 1865. Mustered out at Jeffersonville, Ind., July 8, 1865.

Gould, Robert H. Drafted for 1 year, from Allegan County, age 33. Mustered March 17, 1865. Assigned to Company K. Mustered out at Jeffersonville, Ind., July 8, 1865.

Goulding, Joseph B., Saginaw County. Enlisted in Company D, Aug. 3, 1861, at East Saginaw, for 3 years, age 22. Discharged at Philadelphia, Jan. 13, 1863. Died Sept. 14, 1877. Buried at Saginaw.

Goyer, Richard C. Enlisted in Company C, Jan. 4, 1864, at Flushing, for 3 years, age 44. Discharged at Detroit, May 18, 1865.

Graham, David. Enlisted Jan. 29, 1864, at Plymouth, for 3 years, age 18. No further record.

Graham, John, St. Clair County. Enlisted in Company C, Nov. 18, 1861, at Detroit, for 3 years, age 20. Discharged to date April 30, 1863.

Graham, John. Enlisted in Company I, Feb. 18, 1865, at Pontiac, for 3 years, age 22. Substitute for Charles W. Love, drafted from Putnam, Livingston County. Dropped from rolls June 1, 1865.

Graham, Thomas, Detroit. Enlisted in Company D, Lancers, Nov. 21, 1861, at Detroit, for 3 years, age 26. Transferred to Company K, 16th Michigan, Feb. 28, 1862. Deserted at Detroit, March 20, 1862.

Graham, Ziba, Flint. Enlisted in Company C, Sergeant, Aug. 1, 1861, at Flint, for 3 years, age 22. 1st Sergeant, Sept. 22, 1861. Commissioned 2nd Lieutenant, Aug. 30, 1862. Transferred to Company G, March 1863. Commissioned 1st Lieutenant, Company I, April 22, 1863. Commanding Company Sept. 1863. Wounded in action at Jericho Mills–North Anna River, Va., May 23, 1864. Discharged at expiration of term of service, Sept. 20, 1864.

Granger, James (Veteran), Orleans. Enlisted in Company F, Dec. 20, 1861, at Ionia, for 3 years, age 21. Joined regiment at Hall's Hill, Va., Jan. 11, 1862. Reenlisted Dec. 21, 1863, at Rappahannock Station, Va. Corporal. Sergeant, May 1, 1865. Mustered out at Jeffersonville, Ind., July 8, 1865. Resided Belding, Mich.

Grasuait or **Gravereat, John**, Ontonagon County. Enlisted in Company A, Aug. 3, 1861, at Ontonagon, for 3 years, age 27. Transferred to Gun Boat service on Mississippi River, Feb. 15, 1862. Died Nov. 11, 1862. Buried in Mound City Cemetery, Ill.

Gray, Alphonse R. Drafted for 1 year, from Speaker, Sanilac County, age 40. Mustered Oct. 5, 1864. Assigned to Company K. Deserted at Jeffersonville, Ind., June 28, 1865.

Gray, William. Enlisted in Company F, Feb. 2, 1864, at Bloomfield, for 3 years, age 26. Discharged July 8, 1865. Resided Detroit.

Green, Andrew, Ionia County. Enlisted in Company B, Aug. 2, 1861, at Ionia, for 3 years, age 19. Discharged Dec. 3, 1862.

Green, Cordelle B., Saginaw County. Enlisted in Company D, Sept. 13, 1861, at Detroit, for 3 years, age 17. Wounded in action at second Manassas, Aug. 30, 1862. Discharged at expiration of term of service at Petersburg, Va., Sept. 7, 1864.

Greenberry, Jones. Enlisted in Second Company Sharpshooters, March 26, 1864, at Bridgeport, for 3 years, age 24. Discharged at Detroit, Sept. 2, 1865.

Greene, Orville W. (Veteran), Ann Arbor. Enlisted in Company I, for 3 years. Mustered March 20, 1862. Wounded in action, shrapnel wound, head, at Malvern Hill, July 1, 1862. Wounded in action, back, at second Manassas, Aug. 30, 1862. Reenlisted Dec. 22, 1863, at Rappahannock Station, Va., age 22. Mustered out at Jeffersonville, Ind., July 8, 1865.

Greenhoe, Andrew J. (Veteran), Ionia County. Enlisted in Company B, Aug. 6, 1861, at Ionia, for 3 years, age 22. Reenlisted Dec. 22, 1863, at Rappahannock Station, Va. Sergeant March 1, 1865. Commissioned 2nd Lieutenant, July 7, 1865. Mustered out at Jeffersonville, Ind., July 8, 1865.

Greenhoe, Mathew, Ionia County. Enlisted in Company B, Aug. 6, 1861, at Ionia, for 3 years, age 20. Reported wounded in action Dec. 1863 and listed as absent, wounded. Discharged at expiration of term of service at Detroit, Aug. 17, 1864.

Greenman, Daniel. Enlisted in Company B, Aug. 2, 1861, at Ionia, for 3 years, age 21. Transferred to Company F. Deserted June 16, 1865.

Gridley, William H., Dearborn. Enlisted in First Company Sharpshooters attached to 16th Michigan, Oct. 10, 1861, at Detroit, for 3 years, age 24. Joined regiment at Hall's Hill, Va., Feb. 24, 1862. Wounded in action at Dabney's Mill, Feb. 6, 1865. Commissioned Adjutant July 14, 1865. Mustered out at Jeffersonville, Ind., July 8, 1865.

Grines or **Girmus, Gottlieb**. Enlisted in Second Company Sharpshooters, March 24, 1864, at Saginaw, for 3 years, age 18. Discharged for disability at Satterlee Hospital at West Philadelphia, May 24, 1865.

Griswold, Edward, Adrian. Enlisted in Company F, Lancers, Dec. 21, 1861, at Adrian, for 3 years, age 18. Transferred to Company I, 16th Michigan, Feb. 28, 1862. Deserted at Detroit, March 24, 1862.

Griswold, James R. Drafted for 1 year, from Allegan County, age 30. Mustered March 17, 1865. Assigned to Company C. Mustered out at Jeffersonville, Ind., July 8, 1865.

Griswold, William, Saginaw County. Enlisted in Company F, Aug. 6, 1861, at Plymouth, for 3 years, age 26. Transferred to Company D. Corporal. Wounded and missing in action at Gaines' Mill, June 27, 1862. Discharged for disability, Dec. 22, 1862.

Grubner, August. Enlisted in Company F, Aug. 7, 1861, at Plymouth, for 3 years, age 18. Transferred to Company E. Discharged for disability at Philadelphia, Dec. 4, 1862.

Grubner, Ferdinand. Enlisted in Company F, Aug. 7, 1861, at Plymouth, for 3 years, age 21. Transferred to Company E. Wounded in action at Gaines' Mill, June 27, 1862. Discharged for disability at Baltimore, Nov. 21, 1862.

Grubner, Gottlieb. Detroit. Enlisted in Company F, Aug. 6, 1861, at Plymouth, for 3 years, age 23. Transferred to Company E. Killed in action at Gaines' Mill, June 27, 1862.

Grudel, John. Enlisted April 20, 1864, at Houghton, for 3 years, age 21. No further record.

Guess, Stephen, Wayne County. Enlisted in Company F, Aug. 8, 1861, at Plymouth, for 3 years, age 23. Discharged for disability May 7, 1863.

Guild, William (also given as **George** or **Charles**), Alpena. Enlisted in Company D, March 5, 1864, at Alpena, for 3 years, age 40. Died at Washington, D.C., Nov. 3, 1864, of wounds received in action at Peeble's Farm, Sept. 30, 1864.

Guillotte, Charles F., Saginaw County. Enlisted in Company D, as Musician. Missing in action at Gaines' Mill, June 27, 1862. Discharged for disability Dec. 11, 1862.

Gunn, Stephen I. (Veteran). Enlisted in Company E, Aug. 13, 1861, at Detroit, for 3 years, age 19. Transferred to Company B. Reenlisted Dec. 24, 1863, at Rappahannock Station, Va. Supposedly wounded in action May 1863 or 1864, both years given in different publications; Gunn was listed among the Gettysburg wounded in Washington and Philadelphia hospitals in July 1863 newspaper article. Mustered out at Jeffersonville, Ind., July 8, 1865.

Gunther, John, Ontonagon County. Enlisted in Company A, as Corporal, Aug. 3, 1861, at Ontonagon, for 3 years, age 25. Wounded in action through lungs and chest, at second Manassas, Aug. 30, 1862. Discharged for disability at Washington, D.C., March 2, 1864.

Gurr or **Gunn, Henry**, Saginaw County. Enlisted in Company D, Sept. 14, 1861. Discharged Oct. 3, 1862.

Guthier or **Guthrie, George W.** Drafted for 1 year, from Locke, Ingham County, age 22. Mustered Sept. 27, 1864. Assigned to Company K. Discharged at Washington, D.C., May 30, 1865.

Guthrie, Sanford. Enlisted in Company C, Jan. 4, 1864, at Flint, for 3 years, age 18. Died at a field hospital near Fredericksburg, Va., May 20, 1864, of wounds received in action at Wilderness, May 7, 1864.

Guy or **Grey, Benjamin F.** Enlisted in Company F, Feb. 8, 1865, at Grand Rapids, for 1 year, age 18. Substitute for John Mulholland, drafted. Mustered out at Jeffersonville, Ind., July 8, 1865.

Gwinner, Gotlieb. Enlisted in regimental Band, Sept. 13, 1861, at Detroit, for 3 years, age 30. Mustered out Aug. 11, 1862.

Gwinner, Jacob. Enlisted in regimental Band as Leader, Sept. 13, 1861, at Detroit, for 3 years, age 22. Mustered out Aug. 11, 1862.

Haans, Valerian. Enlisted in Company C, Feb. 23, 1865, at Pokagon, Cass County, for 1 year, age 22. Substitute for John Stretch, drafted. Mustered out at Jeffersonville, Ind., July 8, 1865.

Hack or **Huck, Charles**, Detroit. Enlisted in Company G, Aug. 28, 1862, at Detroit, for 3 years, age 22. Joined regiment at Sharpsburg, Md., Oct. 30, 1862. Taken prisoner at Weldon Railroad, Petersburg, Va., Aug. 21, 1864. Died in prison at Salisbury, N.C., Jan. 14, 1865.

Hadden or **Hedden, Thomas**. Enlisted in Company E, March 28, 1865, at Port Huron, for 3 years, age 23. Substitute for Lewis Azeno, drafted. Discharged at Washington, D.C., June 13, 1865.

Hagar, Harvey, Walled Lake. Enlisted in Company B, Lancers, Dec. 30, 1861, at Walled Lake, for 3 years, age 24. Transferred to Company I, 16th Michigan, Feb. 28, 1862. Regiment's "Roll of Honor" lists him as killed in action, at Malvern Hill, July 1, 1862, while Michigan Adjutant-General's Dept. *Record of Service,* vol. 16 (1905) claims him discharged at expiration of term of service at Detroit, Jan. 16, 1865.

Haggadone or **Haggadorn, William**. Almont. Enlisted in Company K, Feb. 5, 1862, at

Almont, for 3 years, age 35. Wounded in action at Gaines' Mill, June 27, 1862. Transferred to Company D. Discharged at Philadelphia, Jan. 11, 1863, for wounds received in action.

Haggerty, James. Enlisted Feb. 1, 1864, at Detroit, for 3 years, age 31. No further record.

Haines, Jacob, Detroit. Enlisted in Company E, Dec. 16, 1862, at Detroit, for 3 years, age 18. Joined regiment near Falmouth, Va., Jan. 2, 1863. Reportedly lost an arm, "cut off," July 30, 1864, in Petersburg mine explosion, no detail given. Discharged on Surgeon's certificate of disability, Sept. 13, 1865.

Hall, George W., White Pigeon. Enlisted in Company D, Aug. 24, 1861, at White Pigeon, age 20. Killed in action at Gaines' Mill, June 27, 1862.

Hall, George W. Drafted for 1 year, from Bethany, Gratiot County, age 31. Mustered March 17, 1865. Assigned to Company K. Mustered out at Jeffersonville, Ind., July 8, 1865.

Hall or **Hale, Henry W**. Drafted March 15, 1865, for 1 year, from Nelson, Kent County, age 26. Assigned to Company G. Deserted at Jeffersonville, Ind., June 25, 1865.

Hall, James K., Hillsdale County. Enlisted in Company D. Mustered Aug. 24, 1861. Killed in action at Gettysburg, July 2, 1863.

Hall, Jeremiah or **Jerome**. Drafted for 1 year, from Yankee Springs, Barry County, age 44, March 1865. Assigned to Company C. Deserted at Jeffersonville, Ind., June 27, 1865.

Hall, John E., or **L.**, Redford. Enlisted in Company A, Lancers, Oct. 15, 1861, at Detroit, for 3 years, age 18. Transferred to Company K, 16th Michigan, Feb. 28, 1862. Taken prisoner at Hanover Court House, Va., May 27, 1862. Enlisted in Battery M, 5th U.S. Artillery, Oct. 29, 1862.

Hall, Theodore F. Enlisted in Company E, Aug. 15, 1861, at Detroit, for 3 years, age 19. Transferred to Company H. Transferred to Invalid Corps July 1, 1863.

Hall, William H. C. Drafted for 1 year, from Owosso, age 35. Mustered March 16, 1865. Assigned to Company B. Mustered out at Jeffersonville, Ind., July 8, 1865.

Haller or **Heiler, John**. Enlisted in Company I, March 24, 1865, at Detroit, for 1 year, age 21. Substitute for Emile Tapert, drafted. Mustered out at Jeffersonville, Ind., July 8, 1865.

Halstead, Elijah M. (Veteran), Saginaw County. Enlisted in Company D. Missing in action at Gaines' Mill, June 27, 1862. Returned to regiment Aug. 12, 1862. Reenlisted as Corporal Dec. 21, 1863, at Rappahannock Station, Va. Mustered out at Jeffersonville, Ind., July 8, 1865.

Halstead, Samuel. Reportedly an enlistee for 3 years in Company C, mustered in 1861, and wounded, hand, during 1862. Mustered out at expiration of term of service, Sept. 7, 1864.

Hamilton, Elliott A. or **Elias**, Grand Blanc. Enlisted in Company C, Jan. 24, 1865, at Sebewaing, Huron County, for 1 year, age 18. Substitute for Edison Beach, drafted. Discharged at Washington, D.C., May 30, 1865. Died in 1894.

Hamilton James. Enlisted in Second Company Sharpshooters, March 28, 1864, at Spaulding, for 3 years, age 26. Pardoned for deserting upon condition that he return to his Company and faithfully serve his term of enlistment and make good all time lost.

Hamilton, Joshua V. Enlisted in Company F, Aug. 3, 1861, at Plymouth, for 3 years, age 27. Transferred to Company E. No further record.

Handt, Stephen. Enlisted in Company A, Aug. 3, 1861, at Ontonagon, for 3 years, age 25. No further record.

Handy or **Hardy, George**. Enlisted in Company C, Jan. 4, 1864, at Flint, for 3 years, age 18. Killed in action at Laurel Hill–Spotsylvania, Va., May 8, 1864.

Hanford, Benjamin F. Drafted for 1 year, from California, Branch County, age 24. Mustered March 17, 1865. Assigned to Company C. Mustered out at Jeffersonville, Ind., July 8, 1865.

Hanggi, Nimrod, Ontonagon County. Enlisted in Company A, Aug. 3, 1861, at Ontonagon, for 3 years, age 25. Transferred to Company H. Dropped from rolls Feb. 28, 1863.

Hanggi, Otis. Enlisted in Company A, Jan. 27, 1864, at Ann Arbor, for 3 years, age 22. Died of disease at Washington, D.C., Nov. 11 or 15, 1864.

Harbuck, Charles. Enlisted in Company G, Aug. 21, 1861, at Detroit, for 3 years, age 20. Deserted at Detroit, Sept. 6, 1861.

Hardee or **Hardie, William**, Wayne County. Enlisted in Company B, as Sergeant, Aug. 10, 1861, at Ionia, for 3 years, age 42. Wounded in action at Gaines' Mill, June 27, 1862. Discharged for disability at Philadelphia, Nov. 26, 1862.

Hardick, William, Stillwater. Enlisted in Company I, Aug. 10, 1862, at Argentine, for 3 years, age 43. Joined regiment at Antietam, Md., Oct. 12, 1862. Discharged near Washington, D.C., May 29, 1865.

Hardwick, John (Veteran). Enlisted in Company F, Aug. 3, 1861, at Plymouth, for 3 years, age 18. Transferred to Company E. Reenlisted Dec. 21, 1863, at Rappahannock Station, Va. Reported taken prisoner Dec. 10, 1864, in raid on the Weldon Railroad. Returned to regiment Feb. 25, 1865. Mustered out at Jeffersonville, Ind., July 8, 1865.

Hardy, Edwin. Enlisted in regimental Band, Sept. 13, 1861, at Detroit, for 3 years, age 34. Mustered out Aug. 11, 1862.

Harig, Stephen, Ontonagon County. Enlisted in Company A, Aug. 3, 1861, at Ontonagon, for 3 years, age 25. Died of disease at Hall's Hill, Va., Jan. 5, 1862.

Harlin or **Hevlin, Isaac**. Enlisted in Company I, Feb. 27, 1865, at Highland, Oakland County, for 1 year, age 20. Substitute for Thomas Piersons, from Highland. Mustered out at Jeffersonville, Ind., July 8, 1865.

Harmon or **Herman, William**. Drafted March 15, 1865, for 1 year, from Byron, Kent County, age 41. Assigned to Company C. Mustered out at Jeffersonville, Ind., July 8, 1865.

Harrington, Orlan. Enlisted in Company I, March 29, 1865, at Ridgeway, Lenawee County, for 1 year, age 21. Substitute for James Linn, drafted. Mustered out at Jeffersonville, Ind., July 8, 1865.

Harrington, Samuel. Drafted March 15, 1865, for 1 year, from Cascade, Kent County, age 27. Assigned to Company I. Died of disease at Carver Hospital, Washington, D.C., June 1, 1865.

Harrington, Thomas, Ontonagon. Enlisted in Company A, Aug. 3, 1861, at Ontonagon, for 3 years, age 39. Discharged at expiration of term of service, Sept. 6, 1864.

Harris, Charles L., Macomb County. Enlisted in First Company Sharpshooters attached to 16th Michigan, Dec. 5, 1861, at Detroit, for 3 years, age 28. Joined regiment at Hall's Hill, Va., Feb. 14, 1862. Wounded in action at Peeble's Farm, Sept. 30, 1864. Discharged at expiration of term of service at Detroit, Feb. 6, 1865.

Harris, John, Moscow, Hillsdale County. Entered service in Company D, for 9 months. Substitute for A. B. Spencer, drafted. Joined regiment near Falmouth, Va., March 1863.

Discharged at expiration of term of service near Rappahannock Bridge, Va., Dec. 12, 1863.

Harris, Thomas, Wayne County. Enlisted in Company E, Sept. 6, 1861, at Detroit, for 3 years, age 28. Discharged at Washington, D.C., Oct. 6, 1862.

Hart, Edward, Porters Lake. Enlisted in Company D, April 27, 1864, at Houghton, for 3 years, age 27. Reported absent, wounded Nov. 1864. Died at Arlington, Va., March 24, 1865.

Hart, John. Enlisted in Company G, Sept. 10, 1861, at Ann Arbor, for 3 years, age 29. Corporal. Killed in action at Gettysburg, July 2, 1863.

Hartman, George, Ontonagon County. Enlisted in Company A, Aug. 3, 1861, at Ontonagon, for 3 years, age 25. Wounded and missing in action at Gaines' Mill, June 27, 1862. Returned to regiment Nov. 9, 1862. Discharged in Virginia, Nov. 14, 1862, on account of wounds received in action.

Harty or **Hearty, John S**. Canada. Enlisted in Company F, Feb. 6, 1864, at Saginaw, for 3 years, age 20. Captured and died of disease in prison at Andersonville, Ga., May 28 or June 12, 1864. Buried in National Cemetery at Andersonville, Grave No. 1910.

Harvell or **Haswell, Richard**. Enlisted in Company K, Jan. 25, 1865 at Charleston, Kalamazoo County, for 3 years, age 22. Substitute for Horace W. Clark, drafted. Corporal May 14, 1865. Mustered out at Jeffersonville, Ind., July 8, 1865. Resided Marcellus, Mich.

Harz or **Hartz, Frederick**, Ontonagon County. Enlisted in Company A, as Sergeant, Aug. 3, 1861, at Ontonagon, for 3 years, age 34. Wounded in action at Malvern Hill, July 1, 1862. Discharged for disability Nov. 16, 1862.

Haschor, Henry. Enlisted in Company I, Jan. 21, 1865, a substitute, at Grand Rapids, for 1 year, age 18. Deserted.

Haskins, Francis. Drafted March 15, 1865, for 1 year, from Odessa, Ionia County, age 25. Assigned to Company D. Mustered out at Jeffersonville, Ind., July 8, 1865.

Hass or **Haas, John**, White Pigeon. Enlisted in Company D, Aug. 24, 1861, at White Pigeon, age 18. Wounded and taken prisoner at Gaines' Mill, June 27, 1862. Died in the hands of the enemy, Richmond.

Hatfield, Nathaniel. Enlisted in Company B, Jan. 15, 1865, at North Star, Gratiot County, 3 years, age 21. Substitute for John F. Henry, drafted from North Star. Discharged at Jeffersonville, Ind., June 29, 1865.

Hathen, Warren. Enlisted in Company E, Aug. 17, 1861, at Detroit, for 3 years, age 25. Transferred to Company H. Died of wounds received in action at Gaines' Mill, June 27, 1862. Buried in National Cemetery at Philadelphia, Grave No. 8.

Hatherly, Joseph L. Drafted for 1 year, from Kingston, Tuscola County, age 37. Mustered March 17, 1865. Assigned to Company K. No further record.

Hattis, William, Ionia County. Enlisted in Company B, Aug. 6, 1861, at Ionia, for 3 years, age 43. Missing in action at Gaines' Mill, June 27, 1862. Discharged March 28, 1863.

Hatton, George. Enlisted in Company E, March 3, 1865, at Pontiac, for 3 years, age 32. Substitute for Thomas S. Skinner, drafted. Mustered out at Jeffersonville, Ind., July 8, 1865.

Hausler or **Housler** or **Gowsler, Gotlieb**, Ann Arbor. Enlisted in Company G, Sept. 10, 1861, at Ann Arbor, age 34. Killed in action at Gaines' Mill, June 27, 1862.

Hawkins, William. Enlisted in Company E, Aug. 13, 1861, at Detroit, for 3 years, age 43. No further record.

Hawksley, William H. Enlisted in Company A, Feb. 2, 1864, at Ann Arbor, for 3 years, age 21. Deserted at Ann Arbor, Feb. 12, 1864.

Hawley, James. Enlisted in Company F, Aug. 8, 1861, at Plymouth, for 3 years, age 31. Transferred to Company E. Killed in action at Gaines' Mill, June 27, 1862.

Hayden, Alexander. Enlisted in Company C, Jan. 21, 1865, at Watson, Allegan County for 2 years, age 18. Substitute for William McLoughland, drafted. Mustered out at Jeffersonville, Ind., July 8, 1865.

Hayes, Edmond, or **Edward**. Enlisted in Company G, Feb. 20, 1865, at Adrian, for 3 years, age 26. Discharged June 8, 1865.

Haynes, James B. Enlisted in Company K, March 28, 1865, at Ionia, for 1 year, age 18. Substitute for John C Houseman, drafted. Discharged at Detroit, June 15, 1865.

Haywood, Aaron L., Hadley. Enlisted in Company C as Corporal, July 30, 1861, at Flint, for 3 years, age 32. Discharged for disability at Detroit, Aug. 18, 1862. Resided Hadley.

Heald, Warren E., Ionia County. Enlisted in Company B, Aug. 5, 1861, at Ionia, for 3 years, age 22. Discharged for disability at Washington, D.C., Nov. 17, 1862.

Heath, Martin (Veteran), Saginaw County. Enlisted in Company D, Aug. 5, 1861, at East Saginaw, for 3 years, age 19. Reenlisted as Corporal Dec. 24, 1863, at Rappahannock Station, Va. Wounded in action at Bethesda Church–Cold Harbor, June 2, 1864. Sergeant May 1, 1865. Mustered out at Jeffersonville, Ind., July 8, 1865.

Heileg or **Heiley, Jacob**, Detroit. Enlisted in Company G, Sept. 15, 1862, at Detroit, for 3 years, age 29. Joined regiment at Sharpsburg, Md., Oct. 30, 1862. Wounded in action, ankle, Laurel Hill–Spotsylvania Court House, May 8, 1864. This soldier may also be listed as **Jacob Heeley** of Company G, who was reported missing in action at the Weldon Railroad, Petersburg, Va., Aug. 21, 1864. Heileg or Heily was discharged at Camp Chase, Ohio, June 16, 1865.

Heinburg, Helmburg, or **Himburg, Ferdinand**, Detroit. Enlisted in Company K, Jan. 19, 1864, at Detroit, for 3 years, age 30. Killed in action at Peeble's Farm, Sept. 30, 1864.

Heinlin, John. Enlisted in Company A, Feb. 12, 1864, at East Saginaw, for 3 years, age 19. Wounded in action at Petersburg, Va., June 23, 1864. Mustered out at Jeffersonville, Ind., July 8, 1865.

Heisa, Frederick (Veteran). Enlisted in Company F, Aug. 4, 1861, at Plymouth, for 3 years, age 33. Transferred to Company E. Paroled prisoner Aug. 1862. Reenlisted Dec. 21, 1863, at Rappahannock Station, Va. Wounded in action near Cold Harbor, June 7, 1864. Discharged at Camp Chase, Ohio, June 10, 1865.

Heisa, Martin (Veteran), Plymouth. Enlisted in Company F, Aug. 4, 1861, for 3 years, age 33. Mustered Sept. 7, 1861. Transferred to Company E. Reenlisted Dec. 21, 1863, at Rappahannock Station, Va. Wounded in action, right hand, withdrawal from Cold Harbor, June 7, 1864. Mustered out at Jeffersonville, Ind., July 8, 1865. Resided Negaunee, Mich.

Heisa, William, Plymouth. Enlisted in Company F, Aug. 3, 1861, for 3 years, age 35. Transferred to Company E. Missing near Antietam, Md., Oct. 9, 1862, but regiment's "Roll of Honor" states he died of disease in 1864, with no further record.

Heldrith, Alonzo S. Drafted March 15, 1865, for 1 year, from Sparta, Kent County, age 38.

Assigned to Company E. Mustered out at Jeffersonville, Ind., July 8, 1865.

Hemstead, James (Veteran), Genesee County. Enlisted in Company C, Aug. 1, 1861, at Flint, for 3 years, age 19. Reenlisted Dec. 24, 1863, at Rappahannock Station, Va. Corporal, May 31, 1865. Mustered out at Jeffersonville, Ind., July 8, 1865. Resided Flint, Mich.

Henasey, Cornelius. Drafted March 15, 1865, for 1 year, from Cascade, Kent County, age 28. Assigned to Company B. Discharged at Jeffersonville, Ind., June 29, 1865.

Hendee, Sherman H. Enlisted in Company K, March 27, 1865, at Liberty, Jackson County, for 1 year, age 17. Substitute for Jonathan Haines, drafted. Mustered out at Jeffersonville, Ind., July 8, 1865.

Henderson, John. Enlisted in Company F, March 21, 1865, at Detroit, for 3 years, age 19. Substitute for Walter C. Skiff, drafted. Mustered out at Jeffersonville, Ind., July 8, 1865.

Henderson, Martin, Ontonagon County. Enlisted in Company A, Aug. 3, 1861, at Ontonagon, for 3 years, age 33. John Berry wrote Henderson, a teamster, was hung by Rebel cavalrymen when he shot a Confederate officer during Mine Run campaign, Nov. 1863. But Michigan Adjutant-General's Dept. *Record of Service* (1905) states he died of disease at Washington, D.C., Nov. 8, 1863.

Hendrix or **Hardie, Charles**. Enlisted in Company B, Feb. 3, 1864, at Bridgeport, for 3 years, age 43. Discharged for disability at Philadelphia, Dec. 10, 1864.

Hennessy, John F., Kent County. Enlisted in First Company Sharpshooters attached to 16th Michigan, Jan. 8, 1862, at Grand Rapids, for 3 years, age 27. Joined regiment at Hall's Hill, Va., Feb. 14, 1862. Discharged for disability near Falmouth, Va., April 7, 1863.

Henry, Christian. Drafted for 1 year, from Brady, Kalamazoo County, age 46. Mustered March 15, 1865. Assigned to Company I. Mustered out at Jeffersonville, Ind., July 8, 1865.

Henry, William, or **Williams, Henry**. Enlisted in Company C, March 3, 1865, at Pontiac, for 3 years, age 20. Substitute for Joseph A. Durkee, drafted. Reported as absent, wounded in June 1865 and died at Carver Hospital, Washington, D.C., June 16, 1865.

Henskee, Charles, Plymouth. Enlisted in Company F, Aug. 3, 1861, for 3 years, age 40. Transferred to Company E. Taken prisoner at Mine Run, Va., Nov. 27, 1863. Reportedly discharged at expiration of term of service at Weldon Railroad, Petersburg, Va., Nov. 29, 1864.

Henstelbeck, Henry, Eagle River. Enlisted in Company H, Aug. 6, 1861, age 38. Wounded in action at Gaines' Mill, June 27, 1862. Discharged for disability near Falmouth, Va., March 21, 1863.

Herot or **Herst, Robert**. Drafted for 1 year, from Ovid, Branch County, age 32. Mustered March 17, 1865. Assigned to Company G. Mustered out at Jeffersonville, Ind., July 8, 1865. Resided Bronson.

Herrick, Elijah, Rochester, N.Y. Enlisted in Company C, Feb. 22, 1862, at Detroit, for 3 years, age 18. Deserted April 30, 1862.

Hesler, Christ. Drafted March 15, 1865, for 1 year, from Courtland, Kent County, age 28. Assigned to Company C. Mustered out at Jeffersonville, Ind., July 8, 1865.

Hess, Joseph, Amboy. Drafted Feb. 10, 1863, for 9 months, from Amboy, Hillsdale County, age 31. Assigned to Company D, Joined regiment near Falmouth, Va., March 18, 1863. Discharged at expiration of term of service, Nov. 11, 1863.

Hesse, Augustus. Enlisted in Company E, Aug. 13, 1861, at Detroit, for 3 years, age 36. Deserted at Detroit, Sept. 9, 1862.

Hessler, Christian (Veteran), Detroit. Enlisted in Company A, Aug. 25, 1862, at Detroit, age 25. Joined regiment at Antietam, Md., Oct. 26, 1862. Reenlisted Dec. 21, 1863, at Rappahannock Station, Va. Wounded in action, right shoulder, June 2, 1864, at Bethesda Church. Corporal, May 1, 1865. Mustered out at Jeffersonville, Ind., July 8, 1865.

Hesterbar, Henry. Enlisted in Company F, Aug. 9, 1861, at Plymouth, for 3 years, age 38. No further record.

Hetsler or **Hetzler, Charles**, Utica. Enlisted in Company I, March 22, 1862, at Utica, for 3 years, age 22. Corporal. Wounded in action, hand, Wilderness, May 7, 1864. Discharged at expiration of term of service at Detroit, April 7, 1865.

Hetsler, Jefferson L., Utica. Enlisted in Company I, March 20, 1862, at Utica, for 3 years, age 25. Discharged for disability at Detroit, July 1, 1863.

Hett or **Hatt, John**. Enlisted in Company G, Sept. 10, 1861, at Detroit, for 3 years, age 40. Discharged for disability at David's Island, New York Harbor, Oct. 1862.

Hewlett, Ephraim H., Adrian. Enlisted in Company F, Aug. 8, 1861, at Plymouth, for 3 years, age 25. Transferred to Company B, June 1862. Wounded and taken prisoner at Gaines' Mill, June 27, 1862. Died at Annapolis, Md., Oct. 11, 1862.

Heydlauff, Gotlieb (Veteran), Ionia County. Enlisted in Company B, Aug. 3, 1861, at Ionia, for 3 years, age 23. Reenlisted Dec. 24, 1863, at Rappahannock Station, Va. Corporal, May 17, 1865. Mustered out at Jeffersonville, Ind., July 8, 1865.

Hicks, Edgar G., Argentine, Genesee County. Enlisted in Company I, Aug. 9, 1862, at Argentine, for 3 years, age 39. Joined regiment at Antietam, Md., Oct. 12, 1862. Discharged near Falmouth, Va., Jan. 15, 1863.

Higgins, Owen M., Macomb County. Enlisted in First Company Sharpshooters attached to 16th Michigan, Dec. 3, 1861, at Detroit, for 3 years, age 21. Joined regiment at Hall's Hill, Va., Feb. 14, 1862. Discharged at Antietam, Md., Oct. 25, 1862.

Higgins, Patrick. Enlisted in Company D, Feb. 6, 1864, at Saginaw, age 39. Listed as absent wounded, Nov. 1864. Transferred to Veteran Reserve Corps March 25, 1865. Discharged on Surgeon's certificate of disability at Washington, D.C., March 17, 1865. Died March 27, 1892. Buried at Saginaw.

Higgins, William, Saginaw County. Enlisted in Company D, Aug. 5, 1861, at East Saginaw, for 3 years, age 18. Wounded in action, head, at Gettysburg, July 2, 1863. Discharged at expiration of term of service at Detroit, Sept. 17, 1864.

Hill, Edward, Detroit. Entered service in Company D, Lancers, at organization as 1st Lieutenant, Oct. 16, 1861, at Detroit, for 3 years, age 27. Mustered out at Detroit, March 20, 1862. Reentered service in Company K, 16th Michigan at Company organization as 2nd Lieutenant; commissioned 1st Lieutenant, July 29, 1862. Wounded in action at second Manassas, Aug. 30, 1862. Commissioned Captain, Company H, April 17, 1863. Transferred to Company K, Oct. 1, 1863. Wounded in action at Bethesda Church–Magnolia Swamp, Va., June 1, 1864. Unable to serve with the regiment in the field, he was commissioned Major, Sept. 30, 1864, and Lieutenant Colonel, May 8, 1865. Rejoined the regiment near Washington, D.C. Division

Inspector, June 1865. Discharged at Jeffersonville, Ind., July 1, 1865. Awarded the Medal of Honor Dec. 14, 1893, for distinguished gallantry in action near Cold Harbor, June 1, 1864.

Hillaker or **Hallaker, John A.**, Greenbush. Enlisted in Company H, Aug. 20, 1861. Bugler. Deserted at Detroit, Jan. 31, 1862.

Hillard or **Hilliard, Charles M.** Enlisted in Company F, Aug. 8, 1861, at Plymouth, for 3 years, age 24. Transferred to Company G. Wounded in action, leg, at Gettysburg, July 2, 1863. Corporal. Discharged at expiration of term of service at Petersburg, Va., Sept. 7, 1864. Resided Lansing, Mich.

Hilliard, Lee. Enlisted in Company G, Sept. 10, 1861, at Detroit, for 3 years, age 23. Captured, probably in the Seven Days' battles; paroled Aug. 1862. Discharged at expiration of term of service at Petersburg, Va., Sept. 7, 1864.

Hilliker, Loren W., Williamston. Enlisted in Company K, Feb. 10, 1863, at Williamston, for 9 months, age 18. Substitute for Simon Howe, drafted. Listed in newspaper with Gettysburg wounded, in the side, July 1863, Philadelphia. Discharged at expiration of term of service at Kelly's Ford, Va., Nov. 21, 1863. Reentered service in Company K, 14th Michigan Infantry, March 1, 1864, at Williamston for 3 years. Discharged at Jefferson Barracks, Mo., Aug. 21, 1865, for wounds received in action at Chattahoochee River, Ga., July 5, 1864.

Hilsendegen, John H. (Veteran), Detroit. Enlisted in Company F, Oct. 3, 1862, at Detroit, age 18. Joined regiment at Antietam, Md., Oct. 30, 1862. Reenlisted Dec. 21, 1863, at Rappahannock Station, Va. Died at Washington, D.C., Nov. 6, 1864, of wounds received in action at Peeble's Farm, Sept. 30, 1864.

Hilsinger, John, Wayne County. Enlisted in Company A, Sept. 10, 1861, at Detroit, for 3 years, age 42. Killed in action at Gaines' Mill, June 27, 1862.

Hilton, George W., Genesee County. Enlisted in Company C, Aug. 4, 1861, at Flint, for 3 years, age 26. Wounded in action, head, at Gaines' Mill, June 27, 1862. Sergeant. Wounded in action, severely in head, Middleburg, Va., June 21, 1863. Discharged on Surgeon's certificate of disability at Washington, D.C., April 12, 1864. Resided Flint, Mich.

Hilton, Roswell N., Genesee County. Enlisted in Company C, Aug. 4, 1861, at Flint, for 3 years, age 21. Wounded in action at Malvern Hill, July 1, 1862. Discharged Nov. 13, 1862, at David's Island, New York Harbor, for wounds.

Hinds, John. Enlisted in Second Company Sharpshooters, April 28, 1864, at Vernon, for 3 years, age 19. Discharged at Washington, D.C., June 7, 1865.

Hinkley, Andrew J., Plymouth. Enlisted in Company F, Aug. 8, 1861, at Plymouth, for 3 years, age 24. Killed in action at Gaines' Mill, June 27, 1862.

Hirschman, Martin, Plymouth. Enlisted in Company F, Aug. 3, 1861, for 3 years, age 40. Transferred to Company E. Discharged for disability at Detroit, Dec. 31, 1862, for wounds received in action, left ankle, but no date given.

Hodge, Henry W., Disco. Enlisted in Company E, as Sergeant, Aug. 13, 1861, at Detroit, for 3 years, age 22. Wounded and missing in action at Gaines' Mill, June 27, 1862. Died at Washington, D.C., June 17, 1864, of wounds received in action at near Bethesda Church–Cold Harbor, June 3, 1864.

Hodge, James. Drafted for 1 year, from Watervliet, Berrien County, age 27. Mustered Sept. 27,

1864. assigned to Company I. Discharged at Washington, D.C., May 30, 1865.

Hodge, John M., Ionia County. Enlisted in Company B, Aug. 5, 1861, at Ionia, for 3 years, age 22. Discharged for disability at Detroit July 26, 1862.

Hodges, Arthur M. (Veteran), Livingston County. Enlisted in Company C, Aug. 2, 1861, at Flint, for 3 years, age 24. Reenlisted Dec. 24, 1863, at Rappahannock Station, Va. Wounded in July 1864 in the siege of Petersburg. Corporal April 1, 1865. Absent with leave at muster out of his company, July 8, 1865.

Hodgkins, John, Lapeer. Enlisted in Company K, Feb. 5, 1862, at Almont, for 3 years, age 29. Transferred to Company D. Discharged Aug. 1862.

Hoeninghausen, Theodore. Enlisted in Company E, Jan. 23, 1864, at Detroit, for 3 years, age 18. Bugler. Mustered out at Jeffersonville, Ind., July 8, 1865. Died at Detroit, July 25, 1902.

Hogan, William. Enlisted March 31, 1864, at Ovid, for 3 years, age 24. No further record.

Hohman, Frederick, Detroit. Enlisted in Company K, March 27, 1862, at Detroit, for 3 years, age 33. Discharged for disability at Kelly's Ford, Va., Oct. 29, 1863.

Hollis, Hiram. Enlisted in Company A, Aug. 3, 1861, at Ontonagon, for 3 years, age 20. Transferred to Company G, May 1862. Corporal. Discharged at Falmouth, Va., Feb. 27, 1863.

Hollister, James M., Utica. Enlisted in Company H, Lancers, Dec. 10, 1861, at Utica, for 3 years, age 20. Transferred to Company I, 16th Michigan Infantry, Feb. 28, 1862. Discharged for disability Dec. 1862.

Hollister, Thomas J., Utica. Enlisted in Company I, March 20, 1862, at Utica, for 3 years, age 22. Transferred to Invalid Corps July 1, 1863.

Holloran, Michael, Wayne. Enlisted in Company E, Sept. 12, 1861, at Detroit, for 3 years, age 35. Transferred to Invalid Corps July 1, 1863.

Holmes, Morsena, Deerfield. Enlisted in Company G, Feb. 24, 1863, at Deerfield, for 3 years, age 22. Joined regiment near Falmouth, Va., March 1863. Mustered out at Jeffersonville, Ind., July 8, 1865.

Holsted, Samuel, Hillsdale County. Enlisted in Company C, Aug. 24, 1861, at Hillsdale, for 3 years, age 25. Wounded in action in 1862. Discharged at expiration of term of service at Petersburg, Va., Sept. 7, 1864. Resided Cedar Falls, Mich.

Hoof, John. Drafted for 1 year, from Salem, Allegan County, age 34. Mustered March 17, 1865. Assigned to Company B. Mustered out at Jeffersonville, Ind., July 8, 1865.

Hopkins, John S., Ottawa County. Enlisted in First Company Sharpshooters attached to 16th Michigan, Oct. 25, 1861, at Detroit, for 3 years, age 21. Joined regiment at Hall's Hill, Va., Feb. 14, 1862. Discharged for disability Dec. 1862. Died Dec. 14, 1862.

Hopkins, Lorenzo, Argentine. Enlisted in Company I, Aug. 9, 1862, at Argentine, for 3 years, age 30. Joined regiment at Antietam, Md., Oct. 12, 1862. Wounded in action June 1863. Deserted July 31, 1863.

Hopkins, Oliver J., Macomb County. Enlisted in Company E, Aug. 13, 1861, at Detroit, for 3 years, age 23. Transferred to Company C. Discharged for disability at Hall's Hill, Va., Feb. 24, 1862.

Hopkins, Orrin K., St. Clair County. Enlisted in First Company Sharpshooters attached to 16th Michigan, Oct. 5, 1861, at Detroit, for 3 years, age 26. Joined regiment at Hall's Hill,

Va., Feb. 14, 1862. Wounded in action Malvern Hill, July 1, 1862. Wounded accidentally in camp near Fredericksburg, Va., spring 1863. Discharged for disability at Washington, D.C., Aug. 3, 1863.

Hopkins, Thomas, Jr., Argentine. Enlisted in Company I, Aug. 9, 1862, at Argentine, for 3 years, age 33. Joined regiment at Antietam, Md., Oct. 12, 1862. Corporal. Discharged near Falmouth, Va., March 5, 1863.

Hopper, Edward. Drafted for 1 year, from Hartland, Livingston County, age 26. Mustered March 29, 1865. Assigned to Company D. Mustered out at Jeffersonville, Ind., July 8, 1865.

Horan or **Hooraen, Michael F.**, Houghton County. Enlisted in Company A, May 10, 1864, at Saginaw, for 3 years, age 27. Corporal. Died at Washington, D.C., July 7, 1864, of wounds received before Petersburg, Va., June 23, 1864.

Horton, Benjamin. Drafted for 1 year, from Flowerfield, St. Joseph County, age 32. Mustered March 16, 1865. Assigned to Company I. Mustered out at Jeffersonville, Ind., July 8, 1865.

Horton, James. Enlisted in Second Company Sharpshooters, March 28, 1864, at Frankenmuth, for 3 years, age 18. Mustered out at Jeffersonville, Ind., July 8, 1865.

Horton. Thomas. Enlisted in Company F, Aug. 9, 1861, at Plymouth, for 3 years, age 30. No further record.

Hosford, Edgar, Hubbardston. Enlisted in Company H, Aug. 14, 1861, at Detroit, for 3 years, age 24. Discharged at Harrison's Landing, Va., July 8, 1862.

Hoskins, Franklin S., Flushing. Enlisted in Company C, as Corporal, July 30, 1861, at Flint, for 3 years, age 19. Died of disease at Alexandria, Va., Oct. 26, 1862.

Hough, Alvin. Reported in regiment's "Roll of Honor" to be a private in the First Company Sharpshooters, wounded in action during the Overland Campaign, May 1864. No report of discharge.

Hough, James, Jr., Detroit. Enlisted in Company A, 1st Michigan Infantry, April 18, 1861, at Detroit, for 3 months, age 21. Mustered out at Detroit, Aug. 7, 1861. Reentered service in Company E, 16th Michigan as 1st Sergeant, Aug. 13, 1861. Commissioned 2nd Lieutenant, Aug. 30, 1862. Wounded in action at second Manassas, Aug. 30, 1862. Transferred to Invalid Corps June 29, 1863. Discharged for disability June 27, 1863.

Hough, Joseph A. Enlisted in Company B, Jan. 24, 1864, at Flint, for 3 years, age 38. Discharged at Washington, D.C., July 6, 1865.

Hough, Warren J. Enlisted in Company D, Aug. 3, 1861, at East Saginaw, for 3 years, age 26. Deserted at Detroit.

House, Peter. Drafted for 1 year, from Fremont, Sanilac County, age 30. Mustered Feb. 9, 1865. Assigned to Company C. Wounded in action March (25?) 1865—likely at second Hatcher's Run, Va. Died at City Point, Va., April 1865.

Howard, John B. Enlisted in Company E, Aug. 17, 1861, at Detroit, for 3 years, age 29. Reported in Company G, June 1, 1862. Sergeant. Discharged July 5, 1862.

Howard, William H. Enlisted in Company I, Feb. 21, 1865, at Bloomfield, Oakland County, for 3 years, age 25. Substitute for Daniel Whitefield, drafted. Mustered out at Jeffersonville, Ind., July 8, 1865.

Howarth, John W., Montcalm. Enlisted in Company B, Aug. 7, 1861, at Ionia, for 3 years, age

20. Transferred to Invalid Corps. Discharged at expiration of term of service at Washington, D.C., Aug. 12, 1864, from Company F, 19th Regiment, Veteran Reserve Corps. Resided Bloomer, Mich.

Howarth, Joseph S., Bushnell. Enlisted in Company B, Dec. 27, 1861, at Ionia, for 3 years, age 22. Died of disease at Washington, D.C., Nov. 5, 1862.

Hower, Adam. Drafted for 1 year, from Ovid, Branch County, age 37. Mustered March 17, 1865. Assigned to Company G. Mustered out at Jeffersonville, Ind., July 8, 1865.

Hoyt, Samuel, Ionia County. Enlisted in Company B, Aug. 6, 1861, at Ionia, for 3 years, age 24. Wounded in action and taken prisoner at Gaines' Mill, June 27, 1862. Paroled Aug. 1862. Discharged at Philadelphia, Aug. 22, 1864.

Hubbard, Alanson, Midland. Enlisted in Company D, Sept. 10, 1861, at East Saginaw, age 25. Killed in action at Gaines' Mill, June 27, 1862.

Hubbard, Alexander (Veteran). Midland County. Enlisted in Company D, mustered Sept. 14, 1861, probably age 19. Missing in action at Gaines' Mill, June 27, 1862. Reenlisted as Corporal Dec. 21, 1863, at Rappahannock Station, Va., age 21. Wounded in neck in action June 7, 1864, near Cold Harbor. Died from wound March 5, 1865.

Hubbard, David. Enlisted in Company F, Jan. 24, 1864, at Montrose, for 3 years, age 26. Wounded in action, Feb. 1865, likely at Dabney's Mill, Va. Discharged at Philadelphia, June 13, 1865.

Hubbard or **Hurbert, Levi W.**, Saginaw. Enlisted in Company K, Feb. 1864, at Saginaw, for 3 years, age 48. Entered Satterlee Hospital, Philadelphia, Sept. 1, 1864. No further record.

Huckleberry, John, Ionia County. Enlisted in Company B, Aug. 5, 1861, at Ionia, for 3 years, age 18. Discharged at New York, Jan. 12, 1863.

Huff or **Hough, Alvin**. Enlisted in First Company Sharpshooters attached to 16th Michigan, Feb. 15, 1864, at Saginaw, for 3 years, age 25. Wounded in action July 1864, Petersburg, Va. No further record.

Hughes, James, New Hudson. Enlisted in Company B. Lancers, Oct. 24, 1861, at New Hudson, for 3 years, age 30. Transferred to Company I, 16th Michigan, Feb. 28, 1862. Deserted at Detroit, March 24, 1862.

Hughes, Thomas. Enlisted in Company G, Feb. 16, 1865, at Bloomfield, Oakland County, for 3 years, age 40. Substitute for Lucien D. Jenks, drafted. Deserted May 17, 1865.

Hughes, Thomas F., Detroit. Entered service in Company H, as 1st Lieutenant, Aug. 9, 1861. Commissioned Captain, Company K, Dec. 11, 1862. Wounded in action at Fredericksburg, Va., Dec. 13, 1862. Discharged Aug. 15, 1863, to accept appointment as 1st Lieutenant in Invalid Corps. Resigned Oct. 27, 1863.

Hulinguist or **Holliguist, Charles A. M.** Enlisted in Company I, March 28, 1865, at Port Huron, for 1 year, age 28. Substitute for Maynard Hogadone, drafted. Mustered out at Jeffersonville, Ind., July 8, 1865.

Hull, Sanford (Veteran), Jackson. Enlisted in Company F, Aug. 8, 1861, at Plymouth, for 3 years, age 23. Wounded in action at Gaines' Mill, June 27, 1862. Reenlisted Dec. 21, 1863, at Rappahannock Station, Va. Corporal April 1, 1865. Mustered out at Jeffersonville, Ind., July 8, 1865. Buried at North Star, Mich.

Hull, William E., Oakland County. Enlisted in First Company Sharpshooters attached to 16th Michigan, as Corporal, Oct. 8, 1861, at Detroit, for 3 years, age 27. Deserted at Detroit, Feb. 3, 1862.

Humiston, Henry. Enlisted in Company G, Feb. 10, 1863, at Flint, for 3 years, age 35. Discharged for disability April 22, 1863.

Humphrey, Richard, Howell. Entered service in the regiment as substitute for Philo B. Curtis, drafted Feb. 13, 1863, for 9 months, from Howell. No further record.

Hunt, Charles. Enlisted in Second Company Sharpshooters, April 27, 1864, at Spaulding, for 3 years, age 26. Deserted at Saginaw, May 3, 1864.

Hunt, William B. Enlisted in Company G, at White Pigeon, for three years, Aug. 18, 1861, age 18. Killed in action, Gettysburg, July 2, 1863.

Hunter, Edwin R. Kent County. Enlisted in Company B, Aug. 8, 1861, at Ionia, for 3 years, age 21. Paroled prisoner at Annapolis, Md., Aug. 1862. Transferred to U.S. Army.

Hunter, Frank. Enlisted in Company F, March 28, 1865, at Liberty, Jackson County, for 3 years, age 19. Substitute for Henry Rhodes, drafted. No further record.

Huston, Dwight, Plymouth. Enlisted in Company E, as Corporal, Aug. 18, 1861, for 3 years, age 24. Corporal. Sergeant Aug. 30, 1862. Died of disease at Fortress Monroe, Va., Sept. 20, 1862.

Hutten, Wilfred. Enlisted in Company I, Feb. 24, 1865, at Port Huron, for 3 years, age 24. Substitute for Herman W. Stevens, from Port Huron. Mustered out at Jeffersonville, Ind., July 8, 1865.

Hynes or **Haynes, Stephen**. Drafted March 15, 1865, for 1 year, from Wyoming, Kent County, age 39. Assigned to Company A. Mustered out at Jeffersonville, Ind., July 8, 1865.

Ingham, Albert A., Saginaw County. Enlisted in Company C, as Corporal, Aug. 2, 1861, at Flint, for 3 years, age 26. Sergeant Dec. 25, 1861. Wounded and taken prisoner Gaines' Mill, June 27, 1862. Exchanged, and discharged at Philadelphia, Sept. 9, 1862.

Irving, James. Enlisted in Second Company Sharpshooters, April 30, 1864, at Saginaw, for 3 years, age 30. Deserted Aug. 8, 1864.

Ish, James N., Hillsdale County. Enlisted in Company D and mustered Aug. 24, 1861. Discharged Feb. 26, 1863.

Isham, Lester B., Wayne County. Enlisted in Company C, Aug. 17, 1861. Killed in action at Gaines' Mill, June 27, 1862.

Jacka, John, East Saginaw. Enlisted in Company A, Feb. 12, 1864, at East Saginaw, for 3 years, age 34. Wounded in foot in action at Peeble's Farm, Sept. 30, 1864. Entered hospital Nov. 28, 1864. Discharged at Satterlee U.S. Hospital, West Philadelphia, June 9, 1865. Died July 5, 1901, buried at Saginaw.

Jacklin, Rufus W., Detroit. Enlisted in First Company Sharpshooters attached to 16th Michigan as 1st Sergeant, Feb. 1, 1862, at Detroit, for 3 years, age 20. Joined regiment at Hall's Hill, Va., Feb. 14, 1862. Commissioned 2nd Lieutenant, May 18, 1862. Commissioned 1st Lieutenant and Adjutant, Nov. 1, 1862. Taken prisoner at Laurel Hill, May 8, 1864. Rescued by Custer's Brigade May 9, 1864. Returned to regiment May 25, 1864. Commissioned Captain, Company D, June 22, 1864. Commissioned Major May 8, 1865. Brevet Major, U.S. Volunteers, March 13, 1865, for gallant and meritorious services. Discharged at Jeffersonville, Ind., July 1, 1865.

Jackson, Lewis. Enlisted in Company H, March 28, 1865, at Detroit, for 1 year, age 20. Substitute for Patrick McGraw, drafted. Mustered out at Jeffersonville, Ind., July 8, 1865.

Jacobs, George A. Enlisted Jan. 29, 1864, at Saginaw, for 3 years, age 26. No further record.

Jacobs, Henry. Drafted for 1 year, from Climax, age 32. Mustered March 15, 1865. Assigned to Company C. Mustered out at Jeffersonville, Ind., July 8, 1865.

Jacobs, William. Enlisted in Second Company of Sharpshooters, April 27, 1864, at East Saginaw, for 3 years, age 28. Deserted at Saginaw, May 3, 1864.

Jacobs, William E., Flushing. Enlisted in Company K, March 26, 1862, at Detroit, for 3 years, age 22. Discharged for disability at Fortress Monroe, Va., March 22, 1863.

Jardine, George, Saginaw. Entered service in Company F, Lancers, at organization, as Captain, Nov. 18, 1861, at Detroit, for 3 years, age 37. Mustered out at Detroit, March 20, 1862. Reentered service in Second Company Sharpshooters for the 16th Michigan at organization, as Captain, at Saginaw. Commissioned May 1, 1864. Discharged April 4, 1865.

Jellman or **Jellener, William**. See **Gelenaw, William**.

Jenker or **Jonke, Henry**, Detroit. Enlisted in Company H, Lancers, Dec. 10, 1861, at Detroit, for 3 years, age 25. Transferred to Company I, 16th Michigan, Feb. 28, 1862. Wounded in action at Gaines' Mill, June 27, 1862. Discharged at Antietam, Md., Oct. 2, 1862. Died Nov. 18, 1898. Buried at Mt. Clemens.

Jenkins, Charles. Enlisted March 9, 1863, at Locke, for 3 years, age 27. Substitute for James McKie, drafted for 9 months. No further record.

Jenkins, William A. Enlisted in Second Company Sharpshooters March 30, 1864, at Saginaw, for 3 years, age 20. Corporal. Died in the field Oct. 1, 1864, of wounds received in action at Peeble's Farm, Sept. 30, 1864.

Jennings, Thomas J. Enlisted in regimental Band, Sept. 13, 1861, at Detroit, for 3 years, age 21. Mustered out Aug. 11, 1862.

Jevaux, Alexander. Enlisted in Second Company Sharpshooters, April 29, 1864, at Saginaw, for 3 years, age 25. Deserted at Saginaw, May 3, 1864.

Jewell, Charles H. (Veteran). Enlisted in Company C, Aug. 4, 1861, at Flint, for 3 years, age 18. Transferred to Company F. Reenlisted Dec. 21, 1863, at Rappahannock Station, Va. Mustered out at Jeffersonville, Ind., July 8, 1865.

Jewett, Wallace E., Saginaw. Enlisted in Company E, Lancers, as 1st Sergeant, Oct. 7, 1861, at Saginaw, for 3 years, age 21. Transferred to Company K, 16th Michigan, Feb. 28, 1862. Sergeant Major July 1, 1862. Commissioned 2nd Lieutenant, Company K, July 29, 1862. Commissioned 1st Lieutenant, Company H, Feb. 1, 1863. Acting Aide-de-Camp to Colonel commanding Third Brigade, First Division, Fifth Army Corps. Killed in action at Gettysburg, July 2, 1863. Interred in the National Cemetery there.

Johnson, Albert. Enlisted in Company B, Aug. 6, 1861, at Ionia, for 3 years, age 21. Transferred to Company C. Deserted at Detroit, Aug. 30, 1861.

Johnson, Charles. Enlisted in Company G, Feb. 2, 1865, at Putnam, for 3 years, age 28. Substitute for John R. Tibbits from Berlin. Mustered out at Jeffersonville, Ind., July 8, 1865.

Johnson, Elisha M. Drafted from Leonidas, age 37. Mustered March 16, 1865. Assigned to Company H. Mustered out at Jeffersonville, Ind., July 8, 1865.

Johnson, Hiram, Corunna. Enlisted in Company H, Aug. 10, 1861, at Detroit, for 3 years, age 22. Wounded in action at Gaines' Mill, June 27, 1862. Discharged for disability at Washington, D.C., Aug. 17, 1864.

Johnson, John H., Wheatfield, Ingham County. Enlisted in Company B, Lancers, Dec. 18, 1861, at Wheatfield, for 3 years, age 23. Transferred to Company I, 16th Michigan, Feb. 28, 1862. Killed in action at second Manassas, Aug. 30, 1862.

Johnson, Joseph or **Jacob**. Drafted March 15, 1865, for 1 year, from Grattan, age 25. Assigned to Company G. Mustered out at Jeffersonville, Ind., July 8, 1865.

Johnson, Orrin. Enlisted in Company B, Aug. 3, 1861, at Ionia, for 3 years, age 27. Transferred to Company C. Discharged for disability at Washington, D.C., May 11, 1862.

Johnson or **Johnston, Samuel** (Veteran), Detroit. Enlisted in Company E, Lancers, Nov. 19, 1861, at Bay City, for 3 years, age 36. Transferred to Company K, 16th Michigan, Feb. 28, 1862. Transferred to Company I. Reenlisted as Sergeant, Dec. 22, 1863, at Rappahannock Station, Va. Killed in action at Peeble's Farm, Sept. 30, 1864.

Johnson, Sears S. Drafted March 15, 1865, for 1 year, from Grattan, age 33. Assigned to Company G. No further record.

Johnson, William G. Enlisted in Company F, at Jackson, Sept. 24, 1864, age 22. Discharged for disability from Howard Hospital, Washington, D.C., July 1, 1865. Resided Muskegon, Mich.

Jones, Edmond F. Enlisted in Company D, March 14,1865, at Sanilac, for 1 year, age 18. Substitute for James H. Hunter, drafted. Mustered out at Jeffersonville, Ind., June 8, 1865.

Jordan, Jeremy T. or **Jeremiah F**. Enlisted in Company B, Jan. 28, 1865, at Polkton, for 1 year, age 33. Substitute for Amos Taylor, drafted. Mustered out at Jeffersonville, Ind., July 8, 1865.

Josefs or **Josephie, Oscar**, Detroit. Enlisted in Company A and mustered, June 30, 1863, at Detroit, for 3 years, age 19. Corporal. Wounded in action at Spotsylvania Court House May 18, 1864, and at Peeble's Farm, Sept. 30, 1864. Discharged at Wilmington, Del., May 31, 1865.

Joyce, Andrew J., Wayne County. Enlisted in Company E, Aug. 20, 1861, at Detroit, for 3 years, age 20. Wounded in action, right leg, Gettysburg July 2, 1863, later amputated. Discharged for disability at Baltimore, March 17, 1864.

Joyce, Thomas, Wayne County. Enlisted in Company H, as Sergeant, July 25, 1861, at Detroit, for 3 years. Discharged for disability at Yorktown, Va., April 21, 1862.

Judd, Edward. Enlisted in Company E, Lancers, Nov. 18, 1861, at Saginaw for 3 years, age 21. Transferred to Company K, 16th Michigan, Feb. 28, 1862. Discharged at Falmouth, Va., Dec. 24, 1862.

Kapp, Martin. Enlisted April 4, 1865, at Jackson, for 1 year, age 19. Discharged at Jackson, May 6, 1865.

Keel, Lewis E. B. or **Levi,** Lockport. Drafted for 1 year, from Lockport, St. Joseph County, age 27. Mustered March 16, 1865. Assigned to Company K, 16th Michigan. Mustered out at Jeffersonville, Ind., July 8, 1865.

Keeler, Frank D., East Saginaw. Enlisted in Company D, as Corporal, Aug. 1, 1861, at East Saginaw, for 3 years, age 20. Sergeant. Commissary Sergeant Nov. 3, 1862. Commissioned 2nd Lieutenant, Company E, April 26, 1863. Discharged at expiration of term of service, Sept. 10, 1864. Resided Saginaw.

Kehoe, John. Enlisted in Company C, Aug. 8, 1861, at Flint, for 3 years, age 22. Transferred to Company H. Died at York, Pa., Dec. 25, 1862, of wounds received in action at second Manassas, Sept. 30, 1862.

Keiffer, Christian, Wayne County. Enlisted in Company E, Sept. 6, 1861, at Detroit, for 3 years, age 33. Wounded in action, loss of left leg, at second Manassas, Aug. 30, 1863. Discharged for disability at Washington, D.C., Oct. 15, 1863.

Keiffer or **Kieff, Isaac**. Enlisted in Company F, Aug. 4, 1861, at Plymouth, for 3 years, age 21. Transferred to Company E, June 1862. Wounded in action at Gaines' Mill, June 27, 1862. Discharged for disability at Philadelphia, Feb. 6, 1863.

Keigler or **Kugler, John**, Detroit. Enlisted in Company K, Jan. 18, 1864, at Detroit, for 3 years, age 36. Died at Washington, D.C., Oct. 20, 1864, of wounds received in action at Peeble's Farm, Sept. 30, 1864.

Keilizher, James. Enlisted in Company H, Oct. 6, 1861, at Detroit, for 3 years, age 36. Deserted Oct. 11, 1861.

Kelley or **Kelly, James** (Veteran). Enlisted in Company F, Aug. 4, 1861, at Plymouth, for 3 years, age 22. Transferred to Company E. Wounded in action at Gettysburg, July 2, 1863. Reenlisted Dec. 21, 1863, at Rappahannock Station, Va. Mustered out at Jeffersonville, Ind., July 8, 1865.

Kelley or **Kelly, Peter** (Veteran), Houghton County. Enlisted in Company E, Aug. 16, 1861, at Detroit, age 22. Wounded in action at Gettysburg, July 2, 1863. Reenlisted as Sergeant Dec. 21, 1863, at Rappahannock Station, Va. Fatally wounded in left breast in action at Po River–Spotsylvania Court House, May 10, 1864, and died July 6, 1864, near Fredericksburg, Va.

Kelley or **Kelly, William F.**, Ransom. Enlisted in Company G, Aug. 19, 1861, at Hillsdale, age 48. Died at David's Island, New York Harbor, Aug. 1862, of wounds received in action at Malvern Hill, July 1, 1862. Buried in National Cemetery at Brooklyn, N.Y., Grave No. 221.

Kellogg, Rodney (Veteran), Ionia County. Enlisted in Company B, Aug. 10, 1861, at Ionia, for 3 years, age 39. Reenlisted Dec. 24, 1863, at Rappahannock Station, Va. Mustered out at Jeffersonville, Ind., July 8, 1865.

Kellogg, William J. Enlisted in Company C. Discharged for disability at Detroit, May 7, 1863.

Kelloher, John (Veteran). Enlisted in Company F, Aug. 6, 1861, at Plymouth, for 3 years, age 26. Transferred to Company E. Reenlisted Dec. 21, 1863, at Rappahannock Station, Va. Mustered out at Jeffersonville, Ind., July 8, 1865.

Kelly, Dennis A. Enlisted in Company F, Lancers, Nov. 5, 1861, at Marquette, for 3 years, age 25. Transferred to Company H, 16th Michigan, Feb. 28, 1862. Eventually deserted.

Kelly, Edward, Detroit. Enlisted in First Company Sharpshooters attached to 16th Michigan, Dec. 2, 1862, at Detroit, for 3 years, age 18. Joined regiment near Falmouth, Va., Jan. 2, 1863. Regiment's "Roll of Honor" lists him absent, wounded on Sept. 16, 1862, but this is an error and likely means 1863 or 1864. Taken prisoner while on picket Nov. 17, 1864, and reportedly escaped, returned to regiment Dec. 10, 1864. Mustered out at Jeffersonville, Ind., July 8, 1865.

Kelly, James or **John**. Enlisted in Company D, Feb. 3, 1864, at Saginaw, for 3 years, age 22. Discharged at West Philadelphia, June 9, 1865.

Kelly, Patrick. Enlisted in Company F, Feb. 25, 1865, for 3 years, age 27. Substitute for one Heinback, drafted from Park, St. Joseph County. No further record.

Kendall, Fischer, or **Fischer, Bendell**. Enlisted in Company K, March 29, 1862, at Detroit, for 3 years, age 24. Discharged at Yorktown, Va., May 4, 1862.

Kennedy, George. Enlisted in Company C, Jan. 4, 1864, at Flint, for 3 years, age 18. Wounded in action at Petersburg, Va., June 19, 1864. Mustered out at Jeffersonville, Ind., July 8, 1865.

Kennedy, Norman. Enlisted April 10, 1865, at Detroit, for 1 year, age 24. Discharged at Jackson, May 6, 1865.

Kennett, Edmund or **Edward**, North Plains. Enlisted in Company B, Aug. 6, 1861, at Ionia, for 3 years, age 25. Died at Hall's Hill, Va., Nov. 5, 1861.

Kennicott, Henry S., Keelerville. Enlisted in Company I, March 20, 1862, at Keelerville, for 3 years, age 29. Killed in action at second Manassas, Aug. 30, 1862.

Kent, Albert. Drafted March 15, 1865, for 1 year, from Caledonia, Kent County, age 21. Assigned to Company I. Discharged at Washington, D.C., June 23, 1865.

Kent, Stephen M. (Veteran), Flushing. Enlisted in Company K, as Corporal. March 22, 1862, at Detroit, for 3 years, age 21. Reenlisted Dec. 21, 1863, at Rappahannock Station, Va. Sergeant. Commissioned 2nd Lieutenant May 8, 1865. Commissioned 1st Lieutenant July 7, 1865. Mustered out at Jeffersonville, Ind., July 8, 1865. Resided Grand Rapids, Mich.

Kentner, Silas. Enlisted in Company F, Jan. 19, 1864, at Detroit, for 3 years, age 20. Discharged for disability at Philadelphia, Sept. 29, 1864.

Kenyon, Hazelton M. Enlisted in Company G, March 3, 1862. Discharged for disability at Washington, D.C., Jan. 12, 1863.

Kern, Charles, Ontonagon County. Enlisted in Company A, Sept. 4, 1861, at Detroit, for 3 years, age 42. Wounded and missing in action at Gaines' Mill, June 27, 1862. Discharged at expiration of term of service, Sept. 6, 1864.

Kerr, Malcolm. Enlisted in Company I, March 27, 1865, at Grattan, Kent County, for 1 year, age 28. Substitute for John Mooney, drafted. Mustered out at Jeffersonville, Ind., July 8, 1863.

Kerschner or **Kieshner, George** (Veteran). Enlisted in Company F, 1st Michigan Infantry, April 20, 1861, at Detroit, for 3 months, age 20. Mustered out at Detroit, Aug. 7, 1861. Reentered service, enlisting in Company G, 16th Michigan, Aug. 24, 1861. Wounded in action at Gaines' Mill, June 27, 1862. Reenlisted Dec. 21, 1863. Corporal April 1, 1865. Mustered out at Jeffersonville, Ind., July 8, 1865.

Kilets, George F., Lexington. Enlisted in Company K, 22nd Michigan, July 31, 1862, at Lexington, for 3 years, age 29. Mustered as 2nd Lieutenant Aug. 22, 1862. Discharged at Detroit, Sept. 3, 1862. Reentered service in Company E, 16th Michigan, Nov. 15, 1862, at Lexington. Joined regiment near Falmouth, Va., Jan. 2, 1863. Commissioned and mustered 1st Lieutenant, Company E, Jan. 20, 1864. Appointed Adjutant July 20, 1864. Commissioned Captain, Company I, July 16, 1864. Brevet Captain, U.S. Volunteers, July 6, 1864, for gallant and distinguished services at the battle of the Wilderness, and during the campaign before Richmond. Discharged for disability, March 14, 1865.

Killen, Nathaniel (Veteran). Enlisted in Company F, Aug. 4, 1861, at Plymouth, for 3 years, age 31. Transferred to Company E. Reenlisted Dec. 21, 1863, at Rappahannock Station, Va.

Corporal. Wounded in action, left breast, Petersburg, Va., June 23, 1864. Sergeant June 10, 1865. Mustered out at Jeffersonville, Ind., July 8, 1865. Died Oct. 13, 1899. Buried at Saginaw.

King, Andrew, Ontonagon County. Enlisted in Company A, Aug. 3, 1861, at Ontonagon, for 3 years, age 45. Michigan Adjutant-General's Dept. *Record of Service,* vol. 6 (1905), states King was discharged for disability at Hall's Hill, Va., Feb. 25, 1862, while the regiment's "Roll of Honor" reports him wounded in action at Gaines' Mill, June 27, 1862. Resided Soldiers' Home, Milwaukee, Wis.

King, Carlos B. Enlisted as corporal in Company B, Ionia for 3 years, age 19, Aug. 8, 1861. 1st sergeant, Dec. 23, 1863, Rappahannock Station, Va. Wounded in action, thigh, at Bethesda Church, June 1, 1864. Discharged Sept. 8, 1864 to accept commission as Captain, Company C, (reorganized) 3rd Michigan Infantry. Discharged for disability July 20, 1865. Murdered Sept. 23, 1871, while serving as marshal, Newton, Kans.

King, Dennis. Enlisted in Company I, March 21, 1865, at Detroit, for 1 year, age 42. Substitute for Patrick J. Melody, drafted. Mustered out at Jeffersonville, Ind., July 8, 1865.

King, Seth. Drafted March 15, 1865, for 1 year, from Brady, Kalamazoo County, age 33. Assigned to Company I. Mustered out at Jeffersonville, Ind., July 8, 1865.

King, Thomas. Enlisted in Company I, Feb. 27, 1865, at Assyria, Barry County, for 1 year, age 18. Substitute for William Horton, drafted. Corporal. Mustered out at Jeffersonville, Ind., July 8, 1865.

King, William R. Enlisted in Company G, Aug. 21, 1861, at Detroit, for 3 years, age 19. Deserted at Detroit, Nov. 6, 1861.

Kingsley, Guy. Enlisted in Company G, Aug. 5, 1861, at Detroit, for 3 years, age 21. Wounded in action, at Gettysburg, July 2, 1863. Discharged at expiration of term of service at Petersburg, Va., Sept. 7, 1864.

Kinne, Elliott B. Enlisted in Company K, March 23, 1865, at Leroy for 1 year, age 18. Substitute for William A. Davis, drafted. Mustered out at Jeffersonville, Ind., July 8, 1865. Resided Scottsville, Mich.

Kipp or **Tripp, Conrad** or **Coral**. Drafted for 1 year, from North Shade, Gratiot County, age 32. Mustered March 17, 1865. Assigned to Company F. Discharged for disability at Washington, D.C., June 8, 1865.

Kirby, Charles, Ann Arbor. Enlisted in Company A, Aug. 18, 1862, at Ann Arbor, for 3 years, age 25. Joined regiment near Falmouth, Va., Nov. 26, 1862. Discharged May 30, 1865.

Kitchen, Andrew, Saginaw County. Enlisted in Company D, May 13, 1864, at Saginaw, for 3 years, age 18. Reportedly wounded at Petersburg and died from wounds/disease at Point Lookout, Md., Nov. 9, 1864.

Kitchen, Jeremiah C., Detroit. Enlisted in Company H, Lancers, Oct. 5, 1861, at Detroit, for 3 years, age 26. Transferred to Company I, 16th Michigan, Feb. 28, 1862. Corporal. Color Guard July 1862. Killed in action at second Manassas, Aug. 30, 1862.

Klees, Peter. Drafted Dec. 29, 1864, for 1 year, from Ferris, Montcalm County, age 30. Assigned to Company I. Mustered out at Jeffersonville, Ind., July 8, 1865. Resided Sumner, Mich.

Kline, John W. Drafted March 16, 1865, for 1 year, from Bowne, Kent County, age 37. Assigned to Company E. Mustered out at Jeffersonville, Ind., July 8, 1865.

Knapp, Charles (Veteran), Genesee County. Enlisted in Company C, Aug. 8, 1861, at Flint, for 3 years, age 22. Reenlisted Dec. 24, 1863, at Rappahannock Station. Mustered out at Jeffersonville, Ind., July 8, 1865.

Knight, Seymour H. or **Samuel H.** Enlisted in Company G, Aug. 26, 1861, at Detroit, for 3 years, age 28. Listed as absent, wounded, and discharged at Washington, D.C., Dec. 13, 1862.

Knights, John. Enlisted in Company C, Aug. 7, 1861, at Flint, for 3 years, age 24. Transferred to Company G. Discharged at Washington, D.C., March 17, 1863. Died Oct. 5, 1899 and buried at Flint.

Knoth, Nicholas. Enlisted in Company H, Lancers, Dec. 28, 1861, at Detroit, for 3 years, age 40. Transferred to Company I, 16th Michigan, Feb. 28, 1862. Reported in Company K. Listed in 1863 casualties as absent, wounded, but no date given. Transferred to Veteran Reserve Corps Dec. 9, 1863. Discharged at expiration of term of service.

Know, Herman, Ontonagon County. Enlisted in Company A, Aug. 1, 1861, at Ontonagon, for 3 years, age 23. Discharged at expiration of term of service, Sept. 6, 1864.

Koblansky or **Koplansky, Julius**, Ontonagon County. Enlisted in Company A, Aug. 3, 1861, at Ontonagon, for 3 years, age 22. Killed in action at Gaines' Mill, June 27, 1862.

Koerner or **Komer, Simon**, Ontonagon County. Enlisted in Company A, as Musician, Aug. 3, 1861, at Ontonagon, for 3 years, age 25. Brigade Bugler, April 1863. Wounded in action at Rappahannock Station, Nov. 7, 1863. Reenlisted there Dec. 21, 1863. Mustered out at Jeffersonville, Ind., July 8, 1865. Died March 1902 and buried at Houghton, Mich.

Kohler, Michael, Ontonagon County. Enlisted in Company A, Aug. 3, 1861, at Ontonagon, for 3 years, age 28. Killed in action at Gaines' Mill, June 27, 1862.

Kohler, Mathias, Ontonagon County. Enlisted in Company A, Aug. 3, 1861, at Ontonagon, for 3 years, age 23. Wounded and taken prisoner at Gaines' Mill, June 27, 1862. Discharged at expiration of term of service, Sept. 6, 1864.

Kommers, Adolph (Veteran). Enlisted in Company A, as Corporal, Aug. 1, 1861, at Ontonagon, for 3 years, age 19. Wounded in action, Rappahannock Station, Va., Nov. 7, 1863. Reenlisted Dec. 21, 1863, at Rappahannock Station. Listed in newspaper in Washington hospital with Gettysburg wounded, July 1863. Wounded May 18, 1864, at Spotsylvania Court House. Sergeant May 15, 1865. Mustered out at Jeffersonville, Ind., July 8, 1865.

Kort, Anthony, Eagle Harbor. Enlisted in Company H, Aug. 6, 1861, age 35. Discharged for disability, June 27, 1865.

Korie, Stephen. Enlisted in Company E, Aug. 17, 1861, at Flint, for 3 years, age 40. Transferred to Company A. Wounded in action at Gaines' Mill, June 27, 1862. Discharged for disability at Providence, R.I., Jan. 12, 1863.

Koster, John (Veteran), Ontonagon County. Enlisted in Company A, Aug. 3, 1861, at Ontonagon, for 3 years, age 26. Reenlisted Dec. 21, 1863, at Rappahannock Station, Va. Wounded in action at Magnolia Swamp–Bethesda Church, June 1, 1864. Mustered out at Jeffersonville, Ind., July 8, 1865.

Kriest, Joseph. Enlisted in Company A, March 23, 1865, at Detroit, for 1 year, age 32. Substitute for Benton Crosby, drafted. Mustered out at Jeffersonville, Ind., July 8, 1865.

Kriser or **Kaiser, Peter**. Enlisted in Company A, March 23, 1864, at Houghton, for 3 years, age

26. Died Nov. 29, 1864, but no information given.

Kruger, Carl or **Charles** (Veteran), Detroit. Enlisted in Company F, Nov. 15, 1861, at Detroit, for 3 years, age 36. Joined regiment at Hall's Hill, Va., Jan. 11, 1862. Reported in Company G. Reenlisted Feb. 26, 1864, at Bealton, Va. Died May 28, 1864, at Baltimore of wounds received in action at Wilderness, May 7, 1864.

Kuehn, John (Veteran), Ontonagon County. Enlisted in Company A, Corporal, Aug. 3, 1861, at Ontonagon, for 3 years, age 25. Wounded in action at Gaines' Mill, June 27, 1862. Reenlisted Dec. 21, 1863, at Rappahannock Station, Va. Sergeant. Killed in action at Laurel Hill–Spotsylvania Court House, May 8, 1864.

Kugler, John. Reportedly enlistee in Company K, no date given. Wounded in action, shell wound in right thigh, at Peeble's Farm, Sept. 30, 1864. Died from wound Oct. 20, 1864, at Harwood Hospital, Washington, D.C.

Kydd, William, Detroit. Enlisted in Company A, 1st Michigan Infantry, April 18, 1861, at Detroit, for 3 months, age 22. Wounded and in Washington Hospital July 1861. Mustered out Aug. 7, 1861. Reentered service in Stockton's 16th Michigan as Sergeant Major, Aug. 12, 1861, at Detroit, for 3 years. Commissioned 2nd Lieutenant, Company C, Nov. 3, 1862. Assigned to Company G, Nov. 18, 1862. Commissioned 1st Lieutenant Nov. 3, 1862. Chief of Pioneers, Third Brigade, First Division, Fifth Army Corps, April 1864. Discharged at expiration of term of service, Sept. 7, 1864.

Lackey, James. Enlisted in Company F, Aug. 6, 1861, at Plymouth, for 3 years, age 40. Transferred to Company G, July 1862. Discharged for disability at Hall's Hill, Va., April 1862. Died Nov. 18, 1892.

Lackie, Thomas R. (Veteran), Detroit. Enlisted in Company E. Aug. 29, 1861. Wounded in action, left forearm, at Malvern Hill, July 1, 1862. Wounded in action, contusion to chest, at second Manassas, Aug. 30, 1862. Reenlisted Dec. 21, 1863, at Rappahannock Station, Va. Sergeant. Wounded in action, right shoulder, at Jericho Mills–North Ana River, May 23, 1864. Wounded in action, right leg and thigh by shell explosion, at Peeble's Farm, Sept. 30, 1864. Commissioned 2nd Lieutenant, July 7, 1865. Mustered out at Jeffersonville, Ind., July 8, 1865. Died at Detroit, March 13, 1904.

Laclare, Peter. Enlisted in Second Company Sharpshooters, March 28, 1864, at Spaulding, for 3 years, age 19. Discharged for disability at Philadelphia, Aug. 10, 1864.

Lacombe, Maxim. Enlisted in Company F, Lancers, Nov. 16, 1861, at Marquette, for 3 years, age 24. Transferred to Company K, 16th Michigan, Feb. 28, 1862. Deserted at Detroit, March 22, 1862.

La Duc or **Le Duc, Baptiste** or **Batiste**, Detroit. Enlisted in Company G, Jan. 6, 1862, at Detroit, age 24. Joined regiment at Hall's Hill, Va., Feb. 14, 1862. Killed in action at Gaines' Mill, June 27, 1862.

Laduke, William. Enlisted in Company G, Jan. 6, 1862, at Detroit, for 3 years, age 26. Missing in action at Gaines' Mill, June 27, 1862. No further record.

Lago, Thomas, Detroit. Enlisted in Company E, Sept. 6, 1861, at Detroit, age 39. Killed in action at Gaines' Mill, June 27, 1862.

Laher, Gilbert, Ontonagon County. Enlisted in Company A, Aug. 1, 1861, at Ontonagon, for 3 years, age 38. Transferred to Gun Boat service on Mississippi river, Feb. 15, 1862.

Laird, James S. (Veteran). Enlisted in Company G, Aug. 24, 1861. Wounded in action and taken prisoner at Gaines' Mill, June 27, 1862. Paroled Oct. 1862. Reenlisted as Sergeant Dec. 21, 1863, at Rappahannock Station, Va. 1st Sergeant. Commissioned 2nd Lieutenant, Company B, Sept. 14, 1864. Commissioned 1st Lieutenant, Company G, to date Dec. 16, 1863. Reported wounded, shot through the body, no date given. Commissioned Captain, May 7, 1865. Mustered out at Jeffersonville, Ind., July 8, 1865.

Lake, John C., Detroit. Enlisted in Company I, Sept. 4, 1862, at Detroit, for 3 years, age 18. Joined regiment at Antietam, Md., Oct. 12, 1862. Discharged near Washington, D.C., May 29, 1865.

Lamberton, Warren, Kent County. Enlisted in First Company Sharpshooters attached to 16th Michigan as Corporal, Oct. 4, 1861, at Detroit, for 3 years, age 28. Joined regiment at Hall's Hill, Va., Feb. 14, 1862. Discharged for disability at Georgetown, April 19, 1862.

Lamkie or **Lempke, William** (Veteran), Eagle Harbor. Enlisted in Company H, as Corporal, Aug. 6, 1861. Wounded in action at Fredericksburg, Va., Dec. 13, 1863. Reenlisted Dec. 24, 1863, at Rappahannock Station, Va. Wounded in action at Weldon Railroad, Petersburg, Va., Aug. 21, 1864. Sergeant May 1, 1865. No further record.

Lamott, John. Enlisted in Second Company Sharpshooters, March 29, 1864, at Saginaw, for 3 years, age 19. Deserted.

Lander, George. Enlisted in Company F, Aug. 6, 1861, at Plymouth, for 3 years, age 23. Transferred to Company E. Corporal. Killed in action at Gaines' Mill, June 27, 1862.

Lane, Bradley L. Enlisted in Company I, March 29, 1865, at Flowerfield, St. Joseph County, for 1 year, age 19. Substitute for George Bartlett, drafted. Mustered out at Jeffersonville, Ind., July 8, 1865.

Lane, Frank, Ontonagon County. Enlisted in Company A, Aug. 1, 1861, at Ontonagon, for 3 years, age 27. Killed in action at second Manassas, Aug. 30, 1862.

Lane, Morris McHenry, Saginaw County. Enlisted in Company D. Mustered, Sept. 14, 1861. Discharged for disability June 20, 1862.

Lane or **Lang, John.** Enlisted in Company K, Jan. 5, 1864, at Detroit, for 3 years, age 47. Listed as absent, wounded from Sept. 1, 1864, to March 1865. Discharged at Philadelphia. May 18, 1865.

Lang, Peter (Veteran). Enlisted in Company H, Lancers, Dec. 14, 1861, at Detroit, for 3 years, age 30. Transferred to Company I or K, 16th Michigan, Feb. 28, 1862. Taken prisoner at second Manassas, Aug. 30, 1862. Paroled Sept. 1862. Reenlisted Dec. 21, 1863, at Rappahannock Station, Va. Corporal, Aug. 1862. Sergeant. Wounded in action, at Magnolia Swamp–Bethesda Church, June 1, 1864. Mustered out at Jeffersonville, Ind., July 8, 1865.

Lang, Reinhold. Enlisted in Company A, Jan. 23, 1864, at Blumfield, for 3 years, age 37. Mustered out at Jeffersonville, Ind., July 8, 1865.

Langley, George. Enlisted in Company A, March 7, 1864, at Rockland, for 3 years, age 18. Wounded in action at Bethesda Church, June 2, 1864. Wounded in action at Dabney's Mill, Feb. 6, 1865. Discharged at Wilmington, Del., May 31, 1865.

Langley, Henry W. (Veteran), Wayne County. Enlisted in Company F, Aug. 6, 1861, at Plymouth, for 3 years, age 21. Sergeant. Transferred to Company E, Oct. 1862. Reenlisted Dec. 21, 1863, at Rappahannock Station, Va. Discharged at Camp Chase, Ohio, June 10, 1865. Resided Detroit.

Lannon or **Luman, Conrad.** Enlisted in Second Company Sharpshooters, April 8, 1864, at Spaulding, for 3 years, age 18. Wounded in action at Peeble's Farm, Sept. 30, 1864. Mustered out at Jeffersonville, Ind., July 8, 1865. Resided Montrose.

Laplant, Michael. Enlisted in Second Company Sharpshooters, March 24, 1864, at Ingersoll, for 3 years, age 25. Killed in action at Peeble's Farm, Sept. 3, 1864.

Lappens or **Lappius, Squire** (Veteran), Wayne County. Enlisted in First Company Sharpshooters, attached to 16th Michigan, as Corporal, Nov. 1, 1861, at Detroit, for 3 years, age 27. Joined regiment at Hall's Hill, Va., Feb. 14, 1862. Wounded in action, head, in 1862, date not given. Reenlisted Dec. 22, 1863, at Rappahannock Station, Va. Sergeant. Mustered out at Jeffersonville, Ind., July 8, 1865.

Laprott, Gilbert. Enlisted in Company G, Jan. 4, 1864, at Saline, for 3 years, age 19. Wounded in action, July 1864, probably at Petersburg, Va. Discharged at Detroit, May 10, 1865.

Larkin, John (Veteran). Enlisted in Company D, Sept. 5, 1861, at East Saginaw, for 3 years, age 35. Transferred to Company E. Reenlisted as Wagoner, Dec. 21, 1863, at Rappahannock Station, Va. Mustered out at Jeffersonville, Ind., July 8, 1865.

Larkworthy, William (Veteran), Canada West. Enlisted in Company B, Aug. 2, 1861, at Ionia, for 3 years. Hospital Steward, Dec. 9, 1861. Reenlisted Dec. 24, 1863, at Rappahannock Station, Va. Commissioned Assistant Surgeon, April 18, 1864. Discharged at Jeffersonville, Ind., July 1, 1865.

Lary or **Leary, Charles**, Ontonagon County. Enlisted in Company A, Aug. 1, 1861, at Ontonagon, for 3 years, age 35. Deserted at Detroit, Aug. 10, 1861.

Lashley, Alexander, Jackson. Enlisted in Company E, Aug. 13, 1861, at Detroit, for 3 years, age 19. Transferred to Company F. Killed in action at Gaines' Mill, June 27, 1862.

Laughlin, James A. or **John**, Detroit. Enlisted in Company D, Dec. 4, 1861, at Detroit, for 3 years, age 20. Discharged for disability at Hall's Hill, Va., Feb. 25, 1862.

Laughlin, Moses E., Coldwater. Enlisted in Company G, Lancers, Dec. 7, 1861, at Coldwater, for 3 years, age 19. Transferred to Company I, 16th Michigan, Feb. 28, 1862. Discharged for disability.

Laughlin, Patrick. Enlisted Feb. 17, 1865, at Bloomfield, Oakland County, for 3 years, age 20. Substitute for James Van Every, drafted. No further record.

Laurence, Stephen H. Enlisted in Company I, Feb. 18, 1865, at Independence, Oakland County, for 2 years, age 18. Substitute for Guy W. Selden, drafted. Mustered out at Jeffersonville, Ind., July 8, 1865.

Lawke, William. Enlisted in Company C, Aug. 4, 1861, at Flint, for 3 years, age 23. No further record.

Lawler, John, Ontonagon County. Enlisted in Company A, Aug. 3, 1861. Deserted at Detroit, Aug. 10, 1861.

Le Charité, Enseb, East Saginaw. Enlisted in Company D, Aug. 3, 1861, at East Saginaw, age 21. Killed in action at second Manassas, Aug. 30, 1862.

Lee, Benjamin. Enlisted in Company E, Aug. 15, 1861, at Detroit, for 3 years, age 21. Transferred to Company G. Discharged for disability at Hall's Hill, Va., Feb. 25, 1862.

Lee, Geary, Macomb County. Enlisted in First Company Sharpshooters attached to 16th Michigan, Dec. 3, 1861, at Detroit, for 3 years, age 21. Joined regiment at Hall's Hill, Va., Feb. 14, 1862. Discharged at Antietam, Md., Oct. 25, 1862.

Lee, Henry G. (Veteran), Macomb County. Enlisted in First Company Sharpshooters attached to 16th Michigan, as Corporal, Oct. 12, 1861, at Detroit, for 3 years, age 22. Joined regiment at Hall's Hill, Va., Feb. 14., 1862. Reenlisted as Sergeant Dec. 22, 1863, at Rappahannock Station, Va. Wounded in action at Petersburg, Va., June 19, 1864. Commissioned 2nd Lieutenant, July 7, 1865. Mustered out at Jeffersonville, Ind., July 8, 1865.

Lee, Samuel O., Wayne County. Enlisted in Company F, as Corporal, Sept. 12, 1861, at Plymouth, for 3 years, age 28. Reportedly wounded in action, at Hanover Court House, Va., May 27, 1862, and discharged at Gaines' Mill, June 1862.

LeFroy, William H. Enlisted in Company K, March 28, 1865, at Dexter, Washtenaw County, for 1 year, age 22. Substitute for Benjamin H. Glenn, drafted from Dexter. Mustered out at Jeffersonville, Ind., July 8, 1865.

Lehman or **Leahman, William**. Detroit. Enlisted in Company I, March 24, 1862, at Detroit, age 25. Killed in action at Gaines' Mill, June 27, 1862.

Lehr, William. Drafted for 1 year, from Lockport, St. Joseph County, age 31. Mustered March 16, 1865. Assigned to Company B. Deserted near Louisville, Ky., June 25, 1865.

Leighton, William, Trenton. Enlisted in Company H, Lancers, Nov. 21, 1861, at Trenton, for 3 years, age 18. Transferred to Company I, 16th Michigan, Feb. 28, 1862. Died Dec. 24, 1862, at Falmouth, Va., of wounds received in action at Fredericksburg, Va., Dec. 13, 1862.

Lein or **Lievee, Charles**. Enlisted in Company A, Jan. 24, 1864, at East Saginaw, for 3 years, age 18. Mustered out at Jeffersonville, Ind., July 8, 1865.

Lemu or **Lenner, John**. Enlisted in Company E, Aug. 14, 1861, at Detroit, for 3 years, age 21. No further record.

Leonard, Elias. Drafted for 1 year, from Dorr, Allegan County, age 28, March 1865. Assigned to Company B. Mustered out at Jeffersonville, Ind., July 8, 1865.

Leonard, Francis O. N. (Veteran), Assyria, Mich. Enlisted in Company K, March 1, 1862, at Detroit, for 3 years, age 21. Reenlisted March 1, 1864, at Bealton, Va. Corporal. Mustered out near Jeffersonville, Ind., July 8, 1865. Resided Assyria, Mich.

Leonard, John. Enlisted in Company A, Feb. 10, 1864, at Ann Arbor, for 3 years, age 18. Severely wounded in action, arm, at Totopotomoy, Va., May 30, 1864. Discharged at Detroit, May 18, 1865.

Leonard, John T. Enlisted in Second Company Sharpshooters, March 26, 1864, at Frankenmuth, for 3 years, age 28. Discharged at Satterlee Hospital, West Philadelphia, June 9, 1865.

Leonard, Martin. Enlisted in Second Company Sharpshooters, May 2, 1864, at Birch Run, for 3 years, age 32. Mustered out at Jeffersonville, Ind., July 8, 1865.

Lerity, Frederick, Portage Lake. Enlisted in Company H, Aug. 15, 1861. Discharged for disability at Washington, D.C., April 24, 1862.

Lewis, Charles A. Enlisted in Company D, March 27, 1865, at Saginaw, for 1 year, age 25.

Substitute for Norman L. Miller, drafted. Mustered out at Jeffersonville, Ind., July 8, 1865.

Lewis, Timothy, Delhi. Enlisted in Company F, Aug. 6, 1861, at Plymouth, for 3 years, age 19. Transferred to Company G. Died of disease at Hall's Hill, Va., Nov. 6, 1861.

Lewis, William. Enlisted in Company F, Aug. 6, 1861, at Plymouth, for 3 years, age 43. No further record.

Lidler or **Lindler, Philip** (Veteran), Ontonagon County. Enlisted in Company A, Aug. 1, 1861, at Ontonagon, for 3 years, age 30. Reenlisted Dec. 21, 1863, at Rappahannock Station, Va. Mustered out at Jeffersonville, Ind., July 8, 1865.

Lighthall, Edward. Enlisted in Company F, March 22, 1865, at Howell, for 1 year, age 19. Substitute for Franklin E. Steward, or Stewart, drafted. Died of disease at City Point, Va., April 21, 1865.

Likoyon or **Likam, John**, Saginaw County. Enlisted in Company F, Feb. 1, 1864, at Saginaw, for 3 years, age 15. Discharged at Washington, D.C., June 14, 1865.

Lindsay, John. Enlisted in Company B, Aug. 2, 1861, at Ionia, for 3 years, age 21. Discharged for disability at Washington, D.C., April 14, 1862.

Linn, Artemes M. Enlisted in Company H, Sept. 26, 1861, at Detroit, for 3 years, age 35. Deserted Oct. 25, 1861.

Lipscum, Ezekiel, Saginaw County. Enlisted in Company D, Aug. 5, 1861, at East Saginaw, for 3 years, age 32. Discharged March 4, 1863.

Liscombe, Lyman W., Ionia County. Enlisted in Company B, July 31, 1861, at Ionia, for 3 years, age 29. Discharged at expiration of term of service at Petersburg, Va., Sept. 6, 1864. Resided Otisco, Mich.

Littlejohn, William. Enlisted in Company E, Jan. 25, 1864, at Detroit, for 3 years, age 45. Wounded in action at Wilderness, May 7, 1864. Mustered out at Jeffersonville, Ind., July 8, 1865.

Livingston, Charles J. Enlisted in Second Company Sharpshooters, March 28, 1864, at Spaulding, for 3 years, age 23. Deserted Aug. 22, 1864.

Livingston, John. Enlisted in Second Company Sharpshooters, April 5, 1864, at Bridgeport, for 3 years, age 22. Died of disease at City Point, Va., July 25, 1864.

Lobdell, Leroy, Kent County. Enlisted in First Company Sharpshooters attached to 16th Michigan, Jan. 25, 1862, at Grand Rapids, for 3 years, age 24. Joined regiment at Hall's Hill, Va., Feb. 14, 1862. Wounded in action, head, Petersburg, Va., June 20, 1864. Discharged at expiration of term of service, Jan. 20, 1865.

Lockhart, Allen W., St. Joseph County. Enlisted in Company E, Aug. 24, 1861, at Ransom, for 3 years, age 22. Discharged for disability at Washington, D.C., Dec. 22, 1862.

Lockwood, Oscar. Drafted for 1 year, from Lockport, St. Joseph County, age 26. Mustered March 16, 1865. Assigned to Company H. Died of disease at City Point, Va., April 18, 1865.

Lockwood, William J. Enlisted in Second Company Sharpshooters, March 28, 1864, at Spaulding, for 3 years, age 37. In hospital at Philadelphia, Aug. 11, 1864. No further record.

Lohman, John, Ontonagon County. Enlisted in Company A, as Sergeant, Aug. 3, 1861, at Ontonagon, for 3 years, age 24. Wounded in action at Malvern Hill, July 1, 1862; killed in action at second Manassas, Aug. 30, 1862.

Loman or **Toman, Amos B.** Enlisted in Company F, Aug. 8, 1861, at Plymouth, for 3 years, age 30. Transferred to Company G, Jan. 1862. Wounded in action at Gaines' Mill, June 27, 1862. Wounded in action at second Manassas, Aug. 30, 1862. Discharged for disability at Washington, D.C., Oct. 12, 1862. Reentered service in Company E, 7th Michigan Cavalry, Sept. 9, 1864, at Jackson, for 1 year. Discharged at expiration of term of service at Fort Leavenworth, Kans., Sept. 11, 1865. Resided Harrison, Mich.

Long, James B., Van Buren County. Enlisted in First Company Sharpshooters attached to 16th Michigan, Oct. 16, 1861, at Detroit, for 3 years, age 24. Joined regiment at Hall's Hill, Va., Feb. 14, 1862. Discharged at expiration of term of service, Oct. 15, 1864.

Long, John P., Detroit. Entered service in Company H, as 2nd Lieutenant. Commissioned Aug. 9, 1861. Wounded in action at Malvern Hill, July 1, 1862. Discharged for disability at Falmouth, Va., Dec. 4, 1862.

Long, John R. Drafted March 15, 1865, for 1 year, from Byron, Kent County, age 40. Assigned to Company A. Discharged at Washington, D.C., May 16, 1865.

Longen, Dolphus. Enlisted April 13, 1864, at Houghton, for 3 years, age 21. No further record.

Lorenzer, Henry, Ontonagon County. Enlisted in Company A, Aug. 1, 1861, at Ontonagon, for 3 years, age 30. Discharged at expiration of term of service, Aug. 9, 1864.

Loron or **Lown, Sebastian**. Drafted for 1 year, from Sparta, Kent County, age 44. Mustered March 27, 1865. Assigned to Company B. Mustered out at Jeffersonville, Ind., July 8, 1865.

Love, George A. Enlisted in Company F, March 27, 1865, at Grattan, Kent County, for 1 year, age 23. Substitute for Owen Mayer, drafted. Discharged at Washington, D.C., July 6, 1865.

Lovette, P. S. or **Louth, Peter**, Chesaning. Entered service in Company D, for 9 months. Substitute for Hiram A. Tobias, drafted. Joined regiment near Falmouth, Va., March 18, 1863. Discharged at expiration of term of service, Nov. 11, 1863.

Low, James. Enlisted in Second Company Sharpshooters, March 25, 1864, at Saginaw, for 3 years, age 28. Deserted at Saginaw, May 3, 1864.

Lowry, Ebenezer N. (Veteran), Ionia County. Enlisted in Company B, Aug. 6, 1861, at Ionia, for 3 years, age 19. Missing in action at Gaines' Mill, June 27, 1862. Reenlisted as Corporal Dec. 24, 1863, at Rappahannock Station, Va. Wounded in neck in action at Bethesda Church, June 2, 1864. Mustered out at Jeffersonville, Ind., July 8, 1865. Resided Saranac, Mich.

Lucas, Alfred. Drafted March 15, 1865, for 1 year, from Paris, Kent County, age 35. Assigned to Company A. Mustered out at Jeffersonville, Ind., July 8, 1865.

Ludenus, Frederick P., Detroit. Enlisted in Company F, Oct. 3, 1862, at Detroit, for 3 years, age 18. Joined regiment at Warrenton, Va., Nov. 12, 1862. Killed in action at Fredericksburg, Va., Dec. 13, 1862.

Ludlow, Frank, Parma. Enlisted in Company K, March 1, 1862, at Detroit, for 3 years, age 21. Discharged at expiration of term of service at Washington, D.C., May 3, 1865.

Ludwig, Christopher, Ontonagon County. Enlisted in Company A, Aug. 1, 1861, at Ontonagon, for 3 years, age 25. Wounded in action, Gaines' Mill, June 27, 1862. Died Sept. 18, 1862, at Washington, D.C., of wounds received in action at second Manassas, Aug. 30, 1862.

Lugensland, Jacob. Enlisted in Company A, March 4, 1865, at Allegan, for 1 year, age 25. Substitute for Philander Chaffer, drafted. Mustered out at Jeffersonville, Ind., July 8, 1865.

Lutenbatcher, Joseph, Farmington. Enlisted in Company F, Aug. 28, 1861, at Farmington, for 3 years, age 23. Killed in action at Gaines' Mill, June 27, 1862.

Luther, Gotlieb, Ontonagon County. Enlisted in Company A as Drummer, Aug. 4, 1861, at Ontonagon, for 3 years, age 25. Wounded in action at Gettysburg July 2, 1863. Transferred to Invalid Corps Sept. 1, 1863.

Lyford, Charles. Enlisted in Company E, Aug. 14, 1861, at Detroit, for 3 years, age 23. Wounded in action and taken prisoner at Gaines' Mill, June 27, 1862. Discharged near Falmouth, Va., March 17, 1863.

Lyman, Henry, Bay City. Enlisted in Company E, Lancers, Oct. 26, 1861, at Saginaw, for 3 years, age 24. Transferred to Company I, 16th Michigan, Feb. 28, 1862. Killed in action at Gaines' Mill, June 27, 1862.

Lymann, Charles or **John C**. Enlisted in Company K, Feb. 5, 1862, at Detroit, for 3 years, age 44. Transferred to Company D. Discharged April 24, 1862.

Lynch, Michael. Enlisted in Company A, April 29, 1864, at Houghton, for 3 years, age 33. Mustered out at Jeffersonville, Ind., July 8, 1865.

Lynch, Stephen (Veteran). Enlisted in Company F, Aug. 6, 1861, at Plymouth, for 3 years, age 18. Transferred to Company E, May 1862. Reenlisted Dec. 21, 1863, at Rappahannock Station, Va. Discharged for disability at Washington, D.C., June 21, 1865.

Lynd, John. Drafted March 15, 1865, for 1 year, from Grand Rapids, age 23. Assigned to Company E. Died of disease at Washington, D.C., June 4, 1865.

Lyon, Albert O. Enlisted in Company F, Aug. 17, 1864, at Plymouth, for 3 years, age 19. Corporal May 1, 1865. Mustered out at Jeffersonville, Ind., July 8, 1865.

Lyon, Daniel (Veteran), St. Johns. Enlisted in Company H, as Corporal, Aug. 15, 1861, at St. Johns, for 3 years, age 21. Wounded in action at Malvern Hill, July 1, 1862. Reenlisted as 1st Sergeant Dec. 24, 1863, at Rappahannock Station, Va. Wounded in action, both hips, at Laurel Hill–Spotsylvania Court House, May 8, 1864. Commissioned 1st Lieutenant, Sept. 27, 1864. Discharged for disability May 15, 1865, for wounds received in action at Dabney's Mill, Feb. 6, 1865.

Lyon, Jacob, Wayne County. Enlisted in Company F, April 1, 1862, at Plymouth, for 3 years, age 55. Joined regiment at Yorktown, Va., May 1, 1862. Corporal Aug. 1862. Discharged on Surgeon's certificate of disability at Philadelphia, Aug. 30, 1862.

Lyon, Luther. Enlisted in Company F, Jan. 8, 1864, at Plymouth, for 3 years, age 21. Corporal May 1, 1865. Mustered out at Jeffersonville, Ind., July 8, 1865. Resided Plymouth, Mich.

Lyons, Hiram, Delhi, Ingham County. Enlisted in Company E, Dec. 30, 1862, at Detroit for 3 years, age 21. Joined regiment at Falmouth, Va., Jan. 2, 1863. Listed in hospital after Gettysburg, July 2, 1863, but no wound described. Discharged for disability at Philadelphia, May 17, 1864.

Lyons, John, Almont, Lapeer County. Enlisted in Company K, Feb. 5, 1862, at Almont, for 3 years, age 35. No muster out given. Died June 25, 1894, and buried in Saginaw.

Lyons, John. Enlisted in Company E, Aug. 15, 1861, at Detroit, for 3 years, age 18. Transferred to Company D. Wounded in action at Gaines' Mill, June 27, 1862. Discharged for disability Nov. 15, 1862.

Lyons, Lewis. Enlisted in Company C, Aug. 4, 1861 at Flint, for 3 years, age 31. No further record.

Lyons, Walter S., Lapeer County. Enlisted in Company D. Mustered Feb. 5, 1862. Joined regiment at Hall's Hill, Va., Feb. 14, 1862. Discharged on Surgeon's certificate of disability Nov. 15, 1862.

Lyons, William. Enlisted in Feb. 14, 1865, at Dallas, Clinton County, for 1 year, age 18. Substitute for William Miller, drafted. No further record.

McAllum or **McCallum, Malcolm**. Enlisted in Second Company Sharpshooters March 29, 1864, at Thomastown, Saginaw County, age 21. In hospital at Fort Schuyler, N.Y., June 19, 1864. No further record.

McArthur or **McCarthy, James**. Enlisted in Company B, Feb. 24, 1865, at Port Huron, for 3 years, age 28. Substitute for John W. Lewis, drafted from Port Huron. Deserted Washington, D.C., June 10, 1865.

McArthur, James. Enlisted in Second Company Sharpshooters March 30, 1864, at Thomastown, for 3 years, age 40. Deserted July 10, 1865.

McBaine, John. Enlisted in Second Company Sharpshooters March 28, 1864, at Nashville, for 3 years, age 19. Deserted.

McBratner or **McBratine, Charles**, Saginaw County. Enlisted in Company D, Aug. 2, 1861, at East Saginaw, for 3 years, age 30. Corporal. Killed in action at Gettysburg, July 2, 1863.

McCam, McCarn, or **McCann, James**, Ionia County. Enlisted in Company B, Aug. 2, 1861, at Ionia, for 3 years, age 18. Discharged for disability at Philadelphia, Sept. 16, 1862.

McCann, Patrick. Enlisted in Company D, April 14, 1864, at Detroit, for 3 years, age 35. Mustered out at Jeffersonville, Ind., July 8, 1865.

McCarn, William R. (Veteran). Enlisted in Company G as Musician, Aug. 22, 1861. Reenlisted Dec. 21, 1863, at Rappahannock Station, Va. Drum Major, Feb. 1, 1865. Mustered out at Jeffersonville, Ind., July 8, 1865. Died Feb. 28, 1902, at Soldiers' Home, Grand Rapids.

McClellan or **McLelland, Malcolm**, Jonesville. Enlisted in Company E, Aug. 20, 1861, at Jonesville, for 3 years, age 32. Killed in action at Gaines' Mill, June 27, 1862.

McClellan, Albert E., Genesee County. Enlisted in Company C, Jan. 15, 1862, for 3 years, age 18. Joined regiment at Hall's Hill, Va., Feb. 14, 1862. Discharged on Surgeon's certificate of disability at Yorktown, Va., April 18, 1862.

McCreary, John, Diamond Springs. Drafted for 1 year, from Heath, Allegan County, age 40. Mustered March 17, 1865. Assigned to Company B. Mustered out at Jeffersonville, Ind., July 8, 1865. Deceased.

McCrony, Ackland (Veteran), Ottawa County. Enlisted in First Company Sharpshooters attached to 16th Michigan, Dec. 20, 1861, at Grand Rapids, for 3 years, age 26. Joined regiment at Hall's Hill, Va., Feb. 14, 1862. Missing in action at second Manassas, Aug. 30, 1862. Reenlisted Dec. 22, 1863, at Rappahannock Station, Va. Sergeant, July 1, 1865. Mustered out at Jeffersonville, Ind., July 8, 1865.

McDonald, Bosiel, Wayne County. Enlisted in Company E, Aug. 30, 1861, at Detroit, for 3 years, age 41. Discharged for disability at Hendricks Hall, Va., Dec. 1, 1861.

McDonald. John. Enlisted in Company K, Feb. 23, 1865, at Port Huron, for 3 years, age 29. Substitute for Albert B. Cummings, drafted. Joined regiment March 14, 1865. Mustered out at Jeffersonville, Ind., July 8, 1865.

McDonough, Andrew, Sr., Detroit. Enlisted in Company H, Oct. 18, 1861, at Detroit, for 3 years, age 41. Discharged for disability at Fortress Monroe, Va., Dec. 4, 1862.

McDonough, Andrew, Jr. (Veteran), Detroit. Enlisted in Company H, Sept. 5, 1861, age 18. Reenlisted Feb. 27, 1864, at Bealton, Va. Wounded in action at Weldon Railroad, Petersburg, Va., Aug. 21, 1864. Discharged for disability at Detroit, Jan. 29, 1865.

McDonough, John (Veteran), Detroit. Enlisted in Company H, Oct. 29, 1861, at Detroit, for 3 years, age 18. Reenlisted Dec. 24, 1863, at Rappahannock Station, Va. Corporal, May 1, 1865. Mustered out at Jeffersonville, Ind., July 8, 1865.

McDougall, Alexander. Enlisted in Second Company Sharpshooters March 28, 1864, at Saginaw, for 3 years, age 25. Deserted at Saginaw, May 3, 1864.

McDowell, Andrew J., Genesee County. Enlisted in Company C, Aug. 9, 1861, at Flint, for 3 years, age 42. Discharged on Surgeon's certificate of disability at Gaines' Mill, June 17, 1862.

McDowell or **McDonald, James**. Wayne County. Enlisted in Company B, Jan. 14, 1862, at Detroit, for 3 years, age 31. Joined regiment at Hall's Hill, Va., Feb. 14, 1862. Discharged for disability at West Philadelphia, Oct. 22, 1862.

McDuire or **Maguire, Philip**. Enlisted in Company K, Feb. 11, 1864, at Saginaw, for 3 years, age 24. Deserted Sept. 11, 1864.

McEwen, Michael. Enlisted in Company F, Jan. 21, 1865, at Park, St. Joseph County, for 3 years, age 27. Substitute for J. M. Salisbury, drafted. Mustered out at Jeffersonville, Ind., July 8, 1865.

McFall, Jonas or **Joseph**. Algoma. Drafted for 1 year, from Algoma, Kent County, age 38. Mustered March 28, 1865. Assigned to Company H. Died of disease at Washington, D.C., April 30, 1865.

McFarlin, Harrison E., Plymouth. Enlisted in Company F, as Sergeant, July 31, 1861, at Plymouth, for 3 years, age 20. Died at Carver Hospital, Washington, D.C., Sept. 25, 1862, of wounds received in action at second Manassas, Aug. 30, 1862.

McGinnis, Frank (Veteran). Enlisted in Company D, Aug. 6, 1861, at East Saginaw, for 3 years, age 25. Mustered Sept. 7, 1861. Reported as of Company E. Part of the color guard, he was wounded in action, shot through the lungs, at second Manassas, Aug. 30, 1862. Returned to duty with his regiment after 6 months. Reenlisted as Sergeant Dec. 21, 1863, at Rappahannock Station, Va. Corporal, March 1, 1865. Mustered out at Jeffersonville, Ind., July 8, 1865, but was hospitalized in Detroit and died two weeks after his discharge.

McGinnis or **McInnis, Peter**. Enlisted in Second Company Sharpshooters, April 27, 1864, at Bridgeport, for 3 years, age 44. Captured after joining the regiment, date unknown. Died of disease in prison at Andersonville, Ga., Sept. 12, 1864. Buried in National Cemetery at Andersonville, Grave No. 8590.

McGrath, Patrick. Enlisted in Company E, March 25, 1865, at Detroit, for 1 year, age 23. Substitute for Samuel F. Hodge, drafted. Mustered out at Jeffersonville, Ind., July 8, 1865.

McGraw, Byron, Pontiac. Enlisted in Company D, 5th Michigan Infantry, as Sergeant, June 19, 1861, at Fort Wayne, for 3 years, age 22. 1st Sergeant Nov. 1, 1861. Commissioned 2nd Lieutenant, Company I, 16th Michigan, March 22, 1862. Died June 30, 1862, at Savage's

Station, of wounds received in action at Gaines' Mill, June 27, 1862.

McGraw, Thomas S., Detroit. Enlisted in Company I as Corporal, March 13, 1862, at Detroit, for 3 years, age 19. Corporal. Wounded in action and captured at Gaines' Mill, June 27, 1862. Exchanged. Discharged on Surgeon's certificate of disability at Bellevue Hospital, New York City, Sept. 1, 1862.

McGuire, Michael. Drafted for 1 year, from Kalamazoo, age 45. Mustered March 15, 1865. Assigned to Company E. Mustered out at Jeffersonville, Ind., July 8, 1865.

McIlvane or **Mulvena, John**, Ontonagon County. Enlisted in Company A, Aug. 1, 1861, at Ontonagon, for 3 years, age 30. Records state he was discharged for disability April 9, 1863, but the regiment's "Roll of Honor" states he was wounded in action at Chancellorsville, Va., a month later.

Mcintosh, Hugh. Enlisted in Second Company Sharpshooters, March 27, 1864, at Saginaw, for 3 years, age 24. Deserted at Saginaw, May 3, 1864.

Mcintosh, James or **William**, St. Clair County. Enlisted in Company K, Feb. 28, 1862, at St. Clair, for 3 years, age 18. Taken prisoner at White Oak Swamp, Va., June 30, 1862. Paroled Nov. 1862. No further record.

Mcintosh, John. Enlisted in Company E, March 28, 1865, at Detroit, for 1 year, age 19. Substitute for John Vandermulen, drafted. Mustered out at Jeffersonville, Ind., July 8, 1865.

McKay or **McCoy, Daniel**. Enlisted in Company G, March 16, 1865, at Port Huron, for 3 years, age 31. Substitute for William Stewart, drafted. Mustered out at Jeffersonville, Ind., July 8, 1865.

McKay, Hector. Enlisted in Company F, March 22, 1865, at Brady, Kalamazoo County, for 3 years, age 20. Substitute for Herman Potter, drafted. Mustered out at Jeffersonville, Ind., July 8, 1865.

McKay, McKey, or **McKee, James** (Veteran), Genesee County. Enlisted in Company C, as Corporal, Aug. 3, 1861, at Flint, for 3 years, age 18. Wounded in action, head, at Gaines' Mill or Malvern Hill, June 27 or July 1, 1862. Listed in newspaper among Gettysburg wounded in Germantown Hospital, July 1863, though not in regimental casualty report. Reenlisted Dec. 24, 1863, at Rappahannock Station, Va. Mustered out at Jeffersonville, Ind., July 8, 1865.

McKay, Robert. Enlisted in Company I, March 28, 1865, at Detroit, for 1 year, age 19. Substitute for Edward S. Bush, drafted. Mustered out at Jeffersonville, Ind., July 8, 1865.

McKeever, Peter. Enlisted in Second Company Sharpshooters, April 20, 1864, at Richland, for 3 years, age 31. Missing in action, at raid on Weldon Railroad, Petersburg, Va., Dec. 10, 1864. Discharged at Detroit, Sept. 21, 1865.

McKendrie, Edward J. (Veteran), Detroit. Enlisted in Company G, as Sergeant, Aug. 12, 1861, age 27. Reenlisted as 1st Sergeant Dec. 21, 1863, at Rappahannock Station, Va. Commissioned Captain, Company E, 1st Colored Infantry, at organization, Feb. 4, 1864. Mustered out at Charleston, S.C., Sept. 30, 1865.

McKenney, Robert, Redford. Enlisted in Company K, as Sergeant, Feb. 10, 1862, at Detroit, for 3 years, age 22. Discharged for disability May 2, 1862.

McKnight, James A., Ann Arbor. Enlisted in Company I, Aug. 9, 1862, at Argentine, for 3 years, age 30. Joined regiment at Antietam, Md., Oct. 12, 1862. Discharged for promotion Dec.

8, 1863, in 1st Colored Infantry at organization, as 1st Lieutenant and Adjutant. Mustered out at Charleston, S.C., Sept. 30, 1865. Resided Bay City, Mich.

McLaughlin, Patrick, Detroit. Entered service in Company E, at organization, as 1st Lieutenant, Aug. 13, 1861, at Detroit, age 24. Commissioned Captain, Company C, Nov. 3, 1862. Regimental roster reports he resigned April 16, 1863, though in fact he was court-martialed for striking a soldier. Reentered service in 1st Colored Infantry as 1st Lieutenant and Quartermaster. Commissioned Nov. 6, 1863. Killed in action at Salkehatchie, S.C., Feb. 8, 1865.

McLean, Peter. Enlisted in Company H, Feb. 17, 1864, at Detroit, for 3 years, age 25. Died of accidental wound while cleaning rifle near Bealton, Va., March 19, 1864.

McLenithan, Samuel. Enlisted in Company D, Dec. 30, 1863, at St. Charles, for 3 years, age 16. Mustered out at Jeffersonville, Ind., July 8, 1865.

McLennon, John. Enlisted in Company D, Feb. 4, 1864, at Portsmouth, for 3 years, age 18. Reported as absent wounded in Nov. 1864 and March 1865. No further record.

McLeod, Donald (Veteran), Ontonagon County. Enlisted in Company A, Aug. 1, 1861, at Ontonagon, for 3 years, age 31. Wounded in action at Malvern Hill, July 1, 1862. Reenlisted as Corporal Dec. 21, 1863, at Rappahannock Station, Va. Sergeant May 1, 1865. Mustered out at Jeffersonville, Ind., July 8, 1865.

McMullen, Henry J. Enlisted Feb. 15, 1865, at Pontiac, for 3 years, age 19. Substitute for Gilbert O. Graves, drafted from Oregon, Lapeer County. No further record.

McMullen, Lawrence, Detroit. Enlisted in Company H, Oct. 29, 1861, at Detroit, for 3 years, age 18. Discharged at expiration of term of service at Detroit, Nov. 11, 1864.

McMurtine, John H. Drafted for 1 year, from Lockport, St. Joseph County, age 35. Mustered March 16, 1865. Assigned to Company I, transferred to Company K. Mustered out at Jeffersonville, Ind., July 8, 1865.

McNall, Benson, Romeo. Enlisted in Company H, Nov. 5, 1861, at Romeo, for 3 years, age 28. Discharged to date June 30, 1862.

McNall, Joseph, Romeo. Enlisted in Company H, Oct. 5, 1861, at Romeo, for 3 years, age 23. Killed in action at Gaines' Mill, June 27, 1862.

McNaughton, Duncan, Bay City. Enlisted in Second Company Sharpshooters, March 31, 1864, at Spaulding, for 3 years, age 31. Sergeant. 1st Sergeant; Sergeant Major. Commissioned 1st Lieutenant and Adjutant, Oct. 15, 1864. Commissioned Captain, Company E, May 7, 1865. Mustered May 14, 1865. Mustered out at Jeffersonville, Ind., July 8, 1865.

McNeil, John A., Grand Rapids. Entered service in First Company Sharpshooters attached to 16th Michigan, Sept. 16, 1861, at 1st Lieutenant, age 44. Resigned May 17, 1862.

McNitt, Benjamin, Kent County. Enlisted in First Company Sharpshooters attached to 16th Michigan, Dec. 30, 1861, at Grand Rapids, for 3 years, age 26. Joined regiment at Hall's Hill, Va., Feb. 14, 1862. Transferred to 12th U.S. Infantry Jan. 24, 1863.

McRoberts, William H., Milford. Enlisted in Company B, Lancers, Oct. 19, 1861, at Milford, for 3 years, age 18. Transferred to Company I, 16th Michigan, Feb. 28, 1862. Wounded in action, shrapnel, at Malvern Hill, July 1, 1862. Wounded in action, right thigh, at Gettysburg, July 2, 1863. Corporal. Killed in trenches, Petersburg, Va., June 20, 1864.

McSouth or **McLouth, John**, Wayne County. Enlisted in Company F, Aug. 2, 1861, at Plymouth, for 3 years, age 18. Deserted.

Maag, Frank, Ontonagon County. Enlisted in Company A, Aug. 1, 1861, at Ontonagon, for 3 years, age 22. Killed in action at Gaines' Mill, June 27, 1862.

Mack, Patrick, Kent County. Drafted March 15, 1865, for 1 year, from Caledonia, Kent County, age 37. Assigned to Company K. Mustered out at Jeffersonville, Ind., July 8, 1865.

Mack, William L., Wayne County. Enlisted in Company K, March 20, 1862, at Detroit, for 3 years, age 24. Listed as missing in action Aug. 15, 1862, though in fact the regiment was not in battle, but on the march. Missing in action at Weldon Railroad, Petersburg, Va., Aug. 21, 1864. Nothing more was heard from him.

Mackrelly or **Mackerell, Solomon**. Enlisted in Company D, Aug. 2, 1861, at East Saginaw, for 3 years, age 37. Transferred to Company G. Discharged for disability at Washington, D.C., Jan. 12, 1863.

Macomber or **Macumber, Alonzo**. Enlisted in Second Company Sharpshooters, April 20, 1864, at Bridgeport, for 3 years, age 18. Died Nov. 4, 1864, of wounds received in action at Peeble's Farm, Sept. 30, 1864.

Madigan, Michael. Enlisted in Company K, Feb. 15, 1865, at Eddy, for 1 year, age 39. Substitute for Edward Clements, drafted. Mustered out at Jeffersonville, Ind., July 8, 1865.

Magoon, Philander, Algoma. Drafted March 15, 1865, for 1 year, from Algoma, Kent County, age 33. Assigned to Company B. Died of disease at Carver Hospital, Washington, D.C., May 8, 1865.

Maguire, James (Veteran), Ontonagon County. Enlisted in Company A, as Corporal, Aug. 2, 1861, at Ontonagon, for 3 years, age 21. Reenlisted as Sergeant Dec. 21, 1863, at Rappahannock Station, Va., 1st Sergeant. Wounded in action May 10, 1864, at Po River–Spotsylvania Court House. Commissioned 2nd Lieutenant, June 6, 1864. Commissioned 1st Lieutenant, Sept. 7, 1864. Wounded in action at Peeble's Farm, Sept. 30, 1864. Commissioned Captain, Company K, May 8, 1865. Mustered out at Jeffersonville, Ind., July 8, 1865.

Maguire, Philip. Reportedly a private in Company K, enlistment date and place not given. Reported as absent, wounded in Jan.–Feb. 1865. No mention of where he was wounded or a report of muster out.

Mahan, Theodore S., Adrian. Entered service in Company D, at organization, as 1st Lieutenant, July 30, 1861, at East Saginaw, for 3 years, age 24. Commissioned Captain Aug. 23, 1862. Wounded in action at Fredericksburg, Va., Dec. 13, 1862. Resigned April 17, 1863.

Maher, Thomas, Detroit. Enlisted in Company H, Oct. 1861, at Detroit, for 3 years, age 44. Discharged for disability at New York Jan. 18, 1863.

Maley, James. Enlisted in Company H, Feb. 27, 1864, at Detroit, for 3 years, age 18. Discharged at Detroit, July 26, 1865.

Managhen, Patrick. Enlisted in Company B, Lancers, Oct. 24, 1861, at Milford, for 3 years, age 45. Transferred to Company K, 16th Michigan, Feb. 28, 1862. Deserted March 22, 1862.

Manchen, Daniel, Dearborn. Enlisted in Company E, Sept. 6, 1861, at Dearborn, for 3 years, age 25. Accidentally wounded, discharge of pistol, at Yorktown, Va., April 28, 1862. Discharged for disability at Detroit, June 25, 1862. Reentered service, enlisting in Company F, 1st Michigan Sharpshooters, May 12, 1863, at Dearborn, for 3 years, age 23. Discharged on

Surgeon's certificate of disability at Camp Douglas, Ill., April 9, 1864.

Manley, William. Enlisted in Second Company Sharpshooters, April 6, 1864, at Saginaw, for 3 years, age 25. Discharged for disability June 5, 1865.

Mann, Rodger, Detroit. Enlisted in Company H, Nov. 4, 1861, at Detroit, for 3 years, age 40. Killed in action at second Manassas, Aug. 30, 1862.

Manning, John. Drafted for 1 year, from Dayton, Newaygo County, age 43. Mustered March 25, 1865. Discharged at Washington, D.C., June 7, 1865.

Manson or **Maxson, William**. Enlisted in Company E, Aug. 17, 1861, at Detroit, for 3 years, age 24. No further record.

Manwell, Henry A. Enlisted in Company D, Jan. 9, 1864, at Saginaw, for 3 years, age 25. Mustered out at Jeffersonville, Ind., July 8, 1865. Resided Tittabawassee, Saginaw County.

Marcette or **Market, Charles**. Enlisted in Company D, Jan. 24, 1864, at Saginaw, for 3 years, age 23. Reported absent, wounded Sept. 1864. Mustered out at Jeffersonville, Ind., July 8, 1865.

Marion, Charles. Enlisted in Company B, Aug. 3, 1861, at Ionia, for 3 years, age 35. Reported in Company C. Discharged on Surgeon's certificate of disability Feb. 26, 1863.

Marry, William B. Enlisted in Company F, as Corporal, Aug. 3, 1861, at Plymouth, for 3 years, age 21. Deserted.

Marsh, Martin, New Hudson. Enlisted in Company B, Lancers, as Corporal, Nov. 23, 1861, at New Hudson, for 3 years, age 21. Transferred to Company I, 16th Michigan, Feb. 28, 1862. Sergeant. Michigan Adjutant-General's Dept. *Record of Service,* vol. 16 (1905), states he died of disease at Harrison's Landing, Va., Aug. 6, 1862, though the regiment's "Roll of Honor" states he died from wounds in action, shrapnel, at Malvern Hill, July 1, 1862. These causes of death are not mutually exclusive and the combination of wound and illness may have killed him.

Martain, Anthony, Detroit. Enlisted and mustered in Company G, Aug. 27, 1862, at Detroit, for 3 years, age 27. Joined regiment at Sharpsburg, Md., Oct. 30, 1862. Deserted at Bealton, Va., April 1, 1864.

Martin, Charles A., Genesee County. Enlisted in Company C, Jan. 12, 1862, at Detroit, for 3 years, age 19. Joined regiment at Hall's Hill, Va., Feb. 14, 1862. Wounded in hand in action at Gaines' Mill or Malvern Hill. Died at Gettysburg, July 21, 1863, of wounds received in action July 2, 1863.

Martin, John, Detroit. Enlisted in Company H, as Sergeant, Oct. 1, 1861, at Detroit, for 3 years, age 18. 1st Sergeant March 18, 1862. Commissioned 2nd Lieutenant April 11, 1863. Discharged at expiration of term of service, Sept. 30, 1864. Resided Detroit.

Martin, John. Enlisted in Second Company Sharpshooters, April 28, 1864, at Bloomfield, Oakland County, for 3 years, age 28. Corporal. Mustered out at Jeffersonville, Ind., July 8, 1865.

Martin, Robert. Enlisted in Company F, Feb. 13, 1865, at Bloomfield, Oakland County, for 3 years, age 23. Substitute for Edward Hazen, or Harger, drafted. Mustered out at Jeffersonville, Ind., July 8, 1865.

Martin, Stephen, Detroit. Entered service in Company H, at organization, as Captain, July 25, 1861, at Detroit, for 3 years, age 42. Wounded in action at Gaines' Mill, June 27, 1862.

Reportedly wounded, struck by piece of spent shell, second Manassas, Aug. 30, 1862. Resigned on account of disability at Falmouth, Va., April 22, 1863. Died April 4, 1890.

Martinstein, Lester or **Nestor**, Detroit. Enlisted in Company K, March 1, 1862, at Detroit, for 3 years, age 21. Killed in action at second Manassas, Aug. 30, 1862.

Mason, Jesse. Drafted for 1 year, from Coldwater, Branch County, age 38. Mustered March 17, 1865. Assigned to Company H. Mustered out at Jeffersonville, Ind., July 8, 1865.

Mason, John M. Enlisted in Company A, Feb. 2, 1864, at Ann Arbor, for 3 years, age 22. Deserted at Ann Arbor, Feb. 12.

Mason, Silas, Camden, Hillsdale County. Entered service in Company D, at Camden, for 3 years. Substitute for James R. Mason, drafted Feb. 1863, for 9 months. Joined regiment at Falmouth, Va., March 18, 1863. Killed in action at Gettysburg, July 2, 1863.

Massey, Henry R. Enlisted in Company C, March 29, 1865, at Hartland, Livingston County, for 1 year, age 23. Substitute for John Scollon, drafted. Mustered out at Jeffersonville, Ind., July 8, 1865.

Matherson, James W. Enlisted in Company E, Lancers, Nov. 19, 1861, at Bay City, for 3 years, age 22. Transferred to Company K, 16th Michigan, Feb. 28, 1862. Deserted at Detroit, March 25, 1862.

Mathews, Theodore (Veteran), Almont. Enlisted in Company K, Feb. 5, 1862, at Almont, for 3 years, age 20. Transferred to Company H. Reenlisted Dec. 27, 1863, at Rappahannock Station, Va. Wounded in action at Petersburg, Va., June 19, 1864. No further record.

Matney, Nathan S. Drafted March 16, 1865, for 1 year, from Hart, Oceana County, age 34. Assigned to Company A. Died of disease at Washington, D.C., June 18, 1865.

Matteson, John C., Lapeer County. Enlisted in First Company Sharpshooters attached to 16th Michigan, Dec. 19, 1861, at Detroit, for 3 years, age 24. Joined regiment at Hall's Hill, Va., Feb. 14, 1862. Deserted near Falmouth, Va., Dec. 11, 1862.

Matteson or **Mattison, Norman S.** (Veteran), Lapeer County. Enlisted in Company D, Aug. 2, 1861, at East Saginaw, for 3 years, age 22. Wounded in action at Malvern Hill, July 1, 1862. Reenlisted as Corporal Dec. 21, 1863, at Rappahannock Station, Va. Mustered out at Jeffersonville, Ind., July 8, 1865. Died Sept. 6, 1892.

Mattis, Augustus. Enlisted in Company A, Jan. 28, 1865, at Jackson, for 1 year, age 18. Absent without leave June 25, 1865. No further record.

Mattison, Harvey. Drafted for 9 months, from Brady, Saginaw County, age 29. Mustered Feb. 26, 1863. Assigned to Company D. Joined regiment near Falmouth, Va., March 18, 1863. Discharged at expiration of term of service, Dec. 17, 1863.

Mattison or **Mallion, Robert**. Drafted Oct. 30, 1863, for 3 years, from Jackson, age 22. Assigned to Company C. Deserted near Jeffersonville, Ind., June 26, 1865.

Matureau or **Maturin, Moses**. Enlisted in First Company Sharpshooters attached to 16th Michigan, Feb. 15, 1864, at Saginaw, for 3 years, age 24. Wounded in action, at White Oak Road, Va., May 31, 1865. Discharged July 8, 1865. Resided Marlette, Mich.

Maulding, John. Enlisted in Company I, March 28, 1865 at Hartland, Livingston County for 1 year, age 38. Substitute for Edwin M. Clark, drafted. Mustered out at Jeffersonville, Ind., July 8, 1865.

Maulenbry, Mullenberg or **Mullenbray, Joseph**, Washtenaw County. Enlisted in Company B, as Corporal, Sept. 4, 1861, at Ionia, for 3 years, age 22. Wounded in action at second Manassas, right side and arm, Aug. 30, 1862. Sergeant. Died July 18, 1863, of wounds received in action, left arm and chest, at Gettysburg, July 2, 1863.

Maxfield, George. Drafted for 1 year, from Hartland, Livingston County, age 26. Mustered March 29, 1865. Assigned to Company D. Mustered out at Jeffersonville, Ind., July 8, 1865.

Maxon, Calvin. Reported in regimental "Roll of Honor" as private enlisted in Company E and missing in action at Charles City Crossroads near Malvern Hill, June 30, 1862. Other sources reflect the regiment came under artillery fire that day. No record of a mustering out, though he may have been wounded July 1, at Malvern Hill.

Maxon, W., Almont. Enlisted in Company K, Feb. 5, 1862, at Almont, for 3 years, age 40. Transferred to Company E. No further record.

May, Nelson, Delhi. Enlisted in Company E, Dec. 30, 1862, at Delhi, for 3 years, age 18. Joined regiment at Falmouth, Va., Jan. 2, 1863. Wounded in action, chest and hip, withdrawal from Cold Harbor, June 8, 1864. Discharged at Detroit, March 9, 1865, for wounds received in action.

Mead, Henry. Enlisted in regimental Band, Sept. 13, 1861, at Detroit, for 3 years, age 32. Taken prisoner at Gaines' Mill, June 27, 1862. Discharged at New York Oct. 6, 1862.

Mead, Joseph. Drafted for 1 year, from Climax, Kalamazoo County, age 22. Mustered March 15, 1865. Assigned to Company C. Mustered out at Jeffersonville, Ind., July 8, 1865.

Mead, Lorenzo L. Enlisted in Company K, Feb. 26, 1865, at Escanaba, for 1 year, age 18. Substitute for John N. Hiller, drafted. Mustered out at Jeffersonville, Ind., July 8, 1865.

Meehan, Patrick, Hillsdale County. Enlisted in Company E, Aug. 20, 1861, at Detroit, for 3 years, age 35. Wounded in action at Gaines' Mill, June 27, 1862. Discharged at a convalescent camp for disability Jan. 21, 1863.

Meeley or **Maley, John**. Enlisted in Company E, Feb. 4, 1865, at Holland, for 2 years, age 28. Substitute for Komer Schadder, drafted. Mustered out at Jeffersonville, Ind., July 8, 1865.

Mellany or **Molaney, John**, Detroit. Enlisted in Company E, Sept. 6, 1861, at Detroit, for 3 years, age 31. Killed in action at Gaines' Mill, June 27, 1862.

Melvin, S. or L. Enlisted in Company G. Aug. 18, 1861. Mustered Aug. 24, 1861. No further record.

Merchant, George. Enlisted in Company D, Aug. 5, 1861, at East Saginaw, for 3 years, age 18. No further record.

Merrifield, William H. Enlisted in Company C, Aug. 3, 1861, at Flint, for 3 years, age 18. No further record.

Merritt, Abraham. Enlisted in Company C, Aug. 9, 1861 at Detroit, for 3 years, age 19. Discharged on Surgeon's certificate of disability.

Merritt, Peter. Enlisted in First Company Sharpshooters, attached to 16th Michigan Jan. 20, 1864, at Detroit, for 3 years, age 38. Wounded in action, right shoulder, at Bethesda Church, June 2, 1864. No further record.

Merrygold, Amos. Enlisted in Company D, May 6, 1864, at Saginaw, for 3 years, age 16. Discharged at Washington, D.C., July 17, 1865.

Messer, Samuel E., Ionia County. Enlisted in Company H, as Corporal, Aug. 17, 1861, at Hubbardston, for 3 years, age 21. Regiment's "Roll of Honor" states he was killed in action at Gaines' Mill, June 27, 1862, while Michigan Adjutant-General's Dept. *Record of Service,* vol. 16 (1905), states he became 1st Sergeant and was discharged at Detroit, April 1, 1863.

Metz, Albert L., Argentine. Enlisted in Company I, Aug. 25, 1862, at Argentine, for 3 years, age 27. Joined regiment at Antietam, Md., Oct. 12, 1862. Discharged at Washington, D.C., May 29, 1865.

Meyers or **Myers, Alonzo**. Drafted for 1 year, from Algansee, Branch County, age 31. Mustered March 17, 1865. Assigned to Company C. Died of disease at Davis Hospital, N.Y., May 21, 1865.

Meyers, Charles, Detroit. Initially enlisted in 90-day 1st Michigan Infantry, Sergeant. Entered service in Company G at organization of Stockton's regiment as Captain, July 26, 1861. Wounded in action at Gaines' Mill, June 27, 1862. Discharged for disability Oct. 31, 1863. Died Jan. 15, 1900.

Meyer or **Myers, Henry J.** Enlisted in Company E, Aug. 13, 1861, at Detroit, for 3 years, age 38. Transferred to Company H. Wounded in action at Gaines' Mill, June 27, 1862. Wounded in action at Po River–Spotsylvania Court House, May 10, 1864. Michigan's roster states "No further record."

Meyers, Henry J. Jr., Sparta Center, Kent County. Drafted March 15, 1865, for 1 year, age 30. Assigned to Company B. Died of disease at Arlington, Va., June 8, 1865.

Meyers, John, Jr. Drafted March 16, 1865, for 1 year, from Woodland, Barry County, age 40. Assigned to Company D. Died of disease at Alexandria, Va., June 18, 1865. Buried in National Cemetery at Arlington Heights, Va.

Michael, Christian (Veteran). Enlisted in Company K, Feb. 8, 1862, at Detroit, for 3 years, age 23. Transferred to Company A. Reenlisted Dec. 21, 1863, at Rappahannock Station, Va. Wounded in action at Peeble's Farm, Sept. 30, 1864. Discharged at Philadelphia. July 17, 1865. Died Sept. 5, 1896.

Millard, Nathaniel D., Hillsdale. Enlisted in Company E, Aug. 23, 1861, at Hillsdale, for 3 years, age 20. Discharged for disability at Portsmouth Grove, R.I., April 16, 1863. Reentered service in Company G, 27th Michigan Infantry, Dec. 28, 1863, at Woodbridge, for 3 years. Admitted to Harper Hospital March 14, 1865. Discharged at Detroit, July 28, 1865.

Miller, Alfred, Chesaning. Enlisted in Company D, Aug. 3, 1861, at East Saginaw, for 3 years, age 19. Killed in action at Gaines' Mill, June 27, 1862.

Miller, Charles (Veteran), Detroit. Enlisted in Company A, July 25, 1862, age 21. Joined regiment at Antietam, Md., Oct. 12, 1862. Reenlisted Dec. 21, 1863, at Rappahannock Station, Va. Deserted at Detroit, May 6, 1864.

Miller or **Wilber, Charles** or **Karl**. Enlisted in Company B, Feb. 14, 1865, at Marshall, for 3 years, age 19. Substitute for Nicholas Voght drafted from Marshall. Absent sick, June 1865. No further record.

Miller, George F., Bay City. Enlisted in Company E, Lancers, Oct. 18, 1861, at Bay City, for 3 years, age 28. Transferred to Company K, 16th Michigan, Feb. 28, 1862. Discharged for disability at Washington, D.C., March 17, 1863.

Miller or **Mueller, Herman** or **Hilliard**, Ontonagon County. Enlisted in Company A, Feb. 12, 1864, at Blumfield, for 3 years, age 26. Captured. Died of starvation in prison at Andersonville, Ga., Aug. 15, 1864. Buried in National Cemetery at Andersonville, Grave No. 5328.

Miller, Jacob, Ann Arbor. Enlisted in Company G, Oct. 13, 1862, at Ann Arbor, age 38. Joined regiment at Falmouth, Va., Nov. 26, 1862. Taken prisoner Dec. 13, 1862, seemingly at Fredericksburg, Va. Paroled Jan. 1863. No further record.

Miller, James, Saginaw County. Enlisted in Company D, Aug. 4, 1861, at East Saginaw, for 3 years, age 31. Discharged for disability at Harrison's Landing, Va., June 1862.

Miller, James M. Enlisted in Company G, Aug. 24, 1861, at White Pigeon, for 3 years, age 29. Died of disease Jan. 29, 1863.

Miller, John. Drafted March 15, 1865, for 1 year, from Sparta, Kent County, age 35. Assigned to Company A. Mustered out at Jeffersonville, Ind., July 8, 1865.

Miller, John J. Enlisted in Company G, Sept. 10, 1861, at Detroit, for 3 years, age 39. Discharged Dec. 2, 1862.

Miller, Milton (Veteran), Genesee County. Enlisted in Company C, Aug. 5, 1861, at Flint, for 3 years, age 21. Wounded in action, at Gaines' Mill, June 27, or Malvern Hill, July 1, 1862. Reenlisted as Sergeant Dec. 24, 1863, at Rappahannock Station, Va., 1st Sergeant. Killed in action, at Po River–Spotsylvania Court House, May 10, 1864.

Millner, William J. Enlisted in Company G, Aug. 24, 1861, at Coldwater, for 3 years, age 21. Sergeant. Wounded in action at Bethesda Church–Cold Harbor, June 3, 1864. Discharged at expiration of term of service at Detroit, Sept. 7, 1864.

Mills, Ansel or **Amos**. Enlisted in Company B, Jan. 18, 1865, at Sturgis, for 1 year, age 19. Substitute for J. Heiling, drafted from Fawn River, St. Joseph County. Mustered out at Jeffersonville, Ind., July 8, 1865.

Mills, Ellson or **Allson M**., Ionia County. Enlisted in Company B, Aug. 6, 1861, at Ionia, for 3 years, age 22. Joined regiment at Harrison's Landing, Va., July 20, 1862. Discharged for disability at Philadelphia, Dec. 27, 1862.

Mills, Lucius E. Drafted for 1 year, from Casnovia, Muskegon County, age 41. Mustered Oct. 4, 1864. Assigned to Company K. Mustered out at Jeffersonville, Ind., July 8, 1865.

Mills, Stephen (Veteran), Saginaw County. Enlisted in Company D, Aug. 2, 1861, at East Saginaw, for 3 years, age 32. Corporal Aug. 1862. Reenlisted as Sergeant Dec. 21, 1863, at Rappahannock Station, Va. Wounded in action, right leg, Petersburg, Va., June 20, 1864. Discharged at Harper Hospital, Detroit, July 31, 1865, for wounds.

Minikee or **Minka, William**, Wayne County. Enlisted in Company F, Sept. 13, 1861, at Plymouth, for 3 years, age 30. Discharged for disability.

Minnis, Frederick E. (Veteran), Decatur. Enlisted in First Company Sharpshooters attached to 16th Michigan as Corporal, Oct. 16, 1861, at Detroit, for 3 years, age 26. Joined regiment at Hall's Hill, Va., Feb. 14, 1862. Reenlisted Dec. 22, 1863, at Rappahannock Station, Va. Wounded in action, left hand, at Wilderness, May 6, 1864. Transferred to Veteran Reserve Corps Feb. 10, 1865. Discharged at Washington, D.C., July 24, 1865. Resided St. Joseph, Mich.

Minor, George. Enlisted in Second Company Sharpshooters, March 21, 1864, at Saginaw, for

3 years, age 18. Mustered out at Jeffersonville, Ind., July 8, 1865.

Minto, Robert. Enlisted in Company E, Feb. 1, 1865, at Arcada, Gratiot County, 3 years, age 38. Substitute for Francis Gilkins, drafted. Mustered out at Jeffersonville, Ind., July 8, 1865.

Missner, Frederick (Veteran). Enlisted in Company H, Lancers, Jan. 1, 1862, at Detroit, for 3 years, age 36. Transferred to Company I, 16th Michigan, Feb. 28, 1862. Wounded in action in 1862. Reenlisted Dec. 22, 1863, at Rappahannock Station, Va. Corporal, May 1, 1865. Mustered out at Jeffersonville, Ind., July 8, 1865.

Mitchell, Frederick, Detroit. Enlisted in Company K, March 22, 1862, at Detroit, for 3 years, age 22. Sergeant. Wounded in action July 18, 1863. Transferred to Invalid Corps Feb. 15, 1864. Discharged at Elmira, N.Y., Nov. 14, 1865, from Company H, 1st Regiment, Veteran Reserve Corps.

Mittemire, John. Enlisted in Company A, Jan. 14, 1864, at Taymouth, Saginaw County, for 3 years, age 30. Corporal. Wounded in action at Peeble's Farm, Aug. 30, 1864. Died Feb. 8, 1865, at City Point, Va., of wounds received in action at Dabney's Mill, Feb. 6, 1865.

Mizner, George. Enlisted in Company C, Aug. 3, 1861, at Flint, for 3 years, age 20. Transferred to Company F. Discharged Nov. 26, 1862. Enlisted in 2nd U.S. Cavalry Nov. 26, 1862.

Mizner, William (Veteran), Wayne County. Enlisted in Company F, Aug. 6, 1861, at Plymouth, for 3 years, age 18. Reenlisted as Sergeant Dec. 21, 1863, at Rappahannock Station, Va. Commissioned 2nd Lieutenant, May 8, 1865. Commissioned 1st Lieutenant, July 7, 1865. Mustered out at Jeffersonville, Ind., July 8, 1865.

Moffitt, Lester C. Drafted March 15, 1865, for 1 year, from Cascade, Kent County, age 24. Assigned to Company I. Mustered out at Jeffersonville, Ind., July 8, 1865.

Mohn, George H. (Veteran), Genesee County. Enlisted in Company C, Aug. 3, 1861, at Flint, for 3 years, age 20. Reenlisted Dec. 24, 1863, at Rappahannock Station, Va. Corporal. Wounded in action May 31, 1864, at Totopotomoy Creek–Bethesda Church. Sergeant April 1, 1865. Mustered out at Jeffersonville, Ind., July 8, 1865.

Monan, Frank. Enlisted Jan. 12, 1864, at Erie, for 3 years, age 38. No further record.

Monroe, George W., Genesee County. Enlisted in Company C, Aug. 3, 1861, at Flint, for 3 years, age 22. Killed in action at Gaines' Mill, June 27, 1862.

Monroe, Henry F. Drafted for 1 year, from Owosso, age 30. Mustered March 16, 1865. Assigned to Company B. Mustered out at Jeffersonville, Ind., July 8, 1865.

Monroe, Jerry. Enlisted in Company I, Jan. 28, 1865, at Wayland, Allegan County, for 1 year, age 18. Substitute for Abram Berry, drafted. Discharged at Washington, D.C., May 30, 1865.

Monroe, Milo G., Wayne. Enlisted in Company F, Sept. 6, 1861, at Wayne, for 3 years, age 20. Died of disease at Fortress Monroe, Va., Sept. 10, 1862.

Monroe, William, Ottawa County. Enlisted in First Company Sharpshooters attached to 16th Michigan, Dec. 14, 1861, at Grand Rapids, for 3 years, age 21. Joined regiment at Hall's Hill, Va., Feb. 14, 1862. Wounded in action, at second Manassas, Aug. 30, 1862. Discharged for disability at Alexandria, Va., June 1863.

Moon, Russel C., or **Roswell**. Genesee County. Enlisted in Company C, Aug. 7, 1861, at Flint, for 3 years, age 30. Discharged on Surgeon's certificate of disability Feb. 20, 1863.

Moore, Charles. Enlisted in Company G, March 28, 1865, at Howell, for 1 year, age 18. Substitute for Perle Shelbeck, drafted from Howell. Mustered out at Jeffersonville, Ind., July 8, 1865.

Moore, Joseph. Enlisted in Company D, Jan. 21, 1864, at Saginaw, for 3 years. Discharged at Baltimore, June 12, 1865.

Moore, William. Enlisted in Company G, March 28, 1865, at Cohoctah, Livingston County, for 1 year, age 19. Substitute for James McKean, drafted. Mustered out at Jeffersonville, Ind., July 8, 1865.

Moran, Edward, Wayne County. Enlisted in Company E, Aug. 19, 1861, at Detroit, for 3 years, age 43. Discharged at Philadelphia, Feb. 10, 1863.

Moran, Michael, Wayne County. Enlisted in Company E, Aug. 16, 1861, at Detroit, for 3 years, age 25. Discharged for disability at Georgetown, May 22, 1862.

Moran, Thomas. Enlisted in Company F, March 10, 1865, at Pontiac, for 3 years, age 28. Substitute for N. Buell Eldridge, drafted. No further record.

Morey, Samuel A., Kent County. Enlisted in First Company Sharpshooters attached to 16th Michigan, Jan. 29, 1862, at Grand Rapids, for 3 years, age 39. Discharged for disability March 9, 1862.

Morgan or **Maguire, James**. Enlisted in Company B, Feb. 25, 1865, at Bloomfield, Oakland County, for 3 years, age 28. Substitute for Jesse Nichols, drafted from Bloomfield. Deserted at Louisville, Ky., June 27, 1865.

Morisette, Joseph (Veteran), Wayne County. Enlisted in Company E, Sept. 7, 1861, age 23. Reenlisted Dec. 21, 1863, at Rappahannock Station, Va. Mustered out at Jeffersonville, Ind., July 8, 1865.

Morland, James R., Macomb County. Enlisted in First Company Sharpshooters attached to 16th Michigan, Jan. 9, 1862, at Detroit, for 3 years, age 23. Joined regiment at Hall's Hill, Va., Feb. 14, 1862. Discharged at expiration of term of service, Jan. 16, 1865.

Morris, Charles G., Washington, Macomb County. Enlisted in First Company Sharpshooters attached to 16th Michigan, Oct. 29, 1861, at Detroit, for 3 years, age 33. Joined regiment at Hall's Hill, Va., Feb. 14, 1862. Died of disease at Camp Lester, Va., Feb. 21, 1862; his remains were sent home.

Morris, James. Enlisted in Company C, Jan. 25, 1865, at Jasper, for 1 year, age 21. Mustered Jan. 25, 1865. Substitute for Isaac Ball, drafted. Mustered out at Jeffersonville, Ind., July 8, 1865.

Morris, Thomas E., East Saginaw. Entered service in regiment at organization as 1st Lieutenant and Adjutant, Aug. 22, 1861, for 3 years, age 26. Commissioned Major, 15th Michigan, Aug. 21, 1862. Resigned May 31, 1863.

Morrison, John G. Enlisted in Company A, Feb. 2, 1864, at Ann Arbor, for 3 years, age 45. Mustered out at Jeffersonville, Ind., July 8, 1865.

Morse, Allen Benton, Ionia. Enlisted in Company B, as Sergeant, July 30, 1861, at Ionia, for 3 years, age 22. Discharged and joined the 21st Michigan Infantry, commissioned 1st Lieutenant, Dec. 16, 1862. Wounded in action at Mission Ridge, Tenn., resulting in amputation of arm Nov. 25, 1863. Resigned Sept. 1, 1864.

Morton or **Martin, James**. Enlisted in Company E, Dec. 13, 1861, at Detroit, for 3 years, age 22. Joined regiment at Hall's Hill, Va., Jan. 11, 1862. Wounded in action at Gaines' Mill, June 27, 1862. Corporal. Discharged at expiration of term of service at Petersburg, Va., Nov. 18, 1864.

Morton, Sanford G., Corunna. Enlisted in Company H, Aug. 21, 1861, at Corunna, for 3 years, age 19. Listed in newspaper reports with Gettysburg wounded in Philadelphia and Washington hospitals, July 1863. Taken prisoner Aug. 21, 1864 at Petersburg. Corporal. Discharged at expiration of term of service at Detroit, May 10, 1865.

Morton, Thomas (Veteran), Detroit. Enlisted in Company A, Lancers, Oct. 21, 1861, at Plymouth, for 3 years, age 23. Transferred to Company K, 16th Michigan, Feb. 28, 1862. Corporal. Wounded in action, ankle, at Gettysburg, July 2, 1863. Reenlisted Dec. 21, 1863, at Rappahannock Station, Va. Corporal. Mustered out at Jeffersonville, Ind., July 8, 1865.

Moses, Elisha A., Mundy, Genesee County. Enlisted in Company C, Jan. 12, 1862, at Detroit, for 3 years, age 24. Joined regiment at Hall's Hill, Va., Feb. 14, 1862. "Roll of Honor" states he was wounded in leg in 1862, and in right arm in 1863, but no battles given. Discharged on Surgeon's certificate of disability at Detroit, April 1, 1863, for wounds received in action.

Mosher, George D. Drafted March 15, 1865, for 1 year, from Algoma, Kent County, age 44. Assigned to Company A. Mustered out at Jeffersonville, Ind., July 8, 1865.

Mosher, Jonathan, Bay City. Enlisted in Company E, Lancers, Oct. 13, 1861, at Bay City, for 3 years, age 20. Transferred to Company I, 16th Michigan, Feb. 28, 1862. Died July 9, 1862. Buried in National Cemetery at Brooklyn, N.Y., Grave No. 180.

Mosier, Abram S. Drafted for 1 year, from Kinderhook, Branch County, age 36. Mustered March 17, 1865. Assigned to Company C. Mustered out at Jeffersonville, Ind., July 8, 1865.

Mott, John F., or T. Enlisted in Company F, as Sergeant, Aug. 7, 1861, at Plymouth, for 3 years, age 20. Transferred to Company E. Discharged at Snicker's Gap, Nov. 1, 1862, to accept promotion, but no further information given.

Mott, Judd M., Detroit. Entered service in Company B, Lancers, as Captain, Sept. 30, 1861, at Detroit, for 3 years, age 27. Mustered out March 20, 1862. Reentered service in Company I, 16th Michigan at organization, as Captain, his commission backdated to Sept. 30, 1861. Captured and wounded in action at Gaines' Mill, June 27, 1862; released Aug. 12, 1862. Died June 28, 1863, of wounds received in action at Middleburg, Va., June 20, 1863.

Moutny, Levi. Enlisted in Second Company Sharpshooters, March 27, 1864, at Bridgeport, for 3 years, age 20. Corporal May 17, 1865. Mustered out at Jeffersonville, Ind., July 8, 1865.

Moynahan, Peter, Detroit. Enlisted in First Company Sharpshooters attached to 16th Michigan, Dec. 16, 1862, at Detroit, for 3 years, age 18. Joined regiment near Falmouth, Va., Jan. 2, 1863. Died of disease Oct. 22, 1863, Baltimore.

Muir, Lyndock B., Detroit. Enlisted in Company E. Aug. 27, 1862, at Detroit, for 3 years, age 43. Joined regiment at Falmouth, Va., Jan. 2, 1863. 1st Sergeant. Wounded in action at Gettysburg, July 2, 1863. Discharged for disability by order at Washington, D.C., May 30, 1865.

Mulosh, Molosh or **Malosh, Peter.** Enlisted in Company B, March 23, 1865, at Howell, for 1 year, age 22. Substitute for Zenas F. Crossman, drafted from Howell. Mustered out at Jeffersonville, Ind., July 8, 1865.

Munn, William. Enlisted in Company A, May 18, 1864, at Houghton, for 3 years, age 22. Wounded in action Jericho Mills, Va., May 23, 1864. Mustered out at Jeffersonville, Ind., July 8, 1865.

Munson, Marion (Veteran), Oakland County. Enlisted in Company E, Aug. 20, 1861, age 18. Reenlisted Dec. 21, 1863, at Rappahannock Station, Va. Wounded in action, left hand, June 2, 1864, at Bethesda Church. Corporal. Wounded in action, left arm, Dabney's Mill, Feb. 6, 1865. Discharged at Philadelphia, July 6, 1865.

Murphy, Daniel, Redford. Enlisted in Company A, Lancers, Oct. 20, 1861, Willow Creek, for 3 years, age 20. Transferred to Company K, 16th Michigan, Feb. 28, 1862. Deserted at Detroit, March 24, 1862.

Murphy, Henry T. Enlisted in First Company Sharpshooters attached to 16th Michigan, Jan. 16, 1862, at Detroit, for 3 years, age 27. Deserted at Detroit, Feb. 3, 1862.

Murphy, Patrick. Enlisted in Company B, March 23, 1865, at Detroit, for 3 years, age 25. Substitute for James Battle, or Patrick Humphrey, drafted from Detroit. Deserted near Parkersburg, Va., June 19, 1865.

Murphy, Patrick (Veteran), Flint. Enlisted in Company C, Aug. 19, 1861. Reenlisted as Corporal Feb. 27, 1864, at Bealton, Va. 1st Sergeant. Commissioned 1st Lieutenant, July 7, 1865. Mustered out at Jeffersonville, Ind., July 8, 1865.

Murphy, William. Enlisted in Company H, Feb. 9, 1864, at Detroit, for 3 years, age 19. Corporal May 1, 1865. Mustered out at Jeffersonville, Ind., July 8, 1865.

Murray, John. Enlisted in Company I, March 18, 1865, at Dryden, Lapeer County, for 3 years, age 39. Substitute for Horace Bartlett, drafted. Mustered out at Jeffersonville, Ind., July 8, 1865.

Myers, Daniel. Drafted March 16, 1865, for 1 year, from Woodland, Barry County, age 35. Assigned to Company D. Mustered out at Jeffersonville, Ind., July 8, 1865.

Nahorn or **Nayhorn, William** (Veteran), Dearborn. Enlisted in First Company Sharpshooters attached to 16th Michigan, Oct. 28, 1861, at Detroit, for 3 years, age 18. Joined regiment at Hall's Hill, Va., Feb. 14, 1862. Reenlisted Dec. 22, 1863, at Rappahannock Station, Va. Corporal. Killed in action at Pole Cat Creek, Va., May 22, 1864.

Nash, Robert W. (Veteran), Detroit. Enlisted in Company H, Nov. 8, 1861, at Detroit, for 3 years, age 27. Wounded in action at second Manassas, Aug. 30, 1862. Wounded in action at Fredericksburg, Dec. 13, 1862. Reenlisted as Corporal Feb. 27, 1864, at Bealton, Va. Died May 23, 1864, from wounds received in action at Wilderness, May 7, 1864.

Nathan, Charles W. Enlisted in Company E, Lancers, as corporal, Oct. 3, 1861, at Milwaukee, Wis., for 3 years, age 25. Transferred to Company I or K, 16th Michigan, Feb. 28, 1862. Sergeant. Killed in action at second Manassas, Aug. 30, 1862.

Naylor, Samuel J. Enlisted in Company K, Feb. 5, 1864, at Ann Arbor, for 3 years, age 37. Corporal. Wounded in action, Wilderness, May 7, 1864. Michigan Adjutant-General's Dept. *Record of Service,* vol. 16 (1905), states he deserted May 18, 1864, but regiment's "Roll of Honor" states he died of wounds in the field near Spotsylvania Court House.

Nellis, James J. (Veteran). Enlisted in Company C, Lancers, as Sergeant, Sept. 30, 1861, at Lowell, for 3 years, age 30. Transferred to Company I, 16th Michigan, Feb. 28, 1862. Reenlisted Dec. 22, 1863, at Rappahannock Station, Va. Wounded in action May 7, 1864, Wilderness. 1st Sergeant. Commissioned 1st Lieutenant, Aug. 3, 1864. Slightly wounded in action at second Hatcher's Run, March 25, 1865. Commissioned Captain, July 7, 1865. Mustered out at Jeffersonville, Ind., July 8, 1865.

Nelson, Adna or **Adnor,** Corunna. Enlisted in Company E, Aug. 16, 1861, at Detroit, for 3 years, age 18. Transferred to Company H. Killed in action at Gaines' Mill, June 27, 1862.

Nelson, George. Enlisted in First Company Sharpshooters attached to 16th Michigan, Feb. 9, 1864, at Saginaw, for 3 years, age 31. Discharged at Detroit, June 8, 1865.

Nero, William. Enlisted in Company H, March 28, 1865, at Liberty, for 3 years, age 19. Substitute for Noah Tuttle, drafted. Mustered out at Jeffersonville, Ind., July 8, 1865.

Nesmith, John W., Detroit. Enlisted in Company K, Feb. 11, 1862, at Detroit, for 3 years, age 22. Transferred to Company G. Killed in action at Gaines' Mill, June 27, 1862.

Nestor, John M., Detroit. Enlisted in Company A, July 24, 1862, at Detroit, for 3 years, age 28. Joined regiment at Falmouth, Va., Nov. 26, 1862. Corporal. Killed in action at Gettysburg, July 2, 1863.

Netherway, Emanuel. Enlisted in Company G, March 24, 1865, at Dover, for 1 year, age 28. Substitute for Dewitt F. Ireland, drafted. Mustered out at Jeffersonville, Ind., July 8, 1865. Resided Lenoir, Tenn.

Neuman, Henry. Enlisted in Company A, Jan. 25, 1864, at Blumfield, Saginaw County, for 3 years, age 21. Wounded in action at Spotsylvania Court House, May 10, 1864. Discharged on Surgeon's certificate of disability at Detroit, June 30, 1865, for wounds received in action.

Never, George A., Saginaw County. Enlisted in Company D. Mustered Sept. 14, 1861. Discharged June 1862.

Never, Henry H., Chesaning. Enlisted in Company D, Aug. 3, 1861, at East Saginaw, for 3 years, age 24. Died of disease at Baltimore, Nov. 1, 1861.

Never, John. Enlisted in Company C, Aug. 6, 1861, at Flint, for 3 years, age 24. No further record.

Neview, John (Veteran), Ontonagon County. Enlisted in Company A, Aug. 3, 1861. Reenlisted Dec. 21, 1863, at Rappahannock Station, Va. Wounded in action in left arm, May 10 or May 18, 1864, at Spotsylvania Court House. Mustered out at Jeffersonville, Ind., July 8, 1865.

Newell, John T., St. Johns. Enlisted in Company H, as Corporal, Aug. 11, 1861, at Detroit, for 3 years, age 36. Killed in action at Gaines' Mill, June 27, 1862.

Newell, Miner S., Flushing. Entered service in Company C at organization, as 1st Lieutenant, July 30, 1861, at Flint, for 3 years, age 32. Quartermaster Aug. 9, 1861. Acting Brigade Quartermaster, Third Brigade, First Division, Fifth Army Corps, Dec. 1, 1862. Discharged at expiration of term of service, Sept. 7, 1864. Died at Flint, Nov. 30, 1889.

Newman, George. Enlisted in Company G, Aug. 22, 1861, at Detroit, for 3 years, age 25. Discharged at Hall's Hill, Va.

Newman, Joachin. Enlisted in Company K, March 29, 1865, at Macomb, for 1 year, age 22. Substitute for Jacob Ransehart, drafted. Mustered out at Jeffersonville, Ind., July 8, 1865.

Newman, John. No record of enlistment in Michigan Adjutant-General's Dept. *Record of Service,* vol. 16 (1905), but listed in regimental "Roll of Honor" in Company A, severely wounded in chest in action near Po River–Spotsylvania Court House, May 10, 1864. No other information.

Newman, John S., Wayne County. Enlisted in Company F, Aug. 7, 1861, at Plymouth, for 3 years, age 27. Deserted Sept. 13, 1861.

Nichols, Charles A., Kent County. Enlisted in Company I, Feb. 15, 1865 (probably 1864) at

Talmadge, for 1 year, age 19. Substitute for Tindal Baxter, drafted. Alternately reported as having been wounded in action, Wilderness, May 7, 1864 and discharged by order May 1865; or, discharged at Detroit, June 9, 1865. Resided Luther, Mich.

Nichols, George D. See **Ameigh, George D.**

Nichols, Henry. Enlisted and mustered in Company H, March 21, 1865, at Detroit, for 1 year, age 25. Substitute for Antoine Pope, drafted. Mustered out at Jeffersonville, Ind., July 8, 1865.

Nichols, James H. See **Ameigh, James H.**

Niles, Arza N., Genesee County. Enlisted in Company C, as Corporal, Aug. 1, 1861, at Flint, for 3 years, age 21. Sergeant Sept. 22, 1861. Wounded and taken prisoner Gaines' Mill, June 27, 1862. Discharged at Philadelphia, Sept. 9, 1862.

Niles, Jerome R. Enlisted in Company I, March 13, 1865, at Kalamazoo, for 1 year, age 19. Substitute for Abner Lewis, Wayland. Mustered out at Jeffersonville, Ind., July 8, 1865. Resided Breedsville, Mich.

Nisbett, Charles A. Enlisted in Company F, Feb. 15, 1865, at Pontiac, for 3 years, age 18. Substitute for Albert Buckle, drafted. Mustered out at Jeffersonville, Ind., July 8, 1865. Resided Big Rapids, Mich.

Nixon, Henry M. or **John**. Enlisted in Company A, Feb. 2, 1864, at Ann Arbor, for 3 years, age 22. Deserted May 6, 1864.

Nobles, Stephen L. Enlisted in Company G, as Sergeant, Aug. 24, 1861, at White Pigeon, for 3 years, age 20. Discharged at Philadelphia, Nov. 27, 1862. Resided Adrian, Mich.

Noker or **Noeker, August** (Veteran), Ontonagon County. Enlisted in Company A, Aug. 1, 1861, at Ontonagon, for 3 years, age 23. Reenlisted Dec. 21, 1863, at Rappahannock Station, Va. Wounded at Petersburg, Va., June 17, 1864. Corporal May 1, 1865. Mustered out at Jeffersonville, Ind., July 8, 1865.

Norris, John, East Saginaw. Enlisted in Company D, Aug. 4, 1861, at East Saginaw, for 3 years, age 23. Severely wounded and taken prisoner in action at Gaines' Mill, June 27, 1862. Died in prison at Richmond.

Norris, Phillip, St. Joseph County. Enlisted in Company E, Aug. 20, 1861, at Jonesville, for 3 years, age 50. Discharged for disability July 12, 1863.

Northrop, Charles J. (Veteran), Van Buren. Enlisted in First Company Sharpshooters attached to 16th Michigan, Nov. 17, 1861, at Detroit, for 3 years, age 22. Joined regiment at Hall's Hill, Va., Feb. 14, 1862. Reenlisted Dec. 22, 1863, at Rappahannock Station, Va. Corporal. Wounded in action, Bethesda Church–Cold Harbor, June 3, 1864. Transferred to Veteran Reserve Corps Jan. 4, 1865. Discharged at Detroit, July 14, 1865, from Company B, 2nd Regiment, Veteran Reserve Cops.

Northwood, John. Enlisted in Company B, Aug. 3, 1861, at Ionia, for 3 years, age 23. Transferred to Company C. Wounded in both arms at Gaines' Mill, right arm amputated. Taken prisoner at Savage's Station. Confined at Richmond and released. Discharged on Surgeon's certificate of disability at Philadelphia, Aug. 18, 1862. Resided New Lothrop, Mich.

Norton, George. Enlisted in Company D, March 1, 1865, at Kalamazoo, for 3 years, age 25. Substitute for George F. Good, drafted. Mustered out at Jeffersonville, Ind., July 8, 1865.

Norton, Windsor. Macomb County. Enlisted in First Company Sharpshooters attached to 16th

Michigan, Dec. 3, 1861, at Detroit, for 3 years, age 21. Joined regiment at Hall's Hill, Va., Feb. 14, 1862. Discharged at Antietam, Md., Oct. 25, 1862.

Norwood, Wallace N., Ionia County. Enlisted in Company H, as Sergeant, Aug. 13, 1861, at Detroit, for 3 years, age 25. Wounded in action at Gaines' Mill, June 27, 1862. Discharged at expiration of term of service at Petersburg, Va., Sept. 8, 1864.

Noyce, Allen L., Adams. Enlisted in Company G, Aug. 24, 1861, at Hillsdale, for 3 years, age 18. Wounded in action at Gaines' Mill, June 27, 1862. Wounded and taken prisoner in action at Malvern Hill, July 1, 1862. Died in Libby prison at Richmond, July 24, 1862.

Noyes, George W. Enlisted in Company D, Jan. 25, 1864, at Fenton, for 3 years, age 17. Discharged on Surgeon's certificate of disability at Alexandria, Va., Sept. 26, 1864.

Nye, Harrison, Blissfield. Enlisted in Company I, March 22, 1862, at Blissfield, for 3 years, age 44. Deserted at Detroit, March 24, 1863.

Nye, James H. Drafted for 1 year, from Ovid, Branch County, age 34. Mustered March 17, 1865. Assigned to Company G. Mustered out at Jeffersonville, Ind., July 8, 1865.

Nye, Ludivie M. Drafted March 17, 1865, for 1 year from Ovid, Branch County, age 24. Assigned to Company H. Mustered out at Jeffersonville, Ind., July 8, 1865.

Oakley, James O. Enlisted and mustered in Company D, March 28, 1865, at Highland, Oakland County, for 1 year, age 19. Substitute for John Powers, drafted. Mustered out at Jeffersonville, Ind., July 8, 1865.

O'Brian, John. Enlisted in Company E, Feb. 9, 1865, at Oakfield, for 1 year, age 22. Substitute for Nathan H. Gould, drafted. Mustered out at Jeffersonville, Ind., July 8, 1865.

O'Brien, James. Enlisted in Company C, Jan. 17, 1865, at Trowbridge, for 1 year, age 31. Substitute for Albert Mallory, drafted. Mustered out at Jeffersonville, Ind., July 8, 1865.

O'Connell, Joseph. Enlisted in Company C, Aug. 3, 1861, at Flint, for 3 years, age 29. No further record.

O'Connor, James. Enlisted in Company F, Feb. 4, 1864, at Saginaw, for 3 years, age 18. Wounded in action, leg, Bethesda Church–Cold Harbor, June 2, 1864. Transferred to Veteran Reserve Corps Dec. 27, 1864. Discharged on Surgeon's certificate of disability July 15, 1865.

Oddy, William. Enlisted in Company E, Aug. 17, 1861, at Detroit, for 3 years, age 33. Deserted at Detroit, Sept. 1861.

Odell, Charles, Plymouth. Enlisted in Company K, March 21, 1862, at Detroit, for 3 years, age 40. Discharged for disability at Yorktown, Va., May 8, 1862.

O'Keefe, Nicholas (Veteran). Enlisted in Company E, Sept. 12, 1861. Prisoner, probably captured at Gaines' Mill, paroled Aug. 1862. Reenlisted as Corporal Dec. 21, 1863, at Rappahannock Station, Va. Wounded in action near Cold Harbor, left knee, June 7, 1864. Transferred to Veteran Reserve Corps. Discharged at Washington, D.C., by order, July 20, 1865, from Company A, 24th Regiment, Veteran Reserve Corps.

O'Keif, William. Enlisted in Second Company Sharpshooters, April 23, 1864, at Spaulding, for 3 years, age 24. Taken prisoner on the raid on the Weldon Railroad, Petersburg, Va., Dec. 10, 1864. Released June 1865. No further record.

Oleman, Peter, Wayne County. Enlisted in Company A, Aug. 3, 1861, at Ontonagon, for 3 years, age 40. Died of disease at Washington, D.C., or Alexandria, Va., Nov. 11, 1862.

O'Neil, Daniel, Detroit. Enlisted in Company H, Sept. 4, 1861, at Detroit, for 3 years, age 36. Severely wounded in action, hand, Fredericksburg, Dec. 13, 1862. Transferred to Invalid Corps at Washington, D.C., Sept. 1, 1863. Transferred from Invalid Corps, Feb. 23, 1864. Discharged at expiration of term of service at Petersburg, Va., Sept. 7, 1864.

O'Neil, Henry R. Enlisted in Company G, Feb. 15, 1864, at Bridgeport, for 3 years, age 25. Wounded in action, neck, Petersburg, Va., June 19, 1864. Discharged Oct. 16, 1864.

Oppen or **Opfer, John** (Veteran), Macomb. Enlisted in Company E, Aug. 16, 1861, at Detroit, for 3 years, age 19. Reenlisted Dec. 21, 1863, at Rappahannock Station, Va. Mustered out at Jeffersonville, Ind., July 8, 1865. Resided Detroit.

O'Riley, George. Enlisted in Company B, Feb. 4, 1865, at Prairie Ronde, for 3 years, age 29. Substitute for George Bisbun, drafted. Deserted at Washington, D.C., June 15, 1865.

O'Riley, Patrick. Enlisted in Company D, March 19, 1864, at Houghton, for 3 years, age 24. Wounded and missing in action at Peeble's Farm, Sept. 30, 1864. No further record.

Ormsbee, Ira G., Saginaw. Enlisted in Company C, Jan. 11, 1864, at Maple Grove, for 3 years, age 19. Wounded in action at Wilderness, May 7, 1864. Transferred to Veteran Reserve Corps Dec. 24, 1864. Discharged at Washington, D.C., July 26, 1865, from Company B, 14th Regiment, Veteran Reseve Corps. Resided in Flint.

Ormsby, Alfred W. Enlisted in regimental Band, Sept. 13, 1861, at Detroit, for 3 years, age 20. Discharged at Hall's Hill, Va., Feb. 25, 1862.

Orten or **Orton, George A.** (Veteran). Enlisted in Company D, Aug. 5, 1861, at East Saginaw, for 3 years, age 35. Wounded in action at Gaines' Mill, June 27, 1862. Reenlisted Feb. 24, 1864, at Rappahannock Station, Va. Wounded in action, right leg, Petersburg, Va., June 19, 1864. Discharged by order at Detroit, July 26, 1865.

Ortwine, William, Detroit. Enlisted in Company E, Oct. 3, 1862, at Detroit, for 3 years, age 21. Joined regiment at Antietam, Md., Oct. 30, 1862. Corporal. Reported as wounded in action, Wilderness, May 7, 1864; regiment's roster states he was wounded, Feb. 1865, probably Dabney's Mill. Mustered out at Jeffersonville, Ind., July 8, 1865. Died Nov. 2, 1888.

Ostrander, Sylvester, Redford. Enlisted in Company G, as Sergeant, Aug. 28, 1861, at Detroit, for 3 years, age 25. Wounded in action, arm, Fredericksburg, Va., Dec. 15, 1862. Transferred to Invalid Corps Sept. 1, 1863. Discharged at expiration of term of service at Washington, D.C., Aug. 22, 1864. Died Aug. 14, 1899 and buried at Redford.

O'Sullivan, Cornelius. Enlisted in Company F, Aug. 7, 1861, at Plymouth, for 3 years, age 25. Transferred to Company E. Discharged at Philadelphia, Nov. 25, 1862, for wounds received in action at Gaines' Mill, June 27, 1862.

Overton, Nathaniel B., Corunna. Enlisted in Company E, Aug. 15, 1861, at Detroit, for 3 years, age 22. Transferred to Company H. Killed in action at Gaines' Mill, June 27, 1862.

Owen, Isaac N., Macomb County. Enlisted in First Company Sharpshooters attached to 16th Michigan as Corporal, Oct. 12, 1861, at Detroit, for 3 years, age 35. Joined regiment at Hall's Hill, Va., Feb. 14, 1862. Discharged for disability at Falmouth, Va., Feb. 18, 1863.

Owen, John A. (Veteran). Enlisted in Company E, Aug. 16, 1861, at Detroit, for 3 years, age 34. Transferred to Company H, July 1862. Missing in action at Gaines' Mill, June 27, 1862. Reenlisted Dec. 24, 1863, at Rappahannock Station, Va. Killed in action before Petersburg,

Va., June 20, 1864.

Paddock, James. Enlisted in Company G, Sept. 13, 1861, at Detroit, for 3 years, age 38. Transferred to Invalid Corps Aug. 1, 1863 and discharged that year.

Paine or **Payne, Adoniram J**., St. Johns. Enlisted in Company E, Aug. 14, 1861, at Detroit, for 3 years, age 27. Transferred to Company H. Died of disease at Washington, D.C., Oct. 2, 1861.

Palmer, Alonzo J. Drafted March 15, 1865, for 1 year, from Byron, Kent County, age 30. Assigned to Company I. Mustered out at Jeffersonville, Ind., July 8, 1865.

Palmer, Elias or **Silas**, Genesee County. Enlisted in Company C, Aug. 8, 1861, at Flint, for 3 years, age 28. Discharged on Surgeon's certificate of disability at Hall's Hill, Va., Feb. 24, 1862.

Palmer, Gershon, Genesee County. Enlisted in Company C, Aug. 2, 1861, at Flint, for 3 years, age 40. Died of disease at Gaines' Mill, June 11, 1862.

Palmer, Henry C. (Veteran), Chelsea. Enlisted in Company D, Lancers, Oct. 21, 1861, at Chelsea, for 3 years, age 18. Transferred to Company I, 16th Michigan, Feb. 28, 1862. Wounded in action at Gaines' Mill, June 27, 1862. Wounded in action at Gettysburg, July 2, 1863. Reenlisted Feb. 26, 1864, at Bealton, Va. Discharged for disability April 26, 1865. Died Sept. 10, 1891. Buried at Grass Lake.

Palmer, John. Enlisted in Company C, Aug. 2, 1861, at Flint, for 3 years, age 26. Transferred to Company F. Killed in action at Gaines' Mill, June 27, 1862.

Palmer, Robert, Detroit. Enlisted in Company E, Oct. 10, 1862, at Detroit, for 3 years, age 43. Joined regiment at Antietam, Md., Oct. 30, 1862. Discharged at Washington, D.C., July 20, 1863.

Palmer, William, Milford. Enlisted in Company B, Lancers, Oct. 19, 1861, at Milford, for 3 years, age 23. Transferred to Company I, Feb. 28, 1862. Corporal. Discharged for disability March 27, 1863.

Parker, Hollis M., Argentine, Genesee County. Enlisted in Company A at Argentine, for 3 years, age 18. Joined regiment at Antietam, Md., Oct. 12, 1862. Died of disease at Falmouth, Va., Dec. 6, 1862.

Parker, James (Veteran), Saginaw County. Enlisted in Company D, Aug. 5, 1861, at East Saginaw, for 3 years, age 20. Reenlisted Dec. 21, 1863, at Rappahannock Station, Va. Mustered out at Jeffersonville, Ind., July 8, 1865.

Parker, James E., Hillsdale County. Enlisted in Company E, Aug. 24, 1861, at Hillsdale, for 3 years, age 19. Discharged for disability at Philadelphia, Jan. 15, 1863.

Parker, John F. (Veteran). Enlisted in Company A, Aug. 1, 1862, at Argentine, Genesee County, age 20. Joined regiment at Antietam, Md., Oct. 12, 1862. Reenlisted Dec. 21, 1863, at Rappahannock Station, Va. Wounded in action, shoulder, May 7, 1864, Wilderness. Corporal, May 1, 1865. Mustered out at Jeffersonville, Ind., July 8, 1865.

Parkhurst, Freeman S. or **Truman A.**, Saginaw. Enlisted in Company D, Feb. 7, 1864, at Saginaw, for 3 years, age 20. Died of disease at Philadelphia, July 12, 1864. Buried in National Cemetery at Philadelphia.

Parmenter, Jesse (Veteran), Corunna. Enlisted in Company H, as Wagoner, Aug. 21, 1861, at Corunna, for 3 years, age 22. Reenlisted Dec. 24, 1863, at Rappahannock Station, Va.

Wounded in action, shoulder, Wilderness, May 7, 1864. Discharged for disability at Detroit, Feb. 20, 1865, for wounds received in action.

Parmlee, Charles, Wayne County. Enlisted in First Company Sharpshooters attached to 16th Michigan, Nov. 1, 1861, at Detroit, for 3 years, age 25. Joined regiment at Hall's Hill, Va., Feb. 14, 1862. Discharged at expiration of term of service, Nov. 1, 1864. Resided Ingersoll, Mich.

Parrish, Amos, Ottawa County. Enlisted in First Company Sharpshooters attached to 16th Michigan, Nov. 12, 1861, at Grand Rapids, for 3 years, age 41. Joined regiment at Hall's Hill, Va., Feb. 14, 1862. Discharged at Fortress Monroe, Va., Oct. 2, 1862.

Parsons, Harvey S. (Veteran). Isabella County. Enlisted in Company B, Aug. 7, 1861, at Ionia, for 3 years, age 18. Wounded in action at Middleburg, Va., June 21, 1863. Reenlisted Dec. 24, 1863, at Rappahannock Station, Va. Mustered Dec. 24, 1863. Corporal May 14, 1865. Mustered out at Jeffersonville, Ind., July 8, 1865.

Partello, John J. Enlisted in Company E, Aug. 13, 1861, at Detroit, for 3 years, age 24. Transferred to Company H. Missing in action at Gaines' Mill, June 27, 1862. Discharged at expiration of term of service, at Petersburg, Va., Sept. 6, 1864.

Partridge, Benjamin F., Bay City. Entered service in Company H, Lancers, at organization, as 2nd Lieutenant, Oct. 12, 1861, at Bay City, for 3 years, age 38. Reentered service in Company I, 16th Michigan, at organization as 1st Lieutenant. Commissioned Oct. 12, 1861. Wounded in action at Malvern Hill, July 1, 1862. Commissioned Captain, Company C, April 16, 1863. Wounded in action at Gettysburg, July 2, 1863. Transferred to Company I, Oct. 1, 1863. Commissioned Major June 1, 1864. Wounded in action at Peeble's Farm, Sept. 30, 1864. Brevet Colonel, Sept. 30, 1864, for distinguished gallantry at the battle. Commissioned Lieutenant Colonel, Sept. 30, 1864. Commissioned Colonel Dec. 17, 1864. Wounded in action at Dabney's Mill, Feb. 6, 1865. Wounded in action at White Oak Road, March 31, 1865. Brevet Brigadier General. March 31, 1865, for gallant conduct in action at White Oak Road (Quaker Road), March 29, 1865. Mustered out at Jeffersonville, Ind., July 1, 1865. Died Oct. 20, 1892.

Partridge, Hiram D. Enlisted in Company E, Lancers, Nov 27, 1861, at Saginaw, for 3 years, age 39. Transferred to Company K, 16th Michigan, Feb. 28, 1862. Deserted at Detroit, March 26, 1862. Partridge apparently enlisted again in First Company Sharpshooters attached to 16th Michigan, Feb. 13, 1864, at Midland, for 3 years, age 42. Mustered Feb. 13, 1864. Wounded Sept. 1864, no date, probably Peeble's Farm. Mustered out at Jeffersonville, Ind., July 8, 1865.

Partridge, John W. Enlisted in First Company Sharpshooters attached to 16th Michigan, Feb. 13, 1864, at Midland, for 3 years, age 18. Wounded Sept. 1864. Mustered out at Jeffersonville, Ind., July 8, 1865.

Passage, Edward W. M., Wayne. Enlisted in Company F, as Sergeant, July 31, 1861, at Plymouth, for 3 years, age 30. Discharged for disability April 30, 1863. Resided Ypsilanti.

Patterson, Alexander. Enlisted in Company H, as Corporal, Sept. 11, 1861, at Detroit, for 3 years. Missing in action at Gaines' Mill, June 27, 1862. Sergeant. Died at Philadelphia, Nov. 18, 1863, of wounds received in action at Gettysburg, July 2, 1863. Buried in National Cemetery, Philadelphia, Grave No. 553.

Patterson, Andrew, Canada. Enlisted in Company D, Lancers, Oct. 5, 1861, at Detroit, for 3 years, age 24. Transferred to Company K, 16th Michigan, Feb. 28, 1862. Deserted at Detroit, March 10, 1862.

Patterson, Edward, Saginaw County. Enlisted in Company D, Aug. 5, 1861, at East Saginaw, for 3 years, age 20. Discharged at expiration of term of service at Petersburg, Va., Sept. 17, 1864.

Patterson, Ira, Forest, Genesee County. Enlisted in Company C, Aug. 4, 1861, at Flint, for 3 years, age 31. Corporal. Wounded and taken prisoner at Gaines' Mill, June 27, 1862. Died at Richmond, July 4, 1862.

Patterson, J. M., Detroit. Enlisted in Company K, March 1, 1862, at Detroit, for 3 years, age 22. Deserted at Detroit, March 1862.

Patterson, Thomas (Veteran). Enlisted in Company F, Aug. 7, 1861, at Plymouth, for 3 years, age 21. Transferred to Company B. Reenlisted Dec. 24, 1863, at Rappahannock Station, Va. Discharged for disability at Detroit, Dec. 29, 1864.

Patterson, William (Veteran), Ottawa County. Enlisted in First Company Sharpshooters attached to 16th Michigan, Jan. 15, 1862, at Grand Rapids, for 3 years, age 22. Joined regiment at Hall's Hill, Va., Feb. 14, 1862. Wounded in action at Gaines' Mill, June 27, 1862. Reenlisted March 30, 1864, at Bealton, Va. Corporal, May 1, 1865. Mustered out at Jeffersonville, Ind., July 8, 1865.

Patton, William, Wayne. Enlisted in Company E, Aug. 21, 1861, at Detroit, for 3 years, age 25. Sergeant. Killed in action at Fredericksburg, Va., Dec. 13, 1862.

Payne, Charles D. Not listed in regimental roster, but in regiment's "Roll of Honor" as private, Company E, and wounded in action at second Manassas, Aug. 30, 1862. Wounded in action again near Cold Harbor, in hand, June 7, 1864. Mustered out July 8, 1865.

Payne, Emmet, Oakland County. Enlisted in Company K, as Corporal, March 22, 1862, at Detroit, for 3 years, age 23. Discharged for disability in 1863.

Payne, Harrison E., Oakland County. Enlisted in Company K, March 31, 1862, at Detroit, for 3 years, age 20. Discharged for disability at Fortress Monroe, Va., Jan. 17, 1863.

Payne, Philander G., Genesee County. Enlisted in Company C, Aug. 2, 1861, at Flint, for 3 years, age 28. Discharged at expiration of term of service at Petersburg, Va., Sept. 16, 1864.

Peck, Charles. Enlisted in Company H, Aug. 30, 1864, at Redford, for 1 year, age 18. Discharged at Washington, D.C., May 29, 1865.

Peck, Henry, Hillsdale County. Enlisted in Company E, Aug. 20, 1861, at Hillsdale. Died of disease at Hampton, Va., Nov. 19, 1862.

Peck, Myron, Hope. Drafted Feb. 10, 1863, for 9 months, from Hope. Assigned to Company D. Joined regiment at Warrenton, Va., July 30, 1863. Discharged at expiration of term of service at Petersburg, Va., July 6, 1864.

Peltier, Eli. Drafted for 1 year, from Chesterfield, March 23, 1865, for 3 years, age 22. Assigned to Company G. Mustered out at Jeffersonville, Ind., July 8, 1865. Resided Mt. Clemens.

Peltz, George, Ontonagon County. Enlisted in Company A, Aug. 3, 1861, at Ontonagon, for 3 years, age 40. Discharged for disability at Washington, D.C., April 1, 1862.

Perkins, George W. (Veteran). Enlisted in Company C, Lancers, Oct. 15, 1861, at Saginaw, for 3 years, age 21. Transferred to Company K, 16th Michigan, Feb. 28, 1862. Reenlisted Dec.

21, 1863, at Rappahannock Station, Va. Corporal. Listed as absent, wounded from Sept. 1864 to March 1865. Mustered out at Jeffersonville, Ind., July 8, 1865.

Perkins, James N., or M. Enlisted in Company D, March 22, 1865, at Lockport, for 1 year, age 35. Substitute for Julius F. Thompson, drafted. Mustered out at Jeffersonville, Ind., July 8, 1865.

Perrin or **Porter, Daniel**. Enlisted in Company H, March 24, 1865, at Kalamazoo, for 1 year, age 19. Substitute for John D. Curtis, drafted. Mustered out at Jeffersonville, Ind., July 8, 1865.

Perrin, Thomas, Detroit. Enlisted in Company I, March 10, 1862, age 39. Deserted March 25, 1862.

Perry, Charles J., Muir. Enlisted in Company H, Aug. 20, 1861, at Detroit, for 3 years. Sergeant. Discharged at Detroit, Oct. 13, 1863, for wounds received in action at Gettysburg, July 2, 1863.

Perry, David B., Mottville, Mich. Enlisted in Company E, March 27, 1865, at White Pigeon, for 1 year, age 25. Substitute for Isaac Klickner, drafted. Mustered out at Jeffersonville, Ind., July 8, 1865. Resided Mottville, Mich.

Perry, James. Enlisted in Company D, Jan. 25, 1864, at Au Sable, for 3 years, age 26. Failed to report from furlough.

Perry, Seth W. Enlisted in Company A, March 30, 1865, at Dexter, for 3 years, age 18. Substitute for Herman Backus, drafted. Mustered out at Jeffersonville, Ind., July 8, 1865.

Perry, Thadeus A. (Veteran), Saginaw County. Enlisted in Company D, Aug. 6, 1861, at East Saginaw, for 3 years, age 27. Corporal. Wounded in action at Malvern Hill, July 1, 1862. Reenlisted as Sergeant Dec. 21, 1863, at Rappahannock Station, Va. Died Nov. 21, 1864, at Washington, D.C., from gunshot wound received in action at Peeble's Farm, Sept. 30, 1864.

Persons, Abraham, Flushing. Enlisted in Company C, Aug. 19, 1861, at Flint, age 35. Died of disease at Georgetown, April 15, 1862.

Peterhans, George C., Wayne County. Enlisted in Company F, Sept. 16, 1861, at Plymouth, for three years, age 22. Discharged at expiration of term of service at Petersburg, Va., Sept. 7, 1864. Resided Plymouth, Mich.

Peterhans, John C., Wayne County. Enlisted in Company F, Sept. 16, 1861, at Plymouth, for 3 years, age 22. Discharged on Surgeon's certificate of disability at Antietam, Md., Oct. 25, 1862.

Peters, Alexander. Enlisted in Company K, March 4, 1862, at Detroit, for 3 years, age 19. Discharged at Yorktown, Va., May 4, 1862.

Peters, Franklin. Enlisted in First Company Sharpshooters attached to 16th Michigan, Feb. 16, 1864, at Kochville, for 3 years, age 20. Wounded in action, face, Petersburg, Va., June 19, 1864. Discharged by order April 6, 1865.

Pettibone, Harry or **Harvey**. Enlisted in Company B, March 27, 1865, at Wright, for 3 years, age 20. Substitute for Edward Wetherington, drafted from Wright. Absent sick, June 1865. No further record.

Pfifer, Anthony. Enlisted in Company G, Sept. 13, 1861, at Detroit, for 3 years, age 48. Mustered Sept. 14, 1861. Discharged for disability March 17, 1863. Entered 73rd Company, 2nd Battalion, Veteran Reserve Corps, Aug. 28, 1863, at Detroit. Discharged on Surgeon's certificate of disability July 6, 1865.

Phillips, Myron B. Enlisted in Company G, Jan. 28, 1865, at Park, for 3 years, age 21. Substitute for James Boardman, drafted. Mustered out at Jeffersonville, Ind., July 8, 1865.

Phillips, Spary, Kent County. Enlisted in First Company Sharpshooters attached to 16th Michigan, Jan. 7, 1862, at Grand Rapids, for 3 years, age 18. Joined regiment at Hall's Hill, Va., Feb. 14, 1862. Transferred to Invalid Corps, Feb. 15, 1864.

Phipps, Andrew. Enlisted in Company I and mustered March 20, 1862. Killed in action at Gaines' Mill, June 27, 1862.

Phipps, Henry, Portage Lake. Enlisted in Company I, Oct. 26, 1861, at Portage, age 45. Died at Rebel prison, Richmond, of wounds received in action at Gaines' Mill, June 27, 1862.

Pibramsky, Frank. Enlisted and mustered in Company K, March 30, 1865, at Volinia, Cass County, for 1 year, age 36. Substitute for David A. Squires, drafted. Mustered out at Jeffersonville, Ind., July 8, 1865.

Piche, Arcule. Enlisted in Second Company Sharpshooters, March 30, 1864, at Kochville, for 3 years, age 21. Deserted July 10, 1865.

Pickley, William. Enlisted in Company F, Aug. 7, 1861, at Plymouth, for 3 years, age 34. Transferred to Company E. Missing in action at Gaines' Mill, June 27, 1862. Discharged for disability Jan. 9, 1863. Died Oct. 8, 1895.

Pidoux, Alfred, Detroit. Enlisted in Company E, Aug. 18, 1861, at Detroit, for 3 years, age 24. Corporal. Killed in action at Gaines' Mill, June 27, 1862.

Pier, William D. Enlisted in Company B, 4th Michigan Infantry, June 20, 1861, at Adrian, for 3 years, age 25. Discharged for disability at Falmouth, Va., Jan. 2, 1863. Reentered service. Enlisted in Second Company Sharpshooters, April 25, 1864, at Bridgeport. Wounded Oct. 1864, no date or place given. Discharged at Washington, D.C., June 28, 1865.

Pierce, Franklin. Enlisted in Company E, Aug. 20, 1861, at Adrian, for 3 years, age 19. Wounded in action at Gaines' Mill, June 27, 1862. Deserted March 3, 1863.

Pierce, William B. Enlisted in regimental Band, Sept. 13, 1861, at Detroit, for 3 years, age 21. Mustered out Aug. 11, 1862.

Pitcher, Charles E., Wayne County. Enlisted in Company F, Sept. 6, 1861, at Plymouth, for 3 years, age 18. Discharged for disability at Antietam, Md., Oct. 28, 1862. Resided Plymouth, Mich.

Plank, Jacob C. Enlisted in Company B, March 28, 1865, at Comstock, for 1 year, age 19. Substitute for Jacob Hill, drafted. Mustered out at Jeffersonville, Ind., July 8, 1865. Resided Ithaca, Mich.

Plumb, Byron, Kent County. Enlisted in First Company Sharpshooters attached to 16th Michigan, Nov. 2, 1861, at Detroit, for 3 years, age 26. Joined regiment at Hall's Hill, Va., Feb. 14, 1862. Missing in action at Gaines' Mill, June 27, 1862. Discharged at expiration of term of service, Nov. 1, 1864.

Pond, Darius A., Ionia County. Enlisted in Company B, Aug. 8, 1861, at Ionia, for 3 years, age 18. Missing in action at Gaines' Mill, June 27, 1862. Discharged for disability at Newport News, Va., Jan. 31, 1863.

Pond, Jared, Washtenaw County. Enlisted in Company A, Aug. 3, 1861, at Detroit, for 3 years, age 32. Sergeant. Killed in action at Gaines' Mill, June 27, 1862.

Pope, William H. Drafted for 1 year, from Climax, age 29. Mustered March 15, 1865. Assigned to Company G. Discharged at Washington, D.C., June 12, 1865.

Postle, George. Drafted March 15, 1865, for 1 year, from Odessa, age 30. Assigned to Company D. Discharged at Detroit, Nov. 18, 1865.

Potley, Charles. Reportedly a private in Company E, died of fever near Falmouth, Va., April 13, 1863.

Potter, Drowne, Saginaw County. Enlisted in Company E, Lancers, Nov. 2, 1861, at Saginaw, for 3 years, age 23. Transferred to Company K, 16th Michigan, Feb. 28, 1862. Quartermaster Sergeant May 26, 1862. Killed by Confederates at Garlick's Landing, Va., June 13, 1862. Buried in National Cemetery at Yorktown, Va., Grave No. 224, Division A.

Potter, Elbridge, Detroit. Enlisted in Company C, Lancers, as Corporal, Oct. 22, 1861, at Detroit, for 3 years, age 20. Transferred to Company I, 16th Michigan, Feb. 28, 1862. Wounded in action at Gaines' Mill, June 27, 1862. Color Sergeant. Sergeant. Wounded in the right leg carrying the colors at Gettysburg, July 2, 1863, reluctantly giving them up to another soldier. Discharged Aug. 1864, for wounds received in action.

Pottery, Charles, Delhi. Enlisted in Company E, Dec. 30, 1862, at Delhi, age 18. Joined regiment at Falmouth, Va., Jan. 2, 1863. Died of disease at Falmouth, Va., April 13, 1863.

Potts, Joseph. Enlisted in Second Company Sharpshooters, March 18, 1864, at Kochville, for 3 years, age 18. Sergeant. Mustered out at Jeffersonville, Ind., July 8, 1865.

Powers, Abraham. Drafted for 1 year, from Climax, age 20. Mustered March 15, 1865. Assigned to Company C. Mustered out at Jeffersonville, Ind., July 8, 1865.

Powers, Thomas Frank. Enlisted in Company E, Lancers, as Sergeant, Nov. 7, 1861, at Detroit, for 3 years, age 23. Transferred to Company K, 16th Michigan, Feb. 28, 1862. 1st Sergeant. Wounded in action at second Manassas, Aug. 30, 1863. Commissioned 2nd Lieutenant, Company A, Nov. 3, 1862. Transferred to Company B, May 1864. Commissioned 1st Lieutenant June 21, 1864. Acting Quartermaster Sept. 1864. Commissioned Captain Aug. 3, 1864. Mustered out at Jeffersonville, Ind., July 8, 1865.

Potter, William. Enlisted in Company H, Feb. 21, 1865, at Bloomfield, for 3 years, age 20. Substitute for Norton J. McHenry, drafted. Mustered out at Jeffersonville, Ind., July 8, 1865.

Prame or **Pranse, William**, Ontonagon County. Enlisted in Company A, Aug. 3, 1861, at Ontonagon, for 3 years, age 25. Wounded and missing in action at Gaines' Mill, June 27, 1862. Discharged at expiration of term of service, Sept. 6, 1864.

Pranchard, George. Enlisted in Company B, Feb. 25, 1865, at Orange, for 1 year, age 30. Substitute for John Mathews, drafted. Mustered out at Jeffersonville, Ind., July 8, 1865.

Prentice, Henry. Enlisted in Company G, Aug. 21, 1861, at White Pigeon, for 3 years, age 22. Missing in action Aug. 30, 1862. Enlisted in 11th U.S. Infantry at Detroit, Dec. 1862. Discharged at expiration of term of service.

Prentiss, George, Detroit. Entered service in Company A at organization, as 2nd Lieutenant, Aug. 1, 1861, for 3 years, age 24. Acting Adjutant July 1862. Commissioned and mustered 1st Lieutenant to date June 27, 1862. Resigned and discharged Jan. 19, 1863.

Preston, Daniel. Enlisted in Company G, as Musician, Aug. 26, 1861, at Detroit, age 44. Transferred to Invalid Corps Nov. 1, 1863. Discharged in hospital.

Preston, John. Enlisted Jan. 18, 1864, at Detroit, for 3 years, age 23. Deserted at Detroit, Feb. 5, 1864.

Price, George. Enlisted in Company G, Aug. 20, 1861, at White Pigeon, for 3 years, age 18. Wounded in action at Malvern Hill, July 1, 1862. Discharged at Baltimore, Dec. 4, 1862. Resided Mason, Mich.

Provee, Felix, Walled Lake. Enlisted in Company B, Lancers, Oct. 28, 1861, at Walled Lake, for 3 years, age 26. Transferred to Company I, 16th Michigan Feb. 28, 1862. Wounded in action at Gaines' Mill, June 27, 1862. Discharged at Fortress Monroe, Va., Oct. 8, 1862.

Pulver, Byron. Enlisted in Company C, Feb. 8, 1865, at Brandon, Oakland County, for 3 years, age 18. Substitute for Elisha Bird, drafted. Mustered out at Jeffersonville, Ind., July 8, 1865. Resided Jackson, Mich.

Purcell, John. Enlisted in Company D, May 9, 1864, at Saginaw, for 3 years, age 20. Sergeant May 16, 1865. Mustered out at Jeffersonville, Ind., July 8, 1865.

Purchase, Oliver A., Saginaw County. Enlisted in Company D as Sergeant, Aug. 1, 1861, at East Saginaw, for 3 years, age 29. Wounded in action at Hanover Court House, May 27, 1862 by concussion of an exploding shell causing severe vision damage. Discharged at Philadelphia, Dec. 15, 1862.

Purdue, James (Veteran), Plymouth. Enlisted in Company F, Sept. 13, 1861. Reenlisted as Sergeant Dec. 21, 1863, at Rappahannock Station, Va. 1st Sergeant. Commissioned 1st Lieutenant, June 21, 1864. Commissioned Captain, July 7, 1865. Mustered out at Jeffersonville, Ind., July 8, 1865.

Purdy, Judson (Veteran), Wayne County. Enlisted in First Company Sharpshooters attached to 16th Michigan as Sergeant, Oct. 24, 1861, at Detroit, for 3 years, age 21. Joined regiment at Hall's Hill, Va., Feb. 14, 1862. Reenlisted Dec. 22, 1863, at Rappahannock Station, Va. Mustered out at Jeffersonville, Ind., July 8, 1865.

Purdy, Richard. Drafted for 1 year, from Clyde, Allegan County, age 35. Mustered Oct. 22, 1864. Assigned to Company C. Mustered out at Jeffersonville, Ind., July 8, 1865

Putnam, Joseph (Veteran), Nankin, Wayne County. Enlisted in Company F, Sept. 9, 1861, age 18. Reenlisted Dec. 21, 1863, at Rappahannock Station, Va. Corporal. Killed in action at Wilderness, May 6, 1864.

Quackenbush, Sylvester W., Rochester. Enlisted in Company H, Aug. 31, 1861, at Detroit, for 3 years, age 25. Discharged for disability at Georgetown, April 24, 1862. Reentered service in Company E, 12th Michigan Infantry. Enlisted March 17, 1864, at Niles. Mustered out at Camden, Ark., Feb. 15, 1866.

Quackenbush, William N. Enlisted in Company G as Corporal, Aug. 24, 1861, at White Pigeon, for 3 years, age 26. Wounded in action at second Manassas, Aug. 30, 1862. Discharged at Washington, D.C., Nov. 13, 1862.

Ranger, Marshall J., or T. (Veteran), Smyrna. Enlisted in Company B, Aug. 7, 1861, at Ionia, for 3 years, age 24. Reenlisted Dec. 24, 1863, at Rappahannock Station, Va. Killed in action at Jericho Mills–North Anna River, Va., May 26, 1864.

Ranger, William H. H. (Veteran), Ionia County. Enlisted in Company B, Aug. 7, 1861, at Ionia, for 3 years, age 19. Reenlisted Dec. 24, 1863, at Rappahannock Station, Va. Mustered out at Jeffersonville, Ind., July 8, 1865.

Ransom, Randolph W., Flushing. Entered service in Company C at organization, as 2nd Lieutenant, July 30, 1861, at Flint, for 3 years, age 32. Commissioned Captain June 27, 1862. Killed in action at second Manassas, Aug. 30, 1862.

Rapp, George. Enlisted in Company C, Feb. 13, 1865, at Pokagon, for 1 year, age 18. Substitute for Israel P. Hutton, drafted from Pokagon. Mustered out at Jeffersonville, Ind., July 8, 1865.

Rathbun or **Rathburn, Frederick**, Wayne County. Enlisted in Company F, April 1, 1862, at Plymouth, for 3 years, age 37. Joined regiment at Yorktown, Va., May 1, 1862. Discharged for disability at Washington, D.C., Feb. 26, 1863.

Rathbun, Oscar, Ionia County. Enlisted in Company B, Aug. 8, 1861, at Ionia, for 3 years, age 25. Discharged for disability at Philadelphia, Nov. 24, 1862.

Ratz or **Roatz, Jacob**, Detroit. Enlisted in Company A, July 27, 1863, at Detroit, for 3 years, age 21. Substitute for John Way, drafted Feb. 17, 1863, for 9 months, from Erin. Joined regiment April 23, 1863. Corporal. Missing in action at Laurel Hill–Spotsylvania Court House, May 8, 1864. Reportedly severely wounded and absent from September 1864 to May 1865, and dropped by order of War Department May 1, 1865.

Rau or **Raw, Henry**, Detroit. Enlisted in Company H, Lancers, as Corporal, Dec. 28, 1861, at Detroit, for 3 years, age 20. Transferred to Company I, 16th Michigan, Feb. 28, 1862. Sergeant. Killed in action at Gettysburg, July 2, 1863. Buried in National Cemetery at Gettysburg, Grave No. 21, Section D.

Ray, Francis. Enlisted Feb. 15, 1864, at Saginaw, for 3 years, age 20. No further record.

Ray, John, Woodstock. Enlisted March 3, 1863, at Moscow, for 3 years, age 23. Substitute for John Saurman, drafted Feb. 10, 1863, for 9 months. Sent to regiment March 11, 1863. No further record.

Raymond, Alexander (Veteran), Midland County. Enlisted in Company D, Aug. 2, 1861, at East Saginaw, for 3 years, age 23. Wounded in action at Gaines' Mill, June 27, 1862. Reenlisted as Sergeant Dec. 21, 1863, at Rappahannock Station, Va. 1st Sergeant May 1, 1865. Mustered out at Jeffersonville, Ind., July 8, 1865.

Raynor, George W. (Veteran), Osseo. Enlisted in Company G, Aug. 20, 1861, age 17. Reenlisted Dec. 21, 1863, at Rappahannock Station, Va. Killed in action at Wilderness, May 7, 1864.

Recht or **Wright, Lewis**. Enlisted in Company C, Aug. 3, at Flint, for 3 years, age 30. Transferred to Company H. Killed in action at Fredericksburg, Va., Dec. 13, 1862.

Redding, John W. Enlisted in Company H, March 23, 1865, at Bertrand, for 1 year, age 17. Substitute for Michael Herkimer, drafted. Discharged at Baltimore, May 12, 1865.

Reed, Benjamin. Enlisted in Company E, Feb. 2, 1864, at Nankin, Wayne County, for 3 years, age 19. Listed wounded in action at Wilderness, May 7, 1864, in regimental "Roll of Honor," but reported in regiment's roster as wounded in Oct. 1864 (both could be correct). Discharged on Surgeon's certificate of disability at Detroit, Feb. 27, 1865.

Reed, George W., Howell. Enlisted in Company B, Lancers, Dec. 11, 1861, at Howell, for 3 years, age 18. Transferred to Company I, 16th Michigan, Feb. 28, 1862. Discharged Feb. 18, 1863. Resided Stanwood, Mich.

Reed or **Reid, John**. Enlisted in Second Company Sharpshooters, April 10, 1864, at Thomastown,

Saginaw County, for 3 years, age 26. Taken prisoner Aug. 16, 1864. No further record.

Reed, William F. Enlisted in Company B, Jan. 20 1865, for 1 year, age 18. Substitute for Samuel H. Bell, drafted from Calvin. Mustered out at Jeffersonville, Ind., July 8, 1865. Resided Bellevue, Mich.

Reeke, August, Ontonagon County. Enlisted in Company A, Aug. 3, 1861, at Ontonagon, for 3 years, age 22. Wounded in action, ankle, at Middleburg, Va., June 21, 1863. Wounded in action in the withdrawal from Cold Harbor, June 6, 1864. Discharged at expiration of term of service, Sept. 6, 1864.

Refferman, Refner, or **Rifer, Charles**. Drafted for 1 year, from Camden, age 25. Mustered Oct. 6, 1864. Assigned to Company K. Died of disease at Washington, D.C., April 28, 1865.

Renegar, Francis, or **Rinegar, Franz** (Veteran), Wayne County. Enlisted in Company E, Sept. 5, 1861, age 19. Wounded in action, second Manassas, Aug. 30, 1862. Reenlisted Dec. 21, 1863. Deserted at Jeffersonville, Ind., June 26, 1865.

Renick, William, Detroit. Enlisted in Company E, Oct. 8, 1862, at Detroit, for 3 years, age 18. Joined regiment at Antietam, Md., Oct. 30, 1862. Mustered out at Jeffersonville, Ind., July 8, 1865.

Renkle or **Reuhle** or **Reuker, George** (Veteran). Enlisted in Company C, Aug. 4, 1861, at Flint, for 3 years, age 30. Transferred to Company H. Wounded in action in 1862, no date, but hit in the chest. Reenlisted Dec. 24, 1863, at Rappahannock Station, Va. Corporal, May 1, 1865. Mustered out at Jeffersonville, Ind., July 8, 1865.

Reorden, William. Enlisted in Second Company Sharpshooters May 2, 1864, at East Saginaw, for 3 years, age 42. Absent sick May 4, 1865. Died July 21, 1873 and buried at Saginaw.

Resseguire, John. Enlisted in Company E, Aug. 17, 1861, at Detroit, for 3 years, claimed to be 18. Transferred to Company H. Discharged because he was a minor, Sept. 5, 1861.

Retan, Henry C. Enlisted in Company G, Aug. 19, 1861, at White Pigeon, for 3 years, age 18. Wounded in action at Gaines' Mill, June 27, 1862. Discharged on Surgeon's certificate of disability at Philadelphia, Dec. 18, 1862. Right arm amputated.

Reveney, Victor C. Enlisted in Company G, Jan. 6, 1862, at Detroit, for 3 years, age 22. Joined regiment at Hall's Hill, Va., Feb. 14, 1862. Discharged for disability at Washington, D.C., Dec. 25, 1862.

Reverer or **Reafer, Andrew**, Ontonagon County. Enlisted in Company A, Aug. 3, 1861, at Ontonagon, for 3 years, age 36. Reenlisted Dec. 21, 1863, at Rappahannock Station, Va. Wounded in action at Bethesda Church, June 2, 1864. Mustered out at Jeffersonville, Ind., July 8, 1865.

Reynolds, John, Kent County. Enlisted in First Company Sharpshooters attached to 16th Michigan, Nov. 16, 1861, at Grand Rapids, for 3 years, age 35. Joined regiment at Hall's Hill, Va., Feb. 14, 1862. Discharged for disability at Alexandria, Va., May 19, 1863.

Rhoads or **Rhodes, William**, Plymouth. Enlisted in Company D, Aug. 4, 1861, at East Saginaw, for 3 years, age 23. Transferred to Company F. Died of disease at Gaines' Mill, June 16, 1862.

Rhodes, John H. (Veteran), Kent County. Enlisted in First Company Sharpshooters, attached to 16th Michigan, Jan. 17, 1862, at Grand Rapids, for 3 years, age 30. Joined regiment at Hall's Hill, Va., Feb. 14, 1862. Listed as missing in action Aug. 13, 1862, though the regiment was not in battle that day. Reenlisted Feb. 26, 1864, near Bealton, Va. Corporal, May 1, 1865. Mustered out at Jeffersonville, Ind., July 8,1865. Died June 2, 1896, and buried at Spencer Mills, Mich.

Rice, Charles L., Detroit. Enlisted in First Company Sharpshooters attached to 16th Michigan, as Sergeant, Sept. 16, 1861, at Detroit, for 3 years, age 22. Joined regiment at Hall's Hill, Va., Feb. 14, 1862. 1st Sergeant. Commissioned 2nd Lieutenant Nov. 1, 1862. Commissioned 1st Lieutenant Jan. 15, 1863. Discharged on Surgeon's certificate of disability Aug. 14, 1863.

Rice, Lorenzo (Veteran), Stockbridge. Enlisted in Company K, March 1, 1862, at Detroit, for 3 years, age 21. Reenlisted March 1, 1864, at Bealton, Va. Wounded in action at Wilderness, May 7, 1864, loss of leg. Discharged for disability March 21, 1865. Resided Stockbridge.

Richards, Davis M. (Veteran), Wayne County. Enlisted in First Company Sharpshooters attached to 16th Michigan, Dec. 12, 1861, at Detroit, for 3 years, age 23. Joined regiment at Hall's Hill, Va., Feb. 14, 1862. Missing in action at Gaines' Mill, June 27, 1862. Reenlisted Dec. 22, 1863, at Rappahannock Station, Va. Killed in action at Bethesda Church, June 1, 1864.

Richards, George M., Richmond. Enlisted in Company I, Feb. 13, 1862, at Richmond, for 3 years, age 18. Wounded in action at second Manassas, Aug. 30, 1862. Taken prisoner, date unknown. Died of disease in prison at Andersonville, Ga., Aug. 6, 1864. Buried in National Cemetery at Andersonville, Grave No. 4918.

Richards, James, Flushing. Enlisted in Company C, Aug. 2, 1861, at Flint, for 3 years, age 40. Wounded and taken prisoner at Gaines' Mill, June 27, 1862. Died at Annapolis, Md., Aug. 31, 1862.

Richardson, Charles A. Enlisted in Company B, Feb. 5, 1864, at East Saginaw, for 3 years, age 21. Wounded in action at Wilderness, May 7, 1864. Mustered out at Jeffersonville, Ind., July 8, 1865.

Richardson, John J. (Veteran), Wayne County. Enlisted in Company E, Sept. 11, 1861, age 30. Paroled prisoner at Annapolis, Md., Sept. 1862. Reenlisted as Corporal Dec. 21, 1863, at Rappahannock Station, Va. Sergeant. Transferred to U.S. Navy May 2, 1864.

Richardson, John W. Enlisted in Company B, Feb. 27, 1864, at East Saginaw, for 3 years, age 18. Mustered out at Jeffersonville, Ind., July 8, 1865.

Richey, Samuel. Enlisted March 25, 1864, at Houghton, for 3 years, age 36. No further record.

Ricketts or **Richets, Michael**. Enlisted in Company G, Feb. 6, 1865, at Charleston, for 1 year, age 18. Substitute for Edward Woodruff, drafted. Mustered out at Jeffersonville, Ind., July 8, 1865.

Rider, Stephen V. Enlisted in Company B, Aug. 6, 1861, at Ionia, for 3 years, age 27. Discharged for disability at Hall's Hill, Va., April 14, 1862. Reentered service, enlisting in Company C, 2nd Michigan, March 19, 1864, at St. Johns, for 3 years, age 29. Missing in action July 30, 1864. Returned to regiment at Petersburg, Va., April 19, 1865. Admitted to U.S. General Hospital May 23, 1865. Mustered out at Detroit, Aug. 16, 1865.

Right or **Wright, Peter**. Enlisted in Company G, Aug. 20, 1861, at Hillsdale, for 3 years, age 26. Died of disease at Gaines' Mill, June 13, 1862.

Riply, James, Genesee County. Enlisted in Company C, Aug. 3, 1861, at Flint, for 3 years, age

20. Discharged on Surgeon's certificate of disability Feb. 24, 1863. Resided Fenton, Mich.

Robbins, Alexander. Enlisted in Company B, Feb. 9, 1864, at Saginaw, for 3 years, age 19. Wounded in action at Jericho Mills–North Ana River, Va., May 23, 1864. Mustered out at Jeffersonville, Ind., July 8, 1865.

Roberts, Cloris or **Clovis**, Detroit. Enlisted in Company E, Aug. 30, 1862, at Detroit, for 3 years, age 28. Joined regiment at Sharpsburg, Md., Oct. 30, 1862. Died April 1, 1865, from wounds received in action at White Oak Road or skirmish at Gravelly Run, Va., March 31, 1865.

Robinson, Alexander. Enlisted in Company G, Jan. 4, 1864, at Saline, for 3 years, age 18. Wounded in action, Wilderness, May 1864. Mustered out at Jeffersonville, Ind., July 8, 1865.

Robinson, John, Wayne County. Enlisted in Company E, Dec. 7, 1861, at Detroit, for 3 years, age 43. Discharged for disability at Philadelphia, Jan. 7, 1863.

Robinson, William, Lowell. Enlisted in Company C, Lancers, Dec. 9, 1861, at Lowell, for 3 years, age 30. Transferred to Company I, 16th Michigan, Feb. 28, 1862. Missing in action at Gaines' Mill, June 27, 1862. Discharged for disability June 29, 1862.

Robinson, William. Enlisted in Company G, March 18, 1865, for 1 year, age 36. Substitute for William H. Clark, drafted from Howell. Mustered out at Jeffersonville, Ind., July 8, 1865.

Rockwood, Edwin, Plymouth. Enlisted in Company F, Sept. 12, 1861, at Plymouth, age 26. Alternately reported as missing in action (regimental roster) or as wounded in action (regiment's "Roll of Honor") on June 30, 1862 at Charles City Crossroads, the day before Malvern Hill. Further reports alternatively say he died of disease in Detroit, Aug. 2, 1862 (regimental roster) or that he died of wounds ("Roll of Honor.")

Roctor, John. Enlisted and mustered Jan. 18, 1864, at Detroit, for 3 years, age 23. No further record.

Rodgers, Levi B., Saginaw County. Enlisted in Company D, 16th Michigan, Aug. 6, 1861, at East Saginaw, for 3 years, age 21. Wounded in action at Gaines' Mill, June 27, 1862. Discharged on Surgeon's certificate of disability April 15, 1863.

Roe, Chauncey C. Enlisted and mustered Jan. 1864, at Jackson, for 3 years, age 30. Discharged at Jackson, May 6, 1865.

Roe, William B., Plymouth. Entered service in Company F, at organization, as 1st Lieutenant, July 30, 1861, at Plymouth, for 3 years, age 30. Commissioned Captain, Nov. 3, 1862. On detached service with Signal Corps, Dec. 1862. Discharged for disability May 10, 1865.

Roe, William H. (Veteran). Enlisted in Company A, 16th Michigan, Aug. 3, 1861, at Ontonagon, for 3 years, age 21. Transferred to Company F, July 1862. Reenlisted as Corporal Dec. 21, 1863, at Rappahannock Station, Va. Discharged at Detroit, Aug. 22, 1865. Resided Millington, Mich.

Rogers, Mica R., Almont. Enlisted in First Company Sharpshooters attached to 16th Michigan, Dec. 18, 1861, at Detroit, for 3 years, age 39. Wounded and taken prisoner at Gaines' Mill, June 27, 1862. Died in prison at Richmond, July 8, 1862, of wounds received in action at Gaines' Mill, June 27, 1862.

Rogers, William A., Wayne County. Enlisted in Company F, as Corporal, Aug. 2, 1861, at Plymouth, for 3 years, age 19. Deserted.

Rolfe, Thomas, Elk. Enlisted in Company C, Jan. 14, 1864, at Maple Grove, for 3 years, age 31.

Died in the field May 8, 1864, of wounds received that night, at Laurel Hill–Spotsylvania Court House.

Rolfe, William. Enlisted in Company C, Jan. 11, 1864, at Maple Grove, for 3 years, age 19. Wounded in action at Laurel Hill–Spotsylvania Court House May 8, 1864. Discharged from wounds July 14, 1865.

Rolls, James, St. Clair County. Enlisted in 7th Michigan Infantry, age 19, for 3 years. Wounded in action June 30, 1862 at Glendale, Va., and discharged Dec. 1863. Enlisted in one of the Sharpshooters companies in the 16th Michigan at Kochville, Saginaw County, March 26, 1864, but no information about his service is given.

Rommel, George. Enlisted in Company K, March 28, 1865, for 1 year, age 40. Substitute for Thomas Wass Jr., drafted from White Pigeon. Admitted to Harper Hospital July 28, 1865. Discharged at Detroit, Aug. 19, 1865.

Rood, Henry, Mt. Clemens. Enlisted in Company C, Lancers, Jan. 6, 1862, at Mt. Clemens, for 3 years, age 37. Transferred to Company I, 16th Michigan, Feb. 28, 1862. Wounded in action at Gaines' Mill, June 27, 1862. Discharged for disability at Alexandria, Va., Nov. 28, 1862. Died March 2, 1893. Buried at Mt. Clemens.

Rooick, James. Enlisted Jan. 19, 1864, at Detroit, for 3 years, age 21. No further record.

Root, Charles H., Fenton. Enlisted in Company C, Aug. 3, 1861, at Flint, for 3 years, age 20. Discharged on Surgeon's certificate of disability at Detroit, Nov. 26, 1862. Reentered service in Battery E, 1st Michigan Light Artillery, Jan. 15, 1864, at Grand Rapids, for 3 years, age 22. Transferred to Battery A, Aug. 11, 1864. Mustered out at Jackson, Mich., July 28, 1865.

Rosa, Daniel (Veteran), Saginaw County. Enlisted in Company D, Aug. 6, 1861, at East Saginaw, for 3 years, age 36. Reenlisted Dec. 21, 1863, at Rappahannock Station, Va. Reportedly wounded during the Petersburg campaign and died Oct. 27, 1864, at Alexandria, Va.

Rose, Francis M., Wayne County. Enlisted in Company F, Aug. 24, 186 1, at Plymouth, for 3 years, age 18. Discharged for disability March 17, 1863.

Rose, John, Saginaw County. Enlisted in Company D, Aug. 6, 1861, at East Saginaw, for 3 years, age 40. Wounded in action at Gaines' Mill, June 27, 1862. Transferred to Invalid Corps Sept. 1, 1863.

Rose or **Roe, Silas E.**, Amboy. Enlisted in Company G, Aug. 21, 1861, at Hudson, for 3 years, age 18. Died of disease at Hall's Hill, Va., Feb. 6, 1862.

Ross, David. Enlisted in Second Company Sharpshooters, March 30, 1864, at Taymouth, for 3 years, age 18. Corporal May 1, 1865. Mustered out at Jeffersonville, Ind., July 8, 1865.

Ross, Hugh. Enlisted in Second Company Sharpshooters, March 31, 1864, at Albee, for 3 years, age 40. Mustered out at Jeffersonville, Ind., July 8, 1865.

Ross, Russel B. Enlisted in Company H, Lancers, Nov. 4, 1861, at Waltersville, for 3 years, age 24. Transferred to Company K, 16th Michigan, Feb. 28, 1862. Deserted March 22, 1862.

Roth, George (Veteran), Assyria. Enlisted in Company K, March 1, 1862, at Detroit, for 3 years, age 23. Wounded in action at Gettysburg, July 2, 1863. Reenlisted March 1, 1864, at Bealton, Va. Corporal. Mustered out at Jeffersonville, Ind., July 8, 1865.

Rottman, Louis (Veteran), Mt. Clemens. Enlisted in Company H, Lancers, Dec. 28, 1861, at Detroit, for 3 years, age 29. Transferred to Company I, 16th Michigan, Feb. 28, 1862.

Reenlisted Dec. 22, 1863, at Rappahannock Station, Va. Corporal. Wounded on the Petersburg front, Sept. 1864 or earlier; listed as absent wounded Aug.–Dec. 1864. Killed in action at Dabney's Mill, Feb. 6, 1865.

Roubleman or **Reubelmann, John**, Detroit. Enlisted in Company A, Aug. 3, 1861, at Ontonagon, for 3 years, age 23. Wounded in action at Gaines' Mill, June 27, 1862. Reenlisted as Corporal Dec. 21, 1863, at Rappahannock Station, Va. Sergeant. Killed in action at Peeble's Farm, Sept. 30, 1864.

Rouge, Joseph. Enlisted in Company G, March 27, 1865, at Girard, for 1 year, age 33. Substitute for William Rose, drafted from Girard. Discharged at Philadelphia, June 13, 1865.

Rouse, Allen, Saginaw County. Enlisted in Company D, Aug. 3, 1861, at East Saginaw, for 3 years, age 20. Deserted at Detroit.

Rowley, Dennis. Enlisted in Company K, Feb. 17, 1865, at Shelby, for 2 years, age 33. Substitute for John W. Young, drafted. Discharged at Philadelphia, June 13, 1865. Resided New Haven.

Rowley, George, Ionia County. Enlisted in Company B, Aug. 7, 1861, at Ionia, for 3 years, age 22. Discharged for disability at Philadelphia, Nov. 24, 1862.

Ruby, John, Plymouth. Enlisted in Company F, as 1st Sergeant, July 30, 1861, at Plymouth, for 3 years, age 26. Commissioned 2nd Lieutenant July 1, 1862. Killed in action at second Manassas, Aug. 30, 1862.

Ruehle, John V., Detroit. Entered service in 1st Michigan Infantry, Mexican War, as Major, Oct. 18, 1847. Mustered out July 23, 1848. Reentered service in 16th Michigan at organization as Lt. Colonel, Aug. 22, 1861, at Detroit, for 3 years, age 49. Commissioned to date Aug. 21, 1861. Resigned July 6, 1862. Died Dec. 12, 1891.

Rushton, Richard W., Saginaw County. Enlisted in Company D, Aug. 3, 1861, at East Saginaw, for 3 years, age 26. Corporal. Discharged Dec. 23, 1862.

Russell, James S., Utica. Enlisted in Company I, March 2, 1862, at Utica, for 3 years, age 18. Discharged for disability.

Ryan, Edward. Enlisted in Company H, Sept. 28, 1861, at Detroit, for 3 years, age 19. 1861. Deserted Oct. 1, 1861.

Ryan, William. Enlisted in Company C, Jan. 20, 1865, at Amboy, for 3 years, age 35. Substitute for Henry Zuber, drafted. Mustered out at Jeffersonville, Ind., July 8, 1865.

Sackrider, Charles, Adrian. Enlisted in Company F, Lancers, Dec. 20, 1861, at Adrian, for 3 years, age 19. Transferred to Company I, 16th Michigan, Feb. 28, 1862. Deserted at Detroit, March 24, 1862.

Sailer, John Q. A. Enlisted in Company E, Aug. 19, 1861, at Detroit, for 3 years, age 25. Transferred to Company H. Deserted Dec. 1862.

St. Clair, William W. Enlisted in Company B, Feb. 9, 1864, at Fenton, for 3 years, age 30. Mustered out at Jeffersonville, Ind., July 8, 1865.

St. Marie, Francis, Saginaw County. Enlisted in Company D, Aug. 5, 1861, at East Saginaw, for 3 years, age 35. Deserted at Detroit.

Sage, Thomas. Reportedly enlisted as a private in Company E, according to regimental "Roll of Honor," and killed in action at Gaines' Mill, June 27, 1862. He was not listed in the state's roster, which is not comprehensive.

Salter, Charles H., Detroit. Enlisted in Company A, 90-day 1st Michigan Infantry, April 18, 1861, at Detroit, for 3 months, age 21. Mustered out at Detroit, Aug. 7, 1861. Reentered service in Company E of Stockton's regiment at organization as 2nd Lieutenant, Aug. 13, 1861, at Detroit. Commissioned 1st Lieutenant, Company B, Aug. 30, 1862. Commissioned Captain, Company E, Dec. 16, 1863. Acting Brigade Inspector, Sept. 14, 1864. Brevet Major, U.S. Volunteers, Sept. 30, 1864, for conspicuous bravery during the entire campaign. Discharged at expiration of term of service at Petersburg, Va., Jan. 13, 1865. Died March 23, 1892.

Saltmarsh, Samuel. Enlisted in Company E, March 28, 1865, at Sheridan, for 1 year, age 19. Substitute for Gotfried Herie, drafted. Mustered out at Jeffersonville, Ind., July 8, 1865. Died at Detroit, July 22, 1865.

Sanborn, Lucius (Veteran), Lapeer County. Enlisted in Company C as Corporal, Aug. 2, 1861, at Flint, for 3 years, age 18. Wounded in action at Gaines' Mill, June 27, 1862. Reenlisted Dec. 24, 1863, at Rappahannock Station, Va. Sergeant. Mustered out at Jeffersonville, Ind., July 8, 1865. Resided Hadley, Mich.

Sands, James H., Bruce. Enlisted in Company H, Nov. 5, 1861, at Romeo, for 3 years, age 23. Discharged for disability at Philadelphia, Sept. 13, 1862. Resided Lee, Mich.

Sanzie or **Sarzie, Christian** (Veteran). Enlisted in Company G as Corporal, Sept. 10, 1861, age 20. Reenlisted Dec. 21, 1863, at Rappahannock Station, Va. Wounded in action at Petersburg, Va., June 18, 1864. Sergeant, April 1, 1865. Mustered out at Jeffersonville, Ind., July 8, 1865. Died Jan. 19, 1890. Buried at Saline, Mich.

Savage, Augustus C. (Veteran), Ionia County. Enlisted in Company B as Corporal, July 30, 1861, at Ionia, for 3 years, age 41. Reenlisted Dec. 24, 1863, at Rappahannock Station, Va. Acting Hospital Steward, May 1865. Promoted Hospital Steward June 29, 1865. Discharged at Jeffersonville, Ind., July 1, 1865.

Sayles, Cyrenus C. (Veteran), Ionia County. Enlisted in Company B, Aug. 7, 1861, at Ionia, for 3 years, age 21. Reenlisted Dec. 24, 1863, at Rappahannock Station, Va. Wounded in action May 18, 1864, Spotsylvania Court House. Corporal May 1, 1865. Mustered out at Jeffersonville, Ind., July 8, 1865. Resided Langston, Mich.

Scagle or **Skagle, Dennis**. Enlisted in Company B, Feb. 14, 1865, at Algoma, for 1 year, age 19. Substitute for Jackson Coon, drafted. Killed in action at Gravelly Run, Va., March 31, 1865.

Scanlon, Michael (Veteran), Detroit. Enlisted in Company C as Musician, Sept. 1, 1861, at Flint, age 16. Reenlisted Dec. 24, 1863, at Rappahannock Station, Va. Mortally wounded in action at Weldon Railroad, Petersburg, Va., July 23, 1864, dying the next day.

Schaffer or **Shaffer, William**, Oakland County. Enlisted in First Company Sharpshooters attached to 16th Michigan, Dec. 2, 1861, at Detroit, for 3 years, age 24. Joined regiment at Hall's Hill, Va., Feb. 14, 1862. Wounded in action at second Manassas, Aug. 30, 1862. Discharged for disability at Philadelphia, Jan. 12, 1863.

Schaible, Charles, Detroit. Enlisted in Company G, July 25, 1862, at Detroit, age 39. Joined regiment at Sharpsburg, Md., Oct. 30, 1862. Killed in action at Fredericksburg, Va., Dec. 13, 1862.

Schannon, Patrick H., Detroit. Enlisted in Company D, Lancers, as Corporal, Oct. 5, 1861, at Detroit, for 3 years, age 30. Transferred to Company K, 16th Michigan, Feb. 28, 1862. In hospital at Detroit, March 30, 1862. No further record.

Schier, Peter, Detroit. Enlisted in Company D, Lancers, Nov. 19, 1861, at Detroit, for 3 years, age 22. Transferred to Company K, 16th Michigan, Feb. 28, 1862. Deserted at Detroit, March 28, 1862.

Schinderwent or **Schneidewind, Otto** (Veteran). Enlisted in Company G, Aug. 24, 1861, age 24. Wounded in action at Shepherdstown Ford, Sept. 20, 1862. Reenlisted Feb. 26, 1864, at Bealton, Va. Corporal, May 1, 1865. Mustered out at Jeffersonville, Ind., July 8, 1865. Resided Omaha, Neb.

Schlotterbeck, Gustavus. Enlisted in regimental Band, Sept. 13, 1861, at Detroit, for 3 years, age 23. Mustered out Aug. 11, 1862.

Schneider or **Snyder, Jacob**, Detroit. Enlisted in Company H, Oct. 11, 1861, at Detroit, for 3 years, age 43. Killed in action at Gaines' Mill, June 27, 1862.

Schoff, Henry. Enlisted in Company A, Aug. 3, 1861, at Ontonagon, for 3 years, age 21. Transferred to Company F. Corporal 1862. Discharged for disability at Alexandria, Va., Dec. 11, 1862.

Schonite, Frederick. Enlisted in Company E, Feb. 13,1864, at Detroit, for 3 years, age 19. Mustered Feb. 13, 1864. Prisoner Aug. 1864. Discharged on Surgeon's certificate of disability July 28, 1865.

Schradt or **Schadt, George**, Ontonagon County. Enlisted in Company A, Aug. 3, 1861, at Ontonagon, for 3 years, age 20. Killed in action at Gaines' Mill, June 27, 1862.

Schramm, Julius (Veteran), Ontonagon County. Enlisted in Company A, Aug. 3, 1861, at Ontonagon, for 3 years, age 19. Wounded in action, head, at Gettysburg, July 2, 1863. Reenlisted Dec. 21, 1863, at Rappahannock Station, Va. Wounded in action Aug. 30, 1864, Weldon Railroad, Petersburg, Va. Corporal, May 1, 1865. Mustered out at Jeffersonville, Ind., July 8, 1865.

Schrieve, Joseph, Detroit. Enlisted in Company K, April 5, 1862, at Detroit, for 3 years, age 23. Wounded in leg and taken prisoner at second Manassas, Aug. 30, 1862. Paroled. Discharged for disability in 1862.

Schwinden, Tebo. Enlisted in Company I as Drummer, Jan. 1, 1862, at Gaines' Mill, for 3 years, age 16. Discharged at Detroit, Feb. 24, 1863.

Scott, David. Enlisted in Company I, Feb. 13, 1864. At Saginaw, for 3 years, age 18. Wounded in action at Wilderness, May 7, 1864. Transferred to Veteran Reserve Corps Feb. 16, 1865. Discharged at Washington, D.C., July 18, 1865, from Company K, 24th Regiment, Veteran Reserve Corps. Resided Carrollton, Mich.

Scott, Isaac H. Enlisted in Company H, Lancers, Dec. 28, 1861, at Detroit, for 3 years, age 18. Transferred to Company K, 16th Michigan, March 1, 1862. Killed in action at Gettysburg, July 2, 1863.

Scott, Joseph. Enlisted in Second Company Sharpshooters, April 29, 1864, at Saginaw, for 3 years, age 20. Deserted at Saginaw, May 3, 1864.

Scott, Joseph G., or Jacob. Enlisted in Company E, Lancers, Oct. 25, 1861, at Saginaw City, for 3 years, age 24. Transferred to Company K, 16th Michigan, Feb. 28, 1862. Died of disease at Washington, D.C., March 31, 1862.

Scott, Walter (Veteran), Wayne County. Enlisted in First Company Sharpshooters attached to 16th Michigan, Oct. 28, 1861, at Detroit, for 3 years, age 18. Joined regiment at Hall's Hill, Va., Feb. 14, 1862. Reenlisted Feb. 26, 1864, at Bealton, Va. Wounded at Peeble's Farm, Sept. 30, 1864. Mustered out at Jeffersonville, Ind., July 8, 1865.

Scott, William, Buena Vista, Saginaw County. Enlisted in Company D, March 19, 1864, at Houghton, for 3 years, age 21. Mustered out at Jeffersonville, Ind., July 8, 1865.

Scratch, Sidney. Enlisted in Second Company Sharpshooters, April 17, 1864, at Spaulding, for 3 years, age 18. Died of disease at Philadelphia, July 25, 1864.

Searles, Henry D. (Veteran), Wayne County. Enlisted in Company E as Corporal, Aug. 13, 1861, at Detroit, for 3 years. Reenlisted as Sergeant Dec. 21, 1863, at Rappahannock Station, Va. Mustered out at Jeffersonville, Ind., July 8, 1865.

Sebring, William H., Saginaw County. Enlisted in Company D, Aug. 3, 1861, at East Saginaw, for 3 years, age 26. Discharged at expiration of term of service at Petersburg, Va., Sept. 7, 1864.

Seely, Edwin B., Detroit. Enlisted in Company K, March 17, 1862, at Detroit, for 3 years, age 27. Discharged for disability May 12, 1862. Died June 4, 1896, and buried at Byron, Mich.

Seidler, Henry, Wayne County. Enlisted in Company A, Jan. 22, 1862, at Detroit, for 3 years, age 21. Joined regiment at Hall's Hill, Va., Feb. 14, 1862. Wounded in action at Gaines' Mill, June 27, 1862. Wounded in action at Spotsylvania Court House May 18, 1864. Wounded in action in raid on Weldon Railroad, Petersburg, Va., Dec. 10, 1864. Discharged at expiration of term of service at Petersburg, Va., Jan. 22, 1865.

Seiger, James, or **John**. Enlisted in Company K, Jan. 18, 1864, at Detroit, for 3 years, age 20. Severely wounded in action, right leg, Laurel Hill–Spotsylvania Court House, May 8, 1864. Discharged on Surgeon's certificate of disability at Washington, D.C., Feb. 19, 1865.

Senna, Heuse. Enlisted in Company I, March 22, 1865, at Kalamazoo, for 1 year, age 19. Substitute for Noah Roe, drafted from Waukeshma. Mustered out at Jeffersonville, Ind., July 8, 1865.

Sessions, Hiram M., Meridian. Drafted Feb. 10, 1863, for 9 months, from Meridian, age 30. Joined regiment at Falmouth, Va., March 19, 1863. Discharged at expiration of term of service at Kelly's Ford, Va., Nov. 21, 1863.

Severance, Nathan E., Lansing. Enlisted in Company C, Jan. 9, 1863, at Lansing, for 3 years, age 18. Alternate records state he died of disease at Camp Parole, Va., Aug. 9, 1864 or that he died Sept. 29, 1864 at Naval School Hospital, Annapolis, Md.

Seymour, George, Argentine. Enlisted in Company I, Aug. 14, 1862, at Argentine, for 3 years, age 18. Joined regiment at Antietam, Md., Oct. 12, 1862. Wounded in action, chest, Gettysburg, July 2, 1863. Wounded in action, thigh, Wilderness, May 7, 1864. Corporal, March 1, 1865. Discharged at Washington, D.C., May 29, 1865. Resided Saginaw, Mich.

Seymour, James B. Enlisted in Company D, Jan. 22, 1864, at Benton, for 3 years, age 23. Wounded in action, arm and side, June 4, 1864 Bethesda Church–Cold Harbor area. Mustered out at Jeffersonville, Ind., July 8, 1865.

Shaker, John. Enlisted in Company A, Feb. 11, 1864, at East Saginaw, for 3 years, age 32. Wounded in action at Spotsylvania Court House, May 10, 1864. Discharged at Washington, D.C., May 31, 1865.

Shank, James. Enlisted in Company C, Dec. 17, 1863, at Montrose, for 3 years, age 44. Discharged on Surgeon's certificate of disability at Washington, D.C., May 24, 1865.

Shanks, Alexander, Wayne County. Enlisted in Company E, Aug. 14, 1861, at Detroit, for 3 years, age 22. Transferred to Company C. Deserted at Detroit, Sept. 6, 1861.

Shannon, James (Veteran), Wayne County. Enlisted in First Company Sharpshooters attached to 16th Michigan, Sept. 25, 1861, at Detroit, for 3 years, age 24. Joined regiment at Hall's Hill, Va., Feb. 14, 1862. Reenlisted Dec. 24, 1863, at Rappahannock Station, Va. Wounded in action at Hatcher's Run, Oct. 27, 1864. Corporal May 1, 1865. Mustered out at Jeffersonville, Ind., July 8, 1865.

Sharpe, John. Enlisted in Second Company Sharpshooters, April 27, 1864, at East Saginaw, for 3 years, age 35. Deserted at Saginaw, May 3, 1864.

Sharpe, Samuel. Enlisted in Second Company Sharpshooters, April 27, 1864, at East Saginaw, for 3 years, age 39. Deserted at Saginaw, May 3, 1864.

Sharpe, Thomas. Enlisted in Second Company Sharpshooters, April 27, 1864, at East Saginaw, for 3 years, age 18. Deserted at Saginaw, May 3, 1864.

Sharritts, Jacob, Ottawa County. Enlisted in First Company Sharpshooters attached to 16th Michigan, Jan. 7, 1862, at Grand Rapids, for 3 years, age 43. Joined regiment at Hall's Hill, Va., Feb. 14, 1862. Missing in action at Gaines' Mill, June 27, 1862. Discharged at Washington, D.C., Jan. 21, 1863 and joined 1st Michigan Engineers and Mechanics. Mustered out Sept. 22, 1865, Nashville, Tenn. Resided Centreville, Mich.

Shaw, John, New Jersey. Enlisted in Company F, Feb. 6, 1864, at Saginaw, for 3 years, age 18. Killed in action near Bethesda Church–Cold Harbor, June 3, 1864.

Shay or **Shea, Dennis D.**, or **Daniel**. Enlisted in Company A, March 31, 1864, at Houghton, for 3 years, age 21. Wounded and taken prisoner at Dabney's Mill, Feb. 6, 1865. Reported to have died at Andersonville Prison, no date given.

Shay or **Shea, Michael**, Houghton County. Enlisted in Company A, March 19, 1864, at Houghton, for 3 years, age 26. Killed at the raid on the Weldon Railroad, Petersburg, Va., Dec. 10, 1864, reportedly shot after surrendering to Rebels.

Shay, or **Shea, Michael** (Veteran), Wayne County. Enlisted in Company E, Aug. 16, 1861, at Detroit, age 23. Wounded in action, left arm, July 2, 1863, Gettysburg. Reenlisted Dec. 21, 1863, at Rappahannock Station, Va. Died of disease at Washington, D.C., Nov. 24, 1864.

Shearer, John, Albion. Enlisted in Company F, Aug. 8, 1861, at Plymouth, for 3 years, age 18. Killed in action at Gaines' Mill, June 27, 1862.

Sheldon, George C., Houghton. Enlisted in Company E, 4th Michigan Cavalry, Oct. 23, 1863, at Detroit, for 3 years, age 19. Reentered service as 2nd Lieutenant, Company D, 16th Michigan, May 25, 1864. Commanding Company Aug. and Sept. 1864. 1st Lieutenant, Sept. 7, 1864, commanding Company from Nov. 1864 to March 1865. Captain, July 7, 1865. Mustered out at Jeffersonville, Ind., July 8, 1865. Died Oct. 4, 1896, and buried at Houghton, Mich.

Sheldon, Patrick. Enlisted in Company D, March 31, 1864, at Wright, for 3 years, age 23. Wounded in action June 8, 1864, near Cold Harbor. Failed to report from furlough.

Shellinbarger, Nicholas. Drafted March 15, 1865, for 1 year, from Sebewa, Ionia County, age 34. Assigned to Company D. Mustered out at Jeffersonville, Ind., July 8, 1865.

Sherida, Uzerbla. Enlisted in Company D, Aug. 3, 1861, at East Saginaw, for 3 years, age 21. No further record.

Sherman, Charles, Saginaw County. Enlisted in Company D, Aug. 5, 1861, at East Saginaw, for 3 years, age 23. Corporal. Wounded in action at Gaines' Mill, June 27, 1862. Wounded in action again at Malvern Hill, July 1, 1862. Discharged at expiration of term of service at Petersburg, Va., Sept. 7, 1864. Resided Owosso, Mich.

Sherman, Henry D. (Veteran), Wayne County. Enlisted in Company F, Sept. 5, 1861, age 18. Reenlisted Dec. 21, 1863, at Rappahannock Station, Va. Corporal, May 1, 1865. Mustered out at Jeffersonville, Ind., July 8, 1865.

Shoemaker, Leir or **Levi**. Enlisted in Company A, Aug. 3, 1861, at Ontonagon, for 3 years, age 25. Transferred to Company F, May 1862. Discharged to enlist in Company D, 11th U.S. Army Infantry, Feb. 29, 1862.

Shout, John, Argentine. Enlisted in Company C, Aug. 6, 1861, at Flint, for 3 years, age 21. Died of disease at Hall's Hill, Va., March 1, 1862.

Showers, Oliver P. (Veteran), Wayne County. Enlisted in Company A, Sept. 6, 1861. Reenlisted Dec. 21, 1863, at Rappahannock Station, Va. Wounded in action at Laurel Hill–Spotsylvania Court House May 8, 1864. Mustered out at Jeffersonville, Ind., July 8, 1865. Resided Fowlerville, Mich.

Shroy, Samuel. Drafted for 1 year, from Seville, age 42. Mustered Dec. 20, 1864. Assigned to Company I. Mustered out at Jeffersonville, Ind., July 8, 1865.

Shultiff, Frank, Portage County, Ohio. Enlisted in First Company Sharpshooters attached to 16th Michigan, Nov. 2, 1861, at Detroit, for 3 years, age 21. Joined regiment at Hall's Hill, Va., Feb. 14, 1862. Missing in action Sept. 17, 1862, though the regiment was not in battle. Corporal, Nov. 2, 1864. Discharged at expiration of term of service, Nov. 1, 1864.

Sibley, Henry H., Ionia. Entered service in Company B at organization, as Captain, July 30, 1861, at Ionia, for 3 years, age 27. Resigned Sept. 28, 1862.

Sidman, George D., Shiawassee County. Enlisted in Company C, as Drummer, Aug. 1, 1861, at Flint, for 3 years, claiming to be 18 but was 16. Wounded, hip, and taken prisoner at Gaines' Mill, June 27, 1862. Corporal. Wounded in action, foot, at Middleburg, Va., June 21, 1863. Transferred to Invalid Corps Dec. 9, 1863. Discharged Nov. 14, 1865, from Company D, 12th Regiment, Veteran Reserve Corps.

Siel, James, Saginaw County. Enlisted in Company D, Aug. 5, 1861, at East Saginaw, for 3 years, age 28. Deserted at Detroit.

Sifton, or **Lefton, Robert**. Enlisted in Company E, March 15, 1865, at Port Huron, for 3 years, age 31. Substitute for W. Pitt Edison, drafted. Deserted at Jeffersonville, Ind., June 27, 1865.

Silk, Thomas. Enlisted in Company H, Lancers, Dec. 9, 1861, at Plymouth, for 3 years, age 33. Transferred to Company I, 16th Michigan. No further record.

Silliman, Sheffield B., Saginaw County. Enlisted in Company D, as 1st Sergeant, July 31, 1861, at East Saginaw, for 3 years. Commissary Sergeant, May 24, 1863. Transferred to Company D, March 1, 1864. Discharged at expiration of term of service at Detroit, Aug. 15, 1864.

Simmons, Charles, Midland County. Enlisted in Company D, Aug. 4, 1861, at East Saginaw, for 3 years, age 23. Deserted at Malvern Hill, July 1, 1862.

Simmons, Schuyler P., Moscow. Entered service in Company D, from Moscow, for 9 months. Substitute for William H. Combs, drafted Feb. 10, 1863, for 9 months. Joined regiment at Falmouth, Va., March 18, 1863. Discharged at expiration of term of service, Dec. 17, 1863.

Simmons, William, Quincy. Enlisted in Company E, Aug. 17, 1861, at Quincy, age 18. Died Sept. 14, 1862, at Alexandria, Va., of wounds received in action at second Manassas, Aug. 30, 1862.

Simonson, George W. (Veteran), Montcalm County. Enlisted in Company B, as Corporal, Aug. 5, 1861, at Ionia, for 3 years, age 21. Reenlisted Dec. 24, 1863, at Rappahannock Station, Va. Wounded in action at Laurel Hill–Spotsylvania Court House, May 8, 1864. Discharged at Harper Hospital, Detroit, June 20, 1865. Resided Kalkaska.

Simpson, James. Enlisted in Second Company Sharpshooters, March 30, 1864, at Spaulding, for 3 years, age 45. Discharged for disability at Washington, D.C., May 30, 1865.

Sinclair, Neil. Enlisted in Company C, Jan. 26, 1865, at Eagle Harbor, for 3 years, age 20. Substitute for William P. Bailey, drafted. Mustered out at Jeffersonville, Ind., July 8, 1865.

Sinkey, Henry. Enlisted in Company E, Aug. 17, 1861, at Detroit, for 3 years, age 28. Transferred to Company H, July 1862. Died of fever at Harrison's Landing, Va., July 28, 1862.

Skillen, William, Saginaw County. Enlisted in Company D, Aug. 2, 1861, at East Saginaw, for 3 years, age 21. Discharged at Philadelphia, Feb. 5, 1863, for wounds received in action at Gaines' Mill, June 27, 1862.

Slack, Joseph B., East Saginaw. Enlisted in Company D as Corporal, Aug. 1, 1861, at East Saginaw, for 3 years, age 25. 1st Sergeant. Commissioned 2nd Lieutenant, April 22, 1863. Transferred to Company K, May 1864. Discharged at expiration of term of service, Sept. 9, 1864.

Slingerland, Abraham. Enlisted in Company I, Jan. 24, 1865, at Tawas, for 1 year, age 20. Substitute for Benjamin W. Slingerland, drafted. Mustered out at Jeffersonville, Ind., July 8, 1865.

Sloan, William, Ionia County. Enlisted in Company B, Aug. 6, 1861, at Ionia, for 3 years, age 20. Discharged for disability Dec. 2, 1862.

Slocum, Edward H. Enlisted in Company C, Dec. 17, 1863, at Montrose, for 3 years, age 20. Severely wounded in action at Wilderness, May 7, 1864. Discharged to date July 31, 1864. Resided Fenton, Mich.

Small, Nathan (Veteran), Genesee County. Enlisted in Company C, Aug. 5, 1861, at Flint, for 3 years, age 25. Reenlisted Dec. 24, 1863, at Rappahannock Station, Va. Sergeant April 1, 1865. Mustered out at Jeffersonville, Ind., July 8, 1865. Resided Petoskey.

Small, William. Enlisted in Company G, March 20, 1865, at Algoma, for 1 year, age 26. Substitute for Berrong B. Briggs, drafted. Mustered out at Jeffersonville, Ind., July 8, 1865.

Smith, Amos. Enlisted in Company G, Aug. 24, 1861, at White Pigeon, for 3 years, age 22. Wounded in action at Gaines' Mill, June 27, 1862. Discharged at Annapolis, Md., Aug. 30, 1862.

Smith, Charles (Veteran), Saginaw County. Enlisted in Company D, Dec. 17, 1861, at East Saginaw, for 3 years, age 31. Missing in action at Gaines' Mill, June 27, 1862. Reenlisted Dec. 21, 1863, at Rappahannock Station, Va. Absent April 30, 1864. No further record.

Smith, Daniel E., Jackson County. Enlisted in Company F, Aug. 15, 1861, at Jackson, age 21.

Killed in action at Gaines' Mill, June 27, 1862.

Smith, David. Enlisted in First Company Sharpshooters attached to 16th Michigan, Feb. 1864, at Detroit, for 3 years, age 37. Died June 23, 1864, in the field of wounds received in action at Petersburg, June 20, 1864.

Smith, Denton, Sparta. Drafted March 15, 1865, for 1 year, from Sparta, age 42. Assigned to Company A. Died of spinal meningitis at Washington, D.C., June 6, 1865.

Smith, Dewitt C. (Veteran). Watrousville, Tuscola County. Enlisted in Company H, Lancers, Nov. 4, 1861, at Watrousville, for 3 years, age 18. Transferred to Company I, 16th Michigan. Wounded in action at Gaines' Mill June 27, 1862. Reenlisted Dec. 22, 1863, at Rappahannock Station, Va. Taken prisoner on skirmish line, Weldon Railroad, Petersburg, Va., Aug. 21, 1864. No further record.

Smith, Edward, Grass Lake. Enlisted in Company E, March 18, 1862, at Detroit, age 21. Corporal. Joined regiment at Yorktown, Va., May 5, 1862. Killed in action at second Manassas, Aug. 30, 1862, shot in the head.

Smith, Edward H. (Veteran), Kent County. Enlisted in Company B, Aug. 1, 1861, at Ionia, for 3 years, age 19. Missing in action at Gaines' Mill, June 27, 1862. Reenlisted as Sergeant Dec. 22, 1863, at Rappahannock Station, Va. 1st Sergeant. Sergeant Major, Nov. 1, 1864. Commissioned 1st Lieutenant, Company C, May 8, 1865. Commissioned Captain, July 7, 1865. Mustered out at Jeffersonville, Ind., July 8, 1865.

Smith, Francis, Perrinsville. Enlisted in Company F, Sept. 1, 1861, at Plymouth, for 3 years, age 18. Listed in March 1863 as in hospital, wounded. Discharged for disability, hip, at Detroit, April 22, 1863. Resided Decatur, Mich.

Smith, Frederick A., Macomb County. Enlisted in First Company Sharpshooters attached to 16th Michigan, Jan. 7, 1862, at Detroit, for 3 years, age 24. Joined regiment at Hall's Hill, Va., Feb. 14, 1862. Sergeant. Killed in action at Chancellorsville, Va., May 4, 1863.

Smith, George S., or C., Calhoun County. Enlisted in Company F, Aug. 1, 1861, at Plymouth, for 3 years, age 19. Discharged for disability at Hall's Hill, Va., Jan. 22, 1862. Resided Marshall, Mich.

Smith, Henry E., East Saginaw. Enlisted in Company D, Aug. 3, 1861, at East Saginaw, for 3 years, age 32. Killed in action at Gaines' Mill, June 27, 1862.

Smith, Henry F. Enlisted in Company B, Feb. 24, 1865, at Oxford, for 3 years, age 22. Substitute for Isaac Elwell, drafted. Mustered out at Jeffersonville, Ind., July 8, 1865.

Smith, Homer E. (Veteran), Wayne County. Enlisted in Company F, Sept. 16, 1861, age 28. Corporal Aug. 1862. Reenlisted Dec. 21, 1863, at Rappahannock Station, Va. Sergeant. Mustered out at Jeffersonville, Ind., July 8, 1865.

Smith, Jacob, Saginaw County. Enlisted in Company D as Sergeant, Aug. 1, 1861, at East Saginaw, for 3 years, age 24. Missing in action at Gaines' Mill, June 27, 1862. Discharged at Falmouth, Va., Dec. 31, 1862.

Smith, James. Enlisted in Company H, Feb. 27, 1865, at Holly, for 3 years, age 25. Substitute for Richard D.W. Pelton, drafted. Mustered out at Jeffersonville, Ind., July 8, 1865.

Smith, John, Detroit. Enlisted in Company E, Dec. 16, 1862, at Detroit, for 3 years, age 19. Joined regiment at Falmouth, Va., Jan. 2, 1863. Wounded in action, back, at Magnolia

Swamp–Bethesda Church, June 1, 1864. Corporal June 10, 1865. Mustered out at Jeffersonville, Ind., July 8, 1865.

Smith, John. Enlisted in Company H, Feb. 24, 1865, at Warren, for 3 years, age 24. Substitute for John Teison, drafted. Admitted to Harper Hospital July 25, 1865. Discharged at Detroit, Aug. 19, 1865.

Smith, John. Enlisted in Company I, Feb. 27, 1865, at Pontiac, for 3 years, age 18. Substitute for Henry J. Love, Putnam. Discharged at Washington, D.C., June 8, 1865.

Smith, John W., Detroit. Enlisted in Company G, Dec. 16, 1861, at Detroit, for 3 years, age 19. Killed in action at Gaines' Mill, June 27, 1862.

Smith, Joseph W., Wayne County. Enlisted in Company A, Aug. 9, 1861. Deserted at Detroit, Aug. 12, 1861.

Smith, Lucas M., Kent County. Enlisted in First Company Sharpshooters attached to 16th Michigan, Dec. 30, 1861, at Grand Rapids, for3 years, age 38. Joined regiment at Hall's Hill, Va., Feb. 14, 1862. Reenlisted Dec. 22, 1863, at Rappahannock Station, Va. Died of disease June 2, 1864. Buried in National Cemetery at Philadelphia, Grave No. 455.

Smith, Orson, Adrian. Enlisted in Company F, Lancers, as Corporal. Nov. 19, 1861, at Adrian, for 3 years, age 19. Transferred to Company I, 16th Michigan, Feb. 28, 1862. Deserted at Detroit, March 24, 1862.

Smith, Reuben. Entered service in Company H, for 1 year. Mustered March 28, 1865, as substitute. Mustered out at Jeffersonville, Ind., July 8, 1865.

Smith, Richard R. Enlisted in Company D, Feb. 13, 1864, at Tittabawassee, for 3 years, age 19. Wounded in action June 7, 1864 near Cold Harbor. Discharged at Washington, D.C., June 13, 1865. Died Nov. 2, 1892.

Smith, Samuel P. (Veteran), Genesee County. Enlisted in Company C, Aug. 4, 1861, at Flint, for 3 years, age 19. Reenlisted Dec. 24, 1863, at Rappahannock Station, Va. Corporal, April 1, 1865. Mustered out at Jeffersonville, Ind., July 8, 1865. Died Feb. 7, 1892.

Smith, Thomas (Veteran). Enlisted in Company G, Sept. 10, 1861, age 33. Reenlisted Dec. 21, 1863, at Rappahannock Station, Va. Mustered out at Jeffersonville, Ind., July 8, 1865.

Smith, Truman F. Enlisted in Company E, Aug. 13, 1861, at Detroit, for 3 years, age 18. Transferred to Company F. Discharged on Surgeon's certificate of disability April 22, 1863.

Smith, William. Enlisted in Company F, Aug. 8, 1861, at Plymouth, for 3 years, age 20. No further record.

Smith, William. Enlisted in Company H, Feb. 21, 1865, at Lafayette, for 3 years, age 24. Substitute for Bela M. Lewis, drafted. Mustered out at Jeffersonville, Ind., July 8, 1865.

Smith, William, Eagle River. Enlisted in Company H, Aug. 16, 1861. Deserted.

Smith, William S. (Veteran), Akron. Enlisted in Company H, Lancers, Nov. 18, 1861, at Akron, for 3 years, age 23. Transferred to Company I, 16th Michigan. Transferred to 14th Regiment, Veteran Reserve Corps, July 1, 1863. Reenlisted April 12, 1864. Died of disease in Washington, D.C., March 31, 1865.

Snay, Moses. Enlisted in Second Company Sharpshooters March 21, 1864, at Saginaw, for 3 years, age 20. Corporal May 1, 1865. Mustered out at Jeffersonville, Ind., July 8, 1865

Snyder, John. Enlisted in Company E, Aug. 14, 1861, at Detroit, for 3 years, age 36. Transferred to Company G. Sergeant. Discharged for disability Dec. 26, 1861.

Snyder, Joseph (Veteran), Detroit. Enlisted in Company D, Lancers, Nov. 27, 1861, at Detroit, for 3 years, age 45. Transferred to Company I, 16th Michigan, Feb. 28, 1862. Reenlisted Dec. 22, 1863, at Rappahannock Station, Va. Mustered out at Jeffersonville, Ind., July 8, 1865.

Sontag, Frederick W. Enlisted in Company E, Aug. 14, 1861, at Detroit, for 3 years, age 38. Transferred to Company H, June 1862. Killed in action at Gaines' Mill, June 27, 1862.

Soule, Lewellyn, Chesaning. Enlisted in Company D, Aug. 3, 1861, at East Saginaw, for 3 years, age 18. Killed in action at Gaines' Mill, June 27, 1862.

Souler, Daniel. Enlisted in Company G, Sept. 5, 1861, at Detroit, for 3 years, age 21. Deserted at Detroit, Sept. 16, 1861.

Spatch, James (Veteran), Hillsdale County. Enlisted in Company E, Aug. 22, 1861, age 16. Reenlisted Dec. 21, 1863, at Rappahannock Station, Va. Wounded in action, left leg, Cold Harbor area, June 7, 1864. Corporal May 29, 1865. Mustered out at Jeffersonville, Ind., July 8, 1865. Resided McBride, Montcalm County.

Spear, Hiram. Enlisted in Company E, Feb. 1, 1865, at Homer, Calhoun County, for 3 years, age 43. Substitute for Henry H. Parks, drafted. Mustered out at Jeffersonville, Ind., July 8, 1865.

Spencer, Andrew J. (Veteran), Newaygo County. Enlisted in First Company Sharpshooters attached to 16th Michigan, Oct. 24, 1861, at Detroit, for 3 years, age 33. Joined regiment at Hall's Hill, Va., Feb. 14, 1862. Reenlisted Dec. 22, 1863, at Rappahannock Station, Va. Transferred to U.S. Navy May 2, 1864.

Spitz or **Speitzler, Casper**, Wayne County. Enlisted in Company E Aug. 21, 1861, at Detroit, for 3 years, age 23. Transferred to Company A. Deserted at Detroit, Sept. 6, 1861.

Sprague, John. Enlisted in Company C, March 27, 1865, at Fredonia, Calhoun County, for 3 years, age 24. Substitute for John P. Fox, drafted. Mustered out at Jeffersonville, Ind., July 8, 1865.

Stadler, Joseph. Enlisted in Company E, Jan. 27, 1864, at Detroit, for 3 years, age 18. Mustered out at Jeffersonville, Ind., July 8, 1865.

Stadt, George. No record in *Record of Service* vol. 16, but listed in regimental "Roll of Honor" as an enlistee in Company A, killed in action at Gaines' Mill, June 27, 1862.

Stafford, Charles. Enlisted in Company H, as Corporal, Sept. 12, 1861, at Grand Traverse, for 3 years, age 30. Killed in action at second Manassas, Aug. 30, 1862.

Stafford, Daniel C. Enlisted in Company I, March 13, 1865, at Pontiac, for 3 years, age 20. Substitute for Richard J. Marsh, drafted. Mustered out at Jeffersonville, Ind., July 8, 1865.

Stafford, William H., or A., Redford. Enlisted in Company E, Lancers, Dec. 25, 1861, at Detroit, for 3 years, age 33. Transferred to Company K, 16th Michigan, Feb. 28, 1862. Discharged for disability at Detroit, June 25, 1862.

Stanfield, Joseph, Ann Arbor. Enlisted in Company D, Lancers, Oct. 29, 1861, at Ann Arbor, for 3 years, age 25. Transferred to Company I, 16th Michigan, Feb. 28, 1862. Corporal. Killed in action at Gaines' Mill, June 27, 1862.

Stark, Mathias, Ontonagon County. Enlisted in Company A, as Corporal, Aug. 8, 1861, at Ontonagon, for 3 years, age 40. Killed in action at Gaines' Mill, June 27, 1862.

Stark, Alfred, Argentine. Enlisted in Company I, Aug. 18, 1862, at Argentine, for 3 years, age 18. Joined regiment at Antietam, Md., Oct. 12, 1862. Wounded in action, right hand, Gettysburg, July 2, 1863. Discharged by order to date Sept. 24, 1864.

Starks, Charles, Genesee County. Enlisted in Company C, Aug. 4, 1861, at Flint, for 3 years, age 18. Died in hospital Sept. 1862.

Starks, Elam or **Elin**, Argentine. Enlisted in Company I, Aug. 1, 1862, age 24. Joined regiment at Antietam, Md., Oct. 12, 1862. Died of disease at Falmouth, Va., April 17, 1863.

Starks, Wellington, Argentine. Enlisted for 3 years as substitute for Aaron A. Dorrance, drafted Feb. 13, 1863, for 9 months, from Howell. No further record.

Starr, Robert, Macomb County. Enlisted in Company E, Aug. 19, 1861. Wounded in action, head, at Gettysburg, July 2, 1863. Discharged at expiration of term of service at Philadelphia, Nov. 10, 1864. Died June 26, 1895.

Stearns, George W. or M. Enlisted in Company B, Jan. 26, 1865, at Hamlin, for 1 year, age 18. Substitute for George Needham, drafted. Mustered out at Jeffersonville, Ind., July 8, 1865.

Steel or **Steele, John**, Detroit. Enlisted in Company A, Lancers, Oct. 28, 1861, at Detroit, for 3 years, age 24. Transferred to Company K, 16th Michigan, Feb. 28, 1862. Wounded in action in Middleburg, Va., June 21, 1863; arm amputated. Discharged for disability at Washington, D.C., Aug. 17, 1863. Died at Fortress Monroe, Va., Sept. 25, 1877.

Steele, Cyrus B., or **Silas**, Grattan. Drafted March 15, 1865, for 1 year, from Grattan, age 37. Assigned to Company G. Died of disease at Washington, D.C., June 27, 1865.

Steele, Oscar or **Osmer G**., or N., Ionia County. Enlisted in Company B, Aug. 6, 1861, at Ionia, for 3 years, age 20. Died of illness at Finley Hospital, Washington, D.C., Sept. 9, 1862.

Steffie or **Steffs, Adam** (Veteran). Enlisted in Company C Aug. 9, 1861, at Flint, for 3 years, age 21. Wounded in action at second Manassas, Aug. 30, 1862. Transferred to Company H, Sept. 1862. Reenlisted Dec. 24, 1863, at Rappahannock Station, Va. Corporal, May 1, 1865. Mustered out at Jeffersonville, Ind., July 8, 1865.

Steffie or **Steffy, Henry** (Veteran), Chelsea. Enlisted in Company I, Oct. 21, 1861. Reenlisted Dec. 22, 1863, at Rappahannock Station, Va. Wounded in action, hand and leg, at Wilderness, May 7, 1864. Sergeant, May 1, 1865. Mustered out at Jeffersonville, Ind., July 8, 1865. Resided Eaton Rapids, Mich.

Steinhardt, Theodore. Enlisted in Company C, Aug. 2, 1861, at Flint, for 3 years, age 24. Transferred to Company G, June 1862. Wounded in action at Gaines' Mill, June 27, 1862. Transferred to Invalid Corps Dec. 31, 1863. Resided DeWitt, Mich.

Stevens, Aaron L. Enlisted in Company C, March 4, 1865, at Kalamazoo, for 1 year, age 27. Substitute for Emanuel Himebaugh, drafted, Bronson. Deserted at Jeffersonville, Ind., June 18, 1865.

Stevens, Charles D. Drafted Feb. 15, 1863, for 9 months, from St. Charles, Saginaw County Assigned to Company D. Joined regiment at Falmouth, Va., March 18, 1863. Discharged for disability at Washington, D.C., Sept. 12, 1863.

Stevens, George W. Drafted Feb 15, 1863, for 9 months, from St. Charles, Saginaw County. Assigned to Company D. Joined regiment at Falmouth, Va., March 18, 1863. Mortally wounded in action, right lung, at Gettysburg, July 2, 1863, and died July 10 at First Division Hospital.

Stevens, James M., Macomb County. Enlisted in Company F, Aug. 8, 1861, at Plymouth, for 3 years, age 21. Transferred to Company E. Corporal July 1862. Sergeant. Killed in action at Gettysburg, July 2, 1863.

Stevens, Oliver W., Saginaw County. Enlisted in Company D, Aug. 3, 1861, at East Saginaw, for 3 years, age 22. Discharged on Surgeon's certificate of disability at Philadelphia, Oct. 15, 1862, for wound, wrist, received in action at Gaines' Mill, June 27, 1862.

Stewart, George H. Enlisted in Company D, Aug. 7, 1861, at East Saginaw, for 3 years, age 18. Transferred to Company F. Killed in action at Gaines' Mill, June 27, 1862.

Stewart, Henry D., Ontonagon County. Enlisted in Company A, Aug. 3, 1861, at Ontonagon, for 3 years, age 24. Corporal. Wounded with loss of left hand, July 18, 1864, in trenches before Petersburg, Va. Discharged at expiration of term of service at Petersburg, Va., Sept. 7, 1864.

Stewart, James. Enlisted Jan. 22, 1864, at Detroit for 3 years, age 39. No further record.

Stewart, James. Enlisted in Company K, Aug. 24, 1861, at White Pigeon, for 3 years, age 18. (Note: There was no Company K in the formation of Stockton's regiment, possibly meaning Stewart enlisted in Col. William May's unsuccessful independent regiment, and was among the men transferred to Stockton.) Transferred to Company E, Dec. 1, 1861. Died Sept. 3, 1862, at Washington, D.C., of wounds received in action, to the head, second Manassas, Aug. 30, 1862.

Stewart, John. Enlisted in Company D, Aug. 3, 1861, at East Saginaw, for 3 years, age 18. Reported as of Company C. No further record.

Stewart, John M. (Veteran), Wayne County. Enlisted in Company C, Aug. 2, 1861, at Flint, for 3 years, age 18. Transferred to Company E. Reenlisted as Drummer Dec. 21, 1863, at Rappahannock Station, Va. Deserted at Detroit, Sept. 1864.

Stickney, Jerome. Enlisted in Company I, Feb. 1, 1865, at Ashland, Newaygo County, for 1 year, age 17. Substitute for Charles Blood, drafted. Died of disease at Washington, D.C., June 13, 1865.

Stocking, Merritt D. Drafted March 15, 1865, for 1 year, from Grattan, age 30. Assigned to Company G. Mustered out at Jeffersonville, Ind., July 8, 1865.

Stockton, Thomas B. W., Flint. Cadet, Military Academy, July 1, 1823. Brevet 2nd Lieutenant, 1st U.S. Army Infantry Regiment, July 1, 1827. 2nd Lieutenant, July 1, 1827. Acting Quartermaster July 11, 1832. 1st Lieutenant March 4, 1833. Resigned Nov. 30, 1836. Colonel, 1st Michigan Infantry, Mexican War, Oct. 18, 1847. Mustered out July 23, 1848. Entered service in his own regiment, later enrolled as the 16th Michigan Infantry, at organization as Colonel, Aug. 22, 1861, for 3 years. Later commissioned to date July 21, 1861. Taken prisoner at Gaines' Mill, June 27, 1862. Exchanged Aug. 12, 1862. Commanding Third Brigade, First Division, Fifth Army Corps. Resigned May 18, 1863. Died Dec. 9, 1890.

Stoddard, George, Saginaw County. Enlisted in Company D, Aug. 7, 1861, at East Saginaw, for 3 years, age 20. Wounded and missing in action at Gaines' Mill, June 27, 1862. Discharged in hospital, Nov. 4, 1862.

Stone, John B. or **D.**, Midland. Enlisted in Company D, Aug. 7, 1861, at East Saginaw, for 3 years, age 21. Died of disease at Hall's Hill, Va., Jan. 3, 1862.

Stowe, Edwin H. or **Edward.** Drafted for 1 year, from Newark, Gratiot County, age 34. Mustered

Dec. 20, 1864. Assigned to Company C. Mustered out at Jeffersonville, Ind., July 8, 1865.

Straub, John A. (Veteran). Enlisted in Company A, Sept. 5, 1861. Reenlisted Dec. 21, 1863, at Rappahannock Station, Va. Wounded in action at Laurel Hill–Spotsylvania Court House May 8, 1864. Mustered out at Jeffersonville, Ind., July 8, 1865.

Streeter, Lloyd G. (Veteran), Flint. Enlisted in Company B, Aug. 6, 1861, at Ionia, for 3 years, age 21. Paroled prisoner Aug. 1862. Reenlisted as Corporal Dec. 22, 1863, at Rappahannock Station, Va. Sergeant, March 1, 1865. Commissioned 2nd Lieutenant, July 7, 1865. Mustered out at Jeffersonville, Ind., July 8, 1865.

Streeter or **Strever** or **Sheever, William H.** (Veteran), Ionia County. Enlisted in Company B, Aug. 7, 1861, at Ionia, for 3 years, age 19. Reenlisted Dec. 22, 1863, at Rappahannock Station, Va. Sergeant, May 14, 1865. Mustered out at Jeffersonville, Ind., July 8, 1865.

Strong, Edward P., Ionia County. Enlisted in Company B, Aug. 6, 1861, at Ionia, for 3 years, age 24. Corporal. Wounded in action at second Manassas, Aug. 30, 1862. Transferred to Invalid Corps Aug. 5, 1863. Discharged at expiration of term of service at Washington, D.C., Aug. 12, 1864, from 14th Regiment, Veteran Reserve Corps.

Strover, Emile, Detroit. Enlisted in Company G, Sept. 16, 1861, at Detroit, age 22. Died Sept. 5, 1862, of wounds received in action at second Manassas, Aug. 30, 1862.

Sullivan, John T., Houghton. Enlisted in Company E, Aug. 28, 1861, at Hancock, for 3 years, age 21. Dropped from rolls Oct. 9, 1862.

Surine, Peter. Enlisted in Company H, Lancers, Nov. 4, 1861, at Geneva, for 3 years, age 21. Transferred to Company I, 16th Michigan. Discharged for disability after battle of Gaines' Mill, June 27, 1862.

Surrarer, George. Enlisted in Company G, Aug. 24, 1861, at Detroit, for 3 years, age 38. Discharged for disability at Washington, D.C., March 5, 1863.

Sutherland, William, Saginaw County. Enlisted in Company D, Sept. 7, 1861. Discharged April 18, 1863. Present residence, Eagle, Mich.

Sutherly, Charles. Wayne County. Enlisted in Company E, Aug. 17, 1861, at Detroit, for 3 years, age 22. Discharged May 1863.

Sutton, Andrew J. Enlisted in Company E, Aug. 17, 1861, at Detroit, for 3 years, age 24. Transferred to Company G, May 1862. Discharged at expiration of term of service at Petersburg, Va., Sept. 7, 1864.

Swan, George H., Detroit. Entered service in Company A, at organization, as 1st Lieutenant, Aug. 1, 1861, at Ontonagon, for 3 years, age 23. Commissioned Captain, Company C, June 27, 1862. Wounded, face and mouth, in action at Manassas, Aug. 30, 1862. Transferred to Company A, Dec. 22, 1862. Cashiered July 16, 1864.

Swart or **Swartz, Menzo**, Flushing. Enlisted in Company C, as Sergeant, July 30, 1861, at Flint, for 3 years, age 20. 1st Sergeant. 2nd Lieutenant, April 27, 1863. Wounded in action near Bethesda Church, June 1, 1864. Commissioned 1st Lieutenant Aug. 3, 1864. Discharged at expiration of term of service, Sept. 26, 1864. Died at Turner, Mich., June 2, 1904.

Sweatland, Elijah M., or Elisha (Veteran), Ottawa County. Enlisted in First Company Sharpshooters attached to 16th Michigan as Corporal, Oct. 21, 1861, at Detroit, for 3 years, age 36. Joined regiment at Hall's Hill, Va., Feb. 14, 1862. Reenlisted Dec. 22, 1863, at Rappahannock

Station, Va. Reported to have been wounded, but another record states he died of disease at St. Mary's Hospital, Detroit, Aug. 24, 1864.

Swix, William (Veteran), Wayne County. Enlisted in Company D, Aug. 3, 1861, at East Saginaw, for 3 years, age 20. Transferred to Company F, July 1862. Reenlisted Dec. 21, 1863, at Rappahannock Station, Va. Mustered out at Jeffersonville, Ind., July 8, 1865.

Syers, John. Enlisted in Company H, Feb. 27, 1865, at Grand Rapids, for 1 year, age 17. Substitute for Albert G. Kent, from Assyria. Mustered out at Jeffersonville, Ind., July 8, 1865.

Synold, Charles F., Ionia County. Enlisted in Company B, Aug. 5, 1861, at Ionia, for 3 years, age 45. Discharged.

Tack, James. See **Vack, James.**

Taggart, Henry, Lapeer County. Enlisted in Company B, Feb. 5, 1862, at Flint, for 3 years, age 18. Joined regiment at Hall's Hill, Va., Feb. 14, 1862. Killed in action at Gettysburg, July 2, 1863.

Taggart, John. Enlisted Feb. 22, 1864, at Detroit, for 3 years, age 43. No further record.

Talon or **Taylor, Dennis**. Enlisted in Company D, Aug. 9, 1861, at East Saginaw, for 3 years, age 43. Mustered Sept. 7, 1861. Transferred to Company F. Discharged for disability.

Tanner, Marshall, Ionia County. Enlisted in Company B, Aug. 7, 1861, at Ionia, for 3 years, age 20. Discharged at Philadelphia, Oct. 24, 1862. Died Aug. 1894. Buried at Saranac, Mich.

Tawhy or **Tawley, John**. Enlisted in Company F, Aug. 2, 1861, at Plymouth, for 3 years, age 25. Died at Washington, D.C., April 2, 1862.

Taylor, Charles G., Saginaw. Enlisted in Company D, Aug. 3, 1861, at East Saginaw, for 3 years, age 19. Discharged at expiration of term of service at Petersburg, Va., Sept. 7, 1864.

Taylor, George. Enlisted in Company B, Aug. 5, 1861, at Ionia, for 3 years, age 18. No further record.

Teachout, William. Enlisted in Company C, Jan. 18, 1864, at Richfield, for 3 years, age 27. Mustered out at Jeffersonville, Ind., July 8, 1865.

Teal, Archer M., Saginaw County. Enlisted in Company D, Aug. 5, 1861, at East Saginaw, for 3 years, age 42. Discharged for disability at Hall's Hill, Va.

Teeple, Albert B. Drafted March 15, 1865, for 1 year, from Cascade, Kent County, age 32. Assigned to Company B. Discharged at Washington, D.C., May 30, 1865.

Teeple, Seneca. Drafted March 15, 1865, for 1 year, from Cascade, Kent County, age 34. Assigned to Company K. Mustered out at Jeffersonville, Ind., July 8, 1865.

Terry, Francis. Enlisted in Company H, Feb. 17, 1865, at Springfield, Oakland County, for 3 years, age 23. Substitute for James Harrison, drafted. Deserted June 26, 1865.

Terry or **Ferry, Samuel**. Drafted for 1 year, from Lake, Berrien County, age 38. Mustered Nov. 4, 1864. Assigned to Company C. Mustered out at Jeffersonville, Ind., July 8, 1865.

Thier or **Thies, Henry**. Enlisted in Company G, Aug. 18, 1861, at Detroit, for 3 years, age 24, 1861. Wounded in action at Malvern Hill, July 1, 1862; wounded in action, arm, at Gettysburg, July 2, 1863. Transferred to Invalid Corps Nov. 1, 1863. Discharged at expiration of term of service.

Thody or **Thoda, Thomas D.**, or C. Enlisted in Company B, Feb. 16, 1865, for 1 year, age 18. Substitute for Henry S. Pattee, or Potter, drafted, Port Huron. Mustered out at Jeffersonville,

Ind., July 8, 1865.

Thomas, Alfred P., Watrousville, Tuscola County. Enlisted in Company H, Lancers, Dec. 15, 1861, at Watrousville, for 3 years, age 21. Transferred to Company I, 16th Michigan, Feb. 28, 1862. Reported absent, wounded, June–Aug. 1863. Transferred to Invalid Corps at Alexandria, Va., July 1, 1863. Discharged Sept. 1, 1863.

Thomas, Jesse. Enlisted in Company F, March 24, 1865, at Detroit, for 1 year, age 20. Substitute for Lucien Wellon, drafted. Died of disease at City Point, Va., May 8, 1865.

Thomas, John. Enlisted in Company C, Feb. 1, 1865, at Wayland, for 1 year, age 33. Substitute for Ely P. Clark, drafted. Mustered out at Jeffersonville, Ind., July 8, 1865.

Thomas, John J. Enlisted in Company B, Feb. 17, 1865, at Bloomfield, for 3 years, age 28. Substitute for Travis Shaw, drafted. Deserted at Washington, D.C., June 15, 1865.

Thompson, Benjamin E. (Veteran), Detroit. Enlisted in Company K, March 31, 1862, at Detroit, for 3 years, age 18. Reenlisted March 26, 1864, at Bealton, Va. Wounded in action at Petersburg, Va., July 20, 1864. Discharged at Detroit, July 15, 1865.

Thompson, David. Enlisted in Company G, Jan. 23, 1865, at Pokagon, for 3 years, age 19. Substitute for Osborne Silver, drafted. Deserted June 29, 1865.

Thompson, Eugene (Veteran), Easton, Ionia County Enlisted in Company B, Aug. 3, 1861, at Ionia, for 3 years, age 18. Reenlisted Dec. 24, 1863, at Rappahannock Station, Va. Killed in action at Wilderness, May 6, 1864.

Thompson, George L., Lapeer County. Enlisted in Company C, as Corporal, Aug. 2, 1861, at Flint, for 3 years, age 21. Sergeant. Discharged on Surgeon's certificate of disability Jan. 9, 1863. Resided Hadley, Mich.

Thompson, John. Enlisted in Company E, Jan. 21, 1865, at Lake, for 3 years, age 22. Substitute for Gabriel Starr, drafted from Lake. Discharged at Washington, D.C., June 15, 1865.

Thompson, Lorenzo (Veteran), Kent County. Enlisted in First Company Sharpshooters attached to 16th Michigan, Dec. 16, 1861, at Grand Rapids, for 3 years, age 38. Joined regiment at Hall's Hill, Va., Feb. 14, 1862. Missing in action Sept. 17, 1862. Reenlisted Dec. 22, 1863 at Rappahannock Station, Va. Wounded in action at Noel's Turn, Va., May 26, 1864, near North Ana River. No further record.

Thompson, Peter. Enlisted Jan. 25, 1864, at Detroit, for 3 years, age 22. No further record.

Thompson, Thomas. Enlisted in Company C, Jan. 4, 1864, at Flint, for 3 years, age 18. Corporal April 1, 1865. Mustered out at Jeffersonville, Ind., July 8, 1865.

Thompson, Thomas D., Saginaw County. Enlisted in Company D, Aug. 9, 1861, at East Saginaw, for 3 years, age 20. Deserted at Detroit.

Thomson, David. Enlisted in Second Company Sharpshooters, April 28, 1864, at Tittabawassee, Saginaw County, for 3 years, age 19. Mustered out at Jeffersonville, Ind., July 8, 1865.

Thorpe, Franklin. Enlisted in Company K, Jan. 24, 1865, at Sebewaing, for 1 year, age 18. Substitute for Andrew Beck, drafted. Mustered out at Jeffersonville, Ind., July 8, 1865. Died in 1893. Buried at Owosso.

Thrasher, Lyman, Wayne County. Enlisted in Company C, Sept. 14, 1861, at Detroit, for 3 years, age 18. Discharged at Alexandria, Va., Dec. 24, 1862, to enlist in U.S. Army.

Thurston, Theron, Macomb County. Enlisted in First Company Sharpshooters attached to 16th

Michigan, Oct. 10, 1861, at Detroit, for 3 years, age 33. Deserted at Detroit, Feb. 3, 1862.

Tidwell, Francis L. M. Enlisted in Company G, Jan. 27, 1865, at LaSalle, for 3 years, age 23. Substitute for Jacob Moore, drafted from LaSalle. Mustered out at Jeffersonville, Ind., July 8, 1865.

Tiff, Henry H., Ionia. Enlisted in Company B, as Sergeant, Aug. 1, 1861, at Ionia, for 3 years, age 21. Wounded in action at Gettysburg, July 2, 1863, or on July 14, 1863. Transferred to Invalid Corps April 10, 1864. Died Dec. 30, 1903.

Tillman, William, Argentine. Enlisted in Company I, Aug. 9, 1862, at Argentine, for 3 years, age 24. Joined regiment at Antietam, Md., Oct. 12, 1862. Discharged at Falmouth, Va., Feb. 9, 1863.

Tisler, John, Ontonagon County. Enlisted in Company A, Aug. 3, 1861, at Ontonagon, for 3 years, age 23. Discharged at Philadelphia, Jan. 24, 1863, for wounds received in action at Gaines' Mill, June 27, 1862.

Titchworth, Caspar, Wayne County. Enlisted in Company F, Aug. 8, 1861, at Plymouth, for 3 years, age 18. Wounded and missing in action at Gaines' Mill, June 27, 1862. Discharged at Washington, D.C., Nov. 28, 1862.

Titus, Jonas H., Jr., Detroit. Entered service in First Company Sharpshooters attached to 16th Michigan, as 2nd Lieutenant, Sept. 16, 1861, at Detroit, for 3 years, age 30. Joined regiment in Virginia, Feb. 1862. Commissioned 1st Lieutenant, May 18, 1862. Resigned Jan. 14, 1863.

Topping, James L., Fenton. Entered service in Company I, 16th Michigan, as 2nd Lieutenant, age 37. Commissioned Sept. 4, 1862. Resigned March 28, 1863.

Totten, Joseph G. Drafted March 15, 1865, for 1 year, from Sparta, age 39. Assigned to Company A. Mustered out at Jeffersonville, Ind., July 8, 1865.

Tower, Henry S., Saginaw County. Enlisted in Company D, Aug. 6, 1861, at East Saginaw, for 3 years, age 19. Died of disease at Georgetown, Oct. 19, 1861.

Town, Richard M., Orleans. Enlisted in Company B, Aug. 6, 1861, at Ionia, for 3 years, age 19. Died in hospital at Fortress Monroe, Va., Sept. 13, 1862.

Townsend, Bervinus. Enlisted in Company D, Aug. 3, 1861, at East Saginaw, for 3 years, age 19. Discharged by writ of habeas corpus at Detroit, Mich.

Trahey, Thomas, Ann Arbor. Enlisted in Company E, Lancers, Oct. 17, 1861, at Bay City, for 3 years, age 18. Mustered out at Detroit, March 19, 1862. Reentered service in Company H, 16th Michigan, Oct. 13, 1862, at Ann Arbor, for 3 years. Joined regiment at Falmouth, Va., Nov. 26, 1862. Wounded in action, chest contusion from exploding shell, at Fredericksburg, Va., Dec. 13, 1862. Promoted Sergeant May 1, 1865. Mustered out at Jeffersonville, Ind., July 8, 1865. Resided St. Louis, Mo.

Trail, Beverly L. Enlisted in Company D, Feb. 23, 1865, at Jackson, for 3 years, age 30. Substitute for Thomas O'Brien, drafted from Marshall. Deserted at Jeffersonville, Ind., July 29, 1865.

Trask, Lafayette L., St. Johns. Enlisted in Company H, as Corporal, Aug. 13, 1861, at St. Johns, for 3 years, age 20. Discharged for disability Jan. 2, 1863.

Travessy, Henry. Enlisted in Second Company Sharpshooters, March 30, 1864, at Saginaw, for 3 years, age 21. Deserted at Saginaw, May 3, 1864.

Travis, James W., Almont. Enlisted in Company K, Feb. 5, 1862, at Almont, for 3 years, age

22. Transferred to Company D. Joined regiment at Hall's Hill, Va., Feb. 14, 1862. Wounded and taken prisoner at Gaines' Mill, June 27, 1862. Died in prison at Richmond, July 1862.

Travis, William J., or A., Detroit. Enlisted in Company H, Jan. 3, 1862, at East Saginaw, for 3 years, age 21. Joined regiment at Hall's Hill, Va., Jan. 11, 1862. Wounded in action at Malvern Hill, July 1, 1862. Transferred to Invalid Corps, Dec. 15, 1863.

Travoss, John. Enlisted in Company A, Jan. 25, 1864, at Bloomfield, for 3 years, age 30. Mustered out July 8, 1865.

Tromley, Alexander. Enlisted in Second Company Sharpshooters April 4, 1864, at Saginaw, for 3 years, age 27. Discharged on Surgeon's certificate of disability at Washington, D.C., July 25, 1865. Died April 23, 1890.

Trowbridge, Warren (Veteran). Enlisted in Company E, Sept. 6, 1861, age 16. Reenlisted Dec. 21, 1863, at Rappahannock Station, Va. Corporal. Wounded in action at Petersburg, Va., June 20, 1864. Mustered out at Jeffersonville, Ind., July 8, 1865.

Troxel or **Truxel, Solomon**. Enlisted in Company I, March 20, 1865, at Marshall, for 1 year, age 18. Substitute for Jesse Chance, drafted, Vermontville. Mustered out at Jeffersonville, Ind., July 8, 1865.

Tripp, Conrad, or **Coral**. See **Kipp, Conrad**, or **Coral**.

Truesdale, Henry, Ontonagon County. Enlisted in Company A, Aug. 3, 1861, at Ontonagon, for 3 years, age 28. Michigan Adjutant-General's Dept. *Record of Service,* vol. 16 (1905), states he was discharged for disability at Washington, D.C., Oct. 12, 1862, though the regiment's "Roll of Honor" lists him as wounded in action at Fredericksburg, Va., Dec. 13, 1862, and then discharged.

Truesdale, Horace E. (Veteran), Wayne County. Enlisted in Company F, Aug. 5, 1861. Reenlisted Dec. 21, 1863, at Rappahannock Station, Va. Corporal. Wounded in action, neck, Petersburg, Va., June 20, 1864. Commissioned 2nd Lieutenant, Company E, May 8, 1865. Commissioned 1st Lieutenant, July 7, 1865. Mustered out at Jeffersonville, Ind., July 8, 1865.

Tucker, Morris W., Lapeer County. Enlisted in Company C, as Sergeant, July 30, 1861, at Flint, for 3 years, age 21. Wounded in action, concussion from exploding shell, at Malvern Hill, July 1, 1862. Taken prisoner, at Snicker's Gap, Nov. 4, 1862, and paroled, rejoining regiment in April 1863, Stoneman's Station, Va. Captured again near Mine Run, Va., Nov. 27, 1863, and escaped Castle Pemberton, Richmond, Feb. 17, 1864, entering Union lines at Gloucester, Va., and ultimately rejoined regiment. Discharged at expiration of term of service at Detroit, Sept. 16, 1864, having served as orderly sergeant and acting ordnance sergeant for his division.

Tupper, Garwood S. (Veteran), Genesee County. Enlisted in Company C, Aug. 9, 1861, at Flint, for 3 years, age 24. Reenlisted Dec. 24, 1863, at Rappahannock Station, Va. Mustered out at Jeffersonville, Ind., July 8, 1865. Died July 13, 1893.

Turk, Ira, Bay City. Enlisted in Company E, Lancers, Nov. 5, 1861, at Bay City, for 3 years, age 40. Transferred to Company I, 16th Michigan, Feb. 28, 1862. Discharged.

Turner, George, Genesee County. Enlisted in Company F, Aug. 8, 1861, at Plymouth, for 3 years, age 44. Transferred to Company C, June 1862. Discharged at Yorktown, Va., May 8, 1862.

Turner, Jerome. Enlisted in Company F, March 28, 1865, at Fulton, for 1 year, age 18. Substitute for George T. Wilcox, drafted. No further record.

Turner, Joseph N. Enlisted in Company E, Aug. 21, 1861, at Detroit, for 3 years, age 24. Transferred to Company B. Discharged at Hall's Hill, Va., March 1, 1862.

Turner, William. Enlisted in Company E, Feb. 2, 1864, at Flint, for 3 years, age 31. Wounded in action, in the face, near Cold Harbor, June 7, 1864. Discharged on Surgeon's certificate of disability at Washington, D.C., March 17, 1865.

Turrell, or **Farrell, Norman**. Enlisted in Company C, Aug. 3, 1861, at Flint, for 3 years, age 20. Deserted at Detroit, Sept. 9, 1861.

Turrell, Reuben (Veteran), Hubbardston. Enlisted in Company E, Aug. 20, 1861, at Detroit, for 3 years, age 24. Reported in Company H. Wounded in action, at second Manassas, Aug. 30, 1862. Reenlisted as Sergeant Dec. 24, 1863, at Rappahannock Station, Va. Commissioned 1st Lieutenant, Company B, May 8, 1865. Mustered out at Jeffersonville, Ind., July 8, 1865.

Tuttle, Emory, Ionia County. Enlisted in Company B, Sept. 4, 1861, at Ionia, for 3 years, age 18. Killed in action at Gettysburg, July 2, 1863.

Uberoth, Charles. Enlisted in Company A, Aug. 3, 1861, at Ontonagon, for 3 years, age 32. Wounded in action at Gaines' Mill, June 27, 1862. Discharged for disability Oct. 9, 1862. Reentered service in 2nd Regiment, Veteran Reserve Corps, Aug. 18, 1864, at Detroit, for 3 years. Discharged at Detroit, Nov. 10, 1865.

Vack, or **Tack, James** (Veteran), Milwaukee. Enlisted in Company E, Lancers, Nov. 25, 1861, at Franklin, for 3 years, age 18. Transferred to Company K, 16th Michigan, Feb. 28, 1862. Reenlisted Dec. 21, 1863, at Rappahannock Station, Va. "Roll of Honor" states he was listed as absent, wounded, no date given. Corporal May 1, 1865. Sergeant. Mustered out at Jeffersonville, Ind., July 8, 1865.

Valentine, George W. (Veteran). Enlisted in Company C, Aug. 4, 1861, at Flint, for 3 years, age 23. Transferred to Company F. Reenlisted as Drummer, Dec. 21, 1863, at Rappahannock Station, Va. Admitted to Harper Hospital, Detroit, Aug. 18, 1865. Discharged at Detroit, Aug. 25, 1865.

Valentine, James M. Enlisted in First Company Sharpshooters attached to 16th Michigan, Feb. 11, 1864, at Van Buren, for 3 years, age 45. Died of disease at Lincoln Hospital, Washington, D.C., July 20, 1865.

Valiant, Alexander, Portage Lake. Enlisted in Company F, Lancers, as Corporal, Oct. 24, 1861, at Portage Lake, for 3 years, age 32. Transferred to Company I, 16th Michigan, Feb. 28, 1862. Killed in action at Gaines' Mill, June 27, 1862.

Valkenstine, Frank. Enlisted in Company K, Jan. 18, 1864, at Ecorse, for 3 years, age 20. Wounded in action at Petersburg, Va., July 9, 1864. Admitted to Harper Hospital, Detroit, Oct. 15, 1864. Discharged at Detroit, June 15, 1865.

Vanakin, Francis, Hillsdale County. Enlisted in Company G, Infantry, as Wagoner, Aug. 10, 1861, at White Pigeon, for 3 years, age 26. Taken prisoner at Mine Run, Va., Nov. 27, 1863. Died in prison at Andersonville, Ga., Sept. 16, 1864. Buried in National Cemetery at Andersonville, Grave No. 8958.

Vanamburgh, Alonzo E., or **Edward**. Enlisted in Company G, Aug. 12, 1861, at White Pigeon, for 3 years, age 18. Missing in action at Gaines' Mill, June 27, 1862.

Vanarsdall, James, Lansing. Enlisted in Company F, July 30, 1861, at Plymouth, for 3 years, age 24. Transferred to Company G. Killed in action at Gaines' Mill, June 27, 1862.

Vance, James G. Drafted for 1 year, from North Star, age 40. Mustered March 16, 1865. Assigned to Company K. Mustered out at Jeffersonville, Ind., July 8, 1865. Resided Ithaca, Mich.

Van Dusan, James. Enlisted in Company F, March 6, 1865, at Orange, Ionia County, for 1 year, age 19. Substitute for George Keifer. Discharged at Washington, D.C., June 26, 1865.

Vanduzen, Leander W., or A. Enlisted in Company E, 15, 1861, at Detroit, for 3 years, age 18. Transferred to Company H, Oct. 1861. Discharged at expiration of term of service at Petersburg, Va., Sept. 7, 1864.

Van Horn, Cornelius, Pontiac. Enlisted in Company H, Nov. 7, 1861, at Pontiac, for 3 years, age 19. Wounded in action at Manassas, Aug. 30, 1862; arm amputated. Discharged at Washington, D.C., Feb. 23, 1863.

Van Horn, Henry. Enlisted in Company C, Jan. 30, 1864, at Saginaw, for 3 years, age 18. Mustered out at Jeffersonville, Ind., July 8, 1865.

Van Horn, John, Plymouth. Enlisted in Company F, July 30, 1861, at Plymouth, for 3 years, age 31. Corporal. Killed in action at second Manassas, Aug. 30, 1862.

Van Houghton or **Van Houten, David**, Plymouth. Enlisted in Company C, Aug. 6, 1861, at Flint, for 3 years, age 21. Transferred to Company F, June 1862. Killed in action at Gaines' Mill, June 27, 1862.

Vankuren, Charles. Enlisted in Second Company Sharpshooters, April 23, 1864, at Linden, for 3 years, age 17. Deserted at Saginaw, May 3, 1864.

Vankuren, Joseph C., or **James C**. Enlisted in Company I, March 27, 1865, at Dexter, for 1 year, age 19. Substitute for William Glenn, drafted. Discharged at Washington, D.C., May 30, 1865.

Van Riper, Myron, Genesee County. Enlisted in Company C, Aug. 8, 1861, at Flint, for 3 years, age 30. Discharged on Surgeon's certificate of disability at Washington, D.C., Dec. 4, 1862.

Vanscoy, William F. P. Enlisted in Company G, March 28, 1865, at Arlington, for 1 year, age 20. Substitute for Miles Monroe, drafted. Mustered out at Jeffersonville, Ind., July 8, 1865.

Vantecilt, John B. Enlisted in Company E, Aug. 20, 1861, at Detroit, for 3 years, age 28. No further record.

Vantine, Elias. Enlisted in Company E, Aug. 20, 1861, at Detroit, for 3 years, age 22. Transferred to Company H. Discharged on Surgeon's certificate of disability Sept. 27, 1861.

Van Veckten, Josephus or **Joseph**. Enlisted in Company E, Aug. 17, 1861, at Detroit, for 3 years, age 34. Corporal. Transferred to Company H, Oct. 1861. Killed in action at second Manassas, Aug. 30, 1862.

Van Wagoner, George H. Enlisted in Company H, Feb. 16, 1865, at Holly, for 3 years, age 23. Substitute for Samuel Green, drafted. Mustered out at Jeffersonville, Ind., July 8, 1865.

Vanwyck, John F. Drafted Dec. 29, 1864, for 1 year, from Orange, age 40. Assigned to Company E. Discharged at Washington, D.C., June 16, 1865.

Vassan, Silas. Enlisted in Company E, Aug. 16, 1861, at Detroit, for 3 years, age 37. Transferred to Company D. Discharged March 25, 1863.

Vaughn, Tracey (Veteran), Branch County. Enlisted in Company B, 11th Michigan Infantry,

Aug. 24, 1861, at Quincy, for 3 years, age 20. Transferred to Company G, 16th Michigan, Sept. 20, 1861. Reenlisted Dec. 21, 1863, at Rappahannock Station, Va. Mustered out at Jeffersonville, Ind., July 8, 1865.

Vaux, Alfred. Enlisted and mustered in Company I, March 24, 1865, at Detroit, for 1 year, age 22. Substitute for William M. Fenton, drafted. Mustered out at Jeffersonville, Ind., July 8, 1865.

Veeder, Charles (Veteran), Genesee County. Enlisted in Company G, Aug. 24, 1861. Reenlisted as Corporal, Dec. 21, 1863, at Rappahannock Station, Va. Sergeant. Commissioned 1st Lieutenant, Company E, May 8, 1865. Mustered out at Jeffersonville, Ind., July 8, 1865.

Vibber, Sylvester. Enlisted in Company D, Aug. 9, 1861, at East Saginaw, for 3 years, age 18. Discharged at expiration of term of service, Aug. 23, 1863.

Vincent, Robert E., Ionia County. Enlisted in Company B, Aug. 6, 1861, at Ionia, for 3 years, age 24. Transferred to Invalid Corps at Bealton, Va., May 2, 1864.

Visscher, William. Enlisted in Company K, Feb. 20, 1865, at Holland, for 1 year, age 33. Substitute for Ame Vanernd, drafted from Holland. Absent sick June 1865. Died of smallpox, Brooklyn, N.Y., Feb. 11, 1872.

Vose, Henry A. Drafted for 1 year, from Hartland, age 38. Mustered March 29, 1865. Assigned to Company D. Mustered out at Jeffersonville, Ind., July 8, 1865. Died Jan. 3, 1891. Buried at Owosso, Mich.

Vought, John C., Decatur. Enlisted in First Company Sharpshooters attached to 16th Michigan, Oct. 16, 1861, at Detroit, for 3 years, age 22. Joined regiment at Hall's Hill, Va., Feb. 14, 1862. Died of disease at Washington, D.C., March 2, 1863.

Vrooman, Peter, Owosso. Enlisted in Company H, Nov. 1, 1861, at Owosso, for 3 years, age 40. Discharged for disability at Washington, D.C., April 24, 1862.

Wachter or **Watcher, Henry** (Veteran), Ontonagon County. Enlisted in Company A, Aug. 3, 1861, at Ontonagon, for 3 years, age 22. Wounded in action, at Gettysburg, July 2, 1863. Reenlisted Dec. 21, 1863, at Rappahannock Station, Va. Wounded in action, hand and knee, in withdrawal from Cold Harbor, June 1864. Mustered out at Jeffersonville, Ind., July 8, 1865. Died Feb. 28, 1891.

Wade, John, Kent County. Enlisted in First Company Sharpshooters attached to 16th Michigan, Dec. 2, 1861, at Grand Rapids, for 3 years, age 35. Joined regiment at Hall's Hill, Va., Feb. 14, 1862. Discharged at expiration of term of service at Detroit, Feb. 15, 1865.

Wadsworth, Josiah. Saginaw County. Enlisted in Company D, as Teamster, Aug. 1, 1861, at East Saginaw, for 3 years, age 22. Killed in action at Malvern Hill, July 1, 1862.

Wagar, Jacob F. Enlisted in First Company Sharpshooters attached to 16th Michigan, Feb. 4, 1864, at Caledonia, for 3 years, age 27. Mustered out at Jeffersonville, Ind., July 8, 1865.

Wagner, August, Ontonagon County. Enlisted in Company A, Aug. 4, 1861, at Ontonagon, for 3 years, age 26. Wounded in action at Gaines' Mill, June 27, 1862. Discharged for disability at Philadelphia, Jan. 26, 1863.

Wagner John (Veteran), Ontonagon County. Enlisted in Company A, Aug. 3, 1861, at Ontonagon, for 3 years, age 28. Wounded right hand, Gaines' Mill, June 27, 1862; wounded right knee, Gettysburg, July 2, 1863. Reenlisted as Sergeant Dec. 21, 1863, at Rappahannock Station, Va. 1st Sergeant, Sept. 1, 1864. Wounded right breast, Dabney's Mill, Feb. 6, 1865.

Mustered out at Jeffersonville, Ind., July 8, 1865. Resided Port Huron, Mich.

Wainright, David N. Enlisted in Company E, Aug. 17, 1861, at Detroit, for 3 years, age 18. Transferred to Company H. Discharged for disability at Fortress Monroe, Va.

Wait, Benjamin F. (Veteran), Ionia County. Enlisted in Company C, Jan. 1, 1862, at East Saginaw, for 3 years, age 27. Joined regiment at Hall's Hill, Va., Jan. 11, 1862. Wounded in action and captured, Gaines' Mill, June 27, 1862. Reenlisted Dec. 24, 1863, at Rappahannock Station, Va. Corporal. Wounded in action at Weldon Railroad, Petersburg, Va., Aug. 20, 1864. Died Sept. 18, 1864, at City Point, Va., of wounds.

Wakazoo or **Wau-ka-zoo, Joseph**, Grand Traverse. Enlisted in Company H, Nov. 8, 1861, at Hall's Hill, Va., age 23. Missing in action Aug. 27, 1862. Transferred to Company K, 1st U.S. Sharpshooters, Nov. 27, 1863. Discharged at Detroit, Feb. 15, 1865.

Walker, George. Enlisted in Company B, Aug. 5, 1861, at Ionia, for 3 years, age 27. Mustered Sept. 7, 1861. No further record.

Walker, Jeremiah, Imlay, Lapeer County. Enlisted in Company K, Feb. 5, 1862, at Almont, for 3 years, age 18. Transferred to Company F. Corporal. Died of disease at Baltimore, Md., Nov. 20, 1862.

Walker, William, Detroit. Enlisted in Company H, Oct. 4, 1861, at Detroit, for 3 years, age 28. Wounded in action at Malvern Hill, July 1, 1862. Discharged for disability at Philadelphia, Sept. 26, 1862.

Walker, William A., Wayne County. Enlisted in First Company Sharpshooters attached to 16th Michigan, Sept. 25, 1861, at Detroit, for 3 years, age 20. Joined regiment at Hall's Hill, Va., Feb. 14, 1862. Wounded in action at Petersburg, Va., June 18, 1864. Discharged at expiration of term of service at Detroit, Nov. 25, 1864.

Walker, William H., New Hudson. Enlisted in Company B, Lancers, Oct. 30, 1861, at New Hudson, for 3 years, age 20. Transferred to Company I, 16th Michigan, Feb. 28, 1862. Killed in action at Gaines' Mill, June 27, 1862.

Wallace, George S. See **Walles, George S.**

Wallace, Thomas, Wayne County. Enlisted in Company E, Aug. 19, 1861, at Detroit, for 3 years, age 29. Discharged for disability at Washington, D.C., June 20, 1862.

Wallace, William, or **Williams, Wallace**. Enlisted in Company D, Feb. 8, 1864, at Saginaw, for 3 years, age 17. Wounded in action June 10, 1864, near Cold Harbor. Mustered out at Jeffersonville, Ind., July 8, 1865.

Walles, or **Wallace, George S**. Enlisted in Company C, March 23, 1865, at Detroit, for 1 year, age 22. Substitute for William I. Nesbit, drafted. Mustered out at Jeffersonville, Ind., July 8, 1865.

Walters. Jacob. Enlisted in Company A, March 27, 1865, at Concord, for 1 year, age 22. Substitute for Hiram R. Billings, drafted. Mustered out at Jeffersonville, Ind., July 8, 1865.

Walton, William. Enlisted in Company G, Jan. 4, 1865, at Unadilla, Livingston County, for 3 years, age 39. Substitute for John Van Sickle, drafted. Deserted June 11, 1865.

Waltz, George, Wayne County. Enlisted in Company F, Aug. 8, 1861, at Plymouth, for 3 years, age 27. Wounded in action at Malvern Hill, July 1, 1862. Transferred to Veteran Reserve Corps. Discharged Aug. 15, 1864, from Company A, 16th Regiment, VRC.

Ward, Ellis, or **Elias**, Lockwood. Drafted for 1 year, from Lockwood, age 28. Mustered March 16, 1865. Assigned to Company K, 16th Michigan. Discharged at Washington, D.C., June 20, 1865.

Ward, George S., Saginaw County. Enlisted in Company D, Sept. 4, 1861, at Detroit, age 21. Discharged at expiration of term of service at Petersburg, Va., Sept. 7, 1864.

Ward, John, Saginaw County. Enlisted in Company D, Aug. 3, 1861, at East Saginaw, for 3 years, age 28. Wounded and missing in action at Gaines' Mill, June 27, 1862. Discharged at Warrenton, Va., Nov. 14, 1862.

Ward, John W. (Veteran), Ionia County. Enlisted in Company B, as Wagoner, Aug. 29, 1861, at Ionia, for 3 years, age 29. Reenlisted as Sergeant Dec. 24, 1863, at Rappahannock Station, Va. Commissioned 2nd Lieutenant, May 8, 1865. Commissioned 1st Lieutenant, July 7, 1865. Mustered out at Jeffersonville, Ind., July 8, 1865.

Ward, Stephen. Saginaw County. Enlisted in Company D, Aug. 7, 1861, at East Saginaw, for 3 years, age 24. Discharged for disability at Hall's Hill, Va., Feb. 25, 1862.

Ward, William P., or R., Greenville. Enlisted in Company B, Jan. 26, 1864, at Grand Rapids, for 3 years, age 40. Wounded in action at Wilderness, May 1864. Died at Washington, D.C., June 7, 1864, from wounds.

Ward, William S., Detroit. Enlisted in Company C, Lancers, Nov. 20, 1861, at Detroit, for 3 years, age 18. Transferred to Company I, 16th Michigan, Feb. 28, 1862. Discharged on account of wounds received in action at Gaines' Mill, June 27, 1862.

Warren, Frederick. Enlisted in Company G, Aug. 22, 1861. Wounded Oct. 1862. Discharged for disability at Fortress Monroe, Va., Jan. 22, 1863.

Warren, George M. Enlisted in Company E, Aug. 22, 1861, at Detroit, for 3 years, age 20. Transferred to Company F. Discharged at expiration of term of service at Petersburg, Va., Sept. 7, 1864.

Warren, John H. Drafted for 1 year, from Coldwater, age 27. Mustered March 17, 1865. Assigned to Company F, 16th Michigan. Mustered out at Jeffersonville, Ind., July 8, 1865.

Warren, Moses, Genesee County. Enlisted in Company C, Aug. 1, 1861, at Flint, for 3 years, age 40. Deserted at Hall's Hill, Va., Nov. 30, 1861.

Waterman, Solomon H. (Veteran), Ionia County. Enlisted in Company B, Aug. 4, 1861, at Ionia, for 3 years, age 18. Reenlisted Dec. 22, 1863, at Rappahannock Station, Va. Wounded in action at Dabney's Mill, Feb. 6, 1865. Mustered out at Jeffersonville, Ind., July 8, 1865.

Waters, Charles H., Detroit. Enlisted in Company I, March 24, 1862, at Utica, for 3 years, age 19. Discharged for disability at Antietam, Md., Oct. 25, 1862. Resided Hastings, Mich.

Watson, David G., Saginaw County. Enlisted in Company D, as Corporal, Aug. 1, 1861, at East Saginaw, for 3 years, age 26. Died of disease at Baltimore, Oct. 10, 1862.

Watts, Martin (Veteran), Ontonagon County. Enlisted in Company A, Aug. 4, 1861, at Ontonagon, for 3 years, age 25. Reenlisted Dec. 21, 1863, at Rappahannock Station, Va. Killed in action before Petersburg, Va., June 20, 1864.

Way, Abram, or **Abraham** (Veteran), Flushing. Enlisted in Company C, Aug. 1, 1861, at Flint, for 3 years, age 28. Reenlisted Dec. 24, 1863, at Rappahannock Station, Va. Corporal. Severely wounded in action May 7, 1864, Wilderness, and died May 12 near Spotsylvania

Court House, May 7, 1864.

Way, Harrison. Enlisted in Company C, as Sergeant, Aug. 1, 1861, at Flint, for 3 years, age 21. Discharged for disability Dec. 12, 1861.

Weatherton, Francis M. Enlisted Jan. 20, 1865, for 3 years, age 24. Substitute for Samuel Sheiner, drafted from California, Branch County. No further record.

Weaver, David T., Genesee County. Enlisted in Company C, Aug. 4, 1861, at Flint, for 3 years, age 42. Discharged on Surgeon's certificate of disability at Georgetown, April 19, 1862. Reentered service in 13th Michigan Battery, Sept. 14, 1863, at Montrose. Mustered Oct. 2, 1863. Discharged on Surgeon's certificate of disability, Aug. 22, 1864.

Weaver, Frank, Walled Lake. Enlisted in Company I, as Corporal, March 1, 1862, at Walled Lake, for 3 years, age 25. Killed in action at Gaines' Mill, June 27, 1862.

Weaver, Peter. Enlisted in Second Company Sharpshooters attached to 16th Michigan, May 21, 1864, at Spaulding, for 3 years, age 17. Died of disease at Petersburg, Va., July 30, 1864.

Webb, Joseph, Mattison, Branch County. Drafted for 1 year, from Mattison, age 32. Mustered March 17, 1865. Assigned to Company C. Mustered out at Jeffersonville, Ind., July 8, 1865. Resided Colon, Mich.

Webber, Jacob, Lansing. Entered service in at organization of the regiment as 1st Lieutenant, Aug. 6, 1861, in Company G. Resigned Jan. 19, 1863.

Webster, Lewis. Entered service in Company E, Lancers, at organization, as 1st Lieutenant, Oct. 7, 1861, at Detroit, for 3 years, age 32. Commissioned 1st Lieutenant, Company K, 16th Michigan, March 19, 1862. Commissioned Captain July 29, 1862. Resigned Dec. 11, 1862.

Webster, Riley O. Enlisted in Company D, Feb. 12, 1864, at Saginaw, for 3 years, age 20. Wounded in action, left arm, June 10, 1864, Cold Harbor area. Corporal May 1, 1865. Mustered out at Jeffersonville, Ind., July 8, 1865.

Wedemeyer or **Weidmier, Frederick** (Veteran). Enlisted in Company D, July 3, 1861, at East Saginaw, for 3 years, age 25. Transferred to Company G. Reenlisted Dec. 21, 1863, at Rappahannock Station, Va. Wounded in action at Gettysburg, ankle, July 2, 1863. Died of disease at Washington, D.C., March 11 or 16, 1865.

Weckesser or **Weekessen, John**. Enlisted in Company A, Feb. 23, 1864, at Livonia, for 3 years, age 29. Wounded in action at Laurel Hill–Spotsylvania Court House, May 8, 1864. Mustered out at Jeffersonville, Ind., July 8, 1865.

Weeks, Melville R. (Veteran), Plymouth. Enlisted in Company H, Lancers, Dec. 14, 1861, at Plymouth, for 3 years, age 18. Transferred to Company I, 16th Michigan, Feb. 28, 1862. Reenlisted Dec. 22, 1863, at Rappahannock Station, Va. Corporal, May 1, 1865. Mustered out at Jeffersonville, Ind., July 8, 1865. Resided Plymouth, Mich.

Weiler, Safron. See **Wylam, Safron**.

Weitz, Adam, Detroit. Enlisted in Company K, March 21, 1862, at Detroit, for 3 years, age 37. Wounded and taken prisoner at the battle of Gaines' Mill, June 27, 1862. Paroled Oct. 1862. Discharged for disability April 14, 1863. Died May 26, 1889.

Welbon, Henry A. (Veteran), Detroit. Enlisted in Company F, Sept. 29, 1862, at Detroit, age 21. Joined regiment at Antietam, Md., Oct. 30, 1862. Wounded in action at Gettysburg, July 2, 1863. Reenlisted as Sergeant Dec. 21, 1863, at Rappahannock Station, Va. Deserted

April 1, 1864.

Welbon, Isaac (Veteran), Detroit. Enlisted in Company F, Sept. 29, 1862, at Detroit, age 22. Joined regiment at Antietam, Md., Oct. 30, 1862. Reenlisted Dec. 21, 1863, at Rappahannock Station, Va. Corporal, May 1, 1865. Mustered out at Jeffersonville, Ind., July 8, 1865.

Welch, Edward G. (Veteran), Ann Arbor. Enlisted in Company A, Oct. 1, 1862, at Ann Arbor, age 21. Joined regiment at Falmouth, Va., Nov. 26, 1862. Reenlisted Dec. 21, 1863, at Rappahannock Station, Va. Commissary Sergeant, March 1, 1864. Commissioned 2nd Lieutenant, Company A, May 8, 1865. Acting Quartermaster, May 1865. Commissioned 1st Lieutenant, July 7, 1865. Mustered out at Jeffersonville, Ind., July 8, 1865.

Welch, Norval E., Ann Arbor. Entered service in at the organization of regiment as Major, Aug. 22, 1861, at Detroit, for 3 years, age 26. Commissioned Lieutenant Colonel, July 6, 1862. Commissioned Colonel, May 18, 1863. Killed in action at Poplar Grove Church, Sept. 30, 1864.

Welch, Vine E., Ionia County. Enlisted in Company B, as Drummer, Aug. 9, 1861, at Ionia, for 3 years, age 24. Discharged for disability at Detroit, Sept. 1862. Reentered service in Company C, reorganized 3rd Michigan Infantry, as Corporal, Sept. 3, 1864, at Grand Rapids, for 3 years. Transferred to Company F, Oct. 8, 1864. Sergeant. Admitted to Harper Hospital June 2, 1865. Discharged at Detroit, July 27, 1865. Deceased.

Welch, Wallace (Veteran), Ypsilanti. Enlisted in Company A, Sept. 14, 1861, at Detroit, for 3 years, age 23. Quartermaster Sergeant July 1, 1862. Reenlisted Dec. 24, 1863, at Rappahannock Station, Va. Commissioned 1st Lieutenant and Quartermaster, Sept. 8, 1864. Acting Quartermaster, Third Brigade, Jan. 1865. Mustered out at Jeffersonville, Ind., July 8, 1865.

Weller, John, Saginaw County. Enlisted in Company D, as Corporal, Aug. 1, 1861, at East Saginaw, for 3 years, age 21. Sergeant Aug. 1862. 1st Sergeant. Wounded in action at Petersburg, Va., June 20, 1864. Discharged at expiration of term of service at Petersburg, Va., Sept. 7, 1864. Died at Saginaw, Jan. 9, 1904.

Wellington, Alfred, Saginaw County. Enlisted in Company D, July 30, 1861, at East Saginaw, for 3 years, age 18. Died of disease at Hall's Hill, Va., Nov. 9, 1861.

Wellington, Frederick. Enlisted and mustered in First Company Sharpshooters, Feb. 14, 1864, at Saginaw, for 3 years, age, 19. Commissary Sergeant March 14, 1865. Wounded in action, Dabney's Mill, Feb. 6, 1865. Discharged at Jeffersonville, Ind., July 1, 1865. Resided Saginaw.

Wellington, James H. Enlisted in Company B, March 1865, at Saginaw, for 1 year, age 26. Mustered out at Jeffersonville, Ind., July 8, 1865. Resided Saginaw.

Wellington, Samuel F., Saginaw County. Enlisted in Company D, July 30, 1861, at East Saginaw, for 3 years, age 25. Corporal. Died of disease at Georgetown, Oct. 23, 1861.

Wellman, Curtis K., or **Cyrus R.**, Spaulding. Enlisted in Second Company Sharpshooters April 5, 1864, at Spaulding, for 3 years, age 38. Commissioned 2nd Lieutenant, April 1, 1864. Transferred to Company E, Sept. 21, 1864. Dismissed Feb. 14, 1865. Died July 21, 1895.

Wells, Arlington, Ottawa County. Enlisted in First Company Sharpshooters attached to 16th Michigan, Dec. 17, 1861, at Grand Rapids, for 3 years, age 26. Joined regiment at Hall's Hill, Va., Feb. 14, 1862. Discharged for disability April 12, 1862.

Wells, James. Enlisted in Company F, Sept. 23, 1862, at Detroit, for 3 years, age 22. Joined regiment at Antietam, Md., Oct. 30, 1862. Deserted July 12, 1863.

Wells, John H. (Veteran), Wayne County. Enlisted in Company E, Aug. 18, 1861, at Detroit, for 3 years, age 19. Reenlisted Dec. 21, 1863, at Rappahannock Station, Va. Sergeant. Wounded in action at Peeble's Farm, Sept. 30, 1864. Mustered out at Jeffersonville, Ind., July 8, 1865.

Wells, Morris B., Ionia. Joined Company B as 2nd Lieutenant, age 27, July 31, 1861. Resigned Dec. 20, 1862. Commissioned 1st Lieutenant and Adjutant, 21st Michigan Infantry Regiment, at its organization, July 26, 1862. Wounded in action, Stone River, Tenn., Dec. 31, 1862. Commissioned Lt. Colonel, Feb. 3, 1863; killed in action Chickamauga, Ga., Sept. 20, 1863.

Welsh, William H., Wayne County. Enlisted in Company A, Sept. 16, 1861. Wounded in action at Bristow Station, Oct. 14, 1863. Reenlisted Dec. 21, 1863, as Musician, at Rappahannock Station, Va. Mustered out at Jeffersonville, Ind., July 8, 1865.

Wendell, Peter, Ontonagon County. Enlisted in Company A, Aug. 3, 1861, at Ontonagon, for 3 years, age 32. Wounded in action at Gaines' Mill, June 27, 1862. Discharged for disability at Fortress Monroe, Va., Jan. 22, 1863. Resided Hancock, Mich.

Wendell, Richard, Ontonagon County. Enlisted in Company A, as Sergeant, Aug. 3, 1861, at Ontonagon, for 3 years, age 30. Wounded in action at Gaines' Mill, June 27, 1862. Discharged for disability at Portsmouth Grove, R.I., March 21, 1863.

Wenner, Michael (Veteran), Van Buren County. Enlisted in First Company Sharpshooters attached to 16th Michigan, March 18, 1862, age 33. Reenlisted March 30, 1864, at Bealton, Va. Brigade Saddler, Sept. 1864. Corporal, May 1, 1865. Mustered out at Jeffersonville, Ind., July 8, 1865.

West, Arnold J., Saginaw. Enlisted in Second Company Sharpshooters, May 3, 1864, at Spaulding, for 3 years, age 23. Commissioned 1st Lieutenant, May 1, 1864. Wounded in action at Peeble's Farm, Sept. 30, 1864. Commissioned Captain, May 8, 1865. Discharged for disability May 15, 1865.

Western, Reuben (Veteran), Hillsdale County. Enlisted in Company F, Aug. 16, 1861. Reenlisted as Corporal Dec. 21, 1863, at Rappahannock Station, Va. Sergeant. Mustered out at Jeffersonville, Ind., July 8, 1865.

Westfall, Louis A. Enlisted in regimental Band, Sept. 13, 1861, at Detroit, for 3 years, age 23. Mustered out Aug. 11, 1862.

Westgate, Nelson. Enlisted in Company F, Lancers, as Corporal, Nov. 18, 1861, at Wellsville, for 3 years, age 24. Transferred to Company I, 16th Michigan, Feb. 28, 1862. Deserted at Detroit, March 24, 1862.

Weyermiller, Philip, Ontonagon County. Enlisted in Company A, Corporal, Aug. 5, 1861, at Ontonagon, for 3 years, age 25. Wounded in action at Gaines' Mill, June 27, 1862. Discharged at expiration of term of service, Sept. 6, 1864.

Weyner, Charles. Enlisted in Company G, Sept. 9, 1861. Mustered Sept. 14, 1861. Wounded (by accident?) Oct. 1862. Discharged Feb. 27, 1863.

Wheaton, Joseph F., or **J.** Drafted for 1 year, age 35. Mustered Nov. 17, 1864. Assigned to Company K. Deserted at Jeffersonville, Ind., June 28, 1865.

Wheaton, Timothy J., St. Clair County. Enlisted in Company D, as Corporal. Discharged for disability at Detroit, Sept. 1862.

Wheeler, John H. Enlisted in Company F, Jan. 27, 1864, at Plymouth, for 3 years, age 18. Wounded Sept. 1864, no detail given but likely at Peeble's Farm. Mustered out at Jeffersonville, Ind., July 8, 1865.

Wheelock, Alfred. Enlisted in Company F, July 31, 1861, at Plymouth, for 3 years, age 18. No further record.

Whipple, Alson A., Lapeer County. Enlisted in Company D, July 31, 1861, at East Saginaw, for 3 years, age 20. Wounded in action at Malvern Hill, July 1, 1862. Corporal Aug. 1862. Discharged at Antietam, Md., Oct. 25, 1862.

Whitbeck, Abraham (Veteran), Hillsdale County. Enlisted in Company C, Aug. 22, 1861, age 19. Wounded and taken prisoner at Hanover Court House, Va., May 27, 1862. Reenlisted Dec. 24, 1863, at Rappahannock Station, Va. Wounded in action at Magnolia Swamp–Bethesda Church, June 1, 1864. Discharged to date May 25, 1865.

Whitbeck, Clark W. (Veteran), Ionia County. Enlisted in Company B, Aug. 6, 1861, at Ionia, for 3 years, age 20. Reenlisted Dec. 22, 1863, at Rappahannock Station, Va. Wounded in action at Peeble's Farm, Sept. 30, 1864. Corporal March 1, 1865. Mustered out at Jeffersonville, Ind., July 8, 1865.

White, Charles. Enlisted in Jan. 4, 1865, at Arlington, Van Buren County, for 3 years, age 26. Substitute for Phillip Nichols, drafted. No further record.

White, Daniel. Enlisted in Company B, Lancers, Nov. 21, 1861, at Walled Lake, for 3 years, age 19. Transferred to Company I, 16th Michigan, Feb. 28, 1862. Killed in action at second Manassas, Aug. 30, 1862.

White or **Whyte, John.** Enlisted in Second Company Sharpshooters April 23, 1864, at Spaulding, for 3 years, age 22. Sergeant. Killed in action at Peeble's Farm, Aug. 30, 1864.

White, Joseph. Enlisted in Company H, Jan. 13, 1865, at Oronoco, for 3 years, age 18. Substitute for John Feather, drafted. Mustered out at Jeffersonville, Ind., July 8, 1865.

White, Philo, Argentine. Enlisted in Company K, Aug. 23, 1862, at Argentine, for 3 years, age 18. Joined regiment at Antietam, Md., Oct. 3, 1862. Wounded in action May 10, 1864, at Po River–Spotsylvania Court House. Discharged at Washington, D.C., April 30, 1865. Deceased.

Whitehead, Hiram, Bridgeport. Enlisted in Second Company Sharpshooters, April 4, 1864, at Spaulding, for 3 years, age 28. Died July 1, 1864, of wounds, amputation of foot, received in action June 9, 1864, on the withdrawal from Cold Harbor.

Whitfield, Charles W., Ionia County. Enlisted in Company B, Aug. 6, 1861, at Ionia, for 3 years, age 24. Wounded in action at Gaines' Mill, June 27, 1862. Discharged for disability at Washington, D.C., December 1862.

Whitfield, Nathaniel, Ionia County. Enlisted in Company B, Aug. 6, 1861, at Ionia, for 3 years, age 18. Wounds in action at Gaines' Mill, June 27, 1862. Reported taken prisoner and paroled July 22, 1862. Discharged Dec. 18, 1862, for disability on account of wounds.

Whitfield, Thomas N., Lowell. Enlisted in Company C, Lancers, Nov. 12, 1861, at Lowell, for 3 years. Transferred to Company I, 16th Michigan, Feb. 28, 1862. Wounded and taken prisoner June 27, 1862. Paroled prisoner at Annapolis, Md., Sept. 1862. Transferred to Invalid Corps at Washington, D.C., Dec. 15, 1863. Corporal. Died of disease at Baltimore, Dec. 18, 1864.

Whiting, Lewis. Enlisted in Company F, March 29, 1865, at Fredonia, for 1 year, age 18. Substitute for John Fredinburg, drafted from Fredonia. Mustered out at Washington, D.C., July 8, 1865.

Whitman, Henry. Enlisted in Company H, Feb. 28, 1865, at Solon, for 1 year, age 18. Substitute for Melvin J. Park, drafted from Grand Rapids. Mustered out at Jeffersonville, Ind., July 8, 1865.

Whitney, Albert H., Lapeer County. Enlisted in Company D, July 31, 1861, at East Saginaw, for 3 years, age 26. Wounded and missing in action at Gaines' Mill, June 27, 1862. Returned to regiment Aug. 12, 1862. Discharged for disability Feb. 25, 1863.

Whitney, Bradley S., or **Bradney P.** Drafted for 3 years, from Corunna, age 31. Mustered Oct. 27, 1863. Assigned to Company K. Mustered out at Jeffersonville, Ind., July 8, 1865.

Whitney, George, Oakland County. Enlisted in Company I, March 1, 1862, at Walled Lake, for 3 years, age 22. Paroled prisoner July 1863. Discharged for disability Dec. 1863.

Whitty, Phillip, Detroit. Enlisted in Company H, Aug. 25, 1861, at Detroit, for 3 years, age 30. Wounded in action at second Manassas, Aug. 30, 1862. Transferred to Invalid Corps Sept. 1, 1863.

Wickham, Lorenzo D., Flushing. Enlisted in Company C, Aug. 6, 1861, at Flint, for 3 years, age 26. Wounded in action at Malvern Hill, July 1, 1862. Killed in action at Manassas, Aug. 30, 1862.

Wickman, William (Veteran), Ionia County. Enlisted in Company B, Aug. 6, 1861, at Ionia, for 3 years, age 22. Reenlisted Dec. 22, 1863, at Rappahannock Station, Va. Mustered out at Jeffersonville, Ind., July 8, 1865.

Wiess or **Weise, Henry**, Ontonagon County. Enlisted in Company A, Aug. 4, 1861, at Ontonagon, for 3 years, age 34. Corporal. Killed in action at Gaines' Mill, June 27, 1862.

Wigman, Henry I., or J., Ontonagon County. Enlisted in Company A, Aug. 4, 1861, at Ontonagon, for 3 years, age 24. Color Bearer Nov. 1862. Sergeant. Killed in action carrying regimental colors at Fredericksburg, Va., Dec. 13, 1862.

Wilber, Charles or **Karl**. See **Miller, Charles** or **Karl**.

Wilber, Silas (Veteran). Clarence. Enlisted in Company K, March 1862, at Detroit, for 3 years, age 27. Reenlisted March 1, 1864, at Bealton, Va. Wounded in action at Wilderness, May 7, 1864. Transferred to Veteran Reserve Corps Feb. 10, 1865. Discharged at Washington, D.C., July 24, 1865.

Wilcoxson, John R., Wayne County. Enlisted in Company E, Aug. 30, 1861, at Detroit, for 3 years, age 43. Discharged for disability at Hall's Hill, Va., Dec. 23, 1861.

Wilder, Harry M. (Veteran), Wayne. Enlisted in Company D, July 1861, at East Saginaw, for 3 years, age 24. Reported in Company F, Oct. 1861. Reenlisted Dec. 21, 1863, at Rappahannock Station, Va. Mustered out at Jeffersonville, Ind., July 8, 1865. Resided Muir, Mich.

Wilder, William, Metamora. Enlisted in Company C as Corporal, Aug. 2, 1861, at Flint, for 3 years, age 28. Wounded and taken prisoner Gaines' Mill, June 27, 1862. Died at Richmond, July 19, 1862.

Wilkey or **Wilkie, Archie** (Veteran), White Pigeon. Enlisted in Company F, Aug. 24, 1861. Reenlisted Feb. 26, 1864, at Bealton, Va. Wounded in action, right shoulder, at Spotsylvania

Court House, May 20, 1864. Mustered out at Jeffersonville, Ind., July 8, 1865.

Wilkinson, Albert R., Detroit. Enlisted in Company H, Nov. 6, 1861, at Detroit, for 3 years, age 34. Wounded in action at Petersburg, Va., June 20, 1864. Discharged at expiration of term of service, Nov. 8, 1864.

Wilkinson, Ernest S. Enlisted in Company I, March 20, 1865, at Kalamazoo, for 1 year, age 18. Substitute for Menzo Best, drafted. Mustered out at Jeffersonville, Ind., July 8, 1865.

Wilkinson, Isaac B., Wayne County. Enlisted in Company F, Sept. 11, 1861, at Plymouth, for 3 years, age 18. Discharged for disability at Hall's Hill, Va., Feb. 25, 1862.

Wilkinson, John. Enlisted in Company C, Aug. 3, 1861, at Flint, for 3 years, age 18. Wagoner. Transferred to Company F, Jan. 1862. Wounded in action at Malvern Hill, July 1, 1862. Wounded in action, at Gettysburg, July 2, 1863. Discharged for disability Sept. 3, 1863.

Wilkinson, Robert. Enlisted in Second Company Sharpshooters, attached to 16th Michigan, April 4, 1864, at Saginaw, for 3 years, age 28. Deserted at Saginaw, May 3, 1864.

Wilkinson, William S., Corunna. Enlisted in Company H, Sept. 2, 1861, at Meridian Hill, for 3 years, age 19. Wounded in action, in the mouth, at Gaines' Mill, June 27, 1862. Discharged at Antietam, Md., Sept. 26, 1862. Died at Bloomingdale, Mich.

Willey, John, Wayne County. Enlisted in First Company Sharpshooters, attached to 16th Michigan, Oct. 10, 1861, at Detroit, for 3 years, age 20. Joined regiment at Hall's Hill, Va., Feb. 14, 1862. No further record.

Williams, Adelbert D. (Veteran), Ionia County. Enlisted in Company B, as Corporal, Aug. 5, 1861, at Ionia, for 3 years, age 21. Reenlisted Dec. 22, 1863, at Rappahannock Station, Va. Mustered out at Jeffersonville, Ind., July 8, 1865.

Williams, Charles W. Enlisted Feb. 17, 1865, at Bloomfield, for 3 years, age 20. Substitute for James Beatty or John A. Young, drafted from Bloomfield. No further record.

Williams, DeWitt C., Genesee County. Enlisted in Company C, Aug. 4, 1861, at Flint, for 3 years, age 26. Discharged at expiration of term of service at Petersburg, Va., Sept. 16, 1864.

Williams, Dudley J., Detroit. Enlisted in Company D, mustered May 14, 1862. Missing in action at Gaines' Mill, June 27, 1862. Dropped from rolls May 8, 1863.

Williams, Grant E. (Veteran), Wayne County. Enlisted in Company F, Aug. 6, 1861, age 18. Wounded in action at Gaines' Mill, June 27, 1862. Reenlisted Dec. 21, 1863, at Rappahannock Station, Va. Wounded in action, head, at Laurel Hill–Spotsylvania Court House, May 8, 1864. Corporal. Missing in action Nov. 1864. Joined regiment May 14, 1865. Mustered out at Jeffersonville, Ind., July 8, 1865.

Williams, Henry. See **Henry, William**.

Williams, Henry, Mt. Morris. Enlisted and mustered in Company B, March 1, 1865, at Port Huron, for 3 years, age 25. Substitute for Sewell Avery, drafted. Discharged July 8, 1865.

Williams, Hiram N. Enlisted in Company D, July 4, 1861, at East Saginaw, for 3 years, age 18. Transferred to Company F, June 1862. Wounded in action at Gaines' Mill, June 27, 1862. Discharged at expiration of term of service at Detroit, Aug. 15, 1864.

Williams, James R. (Veteran), Detroit. Enlisted in Company D, Dec. 4, 1861, at Detroit, for 3 years, age 18. Wounded and missing in action at Gaines' Mill, June 27, 1862. Reenlisted as Corporal Dec. 21, 1863, at Rappahannock Station, Va. Sergeant. Sergeant Major, May

14, 1865. 2nd Lieutenant, July 7, 1865. Mustered out at Jeffersonville, Ind., July 8, 1865.

Williams, John W., Convis. Enlisted in Company C, March 24, 1865, at Convis, for 1 year, age 27. Substitute for Richard S. Molsey, drafted. Mustered out at Jeffersonville, Ind., July 8, 1865.

Williams, Orange, or **Orange, William**, Saginaw County. Enlisted in Company D, July 1, 1861, at East Saginaw, for 3 years, age 18. Deserted at Detroit.

Williams, Richard, East Saginaw. Enlisted in Company A, as 1st Sergeant, Aug. 1, 1861, at Ontonagon, for 3 years, age 24. Eventually became 2nd Lieutenant, Company H. Transferred to Company C, June 18, 1862. Killed in action at Gaines' Mill, June 27, 1862.

Williams, Wallace. See **Wallace, William**.

Williams, William. Enlisted March 9, 1863, at Allison, age 28. Substitute for Duncan Hossack, drafted Feb. 10, 1863, for 9 months. No further record.

Williamson, John, Calhoun County. Enlisted in Company F, Aug. 2, 1861, at Plymouth, for 3 years, age 21. Discharged at expiration of term of service at Petersburg, Va., Sept. 7, 1864.

Willoughby, Urial, Wayne County. Enlisted in Company D. Mustered Aug. 31, 1861. Discharged at Washington, D.C., Feb. 4, 1863.

Willson, Charles (Veteran), Wayne County. Enlisted in Company F, as Fifer, Aug. 4, 1861, at Plymouth, for 3 years, age 18. Listed as missing in action Sept. 19, 1862, though the regiment was not involved in combat on that date. Reenlisted Feb. 26, 1864, at Bealton, Va. Transferred to Veteran Reserve Corps Nov. 23, 1864. Discharged at Detroit, July 15, 1865, from Company A, 2nd Regiment, Veteran Reserve Corps.

Willson, Elijah. Enlisted in Company G, Aug. 22, 1861, at White Pigeon, for 3 years, age 18. Wounded in action, second Manassas, Aug. 30, 1862. Discharged at expiration of term of service at Washington, D.C., Aug. 24, 1864, from Company H, 10th Regiment, Veteran Reserve Corps.

Willson, Henry, Wayne. Enlisted in Company I, March 21, 1862. Deserted at Detroit, March 23, 1862.

Wilson, Christopher. Enlisted in Second Company Sharpshooters, attached to 16th Michigan, March 24, 1864, at Bridgeport, for 3 years, age 22. Missing in action Aug. 21, 1864. Returned to regiment April 14, 1865. Mustered out at Jeffersonville, Ind., July 8, 1865.

Wilson, Frank (Veteran), Ionia County. Enlisted in Company B, Aug. 10, 1861, age 18. Reenlisted Dec. 24, 1863, at Rappahannock Station, Va. Mustered out at Jeffersonville, Ind., July 8, 1865.

Wilson, Henry, Detroit. Enlisted in Company K, March 31, 1862, at Detroit, for 3 years, age 29. Deserted at Detroit, March 31, 1862.

Wilson, Henry M. Enlisted in Company G, Jan. 4, 1865, at Unadilla, for 3 years, age 21. Substitute for Edgar Vansickle, drafted from Unadilla. Deserted June 13, 1865.

Wilson, John P. Enlisted in Company F, Lancers, as 1st Sergeant, Sept. 30, 1861, at Detroit, for 3 years, age 30. Transferred to Company K, 16th Michigan, Feb. 28, 1862. Deserted March 22, 1862.

Wilson, William H. Enlisted in Company I, March 21, 1865, at Port Huron, for 3 years, age 24. Substitute for William Wastell, drafted. Mustered out at Jeffersonville, Ind., July 8, 1861.

Wiltse, George B. Enlisted in Company I, Feb. 21, 1865, at Three Oaks, for 1 year, age 20.

Substitute for Henry H. Pike, drafted from Kalamazoo. Mustered out at Jeffersonville, Ind., July 8, 1865.

Windle, William C., Jackson. Enlisted in Company F, July 31, 1861, at Plymouth, for 3 years, age 22. Discharged for disability at Washington, D.C., May 2, 1862.

Winn, Archey. Enlisted in Company F, March 25, 1865, at Meridian, for 3 years, age 20. Substitute for Charles E. Servis, drafted from Meridian. No further record.

Winn, Owen (Veteran). Wayne. Enlisted in Company E, Aug. 31, 1861. Wounded in action at second Manassas, Aug. 30, 1862. Reenlisted Dec. 21, 1863, at Rappahannock Station, Va. Mustered out at Jeffersonville, Ind., July 8, 1865. Died Oct. 20, 1894.

Winne, George. Enlisted March 2, 1864, at Houghton, for 3 years, age 21. No further record.

Winters, John. Enlisted in Company D, March 25, 1865, at Eureka, for 1 year, age 22. Substitute for Elijah T. Miller, drafted from Eureka. Mustered out at Jeffersonville, Ind., July 8, 1865.

Witte, Albert (Veteran). Enlisted in Company A, Aug. 3, 1861, at Ontonagon, for 3 years, age 20. Wounded and missing in action at Gaines' Mill, June 27, 1862. Wounded in action at Wilderness, May 6, 1864. Reenlisted as Corporal Dec. 21, 1863, at Rappahannock Station, Va. Sergeant. Wounded June 19, 1864, at Petersburg, Va. Mustered out at Jeffersonville, Ind., July 8, 1865.

Wittman or **Whitman, John** (Veteran), Detroit. Enlisted in Company A, Aug. 12, 1861, at Detroit, age 21. Joined regiment at Antietam, Md., Oct. 12, 1862. Reenlisted Dec. 21, 1863, at Rappahannock Station, Va. Died May 27, 1864, from wounds received in action at Po River–Spotsylvania Court House, May 10, 1864.

Wixom, Dr. Isaac, Argentine. Entered service at organization, as Surgeon, Aug. 17, 1861, at Detroit, for 3 years, age 58. Dismissed by General Court Martial April 18, 1863.

Wolcott, Henry, Wayne County. Enlisted in Company E, Sept. 4, 1861, at Detroit, for 3 years, age 24. Discharged Jan. 30, 1863.

Wood, John (Veteran). Enlisted in Company G, Aug. 22, 1861. Reenlisted Dec. 21, 1863, at Rappahannock Station, Va. Mustered out at Jeffersonville, Ind., July 8, 1865.

Woodard, Silliman. Drafted for 1 year, from California, Branch County, age 20, March 1865. Assigned to Company F. Died of disease at City Point, Va., May 8, 1865.

Woodruff, Albert O., Saginaw County. Enlisted in Company D, as Sergeant, Aug. 1, 1861, at East Saginaw, for 3 years, age 21. Severely wounded in action, shot through both legs, at Gettysburg, July 2, 1863; one leg amputated. Discharged at expiration of term of service, Sept. 1864.

Woodruff, Francis M., Saginaw County. Enlisted in Company D, as Corporal, Aug. 1, 1861, at East Saginaw, for 3 years, age 24. Discharged at expiration of term of service, at Petersburg, Va., Sept. 7, 1864.

Woodruff, Heber H., Wayne County and East Saginaw. Enlisted in Company D, as Corporal, Aug. 1, 1861, at East Saginaw, for 3 years, age 20. 2nd Lieutenant, Aug. 23, 1862. Commissioned 1st Lieutenant, April 11, 1863. Commanding Company, Oct. 1, 1863. Discharged at expiration of term of service, Sept. 10, 1864.

Worden, Alvin B., Deerfield, Livingston County. Enlisted in Company I, March 24, 1862, at Deerfield, for 3 years, age 18. Wounded in action at Malvern Hill, July 1, 1862. Corporal.

Wounded in action at Wilderness, May 6 or 7, 1864. Discharged at expiration of term of service at Detroit, April 7, 1865.

Worden, Anson E., Deerfield, Livingston County. Enlisted in Company B, Lancers, Oct. 26, 1861, at Milford, for 3 years, age 19. Transferred to Company I, 16th Michigan, Feb. 28, 1862. Corporal. Died Dec. 19, 1862, at Falmouth, Va., of wounds received in action at Fredericksburg, Va., Dec. 14, 1862.

Worden, Edward, Saginaw County. Enlisted in Company D. Mustered Sept. 13, 1861. Wounded and missing in action at, Gaines' Mill, June 27, 1862. Discharged on Surgeon's certificate of disability Dec. 13, 1862. Resided Lyons, Mich.

Worth, Adoniram, or **James**, Flushing. Enlisted in Company C, Aug. 4, 1861, at Flint, for 3 years, age 22. Died of heart disease at Yorktown, Va., May 1, 1862.

Worts, Robert C. (Veteran), Macomb County. Enlisted in First Company Sharpshooters Nov. 13, 1861, at Detroit, for 3 years, age 22. Joined at Hall's Hill, Va., Feb. 14, 1862. Reenlisted Dec. 24, 1863, at Rappahannock Station, Va. Mustered out at Jeffersonville, Ind., July 8, 1865.

Wright, Charles. Enlistee in Company G, date unknown. Reported in regiment's "Roll of Honor" to have died July 13, 1862, at Harrison's Landing, Va.

Wright, Cyrus M., Wayne County. Enlisted in Company E, Dec. 5, 1861, at Detroit, for 3 years, age 24. Wounded in action, thigh, at Gettysburg, July 2, 1863. Transferred to Invalid Corps, July16, 1864.

Wright, Ethan Allen. Enlisted in Company K, Jan. 28, 1864, at Flint, for 3 years, age 29. Wounded in action Feb. 1865, probably at Dabney's Mill, Va. Discharged at Washington, D.C., July 10, 1865.

Wright, Henry (Veteran), Ontonagon County. Enlisted in Company A, Aug. 3, 1861, at Ontonagon, for 3 years, age 22. Reenlisted Dec. 21, 1863, at Rappahannock Station, Va. Killed in action at Laurel Hill–Spotsylvania Court House, May 8, 1864.

Wright, Hoel C., Berrien County. Enlisted in First Company Sharpshooters, Nov. 28, 1861, at Grand Rapids, attached to 16th Michigan 1861, for 3 years, age 27. Joined regiment at Hall's Hill, Va., Feb. 14, 1862. Missing in action June 27, 1862. Discharged at Fortress Monroe, Va., Oct. 9, 1862. Resided Buchanan, Mich.

Wright, Lewis. Enlisted in Company H, date not given. Recorded in regimental "Roll of Honor" as killed in action at Fredericksburg, Va., Dec. 13, 1862.

Wright, Peter. Enlisted in Company G, date unknown, but reported in regiment's "Roll of Honor" to have died of fever June 19, 1862, in the field near Gaines' Mill.

Wright, Sydney I. Enlisted in Company E, Aug. 21, 1861, at Detroit, for 3 years, age 23. No further record.

Wright, William, Berlin. Enlisted in Company B, Aug. 5, 1861, at Ionia, for 3 years, age 22. Killed in action at Gaines' Mill, June 27, 1862.

Wurmeling, Theodore. Wayne County. Enlisted in Company F, Sept. 12, 1861, at Plymouth, for 3 years, age 24. Discharged for disability.

Wygant, Charles. Enlisted in Company C, Feb. 23, 1865, at Park, for 3 years, age 20. Substitute for John Branner, drafted. Died of disease at Alexandria, Va., June 1, 1865.

Wylan or **Wylon, Safron** or **Severn** (Veteran). Enlisted in Company G, Sept. 16, 1861, age 26.

Wounded in action, face, at Gettysburg, July 2, 1863. Reenlisted Dec. 21, 1863, at Rappahannock Station, Va. Corporal, April 1, 1865. Mustered out at Jeffersonville, Ind., July 8, 1865.

Wyman or **Wegman, John**. Enlisted in Company A, Aug. 3, 1861, at Ontonagon, for 3 years, age 33. Discharged Oct. 15, 1862, for wounds received in action at Gaines' Mill, June 27, 1862.

Wyse, Patrick. Enlisted in Company E, Lancers, Oct. 24, 1861, at Fox Lake, Wis., for 3 years, age 20. Transferred to Company K, 16th Michigan, Feb. 28, 1862. Killed in action at Manassas, Aug. 30, 1862.

Yates, Carl. Wayne County. Enlisted in Company F, Sept. 12, 1861, at Plymouth, for 3 years, age 25. Missing in action June 30, 1862 near Malvern Hill. Discharged for disability at Washington, D.C., Nov. 3, 1862.

Yates, Isaac. Enlisted in Company K, Feb. 13, 1864, at Saginaw, for 3 years, age 43. Listed as absent, wounded, Jan. 1865. Admitted to Harper Hospital May 11, 1865. Discharged at Detroit, May 20, 1865.

Young, Allen A. (Veteran), Hubbardston. Enlisted in Company H, Aug. 18, 1861, age 21. Wounded in action at Gaines' Mill, June 27, 1862. Reenlisted Dec. 24, 1863, at Rappahannock Station, Va. Deserted at Detroit, Feb. 26, 1864.

Young, David F. (Veteran). Enlisted in Company D, July 6, 1861, at East Saginaw, for 3 years, age 33. Wounded and missing in action at Gaines' Mill, June 27, 1862. Reenlisted Feb. 26, 1864, at Rappahannock Station, Va. Reportedly wounded again, Nov. 1864. Discharged for disability at Washington, D.C., June 6, 1865.

Young, George. Enlisted in Company G, Jan. 30, 1865, at Concord, for 3 years, age 19. Substitute for Henry A. Weimar, or Wetmore, drafted. Deserted June 15, 1865.

Young, Henry. Enlisted in Company C, Feb. 17, 1865, at Washington, Macomb County, for 3 years, age 25. Substitute for Mason Price, drafted. Mustered out at Jeffersonville, Ind., July 8, 1865.

Young, Montgomery V. Enlisted in Company F, July 30, 1861, at Plymouth, for 3 years, age 18. Transferred to Company G, June 1862. Wounded in action at Gaines' Mill, June 27, 1862. Enlisted in 1st U.S. Cavalry at Baltimore, Sept. 1862.

Young, Peter, Ionia County. Enlisted in Company B, Aug. 6, 1861, at Ionia, for 3 years, age 41. Wounded and missing in action at Gaines' Mill, June 27, 1862. Transferred to Invalid Corps Oct. 30, 1863. Transferred back from 58th Company, 2nd Battalion, Veteran Reserve Corps, June 11, 1864. Discharged. Died April 27, 1890.

Zeese, Adolph. Reported to be enlisted in Company A. Wounded in action at Gettysburg, July 2, 1863. Wounded in action at Peeble's Farm, Sept. 30, 1864. Mustered out for wounds, by order, June 2, 1865

Zeran, William. Enlisted in Company G, Feb. 1, 1865, at Detroit, for 3 years, age 18. Substitute for John Boughton. Mustered out at Jeffersonville, Ind., July 8, 1865.

NOTES

CHAPTER 1. APRIL–SEPTEMBER 1861: THE TIME FOR ACTION HAS ARRIVED

1. Flint *Wolverine Citizen,* April 20, 1861.
2. Stockton's description comes from muster records, letters, and biographical materials in his family papers at the Perry Archives of the Sloan Museum and from Theodore Gerrish, *Army Life: A Private's Reminiscences of the Civil War* (Portland: Hoyt, Fogg, & Donham, 1882), p. 24; Stockton to Blair, with endorsement enclosed, April 16, 1861, Austin Blair Papers, Burton Historical Collection, Detroit Public Library. Though Stockton was a major in the Michigan militia at that time, he was referred to as "Colonel Stockton" because of the commission he held during the Mexican War.
3. *Biographical History of Genesee County, Michigan* (Indianapolis: B. F. Bowen, 1908), p. 218; Dennis McMullen, *Col. T. B. W. Stockton: Soldier, Engineer, Businessman* (Flint: University of Michigan-Flint, 1988), pp. 1, 2.
4. *Biographical History of Genesee County, Michigan;* McMullen, *Col. T. B. W. Stockton;* Kim Crawford, *The Daring Trader* (East Lansing: Michigan State University Press, 2012), p. 125; *Flint* (Michigan) *Evening Journal,* Dec. 11, 1890.
5. William D. Green, *A Peculiar Imbalance: The Rise and Fall of Racial Equality in Minnesota, 1837–1869* (Minneapolis: University of Minnesota Press, 2015), p. 13; Stockton letter, *Rachel v. Walker,* Case No. 83, Circuit Court Files, Office of the City Clerk, City of St. Louis, http://stlcourtrecords.wustl.edu.
6. McMullen, *Col. T. B. W. Stockton,* pp. 2–11; *Biographical History of Genesee County,* pp. 218–19. For a detailed account of Jacob Smith's work for the United States among the Chippewa, and securing land for his children, see Crawford, *The Daring Trader.*
7. Green, *A Peculiar Imbalance,* p. 14; *Rachel v. Walker,* Case No. 83; Paul Finkelman, ed., *Encyclopedia of American Civil Liberties* (Abingdon, UK: Routledge, 2006), vol. 1, p. 481.
8. LeRoy Barnett and Roger Rosentreter, *Michigan's Early Military Forces* (Detroit: Wayne State

University Press, 2003), pp. 338, 339; Wm. Hugh Roberts, *Mexican War Veterans* (Washington, D.C.: Bretano's, 1887), pp. 20, 24; The connections by marriage of Garland, Stockton, Longstreet, and Deas in *Flint Journal,* Aug. 9, 1936; Francis B. Heitman, *Historical Register and Dictionary* (Washington, D.C.: U.S. Printing Office, 1965), p. 363; Ralph Selph Henry, *The Story of the Mexican War* (Indianapolis: Bobbs-Merrill, 1950), p. 361; Karl Jack Bauer, *The Mexican War, 1846–1848* (Lincoln: Bison Books, University of Nebraska Press, 1992), p. 322. The marriages of Longstreet and Deas to Garland's daughters are mentioned briefly in *Michigan Pioneer and Historical Collections (MPHC),* 40 vols. (Lansing: Michigan Historical Commission/Pioneer Society of Michigan, 1877–1929), vol. 5, p. 545, and vol. 22, pp. 365–66. Of course, Longstreet and Deas married into the clan of Jacob Smith and John Garland by wedding Maria Stockton's nieces. The word "brevet" before the ranks of these officers means they were honorary or temporary positions. Longstreet and Deas won their promotions for bravery in battle.

9. Benjamin C. Howard, *A Report of the Decision of the Supreme Court of the United States and the Opinions of the Judges Thereof in the Case of Dred Scott Versus John F. A. Sanford, December Term, 1856* (New York: D. Appleton, 1857), p. 551.
10. *Wolverine Citizen,* April 20, 1861; Stockton to J. Robertson, April 22, 1861, Military establishment, RG 59–14, Box 108, 16th Michigan Records, Archives of Michigan, Lansing. In this letter, Stockton quoted Blair's reply to his offer of April 16. In my research, I did not find a "smoking gun" letter or document in the governor's papers that specifically showed Stockton's slave ownership was the source of Blair's enmity, but it is difficult to imagine the governor was unaware of this history.
11. Stockton to Robertson, April 22, 1861, 16th Michigan Records, Archives of Michigan.
12. Robertson to Stockton, April 26, 1861, Letter book of the Michigan Adjutant General, Archives of Michigan.
13. Stockton to Blair, May 14, 1861, Blair Papers, Burton Historical Collection, Detroit Public Library.
14. News of the death of John Garland appeared in the *National Intelligencer* and other Washington newspapers, and was reprinted in the *Wolverine Citizen* on June 15, 1861. Longstreet and Deas married the daughters of John and Harriet Garland after the Mexican War; these links to Stockton, his wife, and her father, Jacob Smith, are mentioned in the *Flint Journal,* Aug. 9, 1936, and mentioned in *MPHC,* vol. 5, p. 545, and vol. 22, pp. 365–66. The federal confiscation of the interest of Longstreet and Deas in land in Flint, Genesee County, and Livingston County is in 1863 and 1864 orders from the U.S. District Court in Detroit, copied into the Genesee County Register of Deeds office, Book of Levies, vol. 1, p. 7, 9, 10.
15. *Wolverine Citizen,* June 15, 1861.
16. United States War Department, *The War of the Rebellion: A Compilation of the Official Records of the Union and Confederate Armies,* 70 vols. in 128 parts (Washington, D.C.: Government Printing Office, 1880–1901), ser. 3, 1: 241; William Constantine Beecher and Samuel Scoville, *A Biography of Rev. Henry Ward Beecher* (New York: C. L. Wesbster, 1888), p. 443.
17. *OR,* ser. 3, 1: 269.
18. Franklin Ellis, *History of Genesee County,* Michigan (Philadelphia: Everts & Abbott, 1879), pp. 85–86. A complaint by Stockton about Blair and his obstacles is in Stockton to Lincoln, Feb. 24, 1862, Blair Papers.

19. A hand-written copy of the telegram to Stockton, July 22, 1861, from the War Department, is in the Blair Papers.
20. *Detroit Free Press,* July 26 and Aug. 2, 1861.
21. Ibid.; Barry to Robertson, April 17, 1862, 16th Michigan Records, Archives of Michigan. In this letter, Capt. Barry said that Stockton specifically asked him to raise a company for the regiment.
22. *Detroit Free Press,* Aug. 4, 1861; *Wolverine Citizen,* Aug. 10, 1861. Even the Republican publisher of the Flint *Wolverine Citizen* wrote privately to Blair, concerned that Stockton and his friends were extremely critical of his treatment of the colonel and asking whether Blair had any material he could use against Stockton. However, no further editorials attacking Stockton appear in the paper. F. H. Rankin to Blair, Aug. 19, 1861, Blair Papers.
23. Cameron/Blair telegrams, *OR,* ser. 3, 1: 426, 428. These were dated Aug. 19, 1861.
24. Bruce Catton, *The Civil War* (Boston: Houghton Mifflin Co., 1960), p. 53.
25. *Free Press,* July 26, 27, Aug. 6, 1861; Ellis, *History of Genesee County,* p. 86.
26. Sidman Papers, Archives of Michigan; 16th Michigan postwar reunion clippings in the "miscellaneous" Civil War file (newspaper clippings), Burton Historical Collection; *Owosso (Michigan) Evening Argus,* Aug. 22, 1912; E. Sidman Wacther, *Sidman–Sidman Families of Upstate New York* (Baltimore: Gateway Press, 1981), pp. 248–55.
27. Letter by Edward Hill to 16th Michigan reunion in Flint, *Wolverine Citizen,* Oct. 6, 1888; *Detroit Free Press,* Aug. 9, 1861; Charles Willman, *Ontonagon County in the Civil War* (n.p., 1961), pp. 5, 6; Entry for John Berry in the U.S. census, 1860.
28. Fisher to Robertson, July 16, 1861, 16th Michigan Records, Archives of Michigan; James R. Wilson, *The Fishers of Saginaw and Zilwaukee* (Bellaire, Mich.: n.d.); reunion letter in *Wolverine Citizen,* Oct. 6, 1888; *Wolverine Citizen,* Aug. 17, 1861.
29. Francis D. "Frank" Keeler, *War Letters Written During the Rebellion* (Saginaw, Mich.: Julian A. Keeler, 1895), pp. iv–vi, with letter to parents. Aug. 12, 1861. Keeler's son Julian transcribed and printed these letters after the war, though he apparently edited them; to what extent is impossible to judge.
30. Ibid.; A. Wellington to family, Aug. 18, 1861, Wellington Family Papers, Hoyt Main Library, Public Libraries of Saginaw.
31. Martin recruiting: *Detroit Free Press,* July 26, 1861. The *Free Press* reported on Sept. 17, 1861, that the captain of Company H was a W. W. Flagler, and he was recorded as Ervay's captain on a government form filled out later by Ervay's father. Yet according to Ervay, Flagler resigned from the service in November or December, as did one of his lieutenants, Charles D. Fox, whom Ervay wrote was jailed for trying to defraud the army over pay.

    In any event, Flagler and Fox seemed to have been later excised out of the regiment's history as published by the state of Michigan. Ervay information: George Washington Ervay, *George W. Ervay, 1845–1863, Civil War Letters* (Marietta, Ga.: self-pub., 1986). These letters were transcribed and self-published by Ervay's relatives in a kind of notebook or booklet in the 1980s. A copy of this booklet is on file with the Kennesaw Mountain National Battlefield Park.
32. Salter biography: Salter briefly told of his childhood in a letter to a friend's mother, Salter to Isabella Bethune Duffield, May 24, 1863, Duffield Papers, Burton Historical Collection, Detroit Public Library. According to Frederic Isham, author of *History of the Detroit Light Guard* (Detroit:

Light Guard, 1896), Stockton regiment officers who had served in the ninety-day 1st Michigan Infantry included Robert Elliott, Thomas Barry, Edward Hill, William Kydd, and others.

33. *Free Press,* Aug. 10, Aug. 21, 1861; *Wolverine Citizen,* Oct. 6, 1888; Hopper, "From Beverly Ford to Bottoms Bridge with the First Michigan Infantry," MOLLUS Papers, Michigan Commandery, p. 8, Bentley Historical Library, University of Michigan.
34. Company F: Jno. Robertson, *Michigan in the War* (Lansing: W. S. George, 1882), 359. The spelling of the name of Capt. James Dafoe is in some places given incorrectly as Defoe. Stockton recorded in his diary on April 18, 1862, that Dafoe resigned for illness. But a letter from Senator Jacob Howard in late May 1862 to Gov. Blair in the Blair Papers states that the "pro-slaveryism" of Stockton and anti-Republican sentiments of other officers caused Dafoe to leave. That fall, Dafoe was made a captain in the 27th Michigan Infantry.

    Also, Brown to Robertson, Aug. 2, 1861, 16th Michigan Records, Archives of Michigan; *Hillsdale Standard,* July 28, 1863; Robertson, *Michigan in the War,* p. 311. Blair blocked the formation of Col. May's independent regiment that summer, but authorized May some weeks later to form a state regiment, the 11th Michigan Infantry.
35. *Wolverine Citizen,* Oct. 6, 1888; Weber to Robertson, April 26, 1861, 16th Michigan Records, Archives of Michigan. Though this officer's signature appears written as "Weber," it is routinely spelled Webber in regimental records.
36. T. Morris to G. Bates, July 24, 1861, 16th Michigan Records, Archives of Michigan.
37. Chittick petition, July 25, 1861, 16th Michigan Records, Archives of Michigan; Michigan Adjutant-General's Dept., *Record of Service of Michigan Volunteers in the Civil War, 1861–1865* (Kalamazoo: Ihling Bros. & Everard, 1905), vol. 16, p. 35; *Free Press,* Aug. 4, 1861; *Wolverine Citizen,* Oct. 6, 1888.
38. *Free Press,* Sept. 6, 1861; Keeler, *War Letters,* Sept. 15, 1861; Munson to Van Hoosen, Oct. 27, 1861, Van Hoosen Papers, Bentley Historical Library. Munson was reported as being 21 in the 1860 census, but said he was 18 when he enlisted in August 1861. Avon Township is now called Rochester Hills. Van Hoosen lived and farmed near an unincorporated hamlet called Stony Creek.
39. *Free Press,* Aug. 13, 15, 1861.
40. References to the "Cass regiment" in the *Free Press,* Aug. 13 and 15, 1861. Naming the regiment: Ellis, *History of Genesee County,* p. 86; Both Stockton and Martin were living when this account was published and could have been sources of the anecdote.
41. *East Saginaw Courier,* Aug. 1, 1861; *Detroit Daily Advertiser,* Aug. 17, 1861; C. B. Burr, ed., *Medical History of Michigan,* 2 vols. (Minneapolis: Michigan State Medical Society and Bruce Publishing Co., 1930), vol. 1, p. 349, vol. 2, p. 855; articles and biographical material in the Wixom family file: Court-martial of Isaac Wixon, Eileen Roddy, transcriber, Fenton Historical Museum, from the records of the Adjutant General, National Archives.
42. Name of Stockton's major left blank in *Detroit Daily Advertiser,* Aug. 16, 1861; Welch's name appeared as major in an order dated Aug. 21, in an undated newspaper clipping that was apparently saved in a personal scrapbook, perhaps by Stockton himself or his wife. Stockton Papers, Buick Research Gallery and Perry Archives, Sloan Museum, Flint.
43. James Kidd, *Personal Recollections of a Cavalryman* (Ionia, Mich.: Sentinel Printing Co., 1908), pp. 19–29; Pension application of Cecilia Welch (photocopy of documents in the National Archives) in 16th Michigan file, Gettysburg National Military Park.

44. *Detroit Free Press,* July 27, 1861, said that Fred W. Backus was to be Stockton's major, but that was not the case.
45. *Detroit Daily Advertiser,* Aug. 12, 1861. Alfred Wellington of Company D noted that a Saturday horse race, on the fairgrounds where the regiment was being formed, meant "there was no drilling." Wellington to family, Aug. 18, 1861, Wellington Family Papers, Hoyt Main Library, Public Libraries of Saginaw.
46. Keeler, *War Letters,* Aug. 15, 1861; Stockton's orders and rules, Aug. 28, 1861, in an unidentified Detroit newspaper clipping, Stockton Papers.
47. *Detroit Free Press,* Aug. 10 and Sept. 12, 1861; *Wolverine Citizen,* Aug. 24 and Sept. 21, 1861; Keeler, *War Letters,* Aug. 25, 1861.
48. Unidentified Detroit newspaper clipping, September 1861, Stockton Papers. The Union army moved to blue uniforms after gray uniforms, which caused confusion at the battle of Bull Run.
49. Keeler, *War Letters,* Aug. 15 and 25, 1861.
50. Keeler, *War Letters,* Aug. 25, 1861.
51. Sword presentations in *Detroit Daily Advertiser,* Sept. 7, 1861; unidentified Detroit newspaper clippings, September 1861, Stockton Papers.
52. Order dated Sept. 12, 1861, unidentified newspaper clipping, Stockton Papers.
53. Telegrams between Cameron and Blair, *OR,* ser. 3, 1: 450–501, 501, 508; Cameron to Blair, Sept. 14, 1861, 16th Michigan Records, Archives of Michigan.
54. Robertson to Stockton, Sept. 15, 1861, and Stockton to Robertson, Sept. 19, 1861, 16th Michigan Records, Archives of Michigan; *Detroit Free Press,* Sept. 17, 1861. It seems that Blair managed to stop Col. May from organizing his independent regiment, but would soon appoint him to command the 11th Michigan Infantry Regiment.
55. Keeler, *War Letters,* Sept. 15, 1861.
56. Salter to I. Duffield, Oct. 14, 1861, Duffield Papers; *Free Press,* Sept. 17, 1861.
57. *Free Press,* Sept. 17, 1861. Though there is no mention of a traditional "stars and stripes" flag in this ceremony, a letter by a soldier in the regiment, published in the same paper on Dec. 10, 1862, said the regiment had another silk banner as it left Detroit—an apparent reference to a national flag, though where it came from or who provided it was not explained. But Stockton must have necessarily had a U.S. flag in his regiment's camp at the fairgrounds.
58. Ibid. Of course, the sergeant was not always the color bearer, and was discharged from the regiment for illness in less than a year.
59. Ibid.

CHAPTER 2. SEPTEMBER 1861–MARCH 1862: STOCKTON'S WORM-EATERS

1. Francis D. Keeler, *War Letters Written During the Rebellion* (Saginaw: Julian A. Keeler, 1895), Sept. 22, 1861; Stockton to Robertson, Sept. 19, 1861, Stockton Papers, Perry Archives, Sloan Museum, Flint.
2. Keeler, *War Letters,* Sept. 22, 1861; Stockton diary, September 1861, Stockton Papers. Two diaries in

Stockton's nearly illegible hand from the fall of 1861 to November 1862 are in the Perry Archives of Flint's Sloan Museum; a poor and unreliable transcription, seemingly made in the 1930s, is in some Michigan libraries, though its errors and jumbled dates and entries make it useless as a source of historical information.

3. Keeler, *War Letters,* Sept. 25, 1861.
4. Ibid.
5. Franklin Ellis, *History of Genesee County, Michigan* (Philadelphia: Everts & Abbott, 1879), pp. 86, 87; Stockton diary, late September 1861; *Official Records* (*OR*), 51, pt. 1: 48–49; *Wolverine Citizen,* Oct. 26, 1861; Salter to I. Duffield, Oct. 14, 1861, Duffield Papers, Burton Historical Collection, Detroit Public Library.
6. *OR,* 51/1: 488–89; Ervay to John Althouse, Oct. 1, 1861, in George Washington Ervay, *George W. Ervay, 1845–1863, Civil War Letters* (Marietta, Ga.: self-pub., 1986).
7. Keeler, *War Letters,* Oct. 6, 1861; *Owosso Evening Argus,* Aug. 22, 1912.
8. Stockton diary, late September 1861; Keeler, *War Letters,* Oct. 6, 1861; Munson to Van Hoosen, Oct. 28, Joshua Van Hoosen Papers, Bentley Historical Library, University of Michigan.
9. Keeler, *War Letters,* Oct. 6, 1861.
10. Oliver W. Norton, *Two Bugle Calls* (n.p., n.d.). Norton probably published this short, undated booklet himself after the war, when former army musicians and soldiers debated where the famous "lights out" bugle call known as "Taps" came from.
11. Salter to I. Duffield, Oct. 14, 1861, Duffield Papers.
12. Keeler, *War Letters,* Oct. 17, 1861; John G. Berry diary (photocopy), Oct. 28, 1861, *Civil War Times Illustrated* Collection, U.S. Army Heritage and Education Center (USAHEC); Oliver W. Norton, *Army Letters, 1861–1865* (Chicago: O. L. Deming, 1903), pp. 32–33.
13. Munson to Van Hoosen, Nov. 13, 1861, Van Hoosen Papers.
14. Salter to Duffield, Oct. 14, 1861, Duffield Papers; Keeler, *War Letters,* Oct. 17, 1861; Stockton diary, Nov. 1, 1861.
15. Keeler, *War Letters,* Oct. 24, 1861.
16. Keeler, *War Letters,* Oct. 24, 1861. He would mention the Harper's Ferry musket issued at that time in another of the *War Letters* on Jan. 1, 1862; Munson to Van Hoosen, Oct. 27, 1861, Van Hoosen Papers.
17. Salter to Duffield, November 1861, Duffield Papers. Two more Wellington brothers, Frederick and John, would serve in the regiment later in the war.
18. Borden to his father, Nov. 24, 1861 (photocopy), from U.S. Pension Office/National Archives, in the 16th Michigan file, Gettysburg National Military Park; Brown discharge, Michigan Adjutant-General's Dept., *Record of Service of Michigan Volunteers in the Civil War, 1861–1865* (Kalamazoo: Ihling Bros. & Everard, 1905), vol. 16, p. 26.
19. Stockton diary, Nov. 6, 1861.
20. Salter to Duffield, November 1861, Duffield Papers.
21. Stockton diary, Nov. 10, 12, 1861.
22. Salter to Duffield, November 1861, Duffield Papers; Munson to Van Hoosen, Nov. 13, 1861, Van Hoosen Papers.
23. Keeler, *War Letters,* Nov. 17 and Dec. 25, 1861.

24. Stockton diary, Nov. 17, 1861.
25. Keeler, *War Letters,* Nov. 26, 1861; Salter to Duffield, November 1861, Duffield Papers; Ervay to family, Nov. 26, 1861, *George W. Ervay;* Stockton diary, Nov. 20, 1861.
26. Keeler, *War Letters,* Nov. 28, 1861; Berry diary, Nov. 24, 1861.
27. Stockton to Robertson, Nov. 25, 1861, 16th Michigan Records, Archives of Michigan.
28. Stockton diary, Nov. 25, 1861; Keeler, *War Letters,* Nov. 28, 1861.
29. Ervay to friends. Nov. 26, 1861, *George W. Ervay;* Borden to his father (photocopy), Nov. 24, 1861, 16th Michigan file, Gettysburg National Military Park (GNMP).
30. Berry diary, Nov. 26, 1861; Keeler, *War Letters,* Nov. 26, 1861.
31. Keeler, *War Letters,* Nov. 26, 1861.
32. Ervay to family, n.d., probably November 1861, *George W. Ervay.*
33. Ibid.; Stockton diary, Nov. 28 and Dec. 1, 1861.
34. Salter to Duffield, December 1861.
35. Ibid.; Keeler, *War Letters,* Dec. 7, 1861; Stockton diary, Dec. 2, 1861.
36. Stockton diary, Dec. 8, 1861; Salter to Duffield, December 1861, Duffield Papers; Aplin to Sarah, Dec. 10, 1861, Aplin Family Papers, Schoff Civil War Collection, William L. Clements Library, University of Michigan.
37. Stockton diary, various December dates, 1861; Salter to Duffield, December 1861, Duffield Papers; Stockton to Cameron, Dec. 17, 1861, Austin Blair Papers, Burton Historical Collection.
38. Stockton to Cameron, Dec. 17, 1861, Blair Papers.
39. Stockton diary, Dec. 19, 1861; Munson to Van Hoosen, Van Hoosen Papers, Dec. 21, 1861.
40. Salter to Duffield, December 1861, Duffield Papers; Keeler, *War Letters,* Dec. 25, 1861.
41. Keeler, *War Letters,* Dec. 25, 1861. For a good account of the mock dress parade, see Eugene Nash, *History of the Forty-fourth Regiment New York Volunteer Infantry* (Chicago: R. R. Donnelley, 1911), pp. 56–57.
42. Salter to Duffield, Jan. 14, 1862, Duffield Papers; Brockway to his brother, Jan. 7, 1862, in *Wolverine Citizen,* Jan. 18, 1862.
43. Keeler, *War Letters,* Dec. 25, 1861.
44. Stockton diary, Dec. 26, 1861; Keeler, *War Letters,* Jan. 1, 1862.
45. Salter to Duffield, Jan. 14, 1862; Stockton diary, Jan. 1, 1862; Keeler, *War Letters,* Jan. 1, 1862; Berry diary, Jan. 1, 1862, USAHEC.
46. Brockway to his brother, in *Wolverine Citizen,* Jan. 18,1862; Salter to Duffield, Jan. 14, 1862;
47. Berry diary, Jan. 2, 3, 1862.
48. Ervay to friends, Jan. 26, 1862, *George W. Ervay;* Munson to Van Hoosen, Jan. 26, 1862, Van Hoosen Papers.
49. Stockton diary, Jan. 26, 1862; Blair to C. Sykes, Jan. 21, 1862, and Blair to L. Witherell, Jan. 22, 1862, Blair Papers. These letters from Blair appear to have been forwarded to Stockton, who then forwarded them to the War Department or perhaps to Lincoln himself, as evidence of Blair's hatred toward Stockton and his regiment. At some point these letters were returned to Blair, possibly as enclosures.
50. Stockton regiment officers' petition, Jan. 30, 1862, Blair Papers.
51. Keeler, *War Letters,* Jan. 10, 1862.

52. Stockton diary, Jan. 27, 1862; Berry diary, Feb. 1, 1862.
53. Ervay to friends, Feb. 3, 1862, *George W. Ervay.* Ervay's story, if not clear to some readers, indicates that the approaching civilian couple fled when they saw the Union pickets, which suggested to the Michigan soldiers they were up to no good, probably Confederate spies. Ignoring Ervay's warning to halt, the pair was shot and wounded by Ervay and his partner, and continued to fight the soldiers until they killed her.
54. Ervay to friends, Feb. 3, 1862, *George W. Ervay.*
55. Graham's explanation of Stockton's Worm-eaters in Ziba B. Graham, *Proceedings of the Third Brigade Association, First Division, Fifth Army Corps, Army of the Potomac, Held at the National Encampment of the G.A.R., Washington, D.C., Sept. 21, 1892.* (New York: River and Driver), p. 25; Stockton's nickname, Norton, *Army Letters,* p. 165.
56. Stockton diary, Feb. 7, 8, 1862; Stockton to A. Blair, June 15, 1862, Blair Papers.
57. Stockton diary, Feb. 10, 1862; *Detroit Daily Tribune,* Sept. 7, 1861; *Michigan Pioneer and Historical Collections,* vol. 13, p. 325; *Detroit Free Press,* Jan. 30 and Feb. 4, 1862; Backus to Robertson, Feb. 5, 1862, 16th Michigan Records, Archives of Michigan. Letters written by Pvt. Edwin Farmer of the Brady Sharpshooters in November 1861 showed that men first thought they were going to be sent to Kentucky and next, to serve in the brigade of Michigan's Brig. Gen. Alpheus S. Williams in Maryland. Of course, the company was sent to neither of those places. See: Farmer to Mother & sister (photocopies), Nov. 4 and Nov. 26, (1861), Farmer Papers, Bentley Historical Library.
58. *Detroit Daily Tribune,* Sept. 7, 1861; Don Farrant, "The Worst Fire a Mortal Endured," *Grand Rapids Press,* April 13, 1984; Farmer to Mother & sister (photocopy), Nov. 26, [1861], Bentley Historical Library; unidentified newspaper clipping on 16th Michigan 1910 regimental reunion in Saginaw, "miscellaneous" Civil War materials, Burton Historical Collection.
59. Rufus W. Jacklin, "Gettysburg: A Paper Prepared and Read before the Michigan Commandery of the Military Order of the Loyal Legion," December 1893, Bentley Library; Farrant, "The Worst Fire a Mortal Ever Endured," *Grand Rapids Press,* April 13, 1984.
60. Stockton diary, Feb. 17, 1862; Keeler, *War Letters,* Feb. 12, Feb. 22, March 9, 1862; Berry diary, Feb. 20, 1862.
61. Munson to Van Hoosen, Feb. 4, 1862, Van Hoosen Papers.

CHAPTER 3. SEPTEMBER 1861–MARCH 1862: THE MICHIGAN LANCERS

1. *Detroit Free Press,* Sept. 13, 1861.
2. Ibid.; *Detroit Free Press,* Sept. 14, Oct. 1, 1861. A lancer volunteer who would soon join Stockton's Independent Regiment recorded that Col. Rankin had planned for them to be called the 1st U.S. Lancers, though clearly these men were not regular army recruits. Joseph Stanfield diary (photocopy), Dec. 5, 1861. The diary is privately owned by John Gibney, and a copy of the diary transcription is in the U.S. Army Heritage and Education Center.
3. *Detroit Free Press,* Sept. 14, 1861.
4. Quebec paper quoted in *Detroit Daily Advertiser,* Oct. 1, 1861; also, *Daily Advertiser* for Oct. 3 and 4,

1861.

5. *Detroit Free Press,* Oct. 8, 9, 11, 16, 20, 1861.
6. *Detroit Daily Advertiser,* Nov. 7, 23, 1861; *Detroit Free Press,* Nov. 13, 23, 1861.
7. Stanfield diary, Nov. 28, 1861.
8. Ervay to family, undated (November 1861), George Washington Ervay, *George W. Ervay, 1845–1863, Civil War Letters* (Marietta, Ga.: self-pub., 1986).
9. *Official Records* (*OR*), series 3, vol. 1, p. 734. Backus's message is dated Dec. 9, 1861, but refers to a previous warning he sent on Nov. 21, warning of the recruitment and transport of Canadian lancer recruits.
10. *Detroit Daily Advertiser,* Dec. 7, 1861; *Detroit Free Press,* Nov. 30, Dec. 3, 7, 8, 10, 1861.
11. *Detroit Daily Advertiser,* Dec. 10, 1861, *Detroit Free Press,* Dec. 11, 1861
12. Mattoon to sister, Dec. 25, 1861 (transcribed copy), Mattoon Family Papers, University Archives and Historical Center, Michigan State University; *Detroit Free Press,* Dec. 17, 24, 1861, and July 13, 1865.
13. *Detroit Free Press,* Dec. 28, 1862; *Detroit Daily Advertiser,* Jan. 3, 1862.
14. *Detroit Daily Advertiser,* Jan. 13, 1862; *Detroit Daily Tribune,* Jan. 14, 1862; *Detroit Free Press,* Jan. 14, 1862.
15. *Detroit Free Press,* Jan. 23, 24, 1862.
16. Stanfield diary, Jan. 21, 1862; *Detroit Free Press,* Jan. 24, 1862; *Detroit Daily Advertiser,* Feb. 3, 1862.
17. *Detroit Free Press,* Jan. 24, 1862; *Detroit Daily Advertiser,* Feb. 3, 1862; Stanfield diary, Jan. 31 and Feb. 1, 1862.
18. *OR,* ser. 3, 1: 876; *Detroit Free Press,* Feb. 9, 11, 1862; *Detroit Daily Advertiser,* Feb. 10, 1861.
19. Mattoon to sister, Feb.16, 1862, Mattoon Family Papers. Mattoon ended up joining the 6th Michigan Cavalry Regiment.
20. *Detroit Free Press,* March 6, 1862; John G. Berry diary (photocopy), March 8, 1862; Francis D. Keeler, *War Letters Written During the Rebellion* (Saginaw: Julian A. Keeler, 1895), March 9, 1862; Stanfield diary, March 9, 1862.
21. *OR,* ser. 3, 1: 885, 898.
22. Stockton to Lincoln, Feb. 24, 1862, with enclosures Blair to Sykes and Blair to Witherell, Burton Historical Collection, Detroit Public Library.
23. Ibid.
24. Ibid. Notes by Porter and others are included with Stockton's appeal to Lincoln.
25. *Detroit Free Press,* March 15, 1862.
26. Ibid.; John Berry diary (photocopy), March 10, 1862, USAHEC.
27. Stockton diary, March 10, 1862.
28. Ibid.; Stockton diary, March 13, 1862,
29. *Detroit Free Press,* March 28, 1862. This article is also on file in the Austin Blair Papers, Burton Historical Collections, with a penciled notation: "Lt. Col. Welch" and "16th Michigan."
30. Blair to Robertson, March 19 and March 26, 1862, 16th Michigan Records, Archives of Michigan.

CHAPTER 4. MARCH–MAY 1862: VICTORIES WITHOUT BLOOD IS MCCLELLAN'S PLAN

1. Stockton diary, March 15, 1862, Stockton Papers, Perry Archives, Sloan Museum, Flint; Aplin to brother, March 18, 1862, Aplin Family Papers, Schoff Civil War Collection, William L. Clements Library, University of Michigan; *Supplement to the Official Records of the Union and Confederate Armies,* part 2, vol. 31 (Wilmington, N.C.: Broadfoot, 1996), pp. 216, 225; Stanfield diary (transcript), March 15, 1862, U.S. Army Heritage and Education Center (USAHEC).
2. Heald to G. Heald, March 20, 1862, and discharge paper, November 1862, Bentley Historical Library, University of Michigan.
3. Aplin to brother, March 18, 1862, Aplin Family Papers, Schoff Civil War Collection, William L. Clements Library, University of Michigan; Berry diary (photocopy), March 19–21, 1862, *Civil War Times Illustrated* collection, USAHEC; *Detroit Free Press,* March 28, 1862.
4. Berry diary, March 19–21, 1862, USAHEC; *Detroit Free Press,* March 28, 1862.
5. Francis D. Keeler, *War Letters Written During the Rebellion* (Saginaw, Mich.: Julian A. Keeler, 1895), March 28, 1862.
6. Berry diary, March 24 and 25, 1862.
7. Stockton diary, March 27, 1862.
8. Stockton diary, April 1–2, 1862; Keeler, *War Letters,* April 3, 1862; Jno. Robertson, *Michigan in the War* (Lansing: W. S. George, 1882), p. 862; Stanfield diary, April 1, 1862, USAHEC.
9. Hill related the anecdote in letter to a regimental reunion in Flint, *Wolverine Citizen,* Sept. 26, 1888.
10. Berry diary, April 5, 1862; Keeler, *War Letters,* April 11, 1862.
11. Stockton diary, April 5, 1862; Rufus Jacklin, "The Famous Old Third Brigade," in *War Papers,* vol. 2 (Detroit: James J. Stone, 1898), pp. 42–43; *Supplement to the Official Records,* part 2, *Record of Events,* vol. 31, p. 241.
12. Berry diary, April 5, 1862; Aplin to brother, April 18, 1862, Aplin Family Papers.
13. Stockton diary, April 5, 1862; Jeffry D. Wert, *Sword of Lincoln: The Army of the Potomac* (New York: Simon & Schuster, 2005), p. 68.
14. Stockton diary, April 7, 1862.
15. Stockton diary, April 10, 1862; Salter to Duffield, April 21, 1862, Duffield Papers, Burton Historical Collection, Detroit Public Library; Keeler, *War Letters,* April 11, 1862.
16. Stockton diary, April 14, 1862; Berry diary, April 14, 1862; Aplin to brother, April 18, 1862, Aplin Family Papers.
17. Berry diary, April 21, 1862; Salter to Duffield, April 21, 1862, Duffield Papers.
18. Keeler, *War Letters,* April 24, 1862; Aplin to Sarah, April 18, 1862, Aplin Family Papers; Stockton diary, April 17, 1862.
19. Barry to Robertson, April 17, 1862, 16th Michigan Records, Archives of Michigan.
20. Ibid.
21. Aplin to his brother, April 18, 1862, Aplin Family Papers, Schoff Civil War Collection.
22. Stanfield diary, April 23, 1862, USAHEC; Munson to Van Hoosen, April 30, 1862, Van Hoosen Papers, Bentley Library, University of Michigan.
23. Berry diary, April 23, 1862; Keeler, *War Letters,* April 24, 1862.

24. Keeler, *War Letters,* April 24, 1862; Michigan Adjutant-General's Dept., *Record of Service of Michigan Volunteers in the Civil War, 1861–1865* (Kalamazoo: Ihling Bros. & Everard, 1905), vol. 16, p. 70. Here the first name is "Cordelle."
25. Stanfield diary, April 26, 1862; Munson to Van Hoosen, April 30, 1862, Van Hoosen Papers; "Roll of Honor, Sixteenth Michigan," in *Proceedings of the Third Brigade Association, First Division, Fifth Army Corps, Army of the Potomac, Held at the National Encampment of the G.A.R., Washington, D.C.* (New York: River and Driver, 1990), vol. 3, p. 128.
26. Keeler, *War Letters,* April 29, 1862; Berry diary, April 29, 1862, USAHEC; Munson to Van Hoosen, Van Hoosen Papers.
27. Berry diary, May 1, 1862, and Stanfield diary, May 1, 1862, both USAHEC; "Roll of Honor, 16th Michigan," *Proceedings of the Third Brigade Association,* vol. 3, p. 122; Stockton to unidentified officer, May 1, 1862, Stockton Papers, Perry Archives, Sloan Museum. Worth's name is given in records as Adoniram J. Worth.
28. Stockton diary, May 2, 1862; Berry diary, May 2, 1862.
29. Stockton diary, May 3, 1862; Keeler, *War Letters,* May 3, 1862; Michigan Adjutant-General's Dept., *Record of Service,* vol. 16, p. 81.
30. Stockton diary, May 3, 1862; Berry diary, May 3, 1862.
31. Keeler, *War Letters,* May 4, 1862; Stockton diary, Mary 4, 1862.
32. Berry diary, May 5–9, 1862; *Supplement to the Official Records,* part 2, vol. 31, p. 240; Keeler, *War Letters,* May 11, 1862.
33. Stockton diary, May 9, 1862; Hollister to sister, May 10, 1862, Michigan Civil War Collection, http://micivilwar.com; *Official Records* (*OR*), ser. 1, vol. 11, pt. 1, pp. 617, 625. Joseph Stanfield also recorded the atrocity story in his diary, stressing it could well be a "camp report."

    As did many other soldiers, Hollister used "we" in his letter, but did he specifically mean comrades in his regiment, or was it an editorial "we," meaning "our side" or "my army comrades"? Other references to the atrocities and subsequent hanging(s) don't mention that Stockton's men were involved, but neither do they report who was; Hollister used "we" from the outset of this letter to describe to the May 7 clash at the landing, which didn't involve his regiment or his brigade. The use of the editorial "we" is common, however, in soldiers' diaries and letters. Yet Hollister's hatred for black soldiers serving the Confederacy (a tiny percentage of the Rebel army, a negligible one in 1862) is strongly expressed, and almost certainly represents a long-standing American tradition of assigning blame and criminality to nonwhites.
34. Partridge to Robertson, Feb. 19, 1865, 16th Michigan Records, Archives of Michigan.
35. Stanfield diary, May 10, 1862, USAHEC.
36. Stockton diary, May 10, 11, and 20.
37. Munson to Van Hoosen, May 13, 1862, Van Hoosen Papers,
38. Keeler, *War Letters,* May 16, 1862.
39. Wert, *Sword of Lincoln,* pp. 79–80.
40. Ervay to friend and parents, May 18, 1862, in George Washington Ervay, *George W. Ervay, 1845–1863, Civil War Letters* (Marietta, Ga.: self-pub., 1986).
41. Berry diary, May 18, 1862, USAHEC; Stockton diary, May 19, 1862.
42. Borden to parents, May 20, 1862 (photocopy), 16th Michigan file, Gettysburg National Military Park.

43. Berry diary, May 20, 1862, USAHEC.
44. Berry diary, May 20–26, 1862; Stockton diary, May 23–24. 1862; Eugene Arus Nash, *A History of the Forty-Fourth Regiment New York Volunteer Infantry in the Civil War, 1861–1865* (Chicago: R. R. Donnelley, 1911), p. 72.
45. Stockton diary, May 22, 1862.
46. Wert, *Sword of Lincoln,* p. 82.
47. Stockton diary, May 26, 1862.
48. *OR,* 11/1: 722; Berry diary, May 27, 1862, USAHEC; Salter to Duffield, June 17, 1862, Duffield Papers.
49. Berry diary, May 27, 1862; Stockton diary, May 27, 1862; Salter to Duffield, June 17, 1862, Duffield Papers.
50. Salter to Duffield, June 17, 1862, Duffield Papers; *OR,* 11/1: 723; Stockton diary, May 27, 1862; Berry diary, May 27, 1862; Stanfield diary, May 29, 1862; Stanfield did not know the name of the 16th Michigan soldier who was wounded at Hanover Court House, but identified him as the man "who was hit at Yorktown" and had just returned to duty. Hodgkins seems to have been the only soldier from the regiment to fit that description, struck by a spent piece of shell. He left the army later that summer, probably discharged for his wound.
51. Salter to Duffield, May 27, 1862; Stockton diary, May 27, 1862; *Detroit Free Press,* July 8, 1862; Munson to Van Hoosen, June 2, 1862, Van Hoosen Papers.
52. *OR,* 11/1: 724; Munson to Van Hoosen, June 2, 1862; Berry diary, May 27, 1862; Powers wrote a sketch about the 16th Michigan that was quoted in Franklin Ellis, *History of Genesee County, Michigan* (Philadelphia: Everts & Abbott, 1879), p. 88.
53. Munson to Van Hoosen, June 2, 1862; Keeler, War Letters, May 30, 1862; Berry diary, May 27, 1862; Stockton diary, May 27, 1862.
54. Stanfield diary, May 28, 1862, USAHEC. African-Americans had been cooking for and serving Stockton's men at the formation of the regiment—Pvt. Alfred Wellington had noted in August 1861 that twenty blacks prepared and served food to the regiment in Camp Backus in Detroit; see Wellington to family, Aug. 18, 1861, Wellington Family Papers, Hoyt Main Library, Public Libraries of Saginaw. Whether Walker was a free black who had come with the regiment from Detroit, or an ex-slave who had liberated himself, is not clear.
55. Salter to Duffield, June 17, 1862, Duffield Papers.
56. Powers, quoted in Ellis, *History of Genesee County,* p. 88; Stanfield diary, May 28, 1862.

CHAPTER 5. MAY–JUNE 1862: THE BULLETS RAINED IN RANKS AROUND ME

1. Stockton diary, May 29, 1862, Perry Archives, Sloan Museum, Flint; Aplin to mother, May 30, 1862, Aplin Family Papers, Schoff Civil War Collection, William L. Clements Library, University of Michigan.
2. Francis D. Keeler, *War Letters Written During the Rebellion* (Saginaw, Mich.: Julian A. Keeler, 1895), May 30, 1862.

3. Berry diary (photocopy), May 31 and June 1, 1862, U.S. Army Heritage and Education Center (USAHEC); Stockton diary, June 1, 1862. A summary of the battle is given in Jeffry D. Wert, *Sword of Lincoln: The Army of the Potomac* (New York: Simon & Schuster, 2005), pp. 83–89.
4. Barrett to friends, June 6, 1862, Bentley Historical Library, University of Michigan; Stockton to Maria, June 7, 1862, Stockton Papers, Perry Archives.
5. Stockton to Maria, June 7, 1862, Stockton Papers.
6. Ibid.
7. Ervay to family, June 7, 1862, in George Washington Ervay, *George W. Ervay, 1845–1863, Civil War Letters* (Marietta, Ga.: self-pub., 1986).
8. Apted diary (transcription), June 8, 1862, Fredericksburg and Spotsylvania National Park; Berry diary, entries from June 6–11, 1862; Stockton diary, entries between June 6–11, 1862.
9. Munson to Van Hoosen, Van Hoosen Papers, Bentley Historical Library, University of Michigan.
10. *Official Records* (*OR*), 11/1: 1038.
11. Ibid.; Stockton diary, June 14, 1862.
12. Hill reunion address in the *Saginaw Evening News,* Sept. 26, 1889; Jewett to *East Saginaw Courier,* July 1, 1862; Stanfield diary (transcript), June 15, 1862, U.S. Army Heritage and Education Center (USAHEC).
13. Stockton diary, June 15, 1862; Salter to Duffield, June 17, 1862, Duffield Papers, Burton Historical Collection, Detroit Public Library.
14. Stockton diary, June 17, 18, 1862; Wert, *Sword of Lincoln,* pp. 93–95; Ervay to family, June 19, 1862, *George Washington Ervay.*
15. Keeler, *War Letters,* June 25, 1862; Apted diary, June 22, 1862; Berry diary, June 21, 24, 1862; Stockton diary, June 19–24, 1862; *Wolverine Citizen,* July 26, 1862 (letter of Capt. Robert Elliot); *Detroit Free Press,* July 8, 1862.
16. Wert, *Sword of Lincoln,* pp. 98–99.
17. Ibid.; Apted diary, June 25, 26, 1862; Berry diary, June 26, 1862.
18. Wert, *Sword of Lincoln,* pp. 101–2; *OR,* 11/2: 322, 323; *Wolverine Citizen,* July 26, 1862.
19. *OR,* 11/2: 322–23; Berry diary, June 26, 1862.
20. *Wolverine Citizen,* July 26, 1862; Wert, *Sword of Lincoln,* p. 102.
21. *Wolverine Citizen,* July 26, 1862; *OR,* 11/2: 316, 323.
22. Salter to Duffield, July 12, 1862, Duffield Papers; *OR,* 11/2: 322.
23. Clifford Dowdey, *The Seven Days* (New York: Little, Brown, 1964), pp. 234–42; *OR,* 11/2: 317, 322; Wert, *Sword of Lincoln,* pp. 103–6.
24. Salter to Duffield, July 12, 1862, Duffield Papers; *OR,* 11/2: 317, 324; Wert, *Sword of Lincoln,* p. 104; *Wolverine Citizen,* July 12 and 26, 1862. Stockton's report states Carr was killed as the regiment was waiting in reserve, but Ziba Graham's letter in the Flint paper and a casualty report in the regimental records in the Archives of Michigan indicate the regiment was moving into battle when the captain was hit. Stockton wrote that Carr was "shot dead." Stockton to wife, June 28, 1862, Stockton Papers.
25. Stockton to Robertson, Sept. 3, 1862, 16th Michigan Records, Archives of Michigan; Wert, *Sword of Lincoln,* p. 105; *OR,* 11/2: 316–17, 322; Salter to Duffield, July 12, 1862, Duffield Papers.
26. Stockton to wife, June 28, 1862, Stockton Papers; Stockton to Robertson, Sept. 3, 1862, 16th

Michigan Records, Archives of Michigan; *Wolverine Citizen,* July 26, 1862

27. *OR,* 11/2: 317, 322–23.
28. Amos M. Judson, *History of the Eighty-Third Regiment Pennsylvania Volunteers* (Erie: B. F. H. Lynn, 1865), pp. 42–43; *OR,* 11/2: 317, 324; Salter to Duffield, July 12, 1862, Duffield Papers.
29. Judson, *History of the Eighty-third Pennsylvania,* pp. 42–43; *OR,* 11/2: 317, 324; Thomas R. Lackie, "Report of Gaines' Mill Affair by a Federal," *Confederate Veteran* (Feb. 1899): 56; Buchanan letter to *Confederate Veteran* (May 1899): 216, 225–26.
30. *Confederate Veteran* (May 1899): 56; Partridge to Robertson, Dec. 28, 1866, 16th Michigan Records, Archives of Michigan; *OR,* 11/2: 323–24.
31. *OR,* 11/2: 273, 317; *Wolverine Citizen,* July 26, 1862; *Hillsdale Standard,* July 28, 1862.
32. Partridge to Robertson Dec. 28, 1866, 16th Michigan Records, Archives of Michigan. In this letter, Partridge gave this account quoting from his 1862 diary; *OR,* 11/2: 324;
33. Salter to Duffield, July 12, 1862, Duffield Papers.
34. *Wolverine Citizen,* July 26, 1862; *Confederate Veteran* (Feb. 1899): 56; Partridge to Robertson, Dec. 28, 1866, 16th Michigan Records, Archives of Michigan; Salter to Duffield, July 12, 1862, Duffield Papers.
35. *OR,* 11/2: 273; wounding of Lt. McGraw is in notes (transcribed) originally found with Alfred Apted's Civil War diaries, and a copy of them is at the U.S. Army Heritage and Education Center. These notes indicate that Apted and Partridge wanted to produce their own history of the 16th Michigan after the war, but did not; *Wolverine Citizen,* July 26, 1862.
36. William F. Fox, *Regimental Losses in the American Civil War* (Albany: Albany Publishing, 1889), p. 387; Wert, *Sword of Lincoln,* p. 105.
37. *Wolverine Citizen,* July 19, 1862; Salter to Duffield, July 12, 1862, Duffield Papers; Keeler to Mrs. Fisher, July 5, 1862, in James R. Wilson, *The Fishers of Saginaw and Zilwaukee,* (genealogy) (Bellaire, Mich.: n.p.), n.d.
38. Keeler, *War Letters,* July 5, 1862; *Wolverine Citizen,* July 12, 1862.
39. Copy of March 1892 application for Medal of Honor for Sidman, Sidman Papers, Archives of Michigan; *Owosso Evening Argus,* Aug. 22, 1912; Minnie Dubbs Millbrook, *A Study in Valor: Michigan Medal of Honor Winners in the Civil War* (Lansing: Michigan Civil War Centennial Observance Commission, 1966), pp. 119–121. Sidman later claimed he was reported as dead at Gaines' Mill, and that his mother held a funeral service for him at the Methodist church in Corunna, Mich.: Evelyn Sidman Watcher, *Sidman–Sidnam Families of Upstate New York* (Baltimore: Gateway Press, 1981), p. 257.
40. *Supplement to the Official Records,* part 2, *Record of Events,* vol. 31, pp. 221, 228; Berry diary, July 21, 1862, and Apted diary notes, USAHEC.
41. Stockton diary, June 27, 1862 (though the actual date was probably June 28); *OR,* 11/2: 323.
42. Stockton to wife, July 1, 1862, Stockton Papers; *OR,* vol. 11, pt. 3, p. 644; *Detroit Free Press,* Aug. 19, 1862, reprinting an article from the *Charleston Mercury* about the captured 16th Michigan (Stockton's regiment) flag. How and when that flag was captured is not clear; Maj. Welch, late in the battle, took "the flag"—seemingly the regiment's national flag—and planted it to gather the regiment. This was after Stockton became separated from the rest of the regiment, as he pursued men who had broken and run. The blue regimental flag was captured, along with Stockton and

others, while the U.S. flag was not. Salter to Duffield, July 12, 1862, Duffield Papers; Wert, *Sword of Lincoln,* pp. 114–17.

43. *Wolverine Citizen,* July 26, 1862; Stockton to wife, July 26, 1862, Stockton Papers.
44. *OR,* 11/2: 318, 327–28, 339.
45. Ibid., 273, 318–19; Keeler, *War Letters,* July 5, 1862; Apted diary notes, USAHEC.
46. Keeler, *War Letters,* July 5, 1862; Salter to Duffield, July 12, 1862, Duffield Papers; Wert, *Sword of Lincoln,* pp. 114–17. Graham to T. Aplin, Aug. 1, 1862, Aplin Family Papers.
47. Apted diary notes and Berry diary, June 28–29, 1862, USAHEC.
48. Salter to Duffield, July 12, 1862, Duffield Papers; Wert, *Sword of Lincoln,* pp. 114–17.
49. Salter to Duffield, July 12, 1862.
50. Salter to Duffield, July 12, 1862, Duffield Papers; Wert, *Sword of Lincoln,* p. 117.
51. *OR,* 11/2: 325, 227–28, 350, 357, 380, 383. The Rebel force that Lt. Salter and Lt. Col. Ruehle said approached that afternoon was under a Gen. Holmes, who had been ordered to seize Malvern Hill before the Union Army reached it; he had 5,820 men and six artillery batteries. Holmes failed to take the hill, but briefly shelled it that afternoon until a massive response by Union artillery and gunboats forced him to withdraw. See C. Clough Buel and Robert Underwood Johnson, *Battles and Leaders of the Civil War: Being for the Most Part Contributions by Union and Confederate Officers,* (New York: Thomas Yoseloff, 1956), vol. 2, *North to Antietam,* pp. 390–91, 411.
52. Salter to Duffield, Duffield Papers; *OR,* 11/2: 325. While Salter was typically an accurate observer who carefully wrote what he experienced, his July 12 description of the events of June 30 at Malvern Hill is at odds with other witnesses, reports, and accounts of this engagement, called Turkey Bend, or Turkey Island Bridge. Salter wrote that a large Confederate infantry attack took place there across an open plain on June 30, and that Union gunboats and artillery left "hundreds" and then "thousands" of them dead on the field. In fact, the brief Confederate shelling and the crushing Union artillery response on the afternoon of June 30 made up a very localized event that killed and wounded a small number of Rebels, though it caused panic and flight among their inexperienced troops there.

CHAPTER 6. JULY–AUGUST 1862: IT WAS AWFUL TO LOOK UPON

1. *Official Records* (*OR*), 11/2: 325; Jeffry D. Wert, *Sword of Lincoln: The Army of the Potomac* (New York: Simon & Schuster, 2005), p. 117.
2. Salter to Duffield, July 12, 1862, Duffield Papers, Burton Historical Collection, Detroit Public Library; *OR,* 11/2: 325.
3. C. Clough Buel and Robert Underwood Johnson, *Battles and Leaders of the Civil War: Being for the Most Part Contributions by Union and Confederate Officers,* (New York: Thomas Yoseloff, 1956), vol. 2, *North to Antietam,* p. 416; Francis D. Keeler, *War Letters Written During the Rebellion* (Saginaw, Mich.: Julian A. Keeler, 1895), July 14, 1862; Berry diary (photocopy), July 1, 1862, U.S. Army Heritage and Education Center (USAHEC). Keeler's use "graybacks" is an insulting reference to the Confederates, since it was also a term used for one of the kinds of lice that plagued soldiers.

4. Salter to Duffield, July 12, 1862, Duffield Papers; *OR*, 11/2: 320, 325, 342.
5. Ibid.
6. Wert, *Sword of Lincoln*, pp. 120–21; Salter to Duffield, July 12, 1862, Duffield Papers; Keeler, *War Letters*, July 12, 1862; William F. Fox, *Regimental Losses in the American Civil War* (Albany: Albany Publishing, 1889), p. 387; Amos M. Judson, *History of the Eighty-Third Regiment Pennsylvania Volunteers* (Erie: B. F. H. Lynn, 1865), p. 48; *Supplement to the Official Records of the Union and Confederate Armies*, part 2, *Record of Events* (Wilmington, N.C.: Broadfoot, 1996), vol. 31, p. 237.
7. Wert, *Sword of Lincoln*, p. 121; Apted diary (transcript), July 1–2, 1862, Fredericksburg and Spotsylvania National Park; Salter to Duffield, July 12, 1862, Duffield Papers; Barrett to parents, Aug. 6, 1862, Bentley Historical Library, University of Michigan. For example, Lt. Salter was just one of the 16th Michigan letter writers and diarists to record that Lee's forces totaled 200,000.
8. Berry diary, July 2, 1862; *Supplement to the Official Records*, part 2, vol. 31, p. 212.
9. Salter to Duffield, July 12, 1862, Duffield Papers.
10. Apted diary (transcript), July 4, 1862, Fredericksburg and Spotsylvania National Park; Berry diary, July 4, 1862.
11. Salter to Duffield, July 12, 1862, Duffield Papers.
12. Ibid.; Barrett to parents, Aug. 6, 1862, Bentley Historical Library.
13. Ervay to parents, July 5, 1862, George Washington Ervay, *George W. Ervay, 1845–1863, Civil War Letters* (Marietta, Ga.: self-pub., 1986).
14. Ibid., July 28, 1862.
15. Munson to Van Hoosen, July 12, 1862, Van Hoosen Papers, Bentley Historical Library.
16. Stockton to wife, June 28, 1862, and July 1, 1862, Stockton Papers, Perry Archives, Sloan Museum, Flint.
17. Stockton to wife, June 28, 1862, Stockton Papers.
18. Stockton to wife, July 13, 1862, Stockton Papers.
19. Stockton to wife, July 16, 1862, Stockton Papers. It appears that Stockton sent this letter by way of one of the Union army surgeons also taken prisoner, perhaps by Dr. Seeley, the 16th Michigan's contract surgeon. Many Union doctors and hospital stewards who remained behind to care for the wounded at Malvern Hill (and also at Savage's Station) were held for a time before being released. Though Stockton mentioned that Longstreet wrote to Maria, there is no letter from Longstreet in Stockton's surviving letters.
20. Stockton to wife, July 26, 1862, Stockton papers. The Confederate secretary of war was then George W. Randolph.
21. Ibid.
22. Deas to Stockton, July 4, 1862 (transcription), Stockton Papers.
23. Stockton to wife, July 26 letter, continued on Aug. 2, 1862; Stockton Papers; Stockton to Robertson, Aug. 2, 1862, 16th Michigan Records, Archives of Michigan, Lansing.
24. According to regimental records, Thomas Barry was commissioned major of the 16th Michigan and Norval Welch was commissioned lieutenant colonel on July 6, 1862, while Col. Stockton was a prisoner in Richmond. See Michigan Adjutant-General's Dept., *Record of Service of Michigan Volunteers in the Civil War, 1861–1865* (Kalamazoo: Ihling Bros. & Everard, 1905), vol. 16, pp. 13, 169.

25. E. Aplin to G. Aplin, Aug. 17, 1862, Aplin Family Papers, Schoff Collection, William L. Clements Library, University of Michigan.
26. *OR,* 11/3: 644 and 51/2: 595.
27. The *Charleston Mercury* story about the 16th Michigan's flag was reprinted in the *Detroit Free Press,* Aug. 19, 1862; *Confederate Veteran* (magazine), May 1899, 226.
28. Keeler, *War Letters,* July 18, 1862; Salter to Duffield August 1862, Duffield Papers.
29. Keeler, *War Letters,* July 18, 1862; Apted diary, July 8, 1862; Ervay to parents, July 29, 1862, *George W. Ervay.*
30. Apted diary, July 9–11, 1862; John Berry diary, July 13, 14, 21, 1862; Oliver W. Norton, *Army Letters, 1861–1865* (Chicago: O. L. Deming, 1903), pp. 323–329. Butterfield later said that he could not read music, but he could play bugle calls; even so, Norton wrote that the general had written his ideas for the bugle call down on paper. Some believe Butterfield's "lullaby" was a variation on a French military bugle call that signaled "lights out."
31. Salter to Duffield, August 1862, Duffield Papers; Borden to parents (photocopy), Aug. 9, 1862, from U.S. Pension Office/National Archives, in 16th Michigan files, Gettysburg National Military Park.
32. Salter to Duffield, August 1862, Duffield Papers; Norton, *Army Letters,* p. 114; Orvey S. Barrett, *The Old Fourth Michigan Infantry* (Detroit: W. S. Ostler, 1888), p. 18; Apted diary, Aug. 7, 1862.
33. Salter to Duffield, August 1862, Duffield Papers; Keeler, *War Letters,* July 13, 1862; Borden to parents (photocopy) Aug. 9, 1862, 16th Michigan file, Gettysburg National Military Park.
34. Wert, *Sword of Lincoln,* pp. 126–28, 132–33.

CHAPTER 7. AUGUST–SEPTEMBER 1862: HURRAH FOR HELL

1. Salter to Duffield, August 1862, Duffield Papers, Burton Historical Collection, Detroit Public Library.
2. Apted diary (transcript), Aug. 3–10, 1862, Fredericksburg and Spotsylvania National Park; Eugene Arus Nash, *A History of the Forty-fourth Regiment New York Volunteer Infantry in the Civil War, 1861–1865* (Chicago: R. R. Donnelley, 1911), p. 94; *Supplement to the Official Records,* part 2, *Record of Events,* vol. 31, p. 208.
3. William F. Breakey, "Recollections and Incidents of Medical Military Service," in *War Papers,* vol. 2, Michigan Commandery Military Order of the Loyal Legion (Detroit: James H. Stone, 1898), pp. 123–25.
4. *Official Records* (*OR*), ser. 2, 4: 437; Stockton to McClellan (transcript), Aug. 14, 1862, Stockton Papers, Perry Archives, Sloan Museum, Flint.
5. Jeffry D. Wert, *Sword of Lincoln: The Army of the Potomac* (New York: Simon & Schuster, 2005), pp. 132–33; Stephen W. Sears, *Lincoln's Lieutenants: The High Command of the Army of the Potomac* (New York: Houghton Mifflin Harcourt, 2017), pp. 290–91, 294–96, 298–99.
6. Francis D. Keeler, *War Letters Written During the Rebellion* (Saginaw, Mich.: Julian A. Keeler, 1895), Aug. 22, 1862; Breakey, "Recollections," p. 126.

7. Breakey, "Recollections," p. 126; Keeler, *War Letters,* Aug. 25,1862; Apted diary, Aug. 17, 1862.
8. Breakey, "Recollections," p. 126.
9. Keeler, *War Letters,* Aug. 22, 1862; Apted diary, Aug. 22, 1862.
10. *OR,* 11/2: 322. For example, the editor of the *Wolverine Citizen,* Aug. 16, 1862, took issue with the *New York Herald* report that stated Welch "led" the regiment through the rest of the Seven Days after Stockton was captured.
11. Salter to Duffield, Sept. 20, 1862, Duffield Papers; Keeler, *War Letters,* Aug. 25, 1862; Keeler seems to have been promoted from corporal to sergeant during that summer; Apted diary, Aug. 24–30, 1862. Copies of Kin Dygert's letters, appeals, and orders regarding his being ruled AWOL and dismissed, from that time on through February 1863, in the 16th Michigan Records, Archives of Michigan, Lansing.
12. Wert, *Sword of Lincoln,* p. 134.
13. Breakey to father-in-law, Sept. 5, 1862, Bentley Historical Library, University of Michigan.
14. Ibid.; Salter to Duffield, Sept. 20, 1862, Duffield Papers; Alpheus S. Williams, *From the Cannon's Mouth: The Civil War Letters of General Alpheus S. Williams* (Detroit: Wayne State University and the Detroit Historical Society, 1959), p. 108.
15. Wert, *Sword of Lincoln,* p. 134; Salter to Duffield, Sept. 20, 1862, Duffield Papers; Breakey to father-in-law, Sept. 5, 1862, Bentley Historical Library; Otto Eisenschiml, *The Celebrated Case of Fitz John Porter* (Indianapolis: Bobbs-Merrill, 1950), pp. 53–58; Sears, *Lincoln's Lieutenants,* p. 319.
16. Keeler, *War Letters,* Sept. 4, 1862; Salter to Duffield, Sept. 20, 1862; Breakey, "Recollections," p. 126.
17. Breakey, "Recollections," p. 126.
18. Breakey, "Recollections," pp. 127–29; Keeler, *War Letters,* Sept. 4, 1862; Salter to Duffield, Sept. 20, 1862, Duffield Papers.
19. Clough Buel and Robert Underwood Johnson, *Battles and Leaders of the Civil War: Being for the Most Part Contributions by Union and Confederate Officers* (New York: Thomas Yoseloff, 1956), vol. 2, p. 474; Wert, *Sword of Lincoln,* p. 174; Eisenschhiml, *The Celebrated Case of Fitz John Porter,* pp. 60–61; Sears, *Lincoln's Lieutenants,* pp. 320–21.
20. Keeler, *War Letters,* Sept. 4, 1862; Breakey to father-in-law, Sept. 5, 1862, Bentley Historical Library; Salter to Duffield, Sept. 20, 1862, Duffield Paspers; Nash, *History of the Forty-fourth,* p. 98.
21. Breakey to father-in-law, Sept. 5, 1862, Bentley Historical Library; Extract of Stephen Martin's diary, Aug. 30, 1862, by Martin, in Martin to Robertson, April 5, 1880, 16th Michigan Records, Archives of Michigan.
22. Eisenschiml, *The Celebrated Case of Fitz John Porter,* pp. 61–64; Salter to Duffield, Sept. 20, 1862, Duffield Papers.
23. Salter to Duffield, Sept. 20, 1862, Duffield Papers.
24. *OR,* 12/1: 476. Hill told the story of Forsyth at Second Bull Run in the *Saginaw Evening News,* Sept. 26, 1889. Forsyth, who also came into the 16th Michigan from the Lancers, claimed to be 44 when he enlisted.
25. Martin to Robertson, April 5, 1880, quoting Martin's diary, 16th Michigan Records, Archives of Michigan; *OR,* 12/1: 475. Capt. Elliott wrote that the regiment formed line when it reached "the swell of ground, some rods beyond which was the rebel line of battle," clearly indicating the men

were not in line of battle when the charge went forward.

26. Prentiss to Martin, June 10, 1882, and Martin diary extract/April 5, 1880, letter, 16th Michigan Records, Archives of Michigan; *OR,* 12/1: 475. The sergeant killed carrying the U.S. flag, whose name Martin could not recall, was probably Utica's Elijah Coffin, in Company E. Since the 16th Michigan's regimental flag had been captured at Gaines' Mill—that is, the blue flag commissioned for Stockton's regiment—the flag referred to here was their national flag brought from Detroit, later replaced in the spring of 1863.
27. Salter to Duffield, Sept. 20, 1862, Duffield Papers; Martin diary abstract/letter, 16th Michigan Records, Archives of Michigan.
28. Keeler, *War Letters,* Sept. 1, 1862; Salter to Duffield, Sept. 20, 1862, Duffield Papers; Martin diary extract/letter, 16th Michigan Records, Archives of Michigan; the regiment's national colors: *Detroit Free Press,* Dec. 10, 1862.
29. Martin diary extract/letter and Prentiss to Martin, June 10, 1882, 16th Michigan Records, Archives of Michigan; Keeler, *War Letters,* Sept. 1, 1862.
30. Martin diary extract/letter to Robertson, 16th Michigan Records, Archives of Michigan. Martin identified William Kydd as a lieutenant, and perhaps Kydd was acting as second lieutenant, but in fact he was a sergeant at the time. Kydd's promotion, when he got it, was dated from June 28 that summer, just after the battle of Gaines' Mill.
31. Ibid.; Stockton's order promoting Fairbanks for bravery at Second Manassas, Oct. 11, 1862, Austin Blair Papers, Burton Historical Collection, Detroit Public Library; Barry to Robertson, May 23, 1882, and Welch to Robertson, April 24, 1863, both in 16th Michigan Records, Archives of Michigan.
32. Salter to Duffield, Sept. 20, 1862, Duffield Papers.
33. Ervay to parents, Sept. 6, 1862, George Washington Ervay, *George W. Ervay, 1845–1863, Civil War Letters* (Marietta, Ga.: self-pub., 1986).
34. Breakey, "Recollections," pp. 129–31.
35. Ibid.
36. Ibid.; Salter to Duffield, Sept. 20, 1863, Duffield Papers; Martin diary extract/letter, 16th Michigan Records, Archives of Michigan.
37. *OR,* 12/1: 475; William F. Fox, *Regimental Losses in the American Civil War* (Albany: Albany Publishing, 1889), p. 387; Wert, *Sword of Lincoln,* p. 136.
38. Breakey, "Recollections," p. 133.
39. Ibid., p. 134.
40. Ibid., p. 135.
41. Salter to Duffield, Sept. 20, 1862, Duffield Papers; Keeler, *War Letters,* Sept. 4, 1862; Breakey, "Recollections," p. 135; Sears, *Lincoln's Lieutenants,* pp. 339–41.
42. Keeler, *War Letters,* Sept. 4, 1862; Apted diary (transcript), Sept. 3, 1862, Fredericksburg and Spotsylvania National Park.
43. Breakey, "Recollections," 135–38; Salter to Duffield, Sept. 20, 1862, Duffield Papers.
44. Apted diary, Sept. 6, 1862; Stockton diary, Sept. 9, 10, 1862.
45. Wert, *Sword of Lincoln,* pp. 142–45; Salter to Duffield, Sept. 20, 1862, Duffield Papers.
46. Ervay, Sept. 13, 1862, *George W. Ervay.*

47. Jno. Robertson, *Michigan in the War* (Lansing: W. S. George, 1882), pp. 375–76; Salter to Duffield, Sept. 20, 1862, Duffield Papers; Stockton diary, Sept. 13–16, 1862.
48. Wert, *Sword of Lincoln,* p. 158; Keeler, *War Letters,* Sept. 19, 1862.
49. Wert, *Sword of Lincoln,* pp. 155–56; Sears, *Lincoln's Lieutenants,* pp. 375–76; Stockton diary, Sept. 17, 1862.
50. Wert, *Sword of Lincoln,* p. 169; Sears, *Lincoln's Lieutenants,* p. 409; Stockton diary, Sept. 19, 1862. With the reinstatement of McClellan, Porter had not yet been removed, despite Pope's complaint.
51. Keeler, *War Letters,* Sept. 19, 1862.
52. Stockton diary, Sept. 20, 1862; *OR,* 19/1: 338–41, 345–49.
53. Stockton diary, Sept. 21, 26, 1862; Ervay to friends and parents, Sept. 23, 1862, *George E. Ervay.*

CHAPTER 8. SEPTEMBER–DECEMBER 1862: FAREWELL, MCCLELLAN, YOU ARE ABOUT PLAYED OUT

1. Apted diary (transcript), Sept. 13, 14, 17, 1862, Fredericksburg and Spotsylvania National Park; Ervay to parents, Sept. 23, 1862, George Washington Ervay, *George W. Ervay, 1845–1863, Civil War Letters* (Marietta, Ga.: self-pub., 1986).
2. E. Aplin to son George, Nov. 23, 1862, Aplin Family Papers, Schoff Civil War Collection, William L. Clements Library, University of Michigan.
3. Stockton diary, Sept. 27, 28, Oct. 1, 12, 1862, Stockton Papers, Sloan Museum, Flint; order (transcribed) allowing Stockton to go to Washington, Oct. 2, 1862, Stockton Papers, Sloan Museum.
4. Stockton to Blair, Oct. 1, 1862, and Stockton to Robertson, Oct. 13, 1862, in 16th Michigan Records, Archives of Michigan, Lansing; Francis D. Keeler, *War Letters Written During the Rebellion* (Saginaw, Mich.: Julian A. Keeler, 1895), Oct. 9,1862.
5. Stockton to Robertson, Oct. 13, 1862, 16th Michigan Records, Archives of Michigan; Michigan Adjutant-General's Dept., *Record of Service of Michigan Volunteers in the Civil War, 1861–1865* (Kalamazoo: Ihling Bros. & Everard, 1905), vol. 16, pp. 14, 20. Information about the relationship of Borgman and Beckett from an interview with Borgman's grandson, the late Donald M. Thurber of Grosse Pointe, Mich.
6. Salter to Duffield, Oct. 1, 1862, Duffield Papers, Burton Historical Collection, Detroit Public Library.
7. Salter to Duffield, Oct. 13, 1862, Duffield Papers.
8. Ibid.
9. Stockton diary, Oct. 19–22, 1862.
10. Ibid., Oct. 24, 1862; Berry diary (photocopy), Oct. 24, 1862, U.S. Army Heritage and Education Center (USAHEC).
11. Stockton diary, Oct. 27, 1862.
12. Keeler, *War Letters,* Nov. 1, 1862; Stockton diary, Oct. 30–Nov. 5, 1862; Berry diary, Oct. 30–Nov. 6, 1862, USAHEC.
13. Keeler, *War Letters,* Nov. 11 and Dec. 15, 1862.

14. Franklin Ellis, *History of Genesee County, Michigan* (Philadelphia: Everts & Abbott, 1879), p. 90; Berry diary, Nov. 3, 1862.
15. Stockton diary, Nov. 9–10, 1862; Keeler, *War Letters,* Nov. 11, 1862; Berry diary, Nov. 11, 1862.
16. Stockton diary, Nov. 10, 1862; Salter to Duffield, Nov. 12, 1862, Duffield Papers.
17. Keeler, *War Letters,* Nov. 11, 1862.
18. Stockton diary, Nov. 12–14, 1862; Salter to Duffield, Nov. 14, 1862, Duffield Papers.
19. Apted diary, Nov. 13, 15, 1862; Salter to Duffield, Nov. 14, 1862, Duffield Papers; Stockton diary, Nov. 14, 15, 1862.
20. Stockton diary, Nov. 14, 15, 1862. An obscure Michigan historical novel titled *Born Strangers,* written by Wixom's granddaughter, purported that Wixom believed slavery was dying in the South and that the Civil War exacerbated the plight of blacks. It is very likely Wixom felt this way.
21. Salter to Duffield, Nov. 27, 1862, Duffield Papers; Stockton diary, Nov. 17, 18, 1862; Berry diary, Nov. 17, 1862.
22. Stockton diary, Nov. 21, 22, 1862.
23. Salter to Duffield, Nov. 27, 1862, Duffield Papers; Berry diary, Nov. 23, 24, 1862.
24. Salter to Duffield, Nov. 27, 1862, Duffield Papers; Keeler, *War Letters,* Nov. 26, 1862.
25. Stockton diary, Nov. 4, 1862; *Detroit Free Press,* Nov. 22, 1862.
26. Salter to Duffield Nov. 27, 1862, Duffield Papers.
27. Ibid.; Stockton diary, Nov. 26–28, 1862; *Detroit Free Press,* Dec. 10, 1862.
28. Stockton diary, Nov. 29, 1862; Apted diary, Nov. 29, Dec. 1, 1862; Dec. 2, 1862, letter by "H," *Detroit Free Press,* Dec. 10, 1862; Berry diary, Dec. 3, 1862.
29. Berry diary, Dec. 6, 1862.
30. Borden to father (photocopy), Dec. 7, 1862, Borden's pension file, National Archives, copy in the 16th Michigan folder, Gettysburg National Military Park.
31. Salter to Duffield, Dec. 21, 1862, Duffield Papers; Berry diary, Dec. 9–11, 1862; John J. Pullen, *The Twentieth Maine* (Philadelphia and New York: J. B. Lippincott, 1957), pp. 46–47.

CHAPTER 9. DECEMBER 1862–JANUARY 1863: A TERRIBLE AND DESTRUCTIVE FIRE

1. Berry diary (photocopy), Dec. 11–12, 1862, U.S. Army Heritage and Education Center (USAHEC); Apted diary (transcript), Dec. 11, 1862, Fredericksburg and Spotsylvania National Park.
2. Salter to Duffield, Dec. 21, 1862, Duffield Papers, Burton Historical Collection, Detroit Public Library; Berry diary, Dec. 12, 1862; John J. Pullen, *The Twentieth Maine* (Philadelphia and New York: J. B. Lippincott, 1957), p. 50.
3. Salter to Duffield, Dec. 21, 1862, Duffield Papers; Jeffry D. Wert, *Sword of Lincoln: The Army of the Potomac* (New York: Simon & Schuster, 2005), p. 197.
4. Salter to Duffield, Dec. 21, 1862, Duffield Papers.
5. Thomas Trahey, "A Sister of Mercy," *National Tribune,* Washington, D.C., May 26, 1904.
6. Ziba B. Graham, "Address of Capt. Graham," in *Proceedings of the Third Brigade Association, First*

Division, Fifth Army Corps, Army of the Potomac, Held at the National Encampment of the G.A.R., Washington, D.C., Sept. 21, 1892 (New York: River and Driver, n.d.), p. 25; Minnie Dubbs Millbrook, *A Study in Valor: Michigan Medal of Honor Winners in the Civil War* (Lansing: Michigan Civil War Centennial Observance Commission, 1966), pp. 119–120. The Maltese cross was the symbol on badges and flags of the Fifth Corps.

7. "Address of Capt. Graham," in *Proceedings of the Third Brigade Association,* p. 25.
8. Edward Hill, "The Last Charge at Fredericksburg," in *Proceedings of the Third Brigade Association, First Division, Fifth Army Corps, Army of the Potomac, Held at the National Encampment of the G.A.R., Washington, D.C., Sept. 21, 1892* (New York: River and Driver); Trahey, "A Sister of Mercy"; Stockton's report, *Official Records* (*OR*), 2: 411.
9. Hill, "The Last Charge at Fredericksburg"; Stephen W. Sears, *Lincoln's Lieutenants: The High Command of the Army of the Potomac* (New York: Houghton Mifflin Harcourt, 2017), p. 463; Wert, *Sword of Lincoln,* pp. 193, 201, 202–3.
10. Hill, "The Last Charge at Fredericksburg"; *OR,* 21: 411.
11. Trahey, "A Sister of Mercy"; Salter to Duffield, Dec. 21, 1862, Duffield Papers; *OR,* 21: 411.
12. Berry diary, Dec. 13, 1862; Hill, "The Last Charge at Fredericksburg"; Stockton to Robertson, Dec. 19, 1862, 16th Michigan Records, Archives of Michigan; *OR,* 21: 411; Salter to Duffield, Dec. 21, 1862, Duffield Papers.
13. Medal of Honor application for George Sidman, Sidman Papers, and Stockton to Robertson, Dec. 19, 1862, 16th Michigan Records, Archives of Michigan; Welch to Fisher, Dec. 18, 1862, transcribed in James R. Wilson, *The Fishers of Saginaw and Zilwaukee* (genealogy) (Bellaire, Michigan: n.d., n.p.); "Roll of Honor, Sixteenth Michigan," *Proceedings of the Third Brigade Association, First Division, Fifth Army Corps, Army of the Potomac, Held at the National Encampment of the G.A.R., Washington, D.C.* (New York: River and Driver, 1900.), vol. 3; Berry diary, Dec. 13, 1862; Hill, "The Last Charge at Fredericksburg."
14. Hill, "The Last Charge at Fredericksburg"; Stockton to Robertson, Dec. 19, 1862, 16th Michigan Records, Archives of Michigan; Berry diary, Dec. 13, 1862.
15. Hill, "The Last Charge at Fredericksburg"; Trahey, "A Sister of Mercy."
16. Charles Lanman, *Red Book of Michigan: A Civil, Military and Biographical History* (Detroit: E. B. Smith, 1871), p. 365. The story was repeated in other books where brief histories of the 16th Michigan appeared.
17. Berry diary, Dec. 14, 1862; Stockton to Robertson, Dec. 19, 1862, 16th Michigan Records, Archives of Michigan; Salter to Duffield, Dec. 21, 1862, Duffield Papers.
18. Hill, "The Last Charge at Fredericksburg"; Stockton to Robertson, Dec. 19, 1862, 16th Michigan Records, and Sidman Medal of Honor application, Sidman Papers, Archives of Michigan; Evelyn Sidman Wachter, *Sidman–Sidnam Families of Upstate New York* (Baltimore: Gateway Press, 1981), p. 260.
19. Hill, "The Last Charge at Fredericksburg"; *OR,* 21: 412; Woodruff to Hall, Feb. 20, 1863, Dale Niesen collection (privately held material); Sidman Medal of Honor application, Archives of Michigan.
20. Wert, *Sword of Lincoln,* p. 202; Salter to Duffield, Dec. 21, 1862, Duffield Papers; Ervay to parents, Dec. 18, 1862, George Washington Ervay, *George W. Ervay, 1845–1863, Civil War Letters* (Marietta,

Ga.: self-pub., 1986).

21. Hill, "The Last Charge at Fredericksburg"; *OR,* 21: 412; Salter to Duffield, Dec. 19, 1862, Duffield Papers.
22. Woodruff to Hall, Feb. 20, 1863, Dale Niesen collection; Salter to Duffield, Dec. 21, 1862, Duffield Papers; Hill, "The Last Charge at Fredericksburg"; Stockton to Robertson, Dec. 19, 1862, 16th Michigan Records, Archives of Michigan.
23. William F. Fox, *Regimental Losses in the American Civil War* (Albany: Albany Publishing, 1889), p. 387; Ostrander's name on Chatham Manor wall is from communication between the author and historian Donald C. Pfanz in 1997.
24. Salter to Duffield, Dec. 21, 1862, Duffield Papers; Stockton to Robertson, Dec. 19, 1862, 16th Michigan Records, Archives of Michigan.
25. Welch to Fisher, Dec. 18, 1862, in Wilson, *The Fishers of Saginaw and Zilwaukee.*
26. Ibid.
27. Berry diary, Dec. 25, 1862.
28. Salter to Duffield, Jan. 4, 1863, Duffield Papers; Sears, *Lincoln's Lieutenants,* pp. 472–473; Survivors' Association, 118th Corn Exchange, Pennsylvania Volunteers, *History of the Corn Exchange Regiment, 118th Pennsylvania Volunteers* (Philadelphia: J. L. Smith, 1888), p. 154.
29. Salter to Duffield, Jan. 4, 1863, Duffield Papers.
30. Stockton to Robertson, Jan. 11, 1863, 16th Michigan Records, Archives of Michigan.

CHAPTER 10. JANUARY–APRIL 1863: THIS CUSSED SOIL OF VIRGINIA

1. Salter to Duffield, Jan. 4 and Jan. 11, 1863, Duffield Papers, Burton Historical Collection, Detroit Public Library.
2. Unidentified newspaper clipping, probably from Owosso, Michigan, April 20, 1911, "miscellaneous" Civil War file, Burton Historical Collection. Versions of the story also appear with accounts of the 16th Michigan in Jno. Robertson, *Michigan in the War* (Lansing: W. S. George, 1882), and Edwin O. Wood, *History of Genesee County, Michigan* (Indianapolis: Federal Publishing Co., 1916).
3. Salter to Duffield, Jan. 18, 1863, Duffield Papers; Apted diary (transcript), Jan. 9, 1863, Fredericksburg and Spotsylvania National Park; Ervay diary, Jan. 10, 1863, Bentley Historical Library, University of Michigan (this original 1863 diary kept by Ervay was donated by Marjorie Neufer, who edited and self-published a transcription/booklet of the diary she titled *March With Me to Gettysburg*); Ervay to parents, Jan. 7, 1863, George Washington Ervay, *George W. Ervay, 1845–1863, Civil War Letters* (Marietta, Ga.: self-pub., 1986); Eaton diary, Jan. 11, 14, 15, 17, 19, Feb. 24, 25, and March 10, 1864, in *This Birth Place of Souls: The Civil War Diary of Harriet Eaton,* ed. Jane E. Schultz (New York: Oxford University Press, 2011), pp. 105, 107, 108–9, 118, 120–21, 127.
4. Salter to Duffield, Jan. 18, 1863, Duffield Papers; Jeffry D. Wert, *Sword of Lincoln: The Army of the Potomac* (New York: Simon & Schuster, 2005), pp. 206–7, 209–11.
5. Salter to Duffield, Feb. 3, 1863, Duffield Papers.

6. Ervay diary, Jan. 23, 1863, Bentley Library; Ervay to parents, Feb. 9, 1863, *George W. Ervay;* Salter to Duffield, Feb. 3, 1863, Duffield Papers; Apted diary, Jan. 24, 1863; Francis D. Keeler, *War Letters Written During the Rebellion* (Saginaw, Mich.: Julian A. Keeler, 1895), January 1863.
7. Craw to Lindley, Jan. 29, 1863, Mattoon Family Papers, University Archives and Historical Center, Michigan State University.
8. *Wolverine Citizen,* Jan. 24, 1863; Berry diary, Feb. 5, 6, 7, 1863, U.S. Arrny Heritage and Education Center (USAHEC).
9. *Detroit Free Press,* Feb. 8, 1863; Borden to parents, Feb. 11, 1863 (copy), from his pension record, National Archives in the 16th Michigan folder, Gettysburg National Military Park (GNMP); Munson to Van Hoosen, Feb. 19, 1863, Van Hoosen Papers, Bentley Historical Library, University of Michigan.
10. Salter to Duffield, Feb. 3, 1863, Duffield Papers.
11. Berry diary, Feb. 3, 1863.
12. James McPherson, *Battle Cry of Freedom* (New York: Oxford University Press, 1988), pp. 600–1.
13. Ervay to parents, Feb. 9 and Feb. 16, 1863, *George W. Ervay.*
14. Berry diary, Feb. 12, 1863; Salter to Duffield, Feb. 21, 1863, Duffield Papers.
15. Woodruff to Hall, Feb. 20, 1863, Dale Niesen (privately held).
16. Salter to Duffield, Feb. 21, 1863, Duffield Papers; Munson to Van Hoosen, Feb. 19, 1863, Van Hoosen Papers.
17. Ervay to parents, Feb. 26, 1863, *George W. Ervay;* Apted diary, Feb. 25, 1863.
18. Berry diary, Feb. 25, 26, 1863; Apted to Stockton, March 2, 1863, letter filed with Welch court-martial, Record of the Adjutant General, National Archives, Washington, D.C.
19. Stockton to Welch, March 6, 1863, filed with Welch court-martial, National Archives; Welch to Stockton, March 7, 1863, Stockton Papers, Perry Archives, Sloan Museum, Flint, Michigan; Welch to Blair, March 4, 1863, Blair Papers, Burton Historical Collection, Detroit Public Library.
20. Salter to Duffield, March 7 and March 20, 1863, Duffield Papers.
21. Ibid. Capt. Judd Mott claimed Welch was behind his court-martial, while other officers who also overstayed their leaves because of the orders of Lt. Col. Smith in Detroit were minimally punished: Mott to Robertson, June 13, 1863, 16th Michigan Records, Archives of Michigan, Lansing. Mott's contention that he alone was cashiered is supported in a letter to Michigan Adjt. Gen. John Robertson, March 16, 1863, 16th Michigan Records, in which 16th Michigan Adjutant Rufus Jacklin put on the record that Maj. Berry and Capt. Elliott had been delayed in returning from leave by the order of Lt. Col. J. R. Smith, the federal military commander in Michigan, with no mention of Capt. Mott, who said he was similarly delayed.
22. Apted diary, March 7 and 12, 1863; Michigan Adjutant-General's Dept., *Record of Service of Michigan Volunteers in the Civil War, 1861–1865,* vol. 16 (Kalamazoo: Ihling Bros. & Everard, 1905), p. 82; Ervay diary, March 12,1863, Bentley Library; Ervay to parents, March 15, 1863, *George W. Ervay;* E. Aplin to G. Aplin, March 23, 1863, Aplin Family Papers, Schoff Civil War Collection, William L. Clements Library, University of Michigan.
23. Keeler, *War Letters,* March 17, 1863; Apted diary, March 18, 1863.
24. Ervay diary, March 19, 1863, Bentley Historical Library, University of Michigan; Ervay to parents, March 24 and 30, 1863, *George W. Ervay;* Apted diary, March 27, 1863.

25. The court-martial of Wixom, from the records of the Judge Advocate General, National Archives, transcribed by Eileen Roddy, Fenton Historical Society.
26. Ibid.
27. Wixom court-martial, National Archives/Fenton Historical Society.
28. This hospital attendant was listed in the state's *Record of Service* volume for the 16th Michigan as William L. Berry, but this was an error; his name was William H. Larkworthy and he became assistant surgeon of the regiment in the spring of 1864.
29. Wixom court-martial, National Archives, transcription by Fenton Historical Society.
30. Ibid; Eaton diary, April 22, 23, 1864, in Schultz, *This Birth Place of Souls,* p. 143.
31. Keeler, *War Letters,* July 13, 1862; *Fenton Courier,* Nov. 13, 1934.
32. Petition or charges against Welch in Stockton Papers.
33. Welch court-martial, National Archives.
34. Ibid.
35. Ibid.
36. Ibid.
37. Stockton to Judge Advocate General, April 25, 1863, Blair Papers; Salter to Duffield, April 20, 1863, Duffield Papers; Michigan Adjutant-General's Dept., *Record of Service,* vol. 16, p. 106. The state's roster for the 16th Michigan states that McLaughlin "resigned" in mid-April 1863, though the letters of Stockton and Salter indicate McLaughlin was dismissed. It is also worth noting that Stockton's letter defending McLaughlin to was sent from the judge advocate general to Gov. Austin Blair, indicating the strong political links between Secretary of War Edwin Stanton's War Department and Radical Republican officials elsewhere.
38. Mott to Robertson, June 13, 1863, 16th Michigan Records, Archives of Michigan; Thos. M. O'Brien and Oliver Diefendorf, eds., *General Orders of the War Department Embracing the Years 1861, 1862, and 1863,* vol. 2 (New York: Derby & Miller, 1864), pp. 164, 166. Lincoln's mitigation of Mott's sentence occurred in the third week of May 1863.
39. Oliver W. Norton, *Army Letters, 1861–1865* (Chicago: O. L. Deming, 1903), p. 147.
40. Craw to Lindleys, March 6, Mattoon Family Papers.
41. Salter to Duffield, April 20, 1863, Duffield Papers; *East Saginaw Courier,* April 14, 1863; Keeler, *War Letters,* Dec. 15, 1862.
42. Berry diary, April 7, 1863; Dygert to Robertson, April 22, 1863, 16th Michigan Records, Archives of Michigan; *Detroit Free Press,* April 19, 1863; Aplin to S. Aplin, April 8, 1863, Aplin Family Papers.
43. Dygert to Robertson, April 22, 1863, 16th Michigan Records, Archives of Michigan.
44. *Detroit Free Press,* April 19, 1863; Ervay diary, April 12, 1863, Bentley Library; John Berry and Alfred Apted also recorded the presentation of the new colors; Salter to Duffield, April 20, 1863, Duffield Papers; Keeler, *War Letters,* March 23, 1863.
45. Ervay to parents, April 5, 1863, *George W. Ervay;* Dygert to Robertson, April 22, 1863, 16th Michigan Records, Archives of Michigan.

CHAPTER 11. APRIL–MAY 1863: ALL THE DEVILS IN HELL

1. Berry diary, April 13, 1863, U.S. Army Heritage and Education Center (USAHEC); Apted diary (transcript), April 13, 1863, Fredericksburg and Spotsylvania National Park.
2. Ervay to parents, April 15, and April 29 (an incorrect date by transcribers) 1863, George Washington Ervay, *George W. Ervay, 1845–1863, Civil War Letters* (Marietta, Ga.: self-pub., 1986). Descendants of Ervay's family misinterpreted the date of the letter as April 29 when he described the lithograph. In fact, the regiment was on the march that day, and not in "camp near Falmouth Va" as Ervay datelined this letter. It is likely that Ervay wrote the letter on April 23 or 25. Also, Salter to Duffield, April 20, 1863, Duffield Papers, Burton Historical Collection, Detroit Public Library.
3. Welch to Martin, April 24, 1863, 16th Michigan Records, Archives of Michigan.
4. Jeffry D. Wert, *Sword of Lincoln: The Army of the Potomac* (New York: Simon & Schuster, 2005), p. 232.
5. Salter to Duffield, April 20, 1863, Duffield Papers; Apted diary, April 27, 28, 1863; Ervay diary, April 29, 1863, Bentley Historical Library, University of Michigan; Borden to parents (photocopy), May 15, 1863, from Borden's pension file, National Archives, in the 16th Michigan file, Gettysburg National Military Park (GNMP).
6. Salter to Duffield, May 16, 1863, Duffield Papers; Wert, *Sword of Lincoln,* p. 238; *Official Records* (*OR*), 25/1: 519. Detailed examinations of the entire Chancellorsville campaign and battle are in Stephen W. Sears's *Chancellorsville* (New York: Houghton Mifflin, 1996) and Ernest Furguson's *Chancellorsville, 1863—The Souls of the Brave.*
7. Salter to Duffield, May 16, 1863, Duffield Papers; Wert, *Sword of Lincoln,* pp. 238, 240–41.
8. Salter to Duffield, May 16, 1863, Duffield Papers; Borden to parents, May 15, 1863, GNMP.
9. Salter to Duffield, May 16, 1863, Duffield Papers; Wert, *Sword of Lincoln,* p. 241; *OR,* 25/1: 519–20; Apted diary, May 1, 2, 3, 1863.
10. Wert, *Sword of Lincoln,* p. 243; Borden to parents, May 15, 1863; Ervay diary, May 3, 1863; Salter to Duffield, May 16, 1863, Duffield Papers.
11. *Detroit Advertiser and Tribune,* May 14, 1863, publication of May 4, 1863 letter of C.H.S. about the 4th and 16th Michigan regiments at Chancellorsville. Salter seems to have sent no other letters to any Detroit newspaper. Whether he sent this directly to the paper or to another person in Detroit, who took his letter to the paper, is not clear, but Salter would tell the Duffields that he did trade letters with a Detroit man whom he never identified.

    Pvt. Apted also mentioned Hooker's visit to the front under his entry for May 2, though it seems clear that the visit took place on the morning of May 3; Apted was on picket duty all night from May 2 through the early morning hours of the 3rd, when Hooker went on a tour of some of his lines.
12. *Detroit Advertiser and Tribune,* May 14, 1863; Salter to Duffield, May 16, 1863, and May 24, 1863, Duffield Papers; Ervay diary, May 4, 1863. Ervay believed those burned in the fire were Union soldiers.
13. Apted diary, May 3, 1863; Wert, *Sword of Lincoln,* p. 244.
14. Apted diary, May 4, 1863; Ervay diary, May 4, 1863; Borden to parents, May 15, 1863, GNMP;

Orvey S. Barrett, *The Old Fourth Michigan Infantry* (Detroit: W. S. Ostler, 1888), pp. 19–20.

15. Salter to Duffield, May 16, 1863, Duffield Papers; Thomas Trahey, "A Sister of Mercy," *National Tribune,* Washington, D.C., May 26, 1904.
16. Wert, *Sword of Lincoln,* pp. 250, 251; Salter to Duffield, May 16, 1863, Duffield Papers; Borden to parents, May 15, 1863, GNMP; Ervay diary, May 6, 1863.
17. Salter to Duffield, May 16, 1863, Duffield Papers; Wert, *Sword of Lincoln,* p. 252; Borden to parents, May 15, 1863, GNMP.
18. Berry diary, May 12 and 18, 1863; Apted diary, May 12, 1863; Ervay diary, May 12, 18, 1863.
19. Joshua L. Chamberlain, *The Passing of the Armies* (New York: G. P. Putnam's Sons, 1915), p. xiv.
20. Dygert wrote of Stockton attempting to get the provost marshal general's post in Michigan in a letter to Michigan Adjutant General John Robertson, April 22, 1863, 16th Michigan Records, Archives of Michigan; Stockton to Butterfield (transcript), May 14, 1863, Stockton Papers, Perry Archives, Sloan Museum, Flint, Michigan.
21. Stockton to Col. Locke (transcript), May 18, 1863, Stockton Papers.
22. *Wolverine Citizen,* May 30, 1863; Salter to Duffield, May 24, 1863, Duffield Papers; Ervay diary, May 22, 1863; Apted diary, May 22, 1863. Stockton's presentation sword is held at the Sloan Museum, Flint, Michigan.
23. Apted diary, May 22, 1863; *Wolverine Citizen,* May 30, 1863.
24. Salter to Duffield, May 24, 1863, Duffield Papers; Ervay diary, May 27, 1863; Berry diary, May 27, 1863; Apted diary, May 24, 27, 1863.
25. Salter to Duffield, May 24, 1863, Duffield Papers; Francis D. Keeler, *War Letters Written During the Rebellion* (Saginaw, Mich.: Julian A. Keeler, 1895), May 23, 1863.
26. E. Aplin to G. Aplin, May 21 and June 11, 1863, Aplin Family Papers, William L. Clements Library, University of Michigan; Ervay to parents, May 22, 1863, *George W. Ervay;* Salter to Duffield, May 24, 1863, Duffield Papers.
27. Wert, *Sword of Lincoln,* p. 259.

CHAPTER 12. MAY–JULY 1863: WE SHALL FIGHT BEFORE THE FOURTH OF JULY

1. Ervay to parents, May 17, 1863, George Washington Ervay, *George W. Ervay, 1845–1863, Civil War Letters* (Marietta, Ga.: self-pub., 1986); Berry diary (photocopy), May 27, 28, 1863, U.S. Army Heritage and Education Center (USAHEC).
2. Ervay to parents May 30, 1863, *George W. Ervay;* Stewart to Dear Cousin, May 27, 1863, Michigan Civil War Collection (online), micivilwar.com; Berry diary, May 30 and June 2, 1863; Salter to Duffield, June 7, 1863, Duffield Papers, Burton Historical Collection, Detroit Public Library.
3. Welch to Dick, May 20, 1863, Austin Blair Papers, Burton Historical Collection.
4. Welch to Howard, June 15, 1863, with notation from Howard, Blair Papers, Burton Historical Collection.
5. Jeffry D. Wert, *Sword of Lincoln: The Army of the Potomac* (New York: Simon & Schuster, 2005), pp. 259–60; Apted diary (transcript), June 4–6, 1863, Fredericksburg and Spotsylvania National Park;

Francis D. Keeler, *War Letters Written During the Rebellion* (Saginaw, Mich.: Julian A. Keeler, 1895), June 8, 1863.

6. Apted diary, June 4–8, 1863; Berry diary, June 4–5, 1863; Keeler, *War Letters,* June 8, 1863; Ervay to parents, June 9, 1863, *George W. Ervay;* Keeler, *War Letters,* June 8, 1863. Apted's earlier note about the rifle disagreement was recorded on March 7, 1863. A clipping from a 1910 unidentified Saginaw newspaper recorded sharpshooter George Bieber about the company's eventual use of Sharps breech-loading weapons, in the miscellaneous Civil War materials, Burton Historical Collection.
7. Ervay diary, June 4, 8–9, 1863, Bentley Historical Library, University of Michigan; Berry diary, May 16, June 9, 11, 1863.
8. Berry diary, June 11, 13–17, 1863; Apted diary, June 13–17, 1863; Ervay diary, June 14–17, 1863, Bentley Historical Library.
9. Berry diary, June 17–20, 1863; Ervay diary, June 16–20, 1863; Apted diary, June 17–20, 1863.
10. Berry diary, June 21, 1863; Salter to Duffield, June 25, 1863; report of Lt. Col. Welch to the Third Brigade, June 23, 1863, and report of Col. Vincent (copy), June 23, 1863, 16th Michigan Records, Archives of Michigan, Lansing.
11. Reports of Vincent and of Welch, June 23, 1863, 16th Michigan Records, Archives of Michigan; *Detroit Free Press,* June 30, 1863.
12. Berry diary, June 21, 1863; Welch's report, June 23, 1863, 16th Michigan Records, Archives of Michigan; Salter to Duffield, June 25, 1863, Duffield Papers; William F. Breakey, "Recollections and Incidents of Medical Military Service," vol. 2, Michigan Commandery Military Order of the Loyal Legion (Detroit: James H. Stone, 1898), p. 138.
13. Welch's report, June 23, 1863, 16th Michigan Records, Archives of Michigan; Michigan Adjutant-General's Dept., *Record of Service of Michigan Volunteers in the Civil War, 1861–1865,* vol. 16 (Kalamazoo: Ihling Bros. & Everard, 1905), p. 89; Keeler, *War Letters,* June 24, 1863.
14. Welch's and Vincent's reports, June 23, 1863, 16th Michigan Records, Archives of Michigan; *Detroit Free Press,* June 30, 1863; Keeler, *War Letters,* June 24, 1863.
15. Stephen W. Sears, *Gettysburg* (New York: Houghton Mifflin, 2003), pp. 100–1
16. Welch's report, June 23, 1863, 16th Michigan Records, and Application for Medal of Honor for George D. Sidman Papers, Archives of Michigan; Jno. Robertson, *Michigan in the War* (Lansing: W. S. George, 1882), p. 372; Michigan Adjutant-General's Dept., *Record of Service,* vol. 16, p. 152; Salter to Duffield, June 25, 1863, Duffield Papers; Keeler, *War Letters,* June 25, 1863.
17. Sears, *Gettysburg,* pp. 83–84, 86–87, 111–12, 118–21; Ervay diary, June 23 and June 26, 1863; Berry diary, June 26, 1863, USAHEC; Ziba B. Graham, "On to Gettysburg: Ten Days from My Diary, 1863," in *War Papers,* vol. 1, Michigan Military Order of the Loyal Legion of the United States (Detroit: Wynn & Hammond, 1889), p. 4; Salter to Duffield, June 29 continuation of letter dated June 25, 1863, Duffield Papers. Though Ziba Graham, presenting his paper decades later, represented it as being his diary entries covering the Gettysburg campaign, details of his paper indicate it is not a straightforward transcription, but an embellished and even romanticized account of his experiences and that of his regiment.
18. Graham, "On to Gettysburg," in *War Papers,* vol. 1, pp. 4–5; Berry diary, June 27, 1863, and Apted diary, June 28, 1863; Ervay diary, June 26, 27, 1863; Regimental return, June 28, 1863, 16th Michigan Records, Archives of Michigan.

19. Graham, "On to Gettysburg," p. 5; Sears, *Gettysburg,* pp. 123–24.
20. Graham, "On to Gettysburg," pp. 5, 6; Berry diary, June 29, 1863; Ervay diary, June 29, 1863.
21. Graham, "On to Gettysburg," p. 6; Berry, Ervay, and Apted diaries, June 30, 1863. The surgeon, Dr. Everett, was a medical school graduate and practicing physician when he signed up at age 21 as a private in the 4th Michigan Infantry in 1861. He was quickly made a hospital steward; an army surgeon in Detroit; and an assistant surgeon in the 5th Michigan Infantry Regiment, before taking the place of the court-martialed Isaac Wixom as surgeon of the 16th Michigan Infantry
22. Graham, "On to Gettysburg," pp. 6–7; Sears, *Gettysburg,* pp. 142–43; Ervay, Apted, and Berry diaries, July 1, 1863; Robert G. Carter, *Four Brothers in Blue* (Norman: University of Oklahoma Press, 1999), pp. 296–98.
23. Graham, "On to Gettysbug," 7; Berry diary, July 1, 1863; Sears. *Gettysburg,* p. 153; *OR,* ser. 1, 27/3: 467, 483; Carter, *Four Brothers in Blue,* pp. 299–300.
24. Ervay diary, July 1, 1863, Bentley Library; Graham, "On to Gettysburg," pp. 7–8; Apted diary, July 1, 2, 1863, Fredericksburg and Spotsylvania National Park; Berry diary, July 2, 1863, USAHEC. For the record, the soldiers' corps commander, Gen. George Sykes, said the Fifth Corps bivouacked early that morning of July 2 at "Bonnaughtown," meaning Bonneauville.
25. Rufus W. Jacklin, *Gettysburg, A Paper Prepared and Read Before the Military Order of the Loyal Legion of the United States,* December 1903, Bentley Historical Library.

CHAPTER 13. JULY 2, 1863: THE MOST DESPERATE FIGHTING I EVER SAW

1. Berry diary (photocopy), July 2, 1863, U.S. Army Heritage and Education Center (USAHEC); Ziba B. Graham, "On to Gettysburg: Ten Days from My Diary, 1863," in *War Papers,* vol. 1, Michigan Military Order of the Loyal Legion of the United States (Detroit: Wynn & Hammond, 1889), p. 8; Harry W. Pfanz, *Gettysburg: The Second Day* (Chapel Hill: University of North Carolina Press, 1987), pp. 62, 77; John J. Pullen, *The Twentieth Maine* (Philadelphia and New York: J. B. Lippincott, 1957), pp. 96–97; Edward P. Coddington, *The Gettysburg Campaign* (Dayton, Ohio: Morningside Books, 1979), p. 334: Oliver W. Norton, *Attack and Defense of Little Round Top* (Dayton, Ohio: Morningside Books, 1983), p. 262.
2. Amos M. Judson, *History of the Eighty-Third Pennsylvania Volunteers* (Erie, Pa.: B. F. H. Lynn, 1865), p. 66; Survivors' Association, 118th Corn Exchange, Pennsylvania Volunteers, *History of the Corn Exchange Regiment, 118th Pennsylvania Volunteers* (Philadelphia: J. L. Smith, 1888), p. 239; Rufus W. Jacklin, *Gettysburg: A Paper Prepared and Read before the Michigan Commandery of the Military Order of the Loyal Legion of the United States,* December 1903, Bentley Historical Library; Graham, "On to Gettysburg," p. 8.

   The accounts of Jacklin and Graham, written long after the war as speeches given before other veterans, are problematic, with some of their statements demonstrably incorrect, while others are confirmed and supported by other sources. For example, their statements on the position of the 16th Michigan in reserve are correct. Jacklin seems to have written and rewritten a speech or paper about Gettysburg after the war with plenty of heroic rhetoric, but almost no specific details of the fight.

3. Ervay to dear parents, July 2, 1863, George Washington Ervay, *George W. Ervay, 1845–1863, Civil War Letters* (Marietta, Ga.: self-pub., 1986). The phrase "We are here now laying in line of battle" appears to refer to the Army of the Potomac being in defensive positions, and not specifically to his own regiment, which at that point was waiting in reserve with the Fifth Corps. In letters home such as this, soldiers like Ervay sometimes used the editorial "we" that could refer to their own platoon or perhaps their entire army.
4. Ibid. The fact that Ervay did not know when he would "have to fall in" again means his regiment was then with its corps in reserve at Powers Hill.
5. Ibid. This was the only letter where George Ervay signed off in this way.
6. Graham, "On to Gettysburg," p. 9; William F. Breakey, "Recollections and Incidents of Medical Military Service," in *War Papers,* vol. 2, *Michigan Commandery Military Order of the Loyal Legion* (Detroit: James H. Stone, 1898), pp. 138–40; Allen C. Guelzo, *Gettysburg: The Last Invasion* (New York: Knopf, 2013), pp. 252–52, 258; *Official Records (OR)*, 27/1: 392.
7. Stephen W. Sears, *Gettysburg* (New York: Houghton Mifflin, 2003), pp. 234, 249–52, 262–63. Historian Edward Coddington wrote that Sickles "put the safety of the whole army in jeopardy," in *The Gettysburg Campaign,* p. 348.
8. Sears, *Gettysburg,* p. 269; Pfanz, *Gettysburg: The Second Day,* p. 201.
9. Norton, *Attack and Defense of Little Round Top,* pp. 238, 264; Norton to Huntington (photocopy), Sept. 28, 1888, Gettysburg National Military Park Library; Norton to Carter (copy), April 11, 1914, Oliver W. Norton Papers, Clarke Historical Library, Central Michigan University.

   Though certain official reports by commanders give a different and incorrect account of how the Third Brigade was sent to Little Round Top (as do the versions given by Ziba Graham and Rufus Jacklin), Norton said he was present and an eyewitness to the conversation between Vincent and Gen. Sykes's aide.
10. Jacklin, "Gettysburg"; Graham, "On to Gettysburg," p. 9; Salter to Duffield, July 12, 1863, Duffield Papers, Burton Historical Collection; Berry diary, July 2, 1863. Berry wrote that Jacklin's horse was "shot under him"; Norton, *Attack and Defense of Little Round Top,* p. 56.
11. Sears, *Gettysburg,* pp. 168–69, 268, 500n. 81, 82, 184; *OR,* 27/1: 518–19; Oliver W. Norton, *Army Letters, 1861–1865* (Chicago: O. L. Deming, 1903), p. 167; Norton, *Attack and Defense of Little Round Top,* p. 264. Norton was specific in his account of the path they took.
12. Salter to Duffield, July 12, 1863, Duffield Papers; Graham, "On to Gettysburg," p. 9; Warren to Farley, July 13, 1872, in Norton, *Attack and Defense of Little Round Top,* pp. 308, 310. First position of the 16th Michigan: Welch's report, *OR,* 27/1: 628; Partridge to Bachelder, March 31, 1866, in *The Bachelder Papers: Gettysburg in Their Own Words,* ed. David L. Ladd and Aubrey J. Ladd, vol. 1 (Dayton, Ohio: Press of Morningside Bookshop, 1994–1995), p. 243; Ellis Spear, "The Left at Gettysburg," *National Tribune,* Washington, D.C., June 13, 1913. It is important to note this because of criticism by Oliver Norton, who denied the 16th Michigan was shifted from the brigade left to the brigade right as the battle began.
13. Third Brigade skirmishers: *OR,* 27/1: 615, 623, 628, 630, 632; Ellis Spear, *The Civil War Recollections of General Ellis Spear* (Orono: University of Maine Press, 1997), pp. 33, 312; Spear, "The Left at Gettysburg"; Report of Capt. Morrill, Co. B, 20th Maine (copy), in *Bachelder Papers,* ed. Ladd and Ladd, vol. 2, p. 1029; Norton, *Attack and Defense of Little Round Top,* p. 258. Movement of the 16th

Michigan to the brigade right: *OR,* 27/1: 628; Partridge to Bachelder, March 31, 1866, *Bachelder Papers,* ed. Ladd and Ladd, vol. 1, p. 243; Spear, "The Left at Gettysburg." Partridge wrote that his regiment joined the 140th New York on the brigade's right, but this was incorrect; the New York regiment hadn't yet arrived on Little Round Top.

14. Judson, *History of the Eighty-Third Pennsylvania,* p. 67. Judson's book was first published in 1865—months after the war ended. Yet Judson was not present for most the battle, since he had been ordered to go find reinforcements, and the source of this story of the order of the regiments in the brigade battle line is unknown; see *OR,* 27/1: 620. Oliver Norton, highly critical of Lt. Col. Norval Welch in his analysis of what happened that day, insisted the 16th Michigan did not send out skirmishers. Again, Norton was wrong.
15. The author paced off the distance from the top of the southern portion of the hill to the regiment's place in the line and observed these battlefield landmarks. Amos Judson, a captain in the 83rd Pennsylvania, gave the brigade strength at 1,141 in his *History of the Eighty-Third Regiment,* p. 69n.

    Since Judson had been sent by Vincent to bring up reinforcements, he was probably in a better position to know the number of troops present for battle. His "exact number" is, I think, far more accurate than modern studies that claim the Third Brigade had a "battle strength" of 1,336. This is too high, especially given that Col. James Rice of the 44th New York, who took command of the brigade after Vincent was wounded, estimated that it had "about 1,000 muskets." See *OR,* 27/1: 616.
16. 16th Michigan's position: Pfanz, *Gettysburg: The Second Day,* pp. 212–13. 16th Michigan's strength: Fox's "218 engaged," from William F. Fox, *Regimental Losses in the American Civil War* (Albany: Albany Publishing, 1889), p. 30; historian James Vanderslice used the same figure in his 1897 book, *Gettysburg Then and Now* (New York: G. W. Dillingham, 1899), p. 96. The numbers given by Fox and Chamberlain are summed up in John W. Busey and David G. Martin, *Regimental Strengths and Losses at Gettysburg* (Highstown, N.J.: Longstreet House, 2006), p. 61. Salter to Duffield, July 12, 1863, Duffield Papers; *OR,* 27/1: 628; Judson, *History of the Eighty-Third Regiment,* p. 67; Graham, "On to Gettysburg," p. 11. Graham gave an incorrect number of the regiment's previous strength in his paper. The regiment's June 28 return in the Archives of Michigan in fact reports 339 men and 17 officers present.

    Chamberlain wrote his claim that the 16th Michigan had 250 men at Gettysburg nine months later, and gave no indication where that number came from. In any event, his number was too high based on what Lt. Salter wrote in the days after the battle—200 men—a number confirmed by Lt. Col. Welch's report.
17. Pfanz, *Gettysburg: The Second Day,* pp. 212–13, 215; *OR,* 27/1: 616–17; 1863, Smither to Dear Mother (typed transcript, photocopy), July 29, 1863, Gettysburg National Military Park (GNMP); Salter to Duffield, July 12, Duffield Papers. Reports by Confederate officers and letters by Texans and Alabamans almost universally refer to Union "breastworks" or stone walls on Little Round Top. Of course, the only stone walls on Little Round Top would have been those set up, with virtually no time, by Vincent's men. Park historians say there were no stone walls on Little Round Top as the battle began.
18. Rufus W. Jacklin, "The Famous Old Third Brigade," in *War Papers,* vol. 1, *Michigan Commandery Military Order of the Loyal Legion of the United States* (Detroit: James H. Stone, 1898), p. 47. Jacklin

presented this paper in 1894; he also wrote and rewrote a speech or paper about Gettysburg after the war with plenty of heroic rhetoric, with no details of the fight. Berry diary, July 2, 1863; Alfred Apted diary (transcript), July 2, 1863, Fredericksburg and Spotsylvania National Park. The writing in the original diary has been described to me as very faded and difficult to read.

Apted's transcriber, his great grandson, was not sure of the word "west" and placed the question mark there. I think it likely Apted wrote "rest" rather than "west," and was referring to these Confederates, who had come around the Third Corps, the Union left. Berry's estimate of moving a half-mile was perhaps too far a distance, but the fact that Michigan skirmishers left the south base of Little Round Top and soon saw the Rebels almost necessarily puts them on Round Top, as Rufus Jacklin maintained later.

19. Letter of Capt. Walter G. Morrill, in *The Bachelder Papers,* ed. Ladd and Ladd, vol. 2, p. 1029; *OR,* 27/1: 623; Spear, *The Civil War Recollections of General Ellis Spear,* p. 33; Judson, *History of the Eighty-Third Regiment,* p. 67; Eugene Arus Nash, *A History of the Forty-fourth Regiment, New York Volunteer Infantry in the Civil War, 1861–1865* (Chicago: R. R. Donnelley, 1911), pp. 144–45, 154.
20. *OR,* 27/2: 391–92, 410–11; Norton, *Attack and Defense of Little Round Top,* pp. 179–80. Norton wrongly maintained the 16th Michigan did not have skirmishers out that day.
21. Ladd and Ladd, eds., *The Bachelder Papers,* vol. 2, pp. 1029; Spear, *The Civil War Recollections of General Ellis Spear,* pp. 35, 313–14; Spear, "The Left at Gettysburg."
22. *OR,* 27/1: 617, 624–25; Ladd and Ladd, eds., *The Bachelder Papers,* vol. 2, p. 1029, Spear, *Civil War Recollections,* pp. 35, 313–17; Spear, "The Left at Gettysburg." Typical accounts of the climax of the fighting on the south side of Little Round are in Sears, *Gettysburg,* pp. 295–96, and Guelzo, *Gettysburg: The Last Invasion,* pp. 271–72. Years later, Ellis Spear gave a very different version of what happened that day, relating that some of the Maine soldiers started down the southern hill of Little Round Top to retrieve wounded comrades just out of reach, thereby igniting spontaneously and unintentionally the famous charge. Of course, Chamberlain said he gave the order for the charge.
23. Berry diary, July 2, 1863,
24. Norton, *Attack and Defense of Little Round Top,* pp. 258–59; *OR,* 27/2: 392–93; Berry diary, July 2, 1863; Apted diary, July 2, 1863. The time element Berry gave here, "about 3 o'clock," is typical of mid-nineteenth-century time keeping, where two different watches or clocks could be set to dramatically different times. In fact, the Confederate infantry attack began about 4 p.m.
25. Nash, *A History of the Forty-fourth New York,* p. 331; Michigan Adjutant-General's Dept., *Record of Service of Michigan Volunteers in the Civil War, 1861–1865,* vol. 16 (Kalamazoo: Ihling Bros. & Everard, 1905), p. 53; published extract of a letter by Capt. Charles W. Gibbs, regarding 44th New York casualties at Gettysburg, 44th New York newspaper clippings, New York State Military Museum, Saratoga Springs.
26. Berry diary, July 2, 1863.
27. Apted diary July 2, 1863; *OR,* 27/2: 393. One historian who drew on the transcribed Apted diary, Glenn LaFantasie, in his *Twilight at Little Round Top,* (New York: Vintage, 2005), p. 146, interpreted the words "And in the short space of 5 minutes lost a great number of men and officers" to mean that the sharpshooter was referring to his own regiment or brigade. Of course, Apted was a skirmisher and not with his regiment in the brigade line that day, and his company did not suffer

such a "great" loss. Nor did his brigade lose "a great number" of personnel in five minutes. This sentence refers to Confederate casualties suffered in the climax of the fighting on the south side of Little Round Top and the saddle between the hills.

28. Company A casualties: 16th Michigan "Roll of Honor," researched after the war by Edward Hill and published in 1900 in *Proceedings of the Third Brigade Association,* vol. 3; it indicates, as do Detroit newspaper reports about the 16th Michigan's wounded men in hospitals after Gettysburg, that two Brady Sharpshooters were wounded in addition to Capt. Dygert being captured. No information about the sharpshooters was included on the regiment's casualty report in the Archives of Michigan, a very incomplete record.
29. Berry diary, July 2, 1863; Oates, "The War Between the Union and the Confederacy," quoted in Norton, *Attack and Defense of Little Round Top,* pp. 85–86, 88, 99; *OR,* 27/1: 518–19; Spear, *The Civil War Recollections of General Ellis Spear,* p. 313.
30. Judson, *History of the Eighty-Third,* pp. 68–69. Oliver Norton, in his *Attack and Defense of Little Round Top,* p. 243, maintained that the 16th Michigan did not send out skirmishers that day. This was just one of the errors the former brigade bugler made about the 16th Michigan at Gettysburg.
31. *OR,* 27/1: 628; Partridge to Batchelder, March 31, 1866, in *The Bachelder Papers,* ed. Ladd and Ladd, vol. 1, p. 243; W. W. Colestock letter, "The 16th Mich. at Little Round Top," *National Tribune,* March 26, 1914.
32. Salter to Duffield, July 12, 1863, Duffield Papers; Norton, *Attack and Defense of Little Round Top,* 258; *OR,* 27/2: 410–12; Landrum to Dear Mother (transcript photocopy), July 15, 1863, Gettysburg National Military Park; William A. Fletcher, *Rebel Private, Front and Rear* (Austin: University of Texas Press, 1954), pp. 59–60; John W. Stevens, *Reminiscences of the Civil War* (Hillsboro, Tex.: Hillsboro Mirror Print, 1902), p. 114.

    Though Salter's accounts are usually clear and almost grammatically correct compared to other Civil War era letter writers, this portion of his letter is a run-on sentence, reading in part: "both sides advancing until down in the hollow, when our brigade succeeded in driving back the rebels, to take refuge behind the rocks, and the ridge opposite us."
33. Fletcher, *Rebel Private,* p. 60; J. Mark Smither to Dear Mother (typed transcript), July 29, 1863, Gettysburg National Military Park; *OR,* 27/2: 412, 413; R. Turrell to D. Ervay, July 28, 1863, and A. Young to D. Ervay, July 29, 1863, in *George W. Ervay.*
34. Graham, "On to Gettysburg," p. 10; *OR,* 27/2: 411, 413; Fletcher, *Rebel Private,* p. 60; Smither to Dear Mother, July 29, 1863, Gettysburg National Military Park. John Stevens of the 5th Texas wrote that while others fell back, his company, at the order of his captain, remained on the hillside, firing. Stevens, *Reminiscences,* p. 114. Oliver Norton believed that the 48th Alabama participated with the Rebels' first attack on Little Round Top, though subsequent historians do not accept that.
35. Graham, "On to Gettysburg," p. 11; Norton, *Attack and Defense of Little Round Top,* pp. 258–59.
36. Pfanz, *Gettysburg: The Second Day,* pp. 223–24; Warren to Farley, July 24, 1872, in Norton, *Attack and Defense of Little Round Top,* pp. 311–12; Edward Hill, "Address of Col. Edward Hill," in *Michigan at Gettysburg,* Michigan Gettysburg Battlefield Commission (Detroit: Winn & Hammond, 1889), p. 108; *Supplement to the Official Records,* part 2, *Record of Events,* vol. 31, p. 219.
37. *OR,* 27/2: 411, 413; Fletcher, *Rebel Private,* p. 60; J. Mark Smither to Dear Mother, July 29, 1863, Gettysburg National Military Park; John C. West, *A Texan in Search of a Fight* (Waco: Press of J. S.

Hill, 1901), p. 86. Fletcher's account sounds very much like sour grapes—an ex-soldier writing after the war that "we Texans didn't take the hill, because we knew we couldn't." Other Texans sounded bitter about the repeated attacks being ordered, but said they carried out their officers' commands.

38. Salter to Duffield, July 12, 1863, and July 29, 1863, Duffield Papers.

39. Partridge to Bachelder, March 31, 1866 in *The Bachelder Papers,* ed. Ladd and Ladd, vol. 1, p. 244; Casualty report of the 16th Michigan, 16th Michigan Records, Archives of Michigan; author's interview with the late Donald M. Thurber, great-grandson of Martin Borgman; Stevens, *Reminiscences of the Civil War,* p. 114; *OR,* 27/2: 411, 413.

40. *OR,* 27/2: 411, 413; Smither to Dear Mother, July 29, 1863, GNMP; Norton, *Attack and Defense of Little Round Top,* pp. 172–73, 259–60; Nash, *History of the Forty-Fourth New York,* p. 145.

41. J. Gary Laine and Morris Penny, *Law's Alabama Brigade in the War Between the Union and the Confederacy* (Shippensburg, Pa.: White Mane, 1996), p. 105; W. F. Perry, "The Devil's Den," *Confederate Veteran,* April 1901, p. 162.

    See Busey and Martin's *Regimental Strengths and Losses at Gettysburg,* p. 280, for figures on the "battle strength" of these individual Confederate regiments that day and the casualties they incurred, but readers should keep in mind these regiments suffered men killed and wounded before their attack even began, when they were hit by Union artillery. Obviously, the Texans experienced casualties in the earlier attacks on Little Round Top, while the Alabamans had been in combat in and around Devil's Den that afternoon.

42. Graham, "On to Gettysburg," p. 10; Salter to Duffield, July 12, 1863, Duffield Papers; Hill, "Address of Col. Edward Hill," p. 108. Reading Salter's letter, one must consider whether his use of "we" in some instances referred to his own regiment, his brigade, or the all Union forces on the left that day. In his first reference to hand-to-hand combat, he clearly wrote, "The brigade lost so many in this close hand to hand fight, that we were unable to pursue the enemy after we drove them back." Obviously, this would mean his regiment and the others in the Third Brigade.

    The 20th Maine's commander would claim the capture of "hundreds" of prisoners, although this was an exaggeration. But it was true that the 16th Michigan, at what was left of their short battle line up the hill, did not capture many prisoners, if any. Salter went on to mention, accurately, hand-to-hand and bayonet fighting in the case of the 4th Michigan in the Wheatfield area, where Col. Harrison Jeffords was fatally wounded, and generally to mention fighting by other elements of the Fifth Corps. The regiment's casualty record for July 1863 notes the names of soldiers killed and wounded, but not specifically how—just the location of the wound, such as "Right hand," "Leg—hosp[ital]," or "Head." It also notes the severity of the wound—"Slight," "Severe," "Arm amput[tated]." Some historians believe that wounds from stabbing weapons in the Civil War were rare, which was why Col. Jeffords's fatal wounding was considered shocking and carefully noted in reports and casualty records.

43. Michigan Adjutant-General's Dept., *Record of Service,* vol. 16, pp. 13, 20, 29–30; Cameron to Robertson, Nov. 17, 1865, 16th Michigan Records, Archives of Michigan.

44. Norton, *Attack and Defense of Little Round Top,* pp. 242–43, 259–60.

45. Partridge to Batchelder, March 31, 1866, in *The Bachelder Papers,* ed. Ladd and Ladd, vol. 1, p. 244; Partridge to Robertson, Aug. 10, 1868, 16th Michigan Records, Archives of Michigan.

46. *OR,* 27/1: 628; Norton, *Attack and Defense of Little Round Top,* pp. 242–43.

47. Hill, "Address of Col. Edward Hill," p. 109; *National Tribune,* March 26, 1914; Norton, *Attack and Defense of Little Round Top,* p. 260. Colestock misspelled Kydd's name and wrongly said he was a captain when he sent his brief account to the *National Tribune.* His comrade Morton suffered a wound to his ankle characterized as "slight." Sgt. Potter's wound and role as flag carrier are given in the "Roll of Honor," *Proceedings of the Third Brigade Association,* vol. 3, p. 138.
48. Colestock letter in *National Tribune,* March 24, 1914; Erin letter, Aug. 14, 1863, in *Wolverine Citizen,* Aug. 24, 1863; Norton, *Attack and Defense of Little Round Top,* p. 260.
49. Sprague to Norton (photocopy), Jan. 16, 1910, 44th New York file, Gettysburg National Military Park.
50. Farley address, Sept. 17, 1889, in *Gettysburg Papers,* vol. 2, compiled by Ken Bandy and Florence Freeland (Dayton, Ohio: Morningside Books, 1978), p. 515; Farley letter to the editor, *Army and Navy Journal,* April 22, 1899; account of the 140th New York by Farley, in Norton, *Attack and Defense of Little Round Top,* pp. 132–35; Taylor, *History of the 48th Alabama Volunteer Infantry Regiment,* p. 18.
51. Barziza diary, July 2, 1863 (transcript), from the Cobb and Hunter Family Papers, Southern Historical Collection, copy in the 4th Texas file, Gettysburg National Military Park; Stevens, *Reminiscences of the Civil War,* pp. 114–15; *OR,* 27/2: 411; Survivors' Association, *History of the Corn Exchange Regiment,* pp. 261–62.
52. Casualty statement of the 16th Michigan, July 29, 1863; Fox, *Regimental Losses,* p. 387; Graham, "On to Gettysburg," pp. 11–12; Salter to Duffield, July 12, 1863, Duffield Papers. Soldier "Erin," who wrote to the Flint newspaper on Aug. 14, said the Gettysburg campaign cost the regiment "thirty killed and since died from wounds received and thirty-four wounded." *Wolverine Citizen,* Aug. 24, 1863.

    But Edward Hill's tabulation of the regiment's casualties, his "Roll of Honor," published in 1900 in the *Proceedings of the Third Brigade,* vol. 3, shows twenty-seven officers and men killed or mortally wounded in the fight for Little Round Top, with more than forty others wounded. This "Roll of Honor" for the regiment is probably the best source of information about the casualties of the 16th Michigan, more comprehensive that the regiment's contemporaneous reports and the Michigan Adjutant-General's Dept. *Record of Service,* vol. 16.
53. Norton, *Attack and Defense of Little Round Top,* p. 244.
54. See Garry Adelman, *The Myth of Little Round Top* (Gettysburg: Thomas Publications, 2003); and Thomas A. Desjardin, *Stand Firm Ye Boys from Maine* (Gettysburg: Thomas Publications, 1995).
55. Spear to Norton, Jan. 18, 1916; Spear, "The Left at Gettysburg—The Men Themselves Started a Decisive Charge," *National Tribune,* June 12, 1913; Spear, *The Civil War Recollections of General Ellis Spear,* pp. 34, 36, 314, 317. For an in-depth discussion of this, see Adelman, *The Myth of Little Round Top.*
56. Adelman, *The Myth of Little Round Top,* p. 85; Salter to Duffield, July 12, 1863, Duffield Papers.
57. Colestock, letter to the editor, "The 16th Mich. at Little Round Top," *National Tribune,* March 24, 1914.
58. Judson, *History of the Eighty-third,* 67; Nash, *History of the Forty-Fourth,* 145; Philander Platt, "On Little Round Top," *National Tribune.* Washington, D.C., April 11, 1907.
59. Fox, *Regimental Losses,* p. 387.

60. Norton to Huntington (photocopy), Sept. 28, 1888, 83rd Pennsylvania file, GNMP; Norton to Gifford (photocopy), Aug. 31, 1911, Norton Papers, Clarke Historical Library, Central Michigan University.
61. Norton, *Attack and Defense of Little Round Top,* 245; *OR,* 27/1: 620; Hill, "Address of Col. Edward Hill," p. 109.

CHAPTER 14. JULY–NOVEMBER 1863: WE ARE NOT FIGHTING FOR GENERALS, BUT OUR COUNTRY

1. *Official Records* (*OR*), 27/1: 618, 625; Salter to Duffield, July 12, 1863, Duffield Papers, Burton Historical Collection, Detroit Public Library; Berry diary (photocopy), July 3, 1863, U.S. Army Heritage and Education Center (USAHEC). Again, the location of the skirmishers' bivouac is not clear, but on July 3, Sgt. Berry wrote, "We find our regiment this morning," clearly indicating his Company A did not reunite with that portion of the 16th Michigan's line left on the western face of Little Round Top.
2. Young to D. Ervay, July 29, 1863, and R. Turrell to D. Ervay, July 28, 1863, in George Washington Ervay, *George W. Ervay, 1845–1863, Civil War Letters* (Marietta, Ga.: self-pub., 1986); William F. Breakey, "Recollections and Incidents of Medical Military Service," in *War Papers,* vol. 2, Michigan Commandery Military Order of the Loyal Legion (Detroit: James H. Stone, 1898), pp. 141–42; John W. Busey, *These Honored Dead: The Union Casualties at Gettysburg* (Hightstown, N.J.: Longstreet House, 1988), p. 40. See also Stephen W. Sears, *Gettysburg* (New York: Houghton Mifflin, 2003), p. 466.
3. Partridge to Robertson, April 10, 1868, 16th Michigan Records, Archives of Michigan, Lansing. Indeed, not Robertson nor any regimental writer or historian seems to have written anything else about Welch's performance and the regiment's break at Gettysburg.
4. Apted diary (transcription), Fredericksburg and Spotsylvania National Park; Ziba B. Graham, "On to Gettysburg: Ten Days from My Diary of 1863," *War Papers,* vol. 1, *Michigan Military Order of the Loyal Legion of the United States* (Detroit: Wynn & Hammond, 1889), p. 12; Berry diary, July 3, 1863, USAHEC.
5. Graham, "On to Gettysburg," p. 12.
6. Ibid., pp. 12–13. Graham obviously misspelled the farm family's last name in his reminiscence.
7. Rufus W. Jacklin, *Gettysburg: A Paper Prepared and Read Before the Michigan Commandery of the Military Order of the Loyal Legion of the United States* (December 1903), Bentley Historical Library; Sears, *Gettysburg,* p. 468.
8. Berry and Apted diaries, July 3, 1863; Sears, *Gettysburg,* pp. 463–64. Of course, Longstreet had not been captured, though the story circulated widely and Union officers and men believed it.
9. Graham, "On to Gettysburg," p. 14; Berry diary, July 4, 1863; Apted diary, July 4, 1863.
10. Breakey, "Recollections and Incidents of Medical Military Service," pp. 143–44; *Detroit Advertiser and Tribune,* Aug. 4, 1863. The use of the name "Round Top" here very likely means "Little Round Top," since the name "Round Top" seems to have been used to refer to either of the hills. In a geological sense, Round Top and Little Round Top are essentially the same rock ridge with two

separate peaks rising from it.

11. Apted diary and Berry diary, July 5, 1863; Graham, "On to Gettysburg," p. 14; Jacklin, *Gettysburg*.
12. Graham, "On to Gettysburg," p. 15; Salter to Duffield, July 12, 1863, Duffield Papers; Berry and Apted diaries, July 5, 1863; Sears, *Gettysburg*, pp. 496–98.
13. Salter to Duffield, July 12, 1863, Duffield Papers; Berry and Apted diaries, July 6–10, 1863.
14. Salter to Duffield, July 12, 1863, Duffield Papers; Berry and Apted diaries, July 11–13, 1863; *OR*, 27/1: 629.
15. Salter to Duffield, July 12 and July 29, 1863, Duffield Papers. Salter's criticism and comparisons between the Michigan regiments exemplify their jealousies and rivalries.
16. Salter to Duffield, July 12, 1863, Duffield Papers.
17. *Hillsdale Standard*, July 28, 1863.
18. Apted and Berry diaries, July 14–17, 1863; *OR*, 27/1: 629; Francis D. "Frank" Keeler, *War Letters Written during the Rebellion* (Saginaw: Julian A. Keeler, 1895), July 20, 1863.
19. Welch addressed this critical letter, signed by an officer in the 16th Michigan, when he wrote to Austin Blair about his desire to be promoted to colonel: Welch to Blair, Sept. 4, 1863, Blair Papers, Burton Historical Collection, Detroit Public Library. A look at Detroit newspapers after Gettysburg shows articles about events, lectures, and fundraisers for the 24th Michigan featuring their Col. Henry Morrow, but there seems to be no such coverage of the fact that Welch had also returned.
20. Keeler, *War Letters*, July 20, 1863.
21. Apted and Berry diaries, July 18–July 22, 1863.
22. Salter to Duffield, July 29, 1863, Duffield Papers; Apted diary, July 23, 1863; Stephen W. Sears, *Lincoln's Lieutenants: The High Command of the Army of the Potomac* (New York: Houghton Mifflin Harcourt, 2017), p. 590.
23. Salter to Duffield, July 29, 1863; Apted diary, July 29, 1863.
24. Young to D. Ervay, July 29, 1863, and Turrell to D. Ervay, July 29, 1863, in *George W. Ervay*.
25. Berry and Apted diaries, Aug. 3–10, 1863.
26. Salter to Duffield, Aug. 6, 1863, Duffield Papers.
27. Apted diary, Aug. 17, 1863.
28. Berry diary, Aug. 12, 14, 18, 20, 24, 1863; Apted diary, Aug. 12, 18, 19, 21, 1863; Salter to Duffield, Aug. 16, 1863, Duffield Papers.
29. Berry diary, Aug. 29, 1863.
30. Apted diary, Aug. 29, 1863. Dramatic accounts of the execution appear in Eugene Arus Nash, *A History of the Forty-fourth Regiment New York Volunteer Infantry in the Civil War, 1861–1865* (Chicago: R. R. Donnelley, 1911), pp. 164–65, and also in John J. Pullen, *The Twentieth Maine* (Philadelphia and New York: J. B. Lippincott, 1957) and Survivors' Association, 118th Corn Exchange, Pennsylvania Volunteers, *History of the Corn Exchange Regiment, 118th Pennsylvania Volunteers* (Philadelphia: J. L. Smith, 1888).
31. Apted diary, Sept. 3, 1863; Welch to Blair, Sept. 4, 1863, 16th Michigan records, Archives of Michigan, Lansing.
32. Apted diary, Sept. 4, 8, 9, 10, 1863; Keeler, *War Letters*, Sept. 7, 1863. Other soldiers questioned Chamberlain's military skills. See Pullen, *The Twentieth Maine*, p. 158. Lt. Salter mentioned that

Major Elliott was sick and injured in a letter, Salter to Duffield, Nov. 6, 1863, Duffield Papers.

33. Jeffry D. Wert, *Sword of Lincoln: The Army of the Potomac* (New York: Simon & Schuster, 2005), pp. 312–13; Apted and Berry diaries, Sept. 13–16, 1863.
34. Apted and Berry diaries, Sept. 17–Oct. 9, 1863; Keeler, *War Letters,* Sept. 20, 1863.
35. Wert, *Sword of Lincoln,* pp. 314–16; Berry diary, Oct. 1–5, 9, 1863; Apted diary, Oct. 1, 7, 1863.
36. Keeler, *War Letters,* Oct. 4, 1863. The furlough given regiments that reenlisted was actually for 30 days rather than 60; three-quarters of a given regiment's men had to sign up in order to receive the bounty and leave benefits.
37. Salter to Duffield, Oct. 22, 1863, Duffield Papers; Berry and Apted diaries, Oct. 10–12, 1863.
38. Berry and Apted diaries, Oct. 13–16; Salter to Duffield, Oct. 22, 1863.
39. Salter to Duffield, Oct. 22, 1863, Duffield Papers; Apted and Berry diaries, Oct. 17–19, 1863.
40. Salter to Duffield, Oct. 22, 1863.
41. Salter to Duffield, Oct. 22, 1863; Apted diary, Oct. 29–31, 1863.
42. Salter to Duffield, Oct. 22, 1863.
43. Salter to Duffield, Nov. 6, 1863; Berry diary, Oct. 23–31, 1863; Michigan Adjutant-General's Dept., *Record of Service of Michigan Volunteers in the Civil War, 1861–1865,* vol. 16 (Kalamazoo: Ihling Bros. & Everard, 1905), pp. 16–17.
44. Apted diary, Oct. 31, 1863; Amos M. Judson, *History of the Eighty-Third Regiment Pennsylvania Volunteers* (Erie: B. F. H. Lynn, 1865), p. 78; Nash, *History of the Forty-fourth New York,* p. 171.
45. *OR,* 29/1: 576–77; Salter to Duffield, Nov. 22, 1863, Duffield Papers.
46. Pullen, *The Twentieth Maine,* 163–65; *OR,* 29/1: 578–81; Salter to Duffield, Nov. 22, 1863; Jno. Robertson, *Michigan in the War* (Lansing: W. S. George), p. 367.
47. Salter to Duffield, Nov. 22, 1863, Duffield Papers; Apted diary, Nov. 7, 1863.

CHAPTER 15. NOVEMBER 1863–MAY 1864: OLD LEE IS A TOUGH CUSS

1. Alfred M. Apted diary (transcript), Nov. 8–9, 1863, Fredericksburg and Spotsylvania National Park; Survivors' Association, 118th Corn Exchange, Pennsylvania Volunteers, *History of the Corn Exchange Regiment, 118th Pennsylvania Volunteers* (Philadelphia: J. L. Smith, 1888), p. 347.
2. Apted diary, Nov. 15–16, 25, 1863; Salter to Duffield, Nov. 22, 1863, Duffield Papers, Burton Historical Collection, Detroit Public Library; Francis D. "Frank" Keeler, *War Letters Written during the Rebellion* (Saginaw: Julian A. Keeler, 1895), Nov. 21, 1863.
3. Stephen W. Sears, *Lincoln's Lieutenants: The High Command of the Army of the Potomac* (New York: Houghton Mifflin Harcourt, 2017), pp. 602–3; Jeffry D. Wert, *Sword of Lincoln: The Army of the Potomac* (New York: Simon & Schuster, 2005), p. 320; Salter to Duffield, Dec. 12, 1863, Duffield Papers.
4. Apted diary, Nov. 27, 1863; Salter to Duffield Dec. 12, 1863; Keeler, *War Letters,* Dec. 5, 1863; "Roll of Honor, Sixteenth Michigan," *Proceedings of the Third Brigade Association, First Division, Fifth Army Corps, Army of the Potomac, Held at the National Encampment of the G.A.R., Washington, D.C.* (New York: River and Driver, 1900), vol. 3, p. 115; Michigan Adjutant-General's Dept., *Record of Service of*

Michigan Volunteers in the Civil War, 1861–1865, vol. 16 (Kalamazoo: Ihling Bros. & Everard, 1905), p. 162; *Official Records* (*OR*), 29/1: 904.

5. Sears, *Lincoln's Lieutenants,* p. 604; Wert, *Sword of Lincoln,* p. 321; Salter to Duffield, Dec. 12, 1863, Duffield Papers.
6. Apted diary Nov. 27–30, 1863; Salter to Duffield, Dec. 12, 1863, Duffield Papers; Sears, *Lincoln's Lieutenants,* p. 605; Wert, *Sword of Lincoln,* p. 321.
7. Apted diary, Dec. 1, 1863; Salter to Duffield, Dec. 12, 1863.
8. Apted diary, Dec. 2–7, 1863; Salter to Duffield, Dec. 12, 1863, Duffield Papers; Keeler, *War Letters,* Dec. 5, 1863.
9. Salter to Duffield, Dec. 12, 1863, and Dec. 21, 1863, Duffield Papers; Apted diary, Dec. 10, 14, 17, 20–21, 23, 26, 28, 1863; T. Aplin to G. Aplin, Feb. 15, 1864, Aplin Family Papers, Schoff Civil War Collection, William L. Clements Library, University of Michigan; Keeler, *War Letters,* Dec. 21, 1863; Wert, *Sword of Lincoln,* p. 323.

   Pvt. Alfred Apted's name is not among the members of the regiment who were listed as signing up for reenlistment offer. Because he joined his company early in 1862, he may not have had the two years of service required for the reenlistment extension offer.
10. Welch to Robertson, Dec. 13, 1863, 16th Michigan Records, Archives of Michigan, Lansing.
11. The 1863 flag sent to Michigan: Welch to Robertson, Dec. 19, 1863, 16th Michigan Records, Archives of Michigan. Another regimental flag is mentioned in the *Detroit Free Press,* Jan. 11, 1864; Salter to Duffield, Dec. 21, 1863 Duffield Papers. Reenlistment: Welch to Robertson, Dec. 26, 1863, 16th Michigan Records, Archives of Michigan.
12. Keeler, *War Letters,* Dec. 28, 1863; Welch to Robertson, Dec. 26, 1863, 16th Michigan Records, Archives of Michigan; Apted diary, Dec. 30–31, 1863; *Supplement to the Official Records,* part 2, *Record of Events,* vol. 31, p. 235.
13. William F. Breakey, "Recollections and Incidents of Medical Military Service," in *War Papers,* vol. 2, Michigan Commandery Military Order of the Loyal Legion (Detroit: James H. Stone, 1898), p. 149.
14. Ibid., p. 150.
15. Ibid., p. 151.
16. Jerome to Roberston, Jan. 5, 1864, 16th Michigan Records, Archives of Michigan.
17. *Detroit Free Press,* Jan. 11, 1864.
18. Ibid.
19. Sarah C. M. Case diary (transcription), Jan. 11, 1864: Sarah C. M. Case, *Diary of Sarah Cushman Miles Case, Dec. 24, 1863–Dec. 13, 1864.* ed. Mrs. James Martin and Mrs. Arthur Davison (Flint: Flint Public Library, 1937).
20. E. Aplin to G. Aplin, Jan. 20, 1864, Aplin Family Papers. Elvira Aplin recorded the wrong date of the regiment's arrival in Detroit.
21. Salter to Duffield, March 1, (1864), Duffield Papers; Breakey, "Recollections and Incidents of Medical Military Service," in *War Papers,* vol. 2, p. 151S; S. Aplin to G. Aplin, Feb. 4, 1864, Aplin Family Papers.
22. Capt. Edward Hill diary, Feb. 16, 1864, Rare Book and Manuscript Collections, St. Mary's College of California; *Detroit Free Press,* Feb. 18, 1864.

23. Vincent to Robertson, Feb. 23, 1864, 16th Michigan Records, Archives of Michigan.
24. Keeler, *War Letters,* Feb. 24, 1864.
25. Salter to Duffield, March 1, (1864), Duffield Papers; Apted diary, [Feb. 23?], 1864. In the case of this particular diary entry, Apted's grandson transcribed this date as "Jan. 12," but this is wrong. Other records show the regiment returned to Bealton on Feb. 23. "Col. Hayes" may have been a commander of a Massachusetts regiment, though why he was making decisions about the Brady Sharpshooters' rifles is not clear.
26. Salter to Duffield, March 1, 1863, Duffield Papers; Munson to Van Hoosen, Feb. 25, 1864, Van Hoosen Papers, Bentley Historical Library, University of Michigan; Keeler, *War Letters,* Feb. 24, 1863.
27. Hill diary, Feb. 24–April 17, 1863; Munson to Van Hoosen, Feb. 25, 1864, Van Hoosen Papers.
28. Salter to Duffield, March 20, 1864; Aplin to S. Aplin, March 13, 1864, Aplin Family Papers; Keeler, *War Letters,* "St. Patrick's Day," 1864.
29. Salter to Duffield, March 20, 1864, Duffield Papers; Aplin to S. Aplin, March 13, 1864, Aplin Family Papers; Breakey, "Recollections and Incidents of Medical Military Service," *War Papers,* vol. 2, pp. 151–52.
30. Keeler, *War Letters,* "St. Patrick's Day," 1864; Salter to Duffield, March 20 and April 1, 1864, Duffield Papers.
31. J. Gibbs to dear friends, March 20, 1864, Van Hoosen Papers.
32. Salter to Duffield, March 20, 1864, Duffield Papers.
33. Keeler, *War Letters,* March 24, 1864; F. Wellington to Dear Sister, April 9, 1864, Hoyt Main Library, Public Libraries of Saginaw.
34. Salter to Duffield, April 1, 1864, Duffield Papers; Wellington to Dear Mother & Father, April 23, 1864, Hoyt Main Library, Public Libraries of Saginaw.
35. Salter to Duffield, April 22, 1864, Duffield Papers.
36. Munson to Van Hoosen, April 6, 1864, Van Hoosen Papers.
37. Keeler, *War Letters,* April 18 and April 30, 1864.
38. Breakey, "Recollections and Incidents," *War Papers,* vol. 2, p. 152.
39. Munson to Van Hoosen, May 1, 1864, Van Hoosen Papers; Apted diary, May 1–2, 1864; Hill diary, May 3, 1864.
40. Apted diary, May 4, 1864; Hill diary, May 4, 1864; Dewitt Clinton Smith diary, May 4, 1864, Special Collections, University of Virginia Library.

CHAPTER 16. MAY–JUNE 1864: BATTLES WITHOUT GAINING GROUND

1. Jeffry D. Wert, *Sword of Lincoln: The Army of the Potomac* (New York: Simon & Schuster, 2005), p. 334; Evander M. Law, "From the Wilderness to Cold Harbor," in *Battles and Leaders of the Civil War,* vol. 4, *The Way to Appomattox* (New York: Thomas Yoseloff, 1956), pp. 119, 122.
2. Apted diary (transcript), May 5, 1864, Fredericksburg and Spotsylvania National Park; Salter to Duffield, May 15, 1864, Duffield Papers, Burton Historical Collection, Detroit Public Library;

Official Records (*OR*), 36/1: 583–84.

3. Apted diary, May 6, 1863; Hill diary, May 6, 1864, Rare Book and Manuscript Collections, St. Mary's College of California Library; Gibbs to sister, May 19, 1864, Van Hoosen Papers, Bentley Historical Library, University of Michigan.
4. Wert, *Sword of Lincoln,* pp. 340–42; Law, "From the Wilderness," p. 126.
5. Apted diary, May 6, 1863; Dewitt Clinton Smith diary, May 6, 1864, Special Collections, University of Virginia Library.
6. Wert, *Sword of Lincoln,* p. 343; *OR,* 36/1: 572, 584; Apted diary, May 7, 1864; William F. Fox, *Regimental Losses in the American Civil War* (Albany: Albany Publishing, 1889), p. 387.
7. Salter to Duffield, May 15, 1864, Duffield Papers; John J. Pullen, *The Twentieth Maine* (Philadelphia and New York: J. B. Lippincott, 1957), p. 193.
8. Apted diary, May 8, 1864; Eugene Arus Nash, *A History of the Forty-Fourth Regiment New York Volunteer Infantry in the Civil War, 1861–1865* (Chicago: R. R. Donnelley, 1911), pp. 188–89.
9. *OR,* 36/1: 584; Ellis Spear, *The Civil War Recollections of Gen. Ellis Spear* (Orono: University of Maine Press, 1997), p. 100; Wert, *Sword of Lincoln,* pp. 346–47.
10. Apted diary, May 8, 1864; Spear, *The Civil War Recollections,* p. 101; Salter to Duffield, May 15, 1864, Duffield Papers; Hill diary, May 9, 1864.
11. Spear, *The Civil War Recollections,* p. 102; Salter to Duffield, May 15, 1864; Apted diary, May 8, 1864; *OR,* 36/1: 584; Hill diary, May 9, 1864.
12. Apted diary, May 9, 1864. The story of the capture and rescue of between 350 and 400 Union soldiers, including Jacklin, was written by Capt. O. L. Munger in Nash, *A History of the Forty-fourth New York,* pp. 250–60.
13. Apted diary, May 10, 1864; *OR,* 36/1: 540, 581, 584; Spear, *The Civil War Recollections,* pp. 104–5; Wert, *Sword of Lincoln,* pp. 358–50.
14. Dewitt Clinton Smith wrote in his diary, held at the Special Collections Library of the University of Virginia, that Barton was killed on May 10, but Alfred Apted's more detailed journal states he and Cowan died on the 11th. Hill diary, May 11, 1864.
15. Wert, *Sword of Lincoln,* pp. 350–54; Apted diary, May 12, 1864; *OR,* 36/1: 584, 638.
16. Hill diary, May 12, 1864; Apted diary, May 12, 1864; *OR,* 36/1: 584; Gordon C. Rhea, *To the North Anna River: Grant and Lee, May 13–25, 1864* (Baton Rouge: Louisiana State University Press), p. 15.
17. Salter to Duffield, May 15, 1864, Duffield Papers.
18. Ibid.; Fox, *Regimental Losses,* p. 387; a May 20 letter from an anonymous sergeant, published in Detroit, reported the 16th Michigan had by that point lost eight men killed, fifty-six wounded, and eight missing: *Detroit Free Press,* May 26, 1864.
19. Rhea, *To the North Anna River,* pp. 67–74, 77; *OR,* 36/1: 584–85; Spear, *The Civil War Recollections,* p. 242; Pullen, *The Twentieth Maine,* p. 202; Apted diary, May 13–14, 1864; Hill diary, May 13–14, 1864.
20. Apted diary, May 14, 1864.
21. Hopper, "From Beverly Ford to Bottoms Bridge with the First Michigan Infantry," MOLLUS Papers, Michigan Commandery, Bentley Historical Library, University of Michigan, p. 8; Apted diary, May 15–16, 1864; Salter to Duffield, May 15 and 16, 1864, Duffield Papers; Dewitt Smith diary, May 15–16, 1864; Hill diary, May 16, 1864.
22. Salter to Duffield, May 19, 1864; Apted diary, May 17–18, 1864; Rhea, *To the North Anna River,* p. 153.

23. J. Gibbs to sister, May 19, 1864, Van Hoosen Papers; Rhea, *To the North Anna River,* pp. 159, 188; Salter to Duffield, May 19, 1864; Apted diary, May 19, 1864; Hill diary, May 17–19, 1864; Dewitt Smith diary, May 17–19, 1864; *Detroit Tribune,* May 25, 1864; Wert, *Sword of Lincoln,* p. 356.
24. Apted diary, May 20–22, 1864; Wert, *Sword of Lincoln,* p. 356; Salter to Duffield, June 7, 1864, Duffield Papers; *OR,* 36/1: 585; Hill diary, May 21, 1864.
25. Apted diary, May 22, 1864; Salter to Duffield, June 7, 1864, Duffield Papers; *OR,* 36/1: 585; Spear, *The Civil War Recollections,* p. 113; Nash, *A History of the Forty-fourth New York,* p. 193; Pullen, *The Twentieth Maine,* p. 204; Amos M. Judson, *A History of the Eighty-Third Regiment Pennsylvania Volunteers* (Erie: B. F. H. Lynn, 1865), p. 99.
26. Rhea, *To the North Anna River,* pp. 282–83, 287, 289–90; William H. Powell, *The Fifth Army Corps* (New York: G. P. Putnam's Sons, 1896), pp. 655–56; Spear, *The Civil War Recollections,* pp. 113–14.
27. Rhea, *To the North Anna River,* pp. 292–94, 306, 309; Spear, *The Civil War Recollections,* p. 114; Hill diary, May 24, 1864; Martin Bertera and Kim Crawford, *The 4th Michigan Infantry in the Civil War,* (East Lansing: Michigan State University Press 2010), p. 217; *OR,* 36/1: 585.
28. *OR,* 36/1: 582, 585, 589; Judson, *A History of the Eighty-Third Regiment,* p. 100; Salter to Duffield, June 7, 1864, Duffield Papers; Powell, *The Fifth Army Corps,* pp. 657–58; Apted diary, May 23–24, 1864; Rhea, *To the North Anna River,* p. 318.
29. Wert, *Sword of Lincoln,* pp. 358–60.
30. Apted diary, May 24–25, 1864; Hill diary, May 24–25, 1864; Salter to Duffield, June 7, 1864, Duffield Papers; *Detroit Advertiser and Tribune,* June 8, 1864; *Ionia Sentinel,* Oct. 14, 1897.

    Jacklin, who became known as one of the regiment's "historians" for the papers he wrote after the war, was not always careful with facts, and he may not have been accurate about the circumstances of his capture. He would state that he was made a prisoner as he was leading his regiment's skirmishers in the night attack in the woods at the rise called "Laurel Hill." Certainly Jacklin had directed his regiment's skirmishers at times, but Ellis Spear of the 20th Maine wrote that the fighting was over when Jacklin volunteered to find his way back to Union lines in the darkness to get orders for his regiment and the others detached that day to support the Third Division. See Spear, *The Civil War Recollections,* pp. 102, 344. Presumably Jacklin thought it was a more exciting tale when he claimed to have been captured in the fighting, rather than as he tried to find his way back after the clash was over.
31. Smith diary, May 26–27, 1864; Hill diary, May 26–27, 1864; Apted diary, May 26–27, 1864; Wert, *Sword of Lincoln,* p. 360; *OR,* 36/1: 585; Gordon C. Rhea, *Cold Harbor: Grant and Lee, May 13–25, 1864* (Baton Rouge: Louisiana State University Press, 2000), p. 58.
32. Apted, Smith, and Hill diaries, May 28, 1864; *OR,* 36/1: 543, 585.
33. Apted diary, May 29, 1864; *OR,* 36/1: 585 and 36/3: 302–4; Smith diary, May 29, 1864; Rhea, *Cold Harbor,* pp. 99–100; Hill diary, May 29, 1864.
34. Rhea, *Cold Harbor,* pp. 107–8, 118–20, 124–25; Powell, *The Fifth Army Corps,* pp. 661, 664–66; Apted diary, May 30, 1864.
35. Rhea, *Cold Harbor,* pp. 132, 139, 141; Powell, *The Fifth Army Corps,* pp. 665–66; *OR,* 36/1: 585; Apted diary, May 30, 1864; Hill diary, May 30, 1864.
36. Judson, *A History of the Eighty-Third Regiment,* p. 102; *OR,* 36/1: 585; Lackie's account of the Elliott's fatal wounding is in *Proceedings of the Third Brigade Association, First Division, Fifth Army Corps, Army*

of the Potomac, Held at the National Encampment of the G.A.R., Washington, D.C., vol. 3 (New York: River and Driver, 1900), p. 95.

37. *Proceedings of the Third Brigade Association,* vol. 3, p. 95; *OR,* 36/1: 585–86; Hill diary, May 31, 1864; Dewitt C. Smith diary, May 30, 1864; Pvt. Smith did nothing like a thorough chronicle of the events this day, and recorded nothing about the heavy skirmish fire as did others. Spear diary, May 30, 1864, in Spear, *The Civil War Recollections,* p. 246; Apted diary, May 30, 1864; Rhea, *Cold Harbor,* pp. 141, 143; Salter to Duffield, June 7, 1864, Duffield Papers; Fox, *Regimental Losses,* p. 387.
38. *OR,* 36/1: 586; Salter to Duffield, June 7, 1864, Duffield Papers; Dewitt C. Smith diary, May 31, 1864; Apted diary, May 31, 1864; Hill diary, May 31, 1864.
39. *OR,* 36/1: 586; Norval Welch explained in a letter sent later that summer to the Michigan Adjutant General that, in his absence, the brigade commander appointed Fuller and Partridge to these command positions: Welch to Robertson, July 23, 1864, 16th Michigan Records, Archives of Michigan, Lansing; Apted diary, June 1, 1864.
40. Hill diary, June 1, 1864; Carl Guarneri and Alyssa Sisco, "When Will the End Come?," essay on Edward Hill, Library of St. Mary's College of California, posted online with the transcription of the Hill diary by the library of St. Mary's College of California.
41. Wert, *Sword of Lincoln,* p. 361; Salter to Duffield, June 7, 1864; Apted diary, June 1, 1864.
42. Rhea, *Cold Harbor,* pp. 209, 213, 267; Powell, *The Fifth Army Corps,* pp. 670–71; Apted diary, June 1, 1864; Salter to Duffield, June 7, 1864.
43. Wert, *Sword of Lincoln,* p. 361; *OR,* 36/1: 586; Apted diary, June 1, 1864; Dewitt C. Smith diary, June 1, 1864.
44. Rhea, *Cold Harbor,* pp. 282–83, 296; Powell, *The Fifth Army Corps,* pp. 671–72.
45. Wert, *Sword of Lincoln,* pp. 362–64; Spear, *The Civil War Recollections,* pp. 116, 247; Salter to Duffield, June 7, 1864; Apted diary, June 2, 1864; *OR,* 36/1: 586.
46. Judson, *A History of the Eighty-Third Regiment,* pp. 102–3; Powell, *The Fifth Army Corps,* p. 673; Jno. Robertson, *Michigan in the War* (Lansing: W. S. George, 1882), p. 372; *OR,* 36/1: 586; Salter to Duffield, June 7, 1864; "Roll of Honor, Sixteenth Michigan," in *Proceedings of the Third Brigade Association,* vol. 3, pp. 118, 140; Apted diary, June 2, 1864; Dewitt C. Smith diary, June 2, 1864.
47. Wert, *Sword of Lincoln,* pp. 364, 366; Rhea, *Cold Harbor,* p. 359; Apted diary, June 3, 1864; *OR,* 36/1: 586; Fox, *Regimental Losses,* p. 387; Salter to Duffield, June 7, 1864.
48. Salter to Duffield, June 7, 1864, Duffield Papers.

CHAPTER 17. JUNE–SEPTEMBER 1864: I AM NOT MUCH MORE THAN A SHADOW

1. Apted diary, June 4, 1864 (transcript), Fredericksburg and Spotsylvania National Park; Michigan Adjutant-General's Dept., *Record of Service of Michigan Volunteers in the Civil War, 1861–1865* (Kalamazoo: Ihling Bros. & Everard, 1905), vol. 16, p. 86. A form sent to the Michigan Adjutant General from the regiment, dated April 28, 1865, told of Jardine's dismissal. This is in 16th Michigan Records, Archives of Michigan, Lansing; it gives no reason as to what Jardine did to warrant his removal from the army.

2. Apted diary, June 5 and 6, 1864; Ellis Spear, *The Civil War Recollections of Gen. Ellis Spear* (Orono: University of Maine Press, 1997), p. 118; *Official Records* (*OR*), 36/1: 540 and 36/3: 666; Salter to Duffield, June 7, 1864, Duffield Papers, Burton Historical Collection, Detroit Public Library.
3. Salter to Duffield, June 7, 1864, Duffield Papers; Francis D. "Frank" Keeler, *War Letters Written during the Rebellion* (Saginaw: Julian A. Keeler, 1895), June 10, 1864; Apted diary, June 7–9, 1864; Gordon C. Rhea, "Grant's Disengagement from Cold Harbor," in *Cold Harbor to the Crater*, ed. Gary W. Gallagher and Caroline E. Janney (Chapel Hill: North Carolina University Press, 2015), pp. 177–78; *OR,* 40/1: 466–67.
4. Salter to Duffield, June 12, 1864, Duffield Papers.
5. Jeffry D. Wert, *Sword of Lincoln: The Army of the Potomac* (New York: Simon & Schuster, 2005), p. 370; *OR,* 40/1: 466–67; Salter to Duffield, June 12, 1864; Rhea, "Grant's Disengagement from Cold Harbor," pp. 188–90, 193–94, 197–98.
6. Salter to Duffield, June 21, 1864, Duffield Papers; Smith diary, June 14, 15, and 16, 1864, Special Collections, University of Virginia Library; William H. Powell, *The Fifth Army Corps* (New York: G. P. Putnam's Sons, 1896), p. 699; Spear, *The Civil War Recollections,* p. 250.
7. Wert, *Sword of Lincoln,* p. 371; Salter to Duffield, June 21, 1864, Duffield Papers; Bruce Catton, *A Stillness at Appomattox,* (Garden City, N.Y.: Doubleday, 1953), p. 191; *OR,* 40/1: 466–67.
8. Salter to Duffield, June 21, 1864, Duffield Papers; Smith diary, June 17 and 18, 1864; *OR,* 40/1: 466–67 and 40/2: 120, 179, 205; Powell, *Fifth Army Corps,* p. 701; Edward G. Longacre, *Joshua Chamberlain: The Soldier and the Man* (Conshohocken, Pa.: Combined Publishing, 1999), pp. 193, 195–96.
9. Horace Porter, *Battles and Leaders of the Civil War* (New York: Thomas Yoseloff, 1956), vol. 4, p. 543; Salter to Duffield, June 24, 1864, Duffield Papers.
10. Kydd to McRoberts (William's brother), (photocopy), June 29, 1864, from U.S. Pension files, copy in 16th Michigan file, Gettysburg National Military Park (GNMP); Smith diary, June 20, 1864.
11. *OR,* 40/1: 454, 467; Salter to Duffield, June 21 (continued on June 22), 1864, Duffield Papers; Smith diary, June 21, 1864; Wert, *Sword of Lincoln,* pp. 376–77.
12. Salter to Duffield, July 4, 1864, Duffield Papers; Smith diary, June 23, 1864.
13. Salter to Duffield, July 4, 1864, Duffield Papers; Keeler, *War Letters,* June 26 and July 5, 1864.
14. Welch to Robertson, July 23, 1864, 16th Michigan Records, Archives of Michigan, Lansing.
15. Ibid.
16. Salter to Duffield, June 21 and July 4, 1864, Duffield Papers; Keeler, *War Letters,* July 5 and July 16, 1864; Willam H. Powell, "The Battle of the Petersburg Crater," in *Battles and Leaders of the Civil War* (New York: Thomas Yoseloff, 1956), vol. 4, pp. 545–46.
17. Salter to Duffield, July 14, 1864; Keeler, *War Letters,* July 16, 1864; Smith diary, June 24, 1864.
18. Craw to Dear Friends, July 14, 1864, Mattoon Family Papers, University Archives and Historical Collections, Michigan State University; Michigan Adjutant-General's Dept., *Record of Service,* vol. 16, p. 42.
19. Salter to Duffield, July 14, 1864, Duffield Papers.
20. Salter to Duffield, July 14 and July 21, 1864; Keeler, *War Letters,* July 17, 1864.
21. Keeler, *War Letters,* July 17, 1864; Salter to Duffield, July 21, 1864, Duffield Papers.
22. Special Order No. 189, Army of the Potomac, July 16, 1864, for raising a First Division

sharpshooters battalion, 44th New York file, Gettysburg National Military Park; Salter to Duffield, July 21, 1864, Duffield Papers; *Detroit Advertiser and Tribune,* Aug. 3, 1864.

23. Keeler, *War Letters,* July 17, 1864.
24. Salter to Duffield, July 28–29, 1864, Duffield Papers; Longacre, *Joshua Chamberlain,* p. 203; *OR,* 40/1: 255 and 40/3: 732; Smith diary, July 22, 1864.
25. Salter to Duffield, Aug. 1, 1864, Duffield Papers; Smith diary, July 30, 1864.
26. Salter to Duffield, Aug. 1, 1864; Wert, *Sword of Lincoln,* pp. 383–84.
27. Salter to Duffield, Aug. 1, 1864.
28. Smith diary, July 31, Aug. 1–13, 1864; Spear, *The Civil War Recollections,* pp. 146, 257.
29. Apted diary (transcript), June 9, 11–13, 1864.
30. Apted diary, July 11–18, Aug. 8, 13, and 14, 1864; Wert, *Sword of Lincoln,* p. 387; William F. Fox, *Regimental Losses in the American Civil War* (Albany: Albany Publishing, 1889), p. 387.
31. Salter to Duffield, Aug. 17, 1864, Duffield Papers.
32. Powell, *Fifth Army Corps,* pp. 710–13; Salter to Duffield, Aug. 23, 1864, Duffield Papers; *OR,* 42/1: 469–70; and 40/2: 250–52; Smith diary, Aug. 18, 1864.
33. Salter to Duffield, Aug. 23, 1864, Duffield Papers; Powell, *Fifth Army Corps,* p. 715; *Wolverine Citizen,* Sept. 3, 1864.
34. Powell, *Fifth Army Corps,* p. 717; Survivors' Association, 118th Corn Exchange, Pennsylvania Volunteers, *History of the Corn Exchange Regiment, 118th Pennsylvania Volunteers* (Philadelphia: J. L. Smith, 1888), pp. 506–7.
35. Salter to Duffield, Aug. 23, 1864, Duffield Papers.
36. Ibid.; Noah Andre Trudeau, *The Last Citadel: Petersburg, Virginia, June 1864–April 1865* (Baton Rouge: Louisiana University Press, 1993), p. 173.
37. Smith diary, Aug. 21, 24, 26 and Sept. 12, 24, 1864, and other dates ending with March 2, (1865); Michigan Adjutant-General's Dept., *Record of Service,* vol. 16, p. 148. In the regiment's postwar "Roll of Honor, Sixteenth Michigan," published in 1900 in vol. 3 of the Third Brigade Association's reunion books, Smith is listed on p. 140 as having been reported in October 1864 as "wounded," and with no record of his being discharged from the army. Of course, Smith was captured in August outside of Petersburg, and did not mention that he was wounded. If Smith survived Confederate prison, perhaps he was never formally discharged.
38. Salter to Duffield, Aug. 23 and Sept. 2, 1864, Duffield Papers; *OR,* 42/1: 469–70; Fox, *Regimental Losses,* p. 387.
39. Salter to Duffield, Sept. 2 and Sept. 12, 1864, Duffield Papers.
40. *Detroit Advertiser and Tribune,* Sept. 15, 1864; Salter to Duffield, Sept. 12, 1864, Duffield Papers.

CHAPTER 18. SEPTEMBER–DECEMBER 1864: THE WORST FIRE A MORTAL EVER ENDURED

1. Salter to Duffield, Sept. 12, 1862, Duffield Papers, Burton Historical Collection, Detroit Public Library.
2. *Wolverine Citizen,* Sept. 17, 1864; S. Aplin to G. Aplin, Oct. 9, 1864, Aplin Family Papers, Schoff

Civil War Collection, William L. Clements Library, University of Michigan.

3. Salter to Duffield, Sept. 20, 1864, Duffield Papers.
4. Apted diary (transcript), Sept. 30, 1864, Fredericksburg and Spotsylvania National Park; Salter to Duffield, Oct. 5, 1864, Duffield Papers; Eugene Arus Nash, *A History of the Forty-fourth Regiment New York Volunteer Infantry in the Civil War, 1861–1865* (Chicago: R. R. Donnelley, 1911), pp. 185–86; Ellis Spear, *The Civil War Recollections of General Ellis Spear* (Orono: University of Maine Press, 1997), p. 150.
5. William H. Powell, *The Fifth Army Corps* (New York: G. P. Putnam's Sons, 1896), pp. 729–31; Noah Andre Trudeau, *The Last Citadel: Petersburg, Virginia, June 1864–April 1865* (Baton Rouge: Louisiana University Press, 1993), p. 212; John J. Pullen, *The Twentieth Maine* (Philadelphia and New York: J. B. Lippincott, 1957), p. 255; Salter to Duffield, Oct. 5, 1864, Duffield Papers; Apted diary, Sept. 30, 1864; Survivors' Association, 118th Corn Exchange, Pennsylvania Volunteers, *History of the Corn Exchange Regiment, 118th Pennsylvania Volunteers* (Philadelphia: J. L. Smith, 1888), p. 514.
6. Apted diary, Sept. 30, 1864; Salter to Duffield, Oct. 5, 1864, Duffield Papers; *Official Records* (*OR*), 42/2: 1132; *Detroit Free Press,* Oct. 5, 1864; Powers's account, signed "Veritas," *Detroit Advertiser and Tribune,* Oct. 6, 1864; "Roll of Honor, 16th Michigan," in *Proceedings of the Third Brigade Association, First Division, Fifth Army Corps, Army of the Potomac, Held at the National Encampment of the G.A.R., Washington, D.C.* (New York: River and Driver, 1900), vol. 3, p. 144.
7. Survivors' Association, *History of the Corn Exchange Regiment,* p. 514. This book was authored by the regiment's Survivors' Association, veterans who experienced the war firsthand. Salter to Duffield, Oct. 5, 1864, Duffield Papers; Lackie's account, *Proceedings of the Third Brigade Association,* vol. 3, p. 91.
8. Salter to Duffield, Oct. 5, and Oct. 23, 1864, Duffield Papers; *Detroit Advertiser and Tribune,* Oct. 6, 1864; Partridge to J. Robertson, Dec. 17, 1865, and a second letter quoting his diary for Sept. 30, 1864, dated Dec. 28, 1866, both in 16th Michigan Records, Archives of Michigan, Lansing. Ellis Spear noted in his diary, and also wrote later, that one of the generals saw Partridge wounded and told Spear he had been killed, as was Welch. Of course, Partridge was not killed. See Spear, *The Civil War Recollections,* pp. 167, 261.
9. Salter to Duffield, Oct. 5, 1864, Duffield Papers; Spear, *The Civil War Recollections,* p. 146. Spear wrote after the war that he declined to take the Lindsay rifle for his men because he had seen it used previously and was aware of its shortcomings, though he did not say by which regiment or in what battle. Today's antique firearms experts and dealers believe the 16th Michigan was the only regiment to have soldiers use it in action. Again, it is not at all clear how many soldiers had the rifle. Experts say only 1,000 of them were made, which would mean that every soldier in the 16th Michigan could have conceivably carried one.
10. Salter to Duffield, Oct. 5, 1864, Duffield Papers. For the record, Gen. Orlando Willcox, Detroiter and commander of a division of the Ninth Corps, said only one of his brigades broke in the fighting and that "the rest of my division held firm." See Robert Garth Scott, ed., *Forgotten Valor: The Memoirs, Journals & Civil War Letters of Orlando B. Willcox* (Kent, Ohio: Kent State University Press, 1999), p. 576.
11. Salter to Duffield, Oct. 5, 1864, Duffield Papers; Apted diary, Sept. 30–Oct. 2, 1864; Don Farrant, "The Worst Fire a Mortal Endured," *Grand Rapids Press,* April 15, 1984; Salter to Duffield, Oct. 5,

1864, Duffield Papers; William F. Fox, *Regimental Losses in the American Civil War* (Albany: Albany Publishing, 1889), p. 387.

12. H. Aplin to S. Aplin (partial letter, Oct. 1864?), Schoff Civil War Collection; Rufus W. Jacklin, "The Famous Old Third Brigade," in *War Papers,* vol. 2, Michigan Commandery Military Order of the Loyal Legion of the United States. (Detroit: James H. Stone, 1898), p. 48; *Detroit Free Press,* Oct. 5, 1864; *Michigan (Ann Arbor) Argus,* Oct. 7, 1864.
13. Salter to Duffield, Oct. 5, 1864, Duffield Papers.
14. Salter to Duffield, Oct. 15, 1864, Duffield Papers; Michigan Adjutant-General's Dept., *Record of Service of Michigan Volunteers in the Civil War, 1861–1865* (Kalamazoo: Ihling Bros. & Everard, 1905), vol. 16, p. 54.
15. Salter to Duffield, Oct. 15, 1864, Duffield Papers. Salter, like many or most Union soldiers, generally referred to Confederate cavalry raiders as guerillas even if they were members of designated troops or regiments; some such attacks were truly mounted by irregulars. The story about the 16th Michigan's fight at Peeble's Farm, written by Capt. Powers under the pseudonym "Veritas," appeared in the *Detroit Advertiser and Tribune*'s p.m. edition on Oct. 6, 1864. In it, the first reference to Salter was written as "Capt. S.," though the later references to Salter were mistakenly rendered as "Capt. H." This was probably an editor's or typesetter's error. There was no "Capt. H." in the regiment at the battle.
16. Salter to Duffield, Oct. 23, 1864, Duffield Papers; Partridge to J. Robertson, Oct. 23, 1864, 16th Michigan Records, Archives of Michigan, Lansing.
17. Powell, *The Fifth Army Corps,* pp. 736–44; Trudeau, *The Last Citadel,* pp. 231–32, 243–44; Salter to Duffield, Nov. 6, 1864, Duffield Papers.
18. Powell, *The Fifth Army Corps,* pp. 736–44; Trudeau, *The Last Citadel,* 243–44; Salter to Duffield, Nov. 6, 1864, Duffield Papers.
19. Salter to Duffield, Nov. 6, 1864, Duffield Papers.
20. Salter to Duffield, Nov. 20, 1864, Duffield Papers; Jeffry D. Wert, *Sword of Lincoln: The Army of the Potomac* (New York: Simon & Schuster, 2005), p. 391.
21. Salter to Duffield, Nov. 20, 1864, Duffield Papers.
22. *Detroit Advertiser and Tribune,* Jan. 23, 1865.
23. Ibid.
24. Ibid.; Michigan Adjutant-General's Dept., *Record of Service,* vol. 16, p. 90.
25. Salter to Duffield, Dec. 4, 1864, Duffield Papers.
26. Salter to Duffield, Dec. 13, 1864, Duffield Papers; Charles F. McKenna, ed., *Under the Maltese Cross, Antietam to Appomattox: The Loyal Uprising in Western Pennsylvania, 1861–1865, Campaigns 155th Pennsylvania Regiment* (Pittsburg: The 155th Regimental Association, 1910), p. 326.
27. Salter to Duffield, Dec. 13, 1864, Duffield Papers; Powell, *The Fifth Army Corps,* pp. 749–51; Spear, *The Civil War Recollections,* p. 159; *OR,* 42/1: 443–45.
28. Pullen, *The Twentieth Maine,* p. 233; McKenna, *Under the Maltese Cross,* pp. 328–30; James I. Robertson Jr., *The Civil War Letters of General Robert McAllister* (New Brunswick: Rutgers University Press, 1965), p. 558; Munson to Van Hoosen, Dec. 30, 1864, Van Hoosen Papers, Bentley Historical Library, University of Michigan. The reported murder (or possible desertion) of Byrman/Dryman and summary execution of Shay/Shea are given in the regiment's "Roll of Honor" in *Proceedings of*

the Third Brigade Association, vol. 3, pp. 115, 117.

29. Salter to Duffield, Dec. 13, 1864, Duffield Papers; Munson to Van Hoosen, Dec. 30, 1864, Van Hoosen Papers.
30. Ellis Spear diary, Dec. 14 and 17, 1864, in Spear, *The Civil War Recollections,* p. 264; Salter to Duffield, Dec. 13, 1864, Duffield Papers.
31. Munson to Van Hoosen, Dec. 30, 1864, Van Hoosen Papers. The Civil War was practically over when Major Hill, having learned that Partridge recommended he be promoted to lieutenant colonel, wrote to the Michigan Adjutant General and asked that his commission be sent to him in Jackson. This is in Hill to Robertson, May 4, 1865, 16th Michigan Records, Archives of Michigan. Hill wrote then that he expected to be leaving shortly to join the regiment in Virginia, where hostilities had ended with Lee's surrender a month before. Other records show he joined the regiment in camp "near Washington" about a week later.

CHAPTER 19. DECEMBER 1864–APRIL 1865: A BLUE WHIPLASH ENCIRCLING LEE

1. Charles F. McKenna, ed., *Under the Maltese Cross, Antietam to Appomattox: The Loyal Uprising in Western Pennsylvania, 1861–1865, Campaigns 155th Pennsylvania Regiment* (Pittsburg: The 155th Regimental Association, 1910), pp. 330–31; *Official Records* (*OR*), 42/1: 443–44; James McPherson, *Battle Cry of Freedom* (New York: Oxford University Press, 1988), pp. 816–19; Survivors' Association, 118th Corn Exchange, Pennsylvania Volunteers, *History of the Corn Exchange Regiment, 118th Pennsylvania Volunteers* (Philadelphia: J. L. Smith, 1888), p. 544.
2. Partridge to Robertson, Dec. 17, 1865, 16th Michigan Records, Archives of Michigan, Lansing; Memorial report, *Michigan Pioneer and Historical Collections* (Lansing: Michigan Historical Commission/Pioneer Society of Michigan, 1877–1929), vol. 26, pp. 32–33; Tim Younkman, "Bay City's Forgotten Hero," *Bay City Times,* Nov. 12, 1989; *Confederate Veteran* 8 (October 1900): 446.
3. *OR,* 46/1: 150–51, 253.
4. Ibid., 149–50, 253–54, 270–71; Noah Andre Trudeau, *The Last Citadel: Petersburg, Virginia, June 1864–April 1865* (Baton Rouge: Louisiana University Press, 1993), pp. 313–16; Survivors' Association, *History of the Corn Exchange Regiment,* pp. 549–20.
5. Survivors' Association, *History of the Corn Exchange Regiment,* p. 549; *OR,* 46/1: 254–55, 270–71.
6. *OR,* 46/1: 254–55, 271; Trudeau, *The Last Citadel,* pp. 318–19; Survivors' Association, *History of the Corn Exchange Regiment,* p. 551.
7. Survivors' Association, *History of the Corn Exchange Regiment,* pp. 552–53; *OR,* 46/1: 271; Trudeau, *The Last Citadel,* p. 320; Partridge to Robertson, Dec. 17, 1865, 16th Michigan Records, Archives of Michigan; *Detroit Advertiser and Tribune,* Feb. 17, 1865.
8. *OR,* 46/1: 271; *Detroit Free Press,* Feb. 17, 1865; McKenna, *Under the Maltese Cross,* pp. 332–33; Amos M. Judson, *History of the Eighty-third Regiment Pennsylvania Volunteers* (Erie: B. F. H. Lynn, 1865), p. 110; John J. Pullen, *The Twentieth Maine* (Philadelphia and New York: J. B. Lippincott, 1957), p. 238.
9. *Detroit Advertiser and Tribune,* Feb. 17, 1865; *OR,* 46/1: 272; Trudeau, *The Last Citadel,* p. 320.

10. *OR,* 46/1: 65, 271–72; William F. Fox, *Regimental Losses in the American Civil War* (Albany: Albany Publishing, 1889), p. 387. While Pearson identified Laird as the 16th Michigan's adjutant, regimental records indicate that a soldier named Duncan McNaughton of Bay City, who had come into the regiment with Jardine's Sharpshooters, was Partridge's adjutant. Lists of the regiment's wounded in this battle, including Munson, appeared in the *Detroit Free Press* and the *Detroit Advertiser and Tribune* on Feb. 17, 1865.
11. McKenna, *Under the Maltese Cross,* pp. 334, 337–38; *OR,* 46/2: 550, 564; Francis Parker, *The Story of the Thirty-second Regiment Massachusetts Infantry, Massachusetts Volunteer Infantry* (Boston: C. W. Calkins, 1880), p. 243.
12. Partridge to Robertson, Feb. 19, 1865, 16th Michigan Records, Archives of Michigan; Visscher, to his mother, Feb. 21, 1865, in Harvey L. Visher, "The Student Volunteer" (n.p., n.d.), Bentley Historical Library, University of Michigan. Two versions of this manuscript article, undated and apparently unpublished, are at the Bentley Historical Library, University of Michigan. The articles are similar in content, drawing from the family genealogy, documents, and the letters of William Visscher.
13. Visscher to family, Feb. 27, 1865, in Visher, "The Student Volunteer."
14. Ibid., March 15, 1865; E. Aplin to G. Aplin, March 28, 1865, Aplin Family Papers, Schoff Civil War Collection, William L. Clements Library, University of Michigan.
15. Jeffry D. Wert, *Sword of Lincoln: The Army of the Potomac* (New York: Simon & Schuster, 2005), pp. 397–98.
16. *OR,* 46/1: 273–76, 675–76, and 46/3: 112–13,
17. Visscher to family, March 25, 1865, in Visher, "The Student Volunteer"; McKenna, *Under the Maltese Cross,* p.339; *OR,* 46/1: 274–75.
18. Visscher to family, March 25, 1865, in Visher, "The Student Volunteer"; McKenna, *Under the Maltese Cross,* 339; *OR,* 46/1: 274–75.
19. Visscher to family, March 25, 1865, in Visher, "The Student Volunteer."
20. Wert, *Sword of Lincoln,* p. 399; William H. Powell, *The Fifth Army Corps* (New York: G. P. Putnam's Sons, 1896), pp. 744–75; Pullen, *The Twentieth Maine,* p. 241; Horace Porter, *Battles and Leaders of the Civil War* (New York: Thomas Yoseloff, 1956), vol. 4, p. 708.
21. Powell, *The Fifth Army Corps,* p. 776; *OR,* 46/1: 799–800, 845–46.
22. *OR,* 46/1: 800–1, 803, 846; Powell, *The Fifth Army Corps,* 777; Fox, *Regimental Losses,* p. 387; McKenna, *Under the Maltese Cross,* p. 345.
23. *OR,* 46/1: 803–10, 846; *Powell, The Fifth Army Corps,* pp. 778–80.
24. Powell, *The Fifth Army Corps,* pp. 780–82; *OR,* 46/1: 813–15; Wert, *Sword of Lincoln,* p. 490; Survivors' Association, *History of the Corn Exchange Regiment,* pp. 568–69.
25. Survivors' Association, *History of the Corn Exchange Regiment,* p. 569; *OR,* 46/1: 846; Powell, *The Fifth Army Corps,* p. 783; Partridge to Robertson, Dec. 17, 1865, 16th Michigan Records, Archives of Michigan; Spear, *The Civil War Recollections,* 167.
26. *OR,* 46/1: 819, 846, 849; Ellis Spear, *The Civil War Recollections of Gen. Ellis Spear* (Orono: University of Maine Press, 1997), p. 168.
27. Horace Porter, "Five Forks and the Pursuit of Lee," in *Battles and Leaders of the Civil War* (New York: Thomas Yoseloff, 1956), vol. 4, pp. 708–11; Wert. *Sword of Lincoln,* p. 400.

28. *OR,* 46/1: 817, 821; Pullen, *The Twentieth Maine,* p. 249; Powell, *The Fifth Army Corps,* pp. 786–87; Survivors' Association, *History of the Corn Exchange Regiment,* pp. 572–73.
29. Powell, *The Fifth Army Corps,* p. 788; *OR,* 46/1: 817–18; Survivors' Association, *History of the Corn Exchange Regiment,* p. 575. It appears that only the 20th Maine was identified in accounts as one of the regiments that moved southwest with Bartlett that evening and skirmished with Confederates north of Dinwiddie Court House.
30. A detailed explanation of the situation confronting Warren as he tried to move his men to Sheridan's aid is in Powell, *The Fifth Army Corps,* pp. 789–99. Warren explained it in *OR,* 46/1: 817–27.
31. Pullen, *The Twentieth Maine,* p. 250; Powell, *The Fifth Army Corps,* p. 797; *OR,* 46/1: 824; Survivors' Association, *History of the Corn Exchange Regiment,* p. 574.
32. *Detroit Free Press,* April 6, 1865; *OR,* 46/1: 827. Streeter's name is also spelled as Strever, Sheever, and even Stubel, while McCrory is listed in the state's *Record of Service* roster of the 16th Michigan as "McCrony."
33. *OR,* 46/1: 825–26, 838; Porter, "Five Forks and the Pursuit of Lee," in *Battles and Leaders of the Civil War,* vol. 4, p. 411.
34. *OR,* 46/1: 829; Powell, *The Fifth Army Corps,* pp. 800, 802–803; Porter, "Five Forks and the Pursuit of Lee," in *Battles and Leaders of the Civil War,* vol. 4, pp. 711–12.
35. Porter, "Five Forks and the Pursuit of Lee," pp. 712–14; Wert, *Sword of Lincoln,* p. 401; *OR,* 46/1: 830.
36. *OR,* 46/1: 330; Powell, *The Fifth Army Corps,* pp. 803–4.
37. Powell, *The Fifth Army Corps,* pp. 805–6; *OR,* 46/1: 861; Pullen, *The Twentieth Maine,* pp. 254–55.
38. Powell, *The Fifth Army Corps,* pp. 805–6; *OR,* 46/1: 866.
39. McKenna, *Under the Maltese Cross,* p. 351; Powell, *The Fifth Army Corps,* pp. 808–9.
40. *OR,* 46/1: 827, 861; Powell, *The Fifth Army Corps,* p. 809; McKenna, *Under the Maltese Cross,* pp. 352–53; Survivors' Association, *History of the Corn Exchange Regiment,* p. 582; Spear, *The Civil War Recollections,* p. 176; Wert, *Sword of Lincoln,* pp. 401–2; Horace Porter, "General Warren at Five Forks and the Court of Inquiry" in *Battles and Leaders of the Civil War* (New York: Thomas Yoseloff, 1956), vol. 4, pp. 723–24.
41. Wert, *Sword of Lincoln,* pp. 403–4; Powell, *The Fifth Army Corps,* pp. 831–32; McKenna, *Under the Maltese Cross,* p. 354; Survivors' Association, *History of the Corn Exchange Regiment,* pp. 583–84.
42. Powell, *The Fifth Army Corps,* pp. 832, 836–837; Survivors' Association, *History of the Corn Exchange Regiment,* p. 584; *OR,* 46/1: 839, 862; McKenna, *Under the Maltese Cross,* p. 356.
43. *OR,* 46/1: 862; Wert, *Sword of Lincoln,* pp. 405–6; Survivors' Association, *History of the Corn Exchange Regiment,* pp. 584–85; McKenna, *Under the Maltese Cross,* pp. 356–57; Powell, *The Fifth Army Corps,* p. 838; Spear, *The Civil War Recollections,* p. 178.
44. *OR,* 46/1: 839, 840–41; Porter, "Five Forks and the Pursuit of Lee," p. 720; Wert, *Sword of Lincoln,* p. 406.
45. Survivors' Association, *History of the Corn Exchange Regiment,* pp. 585–86; McKenna, *Under the Maltese Cross,* p. 357.
46. Survivors' Association, *History of the Corn Exchange Regiment,* pp. 586–87; Wert, *Sword of Lincoln,* p. 406.
47. Thomas R. Lackie, "Reminiscences of Appomattox," *Confederate Veteran* 8 (March 1900): 123; *OR,*

46/1: 841; Spear, *The Civil War Recollections,* pp. 179–80; Survivors' Association, *History of the Corn Exchange Regiment,* p. 587. Lackie's article in *Confederate Veteran* was substantially similar to an account he wrote for the Union veteran's newspaper: "Peace at Appomattox," *National Tribune,* Feb. 18, 1897.

48. Wert, *Sword of Lincoln,* p. 408; McKenna, *Under the Maltese Cross,* p. 359; Alfred Pearson, "Address of Gen. A. L. Pearson," *Proceedings of the Third Brigade Association, First Division, Fifth Army Corps, Army of the Potomac, Held at the National Encampment of the G.A.R., Washington. D.C., Sept. 21, 1892* (New York: River and Driver, n.d.). William Powell, a Union officer and later author of a history of the Fifth Corps, included the anecdote of the soldiers singing "Damn-Dan Butterfield" in *The Fifth Army Corps* (New York: G.P. Putnam's Sons, 1896), p. 849.
49. Joshua L. Chamberlain, "The Third Brigade at Appomattox," reproduced in Oliver W. Norton, *Attack and Defense of Little Round Top* (Dayton: Morningside Books, 1983), p. 333; Pearson, "Address of Gen. A. L. Pearson," p. 53; Powell, *The Fifth Army Corps,* pp. 849–50; Survivors' Association, *History of the Corn Exchange Regiment,* p. 588.
50. Survivors' Association, *History of the Corn Exchange Regiment,* p. 588; Lackie, "Reminiscences of Appomattox," p. 123; Hoeninghausen anecdote, an Ann Arbor newspaper clipping, "miscellaneous" Civil War materials, Burton Historical Collection, Detroit Public Library.
51. Lackie, "Reminiscences of Appomattox," p. 123, and "Peace at Appomattox"; *OR,* 46/1: 841.
52. Lackie, "Reminiscences of Appomattox," 123, and "Peace at Appomattox"; McKenna, *Under the Maltese Cross,* pp. 359–60; Chamberlain, "The Third Brigade at Appomattox," p. 336; *OR,* 46/1: 841, 852; Spear, *The Civil War Recollections,* p. 181; Survivors' Association, *History of the Corn Exchange Regiment,* p. 589; Rufus W. Jacklin, "The Famous Old Third Brigade," in *War Papers,* vol. 2, Michigan Commandery Military Order of the Loyal Legion of the United States (Detroit: James H. Stone, 1898), vol. 2, p. 49.
53. Lackie, "Reminiscences of Appomattox," p. 123, and "Peace at Appomattox."
54. Lackie, "Peace at Appomattox."
55. Sims's letter describing his actions that day is in Survivors' Association, *History of the Corn Exchange Regiment,* pp. 590–591. Confederate flags of truce: Frank P. Cauble, *The Surrender Proceedings, April 9, 1865, Appomattox Court House* (Lynchburg: H. E. Howard, 1987), pp. 31–34.
56. Jacklin, *The Famous Old Third Brigade,* p. 49; Survivors' Association, *History of the Corn Exchange Regiment,* pp. 589–90; McKenna, *Under the Maltese Cross,* pp. 360, 362, 380, 618; Lackie, "Peace at Appomattox."

CHAPTER 20. APRIL–JULY 1865: THINK OF THE NOBLE SPIRITS WE LOST

1. Thomas R. Lackie, "Peace at Appomattox," *National Tribune,* Washington, D.C., Feb. 18, 1897; Ellis Spear, *The Civil War Recollections of General Ellis Spear* (Orono: University of Maine Press, 1997), p. 181; Survivors' Association, 118th Corn Exchange, Pennsylvania Volunteers, *History of the Corn Exchange Regiment, 118th Pennsylvania Volunteers* (Philadelphia: J. L. Smith, 1888), pp. 591–92.
2. Horace Porter, "The Surrender at Appomattox Court House," in *Battles and Leaders of the Civil War*

(New York: Thomas Yoseloff, 1956), vol. 4, p. 737; *Official Records* (*OR*), 46/3: 666–67, 684–85.

3. Joshua L. Chamberlain, "The Third Brigade at Appomattox," reproduced in Oliver W. Norton, *Attack and Defense of Little Round Top* (Dayton: Morningside Books, 1983), p. 337; Visscher to family, April 18, 1865, in Harvey L. Visher, "The Student Volunteer" (n.p., n.d.), Bentley Historical Library, University of Michigan; Survivors' Association, 118th Corn Exchange, Pennsylvania Volunteers, *History of the Corn Exchange Regiment, 118th Pennsylvania Volunteers* (Philadelphia: J. L. Smith, 1888), pp. 592–93. Orders for receiving the surrender: *OR,* 46/3: 684–85 688–89.
4. Apple tree: William W. Blackford, *War Years with Jeb Stuart* (New York: Charles Scribner's Sons, 1946), pp. 291–93; Edward Porter Alexander, *Military Memoirs of a Confederate* (New York: Charles Scribner's Sons, 1907), p. 609; Edward Porter Alexander, *Fighting for the Confederacy* (Chapel Hill: University of North Carolina Press, 1989), p. 537; Survivors' Association, *History of the Corn Exchange Regiment,* p. 597; U. S. Grant, *Personal Memoirs of U. S. Grant,* (New York: Charles L. Webster, 1885), vol. 2, p. 488. John and Hollis Parker: Michigan Adjutant-General's Dept., *Record of Service of Michigan Volunteers in the Civil War, 1861–1865* (Kalamazoo: Ihling Bros. & Everard, 1905), vol. 16, pp. 125, 126; *Flint Journal,* July 7, 1963; 1860 census, Argentine Township, schedule 1, p. 367; "Roll of Honor, Sixteenth Michigan," in *Proceedings of the Third Brigade Association, First Division, Fifth Army Corps, Army of the Potomac, Held at the National Encampment of the G.A.R., Washington, D.C.* (New York: River and Driver, 1900), vol. 3, pp. 117–18.
5. Survivors' Association, *History of the Corn Exchange Regiment,* pp. 592–93; *OR,* 46/3: 691 (order to keep Fifth Corps soldiers from crossing into Confederate camps); Spear, *The Civil War Recollections,* April 10, 1865 diary entry, p. 272; Chamberlain, "The Third Brigade at Appomattox," p. 338; McLean's historic real estate in the Civil War: Porter, "The Surrender at Appomattox Court House," vol. 4, p. 743n.
6. A. S. Drewry, "Experiences on the Battle Line" [letter], *Confederate Veteran,* 8 (October 1900): 445–46.
7. Ibid.
8. Ibid. The surrender terms by the commanders' subordinates clearly stated that Confederate soldiers like Drewry were allowed to keep their privately owned horses. See *OR,* 46/3: 686, and Porter, "The Surrender at Appomattox Court House," p. 740.
9. Partridge to Robertson, Dec. 17, 1865, 16th Michigan Records, Archives of Michigan, Lansing.
10. Chamberlain, "The Third Brigade at Appomattox," p. 340; *OR,* 46/3: 691, 706; Spear diary, April 11, 1865, in Spear, *The Civil War Recollections;* Survivors' Association, *History of the Corn Exchange Regiment,* p. 593.
11. Chamberlain, "The Third Brigade at Appomattox," p. 140; Elizabeth R. Varon, *Appomattox: Victory, Defeat and Freedom at the End of the Civil War* (New York: Oxford University Press, 2013), p. 77; Survivors' Association, *History of the Corn Exchange Regiment,* pp. 594–95; *National Tribune,* March 20, 1913. In postwar letters to Oliver Norton, Spear was highly critical of Chamberlain's accounts, though his criticisms were sometimes themselves wrong. "So far as I have read, 'The Passing of the Armies' is a tissue of lies," Spear wrote about Chamberlain's book: Spear to Norton, Jan. 18, 1916, Oliver W. Norton Papers, Clarke Historical Library, Central Michigan University.
12. *Confederate Veteran,* 7 (Feb. 1899): 56, and (May 1899): 226; Thomas R. Lackie, "Reminiscences of Appomattox," *Confederate Veteran,* 8 (March 1900): 125; Lackie, "Peace at Appomattox." Maguire

was a veteran of Company A who had been wounded in fighting for Rebel rifle pits outside of Spotsylvania Court House; he was promoted to captain in May 1865.

13. Visscher to family, April 18, 1865, in Visher, "The Student Volunteer"; *OR,* 46/3: 734; Survivors' Association, *History of the Corn Exchange Regiment,* p. 593.
14. Roe to Robertson, July 22, 1864, 16th Michigan Records, Archives of Michigan; *OR,* 11/3: 243–44; 19/1: 127, 130; and 19/2: 31.
15. *OR,* ser. 3, 4: 829, 831.
16. Roe to Robertson, July 22, 1864, with enclosure, Maj. Gen. Nathaniel P. Banks to Roe, Feb. 10, 1864, in 16th Michigan Records, Archives of Michigan; Ella Roe Nichols told of her and her husband's life in the Civil War in unidentified newspaper stories dated May 14 and June 12, 1931, in the files of the Plymouth Historical Museum, Plymouth, Michigan. The clippings are identical in wording and content, essentially a historical feature story where the elderly Nichols was interviewed about her memories of the Civil War.
17. Ella Roe Nichols newspaper clippings, Plymouth Historical Museum.
18. Michigan Adjutant-General's Dept., *Record of Service,* vol. 16, p. 146; Evelyn Sidman Wachter, *Sidman–Sidnam Families of Upstate New York* (Baltimore: Gateway Press, 1981), pp. 260–61. There are hundreds of pages of witness statements from the Lincoln assassination and the Seward assassination attempt published and available to the public, but Sidman is not among them.
19. Unidentified newspaper (probably Owosso, Michigan) article about Sidman, April 20, 1911, miscellaneous Civil War file, Burton Historical Collection, Detroit Public Library. The Sidman genealogy quotes other local newspaper articles after 1900 where Sidman recounted his story of the assassination attempt on Seward.
20. Ella Roe Nichols newspaper clippings, Plymouth Historical Museum.
21. Sidman Wachter, *Sidman–Sidnam Families,* p. 262; clipping about Sidman, April 20, 1911, miscellaneous Civil War file, Burton Historical Collection.
22. William H. Powell, *The Fifth Army Corps* (New York: G. P. Putnam's Sons, 1896), pp. 869–70; Survivors' Association, *History of the Corn Exchange Regiment,* pp. 597–99; Spear, *The Civil War Recollections,* p. 185.
23. Visscher to family, April 26, 1865, in Visher, "The Student Volunteer."
24. E. Foster to her husband (photocopy), April 17, 1865, Foster Letters, Haas/Oswalt Collection, Archives and Regional History Collections, Western Michigan University.
25. Ibid.; also Foster marriage records, service records, and other biographical papers and letters part of the collection.
26. Survivors' Association, *History of the Corn Exchange Regiment,* 599–600.
27. Powell, *The Fifth Army Corps,* p. 871; Charles F. McKenna, ed., *Under the Maltese Cross, Antietam to Appomattox: The Loyal Uprising in Western Pennsylvania, 1861–1865, Campaigns 155th Pennsylvania Regiment* (Pittsburg: The 155th Regimental Association, 1910), pp. 377–79; Survivors' Association, *History of the Corn Exchange Regiment,* pp. 601–3.
28. Visscher to family, May 12, 1865, in Visher, "The Student Volunteer"; Spear, *The Civil War Recollections,* p. 189; Hill to Robertson, May 4, 1865, and Hill muster-in, May 11, 1865, "near Washington," in 16th Michigan Records, Archives of Michigan. Jack Wood's description of Hill being disabled from field duty is in Hill's records in the National Archives, quoted in an essay by

Prof. Carl Guarneri of St. Mary's College of California and then-student Alyssa Sisco. Hill's 1864 diary is held at the college's library: Carl Guarneri and Alyssa Sisco, "When Will the End Come?," essay on Edward Hill, Library of St. Mary's College of California.

29. Belcher family entry, genealogy notebooks, Perry Archives of the Sloan Museum, Flint, Michigan; Michigan Adjutant-General's Dept., *Record of Service,* vol. 16, p. 15; Foster to wife, May 20, 1865, Foster Letters, Haas/Oswalt Collection; Visscher to family, May 27, 1865, in Visher, "The Student Volunteer."
30. McKenna, *Under the Maltese Cross,* p. 509; Joshua L. Chamberlain, *The Passing of the Armies* (New York: G. P. Putnam's Sons, 1915), p. 329; Spear, *The Civil War Recollections,* p. 190; Belcher entry, genealogy notebooks, Perry Archives; Belcher gravestone, Glenwood Cemetery, Flint, Michigan. A note pasted into a 16th Michigan quartermaster book at the Bentley Historical Library, University of Michigan, states Belcher died at Ithaca, New York, on this date of "army dysentery."
31. Visscher to family, May 27, 1865, in Visher, "The Student Volunteer"; Foster to wife, May 27, 1865, Haas/Oswalt Collection; McKenna, *Under the Maltese Cross,* pp. 382–83; John J. Pullen, *The Twentieth Maine* (Philadelphia and New York: J. B. Lippincott, 1957), p. 288.
32. Spear, *The Civil War Recollections,* p. 190; *OR,* 46/3: 1255; Jeffry D. Wert, *Sword of Lincoln: The Army of the Potomac* (New York: Simon & Schuster, 2005), p. 413; Lackie postscript in *Confederate Veteran,* 8 (Oct. 1900): 446. Lackie's claim that Partridge caused the regiment to remain in the service after May 1865 cannot be confirmed and sounds like a "camp story."
33. Visscher to family, June 25, 1865, in Visher, "The Student Volunteer."
34. Ibid.; Foster to wife, June 29, 1865, Haas/Oswalt Collection.
35. Foster to wife, June 29, 1865, Haas/Oswalt Collection.
36. Visscher to family, July 5, 1865, in Visher, "The Student Volunteer."
37. Visscher to parents, July 14, in Visher, "The Student Volunteer"; *Detroit Free Press,* July 13, 1865.
38. *Detroit Advertiser and Tribune,* July 25, 1865.
39. Michigan Adjutant-General's Dept., *Record of Service,* vol. 16, p. 105; "Roll of Honor, Sixteenth Michigan," in *Proceedings of the Third Brigade Association,* vol. 3, p. 127; S. Aplin to G. Aplin, July 16, 1865, Aplin Family Papers, William L. Clements Library, University of Michigan.

EPILOGUE. YOUR NAMES ARE AN ETERNAL BENEDICTION

1. Harvey L. Visher, "The Student Volunteer" (n.p., n.d.), Bentley Historical Library, University of Michigan; Visscher obituary in *De Grondet,* Feb. 19, 1872, from the Joint Archives of Holland, Hope College.
2. "Biography" pages of the finding aid for the Aplin Family Papers, William L. Clements Library, University of Michigan; Aplin obituary, *Gladwin (Mich.) Record,* July 28, 1910; "Memoir of Henry Harrison Aplin," *Michigan Pioneer and Historical Collections* (Lansing: Michigan Historical Commission/Pioneer Society of Michigan, 1877–1929), vol. 38, pp. 677–78.
3. Michigan Adjutant-General's Dept., *Record of Service of Michigan Volunteers in the Civil War, 1861–1865* (Kalamazoo: Ihling Bros. & Everard, 1905), vol. 16, p. 122; James Cooke Mills, *History*

of Saginaw County (Saginaw: Seeman & Peters, 1918), p. 359; *Saginaw Courier-Herald,* Sept. 26, 1889; *Portrait and Biographical Record of Saginaw and Bay Counties, Michigan* (Chicago: Biographical Publishing Co., 1892), pp. 783–87.

4. C. B. Burr, *The Medical History of Michigan* (Minneapolis and St. Paul: Michigan State Medical Society and Bruce Publishing, 1930), vol. 2, pp. 394, 799; *Memorial, William F. Breakey, Presented to the University Senate, March 22, 1915,* University of Michigan.
5. Partridge to Robertson, Aug. 10, 1868, 16th Michigan Records, Archives of Michigan, Lansing; Partridge to Bachelder, March 31, 1866, in *The Bachelder Papers: Gettysburg in Their Own Words,* ed. David L. Ladd and Aubrey J. Ladd, vol. 1 (Dayton, Ohio: Press of Morningside Bookshop, 1995–1995), p. 243; *Michigan Pioneer and Historical Collections,* vol. 26, pp. 33–34; Michigan Gettysburg Battlefield Monument Commission, *Michigan at Gettysburg* (Detroit: Winn & Hammond, 1889), pp. 15–16.
6. Alan Naldrett, *Lost Towns of Eastern Michigan* (Mt. Pleasant, S.C.: History Press), 2015, p. 39; *Detroit Free Press,* April 27, 1906; State of Michigan, *Papers in the Matter of the Removal of John W. Jochim, Secretary of State, Joseph Hambitzer, State Treasurer, and John G. Berry, Commissioner of the Land Office, 1894* (Lansing: Robert Smith, 1895); Berry letters to daughter Lettie, Dec. 6, 1905–Jan. 14, 1906, U.S. Army Heritage and Education Center (USAHEC); *Otsego County Record and Herald,* Aug. 2, 1923.
7. Don Farrant, "The Worst Fire a Mortal Endured," *Grand Rapids Press,* April 15, 1984; Apted diary notes, Miscellaneous Civil War Collection, U.S. Army Heritage and Education Center. A reference to Apted having four inches of the bone in his arm removed is in the *Ionia Daily Sentinel,* Oct. 14, 1897.
8. Carl Guarneri and Alyssa Sisco, "When Will the End Come?," essay on Edward Hill, Library of St. Mary's College of California; *Ionia Daily Sentinel,* Oct. 14, 1897; Minnie Dubbs Millbrook, *A Study in Valor: Michigan Medal of Honor Winners in the Civil War* (Lansing: Michigan Civil War Centennial Observance Commission, 1966), pp. 62–63; Hill's compiled "Roll of Honor, Sixteenth Michigan" in *Proceedings of the Third Brigade Association, First Division, Fifth Army Corps, Army of the Potomac, Held at the National Encampment of the G.A.R., Washington, D.C.* (New York: River and Driver, 1900), vol. 3, pp. 112–45; Hill to Richardson, Dec. 1, 1899, 16th Michigan Records, Archives of Michigan; *Wolverine Citizen,* Oct. 6, 1888. Of course, Hill's study of the regiment's casualties is higher, and I think more accurate, than those given in the state's tabulation; those given on the regiment's Gettysburg memorial; and those given by William F. Fox, former officer and compiler of casualties. Fox thought that 247 men and officers from the 16th Michigan had been killed or mortally wounded, and he rated that as the eighth highest combat loss for Union regiments in the war.
9. Sidman nomination and related documents, Sidman Papers, Archives of Michigan; Millbrook, *A Study in Valor,* pp. 119–21.
10. Evelyn Sidman Wachter, *Sidman–Sidnam Families of Upstate New York* (Baltimore: Gateway Press, 1981), pp. 248–49, 262–64.
11. Millbrook, *A Study in Valor,* pp. 62–63; Guarneri and Sisco, "When Will the End Come?" Though Hill's nomination states that his skirmish line assignment was to reveal the location of hidden Confederate batteries that day he was wounded, there is no language reflecting this in existing contemporaneous records or reports.

12. An unidentified newspaper obituary of Hill (late October or November 1900), which attributed his death to heart disease, is attached to a copy of Francis D. "Frank" Keeler, *War Letters Written During the Rebellion* (Saginaw: Julian A. Keeler, 1895), held at the Burton Collection, Detroit Public Library; e-mail communication between the author and Donald Pfanz, historian, Fredericksburg and Spotsylvania National Military Park; Guarneri and Sisco, "When Will the End Come?"
13. Salter's store is listed in Richard Edwards' *Industries of Michigan, City of Detroit for 1880* (New York: Historical Publishing, 1880) p. 233; David Lee Poremba, ed., *If I am Found Dead: Michigan Voices from the Civil War* (Ann Arbor: Ann Arbor Editions, 2006), pp. 235, 239; Michigan Adjutant-General's Dept., *Record of Service,* vol. 16, pp. 140–41. Poremba's book includes transcriptions of Salter's wartime letters to Mrs. Duffield and letters and diaries of other Michigan Civil War veterans.
14. Entries for Munson in the 1870, 1890, and 1900 census; grave marker for Munson, Oakwood Cemetery, Fenton. A brief summary of Munson's record in the Michigan Adjutant-General's Dept. *Record of Service* volume for the 16th Michigan, as well as the regiment's "Roll of Honor, Sixteenth Michigan," mentioned only his first wounding, when he was hit in the hand near Bethesda Church. But the 1890 census and the listing of casualties for the regiment at the battle of Dabney's Mill, in the *Detroit Free Press,* show he suffered a crippling second wound, in the arm.
15. Michigan Adjutant-General's Dept., *Record of Service,* vol. 16, p. 95; *Who Was Who in America Historical Volume, 1607–1896* (Chicago: A. N. Marquis, 1963), p. 301; historical essay by Mark J. Madigan in Willa Cather, *Youth and the Bright Medusa* (Lincoln, Neb.: University of Nebraska Press, 2009), p. 331. American author and novelist Cather never met James Laird but based a character on him, using his real name, in a short story, "The Sculptor's Funeral."
16. That Charles Nisbett was a Democrat, is in *Evening (Owosso) Argus,* Aug. 22, 1912; *Ionia Sentinel,* Oct. 14, 1897; unidentified newspaper clipping (Ann Arbor) about the 16th Michigan reunion in Ann Arbor, Oct 19, 1894, Civil War "miscellaneous" file, Burton Historical Collection, Detroit Public Library.
17. Spear letter quoted in an unidentified clipping of 16th Michigan reunion in Owosso, Oct. 18, 1893; program of the 14th Annual Reunion, 16th Michigan, USAHEC; unidentified clipping, 16th Michigan reunion in Ann Arbor, Oct. 19, 1894, Civil War "miscellaneous" file, Burton Historical Collection.
18. Unidentified clipping, 16th Michigan reunion in Ann Arbor, Oct 19, 1894, Civil War "miscellaneous" file, Burton Historical Collection; John J. Pullen, *The Twentieth Maine* (Philadelphia and New York: J. B. Lippincott, 1957), p. 21.
19. *Flint Journal,* Aug. 9, 1936; *Biographical History of Genesee County, Michigan* (Indianapolis: B. F. Bowen, [1908?]), p. 220; *Michigan Pioneer and Historical Collections,* vol. 22, pp. 365–66; *Flint Daily News,* Sept. 27, 1888; *Saginaw Evening News,* Sept. 26, 1889; *The (Flint) Democrat,* Dec. 13, 1890. The silver water service presented to Stockton is held at the University of Michigan–Flint archive.
20. Unidentified newspaper clipping about the 16th Michigan's reunion in Saginaw, 1910: Civil War "miscellaneous" file, Burton Historical Collection.
21. *Owosso Evening Argus,* Aug. 22, 1912.
22. Unidentified news clipping, 16th Michigan reunion, 1919, in Plymouth, Civil War "miscellaneous" collection, Burton Historical Collection; information about the book of Keeler's letters is from

an unidentified clipping glued on the inside cover of the copy of *War Letters Written During the Rebellion* in the Burton Historical Collection, Detroit Public Library.

23. *Saginaw Evening News,* June 15, 1934, and June 4, 1937.
24. Michigan Gettysburg Battlefield Monument Commission, *Michigan at Gettysburg,* pp. 3–5, 8.
25. Ibid., p. 107.
26. Ibid.
27. Ibid., pp. 108–11.

BIBLIOGRAPHY

ARCHIVES

Archives and Regional History Collections, Western Michigan University: Clarissa Haas/Stanley Oswalt Collection (Herschel Foster letters).

Archives of Michigan, Lansing: George Sidman Papers; Military Establishment, Box 108, 16th Michigan Infantry Regiment Records; Civil War letter and order books of the Michigan Adjutant General.

Bentley Historical Library, University of Michigan: Dr. William F. Breakey letter; George W. Ervay 1863 diary; Farmer Papers; letters of Hubbard Barrett and Warren Heald; Michigan Military Order of the Loyal Legion of the United States (MOLLUS) Papers; Van Hoosen Papers (letters of Marion Munson, Josiah Gibbs).

Burton Historical Collection, Detroit Public Library: Austin Blair Papers; Duffield Papers (letters of Charles L. Salter); "miscellaneous" Civil War file (newspaper clippings).

Clarke Historical Library, Central Michigan University: Oliver W. Norton Papers.

Fredericksburg and Spotsylvania National Park: Alfred M. Apted diary (transcription).

Genesee County Register of Deeds Office. Book of Levies, vol. 1 Transcriptions of 1863 and 1864 federal orders for the seizure of interest from land owned by Mary Louise Longstreet and Bessie Deas.

Gettysburg National Military Park: Transcriptions and copies of letters, pension claims, orders and reports in the files of: 16th Michigan; 83rd Pennsylvania; 44th New York; 20th Maine; 140th New York; 4th Texas; 5th Texas; 44th Alabama; and 48th Alabama.

Hoyt Main Library, Public Libraries of Saginaw: Wellington Family Papers.

Joint Archives of Holland, Hope College, Holland, Michigan: William Visscher family documents and records.

Michigan Civil War Collection (online), micivilwar.com: Letters of James M. Hollister and Hervey D. Stewart.

National Archives, Washington, D.C., Records of the Adjutant General: Court-martial of Norval Welch.

New York State Military Museum, Saratoga Springs: Civil War newspaper clippings.

Perry Archives, Sloan Museum, Flint, Michigan: Flint *Wolverine Citizen* newspaper; Papers of Col. T. B. W. Stockton: diaries, letters, family history documents; Civil War diaries and letters, newspaper clippings, and charges in the court-martial of Norval Welch; 16th Michigan reunion documents and publications.

Plymouth Historical Museum, Plymouth, Michigan: Postwar newspaper articles about William R. and Ella Roe.

St. Mary's College of California Library, Rare Book and Manuscript Collections, Moraga, Ca.: Edward Hill 1864 diary.

United States Army Heritage and Education Center: Alfred M. Apted "diary notes" (transcribed reports and accounts), Miscellaneous Civil War Collection; John G. Berry diary (photocopy), *Civil War Times Illustrated* Collection; Joseph Stanfield diary (transcription), Miscellaneous Civil War Collection.

University Archives and Historical Center, Michigan State University: Mattoon Family Papers (letters of Gershom Mattoon and Jacob Craw).

University of Virginia Library, Special Collections: Dewitt Clinton Smith 1864 diary.

William L. Clements Library, University of Michigan: Schoff Civil War Collection, Aplin Family Papers.

BOOKS AND ARTICLES

Adelman, Garry. *The Myth of Little Round Top*. Gettysburg: Thomas Publications, 2003.

Alexander, Edward Porter. *Fighting for the Confederacy: The Personal Recollections of General Edward Porter Alexander.* Chapel Hill: University of North Carolina Press, 1989.

——. *Military Memoirs of a Confederate*. New York: Charles Scribner's Sons, 1907.

Bandy, Ken, and Florence Freeland, comps. *The Gettysburg Papers*. 2 vols. Dayton: Morningside Books, 1978.

Barnett, Leroy, and Roger Rosentreter. *Michigan's Early Military Forces*. Detroit: Wayne State University Press, 2003.

Barrett, Orvey S. *The Old Fourth Michigan Infantry*. Detroit: W. S. Ostler, 1888.

Bauer, Karl Jack. *The Mexican War, 1846–1848*. Lincoln: Bison Books, University of Nebraska Press, 1992.

Beecher, William Constantine, and Samuel Scoville. *A Biography of Rev. Henry Ward Beecher.* New York: C. L. Webster, 1888.

Bertera, Martin, and Kim Crawford. *The 4th Michigan Infantry in the Civil War.* East Lansing: Michigan State University Press, 2010.

Biographical History of Genesee County, Michigan. Indianapolis: B. F. Bowen, [1908?].

Blackford, William W. *War Years with Jeb Stuart*. New York: Charles Scribner's Sons, 1946.

Breakey, William F. "Recollections and Incidents of Military Medical Service," in *War Papers,* vol. 2, Michigan Commandery Military Order of the Loyal Legion. Detroit: James H. Stone, 1898.

Buel, C. Clough, and Robert Underwood Johnson. *Battles and Leaders of the Civil War: Being for the Most Part Contributions by Union and Confederate Officers*. 4 vols. New York: Thomas Yoseloff, 1956.

Burr, C. B., ed. *The Medical History of Michigan,* 2 vols. Minneapolis and St. Paul: Michigan State Medical Society and Bruce Publishing Co., 1930.

Busey, John W., and David G. Martin. *Regimental Strengths and Losses at Gettysburg*. Hightstown, N.J.: Longstreet House, 2006.

———. *These Honored Dead: The Union Casualties at Gettysburg*. Highstown, N.J.: Longstreet House, 1988.

Carter, Robert G. *Four Brothers in Blue*. Norman: University of Oklahoma Press, 1999.

Case, Sarah C. M. *Diary of Sarah Cushman Miles Case, Dec. 24, 1863–Dec. 13, 1864*. Edited and Transcribed by Mrs. James Martin and Mrs. Arthur Davison. Flint Public Library, 1937.

Catton, Bruce. *A Stillness at Appomattox*. Garden City, N.Y.: Doubleday, 1953.

———. *The Civil War*. Boston: Houghton Mifflin, 1960, and American Heritage, 1987.

Cauble, Frank P. *The Surrender Proceedings, April 9, 1865, Appomattox Court House*. Lynchburg: H. E. Howard, 1987.

Chamberlain, Joshua L. *The Passing of the Armies*. New York: G. P. Putnam's Sons, 1915.

———. "The Third Brigade at Appomattox." Reproduced in Oliver W. Norton, *Attack and Defense of Round Top,* Dayton: Morningside Books, 1983.

Coddington, Edwin P. *The Gettysburg Campaign*. Dayton: Morningside Books, 1979.

Colestock, W. W. "The 16th Michigan at Little Round Top," letter to the editor, *National Tribune,* March 26, 1914.

Court-martial of Isaac Wixon. Eileen Roddy, transcriber, Fenton Historical Museum, from the records of the Adjutant General, National Archives.

Crawford, Kim. *The Daring Trader: Jacob Smith in the Michigan Territory, 1802–1825*. East Lansing: Michigan State University Press, 2012.

Desjardin, Thomas A. *Stand Firm Ye Boys from Maine*. Gettysburg: Thomas Publications, 1995.

Dowdey, Clifford. *The Seven Days*. New York: Little, Brown, 1964.

Drewry, A. S. "Experiences on the Battle Line." *Confederate Veteran*. October 1900.

Edwards. Richard. *Industries of Michigan, City of Detroit for 1880*. New York: Historical Publishing, 1880

Eisenschiml, Otto. *The Celebrated Case of Fitz John Porter*. Indianapolis: Bobbs-Merrill, 1950.

Ellis, Franklin. *History of Genesee County, Michigan*. Philadelphia: Everts & Abbott, 1879.

Ellis, Helen H. *Michigan in the War: A Guide to the Material in Detroit Newspapers 1861–1865*. Lansing: Michigan Civil War Centennial Observance Commission, 1965.

———. *The National Tribune: A Guide to Selected Materials of Civil War Interest*. Burton Historical Collection, Detroit Public Library, 1968–1969.

Ervay, George Washington. *George W. Ervay, 1845–1863, Civil War Letters* (booklet of letter transcriptions). Edited by Blake L. Parrish and Florence Lembeck. Marietta, Ga.: self-pub., 1986.

———. *March with Me to Gettysburg: Diary of a Volunteer*. Edited by Marjorie Neufer. Gainesville, Fla.: self-pub., 1987. Transcription of Ervay's 1863 diary.

Farley, Porter. "Address of Captain Porter Farley" in *The Gettysburg Papers,* vol. 2, compiled by Ken Bandy and Florence Freeland. Dayton: Morningside Books, 1978.

Farrant, Don. "The Worst Fire a Mortal Endured." *Grand Rapids Press,* April 15, 1984.

Finkelman, Paul, ed. *Encyclopedia of American Civil Liberties,* vol. 1. New York: Routledge, 2006.

Fletcher, William A. *Rebel Private, Front and Rear*. Austin: University of Texas Press, 1954.

Fox, William F. *Regimental Losses in the American Civil War*. Albany: Albany Publishing, 1889.

Furguson, Ernest B. *Chancellorsville 1863–The Souls of the Brave*. New York: Alfred A. Knopf, 1992.

Gerrish, Theodore. *Army Life: A Private's Reminiscences of the Civil War*. Portland: Hoyt, Fogg & Donham,

1882.

Graham, Ziba B. "Address of Capt. Graham." *Proceedings of the Third Brigade Association, First Division, Fifth Army Corps, Army of the Potomac, Held at the National Encampment of the G.A.R., Washington, D.C., Sept. 21, 1892.* New York: River and Driver.

——. "On to Gettysburg: Ten Days from My Diary of 1863." *War Papers,* vol. 1. Michigan Military Order of the Loyal Legion of the United States. Detroit: Wynn & Hammond, 1889.

Grant, U.S. *Personal Memoirs of U.S. Grant.* 2 vols. New York: Charles L. Webster, 1885.

Green, William D. *A Peculiar Imbalance: The Rise and Fall of Racial Equality in Minnesota, 1837–1869.* Minneapolis: University of Minnesota Press, 2015.

Guarneri, Carl, and Alyssa Sisco. "When Will the End Come?" Essay on Edward Hill. Library of St. Mary's College of California.

Guelzo, Allen C. *Gettysburg: The Last Invasion.* New York: Knopf, 2013.

Heitman, Francis B. *Historical Register and* Dictionary of *the U.S. Army.* Washington, D.C.: U.S. Government Printing Office, 1903. Urbana: University of Illinois Press, 1965.

Henry, Ralph Selph. *The Story of the Mexican War.* Indianapolis: Bobbs-Merrill, 1950.

Hill, Edward. "Address of Col. Edward Hill." *Michigan at Gettysburg.* Michigan Gettysburg Battlefield Commission. Detroit: Winn & Hammond, 1889.

——. "The Last Charge at Fredericksburg." *Proceedings of the Third Brigade Association, First Division, Fifth Army Corps, Army of the Potomac, Held at the National Encampment of the G.A.R., Washington, D.C., Sept. 21, 1892.* New York: River and Driver.

Hopper, George. "From Beverly Ford to Bottoms Bridge with the First Michigan Infantry." MOLLUS Papers, Michigan Commandery, Bentley Historical Library, University of Michigan.

Howard, Benjamin C. *A Report of the Decision of the Supreme Court of the United States and the Opinions of the Judges Thereof in the Case of Dred Scott Versus John F. A. Sanford, December Term, 1856.* New York: D. Appleton, 1857.

Hoyt, James A. "Anderson's Brigade at Gaines' Mill." *Confederate Veteran,* May 1899.

Isham, Frederic S. *History of the Detroit Light Guard.* Detroit: Detroit Light Guard, 1896.

Jacklin, Rufus W. "The Famous Old Third Brigade," in *War Papers,* vol. 2. Michigan Commandery Military Order of the Loyal Legion of the United States. Detroit: James H. Stone, 1898.

——. *Gettysburg: A Paper Prepared and Read Before the Michigan Commandery of the Military Order of the Loyal Legion of the United States,* December 1903, Bentley Historical Library.

Judson, Amos M. *History of the Eighty-Third Regiment Pennsylvania Volunteers.* Erie: B. F. H. Lynn, 1865.

Keeler, Francis D., "Frank." *War Letters Written during the Rebellion.* Saginaw: Julian A. Keeler, 1895.

Kidd, James. *Personal Recollections of a Cavalryman.* Ionia: Sentinel Printing, 1908.

Lackie, Thomas R. "Peace at Appomattox." *National Tribune,* Washington, D.C.: February 18, 1897.

——. "Reminiscences of Appomattox." *Confederate Veteran,* 8 (March 1900): 123.

——. "Report of Gaines' Mill Affair by a Federal." *Confederate Veteran,* Feb. 1899.

Ladd, David L., and Aubrey J. Ladd, eds. *The Bachelder Papers: Gettysburg in Their Own Words,* vols. 1–3. Dayton: Press of Morningside Bookshop, 1994–1995.

Laine, J. Gary, and Morris Penny. *Laws's Alabama Brigade in the War Between the Union and the Confederacy.* Shippensburg, Pa.: White Mane, 1996.

Lanman, Charles. *Red Book of Michigan: A Civil, Military and Biographical History.* Detroit: E. B. Smith, 1871.

Law, Evander M. "From the Wilderness to Cold Harbor." *The Way to Appomattox,* vol. 4, *Battles and Leaders of the Civil War.* New York: Thomas Yoseloff, 1956.

Longacre, Edward G. *Joshua Chamberlain: The Soldier and the Man.* Conshohocken, Pa.: Combined Publishing, 1999.

May, George S. *Michigan and the Civil War Years 1860–1865: A Wartime Chronicle.* Lansing: Michigan Civil War Centennial Observance Commission, 1964.

McKenna, Charles F., ed. *Under the Maltese Cross, Antietam to Appomattox: The Loyal Uprising in Western Pennsylvania, 1861–1865, Campaigns 155th Pennsylvania Regiment.* Pittsburg: The 155th Regimental Association, 1910.

McMullen, Dennis. *Colonel T.B.W. Stockton: Soldier, Engineer, Businessman* (booklet). Flint: University of Michigan–Flint, 1988.

McPherson, James. *Battle Cry of Freedom.* New York: Oxford University Press, 1988.

Michigan Adjutant-General's Dept. *Record of Service of Michigan Volunteers in the Civil War, 1861–1865,* vol. 16. Kalamazoo: Ihling Bros. & Everard, 1905.

Michigan Gettysburg Battlefield Monument Commission. *Michigan at Gettysburg.* Detroit: Winn & Hammond, 1889.

Michigan Pioneer and Historical Collections. 40 vols. Lansing: Michigan Historical Commission/Pioneer Society of Michigan, 1877–1929.

Millbrook, Minnie Dubbs. *A Study in Valor: Michigan Medal of Honor Winners in the Civil War.* Lansing: Michigan Civil War Centennial Observance Commission, 1966.

Mills, James Cooke. *History of Saginaw County.* Saginaw: Seeman & Peters, 1918.

Naldrett, Alan. *Lost Towns of Eastern Michigan.* Mt. Pleasant, S.C.: History Press, 2015.

Nash, Eugene Arus. *A History of the Forty-fourth Regiment New York Volunteer Infantry in the Civil War, 1861–1865.* Chicago: R. R. Donnelley, 1911.

Norton, Oliver W. *Army Letters, 1861–1865.* Chicago: O. L. Deming, 1903.

———. *Attack and Defense of Little Round Top.* Dayton: Morningside Books, 1983.

———. "Strong Vincent and His Brigade at Gettysburg." Chicago, 1909. Reprinted in *The Gettysburg Papers,* vol. 2. Dayton: Morningside Books, 1978.

———. *Two Bugle Calls.* n.d., n.p.

O'Brien, Thos. M., and Oliver Diefendorf, eds. *General Orders of the War Department Embracing the Years 1861, 1862, and 1863,* vol. 2. New York: Derby & Miller, 1864.

Parker, Francis J. *The Story of the Thirty-second Regiment, Massachusetts Volunteer Infantry.* Boston: C. W. Calkins, 1880.

Pearson, Alfred. "Address of General A. L. Pearson." *Proceedings of the Third Brigade Association, First Division, Fifth Army Corps, Army of the Potomac, Held at the National Encampment of the G.A.R., Washington. D.C., Sept. 21, 1892.* New York: River and Driver, n.d.

Perry, W. F. "The Devil's Den." *Confederate Veteran,* April 1901.

Pfanz, Harry P. *Gettysburg: The Second Day.* Chapel Hill: University of North Carolina Press, 1987.

Platt, Philander. "On Little Round Top." *National Tribune,* Washington, D.C., April 11, 1907.

Poremba, David Lee, ed. *If I Am Found Dead: Michigan Voices from the Civil War.* Ann Arbor: Ann Arbor Editions, 2006.

Porter, Horace. "Five Forks and the Pursuit of Lee," in *Battles and Leaders of the Civil War,* vol. 4. New

York: Thomas Yoseloff, 1956.

——. "General Warren at Five Forks and the Court of Inquiry," in *Battles and Leaders of the Civil War,* vol. 4. New York: Thomas Yoseloff, 1956.

——. "The Surrender at Appomattox Court House," in *Battles and Leaders of the Civil War,* vol. 4. New York: Thomas Yoseloff, 1956.

Portrait and Biographical Record of Saginaw and Bay Counties, Michigan. Chicago: Biographical Publishing, 1892.

Powell, William H. "The Battle of the Petersburg Crater," in *Battles and Leaders of the Civil War,* vol. 4. New York: Thomas Yoseloff, 1956.

——. *The Fifth Army Corps.* New York: G. P. Putnam's Sons, 1896.

Proceedings of the Third Brigade Association, First Division, Fifth Army Corps, Army of the Potomac, Held at the National Encampment of the G.A.R., Washington, D.C., Sept. 21, 1892. New York: River and Driver, n.d.

Proceedings of the Third Brigade Association, First Division, Fifth Army Corps, Army of the Potomac, Held at the National Encampment of the G.A.R., Washington, D.C., vol. 3, New York: River and Driver, 1900.

Pullen, John J. *The Twentieth Maine.* Philadelphia and New York: J. B. Lippincott, 1957.

Rhea, Gordon C. *Cold Harbor: Grant and Lee, May 26–June 3, 1864.* Baton Rouge: Louisiana State University Press, 2002.

——. "Grant's Disengagement from Cold Harbor." *Cold Harbor to the Crater.* Edited by Gary W. Gallagher and Caroline E. Janney. Chapel Hill: North Carolina University Press, 2015.

——. *To the North Anna River: Grant and Lee, May 13–25, 1864.* Baton Rouge: Louisiana State University Press, 2000.

Roberts, William Hugh. *Mexican War Veterans,* Washington, D.C.: Bretano's, 1887.

Robertson, James I., Jr., ed. *The Civil War Letters of General Robert McAllister.* New Brunswick: Rutgers University Press, 1965.

Robertson, Jno. *Michigan in the War.* Lansing: W. S. George, 1882.

"Roll of Honor, Sixteenth Michigan." *Proceedings of the Third Brigade Association, First Division, Fifth Army Corps, Army of the Potomac, Held at the National Encampment of the G.A.R., Washington, D.C.* New York: River and Driver, 1900.

Schultz, Jane E., ed. *This Birth Place of Souls: The Civil War Diary of Harriet Eaton.* New York: Oxford University Press, 2011.

Scott, Robert Garth, ed. *Forgotten Valor: The Memoirs, Journals, & Civil War Letters of Orlando B. Willcox.* Kent, Ohio: Kent State University Press, 1999.

Sears, Stephen W. *Chancellorsville.* New York: Houghton Mifflin, 1996.

——. *Gettysburg.* New York: Houghton Mifflin, 2003.

——. *Lincoln's Lieutenants: The High Command of the Army of the Potomac.* New York: Houghton Mifflin Harcourt, 2017.

Sidman Wachter, Evelyn. *Sidman–Sidnam Families of Upstate New York.* Baltimore: Gateway Press, 1981.

Spear, Ellis. *The Civil War Recollections of General Ellis Spear.* Orono: University of Maine Press, 1997.

——. "The Left at Gettysburg—The Men Themselves Started a Decisive Charge." *The National Tribune,* Washington, D.C., June 13, 1913.

State of Michigan. *Papers in the Matter of the Removal of John W. Jochim, Secretary of State, Joseph Hambitzer,*

State Treasurer, and John G. Berry, Commissioner of the Land Office, 1894. Lansing, Mich.: Robert Smith, 1895.

Stevens, John W. *Reminiscences of the Civil War.* Hillsboro, Tex.: Hillsboro Mirror Print, 1902.

Supplement to the Official Records of the Union and Confederate Armies. 100 vols. Part 2, *Record of Events,* vol. 31. Wilmington, N.C.: Broadfoot Publishing, 1996.

Survivors' Association, 118th Corn Exchange, Pennsylvania Volunteers. *History of the Corn Exchange Regiment, 118th Pennsylvania Volunteers.* Philadelphia: J. L. Smith, 1888.

Taylor, John Dykes. *History of the 48th Alabama Volunteer Infantry Regiment, C.S.A.* Montgomery, Ala. 1902, Reprint. University, Ala.: Confederate Publishing.

Trahey, Thomas. "A Sister of Mercy." *National Tribune,* Washington, D.C., May 26, 1904.

Trudeau, Noah Andre. *The Last Citadel: Petersburg, Virginia, June 1864–April 1865.* Baton Rouge: Louisiana University Press, 1993.

U.S. War Department. *The War of the Rebellion: A Compilation of the Official Records of the Union and Confederate Armies.* 70 vols. in 128 parts. Washington, D.C.: Government Printing Office, 1880–1901.

Vanderslice, James M. *Gettysburg Then and Now.* New York: G. W. Dillingham, 1899.

Varon, Elizabeth R. *Appomattox: Victory, Defeat and Freedom at the End of the Civil War.* New York: Oxford University Press, 2013.

Visher, Harvey L. "The Student Volunteer." n.p., n.d. Bentley Historical Library, University of Michigan.

Wert, Jeffry D. *Sword of Lincoln: The Army of the Potomac.* New York: Simon & Schuster, 2005.

West, John C. *A Texan in Search of a Fight.* Waco: Press of J. S. Hill, 1901.

Who was Who in America Historical Volume, 1607–1896. Chicago: A. N. Marquis, 1963.

Williams, Alpheus S. *From the Cannon's Mouth: The Civil War Letters of General Alpheus S. Williams.* Detroit: Wayne State University and the Detroit Historical Society, 1959.

Willman, Charles. *Ontonagon County in the Civil War* (mimeographed booklet). n.p., 1961.

Wilson, James R. *The Fishers of Saginaw and Zilwaukee* (genealogy). Bellaire, Mich.: n.p., n.d.

Wood, Edwin O. *History of Genesee County, Michigan.* Indianapolis: Federal Publishing Co., 1916.

Younkman, Tim "Bay City's Forgotten Hero." *Bay City Times,* Nov. 12, 1989.

NEWSPAPERS

Detroit Advertiser and Tribune; Detroit Daily Advertiser; Detroit Free Press; East Saginaw Courier; Flint Daily News; (Flint) *Democrat;* (Flint) *Wolverine Citizen; Flint Journal; Gladwin Record; Grand Rapids Press; Hillsdale Sentinel; Hillsdale Standard; Michigan* (Ann Arbor) *Argus; Owosso Evening Argus; Saginaw Courier-Herald; Saginaw Evening News.*

PRIVATELY HELD MATERIAL

John Gibney: Joseph Stanfield diary; Dale Niesen: Heber Woodruff 1863 letter.

INDEX